COMMERCIAL TRANSACTIONS

COMMERCIAL TRANSACTIONS
A Systems Approach

Third Edition

Lynn M. LoPucki
Security Pacific Bank Professor of Law
UCLA Law School

Elizabeth Warren
Leo E. Gottlieb Professor of Law
Harvard University

Daniel Keating
Associate Dean for Academic Affairs and
Tyrrell Williams Professor of Law
Washington University School of Law

Ronald J. Mann
Ben H. & Kitty King Powell Chair in Business
and Commercial Law
University of Texas School of Law

PUBLISHERS

76 Ninth Avenue, New York, NY 10011
http://lawschool.aspenpublishers.com

© 2006 Aspen Publishers, Inc.
a Wolters Kluwer business
http://lawschool.aspenpublishers.com

Aspen Publishers
Attn: Permissions Department
76 Ninth Avenue, 7th Floor
New York, NY 10011-5201

Printed in the United States of America.

2 3 4 5 6 7 8 9 0

ISBN 0-7355-5647-4

Library of Congress Cataloging-in-Publication Data

Commercial transactions : a systems approach / Lynn M. LoPucki ... [et al.].—
3rd ed.
     p. cm.
   Includes index.
   ISBN 0-7355-5647-4
   1. Sales—United States.   2. Negotiable instruments—United States.
3. Credit—Law and legislation—United States.   4. Debtor and
creditor—United States.   I. LoPucki, Lynn M.

   KF914.C59   2006
   346.7307′2—dc22

                                                                2006000917

About Aspen Publishers

Aspen Publishers, headquartered in New York City, is a leading information provider for attorneys, business professionals, and law students. Written by preeminent authorities, our products consist of analytical and practical information covering both U.S. and international topics. We publish in the full range of formats, including updated manuals, books, periodicals, CDs, and online products.

Our proprietary content is complemented by 2,500 legal databases, containing over 11 million documents, available through our Loislaw division. Aspen Publishers also offers a wide range of topical legal and business databases linked to Loislaw's primary material. Our mission is to provide accurate, timely, and authoritative content in easily accessible formats, supported by unmatched customer care.

To order any Aspen Publishers title, go to *http://lawschool.aspenpublishers.com* or call 1-800-638-8437.

To reinstate your manual update service, call 1-800-638-8437.

For more information on Loislaw products, go to *www.loislaw.com* or call 1-800-364-2512.

For Customer Care issues, e-mail *CustomerCare@aspenpublishers.com*; call 1-800-234-1660; or fax 1-800-901-9075.

Aspen Publishers
a Wolters Kluwer business

For Walter O. Weyrauch

—L.M.L.

For Allan Axelrod

—E.W.

For Jane, Amy, Emily, and Matthew

—D.L.K.

For Allison, Alexandra, and Aemilia

—R.J.M.

Summary of Contents

BOOK TWO
Financial Systems   287

Part One
Payment Systems   289

Contents

Chapter 2.   Terms   **115**

Chapter 21. Competitions for Collateral

Acknowledgments

We are deeply indebted to Jay Westbrook, University of Texas School of Law, for his intellectual contributions to this book, not only for his role in developing the "systems approach" used in these materials, but also for his contribution as a teacher to one of us. The following professors provided us with valuable feedback or suggestions about the material:

Allan Axelrod, Rutgers–Newark Center for Law & Justice
John D. Ayer, University of California at Davis Law School
Roger Bernhardt, Golden Gate University School of Law
Roger Billings, Northern Kentucky University College of Law
Amelia H. Boss, Temple University School of Law
Nicholas Brannick, Ohio State University College of Law
Jean Braucher, University of Arizona College of Law
Beth Buckley, SUNY Buffalo School of Law
Scott J. Burnham, University of Montana School of Law
Amy C. Bushaw, Lewis & Clark, Northwestern School of Law
Robert Chapman, Willamette University College of Law
Wilson Freyermuth, University of Missouri–Columbia School of Law
Tracey E. George, Vanderbilt University Law School
Michael Greenfield, Washington University School of Law
Russell Hakes, Widener University School of Law
Kathryn R. Heidt, University of Pittsburgh Law School
John P. Hennigan, Jr., St. John's University School of Law
Margaret Howard, Washington & Lee University School of Law
Sarah Jane Hughes, Indiana University School of Law–Bloomington
Melissa B. Jacoby, University of North Carolina School of Law
Edward Janger, Brooklyn Law School
Avery Katz, Columbia University School of Law
Andrew Kaufman, Harvard Law School
Kenneth C. Kettering, New York Law School
Jason J. Kilborn, Louisiana State University Law Center
Charles Lincoln Knapp, University of California, Hastings College of the Law
F. Stephen Knippenberg, University of Oklahoma Law Center
Michael M. Korybut, Saint Louis University School of Law
Bruce Markell, University of Nevada, Las Vegas, School of Law
Alexander Meiklejohn, Quinnipiac University School of Law
Gary Neustadter, Santa Clara University School of Law
Nancy Ota, Albany Law School, Union University
Katherine Porter, University of Iowa Law School
John A.E. Pottow, University of Michigan Law School
C. Scott Pryor, Regent University School of Law
Robert Rasmussen, Vanderbilt University Law School
Curtis R. Reitz, University of Pennsylvania Law School
Arnold Rosenberg, Thomas Jefferson School of Law
Keith Rowley, University of Nevada, Las Vegas, School of Law

Steven L. Sepinuck, Gonzaga University School of Law
Paul M. Shupack, Yeshiva University, Cardozo School of Law
Lars S. Smith, University of Louisville School of Law
Catherine Tinker, University of South Dakota School of Law
Howard P. Walthall, Cumberland School of Law of Samford University
Stephen J. Ware, University of Kansas School of Law
G. Ray Warner, St. John's University School of Law
Jane Kaufman Winn, University of Washington School of Law
Zipporah B. Wiseman, University of Texas School of Law
William J. Woodward, Jr., Temple University School of Law

We are indebted to them, their students, and our own students at the University of Pennsylvania, Harvard University, Washington University, the University of Texas, the University of Michigan, the University of Wisconsin, Cornell University, and UCLA both for improving the book and for putting up with our errors, both substantive and typographical.

Numerous people who work in the commercial systems discussed in this book were kind enough to answer our questions about the systems and otherwise provide information. They include:

James J. Ahearn, NationsBank (formerly the Boatmen's National Bank of St. Louis)
Buddy Baker, ABN/Ambro
Margie Bezzole, Phoenix International
Mary Binder, Bank One (formerly First National Bank of Chicago)
Naran U. Burchinow, Deutsche Financial Services
Richmond W. Coburn, NationsBank (formerly the Boatmen's National Bank of St. Louis)
Richard A. Cohen, May Department Stores Co.
Joe DeKunder, NationsBank of Texas, N.A.
John Dul, Anixter, Inc.
Paul Easterwood, Dow, Cogburn & Friedman, P.C.
Carl Ernst, UCC Filing Guide, Inc.
Brian M. Foster, Ralcorp Holdings, Inc.
William Geary, Rock-Tenn Co.
Dale R. Granchalek, Bank One (formerly First National Bank of Chicago)
Jerry Grossman, Heller, Ehrman, White, and McAuliffe
Janet L. Haley, NationsBank (formerly the Boatmen's National Bank of St. Louis)
Ed Hand, UCC Filing and Search Services
Carol A. Helmkamp, NationsBank (formerly the Boatmen's National Bank of St. Louis)
James Hinderaker, Bank One (formerly First National Bank of Chicago)
Glen Horton, Washington University
Kenneth Hovorka, Rock-Tenn Co.
Joseph F. Jedlicka III, Anheuser-Busch Companies, Inc.
Linda Jenkins, NationsBank (formerly the Boatmen's National Bank of St. Louis)

John K. Kane, Bryan Cave
Dave Machek, Bank One (formerly First National Bank of Chicago)
Tom McCaffrey, Dow, Cogburn & Friedman, P.C.
Kevin Meyer, Bank One (formerly First National Bank of Chicago)
Mary-Ann Novinsky, Mercantile Bank (formerly Mark Twain Bancshares)
John Podczerwinski, Schnadig Corp.
John Powell, National Cachecard
Mark A. Ptack, Bank One (formerly First National Bank of Chicago)
Mark D. Rabe, McDonnell Douglas Corp.
Frank Ricordati, Bank One (formerly First National Bank of Chicago)
Gayle G. Stratmann, Eveready Battery Company, Inc.
Lester Tober, Tober Industries, Inc.
Steve Volland, Anheuser-Busch Companies, Inc.

The following individuals provided valuable research assistance, and the book was made better by their efforts:

Rebecca Berkeley
Bill Cobb
Bob Droney
Judson Hoffman
Laurel Kolinski
Jennifer Marler
Paul Nalabandian
David Royster
Barbara Smith
Cathy Stites
Heather Suve

Joanne Margherita, Karen Mathews, and Gail Ristow served as desktop publishers and manuscript organizers, and we thank them for their important work in those areas.

The following are acknowledged and have our appreciation for granting permission to reprint:

The Associated Press for permission to reprint a portion of Harry F. Rosenthal, Justice, FTC Oppose Lawyers-Only Real Estate Closings, September 20, 1996.

The St. Petersburg Times for permission to reprint a portion of Amy Ellis, Dream Car Turns Into Nightmare, November 5, 1995.

The Guardian for permission to reprint a portion of Richard Colbey, Extended Warranties Spark New Wave of Complaints, February 17, 1996.

Thomas S. Hemmendinger for permission to reprint a portion of Hillman on Commercial Loan Documentation, published by the Practising Law Institute (New York City).

ICC Publishing, Inc., for permission to reprint a portion of ICC No. 500.

The New York Times for permission to reprint portions of David Margolick, At the Bar, A Maine Lobsterman's Justice, N.Y. Times, Sept. 17, 1993.

Deutsche Financial Services for permission to reprint portions of the Security Agreement and Floorplan Agreement that appear in Assignment 56.

Matthew Bender & Co. for permission to reprint the security agreement default provisions from Howard Ruda, Asset-Based Financing.

Introduction

This book provides a comprehensive introduction to the study of commercial transactions. Our fundamental organizing principle has been that law students learn best if we present the law as one element in a system that includes not only abstract legal rules, but also people who engage in commercial transactions, contracts that are designed to guide those transactions, and physical tools, such as filing, systems and check sorters, that facilitate these transactions. To understand the significance and effectiveness of the legal rules, it is necessary to study them in the context of the law-related systems of which they are but one part.

Our attention to the systems that underpin commercial law has had a pervasive effect on the texture of the assignments in this book. First, to get a sense for how those rules operate in context, we conducted more than forty interviews with business people and lawyers who use the various systems in their daily work. Similarly, to help students get a feel for how the systems operate in practice, we include a substantial number of sample documents and forms. Finally, because we organize our presentation by reference to the systems in which commerce operates—rather than the sections into which statutes are divided or the categories of legal doctrine—our presentation frequently cuts across the arbitrary legal standards that divide commercially similar activities. We want our students to see the close relationships between legal rules for the sale of personal property, leases of personal property, and the sale of real property; the deep structural similarities of all the different payment systems in our economy; and the substantively identical concerns raised by security interests in personal property and mortgages on real property. If our students can understand the connections among those different topics, they will be better prepared to grasp the issues raised by the new institutions and systems that will develop during the course of their careers.

Our attention to the non-doctrinal aspects of commercial transactions also alters the types of issues we include in the book. Most importantly, we are firmly committed to the view that the best way for students to understand how the systems operate is through problems that require them to formulate legal strategies. Accordingly, the book is designed for class sessions devoted exclusively to discussion of problems the students have attempted to solve before class, with no need to spend time on case dissection and similar exercises. Although some instructors may wish to spend some class time summarizing the more difficult parts of the material, the problems included in the book provide plenty of material to fill all of the class sessions.

Conversely, because our problems are designed to present the students with real controversies that could arise between real people, we felt free to omit many of the less significant details of the UCC and the other statutory materials we cover: if we could not think of a plausible controversy that would make an issue of concern to practicing lawyers or judges, we saw no need for the students to spend time considering it.

Our philosophy is that learning proceeds best when students are given all of the information they need to solve the problems. The intellectual task is for them to apply the material. Consequently, the text we provide is considerably more extensive than in traditional casebooks, and at the same time excerpts from cases are considerably less extensive. At bottom, the goal is to maximize the value of each page that the student is asked to read and to minimize the time the student spends studying details of cases that do not directly advance the student's understanding of the system at hand. Given the choice between asking a student to read a lengthy or scholarly opinion that sensitively resolves a difficult legal problem and providing a concise summary of the key points of the analysis, we choose the concise summary every time.

The last major feature of the book is the assignment approach. The material is presented in the form of separate, self-contained assignments. Each assignment is designed to provide adequate material for one 50-60 minute class session. Thus, the 69 assignments in this volume provide separate reading assignments and problem sets for 69 class sessions. Unlike most law-school textbooks, the assignments include no supplementary notes suggesting that the students might profit by consulting cases, law review articles, or other secondary sources. The only things a student needs besides this book and a current statutory supplement are imagination and a sincere interest in learning how law interacts with businesses and their institutions to foster (or retard) economic activity.

Our goal at all points is to provide the students two things: the ability to see the grand structure of the existing systems that we cover and the ability to pick up and use new systems that develop in the years to come.

Good luck. We hope that you enjoy studying the materials as much as we have enjoyed preparing them.

Special Note on the UCC in Transition: One of the hardest dilemmas for the authors of a casebook in a code course arises when the code is in a period of transition. We wish we could say that all of the uncertainty surrounding the revisions of Article 1 and amendments to Articles 2 and 2A of the Uniform Commercial Code have been definitively settled. Unfortunately, however, they have not been. The good news is that revised Article 1 seems to have some momentum, and has been adopted as of this writing in 15 states and has been introduced in the legislatures of seven other states. The new choice-of-law provision of revised Article 1 has not been part of the package in those states moving forward with Article 1, and some of those states have also left out the new good-faith definition.

So what are casebook authors to do? To ignore revised Article 1 and amended Articles 2 and 2A would seem ill-advised, given that revised Article 1 has over a dozen state adoptions and that amended Articles 2 and 2A are (despite their lack of adoptions) the "official" versions of those Articles. On the other hand, to delete current Articles 1, 2, and 2A from the casebook would probably also be foolhardy, since it is still not certain how many, if any, states will adopt revised Article 1 and amended Articles 2 and 2A.

The silver lining here (at least for casebook authors) is that the differences between the amended and current Articles 1, 2, and 2A are not nearly as significant as some earlier revision attempts were. Thus, in this third edition, the base of the book remains current Articles 1, 2, and 2A. When there is a different statutory citation to the same principle in the revised or amended statute, the parallel cite to the revised or amended statute is noted parenthetically. When there is a substantive difference in the revised or amended statute, that is noted with a textual explanation. Our hope (and that of other Commercial Law casebook authors, no doubt) is that by the time of the next edition, things will have sorted themselves out such that a citation to just one version or the other of Articles 1, 2 and 2A will suffice. Stay tuned.

LYNN M. LOPUCKI
ELIZABETH WARREN
DANIEL L. KEATING
RONALD J. MANN

February 2006
St. Louis, Missouri

COMMERCIAL
TRANSACTIONS

BOOK ONE
Sales Systems

Chapter 1. Formation

Assignment 1: The Role and Scope of Codes in Sales Systems

A. Fundamental Aspects of Sales

People have been buying and selling things for just about as long as there have been things to buy and sell. In ancient times, "sales" primarily took the form of what we would think of as trades, but as currency systems developed people began to purchase items with money rather than just with other, directly useful items.

As trade became more and more sophisticated, various social and legal institutions were created to expedite and simplify transfers of ownership within sales systems. Sales "systems" mean all of the people, institutions, laws, and practices that are involved in transfers of ownership for a price. Admittedly, there are different systems for different kinds of goods. But whether a sale involves a corporation buying sophisticated machinery or a consumer buying a DVD player at Sears, sales systems generally perform four functions that facilitate the transfer of ownership from seller to buyer.

First, sales systems bring buyers and sellers together and enable them to create legally enforceable transfers of ownership. In facilitating the formation function, the systems not only provide legal rules to define when formation occurs but also provide people and institutions that help enable formation to happen at all. With higher-value items, there tends to be a layer of employees (often known as brokers) whose sole function is to encourage the formation of additional sales agreements. In the car industry, for example, sellers typically employ an army of individuals who try to convince potential buyers to become actual buyers.

Second, sales systems provide a set of standard terms that govern the transfer of ownership unless the buyer and seller choose to modify the standard terms. Often, but not always, this important gap-filling function of sales systems is performed by a code, most notably the Uniform Commercial Code(UCC). There are other ways that sales systems can fill gaps, however, such as the common law or even standard form contracts that are used by most players in a particular sales industry.

One important caveat at this point is not to confuse the code with the sales system itself. Codes such as the UCC play an important role in law-related sales systems, but they are merely one cog in the bigger machine. Consider, for example, the residential real estate sales system. Here there is no universal code comparable to the UCC, but there are nevertheless institutions and practices within that system which arguably make the real estate sales system an even more sophisticated and unified system than that which exists for the sale of goods.

Anyone who has ever purchased a house knows that this sales transaction will usually involve a broker, an appraiser, an inspector, a title insurance company, and a mortgage lender. And, at the end of it all, the purchaser will participate in a formalistic, almost ritualistic, event known as a "closing." The system is smooth and well functioning, but it does not depend on a code to make it work.

The third function of sales systems is to provide a set of delivery institutions that facilitate the possessory, legal, and symbolic transfer from seller to buyer. For example, the sales system provides a menu of standardized delivery terms that allow parties to select different arrangements with respect to insurance costs, delivery charges, and passage of the risk of loss from seller to buyer.

Fourth, sales systems enforce agreements to transfer ownership by giving the aggrieved buyer or seller various remedies for breach by the other. These remedies might be nonlegal, such as a buyer's refusal to buy in the future from a seller that will not rectify its delivery of a defective product. Or these remedies could consist of the various damage formulas that the UCC provides in a case where informal dispute-resolution breaks down and one party sues the other.

The assignments in this book are organized to correspond with sales systems' four subsystems that are described above: formation, terms, performance, and remedies. Each assignment will address four systems for transfers of ownership, using a hub-and-spoke approach to coverage. The hub will be sales of goods, which are governed by Article 2 of the UCC.

The three spokes that will follow the Article 2 hub in each of the assignments will be personal property leases, international sales of goods, and real estate conveyances. Personal property leases are included because although they do not involve sales, they do involve a very analogous system for the temporary transfer of possession. Furthermore, the rules of UCC Article 2A, which govern leases, borrow heavily from Article 2, and thus there is a particular efficiency in including the 2A spoke on a wheel whose hub is Article 2. A final reason for including coverage of leases is that it is occasionally quite difficult to distinguish a lease from a sale. Both types of transactions involve the exchange of consideration for rights in property; with leases, however, there is not only a physical division of the goods being exchanged, but a temporal division as well.

International sales are generally governed by the Convention on Contracts for the International Sale of Goods (CISG). That code borrows some concepts from the UCC, but in other respects departs significantly from the UCC. The CISG therefore serves as a useful point of comparison to appreciate the workings of the UCC. Finally, the real estate conveyancing system, although it lacks a uniform code, nevertheless contains a good deal of conceptual overlap with the sales of goods system.

B.   The Real World of Sales

This book includes excerpts from extensive interviews with over a dozen buyers and sellers in various industries. Those interviewed included officers in Fortune 50 companies, as well as owners of smaller, privately held enterprises.

The primary purpose in conducting these interviews was to learn how relevant the *law* of sales is to the day-to-day operations of the sales system.

The interviews dealt with issues of contract formation, the statute of frauds, parol evidence, warranties and disclaimers, commercial impracticability, acceptance and inspection, delivery practices, and remedies. For each of these areas, the interviews sought to discover what role, if any, the existing legal rules play in shaping the actual practices of buyers and sellers.

In the assignments to come there will be frequent reference to the results of these interviews, but at this point a few general observations are in order. Probably the most striking finding of this investigation is that there seem to be two, only slightly overlapping, worlds out there: the world of business practice and the world of law. In the world of business practice, law is much less significant than reputation and leverage as forces that govern the day-to-day behavior of the actors.

If a buyer or seller is not acting consistently with the expected norms in an industry, the most common response of an aggrieved party is not to sue, but rather to cease doing business with the violator. Where there is a long-term relationship at stake, both sides have an incentive to compromise and to avoid the litigation world. Even where the relationship is fairly new, the prospect of future business with the other side will often be sufficient to coax parties away from hard-line positions.

These findings about the relative dichotomy between business law and business practice are by no means revolutionary. In an often-cited article that was written more than 30 years ago, Professor Stewart Macaulay discovered the same truths in a wide-ranging empirical study concerning what he called "non-contractual relations in business." Assessing those results more than 20 years later in An Empirical View of Contract, 1985 Wis. L. Rev. 465, 467-468, Professor Macaulay mused:

> Contract planning and contract law, at best, stand at the margin of important long-term continuing business relations. Business people often do not plan, exhibit great care in drafting contracts, pay much attention to those that lawyers carefully draft, or honor a legal approach to business relationships. There are business cultures defining the risks assumed in bargains, and what should be done when things go wrong. People perform disadvantageous contracts today because often this gains credit that they can draw on in the future. People often renegotiate deals that have turned out badly for one or both sides. They recognize a range of excuses much broader than those accepted in most legal systems.

Although excerpts such as that quoted above certainly downplay the significance of sales law in day-to-day sales practice, they do not mean to suggest that the law has no role to play in sales systems. There are at least three ways in which sales law has an impact on sales systems. First, the law of sales will be crucial in those instances where the normal business relationship breaks down and the parties end up in the litigation world. Although this eventuality may be slim for any particular contract, when it does occur the stakes tend to be high. This is also the point at which the lawyers get called into the game.

Second, when parties to a sales agreement negotiate informal settlements to disputes, they will probably do so in the "shadow of the law." In one of the interviews, the general counsel of a computer hardware distributor explained that before his sales people meet with a customer to settle a dispute, they will often request from the general counsel's office "our bottom-line legal position." Although the ultimate legal position of a buyer or seller will not necessarily be the dispositive factor in the resolution of a particular dispute, the legal status of each side's position can at least be an important factor.

Finally, legal rules are important in sales systems because they help dictate the terms of the various forms that business people use in conducting transactions within a given sales system. Lawyers draft these forms — things like purchase orders, distribution agreements, and the like — and business people use them. The forms are the place where lawyers can change the default rules that would otherwise apply in the case of litigation. Forms matter not only because they could be binding in the unlikely event of litigation, but also because business people often act as if the forms are binding and sometimes (but not always) change their behavior to conform to what the forms say.

Professor Russell Weintraub, who conducted an extensive survey of corporate general counsel concerning contract practices, noted the role of legal rules in shaping the content of contracts. In the article where he discusses the results of his survey at 1992 Wis. L. Rev. 1, 5, Professor Weintraub observed:

> Although it is a delusion to assume that commercial conduct is primarily controlled by what is 'legal,' the law should not be contrary to practices that the community perceives as normal and desirable. Laws opposed to practice are unlikely to change practice, but will, when haphazardly and occasionally applied, condemn what should be encouraged.
>
> Moreover, recognizing that legal rules do not control commercial conduct is not the same as saying that rules have no effect on practice. Central to the functional impact of contract law is the fact that legal rules affect not only the parties to litigation, but also the frequency and form of future contracts. The concern with influence on future bargains may call for different rules than if the only concern were past bargains. Once litigation has begun, the siren call for relatively simple, clear rules facilitating settlement becomes especially attractive.

C.   Functions of a Code in Sales Systems

Imagine that you are the president of a manufacturing enterprise that makes clothing of various kinds. You just received yesterday a new purchase order for 20 dozen pairs of blue jeans from an independent retailer, Jeans 'R' Us. You promptly sent the jeans to the store and a week later you got a call from the store's manager, who informed you that two dozen pairs of the jeans that you sent had zippers that did not zip.

The purchase order that the buyer sent to you said nothing about zippers having to zip. And yet you did not hesitate for a moment in apologizing to the Jeans 'R' Us owner and you quickly sent a replacement shipment for the two dozen jeans with the defective zippers.

It so happens that this transaction was a sale of goods and therefore was covered by the UCC. It is also true that you are probably a "merchant" under the UCC with respect to these jeans and therefore you made, whether you intended to or not, a warranty of merchantability to Jeans 'R' Us. That warranty included, among other things, a promise that the jeans would be "fit for [their] ordinary purpose," and jeans with broken zippers are not fit. Thus, under the UCC, you would have been obligated in any event to repair or replace the jeans.

When you immediately agreed to make your buyer whole, how much do you think that the requirements of the UCC were driving your behavior? Probably very little. Even in a world without the UCC, you had plenty of reasons for wanting to send two dozen new pairs of jeans to Jeans 'R' Us.

First, you might be a good person who believes that replacing bad jeans with good ones is the ethically proper thing to do. Second, even if you do not have a strong moral sense, you might have hoped that your new customer would buy more jeans from you in the future, and refusing to replace the bad jeans would make quite dim the prospect of later sales to this buyer. Furthermore, even if you did not care about future deals with Jeans 'R' Us, this disappointed buyer might have friends in the industry who themselves are present or prospective customers of yours. And we all know how people talk.

Finally, even if the UCC did not exist, it is very possible that the common law itself would infer in this sales contract something comparable to the warranty of merchantability. So even if you were not particularly ethical and did not care about your reputation, you still might get sued for breach with respect to the two dozen bad zippers (though the amount at stake seems appropriate only for a suit in small claims court).

When you think about the role of a code in sales systems, you should not overestimate its day-to-day significance on the players in the system. Doubtless there are reputational and ethical concerns that have a more powerful influence on the behavior of buyers and sellers than any code ever could. Nevertheless, a code has an important role to play in sales systems, and that is the role of gap-filling.

Parties to a sales contract cannot think of every contingency in advance. Even if they could, in most sales it would not be worth the time it would take to plan for and agree about the outcome of every possible twist and turn of the sale. With sales of personal property, Article 2 fills the gaps for the parties with a convenient and fairly comprehensive set of default terms on issues such as warranties and remedies.

As hard as a code drafter might try, no code will successfully fill all of the gaps in all of the contracts that the code is intended to cover. That is where the common law comes in, as a kind of back-up gap-filler. Before the first uniform sales act, the common law was the primary gap-filler for sales contracts. The advantage of Article 2 as a gap-filler compared to the common law is that Article 2 is more predictable and generally more uniform from state to state than is the common law.

Nevertheless, even a code as comprehensive and as widely adopted as the UCC must acknowledge the role of the common law. U.C.C. §1-103 tells us that the provisions of the Code displace any common law to the contrary, but that the common law shall continue to supplement the provisions of the Code. There are some common-law doctrines, such as the parol evidence rule, that have clearly been supplanted (at least in sales of goods cases) by Article 2. U.C.C. §2-202.

On the other hand, as we shall see in the material that follows, the common law continues to play at least three roles in law-related sales systems. First, in cases where Article 2 is merely codifying existing law, the common law can help define terms that the UCC has left undefined. For example, nowhere does the UCC define such fundamental terms as "breach," "offer," or "possession," but several UCC provisions use those terms.

Second, in some UCC sections and Official Comments the Code drafters make it clear that the UCC provision in question is not intended to affect certain related common-law doctrine. Thus, parties must still look to the common law to define the parameters of that related doctrine.

Finally, there are a number of common law doctrines that are never referred to explicitly in UCC sections or Comments but that nevertheless continue to operate side-by-side with Code provisions. These include such concepts as mitigation of damages, frustration of purpose for a buyer, and even such related tort theories as intentional interference with contract.

One last general point to remember about the UCC is that the official version of the UCC that you find in your statutory supplement is not necessarily "the law" in every state. Indeed, as of this writing, the official amended version of Article 2 that was promulgated by the American Law Institute and the National Conference of Commissioners on Uniform State Laws has not been enacted in any State. When state legislatures enact articles of the UCC as the law in their state, they often include non-uniform amendments. Thus, you should always check your own state's enactment of the UCC. Furthermore, even where the UCC provision is the same from one state to another, the courts of each state may have interpreted the provision differently. Once again, you need to check the state common law that is controlling in any given case.

D.   Scope of Article 2

In any sales system, there will be some set of rules that will serve as implied terms to agreements when the parties to a sale fail to specify certain terms. The rules might be those of Article 2, but they need not be in order to have a functioning system. Whatever the governing set of rules for the system, it is important that players in the system know whether they will ultimately be subject to those rules or not. The particular default rules that govern the system will affect how the players structure and shape the transactions within the system. That is why it is important to consider the question of the scope of Article 2: what's in and what's out of Article 2's world of default terms.

Our exploration into the scope of Article 2 is not to suggest that Article 2 is the only set of default rules out there in the world of sales. Article 2 is, however, the most prevalent set of default rules for sales of goods. In that respect, it is a set of default rules whose scope is worth studying.

There are at least some discrete sales systems that specifically shun Article 2 and its rules. Professor Lisa Bernstein has done detailed studies of two different sales industries that do not use Article 2 as their governing set of rules: the diamond industry and the grain industry. What was noteworthy to Professor Bernstein about the diamond industry was not merely the set of substantive rules that diamond traders use to govern transactions among its members, but rather the private extralegal system that the industry uses to enforce agreements: "Although many of the shortcomings in the American legal system that make litigation unattractive to diamond dealers are also present in most commercial contexts, the diamond industry is unique in its ability to create and, more important, to enforce its own system of private law." Lisa Bernstein, Opting Out of the Legal System: Extralegal Contractual Relations in the Diamond Industry, 21 J. Legal Stud. 115, 116 (1992).

In Professor Bernstein's study of the grain industry, she highlighted one important contrast between how grain-industry adjudicators use their own set of rules and how courts use Article 2's set of default rules. Article 2 emphasizes the importance of courts enforcing course of performance or course of dealing — that is, the actual practices used by the disputing parties before the relationship broke down — when faced with a sales dispute. The grain industry's private legal system, by contrast, does not seek to explore the actual practices between two contracting parties, or what Professor Bernstein calls "relationship-preserving norms": "[T]ransactors do not necessarily want the relationship-preserving norms they follow in performing contracts and cooperatively resolving disputes among themselves to be used by third-party neutrals to decide cases when they are in an end-game situation . . . [W]hen courts apply the Code's usage of trade, course of dealing, and course of performance provisions, they will often be using relationship-preserving norms to resolve end-game disputes." Lisa Bernstein, Merchant Law in a Merchant Court: Rethinking the Code's Search for Immanent Business Norms, 144 U. Pa. L. Rev. 1765, 1770 (1996).

Thus, Professor Bernstein calls into question one of the fundamental premises that underlies Article 2: that courts should apply the rules in litigation with reference to how the parties acted when they were not in litigation. Having to contend with this umbrella of usage of trade, course of dealing, and course of performance is at least one functional consequence of having a given sale be subject to the rules of Article 2.

Another key functional significance of Article 2 coverage is whether or not the particular transaction will be subject to the gap-filling role of the Code that was discussed above. While there are lots of gap-fillers in Article 2, two of them tend to provide the most common reasons why parties fight about whether or not Article 2 applies to their transaction: the warranty gap-filler and the statute of limitations gap-filler.

One of the most attractive features to a plaintiff of suing on a warranty theory is that the prima facie case is fairly easy to prove. Where the alternative is often a tort suit in negligence, the task in a warranty suit of proving merely the existence of a warranty, causation, and damages seems easy compared to having to show that elusive "lack of due care" required in a tort suit. Furthermore, if the suit is for breach of the warranty of merchantability, then the issue of warranty existence is as simple as demonstrating that this was a sale of goods and the seller was a merchant in goods of the kind.

Whereas the warranty gap-filler often gives the plaintiff a reason to want Article 2 coverage, the Article 2 statute of limitations will sometimes give the plaintiff a reason to want the transaction to be deemed outside of Article 2's scope. U.C.C. §2-725(1) gives a plaintiff four years to commence an action for breach of a sales contract (or up to five years under amended §2-725), but the four years is measured from the time when the cause of action *accrued*, whether or not the plaintiff was aware of it. Many state statutes of limitations for general contract actions, by contrast, do not begin running until the plaintiff actually discovers or should have discovered the breach.

For example, imagine that a contractor agreed to assemble and install a sophisticated product-assembly machine in the buyer's factory. Suppose that the machine contained a latent defect that did not manifest itself until more than four years following the sale. If the transaction were covered under Article 2, then the buyer would be barred by the statute of limitations from bringing a breach of warranty action. If the transaction were considered outside of Article 2, then the buyer could conceivably bring a breach of contract action since the general state statute of limitations would probably not begin to run until the buyer actually discovered or should have discovered the defect.

Although the gap-filling function of the UCC can be very important in many cases, you should also remember that it is truly a last resort. Courts will only look to the UCC gap-filler if they lack a more specific indication of what the parties must have intended with respect to the term in dispute. In other words, we should use UCC gap-fillers only when there is in fact a gap to be filled.

There are at least four ways in which a UCC gap-filler will be superseded. First, the gap-filler will not apply to a particular term if the contract itself specifies what that term should be. U.C.C. §1-102(3) (revised §1-302(a)) makes it clear that the Code drafters desired first and foremost to give effect to private agreements, at least to the extent that those agreements are within the limits of good faith and commercial reasonableness.

Second, even where the parties' written contract is silent on a particular matter, the parties' repeated occasions for performance within that contract may establish an agreement by implication. U.C.C. §2-208(1) (revised §1-303(a)) calls these particular kinds of implicit terms "course of performance."

Third, where parties' past dealings with one another have established a particular way that the parties do business with one another, that history may establish by implication certain standard terms between the parties. U.C.C. §1-205 (revised §1-303(b)) calls such implied terms based on past contracts between the same parties "course of dealing."

Finally, if there is a custom in a particular industry concerning a performance term, that custom will prevail over the UCC gap-filler whenever the two are inconsistent. The UCC calls such customs "usage of trade." U.C.C. §1-205(2) (revised §1-303(c)).

In addition to defining the various ways in which the UCC gap-fillers can be superseded, the Code drafters also created in §1-205(4) (revised §1-303(e)) a hierarchy among these rules: "express terms control both course of dealing and usage of trade and course of dealing controls usage of trade." On the other hand, the statement of this hierarchy begins with the admonition that whenever it is reasonable, we should seek to construe the express terms of an agreement as consistent with course of dealing or usage of trade.

Ragus Co. v. City of Chicago

628 N.E.2d 999 (Ill. App. Ct. 1993)

RIZZI, J.

This action arises out of a contract between Ragus Company (Ragus) and the City of Chicago (City). The contract called for Ragus to supply the City with a certain quantity of rodent traps. As a result of differing interpretations regarding the number of traps specified in the contract, Ragus supplied the City with only half of the rodent traps the City expected. The City refused delivery and suspended Ragus from its bidding process for six months. Ragus subsequently brought a five-count complaint against the City and three of the City's employees, Alexander Grzyb, Walter Brueggen and Mark Pofelski. . . .

The facts of this case are undisputed. In July 1991, the City announced that it was seeking bids from companies to supply the City with Gotcha Glue Boards, a brand of rodent traps. The City's announcement called for the following specifications for the traps:

150 cases of 5 1/2" × 11"; 24/case.

75 cases of 11" × 11"; 12/case.

Ragus submitted a bid offering to supply the City with the traps at a price of $30.00 a case, for a total of $6,750.00. The City awarded the contract to Ragus on August 18, 1991. On October 3 and 4, 1991, Ragus attempted to deliver to the City 150 cases each containing 24 of the bigger [sic] traps and 75 cases each containing 12 of the smaller [sic] traps. The City refused delivery because it was expecting 150 cases containing 24 pairs of the larger [sic] traps and 75 cases containing 12 pairs of the smaller [sic] traps. On October 16, 1991, the City notified Ragus that it had 10 days to cure what it perceived as a defect in Ragus' performance by delivering twice the number of traps. Ragus claimed that it was in compliance with the contract and did not tender the additional traps demanded by the City. On November 7, 1991, the City suspended Ragus from the bidding process until April 26, 1992.

Ragus then filed a five-count complaint seeking declaratory relief and money damages. In count I of the complaint, Ragus asked the court to construe the contract and declare that Ragus had complied with the contract. In count II, Ragus asked the court to declare that defendants wrongfully suspended Ragus from the City's bidding process. . . .

Defendants in turn filed a motion to dismiss the complaint pursuant to §2-619(a)(9) of the Illinois Code of Civil Procedure. A hearing was had on this motion. At the hearing defendants presented affidavits to show that usage of trade demonstrates that "24/case" refers to 24 pairs per case.

The president of the manufacturer of Gotcha Glue Boards averred that for the last 10 years Gotcha Glue Boards have been packaged in pairs. Defendant Alexander Grzyb, the City's purchasing agent averred that once the contract was terminated with Ragus, he awarded a contract for Gotcha Glue Boards to Production Dynamics Company. That contract called for "150 cases of Gotcha Glue Boards, 5 1/2" × 11"; 24/case." Production Dynamics Company supplied the City with 150 cases each containing 24 pairs of traps. Lastly, Tony Proscia, a City employee averred that he oversees goods shipped by various suppliers to the City. Every other case of 5 1/2" × 11" Gotcha Glue Boards he inspected contained 24 pairs of traps.

In an attempt to counter the above affidavits, Ragus presented the affidavit of its president, George L. Lowe. This affidavit, however, simply did not address the factual allegations concerning usage of trade. Accordingly, the factual averments of defendants' affidavits are admitted. . . .

Ragus next argues that the court erred when it referred to usage of trade pursuant to the Uniform Commercial Code §1-205(4) [revised §1-303(e)], in order to interpret the contract where the contract itself was unambiguous. We, however, disagree that the contract was unambiguous. The dispute focused on the interpretation of whether "24/case" and "12/case" refer to individual traps or to pairs of traps. In order to eliminate ambiguity from a contract it is necessary to exclude other reasonable interpretations. The above quoted language does not exclude the reasonable interpretation that 24 pairs and 12 pairs per case are the number of traps called for in the contract. Therefore, reference to usage of trade was proper.

Ragus also argues that defendants failed to present sufficient evidence establishing usage of trade. We disagree. Defendants presented the affidavits of three people who currently deal with Gotcha Glue Boards, including the president of the company that manufactures these traps. Taken together, the affidavits establish that the sole manufacturer of Gotcha Glue Boards packages and sells the traps in pairs, middle men purchase and resell the traps in pairs, and the City buys and receives the traps in pairs. Ragus failed to counter these factual averments. We hold that the trial court had before it sufficient evidence to find that when a party dealing in Gotcha Glue Boards spoke of "24/case" or "12/case," this meant 24 pairs and 12 pairs per case. The trial court properly construed the contract and dismissed count I of Ragus' complaint. . . .

On the issue of scope, Article 2's provisions are most deficient in their coverage of what are commonly known as "mixed contracts": those involving a combination of goods and services, or a combination of goods and something other than services. Article 2 says that it applies to "transactions in goods," U.C.C. §2-102, and then defines goods as "all things (including specially manufactured goods) which are movable at the time of identification to the contract for sale." U.C.C. §2-105(1). Nowhere does either of these provisions suggest how to treat a contract that includes both goods and non-goods aspects.

An example of a mixed goods-services contract would be a carpenter's contract with a homeowner for the carpenter to install new cabinets in the homeowner's kitchen. Whenever someone sells an entire business that consists in part of goods, that is an example of a contract that mixes goods and something other than services, here things like good will or customer lists.

Courts have taken two approaches to these mixed contracts. Most courts apply some version of a predominant purpose test, by which the court decides whether the predominant purpose of the transaction is to sell goods or services. If it is goods, then Article 2 applies to the whole transaction, even the services portion of it. If the predominant purpose is determined to be services, then Article 2 does not apply to any part of the transaction, not even the goods portion.

The other common approach to the mixed contract question has been called the gravamen of the action test. Under that test, the court determines whether the gravamen of the action (the source of the complaint) is with the goods or the services portion of the transaction. If the problem lies with the goods, then Article 2 applies even if the predominant purpose of the transaction is services rather than goods. If the problem lies with the services, then Article 2 does not apply to the dispute even if the predominant purpose of the transaction is goods rather than services.

Each test has its problems. Often it is quite difficult to determine whether the "predominant purpose" of a particular transaction is goods or services. While it might seem easier to decide what is the "gravamen of the action" in a particular case, even that determination can be tricky. For example, suppose you go to an eye doctor to get some medicine for your eyes. Imagine that you have specifically instructed the doctor that you are allergic to sodium-based solutions, but she gives you eye drops that contain sodium. The eye drop container *says* it contains sodium.

When you have an allergic reaction, does the gravamen of your action involve the goods or services portion of your transaction with the doctor? On the one hand, you might say that the gravamen of the action was the goods, since it was the sodium in the solution that caused your allergic reaction. On the other hand, the goods were not inherently defective, and it was only due to the shoddy medical services that you were given a prescription that contained a substance to which you knew you were allergic.

The following case is a reminder that "goods" under Article 2 do not necessarily have to come in the form of solids.

Dakota Pork Indus. v. City of Huron

638 N.W.2d 884 (S.D. 2002)

GORS, ACTING JUSTICE.

Dakota Pork Industries (Dakota Pork) appeals the trial court's grant of summary judgment to the City of Huron (City) on breach of express warranty and breach of implied warranty of fitness for a particular purpose. We affirm.

Dakota Pork operated a pork processing plant in Huron, South Dakota, from 1987 until it ceased operations in July of 1997. In 1991, Dakota Pork entered into an agreement with the City whereby City would provide for Dakota Pork's water needs in exchange for Dakota Pork's water rights in the James River. Negotiations regarding this agreement took place over the course of a year. No special conditions or uses for water were expressed in the written contract.

Prior to May 24, 1994, a foreign substance, later determined to be calcium carbonate, appeared on the meat at Dakota Pork. On May 29, 1998, Dakota Pork filed a complaint against City for negligence, breach of express warranty, and breach of implied warranty of fitness for a particular purpose. City moved for summary judgment and a hearing was held February 26, 2001. The trial court granted City's motion on all counts.

Dakota Pork appeals the issues of breach of express warranty and breach of implied warranty of fitness for a particular purpose. . . .

The primary inquiry is whether City's furnishing of water to Dakota Pork constitutes a sale of goods under Article 2 of the Uniform Commercial Code (UCC). Courts have adopted two conflicting viewpoints.

One viewpoint is expressed in the pre-UCC case of Canavan v. City of Mechanicville, 229 N.Y. 473, 128 N.E. 882 (1920). In *Canavan* the New York Court of Appeals examined the sale of water under the Uniform Sales Act. Under that Act, goods were defined in part as "all chattels personal other than things in action or money." The court held that "[t]he furnishing of water, through a system of waterworks, by a water corporation, either private or municipal, to private consumers, at a fixed compensation, is a sale of goods within the meaning of the statute. . . . It is a sale of goods as if the water were collected and delivered in bottles for a price." *Id.* at 883. See also Gall by Gall v. Allegheny County Health Dep't, 521 Pa. 68, 555 A.2d 786, 789 (1989) (stating "[a]ll who have paid bills for water can attest to its movability"); Zepp v. Mayor & Council of Athens, 180 Ga App. 72, 348 S.E.2d 673, 677 (1986) (stating that it does not find Coast Laundry v. Lincoln City, 9 Or App. 521, 497 P.2d 1224 (1972) compelling, and that "[w]ater, like electricity is a thing; it exists; it is 'fairly identifiable' as a movable at the time of identification to the contract for sale").

The other viewpoint is expressed in Coast Laundry v. Lincoln City, 9 Or. App. 521, 497 P.2d 1224 (1972). In *Coast Laundry* an Oregon court held that the sale of water by a municipality is not governed by the UCC. *Id.* at 1228. The court analyzed *Canavan, supra,* in light of the UCC. The court stated, "[t]he definition of goods is based on the concept of movability and the term 'chattels personal' is not used. It is not intended to deal with things which are not fairly identifiable as movable before the contract is performed." *Id.* (*citing* Official Comment, 1 Uniform Laws Ann. 79, 89 §2-105 (1968)). The *Coast Laundry* court determined that water is not "fairly identifiable as movable before the contract is performed" and concluded that the sale of water does not constitute the sale of goods. *Coast Laundry,* 497 P.2d at 1228.

The UCC defines "goods" as all things "which are movable at the time of identification to the contract for sale[.]" SDCL 57A-2-105(1). Goods "must be both existing and identified before any interest in them can pass." SDCL 57A-2-105(2). "Whatever can be measured by a flow meter has 'movability' as that term is used in connection with the definition of goods." 1 R. Anderson, *Uniform Commercial Code,* §2-105:19, at 560 (3d. ed 1981).

We agree with the conclusion reached in *Canavan* and find that the sale of water by a municipality is the sale of goods and a transaction which is governed by the UCC. . . .

Some courts have assumed that a transaction's failure to qualify under Article 2's scope provision necessarily precludes application of the standards set down in Article 2. There is, however, another way of approaching the matter. Nowhere does it say that a court cannot apply the principles of Article 2 to subjects that are admittedly not within the formal scope of Article 2. Many courts have in fact heeded the admonitions of the UCC drafters, who note with favor in at least one Official Comment those courts that "have recognized the policies embodied in an act as applicable in reason to subject-matter which was not expressly included in the language of the act...where reason and policy so required, even where the subject-matter had been intentionally excluded from the act in general." U.C.C. §1-102, Comment 1 (revised §1-103, Comment 1).

Probably the most significant Article 2 concept for a court to apply by analogy in non-goods transactions is the implied warranty of merchantability. That is the warranty that all merchants create in sales under Article 2, at least where the merchant deals in goods of the kind that are sold. U.C.C. §2-314(1). In a nutshell, the warranty of merchantability promises the buyer that the goods will be fit for their ordinary purpose. It would hardly seem radical (at least in consumer sales) for a court to suggest that even in a non-goods sale, the merchant implicitly promises that whatever it sells will be fit for ordinary uses.

While we are on the subject of the warranty of merchantability, it probably makes sense to deal here with another important scope issue within Article 2: the special default rules that apply only with respect to merchants. Merchants occupy a special place within Article 2. In many parts of the UCC, those qualifying as merchants are held to higher standards than are other players in the system.

Cook v. Downing
891 P.2d 611 (Okla. Ct. App. 1994)

HUNTER, J.

Appellant is a licensed dentist who devotes less than 50% of his practice to fitting and making dentures. Appellee, a patient, sued Appellant in small claims court because of mouth trouble she had on account of the dentures. Appellee alleged the condition was the result of ill-fitting dentures. Appellant testified that the condition was generalized and not consistent with localized sore spots which would result from ill-fitting dentures. Appellant referred Appellee to oral surgeons. The dental specialists' evidence showed that they believed the condition was due to either candidas, an autoimmune reaction or an allergy to the dental material. Although none of the dental evidence pinpointed the source of the problem, it consistently ruled out ill-fitting dentures.

After trial, the court entered judgment in favor of Appellee, setting forth that damages were awarded pursuant to Article 2 of the Oklahoma Uniform Commercial Code, §§2-104, 2-105 and 2-315, "Implied Warranty of Fitness for a Particular Purpose" and that attorney fees were awarded pursuant to 12 O.S.1991 §936. Section 2-104(1) defines merchant as "a person who deals in the goods of the kind or otherwise by his occupation holds himself out as having knowledge or skill peculiar to the practices or goods involved in the transaction or to whom such knowledge or skill may be attributed by his employment of an agent or broker or other intermediary who by his occupation holds himself out as having such knowledge or skill." Section 2-105(1) defines goods as meaning "all things (including specially manufactured goods) which are movable at the time of identification to the contract for sale other than the money in which the price is to be paid, investment securities (Article 8) and things in action. 'Goods' also includes the unborn young of animals and growing crops and other identified things attached to realty . . ." The law of implied warranty in the commercial code is found in §2-315 which states:

> Where the seller at the time of contracting has reason to know any particular purpose for which the goods are required and that the buyer is relying on the seller's skill or judgment to select or furnish suitable goods, there is unless excluded or modified under the next section an implied warranty that the goods shall be fit for such purpose.

We agree with Appellant's position that any claim Appellee might have sounds in tort. In Oklahoma, dentists, professionals who are regulated by the state, furnish dentures. In general, dentists must use ordinary skill in treating their patients. A patient does not establish the elements of legal detriment by only showing nonsuccess or unsatisfactory results.

A dentist is not a merchant and the Uniform Commercial Code is not the law to apply to these facts. Finding no Oklahoma law on point, we align ourselves with the reasoning stated by the Court of Appeals of North Carolina in Preston v. Thompson, 53 N.C. App. 290, 280 S.E.2d 780 (1981). In the Preston case, the patient determined through her research in the yellow pages that the dentist was a specialist in dentures. The patient claimed the doctor made oral assurances that the dentures would fit satisfactorily. The dentures did not fit well and subsequent attempts at correcting the problem were not successful. The patient sued the dentist on an implied warranty theory pursuant to the Uniform Commercial Code. The court held, 280 S.E.2d at 784, that the transaction was not of "goods" and that a dentist was not a "merchant" under the UCC. We adopt the rule as enunciated by the North Carolina court, 280 S.E.2d at 784, that "those who, for a fee, furnish their professional medical services for the guidance and assistance of others are not liable in the absence of negligence or intentional misconduct." (citation omitted). The court further held, 280 S.E.2d at 785, that "the fact that defendant holds himself out as specializing in the preparing and fitting of dentures does not remove him from the practice of dentistry and transform him into a merchant." We hold that under the laws of Oklahoma, a dentist is not a merchant and dentures, furnished by a dentist, are not goods under the UCC.

A dentist could be sued for breach of contract, if such contract were alleged to exist, but that is not the fact as revealed in the record in our case. Appellee presented evidence of an advertisement guaranteeing dentures to fit, but testified that she did not see this ad until after she had begun her treatment with Appellant. The evidence does not support any breach of contract action.

As a matter of law, Appellee erroneously based her cause of action on the Uniform Commercial Code rather than negligence. The court erred in entering judgment in favor of Appellee based on this law. For this reason, we reverse the judgment of the trial court and remand the matter with directions to enter judgment in favor of Appellant.

REVERSED and REMANDED with directions.

JONES, J., dissenting:

As is typical of small claims cases, there were no pleadings here to define the issues. At trial, however, issues were raised as to dental malpractice and breach of implied warranties under the UCC. Although the trial court based its decision on a finding of a breach of the implied warranty of fitness for a particular purpose, §2-315, the trial court's decision must be affirmed if sustainable on any ground.

The decision cannot be affirmed on the basis of professional negligence as the necessary evidence of such negligence was lacking. But neither can the trial court's decision be affirmed on the basis of implied warranty of fitness for a particular purpose. There was no particular or special purpose involved as is required by §2-315. The use Appellee was to make of the dentures was their ordinary use, and that they may not have been suitable for the ordinary purpose for which they were to be used is the concept of "merchantability".

The implied warranty of merchantability is codified at §2-314 and deserves a closer look.

"(1)...a warranty that the goods shall be merchantable is implied in a contract for their sale if the seller is a merchant with respect to goods of that kind. * * * *"

"(2) Goods to be merchantable must be at least such as..."

"(c) are fit for the ordinary purposes for which such goods are used; * * * *."

A "merchant" is defined as:

"...a person who deals in goods of the kind or otherwise by his occupation holds himself out as having knowledge or skill peculiar to the practices or goods involved in the transaction or to whom such knowledge or skill may be attributed by his employment of an agent or broker or other intermediary who by his occupation holds himself out as having such knowledge or skill." §2-104(1).

"Goods" means "all things (including specially manufactured goods) which are movable at the time of identification to the contract for sale other than the money in which the price is to be paid, investment securities...and things in action. * * * *" §2-105(1).

"Dentists" and "dentures" appear to be included in the definitions of merchants and goods.

The transaction of a patient being fitted for and purchasing dentures from a dentist is actually a hybrid. It is not purely a sale of goods by a merchant, nor is it purely the providing of a service by a health care professional. Whether implied warranties under Article 2 of the U.C.C. apply to such a transaction should depend on whether the predominant element of the transaction is the sale of goods or the rendering of services. If the sale of goods predominates, it would be within the scope of Article 2 and the implied warranties contained therein. However, if the service aspect predominates, there would be no implied warranties.

Although the record contains no specific findings of fact, the record does contain evidence from which it could be concluded that this transaction was principally a sale of goods and that the implied warranty of merchantability applies thereto. The evidence was also sufficient that the trier of fact could have concluded that the dentures were not fit for their ordinary purpose as required to establish a prima facie case for breach of the implied warranty of merchantability. We must affirm a law action tried to the court if there is any competent evidence to support the judgment.

In contemporary society the old distinctions separating health care professionals from other businessmen are blurring in many respects. This Court's holding that a dentist is not a merchant, and dentures, furnished by a dentist, are not goods

ignores the fact that nothing excludes them from the statutory definitions of merchant and goods. It also ignores the fact that health care professionals in some
instances are selling goods to their "patients," with the providing of professional
services being secondary to the sale. To such transactions there is no reason Article
2 of the U.C.C should not apply.

I respectfully dissent.

The implied warranty of merchantability is perhaps the most prominent
example of the special responsibility of a merchant. Another instance where
more is expected of merchants than non-merchants is with Article 2's statute
of frauds provision. U.C.C. §2-201(1) provides that sales of goods for at least
$500 require a writing that evidences the contract in order for the contract to
be enforceable. (Amended §2-201 changes $500 to $5,000 and "writing" to
"record," which includes certain retrievable electronic information.) U.C.C.
§2-201(2), however, creates an exception to the writing requirement in the
case where a merchant fails to object to the written confirmation of an oral
contract that is sent by another merchant. Thus, merchants who do not read
their mail can lose their ability to assert the statute of frauds in some situations
where similarly situated non-merchants would retain that defense.

Article 2's merchant definition section is one of those places in the UCC
where the Official Comments tell us much more than the provision itself.
U.C.C. §2-104(1) tells us that a merchant is either a person "who deals in
goods of the kind" or a person who "holds himself out as having knowledge
or skill peculiar to the practices or goods involved in the transaction." What
§2-104(1) does *not* say is that the functional consequences of being a merchant may vary depending on what kind of a merchant a person is.

Comment 2 to §2-104 introduces the concept that there are three different
categories of consequences to being a merchant. The first category of consequences involves the Article 2 rules surrounding general business practices
like answering the mail, giving firm offers, and the like. As the Comment
explains, for this category of consequences "almost every person in business"
would be considered a merchant and therefore subject to the special rules of
those sections.

The second category of consequences covers mainly the implied warranty
of merchantability. The Comment explains that only merchants who deal in
goods of the kind get saddled with that particular responsibility. Thus, for
example, a sporting goods store that made an isolated sale of paint left over
after a store repainting project would not make the implied warranty of merchantability to its paint buyer.

The final category of consequences discussed in Comment 2 deals with the
merchant's general duties of good faith and standards of fair dealing in the
trade. Relevant sections here would include those creating the special duty of
the merchant-buyer to follow a seller's reasonable instructions regarding
goods in the buyer's possession following rejection, as well as the heightened
duty of a merchant to give adequate assurance of future performance. Just like
with the first category of consequences, any person in business will be subject
to the requirements of this group of special merchant provisions.

Problem Set 1

1.1. You just graduated from law school and have taken a job as an associate at a major law firm that is known for its extensive international practice. Your firm receives a call from the Minister of Commerce of a formerly communist country that is now attempting to convert to a free-market economy. This foreign official would like your firm to serve as a consultant on the issue of whether his country should adopt a commercial code. In particular, he would like the firm to consider the following questions: What are the benefits that his country's economy can gain from enacting a commercial code as opposed to letting private agreements handle the details of all commercial dealings? For which subjects (e.g., price, quantity, place of delivery) should the code include gap-fillers? To the extent the code serves a gap-filling function, how do you decide what the gap-fillers should be (e.g., should the default mode for place of delivery be buyer's place or seller's place)? Because you have recently taken several UCC courses, your firm asks you to consider preliminary responses to these questions.

1.2.a. Lumber Works, Inc., makes a contract to sell five separate shipments of lumber to Wooden Play Sets Corporation pursuant to a single contract. The place of delivery for these shipments is not specified in the single contract that governs all five shipments. For the first three deliveries, the seller delivers the lumber to the buyer's place of business. Then the seller's daughter, a first-year law student, tells the seller that the Article 2 gap-filler for place of delivery says that delivery should be at the seller's place — in other words, that the buyer has to come and pick up the goods at the buyer's expense. After hearing this, the seller feels justified in trying to change the delivery mode for the final two deliveries within this contract. The buyer, understandably, is not happy. Does the seller have the right to insist on the buyer picking up the lumber for the last two deliveries? U.C.C. §§2-308(a), 1-201(3) (revised 1-201(b)(3)), 2-208(1) (revised 1-303(a)).

b. Suppose the same facts as part a., except this time there have been no deliveries so far under this particular contract. However, this buyer and seller have done these deals with each other several times in the past. In every prior sale between these parties, the seller has delivered the goods to the buyer. The contract for this particular sale has been signed by both parties, and nowhere does it mention place of delivery. After signing the contract but before the first delivery under this contract, the seller learns of the UCC gap-filler and decides that the buyer should come and pick up the lumber this time. May the seller insist that the buyer pick up the lumber? U.C.C. §§1-205(1) and (3) (revised 1-303(b) & (d)).

c. Suppose again the same buyer and seller of lumber, but now assume that these two parties have had no prior dealings with one another. Imagine, however, that the custom in the lumber industry is that the seller always delivers the lumber to the buyer. The contract has been signed and no place of delivery has been mentioned in the contract. The seller learns of the UCC gap-filler and wants the buyer to come and get the lumber. May the seller insist that the buyer pick up the lumber? U.C.C. §§1-201(3) (1-201(b)(3) as amended), 1-205(2) (revised 1-303(c)).

1.3.   Your favorite aunt just called you because she knows you are the only attorney in the family. It seems that Aunt Millie had taken seven reels of her home movies, representing three decades of family vacations, into the local camera shop to have the shop transfer the movies from the old-fashioned reels onto VHS tapes. Much to Aunt Millie's horror, she got a call from the camera shop yesterday in which the manager explained that a new clerk had messed up the transfer process and destroyed all of Aunt Millie's home movies. Aunt Millie related to you her disgust with the manager's offer to give her new blank movie reels and VHS tapes to make up for the destroyed movies. As you contemplate Aunt Millie's rights against the camera shop, will U.C.C. Article 2 and its warranties be part of the picture? U.C.C. §§2-102, 2-313, 2-314, 2-315.

1.4.   Your law firm was recently retained to represent Kelleher and Associates, a limited liability partnership of optometrists who specialize in making and fitting contact lenses for the "problem wearer." Patients at Kelleher generally pay about three to four times more for their contact lenses than they would at one of the national contact-lens franchises. That price, however, includes the various testing procedures that patients receive before Kelleher custom-designs the lenses. Up to this point, Kelleher has not had its patients sign any kind of contract. One of the partners at Kelleher has a daughter in her second year of law school who suggested to her dad that he might want to have patients sign in advance a form contract that disclaims all of the UCC warranties. The Kelleher partner told you that for reasons of customer good will, he would just as soon not institute that procedure unless "there are compelling reasons to do so." What is your advice? U.C.C. §§2-102, 2-105(1) (amended 2-103(1)(k)), 2-314(1), 2-315.

1.5.   Determine whether U.C.C. Article 2 applies to the following transactions. U.C.C. §§2-102, 2-105(1) (amended 2-103(1)(k)).

a.   The sale by an author of a movable paper certificate representing the author's rights to any future royalties from a book that the author has already written.

b.   The sale of natural gas.

c.   The sale of a compact disc to a consumer by a retail music store.

d.   A recording artist's sale of an original recording on compact disc to a music producer that will produce and distribute the CD.

e.   A publishing company's contract with an author to write a book.

f.   A manufacturer's contract with a merchant buyer to specially manufacture and sell a custom-made machine.

g.   A sculptor's contract with a patron of the arts to create and sell an original sculpture to the patron.

h.   The sale of a raffle ticket in which the holder of the winning ticket gets a new car.

1.6.   At your fifth law school reunion last month, you bumped into classmate Deborah Swift, a one-time law school "gunner" and currently a successful plaintiff's personal injury lawyer. After a few drinks, Deborah began bragging to you about her collection of used Rolls Royces. By the end of the evening she had agreed to sell you the one she had driven that night, a 1983 model, for just $8,000. The deal was that you were to bring her a check and pick the car up at her house at the end of the month. The day after the reunion, just to be safe, you sent Deborah a certified letter that described the terms of the bargain that you had struck. Deborah did not object to or otherwise acknowledge the letter.

Yesterday, some 20 days after the reunion, you went to Deborah's house with a certified check for $8,000. Deborah, who seemed not nearly so friendly as she was to you at the reunion, answered the door and told you that the car you wanted was worth at least $15,000, and that you would have to take her to court to try to enforce the oral contract. Will you succeed? U.C.C. §§2-201(1) and (2), 2-104(1) and (3), Official Comment 2 to §2-104.

Assignment 2: Scope Issues with Leases, CISG, and Real Estate

A. Scope of Article 2A

As far as the UCC goes, Article 2A is one of the new kids on the block. Whereas most of the other articles of the Code were introduced back in the late 1950s, the article on personal property leases was not approved by the American Law Institute(ALI) until 1987. Then, to make matters even more complicated, the ALI, on the recommendation of the National Conference of Commissioners on Uniform State Laws, passed a significant set of amendments to Article 2A in 1990.

Although lease transactions have been around for about as long as sales, favorable tax and accounting treatment caused a significant increase of leases in the United States during the 1950s and 1960s. As the number of leases increased, the common law's longstanding lack of clarity in treating this type of transaction began to become more troublesome. As a result, there was a concerted effort in the early 1980s to clarify and codify the law surrounding leases, culminating in the first and second versions of Article 2A that are noted above. By September 1, 2002, 49 states plus the District of Columbia had adopted the 1990 version of Article 2A, and another state had adopted the 1987 version of 2A.

As we will see over the course of the next several assignments, Article 2A borrows very heavily from the language and concepts of Article 2. Indeed, the Official Comment to U.C.C. §2A-101 says that "the [2A] drafting committee concluded that Article 2 was the appropriate statutory analogue." Most fundamentally, both Article 2 and 2A allow the parties to make their sale or lease contracts more or less as they wish, with gap-fillers provided as back-ups but with very few limits on freedom of contract. U.C.C. §1-102(3) (amended §1-302); Official Comment to §2A-101 ("This codification was greatly influenced by the fundamental tenet of the common law as it has developed with respect to leases of goods: freedom of the parties to contract."). Where there are significant differences between the rules of Article 2 and 2A, those differences stem from the fundamental distinction between a sale and a lease: that the lessor, unlike the seller, has a reasonable expectation of receiving the goods back at a time when the goods still have meaningful economic life.

It is easy enough to state in the abstract what is the distinction between a lease and a sale. Applying that distinction in practice, however, is another matter entirely. If you were to rent a car for $200 a week during your Florida spring break, everyone can see that such a transaction is a true lease. But suppose that you go to your local car dealer and it agrees to "lease" you a new car for five years, at $300 per month. Suppose further that you have no power to terminate your lease at any time during the five years. Finally, imagine that the lease includes a purchase option at the end of the lease for $500 — an option that, by all accounts, seems like it will be an offer that is too good to pass up. So, you might ask yourself, how exactly does this differ from a sale?

Courts have struggled for decades trying to determine whether any given transaction amounts to a "true lease" or "a disguised sale." Lots of different tests have been formulated throughout the years to aid judges in these determinations. The drafters of Article 2A, for their part, specifically endorsed what is known as "the economic realities test."

The economic realities test simply considers the likelihood, at the time the transaction is entered into, that the lessor will receive the goods back at a time when the goods still have meaningful economic life. If there is a reasonable likelihood that the lessor will indeed retain some residual interest in the goods, then the economic realities test deems the transaction to be a true lease. If not, the transaction is considered to be a disguised sale intended for security. A sale intended for security is one in which the seller sells the goods on credit, but retains a special right to foreclose on the goods in the buyer's hands if the buyer fails to pay the price.

In endorsing the economic realities test, the drafters of Article 2A intended to reject any tests that courts had used that focused on the intentions of the parties to the transaction. Some cases had concluded that as long as both parties intended a transaction to be a true lease, then so it was. One of the problems with the intent test is that the characterization of a particular transaction as a lease or sale will have consequences that transcend the two parties to the transaction. As just one example, the lease/sale characterization will determine which party, the lessor or the creditors of the lessee, has priority to the leased goods in the case of default by the lessee on its non-lease obligations.

Although the characterization of a transaction as lease or sale is an important first step in the analysis, ultimately the most crucial question is what are the functional consequences that attach to a true lease, on the one hand, and a disguised sale, on the other. The functional attributes of the distinction are of three types: tax/accounting-related, UCC-related, and bankruptcy-related.

Within the tax and accounting category, significant consequences depend on a transaction's characterization as a lease or a sale. For accounting purposes, the party acquiring goods can treat lease payments as periodic expenses; by contrast, a transaction that is a secured sale will require that the buyer's balance sheet show a debt for the purchase price. In the tax arena, the Internal Revenue Code allows a deduction for amounts paid or accrued to rent property that is used in a trade or business or in the production of income.

In contrast, the purchase of long-lived property is a capital expenditure that is not deductible when paid. If the property is used in a trade or business or in the production of income and wears out over time, its cost may be deducted through depreciation allowances. These depreciation allowances are taken over statutorily prescribed periods that are generally much shorter than the useful economic life of the property. Consequently, an owner of depreciable equipment may obtain a substantial tax advantage (i.e., front-loaded cost-recovery deductions) relative to a lessee. In addition, on the state and local level, the difference between lease tax rates and sales tax rates can be meaningful.

With regard to differences in UCC treatment, the characterization of a transaction as lease or sale will determine whether Article 2A applies or, instead, Articles 2 and 9. Whether Article 2A applies instead of Article 2 will not necessarily bring with it significant consequences. The key article at stake is Article 9. If a purported lease transaction is found to be a sale, typically the "lessor" will at least want the transaction to be treated as a secured sale rather than as an unsecured sale. If the sale is an unsecured sale, then the "lessor" would have no special rights to the leased goods. If the sale is considered a secured sale, the "lessor" would have the chance to qualify for the special Article 9 rights of a secured creditor.

In order for the "lessor" to have the special rights of an Article 9 secured creditor, there are certain hoops that the lessor will have to jump through. If the transaction is found to be a disguised sale, the penalty for the putative lessor for failing to meet the Article 9 requirements is that the lessor may lose certain rights against the lessee as well as against third parties of the lessee. The lessor may lose the ability to repossess the goods or to seize the goods when third parties take them for collection.

Carlson v. Giachetti
616 N.E.2d 810 (Mass. App. 1993)

GILLERMAN, J.

Whether, under the Uniform Commercial Code, an equipment lease is to be treated as a "true lease" or as a security agreement is an issue that has been litigated extensively for more than two decades, but has yet to be discussed in any detail by a Massachusetts appellate court. We must do so now, with the benefit of the findings of fact made by a judge of the Superior Court after a bench trial.

The material facts found by the judge are these. John Carlson manufactures, sells and leases machinery used in the repair of damaged automobile bodies. In April of 1988 Carlson leased a six-tower chassis liner, a machine used in auto body shops to remove dents from damaged cars, together with a complete accessory package, to one Richard A. King, the owner of an auto body repair shop in Quincy. The lease called for a monthly payment of $572.40 for each of sixty months, with two such payments to be made in advance of delivery. The sixty payments came to a total of $34,344. King made the required advance payment for two months, and then defaulted.

In October of 1988, King went out of business and sold the chassis liner to the defendant Louis Giacchetti for $8,600. Giacchetti had no notice of Carlson's interest in the machinery, for it was not until late in December that Carlson filed financing statements in the appropriate public offices. In April, 1989, Carlson brought this action against Giacchetti, who refused to return the chassis liner to Carlson, for conversion and violation of G.L. c. 93A. If the court found the document was a "true lease" and not a security agreement subject to the provisions of article 9 of the Uniform Commercial Code, then King had no power to transfer title to the equipment, and Giacchetti may be liable for conversion.

The judge, however, resolved the issue of ownership in favor of Giacchetti by ruling that the lease agreement between the original parties was not a "true lease," but rather, a security agreement, and that Carlson's failure to perfect his security interest until December was fatal. See §9-301(1)(c) [§9-317(a) as amended]. We disagree with the trial judge and, for the reasons discussed below, we conclude that the lease was not intended as a security agreement.

We look to §§9-102 [§9-109 as amended] and 1-201(37) [§1-203 as amended with respect to the "lease" definition] to determine whether a contract, characterized by the parties as a lease, is a "true lease" or a security agreement. Article 9 applies, except as otherwise provided, to "any transaction (regardless of its form) which is intended to create a security interest in personal property or fixtures. . . ." §9-102(1)(a). Section 9-102(2) provides that article 9 applies to "security interests created by contract including . . . [a] lease . . . intended as security." §9-102(2).

The definition of a security agreement is contained in §1-201(37), which provides in relevant part: "Whether a lease is intended as security is to be determined by the facts of each case; however, (a) the inclusion of an option to purchase does not of itself make the lease one intended for security, and (b) an agreement that upon compliance with the terms of the lease the lessee shall become or has the option to become the owner of the property for no additional consideration or for a nominal consideration does make the lease one intended for security."

The lease in the case before us, the principal provisions of which we summarize in the margin, does not include an option in the lessee to purchase the equipment for no, or nominal, consideration, and thus the instrument does not fall within subparagraph (b) of section 1-201(37). On that basis, the issue which arises under both sections of the Code is whether, on all the facts, the parties intended to create a security interest.

While the Code directs the analysis to what was intended by the parties, it offers no guidelines for deciding the question (other than the rule of law, not applicable to this case, expressed in §1-201[37][b]). Obviously, the declared intention of the parties, standing alone, cannot be decisive. "No one would contend that third parties were bound by the clear intention of the contracting parties to use a device they call a lease if the effect created by the transaction is that of a sale. The test certainly must be applied in accordance with the outward appearance of the facts rather than in accordance with the intent held by one or both of the parties while creating effects contrary to those normally produced by the kind of instrument purportedly employed by the parties." Coogan, Leases of Equipment and Some Other Unconventional Security Devices: An Analysis of UCC Section 1-201(37) and Article 9, 1973 Duke L.J. 909, 916 n.12 (1973). Professor Gilmore, in his treatise on security interests, has also written that the word "intended" in §1-201(37) "has nothing to do with the subjective intention of the parties, or either of them." Gilmore, Security Interests in Personal Property, §11.2, at 338 (1965).

The vagaries inherent in §1-201(37) have obliged the courts to resort to the "facts of each case," as directed by the terms of §1-201(37), with the effect of producing complex guidelines for adjudication which have left judicial decisions entirely unpredictable. The high water mark was reached in the decision of the Bankruptcy Court in In re Brookside Drug Store, Inc., 3 B.R. 120 (Bankr. D. Conn. 1980) where the court, in order to determine the intent of the parties, identified no fewer than sixteen separate factors, having to do with the content of the document and the factual setting of the transaction, as relevant to the ultimate determination. The factors recited by the Bankruptcy Court in *Brookside* include those that focus on whether the lease is a "net lease" (i.e., where the lessee assumes all risk of loss and pays all taxes, insurance, maintenance, and the like), whether the lease is a "full payout lease" (i.e., where the lessee pays an amount equal to or greater than the lessor's cost of the goods or their fair market value), whether the lessor is a financing agency, whether there is an acceleration clause in the lease, whether the lessor has permission to file a financing statement, and whether the lessee has an option to purchase the goods for a nominal consideration. The *Brookside* approach to the problem was adopted by the Bankruptcy Court in In re Mariner Communications, Inc., 76 B.R. 242 (Bankr. D. Mass. 1987), the decision relied upon by Giacchetti and by the trial judge in this case. We believe that a preferable approach to the problem is that proposed by the National Conference of Commissioners on Uniform State Laws and the American Law Institute, the original sponsors of the Uniform Commercial Code. The sponsors approved a revised §1-201(37) in 1987, as well as a definition, for the first time, of "lease" in a new article 2A.

The revised version of §1-201(37) (hereinafter "revised §1-201[37]") deletes all reference to the intent of the parties. It offers, instead, a straightforward economic analysis as the focal point of inquiry: if the obligations of the lessee under the lease are not subject to termination by the lessee, and if the lease is for the full economic life of the goods (or if the lessee may, without further consideration, acquire all rights in the goods for the full economic life of the goods) then a security interest is created. But if the lessor retains the reversionary interest in the goods, then the transaction is a true lease. Revised §1-201(37) also identifies four factors any of which, if included in the lease, do not create a security interest. Two of these factors bear on the facts of this case: the "full payout lease," and the "net lease."

The Legislature has not adopted revised §1-201(37), but that does not preclude this court from looking to the revised section for guidance. [Author's note: In 1996, Massachusetts adopted the revised §1-201(37) and the 1990 version of Article 2A.] We see nothing in the proposed revision which is inconsistent with the existing statutory provision. Construing the phrase "intended as security" to refer principally to the distribution of rights in respect of the economic life of the leased equipment will most likely reveal what was "intended" by the parties. Where, for example, the economic life of the leased equipment plainly will not have been exhausted at the end of the term of the lease, there will be little, if any, justification for the conclusion that the parties intended a security interest incident to a sale, rather than a lease. In our view, the provisions of revised §1-201(37) illuminate, but do not alter, the meaning of the existing provisions of §1-201(37). Further, it facilitates an uncomplicated analysis of the lease in dispute, and thereby enhances for practitioners the predictability of the judicial outcome.

In the document before us the lessee's obligations were non-cancellable by the lessee, and the lease contained no option to purchase by the lessee. Further, the lessee was obligated to keep the leased equipment in good repair and condition and, at the end of the term of the lease, to assemble and deliver the equipment to the lessor. Consistent with these covenants of the lessee was the judge's finding that upon the termination of the lease Carlson "would . . . be entitled to a return of the equipment which still had a significant resale value." This last finding by the judge establishes that Carlson had reserved an economically significant reversionary interest in the lease goods. That finding, in the context of the lease provisions we have just described, requires the conclusion that the lease before us is a true lease and was not intended as a security agreement.

The judge made numerous findings with regard to the terms of the lease, the cumulative effect of which was that the arrangement was found to be both a net lease and a full payout lease to Carlson's substantial benefit. But these provisions, either alone or in combination, do not call for a different result in this case. The contractual arrangements which are so distinctly in favor of Carlson do not uncommonly reflect the relative bargaining positions of the parties, the value of the credit provided by a lease, and the uniqueness of the equipment; consequently, they are as likely to appear in a "true lease" as they are in a secured transaction.

The judgment is vacated and the case remanded to the Superior Court for a trial on the issue of conversion, and, if appropriate, the assessment of the plaintiff's damages, if any.

SO ORDERED.

The property and priority rights that hinge on the characterization of a transaction as a true lease or a disguised sale will become important if the lessee fails to fulfill its obligations under the contract. When that happens, the lessee's bankruptcy filing may not be far behind. If the lessee files for bankruptcy, as the following case shows, still further consequences will depend on the transaction's status as a lease or a secured sale.

In re Bailey

326 B.R. 156 (W.D. Ark. 2005)

MIXON, J.

On May 7, 2004, Keith and Karrie Bailey ("Debtors"), filed a voluntary petition for relief under the provisions of chapter 13 of the United States Bankruptcy Code. On November 16, 2004, Lafayette Investments, Inc. ("Lafayette") filed an objection to confirmation as well as several other pleadings. . . .

Lafayette objects to confirmation on the single ground that it is not a secured creditor, but rather the lessor of two pieces of equipment pursuant to valid leases and that the Debtors must treat its claim in accordance with 11 U.S.C. §365 as an unexpired lease.

The Debtors' first plan was filed on May 7, 2004, and it treated Lafayette's two claims as secured, one in the amount of $22,300.00 secured by collateral valued at $18,000.00 and the other in the amount of $20,800.00 secured by collateral valued at $18,000.00. The 60-month plan proposed identical payments for each claim in the amount of $357.00 per month with interest accruing at the rate of 7% per annum. The plan further proposed that Lafayette retain its lien and be paid over the life of the plan the value of its collateral or the amount of its claim, whichever is less. . . .

The testimony introduced at trial conflicts with some of the documentary evidence. Lafayette called Donald E. Fritsche ("Fritsche") as a witness. On behalf of

Lafayette, Fritsche negotiated the leases of two 2000-model Freightliner over-the-road tractors with Keith Bailey (hereinafter "Debtor"). The lease payments for the two units are $828.00 and $773.00 per month. He stated that Lafayette received a down payment of $2200.00 on the first unit and $3700.00 on the second unit when the leases were executed. (Tr. at 10.) Fritsche testified that the Debtor has made no regular monthly payment on either unit. The leases were executed April 5, 2004, and the Debtor filed a petition for relief under the provisions of chapter 13 on May 7, 2004.

Fritsche testified that the Debtor had an option to purchase the units for an amount equal to 10% of the tractors' fair market value, determined as of the time of the commencement of the leases, less the down payments. (Tr. at 14.) Title to the units remained in the name of Lafayette until the purchase option was exercised. Mid-Am Financial, the bank that financed the transaction, holds a lien in each title, which is evidenced on the face of the titles. The monthly payments the Debtor makes to Lafayette under the leases are equal in amount to the payments Lafayette owes Mid-Am Financial.

According to Fritsche, Lafayette's profit under each lease is the down payment and the 10% buy-out at the end of the lease. (Tr. at 16.) In the event of default, Fritsche stated Lafayette would be entitled to repossess the units and re-lease them, but that the Debtor still owes the balance of the lease payments unless Lafayette can mitigate its damages by re-leasing the units. The Debtor also pays the license fees and the expense of the insurance and repair. Fritsche stated he was unaware of any personal property tax due on the units. He stated the units should be worth approximately $14,000.00 to $15,000.00 at the end of the lease term. When asked why he would trade this value for a small purchase price at the end of the lease, he stated, "Because I get the down payment and the 10% at the end and . . . that's the program that we use." (Tr. at 18.)

The Debtor testified that he thought he was purchasing, not leasing, the units in question. (Tr. at 29.) He stated that he pays personal property taxes on the vehicles.

Exhibit "A" to Creditor's Exhibit 1 is a document styled "Equipment Lease." The lease is an eleven-page document in small print. The document purports to be a true lease. With some exceptions, the lease generally agrees with Fritsche's explanation of the lease terms in his testimony.

The lease has a provision defining "projected residual value" (Creditor's Ex. 1, Ex. "A" at ¶1.30) and a definition of "net sales proceeds," defined as a sum computed as the then fair market value minus lessor's expenses in obtaining possession and selling the equipment at fair market value (Creditor's Ex. 1, Ex. "A" at ¶1.25). The lease contains a provision detailing how the parties will arrive at the "residual value." This provision provides the following:

> Section 3.17 Residual Value. The parties estimate that the Actual Residual Value of the Equipment at expiration of the Term of this lease will be equal to the Projected Residual Value set forth in Schedule 1 hereto. If the Actual Residual Value of the Equipment at expiration of the Term of this Lease exceeds or is less than the Projected Residual Value, the total amount of the rent payable hereunder shall be adjusted accordingly. Within ten (10) days following the final determination of the Actual Residual Value of the Equipment, if the amount thereof exceeds the Projected Residual Value, the difference shall be paid by the Lessor to the Lessee. Conversely, if the Actual Residual Value is less

than the Projected Residual Value, the difference shall be paid by the Lessee to the Lessor within said ten (10) day period.

(Creditor's Ex. 1, Ex. A at ¶3.17.)

Despite this language, the written lease does not contain an option to purchase and specifically states that the transaction is a true lease and that the lessee has no option to purchase. (Creditor's Ex. 1, Ex. 1 at ¶4.13.) Significantly, the sub-section also provides that in the event the document is not construed as a lease by a court of competent jurisdiction, the Lessor shall have a security interest in the equipment. The agreement provides that the law of Missouri shall govern and the testimony of Fritsche was that the lease was executed in Bates City, Missouri.

Debtors' Exhibit No. 1 included a document entitled "Addendum to Equipment Lease Lafayette Investments, Inc. d/b/a Mid Am Truck Center Lease/Purchase Agreement Acceptance Certificate." The addendum stated the following:

I Keith Bailey agree to all terms and conditions of the lease purchase contract. I also understand that at [sic], for any reason during my term of the lease, if I feel that it is necessary to bring the vehicle back, the following conditions will apply:

1. The vehicle will be in road-worthy condition, including the engine, transmission, rear ends, tires in D.O.T. quality, and all other specs that Lafayette Investments, Inc. deems necessary for resale of the truck.
2. Account on lease must be in current condition.
3. Ninety days (3 months) of payments must be submitted at the time of turn-in to ensure the quality of the truck and for time and hardship it creates Mid Am Truck Center.
4. Commencement and Expiration Dates.
   The Commencement Date of the Term of this Lease was April 1, 2004, and the expiration date thereof will be April 1, 2007.

(Debtor's Ex. 1.)

The addendum had other documents attached to it, including a form styled "Uniform Sales & Use Tax Certificate" indicating that Lafayette was the seller and the Debtor, Keith Bailey, was the buyer. The Addendum itself referred to the transaction as a "Lease/Purchase Agreement." (Debtors' Exhibit 1.) The lease was assigned to Mid-Am Financial as collateral for the loan to Lafayette. Debtor's Exhibit 2 is a payment and amortization schedule evidencing a loan at 20% interest per annum from Lafayette to the Debtor of $20,800.00 for 36 months with total principal payments of $20,800.00 and total interest payments of $7,028.09. Similar lease documents were submitted by Lafayette as Creditor's Exhibit 2 and pertained to the second tractor lease, except that no payment and amortization schedule was presented as evidence with regard to the second lease.

If the transaction is construed as a sale of personal property and is secured by a perfected security interest in the property, the Debtor must propose to treat Lafayette's claim as provided in section 1325(a)(4) and (5) of the Bankruptcy Code. If the transaction is a true lease and the Debtor desires to keep the property, then the Debtor must assume the lease, cure all defaults, and perform the lease according to its terms in compliance with sections 1322(b)(7) and 365 of the Bankruptcy Code. In re Sellers, 26 U.C.C. Rep. Serv. 2d 42 (Bankr. N.D. Ala.

1994); In re Taylor, 130 B.R. 849, 853 (Bankr. E.D. Ark. 1991) (citing 11 U.S.C. 365(b)(1); In re Urbanco, Inc., 122 B.R. 513 (Bankr. W.D. Mich. 1991); In re Wallace, 122 B.R. 222 (Bankr. D.N.J. 1990)).

To determine whether an agreement represents a sale or a lease, the bankruptcy court must look to applicable state law. In re Architectural Millwork, Inc., 226 B.R. 551, 553 (Bankr. W.D. Va. 1998) (citing In re Yarbrough, 211 B.R. 654, 656 (Bankr. W.D. Tenn. 1997); In re Nat'l Traveler, 110 B.R. 619, 620 (Bankr. M.D. Ga. 1990)). The parties agree that Missouri law governs the issue of whether this agreement is a sale or a lease.

The briefs filed by the parties are generally unhelpful. . . .

The applicable law is a Missouri statute that mirrors the current version of Section 1-201(37) of the Uniform Commercial Code. The revision of U.C.C. Section 1-201(37) shifts the focus away from the intent of the parties and toward the economic realities of the transaction. In re Yarbrough, 211 B.R. 654 (Bankr. W.D. Tenn. 1997) (citing U.C.C. §1-201(37), cmt.; Laura J. Paglia, Note, U.C.C. Article 2A: Distinguishing Between True Leases and Secured Sales, 63 St. John's L. Rev. 69, 75-76 (1988)). . . .

In 2001, the late Judge Frank Koger of the Bankruptcy Court for the Western District of Missouri decided the issue of whether, under Missouri law as amended in 1992, an agreement was a true lease or security for a conditional sales contract. See In re Hoskins, 266 B.R. 154 (Bankr. W.D. Mo. 2001). . . .

Observing that no Missouri appellate, bankruptcy or Eighth Circuit case had addressed the issue of true lease versus security interest in the context of the amended version of section 400.1-201(37), the court looked for guidance to cases from other jurisdictions with identical U.C.C. provisions. From its examination of those cases, the court developed an analytical framework under the statute.

The court must first ask whether the debtor has a right to terminate the purported lease prior to expiration of its term. *Hoskins,* 266 B.R. at 160. A provision in a contract requiring the lessee to remain financially liable to the lessor for payments that become due after the termination date does not constitute the right to terminate under the statute. *Hoskins,* 266 B.R. at 160. If the debtor does not have a right to terminate, the court then examines whether any of the four enumerated conditions have been satisfied. See Mo. Ann. Stat. §400.1-201(37)(a)-(d) *supra.* If so, the parties have entered into a security agreement as a matter of law. *Hoskins,* 266 B.R. at 160 (quoting In re Owen, 221 B.R. 56, 60-61 (Bankr. N.D.N.Y. 1998) (describing bright-line test for security interest)).

If there is no right to terminate but also none of the four conditions apply, the court cannot find that, as a matter of law, the contract constitutes a security agreement. However, the analysis does not end here. The court must further examine the specific facts of the case to determine whether, despite failing the bright line test, the "economics of the transaction" still suggest a security interest.

In *Hoskins,* there was no right to terminate; however, none of the four additional conditions was satisfied. Therefore, the contract did not pass the bright-line test of a security interest. The court then proceeded to examine the transaction in light of factors relied upon by courts prior to the 1992 amendment to the extent the factors were consistent with the amended statute. Among the relevant factors in *Hoskins* were the facts that the lessee was not under an absolute obligation to purchase the leased property and that the purchase option was not for a nominal sum. These two factors further supported Judge Koger's conclusion that the transaction was a true lease.

Applying this framework to the instant case, the Court finds that because the Debtor does not have a legal right to cease payments and walk away from the lease without liability for the deficiency, the Debtor does not have a right to terminate under the purported lease. According to the Addendum to each lease, the Debtor is liable for three months' lease payments if he chooses to "bring back" the equipment. Lafayette's witness testified that if the Debtor terminates the lease, he is responsible for the remaining lease payments unless Lafayette is successful in releasing the equipment. Under either condition, the Debtor remains financially liable to the lessor for payments that become due after the termination date.

The next step is to determine whether any of the four enumerated conditions listed in the statute apply. The Court finds that the fourth condition is applicable: the lessee has an option to become the owner of the goods for nominal additional consideration upon compliance with the lease agreement. In discussing nominal value, a leading treatise on the Uniform Commercial Code has stated that nominal value is determined by examining the parties' prediction, at the time of the contract, of the concluding value of the goods. The test is whether "the option price is so low that the lessee will certainly exercise it and will, in all plausible circumstances, leave no meaningful reversion for the lessor." James J. White & Robert S. Summers, 4 Uniform Commercial Code §30-3 at 33 (5th ed. 2002).

The question of whether an option price is nominal was recently discussed by the Bankruptcy Court for the Southern District of Illinois. The court stated:

> Section 1-201(37)(x) of Illinois' Uniform Commercial Code strives to delineate whether an option price is nominal. It provides, in pertinent part, that additional consideration is nominal if "it is less than the lessee's reasonably predictable cost of performing under the lease agreement if the option is not exercised." 10 ILCS 5/1-201(37)(x). This section codifies what is traditionally known as the "economic realities" test by focusing on whether the lessee has, given all the facts and circumstances, no reasonable alternative but to exercise the purchase option. See [In re] Taylor, 209 B.R. [482] at 486 [(Bankr. S.D. Ill. 1997)]. In other words, if only a fool would fail to exercise the option, the option price is considered nominal and the transaction revealed to be a disguised sale. Id.; see also 4 J. White & R. Summers, supra, §30-3 at 18. Under this test, it is obvious that an option price constituting merely six percent of the total rentals is so economically compelling that the debtor would be foolish to forego its exercise. The lack of a rational alternative is made more evident still by reviewing the contractual payment schedule. After completion of fifty monthly payments totaling $318,920.00 for Agreement 1 and $230,204.48 for Agreement 2, no reasonable lessee would cede the cows if they could be purchased for a payment equivalent to only three months' rent.

In re Buehne Farms, Inc., 321 B.R. 239, 245-46 (Bankr. S.D. Ill. 2005). . . .

Even though there is no contractual obligation to exercise the option to purchase in this case, the Debtor has no other reasonable alternative. Lafayette's witness testified that at the expiration of the lease the tractors will be worth $15,000.00 each and he will sell them to the Debtor for their projected residual value of approximately $2230.00 and $2080.00. The purchase option in this case is 13% or 14% of what Lafayette estimates the fair market value will be when the lease expires. If the Debtor fails to exercise the option, the Debtor will lose approximately $12,920.00 to $12,770.00 in equipment value (the estimated fair market value less the purchase price) for each tractor. If he does purchase the equipment, he pays only $2200.00 and $2080.00, much less than he will lose if the option is not exercised. Therefore, the additional consideration is nominal because it is less than the Debtor's reasonably predictable cost of performing under the lease but not exercising the option.

Because the Debtor may not terminate the agreements and the consideration to purchase is nominal, the transactions between the Debtor and Lafayette are sales for security and not leases as a matter of law. Additionally, the Court observes that this transaction is characterized by numerous other factors relied upon by other courts to support the conclusion that the transaction was a sale and not a true lease. The court in In re Buehne Farms detailed some of these additional factors:

> Having found that the debtor may not terminate the agreements and that the consideration required to purchase the cows is nominal, the Court finds that the agreements are secured sales *per se.* Given this finding, the Court need not address any of the other arguments of the parties.
>
>   The Court notes, however, the existence of other signposts indicating that the agreements are disguised sales. Under the agreements, the debtor bears all costs of insurance, taxes, upkeep and veterinary care for the cows, as well as the risk of loss if the cows are injured or die. See, e.g., Taylor, 209 B.R. at 487-88. In addition, the debtor was required to pay advance rent of $13,280.00 under Agreement 1, and of $9,583.52 under Agreement 2. See, e.g., Orix [Credit Alliance, Inc. v. Pappas], 946 F.2d [1258] at 1262 [(7th Cir. 1991)] (requirement of a down payment held to be a factor indicating a secured sale). Moreover, movants did not own the cows when they agreed to "lease" them to the debtor. Instead, the cows were supplied by third parties, suggesting that movants were simply financing a sale. *Id.* at 1263. These indicia of a disguised sale are not offset by the presence of language in the agreements providing that movants retain "[a]ll right, title and interest" in the cows. The appearance of such language in a purported lease has been held not determinative of whether the "lessee" is acquiring equity in the "leased" property. Id.

In re Buehne Farms, Inc., 321 B.R. at 246-47.

In the instant case, signposts indicative of a sale include the facts that the Debtor bears the risk of loss, must pay applicable taxes, must maintain insurance with Lafayette as loss payee, is responsible for maintenance and repair of the property, and was required to make a down payment on each piece of equipment before the lease commenced. Furthermore, the Debtor was furnished an amortization schedule that refers to the transaction as a loan and breaks the rent payments into principal and interest.

Also present here is the fact that Lafayette purchased the units and financed them with Mid-Am Financial, paying note payments exactly equal to the lease payments owed by the Debtor to Lafayette. According to Lafayette's own witness, its profits were not derived from the monthly payments but instead from the down payment and the purchase option price. Additionally, the written agreement provided that Lafayette was granted a security interest in the event the transaction was regarded as a sale. (However, there was no evidence that the security interest had been perfected).

For the reasons stated, the Court finds that under Missouri law the agreement between Lafayette and the Debtor was a sale for security and the objection to confirmation is overruled, the motion to assume or reject the unexpired lease is denied, and the motion for relief from stay is denied. . . .

The Missouri code section that was discussed in *In re Bailey* is the 1990 amendment to U.C.C. §1-201(37) (§1-203 as amended with respect to the "lease" definition), which defines "security interest," the Code's chosen term for the flipside to the lessor's interest under a "true lease." Although the UCC also defines "lease" at §2A-103(1)(j) (amended §2A-103(1)(p)), the definition of "security interest" gives much more guidance than the almost tautological definition of "lease" (which includes the quite unhelpful observation that "a sale . . . is not a lease").

The UCC's definition of security interest properly concedes that "[w]hether a transaction creates a lease or a security interest is determined by the facts of each case . . ." U.C.C. §1-201(37) (revised §1-203) does, however, do two useful things. First, it sets out four different scenarios in which the transaction in question *must* be considered a disguised sale. This list is not intended to be exclusive, but it at least gives us some situations in which the statute speaks with certainty on the lease/sale question.

Second, U.C.C. §1-201(37) sets out a number of factors that do not by themselves necessarily create a disguised sale. For example, the subsection says that just because a lease includes a purchase option at fair market value does not of itself turn the lease into a disguised sale. It also says that just because the lessee agrees to assume the risk of loss or to pay insurance or taxes on the goods does not turn the transaction into a disguised sale. These provisions were inserted to reverse some case law that had, in the drafters' view, wrongly concluded that certain transactions were disguised sales merely because of one of the factors that §1-201(37) now rejects as being dispositive on the question.

In addition to providing some guidance as to the distinction between a true lease and a disguised sale, the drafters of Article 2A also created special rules for two distinct kinds of leases: the consumer lease and the finance lease. Most of the provisions in Article 2A assume a basic two-party, arms-length lease transaction in which both parties have roughly equal bargaining power.

With respect to the consumer lease, however, the drafters did not assume equal bargaining power and therefore created some special protections for the consumer lessee. U.C.C. §2A-103(1)(e) defines a consumer lease as a lease transaction between a lessor that is in the business of leasing and an individual lessee who leases goods for personal, family or household use. Amended Article 2A retains the same concept by bifurcating the definition of "consumer lease" now found in §2A-103(1)(e) into a "consumer" portion, §2A-103(1)(e), and a "consumer lease" portion, §2A-103(1)(f). Some of the unique benefits accorded to the consumer lessee include prohibitions against bad-faith accelerations by the lessor, special disclosure requirements, and heightened unconscionability protections. U.C.C. §§2A-109, 2A-208(2), 2A-108(2).

The finance lease departs from the paradigm lease transaction in that it involves three parties rather than two, and the putative "lessor" is really no more than a provider of financing to the lessee. As we will see later, the drafters of Article 2A included a number of provisions that reduce the finance lessor's responsibility for the performance of the leased goods and instead create direct rights for the lessee against the seller, known as the "supplier."

B.   Scope of the CISG

If the task of the UCC drafters seemed daunting, consider what faced those who attempted to create a commercial code that would govern transactions between parties in different countries with widely diverse cultural and legal systems. It is no wonder that the concept of an international commercial code had been tried but had failed several times in the past. Yet with the dizzying increase in the pace of international trade, finally in the 1980s the various barriers were overcome that had previously prevented the widespread adoption of such a code.

In 1980 the United Nations Commission on International Trade submitted the Convention on Contracts for the International Sales of Goods (CISG) to 62 nations in Vienna. Presently over 60 countries have ratified the CISG, including such major world trade players as the United States, China, France, Germany, Canada, and Mexico. Read together, Articles 1 and 6 of the CISG say that unless the parties otherwise specify, the provisions of the CISG will apply to sales of goods contracts between parties with places of business in "Contracting States," i.e., countries that have ratified the CISG. The CISG will only apply, however, if the parties have reason to know by the time of contract formation that they have places of business in different Contracting States. C.I.S.G. Art. 1(2).

The CISG, which became effective in 1988, defines a party's "place of business" as the place "which has the closest relationship to the contract and its performance..." C.I.S.G. Art. 10(a). The CISG provides that it applies to "contracts for the sale of goods," C.I.S.G. Art. 1(1), but then it fails to define just what constitutes "goods." Though the CISG does not define "goods," it does specifically address the issue of mixed goods-and-services contracts by expressly excluding in Article 3(2) contracts where "the preponderant part of [the seller's obligation] consists in the supply of labor or other services."

Viva Vino Import Corp. v. Farnese Vini S.r.l.
2000 WL 1224903 (E.D. Pa. 2000)

DUBOIS, J.

... This case arises out of three alleged agreements between plaintiff, Viva Vino Import Corporation, a Pennsylvania corporation and defendant, Farnese Vini S.r.l., an Italian company. The agreements provided, in essence, for distribution of defendant's wines in Pennsylvania and other parts of the United States by plaintiff.

The Complaint contains four counts: (1) breach of contract; (2) promissory estoppel; (3) unjust enrichment; and (4) interference with business relations. Defendant's Counterclaim is based on breach of contract.

Plaintiff argues that the United Nations Convention on Contracts for the International Sale of Goods, codified at 15 U.S.C.A. App. 1998 (the "CISG"), and/or Pennsylvania law should apply to all of plaintiff's claims and the Counterclaim. Defendant contends that Italian law should apply to all such claims. . . .

The CISG does not apply to tort claims. Consequently, it is inapplicable to plaintiff's claim of interference with business relations.

There is no dispute that both the United States and Italy are signatories to the CISG. When two foreign nations are signatories to the CISG, that Treaty governs contracts for the sale of goods between parties whose places of business are in such nations unless the contract contains a choice of law provision to the contrary. See 15 U.S.C. App. at Art. 1(1)(a); see also Filanto, S.p.A. v. Chilewich Int'l Corp., 789 F. Supp. 1229, 1237 (S.D.N.Y. 1992). The agreements at issue do not contain a choice of law provision.

Defendant challenges the application of the CISG to this case on the ground that none of the agreements at issue had as the subject a particular sale of goods, and none had definite terms regarding quantity and price. See Helen Kaminski Pty. Ltd. v. Marketing Australian Prods., 1997 WL 414137, at *2-3 (S.D.N.Y. July 23, 1997) (refusing to apply the CISG to a distributorship agreement because it did not contain definite terms regarding the price or types of goods to be sold); see also 15 U.S.C.A. App. at Art. 14.

The three agreements between plaintiff and defendant were (1) an exclusive distributorship agreement; (2) an agreement granting plaintiff a 25% interest in defendant; and (3) a sales commission agreement. None of these agreements were for a specific sale of goods, and none had specific terms as to price and quantity. Although exclusive distributorship agreements are considered contracts for the sale of goods under the Uniform Commercial Code adopted in Pennsylvania, this approach has been rejected in connection with the CISG. See *Helen Kaminski,* 1997 WL 414137, at *2.

This Court agrees with the rationale adopted by the court in *Kaminski* and concludes that the CISG does not apply to distributorship contracts that do not cover the sale of specific goods and contain definite terms regarding quantity and price. Because the agreements at issue in this case do not cover the sale of specific goods and set forth definite terms regarding quantity and price, the CISG is inapplicable. . . .

Like Article 2 of the UCC, the CISG is by its terms a default mode that parties may opt out of. C.I.S.G. Art. 6. A comparison of the scope of the CISG with UCC Article 2 reveals at least three key matters included in UCC Article 2 but excluded from the CISG. First, the CISG does not cover the sale of consumer goods, unless the seller neither knew nor should have known that the goods were being purchased for a consumer purpose. C.I.S.G. Art. 2(a). Second, Article 5 says that the CISG does not apply to the liability of the seller for death or personal injury caused by the goods sold. Finally, the CISG specifically excludes from its coverage issues of whether the sale to the buyer cuts off the property interests of third parties in the goods that were sold. C.I.S.G. Art. 4(b).

The gap-filling rules of the CISG were difficult to settle on, given the various legal cultures of the several countries that were involved in the drafting process. Unlike with the UCC, there is no body of "common law" to draw upon where the CISG is silent. In Article 7(1), the CISG says that "[q]uestions concerning matters governed by this Convention which are not expressly settled in it are to be settled in conformity with the general principles on which it is based or, in the absence of such principles, in conformity with the law applicable by virtue of the rules of private international law." The reference to "private international law" is to the choice-of-law rules that will determine whose domestic laws will govern a particular contract dispute.

C.   Real Estate

There is no widely adopted uniform code in the real estate system that plays a role comparable to that played by the UCC in the personal property system. Thus, real estate law is often a function of the geographical idiosyncrasies of particular states or regions of the country. Furthermore, since real estate by definition is not portable, the system does not have the same need for uniform rules governing interstate transactions as does the system for the sale of personal property.

Nevertheless, the common law in most states, plus some individual non-uniform state statutes, have ended up creating default terms that are analogous to some of the most important default terms that are found in Article 2 of the U.C.C. For example, these scattered statutes and the common law will read into most real estate conveyances certain implied warranties.

Later in the book, there will be a discussion of the role of brokers in the real estate system, a role which includes the creation and distribution of local "form contracts" that serve as starting points for parties to various standard, small-sized real estate transactions. These form contracts, because of their wide use in most local markets, serve a default-term function in that their terms will govern unless the parties agree to modify them.

Although U.C.C. Article 2 covers the sale of personal property, it includes one provision that is worth noting in the context of real estate sales. U.C.C. §2-107 attempts to draw a line between the personal property and real property aspects of sales that in some respects affect both. Section 2-107(1) says that a contract for the sale of things which are to be removed from realty, such as minerals, oil and gas, or structures attached to land, is covered by Article 2 if the materials are to be severed by the seller.

Section 2-107(2) covers the sale of timber as well as things not covered in subsection (1) that can be removed from realty without material harm to the realty. A contract for the sale of these readily severable items will be covered by Article 2 whether the buyer or the seller does the severing.

Problem Set 2

2.1. Lou's Used Cars for Less both sells and leases used cars. Determine whether the following transactions, all of which purport to be leases, are in fact true leases or instead are disguised sales. U.C.C. §2A-103(1)(j), Official Comment (j) to §2A-103, §1-201(37), Official Comment 37 to §1-201 (as amended, §2A-103(1)(p), Preliminary Comment (p) to §2A-103, §1-203, Comments 1 & 2 to §1-203).

a.   Martha Keough leases a used Cadillac from Lou. The Cadillac is three years old and its reasonably predicted useful life is 15 years from the lease's inception. Had Martha purchased the car, the cash price would have been $20,000. The terms of the lease are that Martha will pay Lou $300 per month for the next 60 months. At the end of the lease, she has the option to purchase the car for $7,000, which is its predicted fair-market value at the time the option is to be exercised. The lease provides that Martha will pay the insurance on the car and will be responsible for paying for maintenance during the course of the lease. Martha has no option to terminate the lease before the five-year period is up.

b.   Same facts as part a., except Martha agrees to pay Lou $600 per month for 60 months for the same car.

c.   Same facts as part a., except that the car's reasonably predicted useful life is only five-and-a-half years from the lease's inception, and the car is expected to be worth just $500 at the end of the five-year lease term. The purchase option is still $7,000.

d.   Same facts as part a., except that Martha has a ten-year renewal option for $10 per year at the end of the original five-year lease.

e.   Same facts as part a., except that Martha has a ten-year renewal option for $10 per year at the end of the original five-year lease, and she also has a right to terminate the original five-year lease at any time.

f.   Same facts as part a., except that Martha ends up driving the car so much that the car wears out completely in only three years.

g.   Same facts as part a., except the car's reasonably predicted useful life is only five years from the lease's inception, but Martha can terminate the lease at any time by paying a fee of $5,000.

2.2.   Brigid Rogers owns and operates a year-round amusement park. She agrees to lease a new ride, the Portable Death Watch, from Acme Fun Rides, Inc. The terms of the lease are that Brigid will pay $300 per month for 10 years, at which point the Portable Death Watch will be returned to Acme. The expected useful life of the ride is 20 years, and its cash price in a current sale would be $30,000. Brigid can terminate the lease at any time, and the lease includes a purchase option that arises one year into the lease for $10,000. The lease also includes a boldface provision separately signed by both Brigid and Acme which says, "BOTH PARTIES HEREBY INTEND AND AGREE THAT THIS CONTRACT CONSTITUTES A TRUE LEASE AND BOTH PARTIES HEREBY WAIVE ANY RIGHT TO CLAIM OTHERWISE AT ANY TIME."

After signing the lease and making the first payment, Brigid has the new ride delivered to her carnival grounds. Two months later, a new carnival entrepreneur, Joe Bergers, moves to town and tells Brigid how impressed he is by the Portable Death Watch. Deciding she is tired of the carnival business, Brigid agrees to sell the ride to Joe for $30,000 cash. Before buying the ride, Joe checks the appropriate Article 9 files to make sure that there are no recorded interests against the ride. Finding none (since Acme did not believe it needed to file notice of its interest as a lessor), Joe pays $30,000 to Brigid, who then skips town. When Brigid fails to make the next lease payment, Acme locates the Portable Death Watch in Joe's possession and demands its return. Who should prevail in a suit by Acme against Joe? U.C.C. §§1-201(37) (revised 1-203), 9-317(b), 9-505(b).

2.3.   Your law firm represents Jay's Rent-to-Own Pianos, a piano retailer that sells and rents both new and used pianos. The company's owner, Jay Berringer, explained to you that for tax and accounting reasons, he wanted to be certain that all of his rent contracts qualify as true leases rather than as disguised sales. On the other hand, he said, for profit reasons he wanted to structure the rent contracts so that customers would almost always end up buying the pianos.

Jay believes his latest lease creation indeed accomplishes both ends. He calls it the "three-year special": the first month's rent is 50 percent of the piano's purchase price, and each of the remaining 35 monthly payments is just 1.5 percent of the piano's price. The customer may terminate the lease at any time after the first month and may purchase the piano either at the end of the lease or during it, with the customer getting full credit towards the purchase price for all lease payments made up to that point. The store will even extend credit, if necessary, for the first month's rent. Has Jay come up with a winner? If not, can you tinker with the "three-year special" so that Jay achieves what he is after? U.C.C. §§1-201(37) (revised 1-203), 9-505(b).

2.4.   You are the junior member of the Uniform Law Commission's Article 2A revision committee, which is also examining the 1990 amendments to U.C.C. §1-201(37) (revised 1-203). One of the committee's senior members, David Flanders, pulls you aside at a break during your first meeting, and says he has a question for you that he is afraid will sound stupid to the more seasoned members of the committee.

"I don't get it," David tells you. "The second (a) of 1-201(37) says that a transaction is not a disguised sale just because the lessee is obligated to make lease payments that have a present value equal to or greater than the fair market value of the goods. But it seems to me that situation necessarily *would* be a sale, or why else would the lessee enter into a contract with those terms in the first place?"

Do you have any response for David?

2.5.   We Back You Up, Inc. ("WBYU"), is a manufacturer of custom-designed office chairs for highly paid business executives who have back problems. WBYU has its corporate office in Detroit and its only factory in Mexico City, Mexico. Whenever a potential client calls, the WBYU corporate office sends a consultant from Detroit to visit the executive and create specifications for a specially manufactured chair. Those specs are then faxed to Mexico City, which produces the chair and ships it directly to the client. When Carla Icahn, CEO of a small New York City marketing firm, orders two such chairs (one for use in her New York office and one for watching TV in her apartment), will that transaction be covered by the CISG? C.I.S.G. Arts. 1, 10, 2, 3.

2.6.   Miles Farmer lives in the city but also has a summer place in the country that consists of 10 acres of land, an original 1846 farmhouse, and several dozen apple trees. Miles is now hurting for cash and is considering selling all or part of his summer getaway. Which of the following sales by Miles would be covered by Article 2? U.C.C. §2-107.

    a.   A sale of the 1846 farmhouse to be severed from the land.

    b.   The 1846 farmhouse (to remain attached to the land) plus all of the land.

    c.   Six bushels of apples to be picked from the trees on the land.

Assignment 3: The Process of Sales Contract Formation

Hill v. Gateway 2000, Inc.
105 P.3d 1147 (7th Cir. 1997)

EASTERBROOK, C.J.

A customer picks up the phone, orders a computer, and gives a credit card number. Presently a box arrives, containing the computer and a list of terms, said to govern unless the customer returns the computer within 30 days. Are these terms effective as the parties' contract, or is the contract term-free because the order-taker did not read any terms over the phone and elicit the customer's assent?

One of the terms in the box containing a Gateway 2000 system was an arbitration clause. Rich and Enza Hill, the customers, kept the computer more than 30 days before complaining about its components and performance. They filed suit in federal court arguing, among other things, that the product's shortcomings make Gateway a racketeer (mail and wire fraud are said to be the predicate offenses), leading to treble damages under RICO for the Hills and a class of all other purchasers. Gateway asked the district court to enforce the arbitration clause; the judge refused, writing that "[t]he present record is insufficient to support a finding of a valid arbitration agreement between the parties or that the plaintiffs were given adequate notice of the arbitration clause." Gateway took an immediate appeal, as is its right.

The Hills say that the arbitration clause did not stand out: they concede noticing the statement of terms but deny reading it closely enough to discover the agreement to arbitrate, and they ask us to conclude that they therefore may go to court. Yet an agreement to arbitrate must be enforced "save upon such grounds as exist at law or in equity for the revocation of any contract." 9 U.S.C. §2. Doctor's Associates, Inc. v. Casarotto, 116 S. Ct. 1652, 134 L. Ed. 2d 902 (1996), holds that this provision of the Federal Arbitration Act is inconsistent with any requirement that an arbitration clause be prominent. A contract need not be read to be effective; people who accept take the risk that the unread terms may in retrospect prove unwelcome. Terms inside Gateway's box stand or fall together. If they constitute the parties' contract because the Hills had an opportunity to return the computer after reading them, then all must be enforced.

ProCD, Inc. v. Zeidenberg, 86 F.3d 1447 (7th Cir. 1996), holds that terms inside a box of software bind consumers who use the software after an opportunity to read the terms and to reject them by returning the product. Likewise, Carnival Cruise Lines, Inc. v. Shute, 499 U.S. 585 (1991), enforces a forum-selection clause that was included among three pages of terms attached to a cruise ship ticket.

40

ProCD and *Carnival Cruise Lines* exemplify the many commercial transactions in which people pay for products with terms to follow; *ProCD* discusses others. 86 F.3d at 1451-52. The district court concluded in *ProCD* that the contract is formed when the consumer pays for the software; as a result, the court held, only terms known to the consumer at that moment are part of the contract, and provisos inside the box do not count. Although this is one way a contract could be formed, it is not the only way: "A vendor, as master of the offer, may invite acceptance by conduct, and may propose limitations on the kind of conduct that constitutes acceptance. A buyer may accept by performing the acts the vendor proposes to treat as acceptance." Id. at 1452. Gateway shipped computers with the same sort of accept-or-return offer ProCD made to users of its software. ProCD relied on the Uniform Commercial Code rather than any peculiarities of Wisconsin law; both Illinois and South Dakota, the two states whose law might govern relations between Gateway and the Hills, have adopted the UCC; neither side has pointed us to any atypical doctrines in those states that might be pertinent; *ProCD* therefore applies to this dispute.

Plaintiffs ask us to limit *ProCD* to software, but where's the sense in that? *ProCD* is about the law of contract, not the law of software. Payment preceding the revelation of full terms is common for air transportation, insurance, and many other endeavors. Practical considerations support allowing vendors to enclose the full legal terms with their products. Cashiers cannot be expected to read legal documents to customers before ringing up sales. If the staff at the other end of the phone for direct-sales operations such as Gateway's had to read the four-page statement of terms before taking the buyer's credit card number, the droning voice would anesthetize rather than enlighten many potential buyers. Others would hang up in a rage over the waste of their time. And oral recitation would not avoid customers' assertions (whether true or feigned) that the clerk did not read term X to them, or that they did not remember or understand it. Writing provides benefits for both sides of commercial transactions. Customers as a group are better off when vendors skip costly and ineffectual steps such as telephonic recitation, and use instead a simple approve-or-return device. Competent adults are bound by such documents, read or unread. For what little it is worth, we add that the box from Gateway was crammed with software. The computer came with an operating system, without which it was useful only as a boat anchor. Gateway also included many application programs. So the Hills' effort to limit *ProCD* to software would not avail them factually, even if it were sound legally — which it is not.

For their second sally, the Hills contend that *ProCD* should be limited to executory contracts (to licenses in particular), and therefore does not apply because both parties' performance of this contract was complete when the box arrived at their home. This is legally and factually wrong: legally because the question at hand concerns the formation of the contract rather than its performance, and factually because both contracts were incompletely performed. *ProCD* did not depend on the fact that the seller characterized the transaction as a license rather than as a contract; we treated it as a contract for the sale of goods and reserved the question whether for other purposes a "license" characterization might be preferable. All debates about characterization to one side, the transaction in *ProCD* was no more executory than the one here: Zeidenberg paid for the software and walked out of the store with a box under his arm, so if arrival of the box with the product ends the time for revelation of contractual terms, then the time ended in *ProCD* before Zeidenberg opened the box. But of course ProCD had not completed performance with delivery of the box, and neither had Gateway. One element of the transaction was the warranty, which obliges sellers to fix defects in their products. The Hills have invoked Gateway's warranty and are not satisfied with its response, so they are not well positioned to say that Gateway's obligations were fulfilled when the motor carrier unloaded the box. What is more, both ProCD and Gateway promised to help customers to use their products. Long-term service and information obligations are common in the computer business, on both hardware and software sides. Gateway offers "lifetime service" and has a round-the-clock telephone hotline to fulfill this promise. Some vendors spend more money helping customers use their products than on developing and manufacturing them. The document in Gateway's box includes promises of future performance that some consumers value highly; these promises bind Gateway just as the arbitration clause binds the Hills.

Next the Hills insist that *ProCD* is irrelevant because Zeidenberg was a "merchant" and they are not. Section 2-207(2) of the UCC, the infamous battle-of-the-forms section, states that "additional terms [following acceptance of an offer] are to be construed as proposals for addition to a contract. Between merchants such terms become part of the contract unless...". Plaintiffs tell us that ProCD came out as it did only because Zeidenberg was a "merchant" and the terms inside ProCD's box were not excluded by the "unless" clause. This argument pays scant attention to the opinion in *ProCD*, which concluded that, when there is only one form, "sec. 2-207 is irrelevant." 86 F.3d at 1452. The question in *ProCD* was not whether terms were added to a contract after its formation, but how and when the contract was formed — in particular, whether a vendor may propose that a contract of sale be formed, not in the store (or over the phone) with the payment of money or a general "send me the product," but after the customer has had a chance to inspect both the item and the terms. *ProCD* answers "yes," for merchants and consumers alike. Yet again, for what little it is worth we observe that the Hills misunderstand the setting of *ProCD*. A "merchant" under the UCC "means a person who deals in goods of the kind or otherwise by his occupation holds himself out as having knowledge or skill peculiar to the practices or goods involved in the transaction," §2-104(1). Zeidenberg bought the product at a retail store, an uncommon place for merchants to acquire inventory. His corporation put ProCD's database on the Internet for anyone to browse, which led to the litigation but did not make Zeidenberg a software merchant.

At oral argument the Hills propounded still another distinction: the box containing ProCD's software displayed a notice that additional terms were within, while the box containing Gateway's computer did not. The difference is functional, not legal. Consumers browsing the aisles of a store can look at the box, and if they are unwilling to deal with the prospect of additional terms can leave the box alone, avoiding the transactions costs of returning the package after reviewing its contents. Gateway's box, by contrast, is just a shipping carton; it is not on display anywhere. Its function is to protect the product during transit, and the information on its sides is for the use of handlers rather than would-be purchasers.

Perhaps the Hills would have had a better argument if they were first alerted to the bundling of hardware and legal-ware after opening the box and wanted to return the computer in order to avoid disagreeable terms, but were dissuaded by the expense of shipping. What the remedy would be in such a case — could it exceed the shipping charges? — is an interesting question, but one that need not detain us because the Hills knew before they ordered the computer that the carton would include some important terms, and they did not seek to discover these in advance. Gateway's ads state that their products come with limited warranties and lifetime support. How limited was the warranty — 30 days, with service contingent on shipping the computer back, or five years, with free onsite service? What sort of support was offered? Shoppers have three principal ways to discover these things. First, they can ask the vendor to send a copy before deciding whether to buy. The Magnuson-Moss Warranty Act requires firms to distribute their warranty terms on request, 15 U.S.C. §2302(b)(1)(A); the Hills do not contend that Gateway would have refused to enclose the remaining terms too. Concealment would be bad for business, scaring some customers away and leading to excess returns from others. Second, shoppers can consult public sources (computer magazines, the Web sites of vendors) that may contain this information. Third, they may inspect the documents after the product's delivery. Like Zeidenberg, the Hills took the third option. By keeping the computer beyond 30 days, the Hills accepted Gateway's offer, including the arbitration clause.

The Hills' remaining arguments, including a contention that the arbitration clause is unenforceable as part of a scheme to defraud, do not require more than a citation to Prima Paint Corp. v. Flood & Conklin Mfg. Co., 388 U.S. 395, 87 S. Ct. 1801, 18 L. Ed. 2d 1270 (1967). Whatever may be said pro and con about the cost and efficacy of arbitration (which the Hills disparage) is for Congress and the contracting parties to consider. Claims based on RICO are no less arbitrable than those founded on the contract or the law of torts. The decision of the district court is vacated, and this case is remanded with instructions to compel the Hills to submit their dispute to arbitration.

The *Hill* case was decided under the pre-amended Article 2. The amendments to Article 2 include some significant changes to §2-207, which will be discussed in detail later in this assignment. For present purposes, it is worth noting that Official Comment 5 to amended §2-207 demurs on whether the *Hill* case was correctly decided: "This Article takes no position on whether a court should follow the reasoning in Step-Saver Data Systems, Inc. v. Wise Technology, 939 F.2d 91 (3d Cir. 1991) and Klocek v. Gateway, Inc., 104 F. Supp. 2d 1332 (D. Kan. 2000) (original Section 2-207 governs) or the contrary reasoning in Hill v. Gateway 2000, 105 F.3d 1147 (7th Cir. 1997) (original Section 2-207 inapplicable)."

When discussing the process of contract formation in the sales system, it is impossible to do so without some reference to the context of the particular sale. If you go into your local hardware store and buy a rake, it is easy enough to articulate the how and when of contract formation. The "how" is that you take the rake from the shelf, walk it up to the cash register, and hand over your cash or credit card to the clerk. The moment of contract formation is roughly when you hand over your money and the clerk takes it.

If you decided to go out and buy a new car instead of a rake, the contract formation process would be a bit more formal. You would likely test-drive the car, haggle with the car dealer over price, and then sign a sales contract that would purport to detail the terms of your purchase. Even with this larger transaction, however, the contract formation process is still pretty straight-forward.

Now suppose we have two merchants who wish to buy and sell a dozen copy machines. The two parties might sit down and draft a detailed contract that spells out all the terms of the sale. The interviews with buyers and sellers that were conducted for this book, however, suggest that this would be a rare occurrence. As one seller put it, "It usually doesn't make economic sense to try to agree in advance on all of the non-immediate boilerplate terms. In most cases, the stakes are so low and the likelihood that it will ever matter is so low that everyone is really better off ignoring the differences in boilerplate and not trying to come to an agreement on everything."

Rather than the contract being formed pursuant to a formally drafted con-tract, the sale will more likely take place on "open account." In an open account sale, the buyer will make some communication with the seller about what the buyer wishes to purchase. The buyer's communication might be by phone, or it might take the form of a written purchase order. The interviews with buyers and sellers suggest that buyers use purchase orders in at least two different ways.

First, the purchase order might truly serve as the "offer" to the seller. In that case, there is no previously concluded oral contract, although there may have been inquiries by the buyer concerning whether the seller carried the goods that the buyer was interested in purchasing.

Second, the purchase order might be used by the buyer as a way to confirm an oral agreement that has already been reached in a phone call prior to the written purchase order being sent. As one clothing buyer explained, "In the phone call, we agree on the key issues: price, quantity, style, time of delivery. The purchase order will reiterate those key terms, but will also deal with less important, non-negotiated issues."

After the seller receives the buyer's order in an open account sale, the seller will check the buyer's credit with the seller's credit group. Although some parties will arrange for institutional financing that may allow the buyer to defer payment substantially, it is unusual for sellers themselves to extend credit any longer than 30 to 60 days past delivery.

If the buyer's credit is not problematic, the seller will forward the buyer's order to the seller's shipping department, which will then ship the goods to the buyer with a written invoice. Some sellers might also send the buyer an acknowledgement form prior to shipping the buyer the goods, although many sellers will not bother with this step. In any event, the buyer's purchase order and the seller's invoice and acknowledgement form will usually be standard form documents that include lots of boilerplate terms, plus spaces to insert the particulars of any single sale.

To give you a sense of the difference in boilerplate between a buyer's form and a seller's form, consider the following warranty terms used by the same manufacturer, which is sometimes a seller and sometimes a buyer. When this manufacturer is a buyer, its purchase order includes the following:

> Seller warrants that the goods will conform to description and specifications and
> will be free from all defects in material and workmanship and all defects due to

design (other than Buyer's design)...Upon request of Buyer, Seller, at its sole expense, shall repair, or replace f.o.b. Seller's plant, all or any part of any machinery or equipment covered by this order which proves, within one (1) year from the date it is placed in operation but no later than eighteen (18) months from date of shipment, to be defective in material or workmanship...The rights and remedies of Buyer set forth in this order are not exclusive and are in addition to all other rights and remedies of Buyer.

When this manufacturer is seller, its acknowledgement form states the following concerning warranties:

The Company warrants to Purchaser that products furnished hereunder will be free from defects in material, workmanship and title and will be of the kind and quality specified in Seller's quotation of published documents...The warranties and remedies set forth herein are conditioned upon (a) proper storage, installation, use and maintenance, and conformance with any applicable recommendations of the Company and (b) Purchaser promptly notifying the Company of any defects and, if required, promptly making the product available for correction...If any product fails to meet the foregoing warranties (except title), the Company shall thereupon correct any such failure either at its option (1) by repairing any defective or damaged part or parts of the products, or (2) by making available F.O.B. Seller's plant or other point of shipment any necessary repaired or replacement parts, freight allowed to destination within the continental U.S.A. Where a failure cannot be corrected by the Company's reasonable efforts, the parties will negotiate an equitable adjustment in price. The preceding paragraph sets forth the exclusive remedies for claims based on failure of products (except title), whether claims in contract or tort (including negligence), and however instituted and, upon the expiration of the warranty period, all such liability shall terminate. Except as set forth under the heading Patents, the foregoing warranties are exclusive and in lieu of all other warranties whether written, oral, implied or statutory. NO IMPLIED WARRANTY OF MERCHANTABILITY OR FITNESS FOR PURPOSE SHALL APPLY. Seller does not warrant any products of others which Purchaser has designated. In no event will the Company be liable for consequential or special damages.

As this example demonstrates, buyers like to write boilerplate language in their forms that is favorable to them and sellers like to write boilerplate language in their forms that is favorable to them. In the vast majority of cases, these differences simply do not matter, and business people know that. Virtually none of the buyers and sellers that were interviewed for this book actually read the other party's form beyond verifying the key terms of the deal: quantity, type, price, and delivery terms.

As the retired general counsel for a major chemical company put it, "Karl Llewellyn used to say 'nobody ever reads these forms' — he was right. The buyers and the sellers, the marketing guys that were out consummating the transaction, they didn't read the forms....We spent a lot of time preparing forms, both as purchaser and as seller. And we also had seminars for marketing people on what these terms meant. But when the transactions were actually consummated, very rarely would the marketing guys, the sales people, or the purchasing agents read these forms. They were asked to bring to the company's attention any variances that were requested by the other side, the seller or buyer. Sometimes they did do that, sometimes they didn't."

An in-house attorney for a Fortune 500 manufacturing company echoed those sentiments: "It seems to me that the parties sending the forms really don't intend a certain [boilerplate] term which deals with remedies or other things like that — they never thought about it. They will just take their chances and worry about that later, if there is a problem. And a lot of business people think, 'Hey, we're going to work this out, we've got a good relationship' ... and a couple of golf games can get a lot solved, so I don't realistically think the parties have any meeting of the minds on most of this stuff [the boilerplate terms in the forms]."

As you might have guessed by now, the question of contract formation becomes a lot stickier as more steps are added to a particular system's formation process. The drafters of U.C.C. Article 2 hoped that their rules about contract formation would be more functional and less formalistic than what the common law provided. Article 2's formation rules are contained within four consecutive sections: 2-204, 2-205, 2-206, and 2-207.

This book's interviews with buyers and sellers suggested that the issue of whether a contract was formed is typically not important for its own sake. In other words, buyers and sellers usually do not fight about whether a particular exchange of words or forms amounted to a "deal." Somehow business people know whether or not there really has been a deal, and if someone tries to escape a concluded deal they will face the non-legal sanctions of a bad industry reputation and a lack of future business. In a few high-stakes cases, parties might actually litigate whether or not a deal was truly entered into, but those instances will be the exception.

Although formation itself is usually not a fighting issue, the formation rules of Article 2 do take on some significance with respect to figuring out the terms of an agreement. That would occur in those important instances in which the parties actually litigate a "battle of the forms" case. It is difficult to utilize U.C.C. §2-207's machinery for determining terms unless you can first figure out when the contract was formally concluded.

U.C.C. §2-204 sets out three broad principles about sales contract formation: 1. Sales contracts can be made "in any manner sufficient to show agreement," even conduct; 2. Even if we cannot pinpoint the exact moment a sales contract was formed, we may still conclude that a contract existed; and 3. The only substantive detail that is crucial to the formation of a sales contract is that there be some basis for calculating a remedy for breach.

The broad principles of §2-204 are fleshed out somewhat by the more particular offer-and-acceptance rules set down in §2-206. This latter section says that offers to make sales contracts may be accepted "in any manner and by any medium reasonable under the circumstances." More specifically, §2-206 says that when a buyer offers to purchase goods for immediate shipment, the seller may accept such an offer either by shipping the goods or by promising to ship them. Even a shipment of non-conforming goods will count as an acceptance, unless the seller specifically indicates that the non-conforming shipment is offered merely as an accommodation to the buyer (in which case the shipment would constitute a counteroffer).

U.C.C. §2-206 is straightforward enough. U.C.C. §2-207, at least in its pre-amended form, is not. Before tackling the intricacies of pre-amended §2-207, however, let us consider briefly the effect of another formation provision of

Article 2, §2-205. U.C.C. §2-205 creates a limited exception to the common-law rule that "firm offers" are not binding without consideration. Under §2-205, firm offers are binding even in the absence of consideration if the offeror is a merchant and the offer is in writing. Such a firm offer under §2-205, however, is in the absence of a stated time only open for a reasonable time, and in no event would such a gratuitous firm offer remain irrevocable longer than three months.

At least one buyer/manufacturer that was interviewed for this book reported that his company regularly uses the benefits of §2-205. What this buyer does before making a major purchase of supplies is to communicate its standard terms and conditions with potential suppliers. The buyer (which, incidentally, has a lot of leverage because its business is considered very lucrative by vendors) then requires potential vendors to submit "firm offers" to the buyer that incorporate the terms of the buyer's own standard purchase order.

Thus, for example, if one of these suppliers promised in writing that the manufacturer could purchase two tons of steel for a certain price, the supplier could not change its mind if the manufacturer came back the next day ready, willing, and able to make that purchase. The supplier could, of course, limit that firm offer to less than a day, in which case the manufacturer would be out of luck. But if the supplier failed to specify a time, normally if the manufacturer came back the next day that would be considered a "reasonable time" and thus the offer would still have to be kept open.

Now consider U.C.C. §2-207, first in its pre-amended form and then as amended. To understand the situation that §2-207 was meant to address, consider again our two merchants above who want to buy and sell a dozen copy machines. Suppose that the buyer sends a purchase order to the seller that includes, among other things, provisions that indicate that the seller will make certain express and implied warranties to the buyer as part of the sale. Imagine that before shipping the machines, the seller sends its own acknowledgment form to the buyer that purports to disclaim all implied warranties and further, says that all disputes about this sale will be settled by binding arbitration.

Is there a contract at this point? Under the common law, the answer would have been a clear "no." The common law's "mirror image rule" held that unless all of the terms of the purported acceptance agreed with the terms of the offer, then the purported acceptance could not operate as a "true" acceptance. It could not be a true acceptance because it was not a mirror image of the offer.

If the parties nevertheless proceeded to perform the contract, the purported acceptance with the different terms would be considered a "counteroffer" that was accepted by the buyer's performance. Thus, the seller's form would control the terms of the contract since it was the last form sent prior to performance. This was known as the "last shot" doctrine.

Pre-amended U.C.C. §2-207(1) changes that result. That subsection says that an acceptance such as the one described above can indeed count as an acceptance "even though it states terms additional to or different from" those that were offered.

Even under §2-207(1), there are still two ways in which a purported acceptance might not operate as a valid acceptance. The first is if the acceptance is not "a definite and seasonable expression of acceptance." This might be the case, for example, if the acceptance came a long time after the offer was made, or if the terms of the acceptance were wildly and fundamentally different from the terms of the offer. In other words, an offer to buy apples could not be accepted by an acceptance that agreed to sell oranges. Nevertheless, the acceptance may differ in even "material" ways from the offer and still count as an acceptance. Unfortunately, there is no easy way to draw the line between divergent but valid acceptances, on the one hand, and "apples/oranges" invalid acceptances, on the other.

The second way that a purported acceptance might not count as a valid acceptance under §2-207(1) is if the acceptance is "expressly made conditional on assent to the additional or different terms." This could arguably be accomplished by the offeree including conspicuous language in its form that tracks the relevant "expressly made conditional" language of §2-207. On the other hand, if a cautious offeree truly intended not to go forward with the deal except on its own terms, the offeree probably would want to bring that fact home to the offeror in an even more direct way. For example, if the copy-machine seller in our hypothetical did not want to do the deal unless there were no implied warranties, the seller ought to insist that the buyer separately sign a "no implied warranties" letter before shipping the machines.

Ionics, Inc. v. Elmwood Sensors, Inc.
110 F.3d 184 (1st Cir. 1997)

TORRUELLA, CHIEF JUDGE.

Ionics, Inc. ("Ionics") purchased thermostats from Elmwood Sensors, Inc. ("Elmwood") for installation in water dispensers manufactured by the former. Several of the dispensers subsequently caused fires which allegedly resulted from defects in the sensors. Ionics filed suit against Elmwood in order to recover costs incurred in the wake of the fires. Before trial, the district court denied Elmwood's motion for partial summary judgment. The District Court of Massachusetts subsequently certified to this court "the question whether, in the circumstances of this case, [U.C.C.] §2-207 has been properly applied." . . .

The facts of the case are not in dispute. Elmwood manufactures and sells thermostats. Ionics makes hot and cold water dispensers, which it leases to its customers. On three separate occasions, Ionics purchased thermostats from Elmwood for use in its water dispensers. Every time Ionics made a purchase of thermostats from Elmwood, it sent the latter a purchase order form which contained, in small type, various "conditions." Of the 20 conditions on the order form, two are of particular relevance:

18. REMEDIES — The remedies provided Buyer herein shall be cumulative, and in addition to any other remedies provided by law or equity. A waiver of a breach of any provision hereof shall not constitute a waiver of any other breach. The laws of the state shown in Buyer's address printed on the masthead of this order shall apply in the construction hereof.

19. ACCEPTANCE — Acceptance by the Seller of this order shall be upon the terms and conditions set forth in items 1 to 17 inclusive, and elsewhere in this order. Said order can be so accepted only on the exact terms herein and set forth. No terms which are in any manner additional to or different from those herein set forth shall become a part of, alter or in any way control the terms and conditions herein set forth.

Near the time when Ionics placed its first order, it sent Elmwood a letter that it sends to all of its new suppliers. The letter states, in part:

The information preprinted, written and/or typed on our purchase order is especially important to us. Should you take exception to this information, please clearly express any reservations to us in writing. If you do not, we will assume that you have agreed to the specified terms and that you will fulfill your obligations according to our purchase order. If necessary, we will change your invoice and pay your invoice according to our purchase order.

Following receipt of each order, Elmwood prepared and sent an "Acknowledgment" form containing the following language in small type:

THIS WILL ACKNOWLEDGE RECEIPT OF BUYER'S ORDER AND STATE SELLER'S WILL-INGNESS TO SELL THE GOODS ORDERED BUT ONLY UPON THE TERMS AND CON-DITIONS SET FORTH HEREIN AND ON THE REVERSE SIDE HEREOF AS A COUNTEROFFER. BUYER SHALL BE DEEMED TO HAVE ACCEPTED SUCH COUNTER-OFFER UNLESS IT IS REJECTED IN WRITING WITHIN TEN (10) DAYS OF THE RECEIPT HEREOF, AND ALL SUBSEQUENT ACTION SHALL BE PURSUANT TO THE TERMS AND CONDITIONS OF THIS COUNTEROFFER ONLY; ANY ADDITIONAL OR DIFFERENT TERMS ARE HEREBY OBJECTED TO AND SHALL NOT BE BINDING UPON THE PARTIES UNLESS SPECIFICALLY AGREED TO IN WRITING BY SELLER.

Although this passage refers to a "counteroffer," we wish to emphasize that this language is not controlling. The form on which the language appears is labelled an "Acknowledgment" and the language comes under a heading that reads "Notice of Receipt of Order." The form, taken as a whole, appears to contemplate an order's confirmation rather than an order's rejection in the form of a counteroffer.

It is undisputed that the Acknowledgment was received prior to the arrival of the shipment of goods. Although the district court, in its ruling on the summary judgment motion, states that "with each shipment of thermostats, Elmwood included an Acknowledgment Form," Order of the District Court, August 23, 1995, this statement cannot reasonably be taken as a finding in support of the claim that the Acknowledgment and the shipment arrived together. First, in its certification order, the court states that "[t]he purchaser, *after* receiving the Acknowledgment, accepted delivery of the goods without objection." Order Pursuant to 28 U.S.C. §1292(b), Nov. 6, 1995 (emphasis added). This language is clearer and more precise than the previous statement and suggests that the former was simply a poor choice of phrasing. Furthermore, Ionics has not disputed the arrival time of the Acknowledgment. In its Memorandum in Support of Defendant's Motion for Partial Summary Judgment Elmwood stated, under the heading of "Statements of Undisputed Facts," that "for each of the three orders, Ionics received the Acknowledgment prior to receiving the shipment of thermostats." Memorandum in Support of Defendant's Motion for Partial Summary Judgment, at 3. In its own memorandum, Ionics argued that there existed disputed issues of material fact, but did not contradict Elmwood's claim regarding the arrival of the Acknowledgment Form. Furthermore, in its appellate brief, Ionics does not argue that the time of arrival of the Acknowledgment Form is in dispute. Ionics repeats language from the district court's summary judgment ruling that "with each shipment of thermostats, Elmwood included an Acknowledgment Form," Appellee's Brief at 7, but does not argue that the issue is in dispute or confront the language in Elmwood's brief which states that "[i]t is undisputed that for each of the three orders, Ionics received the Acknowledgment prior to receiving the shipment of thermostats." Appellant's Brief at 6.

As we have noted, the Acknowledgment Form expressed Elmwood's willingness to sell thermostats on "terms and conditions" that the Form indicated were listed on the reverse side. Among the terms and conditions listed on the back was the following:

> 9. WARRANTY
> All goods manufactured by Elmwood Sensors, Inc. are guaranteed to be free of defects in material and workmanship for a period of ninety (90) days after receipt of such goods by Buyer or eighteen months from the date of manufacturer [sic] (as evidenced by the manufacturer's date code), whichever shall be longer. THERE IS NO IMPLIED WARRANTY OF MERCHANTABILITY AND NO OTHER WARRANTY, EXPRESSED OR IMPLIED, EXCEPT SUCH AS IS EXPRESSLY SET FORTH HEREIN. SELLER WILL NOT BE LIABLE FOR ANY GENERAL, CONSEQUENTIAL OR INCIDENTAL DAMAGES, INCLUDING WITHOUT LIMITATION ANY DAMAGES FROM LOSS OF PROFITS, FROM ANY BREACH OF WARRANTY OR FOR NEGLIGENCE, SELLER'S LIABILITY AND BUYER'S EXCLUSIVE REMEDY BEING EXPRESSLY LIMITED TO THE REPAIR OF DEFECTIVE GOODS F.O.B. THE SHIPPING POINT INDICATED ON THE FACE HEREOF OR THE REPAYMENT OF THE PURCHASE PRICE UPON THE RETURN OF THE GOODS OR THE GRANTING OF A RESONABLE ALLOWANCE ON ACCOUNT OF ANY DEFECTS, AS SELLER MAY ELECT.

Neither party disputes that they entered into a valid contract and neither disputes the quantity of thermostats purchased, the price paid, or the manner and time of delivery. The only issue in dispute is the extent of Elmwood's liability.

In summary, Ionics' order included language stating that the contract would be governed exclusively by the terms included on the purchase order and that all remedies available under state law would be available to Ionics. In a subsequent letter, Ionics added that Elmwood must indicate any objections to these conditions in writing. Elmwood, in turn, sent Ionics an Acknowledgment stating that the contract was governed exclusively by the terms in the Acknowledgment, and Ionics was given 10 days to reject this "counteroffer." Among the terms included in the Acknowledgment is a limitation on Elmwood's liability. As the district court stated, "the terms are diametrically opposed to each other on the issue of whether all warranties implied by law were reserved or waived." Order of the District Court, August 23, 1995.

We face, therefore, a battle of the forms. This is purely a question of law. The dispute turns on whether the contract is governed by the language after the comma in §2-207(1) of the Uniform Commercial Code, according to the rule laid down by this court in Roto-Lith, Ltd. v. F.P. Bartlett & Co., 297 F.2d 497 (1st Cir. 1962), or whether it is governed by subsection (3) of the Code provision, as enacted by both Massachusetts, Mass. Gen. L. ch. 106, §2-207 (1990 and 1996

Supp.), and Rhode Island, R.I. Gen. Laws §6A-2-207 (1992). We find the rule of *Roto-Lith* to be in conflict with the purposes of §2-207 and, accordingly, we overrule *Roto-Lith* and find that subsection (3) governs the contract. Analyzing the case under §2-207, we conclude that Ionics defeats Elmwood's motion for partial summary judgment.

LEGAL ANALYSIS

Our analysis begins with the statute. Section 2-207 reads as follows:

§2-207. Additional Terms in Acceptance or Confirmation
  (1) A definite and seasonable expression of acceptance or a written confirmation which is sent within a reasonable time operates as an acceptance even though it states terms additional to or different from those offered or agreed upon, unless acceptance is expressly made conditional on assent to the additional or different terms.
  (2) The additional or different terms are to be construed as proposals for addition to the contract. Between merchants such terms become part of the contract unless:
    (a) the offer expressly limits acceptance to the terms of the offer;
    (b) they materially alter it; or
    (c) notification of objection to them has already been given or is given within a reasonable time after notice of them is received.
  (3) Conduct by both parties which recognizes the existence of a contract is sufficient to establish a contract for sale although the writings of the parties do not otherwise establish a contract. In such case the terms of the particular contract consist of those terms on which the writings of the parties agree, together with any supplementary terms incorporated under any other provisions of this chapter. Mass. Gen. L. ch. 106, §2-207 (1990 and 1996 Supp.).

In *Roto-Lith*, Roto-Lith sent a purchase order to Bartlett, who responded with an acknowledgment that included language purporting to limit Bartlett's liability. Roto-Lith did not object. This court held that "a response which states a condition materially altering the obligation solely to the disadvantage of the offeror is an 'acceptance * * * expressly * * * conditional on assent to the additional * * * terms.'" Id. at 500. This holding took the case outside of §2-207 by applying the exception after the comma in subsection (1). The court then reverted to common law and concluded that Roto-Lith "accepted the goods with knowledge of the conditions specified in the acknowledgment [and thereby] became bound." Id. at 500. In other words, the *Roto-Lith* court concluded that the defendant's acceptance was conditional on assent, by the buyer, to the new terms and, therefore, constituted a counter offer rather than an acceptance. When Roto-Lith accepted the goods with knowledge of Bartlett's conditions, it accepted the counteroffer and Bartlett's terms governed the contract. Elmwood argues that *Roto-Lith* governs the instant appeal, implying that the terms of Elmwood's acknowledgment govern.

Ionics claims that the instant case is distinguishable because in *Roto-Lith* "the seller's language limiting warranties implied at law was proposed as an addition to, but was not in conflict with, the explicit terms of the buyer's form. [In the instant case] the explicit terms of the parties' forms conflict with and reject each other." Appellee's Brief at 21.

We do not believe that Ionics' position sufficiently distinguishes *Roto-Lith*. It would be artificial to enforce language that conflicts with background legal rules while refusing to enforce language that conflicts with the express terms of the contract. Every contract is assumed to incorporate the existing legal norms that are in place. It is not required that every contract explicitly spell out the governing law of the jurisdiction. Allowing later forms to govern with respect to deviations from the background rules but not deviations from the terms in the contract would imply that only the terms in the contract could be relied upon. Aside from being an artificial and arbitrary distinction, such a standard would, no doubt, lead parties to include more of the background rules in their initial forms, making forms longer and more complicated. Longer forms would be more difficult and time consuming to read — implying that even fewer forms would be read than under the existing rules. It is the failure of firms to read their forms that has brought this case before us, and we do not wish to engender more of this type of litigation.

Our inquiry, however, is not complete. Having found that we cannot distinguish this case from *Roto-Lith*, we turn to the Uniform Commercial Code, quoted above. A plain language reading of §2-207 suggests that subsection (3) governs the instant case. Ionics sent an initial offer to which Elmwood responded with its "Acknowledgment." Thereafter, the conduct of the parties established the existence of a contract as required by §2-207(3). . . .

We are faced, therefore, with a contradiction between a clear precedent of this court, *Roto-Lith*, which suggests that the language after the comma in subsection (1) governs, and the clear dictates of the Uniform Commercial Code, which indicate that subsection (3) governs. It is our view that the two cannot coexist and the case at bar offers a graphic illustration of the conflict. We have, therefore, no choice but to overrule our previous decision in Roto-Lith, Ltd. v. F.P. Bartlett & Co., 297 F.2d 497 (1st Cir. 1962). Our decision brings this circuit in line with the majority view on the subject and puts to rest a case that has provoked considerable criticism from courts and commentators and alike. . . .

Applied to this case, our holding leads to the conclusion that the contract is governed by §2-207(3). Section 2-207(1) is inapplicable because Elmwood's acknowledgment is conditional on assent to the additional terms. . . . Finally, the conduct of the parties demonstrates the existence of a contract, as required by §2-207(3). Thus, §2-207(3) applies and the terms of the contract are to be determined in accordance with that subsection.

We conclude, therefore, that §2-207(3) prevails and "the terms of the particular contract consist of those terms on which the writings of the parties agree, together with any supplementary terms incorporated under any other provisions of this chapter." Mass. Gen. L. ch. 106, §2-207(3). . . .

CONCLUSION

For the reasons stated herein, the district court's order denying Elmwood's motion for partial summary judgment is affirmed and the case is remanded to the district court for further proceedings.

While we are on the subject of pre-amended §2-207(1), you should note one drafting glitch in that subsection. The subsection begins by saying that "[a] definite and seasonable expression of acceptance *or a written confirmation* which is sent within a reasonable time *operates as an acceptance . . .*" (emphasis added). It makes little sense to say that a confirmation can ever operate as an acceptance. A confirmation by definition presupposes that there has already been a valid offer and acceptance; otherwise, how could there be a pre-existing contract to confirm? Presumably what the drafters meant here is that for purposes of deciding how to treat additional or different terms that appear in a confirmation, we should look to §2-207. That, in turn, leads us to §2-207(2).

Each of the subsections of §2-207 plays a specific role. As we just explored, §2-207(1) determines when a writing with different terms nevertheless constitutes an acceptance. The purpose of §2-207(2) is to tell us what to do with new terms in the acceptance. U.C.C. §2-207(3), which we will consider shortly, covers the situation in which the buyer and seller *act* as if there is a contract even though the purported written acceptance does not qualify as a valid written acceptance under §2-207(1).

Now let us see how §2-207(2) operates in practice. To consider again our example of the copy-machine sale, suppose that the seller sends the acknowledgment form with the arbitration clause and the "no warranties" clause, and then ships the machines. The buyer accepts the machines and begins using them. At some later point, the buyer has complaints about the performance of the machines. Both buyer and seller need to know at this point whether seller has made any implied warranties and whether buyer must bring its complaints to arbitration.

Just like §2-207(1), §2-207(2) suffers from drafting problems. By its terms, §2-207(2) purports to cover only "additional" terms in the acceptance. Official Comment 3 to 2-207, however, says that "[w]hether or not *additional or different terms* will become part of the agreement depends upon the provisions of subsection (2)" (emphasis added). The arbitration clause, as an "additional" term, is clearly covered by §2-207(2). Such additional terms, we are told, are "mere proposals" except that between merchants these additional terms will automatically become part of the contract unless: 1. the offer has clearly limited acceptance to the terms of the offer; 2. the additional terms amount to a material alteration of the offer; or 3. the offeror has objected in advance to the additional terms or objects to them within a reasonable time.

There is a lot of litigation about which additional terms do or do not amount to material alterations of an offer. The various examples of both material and non-material additional terms that are provided in Official Comments 4 and 5 to §2-207 have not been very successful in clarifying the issue. Ultimately, much will depend on whether the additional term is common in the buyer's and seller's industry. The arbitration clause in the copy-machine seller's form, for example, might or might not amount to a material alteration of the buyer's purchase order depending on whether arbitration is a common mode of dispute-resolution in that industry.

How to treat different terms is perhaps even more of a mess than how to treat additional terms. If you believe what Comment 3 says, as some courts do, then different terms as well as additional terms are handled by §2-207(2). If that is true, however, then the different terms in an acceptance should never become part of the contract. That is because the mere fact of their being contrary to a particular term in the offer should mean that the offeror has in effect objected to them in advance.

Most courts handle different terms using what has been called the "knock-out rule," which has no particular statutory basis but which apparently strikes the majority of courts as the proper result. Under the knockout rule, the court will "knock out" the different terms and use the UCC to fill the gap left by the knocked-out terms. In our copy-machine sale, you may recall, our buyer's form said "implied warranties" and our seller's form said "no implied warranties." Under the knockout approach, both terms would drop out and the UCC gap-filler — that there *are* implied warranties — would fill the gap. Thus, in that case, the gap-filler would end up giving the buyer what the buyer wanted: implied warranties.

The final subsection of 2-207, sub (3), covers the following situation: Suppose that our copy-machine buyer's purchase order had said something like "seller must accept all of the terms of this offer or there will be no contract." Imagine also that seller's acknowledgment form, besides including additional and different terms, also included a conspicuous statement that "this acceptance is expressly made conditional on buyer's assent to the additional or different terms contained herein."

Suppose that despite these terms, the seller shipped the machines and the buyer accepted them. Imagine that a few months following the sale, the buyer began having trouble with the machines and wanted to sue the seller on a breach of implied warranty theory. The buyer now needs to know whether there is an implied warranty and whether the warranty claim needs to be brought to arbitration.

This is where §2-207(3) comes in. Where, as in this case, the purported acceptance cannot qualify as a true acceptance even under the liberal standards of §2-207(1), then we do not have a contract by the exchange of writings. Even where the writings get "knocked out" of §2-207(1), we may nevertheless have conduct by both parties which, in the words of §2-207(3), "recognizes the existence of a contract." In this case, we would seem to have such conduct: seller shipped the machines, and buyer accepted them and paid for them. Thus, §2-207(3) would conclude that there is a contract here "although the writings of the parties do not otherwise establish a contract."

In the §2-207(3) case of a contract by "conduct only," we end up with a rule that virtually replicates the judicially created "knockout rule" for different terms under §2-207(2): use the terms on which the writings agree, and add to them the UCC gap-fillers for the terms on which the writings do not agree. The only way that §2-207(3)'s statutory knockout rule differs from the judicially created knockout rule for §2-207(2) is in its treatment of additional terms: the §2-207(3) rule "knocks out" additional terms whereas under §2-207(2) additional terms between merchants will become part of the contract unless one of the three exceptions in §2-207(2) applies.

Thus, in our copy-machine sale, under §2-207(3) the buyer comes out looking like a winner both with respect to the additional term and the different term: the seller's arbitration clause gets tossed out, and as to implied warranties, the UCC gap-filler says that they will exist.

On the subject of §2-207(3), there is a very common conceptual mistake that you should seek to avoid. Where the two parties have exchanged forms and then have proceeded to perform the contract, you should not immediately jump to §2-207(3) to determine the contract's terms. There is a clear temptation to do so: you *know* that there is sufficient conduct to create a contract, and besides, you think to yourself, wouldn't it be great to avoid altogether having to contend with §§2-207(1) & (2)!

Yet the language of §2-207(3) is clear that you only go to that section when *"the writings of the parties do not otherwise establish a contract."* This means that to get to §2-207(3), you must first decide either that the purported acceptance was not a "definite and seasonable expression of acceptance" or that the acceptance was "expressly made conditional on assent to the additional or different terms." Otherwise, you do have a contract by the writings and you must determine its terms under §2-207(2) rather than §2-207(3).

Amended Article 2 makes a valiant attempt to simplify the battle of the forms situation with a thoroughly re-drafted §2-207. The primary goal in the redrafting of §2-207 was to separate the issue of formation from the issue of terms. In pre-amended §2-207, §2-207(1) determined whether a contract was formed, §2-207(2) handled the question of terms, and §2-207(3) affected both formation and terms.

In §2-207 as amended, the formation question is completely removed from that section and is instead handled exclusively by sections 2-204, 2-205, and 2-206. The key amendment here was moving the formation concept that was previously contained in §2-207(1) to §2-206(3), where it now reads: "A definite and seasonable expression of acceptance in a record operates as an acceptance even if it contains terms additional to or different from the offer." Thus, the common law mirror-image rule continues to be rejected by amended Article 2.

The escape clause that was in pre-amended §2-207(1) — "unless acceptance is expressly made conditional on assent to the additional or different terms" — has been deleted as "unnecessary." The idea is that while minor deviations contained in a response to an offer will not prevent the response from constituting an acceptance, the response "must still be reasonably understood as an 'acceptance' and not as a proposal for a different transaction." Official Comment 2 to amended §2-206.

Amended §2-207 is much shorter and simpler than its pre-amended form. It begins with the premise that §2-207 does not apply at all unless there has already been formation of a contract by conduct, by offer and acceptance, or by any other means recognized by the three earlier sections on formation. If a contract has been formed, the role of amended §2-207 is simply to determine the contract's terms. The terms of a contract under amended §2-207 are determined with reference to three fairly straightforward rules. The terms will include: "(a) terms that appear in the records of both parties; (b) terms, whether in a record or not, to which both parties agree; and (c) terms supplied or incorporated under any provision of this Act [in other words, the UCC gap-fillers]."

The functional effects of amended §2-207 will be several. First, that section will now govern the terms of all contracts, not just the terms of contracts that were formed through a classic battle of the forms scenario. Second, amended §2-207 removes any advantage from firing either the "first shot" or the "last shot" in an exchange of forms. With amended §2-207, you can only have your terms become part of the contract if the other side agrees, if the other side has included the same terms in its form, or if your terms happen to coincide with the UCC gap-filler terms. Finally, amended §2-207 intentionally grants a lot more discretion to courts to determine just what constitutes an "agreement" by one party to another's terms: "There is a variety of verbal and nonverbal behavior that may suggest agreement to another's record. This section leaves the interpretation of that behavior to the discretion of the courts." Official Comment 3 to amended §2-207.

Besides the conceptual revamping of §2-207, the other notable change in the formation provisions of amended Article 2 was the explicit recognition of the validity and the enforceability of electronic contracting methods. References to a "writing" throughout Article 2 have all been replaced with references to a "record," which includes not only traditional writings but also electronically stored information that is retrievable.

Amended §2-204's formation rules explicitly recognize in §2-204(4) the formation of sales contracts "by the interaction of electronic agents of the parties" or by "the interaction of an electronic agent and an individual acting on the individual's own behalf or for another person." These rules on electronic contracting were derived from Section 14 of the Uniform Electronic Transactions Act (UETA), and were included in amended Article 2 "to negate any claim that lack of human intent, at the time of contract formation, prevents contract formation." Official Comment 4 to amended §2-204. Thus, for example, the fact that an individual buyer makes its contract by interacting with a website does not make the contract any less binding on either side than if the buyer had interacted directly with an individual seller.

As of August 2005, all states except for Georgia and Washington had adopted UETA. In addition, at the federal level the Electronic Signatures in Global and National Commerce Act ("E-Sign") was signed into law on June 30, 2000. Much like UETA, the federal E-Sign law provides that signatures or contracts are not to be denied legal effect merely because they are in electronic form. Thus, electronic signatures should continue to grow in popularity as a means for effecting contract formation under Article 2 of the UCC. Keep in mind, however, that neither UETA nor E-Sign requires a party to agree to use or accept an electronic signature. The two statutes simply make it clear that parties to a contract can choose to proceed by electronic means if they so desire.

Three brand-new sections in the §2-200's, also derived from UETA, were added to amended Article 2. Section 2-211 prevents a court from denying legal effect or enforceability to a contract just because the contract is in electronic form or uses an electronic record in its formation. Section 2-212 creates a rule of attribution in the electronic contract environment that simply assigns the responsibility of an electronic record or signature to the person who created or generated that record or signature. Section 2-213(1) makes the recipient of an electronic message accountable for the legal effect of its receipt, whether or not the recipient is aware of the receipt. In other words, people who fail to read their e-mail are no better off legally than people who fail to read their snail mail.

An increasing number of merchants have begun transacting their open account sales with a system known as Electronic Data Interchange (EDI). The EDI system transmits the standard purchase order/invoice information by use of electronic mail. In at least some cases a buyer or seller's decision to use EDI with a particular customer also provides an occasion to actually sit down and work out the terms and conditions of the sale with that customer. In some industries, the hard work of creating standard terms that are fair to both buyers and sellers has been accomplished by industry trade associations that include both buyer and seller representation.

Standard EDI forms have been created thus far for grocers, for warehouses, and for general merchandise transactions. By use of these standard forms, the buyer needs merely to fill in certain blanks in the form that are peculiar to the buyer's specific order: the parties, the merchandise, the quantity, the price, and the delivery terms. As noted above, these standard forms will be the product of negotiating between industry representatives for both buyers and sellers. From the buyer's perspective, they will not be as favorable as the buyer's standard purchase order; from the seller's perspective, they will not be as favorable as the seller's standard acknowledgment form.

One obvious business advantage of EDI is that it reduces costs by eliminating the need for the sending and storage of the paper documentation that accompanies traditional open-account transactions. A second clear advantage to EDI is speed: the buyer's purchase order on EDI can be transmitted to the seller in a matter of moments instead of hours or days. Yet these advantages of EDI can be captured even without sitting down and working out all of the terms and conditions of a particular sale. In industries where there are no standard EDI terms and conditions, parties can still get the benefits of EDI without agreeing on terms and conditions.

Several of the buyers and sellers that were interviewed for this book indicated that they use EDI to transact business with certain customers even though they have not worked out the terms and conditions of the sale with those customers. Before doing sales by EDI, a buyer and seller will enter into what is known as an EDI "trading partner agreement." That agreement might include negotiated terms and conditions, or it might simply beg the question by indicating both that "buyer's standard terms and conditions will govern" and that "seller's standard terms and conditions govern," even though both parties know full well that those terms and conditions are quite inconsistent with one another.

While an EDI trading agreement might provide the impetus for a buyer and seller to negotiate terms and conditions, the use of EDI is neither a necessary nor a sufficient condition to resolving the battle of the forms. Buyers and sellers who are involved in either a large single transaction or a long-term series of sales may well conclude that it is worth the sunk cost to work out all of the terms and conditions of their deal. Yet parties can and sometimes do make this investment of time even in cases where no EDI is involved. On the other hand, as noted above, parties that want the time and paper-saving efficiencies of EDI can capture those even where they decide it is not in their interests to negotiate all of the terms and conditions of sale.

In the final analysis, there may be no "solution" to the battle of forms. Rather, the decision of buyers and sellers *not* to sit down and negotiate all of the terms and conditions of a particular sale may well be the most economically rational course to take, even though there will be a small percentage of these deals in hindsight this failure will prove unfortunate.

Problem Set 3

3.1. a.   Suppose that in the *Gateway 2000* case at the beginning of this assignment, the terms and conditions that the Hills failed to read closely also included the following: 1. that the buyers agreed not to use any other printer with the computer except a special Gateway printer (whether or not any other printers were actually compatible); 2. that the seller was not responsible for any consequential damages suffered by the buyers from defects in the computer; and 3. that the buyers' only remedy for any defects in the computer was that buyers would receive a special Gateway baseball cap for their troubles. Would these clauses be just as enforceable against the buyers as the arbitration clause? U.C.C. §§2-206, 2-204, 2-207, Official Comment 1 to §2-207, Official Comment 1 to §2-719.

b.   Suppose that in *Gateway 2000*, following the phone conversation in which the Hills placed their order (and in which the seller promised to send the computer), the seller called the Hills back a week later and said, "We've decided that we cannot sell the computer to you at the price you ordered it; you must agree to pay 10 percent more than that or we won't ship it." Would the seller be able to enforce such a condition on the sale?

3.2.   Your law firm just took on a new client last month, an exercise equipment manufacturer called Heavy Metal, Inc. You were assigned to meet with Heavy Metal's president, Arlene Ledger, to discuss her various legal concerns about certain sales by this company, which she founded herself. Arlene's first concern related to a major order of Stairmaster machines that her company filled last month for Fit for Life, a national health club chain.

Fit for Life's purchase order, which Arlene had not read until recently, indicated that "seller will be liable for all remedies available under the UCC." Heavy Metal's acknowledgment form, by contrast, disclaimed in bold-face language all consequential damages. One other thing troubled Arlene about this transaction: she had meant to send the acknowledgment form before shipping the Stairmasters, but instead she had shipped the Stairmasters and only later did she send the acknowledgment form. Arlene said that she is extremely worried about having all those Stairmasters out there for which her company might be liable for unlimited consequential damages. Are Arlene's fears well grounded? U.C.C. §§2-204, 2-206, 2-207.

3.3. a.   Another recent situation that Arlene wants to ask about relates to a purchase order the company just received from Sportlife, a regional sporting goods chain, to buy a dozen 580XL circuit-trainer weight machines for current shipment. In this case, Arlene said, immediately after receiving the purchase order she did send Sportlife an acknowledgment form *before* shipping the machines. In fact, although she sent the acknowledgment she still has not shipped the machines to Sportlife. What bothers Arlene about this order is that she had a phone conversation yesterday with a friend in the industry who strongly advised Arlene not to do business with Sportlife. "They're more trouble than they're worth," her friend had told her. "They make your life miserable by complaining about problems with the orders that don't even exist."

Arlene wants to know whether it is still too late to get out of this contract. In looking at the purchase order and the acknowledgment form, you notice that Heavy Metal's acknowledgment form requires that all disputes be brought to binding arbitration. The purchase order says nothing about the mode of dispute resolution. Can Arlene still avoid this deal? U.C.C. §§2-204, 2-206, and 2-207. Could she have avoided it under the common law?

b. Same facts as part a., except that Heavy Metal's acknowledgment form purports to accept Sportlife's offer to buy a dozen Lifecycle stationary bikes rather than a dozen 580XL circuit-trainer weight machines. Prior to shipment by Heavy Metal, is there a contract at all? U.C.C. §§2-204, 2-206, and 2-207.

c. Same facts as part a., except that Heavy Metal's acknowledgment form also says that "THIS ACCEPTANCE IS EXPRESSLY MADE CONDITIONAL ON BUYER'S ASSENT TO ANY ADDITIONAL OR DIFFERENT TERMS CONTAINED IN THIS FORM." Prior to shipment of the goods, can Arlene still avoid this deal? U.C.C. §§2-204, 2-206, and 2-207.

d. Same facts as part a., except that Heavy Metal's acknowledgment form also says that "THIS ACCEPTANCE IS EXPRESSLY MADE CONDITIONAL ON BUYER'S ASSENT TO ANY ADDITIONAL OR DIFFERENT TERMS CONTAINED IN THIS FORM" and Arlene has both shipped the goods and accepted payment for them. Now is there a contract? If so, will disputes be subject to arbitration? U.C.C. §§2-204, 2-206, and 2-207. What would the answers to those two questions be under the common law?

3.4. a. The next problem Arlene wants to talk about stems from her company's sale of an industrial-level weight machine to a local Gold's Gym franchise. It turns out that one of the cables on the machine broke during use and severely injured one of the Gold's Gym patrons. The Gold's Gym manager had called Arlene last week and told her that if his patron sued the gym, Gold's Gym would make Heavy Metal responsible for all of the damages.

This transaction had involved a purchase order from Gold's, an acknowledgment form from Heavy Metal, and then shipment of the machine from Heavy Metal to Gold's. Gold's purchase order had specifically reserved all of its remedies and had mentioned nothing about the mode of dispute resolution. Heavy Metal's acknowledgment form had a conspicuous disclaimer of consequential damages and a provision that said that all disputes would be subject to binding arbitration (but no "expressly made conditional" language). Is there a contract at all? Will the consequential damages disclaimer hold? Will disputes be subject to arbitration? U.C.C. §§2-204, 2-206, and 2-207.

b. Same facts as part a., except suppose that Heavy Metal has sold various weight machines to this Gold's Gym franchise during the past several months, with each side always using the same forms. Imagine that when this relationship between buyer and seller was beginning, the manager of the Gold's franchise actually read Heavy Metal's acknowledgment form. At that time, he noticed the arbitration clause, called Arlene, and told her that he didn't like the arbitration clause in her form. Arlene replied, "Take it or leave it." The Gold's manager said, "Well, I guess so." Now Arlene wants to cite that one-time conversation to make the following argument: as far as the arbitration clause goes, this isn't a §2-207 case at all, since the buyer in fact specifically assented to this additional term on Arlene's acknowledgment form. Will this argument work for Arlene?

c.   Same facts as part a., except that this transaction had begun with an oral contract between Arlene and the Gold's manager. The terms of the oral contract included the fact that Heavy Metal would not be responsible for consequential damages. Following the oral contract, Gold's sent Arlene a written confirmation. That confirmation stated the terms of the oral contract, including type of machine and price, but it said that the seller *would* be responsible for consequential damages. Further, the confirmation said that "THIS ACCEPTANCE IS EXPRESSLY MADE CONDITIONAL ON SELLER'S ASSENT TO THE ADDITIONAL OR DIFFERENT TERMS CONTAINED IN THE CONFIRMATION." There has been no performance yet by either side. Arlene comes to you and says that she wants to enforce the oral contract, but only if she is not responsible for consequential damages. (1) What effect, if any, should be given to the "expressly made conditional" clause contained in the confirmation? U.C.C. §§2-204, 2-206, and 2-207. (2) At this point, can Arlene enforce the sale according to the terms of the oral contract (i.e., no consequential damages)? U.C.C. §§2-204, 2-206, and 2-207. (3) What if Gold's confirmation had included not only a different term (seller's responsibility for consequential damages), but also an additional term (e.g., "delivery must take place on a Thursday") — would the additional term become part of the contract? U.C.C. §§2-204, 2-206, and 2-207.

3.5.   Arlene tells you that she is tired of talking about mistakes she may have made in the past. She now wants to know how she can avoid problems in the future. In particular, she wants to know if there is something else she should include in her form or if there is some procedure she should follow to ensure that her exclusion of consequential damages clause becomes a valid term of every sale that she makes. Do you have any suggestions for her? U.C.C. §§2-204, 2-206, and 2-207.

Assignment 4: Formation with Leases, International Sales, and Real Estate

A. Formation of Contracts for Leases

The difference between the formation provisions of U.C.C. Article 2 and those of Article 2A reflects the difference in practice between how sales are formed, on the one hand, and how leases are formed, on the other. For one thing, commercial leases will rarely be concluded through the exchange of forms, in contrast to the case of a merchant-to-merchant sale of goods on open account. Any large commercial lease will likely be the product of a negotiated contract. Because of the lessor's residual interest, it will typically make sense for the two sides to in fact sit down and work out all of the terms and conditions of the lease in advance of entering into the lease. The most important consequence of this difference is that Article 2A has no "battle of the forms" section or even anything that looks remotely like U.C.C. §2-207.

Although the Article 2A drafters did not feel compelled to create a lease analogue to §2-207, they did borrow liberally (and literally, in some cases) from the sales formation rules of §§2-204, 2-205 and 2-206. U.C.C. §§2A-204 and 2A-205 directly steal from their Article 2 cousins, aside from plugging in the word "lease contract" where the word "sales contract" appears in Article 2. Thus, in §2A-204 the general formation rules for leases have the same flexible principles that guide formation for sales: lease contracts may be formed in any manner that shows agreement; we do not need to know exactly when a lease contract is formed in order to conclude that it has been formed; and the only substantive detail needed in a lease contract is "a reasonably certain basis for giving an appropriate remedy." Furthermore, amended §2A-204(4) contains the same new provisions as amended §2-204(4), which allows the formation of a contract through electronic agents. U.C.C. §2A-205 creates for leases the same limited exception to the common law unenforceability of firm offers without consideration as we see in §2-205.

U.C.C. §2A-206 represents a modest reworking of §2-206. The lease version of the offer and acceptance section contains the same proviso that unless otherwise clearly indicated, an offer to make a lease should be construed as inviting acceptance "in any manner and by any medium reasonable in the circumstances." What is missing from §2A-206 are the parts of §2-206 that refer to purchase orders and shipment. Just like the absence of a clone to §2-207, the absence in Article 2A of the §2-206 shipping provisions is a translation from Article 2 that, in the words of the Official Comment to §2A-206, "reflect[s] leasing practices and terminology."

B.   Formation of Contracts for
International Sales

Whereas Article 2A of the UCC did not include §2-207 because leasing formation practices make those issues largely irrelevant, the CISG drafters did not include the rules of §2-207 because they must not have agreed with them. In international sales, just like in domestic sales, there will often be purchase orders and acknowledgment forms. And sometimes these forms will have terms that do not agree.

The way that the CISG handles the "battle of the forms" is something of a cross between U.C.C. §2-207 and the common-law "mirror image" rule. On the one hand, C.I.S.G. Article 19(1) says that purported acceptances that contain additions or modifications are not acceptances, but are instead counteroffers. That sounds like the common-law mirror-image rule. On the other hand, Article 19(2) says that purported acceptances that contain additional or different terms *do* count as valid acceptances as long as the new terms are not material alterations or the offeror does not object to the discrepancy "without undue delay." That sounds a lot like U.C.C. §2-207(1) (and amended U.C.C. §2-206(3)). Yet the CISG's definition of what constitutes a material alteration is fairly broad: any additional or different terms "relating among other things, to the price, payment, quality and quantity of the goods, place and time of delivery, extent of one party's liability to the other or the settlement of disputes." C.I.S.G. Art. 19(3).

There are a number of significant differences between U.C.C. §2-207 and C.I.S.G. Article 19. The first is that §2-207 (and amended U.C.C. §2-206(3)) will clearly allow an acceptance that contains even material alterations of the offer to count as an acceptance. Second, there is nothing in Article 19 that is quite analogous to the offeree's ability in pre-amended §2-207(1) to make its acceptance "expressly . . . conditional on assent to the additional or different terms."

Finally, Article 19 does not contain an analogue to pre-amended §2-207(3) that tells us exactly what happens when a purported acceptance that *does* contain materially different terms is not objected to and then is followed by conduct by both sides which indicates a contract. The seeming result under the CISG in such a scenario would be a return to the common law's "last-shot" doctrine, by which the party who sent the last form would see its terms control as long as buyer and seller both proceeded to act as if there were a contract. Under C.I.S.G. Art. 19(1), the purported acceptance with the materially different terms will be a counteroffer. Under C.I.S.G. Art. 18(1), the original offeror's proceeding to perform under the contract would constitute conduct by which the original offeror will be deemed to have accepted the "counteroffer."

The following is one of the few reported cases so far that have had to deal with the "battle of the forms" in an international context.

Filanto v. Chilewich International Corp.
789 F. Supp. 1229 (S.D.N.Y. 1992)

BRIEANT, CHIEF JUDGE.

... This case is a striking example of how a lawsuit involving a relatively straight-forward international commercial transaction can raise an array of complex questions. Accordingly, the Court will recount the factual background of the case, derived from both parties' memoranda of law and supporting affidavits, in some detail.

Plaintiff Filanto is an Italian corporation engaged in the manufacture and sale of footwear. Defendant Chilewich is an export-import firm incorporated in the state of New York with its principal place of business in White Plains. On February 28, 1989, Chilewich's agent in the United Kingdom, Byerly Johnson, Ltd., signed a contract with Raznoexport, the Soviet Foreign Economic Association, which obligated Byerly Johnson to supply footwear to Raznoexport. Section 10 of this contract — the "Russian Contract" — is an arbitration clause. ...

The first exchange of correspondence between the parties to this lawsuit is a letter dated July 27, 1989 from Mr. Melvin Chilewich of Chilewich International to Mr. Antonio Filograna, chief executive officer of Filanto. This letter refers to a recent visit by Chilewich and Byerly Johnson personnel to Filanto's factories in Italy, presumably to negotiate a purchase to fulfill the Russian Contract. ...

[T]he focus of this dispute, apparent from the parties' submissions, is not on the scope of the arbitration provision included in the Russian contract; rather, the threshold question is whether these parties actually agreed to arbitrate their disputes at all. ...

Not surprisingly, the parties offer varying interpretations of the numerous letters and documents exchanged between them. The Court will briefly summarize their respective contentions.

Defendant Chilewich contends that the Memorandum Agreement dated March 13 which it signed and sent to Filanto was an offer. It then argues that Filanto's retention of the letter, along with its subsequent acceptance of Chilewich's performance under the Agreement — the furnishing of the May 11 letter of credit — estops it from denying its acceptance of the contract. Although phrased as an estoppel argument, this contention is better viewed as an acceptance by conduct argument, e.g., that in light of the parties' course of dealing, Filanto had a duty timely to inform Chilewich that it objected to the incorporation by reference of all the terms of the Russian contract. Under this view, the return of the Memorandum Agreement, signed by Filanto, on August 7, 1990, along with the covering letter purporting to exclude parts of the Russian Contract, was ineffective as a matter of law as a rejection of the March 13 offer, because this occurred some five months after Filanto received the Memorandum Agreement and two months after Chilewich furnished the Letter of Credit. Instead, in Chilewich's view, this action was a proposal for modification of the March 13 Agreement. Chilewich rejected this proposal, by its letter of August 7 to Byerly Johnson, and the August 29 fax by Johnson to Italian Trading SRL, which communication Filanto acknowledges receiving. Accordingly, Filanto under this interpretation is bound by the written terms of the March 13 Memorandum Agreement; since that agreement incorporates by reference the Russian Contract containing the arbitration provision, Filanto is bound to arbitrate.

Plaintiff Filanto's interpretation of the evidence is rather different. While Filanto apparently agrees that the March 13 Memorandum Agreement was indeed an offer, it characterizes its August 7 return of the signed Memorandum Agreement with the covering letter as a counteroffer. While defendant contends that under Uniform Commercial Code §2-207 this action would be viewed as an acceptance with a proposal for a material modification, the Uniform Commercial Code *** does not apply to this case, because the State Department undertook to fix something that was not broken by helping to create the Sale of Goods Convention which varies from the Uniform Commercial Code in many significant ways. Instead, under this analysis, Article 19(1) of the Sale of Goods Convention would apply. That section, as the Commentary to the Sale of Goods Convention notes, reverses the rule of Uniform Commercial Code §2-207, and reverts to the common law rule that "A reply to an offer which purports to be an acceptance but contains additions, limitations or other modifications is a rejection of the offer and constitutes a counter-offer". Sale of Goods Convention Article 19(1). Although the Convention, like the Uniform Commercial Code, does state that non-material terms do become part of the contract unless objected to, Sale of Goods Convention Article 19(2), the Convention treats inclusion (or deletion) of an arbitration provision as "material", Sale of Goods Convention Article 19(3). The August 7 letter, therefore, was a counteroffer which, according to Filanto, Chilewich accepted by its letter dated September 27, 1990. Though that letter refers to and acknowledges the "contractual obligations" between the parties, it is doubtful whether it can be characterized as an acceptance.

More generally, both parties seem to have lost sight of the narrow scope of the inquiry required by the Arbitration Convention. All that this Court need do is to determine if a sufficient "agreement in writing" to arbitrate disputes exists between these parties. Although that inquiry is informed by the provisions of the Sale of Goods Convention, the Court lacks the authority on this motion to resolve all outstanding issues between the parties. Indeed, contracts and the arbitration clauses included therein are considered to be "severable," a rule that the Sale of Goods Convention itself adopts with respect to avoidance of contracts generally. Sale of Goods Convention Article 81(1)....

Since the issue of whether and how a contract between these parties was formed is obviously related to the issue of whether Chilewich breached any contractual obligations, the Court will direct its analysis to whether there was objective conduct evidencing an intent to be bound with respect to the arbitration provision.

The Court is satisfied on this record that there was indeed an agreement to arbitrate between these parties.

There is simply no satisfactory explanation as to why Filanto failed to object to the incorporation by reference of the Russian Contract in a timely fashion. As noted above, Chilewich had in the meantime commenced its performance under the Agreement, and the Letter of Credit it furnished Filanto on May 11 itself mentioned the Russian Contract. An offeree who, knowing that the offeror has commenced performance, fails to notify the offeror of its objection to the terms of the contract within a reasonable time will, under certain circumstances, be deemed to have assented to those terms. The Sale of Goods Convention itself recognizes this rule: Article 18(1), provides that "A statement made by or other conduct of the offeree indicating assent to an offer is an acceptance". Although mere "silence or inactivity" does not constitute acceptance, Sale of Goods Convention Article 18(1), the Court may consider previous relations between the parties in assessing whether a party's conduct constituted acceptance, Sale of Goods Convention Article 8(3). In this case, in light of the extensive course of prior dealing between these parties, Filanto was certainly under a duty to alert Chilewich in timely fashion to its objections to the terms of the March 13 Memorandum Agreement — particularly since Chilewich had repeatedly referred it to the Russian Contract and Filanto had had a copy of that document for some time....

In light of these factors, and heeding the presumption in favor of arbitration, which is even stronger in the context of international commercial transactions, the Court holds that Filanto is bound by the terms of the March 13 Memorandum Agreement, and so must arbitrate its dispute in Moscow....

Besides the different way that the CISG handles the "battle of the forms" which was discussed in *Filanto*, there are a couple of other distinctions worth noting between the CISG formation rules and the Article 2 rules. First, the CISG provides in Article 18(2) that acceptances are effective only when received by the offeror, not when sent as is true under the UCC.

Second, C.I.S.G. Article 16(2) contains an even more liberal exception than U.C.C. §2-205 to the common-law rule that firm offers are not binding unless they are given for consideration. C.I.S.G. Article 16(2) says that offers which indicate that they are irrevocable may not be revoked for the time stated by the offeror. Unlike U.C.C. §2-205, the irrevocability of a firm offer under C.I.S.G. Article 16(2) is not a function of the offer being in writing and is not limited to a period of three months.

C.   Formation of Real Estate Contracts

Understanding the formation of real estate contracts is simplified by the fact that the process typically does not involve the exchange of inconsistent forms as is often true with commercial sales of goods. What complicates the real estate formation process is that there are typically one or more brokers serving as agents or subagents of the seller and, occasionally, the buyer.

With significant commercial real estate sales, the contract formation process will be fairly straightforward. Both buyer and seller will normally be represented by lawyers, and the two sides will hammer out a sales contract that will detail as many of the terms as the two sides can think of and care to resolve.

From a systems perspective, perhaps the most interesting real estate formation process exists in the context of residential real estate sales. With residential sales, there is a very elaborate and developed system in place that includes real estate brokers as key players in the process. Indeed, it is safe to say that the vast majority of residential real estate contracts in this country are formed only with the intervention of real estate brokers.

Consider a typical residential real estate scenario: Steve and Karen Shaughnessy were married soon after both of them graduated from law school, and now the two of them would like to buy a house. A classmate who has lived in the area all his life recommends to them a "great real estate agent," Patty Schaner. Steve and Karen approach Patty, who agrees to "work with" them.

Patty then learns what the Shaughnessys are looking for in a house, and how much they can afford. She begins taking the couple to "showings" of houses on the market that seem to meet the couple's specifications and budget. Unless one of the Shaughnessys took a real estate course or their state has strict agency disclosure requirements, they may not realize that Patty is technically not their agent, but rather is the agent (or sub-agent) of the seller. Although an increasing number of real estate brokers today will offer a true "buyer's agent," the majority of residential sales today are put together solely by agents and sub-agents of the seller.

Patty's ability to quickly find houses on the market that meet the Shaughnessys' requirements will be enhanced by her access to her local multiple listing service (MLS). The MLS is typically formed by the local real estate brokers group for the purpose of sharing listings with each other. The MLS consists of a computer data base that can display home listings according to such parameters as price, location, number of rooms, and the like. In most areas, over 90 percent of homes that are listed with brokers will have a description of the home included in the MLS.

After several dozen showings, the Shaughnessys finally find their "dream home." The home they wish to buy is owned by the Garners, a growing family that has just purchased a new and larger home. When the Garners decided to put their home on the market, they entered into a 90-day "exclusive listing agreement" with Bob Erker, a neighbor who also happened to be a real estate agent. The listing agreement provides that Bob will receive a 6-percent commission upon closing of the sale, even if the Garners decide to ditch Bob during the 90-day period and sell their house through another agent, or even if the Garners are able to sell their house with no agent.

The Shaughnessys tell Patty that they would like to make an offer to the Garners for the house's full asking price, $100,000. Patty supplies the Shaughnessys a form contract on which to make that offer. The contract was drafted as a cooperative effort between the local bar association and the local association of realtors. It contains several boilerplate provisions, plus some blanks for the particulars of each deal and any contingencies that either side would like to insert. The Shaughnessys ask Patty to insert contingencies providing that they will not be obligated to close unless they obtain specified financing and unless the house is found to be in good repair by an inspector to be hired by the Shaughnessys.

Albright v. McDermond

14 P.3d 318 (Colo. 2000)

... On December 6, 1998, Buyers viewed Seller's residence in Denver's Park Hill neighborhood. Buyers placed a bid of $230,000 on the property after another prospective purchaser had placed a bid of $225,000. Seller took the higher bid and executed a contract with Buyers dated December 6, 1998. The parties utilized form No. CBS 1/M-7-96, which the Commission promulgated pursuant to its statutory authority. See §12-61-803(4), 4 C.R.S. (2000). Paragraph 10 of the Contract (Inspection Provision) recited:

> INSPECTION. Seller agrees to provide Buyer on or before [December] 13, 1998, with a Seller's Property Disclosure form completed by Seller to the best of Seller's current actual knowledge. Buyer or any designee, shall have the right to have inspection(s) of the physical condition of the Property and Inclusions, at Buyer's expense. If written notice of any unsatisfactory condition, signed by or on behalf of Buyer, is not received by Seller on or before [December 16], 1998 (Objection Deadline), the physical condition of the Property and Inclusions shall be deemed to be satisfactory to Buyer. *If such notice is received by Seller as set forth above, and if Buyer and Seller have not agreed, in writing, to a settlement thereof on or before [December 17], 1998 (Resolution Deadline), this Contract shall terminate three calendar days following the Resolution Deadline*; unless, within the three calendar days, Seller receives written notice from Buyer waiving objection to any unsatisfactory condition. Buyer is responsible for and shall pay for any damage which occurs to the Property and Inclusions as a result of such inspection. (Emphasis added.)

Initially, the parties specified an Objection Deadline of December 14, 1998, and a Resolution Deadline of December 15, 1998. The parties mutually agreed to extend the Objection Deadline to December 16 and the Resolution Deadline to December 17.

The Contract specified a closing date of December 31, 1998, and an earnest money deposit of $4,000.00 to be held in trust by Seller's real estate agent. The Contract included a liquidated damages provision (paragraph 18(a)(2)), providing for forfeiture of Buyers' earnest money deposit to Seller, as her sole and only remedy, in the event of Buyers' breach.

Pursuant to the Inspection Provision, Buyers hired an inspector, inspected the property, and timely presented Seller with inspection objections. By means of an Inspection Release Addendum they proposed before the Objection Deadline of December 16, Buyers listed ten conditions they deemed unsatisfactory. Buyers' addendum proposed that Seller remedy these ten items prior to closing at her expense, through use of licensed contractors, in conformance with codes, and subject to a walk-through one day prior to closing to verify completion of the work. . . .

Pursuant to Paragraph 10 of the Contract, Buyer has conducted inspection(s) of the Property and has identified certain conditions that do not meet with approval of the Buyer. *Provided the Seller agrees to arrange for and pay the cost of having the following work (Work) performed at the Property, the Buyer agrees to release and waive any objection to the Property and to hold the Contract in full force and effect.* Work is to be performed by licensed contractor(s) in a workmanlike manner and shall meet code requirements when applicable. Seller agrees to deliver to Buyer, on date of closing, following successful transfer of deed, any and all warranties and/or guarantees that may be provided to Seller as a result of having the Work performed. *Buyer shall have the right to walk-through the Property not later than one (1) day prior to date of closing, at a mutually agreeable time, to verify completion of the Work as agreed.* (Emphasis added.)

The trial court found that Seller's agent informed Buyers' agent on December 14, and again on December 15, that Seller was "[n]ot interested in doing the work prior to closing." Buyers' agent responded that Buyers "expected all repairs to be done at the seller's expense and before closing."

On December 16, several exchanges occurred. Instead of signing Buyers' proposed Inspection Release Addendum, Seller wrote on its face that:

> Seller accepts conditions 1-10 with the following notes: 1) I have obtained estimates in the minimum of $2835 and maximum of $3600. *I will escrow $4500 with whomever out of closing proceeds & will have the work done after closing;* & 2) while not a requirement, I would prefer a closing date of 12/21. That will allow me more time to get the work done.

(Emphasis added.) Seller accompanied this writing with a letter providing additional details about her proposed terms.

Also on the 16th, Buyers provided Seller with an additional Inspection Release Addendum, stating that:

> Due to lack of agreement of seller & buyer to prior inspection addendum the contract has failed under paragraph 10. Buyers request release of earnest money. See attached earnest money release addendum.

The earnest money Mutual Release Agreement that Buyers proposed to Seller recited that the parties mutually agreed to terminate the Contract with return of the $4,000.00 earnest money deposit to Buyers. Seller did not execute this release. Finally, Buyers' agent faxed to Seller's agent a handwritten note, reciting that: "As we discussed at 5:00 the buyers don't want to accept [Seller's] proposal of $4,500 as just faxed to me." Although the parties disputed at trial the exact timing of sending and receiving of these documents dated December 16, the County Court found that these instruments and the testimony of witnesses nevertheless demonstrated that the parties did not reach agreement for resolution of the inspection objections by the Resolution Deadline.

On December 17, prior to the close of the Resolution Deadline under the Contract, Buyers entered into a contract for purchase of a house they had viewed prior to entering their bid on Seller's house. On December 18, Seller entered into a contract for sale of her house to the previous prospective purchaser whom the Buyers had outbid. Declaring the occurrence of a material breach, Seller refused to authorize the release of the $4,000.00 earnest money deposit to Buyers. Buyers' agent took the position on behalf of her clients that: (1) Seller had refused to agree to Buyers' terms; and (2) Buyers could terminate the contract for any or no reason.

Buyers brought suit in Small Claims Court for return of their $4,000.00 earnest money deposit. Seller counter-claimed for damages and filed a separate suit against Buyers' agent for tortious interference with contract. By agreement of the parties, the Small Claims Court transferred the suits to the County Court for joint trial.

The County Court found that Buyers and Seller had not reached agreement under the Inspection Provision, and that, consequently, Buyers were entitled to return of their earnest money deposit. The County Court also found that Buyers' agent had not committed tortious interference with the contract by assisting Buyers in entering the contract for purchase of a different house before the Resolution

Deadline. In addition to costs against Seller, the County Court awarded attorney's fees (1) to Buyers under the attorney's fees provision of the Contract; and (2) to Buyers' agent because Seller filed and pursued a frivolous and vexatious claim. . . .

A court's primary obligation is to effectuate the intent of the contracting parties according to the plain language and meaning of the contract. See *Ad Two,* 9 P.3d at 376. A trial court takes evidence regarding the intent and meaning of a contract only in the event of a material term's ambiguity, whereas "[w]ritten contracts that are complete and free from ambiguity will be found to express the intention of the parties and will be enforced according to their plain language." Id.

Here, the Seller and Buyers entered into a residential real estate contract on a Commission-promulgated form. The General Assembly gave the Commission the authority to promulgate rules, consider licensing and examination matters, provide educational materials, review complaints, and take disciplinary action against licensees. . . .

Protection of the public is a primary Commission purpose. . . . To further this purpose, agents must use the Commission's standardized forms. These forms set forth the basic contractual rights and remedies for Buyers and Sellers of real property in Colorado . . . .

In 1989, the Commission added an Inspection Provision to the standard residential real estate form to replace agents' prior practice of inserting their own choice of inspection language. This provision, which the Commission has adjusted from time to time, allows Buyers to inspect, object to, and obtain resolution of their objections concerning the physical condition of the contracted property and inclusions, and in the absence of such resolution, trigger termination of the Contract. See Kent Jay Levine et al., *Guidebook to Colorado Real Estate Contracts & Disclosures* 72 (2d ed. 1995).

Pursuant to the Contract, the Seller supplies Buyer with a copy of Seller's Property Disclosure form. Buyer then has the right to inspect the property and the inclusions. The Objection Deadline is the time by which Buyer must supply written objections to Seller listing the physical conditions of the property or inclusions that are unsatisfactory to Buyer. In the event of no timely written objection, Buyer accepts the physical condition of the property and inclusions. In the event of timely written objection, the parties then have until the Resolution Deadline to reach a written agreement satisfying Buyer's concerns. If the parties reach agreement, they sign an addendum that describes that agreement. If they cannot reach agreement, the Contract terminates three calendar days after the Resolution Deadline, unless Buyer waives the objection. If Buyer withdraws the objection, Seller remains under an obligation to sell to Buyer under the contract terms.

A commentator observes that the Inspection Provision allows Buyer to exercise his or her own discretion in determining whether the physical condition of the property and inclusions is unsatisfactory, thereby triggering termination in absence of reaching agreement:

> Unlike prior approved forms, the current [Commission] Forms contain an inspection provision whereunder the buyer can terminate the contract if the buyer identifies any unsatisfactory physical condition, and the buyer and seller do not reach written agreement in settlement of the condition.

2 Cathy Stricklin Krendl, Colorado Methods of Practice 92 (4th ed. 1998). . . .

...Upon review of the Contract, we read the Inspection Provision as providing that: (1) if Seller did not agree to the Buyers' timely inspection objection proposal made before the Objection Deadline; and (2) the parties did not reach an alternate accommodation by the Resolution Deadline; then (3) the Contract terminated three days after the Resolution Deadline unless (4) the Buyers withdrew their objections. Additionally, an implied duty of good faith and fair dealing applied to the Seller's and Buyers' actions under the Contract. See Bayou Land Co. v. Talley, 924 P.2d 136, 154 (Colo. 1996). Accordingly, we proceed with our review of the record to determine who is entitled to the $4000.00 earnest money deposit....

The record here demonstrates that the sale and purchase of a home can be a stressful and unsuccessful event between the parties to a contract. Buyers' and Seller's difficulties centered primarily on the fact that they mutually agreed in the December 6 Contract to a closing date of December 31. Of course the holiday season intervened; nevertheless, the parties held to their agreed-upon December 31 closing date.

Buyers insisted on the repairs being accomplished no later than the day before closing, in order to verify their completion prior to taking possession. Seller became frustrated by her inability to obtain contractors during the holiday season. Not wishing to extend the closing date and also desiring to circumscribe the amount she would pay for repairs, Seller proposed to escrow a certain amount of money at closing toward accomplishing the repairs after closing. Buyers rejected this proposal. The parties did not pursue an extension of the Resolution Deadline or of the closing date in an effort to reach agreement and accomplish the repairs prior to closing.

As the County Court found — and we agree based on evidence in the record — Buyers and Seller did not enter into a written agreement resolving Buyers' timely inspection objections by the close of the December 17 Resolution Deadline. Accordingly, because Buyers did not withdraw their objections, the Contract terminated by its terms December 20, three days after the Resolution Deadline.

Both Buyers and Seller took separate actions on December 17 and December 18, respectively, to enter into different contracts, thereby abandoning their effort at reaching agreement. Their motivations differed. Buyers believed that Seller did not intend to accomplish the repairs prior to closing, whereas Seller believed that Buyers did not intend to purchase the property on inspection objection terms reasonable to her....

Material to our decision, in accord with same conclusion reached by the County Court and the District Court, is the fact that Seller and Buyers did not agree on a resolution to the inspection objections by the Resolution Deadline, and the Contract terminated by its terms. While the Contract anticipated that Seller and Buyers had until the end of the Resolution Deadline to resolve their differences, it became apparent to the agents and the parties in this case that Buyers and Seller were deadlocked.

Contrary to Seller's contention, there was no anticipatory breach or breach of the implied covenant of good faith and fair dealing on Buyers' part by their action in (1) not agreeing to Seller's proposal to accomplish the repairs after closing and limited in cost to Seller; or (2) entering into another residential contract before the Resolution Deadline. When they realized they could not converge on a resolution, the parties and their agents pursued their respective best interests and promptly accomplished separate transactions with other parties. . . .

The misstatement of Buyers' agent that her clients could terminate the Contract "for any reason" did not prevent Seller from agreeing to Buyers' inspection resolution terms. Had Seller agreed before the Resolution Deadline to Buyers' proposal, Seller would have had a claim to the earnest money deposit, as liquidated damages, upon Buyers' failure to close in accordance with the terms of the Contract. Seller did not agree to Buyers' inspection resolution terms before the Resolution Deadline and Buyers did not withdraw their objections. Thus, the Contract terminated.

Accordingly, we affirm the judgment of the District Court upholding the County Court's judgment.

Returning now to our hypothetical home buyers, Patty brings the signed offer with the financing and inspection contingencies to the Garners. If the Garners choose to accept and sign the Shaughnessys' offer, then a residential sales contract, albeit one with contingencies, will have been formed. If the contract survives all the way through closing, Bob will not end up with as much money as you might think: Bob's 6-percent commission is first split between the listing agent (Bob) and the selling agent (Patty). In most cases, Bob and Patty then split their 3 percent with their respective home offices. Thus, in this $100,000 home sale, Bob, Patty, and each of their offices end up with $1,500 apiece.

It might not surprise you to learn that the litigation which exists surrounding the formation process in residential real estate transactions more often involves issues of broker commissions than it does whether a particular sales contract was formed or not. Perhaps some of this litigation stems from the differing perspectives on the formation process that are held by agents and by sellers: The seller might begrudge the size of the agent's commission, "given how little work she actually did for me"; the agent, on the other hand, cannot forget all of the uncompensated work she did for various other sellers whose house sales never did materialize. Another frequent source of litigation is the tension between the broker's legal role as representative of the seller and its practical role as advisor to the buyer.

Messler v. Phillips

867 P.2d 128 (Colo. Ct. App. 1993)

HUME, J.

In this action premised on claims for fraud, negligence, and theft in regard to a real estate transaction, defendant, Sandra Phillips, doing business as Phillips and Associates, appeals the trial court's judgment finding her to be negligent and awarding compensatory and exemplary damages to plaintiff, Gladys V. Messler. . . .

Defendant entered into a listing contract to act as plaintiff's real estate broker for the sale of her home and the concurrent purchase of a townhome from Lockley Investment Corporation, for which defendant was also the exclusive listing broker. The contract to purchase the townhome was contingent on the sale of plaintiff's home. At the concurrent closings, defendant was present when plaintiff endorsed a proceeds check from the sale of her home directly to developer John Lockley in payment for the townhome.

The townhome was part of a multi-unit development that was subject to certain liens and encumbrances; however, no payment was made to release these encumbrances as they related to the townhome, no title insurance coverage for the townhome was procured, and no deed for that property was delivered or recorded as called for by the purchase contract. Lockley cashed the proceeds check and left Colorado. Subsequently, the property went into foreclosure.

Plaintiff sued both defendant and Lockley alleging negligence, fraud, and theft. Defendant cross-claimed against Lockley for indemnification. Lockley filed answers to plaintiff's complaint and defendant's cross-claim, but failed to appear at trial.

The trial court entered default judgment against Lockley on each of plaintiff's claims. After a bench trial, it also determined that defendant was negligent and awarded compensatory damages equivalent to the purchase price paid by plaintiff, plus attorney fees and costs, jointly and severally between defendant and Lockley. The court also awarded plaintiff exemplary damages against defendant in an amount equal to the compensatory damage award. . . .

Defendant next contends that the trial court erred in determining that she negligently breached a duty of care to the plaintiff. We disagree.

The trial court found that defendant breached a fiduciary duty she owed to plaintiff in her role as broker/agent at both closings by allowing the proceeds check for the purchase of plaintiff's house to be endorsed solely to Lockley without ensuring that plaintiff received title insurance and a deed conveying title to the townhome as called for by the terms of the contract. The trial court found that defendant did not disclose to plaintiff that she was acting as Lockley's agent as listing broker for the townhome and that she could not represent plaintiff's interests in that closing without a written authorization from both principals to act as a dual agent. Rather, defendant told plaintiff that she would represent plaintiff's interests at both closings, without differentiating between whom she represented at each closing.

In so doing, she negligently misrepresented what she could or would do on plaintiff's behalf.

We reject the trial court's finding that defendant had a fiduciary duty to plaintiff with respect to the sale of Lockley's townhome; however, we agree with the trial court's underlying finding that defendant breached a duty of care to the plaintiff.

General agency principles allow an agency relationship to be established by the conduct of the parties as principal and agent. Such a relationship, however, cannot arise by implication between a purchaser and a real estate broker or salesperson if the real estate broker or salesperson also represents the seller.

Under Colorado law and Real Estate Commission rules, in order for a real estate broker to represent both the seller and buyer in a transaction, the broker must put the agency agreement in writing, and the seller and purchaser both must sign it. If there is no such written agreement, the agent is considered only the agent of the seller. The fiduciary duty owed by defendant as a broker, then, is inapplicable in this case.

However, real estate brokers have been held accountable for failure to deal fairly and honestly with a purchaser while serving as the seller's agent. We conclude that defendant's negligent misrepresentation of her ability to represent plaintiff's interests constitutes a violation of the broker's duty of honesty and fair dealing.

Negligent misrepresentation may occur if:

> (1) One who, in the course of his business, profession or employment, . . . supplies false information for the guidance of others in their business transactions, is subject to liability for pecuniary loss caused to them by their justifiable reliance upon the information, if he fails to exercise reasonable care or competence in obtaining or communicating the information.
> (2) . . . [T]he liability stated in Subsection (1) is limited to loss suffered
> > (a) by the person or one of a limited group of persons for whose benefit and guidance he intends to supply the information or knows that the recipient intends to supply it; and
> > (b) through reliance upon it in a transaction that he intends the information to influence or knows that the recipient so intends or in a substantially similar transaction.

Restatement (Second) of Torts §552 (1977).

The standard for negligent misrepresentation considers the care and competence of the actor, who "must utilize with reasonable attention and caution not only those qualities and facilities which as a reasonable [person he or she] is required to have, but also those superior qualities and facilities which [the actor] has." Restatement (Second) of Torts §298 comment d (1965).

Here, defendant's representations implied that she would exercise the level of care that a reasonable real estate broker or salesperson would use in overseeing a closing for a purchaser. We conclude the trial court did not err in determining that defendant assumed a duty of care by these affirmative assertions and that she breached the standard of care applicable to her actions.

Further, even though defendant did not formally contract to act as plaintiff's agent for the purchase of the townhome, she may nevertheless be held responsible for violation of an assumed duty of care in representing plaintiff's interests in the townhome closing.

An assumed duty may arise if 1) a defendant promises or undertakes affirmative acts to render a service to the plaintiff that was reasonably calculated to prevent the type of harm that befell plaintiff, and 2) plaintiff relies on the defendant to perform the service or defendant's undertaking increased plaintiff's risk.

The scope of an assumed duty is limited to the service undertaken. The standard of care, however, as in the case for negligent misrepresentation, is related to the care and competence of the actor.

Here, defendant told plaintiff and her relatives that she would look after plaintiff's interests at both closings, and she assured plaintiff's relatives they did not need to attend. Thus, we perceive no error in the trial court's determination that defendant assumed a duty of care by her promises that she would represent plaintiff's interests at the townhome closing and that she subsequently breached the duty she purported to assume. . . .

Problem Set 4

4.1. a.   You were working out at your health club after work one night last week when who should you run into again but your one-time law school classmate, Deborah Swift (from Problem 1.6). Deborah told you that she was feeling bad about the "misunderstanding" the two of you had at your fifth law school reunion a few weeks ago. She also told you that since the reunion she has quit her job as a lawyer and has started her own business selling and leasing Rolls Royces. In any event, to make amends Deborah said that she would offer to lease you that same 1983 Rolls Royce for two years, for just $150 per month. To avoid any confusion, Deborah said that this time she would put the offer in writing and would keep it open for five months.

You agreed to pay Deborah $100 for "tying up" this car for five months, and she said she would even apply this money toward the first month's lease payment should you choose to lease the car. After you paid Deborah and got her signed writing, you remembered that your Uncle Harry, the auto buff, was due to visit you in four months. You are also a little suspicious about the great lease rate for Deborah's car. Are you safe to wait until Uncle Harry comes and looks at the car before exercising your option? U.C.C. §2A-205.

b.   Same facts as part a., except that you do not pay anything for Deborah's signed writing promising the same lease deal. Are you safe now to wait until Uncle Harry comes to town? U.C.C. §2A-205.

c.   What if under the facts of part b., you did wait four months for Uncle Harry and then Deborah said that the offer was no longer open. Could you come up with another theory of enforcement outside of §2A-205? U.C.C. §1-103.

4.2.   Recall the facts of Problem 3.4.a.: Gym franchise sends purchase order to weight-machine seller; seller responds with acknowledgment form that includes a different term (no consequential damages) and an additional term (arbitration); buyer and seller perform without discussing differences in forms, but later those differences become relevant when a gym patron is injured by the machine. Suppose now that the Gold's Gym franchisee in that problem had been based in Toronto, Canada, rather than in the United States. How would your answers to the three questions in Problem 3.4.a. change: Is there a contract at all? Will the consequential damages disclaimer hold? Will disputes be subject to arbitration? C.I.S.G. Arts. 1(1), 18(1), 19.

4.3.   The following letter appeared in the syndicated real estate column of Robert Bruss:

"Dear Bob: I am selling a house I inherited. I told the Realtor to advertise it 'as is' because it's a fixer-upper. A buyer made a purchase offer I accepted. It contained a contingency for a professional inspection. That was fine with me. But the inspection revealed many defects, as I knew it would. Now the buyer refuses to complete the purchase unless I give her a $7,500 credit for repairs. To me, this looks like a $7,500 price reduction. Can the buyer force me to pay for these repairs?" Assume that the inspection contingency read as follows: "Buyer's purchase offer is contingent on the buyer's approval of a professional inspection report, which the buyer will arrange to have prepared within 14 days of this offer." What would your answer be if you were Robert Bruss?

4.4. Recall our hypothetical home-buyers, the Shaughnessys. On the recommendation of some friends, they approached real estate agent, Patty Schaner, who agreed to "work with" them in their quest to purchase a house. Imagine that when the Shaughnessys found their "dream home," listed by the Garners at $100,000, the Shaughnessys asked Patty if she could advise them on how little they could offer and still get the house. Patty then had a discussion with Bob Erker, the Garners' agent, who told Patty that the Garners had said from the start that though they were listing the home at $100,000, they would be thrilled to get $90,000 for it. In light of this conversation with Bob, what can Patty advise the Shaughnessys concerning their question to her about what offer to make?

Assignment 5: Statute of Frauds with Sales of Goods

When most non-lawyers think of legally enforceable contracts, they think of a writing. The fact is, of course, that under the common law most contracts do not have to be in writing in order to be legally enforceable. In that respect, the requirement of a writing for enforceability is the exception rather than the rule in the world of contracts. The writing requirement has, nevertheless, been made a feature of the system for the sale of goods.

Amended Article 2 of the U.C.C. has replaced the concept of a "writing" with that of a "record." The term "record" is a much broader term than "writing" and specifically encompasses information that is electronically stored as long as it is retrievable. Revised U.C.C. §1-201(31).

Just because there is a legal rule that says that sales contracts must be contained in a signed record or writing to be enforceable, however, does not mean that buyers and sellers will necessarily find it in their interests to put every sales contract in writing. Reducing a sales agreement to a record entails costs in both time and efficiency that do not always justify the benefits gained.

As one furniture manufacturer interviewed for this book put it: "For us, putting contracts into writing is a costly way to do business. We occasionally have buyers back out by claiming that they never made an order when we know they did, but that's still a small enough percentage of our orders that we still don't feel it's worth it to have every contract put in writing."

Another seller, a manufacturer of plastics, described how his company's system for purchasing raw materials from suppliers does not include formalizing their deals with a signed writing: "I handle our buying of raw materials from suppliers, things like rosin and colors. When we need a certain raw material I'll call three or four suppliers to find out whether they've got it and how much they'll sell it for. After that I'll call back the supplier I want and I'll do an oral order for the amount that we need. In that conversation, we'll settle on type, price, quantity, and delivery terms. I'll write that down and send the information to our warehouse people, who will then know what to expect and when to expect it. I never follow these phone calls with a written purchase order, but that's never been a problem. Probably 80 percent of the suppliers we deal with don't bother to send acknowledgment forms, either. If anyone ever tried to renege on one of these oral contracts, we would just stop doing business with them."

The decision about whether or not to include a writing component in one's purchasing system will also be a function of the size of the particular sale, as described by an in-house lawyer at a Fortune 100 company: "There are some purchases where we will deliberately choose not to use a writing, namely when the size of the purchase is small and it's a regular customer. In fact, we have a certain dollar threshold below which we will not insist on a signed writing from the seller, and still a lower threshold below which we won't even bother to send our own signed confirmation. The stakes are low enough in those cases and the likelihood of a problem low enough that we're willing to take our chances just so that we can conduct business more quickly. Besides, we have the business leverage of refusing to buy from a particular supplier in the future."

The above examples demonstrate that many sophisticated buyers and sellers decide that it is not in their interests to put every contract in writing, despite the statute of frauds rule. There are, however, many buyers and sellers who do follow a firm policy of having every sales contract memorialized with a writing. As one lawyer from a major clothing retailer put it: "Although our contracts to purchase clothes from wholesalers or manufacturers are probably formed on the phone, we insist that our purchasing people always follow with a signed written purchase order for at least two reasons: first, for purposes of our internal record-keeping, and second, because it makes me feel comfortable as a lawyer to think that we have something in writing."

In situations where a buyer and seller are engaged in a series of ongoing sales, one approach that is often taken to the writing requirement is that the two parties negotiate and sign at the beginning of their relationship one "master agreement" that outlines all of the terms and conditions of each sale that will take place in the future. All future sales are then conducted without the benefit of individual signed writings, and often the master agreement will specifically state that both parties agree to waive their ability to assert the statute of frauds as a bar to enforceability.

A lawyer that advises several natural gas suppliers described the use of this type of arrangement to handle what are known as "day trades" in the gas industry:

> Contracts that best reflect the reality of the hyperactive day-trading business address management approval through recognition of oral contracts. Because of the current Uniform Commercial Code ("U.C.C.") requirement found at 2-201, there may be an issue as to the enforceability of any contract for the sale of goods in excess of $500 which is not evidenced by writing . . . On the other hand, for a day trade, a company may make the decision to forgo a written contract because of simple economics — the risk of loss for one day's flow of gas may not justify the necessary administration costs.
>
> In order to avoid the potential problems that could result by flowing gas without a written contract, the following language may be used in any master gas contract for swing/interruptible/day-trading activities: "The Parties agree by their execution hereof that transactions will be entered into orally. No written confirmation will be required prior to the time Gas flows under such transaction and, unless otherwise agreed, each Party shall be responsible for making its own communications necessary to effect the flow of Gas. However, for billing and payment purposes, [Buyer] [Seller] will provide a written confirmation of any such oral transaction to [Seller] [Buyer] prior to the date specified herein for billing."
>
> The master contract also would have language indicating that the entire "Contract" is made up of the terms and conditions in the master contract as well as all transactions entered into under the terms of the master contract, whether oral or

written. An example of a clause of this type is: "The contract contemplated by this agreement shall include all transactions entered into by the parties, whether oral (as provided for in the preceding paragraph) or written; and the provisions of this Master Contract and all such transactions shall form a single Contract between the parties." An additional protection would be to allow tape recording of the oral contracts.

"Emphasis on Oral Commitments Advocated for Short-Term Deals," Gas Transactions Report, Vol. 3, No. 11 (1995).

Buyers and sellers that use Electronic Data Interchange, as described in Assignment 3, can similarly use the master EDI trading partner agreement to address questions about whether electronic orders will "count" to satisfy the statute of frauds. Most EDI trading partner agreements will include acknowledgments by both sides to the agreement that each electronic order constitutes a signed writing that is sufficient to satisfy Article 2's statute of frauds requirement.

The goals of the Article 2 drafters in formulating U.C.C. §2-201 were apparently to reconcile two competing dangers: on the one hand, not requiring any writing increases the risk that a party might fabricate the existence of an oral contract that never really existed; on the other hand, creating any writing requirement as a prerequisite for enforceability increases the risk that parties who enter into bona fide oral agreements might renege on them. The way that the drafters attempted to reconcile this tension is to require some tangible evidence that a contract existed, but not too much. In addition, §2-201 provides four different circumstances in which a sales contract is enforceable even without the existence of a writing. Under the UCC approach, then, it would still be difficult for a party to enforce a contract that never existed, but it would not be too onerous to enforce a less-than-fully-documented contract that really did exist.

The Article 2 writing (or "record") requirement does not apply at all where the contract for the sale of goods is for less than $500, and amended §2-201 has raised that amount to $5,000. Even when the requirement does apply, the required writing need contain just three elements under §2-201(1): (1) a sufficient indication that the contract for sale has been made; (2) the signature of the party who is trying to avoid the contract; and (3) a quantity term.

Even where the party seeking to enforce the contract cannot muster the fairly minimal writing that is required by §2-201(1), §2-201 provides other ways in which the writing requirement might be met. One way that is set out in §2-201(3)(a) is for the seller to show that it relied to its detriment on the existence of an oral contract in beginning the manufacture of specially manufactured goods according to that contract. For this exception to operate, the seller must also show that the special manufacture began "under circumstances which reasonably indicate that the goods are for the buyer."

A second and more troublesome exception that is found in §2-201(3)(b) allows enforcement of the sales contract despite the lack of a writing where the party seeking to avoid the contract "admits in his pleading, testimony or otherwise in court that a contract for sale was made." This exception is problematic for a couple of reasons. First, it rewards those who are willing to lie under oath and punishes those who are not. If the whole idea of the statute of frauds is that contracts which are not in writing are unenforceable, shouldn't a party seeking to avoid such a contract be able to freely admit, "Yes, I made this oral agreement, but the system says I don't have to honor it since I never signed anything"?

A second reason that the "admission exception" is troublesome is that it is never clear just how far a plaintiff who does not have a writing should be able to take its case before having its claim rejected. Given the admission exception, a plaintiff could argue that its case must go to trial just so that the plaintiff can have an opportunity to get the defendant to admit in open court that the oral contract did exist. The defendant, on the other hand, can contend that as long as it denies the existence of the oral contract at the pleading stage, there is little point in forcing the defendant to have to deny it again at a later stage in the case. This is particularly true, the defendant might say, given that one of the likely purposes of having a writing requirement is to avoid wasting a court's time litigating about the existence of contracts that are not supported by a writing.

DF Activities Corp. v. Brown

851 F.2d 920 (7th Cir. 1988)

POSNER, J.

This appeal in a diversity breach of contract case raises an interesting question concerning the statute of frauds, in the context of a dispute over a chair of more than ordinary value. The plaintiff, DF Activities Corporation (owner of the Domino's pizza chain), is controlled by a passionate enthusiast for the work of Frank Lloyd Wright. The defendant, Dorothy Brown, a resident of Lake Forest (a suburb of Chicago) lived for many years in a house designed by Frank Lloyd Wright — the Willits House — and became the owner of a chair that Wright had designed, the Willits Chair. This is a stark, high-backed, uncomfortable-looking chair of distinguished design that DF wanted to add to its art collection. In September and October 1986, Sarah-Ann Briggs, DF's art director, negotiated with Dorothy Brown to buy the Willits Chair. DF contends — and Mrs. Brown denies — that she agreed in a phone conversation with Briggs on November 26 to sell the chair to DF for $60,000, payable in two equal installments, the first due on December 31 and the second on March 26. On December 3 Briggs wrote Brown a letter confirming the agreement, followed shortly by a check for $30,000. Two weeks later Brown returned the letter and the check with the following handwritten note at the bottom of the letter: "Since I did not hear from you until December and I spoke with you the middle of November, I have made other arrangements for the chair. It is no longer available for sale to you." Sometime later Brown sold the chair for $198,000, precipitating this suit for the difference between the price at which the chair was sold and the contract price of $60,000. Brown moved under Fed. R. Civ. P. 12(b)(6) to dismiss the suit as barred by the statute of frauds in the Uniform Commercial Code. See U.C.C. §2-201. (The Code is, of course, in force in Illinois, and the substantive issues in this case are, all agree, governed by Illinois law.) Attached to the motion was Brown's affidavit that she had never agreed to sell the chair to DF or its representative, Briggs. The affidavit also denied any recollection of a conversation with Briggs on November 26, and was accompanied by both a letter from Brown to Briggs dated September 20 withdrawing an offer to sell the chair and a letter from Briggs to Brown dated October 29 withdrawing DF's offer to buy the chair.

The district judge granted the motion to dismiss and dismissed the suit. DF appeals, contending that although a contract for a sale of goods at a price of $500 or more is subject to the statute of frauds, the (alleged) oral contract made on November 26 may be within the statutory exception for cases where "the party against whom enforcement is sought admits in his pleading, testimony or otherwise in court that a contract for sale was made." U.C.C. §2-201(3)(b). DF does not argue that Brown's handwritten note at the bottom of Briggs' letter is sufficient acknowledgment of a contract to bring the case within the exemption in §2-201(1).

At first glance DF's case may seem quite hopeless. Far from admitting in her pleading, testimony, or otherwise in court that a contract for sale was made, Mrs. Brown denied under oath that a contract had been made. DF argues, however, that if it could depose her, maybe she would admit in her deposition that the affidavit was in error, that she had talked to Briggs on November 26, and that they had agreed to the sale of the chair on the terms contained in Briggs' letter of confirmation to her.

There is remarkably little authority on the precise question raised by this appeal — whether a sworn denial ends the case or the plaintiff may press on, and insist on discovery. In fact we have found no authority at the appellate level, state or federal. Many cases hold, it is true, that the defendant in a suit on an oral contract apparently made unenforceable by the statute of frauds cannot block discovery aimed at extracting an admission that the contract was made, simply by moving to dismiss the suit on the basis of the statute of frauds or by denying in the answer to the complaint that a contract had been made. There is also contrary authority. . . . We need not take sides on the conflict. When there is a bare motion to dismiss, or an answer, with no evidentiary materials, the possibility remains a live one that, if asked under oath whether a contract had been made, the defendant would admit it had been. The only way to test the proposition is for the plaintiff to take the defendant's deposition, or, if there is no discovery, to call the defendant as an adverse witness at trial. But where as in this case the defendant swears in an affidavit that there was no contract, we see no point in keeping the lawsuit alive. Of course the defendant may blurt out an admission in a deposition, but this is hardly likely, especially since by doing so he may be admitting to having perjured himself in his affidavit. Stranger things have happened, but remote possibilities do not warrant subjecting the parties and the judiciary to proceedings almost certain to be futile.

A plaintiff cannot withstand summary judgment by arguing that although in pretrial discovery he has gathered no evidence of the defendant's liability, his luck may improve at trial. The statement in a leading commercial law text that a defense based on the statute of frauds must always be determined at trial because the defendant might in cross-examination admit the making of the contract, see White & Summers, Handbook of the Law Under the Uniform Commercial Code 67 (1980), reflects a misunderstanding of the role of summary judgment; for the statement implies, contrary to modern practice, that a party unable to generate a genuine issue of fact at the summary judgment stage, because he has no evidence with which to contest an affidavit of his adversary, see Fed. R. Civ. P. 56(e), may nevertheless obtain a trial of the issue. He may not. By the same token, a plaintiff in a suit on a contract within the statute of frauds should not be allowed to resist a motion to dismiss, backed by an affidavit that the defendant denies the contract was made, by arguing that his luck may improve in discovery. Just as summary judgment proceedings differ from trials, so the conditions of a deposition differ from the conditions in which an affidavit is prepared; affidavits in litigation are prepared by lawyers, and merely signed by affiants. Yet to allow an affiant to be deposed by opposing counsel would be to invite the unedifying form of discovery in which the examining lawyer tries to put words in the witness's mouth and construe them as admissions.

The history of the judicial-admission exception to the statute of frauds, well told in Stevens, Ethics and the Statute of Frauds, 37 Cornell L.Q. 355 (1952), reinforces our conclusion. The exception began with common-sense recognition that if the defendant admitted in a pleading that he had made a contract with the plaintiff, the purpose of the statute of frauds — protection against fraudulent or otherwise false contractual claims — was fulfilled. (The situation would be quite otherwise, of course, with an oral admission, for a plaintiff willing to testify falsely to the existence of a contract would be equally willing to testify falsely to the defendant's having admitted the existence of the contract.) Toward the end of the eighteenth century the courts began to reject the exception, fearing that it was an invitation to the defendant to perjure himself. Later the pendulum swung again, and the exception is now firmly established. The concern with perjury that caused the courts in the middle period to reject the exception supports the position taken by Mrs. Brown in this case. She has sworn under oath that she did not agree to sell the Willits Chair to DF. DF wants an opportunity to depose her in the hope that she can be induced to change her testimony. But if she changes her testimony this will be virtually an admission that she perjured herself in her affidavit (for it is hardly likely that her denial was based simply on a faulty recollection). She is not likely to do this. What is possible is that her testimony will be sufficiently ambiguous to enable DF to argue that there should be still further factual investigation — perhaps a full-fledged trial at which Mrs. Brown will be questioned again about the existence of the contract.

With such possibilities for protraction, the statute of frauds becomes a defense of meager value. And yet it seems to us as it did to the framers of the Uniform Commercial Code that the statute of frauds serves an important purpose in a system such as ours that does not require that all contracts be in writing in order to be enforceable and that allows juries of lay persons to decide commercial cases. The methods of judicial factfinding do not distinguish unerringly between true and false testimony, and are in any event very expensive. People deserve some protection against the risks and costs of being hauled into court and accused of owing money on the basis of an unacknowledged promise. And being deposed is scarcely less unpleasant than being cross-examined — indeed, often it is more unpleasant, because the examining lawyer is not inhibited by the presence of a judge or jury who might resent hectoring tactics. The transcripts of depositions are often very ugly documents.

Some courts still allow the judicial-admission exception to be defeated by the defendant's simple denial, in a pleading, that there was a contract; this is the position well articulated in Judge Shadur's opinion in the Triangle Marketing case. To make the defendant repeat the denial under oath is already to erode the exception (as well as to create the invitation to perjury that so concerned the courts that rejected the judicial-admission exception altogether), for there is always the possibility, though a very small one, that the defendant might be charged with perjury. But, in any event, once the defendant has denied the contract under oath, the safety valve of §2-201(3)(b) is closed. The chance that at a deposition the defendant might be badgered into withdrawing his denial is too remote to justify prolonging an effort to enforce an oral contract in the teeth of the statute of frauds. If Dorothy Brown did agree on November 27 to sell the chair to DF at a bargain price, it behooved Briggs to get Brown's signature on the dotted line, posthaste.

AFFIRMED.

FLAUM, J., dissenting.

Because I disagree with the majority's holding that additional discovery is prohibited whenever a defendant raises a statute of frauds defense and submits a sworn denial that he or she formed an oral contract with the plaintiff, I respectfully dissent. Neither would I hold, however, that a plaintiff is automatically entitled to additional discovery in the face of a defendant's sworn denial that an agreement was reached. Rather, in my view district courts should have the authority to exercise their discretion to determine the limits of permissible discovery in these cases. This flexibility is particularly important where, as here, the defendant's affidavit does not contain a conclusive denial of contract formation. While district courts have broad discretion in discovery matters, I believe the district court abused that discretion in the present case.

The purpose of the statute of frauds "is to protect a party from the fraudulent and perjurious claim of another that an oral contract was made and not to prevent an oral contract admittedly made from enforcement." URSA Farmers Coop. Co. v. Trent, 58 Ill. App. 3d 930, 16 Ill. Dec. 348, 350, 374 N.E.2d 1123, 1125 (1978) (citing Cohn v. Fisher, 118 N.J. Super. 286, 287 A.2d 222 (1972)). The statute is also designed to protect innocent parties from the expense of defending against allegations that they breached a contract that is not evidenced by a writing. As the majority notes, there is no Illinois case law conclusively deciding a plaintiff's right to obtain further discovery when a defendant denies the existence of an oral contract in a sworn affidavit. Relevant case law in other jurisdictions is split between the position that the majority adopts today and a rule permitting additional discovery (and in some cases full trials) in statute of frauds cases.

Although it is difficult to give full effect to both the statute of frauds and the admissions exception thereto, that is what we must attempt to do. In my view, these provisions can best be reconciled by allowing district courts to exercise their discretion to determine when additional discovery is likely to be fruitful and when it is being sought just to improperly pursue a defendant who is clearly entitled to the protection of the statute of frauds.

If a denial is a complete bar to additional discovery, the exception to the statute of frauds for admissions made in a "pleading, testimony or otherwise in court that a contract for sale was made" would be rendered virtually meaningless. In Illinois involuntary admissions can satisfy the admissions exception to the statute of frauds. Such involuntary admissions will be almost impossible under the majority's rule because the plaintiff will never have an opportunity to examine the defendant in order to elicit an involuntary admission. Either the defendant will make a fatal admission in his or her affidavit and the statute of frauds exception will be satisfied without resort to the testimony component, or the defendant will deny the contract in his or her pleadings and the case will be dismissed before a testimonial admission is possible. A blanket rule prohibiting any further discovery once the defendant denies under oath that a contract was formed is therefore too inflexible.

Similarly, I would not adopt a rule that requires district courts to allow additional discovery in every one of these cases. I would leave the decision to the discretion of the district judge. In cases where a defendant does not explicitly deny under oath that an oral contract was reached, or where there is some indication that the statute of frauds is being used to perpetrate a fraud, it would be permissible to allow the plaintiff to question the defendant under oath to ensure that he or she personally denies that the parties formed an oral contract. This does not mean, however, that summary judgment is never appropriate when the statute of frauds is raised as an affirmative defense. If a defendant who conditionally denies contract formation in his or her pleadings or affidavit specifically denies that an agreement was reached in a deposition, summary judgment might well be appropriate at that stage of the litigation. A simple denial in an affidavit, however, should not trigger foreclosure of further discovery in every case.

In the present case I think the district court abused its discretion by disallowing any additional discovery once Brown filed her motion to dismiss and accompanying affidavit. The majority argues that it would be futile for DF Activities Corporation ("DF") to take Brown's deposition. Brown is unlikely to admit any facts from which a reasonable trier of fact could conclude that an oral contract was formed because, in the face of her affidavit, such admissions would leave her exposed to perjury charges. In my view, this overstates the content of Brown's affidavit. While Brown denied that any oral or written agreement was reached in both her answer and motion to dismiss, such a blanket denial is curiously missing from her affidavit. Rather, in her affidavit Brown stated only that she did not accept any offer from Domino's Farms or Sarah Briggs for the sale of the Willits chair and that she does not recall having a conversation with Sarah Briggs on November 26, 1988. Deposing Brown therefore would not necessarily be a futile effort. It is possible that under questioning during a deposition Brown would remember the November 26 conversation during which Briggs claims she and Brown reached an agreement for the sale of the chair. Although any convenient prior memory lapse might be viewed with suspicion if a deposition elicited additional information, it is highly unlikely that it would lead to perjury charges. On the facts of this case, I believe the district court abused its discretion when it refused to allow DF to take Brown's deposition.

I share the majority's concern that one of the purposes of the statute of frauds is to protect litigants from the cost of defending breach of contract claims based on alleged agreements that are not supported by written documentation. The statute of frauds, however, contains a specific exception for cases in which a party admits in a pleading, testimony, or otherwise in court that an oral contract was reached, and that provision must be given some effect. The testimonial admissions provision would be virtually meaningless if a district court could never exercise its discretion to permit additional discovery in the face of a defendant's sworn denial in an affidavit.

Because in my view the district court abused its discretion when it prohibited further discovery, I would remand this case to the district court with instructions to permit discovery to continue at least to the point where DF is given an opportunity to depose Brown. If Brown then denies under oath during her deposition that any oral contract was made, summary judgment might well be appropriate at that time.

Amended §2-201(3)(b) now makes it clear that when a defendant admits the existence of an oral contract "under oath" rather than "in court" as under pre-amended §2-201(3)(b), that is sufficient to overcome the statute of frauds defense even in the absence of an authenticated record of the contract. This change in the statute, however, does not completely settle the question that was litigated in the *Brown* case. Where a defendant *denies* the existence of a contract in a sworn affidavit at the pre-trial pleading stage, the plaintiff could still argue that it ought to be given an opportunity to cross-examine the plaintiff in a deposition at least, and ideally in the more formal and perhaps more intimidating context of an actual trial.

Courts and commentators do not agree on just how far a plaintiff without a writing or writing substitute to satisfy the Statute of Frauds should be able to take its case before being dismissed. Most, but not all, courts believe that a plaintiff should at least get to conduct some discovery before having its case dismissed for lack of a writing. Comment 6 to §2-201 says that the writing need not be delivered in order to satisfy the statute, suggesting that plaintiffs ought to at least be able to discover documents in the possession of the defendant that may satisfy the writing requirement of the statute.

A third and more straightforward exception to the writing requirement in §2-201 is what is known as the "part performance" exception. This exception, found in §2-201(3)(c), simply says that to the extent that either the seller receives and accepts payment for the goods or the buyer receives and accepts the goods, neither party can deny the existence of the oral contract. As Official Comment 2 (Official Comment 3 in amended §2-201) to §2-201 puts it, "[r]eceipt and acceptance either of goods or of the price constitutes an unambiguous overt admission by both sides that a contract actually exists."

Easily the most litigated exception to the writing requirement in §2-201 is the so-called "merchant's exception" found in §2-201(2). As the next case demonstrates, it is not always clear what kind of writing will qualify as a "confirmation" to trigger the merchant's exception that is found in §2-201(2).

General Trading Int'l v. Wal-Mart Stores
320 F.3d 831 (8th Cir. 2003)

BOWMAN, J.

General Trading International, Inc. (GTI), sued Wal-Mart Stores, Inc., for breach of contract, action for goods sold, and action on account in a dispute arising out of Wal-Mart's alleged failure to pay for large numbers of decorative "vine reindeer" sold to Wal-Mart for resale to the public during the 1999 Christmas season. Wal-Mart counterclaimed for breach of contract and for fraud. According to Wal-Mart, most of the reindeer, manufactured in Haiti, were "scary-looking" and unsuitable for sale as Christmas merchandise. Wal-Mart claims that GTI orally agreed to absorb $200,000 of the purchase price because of Wal-Mart's dissatisfaction with the quality of the product. GTI, denying the existence of the alleged oral agreement, filed a motion for partial summary judgment, seeking an award of $200,000 of the unpaid balance, by arguing that the alleged oral agreement was unenforceable and violated the statute of frauds. The District Court granted partial summary judgment in favor of GTI and submitted the remaining claims to a jury, which returned a verdict in GTI's favor. Subsequently, the District Court denied Wal-Mart's motion for judgment as a matter of law or for a new trial and GTI's request for attorney fees. Wal-Mart appeals the grant of partial summary judgment and the denial of its motion for a new trial. GTI cross appeals the denial of attorney fees. We affirm.

Although the factual history of this dispute is set forth in detail in the partial summary-judgment opinion of the District Court, see Mem. Op. at 1-17 (Jan. 15, 2002), we will summarize some of the major events, especially as they relate to Wal-Mart's claims on appeal. In February 1999, Beth Gitlin, a seasonal buyer for Wal-Mart, began negotiating with Patrick Francis, the president of GTI (a company that sells seasonal craft items to large retailers) for the purchase of 250,000 vine reindeer for resale to Wal-Mart customers during the 1999 Christmas season. In March 1999, GTI executed Wal-Mart's standard vendor agreement. The vendor agreement provided that any changes in the agreement must be in writing and executed by both parties. Wal-Mart issued separate purchase orders, covering price and quantity terms, to GTI for the purchase of the reindeer.

In mid-August 1999, Wal-Mart noticed serious defects with the reindeer when the first shipments began arriving at its stores and warehouses. Gitlin estimated that, at that time, at least seventy percent of the reindeer were of poor quality. A Wal-Mart employee described the reindeer as "[m]oldy, broken grapevines, shapes that no more resembled a deer than they did a rabbit . . . scary-looking." Id. at 3 (quoting Estes Dep. at 19). During the next few weeks, Gitlin communicated with Francis about quality problems with the product. On September 13, 1999, Wal-Mart directed GTI to cancel all further shipments of the reindeer.

On September 23, 1999, Gitlin met with Francis and Jeff Kuhn, a GTI representative, to discuss the slow sales and quality problems. During that meeting, Wal-Mart agreed to accept delivery of any reindeer GTI had already manufactured (approximately 25,000), but at a lower price than the prior purchase orders. In addition, Gitlin requested that GTI agree to Wal-Mart's withholding of $400,000 owed to GTI for potential claims for defective merchandise. Finally, according to Wal-Mart, GTI orally agreed, at some point before September 30, to reduce the total amount due from Wal-Mart by $200,000 because of Wal-Mart's price markdown of the reindeer at its stores in view of their poor quality. On September 30, 1999, Gitlin sent Francis and Kuhn an e-mail stating that sales of the reindeer were "too low" and that Wal-Mart would take a price markdown on the product within the next two weeks. E-mail from Gitlin to Francis and Kuhn (Sept. 30, 1999) (Gitlin's Sept. 30 e-mail). In that e-mail, Gitlin also stated that she was "also concerned about the defective percentage and claims at the end of the season. You say they normally run less than 10%. I'm going to be conservative and estimate 20%.

I'm going to change the reserve on the account to $600,000 and will release the rest of the payments." Id. Gitlin did not receive a response to this e-mail from Francis or Kuhn.

On November 12, 1999, Kuhn sent Gitlin an e-mail stating GTI's frustration in obtaining payment from Wal-Mart on past-due invoices for the reindeer. In that e-mail, Kuhn noted that Gitlin said Wal-Mart was "going to hold $400,000 against future defective claims." E-Mail from Kuhn to Gitlin (Nov. 12, 1999). Gitlin replied three days later asking Kuhn to call her to discuss the matter. Gitlin and Kuhn spoke on November 19, 1999, and Gitlin sent Kuhn an e-mail that same day in which she stated, "As we both agree, we have $600,000 on hold now. $200,000 was to go to Markdowns and $400,000 was to cover claims. If you are willing to do this, then I will be able to consider reducing the amount on hold from $600,000 to $500,000." E-mail from Gitlin to Kuhn (Nov. 19, 1999) (Gitlin's Nov. 19 e-mail). Counsel for GTI sent Gitlin a facsimile letter that day demanding payment of the entire balance owed to GTI. Kuhn replied to Gitlin on November 22 and stated that "GTI would accept Wal-Mart withholding the amount of $400,000.00 for present and future charge backs." E-mail from Kuhn to Gitlin (Nov. 22, 1999). Kuhn sent Gitlin another e-mail on November 24 and stated that "[t]he principals [sic] of GTI's position is unwavering and non-negotiable. We want a check for $521,429 next week and on 1/15-2/1/2000 the $400,000 reserve will be revisited and adjusted accordingly." E-mail from Kuhn to Gitlin (Nov. 24, 1999). Thereafter, during the next several weeks, Gitlin and Kuhn continued to exchange e-mails, which can be characterized primarily as GTI continuing to demand immediate payment of outstanding invoices, or some settlement thereof, and Wal-Mart reiterating its position that GTI agreed to Wal-Mart's retention of funds for defective merchandise claims and $200,000 for price markdowns. GTI never acknowledged the $200,000 for price markdowns in any of its correspondence with Wal-Mart.

In December 2000, GTI sued Wal-Mart for breach of contract, action for goods sold, and action on account, alleging that GTI had shipped Wal-Mart 176,217 vine reindeer at an agreed price of $1,839,777.96, of which Wal-Mart had only paid $1,444,093.79. Wal-Mart counterclaimed for fraud and breach of contract. On October 1, 2001, GTI filed a motion for partial summary judgment, seeking an award of $200,000 of the unpaid balance, by arguing that the vendor agreement precluded any oral modifications and that the statute of frauds barred the alleged oral agreement to deduct $200,000 for price markdowns. The District Court granted GTI's motion on January 15, 2002, concluding that both the terms of the vendor agreement and the provisions of the statute of frauds barred the oral agreement to reduce $200,000 from the amount owed to GTI. The jury heard the remaining claims the next month and returned a verdict in favor of GTI on its breach of contract claim, awarding GTI $63,280, and in favor of GTI on Wal-Mart's counterclaim for breach of contract. Subsequently, the District Court denied Wal-Mart's motion for judgment as a matter of law or new trial and GTI's request for an award of attorney fees. On appeal, Wal-Mart contends the District Court erred in granting partial summary judgment to GTI on the $200,000 claim and abused its discretion in denying Wal-Mart's motion for a new trial on the ground that the erroneous grant of partial summary judgment prejudiced Wal-Mart in the trial of the remainder of the case. GTI cross appeals, arguing the denial of its request for attorney fees was an abuse of discretion. . . .

Wal-Mart first argues the District Court erred when it granted partial summary judgment in favor of GTI by holding that the oral agreement to reduce $200,000 from the amount owed to GTI for price markdowns was barred by the statute of frauds. Subject to certain limited exceptions, the statute-of-frauds provision of the Arkansas version of the Uniform Commercial Code (U.C.C.) renders unenforceable any unwritten contract for the sale of goods with a value of more than $500 "unless there is some writing sufficient to indicate that a contract for sale has been made between the parties and signed by the party against whom enforcement is sought." Ark. Code Ann. §4-2-201(1) (Michie 2001). Both parties agree the case is governed by the so-called "merchants' exception" to the statute of frauds. Under the merchants' exception, a confirmatory writing setting forth the terms of the agreement is sufficient if the recipient of the writing knows its contents and fails to object in writing within ten days. See §4-2-201(2) (Michie 2001). Here, Wal-Mart claims GTI did not object within ten days of Wal-Mart's sending GTI a confirmatory writing of the oral agreement for the $200,000 allowance. Specifically, Wal-Mart argues Gitlin's September 30 e-mail as well as her other e-mails to Kuhn and Francis are confirmatory memoranda to which GTI did not object in writing.

The question of whether a writing constitutes a confirmation of an oral agreement sufficient to satisfy the statute of frauds is a question of law for the court. See Vess Beverages, Inc. v. Paddington Corp., 886 F.2d 208, 214 (8th Cir. 1989) (whether document satisfies the statute of frauds is a question of law) (applying Missouri U.C.C.). In this case, the District Court concluded that as a matter of law none of Wal-Mart's e-mails were sufficient. We agree.

We turn first to Gitlin's September 30 e-mail to Francis and Kuhn. In that e-mail, Gitlin stated that she was "going to change the reserve on the account to $600,000." Gitlin's Sept. 30 e-mail. According to Wal-Mart, this e-mail clearly indicates that Wal-Mart believed the original contract had been changed. Moreover, Wal-Mart argues that "although the breakdown of the $600,000 into a $400,000 reserve allowance for defective merchandise claims and a $200,000 for a markdown allowance is not explicit, it is strongly implied by the text of the e-mail." Br. of Appellant at 34. GTI does not dispute that it never responded to this e-mail. Instead, GTI argues that Gitlin's September 30 e-mail is not a confirmatory writing under §4-2-201(1).

While the merchants' exception does not require a confirmatory writing to be signed by the party to be charged, see §4-2-201(2), the writing still must satisfy the dictates of §2-201(1). See St. Ansgar Mills, Inc. v. Streit, 613 N.W.2d 289, 294 (Iowa 2000) ("[A] writing is still required [under §2-201(2)], but it does not need to be signed by the party against whom the contract is sought to be enforced."); Howard Constr. Co. v. Jeff-Cole Quarries, Inc., 669 S.W.2d 221, 227 (Mo. Ct. App. 1983) ("[C]ourts have found that the §2-201(2) confirmatory memorandum must satisfy the 'sufficient to indicate' requirement of §2-201(1)"). Under the U.C.C., "[a]ll that is required [for a writing to indicate a contract for sale has been made under §2-201(1)] is that the writing afford a basis for believing that the offered oral evidence rests on a real transaction." U.C.C. §2-201, cmt. 1. Most courts that have interpreted the "sufficient to indicate" requirement "have required that the writing indicate the consummation of a contract, not mere negotiations." Howard Constr. Co., 669 S.W.2d at 227. Thus, writings that contain language evincing a tentative agreement or writings that lack language indicating a binding or complete agreement have been found insufficient. Id.; cf. M.K. Metals, Inc. v. Container Recovery Corp., 645 F.2d 583, 591 (8th Cir.1981) (concluding that the terms of the agreement were so specifically geared to the desires of the party to be charged that the agreement reflected a complete contract) (applying Missouri U.C.C.).

Based upon our review of Gitlin's September 30 e-mail, we agree with GTI that this e-mail fails sufficiently to indicate the formation or existence of any agreement between the parties through inference or otherwise. This e-mail is simply devoid of any language concerning an agreement on the issue of $200,000 for markdowns. While the e-mail references a $600,000 reserve, it does not state what, if any, portion of that amount was agreed to be set aside for markdowns. At most, the e-mail shows Wal-Mart's unilateral effort at taking a markdown on the reindeer and changing the reserve, e.g., "I will be taking a MD on this either next week or the following. . . . I'm going to change the reserve on the account to $600,000." Gitlin's Sept. 30 e-mail. In summary, the language in the e-mail does not constitute a sufficient writing for purposes of the statute of frauds because it does not evince any agreement between the parties on price markdowns. See R.S. Bennett & Co. v. Econ. Mech. Indus., 606 F.2d 182, 186 (7th Cir. 1979) (a §2-201(2) writing must "indicate [ ] that the parties have already made a deal or reached an agreement") (applying Illinois U.C.C.).

Wal-Mart next argues that even if the September 30 e-mail is not a sufficient writing, Gitlin's subsequent e-mails to Kuhn and Francis constitute confirmatory memoranda. In particular, Wal-Mart points to Gitlin's e-mail to Kuhn on November 19 in which she stated, "As we both agree, we have $600,000 on hold now. $200,000 was to go to Markdowns and $400,000 was to cover claims. If you are willing to do this, then I will be able to consider reducing the amount on hold from $600,000 to $500,000." Gitlin's Nov. 19 e-mail. GTI does not directly refute that this or subsequent e-mails from Gitlin could constitute confirmatory memorandums. Instead, GTI argues that it filed timely objections to these writings. Specifically, Kuhn replied on November 22 and 24 and offered to sign a letter authorizing Wal-Mart to retain $400,000 for defective merchandise claims, but he also demanded immediate payment on all outstanding invoices, noting that GTI's position was not negotiable.

Section 4-2-201(2) does not prescribe any particular form for an objection to a confirmatory writing. Nonetheless, both parties agree that courts require an unequivocal objection to a confirmatory writing alleging an oral agreement. See, e.g., M.K. Metals, Inc., 645 F.2d at 592 (holding response to a purchase order was not an adequate objection under §2-201(2) because it did not challenge the price term in the purchase order, but rather stated that "there was someone who was willing to pay more than the amount stated in the purchase order") (applying Missouri U.C.C.). Here, Wal-Mart argues that GTI did not unequivocally object to its confirmatory writing because GTI failed specifically to object to the $200,000 for price markdowns in its November 22 and 24 e-mail responses to Gitlin's e-mails. In analyzing these e-mails, the District Court concluded that GTI's "reply e-mails including different terms and containing demands for payment of the amount due on the invoices, less a reserve, constitute objections under §2-201(2)." Mem. Op. at 26. Though GTI failed to mention the $200,000 in its responses, it is clear when viewing the responses as a whole that GTI never agreed to Gitlin's assertion that they had reached an agreement on markdowns. Instead, GTI's responses, with a demand for full payment, less a reserve for defective merchandise claims, can only be characterized as unequivocal objections to any agreement on markdowns.

On the facts of this case, the merchants' exception to the statute of frauds has not been satisfied. Accordingly, we find the District Court did not err in granting partial summary judgment in favor of GTI on its claim for $200,000 of the unpaid balance of the reindeers' purchase price. . . .

There is one subtle but crucial point worth noting about the operation of the Article 2 writing requirement: The difference in the consequences of meeting vs. not meeting that requirement will tend to make courts liberal in finding that the requirement has been met. If the plaintiff is unable to meet the requirement, that fact spells death for the plaintiff's case — it's all over. On the other hand, if the plaintiff does meet the requirement, all that happens is that the plaintiff gets to continue waging the fight to prove the enforceability of the contract. Given this difference in stakes, it is easy to see why in a close case, courts might be inclined to find that the requirement has been met.

Problem Set 5

5.1. a.   Mike Sims and Sara McCarthy are both in the furniture business. The two of them met at an industry convention where Mike alleges that they made an oral contract in which Mike agreed to sell Sara eight antique oak desks for $12,000 each, delivery to be made in five weeks to Sara's out-of-state place of business. Two days after the oral contract, Mike sent Sara a confirming memorandum on his company's letterhead that outlined the terms of their deal, including quantity. Consistent with normal practice, there was no signature on the memo. When Sara received the confirmation, she immediately called Mike and said, "You promised me that you could send me the desks in three weeks, not five. As far as I'm concerned, our deal is off." If Sara does nothing more, can Mike enforce the oral contract with Sara? U.C.C. §§2-201, 1-201(39), Official Comment 39 to §1-201, revised 1-201(33a).

b.   Same facts as part a., except Sara sends her objection in writing (the contents of which are quoted in part a.). Can Mike enforce the oral contract with Sara? U.C.C. §2-201.

c.   Same facts as part a., except that Mike does not send a confirmation, but Sara sends Mike a check for $20,000, with "downpayment for desk deal" marked on the memo line. To what extent may Mike enforce the oral contract with Sara? U.C.C. §2-201, Official Comment 2 to §2-201 (Official Comment 3 as amended).

d.   Same facts as part a., except that Mike does not send a confirmation. When Mike eventually files a complaint in federal court to enforce the contract, Sara responds with a F.R.C.P. 12(b)(6) motion which says, "Even if everything alleged in plaintiff's complaint is true, the contract is still unenforceable for lack of a writing." Should the trial judge dismiss Mike's complaint at this point? U.C.C. §2-201.

e.   Same facts as part a., except that Mike does not send a confirmation. However, shortly after his oral contract with Sara, Mike enters into a written contract with another furniture seller to buy eight antique oak desks (of the type promised to Sara) for $10,000 each. Now can Mike enforce the oral contract with Sara? U.C.C. §§2-201, 1-103.

5.2.   Arlene Ledger (from Problem 3.2) is back at your law office to ask you about a couple of difficulties that she has had with certain customers of her exercise equipment company, Heavy Metal. Several weeks ago, she had met with Tom Lauder, director of Monticello Senior Center, to discuss the possibility of Heavy Metal manufacturing three identical multi-station weight machines that would be custom-made for the special needs of the residents of his senior center. In particular, the weight stack would have lighter increments than normal and each of the stations on the machine could be used even by residents who were wheel-chair bound.

Arlene said that Lauder had later called her and told her to go ahead and make the three special machines, which the two had agreed would cost $8,000 each. When Heavy Metal had nearly finished the first of these three machines, Lauder called Arlene again and left a message that said, "We won't need the machines after all. So sorry to trouble you." Arlene sheepishly admits to you that she never put this deal in writing. Now, she tells you, she is stuck with one special machine that no other buyer may want, plus a $3,000 bill from a consultant who had helped to draft the plans for the prototype for these three machines. Will Arlene be in a position to enforce this contract with Monticello Senior Center? If so, can she enforce it just for the one machine in process or for all three? U.C.C. §2-201, cf. Official Comment 2 to §2-201.

5.3.   Your law firm just took on a new client, Max Swain, an independent grocery store owner. Max was at an independent grocers' convention last week and he heard a lot about his colleagues' use of Electronic Data Interchange. Max concedes that he is a traditionalist at heart, but he said that he would not mind eliminating all of the paperwork involved with the current method by which he orders groceries from his various suppliers. Max tells you that he thinks he is ready to "take the plunge" and buy a computer that will enable him to transmit orders via the EDI system. He wants to know if this new method of doing business has any increased risks over the old-fashioned way, and whether there are ways that he might reduce those risks. What do you advise him? U.C.C. §§2-201, 1-201(39), 1-201(46), revised 1-201(37), revised 1-201(43) .

Assignment 6: Parol Evidence with Sales of Goods

In the case where parties to a sales contract do bother to memorialize their agreement with a writing, they are thereby limiting their ability to enforce terms that are not contained in that writing. Whereas the UCC's statute of frauds rule bars the enforceability of certain contracts, the parol evidence rule bars the introduction into evidence (and therefore the enforceability) of certain terms that are not put into writing.

In the sales system as it operates in practice, whether or not parties create "side deals" that are not contained in the relevant writing or writings will be a function of how formal they intend for the writing or writings to be. If the particular sales contract is documented by a purchase order alone, or by a purchase order and an acknowledgement form, there may well be nontrivial terms which are not contained in writing.

As one steel manufacturer explained: "Sometimes our sales people will enter into non-written special deals with certain buyers as to matters such as a lower-than-list price or longer-than-usual credit terms. These side deals are noted in our files but we never then formally acknowledge them in writing."

If a particular sale is significant enough for the two sides to sit down and negotiate a full-blown written contract, that contract will almost always include a standard merger clause that reads something like this: "This Agreement constitutes the complete and final agreement and understanding among the parties relating to the subject matter hereof, and supersedes all prior proposals, negotiations, agreements and understandings relating to such subject matter. In entering into this Agreement, Buyer acknowledges that it is relying on no statement, representation, warranty, covenant or agreement of any kind made by the Seller or any employee or agent of the Seller, except for the agreements of Seller set forth herein."

The idea behind the merger clause is that if the two parties are going to spend the sunk cost to sit down and work out all of the terms of their agreement, then it doesn't make sense to leave room for "side deals" that go beyond what the parties agreed to in writing. After all, if "side deals" were going to be the order of the day, then why waste the time to think about and reduce to writing the terms that are to govern the transaction?

Betaco, Inc. v. Cessna Aircraft Co.

103 F.3d 1281 (7th Cir. 1996)

Ilana Diamond Rovner, C.J.

Betaco, Inc. agreed to purchase a six-passenger CitationJet from the Cessna Aircraft Company for $2.495 million. After making deposits totaling $150,000 toward the purchase of the aircraft, Betaco decided that the anticipated range of the plane was unsatisfactory and canceled the contract. Cessna, invoking a contractual provision entitling it to keep deposits as liquidated damages in the event of cancellation, refused to return the $150,000 Betaco had advanced. Betaco filed this diversity action contending, among other things, that Cessna had breached a purported warranty not contained in the signed purchase agreement that the new CitationJet would have "more range" than its predecessor, the Citation I. A jury agreed that Cessna had made and breached the extrinsic warranty, and the district court ordered it to pay damages of $150,000 plus pre- and post-judgment interest.

In a prior appeal, we vacated the award of damages and remanded for the purpose of a bench hearing on whether the parties intended the purchase agreement they signed to be the complete embodiment of their contract. After conducting that hearing, the district court answered this question in the negative. Finding that determination to be clearly erroneous, we reverse and remand with directions to enter a final judgment in favor of Cessna. . . .

In response to Betaco owner J. George Mikelsons' request for information about the CitationJet, Cessna sent Mikelsons a packet of materials including a cover letter from Robert T. Hubbard, a regional manager for Cessna, a twenty-three page executive summary providing general information and performance estimates for the new plane, and an unsigned but otherwise completed purchase agreement. In pertinent part, Hubbard's letter stated: Although a completely new design, the CitationJet has inherited all the quality, reliability, safety and economy of the more than 1600 Citations before it. At 437 miles per hour, the CitationJet is much faster, more efficient, and has more range than the popular Citation I. Its luxurious first-class cabin reflects a level of comfort and quality found only in much larger jets.

The purchase agreement occupied both sides of one sheet of paper. "Exhibit A," attached and incorporated into that agreement, set forth preliminary specifications indicating that at its maximum gross takeoff weight of 10,000 pounds, the CitationJet would have a full fuel range of 1,500 nautical miles, plus or minus four percent, under specified conditions. A highlighted clause in the purchase agreement disclaimed warranties beyond those contained in the preliminary specifications:

> EXCEPT FOR THE EXPRESS TERMS OF SELLER'S WRITTEN LIMITED WARRANTIES PERTAINING TO THE AIRCRAFT, WHICH ARE SET FORTH IN THE SPECIFICATION (EXHIBIT A), SELLER MAKES NO REPRESENTATIONS OR WARRANTIES EXPRESS OR IMPLIED, OF MERCHANTABILITY, FITNESS FOR ANY PARTICULAR PURPOSE, OR OTHERWISE WHICH EXTEND BEYOND THE FACE HEREOF OR THEREOF. . . . NO PERSON OR ENTITY IS AUTHORIZED TO MAKE ANY REPRESENTATIONS OR WARRANTIES OR TO ASSUME ANY OBLIGATIONS ON BEHALF OF SELLER.

The agreement also included an integration clause:

> This agreement is the only agreement controlling this purchase and sale, express or implied, either verbal or in writing, and is binding on Purchaser and Seller, their heirs, executors, administrators, successors or assigns. . . . Purchaser acknowledges receipt of a written copy of this Agreement which may not be modified in any way except by written agreement executed by both parties. . . .

We are satisfied that our first opinion adequately sets out the applicable legal principles, and no more than a modest re-cap is required here. Kansas law, of course, governs this dispute, and section 2-202 of the Kansas Statutes provides that a document intended by the parties as a final expression of their agreement may not be contradicted by evidence of any prior agreement or contemporaneous oral agreement, and may not be supplemented with evidence of consistent additional terms when a court finds that the parties intended the document to be the "complete and exclusive statement of the terms of the agreement." Kan. Stat. Ann. §84-2-202(b). Thus, to the extent that Betaco and Cessna intended for the signed purchase agreement to include each and every term of their agreement, Betaco cannot attempt to establish by parol evidence a term beyond the four corners of that document and seek to recover damages for the purported breach of that term. In assessing the intent of the parties, the following factors should be considered: (1) the inclusion of merger or integration clauses in the document under consideration, (2) the disclaimer of warranties, (3) whether the extrinsic term is one that the parties would certainly have included in the document had it been part of their agreement, (4) the sophistication of the parties, and (5) the nature and scope of both prior negotiations between the parties and any purported extrinsic terms.

The question of the parties' intent is typically a factual one, particularly when it turns not just on the written provisions of their contract but on surrounding events that the parties may have interpreted and recalled differently. In this case, for example, Mikelsons testified that he had one or more conversations with Cessna officials about the relative range of the CitationJet before he received and signed the purchase agreement. Cessna denies that any such conversations took place. The district court credited Mikelsons on this point, and this assessment was obviously key to the district court's determination that the parties did not intend for the purchase agreement to be a fully integrated document. We are loathe to second-guess the district court's factual findings. Yet, the contractual language disavowing terms beyond the face of the purchase agreement is plain and unequivocal, and the evidence that Mikelsons has adduced in an effort to overcome this language is exceedingly weak. Having reviewed the record, we are unable to sustain the district court's ultimate finding that the parties did not intend for the purchase agreement to be fully integrated; that finding was, we believe, clearly erroneous. The analysis which leads us to that conclusion will follow the list of relevant factors we identified above.

As we observed in *Betaco I,* the inclusion of an integration clause in a written document is " 'strong evidence' " that the parties intended that document to represent the entirety of their agreement. The purchase agreement executed by Betaco and Cessna contains such a clause, stating both that the signed agreement "is the only agreement" controlling the purchase of the aircraft, that it "is binding on Purchaser and Seller," and that the agreement "may not be modified in any way except by written agreement executed by both parties." We noted that the language of the clause is simple and straightforward, that it was not buried in fine print, and that it was not otherwise likely to be overlooked in an agreement that covered only two pages. We also pointed out that Mikelsons had signed the agreement containing this clause and that he had had the opportunity to review it before signing.

The integration clause speaks for itself, of course, and nothing adduced on remand has shaken our conviction that it constitutes strong evidence that the parties intended the written purchase agreement to constitute the full embodiment of their contract. On the contrary, although extrinsic evidence ordinarily is unnecessary to establish that the parties to an agreement meant what they said in their contract, Mikelsons' testimony on remand only confirms that the integration clause should be taken seriously. Mikelsons acknowledged that in signing the contract, he verified that he had read it, that he understood it, and that he had full authority to bind Betaco with his signature. He acknowledged what the integration clause said; indeed, when asked by Cessna's counsel what he understood the language to mean, he answered, "Just exactly what it says, Mr. Buehler — that this contract is the only contract between the parties."...

The parties to a contract are presumed to comprehend contract terms in the way those terms are ordinarily used. Thus, the district court's concerns about the lack of clarity notwithstanding, it is entirely reasonable to charge Mikelsons and Betaco with the realization that when the contract spoke of "this Agreement" being the sole agreement between the parties and disclaimed all representations beyond it, it meant that only those terms expressly incorporated within the two-page purchase agreement itself were part of the bargain....

A disclaimer of extrinsic warranties complements and reinforces the integration clause by making clear what is implicit in the notion of a fully integrated contract: that no representation not documented in the written agreement itself is part of the parties' bargain....

The purchase agreement itself was not silent as to the anticipated range of the CitationJet. The preliminary specifications incorporated into that agreement contained a section on "estimated performance" which listed some seven factors, among them the full fuel range of the aircraft; we reproduced that section in full in *Betaco I*. As we pointed out, "[t]his summary of the aircraft's performance is, in stark contrast to [Hubbard's] letter, quite precise and quite explicit about the assumptions underlying each of the estimates." Thus, Cessna clearly was willing to make certain performance estimates part of the contract, but when it did so it gave concrete estimates (a full fuel range of 1,500 nautical miles, for example) and made explicit the conditions under which those estimates would apply.

The fact that the purchase agreement addressed the range and did so with specificity indicates to us that had Cessna and Betaco intended for any additional representations as to the range of the CitationJet to be included in their contract, they would have been made an explicit part of the purchase agreement. It is not as if the relative range of the CitationJet vis-a-vis the Citation I was different from the other types of factors addressed in the preliminary specifications, or one that could not be reduced to the level of detail otherwise reflected in the specifications. In fact, the only sense in which Hubbard's "more range" representation stands apart in kind from the terms expressly included in the contract is its extraordinary ambiguity. Given that the contract otherwise described the expected performance of the aircraft with a high degree of specificity, making all of the assumptions underlying each expectation explicit, it is utterly implausible to think that the parties would have understood the types of casual representations found in Hubbard's letter to be part of the same contract. Indeed, it is hard to believe that a manufacturer of aircraft that had attempted to limit its obligations to a carefully delineated set of performance estimates would substantially increase its exposure with an indefinite term like "more range." Equally implausible is the suggestion that Mikelsons, an experienced and sophisticated purchaser of aircraft with a professed concern about range, and with a staff available to crunch the numbers, would be content to spend nearly two-and-a-half million dollars on a plane on the mere assurance that it had "more range" than an earlier model. The district court thought that the parties treated this transaction more like the purchase of a family car than the purchase of a multi-million dollar jet. It may be that Mikelsons treated the purchase that casually. But we find no evidence in the record that Cessna did, or in particular that Cessna shared Mikelsons' professed expectation that an indefinite, extrinsic term like "more range" would become a term of the contract. . . .

Mikelsons is not, as the district court emphasized, a lawyer; and yet, his familiarity with the types of contract terms at issue here rendered him fully able to appreciate the import of those terms. As we have pointed out, Mikelsons read and understood the language in the purchase agreement disclaiming extrinsic warranties; he likewise read and understood the integration clause. . . .

In sum, we have a purchase agreement which in straightforward language declares itself to be the only agreement between the parties. Its principal provisions occupied a single sheet of paper. It incorporated written specifications as to the expected performance of the new aircraft, including its range. It expressly disclaimed any other warranties beyond these. It was presented to a sophisticated purchaser well grounded in aeronautics, who had purchased aircraft before, who was in the business of buying and leasing aircraft (not to mention running an airline). He read and understood the integration clause, he read and understood the warranty disclaimer clause — he had read such clauses before. He signed the contract at a moment of his own choosing, after making modifications.

All of this weighs heavily in favor of honoring the integration and warranty disclaimer clauses and precluding Betaco's effort to read into the parties' agreement an extrinsic term as to the relative range of the CitationJet. Mikelsons could not have been taken by surprise by the contents of the purchase agreement in any sense of the word. . . .

It is important to recall where our analysis began. The parol evidence rule bars evidence of extrinsic terms where the parties intended for a particular document to embody their complete agreement. The purchase agreement that Cessna and Betaco signed suggests on its face that the parties did intend for that document to represent the sole and exclusive agreement between them: the agreement contained an integration clause, and it also disclaimed any warranties beyond those expressly incorporated into the agreement. These provisions were neither hidden nor incomprehensible. Mikelsons read and understood them before signing the contract.

The question, then, is whether the evidence Betaco adduced on remand is sufficient to overcome the presumption that the contract meant what it said, and that no terms not expressly included within the purchase agreement were made part of the bargain. It is far from sufficient. Although we accept, as we must, the district court's finding that Mikelsons had one or more conversations with Cessna representatives in which he was assured that the CitationJet would have more range than the Citation I, there is a paucity of evidence indicating that the parties shared an intent to make any such representation a part of their bargain. Hubbard's representation that the CitationJet would have "more range" than its predecessor came in the form of a standard promotional letter sent to countless other prospective purchasers. Moreover, if one attributes to "more range" the meaning that phrase typically carries in the aviation industry — more range at gross takeoff weight with a full load of fuel — it was wholly duplicative of the purchase agreement, which specified that the CitationJet would have a range of 1,500 nautical miles at that payload configuration, a range concededly greater than the range of the Citation I. Only if one broadens the meaning of "more range" to connote more range at all payloads does that term add anything to the purchase agreement, and yet there is no evidence that that is what Cessna understood the "more range" reference in Hubbard's letter to mean.

At bottom, what Betaco has attempted to do is to retroactively make part of its bargain with Cessna its own expectations of the aircraft in direct contravention of the terms of the written agreement it signed. This is what the parol evidence rule classically forbids. The district court was in error in concluding that the written agreement was not fully integrated and in permitting extrinsic evidence of an additional term, and accordingly the jury's verdict in favor of Betaco for breach of that term cannot stand.

The district court's finding that the written purchase agreement was not fully integrated, and that proof of an extrinsic term was therefore permissible, is reversed and the case is remanded with directions to vacate the jury's verdict in favor of Betaco on Count II of the complaint and to enter final judgment in favor of Cessna on that count.

REVERSED AND REMANDED.

Most of the buyers and sellers interviewed for this book indicated that if a particular sale was important enough to warrant its own separate contract, then it also made sense to include a merger clause. However, one lawyer who oversees procurement practices in a Fortune 100 company indicated that there are some situations where it is not in his company's interest to include a merger clause in a long-term contract with a supplier: "When we do single large contracts, we may or may not want a merger clause. Sometimes certain of our suppliers give us a lot of side services that we couldn't hope to fully describe or capture in a writing. Frankly, sometimes they'll do a lot more than they're legally obligated to do just to keep us happy as a customer. Therefore, it's not always in our interest to put the merger clause in because it's probably better for us to be able to insist on a supplier's 'customary and ordinary' services rather than a laundry list of particulars in the writing. We're afraid if we undertake to try to list everything and then we leave something out, the supplier might decide only to do those things for us that we specifically outlined in the contract."

Whether or not particular extrinsic evidence is admissible under U.C.C. §2-202 is a function both of the nature of the evidence sought to be introduced and the status of the writing that would serve to keep the evidence out. As tricky and nebulous as §2-202 can be, there are nevertheless a couple of categorical statements that can be made about the issue which that section covers.

First, if the writing that seeks to keep evidence out is not intended by both parties to be a final expression of the parties' agreement with respect to the terms included therein, then it will not serve to keep out any parol evidence. Thus, while a confirmation sent by one party, an offer sheet, or a purchase order are all writings that contain terms, none of these are writings that are intended by both parties to be a final expression of the parties' agreement as to the terms contained in the writing.

Second, even where there is a writing intended by both parties to be a final expression of their agreement, parties may always introduce evidence of side agreements that occurred *after* the writing in question. This is just another way of saying that parties are always free to modify earlier agreements that they made, no matter how comprehensive and final the earlier agreement seemed to be at the time. U.C.C. §2-209.

A third categorical statement that can be made about parol evidence in the sales system is that even where there is a writing intended by both parties to be a final expression of their agreement, a party may always introduce evidence of usage of trade, course of dealing, or course of performance to explain or supplement the writing. The one exception to this statement is that these terms may not explain or supplement a writing if the writing has "carefully negated" that possibility, in the words of Official Comment 2 to §2-202. Even this exception is probably limited to the careful negation of a particular usage of trade, course of dealing, or course of performance; it would seem nearly impossible for a court to read any sales agreement in the complete absence of context to the particular parties' prior dealings and the industry in which they deal.

C-Thru Container Corp. v. Midland Mfg. Co.
533 N.W.2d 542 (Iowa 1995)

TERNUS, J.

This case requires us to interpret and apply the trade-usage exception to the parol evidence rule embodied in Iowa Code chapter 554, Iowa's Uniform Commercial Code (U.C.C.). The trial court held that parol evidence of trade usage was inadmissible and granted summary judgment to the defendant, Midland Manufacturing Company. We agree with the contrary decision of the court of appeals that the challenged evidence was admissible and generated a question of fact that prevented summary judgment. Therefore, we affirm the decision of the court of appeals and reverse the judgment of the district court.

C-Thru Container Corporation entered into a contract with Midland Manufacturing Company in March of 1989. In this contract, Midland agreed to purchase bottle-making equipment from C-Thru and to make commercially acceptable bottles for C-Thru. Midland was to pay for the equipment by giving C-Thru a credit against C-Thru's bottle purchases. The contract stated that C-Thru expected to order between 500,000 and 900,000 bottles in 1989. Finally, the contract also provided that if Midland failed to manufacture the bottles, C-Thru could require Midland to pay the entire purchase price plus interest within thirty days.

Midland picked up the equipment as agreed and later sent a notice to C-Thru that it was ready to begin production. C-Thru never ordered any bottles from

Midland, but instead purchased its bottles from another supplier at a lower price. C-Thru claims that in numerous phone conversations between the parties Midland indicated that it was unable to produce commercially acceptable bottles for C-Thru.

In 1992, Midland gave C-Thru notice that it was rescinding the 1989 contract based on C-Thru's failure to order any bottles. C-Thru did not respond to this notice. Midland later sent C-Thru notice that it was claiming an artisan's lien for the expenses of moving, rebuilding and repairing the machinery. Midland eventually foreclosed the artisan's lien and sold the machinery.

Approximately one month later, C-Thru notified Midland that Midland had failed to comply with the terms of the contract and that the full purchase price plus interest was due and payable within thirty days. When Midland failed to pay C-Thru the amount requested, C-Thru filed a petition alleging that Midland had breached the contract by being incapable of producing the bottles as agreed to in the contract.

Midland filed a motion for summary judgment. It contended that the contract did not require that it demonstrate an ability to manufacture commercially acceptable bottles as a condition precedent to C-Thru's obligation to place an order. Midland asserted that the contract merely required that it manufacture commercially acceptable bottles in response to an order from C-Thru. Because C-Thru never placed an order, Midland argued that it had not breached the contract by failing to manufacture any bottles.

C-Thru resisted Midland's motion. It argued that a material issue of fact existed on whether Midland was unable to manufacture the bottles, thereby excusing C-Thru's failure to place an order. As proof that Midland could not manufacture the bottles, C-Thru pointed to Midland's failure to provide sample bottles. C-Thru relied on deposition testimony that the practice in the bottle-making industry was for the bottle manufacturer to provide sample bottles to verify that it could make commercially acceptable bottles before the purchaser placed any orders.

In ruling on Midland's motion for summary judgment, the trial court found no sample container requirement in the written contract. The court also held that the parol evidence rule precluded consideration of any evidence that the practice in the trade was to provide sample bottles before receiving an order. It concluded that no genuine issue of material fact existed and granted Midland summary judgment. The court of appeals reversed the district court's ruling, concluding that evidence regarding the trade practice should have been considered. We granted Midland's application for further review. . . .

Unlike the common law, parol evidence may be used to supplement a fully integrated agreement governed by the UCC if the evidence falls within the definition of usage of trade.

The Iowa U.C.C. includes the following definition of usage of trade:

> 2.   A usage of trade is any practice or method of dealing having such regularity of observance in a place, vocation or trade as to justify an expectation that it will be observed with respect to the transaction in question. The existence and scope of such a usage are to be proved as facts. . . .

Section 1-205 goes on to provide that any usage of trade of which the parties are or should be aware supplements their agreement.

Midland does not dispute that a trier of fact could find that the alleged practice in the bottling industry of providing samples to a prospective purchaser is a usage of trade. However, Midland argues usage-of-trade evidence may not be used to add a new term to a contract that is complete and unambiguous.

We first reject Midland's argument that evidence of trade usage is admissible only when the contract is ambiguous. There is no such requirement in §2-202. Moreover, the official comment to §2-202 of the Uniform Commercial Code . . . states that this section "definitely rejects" a requirement that the language of the contract be ambiguous as a condition precedent to the admission of trade-usage evidence. U.C.C. §2-202 cmt. 1 (1977).

We also hold that even a "complete" contract may be explained or supplemented by parol evidence of trade usages. As the official comment to §2-202 states, commercial sales contracts "are to be read on the assumption that the course of prior dealings between the parties and the usages of trade were taken for granted when the document was phrased." U.C.C. §2-202 cmt. 2 (1977). Therefore, even a completely integrated contract may be supplemented by practices in the industry that do not contradict express terms of the contract.

That brings us to the remaining argument made by Midland — that C-Thru may not use parol evidence to add a new term to the agreement. Section 2-202 says that when parol evidence shows a usage of trade that does not contradict a contract term, the evidence is admissible to "supplement" the contract. We look to the common meaning of the word "supplement." "Supplement" means "to add . . . to." Webster's Third New Int'l Dictionary 2297 (1993). Consequently, the trade-usage evidence upon which C-Thru relies is admissible even though it adds a new term to the contract.

The usage-of-trade evidence offered by C-Thru does not contradict any explicit contractual term. It supplements the written agreement which is permitted under §2-202. Taking this evidence in a light most favorable to C-Thru, we conclude there exists a genuine issue of fact concerning the performance required of Midland as a prerequisite to C-Thru's obligation to place an order. Therefore, summary judgment is not appropriate. We affirm the decision of the court of appeals, reverse the judgment of the district court and remand for further proceedings.

DECISION OF COURT OF APPEALS AFFIRMED; JUDGMENT OF DISTRICT COURT REVERSED AND REMANDED.

Another issue with the introduction of usage of trade is what constitutes permissible "explaining or supplementing" vs. impermissible "contradicting." Some courts have been very lenient in their definition of "explaining or supplementing." One court allowed a defendant to introduce usage of trade to the effect that in this particular industry, a stated quantity really does not mean a stated quantity but instead means whatever the buyer in fact happens to need. This, the court said, did not "contradict" an express term in the contract (the stated quantity), but instead merely explained or supplemented it.

Beyond these categorical statements about certain kinds of writings or certain kinds of evidence, the general rule about parol evidence in the sales of goods system is this: Prior consistent additional terms may be introduced to explain or supplement any writing except those that are intended by both parties to be a complete and exclusive statement of all the terms of the contract. The "complete and exclusive" nature of the writing might be proven, for example, by the existence of a well-drafted and conspicuous merger clause that screams out the completeness and exclusivity of the writing.

A corollary to the general rule that "consistent additional terms" may be introduced as evidence is that "contradictory" terms may not be. Sometimes the difference between these two kinds of terms is less than obvious. For example, suppose that the seller of a used car told the buyer orally that the buyer could return the car for any reason during the first six months after the sale and receive a full refund. Suppose that this statement were made prior to the execution of a written contract that was found to be a final expression of the parties' agreement, at least with respect to the terms included therein. The writing said nothing about the buyer's right to return the car for a refund.

Is the pre-writing oral statement about buyer's right to return the car a "consistent additional term" or a "contradictory" one? On the one hand, that statement does not directly contradict anything contained in the writing, since the writing is silent about buyer's right to return the car for a full refund. On the other hand, the common understanding in the absence of anything said to the contrary is that all sales are final, and thus a right of the buyer to return the car for up to six months would contradict that unstated assumption.

Problem Set 6

6.1. a. Arlene Ledger (from Problem 3.2) is having difficulty with her company's steel supplier, Wilson Steel. Jake Wilson, president of Wilson Steel, had negotiated a contract with Arlene by which Arlene had agreed to purchase all of her company's requirements for steel over the next year from Wilson at a stated price per ton. In getting Arlene to sign this contract, Jake had assured Arlene that he was so confident of how low his price was, that if she happened to find a lower price during the next year she could buy her steel requirements from the lower-priced competitor. Arlene admits to you that she never did read the contract closely before signing it. Now, Arlene tells you, just two months after signing this contract, she has found a lower-priced steel supplier.

As you look at the contract Arlene signed with Wilson, you notice two things: (1) the contract says nothing about this "low-price guarantee"; and (2) the contract does not contain a merger clause. What do you advise Arlene about her ability to buy her steel requirements from the lower-priced competitor to Wilson? U.C.C. §2-202, Official Comment 3 to §2-202.

b. Same facts as part a., except that the contract does contain a merger clause, and Jake gave Arlene the price guarantee *after* the two had signed the contract. In a suit to enforce the contract, may Arlene introduce evidence of Jake's price guarantee? U.C.C. §§2-202, 2-209(1).

c. Same facts as part a., except that the contract does contain a merger clause, and Jake and Arlene have done these requirements contracts several times in the past. In all of these prior deals, Jake has made the same oral assurances concerning the price guarantee, but Arlene has never had to exercise her rights under the guarantee. In a suit to enforce the contract, may Arlene introduce evidence of Jake's price guarantee? U.C.C. §§1-205 (revised §1-303), 2-202.

   d.   Same facts as part a., except that the contract does contain a merger clause, and the custom in this industry is that for requirements contracts like this one, the price is typically the lowest price that the buyer could get from any other source at the time it requires each steel shipment. In a suit to enforce the contract, may Arlene introduce evidence of Jake's price guarantee? If not, may she nevertheless introduce evidence of the price custom in the industry that in fact is identical to what Jake guaranteed orally? U.C.C. §§1-205 (revised §1-303), 2-202.

   6.2.   You have finally learned your lesson about doing business with your one-time law school classmate and Rolls Royce collector Deborah Swift (from Problem 1.6). Unfortunately, one of your friends has not. Justin Roberts, a non-lawyer and neighbor of yours, comes to you for some friendly advice about a problem that he is having with Deborah. Justin, himself a car buff, had gone with a friend to Deborah's house and had done a "handshake deal" with Deborah to buy Deborah's four '89 Rolls Royces for $17,000 each. According to this oral agreement, Justin was to pick the cars up in 30 days.

   The day after Justin's visit to Deborah's house, he received a signed letter from her purporting to confirm their agreement. Deborah's letter, however, said that their agreement was for Justin to purchase just two of her '89 Rolls Royces, and for $25,000 each instead of $17,000. Following receipt of that letter, Justin tried for two weeks to reach Deborah to clear up what he thought might have been an honest mistake on her part about the terms of their deal. When Justin finally did reach her, Deborah insisted that it was "her way or the highway," even though Justin's friend was willing to swear that Justin's version of the oral agreement was correct.

   If you represent Justin, for what quantity and price will you be able to enforce his deal with Deborah? U.C.C. §§2-201, 2-202, 2-207.

Assignment 7: Requisites to Formalization in Leases, International Sales, and Real Estate Sales

A.   Requisites to Formalization in Leases

When it comes to requisites for formalizing a contract, the system for leases is roughly parallel to that for sales. The rules governing extrinsic evidence for lease contracts in §2A-202 are precisely the same as those found for sales of goods in §2-202. The rules on the necessity for a writing in lease deals, found in §2A-201, differ in a few notable respects from the comparable rules for sales.

First, the necessity for a writing (or "record" as amended) with leases does not kick in unless the total lease payments are at least $1,000. Some states, including California and Florida, have added a non-uniform amendment to §2A-201 that requires a writing to enforce consumer leases no matter how small the amount of total lease payments.

Second, when a writing is required in a lease deal, slightly more must be in that writing than in the writing that §2-201(1) requires for sales of goods. Not only does the lease writing in §2A-201(1) need to include a signature of the party to be charged and an indication that a lease contract has been made, it must also "describe the goods leased and the lease term."

The statutory exceptions to the writing requirement for leases also depart slightly from those available for sales of goods contracts. The main difference is that there is no "merchant's exception" to the writing requirement in the case of leases. The rationale for that omission, we are told by the drafters in the Official Comment to §2A-201, is that "the number of such transactions involving leases, as opposed to sales, was thought to be modest." This echoes the rationale mentioned in Assignment 4 for why Article 2A does not include a "battle of the forms" section: Lessors and lessees do not typically exchange purchase orders and acknowledgement forms, as do buyers and sellers.

The other difference in the exceptions to the writing requirement between leases and sales is the absence in §2A-201(3) of the exception for payment received and accepted by the lessor. As to this change from the sales counterpart, the drafters of Article 2A note in the Official Comment to §2A-201 that the payment typically tendered in a lease deal is only for a relatively small portion of the total lease payments. In light of this reality, the drafters believed that "as a matter of policy, this act of payment is not a sufficient substitute for the required memorandum."

B. Requisites to Formalization in International Sales

In international sales, the requisites to formalization are few and far between. There is no default rule in the CISG that bars the introduction of extrinsic evidence. Instead, C.I.S.G. Article 8(3) tells us that "due consideration is to be given to all relevant circumstances of the case including the negotiations, any practices which the parties have established between themselves, usages and any subsequent conduct of the parties."

MCC-Marble Ceramic Center, Inc. v. Ceramica Nuova D'Agostino, S.p.A.

144 F.3d 1384 (11th Cir. 1998)

BIRCH, C.J.

This case requires us to determine whether a court must consider parol evidence in a contract dispute governed by the United Nations Convention on Contracts for the International Sale of Goods ("CISG"). The district court granted summary judgment on behalf of the defendant-appellee, relying on certain terms and provisions that appeared on the reverse of a pre-printed form contract for the sale of ceramic tiles. The plaintiff-appellant sought to rely on a number of affidavits that tended to show both that the parties had arrived at an oral contract before memorializing their agreement in writing and that they subjectively intended not to apply the terms on the reverse of the contract to their agreements. The magistrate judge held that the affidavits did not raise an issue of material fact and recommended that the district court grant summary judgment based on the terms of the contract. The district court agreed with the magistrate judge's reasoning and entered summary judgment in the defendant-appellee's favor. We reverse. . . .

The plaintiff-appellant, MCC-Marble Ceramic, Inc. ("MCC"), is a Florida corporation engaged in the retail sale of tiles, and the defendant-appellee, Ceramica Nuova D'Agostino S.p.A. ("D'Agostino") is an Italian corporation engaged in the manufacture of ceramic tiles. In October 1990, MCC's president, Juan Carlos Mozon, met representatives of D'Agostino at a trade fair in Bologna, Italy, and negotiated an agreement to purchase ceramic tiles from D'Agostino based on samples he examined at the trade fair. Monzon, who spoke no Italian, communicated with Gianni Silingardi, then D'Agostino's commercial director, through a translator, Gianfranco Copelli, who was himself an agent of D'Agostino. The parties apparently arrived at an oral agreement on the crucial terms of price, quality, quantity, delivery and payment. The parties then recorded these terms on one of D'Agostino's standard, pre-printed order forms and Monzon signed the contract on MCC's behalf. According to MCC, the parties also entered into a requirements contract in February 1991, subject to which D'Agostino agreed to supply MCC with high grade ceramic tile at specific discounts as long as MCC purchased sufficient quantities of tile. MCC completed a number of additional order forms requesting tile deliveries pursuant to that agreement. . . .

MCC brought suit against D'Agostino claiming a breach of the February 1991 requirements contract when D'Agostino failed to satisfy orders in April, May, and August of 1991. In addition to other defenses, D'Agostino responded that it was under no obligation to fill MCC's orders because MCC had defaulted on payment for previous shipments. In support of its position, D'Agostino relied on the pre-printed terms of the contracts that MCC had executed. The executed forms were printed in Italian and contained terms and conditions on both the front and reverse. According to an English translation of the October 1990 contract, the front of the order form contained the following language directly beneath Monzon's signature . . .

[T]he buyer hereby states that he is aware of the sales conditions stated on the reverse and that he expressly approves of them with special reference to those numbered 1-2-3-4-5-6-7-8.

R2-126, Exh. 3 ¶5 ("Maselli Aff."). Clause 6(b), printed on the back of the form states:

> [D]efault or delay in payment within the time agreed upon gives D'Agostino the right to . . . suspend or cancel the contract itself and to cancel possible other pending contracts and the buyer does not have the right to indemnification or damages. Id. ¶6.

D'Agostino also brought a number of counterclaims against MCC, seeking damages for MCC's alleged nonpayment for deliveries of tile that D'Agostino had made between February 28, 1991 and July 4, 1991. MCC responded that the tile it had received was of a lower quality than contracted for, and that, pursuant to the CISG, MCC was entitled to reduce payment in proportion to the defects. D'Agostino, however, noted that clause 4 on the reverse of the contract states, in pertinent part. . . .

Possible complaints for defects of the merchandise must be made in writing by means of a certified letter within and not later than 10 days after receipt of the merchandise. . . .

Maselli Aff. ¶6. Although there is evidence to support MCC's claims that it complained about the quality of the deliveries it received, MCC never submitted any written complaints.

MCC did not dispute these underlying facts before the district court, but argued that the parties never intended the terms and conditions printed on the reverse of the order form to apply to their agreements. As evidence for this assertion, MCC submitted Monzon's affidavit, which claims that MCC had no subjective intent to be bound by those terms and that D'Agostino was aware of this intent. MCC also filed affidavits from Silingardi and Copelli, D'Agostino's representatives at the trade fair, which support Monzon's claim that the parties subjectively intended not to be bound by the terms on the reverse of the order form. The magistrate judge held that the affidavits, even if true, did not raise an issue of material fact regarding the interpretation or applicability of the terms of the written contracts and the district court accepted his recommendation to award summary judgment in D'Agostino's favor. MCC then filed this timely appeal. . . .

The parties to this case agree that the CISG governs their dispute because the United States, where MCC has its place of business, and Italy, where D'Agostino has its place of business, are both States Party to the Convention. See CISG, art. 1. Article 8 of the CISG governs the interpretation of international contracts for the sale of goods and forms the basis of MCC's appeal from the district court's grant of summary judgment in D'Agostino's favor. MCC argues that the magistrate judge and the district court improperly ignored evidence that MCC submitted regarding the parties' subjective intent when they memorialized the terms of their agreement on D'Agostino's pre-printed form contract, and that the magistrate judge erred by applying the parol evidence rule in derogation of the CISG. . . .

Contrary to what is familiar practice in United States courts, the CISG appears to permit a substantial inquiry into the parties' subjective intent, even if the parties did not engage in any objectively ascertainable means of registering this intent. Article 8(1) of the CISG instructs courts to interpret the "statements . . . and other conduct of a party . . . according to his intent" as long as the other party "knew or could not have been unaware" of that intent. The plain language of the Convention, therefore, requires an inquiry into a party's subjective intent as long as the other party to the contract was aware of that intent. . . .

In this case, MCC has submitted three affidavits that discuss the purported subjective intent of the parties to the initial agreement concluded between MCC and D'Agostino in October 1990. All three affidavits discuss the preliminary negotiations and report that the parties arrived at an oral agreement for D'Agostino to supply quantities of a specific grade of ceramic tile to MCC at an agreed upon price. The affidavits state that the "oral agreement established the essential terms of quality, quantity, description of goods, delivery, price and payment." See R3-133 ¶9 ("Silingardi Aff."); R1-51 ¶7 ("Copelli Aff."); R1-47 ¶7 ("Monzon Aff."). The affidavits also note that the parties memorialized the terms of their oral agreement on a standard D'Agostino order form, but all three affiants contend that the parties subjectively intended not to be bound by the terms on the reverse of that form despite a provision directly below the signature line that expressly and specifically incorporated those terms. . . .

The terms on the reverse of the contract give D'Agostino the right to suspend or cancel all contracts in the event of a buyer's non-payment and require a buyer to make a written report of all defects within ten days. As the magistrate judge's report and recommendation makes clear, if these terms applied to the agreements between MCC and D'Agostino, summary judgment would be appropriate because MCC failed to make any written complaints about the quality of tile it received and D'Agostino has established MCC's non-payment of a number of invoices amounting to $108,389.40 and 102,053,846.00 Italian lira.

Article 8(1) of the CISG requires a court to consider this evidence of the parties' subjective intent. Contrary to the magistrate judge's report, which the district court endorsed and adopted, article 8(1) does not focus on interpreting the parties' statements alone. Although we agree with the magistrate judge's conclusion that no "interpretation" of the contract's terms could support MCC's position, article 8(1) also requires a court to consider subjective intent while interpreting the conduct of the parties. The CISG's language, therefore, requires courts to consider evidence of a party's subjective intent when signing a contract if the other party to the contract was aware of that intent at the time. This is precisely the type of evidence that MCC has provided through the Silingardi, Copelli, and Monzon affidavits, which discuss not only Monzon's intent as MCC's representative but also discuss the intent of D'Agostino's representatives and their knowledge that Monzon did not intend to agree to the terms on the reverse of the form contract. This acknowledgment that D'Agostino's representatives were aware of Monzon's subjective intent puts this case squarely within article 8(1) of the CISG, and therefore requires the court to consider MCC's evidence as it interprets the parties' conduct. . . .

Given our determination that the magistrate judge and the district court should have considered MCC's affidavits regarding the parties' subjective intentions, we must address a question of first impression in this circuit: whether the parol evidence rule, which bars evidence of an earlier oral contract that contradicts or varies the terms of a subsequent or contemporaneous written contract, plays any role in cases involving the CISG. We begin by observing that the parol evidence rule, contrary to its title, is a substantive rule of law, not a rule of evidence. See II E. Allen Farnsworth, Farnsworth on Contracts, §7.2 at 194 (1990). The rule does not purport to exclude a particular type of evidence as an "untrustworthy or undesirable" way of proving a fact, but prevents a litigant from attempting to show "the fact itself — the fact that the terms of the agreement are other than those in the writing." Id. As such, a federal district court cannot simply apply the parol evidence rule as a procedural matter — as it might if excluding a particular type of evidence under the Federal Rules of Evidence, which apply in federal court regardless of the source of the substantive rule of decision. Cf. id. §7.2 at 196. . . .

The CISG itself contains no express statement on the role of parol evidence. See Honnold, Uniform Law §110 at 170. It is clear, however, that the drafters of the CISG were comfortable with the concept of permitting parties to rely on oral contracts because they eschewed any statutes of fraud provision and expressly provided for the enforcement of oral contracts. Compare CISG, art. 11 (a contract of sale need not be concluded or evidenced in writing) with U.C.C. §2-201 (precluding the enforcement of oral contracts for the sale of goods involving more than $500). Moreover, article 8(3) of the CISG expressly directs courts to give "due consideration . . . to all relevant circumstances of the case including the negotiations . . ." to determine the intent of the parties. Given article 8(1)'s directive to use the intent of the parties to interpret their statements and conduct, article 8(3) is a clear instruction to admit and consider parol evidence regarding the negotiations to the extent they reveal the parties' subjective intent. . . .

This is not to say that parties to an international contract for the sale of goods cannot depend on written contracts or that parol evidence regarding subjective contractual intent need always prevent a party relying on a written agreement from securing summary judgment. To the contrary, most cases will not present a situation (as exists in this case) in which both parties to the contract acknowledge a subjective intent not to be bound by the terms of a pre-printed writing. In most cases, therefore, article 8(2) of the CISG will apply, and objective evidence will provide the basis for the court's decision. See Honnold, Uniform Law §107 at 164-65. Consequently, a party to a contract governed by the CISG will not be able to avoid the terms of a contract and force a jury trial simply by submitting an affidavit which states that he or she did not have the subjective intent to be bound by the contract's terms. . . . Moreover, to the extent parties wish to avoid parol evidence problems they can do so by including a merger clause in their agreement that extinguishes any and all prior agreements and understandings not expressed in the writing. . . .

Considering MCC's affidavits in this case, however, we conclude that the magistrate judge and the district court improperly granted summary judgment in favor of D'Agostino. Although the affidavits are, as D'Agostino observes, relatively conclusory and unsupported by facts that would objectively establish MCC's intent not to be bound by the conditions on the reverse of the form, article 8(1) requires a court to consider evidence of a party's subjective intent when the other party was aware of it, and the Silingardi and Copelli affidavits provide that evidence. This is not to say that the affidavits are conclusive proof of what the parties intended. A reasonable finder of fact, for example, could disregard testimony that purportedly sophisticated international merchants signed a contract without intending to be bound as simply too incredible to believe and hold MCC to the conditions printed on the reverse of the contract. Nevertheless, the affidavits raise an issue of material fact regarding the parties' intent to incorporate the provisions on the reverse of the form contract. If the finder of fact determines that the parties did not intend to rely on those provisions, then the more general provisions of the CISG will govern the outcome of the dispute. . . .

MCC's affidavits, however, do not discuss all of the transactions and orders that MCC placed with D'Agostino. Each of the affidavits discusses the parties' subjective intent surrounding the initial order MCC placed with D'Agostino in October 1990. The Copelli affidavit also discusses a February 1991 requirements contract between the parties and reports that the parties subjectively did not intend the terms on the reverse of the D'Agostino order form to apply to that contract either. See Copelli Aff. ¶12. D'Agostino, however, submitted the affidavit of its chairman, Vincenzo Maselli, which describes at least three other orders from MCC on form contracts dated January 15, 1991, April 27, 1991, and May 4, 1991, in addition to the October 1990 contract. See Maselli Aff. ¶2, 25. MCC's affidavits do not discuss the subjective intent of the parties to be bound by language in those contracts, and D'Agostino, therefore, argues that we should affirm summary judgment to the extent damages can be traced to those order forms. It is unclear from the record, however, whether all of these contracts contained the terms that appeared in the October 1990 contract. Moreover, because article 8 requires a court to consider any "practices which the parties have established between themselves, usages and any subsequent conduct of the parties" in interpreting contracts, CISG, art. 8(3), whether the parties intended to adhere to the ten day limit for complaints, as stated on the reverse of the initial contract, will have an impact on whether MCC was bound to adhere to the limit on subsequent deliveries. Since material issues of fact remain regarding the interpretation of the remaining contracts between MCC and D'Agostino, we cannot affirm any portion of the district court's summary judgment in D'Agostino's favor. . . .

MCC asks us to reverse the district court's grant of summary judgment in favor of D'Agostino. The district court's decision rests on pre-printed contractual terms and conditions incorporated on the reverse of a standard order form that MCC's president signed on the company's behalf. Nevertheless, we conclude that the CISG, which governs international contracts for the sale of goods, precludes summary judgment in this case because MCC has raised an issue of material fact concerning the parties' subjective intent to be bound by the terms on the reverse of the pre-printed contract. The CISG also precludes the application of the parol evidence rule, which would otherwise bar the consideration of evidence concerning a prior or contemporaneously negotiated oral agreement. Accordingly, we reverse the district court's grant of summary judgment and remand this case for further proceedings consistent with this opinion.

Of course, parties in an international sales contract may always choose to vary the CISG default term on that score and create by contract their own parol evidence rule. A standard merger clause that deems a particular writing complete and exclusive would seem to do the trick. C.I.S.G. Article 6 is clear on the ability of parties to "derogate from or vary the effect of any of [the CISG's] provisions."

C.I.S.G. Article 11 indicates that there is no writing requirement in international sales contracts. This is in accordance with the continental approach, and has the practical advantage of avoiding the need for transnational discovery of documents that may be needed to satisfy a writing requirement if there were one.

The drafters of the CISG did, however, create a compromise provision for those countries which believed that it was important that there should be a statute of frauds. Article 96 allows a country to make a declaration that there *will* be a statute of frauds requirement in any contract involving parties that have their principal place of business in that country. The United States has not chosen to make such a declaration, and therefore international sales contracts involving United States parties will not be subject to the UCC statute of frauds rules.

C.   Requisites to Formalization in
the Real Estate System

Although real estate sales will not be governed by the writing requirement of U.C.C. §2-201, most states have either by common law or statute some form of writing requirement for the sale of real estate. This is hardly surprising, given that sales of real estate were the first category of sales under the law to require some kind of writing to be enforceable.

The writing requirement for the enforceability of real estate sales tends to be stricter than that which exists for the sale of goods. Whereas the Article 2 rules require very little in the way of terms that must be in writing, most of the state statutes of frauds for real estate require that the writing include the "material terms" of the sale. Sometimes the statute will specify which terms are material, and will typically include such terms as party names, identification of the property, the nature of the title to be conveyed, and the price.

Where a party to a real estate contract has not satisfied the statute of frauds, there remains the argument that the plaintiff detrimentally relied on the oral promises made by the defendant. Although not all courts accept that argument, equitable estoppel is one of the commonly accepted exceptions to the usual requirement that a contract to sell real estate must be in writing.

A second common exception to the real estate statute of frauds, which is in some sense a subset of equitable estoppel, is part performance. With the part performance exception, the buyer takes some action in part performance (payment, possession, or improvements) that substitutes for the missing writing.

Holbrook v. Holbrook

474 S.E.2d 900 (W. Va. 1996)

PER CURIAM.

This action is before this Court upon an appeal from the final order of the Circuit Court of Berkeley County, West Virginia, entered on August 23, 1994. Pursuant to that order, the circuit court dismissed the complaint of the appellant, Edwina T. Holbrook, against the appellees, Arthur M. Holbrook, Jr., and Gladys J. Holbrook, in an action in which the appellant sought specific performance to compel the appellees to convey to her a certain interest in real property. The dismissal of the complaint was upon a motion filed by the appellees pursuant to W. Va. R. Civ. P. 12(b)(6). . . .

In June 1985, the appellees purchased a parcel of real property in Arden District, Berkeley County, consisting of 3.978 acres. By deed dated June 13, 1985, the appellees conveyed one acre of that parcel to their son, Arthur M. Holbrook III. A home was constructed upon the one acre which later became the marital domicile of the appellees' son and the appellant.

As alleged in the complaint, prior to the marriage of the appellees' son and the appellant, the appellees orally agreed to convey the remaining 2.978 acres to the son and the appellant for $10,000, plus interest. Specifically, the appellees were to convey the acres upon the completion by the son and the appellant of 120 payments of $132.16 each.

The appellees' son and the appellant were married on February 16, 1986. They separated, however, in March 1992 and subsequently obtained a divorce upon the ground of irreconcilable differences. As part of the divorce settlement, the appellees' son purchased the appellant's interest in the one-acre parcel, upon which the home was located, for $20,000. Nevertheless, neither the divorce decree entered on June 28, 1994, nor the property settlement agreement incorporated therein, mentioned the 2.978 parcel of real property.

On July 1, 1994, the appellant instituted the underlying action in which she claims entitlement to an undivided one-half interest in the 2.978 acres. Importantly, the complaint alleges that, prior to their separation and divorce, the appellees' son and the appellant made substantial payments to the appellees for the property. As the complaint states:

> That [appellant] and Arthur M. Holbrook III jointly made payments for the purchase of said property, principal and interest, from July 1985 through March 1992 . . . [and that] said payments made by the [appellant] and Arthur M. Holbrook III were received and accepted until the parties separated and the said Arthur M. Holbrook III left the marital domicile; that from April 1992 through September 1992 the [appellant] continued to make the said payments to the Defendants, but the Defendants refused to cash or negotiate the check funded them by the [appellant].

In the complaint, the appellant asked the circuit court to permit her to pay any unpaid sums with regard to the appellees' agreement to sell the 2.978 acres. The appellant concluded the complaint by asking the circuit court to compel the appellees to convey to her an undivided one-half interest in the 2.978 acres.

In response, the appellees filed a motion to dismiss the complaint pursuant to W. Va. R. Civ. P. 12(b)(6), alleging that, inasmuch as the action involved an oral agreement for the sale of land, the agreement was unenforceable pursuant to this State's statute of frauds. As reflected in the final order of August 23, 1994, the circuit court agreed with the appellees and dismissed the complaint. This appeal followed. . . .

This State's statute of frauds, embodied in W. Va. Code, 36-1-3 [1931], provides:

> No contract for the sale of land, or the lease thereof for more than one year, shall be enforceable unless the contract or some note or memorandum thereof be in writing and signed by the party to be charged thereby, or by his agent. But the consideration need not be set forth or expressed in the writing, and it may be proved by other evidence.

In Timberlake v. Heflin, 180 W. Va. 644, 648, 379 S.E.2d 149, 153 (1989), this Court noted that the underlying purpose of the statute of frauds "is to prevent the fraudulent enforcement of unmade contracts," rather than the legitimate enforcement of contracts which were, in fact, made. As syllabus point 3 of *Timberlake* observes:

> The statute of frauds, as applicable to contracts for the sale or lease of land, is a procedural bar to prevent enforcement of oral contracts unless the conditions expressed in W.Va.Code, 36-1-3, are met. The operation of the statute of frauds goes only to the remedy; it does not render the contract void.

That distinction between the enforceability and the validity of such contracts, recognized in *Timberlake*, is consistent with the principle that, in some circumstances, considerations of equity may result in the statute not being imposed. As this Court held in syllabus point 1 of Ross v. Midelburg, 129 W. Va. 851, 42 S.E.2d 185 (1947): "A party to an oral contract for the sale of land, to which the statute of frauds is applicable, may, by conduct on his part, be estopped in equity to assert the statute of frauds as a defense to such contract." One such exception, grounded in equity, is the doctrine of part performance.

In Ballengee v. Whitlock, 138 W. Va. 58, 63, 74 S.E.2d 780, 784 (1953), this Court stated, generally, that "[i]f there has been part performance of a contract for the sale of real estate, such contract may be enforced." In particular, this Court has recognized that, although the mere payment of the purchase price may not be sufficient part performance to render an oral agreement for the sale of real property enforceable, syl. pt. 4, Gibson v. Stalnaker, 87 W. Va. 710, 106 S.E. 243 (1921), 8B M.J. Frauds, Statute of §36 (Michie 1994), such payment, in conjunction with possession of the property or improvement thereof by the vendee, is supportive of the application of the doctrine of part performance as an exception to the statute of frauds. . . .

In the action now before this Court, it must be emphasized that our review is upon the limited issue of whether the circuit court committed error in dismissing the complaint pursuant to W. Va. R. Civ. P. 12(b)(6). Stated another way, the question is whether, viewing the complaint liberally, the appellant can prove facts in support of her claim which would entitle her to relief. In that regard, it is not fatal to the complaint that the appellant seeks relief in the form of specific performance under a "resulting trust," rather than a "part performance," theory, even though a "resulting trust" theory would not apply in these circumstances. . . .

Here, the complaint alleges that the appellees' son and the appellant made substantial payments to the appellees for the 2.978 acres, based upon an oral agreement. The payments were allegedly made from July 1985 through March 1992. Although, as indicated above, such payments alone do not constitute part performance as an exception to the statute of frauds, and the appellees have disputed whether the payments were, in fact, for the 2.978 acres, such payments, if established as purchase money, are a factor to be considered under the doctrine of part performance.

Moreover, the complaint indicates that the alleged oral agreement concerning the 2.978 acres did not occur in a vacuum but, instead, occurred as part of an intent by the appellees to transfer the larger 3.978 acres to their son and the appellant in contemplation of marriage. Specifically, the complaint alleges that the appellees purchased the original 3.978 acre parcel because the appellees' son and the appellant "wanted to build a residence upon one (1) acre of said property[.]" According to the appellant, although the one acre was conveyed to the appellees' son separately, the residence was built thereon and became the marital domicile. In that context, the building of the marital domicile and the question of use or possession of the entire 3.978 acres thereafter by the appellees' son and the appellant, become relevant considerations as to whether the oral agreement is enforceable under the doctrine of part performance. Under such a theory, those considerations are relevant even though the appellant sold her interest in the one acre parcel following the divorce. As stated above, neither the divorce decree nor the property settlement agreement mentioned the remaining 2.978 acre parcel.

In summary, although it may be later determined that the one acre conveyance to the appellees' son was unrelated to the alleged oral agreement concerning the 2.978 acres, the complaint's merging of the two transactions, coupled with the allegations of payment of purchase money for the 2.978 acres, render the complaint sufficient to withstand dismissal under W. Va. R. Civ. P. 12(b)(6). . . .

Accordingly, the final order of the Circuit Court of Berkeley County, entered on August 23, 1994, is reversed, and this action is remanded to that court for further proceedings.

REVERSED AND REMANDED.

As far as real estate law's treatment of parol evidence, the rule looks an awful lot like the one you see in U.C.C. §2-202. The reason is that the UCC parol evidence rule was essentially just a codification of the parol evidence rule that governs real estate contracts as well as any other contracts under the common law. In some minor respects, the common-law version of the parol evidence rule can be slightly more restrictive than the UCC version regarding which parol evidence is admissible, depending on which state's common law is at issue.

For example, some courts under the common-law parol evidence rule have required that the contract be "ambiguous" with respect to the term that a party seeks to explain or supplement by the introduction of parol evidence.

The UCC rule, by contrast, does not require ambiguity as a prerequisite to a party's ability to explain or supplement a partially integrated writing with "consistent additional terms."

Problem Set 7

7.1. a.   Jay Berringer, owner of Jay's Rent-to-Own Pianos (Problem 2.3), is back in your office with more questions. It seems that one of Jay's brand-new workers, Sam Clark, did not realize that Jay's policy was that all of his store's leases were to be in writing. As a result, Sam entered into an oral lease contract with Bonnie Kilgen. The terms of that "handshake deal" were that Bonnie would lease a 1982 Steinway upright piano for $75 per month for one year, with an option for $150 to renew the lease for one more year on the same terms. Jay wants to know to what extent this oral lease contract will be enforceable if Bonnie decides she does not want to go forward with it. What do you advise? U.C.C. §2A-201.

b.   Same facts as part a., except that the oral contract required that the first year's rent would be $100 per month and would all be paid upfront in one $1,200 payment, which Bonnie has already made. The one-year lease renewal option is for $50 per month, rent to be paid at the start of each month. To what extent is this oral lease agreement enforceable by Bonnie? U.C.C. §2A-201, Official Comment to §2A-201.

c.   Same facts as part a., except that the first year's rent was $100 per month and Jay's has delivered the piano to Bonnie, who accepted it and began using it. Two months later, however, before any written lease contract is executed, Bonnie enters into a written contract with a neighbor by which Bonnie purports to lease the piano to the neighbor for $200 per month for one year. Jay learns about this and decides that he would like to rent the piano to the neighbor for $200 per month instead of to Bonnie for $100 per month. May Jay's avoid Bonnie's oral lease so that he may enter into a new lease with her neighbor? U.C.C. §2A-201.

7.2. a.   Susan Heil, an authorized sales agent for Ford Motor Co. of Detroit, entered into an oral contract on behalf of Ford Motor with Toronto Ford, a Canadian car dealership. The two sides agreed orally that Ford Motor Co. would sell Toronto Ford 36 Taurus station wagons at the manufacturer's standard dealer price, delivery to take place in one month. The two sides also agreed orally that Michigan law (excluding the CISG) would govern the transaction. Shortly before delivery, Toronto Ford indicates to Susan that it wants out of the deal. Susan eventually files a lawsuit in Detroit to enforce the oral contract. Toronto Ford moves for summary judgment, pleading the statute of frauds defense and attaching a signed affidavit denying that it ever entered into a contract with the plaintiff. If you are the trial judge, should you grant the summary judgment motion? C.I.S.G. Arts. 1(1), 6, 11; U.C.C. §2-201.

b.   Same facts as part a., except that the two parties do have a written sales contract. The contract, which has no merger clause, mentions all of the relevant terms except the fact that Michigan law (excluding the CISG) will govern the transaction. The choice-of-law provision was an oral side agreement that the two parties entered into before the writing was signed. Now Toronto

Ford has breached the contract, and Susan Heil would like to avail her company of the UCC's remedy provisions rather than the CISG's. Will Susan be able to successfully introduce evidence of the side agreement on choice-of-law? C.I.S.G. Arts. 1(1), 6, 8(3); U.C.C. §2-202, Official Comment 3 to §2-202.

7.3. a.   When Pete Smarz's daughter, Denise, got married two years ago, Pete decided that he would help out the newlywed couple by letting them rent his second home in West Virginia. Pete told Denise and her husband, Bill, that the two of them could rent the house for two years at $500 per month. All of the parties agree with that much of the facts. Denise and Bill claim that Pete also told the two of them that if they were still married and had a child at the end of the two years, Pete would let them buy the house for its appraised value less the total of the rent payments they made for two years. Pete denies that he ever gave the couple this purchase option. Denise tells you that her father is just angry because he and Bill had a falling out, and her father just wants to get back at Bill by kicking both of them out of the house. It has now been two years since the lease began, Denise and Bill have a six-month-old son, and the house has been appraised at $150,000. Denise asks you whether she can enforce the purchase option and buy the house from her father for $138,000, which is the appraised value minus the rent payments made. What do you advise her?

b. Same facts as part a., except that Denise and Bill added a two-story addition to the back of the house during their second year in the house for a total cost of $40,000. To what extent does this help their case for enforcement of the purchase option?

Chapter 2.   Terms

Assignment 8: Warranties with Sales of Goods

A.   The Effects of Warranty Law
on Business Practice

From the buyer's perspective, a key feature of any sales transaction is trying to ensure that the goods being purchased will work the way they are supposed to. U.C.C. Article 2 contains a number of provisions that define the nature and scope of the promises the seller makes concerning the quality of goods that the seller is transferring to the buyer. Some of these provisions deal with explicit promises made by the seller, whereas other provisions create certain implicit promises that will become part of the deal unless the seller does something affirmative to disclaim them.

Players in the system are generally not thinking too much about the various warranty rules of Article 2 when they conduct purchase and sale transactions. They are, however, focusing very much on the issue of quality for the sake of future business.

As the president of a medium-sized shoe manufacturer put it: "Nobody bargains over warranties, because it's really pretty simple: Either the shoes are what they are supposed to be, or they're not. If they're not, you're not going to be in business very long. As seller, our incentive for quality is not driven by legal warranties, it's driven by business necessity."

The general counsel for a computer hardware distributor echoed those sentiments: "The warranties we give to retailers are whatever we get from the manufacturers, which is typically limited to repair, replacement, or refund of the hardware. Our real incentive, though, is never the warranty that we give but our philosophy of serving our customers. That's the reason, not warranties, that we try to make something right if one of our buyers gets a bad shipment."

The owner of a medium-sized air tool manufacturer explained how, as seller, he stands behind his products, but he also expects his own suppliers to do the same: "One time a company in Cleveland, Ohio, made some needle tubes not dimensionally correct and they were going to charge us to correct the problem. And they stood by their position, which was that there was a blueprint that did not have that particular dimension on it. And our position was that we are a long-time customer of [theirs], and I've known [their president] for probably 20 years. So I wrote to their president and said, 'Al, fix your own problems, and correct those problems and get those needle tubes to us.' I did that over the fax machine, and they complied with my request."

There are two major issues regarding warranty creation that tend to command the attention of buyers and sellers in the sales system: (1) sellers feel the need for an outside time limit on warranties, but buyers who re-sell do not want any time limits to begin until their resale; and (2) middlemen do not like to give greater warranties to their buyers than they're getting from their own sellers.

As to outside time limits on warranties, sellers are concerned that their responsibility for a particular sale not be completely open-ended. Sellers at least want to know that after a certain passage of time, the goods delivered were in fact acceptable. A furniture manufacturer related a problem that his company had a couple of years ago along these lines: "In a disturbing number of cases the ultimate buyer, the consumer, would ask the retailer to take the furniture back two or three years after the consumer had purchased it. Our retailers, figuring we would take it from them, would agree to do so for the sake of their own business and then would expect us to make them whole. We now make it clear that our warranties run 12 months from the time the retailer gets it from us; we'll honor the warranty within that time period even if the true claimant is the consumer rather than our buyer."

Although sellers may want to cap the length of their exposure for warranty problems, buyers who resell do not want warranty time limits to begin until the goods leave their own hands. One manufacturer described this tension between the desire of the seller for liability that is not open-ended and the desire of the buyer who resells not to get stuck with a warranty problem caused by its supplier: "For reasons of certainty, many of our suppliers want to cap the time during which we can complain about a problem. But the reality is that sometimes a problem won't manifest itself until the product has reached our buyer, and that could take some time. So we always want the warranty to start running from the time when our buyer gets the finished product, not when we get the raw material."

Beyond the timing issues, buyers who resell are very careful as a general matter to make certain that the warranties that they give to their buyers are no greater than the warranties that they are receiving from their own sellers. Otherwise, wholesalers can get stuck in the unenviable position of being responsible to their buyers for problems created by the manufacturer, with no recourse against the manufacturer. As one Fortune 100 manufacturer noted: "Our biggest warranty issue is that we need to make sure that the warranties we're getting from our suppliers are the same warranties that we will have to give to the government when we sell the finished product to it. In fact, we will put clauses in our purchase contracts to that effect, and it's not something that we'll negotiate about since we can't afford to be stuck with a problem in our sale that was created by one of our suppliers."

B.   The Basic UCC Quality Warranties

How the above-described warranty tensions end up being reconciled is typically a product of the leverage and negotiating skills of the players in each discrete transaction. The actual scope of the quality promises that are made in each case will thus come down more to business realities than to legal rules. The legal rules of Article 2 are important, though, in that they provide the structure within which these negotiations take place. In most cases, the default rules of Article 2 provide the starting point for negotiations.

The UCC provides two implied warranties that relate to the performance of the goods sold. There is also an implied title warranty, which is covered by U.C.C. §2-312. Of the two implied warranties of quality, the more important is the implied warranty of merchantability found in U.C.C. §2-314. Unless disclaimed or modified, this implied warranty arises in every sale of goods where the seller is a merchant with respect to goods of the kind being sold. U.C.C. §2-314(1). The two key promises within the implied warranty of merchantability are that the goods being sold are at least as good as other similar goods in the trade, and that the goods are fit for the ordinary purposes for which goods of that description are used. U.C.C. §§2-314(2)(a) & (c).

With the implied warranty of merchantability under Article 2, sometimes the buyer's complaint about the goods relates not to the quality of what was received, but rather to the absence of a particular safety feature in the product.

Phillips v. Cricket Lighters

852 A.2d 365 (Pa. Super. 2004)

MUSMANNO, J.

Gwendolyn Phillips, as administratrix of the estates of Robyn Jorjean Williams, Jerome I. Campbell, and Alphonso Crawford, and as guardian of Neil Curtis Williams, a minor, (collectively, "Phillips"), appealed from the Order granting summary judgment in favor of the Appellees set forth above (collectively, "Cricket"). The Pennsylvania Supreme Court has remanded this matter for this Court's determination of issues based upon Phillips's claim that Cricket breached the implied warranty of merchantability and the claim for punitive damages.

The Pennsylvania Supreme Court summarized the factual and procedural history of the instant case as follows:

> On the night of November 30, 1993, two year old Jerome Campbell ("Jerome") pulled down the purse belonging to his mother, Robyn Williams ("Robyn"), from the top of the family's refrigerator. Jerome retrieved a Cricket disposable butane cigarette lighter from his mother's purse. It is uncontested that this butane lighter lacked any child-resistant feature. Jerome's five year old brother, Neil Williams ("Neil"), observed Jerome use the lighter to ignite some linens. The fire spread to the rest of the family's apartment. After Neil was unsuccessful in his attempts to rouse his mother [from sleep], he was able to get to a window and began screaming; a neighbor rescued him. Tragically, Robyn, Jerome, and another minor child of Robyn's, Alphonso Crawford, died in the fire.
>
> Gwendolyn Phillips ["Phillips"], as administratrix of the estates of the three decedents and as guardian of Neil, instituted this action against the manufacturers and distributors of the Cricket lighter [collectively, "Cricket"]. In her complaint, [Phillips] raised, *inter alia*, claims of design defect sounding in both strict liability and negligence, negligent infliction of emotional distress, breach of the implied warranty of merchantability, and punitive damages. These claims were all predicated on [Phillips's] allegations that [Cricket] should have manufactured and distributed a lighter that had childproof features.
>
> [Cricket] filed for summary judgment. The trial court found in favor of [Cricket], and dismissed all claims against [Cricket]. . . .

Phillips first claims that the trial court erred in granting summary judgment on its cause of action for Cricket's breach of the implied warranty of merchantability. In its Opinion, the trial court explained its rationale as follows:

> The ordinary purpose for which disposable butane lighters are used is to produce a flame. The evidence reveals that the lighter was fit for such a purpose and did not malfunction in any respect. Additionally, in Altronics of Bethlehem, Inc., v. Repco, Inc., 957 F.2d 1102, 1105 (1992), the Third Circuit Court of Appeals noted that under Pennsylvania law, a plaintiff must show a defect in the goods purchased in order to establish a breach of the implied warranty of merchantability. Such has not been demonstrated in the instant case. As the Cricket lighter apparently functioned normally and was of a merchantable quality, we will grant Cricket's Motion for summary judgment on the warranty claim.

Trial Court Opinion, 12/1/98, at 31-32. We disagree with the trial court's interpretation of the implied warranty of merchantability.

Summary judgment is proper where the pleadings, depositions, affidavits and materials of record show that there is no genuine issue of material fact and that the moving party is entitled to judgment as a matter of law. Weiner v. American Honda Motor Co., 718 A.2d 305, 307 (Pa. Super. 1998). We view the record in the light most favorable to the opposing party and resolve all doubts and reasonable inferences about the existence of an issue of fact in favor of the nonmoving party. Telega v. Security Bureau, Inc., 719 A.2d 372, 375 (Pa. Super. 1998).

> Upon appellate review, we are not bound by the trial court's conclusions of law, but may reach our own conclusions. In reviewing a grant of summary judgment, the appellate Court may disturb the trial court's order only upon an error of law or an abuse of discretion. The scope of review is plenary and the appellate Court applies the same standard for summary judgment as the trial court.

Grandelli v. Methodist Hosp., 777 A.2d 1138, 1144 (Pa. Super. 2001).

The implied warranty of merchantability arises by operation of law under the Pennsylvania Commercial Code ("PCC"), 13 Pa. C.S.A. §2314. The warranty serves to protect buyers from loss where the goods purchased are below commercial standards or unfit for the buyer's purpose. Borden, Inc. v. Advent Ink Co., 701 A.2d 255, 258 (Pa. Super. 1997).

The implied warranty of merchantability, set forth in section 2314 of the PCC provides, in relevant part, as follows:

> (a) Sale by merchant. — Unless excluded or modified[,] . . . a warranty that the goods shall be merchantable is implied in a contract for their sale if the seller is a merchant with respect to goods of that kind. . . .
> (b) Merchantability standards for goods. — Goods to be merchantable must be at least such as:
> (3) are fit for the ordinary purposes for which such goods are used.

13 Pa. C.S.A. §2314. In describing the implied warranty of merchantability, our Pennsylvania Supreme Court has stated:

> The concept of "merchantability" does not require that the goods be the best quality, or the best obtainable, but it does require that they have an inherent soundness which

makes them suitable for the purpose for which they are designed, *that they be free from significant defects,* that they perform in the way that goods of that kind should perform, and that they be of reasonable quality within expected variations and for the ordinary purpose for which they are used. The implied warranty of merchantability, as set forth in the [PCC], is "a warranty that the goods will pass without objection in the trade and are fit for the ordinary purposes for which such goods are used."

Gall v. Allegheny County Health Department, 521 Pa. 68, 555 A.2d 786, 789 (1989) (emphasis added). However, a product need not be defective, for purposes of strict products liability, in order to be unfit for ordinary purposes. See *Azzarello,* 391 A.2d at 1026 (recognizing that "defective condition" is a term of art invoked when strict liability is appropriate).

In this case, Phillips claims that the Cricket lighter that started the fire was defective and breached the implied warranty of merchantability because of the absence of childproof features. Cricket counters that the lighter was not defective because it was completely safe for all of those individuals who were intended users. Cricket further asserts that "[a] two-year-old child is incapable of 'using' a disposable butane lighter in the sense the word 'used' is employed in 13 Pa. C.S.A. §§2314 and 2318." Brief for Appellees at 6. We disagree with both contentions.

First, we note that Pennsylvania law does not limit the applicability of the implied warranty of merchantability to the product's intended users. Section 2318 of the PCC states as follows:

Third party beneficiaries of warranties express or implied:
    The warranty of a seller whether express or implied extends to any natural person who is in the family or household of his buyer or who is a guest in his home if it is reasonable to expect that such person may use, consume *or be affected by* the goods and who is injured in person by breach of the warranty. A seller may not exclude or limit the operation of this section.

13 Pa. C.S.A. §2318 (emphasis added). Thus, section 2318 requires only that household members *be affected* by the product. In accordance with section 2318, the warranty of merchantability extends to two-year-old Jerome, a member of the household affected by the product.

In Hittle v. Scripto-Tokai Corp., 166 F. Supp. 2d 142 (W.D. Pa. 2001), the federal district court of the Western District of Pennsylvania addressed a situation involving similar circumstances. In that case, the plaintiffs' four-year-old child started a fire that caused the death of another child in the household and injury to the children's mother. Plaintiffs sued the manufacturer of the lighter alleging, *inter alia,* a breach of the implied warranty of merchantability based upon (a) the malfunction of the on/off switch on the lighter, and (b) the lighter's lack of child-resistant safety features. In denying the defendant manufacturer's motion for summary judgment, the federal district court opined that "[a] reasonable jury could conclude, based on the inference of a malfunction of the 'on/off' switch *and the related factual issue of whether the lighter could have been designed to be more child-resistant,* that the Aim 'N Flame was 'defective' and not merchantable." Id. at 158 (emphasis added). While we are not bound by the decision of the federal district court, we are guided by its sound reasoning. In the instant case, a reasonable jury could conclude, based on the factual issue of whether the lighter could have been designed to be more child-resistant, that the lighter was "defective" and therefore not merchantable. . . .

Phillips next claims that the trial court erred in entering summary judgment against her and in favor of Cricket on her claim for punitive damages. In its Motion for summary judgment, Cricket asserted that "[p]unitive damages are not available under the facts of this case and where the lighter at issue was not defective and met or exceeded all applicable safety standards existing at the time of this incident and at the time of its manufacture and sale." Cricket's Motion for Summary Judgment, at ¶25. The trial court granted summary judgment, concluding that "there was no wanton or willful misconduct." Trial Court Opinion, 12/1/98, at 38. We disagree.

Punitive damages are awarded to punish a defendant for outrageous acts and to deter him or others from engaging in similar conduct. Reading Radio, Inc. v. Fink, 833 A.2d 199, 214 (Pa. Super. 2003).

> The standard under which punitive damages are measured in Pennsylvania requires analysis of the following factors: (1) the character of the act; (2) the nature and extent of the harm; and (3) the wealth of the defendant. . . . Moreover, in Pennsylvania, punitive damages are awarded for outrageous conduct, that is, for acts done with a bad motive or with a reckless indifference to the interests of others. An amount of an award of punitive damages will not be reversed unless it shocks the Court's sense of [conscience].

Id. (quotation omitted).

In response to Cricket's Motion for summary judgment, Phillips filed an expert report prepared by John O. Geremia, Ph.D. Contrary to the trial court's determination, Dr. Geremia's report evidenced Cricket's "reckless indifference to the interests of others." Id. This Court previously summarized the contents of that report as follows:

> Dr. Geremia has consulted extensively in the area of design and safety of disposable butane lighters. Designers, manufacturers, and distributors of Cricket disposable butane lighters have "been well aware, since at least the early 1970's, that there was a potential significant serious hazard of catastrophic injury and death, particularly to the young, as a result of children utilizing or playing with disposable butane cigarette lighters. Plaintiff's response to Motion for Summary Judgment, Expert Report, 9/25/97, at 3. In fact, Dr. Geremia was involved in preparing a 1973 report to the cigarette lighter industry that discussed the hazards.

> * * *

> The Consumer Product Safety Commission did a study of fire hazards involving children playing with cigarette lighters and the results were published in September 1987. That study indicated that during 1980-85, an average of 170 people a year died in cigarette lighter fires and of those 170, 120 died in fires started by children playing with cigarette lighters. Most of those victims were young children. In addition, at least 750 people per year were injured from fires caused by children playing with cigarette lighters. The annual cost of child-play lighter fires during that time was $300-375 million dollars, or sixty to seventy-five cents per lighter sold.

> Disposable butane lighters were involved in ninety-six percent of the fires in which the type of lighter was known. Dr. Geremia also opined that while lighters may not be intended for children, a lighter is an attractive product for children since it produces a flame and since children are naturally curious about fire.

Finally, Dr. Geremia rendered the opinion that "for many years prior to the time of the manufacture of the subject Cricket lighter, it was technologically, commercially and economically feasible to manufacture and distribute a reasonably designed child-resistant lighter." Id. at 11. He stated that the manufacture and distribution of a child-resistant lighter would have entailed "only a nominal additional cost." Id.

Phillips v. Cricket Lighters, 773 A.2d at 814. Contrary to the trial court's determination, Phillips's evidence was sufficient to create a jury question regarding whether Cricket's actions exhibited reckless indifference to the interests of others. On this basis, we reverse the trial court's dismissal of Phillips's claim for punitive damages.

Judgment reversed as to the grant of summary judgment on the issues of (a) breach of the implied warranty of merchantability, and (b) punitive damages.

Even used goods, as long as they are sold by merchants, come with an implied warranty of merchantability. Of course, that does not mean that used goods are warranted to perform as if they were new goods. As noted by Official Comment 3 to §2-314 (Official Comment 4 to §2-314 as amended), "A contract for the sale of second-hand goods, however, involves only such obligation as is appropriate to such goods for that is their contract description."

The other implied warranty is the warranty of fitness for a particular purpose. This implied warranty arises in much more limited circumstances than the warranty of merchantability. Unless disclaimed or modified, the fitness warranty is implied whenever the seller knows that the buyer is buying the goods for a particular purpose and is relying on the seller's expertise to select or furnish the goods. U.C.C. §2-315. The fitness warranty promises that the goods are indeed fit for the buyer's particular purpose. A common situation in which the fitness warranty arises is where the buyer furnishes to the seller certain specifications indicating the particular purpose for which the buyer is purchasing the goods.

Buyers sometimes confuse the two implied warranties by wrongly believing that an implied warranty of fitness arises even in a case where the buyer's contemplated use of the goods is an ordinary one rather than a "particular" purpose. Yet Official Comment 2 to §2-315 makes it clear that the implied warranty of fitness was not intended for the buyer whose use of the goods is ordinary: "For example, shoes are generally used for the purpose of walking upon ordinary ground, but a seller may know that a particular pair was selected to be used for climbing mountains."

Leal v. Holtvogt

702 N.E.2d 1246 (Ohio App. 1998)

FAIN, J.

. . . Joseph and Claudia Holtvogt owned and operated Shady Glen Arabians, a horse barn in Miami County, Ohio. They were experienced in Arabian horse training, breeding, boarding, selling, and showing. In 1992, the Leals, novices in the equine industry, decided to begin raising horses. In April 1993, Ferdinand Leal began visiting Shady Glen Arabians regularly to learn how to ride and handle horses. Before long, a friendship developed between the Holtvogts and Leals, and Ferdinand Leal began spending three to four days each week at the Holtvogts' barn helping Joseph Holtvogt with the horses.

In late 1993, the Leals decided they wanted to start a breeding program by purchasing a stallion to breed with a mare they owned. At first, they were interested in purchasing Procale, a stallion owned by John Bowman. After talking to Mr. Holtvogt about Procale, the Leals decided not to buy him. The Holtvogts then offered the Leals a one-half interest in Mc Que Jabask, an Arabian stallion that the Holtvogts owned. At trial, the Leals testified that before they agreed to invest in Mc Que Jabask, Mr. Holtvogt made a number of statements regarding the stallion, such as Mc Que Jabask was a national top-ten champion in three categories; he was an all-around winning stallion; he earns $20,000 per year in stud fees; he is capable of attaining national show titles again; and his foals were selling for $6,000 to $10,000 each (these statements will be referred to hereinafter as "the five contested statements").

In January 1994, the Leals and Holtvogts entered into a contract of sale for a one-half interest in Mc Que Jabask for $16,000. The contract also established a partnership agreement, which called for the parties to share equally in the expenses and profits arising from their joint ownership of Mc Que Jabask.

There was expert testimony that prior to January 1994, Mc Que Jabask had been treated for lameness and was suffering a chronic lameness condition in his right rear and fore fetlocks. Mr. Holtvogt testified that he had taken the stallion for lameness treatments numerous times. He also stated that he did not disclose this information to the Leals.

By July 1994, the Leals were dissatisfied with the partnership and indicated to the Holtvogts that they wanted either a refund of their money or a remedy for their concerns. In March 1995, the mortality insurance on Mc Que Jabask lapsed when neither the Leals nor the Holtvogts paid the insurance premium.

Mary Leal, a former Dayton police officer, was unhappy with the partnership. She began making disparaging remarks about Joseph Holtvogt's honesty and integrity to the past and present customers of Shady Glen Arabians. As a result of these remarks, Joseph Holtvogt testified that he suffered from depression, had visited some medical doctors, and was on medication. The Holtvogts did stipulate, however, that they could not prove any business or economic damages due to Mary Leal's remarks.

On January 17, 1996, Mc Que Jabask died from stomach ulcer complications. Since neither party had renewed the stallion's mortality insurance, Mc Que Jabask was uninsured. . . .

. . . In its entry, the trial court found the following:

"[T]he information the [Holtvogts] failed to apprise the [Leals] of was the lameness of the horse at the time the contract was executed in January 1994."

"The [Leals] suffered damages in the amount of $16,000.00 as a result of this negligent misrepresentation."

"The *same set of facts* establishes a cause of action for breach of express warranty *on the condition of the horse for the purposes intended * * *.*" (Emphasis added.)

In its entry, the trial court did not just say that an express warranty was breached, but rather said that an "express warranty *on the condition of the horse for the purposes intended*" was breached. (Emphasis added.) We conclude that the trial court intended to say that an implied warranty of fitness for a particular purpose was breached. Our conclusion is supported by the trial court's statement that the same set of facts establishes claims for both a breach of express warranty on the condition of the horse for the purposes intended and negligent misrepresentation. We note that the elements of a claim for negligent misrepresentation and breach of an implied warranty of fitness for a particular purpose are quite similar, while the elements of negligent misrepresentation and breach of an express warranty are not similar. Thus, we conclude that the trial court, in its conclusions of law, intended to say that an implied warranty of fitness for a particular purpose was given and breached by the Holtvogts when they failed to disclose Mc Que Jabask's lameness to the Leals.

An implied warranty of fitness for a particular purpose is covered by the Uniform Commercial Code, Sales, R.C. 1302.28, which provides:

"Where the seller at the time of contracting has reason to know any particular purpose for which the goods are required and that the buyer is relying on the seller's skill or judgment to select or furnish suitable goods, there is unless excluded or modified under section 1302.29 of the Revised Code an implied warranty that the goods shall be fit for such purpose."

Ohio courts have set forth the following test to determine whether an implied warranty of fitness for a particular purpose has been created: (1) the seller must have reason to know of the buyer's particular purpose; (2) the seller must have reason to know that the buyer is relying on the seller's skill or judgment to furnish or select appropriate goods; and (3) the buyer must, in fact, rely upon the seller's skill or judgment. Hollingsworth v. The Software House, Inc. (1986), 32 Ohio App. 3d 61, 65, 513 N.E.2d 1372, 1375-1376; Delorise Brown, M.D., Inc. v. Allio (1993), 86 Ohio App. 3d 359, 362, 620 N.E.2d 1020, 1021-1022.

The first element requires that Mr. Holtvogt knew why the Leals decided to buy an interest in Mc Que Jabask. From our review of the record, we see that Mr. Holtvogt clearly knew that the Leals wanted to buy an interest in the stallion to start a breeding program. Mr. Holtvogt testified:

"* * * [The Leals] had explained what type of horse they were looking for [and] it seemed to me that [Mc Que] Jabask fit the bill [of] what they were looking for and that's why I mentioned to them, uh, to Ferdinand that there might be a possibility that we would be interested in selling part interest in him."

"* * * [T]he things that they were saying, * * * those things were, were present in, in [Mc Que] Jabask * * *."

"* * * [I]t just, it made sense that, you know, in the fact that the Leals could breed to [Mc Que] Jabask * * *. * * * Um, we could, uh, with the experience and the reputation that we had we could help market their foals, um, it was, I really felt that it was something that could work."

Thus, evidence of the first element of an implied warranty of fitness for a particular purpose was presented at trial.

The second element requires that Mr. Holtvogt had reason to know that the Leals were relying on his skill and judgment to select or furnish the appropriate goods. Evidence presented at trial shows that Mr. Holtvogt knew, or at least should have known, that the Leals were relying on his judgment when they purchased an interest in the stallion. The relationship between Mr. Holtvogt and Mr. Leal was like that of a teacher and student. Mr. Leal spent a great deal of time at the Holtvogts' barn, helping Mr. Holtvogt with the horses and learning from Mr. Holtvogt. Mr. Holtvogt testified that he was an expert trainer and breeder with Arabian horses, and the evidence shows that he knew Mr. Leal knew very little about horses. Furthermore, the Leals testified that they were interested in purchasing another horse, Procale, but that Mr. Holtvogt steered them away from that horse, saying that horse was not the type of horse that the Leals wanted to buy. Mr. Holtvogt even testified that he mentioned Mc Que Jabask to the Leals because the stallion was the type of horse that they were looking for. Thus, evidence of the second element of an implied warranty of fitness for a particular purpose was presented at trial.

The third element requires that the Leals actually did rely upon Mr. Holtvogt's skill and judgment when they purchased an interest in the stallion. The trial court found that the Leals justifiably relied upon the Holtvogts' representations regarding the stallion. This finding is not against the manifest weight of the evidence. As stated earlier, there was competent and credible evidence presented at trial to support this finding, as both Leals were novices in the horse industry and they testified that they trusted Mr. Holtvogt and considered him to be the expert. Thus, evidence of the third element was presented at trial.

Because all three elements were proven at trial, we conclude that an implied warranty of fitness for a particular purpose was given by the Holtvogts to the Leals at the time of the sale. There must be evidence that the warranty was breached if the Leals are to recover. Delorise Brown, M.D., Inc., 86 Ohio App. 3d at 363, 620 N.E.2d at 1022. "Whether a warranty has failed to fulfill its essential purpose is ordinarily a determination for the fact finder." Id.

The trial court found that a warranty was breached by the Holtvogts because the horse was lame. As stated above, competent and credible evidence was presented to support the trial court's finding that Mc Que Jabask suffered from chronic lameness at the time of the sale. At trial, Dixie Gansmiller testified that even though a lame stallion could stand for stud, its lameness would affect her decision whether to breed her mares with it. Thus, we conclude that competent and credible evidence in the record does demonstrate that Mc Que Jabask was not fit for the particular purpose intended by the Leals when they invested in him. . . .

Besides outlining the terms and conditions of implied warranties, Article 2 also describes the various ways in which express warranties are created. Express warranties must be affirmatively created by the seller to the immediate buyer through affirmations of fact, promises, descriptions, samples, or models, as long as any of these become "part of the basis of the bargain." U.C.C. §2-313(1) (amended §2-313(2)). In order to create an express warranty a seller need not use any magic words like "guarantee" or "warranty," but if a seller is merely giving its opinion of the goods then such statements are considered "puffing" and do not give rise to a warranty. U.C.C. §2-313(2) (amended §2-313(3)).

The determination whether a particular statement by a seller amounts to a true express warranty or mere "puffing" is very fact-specific. There are a number of particular factors which may be relevant to the inquiry. First, specific language is much more likely to be deemed an express warranty than is vague language. For example, "this car gets 22 miles to the gallon" is a better bet to be an express warranty than "this is a wonderful car."

Second, all other things being equal, a written statement is more likely to be considered an express warranty than is an oral statement. Third, the context in which the seller's statement was made will normally be important in deciding whether the statement is an express warranty rather than puffing. For example, in a context where the seller was making a statement in response to the buyer's request that the seller give his opinion of the product, that is at least a factor that weighs in favor of the seller's statement being considered as puffing.

Ultimately, the express warranty/puffing determination must come down to the reasonableness of the buyer's reliance on the seller's statement. If the buyer's reliance on the seller's statement was reasonable under the circumstances, that argues in favor of an express warranty rather than puffing. If the buyer's reliance was not reasonable, that argues in favor of the seller's statement being characterized as puffing. As Comment 8 to §2-313 (Official Comment 10 to §2-313 as amended) puts it, "Concerning affirmations of value or a seller's opinion or commendation under subsection (2), the basic question remains the same: What statements of the seller have in the circumstances and in objective judgment become part of the basis of the bargain?"

At this point, you should note an interesting anomaly between the law on the books regarding express warranties and the sales system as it actually operates. U.C.C. §2-313 is very clear about the requirement that the seller's promises about the goods must be at least "part of the basis of the bargain" in order to qualify as express warranties. Yet the reality is that in most sales transactions, whether commercial or consumer, the buyer does not even bother to read the terms of the written "warranty," if at all, until some point after paying for the goods.

Does this mean that the written warranty does not in fact amount to a valid express warranty, since the purchaser cannot claim reliance on promises that were not even read before the sale was concluded? In other words, how can something that the buyer never reads be "part of the basis of the bargain" for purposes of U.C.C. §2-313? In practice, it would be rare for a seller to attempt to escape the terms of a written warranty on the grounds that the buyer never read it. Could an unscrupulous seller avoid liability on that basis if it wanted?

An in-house lawyer for a Fortune 100 clothing retailer, which does a significant amount of buying from wholesale clothing vendors, makes the following argument for the legal enforceability of such unread warranties: "It's true that nobody dickers over the terms of warranties. We have fairly extensive warranties in our purchase orders about merchantability, fitness, flammability, and the like. Although nobody reads those before agreeing to sell, our regular vendors get these forms time and time again so they know when we enter into each contract that we are going to be expecting the usual warranties. In that sense we are relying on the existence of those warranties as a basis of our bargain with them."

Whenever a defect in a product causes personal injury, the plaintiff will often bring suit both on a UCC warranty theory and on the tort theories of negligence and strict products liability. The advantage of the warranty theory is that the plaintiff does not need to show lack of due care, as it must in a negligence action. On the other hand, the tort plaintiff does not have to contend with certain privity problems that can sometimes prevent otherwise viable warranty suits. Furthermore, the tort plaintiff is not subject to the strict notice requirements of U.C.C. §2-607(3)(a), nor does the tort plaintiff need to show the reliance element that is necessary for an express warranty claim.

With amended Article 2, the drafters took the opportunity to clarify a conceptual problem with express warranties that had troubled many courts under the pre-amended §2-313. This problem arises when statements relating to goods are made by sellers, such as manufacturers, who typically do not sell their products directly to the ultimate user. These sellers instead sell to wholesalers or retailers who in turn sell to the final buyer in the chain of distribution.

The original seller often makes claims about the product either through public advertising or through records included in the product's package. In doing so, the seller knows full well that remote buyers will likely rely on or at least be influenced by such claims when they choose to buy the product from a retailer further down the chain of distribution. For express warranty purposes, the conceptual problem is that there is no direct bargain between the original seller and the remote buyer. Therefore, under the language of §2-313, the remote buyer cannot claim that the statements made by the original seller were part of "the basis of the bargain" since there is no "bargain" between these two parties. With no "basis of the bargain" affirmations, the ultimate purchaser cannot hold the remote seller liable for breach of an express warranty under §2-313.

Under pre-amended Article 2, courts were uncomfortable with an outcome whereby a manufacturer that made purchase-inducing claims could escape responsibility in express warranty to the remote buyer for the product's nonconformity to those claims. Courts typically found ways to achieve what they viewed as the just result, but it was a difficult task in light of the language of Article 2's express warranty section and the "basis of the bargain" requirement.

The drafters of amended Article 2 took a number of steps to clarify the situation involving a remote purchaser who buys a product in part based on claims about the product that were made by a seller further up the chain of distribution. First, amended §2-313 provides that sellers create express warranties only to their "immediate buyer," defined as the buyer that actually enters into a contract with the direct seller. Therefore, amended §2-313 reinforces the notion that no buyer can bring an express warranty action against a seller other than the seller with whom the buyer directly dealt.

Even though sellers, such as manufacturers, will clearly not be liable for an express warranty to remote purchasers under amended Article 2, such sellers could be liable under a couple of non-warranty causes of action that were created by the amendments. Newly added §2-313A gives rise to an "obligation" (but not a warranty) to a remote purchaser that is based on statements made by the non-immediate seller in any record that accompanies the goods. Newly added §2-313B creates a similar obligation to remote purchasers that arises from communications, such as advertising, that the seller makes to the public.

These two new "obligations" of the seller to remote purchasers mean that sellers that make affirmations of fact concerning the product will not be able to escape liability to a remote purchaser on the basis that the seller had no contract with that purchaser. These new obligations, which do not contain the "basis of the bargain" requirement that their express warranty counterparts do, are nonetheless similar in some respects to express warranties.

First, just as with express warranties, the records or communications must "relate to the goods," and must include either affirmations of fact, descriptions, or promises about the product. U.C.C. §§2-313A(3) and 2-313B(3) as amended. Second, if the affirmations are merely the seller's opinion and a reasonable purchaser should know that, then the seller's statements are "puffing" and do not give rise to the usual obligations. U.C.C. §§2-313A(4) and 2-313B(4) as amended.

Third, the seller can limit or modify the remedies available to the remote purchaser for breach of these obligations as long as the seller does so in a limitation that is furnished to the purchaser "no later than the time of purchase." U.C.C. §§2-313A(5)(a) and 2-313B(5)(a) as amended. Fourth, the seller is only responsible for breach of these obligations when the breach existed at the time the goods left the seller's control. U.C.C. §§2-313A(6) and 2-313B(6) as amended.

The seller's liability for such obligations to remote purchasers is more limited in some respects than is express warranty liability. First, the obligations can arise only with new goods. U.C.C. §§2-313A(2) and 2-313B(2) as amended. Second, the remote purchaser to whom the obligations run must be a purchaser in the normal chain of distribution. Id. Third, although the seller is liable for most incidental and consequential damages absent a valid remedies limitation, the seller will not be liable for lost profits suffered by the remote purchaser from a breach of these obligations. U.C.C. §§2-313A(5)(b) and 2-313B(5)(b) as amended.

With regard to obligations arising from a record included with the product, the seller is only liable to the remote purchaser if the seller reasonably expects the record to be furnished to the remote purchaser and the remote purchaser is in fact furnished with the record. U.C.C. §2-313A(3) as amended. In the analogous context of obligations based on public communications, the remote purchaser must actually have known of the communication by the time of purchase and must have reasonably expected that the goods would conform to the affirmations of fact made in the advertising. U.C.C. §2-313B(3)(a).

Thus, for example, a remote purchaser could not base an action for breach of a remote seller's obligation arising from an ad that the purchaser did not see until after the purchase. Nor, for that matter, would it necessarily be reasonable for a purchaser that saw an ad for a product 10 years ago to expect that the advertised goods today would conform to the affirmations of fact made in that ad. Official Comment 4 to §2-313B as amended. This is particularly true if the product and the product's ad campaign had changed significantly since then.

In amended Article 2, the drafters introduced a separate warranty-related concept known as "the remedial promise." A "remedial promise" is mentioned in amended §§2-313, 2-313A, and 2-313B, and it is defined in amended §2-103(1)(n) as "a promise by the seller to repair or replace the goods or to refund all or part of the price upon the happening of a specified event." Remedial promises by the seller create obligations to and are actionable by buyers, but they do not amount to express warranties as such.

The reason that a remedial promise is not a warranty is that it is not a promise that relates to the quality of the goods, but rather is a commitment by the seller to act in a certain way in the future. A promise that is a warranty would be "The car's engine will run consistently for three years." A promise that is not a warranty but rather a "remedial promise" is "If the car's engine stops running in the next three years, I will repair it immediately or replace it with a new engine if I am unable to repair it."

From a purchaser's perspective, the key functional distinction between a warranty and a remedial promise is how each is treated under the statute of limitations. Because a remedial promise is not a warranty, such a promise is effectively subject to a more generous statute of limitations for the buyer under amended §2-725. With warranty breaches, the plaintiff gets four years from the time when the cause of action accrued (typically the time of tender) plus up to one extra year if the breach was first discovered or should have been discovered in that fourth year after tender. U.C.C. §2-725(1) as amended. Five years from the time of tender, however, is the outer limit even in a case where the buyer could not have known of the seller's breach of warranty within that time period. Thus, it is possible that the statute of limitations for a breach of warranty action may expire even before the purchaser knows or should have known about the breach.

With a remedial promise, the statute of limitations should not expire before the buyer knows or should have known about the breach. The statute of limitations for remedial promises is, at least on the surface, the same as for warranties: the later of either four years from when the cause of action accrued or one year after the buyer knows or should have known of the breach. U.C.C. §2-725 as amended. Because a remedial promise relates to promised action by the seller rather than to a defect in the goods, a right of action does not accrue with a remedial promise until that promise is not performed when due. U.C.C. §2-715(2)(c) as amended.

This difference in the definition of when a right of action accrues ends up being critical. In the warranty arena, a right of action accrues upon the seller's tender of the goods whether or not the warranty breach is evident at that point. Thus, the warranty statute of limitations could expire before the buyer even knows that there is a problem with the goods. By contrast, the statute of limitations clock should not start running in the remedial promise arena without the buyer knowing that the seller has breached its promise. The reason is that the seller's remedial promise will not arise (and the statute of limitations clock will not start running) until there is a discernable problem with the goods.

C.   Extended Warranties and
Maintenance Agreements

In the last decade or two, there has been a proliferation of so-called "extended warranties" or "maintenance agreements." The basic idea behind these extended warranties is that the manufacturer's warranty may be limited in either duration or scope, and the extended warranty provides a relatively cheap form of insurance for the buyer in case there is a problem that is not covered by the basic warranty. Extended warranty programs are most commonly available with major consumer items such as a car or a significant home appliance.

It is not difficult to understand the increased availability of extended warranties. The profit margins on extended warranties are huge, given that about 80 percent of the extended warranties that are sold go unused. Consumer Reports said in a recent study, "Warranty sales often bring in more profit than the merchandise, because for every dollar a retailer makes on a warranty, it spends an average of just 4 to 15 cents fixing the product. Only 12% to 20% of those who buy warranties ever use them."

What the consumer may not realize is that some extended warranties are largely duplicating what the customer is already getting from the manufacturer's warranty. As the purchasing officer for a major university noted: "The big thing now is maintenance agreements. But I tell my departments not to go right out and buy the maintenance agreement until the original warranty is about to run. If the equipment has problems during the original period, some of the manufacturer's warranties will automatically be extended."

Another surprise that consumers may encounter in purchasing extended warranties is that those warranties are often serviced by a third party that has no formal connection to the seller of the goods. The same university purchasing officer quoted above also noted the importance to his organization of having the warranty be serviced by the seller itself rather than some third party: "Once we were buying a multi-million dollar machine from a major manufacturer and they wanted to put the warranty immediately with a third party, but we just wouldn't let them do it. Our people here don't always read the warranties closely before they buy something, but at least if the product doesn't work and we don't get satisfaction, we can threaten not to do business with the seller again. It becomes a much more complicated scenario when you're not even dealing with the seller anymore."

Consumers that end up buying extended warranties that are serviced by third parties quickly come to realize that these third-party servicers have a vested interest in coming up with reasons why claims should not be paid. Like primary-care physicians in health maintenance organizations, third-party warrantors are gate-keepers that attempt to screen out as many complaints as possible before they even reach the paying stage.

Richard Colbey, a British barrister, described his personal experience with a third-party warrantor as follows:

> The words "take out Coverplan Plus and you need only make one simple phone call to ensure a prompt skillful repair" still bring my blood close to boiling point three years after I misguidedly took out a policy on a fax machine I bought from Dixons.

I reasoned it was worth paying a bit extra to be spared the aggravation if the fax did go wrong. When it did, my first attempt to make that phone call resulted in me being cut off. When I finally got through I was told to ring another number to arrange an appointment with a firm of independent engineers. Their number was perpetually engaged. Eventually I gave up and bought a new fax.

Dixons, although willing to refund the insurance premium, needed to be persuaded that I was serious about the threat of legal proceedings before coughing up a further pounds 150 compensation.

Richard Colbey, "Extended warranties spark new wave of complaints," *The Guardian City* Page, February 17, 1996.

Yet another problem consumers have encountered with third-party warrantors arises when the warrantor has an arrangement with the seller whereby the seller agrees to pay the warrantor for each repair that the warrantor completes. In cases where the seller has stopped paying the third-party servicer, the servicer may force the customer to pay for the servicer's repair and then instruct the customer to bill the seller directly. This is exactly what happened to Silo customers who had purchased extended warranties when that store stopped paying its third-party servicer.

In the final analysis, it is probably impossible to say that extended warranties are never a good idea. Like all forms of insurance, they are a gamble, but consumers are often not fully aware of all of the risks involved in that gamble:

An extended warranty or service contract is actually [product] repair insurance. It's a gamble that will pay off only if [the product] needs repairs that cost more than the price of the contract, if the repairs are not already covered under the manufacturers' warranty, and if the warranty company stays in business and agrees that the repairs are covered.

Judy Garnatz Harriman, "A close look at extended warranties," *St. Petersburg Times*, 2D, March 13, 1995

Problem Set 8

8.1. a.   You just sold to your law school classmate a computer that you had owned for three months. A week after the sale, your classmate complains that the characters on the screen fade noticeably after about 20 minutes. You had never noticed this when you used the computer. Have you breached the implied warranty of merchantability? U.C.C. §2-314.

b. Same facts as part a., except that you knew about the fading problem and did not mention it prior to the sale. Have you breached the implied warranty of merchantability? Are you liable on some other theory? U.C.C. §§2-314, 1-203 (revised 1-304), 1-201(19), Official Comment 3 to §2-314 (Official Comment 4 to §2-314 as amended), §2-103(1)(b) (amended §2-103(1)(j)).

c.   Same facts as part a., except that you knew about the fading problem and not only did you not mention it, you told your classmate that this computer was "super." Have you breached an express warranty? Are you liable on some other theory? U.C.C. §2-313, Official Comments 3 and 8 to §2-313 (Official Comments 5 and 10 to §2-313 as amended), §1-103.

d.   Same facts as part a., except your law school classmate bought the used computer from your law school, which makes an annual sale of used computers. Has the law school breached the implied warranty of merchantability? U.C.C. §2-314, Official Comment 3 to §2-314 (Official Comment 4 to §2-314 as amended), §2-104(1), Official Comment 2 to §2-104.

8.2. a. Bob Sinclair owns a used-car lot, Bob's Affordable Wheels. You just graduated from college and visit Bob's with an eye to finding a car in the $5,000 price range. You spot a 1990 Honda Accord for $4,900 and ask Bob about the car. "She's a humdinger, all right," says Bob. If you purchase the Accord, has Bob made an express warranty? If so, what is its content? U.C.C. §2-313.

b. Same facts as part a., except that you are particularly concerned about gas mileage, so you ask Bob what kind of gas mileage the 1990 Accord gets. "You know those Accords," says Bob. "They're like camels." If you purchase the Accord, has Bob made an express warranty? If so, what is its content? U.C.C. §2-313.

c. Same facts as part a., except that you bring your mother with you to Bob's, because your mother knows a lot more about cars than you do. Your mother tells you that the 1990 Accord is a good bet because it gets such good gas mileage. Just to be sure, you ask Bob about this particular Accord's gas mileage, and he gives you the "like camels" line. Has Bob made an express warranty? U.C.C. §2-313.

d. Same facts as part a., except that as soon as you come in, you tell Bob that the most important thing for you is to buy a car that gets good gas mileage. "Then I've got just the car for you, young man," Bob tells you, and shows you the 1990 Accord. Has Bob made an express warranty to you? U.C.C. §2-313. Has he made any other type of warranty? U.C.C. §2-315.

e. Same facts as part a., except that right after you give Bob the check for $4,900 but before you leave his lot, you tell him, "By the way, I forgot to ask you about gas mileage. That's extremely important to me. Does this car get good mileage?" Bob replies, "Son, I promise that this car will give you at least 30 miles per gallon in the city." Has Bob made an express warranty? U.C.C. §§2-313, 2-209, and Official Comment 7 to §2-313 (Preliminary Comment 9 to §2-313 as amended).

f. Same facts as part a., except that before buying the car you ask Bob whether it comes with a warranty. "You bet, son," says Bob, who then hands you a six-page warranty that you do not bother to read on the spot. Two days later as you read the warranty, your eyes light up when you get to the part about gas mileage. "Great," you tell yourself, "this says that the car will get at least 30 miles per gallon in the city." Has Bob made an express warranty concerning the gas mileage? U.C.C. §2-313.

8.3. a. Carol Campbell owns a clothing store, Dress for Success, that sells a variety of men's and women's business attire. Paul Wofsey selected a new suit there, had it altered by the store, bought it, and took the suit home. When he tried the suit on two weeks later, he sat down and discovered to his painful surprise that someone had sewn a rusty tack into the seat of the pants. Is Carol's store liable for breach of warranty? U.C.C. §2-314.

b. Same facts as part a., except that Carol has her workers frisk all of the inventory thoroughly every night to make sure that there are no foreign objects such as pins that are stuck in the clothes. Will this evidence be useful for Carol if nobody knows how and when the rusty tack got into the pants? U.C.C. §2-314 and Official Comment 13 to §2-314 (Official Comment 15 to §2-314 as amended).

   c.   Same facts as part b. Will this evidence be useful for Carol if it is established as a fact that an angry customer placed the rusty tack in the pants a half-
hour before Paul bought them? U.C.C. §2-314 and Official Comment 13 to §2-
314 (Official Comment 15 to §2-314 as amended).

   8.4.   You just began your first job after graduation as in-house counsel for a
major beer manufacturer. Your initial project involves a lawsuit that was filed
against your company by a 62-year-old man who developed cirrhosis of the
liver after several decades of heavy beer-drinking. One of the theories of his
suit, the one that you have been asked to focus on, is that your company
breached its implied warranty of merchantability because beer that causes
cirrhosis of the liver is not fit for its ordinary use. Your general counsel
asked you to think about different arguments that your company can make
in response to this warranty claim. What statutory arguments can you come
up with as to why your company should not be liable on an implied warranty
theory? U.C.C. §2-314(2), Official Comment 13 to U.C.C. §2-314 (Official
Comment 15 to §2-314 as amended).

   8.5.   Your law firm was just retained to represent a car manufacturer that
was sued by a woman who was a passenger in one of your client's newer car
models that the woman had purchased. The woman, who was seriously injured in a car accident, claims that the manufacturer's failure to include a
passenger-side airbag as a standard feature in the car she bought amounted
to a breach of the implied warranty of merchantability. The car, which was
one of the manufacturer's economy models, did have a standard driver's side
airbag. What are the strongest Article 2 arguments your firm can muster to
defend against this lawsuit? How generally should a court decide when the
implied warranty of merchantability must include a particular safety feature?
U.C.C. §2-314(2).

   8.6.   Consider the following actual news story that appeared in the *St.
Louis Post-Dispatch* on June 7, 1997:

> "Dairy Industry Sued Over Man's Ill Health" (SEATTLE) (AP) — Norman Mayo, 61,
> is suing the dairy industry, claiming drinking whole milk contributed to his clogged
> arteries and a minor stroke. He said he might have avoided the problems if he had
> been warned on milk cartons about fat and cholesterol. The federal lawsuit names
> Safeway and the Dairy Farmers of Washington as defendants. Mayo wants warn-
> ings on dairy products. 'If tobacco products can be required to have warning
> labels, why not dairy products?' said Mayo, a former smoker. 'I think milk is
> just as dangerous as tobacco.'

   Suppose that Mr. Mayo's implied warranty theory is not lack of fitness for
ordinary use, like Problem 8.4, but instead that the whole milk was not "adequately contained, packaged and labeled" due to its lack of a warning about
health risks. Should Mr. Mayo prevail on this theory? U.C.C. §2-314(2)(e).

   8.7.   Consider Carol Campbell again, and in particular the facts of Problem
8.3.c., where even her nightly inspections are not enough to catch the angry
customer who put the rusty tack in. Carol now wants to defend by saying that
the cost of avoiding this particular harm would not be worth the benefit, since
Carol's workers would have needed to do clothes inspections every 15 minutes
to avoid this harm. Therefore, says Carol, she should not be liable for an
unavoidable harm. Will this defense work?

Assignment 9: Lease, International, and Real Estate Warranties

A. Lease Warranties: The Case of Finance Leases

Like so many other parts of U.C.C. Article 2A, the provisions on lease warranties sound an awful lot like the comparable provisions in Article 2 for sales of goods. There is, however, one notable exception to the general pattern of lease warranty provisions mimicking the provisions of sale warranties: a leasing device known as the "finance lease."

A finance lease is a lease transaction that involves three parties: the supplier, the lessor, and the lessee. Functionally, a finance lease is very much like a sale of goods from the supplier to the lessee, and the warranty provisions of Article 2A treat a finance lease very much as if it were a sale from the supplier to the lessee. As explained in the Official Comment to §2A-103, most sale-leaseback transactions will qualify as finance leases. Official Comment g to §2A-103.

In a finance lease, the "supplier" is the party that supplies the goods that will be leased to the lessee. The "lessor" in a finance lease is more functionally a financier, typically a bank or other financial institution. In a finance lease, the lessor has nothing to do with the selection, manufacture, or supply of the leased goods, which the lessor purchases (or leases) from the supplier solely in connection with the particular finance lease. The lessee in a finance lease is the party that identifies the goods to be leased, and the lessee will also have an opportunity to review the purchase (or lease) contract between the supplier and the lessor. U.C.C. §2A-103(1)(g) (amended §2A-103(1)(l)).

Because the finance lessor's role is strictly one of financing and because the finance lessor has little to do with the goods themselves, there are a number of special warranty rules that apply in finance leases. From the perspective of the lessee in a finance lease, these special warranty rules include both burdens and benefits.

The disadvantage to the finance lessee is that the finance lessor does not give the normal implied warranties of either fitness or merchantability that non-finance lessors give under Article 2A. U.C.C. §§2A-212(1), 2A-213. To reinforce the finance lessor's lack of accountability to the lessee, §2A-407 provides that in non-consumer finance leases the lessee's promises under the lease contract become irrevocable once the lessee has accepted the goods. This means that the lessee's obligation to pay the lessor continues even if the lessee ends up having problems with the leased goods following acceptance.

The flipside to the reduction in warranty rights that the finance lessee has against its lessor is that the finance lessee gains warranty rights that it would not otherwise have against the supplier. Under U.C.C. §2A-209(1), any warranty rights that the finance lessor gets from the supplier, whether express or implied, run directly to the finance lessee. Thus, if the supplier sells the goods to the finance lessor, the finance lessor would typically receive the Article 2 implied warranty of merchantability. Normal rules of privity would dictate that this sales warranty run only to the buyer, who is the finance lessor; the special rules of the finance lease cause that warranty to run to the lessee as well.

In light of these special warranty rules, it makes sense that the finance lessee must see a copy of the sales or lease contract between the supplier and the finance lessor before signing its own lease contract with the finance lessor. If the supplier has attempted to disclaim or limit warranties in its transaction with the finance lessor, those disclaimers and limitations would directly affect the rights of the finance lessee, whose warranty rights against the supplier are strictly a function of the supplier's contract with the finance lessor.

One last point about finance leases: in order for there to be a finance lease, the transaction between the finance lessor and lessee must in fact be a true lease, rather than merely a disguised sale. The very nature of the finance lease, in which the finance lessor has little interest in the goods, makes it quite possible that the lease transaction will be a sham. The key question to remember on the sale/lease distinction, as was explored in Assignment 2, is whether there is a reasonable likelihood at the inception of the lease that the finance lessor will get the goods back at a time when they still have meaningful value left in them.

B.   Warranties with International Sales

The CISG warranties provision, Article 35, provides in one place a laundry list of warranties that essentially mimics the three major quality warranties that are found in the UCC: express warranty, implied warranty of merchantability, and implied warranty of fitness for a particular purpose. Article 35(1) requires the seller to deliver goods "which are of the quantity, quality and description required by the contract..." Article 35(2)(c), in turn, says that the goods do not conform to the contract unless they "possess the qualities of goods which the seller has held out to the buyer as a sample or model." These two subsections together amount to the express warranty provisions of the CISG.

The CISG also provides the buyer with an implied warranty of merchantability, but the requirements for merchantability include only two elements from the comparable list of six that we see in U.C.C. §2-314(2). Under the CISG, goods must be "fit for the purposes for which goods of the same description would ordinarily be used," C.I.S.G. Art. 35(2)(a), and they must be "contained or packaged in the manner usual for such goods or, where there is no such manner, in a manner adequate to preserve and protect the goods," C.I.S.G. Art. 35(2)(d).

Finally, the CISG provides the buyer with an analogue to the UCC's implied warranty of fitness for a particular purpose. C.I.S.G. Article 35(2)(b) requires that the goods be fit "for any particular purpose expressly or impliedly made known to the seller," as long as the buyer reasonably relied on the seller's skill and judgment in providing the goods for the buyer's particular purpose.

Medical Marketing Int'l v. Internazionale Medico Scientifica

1999 WL 311945 (E.D. La. 1999)

DUVAL, J.

... Plaintiff MMI is a Louisiana marketing corporation with its principal place of business in Baton Rouge, Louisiana. Defendant IMS is an Italian corporation that manufactures radiology materials with its principal place of business in Bologna, Italy. On January 25, 1993, MMI and IMS entered into a Business Licensing Agreement in which IMS granted exclusive sales rights for Giotto Mammography H.F. Units to MMI.

In 1996, the Food and Drug Administration ("FDA") seized the equipment for noncompliance with administrative procedures, and a dispute arose over who bore the obligation of ensuring that the Giotto equipment complied with the United states Governmental Safety Regulations, specifically the Good Manufacturing Practices (GMP) for Medical Device Regulations. MMI formally demanded mediation on October 28, 1996, pursuant to Article 13 of the agreement. Mediation was unsuccessful, and the parties entered into arbitration, also pursuant to Article 13, whereby each party chose one arbitrator and a third was agreed upon by both.

An arbitration hearing was held on July 13-15, July 28, and November 17, 1998. The hearing was formally closed on November 30, 1998. The arbitrators rendered their decision on December 21, 1998, awarding MMI damages in the amount of $357,009.00 and legal interest on that amount from October 28, 1996. The arbitration apportioned 75% of the $83,640.45 cost of arbitration to MMI, and the other 25% to IMS. IMS moved for reconsideration on December 30, 1998, and this request was denied by the arbitrators on January 7, 1999. Plaintiff now moves for an order from this court confirming the arbitral award and entering judgment in favor of the plaintiff under 9 U.S.C. §9. ...

IMS has alleged that the arbitrators' decision violates public policy of the international global market and that the arbitrators exhibited "manifest disregard of international sales law." Specifically, IMS argues that the arbitrators misapplied the United Nations Convention on Contracts for the International Sales of Goods, commonly referred to as CISG, and that they refused to follow a German Supreme Court Case interpreting CISG.

MMI does not dispute that CISG applies to the case at hand. Under CISG, the finder of fact has a duty to regard the "international character" of the convention and to promote uniformity in its application. CISG Article 7. The Convention also provides that in an international contract for goods, goods conform to the contract if they are fit for the purpose for which goods of the same description would ordinarily be used or are fit for any particular purpose expressly or impliedly made known to the seller and relied upon by the buyer. CISG Article 35(2). To avoid a contract based on the non-conformity of goods, the buyer must allege and prove that the seller's breach was "fundamental" in nature. CISG Article 49. A breach is fundamental when it results in such detriment to the party that he or she is substantially deprived of what he or she is entitled to expect under the contract, unless the party in breach did not foresee such a result. CISG Article 25.

At the arbitration, IMS argued that MMI was not entitled to avoid its contract with IMS based on non-conformity under Article 49, because IMS's breach was not "fundamental." IMS argued that CISG did not require that it furnish MMI with equipment that complied with the United States GMP regulations. To support this proposition, IMS cited a German Supreme Court case, which held that under CISG Article 35, a seller is generally not obligated to supply goods that conform to public laws and regulations enforced at the buyer's place of business. Entscheidungen des Bundesgerichtshofs in Zivilsachen (BGHZ) 129, 75 (1995). In that case, the court held that this general rule carries with it exceptions in three limited circumstances: (1) if the public laws and regulations of the buyer's state are identical to those enforced in the seller's state; (2) if the buyer informed the seller about those regulations; or (3) if due to "special circumstances," such as the existence of a seller's branch office in the buyer's state, the seller knew or should have known about the regulations at issue.

The arbitration panel decided that under the third exception, the general rule did not apply to this case. The arbitrators held that IMS was, or should have been, aware of the GMP regulations prior to entering into the 1993 agreement, and explained their reasoning at length. IMS now argues that the arbitration panel refused to apply CISG and the law as articulated by the German Supreme Court. It is clear from the arbitrators' written findings, however, that they carefully considered that decision and found that this case fit the exception and not the rule as articulated in that decision. The arbitrators' decision was neither contrary to public policy nor in manifest disregard of international sales law. This court therefore finds that the arbitration panel did not "exceed its powers" in violation of the FAA. . . .

C.   Real Estate Warranties

1.   *Warranties Generally*

When discussing the subject of real estate warranties, we need to create at least a couple of divisions. First, there is a significant distinction between warranties in commercial real estate sales and warranties in residential sales. With commercial sales, warranties will typically be negotiated carefully and will appear in a written contract. As a general matter, there will not be any implied warranties created in the sale of commercial real estate.

With residential real estate, the warranty rules are different depending on whether the sale is of a new or a resale home. With a new home, most states create either by statute or by common law an implied warranty of habitability, at least where the seller is a professional builder. Such a warranty would include that the home is free from material defects and is fit for its intended purpose, but it does not cover defects that are visible upon a reasonable inspection by the buyer.

States disagree about whether the warranty of habitability for new homes can benefit subsequent purchasers. Some states' laws hold that it can, on the theory that sometimes the subsequent purchaser is really the first person in a position to discover the problem. Other states disagree, on the grounds that the subsequent purchaser lacks privity with the builder who made the implied warranty in the first place.

Hershey v. Rich Rosen Construction Co.

17 P.2d 55 (Ariz. Ct. App. 1991)

JACOBSON, P.J.

This action, brought by a subsequent purchaser of a residential home for damages caused by a builder's faulty stucco application more than twelve years prior to this suit, presents the following issues:

(1) whether the "reasonable inspection of the structure prior to purchase" required to recover for a latent defect under a theory of implied warranty was met by plaintiffs' inspection or whether an inspection by an expert was required; and
(2) whether the time period between the stucco installation and the filing of the complaint is an unreasonable time to extend a home builder's implied warranty of habitability and workmanship for a stucco installation.

Appellant Rich Rosen Construction Co. (defendant) completed construction of the single family residence at issue in this case and sold it to the initial purchaser on April 1, 1976. In 1985 the initial owner sold the house to its second owner, who later added a room onto a western corner of the house. In November 1985, appellees Hershey (collectively, plaintiff) rented the house from the second owner, and lived there for six months prior to purchasing the residence in May 1986. During that tenancy, plaintiff did not experience any problems with the stucco. Prior to the purchase, plaintiff performed a "walk-around inspection," during which he did not see any cracks or defects in the stucco on the exterior of the house.

In April or May 1987, plaintiff first noticed "some bulging of the stucco on the southwest side of the house." He did not do anything about it at that time because "it didn't look to be a major problem." However, after a heavy rainstorm in August 1987, his daughter heard what she thought was water running behind the bedroom wall on the northwest side of the house. Plaintiff thought the roof might be leaking and went out to check the next day. He testified, "it looked as if the stucco was bulging from the wall. And there was a small hole where a piece had dropped out."

Thinking the stucco problem was due to rain damage, plaintiff filed a claim with his homeowner's insurance company, State Farm Fire & Casualty Company. The insurer responded in September 1987, denying the claim based on the opinion of its retained architect, Dwight L. Busby, P.E.:

[I]t is his determination that the various cracks and loose stucco results from the exterior application being improperly done at the time of construction. It is apparent that none of the exterior application of sheathing, building paper and stucco is weather approved, and it does not meet the Scottsdale Building Code (U.B.C.). Also in accordance with the building code, a layer of lath should have been applied prior to the application of the stucco.

Soon thereafter, plaintiff discovered the name of defendant, the builder, from his next door neighbor, who was an original owner and who had a similar problem with his stucco in 1979.

Plaintiff retained his own expert to examine the stucco, C. Randal Rushing, the secretary of Wall & Ceiling Industries of Arizona, a professional trade association. In October 1988, Rushing gave plaintiff the following written opinion:

I would classify the existing Stucco Exterior on your home to be one of the worst examples of material selection and application that I have encountered in the past 10-12 years.

. . . .

There are numerous errors and building code violations in the above assembly.

. . . .

I would categorize the workmanship on this structure (i.e., material selection and workmanship) as below average to almost criminal.

Rushing concluded that the existing construction consisted of gypsum board nailed to the exterior of the wood framing, with a woven fiberglass tape applied vertically to the joints of the gypsum board, with a layer of stucco approximately 1/8 of an inch thick covered with a coating of paint. The City of Phoenix Construction Code required, however, as a minimum, two layers of 15 lb. felt over exterior grade gypsum sheathing, with 1 inch 20 gauge wire mesh in the base coat and approved wall assembly of 3/8 of an inch to 1/2 of an inch thick.

Plaintiff contacted defendant in March 1988, approximately seven months after he had discovered the problem, and requested that defendant repair the damage; defendant declined. Plaintiff filed a complaint against defendant in June 1988, and by an amended complaint alleged a claim for breach of implied warranty, seeking repair costs of $16,500.00 and attorneys' fees and costs.

Defendant answered, denying the allegations and generally asserting the defenses of statute of limitations, failure to state a claim, waiver, estoppel, and failure to make a reasonable inspection of the premises prior to purchase. After filing cross-motions for summary judgment, the parties stipulated to certain facts, and further agreed that the court should decide the case based on that record as well as on the basis of the testimony in plaintiff's deposition and the expert testimony of C. Randal Rushing.

Among the stipulated facts were defendant's admission that "the workmanship was below average," and that "the particular stucco process applied had deficiencies." Defendant also "agree[d] that the stucco process should last in excess of twelve years."

At the hearing on January 24, 1990, Rushing testified that his inspection of the exterior structure revealed "50 to 60 percent complete delamination of the outside base coat skin, paint coating, from the structure," with "bulges all over the building." The separation of the stucco from the building was apparently caused by the lack of internal reinforcement, or stucco netting. The Uniform Building Code, adopted by the City of Phoenix and the State of Arizona, requires "some type of external reinforcing wire." Rushing's subsequent visits to the house showed "extensive damage recurring. It will not stop." The cracks now go through to the interior perimeter, and the exterior sheathing has deteriorated to "basically mush," from water infiltration through the stucco separation into the gypsum board. Besides the lack of reinforcement, Rushing also testified that the lack of depth of the application was also substandard; "the only thing that's been holding that system on has been the paint."

Most significantly, Rushing testified that a properly applied stucco exterior of this type, with repainting every 10 to 15 years, would reasonably be expected to last from 30 to 50 years. Because of the low rainfall level in this area, the water damage would have taken a long time to become evident to a lay person, who would not be able to ascertain the depth of the materials or the structure of the application from a visual inspection.

In rendering judgment for plaintiff, the trial court made the following findings of fact and conclusions of law:

1. That the damage to the stucco was caused solely by poor workmanship;
2. That plaintiff's claim was not barred by the statute of limitations;
3. That the damage was not caused by normal wear and tear;
4. That the room addition [built by the previous owners], although a substantial alteration to the premises, did not void defendant's implied warranty of proper workmanship;
5. That the leak in the roof did not contribute to the damage to the stucco;
6. That plaintiff did conduct a reasonable inspection of the residence prior to purchase;
7. That defendant was not entitled to an award of attorneys' fees;
8. That the condition of the exterior walls of the residence constituted a breach of implied warranty by defendant;
9. That plaintiff's damages were $16,500.00;
10. That plaintiff is entitled to reasonable attorneys' fees and costs.

The court further found that "there was no reasonable indication of a serious stucco problem until 1987, when the stucco first began falling off in large pieces and there was bulging in various spots all over the house. This action was then brought within a year of such notice. It was certainly timely for a breach of the [implied] warranty of habitability and proper workmanship which first reasonably evidenced itself only in 1987."

In its minute entry, the court also made the following findings:

There is no statute of limitations defense because in Arizona the builders' implied warranty of habitability and proper workmanship extends to subsequent purchasers. While not unlimited in time, it extends for a reasonable period of time depending on the component part of the house involved. While five years may be reasonable for a warranty for a septic tank or for termite protection, because they both have a useful life of approximately five years, the component of exterior stucco has a normal expected life of thirty to fifty years. Therefore, an extension of the warranty on it for twelve years is certainly reasonable. In light of Mr. Rushing's testimony as to the reasonable life span of a properly applied stucco application, the Court finds that the warranty life has not run out here and there is no violation of A.R.S. §12-548 and its six year statute of limitations.

. . . .

Another of defendant's suggestions of a defense was that plaintiffs failed to reasonably inspect the home before purchasing. It claims that such an inspection would have revealed the potential of the disastrous defect of workmanship this house had. There is no evidence of such a claim. Plaintiffs bought the home in 1986. At that time, there were a few cracks in the stucco of a normal nature. Not until 1987 did separation of the stucco from the exterior sheathing begin to manifest itself in chunks falling off and bulging. Its rapid acceleration since indicates that only from 1987 would a reasonable purchaser have been put on any kind of notice that a disastrous problem lay hidden beneath the exterior stucco and paint.

Judgment was entered in plaintiff's favor in the sum of $16,500.00 as damages, together with attorneys' fees in the sum of $3,180.00, and costs of $216.13. Defendant timely appealed.

Implied warranties of workmanship and habitability for original owners of residential structures were first recognized by this court in Columbia Western Corp. v. Vela, 122 Ariz. 28, 592 P.2d 1294 (App. 1979), and were extended to subsequent purchasers by our supreme court in Richards v. Powercraft Homes, Inc., 139 Ariz. 242, 678 P.2d 427 (1984). These warranties are limited, however, to latent defects that would not have been discoverable had a "reasonable inspection" been made prior to the purchase.

Here, defendant contends that a reasonable inspection did not occur prior to purchase because the defect would have been easily discoverable by a trained person, engaged in the business of home inspection. Indeed, Rushing testified that such an inspection by a trained person, had that person measured the depth of material and analyzed the mixture, would have indicated "rather quickly" the existence of the defects in the stucco installation.

However, Rushing also testified that a lay person would not "key in on any of these problems until they started to appear the way they are now," and plaintiff testified he made a lay person's inspection of the home prior to purchase. The trial court found that, at the time of the purchase, "there [were] few cracks in the stucco of a normal nature," and "only from 1987 would a reasonable purchaser have been put on any kind of notice that a disastrous problem lay hidden beneath the exterior stucco and paint."

We disagree with defendant's contention that a "reasonable inspection" must include, as one of its components, an inspection by an expert or professional home inspection service to scrutinize the house for internal defects prior to purchase. Rather, under the policies stated in Columbia and Powercraft, an implied warranty should be voided for lack of a "reasonable inspection" only if the defect could have been discovered during an inspection made by the average purchaser, not an expert.

The rule of caveat emptor applies generally to the sale of real estate. However, the general rule is not applied to the construction of residential houses because of the public policy favoring the protection of innocent home purchasers and the accountability of home builders. In Columbia, we recognized the disparity between the expertise of the home builder and the average home purchaser:

Many firms and persons . . . hold themselves out as skilled in home construction and are in the business of building and selling to individual owners. . . . Building construction by

modern methods is complex and intertwined with governmental codes and regulations. The ordinary home buyer is not in a position, by skill or training, to discover
defects lurking in the plumbing, the electrical wiring, the structure itself, all of which
is usually covered up and not open for inspection.

122 Ariz. at 32, 592 P.2d at 1298, quoting Tavares v. Horstman, 542 P.2d 1275,
1279 (Wyo. 1975). The same recognition was extended to subsequent purchasers
in *Powercraft*:

> Home builders should anticipate that the houses they construct will eventually, and
> perhaps frequently, change ownership. The effect of latent defects will be just as
> catastrophic on a subsequent owner as on an original buyer and the builder will be
> just as unable to justify improper or substandard work. Because the builder-vendor
> is in a better position than a subsequent owner to prevent occurrence of major
> problems, the costs of poor workmanship should be his to bear. 139 Ariz. at 245,
> 678 P.2d at 430.

Admittedly, the "reasonable inspection" requirement for subsequent purchasers is necessary to avoid a windfall to the purchaser who negotiates a reduction in the purchase price based upon defects and then subsequently seeks
damages from the builder for the same defects. However, a requirement that
the "reasonable inspection" made prior to purchase be done by an expert rather
than by the purchaser would negate the policy considerations for recognizing an
implied warranty in the first place. In declining to adopt such a rule, we agree with
the observations of the Colorado Supreme Court:

> An experienced builder who has erected and sold many houses is in a far better position
> to determine the structural condition of a house than most buyers. Even if a buyer is
> sufficiently knowledgeable to evaluate a home's condition, he rarely has access to make
> any inspection of the underlying structural work, as distinguished from the merely
> cosmetic features.

Duncan v. Schuster-Graham Homes, Inc., 194 Colo. 441, 578 P.2d 637, 638-39
(1978).

The evidence in this case clearly established that the average purchaser would
not have discovered the defect upon reasonable inspection and that plaintiff made
such an inspection. We thus find no error in the trial court's finding that plaintiff
met the reasonable inspection requirement necessary to an implied warranty of
habitability or proper workmanship.

Defendant also contends that the trial court's extension of an implied warranty
more than twelve years after completion of construction is unreasonable, and fails
to meet the limitations on the warranty set forth by the supreme court in *Powercraft* and followed by Division Two of this court in Sheibels v. Estes Homes, 161
Ariz. 403, 778 P.2d 1299 (App. 1989).

In *Powercraft,* the supreme court adopted the standard of reasonableness first
articulated by the Indiana Supreme Court in Barnes v. Mac Brown & Co., 264 Ind.
227, 342 N.E.2d 619 (1976):

> The standard to be applied in determining whether or not there has been a breach of
> warranty is one of reasonableness in light of surrounding circumstances. The age of a

home, its maintenance, the use to which it has been put, are but a few factors entering into this factual determination at trial.

Powercraft, 139 Ariz. at 245, 678 P.2d at 430, quoting *Barnes,* 342 N.E.2d at 621....

[T]he duration that an implied warranty will exist is a factual determination that will depend, in part, on the life expectancy of the questioned component in a non-defective condition. In making this determination, a fact finder need not decide the outside limits of that life expectancy, but only whether liability is reasonable at the point of the breach under the particular facts of the case.

In this case, the trial court heard expert testimony that a stucco exterior has a normal life expectancy in the Arizona desert of thirty to fifty years, and defendant conceded that the stucco process applied to plaintiff's house could be reasonably expected to last more than the twelve years that it did. The evidence also established that the damage from the defective stucco application was gradual and progressive, occurring over a period of at least ten years, and was not discoverable by reasonable inspection until it actually was discovered. Under these circumstances, we find no error in the trial court's conclusion that, based on the expected life of the defective component of the house, twelve years was not an unreasonable period for an implied warranty of habitability and workmanship to exist.

Based on the foregoing, we affirm the judgment of the trial court....

With the sale of used homes, there are generally no implied warranties, and the homes are sold "as is." That is why with residential resale transactions, most buyers use a professional home inspector to inspect the house before being bound to purchase it. A typical home inspection contingency clause in a residential real estate sales contract would look something like this:

Buyer and Seller agree that the property is being sold in its present, "as is" condition, with no warranties, express or implied, and that conditions of the property that are visible on a reasonable inspection by a prospective Buyer should either be taken into account by the Buyer in the purchase price, or the Buyer should make correction of these conditions by Seller a requirement of the contract. Within fifteen (15) days after the "Acceptance Deadline" date of the sale contract, Buyer, at his option and expense, has the right to obtain written inspection reports from a qualified and reputable engineer, contractor, or home inspection service of the property and improvements limited to structural defects, environmental hazards, termite or other type of infestation and damage, plumbing, wells and sewer systems and equipment, roof, heating, and/or air conditioning systems and equipment, electrical systems and equipment, swimming pool and equipment, exterior drainage, basement leaks, and mechanical equipment including appliances, and shall furnish a copy thereof to Seller or listing agency stating in writing any defects unacceptable to Buyer.

The clause then goes on to state that in the event of such defects, the parties have ten days to agree who will pay for and correct the defects, or to agree instead to a price adjustment in lieu of correction. If those attempts fail, then the contingency clause provides that the deal is off.

2. *Third-Party Home Warranties*

Just as was discussed above with consumer products, there has been an in-crease in the last decade in the use of home warranties in the sale of both new and used homes. Unlike with the sale of goods, in the home sale market the warranty programs are serviced almost exclusively by third parties rather than by the seller itself.

Once more it is important to distinguish between new-home sales and used-home sales. Resale home warranty plans, when they are part of a sale, are typically offered by the seller as an enticement for the buyer. These resale warranties generally consist of a one-year service contract providing for repair or replacement of a home's major systems and appliances if any of those fail during the life of the warranty.

Unlike extended warranties on consumer products, resale home warranties are actually used by the buyer fairly frequently. One survey indicated that the average buyer with a resale home warranty made two uses per year of the warranty. The popularity of resale home warranties varies significantly from state to state. In Texas, only about 6 percent of home resales in a recent year included home warranties. In California, by contrast, the figure has been as high as 76 percent.

New home warranties are normally longer in duration than resale home warranties, sometimes as long as 10 years on certain systems in the house. Partly because of that, some new home warrantors have run into financial difficulty which has caused them to be unable to pay claims in some cases. The most prominent example of a new-home warrantor overextending itself is HOW Insurance Company, a Virginia-based firm that was forced into receiv-ership by Virginia insurance regulators on the grounds that it had not set aside sufficient reserves to pay future claims.

As a result of the action by the Virginia insurance regulators, HOW Insur-ance Company was barred from writing any new policies. Furthermore, pend-ing claims by homeowners against the company are being paid at just 40 cents on the dollar so that there will be some money left for future claimants.

Even when the new-home warrantor is solvent, the policies come with limits:

> Indeed, new-home warranties are sharply limited. Homes with major structural defects, for instance, must be deemed unsafe, unsanitary or unlivable to qualify for repair under most warranties — and it is the warranty company that makes the judgment. Even when claims are declared legitimate, payouts can be months, even years, in coming. And warranty companies frequently provide quick fixes rather than permanent cures for even major problems, such as faulty foundations.
>
> Karen Blumenthal, "Insured warranties attacked; some owners say policies worth-less," *The Cincinnati Enquirer*, H4, January 22, 1995.

Problem Set 9

9.1. a.   First National Bank has a leasing division, First National Leasing, that leased a dozen trailers to a trucking firm, Standard Delivery. Prior to entering the lease, Standard determined the kind of trailer it wanted and identified for First National a company, Billings Equipment Co., that sold this type of trailer. First National then purchased a dozen custom-built trailers from Billings after having Standard sign off on the terms of First National's purchase agreement with Billings, which included various express warranties. Following Standard's approval of the sale terms, First National signed a 10-year lease agreement with Standard. One year into the lease, two of the trailers began leaking when it rained. What rights does Standard have against First National Leasing as to the defective trailers? U.C.C. §§2A-103(1)(g) (amended §2A-103(1)(l)), 2A-212(1), 2A-213(1), 2A-407, Official Comment (g) to §2A-103.

b. Same facts as part a., except that the leasing officer at First National tells the Standard officer in charge of this deal, "I highly recommend that we get the trailers from Billings Equipment Co. We've dealt with them before and their trailers have always been first-rate." Would Standard now have rights against First National Leasing as to the defective trailers? U.C.C. §§2A-103(1)(g) (amended §2A-103(1)(l)), 2A-210, 2A-407(1), Official Comment 2 to §2A-407.

c. Same facts as part a. What rights does Standard have against Billings Equipment as to the defective trailers? U.C.C. §§2A-209(1), 2-313, 2-314, and Official Comment 1 to §2A-209. What if the sales contract contained warranty disclaimers — would those be effective? U.C.C. §2A-209(1).

d. Same facts as part a., except that the Standard officer told the Billings salesman prior to the sale, "We make a lot of deliveries over rugged mountain roads. So we need trailers with good shocks." The Billings salesman then replied, "Might I recommend our Rover XXL model?" It turned out that the Rover XXL had shock absorbers no better than the typical trailer, and so the shocks failed on a number of trailers within the first year of the lease. The written sales contract between Billings and First National said nothing about the durability of the shocks. Does Standard have any rights against Billings regarding the shocks? U.C.C. §§2-315, 2A-213, 2A-209(1).

9.2. In your capacity as in-house counsel for First National Bank, the leasing division has asked you to take a look at its form lease that it uses whenever the bank engages in a finance lease. The leasing officers who do these deals on a regular basis tell you that it's very important that these transactions get characterized as finance leases so that the bank can get all of the benefits of being a finance lessor. What kinds of clauses will you make sure are included in the contract? U.C.C. §2A-103(1)(g) (amended §2A-103(1)(l)), Official Comment (g) to §2A-103, §§2A-212(1), 2A-213, 2A-407(1).

9.3. Steve Stern is a construction worker whose job sometimes takes him out of state for a few weeks at a time. He and his wife, Sandra Werner, have been looking for a few months to buy a house after living in an apartment for the first three years of their marriage. When Sandra found a four-year-old house in an established neighborhood of eighty-year-old houses, she decided to make an offer on the house on the spot, even though Steve was out of town on a job. She included an inspection contingency clause in the contract, which was accepted by the seller. Sandra figured that Steve could do the inspection himself, but he was so exhausted from travelling and working the out-of-town job that he told Sandra that she could do a walk-through on her own. Sandra did not notice anything in her admittedly superficial inspection, and she and her husband purchased the house. Two months after moving in, Steve was fixing the gutters when he noticed that there was something peculiar about the way in which the roof shingles were attached. Upon closer inspection, Steve could see (because of his extensive experience in the construction industry) that the roof work was incredibly shoddy, and he estimated it would cost nearly $5,000 to get the roof done right. May Sandra and Steve recover against the original builder for the cost of the roof repairs?

Assignment 10: Reducing or Eliminating
Warranty Liability: Basics

A.   Warranty Reduction with Sales of Goods

There is a recurring tension that characterizes the issue of warranty disclaimers or limitations in the sales system. On the one hand, all sellers have an incentive to stand behind the quality of their goods for the reason that such an assurance helps future sales either with repeat buyers or with new customers who learn of the seller's good reputation. On the other hand, having unlimited warranty liability can be a very expensive proposition, even if the goods being sold are generally fit for their ordinary purpose.

When it comes to warranty disclaimers, there is a tendency for commercial sellers to care more about the long-term relational aspects of a sale than the money saved by enforcing a warranty disclaimer in a particular context. The one limitation that even commercial sellers will fight for, however, is a disclaimer of consequential damages. Consequential damages, you may recall from your contracts class, are damages that a buyer suffers that are other than to the product itself. Consequential damages, for example, might include a consumer's personal injuries from a defective product or a business' economic loss from a poorly designed machine.

Sellers are particularly wary of accepting unlimited consequential damage liability when the product they are selling is a relatively inexpensive item. As an in-house lawyer for an industrial products manufacturer explained: "When we offer a component of small value that will be put in a much more expensive product, we can't have the potential liability all out of whack with the potential return. It would damage our business. So we're going to take a pretty strong position there. Look, we understand that our little part fails. You may have some significant damages, but you know, we've got to go forward with the understanding we're going to do the best we can and to supply you a good product. But if we don't, we can't have liability that's all out of whack with potential return."

Just as sellers of commercial goods are reluctant to accept the possibility of consequential damages, buyers of commercial goods will not bargain away lightly that category of recovery. As the in-house counsel for a major beer manufacturer put it: "Our equipment suppliers will often want to limit remedies to repair or replacement of defective parts, but we'll resist those efforts because sometimes we will have important and legitimate consequential damages to claim. For example, if a filtration system that we've been sold doesn't work and we lose a lot of beer because of that, we'll want to be reimbursed for the lost beer by the seller who sold us the filtration system. Whether or not the consequential damages disclaimer stays or goes will depend mainly on commercial leverage. In that respect, it has helped us a lot that we're a big company."

Sellers of consumer goods often care about reputational concerns just as much as sellers of commercial goods. There is nevertheless a large class of consumer sales — those in which the size of each transaction is large but repeat business is low, such as used-car sales — where it may be in the seller's interest to care more about the short-term dollar cost of broad warranty protection for its buyers than about the longer-term reputational cost of very limited warranty protection. To complicate the workings of the system even further, the employees of the seller that deal directly with the buyer are often sales people whose incentives are geared almost exclusively toward closing the deal. Even when these sales people are required to sell goods that have very little warranty protection, there is a strong temptation for them to make oral promises about quality to the potential buyer that may or may not become enforceable terms of the sales contract.

The Consumers Digest "Used-Car Buying and Selling Guide" described the following not uncommon scenario along those lines:

> Dishonest dealers may tell consumers that "as is" refers to the equipment or options that come with the car, or that it reflects any warranty terms that may have been offered verbally. Neither is true. More commonly, a dishonest dealer will offer to fix a problem you might discover while examining the vehicle, have you sign the contract that contains the "as is" clause, and then refuse to honor the oral promise after the car changes hands. Although an oral promise technically constitutes an express warranty, it is difficult to prove. In most states, under what's known as the "parol evidence rule," terms in a written agreement always override inconsistent spoken promises. To avoid this pitfall, get all promises in writing.
>
> *Consumers Digest*, Vol. 35, No. 4 (1996).

As the following story from Florida demonstrates, the "as is" used-car sale that is described above is by no means limited to the proverbial "$500 special":

> It was the best looking vehicle Diana Smith had ever owned. The shiny red, used Jeep Grand Cherokee was no steal at $25,300, but Smith pulled together enough for a down payment and traded in her 1988 Ford Thunderbird. Her kids loved it. And Smith, a single mother who works as a secretary in Lecanto, was thrilled to finally have something nice to shuttle them around in. Now, five months after she bought the 2-year-old Jeep at a tent sale in Dunnellon, Smith says she would love nothing more than to have her old car back. That's because the Jeep, sold to her by Rallye Dodge of Ocala, was apparently in a wreck before she bought it.
>
> Smith doesn't have the money to repair the bent frame, flattened brake lines, buckled roof and other damage the Jeep suffered. She said she still drives the car, even though she is concerned about its safety, because she has no choice. Because she signed a contract with a warranty disclaimer, or "as is" clause, the dealership's general manager told her there is nothing he can do. "I am just heartbroken," said Smith, 39. "My 15-year-old won't even get in it. I thought it was the nicest thing I had ever owned. Now, the thrill is completely gone...."
>
> [Smith] said the salesman told her that the vehicle had been repainted only because someone had scratched it. "I asked him specifically if it had been in a wreck because I

noticed there was a bubble in the paint," she said. "Nobody can convince me that they didn't lie to me about it." Smith first learned of the damage when she brought the Jeep into Crystal Chevrolet-Geo in Crystal River for minor repairs after another driver rear-ended her. The manager of the body shop told her about the previous repair work that had been done, including plastic body filler applied to the roof and frame. All together, 15 separate repairs were listed as needed to return the Jeep to pre-wreck condition.

Smith has notified Chrysler Corp., the Florida Department of Consumer Affairs, the Department of Highway Safety and Motor Vehicles and 60 Minutes. A letter from the motor vehicles division states that, because Smith signed an "as is" clause, she has no legal recourse other than a civil suit. A representative from Chrysler told her a complaint would be filed in the company's data base, but beyond that, nothing could be done. The representative told Smith that she should have had the car checked before she bought it. Smith said she believes there are plenty of things she should have done — like shopped at a different dealership. "I figured it was a reputable place," she said. "If Lee Iacocca were still around, I bet he'd do something about this."

Amy Ellis, "Dream car turns into nightmare," *St. Petersburg Times*, November 5, 1995.

Perhaps because of stories like the one above, there is significant regulation at both the state and federal level that governs the mechanics of warranty disclaimers and limitations. At the state level, there is Article 2 of the UCC, which contains a number of provisions that set down specific requirements that must be met in order for warranty disclaimers to be effective.

In addition, nearly all states have some form of "lemon law" that covers the sale of new (and in some cases used) cars. The primary abuse targeted by state lemon laws has been car manufacturers' attempts to limit a buyer's remedy to repair or replacement of defective parts. The problem with such a remedy limit, as most car buyers know, is that with some cars this would mean having to bring the car back for adjustments practically every month. In those cases, what the buyer really wants is a different car. One of the key features of state lemon laws is to limit the number of repair attempts that a car seller has before being required to offer the buyer either a new car or a refund of the purchase price.

At the federal level, the Magnuson-Moss Act includes some regulations that limit the ability of consumer product sellers to disclaim the implied warranty of merchantability. Furthermore, the FTC Used Car Rule mandates conspicuous disclosure of a used car's warranty protections and limitations in plain view of any prospective purchaser.

Before looking in greater detail at these various statutory limits on a seller's ability to disclaim or reduce warranty liability, there is a more general point that needs to be made about this area: When it comes to enforcing warranty limitations, courts will be very tough on the seller, particularly where the buyer is a consumer. This is not to suggest, of course, that properly worded and clearly written warranty disclaimers will never work to do what their drafters intended. The lesson instead is, as the following case shows, that any ambiguity in the language of a warranty disclaimer is likely to be construed strictly against the seller that drafted it.

Wilbur v. Toyota Motor Sales, U.S.A.

86 F.3d 23 (2d Cir. 1996)

OAKES, SENIOR C.J.

Appellant Nicolyn S. Wilbur ("Wilbur") appeals from an order entered on March 27, 1995, by the United States District Court for the District of Vermont, Franklin S. Billings, Jr., Senior Judge, granting summary judgment to Appellee Toyota Motor Sales, U.S.A., Inc. ("Toyota"). Wilbur sued Toyota for violating the Magnuson-Moss Warranty — Federal Trade Commission Improvement Act and the Vermont Consumer Fraud Act ("VCFA"), by refusing to honor its new car warranty on her Toyota Camry. On appeal, Wilbur argues that the district court erred in finding as a matter of law that the warranty excluded damage done to the car before it was purchased. We agree with Wilbur that the damage occurring prior to the date the dealer listed the car as "in service" was not excluded from warranty coverage. Accordingly, we reverse the summary judgment in favor of Toyota and remand to the district court. . . .

On May 18, 1992, Wilbur bought a 1992 Toyota Camry for $18,600 from Tri-Nordic Toyota ("Tri-Nordic") in White River Junction, Vermont. The car had been used as a demonstrator by the dealership and had roughly 5,800 miles on the odometer. Wilbur's Bill of Sale identified the car as a "New Camry Demo."

Before Wilbur bought the car, Tri-Nordic informed her that the car had been in an accident requiring almost $4,000 in repairs. The accident, a rear-end collision, occurred in October 1991 when one of Tri-Nordic's employees was using the car to look at New Hampshire's fall foliage with his relatives. Tri-Nordic told Wilbur that the car had been fully repaired and had sustained no structural damage.

At the time of purchase, Wilbur received a copy of Toyota's "New Vehicle Limited Warranty" which stated that the warranty went into effect "on the date the vehicle is first delivered or put into use (in-service date)." Tri-Nordic filled in the in-service date as 5/18/92, the date Wilbur bought the car. The warranty further stated that "repairs and adjustments required as a result of . . . accident . . . are not covered."

In June 1992, Wilbur drove the Camry to California for the summer. On the way, she discovered that the car's ABS braking system did not work, that the trunk had a major leak, and that the rear of the car made a creaking noise. When she brought the car to a Toyota dealer in California for repairs, the dealer told her that the repairs were excluded from warranty coverage because the vehicle had sustained structural damage in an accident. After making visits to several other dealerships, all of which refused to honor her Toyota warranty, Wilbur obtained an estimate of approximately $9,500 for the repairs. She also had the car appraised and learned that a potential buyer who knew of its condition would not have paid more than $10,000 for it.

Wilbur reported the repair estimate to Tri-Nordic, which offered to make the repairs if Wilbur agreed to split the cost of transporting the car back to Vermont. After refusing to do so, Wilbur made numerous complaints about the denial of warranty coverage to Toyota, Tri-Nordic, and the Attorney General of Vermont.

Wilbur brought suit in Vermont state court against Tri-Nordic and Toyota in February 1994, alleging that Toyota had violated the MMWA, that Tri-Nordic had violated the Vermont Motor Vehicle Manufacturers, Distributors and Dealers Franchising Practices Act, and that both parties had violated the VCFA. The district court held that because the damage from the accident was excluded from coverage under the warranty as a matter of law, Toyota did not violate the MMWA or the VCFA when it refused to repair Wilbur's car. This appeal followed. . . .

Before discussing the merits, it will be helpful to explain how the parties refer to certain aspects of Toyota's warranty. When referencing the date on which the warranty commenced, the parties mean the date that starts the period in which exclusions spelled out in the warranty apply. Though they sometimes speak as if the warranty is not even applicable to the period before it commenced, they do not mean this literally: if a defect resulted from damage that occurred while the vehicle was being manufactured, for example, the warranty would apply to such a defect. Thus, when Toyota contends that the accident occurred during the warranty period and Wilbur says it did not, Toyota means that the accident exclusion in the warranty applied and relieved Toyota of liability, while Wilbur means that the accident exclusion did not apply and that therefore the warranty entitled her to compensation.

In this case, both sides agree that the warranty would cover a defect resulting from an accident that occurred before delivery to Tri-Nordic and would not cover a defect resulting from an accident that occurred after Wilbur bought the car. They dispute whether the warranty covers an accident that occurred during the period the car was used by Tri-Nordic as a demo.

The district court found that the warranty, with its accident exclusion, went into effect at the start of the demo period, that Wilbur "assumed the remainder of the limited factory warranty" when she bought the Camry and that the accident in October "occurred during the course of the warranty," i.e. at a time when the warranty's accident exclusion was applicable. Because the warranty specifically excluded repairs resulting from accidents, the district court concluded that the damage to Wilbur's car was not covered. The MMWA mandated this conclusion, the district court reasoned, because the accident exclusion was clearly and conspicuously disclosed in accordance with the law.

The central issue in this case is whether the warranty, with its accident exclusion, applied to the period before the inservice date when the car was being used as a demo. The district court found, and Toyota argues on appeal, that the warranty had already begun to run when the accident happened, over seven months before Wilbur purchased the car. A review of the warranty in light of the requirements of the MMWA, however, leads us to a different result.

The Toyota New Vehicle Limited Warranty issued to Wilbur at the time of purchase stated that "[t]he warranty period begins on the date the vehicle is first delivered or put into use (in-service date)." The in-service date was filled in by Tri-Nordic as May 18, 1992 — the day Wilbur bought the car. It seems evident, then, that the warranty had not commenced when the accident occurred and that therefore the repairs were not excluded from warranty coverage.

Despite these facts, Toyota claims that a later section of the warranty book entitled "California Emission Control Warranty" makes clear that the warranty period begins on the date the vehicle is first delivered to the ultimate purchaser; or, if the vehicle is first placed into service as "demonstrator" or "company car" prior to delivery, on the date it is first placed into service.

Toyota urges us to treat this isolated language, appearing ten pages later in the warranty book as part of a wholly separate warranty, as a clear indication to Wilbur that the New Vehicle Limited Warranty had commenced at the time of the accident. We are unwilling to do so.

The MMWA grants relief to a consumer "who is damaged by the failure of a...warrantor...to comply with any obligation...under a written warranty." 15 U.S.C. §2310(d)(1) (1994). When drafting a written warranty, Toyota must "fully and conspicuously disclose in simple and readily understood language [its] terms and conditions." 15 U.S.C. §2302(a) (1994). The accompanying regulations define one such term as "[t]he point in time or event on which the warranty term commences, if different from the purchase date." 16 C.F.R. §701.3(a)(4) (1995).

Facially, Toyota's New Vehicle Limited Warranty appears to fulfill the MMWA's clarity requirements: the warranty commences on the in-service date, which is filled in by the dealer when the car is sold. Failure to repair damage sustained before the in-service date therefore puts Toyota in violation of MMWA for breach of warranty. Moreover, Toyota's suggested addition of the California Emission Control Warranty's language renders the time of the warranty's commencement ambiguous at best: Is the "in-service date" the date the car is put into use by the buyer or by the dealer? Under Toyota's own construction, then, the warranty would violate the MMWA because it would not "fully and conspicuously disclose" its commencement date.

Toyota is thus placed in a somewhat uncomfortable position. If it subscribes to a straight reading of its New Vehicle Limited Warranty, it must concede that Wilbur's warranty had not commenced when the accident occurred and that its refusal to repair her car is a breach of warranty. If Toyota stands by the warranty construction it has pressed upon us here, its warranty must be deemed cryptic and unclear. In either case, Wilbur may recover damages under the MMWA.

Concededly, it was the actions of Tri-Nordic, not Toyota, which resulted in the damage to the car that in turn led to this lawsuit. But Toyota provided Wilbur with a new car warranty and gave its dealer the authority to fill in the in-service date. The MMWA, by requiring any warrantor to draft clear warranty terms and conditions, simply incorporates the well-established contract principle of contra proferentem by which a drafting party must be prepared to have ambiguities construed against it. We therefore find that Wilbur's claim under the MMWA cannot be defeated on Toyota's motion for summary judgment and must be allowed to proceed to trial.

Because the district court based its decision in this case on the warranty's accident exclusion and did not address the warranty's commencement date, the court erred in granting summary judgment to Toyota on the MMWA claim. Thus, the district court's grant of summary judgment on Wilbur's state claim, based on its finding that the absence of liability under the MMWA removed any basis for recovery under the VCFA, was also in error. We reverse and remand both claims for reconsideration by the district court.

———————

The above case is a good example of a recurring tension that courts are often forced to resolve in cases involving warranty disclaimers: Was the loss complained of by the buyer due to a conscious allocation of risk by both parties at the time of contracting (in which case the seller should win) or was the buyer's loss due instead to unfair oppression by the seller (in which case the buyer should win)?

The drafters of Article 2 were well aware of this tension when they put together the various rules governing sales warranties and disclaimers. The only problem was, the UCC drafters apparently wanted at the same time to be both pro-freedom of contract and anti-oppression. Consider the following examples of the Code's schizophrenia on this issue:

From Official Comment 1 to §2-302 (unconscionability): "The principle is one of the prevention of oppression and unfair surprise, and not of disturbance of allocation of risk because of superior bargaining power."

From Official Comment 4 to §2-313 (Official Comment 6 to §2-313 as amended) (express warranties): "This is not intended to mean that the parties, if they consciously desire, cannot make their own bargain as they wish. But in determining what they have agreed upon good faith is a factor and consideration should be given to the fact that the probability is small that a real price is intended to be exchanged for a pseudo-obligation."

From Official Comment 3 to §2-719 (limitation of remedies): "Subsection (3) recognizes the validity of clauses limiting or excluding consequential damages but makes it clear that they may not operate in an unconscionable manner. Actually such terms are merely an allocation of unknown or undeterminable risks."

Unfortunately, the Article 2 drafters were better at identifying this tension between freedom of contract and anti-oppression than they were at outlining specific factors to resolve it. When courts are faced with a case highlighting this tension, they tend to consider the following factors either explicitly or implicitly: (1) the relative bargaining power and sophistication of the parties — is the buyer a consumer or a business person?; (2) the price paid — did it appear that the buyer chose to sacrifice greater warranty protection by paying a lower than usual price?; (3) usage of trade, course of dealing, and course of performance — these all provide some clues as to what the parties probably had in mind when they struck their deal; and (4) what the words of the contract actually said, including how clearly the limitation of the usual warranty protection was brought home to the buyer, and how well the provisions complied with the technical requirements of Article 2 on disclaimers and limitations of warranty.

B.   Warranty Reduction with Leases

For the most part, the provisions in U.C.C. Article 2A concerning a seller's ability to reduce its liability for warranties were directly borrowed from Article 2. In that respect, §2A-214 reads almost like a carbon copy of §2-316. There are, however, two notable differences between pre-amended §2-316 and §2A-214.

The first difference is that whereas under §2-316(2) a seller can disclaim the implied warranty of merchantability with a properly worded oral disclaimer, under §2A-214(2) a lessor can only disclaim the implied warranty of merchantability by using a conspicuous written disclaimer. In both §2-316(2) and §2A-214(2), the disclaimer must mention the word "merchantability" to be effective. If the seller chooses to use a written disclaimer of the implied warranty of merchantability under §2-316(2), the disclaimer must be conspicuous, which is consistent with the written disclaimer requirements of §2A-214(2).

The second difference between pre-amended §2-316 and §2A-214 is the example that each provision gives for properly disclaiming the implied warranty of fitness for a particular purpose. Both provisions provide that such a disclaimer must be in writing and must be conspicuous. The example of a sufficient disclaimer of the fitness warranty given in §2-316(2) is the fairly general statement: "There are no warranties which extend beyond the description on the face hereof." Section 2A-214(2), by contrast, provides an example of a sufficient fitness disclaimer that is much more specific: "There is no warranty that the goods will be fit for a particular purpose."

With the simultaneous proposed amendments to both Articles 2 and 2A, §2-316 and §2A-214 are now even more alike than they were prior to the amendments. As amended, the only difference between §2-316 and §2A-214 is that §2A-214 contains more situations where a disclaimer must be in writing in order to be effective. By using "as is" language, a seller can disclaim the implied warranties orally with either consumer or merchant buyers. U.C.C. §2-316(2) as amended. A lessor, by contrast, must put the disclaimer in a record in order to be effective even where the lessor is using "as is" language. U.C.C. §2A-214(2) as amended. Furthermore, with a merchant buyer (but not a consumer buyer), a seller not using "as is" language can still orally disclaim the implied warranty of merchantability or of fitness as long as the seller uses certain other key words ("merchantability") or phrases ("There are no warranties that extend beyond the description on the face hereof"). U.C.C. §2-316(3)(b) as amended. By contrast, even a lessor that uses key words like "merchantability" cannot disclaim implied warranties orally with either consumer lessees or merchant lessees. U.C.C. §2A-214(3)(a).

C. Warranty Reduction with International Sales

As in so many areas, the CISG ends up in much the same place as the UCC with respect to warranty reduction, except by using a lot fewer words. The CISG manages to include in one place, Article 35, virtually all of its rules on both warranty creation and warranty reduction.

There are two points within C.I.S.G. Article 35 where warranty reduction rules can be found. The first is in the introductory clause to Article 35(2). Subsection 35(2) describes four different warranties that arise in a sale of goods covered by the CISG, including the implied warranties of merchantability and fitness for a particular purpose. Those obligations of the seller will not arise, however, "where the parties have agreed otherwise." The just-quoted language is the clause that begins subsection (2) of Article 35 and therefore conditions the seller's liability for the warranties subsequently outlined in Article 35(2).

Supermicro Computer, Inc. v. Digitechnic, S.A.

145 F. Supp. 2d 1147 (N.D. Cal. 2001)

LEGGE, J.

...Plaintiff is a California corporation that manufactures computer parts. Defendant is a French corporation that assembles and sells computer network systems. Defendant made fourteen purchases of computer parts from plaintiff between May 1996 and December 1997. In each of the transactions, defendant placed an order with plaintiff via phone or e-mail, and plaintiff shipped the goods to France. Plaintiff included a sales invoice and a user's manual with each shipment. The sales invoice and user's manual contained certain terms and conditions, including a limited warranty and limitations of liability.

Beginning in 1998, defendant allegedly experienced electrical problems with some of the parts that it had purchased from plaintiff; specifically, some of the parts caught fire. Defendant demanded $200,400 in replacement costs, and consequential damages of approximately $6,000,000. Plaintiff rejected the demand and claimed that, based on the limited warranty contained in the sales invoices and the consequential damages waiver found in the user's manual, defendant's sole remedy was the repair and replacement of any malfunctioning parts.

In December 1998 defendant filed an action in France in the Tribunal de Commerce de Bobginy (the "French Commercial Court"). The French case has been ongoing since that time and plaintiff has been participating in it. The parties disagree on the posture and scope of the French case. Plaintiff contends that it is an "interim relief procedure" that has no judicial effect. Defendant argues that it is a legal proceeding wherein the parties can be afforded complete relief.

Plaintiff filed this action on January 20, 2000, more than a year after the French action began. The complaint seeks a declaration that: (1) the computer parts were not defective; (2) the parts failed as a result of defendant's misuse; and (3) even if plaintiff were at fault, defendant's sole remedy is for repair or replacement....

While there are no "state" law issues present here, there is the analogous situation of issues of international law. The parties agree that the United Nations Convention on Contracts for the International Sale of Goods (hereinafter "CISG") governs their transactions....

Application of the CISG here requires a court to resolve an issue of first impression. To wit, the court must determine whether a warranty disclaimer in a purchase order is valid under the CISG. The court has no controlling authority on this issue. Plaintiff contends that Article 35 of the CISG permits warranty disclaimers such as the one at issue. Article 35 however, deals with a seller's obligation to deliver conforming goods. It does not discuss disclaimers. If anything, a disclaimer in this case might not be valid because the CISG requires a "mirror-image" approach to contract negotiations that allows the court to inquire into the subjective intent of the parties. See CISG, Art. 8; also *MCC-Marble Ceramic,* 144 F.3d at 1389. Here, defendant has submitted evidence that it was not aware of the disclaimer and that it would not have purchased the goods had it been aware of the disclaimer. If the defendant was not aware of the disclaimer, then it may not have been valid. Given that this issue of law is unsettled, this factor weighs against this court exercising its discretion to hear the matter in favor of the French court that already has the issue before it. . . .

The second part of Article 35 that is relevant for warranty reduction purposes is subsection (3). That subsection is similar in many respects to U.C.C. §2-316(3)(b), which says that a seller is not liable for defects that a buyer ought to have discovered in an examination of the goods, if the buyer either actually examined the goods before purchasing them or refused to do so. C.I.S.G. Article 35(3) provides, much along the same lines, that a seller is not liable for any nonconformity in the goods if prior to the formation of the sales contract "the buyer knew or could not have been unaware of such lack of conformity." In comparing these two standards of buyer waiver, note that the CISG does not, like the UCC, impose a duty on the buyer to investigate the goods at the risk of losing warranty rights even if the seller were to make a demand of the buyer.

In general, the CISG seems much more inclined to defer to freedom of contract in the realm of warranty reduction, and also seems much less protective of the buyer on this score than is the UCC. That difference is perfectly understandable if you remember from Assignment 2 that the CISG, unlike the UCC, excludes from its scope the sale of goods to consumers. C.I.S.G. Art. 2(a). The UCC drafters, by contrast, had consumers uppermost on their mind when they set out to articulate which hoops a seller would need to jump through in order to successfully reduce the seller's usual warranty obligations to the buyer.

D.   Disclaiming the Real Estate Implied Warranty of Habitability

As discussed in Assignment 9, most states have created either by statute or by common law an implied warranty of habitability for buyers of new homes that are built by professional builders. Unlike in the comparable case of sales of goods under Article 2, there is no uniform set of rules in the real estate realm that dictate whether and how a home builder might successfully disclaim that implied warranty of habitability.

There is, however, one general observation that can be made about disclaiming the implied warranty of habitability: The builder's only hope for such a disclaimer to work is to put the disclaimer in clear and unmistakable terms. Anything less, as the following case demonstrates, will cause a court to deem the disclaimer ineffective.

Axline v. Kutner
863 S.W.2d 421 (Tenn. Ct. App. 1993)

FARMER, J.

This is an action by a home buyer against the seller/contractor. The trial court granted [the seller's] motion for partial summary judgment. . . .

The implied warranty rule [is] as follows:

> "[w]e hold that in every contract for the sale of a recently completed dwelling, and in every contract for the sale of a dwelling then under construction, the vendor, if he be in the business of building such dwellings, shall be held to impliedly warrant to the initial vendee that, at the time of the passing of the deed or the taking of possession by the initial vendee (whichever first occurs), the dwelling, together with all its fixtures, is sufficiently free from major structural defects, and is constructed in a workmanlike manner, so as to meet the standard of workmanlike quality then prevailing at the time and place of construction; and that this implied warranty in the contract of sale survives the passing of the deed or the taking of possession by the initial vendee." [Hartley v. Ballou 208 S.E. 2d 776 (1974).]
>   *Dixon,* 632 S.W.2d at 541.

The court in *Dixon* further said that this warranty is implied only when the written contract is silent. Builder-vendors and purchasers are free to contract in writing for a warranty upon different terms and conditions or to expressly disclaim any warranty. The written contract contained no reference as to the quality of workmanship.

Defendants contend that the implied warranty doctrine is not applicable here because of the provision in *Dixon* that the warranty is implied only when the written contract is silent, and that this contract limits the warranty to one (1) year. [We have] held:

> Because the buyer is completely relying on the skills of the vendor-builder in this situation, we think that in order to have a valid disclaimer of the implied warranty, it must be in clear and unambiguous language. The buyer must be given adequate notice of the implied warranty protections that he is waiving by signing the contract. In addition, such a "disclaimer" must be strictly construed against the seller. This is generally the law in other jurisdictions which have adopted this, or a comparable, implied warranty of good workmanship and materials.

Plaintiffs contend that the term "one year builder's warranty" is meaningless because there is no indication what the builder is warranting. Construing strictly against the builder/seller, we are inclined to agree.

Appellees further rely upon the following handwritten language to the contract: "PURCHASER ACCEPTS PROPERTY IN ITS EXISTING CONDITION, NO WARRANTIES OR REPRESENTATIONS HAVING BEEN MADE BY SELLER OR AGENT WHICH

ARE NOT EXPRESSLY STATED HEREIN." This exact language was contained in the agreement before the court in Dewberry v. Maddox wherein this court said:

> We do not think that this provision is adequate to disclaim the implied warranty . . . In the setting of the marketplace, the builder or seller of new construction — not unlike the manufacturer or merchandiser of personalty — makes implied representations, ordinarily indispensable to the sale, that the builder has used reasonable skill and judgment in constructing the building. On the other hand, the purchaser does not usually possess the knowledge of the builder and is unable to fully examine a complete house and its components without disturbing the finished product. Further, unlike the purchaser of an older building, he has no opportunity to observe how the building has withstood the passage of time. Thus, he generally relies on those in a position to know the quality of the work to be sold, and his reliance is surely evident to the construction industry.

We conclude that the trial court erred in granting partial summary judgment in this matter and that judgment is reversed. This cause is remanded to the trial court for further proceedings consistent with this opinion.

Another way to view the *Axline* case is as a situation involving the cumulation and conflict of warranties. In other words, when a seller gives both express and implied warranties, how should those warranties be construed in relationship to one another? Although real estate law lacks a widely adopted uniform code like sales, one would suspect that courts considering real estate cases would be guided generally by the cumulation and conflict principles set down in U.C.C. §2-317: (1) Whenever it is reasonable to do so, warranties should be construed as consistent with one another and therefore as cumulative; and (2) Whenever it is unreasonable to construe warranties as consistent with one another, express warranties displace inconsistent implied warranties except for the implied warranty of fitness for a particular purpose.

If the issue in *Axline* had been framed as a case of cumulation and conflict, the builder no doubt would have argued that a one-year express warranty is inherently inconsistent with a more open-ended implied warranty of habitability. Thus, the builder would argue, the one-year express warranty must displace the inconsistent implied warranty of habitability.

The buyers, on the other hand, could have argued that there is nothing inconsistent with cumulating the one-year express warranty, which provides certain rights for a certain length of time, with the lengthier implied warranty of habitability, which provides other rights for a longer period of time. In other words, the buyer could argue that it is not unreasonable to "stack" a limited-duration express warranty with a longer-duration implied warranty.

Problem Set 10

10.1. Fresh out of law school, you have just opened up your own law practice in a storefront in the neighborhood where you grew up. One of your first clients is Mrs. McGillicudy, your former next-door neighbor who remembers you back when "you just barely came up to my knees." It turns out that Mrs. McGillicudy had just bought a 1993 used Cadillac from the local used-car lot, Lou's Used Cars for Less. Three weeks after the purchase, the Cadillac was giving Mrs. McGillicudy a host of problems that she wanted Lou's to repair. When she brought the car back in, Lou pulled out the contract that she had signed and pointed out a clause that said there were no warranties which were included with the sale of this car. You take a look at the contract, which includes the following clause in very fine print: "There are no warranties, express or implied, that are included as a part of this sale." You ask Mrs. McGillicudy if she read that clause before purchasing the car. "Of course, dear," she says. "I always read everything carefully before I sign something." Is there still hope for Mrs. McGillicudy to insist on having her car repaired by Lou's? U.C.C. §§2-316, 1-201(10).

10.2. It seems that Lou's Used Cars for Less is going to be providing your fledgling law practice with a steady source of business. Another dissatisfied customer of Lou's comes to you for advice. Deborah Swift (from Problem 1.6), your erstwhile law school classmate and a current personal-injury lawyer, asks for your advice concerning a recent transaction she had with Lou's. Deborah purchased a 1994 used Jeep Cherokee from Lou's a few weeks ago, and she discovered only yesterday that the vehicle has a serious engine problem. When Deborah brought the Jeep back to Lou's for repair, he pointed out to her that he had asked her to check out the Jeep before buying it and she had refused. "I was in a hurry," Deborah told you. "If I had spent a lot of time examining the car, I might have been able to discover the problem, but that's only because I tinker with used cars as a hobby." Does Deborah have a reasonable basis for demanding that Lou repair her Jeep? U.C.C. §2-316(3)(b) and Official Comment 8 to §2-316 (Official Comment 6 to §2-316 as amended).

10.3. After you won several cases against Lou's Used Cars for Less, Lou convinced his big law firm, Dewey, Cheatem & Howe, to hire you to work for them. Now Lou wants you to look at his standard sales contract with an eye toward your re-drafting it. Based on a couple of your previous victories against him, Lou knows that he needs to increase the prominence of his implied warranty disclaimer and to use the word "merchantability." Lou wonders if there is any mileage (no pun intended, he says) in also including a prominent disclaimer of express warranties as well. "You know those salespeople," he says. "They'll say darn near anything to sell a car, bless their souls." What do you advise Lou? Are there other clauses you recommend including in the contract to prevent the salespeople from "giving away the store"? U.C.C. §§2-316(1), 2-202, Official Comment 2 to §2-316.

10.4. Since joining Dewey, Cheatem & Howe, you seem to be getting as many cases for Lou's Used Cars for Less as you used to have against him when you were on your own. Your next defense for Lou involves a buyer who bought a '91 Ford Taurus wagon from Lou's. A month after the purchase, the brakes failed on the car and the buyer was seriously injured, although the car was not. Lou's sales contract for that sale involved a conspicuous limitation of remedy to repair or replacement of defective parts. Lou says he is happy to repair the car's brakes, but he doesn't feel like paying thousands of dollars in hospital bills. Lou asks you whether the exclusive remedy will be effective here. He also wants to know if it would have helped him in this case if he had included a prominent "AS IS" clause instead of the exclusive remedy. What do you advise Lou on these two questions? U.C.C. §§2-719, 2-316(3)(a), 2-302, Official Comment 2 to §2-316, Official Comments 1 and 3 to §2-719.

10.5.   Dan and Carol Pontello, who had a new home built by Cannon Construction Co. six years ago, recently came to see you in your law office. Their home had come with a written "Builder's Warranty" that provided that "Builder warrants that the home will be free of defects in material and workmanship for a period of five years on the foundation and for a period of two years on all other parts of the home. The five-year foundation warranty includes a warranty against any cracks or water seepage." The contract also contained a merger clause, separately signed by both buyer and seller, which said, "This contract is the complete and final understanding of the agreement between the parties and supersedes any and all other agreements or rights implied by law that are not contained within the four corners of this agreement." Now, six years after signing this contract, the foundation suddenly developed significant cracks leading to costly basement flooding. The Pontellos point out to you that most of their friends who had new houses built got 10-year foundation warranties and, further, that most foundations in new houses around this area will last without problems for at least 10 years. The Pontellos want to know if they have a good cause of action against Cannon Construction for the cracks in their foundation. What do you advise them?

Assignment 11: Commercial Impracticability

A. Commercial Impracticability with Sales of Goods

From the perspective of both the buyer and the seller, every agreement to transfer goods for a price involves various elements of risk. The seller is gambling that it can actually get the goods to be delivered, either by producing the goods itself or by obtaining them from some third party. The seller is also risking that the price for which it has agreed to sell the goods will not prove to be unduly low in light of later market shifts.

The buyer, in turn, accepts the risk that it will not want the goods by the time they are to be delivered. The buyer is also risking that the price it has agreed to pay does not prove to be unreasonably high in light of any post-bargain but pre-performance market movements.

Events don't always turn out the way that the parties to a sales contract want them to. Sometimes the seller is unable to obtain the goods that it thought it could; sometimes the price of goods shifts significantly in a way that makes the original deal very unprofitable for either the buyer or the seller. As a general matter, the sales system says that's too bad for the unlucky buyer or seller. The very nature of a sales contract is that both parties are assuming certain risks, which risks inherently comprise some of the consideration being exchanged by each side to the deal.

Nevertheless, there are some contingencies which are thought to be so out of the realm of what either party could reasonably anticipate that the occurrence of one of these contingencies might excuse performance by the adversely affected party. These special kinds of contingencies generally fall into two categories: first, an unexpected failure of seller's source of supply; and second, a dramatic price fluctuation. The first category would only be a basis for a seller's excuse. The second category might excuse either buyer or seller.

At this point it makes sense to try to clarify two common sources of confusion with respect to the doctrine of commercial impracticability. The first confusing issue is trying to distinguish between the scope of §2-613, Casualty to Identified Goods, and the scope of the more general impracticability provision, §2-615. Section 2-613 applies only where "the contract *requires* for its performance goods identified when the contract is made" (emphasis added), and the goods are damaged or destroyed through no fault of either party before risk of their loss has passed to the buyer. In such a case, the seller is excused from performance although the buyer will then have a specific opportunity to buy the damaged goods at a reduced price.

For a case to qualify under §2-613, it is not enough that the seller happened to identify particular goods for the buyer that end up being destroyed. The nature of the contract must be such that the contract requires for its performance certain goods that are identified when the contract is made: "I'll buy that painting"; "I'll sell you my Prince tennis racket." If a seller earmarks certain fungible goods for the buyer and they end up being destroyed, the seller's only hope for excuse must come from §2-615 rather than §2-613.

Once it is determined that §2-613 applies, that section sets out two possibilities. First, if the loss is "total," then the contract is avoided completely. Second, §2-613(b) says that if the loss is "partial," then "the buyer may nevertheless demand inspection and at his option either treat the contract as avoided or accept the goods with due allowance from the contract price for the deterioration." For example, suppose you contracted to sell your car to a buyer for $5,000 and your car suffered a $1,000 dent prior to your tendering the car to the buyer. Per §2-613(b), your buyer would have the option to either avoid the contract or to buy the car for $4,000 rather than $5,000, with the new price reflecting a "due allowance" for the dent.

The second common source of confusion for students in the excuse area is the functional consequence of a seller qualifying for excuse when goods are destroyed while in the seller's hands. Here one must distinguish between risk of loss, on the one hand, and excuse from performance on the other. If the seller in this case qualifies for excuse, that does not change the risk of loss: the seller still owned the goods at the time of destruction and therefore the seller suffered an economic loss to that extent.

Yet even though the seller still suffers the risk of loss, qualifying for excuse means that the seller will not suffer a still further loss: paying damages to the buyer for seller's delay or nonperformance. These damages to the buyer might include things like loss of a good bargain for buyer or consequential damages that the buyer suffers. These are all items that go beyond the cost of the destroyed goods themselves.

The UCC is not especially helpful in defining what circumstances might excuse a party from its performance obligations. The relevant sections, 2-613 to 2-616, speak strictly in terms of a seller's ability to be excused. Nevertheless, some courts have been willing to consider a buyer's defense of excuse in a sale of goods case, either by analogy to §2-615's "commercial impracticability" rules for sellers or simply by reference to the common law of excuse. Just like with sellers, however, there are very few cases in which buyers successfully use the defense of excuse.

Resources Investment Corp. v. Enron Corp.

669 F. Supp. 1038 (D. Colo. 1987)

KANE, J.

This is an action for breach of contract. . . .

Plaintiffs have instituted this action alleging non-performance of 32 contracts executed over a period of 18 years. These contracts concern gas reserves in three states — Texas, Oklahoma and Kansas. The contracts all contain terms creating what are known as "take-or-pay" obligations. Defendants undertook to purchase a specified quantity of gas each year. If in any year defendants did not accept delivery of the specified amount, the deficiency in purchases would nonetheless be paid for. Provision was made for gas paid for but not used to be carried forward to subsequent years.

Plaintiffs now allege defendants have failed since July, 1980 to comply with the terms of the contracts. They claim damages and seek a declaration that defendants are obligated in the future to perform the take or pay obligations.

Defendants respond asserting fourteen affirmative defenses and ten counterclaims. The matter is before me on plaintiffs' motion to dismiss the counterclaims and to strike all but the first, second, thirteenth and fourteenth affirmative defenses. This motion is granted in part. . . .

In their first, seventh, ninth and tenth counterclaims and fourth, sixth and eighth affirmative defenses defendants argue that events since the execution of the contracts excuse their breach of the contracts in question. This argument assumes a number of forms. Defendants seek to claim price-induced energy conservation, foreign commodity competition, abnormally warm weather during a number of the heating seasons, an economic recession, an unforeseeable change in the natural gas market and the enactment of regulatory state and federal statutes (first counterclaim) resulted in frustration of the underlying contracts (seventh counterclaim and fourth affirmative defense), rendered performance of these contracts impossible or commercially impracticable (ninth counterclaim and sixth affirmative defense) and resulted in suspension of the contracts through the occurrence of a *force majeure* (tenth counterclaim and eighth affirmative defense).

Dealing first with the frustration claim, although plaintiffs seek dismissal of all these claims in their entirety, they take issue in argument only with that element of the frustration defense dependent upon the changes in the natural gas market. In this they are correct. Here, as in United States of America v. Great Plains Gasification Associates, et al., 819 F.2d 831 (8th Cir. May 19, 1987), the parties clearly contemplated the likelihood of changing economic conditions, including alterations in fuel price levels "and such fluctuation was not the kind of completely unforeseeable event required to invoke the doctrine of frustration of purpose", *Great Plains* at p. 835. "This court will not hold a contract to be frustrated merely because of an increase in cost to one of the parties", Ross Industries v. M/V Gretke Oldendorff, 495 F. Supp. 195, 199-200 (E.D.Tex.1980). See also *Universal Resources*, 813 F.2d at 80. This immediately precludes defendants from relying on everything listed above except the warm weather and enactment of state and federal regulatory legislation. Insofar as the claims of frustration depend upon these factors listed in the first counterclaim, they shall stand.

Similar considerations govern the claim based upon impossibility and commercial impracticability. Failure to predict market patterns will not provide a basis for relief under these doctrines, Northern Indiana Public Service Co. v. Carbon County Coal Co., 799 F.2d 265, 276-278 (7th Cir. 1986) and see Sunflower Electric Co-op. v. Tomlinson Oil Company, 7 Kan. App. 2d 131, 638 P.2d 963, 969 (1981). Defendants cannot rely either upon the terms of section 2-615 of the Uniform Commercial Code. The commentary to this, again adopted by each of the states in question clearly asserts at note 4 "Increased cost alone does not excuse performance" and further makes clear that a rise or collapse in the market "is exactly the type of business risk which business contracts made at fixed prices are intended to cover". Insofar as based upon other grounds, however, I see no reason why this claim should not stand. . . .

In practice, buyers and sellers tend to write their own excuse provisions into their contracts, at least when the stakes are fairly high. Such provisions supersede the applicable UCC sections on the subject, although in many cases these "force majeure" clauses end up providing no more guidance on the excuse issue than the fuzzy UCC standard itself.

Consider the following force majeure clause in a long-term natural gas supply contract:

> Suspension for Event of Force Majeure. Except with regard to Buyer's or Seller's obligations to make payments due under this Agreement, in the event that either Party is rendered unable, wholly or in part, by an event of Force Majeure to carry out its obligations under this Agreement, it is agreed that upon such Party's giving notice and full particulars of such event of Force Majeure to the other Party as soon as reasonably possible, such notice to be confirmed in writing, then the obligations of the Party giving such notice, so far as they are affected by such event of Force Majeure, from its inception, shall be suspended during the continuance of any inability so caused. The cause of the Force Majeure event shall be remedied with all reasonable dispatch. Each party shall give the other Party notice of its ability again to perform after the event of Force Majeure has been remedied, and upon such notice, the Parties shall resume their performance as if the Force Majeure had not occurred.
>
> Definition of Force Majeure. In this Agreement the term force majeure ("Force Majeure") means any event which is not within the control of the Party claiming suspension and which by the exercise of due diligence such party could not have prevented and is unable to overcome. It is expressly agreed that neither Buyer's nor Seller's ability to obtain a more favorable price for Gas than the price for Gas purchased under this Agreement shall constitute an event of Force Majeure hereunder.
>
> Third Party Force Majeure. Force Majeure shall include any event of Force Majeure validly claimed by Buyer's Transporter or Seller's Transporter to the extent that such event affects Seller's ability to deliver or Buyer's ability to take delivery of the Gas. Force Majeure shall not include any other curtailment or interruption of service by pipelines or other third parties, including third party producers and suppliers.

The clause quoted above tracks in many respects the default rule that is given in U.C.C. §2-615. The gas supply clause first mentions the duty of the party claiming excuse to give notice to the other side. In §2-615(c), the seller who wishes to claim excuse is required to notify the buyer of any delay or non-delivery occasioned by a justifiable excuse.

U.C.C. §2-615(a) says that for the seller that qualifies for excuse, a delay in delivery (§2-615(a) as amended substitutes "performance" for "delivery") or a complete non-delivery is not a breach of the seller's duty under the contract. The gas supply clause, by comparison, speaks in terms of the excused party's performance being "suspended" during the continuance of the force majeure event.

The definition of force majeure that is provided in the contractual clause emphasizes the fact that the event was not within the control of the party claiming excuse. U.C.C. §2-615(a), by contrast, focuses on the foreseeability of the supervening event: that event must be "a contingency the non-occurrence of which was a basic assumption on which the contract was made." U.C.C. §2-615(a) also mentions specifically the seller's good-faith compliance with applicable governmental regulations as a permissible basis for excuse.

The gas supply clause explicitly notes that either party's ability to get a better price from some other party cannot be an event of force majeure. Although §2-615 itself does not address price fluctuations as a justification for non-performance, Official Comment 4 to 2-615 does, albeit in a very inconclusive way:

> Increased cost alone does not excuse performance unless the rise in cost is due to some unforeseen contingency which alters the essential nature of the performance.

Finally, note that the contractual force majeure clause specifically addresses the issue of supplier problems as a basis for excuse. Essentially, it says that if buyer's or seller's immediate carrier has a valid commercial impracticability defense, then so will buyer or seller. Official Comment 5 to §2-615 speaks to the issue of the seller's source of supply failing unexpectedly. That Comment suggests that unless both buyer and seller had reason to believe that a particular source of supply was to be seller's exclusive source of supply, then the seller should not be able to rely on the inability of a particular supplier as a basis for its own excuse. Thus, the clause as written seems to broaden the buyer's and seller's ability to claim excuse beyond that which they would get from the default rule of Article 2.

In practice, commercial buyers tend not to be as harsh as Comment 5 might suggest they could be when it comes to excusing their seller's inability to deliver goods due to the seller's supply problems. As an in-house lawyer for a Fortune 100 clothing retailer put it: "Whether or not we would let some vendor off the hook when they said that they couldn't supply to us because it was impossible would depend on whether they were somehow able to supply the same goods to one of our competitors. Also, it would depend on the length and nature of our relationship with them and whether we thought they were acting in good faith."

The general counsel for a computer hardware distributor echoed these sentiments as applied to his company's capacity as seller: "There will often be occasions in which we aren't able to fulfill an order, but our buyers will always believe us after they try to go to other manufacturers and suppliers only to realize that there really is nobody out there from whom they can get the item."

As the following case demonstrates, a buyer's willingness to accept supplier-related excuses from the seller may be significantly diminished when the buyer's dealings with the seller are not so much a long-term relationship as they are a one-shot proposition.

Alamance County Bd. of Educ. v. Bobby Murray Chevrolet
465 S.E.2d 306 (N.C. Ct. App. 1996)

JOHN, J.

Defendant Bobby Murray Chevrolet, Inc. ("Bobby Murray") appeals the trial court's entry of summary judgment in favor of plaintiffs, a number of North Carolina school boards ("plaintiffs"; "school boards"), on their respective claims for breach of contract. Defendant contends application of N.C.G.S. §25-2-615 (1995) regarding commercial impracticability operates under the facts of the case sub judice to excuse its performance under the contracts with plaintiffs. We disagree.

Pertinent factual and procedural information is as follows: Bobby Murray, a General Motors franchisee, received an invitation on or about 7 April 1989 to bid on approximately 1200 school bus chassis from the North Carolina Department of Administration's Division of Purchase and Contract ("the Division")....

After consulting with the GMC Truck Division ("GM Truck") of defendant General Motors Corporation ("GM") regarding prices and availability, Bobby Murray proposed to supply several different sizes of chassis at specified prices. The chassis were described as "Chevrolet" brand in the bid, but were to be manufactured by GM Truck....

On 26 July 1990, the Environmental Protection Agency (EPA) enacted Federal Emissions Standards changes for heavy duty diesel engines, thereby rendering the 8.2N diesel engine described in Bobby Murray's bid out of compliance with the regulations effective 1 January 1991....

On 10 August 1990, Bobby Murray received a message from GM through its Dealer Communication System ("DCS"), a computer network linking GM with its dealers, setting the final chassis buildout date at the week of 10 December 1990, but warning that estimated production dates could be pushed back due to a potential shortage of the requisite brand of automatic transmission (Allison automatic transmissions). On 24 August 1990, in a DCS message to Bobby Murray, GM reiterated that due to "the uncertainty of major component availability," no further orders for school bus chassis would be accepted.

On 30 November 1990, another DCS message to Bobby Murray indicated that the chassis orders placed between 1 August and 14 August 1990 would not be filled due to unavailability of Allison automatic transmissions. Bobby Murray contacted GMC Truck on or about 11 December 1990 and learned that none of the chassis were to be built prior to the end of December because the Allison transmissions would not be provided until February or March 1991. At that point, however, installation of the 8.2N diesel engines would be illegal in consequence of the modified EPA regulations. On or about 11 December 1990, Bobby Murray notified the Division the chassis could not be supplied.

On or about 23 January 1991, the Division informed Bobby Murray the chassis were being purchased from another source, and that it intended to hold Bobby Murray liable for any excess in cost. The substitute chassis were later obtained by plaintiffs, who subsequently filed suit against Bobby Murray for a total of $150,152.94, representing the difference between the bid prices and the actual amounts expended by plaintiffs in purchasing similar chassis. In its answer and third-party complaint against GM, Bobby Murray claimed, inter alia, that GM breached its contract with Bobby Murray to provide the chassis at issue and that Bobby Murray had merely been acting as an agent of GM. Thereafter, both the plaintiffs and GM filed motions for summary judgment.

Summary judgment was entered against Bobby Murray and in favor of plaintiffs 18 April 1994 by Judge F. Fetzer Mills in the amount of $150,152.94 plus interest at 8% per annum from 11 December 1990 until paid....

Bobby Murray asserts two arguments based upon [U.C.C. §2-615]. It contends the failure of GM to supply the bus chassis was "a contingency the nonoccurrence of which" was a basic assumption of the underlying contracts between Bobby Murray and plaintiffs. Second, Bobby Murray claims governmental regulation prohibiting the installation of the 8.2N engine after 1 January 1991 was an intervening factor which should operate as an excuse. . . .

In order to be excused under §2-615, a seller of goods must establish the following elements:

(1) performance has become "impracticable";
(2) the impracticability was due to the occurrence of some contingency which the parties expressly or impliedly agreed would discharge the promisor's duty to perform;
(3) the promisor did not assume the risk that the contingency would occur;
(4) the promisor seasonably notified the promisee of the delay in delivery or that delivery would not occur at all[.]

Utilizing the foregoing criteria as well as the official commentary to §2-615 and case law from other jurisdictions, we now consider Bobby Murray's arguments on appeal.

Initially, Bobby Murray contends an implied condition of its contract with plaintiffs was the ability of GM to manufacture and supply the ordered bus chassis. We agree that when an exclusive source of supply is specified in a contract or may be implied by circumstances to have been contemplated by the parties, failure of that source may excuse the promisor from performance. N.C.G.S. §25-2-615, Official Comment 5. However, neither contingency is reflected in the record herein.

Bobby Murray insists in its brief that "[a]ppellant disclosed in the bid that the chassis would be manufactured by Chevrolet and Plaintiff-Appellees had knowledge that Appellant's sole source of supply was General Motors." However, Bobby Murray points to no record evidence of such knowledge on the part of plaintiffs, and appears to rely solely upon its status as a GM franchisee to support its assertion.

By contrast, we note that the "General Contract Terms and Conditions" on Form TC-1, incorporated into the bid document, contain the following section entitled "MANUFACTURER'S NAMES":

Any manufacturers' names, trade names, brand names, information and/or catalog numbers used herein are for purpose(s) of description and establishing general quality levels. Such references are not intended to be restrictive and products of any manufacturer may be offered.

Further, no clause in the contract between plaintiffs and Bobby Murray conditioned the latter's performance on its ability to obtain bus chassis from its manufacturer. See William H. Henning & George I. Wallach, The Law of Sales Under the Uniform Commercial Code, ¶5.10[2], S5-4 (1994 Supplement) (generally, where seller fails to make contract with buyer contingent on adequate supply, courts reluctant to excuse seller). Plaintiffs aptly point to Richard M. Smith and Donald F. Clifford, Jr., North Carolina Practice, Uniform Commercial Code Forms Annotated, Vol. 1, §2-615, Form 3 (1968), which indicates a seller of goods may limit its liability by inclusion of the following "Single Source Clause":

It is expressly understood that the seller has available only one source, [name of single source], of [address], for the [name or identify the raw materials obtained by the seller from the single source] used by the seller in the manufacture of the goods for the buyer under this contract. In the event of any interference or cessation of the supply from the seller's source of supply, the seller shall be temporarily, proportionately, or permanently relieved of liability under this contract, depending upon whether the interruption of the source of supply is a temporary interruption, a reduced delivery of materials, or a permanent cessation of supply . . .

We next examine Bobby Murray's contention its performance should be excused in consequence of intervening governmental regulations. Generally, governmental regulations do not excuse performance under a contract where a party has assumed the risk of such regulation. The contract between the parties sub judice, in its "General Contract Terms and Conditions", Form TC-1, provided as follows:

GOVERNMENTAL RESTRICTIONS: In the event any Governmental restrictions may be imposed which would necessitate alteration of the material, quality, workmanship or performance of the items offered on this proposal prior to their delivery, it shall be the responsibility of the successful bidder to notify this Division at once, indicating in his letter the specific regulation which required such alterations. The State reserves the right to accept any such alterations, including any price adjustments occasioned thereby, or to cancel the contract.

Bobby Murray, by terms of the parties' agreement, accepted responsibility for keeping abreast of governmental regulations bearing upon the contract.

In addition, Bobby Murray was on notice 26 July 1990 that new emissions standards would preclude, effective 1 January 1991, production of bus chassis using the 8.2N engine specified in its bid. Nothing in the record indicates that this information was conveyed to plaintiffs. Bobby Murray was further notified 10 August 1990 that production dates could be pushed beyond December 1990. The record contains no evidence that Bobby Murray explored with plaintiffs, or otherwise, alternative methods of meeting its contractual obligations. Under these circumstances, equity dictates that excuse by governmental regulation be unavailable to Bobby Murray. . . .

In sum, taking the evidence presented in the light most favorable to Bobby Murray, we hold there exists no genuine issue of material fact as to plaintiffs' respective claims of breach of contract against Bobby Murray, and Bobby Murray's arguments to the contrary are unavailing. The trial court thus properly granted plaintiffs' summary judgment motion.

AFFIRMED.

In the *Bobby Murray* case above, the seller was claiming excuse as to its entire ability to perform. (The seller was also suing GM in a separate action for breach of GM's contract to provide the chassis to the seller.) Oftentimes when a seller has problems with obtaining adequate supply, those problems affect only a portion of seller's ability to perform. Or sometimes a seller will have several buyers under contract for the same type of goods but will have a capacity to satisfy only some of those buyers.

In cases where a seller that is claiming excuse under §2-615 has more than one buyer and has a limited capacity to perform, §2-615(b) requires that the seller must allocate production and delivery among its customers in a "fair and reasonable" manner. Section 2-615(b) does not give very much guidance on exactly what constitutes a fair and reasonable allocation; §2-615(b) does, however, provide that a seller may "include regular customers not then under contract as well as his own requirements for further manufacture."

The rules about a seller's allocation in times of shortage became significant in the mid-1970s when there were widespread shortages in the chemical industry. Professor James J. White surveyed 30 people at ten chemical and pharmaceutical companies in the summer of 1977 to determine whether companies that were faced with shortages actually followed the limited allocation guidance given by §2-615(b).

Professor White's first surprise in conducting these surveys was that none of the companies he surveyed had a formal written policy for handling allocations to buyers in a time of shortage. His second surprise was that the informal practices of these companies often deviated in significant and suspicious ways from a pro rata distribution among buyers that were under contract:

> The inarticulate premise of section 2-615 is that a seller should not be free in time of shortage to disregard his long term commitments and favor short term buyers who will pay higher prices. Although it is clear the seller may treat himself as a customer, section 2-615 forbids giving himself an additional, unjustified share. Rarely could one justify the addition of new customers under section 2-615 in time of shortage. Discussions with chemical company lawyers, before and during the interviewing process, disclosed that they were well aware of those problems. The written materials furnished by some lawyers indicates they were careful to point out those difficulties to their sellers. Nevertheless, I received a surprising number of admissions that sellers had engaged in non-pro rata distributions which almost certainly were in violation of section 2-615. In two cases, these admissions were made in the presence of company lawyers who were surprised and obviously discomfited by the admissions.
>
> James J. White, Contract Law in Modern Commercial Transactions, An Artifact of Twentieth Century Business Life?, 22 Washburn L.J. 1 (1982).

Professor White identified a number of questionable ways in which sellers deviated from a pro-rata distribution in their allocations during a time of shortage. First, most sellers admitted diverting a greater than pro-rata share to their internal uses. A second deviation from pro-rata distribution was that some sellers sold to new customers despite not fulfilling all of their obligations to customers that were already under contract. Third, most sellers admitted giving a greater than pro rata share to certain favored customers.

Ten years after Professor White's empirical study was published, Professor Russell Weintraub conducted a survey of general counsel at several dozen major U.S. companies that further shed light on the operation of the commercial excuse doctrine in actual practice. Russell J. Weintraub, A Survey of Contract Practice and Policy, 1992 Wis. L. Rev. 1. Among other topics, Professor Weintraub's survey focused on the willingness of companies to grant a customer's request for a price modification. What Professor Weintraub found was that 95 percent of the companies surveyed would at least sometimes grant such requests for deviations from the contractually agreed-to price. The most common reasons given for granting such requests were that the request was reasonable in the trade or that the customer was a long-time and valued customer.

In another part of Professor Weintraub's survey, he posed a hypothetical that involved a long-term supply contract and a price fluctuation that would put the seller out of business if the contract were enforced against the seller at the original price. Professor Weintraub's question to the general counsel in his survey was what outcome the law *ought to require* in this case.

The greatest percentage of respondents, 46 percent, said that the court should adjust the price so as to avoid ruinous loss to the seller but still give the buyer a significant savings over the current market. Some 35 percent of respondents said that the contract should be enforced according to its original terms even if that would put the seller out of business; 14 percent of respondents said that the seller should be completely excused from performing.

Perhaps "splitting the baby" and having a court re-write the contract is the most intuitively attractive approach to take in the case of a significant price fluctuation with a long-term contract. Nevertheless, American courts rarely believe that it is within their power to adjust the terms of a contract in a case where one party claims excuse on the basis of commercial impracticability.

Not all Western court systems share the American judiciary's aversion to re-writing the parties' contract:

> German law is perhaps the best example of a system that allows the courts to revise a contract based upon impossibility of performance of the existing contract. The origins of the current willingness of the German courts to revise contracts for the parties are found in the economic dislocation caused by World War I and the tremendous inflation that resulted. Initially, the contract revisions were limited to situations in which parties were simply unable to perform their monetary obligations because of the inflation in the German currency. Based upon the German concept of "good faith" found in the civil code and examination of gerschaftsgrundlage, "foundation of the transaction," German law has evolved today to the point where courts now will revise many types of contracts. Today, the standard doctrine of the German courts is to revise by court order those contracts "whose foundations have been destroyed by unexpected events or discoveries" rather than to rescind them.
>
> Daniel T. Ostas & Burt A. Leete, Economic Analysis of Law as a Guide to Post-Communist Legal Reforms: The Case of Hungarian Contract Law, Am. Bus. L.J., Feb. 1, 1995.

There are several possible criticisms to the German approach to contract reformulation. First, judges often lack a sense for the industry in which they will be re-writing the contract. Second, even if a judge knew something about a particular industry, it is doubtful that the judge would know much about the particular context in which the individual contract was negotiated. Finally, the specter of judges re-writing contracts would introduce an element of randomness or uncertainty into the prospect of contract enforcement that would likely complicate the contract formation process.

If judicial contract reformulation is not a viable approach to unexpected price increases, the only other approaches to the price-increase problem would seem to be: (1) never allow any price increase to be the basis for commercial excuse; or (2) allow only very significant price increases to be the basis for excuse.

The second possibility, allowing excuse but only for sufficiently severe price increases, has serious theoretical problems. For example, suppose that a judge determined that the appropriate threshold for allowing a seller's excuse is a 100 percent price increase. That would mean that in a case in which the price increased just 95 percent, the seller would end up assuming all of that risk. Yet in a case in which the price increased 105 percent, the seller would end up assuming none of that risk.

As a way around the theoretical problems suggested above, the judge could of course determine that the seller would be responsible for the first 100 percent price increase and that the buyer would be responsible for anything greater than that. The problem with this approach is that then the judge is merely re-writing the contract, a technique that was discussed and criticized earlier.

Perhaps the most powerful reason for a court to refuse to allow price fluctuation as a basis for excuse in a long-term contract is articulated by Professor Weintraub:

> Only three respondents [in his survey], one of whom sold only services, did not provide some contract protection against market shifts during the performance of long-term contracts. This response suggests that when a contract that is to be performed over a period of more than a year does not contain provisions protecting the parties from market changes, either the parties have acted imprudently when tested by industry standards or the price has taken account of the risk. In either circumstance, a frustration argument based solely on market shift, when there is no reasonable attempt to draft protection into the contract, should not be favorably received.
> Weintraub, 1992 Wis. L. Rev. at 51.

B.   Commercial Impracticability with Leases

The Article 2 rules on commercial impracticability were borrowed almost verbatim by the drafters of Article 2A. The lease analogue to §2-613 on casualty to identified goods is found in §2A-221, the lease version of §2-615 on excused performance is §2A-405, and Article 2A's provision covering the procedure on excused performance is found in §2A-406 rather than §2-616.

Probably the only difference in the lease sections from the comparable sales sections besides minor language changes "to reflect leasing practices and terminology" is the special treatment of nonconsumer finance lessees. Under Article 2, buyers that have contracts with sellers who are excused from performance are given the option to demand a partial performance from the seller at a reduced price. Under §2-613(b), the buyer can choose to accept damaged goods from the seller with "due allowance" against the original purchase price to reflect the damage; similarly, §2-616(1)(b) lets a buyer take its "available quota in substitution" where the seller is unable to make complete delivery.

Lessees under §§2A-221 and 2A-406 are generally given options that are comparable to those available to aggrieved buyers under Article 2. Those options, however, are not available to the nonconsumer finance lessee, whose only choices in these situations are to either terminate the contract or to go forward with the contract with no reduction in rent. U.C.C. §§2A-221(b), 2A-406(1)(b).

The reason that the finance lessee is not given the option to continue the lease contract, albeit at a reduced rent, is that such a right would be inconsistent with the policy behind the automatic "hell or high water clause" of §2A-407(1). Official Comment to §2A-406. That clause, as you may recall from Assignment 9, makes the nonconsumer finance lessee's promises "irrevocable and independent upon the lessee's acceptance of the goods." To give the nonconsumer finance lessee the right to insist on the lessor's partial performance with reduced rent would mean that the finance lessee's obligation to pay full rent upon acceptance would no longer be "irrevocable and independent."

If the nonconsumer finance lessee in the case of lessor excuse wants to call off the whole contract prior to acceptance, it still may do that. But if the nonconsumer finance lessee wants to go forward with the lease contract in a case where the lessor's original performance has been excused, the lessee's decision to accept partial performance will not obviate its usual obligation following acceptance to pay full rent to the finance lessor.

C.   Commercial Impracticability with International Sales

Article 79 of the CISG sets down the principles of commercial impracticability in international sales. Those principles are similar to the U.C.C. Article 2 approach in most respects, but are different in a couple of ways.

The gist of the UCC and CISG approaches to excuse is essentially the same: C.I.S.G. Article 79 excuses a party from performance where the inability was due "to an impediment beyond his control," as long as the impediment was unavoidable and the excused party could not reasonably have been expected to account for the impediment at the time of contract formation. This concept is much like what we see in U.C.C. §2-615(a). Another similarity between C.I.S.G. Article 79 and U.C.C. §2-615 is that both require the excused party to notify the other side of the basis for the excuse and of its effect on the excused party's ability to perform.

There are, however, differences between the CISG approach to commercial impracticability and the UCC approach. The CISG excuse rules are broader in two ways than the UCC's, but narrower in another way. The CISG excuse approach is broader in that it applies to both buyers and sellers rather than just to sellers as is true under U.C.C. §2-615. Second, the CISG excuse rules cover a party's failure to perform "any of his obligations," whereas U.C.C. §2-615(a) allows excuse only with respect to a seller's "[d]elay in delivery or nondelivery in whole or in part."

Practically speaking, neither of these differences should matter much. As we saw earlier in this assignment, most courts will allow buyers to claim excuse in the UCC context, either by assuming that §2-615 must also apply to buyers or by looking to the common law of excuse. Furthermore, there won't be many cases where breach of the seller's obligation is something other than either delay in delivery or non-delivery of the goods in whole or in part.

The one respect in which the CISG excuse approach is arguably stingier than U.C.C. §2-615 arises in the case where a seller's assumed source of supply fails to deliver to the seller, thereby preventing the seller from performing its obligations to the buyer. Under the UCC, Official Comment 5 to §2-615 suggests that as long as the seller's source of supply is assumed by both parties to be the seller's exclusive source, then the seller will be excused when the seller's source fails to deliver. Under C.I.S.G. Article 79(2), by contrast, a party like the seller above is only excused by the failure of a third-party source when the third-party source itself has a valid basis of excuse.

Thus, in a case where the seller's supplier fails to deliver to the seller for no valid reason, the CISG would not excuse the seller's obligation to its own buyer even if both the seller and the buyer assumed that the seller would be getting its goods from this particular supplier. Under the UCC, however, the seller would be off the hook due to its supplier's breach, and the buyer would have to settle for the seller "turning over to the buyer...his rights against the defaulting source of supply to the extent of the buyer's contract in relation to which excuse is being claimed." U.C.C. Official Comment 5 to §2-615.

D.   Commercial Impracticability with Real Estate

In the case of real estate sales, there is no "real estate-specific" doctrine of commercial impracticability that has either been codified in state statutes or that has developed in the common law. Instead, parties to a real estate sales contract that wish to claim excuse from their contractual obligations must look to the general common law of impossibility, which presumably was covered in your contracts course and which (you may recall) sounds a lot like U.C.C. §2-615.

Problem Set 11

11.1.   In your capacity as an associate at Dewey, Cheatem & Howe, you were just handed another case from one of your firm's most active clients, Lou's Used Cars for Less (from Problem 2.1). One of Lou's salespeople, "Slick Rick" Newman, explained to you that he had a contract to sell a used 1993 Cadillac convertible for $15,000 to a very demanding customer, Kristi Aiken. Kristi really wants this particular car because it was once driven by Ann Landers. After the customer paid the price and signed the contract, she arranged to pick up her Cadillac from Lou's the very next day. That evening there was a terrible hailstorm that damaged the body of the Cadillac so badly that it would cost $18,000 to repair it. The car now has a scrap value of $500. Kristi insisted that Lou's should pay for whatever body work it would take to put the car back in the condition it was when she signed the contract. Rick says he wants to know what his obligations and his options are with respect to Kristi's demands. U.C.C. §§2-613, 2-509(3), Official Comment 3 to §2-509.

11.2.   a.   Arlene Ledger, president of Heavy Metal, Inc. (from Problem 3.2), is back in your office. Heavy Metal, as you may recall, is a manufacturer of exercise equipment. Arlene explains to you that last month she agreed to fill a large order for a new local Gold's Gym franchise that is planning its grand opening late next week. The order to Gold's Gym is supposed to be delivered to them tomorrow. The problem, Arlene says, is that a heavy rain late last week caused a flood in the basement of Heavy Metal's building, which is where Arlene had been storing the exercise machines that were earmarked for Gold's Gym. Now those machines are rusty and unsuitable for delivery. As soon as Arlene discovered the problem she notified the president of Gold's Gym, Cory Haney. Cory, however, has told Arlene that Gold's Gym cannot afford to open late, given all of the advance publicity that she has generated so far about the grand opening. Arlene asks you whether she will be able to claim an excuse for a delay in delivering the equipment to Gold's Gym. Arlene says that it would take a few weeks for her company to manufacture replacement equipment for Gold's. Arlene admits that she can buy the same equipment immediately from another manufacturer but at a price that would cause her to lose money on her Gold's Gym contract. In reading the sales contract, you see that it says nothing either about force majeure or about source of supply. What do you tell Arlene? U.C.C. §§2-613, 2-615, Official Comment 5 to §2-615.

b.   Same facts as part a., except the reason for Arlene's failure to perform is that Arlene's steel supplier, which was designated in Arlene's contract with Gold's Gym as Arlene's exclusive source of steel for this contract, reneged on its contract with Arlene. The steel supplier's failure to deliver was due to the destruction of its plant by a fire that was negligently caused by several of its own employees. Will Arlene be excused from her obligations to Gold's Gym? U.C.C. §2-615, Official Comment 5 to §2-615. Would your answer change if this contract were governed by the CISG? C.I.S.G. Art. 79.

c.   Same facts as part a., except that there were 60 machines in the basement, only 30 of which were ruined by the flood. The Gold's Gym order was for 40 machines, but Big Jake's Gym across town also had an order from Heavy Metal for 20 machines for his grand opening on the same day. Arlene would like to allocate 20 of the 30 good machines to Jake's and just 10 to Gold's Gym for at least two reasons: first, because she thinks it is better to have at least one happy customer rather than no happy customers; and second, because she heard from her friends in the industry that Jake's will soon be opening up lots more local branches that she would love to supply with machines. Can Arlene justify her proposed allocation? U.C.C. §2-615(b).

d.   Same facts as part c., except Arlene chooses to allocate the good machines in a pro-rata fashion: Jake's gets 10 and Gold's gets 20. When Arlene gives Gold's Gym notice of the problem and of Gold's share of the good machines, Cory Haney of Gold's says, "We'll take the 20 you have for us right now, and we'll just wait to take the remaining 20 whenever you can make some new ones for us. We don't want to lose that great price we got."

Arlene has to admit that she did undersell herself when she originally made the contract with Gold's; Arlene's strong preference would be to give Cory her fair allocation of 20 machines and be finished for good with the Gold's contract. May Arlene condition her allocation of 20 machines to Gold's on Gold's agreeing to forget the rest of the contract? U.C.C. §§2-615, 2-616(1). Would your answer change if this contract were governed by the CISG? C.I.S.G. Art. 79.

11.3.   The President of Golden Dairy, Ben Able, comes to your office to discuss a long-term supply contract that he is negotiating with a new retirement center. The directors of the retirement center would like to enter into a five-year deal in which Golden Dairy supplies all of the milk for the center's cafeteria. The center would very much like to negotiate a set price for the milk, even if that fixed price increases during each of the five years of the contract. Ben is not averse to that approach, except he is concerned about his dairy's exposure if there is a significant milk shortage during the five-year contract period. Ben would like you to suggest some ways in which the contract could give price certainty to the retirement center, but still limit the dairy's risk in the event that milk prices go through the ceiling. In light of Ben's stated desire, consider the following three possibilities: (1) Completely fixed pricing; (2) Completely variable pricing that ties the price to some objective market measure; and (3) Variable pricing with specific price floors or ceilings. Which option would you recommend? Are there other options you can think of? Official Comments 4 and 8 to §2-615.

Assignment 12: Unconscionability

A. Unconscionability with Sales of Goods

The concept of unconscionability is one of the most amorphous features of the sales system. Like the doctrine of impossibility, unconscionability is a basis by which a party to an otherwise enforceable sales agreement may avoid that agreement. Whereas the impossibility excuse tends to be used most successfully by the commercial seller, the unconscionability excuse tends to be used by the consumer buyer.

Although the drafters of Article 2 chose to include a section on unconscionability, they were not able to agree upon a definition of the term. Section 2-302 itself, the basic unconscionability section, nowhere even pretends to define the concept. Official Comment 1 to §2-302 gives us some hints at a definition of unconscionability, but at times the Comment lapses into tautology: "the basic test is whether, in light of the commercial background and the commercial needs of the particular trade or case, the clauses involved are so one-sided as to be unconscionable under the circumstances existing at the time of the making of the contract..." Probably the best we get from Comment 1 in the way of definition is as follows: "the principle is one of the prevention of oppression and unfair surprise and not of the disturbance of allocation of risks because of superior bargaining power..."

When courts today are faced with claims of unconscionability, they tend to use the definition that was first set down in Williams v. Walker-Thomas Furniture, 350 F.2d 445 (D.C. Cir. 1965): "an absence of meaningful choice on the part of one of the parties together with contract terms which are unreasonably favorable to the other party." Professor Arthur Leff, in a famous article on the subject of unconscionability, echoed the *Walker-Thomas Furniture* definition by noting that a successful unconscionability defense should require that the defendant was the victim of both procedural unconscionability ("an absence of meaningful choice") as well as substantive unconscionability ("unreasonably favorable terms"). Arthur Leff, Unconscionability and the Code — The Emperor's New Clause, 115 U. Pa. L. Rev. 485 (1967). Although most courts today require both procedural and substantive unconscionability, some believe that either one or the other will suffice for a finding of unconscionability.

Although U.C.C. §2-302 does not bother to define unconscionability, that section does give us several useful pieces of information about how the doctrine of unconscionability is to operate in practice. First, §2-302(1) tells us that the unconscionability determination is a matter of law, thus taking this consumer-friendly defense out of the hands of what would likely be a consumer-friendly jury.

Second, §2-302(1) indicates that the appropriate time for measuring the unconscionability of a contract or a clause in the contract is when the contract was made rather than in light of later events. Therefore, the fact that a particular contract turned out to be, in retrospect, a terrible deal for the buyer should not be sufficient grounds for finding substantive unconscionability.

Third, and perhaps most significantly, §2-302(1) indicates the functional consequences of a judge finding that a contract or a clause in the contract was indeed unconscionable. A judge that makes a finding of unconscionability has three options: (1) refuse to enforce the contract at all; (2) enforce the remainder of the contract without the unconscionable clause; or (3) limit the application of any unconscionable clause in order to avoid an unconscionable result.

The final contribution that §2-302 makes to our understanding of unconscionability is to require in §2-302(2) that there be a hearing afforded to the parties that gives them "a reasonable opportunity to present evidence as to its commercial setting, purpose and effect to aid the court in making the [unconscionability] determination." The idea here seems to be that unconscionability is very much contextual and therefore the parties ought to have a specific opportunity to present evidence about context.

Although unconscionability claims rarely succeed, it is by no means a dead letter. As the following case demonstrates, the defense is most likely to be successful in a case involving the combination of an unsophisticated consumer buyer, on the one hand, and an aggressive seller with onerous terms, on the other. As is true in this case, it is not at all uncommon for the "substantive unconscionability" to consist in part of credit terms that strike the court as overreaching.

Maxwell v. Fidelity Financial Services, Inc.

907 P.2d 51 (Ariz. 1995)

FELDMAN, C.J.

... The facts, taken in the light most favorable to Maxwell, against whom summary judgment was granted, are that in December 1984, Elizabeth Maxwell and her then husband, Charles, were approached by Steve Lasica, a door-to-door salesman representing the now defunct National Solar Corporation ("National"). Lasica sold the Maxwells a solar home water heater for a total purchase price of $6,512. Although National was responsible for installation, the unit was never installed properly, never functioned properly, and was eventually declared a hazard, condemned, and ordered disconnected by the City of Phoenix. Thus, although the unit may have been intrinsically worthless, the question of unconscionability is determined as of the time the contract was made.

Financing for the purchase was accomplished through a loan to the Maxwells from Fidelity Financial Services, Inc. ("Fidelity"). The sale price was financed for a ten-year period at 19.5 percent interest, making the total cost nearly $15,000.

At the time of the transaction, Elizabeth Maxwell earned approximately $400 per month working part-time as a hotel maid and her husband earned approximately $1,800 per month working for the local paper. At Fidelity's request, an appraisal was made of the Maxwells' South Phoenix home, where they had resided for the preceding twelve years. The appraisal showed that the Maxwells lived in a modest neighborhood, that their 1,539 square foot home was in need of a significant amount of general repair and maintenance, and that its market value was approximately $40,000.

In connection with the financing transaction, Elizabeth Maxwell signed numerous documents, including a loan contract, a deed of trust, a truth-in-lending disclosure form, and a promissory note and security agreement. The effect of these documents was not only to secure the deferred purchase price with a lien on the merchandise sold, but also to place a lien on Maxwell's house as additional security for payment on the water heater contract. The forms and their terms were unambiguous and clearly indicated that Maxwell was placing a lien on her house ...

Despite the fact that the water heater was never installed or working properly, Maxwell made payments on it for approximately three and one-half years, reducing the deferred purchase balance to $5,733. In 1988, Maxwell approached Fidelity to borrow an additional $800 for purposes unrelated to the original loan. In making this second loan, Fidelity required Maxwell to again sign a bundle of documents essentially identical to those she signed in 1984. Instead of simply adding $800 to Maxwell's outstanding balance on the 1984 contract, Fidelity created a new contract that included the unpaid balance of $5,733 on the 1984 loan, a term life insurance charge of $313, as well as the new $800 loan. In all, Maxwell financed the sum of $6,976 with this second loan. The terms of this latest loan also included interest at 19.5 interest and payments for a period of six years, making Maxwell's new payments, including interest, total nearly $12,000. The combined amount Maxwell would pay under the two contracts for a non-functioning water heater and the additional $800 loan thus totals approximately $17,000, or nearly one-half the value of her home.

Maxwell continued to make payments until 1990, when she brought this declaratory judgment action seeking, inter alia, a declaration that the 1984 contract was unenforceable on the grounds that it was unconscionable. . . .

Many courts, perhaps a majority, have held that there must be some quantum of both procedural and substantive unconscionability to establish a claim, and take a balancing approach in applying them. Other courts have held that it is sufficient if either is shown. . . .

[W]e conclude that under A.R.S. §47-2302, a claim of unconscionability can be established with a showing of substantive unconscionability alone, especially in cases involving either price-cost disparity or limitation of remedies. If only procedural irregularities are present, it may be more appropriate to analyze the claims under the doctrines of fraud, misrepresentation, duress, and mistake, although such irregularities can make a case of procedural unconscionability. However, we leave for another day the questions involving the remedy for procedural unconscionability alone.

We conclude further that this case presents a question of at least substantive unconscionability to be decided by the trial court. From the face of it, we certainly cannot conclude that the contract as a whole is not unconscionable, given the $6,500 price of a water heater for a modest residence, payable at 19.5 percent interest, for a total time-payment price of $14,860.43. These facts present at least a question of grossly-excessive price, constituting substantive unconscionability. This contract is made even more harsh by its security terms, which, in the event of non-payment, permit Fidelity not only to repossess the water heater but fore-close on Maxwell's home. The apparent injustice and oppression in these security provisions not only may constitute substantive unconscionability but also may provide evidence of procedural unconscionability. . . .

Therefore, we vacate the court of appeals' opinion, reverse the trial court's judgment, and remand to the trial court for proceedings consistent with this opinion and A.R.S. §47-2302.

Justice Martone, one of the concurring judges in *Maxwell*, indicated in his concurring opinion that he would not have merely remanded the case to the trial court for an unconscionability determination; he would have held the contracts in question to be unconscionable as a matter of law:

> The facts as outlined by the majority lead to one inescapable conclusion: one of un-conscionability. If these contracts are not unconscionable as a matter of law, what contract would be? . . . On the undisputed facts, the commercial setting, purpose and effect of the contracts are tragically plain. The commercial setting: a "now defunct" entity took advantage of a limited person living on the margin of human existence. The purpose: to extract "$17,000" from a "hotel maid" who earned "$400 per month." The effect: to subject a marginal person to the risk of loss of her home, all for a hot water heater that "was never installed properly, [and] never functioned properly."

When dealing with such subjective concepts as unconscionability, it is hard to contend that the personal views of the judge will have nothing to do with the outcome in a particular case. For example, if you were representing a consumer defendant and were attempting to assert the unconscionability defense, consider whether it would matter to you whether your case were being decided by the likes of Justice Martone, whose concurrence is excerpted above, or instead by Judge Richard Posner of the Seventh Circuit Court of Appeals, who wrote an opinion on unconscionability that included the following observations:

> There can be no objection to using the one-sidedness of a transaction as evidence of deception, lack of agreement, or compulsion, none of which has been shown here. The problem with unconscionability as a legal doctrine comes in making sense out of lack of "meaningful choice" in a situation where the promisor was not deceived or compelled and really did agree to the provision that he contends was uncon-scionable. Suppose that for reasons unrelated to any conduct by the promisee the promisor has very restricted opportunities. Maybe he is so poor that he can be induced to sell the clothes off his back for a pittance, or is such a poor credit risk that he can be made (in the absence of usury laws) to pay an extraordinarily high interest rate to borrow money that he wants desperately. Does he have a "mean-ingful choice" in such circumstances? If not he may actually be made worse off by a rule of nonenforcement of hard bargains; for, knowing that a contract with him will not be enforced, merchants may be unwilling to buy his clothes or lend him money. Since the law of contracts cannot compel the making of contracts on terms favor-able to one party, but can only refuse to enforce contracts with unfavorable terms, it is not an institution well designed to rectify inequalities in wealth.
> Amoco Oil Co. v. Ashcraft, 791 F.2d 519, 522 (7th Cir. 1986).

Whether or not you buy into Judge Posner's world view generally, it is certainly the case that the unconscionability doctrine is not one that courts use lightly. If unconscionability were routinely allowed as a basis for escaping contract liability, the entire sales system would suffer from the effects of the uncertainty that ensued. Consider the following observations from a couple of scholars who were considering the role that excuse doctrines such as unconscionability ought to play in the Hungarian contracts system:

> Finally, contract law reduces transaction costs by assuring propriety in the contract negotiation process. Doctrines of fraud, undue influence, and unconscionability provide the paradigms. In a typical case, one party will assert that a contract reflects a voluntary agreement worthy of judicial enforcement, and the other party will seek to be excused from performing. The court must be alert to two forms of opportunism. Perhaps the first party has misled the second into signing a contract the second did not fully understand. On the other hand, the second party may simply be trying to excuse itself from its own bad bargain. Either type of opportunism increases the costs of conducting exchanges. A court following an economic logic will decide such cases so as to minimize the potential for these two types of costly opportunism, and thereby provide an incentive structure that encourages future parties to bargain more effectively.
>
> Ostas & Leete, Am. Bus. L.J., Feb. 1, 1995.

B.   Unconscionability with Leases

The unconscionability provision of Article 2A, U.C.C. §2A-108, essentially mimics most of the key provisions of §2-302, with a couple of additions that were modeled after the Uniform Consumer Credit Code. There are two major differences between §2-302 and §2A-108. First, §2A-108(2) refers to a lease contract or a clause in a lease contract being induced by "unconscionable conduct," and also grants relief where there is unconscionable conduct in the collection of a claim. Section 2-302 does not use the phrase "unconscionable conduct" nor does it regulate collections of claims.

The second key difference is §2A-108(4), which allows for the possibility of attorneys' fees to the prevailing consumer in an unconscionability action. Section 2A-108(4) also allows for the possibility of attorneys' fees being awarded against the consumer if the consumer's unconscionability action not only loses but is also deemed groundless by the court. Section 2-302 does not provide for attorneys' fees.

BMW Financial Services v. Smoke Rise Corp.
486 S.E.2d 629 (Ga. Ct. App. 1997)

POPE, P.J.

In this action to enforce an excess mileage provision in a motor vehicle lease, the plaintiff lessor appeals from the trial court's denial of its motion for summary judgment. Because there is no question of material fact regarding plaintiff's right to enforce the provision, we granted its application for interlocutory appeal and now reverse.

Defendant Smoke Rise Corporation leased a BMW automobile from plaintiff, and the corporation's president, defendant William Probst, personally guaranteed the lease. The lease, as modified in an extension agreement, provided that at the end of the lease term defendants could purchase the vehicle for $16,863.75, the estimated end-of-term wholesale value of the vehicle. It also provided that if defendants returned the vehicle rather than exercising their option to purchase it, they would have to pay a charge of "up to 15 cents" for each mile the vehicle had been driven in excess of 85,011 miles. Defendants chose not to purchase the vehicle and returned it with an odometer reading of 180,409 miles, but they refused to pay for the excess mileage. Plaintiff seeks $14,309.70, which is 15 cents times 95,398 (the difference between 180,409 and 85,011 miles), plus attorney fees.

In their defense, Smoke Rise and Probst contend the excess mileage provision is unconscionable because the $14,309.70 charge is almost as much as the projected end-of-term value of the car, and is considerably more than their experts say the actual value of the car is with 180,409 miles. Unconscionability is evaluated by looking at the circumstances at the time the contract was originally made, however, and determining whether, in light of the commercial needs of the particular trade involved, the agreement is one which " 'no sane man not operating under a delusion would make and . . . no honest man would take advantage of.' [Cits.]" R.L. Kimsey Cotton Co. v. Ferguson, 233 Ga. 962, 965-66(3), 214 S.E.2d 360 (1975); accord Zepp v. Mayor & Council of Athens, 180 Ga. App. 72, 79(2), 348 S.E.2d 673 (1986). See also OCGA §11-2A-108. In the context of a corporation leasing a luxury vehicle, an excess mileage charge of 15 cents a mile is not unreasonable and certainly does not shock the conscience. Such a charge serves the necessary commercial function of compensating for out-of-the-ordinary usage which will effect the residual value of the car. If at the end of the term defendants discovered the excess mileage charge was too high relative to the value of the car, they could have exercised their option to purchase it. But they did not do so, and now they cannot complain about a charge they agreed to pay.

Defendants' argument that the provision is too indefinite to enforce is also without merit. Plaintiff is entitled to anything up to 15 cents a mile, and that includes 15 cents a mile. And the fact that it was willing to take less earlier in the dispute does not undermine its right to 15 cents a mile.

The excess mileage provision is clear and unambiguous, and must be enforced as written. Accordingly, the trial court erred in denying plaintiff's motion for summary judgment.

JUDGMENT REVERSED.

C.   Unconscionability with International Sales

Although the CISG contains a provision governing commercial impracticability, it does not include any provision that recognizes a doctrine of unconscionability. This is perhaps not too surprising, since the UCC unconscionability section, 2-302, is generally applied with consumers and the CISG specifically excludes from its scope the sale of goods to consumers. C.I.S.G. Art. 2(a). Further, the CISG says that it does not concern itself with the "validity of the contract or of any of its provisions...." C.I.S.G. Art. 4(a). Thus, it would seem unlikely that a court would recognize an unconscionability argument raised in a sales contract covered by the CISG.

D. Unconscionability with Real Estate

There are no statutory or common-law unconscionability doctrines that are peculiar to real estate sales. On the other hand, the common law of contracts generally recognizes the concept of unconscionability, and therefore parties to real estate sales contracts should be able to avail themselves of that doctrine. The common-law doctrine is essentially the same as what we find in U.C.C. §2-302. There should not be much difference, then, between a party's ability to claim unconscionability in a sales of goods context and a party's ability to do so in a real estate context.

Problem Set 12

12.1. Lou's Used Cars is at it again. "Slick Rick" Newman comes to your office to ask you whether a recent customer of his can void a sale that Rick just entered into with her. A newly arrived immigrant, Mary Salvino, came into Lou's last week with the man for whom she cleans house, Paul Leske. Paul is a good friend of Rick's, so when Mary asked Paul where she might buy a used car, Paul suggested Rick. Mary paid $8,000 cash for a 1992 Honda Accord. That was the posted price, although most customers of Lou's Used Cars end up negotiating about 25 percent off of the posted price. Paul read Mary the sales contract before she signed it, since Mary still does not read English well. That contract included a prominent "AS IS" disclaimer on the face of it. The car broke down three days after Mary bought it, and now a legal aid lawyer is threatening to sue Lou's Used Cars unless Mary gets her money back. The legal aid lawyer said he will argue unconscionability. Will he likely succeed? U.C.C. §2-302.

12.2. a. Another of Lou's top salesman, "Fast Eddie" Turner, comes to see you to ask about a recent lease deal that he entered into with Joe Schafer. Joe, it turns out, had a horrible credit record and no other car dealer in town would sell or lease to him on credit. Joe, however, desperately wanted to lease a used purple Cadillac for "fun cruising." Fast Eddie found a '92 purple Cadillac on which he entered into a four-year lease with Joe for $500 per month, twice the rate that would be charged to a lessee with good credit. Further, Fast Eddie put in a special clause in which Joe granted Lou's a security interest in Joe's trailer home in the event that Joe missed a lease payment. The lease also included an acceleration clause, which would cause all future rent payments to accelerate in the event of a single missed payment. Three months into the lease, Joe missed two consecutive payments and is nowhere to be found. Now Fast Eddie wants to accelerate the lease payments and foreclose on Joe's trailer home (where Joe's wife and six hungry children are currently residing). Do you see any problem with Fast Eddie enforcing his lease contract as written? §2A-108. Does it make any difference here whether the contract with Joe is a true lease or a disguised sale?

b.   Same facts as part a., except Joe had a great credit rating. However, Joe did confide to Fast Eddie when he walked into Lou's that he (Joe) had never leased a car before. Because of this information, Fast Eddie offered Joe what Fast Eddie characterized as a "special first-time lessee's rate" of $750 per month for four years. What Fast Eddie did not tell Joe was that the typical rate for a Cadillac this old would be only $250 per month. Much to Eddie's amazement, Joe signed the lease with the "special rate," mumbling something about the fact that he just wasn't a "shop-around guy." If Joe learns later that he got a bum deal, should he be able to void it? §2A-108.

c.   Same facts as part b., except Joe wants to lease not a purple Cadillac, but a down-and-dirty used Ford Pinto for the sole purpose of having a car so that he can drive to work. For that deal, Fast Eddie's "first-time lessee's rate" of $150 is triple the usual $50 per month lease payment for a car like this. If Joe learns later that he got a bum deal, should he be able to void it? §2A-108.

d.   Same facts as part c., except Fast Eddie gives Joe the usual rate of $50 per month on the Ford Pinto. However, a couple of months after the lease is entered into, an investigative report in Consumer Digest suggests that the model of Pinto that Joe has leased contains a gas tank that explodes on impact. In light of that information, the market rate of a lease on a Pinto like Joe's drops to $5 per month. Joe wants to escape the contract on the grounds of unconscionability. May he? §2A-108.

Chapter 3.   Performance

Assignment 13: Closing the Sale with Sales of Goods

Unlike in the real estate context, where the "closing" is a significant event that marks the point when the property is now the buyer's problem rather than the seller's, the closing of a sale of personal property is perhaps as much a journey as it is a destination. The process of closing a sale of personal property begins with the buyer's physical receipt of the goods, but that is by no means the end of the story. The buyer is always given a reasonable opportunity to inspect the goods, before which time the buyer may "reject" the goods and put them back into the seller's hands.

Where the buyer's inspection time has passed and the buyer has accepted the goods, the buyer in many cases will have a second opportunity to unravel the transaction, a right known as revocation of acceptance. The buyer's rights to reject or revoke acceptance, however, are not without limit. If the seller can tender a satisfactory cure of the nonconformity, then the buyer must keep the cured goods and the deal will proceed.

Even after the time for revocation has passed, the buyer has not lost all rights of recourse against the seller when a later problem with the goods arises. For example, any suit for breach of warranty by the buyer is premised on the assumption that the buyer has in fact already accepted the goods. U.C.C. §2–714(1). Thus, the functional consequences for the buyer of acceptance under Article 2 are simply that the buyer has lost one particular remedy (rejection), the buyer now has the burden of proof on non-conformities, and the buyer must give timely notice of a breach in order to recover any damages from the seller.

In practice, buyers are not usually eager to reject shipments from sellers if there is any way in which the goods might be either repaired or replaced with conforming goods.

The general pattern in the sale of goods system is one in which sellers are fairly generous in responding to relatively late complaints by buyers, and buyers inturn are mostly amenable to seller's attempts to cure defects.

The law on the books says that there are three ways in which a buyer will be deemed to have "accepted" goods: (1) an affirmative signification that buyer has accepted; (2) a failure to reject the goods following a reasonable opportunity to inspect them; and (3) an act by the buyer that is inconsistent with the seller's ownership. U.C.C. §2–606(1).

Discussions with parties in the field, however, suggest that in practice neither buyers nor sellers are thinking very much about the point at which the buyer satisfies that standard. If buyers truly worried about the consequences of acceptance, they would probably spend more time and energy on their inspection procedures. Some larger buyers have fairly formal and detailed inspection procedures in which the goods are checked for nonconformities right as they come in. Most smaller manufacturers, however, will not conduct formal inspections of the raw materials they purchase. Their inspections, such as they are, occur when they begin to use those materials for producing the finished product.

As one officer for a medium-sized plastics manufacturer described it: "We don't bother to inspect material as it comes in other than to count and weigh it. Anything more would be too expensive. Instead we just wait until we use the stuff for production to see if there's any problem with it. There has never been an issue about us waiting too long to complain. Sometimes material might sit around for a few months before we begin using it for production, but if what the supplier sent isn't right, then they know they have to fix it no matter when we discover the problem."

The in-house counsel for a Fortune 200 manufacturer echoed those sentiments: "We take the position as buyer that it's never too late to complain about a nonconformity, even if it's not discovered until after it's in a finished product, as long as we're in a position to prove that the problem existed with the material that we received from the supplier. Our quality assurance program would catch most of those problems before that point, but it may not catch all of them all of the time."

Much like manufacturers who buy raw materials from suppliers, wholesalers that buy from manufacturers believe that even if they do not end up discovering a problem with the goods until they have been shipped to the retailers, it should still not be too late for the wholesaler to complain at that point to the manufacturers. Similarly, wholesalers generally are willing to remedy complaints about the goods they sell to retailers for as long as the goods sit on the shelf in the retailer's store. Not surprisingly, retailers have come to expect this accommodation.

As the in-house lawyer for one major retail buyer put it: "Our stores typically don't follow formal inspection procedures when they get the goods. On the other hand, we'll know pretty quickly if there's a problem either because we'll see it when we put clothes out on the shelf or our customers will let us know. Clothes have a relatively short shelf life, but even with a longer-shelf item like a TV, we've never had an issue about it being too late for us to send goods back to our seller on the grounds that the goods were nonconforming."

The typically long period that sellers give buyers to complain about problems with the goods seems to work well generally, although there certainly is occasional abuse. For example, an officer at a medium-sized furniture manufacturer was convinced that a few of his company's retail buyers would damage the goods themselves shortly before the 12-month warranty period expired as a way to return furniture that they had not been able to sell: "In some cases it was pretty obvious — the furniture had punctures in it but the box in which the furniture was shipped did not." Voicing that same desire to dispose of stale merchandise, a lawyer for a retail buyer admitted, "Generally, we'll give sellers a chance to cure, unless we've decided that the merchandise is a dog and we need a reason to justify giving it back to them."

A relatively new feature of the sales system is probably reducing even further the amount of time that buyers spend inspecting the goods when they receive them: supplier certification programs. With a supplier certification program, the buyer devotes a significant amount of time only at the beginning of a relationship with a new seller to determine whether that seller has adequate quality control mechanisms in place. Thus, at the beginning of a relationship, a buyer may perform these supplier certification procedures. Such procedures involve intensive inspections of shipments a buyer receives, and also visits to the seller's factory to insure the quality of the seller's entire operation. Once a particular supplier is certified by a buyer, the buyer will do only spot inspections of that supplier's deliveries.

Although in the vast majority of cases buyers and sellers are able to work out their differences concerning the quality of the goods shipped, there will be occasions in which one or both parties will choose to resort to the legal system. In those situations, the buyer is given a couple of goods-oriented remedies under Article 2: rejection and revocation. Rejection authorizes, but does not require, the buyer to cancel the contract with the seller.

Rejection must occur within a reasonable time after delivery of the goods, and it is ineffective unless the buyer seasonably notifies the seller. U.C.C. §2–602(1). If the buyer fails to state the specific grounds for rejection, then the buyer may lose the ability to use the unstated rejection grounds to justify the rejection. U.C.C. §2–605(1).

The buyer's right to reject technically exists whenever the goods "fail in any respect to conform to the contract," §2–601, but there are a number of exceptions to this so-called "perfect tender" rule. First, if the contract is an installment contract (one in which the contract contemplates a series of separate deliveries), then the buyer may only reject an installment "if the non-conformity substantially impairs the value of that installment and cannot be cured." U.C.C. §2–612(2) (§2–612(2) as amended has removed the phrase "and cannot be cured"). Second, the seller may have contractually limited the buyer's remedies, including the right to reject, thereby obligating the buyer to accept the seller's efforts to repair or replace defective parts.

Third, the seller's right to "cure" (about which more later) can often reverse a buyer's rejection. And finally, concepts such as usage of trade, course of dealing, and course of performance may allow the seller some "commercial leeways in performance" that will preclude the buyer's rejection of a less-than-perfect tender. Official Comment 2 to U.C.C. §2–106.

A buyer that does successfully reject the seller's delivery has very little responsibility for the rejected goods. Non-merchant buyers need merely to hold the goods with reasonable care for the seller for a time sufficient to enable the seller to remove them. U.C.C. §2–602(2)(b). Merchant buyers have a slightly heightened duty with respect to rejected goods. When the goods are in the buyer's possession and the seller has no agent at the place of rejection, the merchant buyer must follow any reasonable instruction of the seller as to resale, storage, or the like. U.C.C. §2–603(1). If the goods are perishable or will lose their value quickly, the buyer must sell them on the seller's behalf. U.C.C. §2–603(1).

When a buyer has accepted the goods, which typically occurs by default when the buyer fails to reject the goods following a reasonable opportunity to inspect, the buyer has lost its legal right to reject the goods. U.C.C. §2–607(2). This does not, however, mean that the buyer has lost all opportunity to put the goods back to the seller. Aside from the practical likelihood that the seller will accept return of defective goods even if it is untimely, the buyer also has the legal right in some cases to revoke acceptance.

The buyer who wishes to revoke acceptance must overcome a number of hurdles that the rejecting buyer does not. First, with a revocation the non-conformity must "substantially impair" the value of the goods to the buyer. U.C.C. §2–608(1). Second, the buyer may only revoke its acceptance in one of two circumstances: where the buyer reasonably believed that the problem with the goods would be cured and it has not been; and where the buyer was unaware of the problem because of seller's assurances or because the problem was too hard to discover before acceptance. U.C.C. §2–608(1).

The revoking buyer also must deal with some time limits. The revocation must occur within a reasonable time after the buyer actually discovered or should have discovered the grounds for the revocation, and it must also occur before there is any substantial change in the goods that was not caused by their own defects. U.C.C. §2–608(2). And, just as with rejection, revocation is not effective until the buyer notifies the seller of it. As the following case demonstrates, that standard gives a buyer that is strung along by the promises of a seller to make things right quite a long window in which to effectively revoke acceptance of the goods.

North American Lighting, Inc. v. Hopkins Manufacturing Corp.

37 F.3d 1253 (7th Cir. 1994)

CUDAHY, C.J.

Hopkins Manufacturing Corporation (Hopkins) appeals from a judgment for North American Lighting, Inc. (NAL) for refund of the partial purchase price of a headlight aiming system. The district court held that NAL had timely revoked its acceptance of the system and was not liable for the rental value of the system during the period prior to revocation. We affirm in part and reverse in part.

Hopkins produces headlight aiming systems and other photometric quality control devices. NAL produces headlamp assemblies for most major automobile manufacturers, including replaceable bulb headlamps. NAL needs to conform its replaceable bulb headlamps both to individual car maker specifications and, as required under the Motor Vehicle Safety Act, to industry standards. 15 U.S.C. §§1391–1426. Consistent with the Act, the Society of Automobile Engineers (SAE) promulgated standards which were then adopted by Federal Motor Vehicle Safety Standard No. 108 (Standard 108)....

... NAL decided to purchase a [Machine Vision System] (MVS), based largely on Hopkins' ongoing promises that software could be added to correct problems experienced with the prototype. The permanent MVS was purchased in June 1989 for an invoice price of $79,548, ten percent of which NAL withheld pending completion of the promised software upgrades — including upgrades to allow testing of the two checkpoints about which NAL's engineer had expressed some concern. The permanent system, which arrived in August 1989, did not perform well. One NAL employee testified that the permanent system sometimes gave readings that varied more than 100% from the known light intensity properties of certified headlamps. On other occasions, the MVS would give a "zero" reading even though a light beam was present. Over the course of 210 days, 74%

of the system's readings fell outside the required 10% accuracy range and the system failed to test at some of the checkpoints required by Standard 108....

Both parties concede that NAL accepted the MVS. They disagree, however, on whether NAL could subsequently revoke its acceptance. Hopkins argues that, since NAL knew the existing capabilities and shortcomings of the MVS, there was no "non-conformity" upon which NAL could base its revocation. Hopkins relies on §2–607(2) of Illinois' version of the Uniform Commercial Code (UCC), which provides:

> (2) Acceptance of goods by the buyer... if made with knowledge of a non-conformity cannot be revoked because of it unless the acceptance was on the reasonable assumption that the non-conformity would be seasonably cured....
>   810 ILCS 5/2–607(2).

Hopkins relies on this provision, as well as cases from this Circuit and from Illinois, to suggest that goods "conform" to the contract whenever the buyer knows or has reason to know that goods will not serve the function for which he bought them.

We, like the district court, reject this argument. The language of §2–607(2) itself makes clear that the buyer can "know" of a non-conformity without destroying his right to revoke acceptance. Id. (buyer with knowledge of non-conformity may revoke where he accepted "on the reasonable assumption that the non-conformity would be ... cured"). And the authorities Hopkins cites in support of its notion of "non-conformity" demonstrate, at most, that, where a buyer accepts goods with an understanding of what they can and cannot do, he cannot later undo the contract, under certain conditions resulting from his acceptance. The condition allegedly precluding revocation of acceptance here is that this preclusion is based solely on the fact that the goods, while performing to his expectations, nevertheless failed to serve the purpose for which the buyer claims to have bought the goods.

But NAL does not seek to revoke based solely on the failure of the MVS to test light intensities at the Standard 108 checkpoints. Rather, NAL seeks to revoke based on what it claims was its reasonable acceptance based on Hopkins' assurances that this failure would be rectified. Indeed, the notion that NAL fully understood the capabilities of the MVS defies common sense. There is no suggestion that NAL failed to make a good faith effort to comply with Standard 108. NAL has repeatedly demonstrated its willingness to comply with the standard: by sending its headlamps to a New York laboratory, by trying to obtain software upgrades on the MVS, by using its sensitive certification equipment to perform due care testing (and thereby risking damage to that equipment) and by attempting to procure a replacement for the MVS as soon as the promised upgrades failed to enable the system to perform the required tests. It would be nonsensical to conclude that NAL acquired the MVS and spent months trying to have it upgraded merely to have the opportunity to sue, as it did below, for a refund of the purchase price and related expenses.

More plausible is NAL's version of the facts, which the district court accepted. NAL claims not to have discovered the non-conformity of which it complains, as indicated by its reliance on [U.C.C.] subsection [2–608(1)(b)]. This is entirely consistent with the record. NAL does not deny that it knew that the MVS was originally intended to serve as an aiming device and it admits that its engineer and other employees expressed at least some doubt as to Hopkins' ability to adapt the MVS for NAL's purposes. As we have indicated, however, these facts do not preclude the existence of a non-conformity. Rather, it follows that the undiscovered non-conformity NAL claims was not that the unmodified MVS could not perform the Standard 108 tests but rather that the system would not perform the tests even after modifications.

We are left, then, with the question whether, given NAL's failure for an extended period to discover that the MVS could not be modified to suit its purposes, NAL properly revoked. Specifically, we must determine whether NAL could, relying on Hopkins' alleged assurances, revoke its acceptance even after it had used the MVS for several months. We conclude that NAL could revoke. . . .

A seller may be found to have given "assurances" within the meaning of §2–608 based on either circumstantial evidence or the seller's explicit language and, where the seller has assured the buyer explicitly, revocation will be available whether or not the seller made the assurances in bad faith. There is ample evidence in the record that Hopkins assured NAL that the MVS could be modified for the purpose of satisfying its due care obligations under Standard 108. Hopkins' written materials support this point, as does testimony by both NAL and Hopkins employees. As indicated, moreover, it would strain credulity to think that NAL would accept the device and expend resources over several months to modify it unless it had been persuaded, presumably by Hopkins, that the device could eventually suit its needs. Further, given the sophistication of the technology involved, the district court did not err in finding that NAL behaved reasonably in relying on Hopkins' assurances. While NAL's engineer and other employees may have alerted it to some limitations of the MVS, it stands to reason that NAL would defer to Hopkins regarding the capabilities of its products, especially since NAL does not itself make headlight aiming or photometric devices.

Whether the value of the product has been impaired is determined subjectively, from the buyer's perspective. Whether such impairment is "substantial," however, is determined based on the objective evidence. There can be little disagreement that NAL purchased the MVS to perform daily testing of its headlight assemblies at sixteen critical checkpoints, a function required of NAL by federal regulations. Nor is there any dispute that the MVS was never able to carry out this function. Indeed, the MVS eventually stopped working altogether. Thus, there was "substantial impairment" of the device's value within the meaning of §2–608.

Section 1–204(2) [1–302(b) as amended] of the U.C.C. indicates that what is a "reasonable time" for revocation depends on the nature, purpose and circumstances of the transaction. In particular, the period where revocation is allowable may be extended where the seller gives continuous assurances, and where the seller fails, after repeated attempts, to repair defects of which the buyer complains. Here, there is substantial evidence that Hopkins made express written and oral assurances, with respect to both the loaned prototype MVS and the permanent system that arrived in August, 1989. These assurances — and Hopkins' failure to make good on them — were sufficient both to cause concern at Hopkins and to induce NAL to continue working with Hopkins to upgrade the system. NAL's responsiveness to such inducement was reasonable for much the same reason that NAL's acceptance of the system was reasonable: NAL could reasonably defer to Hopkins' superior expertise with the device's technology until the promised software upgrades failed to make the device viable. That NAL did not seek to revoke during the several months between delivery of the permanent system and the upgrades attests, perhaps, to NAL's desperation to find a more economical method of satisfying its due care obligations, but such delay did not make NAL's revocation untimely given Hopkins' repeated assurances and the other facts of this case. We reject Hopkins' argument that NAL could not revoke simply because it used the MVS. Consistent with the Code, Illinois courts have rejected the notion that any use by the buyer constitutes an irrevocable acceptance by the buyer, "hav[ing] tempered [this] absolute rule of acceptance with a consideration for the reasonableness of the buyer's conduct." Alden Press, Inc. v. Block & Co., 527 N.E.2d 489, 497 (Ill. App. 1988). It would be inequitable to require NAL to pay for the MVS in full if it reasonably delayed revocation in order to allow Hopkins to make good on its promises. Indeed, given the clear evidence that Hopkins assured NAL that the system could be adapted for due care purposes, Hopkins' product use argument comes dangerously close to suggesting a rule that would allow sellers to "lock in" purchasers of goods by promising them the moon — only to bring them back to earth when they attempted to revoke the acceptance that they were persuaded to give because of their failure to understand fully a substantial defect. Thus, there was timely revocation of acceptance here.

With respect to the [MVS,] we conclude that some compensation is due Hopkins. As indicated, where revocation of acceptance has been established, the aggrieved buyer's remedies are the same as those afforded a buyer who has rejected the goods. These remedies are set out at U.C.C. §2–711, which does not specifically provide for an offset for beneficial use prior to revocation of acceptance. However, the Code does state: "Unless displaced by the particular provisions of this Act, the principles of law and equity . . . shall supplement its provisions." U.C.C. §1–103. Such supplementary principles include quantum meruit recovery. In order to be successful on a theory of quantum meruit under Illinois law, a party must prove performance of the services, reasonable value of the services, and the receipt by the defendant from the plaintiff of a benefit which it would be unjust for him to retain without paying the complaining party.

As indicated, there is substantial evidence that NAL knew that there were problems in adapting the MVS to enable NAL to satisfy its due care obligations. Thus, even though it would appear that NAL was not aware that the MVS would not suit its needs even after the promised software upgrades were finally made, it seems equally clear that NAL purchased the device knowing that its performance would be, at least initially, suboptimal. That NAL continued to use the device instead of finding alternative methods of testing the bulbs — but, as we have indicated, there is no indication of bad faith on NAL's part — indicates that the device served some beneficial use. The fairness of this result is supported by the fact that NAL, at the time of its revocation, itself proposed that NAL pay rental fees through July, 1990 in exchange for a refund of the portion of the purchase price already paid. Further, Hopkins presented testimony that another of Hopkins' devices with similar capabilities was on lease for $3,300 per month and that, based on this figure and the amount that NAL was spending to send its assemblies to the New York laboratory, a reasonable rental figure for the MVS would be $1,600 per month. These facts, while sparse, seem to satisfy the general requirements for quantum meruit recovery. Thus, we remand to the district court to consider — based on these facts and whatever other evidence the district court, in its discretion, deems appropriate — what rental value would be reasonable compensation for NAL's use of the permanent MVS from the time of its arrival in August, 1989 until the time of NAL's timely revocation some months later.

One revocation issue that the court in *North American Lighting* did not have to discuss is whether a seller has a right to cure in the case of a revoking buyer. Suppose, for example, that a buyer ordered a machine, used it for awhile, and then discovered that the machine had a defect that could not have been discovered until the machine had been used for at least a short time.

At this point, it would probably be too late for the buyer to reject the machine, since the buyer has taken acts inconsistent with the seller's ownership of the machine and a reasonable time for inspection has seemingly passed. Nevertheless, the buyer could argue that it still had a right to revoke its acceptance under U.C.C. §2–608(1)(b), since the buyer could argue that it accepted the goods without discovery of the non-conformity because of the difficulty of its discovery before acceptance.

Suppose that in response to the buyer's announcement that it intended to revoke its acceptance, the seller told the buyer that it wished to cure the problem by repairing the machine. Would the buyer in that case be obligated to accept the seller's cure attempt, or could the buyer decide that it simply wanted to undo the transaction for good?

Berning v. Drumwright

832 P.2d 1138 (Idaho App. 1992)

Silak, J.

This appeal arises from a dispute between a mechanic, Bill Drumwright, and automobile owners Annet and Marvin Berning. The central issue on appeal is whether the magistrate correctly determined the amount of damages Drumwright owed to the Bernings. We also address whether the magistrate correctly concluded that the Bernings had given adequate notice of their intention to revoke the contract. We affirm the judgment of the magistrate.

The essential facts are as follows. The Bernings live in the Virgin Islands, spend part of the summer in north Idaho, and own a Chevrolet van which they keep in Idaho. The van was in good condition and had been driven only 40,000 miles. In the late spring of 1988, they discovered that the van had water in the oil. They were unable to start the engine and had the van towed to Bill Drumwright, a local mechanic, for repairs. Drumwright was unable to start the engine and told the Bernings that he would have to remove the engine to determine what the problem was. On June 29 or 30, Drumwright gave the Bernings three options: (1) to have the engine rebuilt at a cost of $1,200; (2) to have Drumwright work on the engine at an hourly rate without a price estimate; and (3) to find a second-hand engine that could be put in the van. The Bernings decided to think over their options.

The next day, Drumwright called the Bernings and told them that he had located a second-hand engine which had good compression and that he could put it in their vehicle for around $700 to $800. The Bernings decided to have Drumwright install the second-hand engine. Marvin paid Drumwright a $400 deposit in travelers(checks and asked him to try to get the work done quickly because the van was the main source of transportation for the family.

The work on the van was not completed until early August. Marvin Berning had by then returned to the Virgin Islands. On August 3rd, Annet Berning called her husband to tell him that the van would be ready the next day, but that, in order to check the oil, they would have to access the dipstick from the passenger compartment. To do this, they would have to remove the firewall, the radio and other equipment. Marvin Berning called Drumwright from the Virgin Islands and told him that this arrangement would be unacceptable. During their conversation, Drumwright told Marvin that the engine was for an older model which had the dipstick in a different place. Later, during the trial before the magistrate, Drumwright testified that the engine was not even a van engine but was, in fact, a truck engine.

After their August, 1988, conversation, Drumwright tried to fix the problem with the dipstick by placing a copper tube which could be used to access the dipstick from the front of the engine. Annet Berning picked up the car after the work was finished and paid Drumwright an additional $700. The engine smoked, overheated, and appeared to be burning oil. She took the van back to Drumwright who told her that it was customary for a new engine to use more oil at first. The van continued to use oil at the rate of one quart every forty to fifty miles. Two days after she picked up the van, Annet Berning tried to drive the van on a short trip. The van overheated and stopped four times in four miles. She called Drumwright who came to get the van and performed additional repairs. The van stopped overheating but continued to consume oil. The Bernings decided to take the van to a different garage and have the engine replaced. Because the engine that Drumwright had put in the car was not the correct engine for the vehicle, the garage did not try to repair it. The Bernings had a newly rebuilt engine and a new manifold installed; they also had the carburetor rebuilt. They paid $1,951.79 for the additional work.

The Bernings filed a small claims complaint on May 15, 1989, alleging that Drumwright "performed grossly incompetent auto repair." Though Drumwright now contends that he never gave the Bernings the final bill for his work and that the Bernings never paid him for the used engine he installed, he did not file an opposing action and made no claim for monetary damages. The small claims court held a trial in July, 1989, and entered judgment in favor of the Bernings for $1,100 minus a deposit on the second-hand engine of $250. The court also awarded the Bernings costs, filing fees, and statutory attorney fees in the amount of $25. Drumwright appealed the judgment. On appeal, Drumwright claimed that he should be paid for his labor for installing the new engine. Drumwright also claimed that the Bernings should pay for the used engine which was installed in their van. Drumwright did not raise any defenses to the breach of warranty action, nor did he raise the issue of lack of notice of revocation of the contract.

In July, 1990, the magistrate division held a trial de novo. The magistrate ruled that a contract existed between the Bernings and Drumwright for the sale and installation of the second-hand engine. The magistrate found that Drumwright was a merchant, and that the sale was subject to the Uniform Commercial Code (UCC). The magistrate held that the engine was defective. Applying the relevant sections of the UCC, the magistrate determined that, because the engine was defective, Drumwright had breached the implied warranty of merchantability and the implied warranty of fitness for a particular purpose. The magistrate also found that the Bernings had a duty to mitigate their damages. The magistrate held that the Bernings had performed that duty in part by trying to fix the engine; however, the magistrate also concluded that the Bernings had a duty to return the second-hand engine to Drumwright. The magistrate awarded the Bernings $1,100 in damages, but deducted a deposit for the second-hand engine in the amount of $250. The court also awarded costs and statutory attorney fees.

Drumwright appealed to the district court. The district court affirmed the magistrate's decision. Drumwright then filed an appeal which was assigned to this Court. On this appeal, Drumwright argues that the magistrate erred by refusing to accept testimony regarding the value of the second-hand engine and the rental value for the use of the second-hand engine based on the number of miles it had been driven before being removed. He also argues that the magistrate erred by failing to credit him with the value of the labor spent removing the original engine and trying to repair it. He further claims that the magistrate erred by failing to require that the Bernings return the second-hand engine. Finally, he argues that the magistrate erred by entering judgment in favor of the Bernings where they failed to timely revoke acceptance of the defective second-hand engine. . . .

The UCC allows a buyer to revoke acceptance if a product's "non-conformity substantially impairs its value to him" and if the buyer accepted it "on the reasonable assumption that its nonconformity would be cured and it has not been seasonably cured." I.C. §28-2-608(1); Lee v. Peterson, 110 Idaho 601, 603, 716 P.2d 1373, 1375 (Ct. App. 1986). The magistrate made no specific determination that the Bernings revoked acceptance; however, the record clearly shows that the defect in the engine substantially impaired its value and that the Bernings retained possession of it while reasonably assuming that Drumwright would repair the engine. Based on these facts, we hold that the Bernings revoked their acceptance of the second-hand engine. See Pope v. Intermountain Gas Co., 103 Idaho 217, 225, 646 P.2d 988, 996 (1982) (appellate court may disregard absence of finding by trial court where record is clear and yields obvious answer).

Under I.C. §28-2-711, a buyer who justifiably revokes his acceptance of goods may cancel the purchase and recover as much of the purchase price as had been paid. Lee, 110 Idaho at 604, 716 P.2d at 719. In Lee, the buyer of a defective copy machine revoked his acceptance of the machine because it breached the implied warranty of merchantability. This Court found no error in the remedy selected by the lower court — return of the machine, and recovery of the purchase price and cost of chemicals. In the present case, the Bernings revoked the "whole contract" which included not only the cost of the second-hand engine, but also the cost of removing the original engine and installing the second-hand engine.

Drumwright further claims that the magistrate erred by failing to require that the Bernings return the second-hand engine. As noted above, I.C. §28-2-711 gives a buyer who has justifiably revoked acceptance of goods a security interest in those goods and allows the buyer to retain the goods and resell them. In this case, the Bernings retained the second-hand engine, but did not resell it. The deposit for the engine, which Drumwright claimed was $250, was offset against the damages which were awarded to the Bernings following the trial. Based on this fact, we find no error in the remedy selected by the magistrate because

Drumwright is in no worse position than he would have been if the Bernings had resold the engine and deducted the resale price from their damages pursuant to I.C. §28–2–706.

Drumwright has also loosely framed an issue regarding the Bernings' refusal to allow him to correct the problems with the engine. A right to cure is relevant only when a buyer has rejected goods prior to a formal acceptance; the UCC does not allow a seller the right to cure defects following a buyer's acceptance of the goods. Jensen v. Seigel Mobile Homes Group, 105 Idaho 189, 193, 668 P.2d 65, 69 (1983). In this case, the Bernings had already accepted the second-hand engine; therefore, Drumwright had no right to cure. Though the Bernings gave Drumwright two opportunities to repair the engine, he was unable to repair it to their satisfaction. The Bernings were under no obligation to give Drumwright unlimited opportunities to fix the problem. See Jensen, 105 Idaho at 194, 668 P.2d at 70 (though buyer may notify seller of defects and attempt to obtain cures therefor, buyer thereby gives seller right to cure only until buyer finds seller(s efforts to be unsatisfactory).

Drumwright's final argument is that he did not receive timely notice of the Bernings(intent to revoke their acceptance of the contract. Drumwright did not raise this argument below and is thus foreclosed from raising it on appeal. . . .

Pre-amended U.C.C. §2–508 is clear that where the buyer *rejects* the seller's tender, the buyer must allow the seller an opportunity to cure where either 1.) the time for performance has not yet expired (i.e., if there was a set delivery deadline and the seller delivered early) or 2.) the seller had reasonable grounds to believe that its rejected tender would be acceptable to the buyer. What pre-amended U.C.C. §2–508 is not clear on is whether the revoking buyer, as opposed to the rejecting buyer, has the same responsibility to give the seller a chance to cure. Amended §2–508 settles a split in the case law by granting sellers nearly the same rights to cure in a revocation situation as they have in the case of a rejection. With consumer buyers, however, sellers do not have the right to cure following revocation under §2–508 as amended.

A common point of contention in cure situations is determining what should count as an acceptable cure, and who should define what that is. Explains an officer for a medium-sized furniture manufacturer: "If furniture has minor defects, we authorize the retailers who have repair capabilities to repair the furniture themselves and then bill us according to an hourly rate that we have agreed to in advance. But we have one retailer who simply refuses to accept repair as a cure. For that retailer, we always have to send brand-new furniture. Most of the other buyers will accept repair as a valid cure as long as the defect is only minor."

Oftentimes the dynamics of the cure details will come down to who has more leverage as between buyer and seller. And while leverage will be a function of a number of things, one factor that can affect leverage in the cure setting is the schedule for buyer's payment of the purchase price. One institutional buyer noted that he specifically arranges for a holdback just for the purposes of retaining leverage in cure situations: "I like to set up a payment system that holds back money until we've had a chance to test the machine that we've purchased, particularly an expensive piece of lab equipment. I might pay a quarter of the purchase price at the signing of the contract, a quarter more at delivery, and then hold back the other half until the researcher has had an adequate opportunity to really test the machine."

One argument that buyers sometimes make is known as the "Shaken Faith Doctrine." The Shaken Faith Doctrine was first used in Zabriskie Chevrolet, Inc. v. Smith, 240 A.2d 195 (N.J. 1968), where an auto dealer attempted to cure the buyers' defective new car by replacing the transmission in that very car rather than giving the buyers a new car. The court in *Zabriskie* said that the cure attempt was ineffective because the nature of the defect was such that the buyers' faith in that particular car was legitimately shaken. Similarly, the buyers in *Bowen* might have said that having bought one heating and cooling system from this dealer, their faith was so shaken in the trustworthiness of the dealer that they should not have to accept a substitute system from the same dealer.

Another way to view the "Shaken Faith" case is this: The case does not really create a new doctrine after all. Instead, it simply makes the point that the seller cannot unilaterally define what constitutes an acceptable cure under §2–508. Therefore, the cure that is tendered must be at least enough to satisfy a reasonable person in the buyer's position.

Problem Set 13

13.1. a. Kim McNicholas orders a home computer from Computers By Mail, Inc. When the computer arrives, she takes it out of the box and uses it for about 10 minutes before she discovers that the left side of the screen's frame is cracked. At this point, has Kim accepted the computer? U.C.C. §2–606, Official Comment 4 to §2–606.

b. Same facts as part a., except that as soon as Kim takes the computer out of the box, she drills several holes in its plastic base and screws it onto her desk. Then she uses it for about 10 minutes before she discovers that the left side of the screen's frame is cracked. At this point, has Kim accepted the computer? U.C.C. §2–606.

c. Same facts as part a., except that Kim sees the crack in the frame as soon as she takes the computer out of the box. Nevertheless, she proceeds to use the computer for 10 minutes. At this point, has Kim accepted the computer? U.C.C. §2–606.

d. Same facts as part a., except that Kim sees the crack in the frame as soon as she takes the computer out of the box. She immediately calls the seller, Computers by Mail, and tells them that she is rejecting the computer. Nevertheless, she proceeds to use the computer for 10 minutes. At this point, has Kim accepted the computer? U.C.C. §2–606.

e. Same facts as part a., except that Kim's contract with Computers by Mail is for a series of four computers, one to be shipped at the beginning of each month. When the first computer arrives, Kim takes it out of the box and immediately notices a crack on the left side of the screen's frame. May Kim reject this installment? May the seller cure the defective installment? May Kim cancel the remainder of the contract? U.C.C. §§2–612, 2–508; cf. §2–601.

f. Same facts as part a., except that Kim's contract with Computers by Mail is for a series of four computers, one to be shipped at the beginning of each month. When the first computer arrives, Kim takes it out of the box, plugs it in, and the computer explodes. Kim is frightened, but she is not injured by the blast. May Kim reject this installment? May the seller cure the defective installment? May Kim cancel the remainder of the contract? U.C.C. §§2–612, 2–508.

g. As a general proposition, once Kim accepts the goods has she precluded herself from any remedy for the computer's defects? U.C.C. §§2–607(2) and (3)(a), 2–608(1).

13.2. Arlene Ledger, president of Heavy Metal, Inc. (from Problem 3.2), has come to your office with what she describes as an "ethical dilemma." She also wonders whether her problem has legal implications. Last week Arlene received a shipment of raw steel from a new steel supplier, Nielson Steel. In conducting a spot inspection, Arlene discovered that the steel had a slight impurity that would make it somewhat more expensive for Heavy Metal to use the steel in manufacturing the circular weight plates that Heavy Metal sold to sporting goods stores. Accordingly, Arlene immediately called Nielson and told its president that Heavy Metal was rejecting the ten-ton shipment of raw steel. Heavy Metal kept possession of the steel while it waited for Nielson to pick it up. Two days ago, the price of raw steel suddenly shot up and now Arlene wants to know whether her company, which still has the steel, could simply begin using it in production and thereby effectively "un-reject" the goods so as to take advantage of what now seems like a good deal. Arlene also tells you that Nielson is on the verge of filing for bankruptcy, so that the likelihood is slim that Arlene could recover damages from Nielson. What do you advise Arlene? U.C.C. §2–606(1), Official Comment 4 to §2–606, §2–602(2)(a), Official Comment 2 to §2–601.

13.3. Lou from Lou's Used Cars (Problem 2.1) has come to you to talk about "quality control" problems that he has been having with his used-car business. When Lou obtains a fresh "pre-owned" vehicle, his company's current procedure is to spend about six or seven hours of a mechanic's time inspecting the car for any major problems. "Do you know what mechanics cost these days?" Lou asks you rhetorically. Lou's brilliant idea for saving money is to just wax and shine the cars as they come in, drive them around for 10 minutes, and then put them on the lot to sell. Lou explains that with the money he saves from mechanic inspection time, he will be more than happy to cure any problems that dissatisfied customers bring to him after they have owned the car for a time (these cars are not being sold "as is"). "I just need to know that I'll still have the right to fix the car, and that no buyer can kill the deal and get their money back just because of some problem we didn't discover," Lou tells you in earnest. What do you advise Lou about his new plan? U.C.C. §2–508.

13.4. Your firm does occasional work for a local small college, Mammoth College, that has a full Division III sports program. Mammoth's athletic director, Shelly Stone, comes to see you about her school's purchase of a used bus last week for the purpose of transporting school teams to away games. Mammoth purchased the bus from Big Al's, a used-bus dealer in town, who promised in writing that the bus did not burn oil. After paying for the bus, the school learned that contrary to Big Al's warranty the bus was a true oil-guzzler:

on its first team trip, a mere 100 miles away, the bus consumed six quarts of oil. Shelly now has four questions about the bus purchase: (1) May the school avoid its deal with Big Al's and get its money back?; (2) If so, can the school keep possession of the bus until Big Al's gives the school its money back?; (3) Even though Shelly wants to undo the deal, she would desperately like to use the bus one last time this weekend, oil problems and all, for her school's conference track meet that is about 150 miles away. She wants to know whether this final use would hurt her school's ability to give the bus back to Big Al's and undo the deal; and (4) Shelly wants to know whether her school would have to accept an offer by Big Al's, should he make one, to fix the oil-guzzling problem as an alternative to avoiding the whole deal. What do you advise? U.C.C. §§2–508, 2–602, 2–606, 2–608, 2–711(3).

13.5. Hi Tech Corp. was a Chicago retailer in the business of selling office computers. Danker & Kodner was a 10-lawyer partnership that was also located in Chicago. Don Danker, managing partner of the law firm, negotiated a contract with Hi Tech for the purchase of six computers. The contract indicated that Hi Tech would deliver the six machines to the Danker firm for a total price of $16,000. The contract said that the computers would be installed at no extra charge. On the date of performance, the six computers arrived to the law firm's offices and Don paid the agreed purchase price. When Don called Hi Tech president Harold Scott to ask about installation, Harold said, "We'll get to it eventually." Disgusted, Don told Gretchen Giltner, a new associate who was the office computer whiz, to try to install the computers. Gretchen gave it her best shot, but during the next week both lawyers and secretaries at Danker experienced assorted difficulties with the computers. An angry Don once again called Harold, this time telling him that he was going to send back all of the computers and demand a refund of the purchase price. In response, Harold sent out one of his technicians, who concluded that the computers themselves each had a slight keyboard problem. The technician added, however, that almost all of the difficulties Danker workers had experienced the previous week were due to a faulty installation job. Discuss whether Danker & Kodner has the right at this point to send the computers back to Hi Tech for a refund. U.C.C. §§2–508, 2–601, 2–602, 2–606, 2–608, Official Comments 3 and 4 to §2–606, Official Comment 2 to §2–106.

Assignment 14: Closing with Leases, International Sales, and Real Estate

A. Closing with Leases

The provisions in U.C.C. Article 2A on acceptance, rejection, revocation, and cure mainly mirror the comparable provisions in Article 2. The one major exception to that similarity is the case of finance leases. Finance leases, you may recall from Assignment 9, are three-party deals in which the lessor's principal connection with the lease transaction is to provide the financing to make it happen.

Colonial Pacific Leasing Corp. v. J.W.C.J.R. Corp.
977 P.2d 541 (Utah App. 1999)

BILLINGS, J.

...JWCJR, an auto body shop, sought a computer and software package that would facilitate the generation of estimates for insurance companies and improve internal shop management. JWCJR was approached by Bottomline Systems, Inc. (Bottomline), who demonstrated a computer and software system. To obtain the demonstrated system, JWCJR entered into a finance lease agreement with Colonial Pacific, the lessor. JWCJR's owner, Cumberledge, signed the lease both as an agent of JWCJR and as a personal guarantor. Colonial Pacific purchased the equipment from Bottomline. Under the finance lease agreement, JWCJR was to make monthly payments to Colonial Pacific.

A few days before JWCJR received the computer and software package from Bottomline, Colonial Pacific required Cumberledge to sign an "acceptance and acknowledgment" form that stated the equipment had been received from Bottomline and was satisfactory. Cumberledge signed the acceptance and acknowledgment form and made an initial lease payment. On the day JWCJR received the equipment, Colonial Pacific contacted Cumberledge seeking a verbal verification that the equipment was acceptable. Cumberledge told Colonial Pacific's representative that JWCJR had received the equipment, but it was not yet operational.

Cumberledge had difficulty getting the computer system to function properly and repeatedly contacted Bottomline with his concerns. On the second day JWCJR had the computer equipment, Colonial Pacific again contacted Cumberledge to inquire whether the system was operational; Cumberledge responded that the system was working. Colonial Pacific then paid Bottomline for the equipment.

197

Later that day the system crashed, and despite repeated calls to Bottomline and many attempts to get it functioning, Cumberledge could not get the system to work.

Soon after, Cumberledge phoned Colonial Pacific and informed it the computer equipment was not functioning and never had functioned properly. Cumberledge boxed up the equipment and contacted Bottomline to pick it up. Within the next few weeks, Cumberledge again phoned Colonial Pacific to tell it of his problems with the computer system and to cancel the lease. From his conversation with a Colonial Pacific representative, Cumberledge believed the lease was canceled and that he was no longer obligated to make lease payments. Colonial Pacific had no record of the telephone calls.

More than two years later, Colonial Pacific sought to recover the unpaid lease payments. JWCJR, and Cumberledge as guarantor of the lease, refused to pay. Colonial Pacific brought this action to recover the full lease amount. The trial judge concluded JWCJR had breached the lease agreement by failing to make the required lease payments and awarded Colonial Pacific a judgment for $21,275.30. JWCJR and Cumberledge now appeal. . . .

On appeal JWCJR argues the trial court erred in enforcing the lease agreement because JWCJR never accepted the goods covered by the lease. JWCJR contends any alleged acceptance took place before it had a reasonable opportunity to inspect the computer equipment.

Under Article 2A of the Uniform Commercial Code (UCC), which governs enforcement of financing leases, we must determine if a lessee has accepted the goods, and therefore, has agreed to the lease. Once a lessee has accepted the goods, the lessee's promises are deemed irrevocable. . . .

Because it is generally accepted that UCC sections 2–606 and 2A–515 are analogous, we look to case law interpreting both provisions to help us determine whether JWCJR had a reasonable opportunity to inspect the computer equipment, and thus by its acts accepted the equipment. . . .

Whether a party has had a "reasonable opportunity to inspect," and thus whether an acceptance has occurred, is a question of fact. . . .

Taking possession of the goods is not determinative of acceptance, nor is the signing of a form acceptance before receipt of the goods, nor the making of a lease payment. . . .

In this case, the trial judge failed to make findings of fact on the pivotal issue of whether JWCJR had a reasonable opportunity to inspect the computer and software package, or even on the ultimate issue of whether JWCJR accepted the goods. . . .

In this case, the trial court's failure to make findings on whether JWCJR had a reasonable opportunity to inspect the goods, and thus by its acts accepted the goods, is not harmless error. . . . Cumberledge, on the second day after he received the computer equipment, told Colonial Pacific that the equipment was operational. However, soon after, Cumberledge made repeated telephone calls to Colonial Pacific telling it that the equipment was inoperative. Cumberledge also testified he was unfamiliar with the computer system and needed assistance in installing the programs and learning how to use the system. Finally, Cumberledge spoke with a representative of Colonial Pacific and understood from this conversation that the lease was canceled.

In contrast, Colonial Pacific relies on the "acceptance and acknowledgment" form, signed by Cumberledge before the equipment was delivered, to establish acceptance. Further, it claims that to the best of its knowledge the computer and software package were operational, and that Cumberledge never contacted Colonial Pacific in the initial weeks of the lease. The trial court was thus faced with disputed evidence but never made the critical finding that JWCJR, after having a "reasonable opportunity to inspect" the computer equipment, had "accepted it."

Similarly, because it cannot reasonably be implied that JWCJR had a "reasonable time for inspection," and thus accepted the computer and software system, the second alternative for affirming the trial court's ruling also fails. The trial court heard conflicting testimony as to Cumberledge's ability to get the computer and software equipment to function properly. Colonial Pacific contended that only two to three days after the computer equipment's delivery, it contacted Cumberledge to determine if the equipment was operational. Based upon his affirmative answer, Colonial Pacific funded the lease. However, Cumberledge testified the computer system crashed that same day, and that he telephoned Colonial Pacific twice, once soon after the system crashed and again within about ten days of its failure. Both times Cumberledge told Colonial Pacific the equipment was not operating and had never operated properly. Indeed, the trial court's findings of fact suggest that JWCJR did not have a reasonable opportunity to inspect the leased equipment and did not signify acceptance by its acts:

4.   The equipment was delivered and installed at Defendant [JWCJR's] place of business by Bottomline Systems, Inc., but it did not function properly.
5.   Defendant John Cumberledge informed [Colonial Pacific] on two occasions that the equipment was not operational.
6.   The equipment was returned to Bottomline Systems, Inc. subsequent to the signing and execution of the finance lease.
7.   [Cumberledge and JWCJR] were not contacted by [Colonial Pacific] until approximately two years thereafter, at which time [Colonial Pacific] sought payment in full from [JWCJR].

In sum, a finding that JWCJR had a reasonable opportunity to inspect the computer equipment, and thus by its actions accepted the equipment, cannot be reasonably implied "where there is a 'matrix of possible factual findings' and we cannot ascertain the trial court's actual findings." Hall, 858 P.2d at 1025–26. We conclude the trial court's failure to expressly make the findings of fact whether JWCJR had a reasonable opportunity to inspect the equipment, and whether it signified acceptance of the equipment by its actions, is not harmless error. We therefore reverse and remand for the trial court to consider these critical issues in light of our opinion, and to make the necessary findings to support its conclusion. . . .

JWCJR also argues the trial court erred in concluding it breached the lease agreement because JWCJR contends it rejected the computer equipment. The concept of rejection is intertwined with acceptance. "Acceptance of goods occurs after: the lessee fails to make an effective rejection of the goods as provided in Subsection 70A-2a-509(2)." Utah Code Ann. §70A-2a-515(1)(b) (1997). Section 70A-2a-509(2) explains when a lessee has rejected leased goods: "Rejection of goods is ineffective unless it is within a reasonable time after tender or delivery of the goods and the lessee seasonably notifies the lessor." Utah Code Ann. §70A–2a–509(2) (1997). . . .

Assuming the goods do not conform to the lease contract, section 2A–509(2) places the lessee under an affirmative duty to reject them on pain of being deemed to have accepted them. . . . Because failure to make a proper rejection amounts to an acceptance, section 2A–509(2) is closely related to section 2A–515(1)(b), which deals with acceptance and cross-references section 2A–509(2).

To make an effective rejection, the rejection must occur within a reasonable time after the tender or delivery of the goods. The duration of the reasonable time in which the lessee has the right to reject will vary with the circumstances. . . . It should be remembered that the lessee has a reasonable opportunity to inspect the goods before the lessee is deemed to have accepted them under section 2A–515(1). *The affirmative duty to reject on pain of being deemed to have accepted does not arise until the time given the lessee to inspect has ended.* 2A Hawkland and Miller §2A–509:08, at 780–81 (citations and footnotes omitted) (emphasis added).

Accordingly, the factual determination as to whether JWCJR had a reasonable opportunity to inspect the computer equipment must be made before the question of whether JWCJR properly rejected the goods can be answered. Having concluded that the trial court failed to make this critical factual determination, we remand to the trial court to make appropriate findings as to whether JWCJR had a reasonable opportunity to inspect the goods, and thus whether JWCJR timely rejected them. . . .

Additionally, JWCJR argues, even assuming the trial court determines it accepted the leased goods, the trial court's conclusion that JWCJR breached the finance lease agreement is nevertheless in error because Colonial Pacific consented to cancel the lease. We note that even the "hell or high water" provision provides a mechanism by which a lessee can escape its harsh strictures. "A promise that has become irrevocable and independent under Subsection (1): is not subject to cancellation, termination, modification, repudiation, excuse, or substitution *without the consent of the party to whom the promise runs.*" Utah Code Ann. §70A–2a–407(2)(b) (1997) (emphasis added). One commentator has explained what constitutes consent under this section:

> The waiver that is inherent in the independence-irrevocability concept of UCC §2A–407 is itself declared to be irrevocable. The Code declares that the lessee cannot be released from the consequence of the lessee's acceptance of goods "without the consent of the party to whom the promise (that has become irrevocable and independent) runs." It is specifically stated that it "is not subject to cancellation, termination, modification, repudiation, excuse, or substitution" without such consent. Nothing is stated as to the form or content of the consent. It is to be concluded that the consent may be oral and may be established by conduct that reasonably manifests an intent to consent. With respect to the content of the consent, it is not necessary that reference be specifically made to UCC §2A– 407. Any manifestations that the obligation of the lessee will not be enforced independently of the obligation that runs to the consenting party is sufficient.
>
> 5 Anderson §2A–407:7, at 607 (footnote omitted).

Though we have not found any case law to help us determine when a lessor consents to the cancellation of a lease, this question is comparable to whether parties have agreed to an oral modification of a lease. In Richard Barton Enterprises, Inc. v. Tsern, 928 P.2d 368 (Utah 1996), our supreme court explained a prerequisite for a contract or lease modification. "A valid modification of a contract or lease requires 'a meeting of the minds of the parties, which must be spelled out, either expressly or impliedly, with sufficient definiteness.'" Id. at 373 (quoting Valcarce v. Bitters, 12 Utah 2d 61, 63, 362 P.2d 427, 428–29 (1961)) (additional citation omitted); accord Fisher v. Fisher, 907 P.2d 1172, 1177 (Utah Ct. App. 1995) (same); see also Dennett v. Kuenzli, 130 Idaho 21, 936 P.2d 219, 224 (Ct. App. 1997) (stating modification of an agreement "'may be implied from a course of conduct in accordance with its existence and assent may be implied from the acts of one party in accordance with the terms of the change proposed by the other'" (citation omitted)). . . .

Further, the question of whether an "oral modification has been proven is one for the trier of fact." Kuenzli, 936 P.2d at 224. . . .

In this case, the trial court made findings of fact regarding Cumberledge's two telephone calls to Colonial Pacific:

5. Defendant John Cumberledge informed [Colonial Pacific] on two occasions that the equipment was not operational. . . .
7. The Defendants were not contacted by [Colonial Pacific] until approximately two years thereafter, at which time [Colonial Pacific] sought payment in full from Defendants.

Additionally, the trial court's ruling from the bench acknowledges Cumberledge's understanding that the lease was canceled after the second conversation: . . .

> Mr. Cumberledge contacted Colonial Pacific Leasing and advised them of the problem. Two to three weeks later, he contacted Colonial again and advised them of the problem. *He was under the impression that if he didn't hear from Colonial, everything was okay regarding the lease.* Mr. Cumberledge did not hear from Colonial for about two years when it initiated this case against the corporation and himself for failing to make the payments on the lease. (Emphasis added.)

The trial court's findings of fact and conclusions of law fail to make the critical determination as to whether Colonial Pacific consented to cancel the finance lease agreement. As we have noted above, absent adequate factual findings, the question is whether "the failure to make the missing findings can be viewed as harmless error." Hall, 858 P.2d at 1025.

We conclude the trial court's failure to determine whether Colonial Pacific consented to cancel the lease is not harmless error. Though the trial court found that Cumberledge made two telephone calls to Colonial Pacific concerning the problems he was having with the equipment, and that Cumberledge believed the lease was effectively canceled after the second telephone conversation, it made no findings concerning Colonial Pacific's refusal to cancel the lease. Cumberledge testified that he expected to be invoiced or to receive payment books on a monthly basis, and that he took the absence of such invoices and contact from Colonial Pacific as further evidence the lease was canceled.

In opposition, a Colonial Pacific representative testified to the following: that Colonial Pacific had no record of Cumberledge's telephone calls; that Colonial

Pacific was under no obligation to send Cumberledge payment books or invoices; and that because Colonial Pacific switched computer systems, JWCJR's lease "fell through the cracks," and this accounted for the two year lapse in its pursuit of lease payments. The trial court was thus faced with disputed evidence on whether Colonial Pacific consented to cancel its finance lease, but never made the critical finding on consent.

Also, because it cannot be reasonably implied that Colonial Pacific did not consent to the cancellation of the lease, the second alternative for affirming the trial court's ruling as harmless error also fails. We thus remand for the trial court to make the necessary finding of fact on whether Colonial Pacific consented to cancel the finance lease. . . .

Whenever the lease transaction is a finance lease, the finance lessee's ability to revoke acceptance of the leased goods is much narrower than the revocation rights of an ordinary buyer or of a non-finance lessee. In fact, the only situation in which a finance lessee may revoke acceptance of the leased goods is where the finance lessee's failure to discover the nonconformity before acceptance was reasonably induced by the *lessor's* assurances. Since the finance lessor is typically not going to be making many assurances (the finance lessee, after all, selected the goods), it will be an unusual case in which the finance lessee may revoke acceptance.

Given certain other attributes of the finance lease, however, failing to give the finance lessee broad revocation rights is not nearly as draconian as it might seem. For example, suppose that there is a finance lease of a drill press. Imagine that the finance lessee accepts the drill press and then later discovers a nonconformity that was virtually impossible to discover prior to acceptance. U.C.C. §2A–517(1)(b) states clearly that the finance lessee may not revoke acceptance of the leased goods in this situation.

Is the finance lessee, then, stuck with no recourse? Although the finance lessee does not retain the goods-oriented remedy of revocation in this situation, it does nevertheless remain eligible for its breach of warranty rights against the supplier. As you may recall from Assignment 9, the finance lessee gets the benefit of all the warranties that were made by the supplier to the lessor. Thus, the finance lessee may demand that the supplier make things right or pay damages. As Official Comment 1 to §2A–516 notes about the narrowing of the finance lessee's revocation rights, "this is not inequitable as the lessee has a direct claim against the supplier."

B.   Closing with International Sales

Probably the broadest statement that one could make about the difference in "closing" concepts between the international sales system and the domestic sales system is that the international system is much more averse to letting buyers use goods-oriented remedies. This reluctance is perhaps understandable given that delivery costs are generally higher in international sales than in domestic sales and therefore there is more dead-weight loss that is suffered in an international sale if the sales transaction must be physically reversed.

The CISG recognizes only two situations in which the buyer may "avoid" its contract with the seller. C.I.S.G. Art. 49(1). The first is where the seller has committed a "fundamental breach" of contract. C.I.S.G. Art. 49(1)(a). A fundamental breach is a breach that amounts to a substantial deprivation of the aggrieved party's benefit of the bargain. C.I.S.G. Art. 25. Where the buyer wishes to declare a fundamental breach, it must give notice to the seller no later than a reasonable period following when the buyer knew or ought to have known of the defect. C.I.S.G. Art. 49(2)(b)(i).

Delchi Carrier SpA v. Rotorex Corp.
71 F.3d 1024 (2d Cir. 1995)

WINTER, C.J.

Rotorex Corporation, a New York corporation, appeals from a judgment of $1,785,772.44 in damages for lost profits and other consequential damages awarded to Delchi Carrier SpA following a bench trial before Judge Munson. The basis for the award was Rotorex's delivery of nonconforming compressors to Delchi, an Italian manufacturer of air conditioners....

In January 1988, Rotorex agreed to sell 10,800 compressors to Delchi for use in Delchi's "Ariele" line of portable room air conditioners. The air conditioners were scheduled to go on sale in the spring and summer of 1988. Prior to executing the contract, Rotorex sent Delchi a sample compressor and accompanying written performance specifications. The compressors were scheduled to be delivered in three shipments before May 15, 1988.

Rotorex sent the first shipment by sea on March 26. Delchi paid for this shipment, which arrived at its Italian factory on April 20, by letter of credit. Rotorex sent a second shipment of compressors on or about May 9. Delchi also remitted payment for this shipment by letter of credit. While the second shipment was en route, Delchi discovered that the first lot of compressors did not conform to the sample model and accompanying specifications. On May 13, after a Rotorex representative visited the Delchi factory in Italy, Delchi informed Rotorex that 93 percent of the compressors were rejected in quality control checks because they had lower cooling capacity and consumed more power than the sample model and specifications. After several unsuccessful attempts to cure the defects in the compressors, Delchi asked Rotorex to supply new compressors conforming to the original sample and specifications. Rotorex refused, claiming that the performance specifications were "inadvertently communicated" to Delchi.

In a faxed letter dated May 23, 1988, Delchi cancelled the contract. Although it was able to expedite a previously planned order of suitable compressors from Sanyo, another supplier, Delchi was unable to obtain in a timely fashion substitute compressors from other sources and thus suffered a loss in its sales volume of Arieles during the 1988 selling season. Delchi filed the instant action under the United Nations Convention on Contracts for the International Sale of Goods

("CISG" or "the Convention") for breach of contract and failure to deliver con-forming goods. . . .

The district court held, and the parties agree, that the instant matter is governed by the CISG, reprinted at 15 U.S.C.A. Appendix (West Supp. 1995), a self-execut-ing agreement between the United States and other signatories, including Italy. Because there is virtually no caselaw under the Convention, we look to its language and to "the general principles" upon which it is based. See CISG art. 7(2). The Convention directs that its interpretation be informed by its "international char-acter and . . . the need to promote uniformity in its application and the observance of good faith in international trade." See CISG art. 7(1). Caselaw interpreting analogous provisions of Article 2 of the Uniform Commercial Code ("UCC"), may also inform a court where the language of the relevant CISG provisions tracks that of the UCC. However, UCC caselaw "is not per se applicable." Orbisphere Corp. v. United States, 726 F. Supp. 1344, 1355 (Ct. Int'l Trade 1989).

We first address the liability issue. . . . Under the CISG, "[t]he seller must deliver goods which are of the quantity, quality and description required by the contract," and "the goods do not conform with the contract unless they . . . [p]ossess the qualities of goods which the seller has held out to the buyer as a sample or model." CISG art. 35. The CISG further states that "[t]he seller is liable in accordance with the contract and this Convention for any lack of conformity." CISG art. 36.

Judge Cholakis held that "there is no question that [Rotorex's] compressors did not conform to the terms of the contract between the parties" and noted that "[t]here are ample admissions [by Rotorex] to that effect." We agree. The agree-ment between Delchi and Rotorex was based upon a sample compressor supplied by Rotorex and upon written specifications regarding cooling capacity and power consumption. After the problems were discovered, Rotorex's engineering repre-sentative, Ernest Gamache, admitted in a May 13, 1988 letter that the specification sheet was "in error" and that the compressors would actually generate less cooling power and consume more energy than the specifications indicated. Gamache also testified in a deposition that at least some of the compressors were nonconform-ing. The president of Rotorex, John McFee, conceded in a May 17, 1988 letter to Delchi that the compressors supplied were less efficient than the sample and did not meet the specifications provided by Rotorex. Finally, in its answer to Delchi's complaint, Rotorex admitted "that some of the compressors . . . did not conform to the nominal performance information." There was thus no genuine issue of material fact regarding liability, and summary judgment was proper.

Under the CISG, if the breach is "fundamental" the buyer may either require delivery of substitute goods, CISG art. 46, or declare the contract void, CISG art. 49, and seek damages. With regard to what kind of breach is fundamental, Article 25 provides:

> A breach of contract committed by one of the parties is fundamental if it results in such detriment to the other party as substantially to deprive him of what he is entitled to expect under the contract, unless the party in breach did not foresee and a reasonable person of the same kind in the same circumstances would not have foreseen such a result.

CISG art. 25. In granting summary judgment, the district court held that "[t]here appears to be no question that [Delchi] did not substantially receive that which [it] was entitled to expect" and that "any reasonable person could foresee that shipping non-conforming goods to a buyer would result in the buyer not receiving that which he expected and was entitled to receive." Because the cooling power and energy consumption of an air conditioner compressor are important determinants of the product's value, the district court's conclusion that Rotorex was liable for a fundamental breach of contract under the Convention was proper. . . .

Besides the "fundamental breach" scenario, the second situation in which the buyer may avoid the contract under the CISG is where the seller's delivery is later than the agreed due date plus any additional time that the buyer has agreed to give the seller to deliver. C.I.S.G. Art. 49(1)(b). Where a buyer agrees to give the seller additional time to deliver, the buyer does not thereby prejudice its right to damages for the delay. C.I.S.G. Art. 47(2).

The functional consequences of avoidance by the buyer are that both parties are relieved of their obligations, but the buyer may sue for damages. C.I.S.G. Art. 81(1). Either party may claim restitution if their partial performance has resulted in a benefit to the other party. C.I.S.G. Art. 81(2). If the buyer has already received delivery of the goods, the buyer has an obligation to return the goods to the seller in substantially the same condition as the buyer received them. C.I.S.G. Art. 82(1).

Where the seller's breach is less than "fundamental," the buyer must keep the goods but retains its rights to sue for any of the non-avoidance remedies under the CISG. These could include monetary damages, C.I.S.G. Arts. 74-77, or a demand by the buyer that the seller cure the problem. C.I.S.G. Art. 46. The seller is also given the right to core any non-fundamental branches. C.I.S.G. Art. 48.

C.   Real Estate Closings

THE RITUAL CLOSING CEREMONY

This is an important and highly traditional part of the homebuying process, the last major hurdle you must clear before you become an official homeowner. Essentially what you must do, in the Ritual Closing Ceremony, is go into a small room and write large checks to total strangers. According to tradition, anybody may ask you for a check, for any amount, and you may not refuse. Once you get started handing out money, the good news will travel quickly through the real estate community via joyful shouts: "A Closing Ceremony is taking place!"

Soon there will be a huge horde of people — lawyers, bankers, insurance people, termite inspectors, caterers, photographers, people you used to know in high school — crowding into the closing room and spilling out into the street. You may be forced to hurl batches of signed blank checks out the window, just to make sure that everyone is accommodated in the traditional way.

Another ritual task you must perform during the Closing Ceremony is to frown with feigned comprehension at various unintelligible documents that will be placed in front of you by random individuals wearing suits.

RANDOM INDIVIDUAL:	Now, as you can see, this is the declaration of your net interest accrual payments of debenture.
YOU (frowning):	Yes.
RANDOM INDIVIDUAL:	And this is the notification of your Pro Rata Indemnities of Assumption.
YOU:	Certainly.
RANDOM INDIVIDUAL:	And this is the digestive system of a badger.
YOU:	Of course.

Dave Barry, Homes and Other Black Holes, 45–47 (1988).

To anyone who has ever gone through the process, a real estate closing does seem to take on the aura of an ancient ritual. Much of what goes on passes for federally mandated "disclosure," but as the hypothetical story above suggests, disclosure and comprehension are two completely different things.

In the midst of all of the papers being signed at a typical house closing, the fundamental exchange taking place is that the buyer is giving a check for the purchase price and the seller is giving the deed to the property. The legal transfer of ownership from the seller to the buyer takes place when the seller "delivers" the deed to the buyer. Delivery requires both a physical transfer of the deed from the seller to the buyer as well as an intent on the seller's part to create a present ownership interest in the buyer as a result of the physical delivery.

In contrast to the sales of goods system, there is a true functional significance to the moment of the "closing" in real estate sales. Following the closing, there is very little chance absent some fundamental fraud or mistake in the transaction that the buyer would be able to reject or revoke acceptance of the real estate and rescind the entire contract.

Gray v. First NH Banks

640 A.2d 276 (N.H. 1994)

BATCHELDER, J.

The plaintiffs appeal the decision of the Superior Court (O'Neil, J.) dismissing their suit for rescission of a real estate purchase. They argue that the trial court erred: (1) in finding that the defendants' violation of RSA 485–A:39 (1992) did not provide the basis for a cause of action; (2) in failing to rule that the lack of signatures on the site assessment study constituted per se liability; (3) in finding that the realtor was acting as an intermediary, rather than as the bank's agent; and (4) because its findings on each theory of recovery were clearly erroneous. We affirm.

In July 1990, the plaintiffs, Peter Gray, his wife, Sandra, and his parents, Henry and Shirley, learned of the availability of a bowling alley, Lakeview Lanes, on the shore of Little Squam Lake in Holderness. Defendant First NH Banks, formerly First Central Bank (the bank), had acquired title to the bowling alley by virtue of a deed in lieu of foreclosure against the previous owner. Peter Gray contacted the bank about the property. Shortly thereafter, Rod Donaldson, a real estate agent associated with defendant La-Sal Properties of New Hampshire, Inc. (La-Sal) who had worked with Gray in unsuccessful negotiations for another property, became involved in the negotiations for Lakeview Lanes on Gray's behalf. After viewing the property with Gwendolyn Davis, a bank representative, Peter Gray offered to buy it for $225,000. The bank made a counteroffer of $325,000, and the parties failed to reach agreement.

Following the initial offer, Peter Gray spoke with a co-worker, Philip Stone, who had worked for several summers at Lakeview Lanes. Stone told Gray that he "had heard that there were problems with the septic system," that the son of a former owner had been deterred from purchasing the property because "there were significant problems with the septic system," and that he should have the system checked. Gray responded that he intended to use the septic problems "as a negotiating tool with the bank to lower the purchase price." The system was never inspected.

On October 17, 1990, Peter Gray offered $275,000 for the property, requesting a warranty deed. The proposal to purchase contained the following paragraph: "4. Buyers and Sellers recognize that there is a present and potential problem with subject property's well and septic systems." The parties ultimately entered into a sales agreement on October 23, 1990, which provided that the property would be transferred by quitclaim deed and made no reference to the septic system. The Grays and the bank closed the sale and transferred title on November 16, 1990.

When the Grays began operating the bowling alley and restaurant, the septic problems surfaced. The system needed frequent pumping and emitted noxious odors. After learning that RSA 485–A:39 (1992) (current version at RSA 485–A:39 (Supp. 1993)) required the preparation of a site assessment study evaluating the sewage system of developed waterfront property before it could be offered for sale, Shirley Gray contacted Donaldson and requested a copy of the document. Although the Grays maintain that they had no knowledge of the site assessment until Shirley Gray received a copy from Donaldson in January 1991, the bank contends that the Grays were given a copy of the document at the closing.

The Grays filed suit against the bank and La-Sal, contending that the bank's failure to procure a site assessment until the day before the closing violated RSA 485–A:39, entitling them to rescission of the contract, and that the negligent or fraudulent misrepresentations of the bank and La-Sal entitled them to money damages. . . .

The plaintiffs' first two arguments raise the consequences of a violation of the site assessment statute. RSA 485–A:39 requires the owner of developed waterfront property, prior to offering it for sale, to procure a site assessment study on the sewage disposal system. In this case, the site assessment study was dated the day before the closing and was not signed by the buyers as required. That the requirements of the site assessment statute were not met is not in dispute. Rather, it is the remedy for failure to strictly comply with the statutory mandate that is at stake. The plaintiffs contend that the failure to comply creates per se liability, entitling them to rescission of the purchase. We disagree.

Although a violation of RSA 485–A:39 occurred, evidence at trial refuted the plaintiffs' argument that the violation in any way caused their injuries. The trial court found that "[t]he plaintiffs were aware of significant problems with the septic system prior to the sale." In addition to Stone's testimony that he had warned Peter Gray of the problems with the septic system, the initial proposal to purchase contained an express acknowledgement that there was "a present and potential problem with subject property's well and septic systems." Further, Gray testified that this language was included because "the bank wanted to be sure that I wouldn't come back later on and say I've got no water and my leach field is not working."

The evidence that is most damaging to the plaintiffs is Peter Gray's admission that he intended to use the septic problems "as a negotiating tool with the bank to lower the purchase price." The purpose of the site assessment study is "to determine if the site meets the current standards of sewage disposal systems established by the division [of water supply and pollution control, department of environmental services]." RSA 485–A:39, I; see RSA 485–A:2, III. Thus the statute serves to inform a prospective buyer of the condition of the sewage system, information not readily apparent from a site inspection of the property. Here, however, the plaintiffs knew of the problems yet chose to utilize them as a bargaining chip in negotiations for the purchase of the property. Accordingly, because the plaintiffs failed to prove that the statutory violation, rather than their chosen negotiation strategy, caused their injuries, the trial court's ruling was not contrary to the evidence or erroneous as a matter of law.

We recognize that the material required by the statute to be disclosed to the potential purchaser is broader than the information that the plaintiffs acknowledged they received. The trial court specifically found, however, that "[t]here was nothing new in the way of septic system information in the [site assessment] report." Because this factual finding was not clearly erroneous, we will not overrule it. We note that in future cases, the lack of strict compliance with the statutory mandate may give rise to the remedy sought by the plaintiffs here. . . .

The plaintiffs finally contend that the trial court's findings on each of its theories of recovery were so against the weight of the evidence as to constitute an abuse of discretion. With respect to the plaintiffs' count based on negligent or fraudulent misrepresentation, "[o]ne who fraudulently makes a misrepresentation . . . for the purpose of inducing another to act or to refrain from action in reliance upon it, is subject to liability to the other in deceit for pecuniary loss caused to him by his justifiable reliance upon the misrepresentation." Restatement (Second) of Torts §525 (1976). Similarly, "[o]ne who, in the course of his business . . . supplies false information for the guidance of others in their business transactions, is subject to liability for pecuniary loss caused to them by their justifiable reliance upon the information, if he fails to exercise reasonable care or competence in obtaining or communicating the information." Id. §552. The plaintiffs failed to meet their burden on both theories.

The trial court found that no misrepresentation occurred. Further, based on evidence that included Peter Gray's own testimony, the court found that the plaintiffs were aware of the problems with the sewer system early on in the negotiations, thus negating any argument that they relied on the bank's or realtor's statements. Finally, Peter Gray testified that he had no evidence that the value of the property is substantially less than that bargained for with the defendants. Because there was evidence on which the trial court could reasonably base its finding that no misrepresentation occurred, it did not err in dismissing this count.

Finally, the plaintiffs maintain that the trial court erred in dismissing its count seeking restitution by rescission for mutual mistake. "Where a mistake of both parties at the time a contract was made as to a basic assumption on which the contract was made has a material effect on the agreed exchange of performances, the contract is voidable by the adversely affected party." Restatement (Second) of Contracts §152(1) (1979). Because the trial court found that "[t]he plaintiffs were aware of significant problems with the septic system prior to the sale" and because there was ample evidence to support this finding, no mistake occurred. Consequently, we find no abuse of discretion in the trial court's ruling.

AFFIRMED.

In the real estate system, the buyer has had its opportunity to inspect the property and negotiate for repairs during the executory period between the signing of the contract and the closing of the sale. Typically the buyer will do a final "walk through" of the property on the day before or the day of closing just to make sure that no changes have occurred following the buyer's earlier formal inspection.

In many states in the western United States, the use of escrow agents takes the place of a formal closing. In those states, the parties will agree on escrow instructions that will bind the escrow's ability to deliver the deed to the buyer and the purchase price to the seller.

In states where the more standard closings still take place, the parties that attend the closing will vary from state to state. In some states both the buyer and the seller will always attend in person; in other states they may not. In most states, the broker almost always attends (perhaps to make sure it gets its commission check!). In some states lawyers are typically used by the two sides at a closing, whereas in other states lawyers are rarely involved and most of the details and documents are handled by the title company.

As a future lawyer, consider the following:

WASHINGTON (AP) — Lawyers at the Justice Department and the Federal Trade Commission think a proposal to allow only lawyers to conduct real estate closings in Virginia is a rotten idea.

"It's difficult enough trying to buy a home," said Anne K. Bingaman, who heads Justice's antitrust division. "Let's not make it even more costly or difficult for those trying to grab a piece of the American dream."

She and Director William J. Baer of the Federal Trade Commission sent a stiff letter to Thomas A. Edmonds, director of the Virginia State Bar Association on Friday.

A committee of the association said in an opinion that real estate closings by anyone other than a lawyer should be considered an unauthorized practice of law. The committee stressed the risk that a lay person will make a mistake that a lawyer would not and that the consumer would be hurt.

The opinion eventually may see action by the legislature or the state Supreme Court or both. The Justice-FTC letter will become part of a comment package to be considered by the Virginia State Bar Council.

The Justice Department said lay settlement services and attorneys compete in real estate closings in many states, including in New Jersey where the state Supreme Court ruled last year that non-lawyers may conduct closings and settlement.

The court found that in the southern part of the state, where lay settlements were commonplace, buyers paid $350 on average to non-lawyers and $650 to lawyers, the department said. In northern New Jersey, where lawyers handle most such transactions, sellers paid $750 in lawyers fees on average and buyers $1,000.

Harry F. Rosenthal, "Justice, FTC Oppose Lawyers-Only Real Estate Closings," September 20, 1996, Associated Press.

Problem Set 14

14.1. a. Not quite a month following her last visit to your law office, Mammoth College athletic director Shelly Stone (from Problem 13.4) is back to see you again — with more bus problems. After unloading Big Al's bus back to him, Shelly discovered that a local bank, First National, had a leasing division that leased buses. A leasing officer there, Mark Archer, had convinced Shelly of the benefits of a finance lease. Shelly had agreed to a five-year finance lease of a two-year-old bus that she had personally selected from the fleet at Little Sal's, a local bus dealer who happened to be Big Al's younger sister. Shelly had intended to have a mechanic check out the bus before accepting it, but Mark Archer convinced her that his bank's experience with Little Sal's was so consistently positive that Shelly should not waste her time and money getting a mechanic. Unfortunately, when the bus took its first long trip with the women's volleyball team, the bus turned out to be an even worse oil-guzzler than the one Shelly had dumped back to Big Al's. The lease contract that Shelly signed with First National had a clause that said, "The lessee's promises under the lease contract become irrevocable and independent upon the lessee's acceptance of the goods, AND THERE SHALL BE NO EXCEPTIONS TO THE EFFECTIVENESS OF THIS CLAUSE." Shelly now wants to know if she can revoke acceptance of the bus and, if she cannot, what other recourse she has and against whom. What do you advise? U.C.C. §2A–407, Official Comments 1 and 2 to §2A–407, §2A–517(1), Official Comment 1 to §2A–516, §1–102(3) (§1–302 as amended).

b. Same facts as part a., except that the lease contract did not contain the clause that was quoted in part a. Can Shelly revoke acceptance of the bus? U.C.C. §2A–407, Official Comments 1 and 2 to §2A–407, §2A–517(1), Official Comment 1 to §2A–516, §1–102(3) (§1–302 as amended).

c. Same facts as part a., except instead of a bus for Mammoth College, Shelly was leasing a van from Little Sal's for her personal use, and the lease contract did not contain the clause that was quoted in part a. Further, Mark Archer gave no assurances to Shelly in this case. When it turns out that the van is an oil-guzzler, can Shelly revoke acceptance of the van? If not, what recourse does Shelly have and against whom? U.C.C. §§2A–407(1), 2A–517, 2A–209(1), 2A–212(1).

d. Same facts as part a., except instead of a bus for Mammoth College, Shelly was leasing a van from Little Sal's for her personal use. The lease contract contained the same clause as in part a., but Mark Archer gave no assurances to Shelly in this case. When it turns out that the van is an oil-guzzler, can Shelly revoke acceptance of the van? If not, what recourse does Shelly have and against whom? U.C.C. §§2A–407(1), 2A–517, 2A–209(1), 2A–212(1), Official Comment 6 to §2A–407.

e. Same facts as part a., except that the problem with the bus was not oil-guzzling but a defective steering wheel that Shelly discovered even before leaving Little Sal's lot (but after signing the lease with the bank). (1) Must Shelly go through with the lease? (2) What if the clause had said that Shelly's obligations under the lease became irrevocable and independent "upon the lessee's signing of the lease contract" instead of "upon the lessee's acceptance of the goods"? §§2A–515, 2A–108, 1–102(3) (§1–302 as amended).

14.2. a. Mal's Shop for Men, a Chicago suit retailer, made a contract to buy four dozen men's suits from Italy's Best, a suit manufacturer headquartered in Italy. Mal's received the suits on time and, as was the store's practice, simply put the suits on the racks. The suits sat there for a couple of months before anyone bought them. When customers finally started buying the suits, virtually every customer who had purchased those suits complained about the suit's "cheap material," which frayed significantly. At this point, which was about three months after the store had received delivery of the suits, Mal's announced to Italy's Best that Mal's was sending back all of the suits for a refund. Does Mal's have a right to void this contract? Does Italy's Best have a right to cure? C.I.S.G. Arts. 25, 39, 49, 48, 46.

b. Same facts as part a., except that the suit's material was fine, but the sleeves on a few of the suits were missing one or both buttons. Once again, Mal's does not discover these defects until customers start complaining later on. Does Mal's have a right to void this contract? Does Italy's Best have a right to cure? C.I.S.G. Arts. 25, 49, 48, 46.

c. Same facts as part a., except that Italy's Best delivers the suits three weeks before the contractual delivery date and Mal's discovers the fraying material by inspecting the suits immediately. Mal's then calls Italy's Best to complain about the material. Does Mal's have a right to avoid this contract? Does Italy's Best have a right to cure? C.I.S.G. Arts. 25, 37, 49, 48, 46.

14.3. After three years of living in an apartment, Mike and Dayna Wellston had finally put together enough funds to purchase their first home in a modest section of Manchester, New Hampshire. Mike was an engineer for an environmental auditing firm and Dayna was a reporter for a suburban newspaper. Together their salaries were just enough to qualify for the mortgage necessary to finance the $170,000 home. Two months after the closing, Mike was digging a hole in his backyard to put in a pole for a basketball hoop when he happened upon a buried gas tank. Mike believed the sellers when they told him they knew nothing about the tank, but when Mike learned of the $40,000 cost of removal he and Dayna came to see you about a possible rescission action. Mike and Dayna had commissioned a standard inspection of the home that, not surprisingly, did not discover the tank. Mike was aware from his work that occasionally prospective home buyers would commission an environmental audit of the land they were going to buy, but such audits were rare given the tremendous expense. What do you advise Mike and Dayna about the likelihood of a successful rescission of their home purchase?

Assignment 15: Risk of Loss with Sales of Goods

In Assignment 13, we explored the vagaries of the "closing" concept in the sale of goods system. An issue that is closely related to closing is risk of loss. Risk of loss rules define which party, as between the buyer and the seller, is responsible for the destruction of or damage to goods that occurs between the time that the contract is entered into and the time that the buyer receives possession of the goods.

Risk of loss issues can arise in two-party cases where the seller itself delivers the goods or the buyer comes and picks up the goods at the seller's place of business. Most of the action in risk of loss, however, occurs in the very common three-party situation, in which the seller makes arrangements to have the goods delivered to the buyer by a third-party common carrier such as a truck, plane, or boat.

Before getting into some of the complicated rules governing risk of loss, you should consider a couple of more general points about the subject. The first point is that if the destruction or damage to goods occurs through the fault of either the buyer or the seller, then the negligent party must bear the loss and the usual risk of loss rules do not come into play. In other words, the risk of loss rules were designed to cover only the case in which the destruction or damage to the goods occurs other than through the fault of either buyer or seller.

Second, risk of loss fights in actual practice tend to involve insurance companies, either against each other or against the buyer or seller. In three-party transactions where the seller uses a common carrier, the carrier will almost always have insurance to cover losses in transit. Similarly, the buyer and seller will usually both have their own backup insurance policies that may cover any losses that occur during the executory period between contracting and buyer acceptance. Some larger companies will effectively self-insure at the lower levels by having insurance policies with huge deductibles.

The purchasing agent for a medium-sized plastics manufacturer, which does not insure its orders in transit, described the risk of loss issue this way: "The real question in risk of loss situations is not which party, the buyer or seller, will bear the loss. Rather, the issue is usually which party, the buyer or seller, will have to deal with the hassle of going against the carrier's insurance company." The in-house attorney for a Fortune 500 seller that does insure its deliveries in transit described the risk of loss issue as involving little more than getting paid for the loss by its own insurance company, which then goes after the carrier's insurance.

The third more general point to make about risk of loss is a point that we have made in other contexts as well: Even where the legal rule would seem to dictate one result, business considerations may cause parties to agree to another result that is technically inconsistent with their legal obligations. For example, one medium-sized furniture manufacturer will include in its contracts a provision that shifts risk of loss to the buyer as soon as the furniture leaves the seller's factory, but when there is a problem in transit the seller almost always makes the buyer whole anyway. As the operations manager for that manufacturer explained: "Officially, we say that risk of loss passes from us to the buyer as soon as we load the goods onto the truck. In fact, though, if there is a problem that occurs during delivery our customers expect us to pay them and then go against the carrier ourselves. If they're good customers, we will almost always do that for them."

Most high-volume sellers will have their own dedicated third-party carriers that they will use to deliver shipments even where the buyer is contractually obligated to pay for the cost of freight. The seller in those cases will arrange for the transportation and then charge the buyer for use of the seller's captured carrier. In setting the delivery fee for buyers, sellers will charge not only for the actual cost of the third-party carrier but also a profit to account for seller's time in arranging the delivery details. Some large buyers will have their own dedicated fleets that come to the seller's place of business and pick up the goods.

Whenever there is a third-party carrier involved, seller and buyer will almost always specify when risk of loss passes. In practice, parties to domestic sales transactions almost always use just two basic delivery terms: FOB Seller's Place (a "shipment" contract) and FOB Buyer's Place (a "destination" contract). (FOB is short for "free on board" and literally means seller must pay all charges necessary for the merchandise to arrive, on board, at the designated location, free of charge to the buyer.) If the parties fail to specify a delivery term, Article 2's default rule is for a shipment contract. U.C.C. §2–308(a), Official Comment 5 to §2–503.

With a shipment contract, risk of loss shifts to the buyer when the goods are delivered to the carrier, and the buyer is responsible for paying the cost of freight. §2–509(1)(a). With a destination contract, risk of loss does not shift to the buyer until the goods are tendered to the buyer at the stated destination, and the seller is responsible for paying the cost of freight. §2–509(1)(b). Whether the delivery ends up as a shipment or destination kind will be a function of both negotiation and the relative leverage of the parties. Some sellers with significant leverage make it non-negotiable that all of their sales be shipment contracts so that those sellers never have to contend with insuring risk of loss in transit.

Both the shipment contract and the destination contract contain some additional requirements for the seller that are incorporated by reference to other provisions in Article 2. In a destination contract, the Code says that the seller must "tender" the goods to the buyer at the stated destination. The requirements of "tender," in turn, are set out in §2–503. Most significantly, tender requires that the seller: (1) put and hold the goods at the buyer's disposition for the period necessary for the buyer to take possession; (2) give the buyer notice of tender; and (3) give the buyer any documents that are needed for the buyer to take delivery.

In a shipment contract, the seller must "deliver" the goods to the carrier in order for risk of loss to pass to the buyer. The specific requirements that the seller must meet in order to shift risk to the buyer are set out in §2–504. Those requirements are that the seller: (1) put the goods in possession of the carrier; (2) make a reasonable contract for their transportation; (3) deliver any document necessary to enable the buyer to take delivery; and (4) promptly notify the buyer of shipment.

What counts as a "reasonable contract" for the goods' transportation is not always clear, as the following case demonstrates.

<u>**Cook Specialty Co. v. Schrlock**</u>

772 F. Supp. 1532 (E.D. Pa. 1991)

WALDMAN, J.

Defendant Machinery Systems, Inc. ("MSI") contracted to sell plaintiff a machine known as a Dries & Krump Hydraulic Press Brake. When the machine was lost in transit, plaintiff sued defendants to recover for the loss. Presently before the court is plaintiff's Motion for Summary Judgment and defendant MSI's Cross-Motion for Summary Judgment. . . .

Plaintiff entered into a sales contract with defendant MSI for the purchase of a Dries & Krump Press Brake in August of 1989 for $28,000. The terms of the contract were F.O.B. MSI's warehouse in Schaumburg, Illinois. Defendant R.T.L., also known as Randy's Truck Lines, ("the carrier") was used to deliver the press brake from the defendant's warehouse to the plaintiff in Pennsylvania. MSI obtained a certificate of insurance from the carrier with a face amount of $100,000 and showing a $2,500 deductible.

On October 20, 1989, the carrier took possession of the press brake at MSI's warehouse. While still in transit, the press brake fell from the carrier's truck. The carrier was cited by the Illinois State Police for not properly securing the load. Plaintiff has recovered damages of $5,000 from the carrier's insurer, the applicable policy limit for this particular incident. The machine was worth $28,000. . . .

The term "F.O.B., place of shipment," means that "the seller must at that place ship the goods in the manner provided in this Article (section 2–504) and bear the expense and risk of putting them into the possession of the carrier." [U.C.C. §2–319] [§2–319 has been eliminated under Article 2 as amended]. Thus, MSI bore the expense and risk of putting the machine into the carrier's possession for delivery. At the time the carrier takes possession, the risk of loss shifts to the buyer. The UCC provides:

> Where the contract requires or authorizes the seller to ship the goods by carrier
>   a) if it does not require him to deliver them at a particular destination, the risk of loss passes to the buyer when the goods are duly delivered to the carrier. . . .
>   [U.C.C. §2-509].

Goods are not "duly delivered" under §2–509, however, unless a contract is entered which satisfies the provisions of Section 2–504. [See U.C.C. §2–509, Official Comment 2]. Section 2–504, entitled "Shipment by Seller" provides that:

Where the seller is required or authorized to send the goods to the buyer and the contract does not require him to deliver them at a particular destination, then unless otherwise agreed he must

a) put the goods in the possession of such a carrier and make such a contract for their transportation as may be reasonable having regard to the nature of the goods and other circumstances of the case.

[U.C.C. §2–504].

Plaintiff argues that the contract MSI made for the delivery of the press brake was not reasonable because defendant failed to ensure that the carrier had sufficient insurance coverage to compensate plaintiff for a loss in transit. Plaintiff thus argues that the press brake was never duly delivered to a carrier within the meaning of section 2–509 and accordingly the risk of loss never passed to plaintiff. . . .

The dearth of support for plaintiff's position is instructive. A leading UCC authority has remarked: "Under this subsection [§2–504], what constitutes an 'unreasonable' contract of transportation? Egregious cases do arise." See J. White and R. Summers, Uniform Commercial Code §5–2 (1988). The only such "egregious case" identified by White and Summers is [one in which] "the package was underinsured, misaddressed, shipped by fourth class mail, and bore a 'theft-tempting' inscription." White and Summers, supra, at §5–2.

The actions taken by the defendant in [that case] were utterly reckless. Moreover, unlike the defendant in that case, MSI did not undertake the responsibility to insure the shipment, and did not ship the press brake at a lower cost than the plaintiff expressly authorized it to pay.

Plaintiff also relies on Miller v. Harvey, 221 N.Y. 57, 116 N.E. 781 (1917). This pre-Code case is inapplicable. In *Miller*, by failing to declare the actual value of goods shipped on a form provided for that purpose, the seller effectively contracted away the buyer's rights against the carrier. Official Comment 3 to section 2–504 states:

[i]t is an improper contract under paragraph (a) for the seller to agree with the carrier to a limited valuation below the true value and thus cut off the buyer's opportunity to recover from the carrier in the event of loss, when the risk of shipment is placed on the buyer.

Thus, a contract is improper if the seller agrees to an inadequate valuation of the shipment and thereby extinguishes the buyer's opportunity to recover from the carrier. That is quite different from a seller's failure to ensure that a carrier has sufficient insurance to cover a particular potential loss, in which case the carrier is still liable to the buyer.

Plaintiff's focus on a single sentence of Official Comment 3 ignores the explicit language of the statute which defines reasonable in the context of "having regard to the nature of the goods," [U.C.C. §2–504], and the portion of the Comment which states:

Whether or not the shipment is at the buyer's expense the seller must see to any arrangements, reasonable in the circumstances, such as refrigeration, watering of live stock, protection against cold . . . and the like. . . .

[U.C.C. §2–504], Official Comment 3.

The clear implication is that the reasonableness of a shipper's conduct under §2–504 is determined with regard to the mode of transport selected. It would be unreasonable, for example, to send perishables without refrigeration. No inference fairly can be drawn from the section that a seller has an obligation to investigate the amount and terms of insurance held by the carrier.

The court finds as a matter of law that MSI's conduct was not unreasonable under section 2–504. MSI obtained from the carrier a certificate of insurance and did nothing to impair plaintiff's right to recover for any loss from the carrier. Accidents occur in transit. For this reason, the UCC has specifically established mercantile symbols which delineate the risk of loss in a transaction so that the appropriate party might obtain insurance on the shipment. The contract in this case was "F.O.B." seller's warehouse. Plaintiff clearly bears the risk of loss in transit.

There are no material facts in dispute and MSI is entitled to judgment as a matter of law.

There are other ambiguities in §2–504 besides what does or does not constitute a "reasonable" contract for shipment by the seller. Much of the additional uncertainty about the operation of §2–504 stems from the last sentence in that section: "Failure to notify the buyer under paragraph (c) or to make a proper contract under paragraph (a) is a ground for rejection only if material delay or loss ensues."

This sentence raises the question of whether the requirements for a proper shipment by seller under §2–504 are truly prerequisites for passing risk of loss to the buyer or whether instead they are merely requirements on which buyer can rely to recover damages that are directly related to seller's inability to fulfill them. For example, suppose that buyer purchased twelve dozen crystal vases from seller, "FOB Seller's Factory." Without consideration for the fragile nature of the goods, seller arranges delivery with a fly-by-night carrier that has a terrible record of damaging goods in transit. Seller promptly notifies buyer that the vases are on their way.

Suppose that halfway to the buyer's destination and with no damage yet to the vases, the delivery truck gets hit by lightning and all of the vases are destroyed. Can seller argue that buyer has risk of loss here since seller delivered the goods to the carrier and promptly notified buyer? Can buyer argue that seller still has the risk since seller did not make a reasonable contract of transportation for the vases as seller is required to do under §2–504(a)? Can seller counter that even if it failed to fulfill that obligation, its failure to do so was not the cause of the loss and therefore, under the "no harm, no foul" concept of the last sentence in §2–504, buyer cannot complain?

These are questions that have not been met with a clear answer in the case law. In one oft-cited case, the North Carolina Court of Appeals held that even though the parties in that case agreed to a shipment contract, risk of loss for the crates of wine being sold did not pass to the buyer after the carrier received them because the seller failed to give the buyer prompt notice of shipment. Rheinberg-Kellerei GmbH v. Vineyard Wine Co., 281 S.E.2d 425 (N.C. App. 1981). The court reasoned that had the buyer received prompt notice of shipment, the buyer might have insured the wine and therefore avoided the loss that occurred when the wine was lost at sea by the carrier. In this sense, the court said, the seller's failure to notify the buyer caused the buyer's loss to "ensue" as is required by the last sentence of §2–504.

Up to this point, we have been looking at cases in which neither the buyer nor the seller are in breach of their substantive obligations under the sales contract, as opposed to their more procedural obligations related to delivery. In a case where either the buyer or the seller is in breach of the underlying contract, the various delivery codes created by Article 2 give way to a special set of rules governing risk of loss.

Section 2–510 covers the effect of breach by either the buyer or seller on the passage of the risk of loss. Section 2–510(1) provides that "[w]here a tender or delivery of goods so fails to conform to the contract as to give a right of rejection the risk of their loss remains on the seller until cure or acceptance." Thus, for example, suppose seller agrees to ship the buyer two dozen model 110Z Stairmasters, "FOB Seller's Factory." Imagine that seller inadvertently sends two dozen model 104X Stairmasters. If that delivery is destroyed in transit through no fault of either party, the seller keeps the risk of loss since the goods delivered "so failed to conform to the contract as to give a right of rejection."

Section 2–510(2) provides that when a buyer rightfully revokes acceptance, the buyer may treat the risk of loss as if it had rested on the seller from the beginning, but only to the extent of a deficiency in the buyer's insurance coverage. Therefore, suppose in the Stairmaster case above with the same term of FOB shipment, the buyer received the machines, accepted them without discovery of the nonconformity (which was difficult to discover), and then revoked its acceptance by notifying the seller. While waiting for the seller to pick up the Stairmasters, the machines were destroyed through no fault of the buyer.

Under §2–510(2), if the buyer had insurance that covered the destroyed machines, the insurer would pay for the loss. If the buyer did not have insurance, then risk of loss would be with the seller even though this was a shipment contract that would normally put risk with the buyer as soon as the seller delivered the goods to the carrier.

Section 510(3) covers the effect of breach by the buyer on risk of loss. That section says that where the buyer repudiates as to conforming goods already identified to the contract, risk of loss will be on the buyer for a commercially reasonable time to the extent of any deficiency in the seller's insurance coverage. Thus, suppose our Stairmaster seller (with the same FOB shipment term) had identified to the contract twelve dozen machines that conformed to its contract with buyer. Imagine buyer called seller before the machines left seller's warehouse and told seller that the deal was off.

If shortly after that call the Stairmasters were destroyed in a fire at seller's warehouse, buyer would have the risk of loss if seller's insurance were deficient. This is true even though seller never delivered the goods to the third-party carrier, which would normally be required for seller to pass the risk to buyer even in a shipment contract such as this one.

You have probably sensed by now that the drafters of Article 2 generally liked to let losses rest with an insurer whenever possible, even where one of the two parties was in breach of the contract. As the next case reminds us, however, oftentimes insurance companies will have their own arguments for denying coverage for these losses.

Design Data Corp. v. Maryland Casualty Co.

503 N.W.2d 552 (Neb. 1993)

HASTINGS, C.J.

This action was brought by the insured, Design Data Corporation, upon the denial of a claim made on a commercial insurance policy issued by defendant and third-party plaintiff Maryland Casualty Company. Design Data sought the recovery of damages to a computer plotter shipped by third-party defendant Consolidated Freightways, Inc., from the insured to a customer, HHB Drafting, Inc....

Design Data operates a computer services company in Lincoln, Nebraska. Design Data purchased from Maryland Casualty a policy of commercial insurance for its operations which was in effect at the time of the loss at issue here. In relevant part, the policy provides:

Property Insured

....

We'll cover equipment you own, rent, or for which you are legally responsible. We'll consider all of these to be yours in this agreement.

....

Where Insurance Applies

We'll cover losses that occur at the locations shown in the Declarations, or while in transit in the United States of America excluding Hawaii and Alaska.

Causes of Loss Insured

....

We'll cover losses that occur at the locations shown in the Declarations, up to the limit of coverage that applies. Losses that occur while property is in transit are covered up to the transit limit. If no transit limit is shown, these losses won't be covered.

The schedule of covered premises in the "Declarations" shows the address of the location as 1033 O Street, Lincoln, NE 68508. The limits of insurance in the "Declarations" disclose: "G. Property in Transit $_____." In November 1988, Design Data sold a "Hewlett Packard 7586B Roll-Feed 8-Pen Drafting Plotter," as part of a structural steel design computer system, to HHB. Design Data arranged for shipment to the purchaser in Pevely, Missouri, via Consolidated. In a deposition, Design Data's vice president of sales, Ed Bruening, stated that the plotter was in good condition when tendered to Consolidated and that the carton it was packaged in showed no evidence of damage or perforation. However, HHB employee Harold Glamann, who received the shipment, testified by deposition that when the plotter arrived, he noticed that there had been some damage to the cardboard container. Glamann stated: "The wheels of the plotter were actually protruding through a hole in the container. When the driver drug [sic] it off or dropped it to the ground, that may or may not have created more damage. It dropped rougher than I would like to see computer equipment handled."

When Glamann was asked if there was any other noticeable damage to the carton, he replied that it appeared that "something had either fallen on it or something heavy put on it that it was caved in." Upon opening the carton and examining the plotter, Glamann noticed that it had been "cracked and chipped in a couple of different places" and that the paper tray was bent or not positioned properly.

Howard Becker, president of HHB, stated in a deposition that at the time he learned of the damage to the plotter upon his return to his plant, a Design Data representative was present. Becker testified that the individual from Design Data hooked up the plotter and "tried to get it to work," but that it just made a loud noise and was not operable. . . .

In a letter to Design Data dated February 21, 1989, Maryland Casualty acknowledged the receipt of a loss notice regarding the damaged plotter and stated:

> It is our position that Design Data Inc. no longer owned the equipment purchased and accepted by HHB Drafting Inc. Therefore, your Electronic Data Processing form would not cover any equipment since you did not own[,] rent or have legal responsibility for same. We must respectfully deny coverage on this claim.

In its amended answer, Maryland Casualty alleged that Design Data had delivered the computer to the purchaser, which had accepted the goods. . . .

Maryland Casualty contends that under [U.C.C. §2–509], the risk of loss had passed to the buyer upon the buyer's acceptance of the plotter and that Design Data had no insurable interest at the time the damage was discovered. In pertinent part, §2–509 provides:

> (1) Where the contract requires or authorizes the seller to ship the goods by carrier . . .
>   (b) if it does require him to deliver them at a particular destination and the goods are there duly tendered while in the possession of the carrier, the risk of loss passes to the buyer when the goods are there duly so tendered as to enable the buyer to take delivery.

* * *

[U.C.C. §2–510] deals with the effect of a breach on the risk of loss, stating in pertinent part:

> (1) Where a tender or delivery of goods so fails to conform to the contract as to give a right of rejection the risk of their loss remains on the seller until cure or acceptance.
> (2) Where the buyer rightfully revokes acceptance he may to the extent of any deficiency in his effective insurance coverage treat the risk of loss as having rested on the seller from the beginning.

* * *

Maryland Casualty argues that HHB's rejection was untimely and, thus, an ineffective transfer of the risk of loss, since the buyer's onsite manager had reason to suspect that the plotter had been damaged when the shipment arrived. Although HHB employee Glamann noticed that the container was damaged when the shipment arrived, he testified that at the time he signed the delivery receipt, the plotter was still in the box and he did not know that there was any physical damage to the plotter. After he discovered the damage he reported it to his supervisor, Becker, when Becker returned to the office.

Becker testified that he had been in Lincoln for a training session with Design Data and learned of the damage to the plotter upon his return to the office on Sunday. As we have previously stated, Becker said that he had made arrangements for a Design Data representative to be at HHB's plant on Sunday to install the equipment so that it could be used on Monday. Becker and the Design Data representative learned of the damage to the plotter at approximately the same time. Becker stated that the Design Data representative was to return to Lincoln on Monday morning and report the damage to his supervisor and would send another plotter to HHB as soon as possible. Becker further testified that he was to pay the balance due on the equipment after it was installed in his office, but that he withheld payment that day because the system was not working.

While HHB had reason to suspect that the plotter was damaged, the nature of the damage was not known until the carton was opened and inspection was made. It was reasonable under the circumstances forBecker to allow the Design Data representative who was present to install the plotter to ascertain the extent of the damage. The revocation of acceptance was timely, and thus, the risk of loss remained with the seller, Design Data. Under the terms of its policy, Maryland Casualty was to provide coverage for equipment which Design Data owned, rented, or for which it was legally responsible. Design Data had an insurable interest in the plotter at the time the damage was discovered, and therefore Maryland Casualty's first assignment of error is without merit. . . .

Because of the transit limit in the policy, the insurance company in *Design Data* ended up not having to pay. Nevertheless, the *Design Data* case highlights some of the proof problems that are inherent in a system where risk of loss can sometimes hinge on the condition of goods while they are still inside of a box. For example, if goods in a shipment contract are destroyed while in transit, how will the buyer know as it must under §2–510(1) whether the goods were so nonconforming when they reached the carrier "as to give a right of rejection"?

One possible answer is that many carriers will take their own inventory of the goods when they receive them from the seller. The nature of such an inventory is limited, of course, if the goods are sealed inside of a box, but at least a carrier can record things like color, style, or quantity that are indicated on the packaging. Any of these pieces of information might be sufficient for the buyer to claim that the goods did not conform to the contract and therefore that risk of loss never passed to the buyer.

Also on the subject of proof, most sellers require the carrier to have the buyer sign an invoice upon receiving the goods which verifies that the goods in fact were delivered. The seller will then receive a copy of this invoice from the carrier in case the buyer later tries to claim that it never received the goods.

This fairly simple system of having the buyer sign an invoice upon receipt prevents fraud in most cases, but not all. Consider this tale from the general counsel of a computer hardware distributor: "We had a delivery scam recently where somebody called us with a real customer number but with what turned out to be a fictitious address. When the goods proved to be undeliverable because of the fictitious address, our carrier brought the goods back to the carrier's own trucking depot. Then the thief called the depot and said he would pick the goods up at the depot's will call. After the carrier let the goods go to the thief and we learned about it, we pointed out to them that their contractual responsibility was to call us first whenever any goods proved to be undeliverable. They weren't too happy to hear that, but this was only a $50,000 loss for a carrier that we give $3 million worth of business every year."

Up to this point, our discussion about risk of loss has been limited to the common situation in which the contract requires or authorizes the seller to ship the goods by carrier. Risk of loss issues can arise in other situations as well, and Article 2 has special rules for those.

In a case where the seller is using a third-party bailee to hold the goods for the buyer, such as a meat seller that stores its goods in a refrigerated third-party warehouse, risk of loss passes to the buyer at the first of three events: (1) when the buyer receives a negotiable document of title covering the goods; (2) when the bailee acknowledges to the buyer the buyer's right to possession of the goods; or (3) when the buyer receives a non-negotiable document of title or other written direction to the bailee to deliver. U.C.C. §2–509(2).

The default rule on risk of loss for cases involving neither a third-party carrier nor a bailee (such as a case where the buyer is coming to the seller's place to pick up the goods) is that risk passes to the buyer on receipt of the goods if the seller is a merchant, and if the seller is not a merchant then risk passes to the buyer when the seller tenders delivery of goods to the buyer. §2–509(3).

Remember again that all of these risk of loss rules, just like the rules for risk of loss in cases involving a carrier, are subject to three important qualifications: (1) if the parties specifically agree when risk of loss will pass, that agreement governs; (2) if one of the parties causes the loss in question, the negligent party assumes that loss; and (3) if one of the parties is in breach of its obligations under the contract, then the special rules of §2–510 will determine when risk of loss passes from seller to buyer.

Problem Set 15

15.1. Lou from Lou's Used Cars (Problem 2.1) stops by your office with a problem that he says he has never seen before. Two weeks ago, a new customer came in and agreed to buy a 1993 Chevy Camaro that Lou had on his lot. The next day, the customer sent Lou a cashier's check for the full amount of the price and told Lou that he would be in during the next couple of days to pick up his car. A week later, when the customer still had not picked up the car, Lou unsuccessfully tried to phone the customer several times. The car is still sitting on Lou's lot "taking up space," as Lou put it. Lou has a couple of questions for you. (1) First, would Lou be responsible if the car were damaged or stolen? (2) Second, what can Lou do in this case and in the future to ensure that customers pick up their cars after they purchase them? U.C.C. §§2–509(3),

2–509(4), 2–103(1)(c) (§2–103(1)(n) as amended), 2–509(2)(b), 2–510(3), Official Comment 3 to §2–509.

15.2. Before Lou leaves your office, he has one more "problem customer" that he needs to discuss. It turns out that the customer, Karen Frederick, is a law student ("or so she tells me," says Lou). Karen had purchased a 1995 Ford Taurus from Lou and brought the car back a couple of weeks later because of a major problem with the car's brake system. Karen (who still had not purchased insurance on the car) had told Lou upon returning the car, "If you don't fix the brake problem in two days, I will revoke my acceptance of the car and demand my money back." The next night, before the brakes were fixed, vandals entered Lou's lot after it closed (through no fault of Lou's) and caused $3,000 worth of body damage to the car. Lou tells you he has fixed the brakes, but needs to know whether he is also responsible for fixing the extensive body damage. (1) What do you advise? (2) Would your answer be different if Karen had said, "I hereby revoke until you get the brake system working properly"? U.C.C. §§2–510(1), 2–510(2), 2–608(2), Comment 3 to §2–510.

15.3. Arlene Ledger, president of Heavy Metal, Inc. (from Problem 3.2), is having another run-in with Gold's Gym. Gold's had signed a contract for an order of ten tons of assorted free weights, all painted gold, for one of its franchisees that was expanding the size of its operations. The contract said that the order would be sent, "FOB Seller's Factory." Arlene had Heavy Metal's usual carrier, Dependo, come and pick up the weights, and Arlene had notified Gold's Gym of the shipment. The first problem was, Arlene neglected to tell her shipping department that these were to be gold-painted weights rather than the standard black-painted weights. Thus, the weights that were given to the carrier were black instead of gold and the shipping boxes indicated that fact. The second problem was that the two trucks carrying the shipment were stolen during transit while they were parked overnight. The third problem was that the carrier's insurance, unknown to Arlene, had lapsed last month for failure to pay the premium. (1) What Arlene would like to know is who, as between Heavy Metal and Gold's Gym, has the burden of pursuing the carrier for the loss? (2) Would your answer change if the sales contract had included a conspicuous exclusive remedy clause that limited Gold's Gym's remedies to repair or replacement of defective weights? U.C.C. §§2–509(1)(a), 2–509(4), 2–510(1), 2–601, 2–719.

15.4. Same facts as Problem 15.3, except suppose that the weights Heavy Metal sent were conforming, but Arlene had neglected to give notice to Gold's Gym of the shipment when it was made. Gold's Gym was therefore not able to insure the goods in transit. (1) Which party, as between Heavy Metal and Gold's Gym, would bear the risk of loss in this situation? (2) Would your answer change if Gold's Gym had happened to learn from third-party sources that the shipment was made, but still never bothered to insure the goods in transit? U.C.C. §§2–509(1)(a), 2–504, Official Comment 2 to §2–509, Official Comment 6 to §2–504.

15.5. a. Frank Ziegler decided to sell his used rider-mower through the classified ads. Frank was asking $3,000 for the mower, which he had purchased in 1992. Not long after the ad appeared Frank had a potential buyer, Ed Kinman, out to see the mower. Ed told Frank he would buy it for $3,000, and Frank had Ed sign a handwritten contract that Frank had prepared. The contract said nothing about risk of loss. Ed promised Frank that he would be back with his pick-up truck and a cashier's check for $3,000 "in the next couple of days." The next day, Frank discovered that the rider-mower had been stolen from Frank's garage. Who had risk of loss as to the stolen mower? U.C.C. §§2–509(3), 2–503(1).

b. Same facts as part a., except that a week passed with no word from Ed, and then the mower was stolen from Frank's garage. Who had risk of loss as to the stolen mower? U.C.C. §§2–509(3), 2–503(1), 2–510(3).

c. Same facts as part a., except that six months passed with no word from Ed, and then the mower was stolen from Frank's garage. Who had risk of loss as to the stolen mower? U.C.C. §§2–509(3), 2–503(1), 2–510(3), 2–709(1)(a), 1–103.

d. Same facts as part a., except that Ed had paid Frank with a $3,000 cashier's check the first night that he looked at the mower, promising to come back with his pick-up truck "in the next couple of days." When the rider-mower was stolen the next day, who had risk of loss? U.C.C. §§2–509(3), 2–503(1).

e. Same facts as part d., except that after paying the $3,000 check, Ed never picks up the mower. Then, six months later the rider-mower is stolen from Frank's garage. Who had risk of loss as to the mower? U.C.C. §§2–509(3), 2–503(1), 2–510(3), 2–709(1)(a), 1–103.

15.6. a. Grandma's Superstore in Boise, Idaho, decided that it wanted to start carrying frozen steaks to complement its wide inventory of non-food items. Grandma's made a contract with Enos' Slaughterhouse in Missoula, Montana, in which Enos was to ship 500 8-ounce filet mignons to Grandma's, "FOB Missoula." Because it was cheaper, Enos had the goods shipped by a non-refrigerated truck from Dependo Carriers, Inc. Dependo, as its name suggests, had an excellent reputation for reliability. The steaks were fine when they were loaded on the truck for the 400-mile journey to Boise, but 10 miles into the journey the truck was run off the road and into a lake, where the steaks were destroyed. Enos had given Grandma's timely and proper notice of shipment. Who had risk of loss as to the steaks? U.C.C. §§2–509(1), 2–504, Official Comment 2 to §§2–509, 2–510(1).

b. Same facts as part a., except that Enos did use a refrigerated truck and there was no accident on the way. However, 40 of the steaks were ruined during the trip when some rodents hopped aboard the truck midway through the journey. May Grandma's reject some or all of the steaks when they arrive? U.C.C. §§2–509(1), 2–601.

c. Same facts as part a., except that Enos did use a refrigerated truck and there was no accident on the way. However, 30 of the steaks were already bad when Enos had them loaded on the truck, and another 40 were ruined during the trip when some rodents hopped aboard the truck midway through the journey. May Grandma's reject some or all of the steaks when they arrive? U.C.C. §§2–509(1), 2–601, 2–510(1).

d. Same facts as part a., except that Enos did use a refrigerated truck and there was no accident on the way. After Enos had selected the steaks and was about to load them on the truck, Grandma's called and said that it was cancelling its order. Enos told Grandma's that Enos was not waiving its right to sue for the breach. A week later, the 500 steaks that had been earmarked for

Grandma's were destroyed in a fire at Enos' Slaughterhouse through no fault of Enos. Enos had insurance, but it came with a $1,000 deductible. Enos lost a total of $15,000 worth of meat in the fire, including the 500 steaks that had been ordered by Grandma's, for which Grandma's had agreed to pay $6,000. Who had risk of loss as to the 500 steaks that had been earmarked for Grandma's? U.C.C. §§2–510(3), 2–709(1).

e. Same facts as part d., except Enos' insurance policy included the following clause: "Insurance Company reserves the right to recover any amounts paid under this policy from parties that would have had the risk of loss as to the destroyed goods, but for the existence of this policy." How would this clause affect Grandma's liability for the destroyed steaks? U.C.C. §2–510(3), Official Comment 3 to §2–510.

Assignment 16: Risk of Loss with Leases, International Sales, and Real Estate

A. Risk of Loss with Leases

The passage of the risk of loss with leases more or less tracks the system for passage of risk with sales of goods. There is, however, one important exception to that similarity. Article 2A sets out a default rule which says that risk of loss never passes from the lessor to the lessee except with finance leases. U.C.C. §2A–219(1). This is in contrast to the default rule on passage of risk in sales, where (at least in the absence of breach) risk eventually does pass to the buyer at some point, whether the seller is itself delivering the goods, a third party is delivering the goods, or the buyer is picking up the goods.

After setting out the broad default rule of "no passage of risk to lessee in non-finance leases," the Article 2A drafters then mimic the provisions of §§2–509 and 2–510 for all those cases where "risk of loss is to pass to the lessee and the time of passage is not stated." §§2A–219, 2A–220. Thus, for example, if lessor and lessee agreed to a five-year lease of a printing press, "FOB Lessor's Place of Business" then the provisions of §2A–219(2)(a) would dictate that risk would pass to the lessee at the point when the lessor delivers the goods to the carrier, just as would be the case under §2–509(1)(a) with a sale of the same goods.

B. Risk of Loss with International Sales

The CISG has a fairly organized set of default rules to govern when risk of loss passes from seller to buyer in an international sale covered by its provisions. However, the most important information to know about passage of risk in an international sale is the standard "Incoterms," which if included in the contract will govern passage of the risk of loss. Recall that C.I.S.G. Article 6 allows the parties to an international contract to vary the provisions of the CISG. As a result, parties can agree to use a standard shipping term to contract around the CISG's default rules for risk of loss.

BP Oil Int'l v. Empresa Estatal Petroleos de Ecuador

332 F.3d 333 (5th Cir. 2003)

SMITH, J.

Empresa Estatal Petroleos de Ecuador ("PetroEcuador") contracted with BP Oil International, Ltd. ("BP"), for the purchase and transport of gasoline from Texas to Ecuador. PetroEcuador refused to accept delivery, so BP sold the gasoline at a loss. BP appeals a summary judgment dismissing PetroEcuador and Saybolt, Inc. ("Saybolt"), the company responsible for testing the gasoline at the port of departure. We affirm in part, reverse in part, and remand.

PetroEcuador sent BP an invitation to bid for supplying 140,000 barrels of unleaded gasoline deliverable "CFR" to Ecuador. "CFR," which stands for "Cost and Freight," is one of thirteen International Commercial Terms ("Incoterms") designed to "provide a set of international rules for the interpretation of the most commonly used trade terms in foreign trade." Incoterms are recognized through their incorporation into the Convention on Contracts for the International Sale of Goods ("CISG"). St. Paul Guardian Ins. Co. v. Neuromed Med. Sys. & Support, GmbH, 2002 WL 465312, at *2, 2002 U.S. Dist. LEXIS 5096, at *9–*10 (S.D.N.Y. Mar. 26, 2002).

BP responded favorably to the invitation, and PetroEcuador confirmed the sale on its contract form. The final agreement required that the oil be sent "CFR La Libertad-Ecuador." A separate provision, paragraph 10, states, "Jurisdiction: Laws of the Republic of Ecuador." The contract further specifies that the gasoline have a gum content of less than three milligrams per one hundred milliliters, to be determined at the port of departure. PetroEcuador appointed Saybolt, a company specializing in quality control services, to ensure this requirement was met.

To fulfill the contract, BP purchased gasoline from Shell Oil Company and, following testing by Saybolt, loaded it on board the M/T TIBER at Shell's Deer Park, Texas, refinery. The TIBER sailed to La Libertad, Ecuador, where the gasoline was again tested for gum content. On learning that the gum content now exceeded the contractual limit, PetroEcuador refused to accept delivery. Eventually, BP resold the gasoline to Shell at a loss of approximately two million dollars.

BP sued PetroEcuador for breach of contract and wrongful draw of a letter of guarantee. After PetroEcuador filed a notice of intent to apply foreign law pursuant to Fed. R. Civ. P. 44.1, the district court applied Texas choice of law rules and determined that Ecuadorian law governed. BP argued that the term "CFR" demonstrated the parties' intent to pass the risk of loss to PetroEcuador once the goods were delivered on board the TIBER. The district court disagreed and held that under Ecuadorian law, the seller must deliver conforming goods to the agreed destination, in this case Ecuador. The court granted summary judgment for PetroEcuador.

BP also brought negligence and breach of contract claims against Saybolt, alleging that the company had improperly tested the gasoline. Saybolt moved for summary judgment, asserting a limitation of liability defense and waiver of claims based on the terms of its service contract with BP. The court granted Saybolt's motion, holding that BP could not sue in tort, that BP was bound by the waiver provision, and that Saybolt did not take any action causing harm to BP. Pursuant to Fed. R. Civ. P. 54(b), the court entered final judgment in favor of PetroEcuador and Saybolt. . . .

The CISG incorporates Incoterms through article 9(2), which provides:
The parties are considered, unless otherwise agreed, to have impliedly made applicable to their contract or its formation a usage of which the parties knew or ought to have known and which in international trade is widely known to, and regularly observed by, parties to contracts of the type involved in the particular trade concerned.

CISG art. 9(2). Even if the usage of Incoterms is not global, the fact that they are well known in international trade means that they are incorporated through article 9(2).

PetroEcuador's invitation to bid for the procurement of 140,000 barrels of gasoline proposed "CFR" delivery. The final agreement, drafted by PetroEcuador, again specified that the gasoline be sent "CFR La Libertad-Ecuador" and that the cargo's gum content be tested pre-shipment. Shipments designated "CFR" require the seller to pay the costs and freight to transport the goods to the delivery port, but pass title and risk of loss to the buyer once the goods "pass the ship's rail" at the port of shipment. The goods should be tested for conformity before the risk of loss passes to the buyer. *Folsom, supra,* at 41. In the event of subsequent damage or loss, the buyer generally must seek a remedy against the carrier or insurer. In re Daewoo Int'l (Am.) Corp., 2001 WL 1537687, 2001 U.S. Dist. LEXIS 19796, at * 8 (S.D.N.Y. Dec. 3, 2001).

In light of the parties' unambiguous use of the Incoterm "CFR," BP fulfilled its contractual obligations if the gasoline met the contract's qualitative specifications when it passed the ship's rail and risk transferred to PetroEcuador. CISG art. 36(1). Indeed, Saybolt's testing confirmed that the gasoline's gum content was adequate before departure from Texas. Nevertheless, in its opposition to BP's motion for summary judgment, PetroEcuador contends that BP purchased the gasoline from Shell on an "as is" basis and thereafter failed to add sufficient gum inhibitor as a way to "cut corners." In other words, the cargo contained a hidden defect.

Having appointed Saybolt to test the gasoline, PetroEcuador "ought to have discovered" the defect before the cargo left Texas. CISG art. 39(1). Permitting PetroEcuador now to distance itself from Saybolt's test would negate the parties' selection of CFR delivery and would undermine the key role that reliance plays in international sales agreements. Nevertheless, BP could have breached the agreement if it provided goods that it "knew or could not have been unaware" were defective when they "passed over the ship's rail" and risk shifted to PetroEcuador. CISG art. 40.

Therefore, there is a fact issue as to whether BP provided defective gasoline by failing to add sufficient gum inhibitor. The district court should permit the parties to conduct discovery as to this issue only.

BP raises negligence and breach of contract claims against Saybolt, alleging that the company improperly tested the gasoline's gum content before shipment. These claims amount to indemnification for BP's losses suffered on account of PetroEcuador's refusal to accept delivery. Our conclusion that PetroEcuador is liable so long as BP did not knowingly provide deficient gasoline renders these claims moot. Summary judgment was therefore proper, though we need not review the district court's reasoning. . . .

Incoterms are international trade delivery terms that are understood well by any player in that system. These 13 codes, which delineate the respective responsibility of seller and buyer as to various shipping matters, are published periodically by the International Chamber of Commerce in Paris. The first publication of them occurred in 1936 and the most recent in 1990.

Buyers or sellers that engage in international transactions with ignorance of the Incoterms are proceeding at their own peril:

> An exporter who ignores Incoterms may watch a profitable export become a horrendous loss. Consider the case of the Kumar Corp., a Florida business that sold electronic goods to South America. Kumar's shipping documents included an Incoterm that required Kumar to provide transit insurance. Kumar failed to insure the shipment, and then it disappeared after it was delivered to the freight handler. By failing to provide insurance for that risk, as the Incoterm required, Kumar became the self-insurer for the loss.
>
> Frank G. Long, "Shipments Often Vanish; Know If Buyer or Seller Pays," *Ariz. Bus. Gazette*, Sept. 19, 1996, p. 5.

Although there are 13 different Incoterms, they can be divided into four functional categories based on the first letter in the code. An E Incoterm creates the lowest level of responsibility for the seller. For example, with the EXW term, the seller must merely pack the goods and store them at the point of origin. The buyer assumes the risk of loss from that point and must also pay for shipping and insurance.

An F Incoterm represents a slightly higher level of responsibility for the seller. With an FOB term, for example, the seller at least has the responsibility of delivering the goods to the carrier, after which point the buyer will have risk of loss and responsibility for paying the cost of carriage.

The next level of Incoterm, C, will often require the seller to pay for certain shipping and insurance charges. With the CIF term, for instance, the seller will have the responsibility of paying for the shipping and insurance charges to the port of destination, but risk of loss will still pass to the buyer once the goods are loaded onto the carrier.

The final category, D Incoterms, puts the greatest responsibility and risk onto the seller. For instance, a DDP term means that the seller must pay all insurance, delivery, loading, and unloading costs. Furthermore, with the DDP term, risk of loss does not pass to the buyer until the goods are tendered at the stated destination.

In setting out default rules for the passage of risk of loss, the CISG provides rules for three different situations: (1) where the goods are to be delivered to buyer but the goods are not in transit at the time the contract is entered into; (2) where the goods are already in transit when the contract is made; and (3) where the buyer is to pick up the goods from the seller or from some third party.

For the first category, risk of loss passes to the buyer when the seller delivers the goods to the first carrier. C.I.S.G. Art. 67(1). This is similar to the default rule of U.C.C. Article 2, where in the absence of anything stated explicitly, the UCC presumes a shipment contract.

If the goods in an international sale are already in transit when the parties enter into a contract for those goods, risk passes to the buyer at the time the contract is concluded. C.I.S.G. Art. 68. However, risk in the transit case may pass to the buyer retroactively from the point when the goods were handed over to the carrier "if the circumstances so indicate" and if the seller did not know or have reason to know that the goods were lost or damaged at the time the contract was concluded. C.I.S.G. Art. 68.

Where the buyer is to pick up the goods from the seller's place or from some third party, risk passes to the buyer when it "takes over the goods" or when its failure to pick up the goods amounts to a breach of the contract. C.I.S.G. Art. 69(1). In a case where the buyer's pick-up will take place at a third-party location, the standard is stricter for the buyer: risk will then pass to the buyer "when delivery is due and the buyer is aware of the fact that the goods are placed at his disposal at that place." C.I.S.G. Art. 69(2).

When the seller has committed a "fundamental breach" of its obligations under the contract, the buyer retains all of its remedies for the seller's breach, including the right to "avoid" the contract. C.I.S.G. Arts. 70, 82. This result is similar to U.C.C. Article 2, where nonconformity in the goods will prevent passage of the risk of loss to the buyer, even where the nonconformity has nothing to do with the damage or destruction of the goods that occurs. The difference between the CISG and the UCC on this score is that the UCC prevents passage of the risk with merely any nonconformity that would give buyer a right to reject; for the buyer in the CISG to avoid the contract and effectively prevent passage of risk, there must be a fundamental breach of the contract.

C. Risk of Loss with Real Estate

With the sale of real estate, the common-law default rule in most states today is that the risk of loss during the period between the signing of the contract and closing is on the buyer. The real estate risk of loss rule has been justified by reference to the obscure doctrine of equitable conversion, which says that once an enforceable sales contract has been signed by both parties, the buyer has equitable title in the property from that point forward and the seller is merely holding the property in trust for the buyer during the executory period.

The problem with this theory today as a justification for the risk of loss rule is that the modern real estate sales contract is rife with conditions and qualifications of various sorts that make the contract's true "enforceability" virtually coterminous with the closing itself. Accordingly, it should come as no surprise that the risk of loss default rule has had only a limited practical effect in modern real estate practice, for at least two important reasons.

First, and most importantly, courts almost always require the seller to hold any insurance proceeds in trust for the buyer, thus limiting the significance of the default rule to cases of inadequate insurance. Second, most standard real estate sales contract forms include an express provision contracting around the common-law rule. Such a provision will look something like this in a simple residential transaction:

> Risk of loss to the improvements on the property shall be borne by Seller until title is transferred. If any improvements covered by this contract are damaged or destroyed, Seller shall immediately notify Buyer in writing of the damage or destruction, the amount of insurance proceeds payable, if any, and whether Seller intends, prior to closing, to restore the property to its condition at the time of the contract. In the event Seller restores the property to its prior condition before scheduled closing, Buyer and Seller shall proceed with closing. In the event the property is not to be restored to its prior condition by Seller before closing, Buyer may either (a) Proceed with the transaction and be entitled to all insurance money, if any, payable to Seller under all policies insuring the improvements, or (b) rescind the contract, and thereby release all parties from liability hereunder. Buyer shall give written notice of his election to Seller or listing agent within ten (10) days after Buyer has received written notice of such damage or destruction and the amount of insurance proceeds payable, and closing will be extended accordingly, if required. Failure by Buyer to so notify Seller shall constitute an election to rescind the contract. A rescission hereunder does not constitute a default by Seller.

Commercial transactions will frequently include similar provisions concerning allocation of the risk of loss. However, buyers in commercial transactions will often retain the right to walk away if the damage is severe, reflecting the subjectivity of damage assessment in that context.

Even when the parties bother to specify in their agreement what should happen in the event of loss or damage to the property during the executory period, the provisions they draft do not always settle the matter, as the following case demonstrates.

Voorde Poorte v. Evans

832 P.2d 105 (Wash. Ct. App. 1992)

SWEENEY, J.

Art and Ann Voorde Poorte brought this action for damages against William and Jeannette Evans following a fire which resulted in the loss of their mobile home. The Evanses were in the process of purchasing the home when the fire occurred. On the Evanses' motion for summary judgment, the court dismissed the Voorde Poortes' complaint. The Voorde Poortes appeal. We affirm in part, reverse in part and remand for further proceedings.

In July 1987, the Voorde Poortes and the Evanses executed a real estate purchase and sale agreement for the sale of land and a mobile home owned by the Voorde Poortes. The mobile home was vacant and the utility services had been disconnected.

The sale agreement provided in part that: closing was to occur on or before August 15, 1987; the buyers (Evanses) were entitled to possession on closing; and if the property was destroyed by fire, the buyers (Evanses) could terminate the agreement. The sale was originally set to close on July 26, 1987, but closing was delayed by agreement of the parties because the Voorde Poortes could not provide clear title.

Prior to closing, the Evanses took possession, moved employees into the mobile home and restored electrical service to the mobile home. On September 16, 1987, after the Evanses' employees had just finished lunch in the mobile home, they noticed smoke coming from somewhere in the mobile home. The local fire department responded, but the mobile home was destroyed by the fire.

Following his investigation, Grant County Fire Marshall Sam Lorenz concluded that the fire probably started in the kitchen and most likely involved the electrical system. He did not know the exact cause of the fire. There was no evidence that the fire was caused by incendiaries, chemicals, lightning or smoking. Fireman Steven Mitchell helped extinguish the fire and also investigated its cause. He believed the fire was caused by an electrical device that overheated or shorted out. The employees occupying the mobile home were transient workers who could not be located and therefore were not questioned.

After the fire, the Evanses terminated the sale agreement. The Voorde Poortes brought causes of action based on contract, tort and trespass. . . .

Contractual provisions allocating the risk of loss will generally be enforced in Washington. In [one Washington Supreme Court case, for example,] the court enforced a contract provision placing risk of loss prior to closing on the seller. It held the seller liable for damage to an orchard which had occurred prior to closing.

The Voorde Poortes contend that risk of loss should follow possession. While their position has a certain equitable appeal, it is against the weight of authority.

Phillips v. Bacon, 267 S.E.2d 249 (1980), presents a fact pattern similar to the case before us. There, the sale contract gave the purchaser the option of canceling the contract if the property was destroyed prior to closing. The purchaser improved and occupied the property before closing. The closing did not occur as scheduled because of a problem with the title. Before the closing could be completed, the house was destroyed by fire. The Georgia Supreme Court affirmed a summary judgment dismissing the seller's action for specific performance concluding that the risk of loss provision controlled.

Here, there is a disagreement whether the Voorde Poortes knew or consented to the Evanses' early possession of the mobile home. However, that dispute is not a genuine issue of material fact. Risk of loss remained with the sellers even if we assume the Evanses' occupancy was nonpermissive. Early possession of the mobile home did not affect the contract provision that placed the risk of loss with the sellers.

If a contract is unambiguous, summary judgment is proper even if the parties dispute the legal effect of a certain provision. Interpretation of an unambiguous contract is a question of law.

Here, the only dispute involved the legal effect of early possession. The court correctly decided as a matter of law that the risk of loss remained with the sellers. . . .

In *Voorde Poorte*, the court stressed that even if the Evanses' early possession amounted to a breach of the sales contract, that would not affect the risk of loss since their early possession had nothing to do with the loss that occurred.

Contrast this result to that which U.C.C. §2–510(1) gives us in the sales system, where any nonconformity that would give the buyer a right to reject will delay the passage of risk to the buyer. Thus, in the UCC system the seller can suffer a loss that occurs in transit merely because the goods were nonconforming, even though the nonconformity had no connection to the loss.

One aspect of the real estate risk of loss system that is raised but not discussed much in *Voorde Poorte* is that if the loss in question is caused by either party, then that party must suffer the loss despite what the usual risk of loss rule would be. Thus, had there been any evidence that the Evanses or their employees had started the fire negligently or otherwise, then that would be a triable factual dispute that would bear on the risk of loss issue. Given what was reported by the fire department, however, the court in *Voorde Poorte* did not believe that there was any evidence to support the notion that the Evanses or their employees were responsible for starting the fire.

Problem Set 16

16.1. a. State Law School leased a hi-tech photocopying machine for use in its mailroom. The lessor was Ted's Copy Shop. The lease was for five years at $2,000 per year, and the lease said nothing about the risk of loss. Steve Manion, a disgruntled mailroom employee, acts out his frustrations one night by taking an ax to the photocopying machine, which he thoroughly destroys. The parties were in the third year of the lease when the machine was destroyed. When Steve is caught, he loses his job and is more broke than ever. Neither the lessor nor the lessee had insured the goods. Who has risk of loss as to the destroyed machine? U.C.C. §2A-219(1).

b. Same facts as part a., except that the machine is destroyed by an accidental fire, and the lease is a finance lease. The lessor is First National Bank, and the supplier is Ted's Copy Shop. Who has risk of loss as to the destroyed machine? U.C.C. §2A–219(1).

c. Same facts as part a., except the machine is destroyed by an accidental fire, and at the time of the machine's destruction State Law School was two months behind in its lease payments. Who has risk of loss as to the destroyed machine? U.C.C. §2A–220(2).

d. Same facts as part a., except the machine is destroyed by an accidental fire, and State Law School had promised in the lease contract that it would insure the machine. At the time of the machine's destruction, State Law School had never taken out an insurance policy on the machine. Who has risk of loss as to the destroyed machine? U.C.C. §2A–220(2).

16.2. Recall the facts of Problem 15.3: Heavy Metal signs a contract to sell Gold's Gym ten tons of assorted free weights, painted gold. The contract said that the order would be sent, "FOB Seller's Factory." Arlene had Heavy Metal's usual carrier, Dependo, come and pick up the weights, and Arlene had notified Gold's Gym of the shipment. However, the weights that were given to the carrier were black instead of gold and the two trucks carrying the shipment were stolen during transit. Finally, the carrier had no insurance. Assuming that this shipment was to a Gold's Gym franchise in Canada, who would have risk of loss as to the stolen weights? C.I.S.G. Arts. 66, 67, 70, 82, 49, 25, 58(3).

16.3. a. Take a look at the sample risk-of-loss real-estate clause that is excerpted earlier in this assignment. Mary Russell and David Gavin, a newly married couple and your clients, signed a purchase contract with this clause on a house that was being sold by David's one-time neighbor, Mary Ellen O'Neill. Mrs. O'Neill is a widow who used to be a next-door neighbor to David when David was growing up. When Mrs. O'Neill decided that she needed to move to a retirement center, she gave David and Mary the opportunity to buy her house for $120,000, which David believed was at least $15,000 below market. In between the signing of the contract and the scheduled closing, there was an electrical fire at the house that caused $20,000 worth of damage. Mrs. O'Neill had fire insurance, but the policy had a $5,000 deductible. Mrs. O'Neill through her lawyer notified David and Mary that she would neither restore the property nor lower the price, although she was perfectly willing to proceed with the closing as scheduled. David and Mary come to you and ask you what their options are at this point, and which option you would advise them to take. What do you tell them?

b. Same facts as part a., except that the electrical fire was caused after David went through the house to do some last-minute inspection. He left one of the lamps on, which normally would not cause a fire, except this lamp had a faulty cord. David was actually in the house without permission, but Mrs. O'Neill had already moved to the nursing home, and David knew from growing up next door that Mrs. O'Neill always kept a spare house key under the bush near the front porch. How would these additional facts change the advice that you gave David and Mary in part a.?

Chapter 4.   Remedies

Assignment 17: Seller's Remedies with Sales of Goods

1.   *Why Do Legal Remedies Matter at All?*

When thinking about remedies in the sales of goods system, you need at the outset to keep in mind two important but seemingly contradictory truths: (1) The players in the system rarely resort to the legal remedies available to them for breaches by the other side; and (2) The existence of the legal remedies is nevertheless a crucial feature of the system.

As to the first point, the general pattern in the system when there are disagreements about a particular transaction is that the business people work out those disagreements. If the disagreements arise in the context of a long-term relationship, both sides realize that they have much to lose if they are unable to settle the problem and for that reason both sides have a great incentive to compromise. Even where the problem arises in a context where "relational" considerations are not as great, the parties still have to consider how costly and time-consuming it will be, if only in the short term, to fail to resolve the dispute.

Even where one or both sides finally conclude that the other side is being completely unreasonable and that the dispute cannot be resolved consensually, the most common remedies that are employed do not involve resort to the legal system. For the aggrieved seller, perhaps the most common remedy for a breach by the buyer is simply to refuse to sell to that buyer ever again. The seller may also take informal steps, short of business slander, that will make it more difficult for the buyer to transact business in the relevant trade community. Unless the stakes are very high and victory seems sure, the aggrieved seller will normally eschew resort to a litigation system that is costly, time-consuming, and uncertain.

Even though so few sales disputes make it to litigation, the formal legal remedy structure available to aggrieved parties is still a crucial feature of the sales system. One way to explain this seeming anomaly is to think of the legal remedies structure as a kind of shadow that lurks behind all negotiations involving disputes between buyers and sellers. As the general counsel for a computer hardware distributor described it: "When our business people get ready to meet with a customer with whom we have a dispute, they will always first come to the legal department just to know what their legal bottom line is coming into those dispute-resolution meetings."

Another way to justify the significance of legal remedies is to say that while access to formal legal remedies will not matter that much in most disputes, the cases where it does matter tend to have very high stakes. It is true that with most disputes, either the stakes will be too low to justify litigation, or there will be non-legal incentives, either relational or reputational, that will reduce the likelihood of advantage-taking by either side. On the other hand, there will be some cases where the amount in controversy is so large, or where the non-legal sanctions will be so small for a particular party, that the possibility of bad faith and opportunism would be much greater in the absence of a legal remedy for the aggrieved party.

In Professor Russell Weintraub's extensive survey of general counsels for major U.S. companies, one question he posed was, "If there were no legal sanctions for breach of contract and compliance depended on nonlegal sanctions (e.g., reputation in the business community, intra-corporate incentives for good performance), what is your estimate of how business operations would be affected?" Roughly two-thirds of the general counsel responded that there would be a "substantial detrimental effect." Russell J. Weintraub, A Survey of Contract Practice and Policy, 1992 Wis. L. Rev. 1, 24.

As one respondent put it: "Our conduct would change very little because our reputation is critical on a long term basis. My concern would be that smaller companies and start up operations would be substantially disadvantaged. We would be less inclined to take service or products from them. They have no reputation and [there would be] no legal penalty for non-performance." Id.

Another respondent noted: "I suspect that business in general would tend to the lowest common denominator. Probably would be more uncertainty and sharp practices. Legal sanctions for breach of contract are absolutely essential to business. A contract sets the rules for virtually every transaction." Id. at 24-25.

It is perhaps a tribute to the default remedies for sellers set out in Article 2 of the UCC that few sales contracts in practice change those standard remedies. The main tinkering with remedies that one tends to see in sales contracts is tinkering that affects the buyer's remedies: limitations of remedies to repair or replacement of defective parts, or separate exclusions of consequential damages. If a contract included a liquidated damages provision, that could affect the seller's remedies as well, but liquidated damages provisions are not prevalent in most sales contracts.

2.   What Are a Seller's Legal Remedies?

Before exploring in any detail the standard seller's remedies under Article 2, one needs first to consider two more general provisions in the UCC that relate to seller's remedies. The first of these is §1-106 (revised §1-305), a provision that you might think of as "the spirit of the remedies" section. Section 1-106(1) (revised §1-305(a)) sets down two principles that are significant for a seller's remedies: (1) that the goal of all the remedy provisions in the Code is "that the aggrieved party may be put in as good a position as if the other party had fully performed"; and (2) that consequential damages are not allowed unless there is specific provision made for them in the Code.

The first principle, the "benefit of the bargain" idea, can often be a useful gauge against which to measure conflicting interpretations of individual seller's remedies in various contexts. The second principle meant that sellers were not eligible for consequential damages under pre-amended Article 2 since there was no provision in Article 2 which gave them such. Sellers under amended Article 2 continue to be eligible for "incidental damages" under §2-710, and as the *Firwood* case demonstrates later in this assignment, sellers under pre-amended Article 2 would sometimes argue hard for a broad definition of incidental damages that became hard to distinguish from consequential damages. Section 2-710(2) as amended allows sellers to recover consequential damages in any appropriate case except that which involves a consumer contract.

Besides §1-106 (revised §1-305), the other general Code section on seller's remedies that is worth noting at the outset is §2-703. Section 2-703 serves as a convenient catalog for two different things: (1) the various ways in which a buyer might breach its contract with the seller; and (2) the possible remedies available to the seller.

Section 2-703 gives four different ways in which a buyer might breach: (1) wrongfully reject goods; (2) wrongfully revoke acceptance; (3) fail to make a payment when due; or (4) anticipatorily repudiate the contract. The one characteristic that all four types of breach have in common is that the buyer is failing to timely pay the seller the full price for the goods purchased. Presumably the seller will not care much what the buyer does as long as the buyer has paid the full price on time and is not asking for its money back. Amended §2-703 adds a fifth way for buyer to breach: "wrongful failure to perform a contractual obligation."

Section 2-703 lists seven different possible remedies that an aggrieved seller might pursue: (1) withhold delivery; (2) stop delivery by any bailee; (3) identify goods to the contract in the case of an anticipatory repudiation; (4) resell and recover damages under §2-706; (5) recover contract-market damages (or lost profits) under §2-708; (6) sue for the price under §2-709; or (7) cancel the contract. Amended §2-703 adds to the laundry list specific performance, liquidated damages, and a catch-all category, any damages "reasonable under the circumstances." Note that the first three remedies listed are really just actions that the seller may take to limit damages; the last four remedies represent various measures of damages, which we will cover below in order.

The remedy possibilities that are set out in §2-703 are probably intended to encompass all of the seller's remedies, but are clearly not meant to be mutually exclusive of one another. For instance, in a case where a buyer anticipatorily repudiated a contract with the seller before the seller even identified the goods to the contract, the seller could theoretically pursue four of the listed remedies: (1) withhold delivery of the goods; (2) identify them to the contract; (3) resell them to a third-party buyer and sue for resale damages; and (4) cancel the original contract (since the "cancelling" party always retains the right to sue for breach, §2-106(4)).

Whether the pursuit of one remedy by the seller should bar another is not always as simple as the above example suggests. For instance, if an aggrieved seller prior to the original performance date resells goods that were intended for the original contract, can the seller later choose to pursue contract-market damages rather than resale damages if the former end up being more lucrative than the latter? The guidance that the Code gives us on this issue, found in Comment 1 to §2-703, is cryptic at best: "This Article rejects any doctrine of election of remedy as a fundamental policy and thus the remedies are essentially cumulative in nature and include all of the available remedies for breach. Whether the pursuit of one remedy bars another depends entirely on the facts of the individual case."

1. *Action for the Price.* In discussing particular seller remedies, probably as good a place as any to begin is the seller's action for the price under §2-709. This remedy is in effect the seller's right of specific performance: it allows the seller to file suit forcing the buyer to pay the agreed-upon price. It is not, however, universally available. The seller is eligible to sue for the price in any of the following three circumstances (all of which assume that the buyer has not yet paid the price): (1) where the buyer has accepted the goods; (2) where conforming goods, whether or not accepted, have been lost or damaged "within a commercially reasonable time after risk of their loss has passed to the buyer"; and (3) where the seller has identified goods to the contract and there is no reasonable prospect of reselling them to a third party for a reasonable price. U.C.C. §2-709(1). If none of those three circumstances exists, the seller cannot sue for the price.

Sack v. Lawton

2003 WL 22682043 (S.D.N.Y. 2003)

Fox, J.

In this action, plaintiffs Shirley D. Sack ("Sack") and Shirley D. Sack, Ltd. ("Sack, Ltd.") (collectively "plaintiffs") allege breach of contract against Kenneth Lawton ("Lawton" or "defendant") and Salvatore Romero ("Romero"). Upon Lawton's failure to answer or otherwise respond to the complaint, United States District Judge Allen G. Schwartz ordered that a default judgment be entered against him. Judge Schwartz then referred the matter to the undersigned to conduct an inquest and to report and recommend the amount of damages, if any, to be awarded to plaintiffs against the defendant. . . .

Sack is a citizen of the state of New York and the president of Sack, Ltd. Sack, Ltd. is a corporation organized and existing under the laws of the state of New York. Lawton is a citizen of the state of North Carolina.

Plaintiffs are the owners of a drawing by the Italian Renaissance artist Raphael, entitled "St. Benedict Receiving Mauro and Placido." The drawing is referred to, by the plaintiffs and others, as the "Modello." Sack avers that the Modello is a unique work of art: an original drawing, with provenance proven beyond question, executed solely by Raphael, and dated 1503-1504 by New York's Metropolitan Museum of Art.

The plaintiffs acquired the work approximately ten years ago; in or about July 2000, plaintiffs offered the Modello for sale. At the time of the offering, the Modello was appraised and determined to be authentic. The work is insured for $12,000,000 by Lloyds of London. Several prospective buyers, including a museum, expressed interest in the Modello; in addition, the plaintiffs received several offers for the drawing. On August 23, 2000, the plaintiffs, acting through their agent, Alan M. Stewart ("Stewart"), entered into an agreement with Lawton whereby Lawton agreed to purchase the Modello for $12,000,000. According to Sack, there was no indication from Lawton that the sale was subject to any further agreement or conditions, and Lawton agreed that the purchase price would be transferred by wire to Stewart's International Capital Management ("ICM") account in New York City.

The sale of the Modello was memorialized in a document entitled "Bill of Sale," dated August 23, 2000, and executed by Stewart and Lawton. The Modello remained in the possession of the plaintiffs pending payment by Lawton of the purchase price. However, Lawton failed to pay any part of the purchase price, despite numerous demands by the plaintiffs, as well as representations by Lawton that the funds were, or would be, forthcoming.

According to Sack, when it became clear that Lawton would not pay the purchase price for the Modello, she attempted to find other buyers for the work. To this end, she displayed the work at a gallery in New York City and publicized its availability among art dealers and members of the art community. However, she was unable to find another buyer for the work at a price comparable to the price agreed upon by Lawton. In addition, Sack contends, since the bill of sale to Lawton is fully executed and has never been cancelled, she may be unable to convey clear title to the work, in the event that she finds a buyer and attempts to consummate an unconditional sale.

At the time Stewart was negotiating the sale of the Modello on behalf of the plaintiffs, Lawton offered to sell plaintiffs a work by the artist Giovanni Bellini, entitled "Madonna and Child." This work is referred to by the plaintiffs as the "Bellini." On or about August 30, 2000, Lawton entered into an agreement with Stewart whereby Stewart became his exclusive agent with respect to the sale of the Bellini. The terms of their agreement were set forth in a commission agreement dated September 18, 2000, and executed by Stewart and Lawton. The commission agreement stated, among other things, that Lawton and Romero were the sole lawful owners of the Bellini and, as such, possessed the legal right to sell, convey and transfer the work without restriction.

Sack states that it was her intention to resell the Bellini immediately after purchasing it, and that she agreed to pay Lawton $10,000,000 for the Bellini after ascertaining that she could resell the work to prospective buyers for $15,000,000. However, according to Sack, after Lawton agreed to sell the Bellini, she was informed that Lawton was not the owner of the work and was not authorized to offer it for sale, and, furthermore, that the true owner did not wish to sell the work to Sack. As a result, Lawton failed to surrender the Bellini to the plaintiffs or to accept payment in connection with their agreement to purchase the work.

Plaintiffs aver that Lawton breached his contract with them for the sale of the Modello and that, although they have reasonably attempted to resell the drawing in order to mitigate the damages caused by the breach, they have been unable to do so, in whole or in part. Plaintiffs also contend that Lawton breached his contract with them concerning the purchase of the Bellini and that they have sustained damages in connection with the breach in the amount of their anticipated profit upon resale of the work. Thus, plaintiffs seek damages in connection with the contract for the sale of the Modello in an amount equal to the purchase price, that is, $12,000,000, as well as interest, and consequential damages in the amount of $3,000,000. In connection with the contract for the purchase of the Bellini, plaintiffs seek damages equal to their anticipated profit, that is, $5,000,000.

Lawton has opposed plaintiffs' claims for damages. In a letter dated February 18, 2002, Lawton denied having breached the contracts at issue in this case and asserted that the Modello was "last traded publicly in London at a Christie's sale in 1989, for under $60K." Lawton also submitted what purports to be a declaration, setting forth essentially the same contentions concerning plaintiffs' damages claims as those contained in his earlier letter. However, the "declaration" is neither signed nor attested.

In support of their application for damages, plaintiffs submitted, *inter alia:* (i) a copy of the August 23, 2000 bill of sale conveying the Modello to Lawton for a sum of $12,000,000; (ii) a copy of the September 18, 2000 commission agreement setting forth the terms of Stewart's agency arrangement with Lawton with respect to the sale of the Bellini; (iii) the declaration of Stewart in support of plaintiffs' motion for a default judgment against Lawton; and (iv) a statement of the interest claimed to be due on plaintiffs' contractual damages. . . .

The general rule for measuring damages for a breach of contract is "the amount necessary to put the plaintiff in the same economic position he would have been in had the defendant fulfilled his contract." Indu Craft, Inc. v. Bank of Baroda, 47 F.3d 490, 495 (2d Cir. 1995). Under New York law, which governs this diversity action, in a case involving the breach of a contract for the sale of goods, a seller may recover the entire contract price, "if the seller is unable to resell [the goods] at a reasonable price or the circumstances reasonably indicate that such effort will be unavailing." Uniform Commercial Code ("UCC") §2-709(1)(b); see also Hyosung America, Inc. v. Sumagh Textile Co., Ltd., 137 F.3d 75, 80-81 (2d Cir. 1998); Creations by Roselynn v. Costanza, 189 Misc. 2d 600, 601, 734 N.Y.S.2d 803, 804-805 (App. Term 2d Dep't 2001).

An aggrieved seller may also recover incidental damages, that is, "commercially reasonable charges incurred in [for example] stopping delivery [or] in the transportation, care and custody of goods after the buyer's breach. . . ." UCC §2-710; see also UCC §§2-708 and 2-709. Since the purpose of providing incidental damages "is only to put the seller in as good a position as performance would have done," incidental damages under the UCC "are limited to out-of-pocket expenses." Ernst Steel Corp. v. Horn Constr. Div., Halliburton Co., 104 A.D.2d 55, 64, 481 N.Y.S.2d 833, 840 (App. Div. 4th Dep't 1984).

Although New York's commercial code provides for incidental damages in the event of a breach by a buyer, there is no comparable provision allowing an aggrieved seller to recover consequential damages. See Associated Metals & Minerals Corp. v. Sharon Steel Corp., 590 F. Supp. 18, 21 (S.D.N.Y. 1983) (citing Petroleo Brasileiro, S.A., Petrobras v. Ameropan Oil Corp., 372 F. Supp. 503, 508 [E.D.N.Y. 1974]). . . .

Based on a review of the parties' submissions in this case, the Court finds that plaintiffs have provided sufficient documentary proof to establish that they are entitled to the amount claimed to be owed for Lawton's breach of the contract for the sale of the Modello. Furthermore, plaintiffs are entitled to prejudgment interest under New York law. However, the Court is not persuaded that plaintiffs are entitled to recover the amount claimed to be owed as consequential damages.

The material submitted by plaintiffs in connection with this inquest establishes that plaintiffs entered into a contract with Lawton for the sale of the Modello for a sum of $12,000,000 and that Lawton failed to pay any part of the purchase price. There is no evidence that the Modello has been resold. Moreover, plaintiffs have established that, under the circumstances, they are unable to resell the Modello at a reasonable price. Accordingly, based on the record evidence, Lawton owes the plaintiffs $12,000,000, the contract price of the Modello....

For the reasons set forth above, I recommend the plaintiffs be awarded damages in the amount of $12,000,000 on their claim for breach of the contract for the sale of the Modello, and prejudgment interest, to be calculated by the Clerk of Court at a rate of 9% per year, on $12,000,000, accruing on August 23, 2000....

If the seller sues for the price, not surprisingly the seller must hold for the buyer the goods that are the subject of the contract. §2-709(2). If the buyer ultimately pays the judgment for the price, the buyer is entitled to the goods. If while the seller is holding the goods for the buyer, resale becomes possible, then the seller may resell and must deduct from its action for the price any proceeds of resale. §2-709(2).

The seller who sues for the price is also eligible to recover incidental damages (and under amended §2-709, consequential damages as well). Incidental damages are defined under §2-710 to include "any commercially reasonable charges, expenses or commissions incurred in stopping delivery, in the transportation, care and custody of goods after the buyer's breach, in connection with return or resale of the goods or otherwise resulting from the breach." A seller's consequential damages are defined in amended §2-710 in the same way as buyer's consequential damages in §2-715(2)(a): any loss resulting from the breach that the breaching party had "reason to know" at the time of contracting and that could not be prevented by the aggrieved party.

2. *Resale Damages.* Besides the seller's action for the price, a second standard seller's remedy available under the Code is the seller's right to resale damages. The seller is eligible for these damages whenever the buyer breaches, the seller reasonably identifies the goods being resold as referring to the broken contract, the seller gives the buyer notice of resale, and the seller resells the goods at either a public or private resale. U.C.C. §2-706. The damages formula for the reselling seller that is given under §2-706(1) is $KP - RP + ID - ES$, where KP = contract price, RP = resale price, ID = incidental damages, and ES = expenses saved as a consequence of buyer's breach (under amended §2-706 the formula also includes "+ CD" to represent a seller's eligibility for consequential damages). To give the seller an incentive to obtain the highest possible price, the Code provides that the seller is not liable to account to the breaching buyer for any profit that it makes on a resale. §2-706(6).

When the seller's resale takes place over an extended period of time, as in the following case, at least a couple of issues are raised: (1) May the seller's resale still be considered commercially reasonable?; and (2) Will the seller be compensated for the time value of money lost to the delay?

Firwood Mfg. Co. v. General Tire
96 F.3d 163 (6th Cir. 1996)

KENNEDY, C.J.

Defendant General Tire, Inc. appeals the District Court's...judgment ...awarding plaintiff Firwood Manufacturing Company, Inc. $187,513 in resale damages and $100,476 in interest in this breach of contract dispute....For the following reasons, we AFFIRM the liability award but REVERSE the award of interest.

This dispute arises from a contract between Firwood and General Tire in which General Tire allegedly agreed to purchase fifty-five model 1225 post-cure inflators (PCIs), thirty-thousand dollar machines used by General Tire in its manufacturing process....

By April 1990, General Tire had purchased twenty-two PCIs from Firwood under the contract. General Tire closed its Barrie plant soon thereafter.

On April 11, 1991, Firwood wrote General Tire to remind it of its obligation to purchase fifty-five PCIs. Firwood informed General Tire that the thirty-three remaining PCIs were in the following stages of production: eight units, 100 percent complete; five units, 95 percent complete; and twenty units, 65 percent complete.

After learning that General Tire did not intend to complete the purchase of the remaining thirty-three PCIs at issue in this dispute, Firwood began looking for alternative buyers. Firwood contacted every major tire company in the United States. General Tire also sought alternative buyers for the PCIs. After three years of searching for alternative buyers, during which it sold a few machines, Firwood was ultimately able to sell the balance of the thirty-three PCIs intended for General Tire, but at a price below that called for in the contract with General Tire.

While looking for buyers, Firwood filled some of its ongoing orders for spare parts with parts that already had been installed in the thirty-three PCIs intended for General Tire. Although the PCIs themselves were specially made for General Tire, the parts taken from the General Tire PCIs and sold as spare parts were fungible parts regularly sold in Firwood's spare parts business.

Following a jury trial, the jury awarded Firwood $287,989 in damages, of which $187,513 represented the difference between resale price and contract price, and $100,476 represented interest. Following trial, General Tire filed a motion seeking judgment as a matter of law, a new trial, or remittitur. The District Court denied General Tire's post-trial motions, and this appeal followed....

General Tire argues that Firwood cannot recover under [U.C.C. §2-706] because it did not comply with this section's requirements. General Tire argues that Firwood did not reasonably identify the goods under the contract because the thirty-three PCIs ultimately sold contained parts not originally included in the machines at the time of the breach. There is also a question whether the resale was commercially reasonable where twenty-nine of the thirty-three machines were sold three years after the breach.

We must first decide whether a seller may substitute fungible goods for those identified to the contract at the time of the breach. Here, identical parts were used to replace the parts which had been sold in the interim. On this question, we find persuasive the reasoning of those courts that allow sellers to substitute fungible goods for purposes of resale so long as the goods truly are fungible and the resale itself is commercially reasonable. In Servbest Foods, Inc. v. Emessee Indus., Inc., 82 Ill. App. 3d 662, 37 Ill. Dec. 945, 403 N.E.2d 1 (1980), the Court allowed a seller to recover damages under §2-706 of the U.C.C. when the resale included different meat than that specifically identified to the contract at the time of the breach:

> the nature of fungible goods suggests no reason why, where a contract involving fungible goods is breached by the buyer, a seller could not recover a deficiency award under section 2-706 based upon a resale of goods other than those identified to the contract inasmuch as such a sale would not affect or alter the price received for the goods in either a private or public sale.

Servbest, 37 Ill. Dec. 945, 403 N.E.2d at 9. The Second Circuit adopted the Servbest rule in a case considering whether a heating oil seller could receive damages under §2-706 when the oil ultimately resold was different from the oil originally identified to the contract. Apex Oil Co. v. Belcher Co. of New York, Inc., 855 F.2d 997, 1005 (2d Cir. 1988). The resold model 1225 post-cure inflators remained reasonably identified to the contract. Thus Firwood is not barred from recovery simply because the PCIs it ultimately sold contained parts different than those at the time General Tire breached. The parts were fungible, and the PCIs into which they were placed were essentially the same PCIs specially made for General Tire.

However, Apex Oil and Servbest identified another important consideration for analyzing whether resales involving substituted fungible goods are commercially reasonable. In Apex Oil, the court noted that "[t]he most pertinent aspect of reasonableness with regard to identification and resale involves timing." Apex Oil, 855 F.2d at 1006. Noting that §2-706 is designed to provide the seller the difference between market value and the contract price, and that resale is designed to determine market price, the court cautioned that timely resale was particularly important in cases involving substituted goods:

> The rule that a "resale should be made as soon as practicable after . . . breach" should be stringently applied where, as here, the resold goods are not those originally identified to the contract. In such circumstances, of course, there is a significant risk that the seller, who may perhaps have already disposed of the original goods without suffering any loss, has identified new goods for resale in order to minimize the resale price and thus to maximize damages.

Apex Oil, 855 F.2d at 1007 (citation omitted); see also McMillan v. Meuser Material & Equip. Co., Inc., 260 Ark. 422, 541 S.W.2d 911, 913 (1976) (finding resale commercially unreasonable because "the resale of [a] bulldozer, in excess of fourteen months after the alleged breach, will be of 'slight probative value' as an indication of the market price at the time of the breach.").

We must decide whether Firwood's resale of PCIs may not serve as the basis of the damage award because sales three years after a breach are not commercially reasonable. There is significant support for the view that three years is unreasonable. See Apex Oil, 855 F.2d at 1006-07 (finding that six-week delay between breach and resale of heating oil, when market volatility over that period was considered, prevented resale from accurately reflecting the market value of the oil); Meuser Material, 541 S.W.2d at 913.

Nevertheless, as the Second Circuit recognized in *Apex Oil,* sellers ought not to be precluded from recovering damages in every case in which resale does not occur immediately:

> "If no reasonable market existed at [the] time, no doubt a delay may be proper and a subsequent sale may furnish the best test, though confessedly not a perfectly exact one, of the seller's damages."

Apex Oil, 855 F.2d at 1006, quoting 4 Anderson on the Uniform Commercial Code §2-706:25 (3d ed. 1983). Indeed, Comment Five to [U.C.C. §2-706] notes that "[w]hat is such a reasonable time depends upon the nature of the goods, the condition of the market and the other circumstances of the case; its length cannot be measured by any legal yardstick or divided into degrees." Even though there was a three-year delay between breach and resale here, we cannot say that the jury was required to find that the resale was commercially unreasonable. At the time of the breach, there was no market for PCIs, machines costing over thirty-thousand dollars that have a very specialized use. Moreover, Firwood made a continuing good faith effort to locate other purchasers. While a three-year delay is suboptimal, we are mindful that UCC remedies are to be liberally construed to ensure that the aggrieved party is "put in as good a position as if the other party had fully performed...." [U.C.C. §1-106] [§1-305(a) as amended]. Accordingly, we hold that the District Court did not err when it denied General Tire's motion for judgment as a matter of law.

Finally, defendant argues that the District Court erred in denying its remittitur motion to eliminate the interest portion of the damage award. Defendant argues that the District Court abused its discretion because, under the UCC, sellers are not entitled to interest damages when buyers breach the contract, and interest is a consequential, not incidental, damage. The District Court denied defendant's motion on the ground that, since courts have required breaching buyers to compensate sellers for extra interest payments made on loans as a result of a breach, plaintiff should be allowed to collect its lost use of money due to the breach. We review a district court's denial of a remittitur motion for abuse of discretion, reviewing the legal component of such denial de novo.

Resolution of this question rests on the distinction between incidental and consequential damages, for sellers are entitled to incidental, but not consequential damages, under the UCC. Michigan defines a seller's incidental damages to include any commercially reasonable charges, expenses or commissions incurred in stopping delivery, in the transportation, care and custody of goods after the buyer's breach, in connection with return or resale of the goods or otherwise resulting from the breach. [U.C.C. §2-710]. The District Court held that "commercially reasonable charges ... resulting from the breach" include interest on the lost use of money caused by the breach. The District Court drew support for its expansive interpretation of "commercial reasonable charges" from Bulk Oil (U.S.A.), Inc. v. Sun Oil Trading Co., 697 F.2d 481 (2d Cir. 1983), in which the seller, Bulk Oil, was awarded post-breach interest payments on a loan taken out to finance its $4,000,000 fuel oil purchase. 697 F.2d at 482. The District Court implicitly held that lost use of money was "related to the concept of interest paid on a loan that would not have been taken out absent breach." Since interest payments constituted incidental damages under *Bulk Oil,* the District Court reasoned, Firwood could recover an analogous incidental damage, viz. its lost use of money caused by General Tire's breach....

Although New York has interpreted incidental damages broadly to include interest payments attributed to the breach under its version of the UCC, Michigan defines incidental damages much more narrowly. In S.C. Gray, Inc. v. Ford Motor Co., 92 Mich. App. 789, 286 N.W.2d 34 (1979), the Michigan Court of Appeals held that a seller could not recover "interest it paid on loans taken out to maintain the business when Ford failed to pay" as incidental damages because interest payments constitute consequential damages. *S.C. Gray,* 286 N.W.2d at 43.

Moreover, Michigan courts have impliedly rejected sellers' claims to the lost use of money by treating interest payments as consequential damages. In Sullivan Indus., Inc. v. Double Seal Glass Co., Inc., 192 Mich. App. 333, 480 N.W.2d 623 (1991), appeal denied, 441 Mich. 931, 498 N.W.2d 737 (1993), the Court of Appeals noted: "Examples of consequential damages include lost profits and interest paid on loans taken out to maintain business operations, see *S.C. Gray,* 92 Mich. App. at 811-812, 286 N.W.2d 34." *Sullivan Indus.,* 480 N.W.2d at 631 (citations omitted); see also id. 480 N.W.2d at 633 ("Interest paid on loans taken out to maintain the business, if foreseeable, falls within the category of consequential damages as prescribed by the UCC."). Since Michigan considers interest paid on loans to be a consequential damage, not an incidental damage, and since sellers may not seek consequential damages, Firwood could not have sought to collect interest payments on a loan to pay for the raw materials in the machines it was to build for General Tire. Nor could it seek the economic equivalent — its lost use of money. . . .

Moreover, even if lost use of money were somehow economically distinguishable from interest payments on a loan, we are inclined to agree with the Seventh Circuit's view that sellers are not entitled to the former as an element of the damage award because lost use of funds is a consequential damage. In Afram Export Corp. v. Metallurgiki Halyps, S.A., the Seventh Circuit rejected a seller's claim for interest payments. 772 F.2d 1358 (7th Cir. 1985). Noting that

> a foregone profit from exploiting a valuable opportunity that the breach of contract denied to the victim of the breach fits more comfortably under the heading of consequential damages than of incidental damages

it held that "the interest or profit [plaintiff] could have obtained from investing, or using elsewhere in its business, the money that it would have gotten [if defendant had not breached]" was a consequential damage. *Afram Export,* 772 F.2d at 1369-70. Since sellers may receive only incidental damages, not consequential damages, and since the lost use of money is a consequential damage, Firwood was not entitled to receive interest as a measure of the damage award. . . .

Nevertheless, Firwood was entitled to claim statutory interest from the date on which suit was filed under Mich. Comp. Laws Ann. §600.6013 even if, as a seller, it was not entitled to interest as a measure of damages under the UCC.

For the foregoing reasons, the District Court is AFFIRMED in all respects except: the award of interest as an element of damages is VACATED, and the case is REMANDED to the District Court for calculation of prejudgment interest under Mich. Comp. Laws Ann. §600.6013.

The result in *Firwood* suggests the wisdom of allowing sellers to be eligible for consequential damages under Article 2 as amended. Suppose that instead of waiting around three years to ultimately find a buyer for these specialized machines, the seller in *Firwood* had chosen instead to sue immediately (or at least right after it struck out despite contacting all of the major tire companies) for the price under §2-709(1)(b) ("if the seller is unable after reasonable effort to resell [the goods] at a reasonable price or the circumstances reasonably indicate that such effort will be unavailing"). Given the very specialized nature of these expensive machines, it would not have seemed much of a stretch for the seller to argue that circumstances reasonably indicate here that efforts to resell would be unavailing.

Had the seller in *Firwood* sued immediately for the price, then under Michigan law it would have been able to claim statutory interest on that amount from the date the suit was filed. Instead, the seller diligently tried for three years to sell all of the machines and finally was able to. Yet despite these good-faith efforts that mainly benefitted the breaching buyer, the Sixth Circuit was not willing to give the seller the time value of its money, a value that the seller certainly would have been able to capture in a successful action for the price. Given the Sixth Circuit's position on this matter, what incentive will a seller in Firwood's position have in the future when faced with a similar breach by a buyer: try long and hard to resell, or look for the first opportunity to sue for the price?

One reason that the incentives created by the *Firwood* case should be troubling for the larger sales system is that as a general matter, the seller is in a much better position than the breaching buyer to dispose of goods for the highest possible price. If sellers are encouraged to immediately sue for the price rather than wait to resell, then it will be the buyer rather than the seller that will ultimately have to dispose of the goods in any case where the seller actually recovers the price from the buyer.

3. *Contract-Market Difference (Without Resale).* Besides the contract-resale difference and an action for the price, another basic seller's remedy is the contract-market difference under §2-708(1). Whenever the buyer repudiates or wrongfully fails to accept, the seller's damages under §2-708(1) equal KP − MP + ID − ES, where KP = contract price, MP = market price, ID = incidental damages, and ES = expenses saved as a consequence of buyer's breach (under §2-708 as amended the formula also includes "+ CD" to represent a seller's eligibility for consequential damages).

   The market price under §2-708(1) is measured as of the time and place for tender, both of which are defined by the contract. The time for tender will be the stated performance date in the contract, and the place for tender will be a function of the delivery term. Thus, an "FOB shipment" term would measure the market price at the seller's location; an "FOB destination" term would measure the market price at the buyer's location. Under amended §2-708(1), the time for measuring market price in the case of repudiation (as opposed to non-acceptance) is "at the expiration of a commercially reasonable time after the seller learned of the repudiation, but no later than the time [for tender]."

4. *Lost Profits.* The last major route that the aggrieved seller may pursue to recover damages is the "lost profits" measure of §2-708(2). Think of the lost-profits seller as one who, had the buyer not breached, would have sold those same goods to another buyer and made an additional profit. Thus, such a seller will have lost a profit by the buyer's breach, and neither the contract-resale nor contract-market damage measures truly puts this seller in the same position the seller would have been in had the buyer not breached.

Problem Set 17

17.1. a. Specialty Dolls, Inc., is in the business of manufacturing children's dolls and stuffed animals. At the height of the "Beanie Baby" craze, Specialty Dolls made a contract to sell 2,000 Beanie Babies to a retailer, Kid Knacks, for a total price of $10,000. The contract said that the 2,000 Beanie Babies would come from "the stock of 8,000 Beanie Babies currently stored in the Specialty Dolls warehouse." When suddenly the Beanie Baby mania died out, Kid Knacks repudiated its contract with Specialty Dolls and told it not to ship the Beanie Babies. At this point, the dolls intended for the Kid Knacks contract had not been set apart from the other 6,000 dolls in the Specialty Dolls warehouse. Specialty Dolls spent lots of time during the next couple of days calling around for another buyer. The only one it found, however, was the Everything Is a Dollar store, which was willing to pay just $1,000 for a shipment of 2,000 Beanie Babies. If Specialty Dolls declines the offer from the Everything Is a Dollar store, may it recover the price from Kid Knacks? U.C.C. §§2-704(1)(a), 2-709.

b. Same facts as part a., except that after turning down the offer from Everything Is a Dollar, the goods are completely destroyed in a fire through no fault of Specialty Dolls. Unfortunately, Specialty Dolls has no fire insurance. May Specialty Dolls recover the price from Kid Knacks? U.C.C. §§2-510(3), 2-709, 2-501(1), Official Comment 5 to §2-501, §§2-105(4), 1-201(17) (revised 1-201(18)).

c. Same facts as part a., except that after turning down the offer from Everything Is a Dollar, Specialty Dolls sends one of its representatives to a local flea market in an attempt to sell its last stock of Beanie Babies, including those intended for Kid Knacks. The Specialty Dolls rep brings three identical boxes of 2,000 Beanie Babies each, including one that has Kid Knacks' name on it. The first buyer at the flea market agrees to pay $6,000 for one of the boxes, so the Specialty Dolls rep gives the buyer the box with Kid Knacks' name on it. The second buyer agrees to buy one of the two remaining boxes for $7,000, and the third buyer buys the last box for $4,000. Assuming that Specialty Dolls gave Kid Knacks proper notice of its intent to re-sell at the flea market, for what amount may Specialty Dolls recover from Kid Knacks? U.C.C. §2-706.

d. Same facts as part a., except suppose that originally the parties had two separate contracts: one for a box of 1,000 "Dobie Dog" dolls for $5,000 and the second for a box of 1,000 "Digger Frog" dolls for $5,000. When Specialty Dolls goes to the flea market to sell its last stock of these dolls, it ends up selling the box of Dobie Dogs for $8,000 and the box of Digger Frogs for $3,000. Assuming proper notice of the resale, for what amount may Specialty Dolls recover from Kid Knacks? U.C.C. §2-706.

17.2. a. Mel's Furniture for Less makes a contract with Kathy Levine to sell her an oak desk for Kathy's home office that she just had built in her basement. Payment was due a month after delivery. Kathy receives the desk and immediately notices that there is significant water damage on the surface of the desk. She intends to call Mel's to complain, but she gets busy with other things. When Mel's sends the bill a month later, Kathy announces to Mel's that she is not going to pay for the desk and Mel's should come and pick it up. Should Mel's be allowed to recover from Kathy in a suit for the price? U.C.C. §§2-709, 2-606, 2-607(2) and (3), 2-602(1).

b. Same facts as part a., except that the desk was perfectly fine, but Kathy decided on the day that she received it that she did not like how it looked in her basement. She immediately called Mel's and told the manager there, "Come get your desk. I've decided I don't want it after all, and I'm not paying for it." Should Mel's be allowed to recover from Kathy in a suit for the price? U.C.C. §§2-709, 2-606, 2-602.

c. Same facts as part a., except that the desk was perfectly fine, but Kathy decided two weeks after she received it that she did not like how it looked in her basement. She then called Mel's and told the manager there, "Come get your desk. I've decided I don't want it after all, and I'm not paying for it." Should Mel's be allowed to recover from Kathy in a suit for the price? U.C.C. §§2-709, 2-608, Official Comment 5 to §2-709.

17.3. Shoe Works was a Boston manufacturer of athletic footwear. Foot Locker was a Chicago retailer that sold shoes of all kinds, including sports shoes. On May 1, Shoe Works and Foot Locker entered into a contract in which Shoe Works agreed to sell Foot Locker 500 pairs of "Sambas," a trendy brand of children's gym shoes. The price was $7,500, the delivery date was "on or before June 1," and the delivery term was "FOB Seller's Plant." Delivery costs from Boston to Chicago were $300, which the buyer paid in advance. Shoe Works put the shoes into the possession of a carrier in Boston on May 25, and the shoes arrived at Foot Locker on June 1. By that point, Foot Locker had concluded that Sambas were no longer "hot," so the Foot Locker manager immediately called the Shoe Works president and told her that the Foot Locker was rejecting the order. Shoe Works quickly arranged to have the shoes sold to Hermann's Sporting Goods in the Chicago suburb of Oak Lawn. Hermann's paid $6,000 for the shoes and picked up the shoes itself from Foot Locker. Unfortunately for Shoe Works, it forgot to give Foot Locker notice of this resale. The market price of 500 Sambas was $6,000 in Chicago on June 1 and $6,500 in Boston on the same date. On May 1, the market price was $7,000 in Chicago and $7,500 in Boston. On May 25, the price was $6,200 in Chicago and $6,700 in Boston. In a suit against Foot Locker, how much may Shoe Works recover (assuming Shoe Works is not a lost-volume seller)? U.C.C. §§2-509(1)(a), Official Comment 2 to §2-706 (Official Comment 11 to §2-706 as amended),

2-706, 2-708(1), 2-503(2), 2-504, Official Comment 1 to §2-708 (Official Comment 3 to §2-708 as amended).

17.4. a. Ben Farmer, a local cattle rancher, is visiting your office for the first time. It turns out that earlier this year Ben had agreed to sell 100 cattle (the last 100 Ben had available for sale) to Mel's Meat For Less (MMFL) for $50,000, "buyer to pick up on May 1." On May 1, MMFL called Ben and repudiated the contract. The market price for 100 cattle on May 1 was $45,000. On June 15, without ever giving notice to MMFL, Ben sold the 100 cattle to a third party for $49,000. It cost Ben roughly $400 per month to feed these cattle. Ben would like to know what his damages against MMFL will be. What do you advise? U.C.C. §§2-708(1), 2-706, 1-106(1) (revised 1-305(a)), Official Comment 1 to §2-703.

b. Same facts as part a., except Ben's resale had been for just $40,000. What would Ben's damages be then? Official Comment 2 to §2-706 (Official Comment 11 to §2-706 as amended).

c. If Ben's resale had been for $40,000, except this time he had given proper notice of the resale, what would Ben's damages be then? Official Comment 5 to §2-706.

d. Suppose now that MMFL had repudiated on March 1, and then on March 15 Ben gave MMFL notice of resale, identified the cattle as the subject of resale, and resold the cattle for $48,000. If the market price of the cattle on May 1 were $45,000, would Ben still be eligible for §2-708(1) damages? If not, why not? U.C.C. §§2-708(1), 2-706, 1-106(1) (revised 1-305(a)), Official Comment 1 to §2-703.

e. Suppose that MMFL had repudiated on March 1, and then on March 15 Ben identified the cattle as the subject of resale and resold the cattle for $48,000. But this time Ben, though he intended otherwise, completely forgot to give notice of the resale to MMFL. If the market price of the cattle on May 1 were $45,000, would Ben still be eligible for §2-708(1) damages? If not, why not? U.C.C. §§2-708(1), 2-706, 1-106(1), (revised 1-305(a)), Official Comment 1 to §2-703.

17.5. Super Dave's Ford Dealership in Waterloo, Iowa, was participating in a manufacturer's incentive program whereby Ford would give a $20,000 bonus to any dealership that sold 100 new Ford Aerostar mini-vans in one calendar year. In late November, Super Dave's had sold 87 new Aerostars when the Waterloo School District made a contract with Dave's to purchase 15 Aerostars for delivery on December 20. Immediately before the district signed the contract, Super Dave told the district representative, "The reason I am able to give you such a great price on these vans is that the 15 vans that you're buying brings our total Aerostar sales to 102 for the year, and we get a $20,000 bonus from Ford if we sell over 100 Aerostars for the year." On December 18, the superintendent of the school district calls Super Dave's to tell him that the district had found a different dealership with a better price on the mini-vans, and thus it would not be buying the vans from Super Dave's. On December 31, Super Dave's had sold a total of 91 Aerostars for the year and therefore did not qualify for the $20,000 incentive payment. When Super Dave's sues the school district for breach, may Super Dave's include in its damages the $20,000 manufacturer's incentive? U.C.C. §§2-710, 1-106(1) (revised 1-305(a)), 2-706(1), 2-708, 2-709(1), cf. §2-715(2)(a).

Assignment 18: Lessor's and Seller's Remedies with Leases, International Sales, and Real Estate

A. Lessor's Remedies

Although the UCC drafters clearly used the Article 2 remedy structure as a foundation for drafting the remedy provisions of Article 2A, there are a number of fundamental differences between a sale and a lease that in turn create major differences between the remedies of a seller and those of a lessor.

The fundamental difference between a sale and a lease is that the lessor has a residual interest in the goods that are leased; the seller has no continuing interest in the goods that are sold. As a result, the lessor and lessee realize at the outset that their contract is necessarily in the nature of a long-term relationship, whereas the seller and buyer may view their contract as a one-shot deal.

The functional significance of the long-term nature of the lessor-lessee relationship is that parties to a lease contract are more likely than buyers and sellers to specify in the lease contract just what the lessor's remedies will be in the event of a default. Similarly, the lessor and lessee are more likely to articulate in their contract exactly what constitutes an event of default. The seller and buyer, by contrast, know that ordinarily the only way that the buyer can breach is by failing to pay the price.

Section 2A-523 categorizes both the lessor's remedies and the various ways in which the lessee can breach. In comparing §2A-523 with §2-703 (listing seller's remedies), two differences are apparent. The first is that the lessor, unlike the seller, is given the right to repossess the goods as one of its standard remedies in §2A-523. Unless the seller has a security interest in the goods it sells on credit, the seller will not normally have a right to repossess upon the buyer's failure to pay the price (and even then the right to repossess arises under Article 9 and the parties' agreement, not Article 2). Because the lessor has a residual interest, however, a default by the lessee can trigger the lessor's right to repossess, which helps the lessor preserve the value of its residual interest.

The second difference between the lessor's listed remedies and those of the seller is that §2A-523(1)(f) (amended §2A-523(1)(i)) specifically mentions that the lessor may "exercise any other rights or pursue any other remedies provided in the lease contract." This is a recognition of the practice described above of the lessor and lessee often spelling out in their lease contract the various ways in which the lessee might be in default of its obligations to the lessor.

The lessor's analogous remedy to the seller's action for the price is the lessor's action for the rent under §2A-529. The lessor's "price" equivalent consists of both unpaid past rent plus the present value of any future rent. §2A-529(1). Once the lessor sues for the rent, it must hold the leased goods for the lessee for the remaining term of the lease. §2A-529(2). If the lessor re-leases the goods before the end of the lease term, then the original lessee gets credit for the revenue gained on the re-lease. §2A-529(3). If the lessee pays the judgment for the rent, it is entitled to possession and use of the leased goods for the remainder of the term. §2A-529(4).

The lessor who sues for the rent is also eligible for incidental damages under §2A-530. Under amended §2A-530, lessors are also eligible to recover consequential damages, just as sellers now can under amended Article 2.

The lessor's analogue to contract-resale damages is found in §2A-527. If the lessor re-leases the goods in a lease agreement that is "substantially similar" to the original lease agreement, the lessor is entitled to $UR + (PVOL - PVNL) + ID - ES$, where UR = accrued but unpaid rent on the original lease as of the date of the new lease term, $PVOL$ = the present value, as of the same date, of the total remaining lease payments for the original lease, $PVNL$ = the present value, as of the same date, of the total lease payments in the new lease for the term that is comparable to the remainder of the original lease, ID = incidental damages, and ES = expenses saved as a consequence of the lessee's breach (under amended §2A-527 the formula also includes "+ CD" to represent a lessor's eligibility for consequential damages).

Note why the "substantially similar" limitation exists for re-leases but not for resales: whereas with lease agreements the lease terms can vary in length, with sales agreements the transfer of ownership from seller to buyer is always intended to be final. If the lease agreement in the re-lease is not "substantially similar" to the original lease, then the lessor must seek damages under §2A-528, Article 2A's contract-market measure. The formula under §2A-528 is $UR + (PVOL - PVML) + ID - ES$, where UR = accrued but unpaid rent for the original lease (measured as of the default where lessor has not repossessed or the date of repossession where the lessor has repossessed), $PVOL$ = the present value, as of the same date, of the total remaining lease payments for the original lease, $PVML$ = the present value, as of the same date, of the market rent for such a remaining term at the place where the goods are located, ID = incidental damages, and ES = expenses saved (under amended §2A-528 the formula also includes "+ CD" to represent a lessor's eligibility for consequential damages).

Section 2A-528(2) also provides a "lost profits" alternative for the aggrieved lessor when the lessor can show that the other measures of damages do not place it in the same position that performance by the lessee would have.

C.I.C. Corp. v. Ragtime, Inc.

726 A.2d 316 (N.J. App. 1999)

PRESSLER, J.

. . . Plaintiff C.I.C. Corp., a New Jersey corporation, appeals from a judgment entered upon a jury verdict awarding it damages of one dollar on its contract claim against defendants, Ragtime, Inc., and Donald Tabatneck. It also appeals from the subsequent order of the trial court denying its motion for a new trial on damages. We find plain error in the court's instructions to the jury respecting damages and accordingly reverse and remand for a new damages trial.

Plaintiff is in the vending machine business. Pursuant to written contracts with owners of various types of retail establishments, it places a variety of coin-operated machines, which it owns, on their premises, including cigarette machines, jukeboxes and game machines. If the machine sells a product, plaintiff keeps the machine stocked. It also services the machines on an on-call basis. The coins are removed by its collectors on a bi-weekly basis and the revenue is shared between plaintiff and the owner of the premises in accordance with the terms of their agreement. Defendant Donald Tabatneck is the proprietor of a so-called go-go bar in West Paterson owned by his corporation, 821 McBride Avenue Corporation, and operated under the trade name Ragtime. He had had plaintiff's coin-operated machines on his premises since the late 1970s or early 1980s under a series of consecutive contracts.

The controversy between the parties arose out of the five-year contract executed by them on October 13, 1994. The agreement covered a cigarette machine, a jukebox, a pool table, and a pinball machine, which had been on the premises for some time. Pursuant to the terms of the agreement, and at defendant's request, plaintiff also loaned defendant $3,500 by way of an advance on his portion of the future revenues at ten percent interest. In the following month, defendant repaid the loan and the four machines were removed. . . .

The problem here is only as to damages. Plaintiff's Office Manager Kathleen Strojny explained plaintiff's computerized record-keeping system and its printouts by which she was able to determine the average net monthly revenue earned by plaintiff from each of the four machines that it had placed in defendant's premises during the twelve-month period preceding the breach. Its net average monthly revenue from the cigarette machine, based on an average monthly sale of 242 packs, was $254. The arrangement with respect to the jukebox was a flat $15 weekly rental sum paid by defendant to plaintiff or, roughly, a monthly net revenue of $60. The monthly revenue from the pinball machine and the pool table was shared between the parties, and plaintiff's average total net for the two machines totaled $386. Strojny therefore calculated plaintiff's net lost monthly revenue over the life of the contract at $700. Over the course of the 59 months of the term remaining on the lease at the time of the breach, the total loss of net revenue was, therefore, $41,000. That was the sum plaintiff sought to recover.

Defendant did not dispute Strojny's calculations respecting the revenue earned by the four machines during the year prior to the breach. The thrust of his defense to the damages claim was his assertion that plaintiff was required to mitigate damages and had failed to do so. And therein lies the error that tainted this damages verdict. In sum, as a matter of law, plaintiff was not required to mitigate.

We consider that legal issue in the context of this record. First, defendant, on his cross-examination of Strojny, attempted to elicit from her information as to what had happened to the four machines after they were removed from his premises. All she could say is that they had been taken to plaintiff's warehouse and that another customer would, in the normal course of business, have been sought for them. She was unable to say, beyond speculation, if these machines had ever been placed with another customer and, if so, how long it had taken to do so. The mitigation issue was next referred to by the court in overruling defendant's objection to the admission into evidence of Strojny's computer printout respecting the average monthly revenue earned by each machine in the year preceding the breach. Although permitting its admission, the court noted that:

> It can be argued that there were very effective arguments made against it, for example, that the equipment was used by somebody else within a few months and the [defense] hasn't been able to say, you know, what happened to the equipment and whether it was used by another company or not.

Evidently, then, the judge was of the view that mitigation was an applicable doctrine here, and plaintiff did not take exception to these comments, perhaps because he had prevailed on the evidence issue that provoked those comments.

The mitigation issue was again referred to in both summations. Defendant's attorney told the jury that he believed the judge would instruct it on mitigation of damages and then referred to Strojny's testimony respecting her lack of knowledge as to the disposition of the equipment after its removal from defendant's premises. He concluded these remarks with this argument:

> Because they want $41,400 from Mr. Tabatneck, if you find he breached his contract, and it didn't work — didn't go as Mr. Tabatneck said. They want you to give them 41,000 — what is it again? Four hundred dollars. But they don't tell you whether they made earnings and what earnings they made on those machines when they took them out of there or when it all started. They're going to ask you to take a shot in the dark. That's what they're asking you. Pick a number, pick 41,400, pick any number you want. Do you understand what I'm saying? Put in the position that this defendant is put in, he's asked to pay forty-one.

In his ensuing summation, plaintiff's attorney argued that there was no duty to mitigate. This is what he said:

> But let's assume that eventually we were able to do that [place the equipment elsewhere]. Does that mean that we don't have losses? Of course not. We have the right to have two establishments, Ragtime plus the next one, a thousand establishments. Now granted, we would have to buy a couple more machines to put into these other establishments, but he is asking you to believe that, if we found another establishment, that wipes out our monetary losses. His position is completely wrong. It's as wrong as, if somebody signs a contract to buy a television set and refuses to pay for it and doesn't want the TV set, if the television seller wants to sue him, they can't say, well, you probably sold your new TV set to someone else. The response is going to be the same as I'm telling you. But what if we did sell that TV to someone else? We have a right to sell TVs to two people, so we want our lost profits from your transaction, Mr. Tabatneck.

Unfortunately, neither attorney requested a charge respecting the duty to mitigate despite defendant's clear assertion that there was such a duty as a matter of law and plaintiff's equally clear assertion that there was not. The judge then instructed the jury generally as to the primary function of compensatory damages, namely, making the injured party whole, and then had this to say:

> The plaintiff presented the testimony of Miss Strojny with regard to the records of the corporation and what the losses were with regard to each machine. You have an exhibit

that goes through that testimony, which reveals that testimony, that testimony as to what the end result was with regard to each machine. *You also have the cross-examination of the defendant, which pointed out ways which may or may not have mitigated or lessened those damages. So what those damages are is for you to decide, according to the law that I just described.* Now in arriving at an amount of any loss of profits sustained by the plaintiff, you may consider any past earnings of the plaintiff in its business, as well as any other evidence bearing upon the issue. So you-the testimony that you heard from Miss Strojny about what happened in the immediate past and you have to make a determination as to whether that can be projected reasonably into the future or not. That's the kind of determination that you have to make if you get to the issue of damages in this case. [Emphasis added.]

Thus, although not expressly instructing the jury with respect to the doctrine of mitigation or its applicability here, the court nevertheless clearly advised the jury that in fixing damages, it could consider what plaintiff did or should have done to "mitigate or lessen damages."

That instruction was in error. This is clearly a "lost volume" situation or, at least, the jury could have so found. As explained by Restatement (Second) of Contracts §347 comment f (1981):

Whether a subsequent transaction is a substitute for the broken contract sometimes raises difficult questions of fact. If the injured party could and would have entered into the subsequent contract, even if the contract had not been broken, and could have had the benefit of both, he can be said to have "lost volume" and the subsequent transaction is not a substitute for the broken contract. The injured party's damages are then based on the net profit that he has lost as a result of the broken contract. Since entrepreneurs try to operate at optimum capacity, however, it is possible that an additional transaction would not have been profitable and that the injured party would not have chosen to expand his business by undertaking it had there been no breach. It is sometimes assumed that he would have done so, but the question is one of fact to be resolved according to the circumstances of each case.

And as further explicated by the Restatement, supra, §350 comment d (1981):

The mere fact that an injured party can make arrangements for the disposition of the goods or services that he was to supply under the contract does not necessarily mean that by doing so he will avoid loss. If he would have entered into both transactions but for the breach, he has "lost volume" as a result of the breach. See Comment f to §347. In that case the second transaction is not a "substitute" for the first one.

We adopted the Restatement view in Locks v. Wade, 36 N.J. Super. 128, 114 A.2d 875 (App. Div. 1955), a case involving the remarkably similar circumstance of a jukebox rental. Relying on the analogous section of the first Restatement of Contracts §336 comment c, we held that:

We think the position plaintiff takes on the matter is sound. Where, as here, a plaintiff lessor agrees to lease an article of which the supply in the market is for practical purposes not limited, then the law would be depriving him of the benefit of his bargain if on the breach of the agreement, it required his claim against the lessee to be reduced by the amount he actually did or reasonably could realize on a re-letting of the article. For if there had been no breach and another customer had appeared, the lessor could as well have secured another such article and entered into a second lease. In case of the breach of the first lease, he should have the benefit of both bargains or not-in a situation where the profit on both would be the same-be limited to the profit on the second of them. Id. at 130-131, 114 A.2d 875.

As we further pointed out in *Locks,* the lost-volume rule has been recognized throughout the country. Id. at 132, 114 A.2d 875.... Moreover, although the parties have not raised the issue, we note that by L. 1994, c. 114, §1 effective January 10, 1995, the Legislature adopted the Uniform Commercial Code — Leases, N.J.S.A. 12A:2A-101 to -532. Its provisions are instructive here. We acknowledge that Chapter 2A of the Code is not applicable to leases of goods entered into prior to its effective date and is hence not applicable to this lease. Nevertheless, we note that the lessor's remedies in the event of default provided for by N.J.S.A. 12A:2A-528(1) expressly include the present value of the total rent for the remaining term. N.J.S.A. 12A:2A-528(2) further provides that:

> If the measure of damages provided in subsection (1) is inadequate to put a lessor in as good a position as performance would have, the measure of damages is the present value of the profit, including reasonable overhead, the lessor would have made from full performance by the lessee, together with any incidental damages allowed under 12A:2A-530, due allowance for costs reasonably incurred and due credit for payments or proceeds of disposition.

We think it plain that the proofs here would have supported a jury finding that plaintiff had a warehouse full of a variety of coin-operated machines and could have placed as many as it could have found customers for. Thus, even if it eventually placed with another customer the machines removed from defendant's premises, it still would have lost the benefit of its bargain with defendant since, in that case, it would have made two deals, not just the second. We also think it plain that the judge's charge, to the extent it referred to mitigation and failed to explain the lost-volume rule, clearly misled and misinformed the jury.

We recognize that plaintiff failed to request a lost-volume instruction and failed, as well, to object to the instructions given. The plain-error rule, therefore, applies, and we must determine whether the erroneous instructions produced an unjust result or prejudiced substantial rights.... Obviously a charge that has the capacity to mislead, misinform and confuse the jury with respect to the measurement of damages — and it evidently did so here — meets the plain-error standard....

We need not speculate as to why the jury awarded plaintiff only one dollar in damages. We are, however, persuaded that the error in the instructions deprived plaintiff of its right to have a properly informed jury address the damages issue. It is, therefore, entitled to a new trial on damages.

A final remedy for the lessor, which has no analogue in Article 2, is found in §2A-532, entitled "Lessor's Rights to Residual Interest." This remedy, which is in addition to other remedies that the lessor may exercise, compensates the lessor for "any loss or damage to the lessor's residual interest in the goods caused by the default of the lessee." This remedy protects the lessor against, among other things, damage by the lessee of the leased goods. For example, if a lessee in a two-year lease failed to pay the final four months' rent and also negligently damaged the leased goods, the lessor could sue not only for the unpaid rent but also for the value of the damage to its residual interest in the leased goods.

B.   Seller's Remedies with International Sales

To understand the world of a seller's remedies under the CISG, one must appreciate a major distinction that the CISG draws at the outset: the difference between the seller that "avoids" the contract and the seller that chooses not to avoid the contract. A seller may avoid a contract only when the buyer commits a "fundamental breach," C.I.S.G. Art. 64(1)(a), which is in turn defined by Article 25 as a breach that substantially deprives the other party of "what he is entitled to expect under the contract."

Under Article 81(1), avoidance of a contract by either party releases both parties of their obligations thereunder, although the avoiding party retains its right to sue for damages. What this means for the seller that chooses to avoid the contract is that if the seller does so, it no longer may bring what we think of as "an action for the price," since the buyer is no longer obligated to pay the price. The avoiding seller may, however, sue the buyer for contract-resale damages under Article 75 or contract-market damages under Article 76. Under either article, the seller may also recover what we think of in the UCC as either incidental or consequential damages. C.I.S.G. Art. 74. Thus, in international sales, the seller can get both incidental and consequential damages, but only to the extent that they are reasonably foreseeable by the buyer at the time of contract formation.

There are two interesting features to note at this point about the CISG remedies structure. First, the CISG combines the buyer's "cover" remedy (about which more in Assignment 20) with the seller's resale remedy in a single Article, 75, and also combines in Article 76 both the buyer's and the seller's contract-market damages. Second, the CISG combines in a single article, 74, the buyer's incidental and consequential damages with the seller's incidental and consequential damages (including "lost profit"). Article 74 describes the damages solely as consequential damages and contains the Hadley v. Baxendale limit on the foreseeability of the harm ultimately suffered by the aggrieved party.

If the seller in an international transaction does wish to sue the buyer for the price, the seller's ability to do so seems at first greater than that of a seller under the UCC. Article 62 says quite simply, "The seller may require the buyer to pay the price, take delivery or perform his other obligations, unless the seller has resorted to a remedy which is inconsistent with this requirement."

This right of the seller under the CISG to demand specific performance of the buyer does, however, come with some limits. First, Article 77 sets up a general mitigation rule by which a party that fails to reasonably mitigate the damages of the breaching party may see its own claim for damages reduced accordingly. Second, in the case where the seller is still in possession of the goods, Article 88(2) creates a duty on the seller's part to resell the goods for the buyer's benefit in any case where the goods are subject to rapid deterioration. Third, and most significantly, Article 28 says that in a dispute under the CISG, the forum court "is not bound" to require specific performance of a particular party unless the forum court's domestic sales law would similarly require specific performance of that same party. Thus, in a CISG case before an American court, the seller's action for the price might be limited, depending on the court's interpretation of Article 28, to the situations that are enumerated in U.C.C. §2-709. As a practical matter, then, the international action for the price may not be significantly broader than the domestic one.

C.   Seller's Remedies with Real Estate Sales

When a buyer breaches its agreement in a real estate sale, the breach will almost always take the form of an anticipatory repudiation. Typically, the seller will not deliver title to the buyer until the seller receives cash from the buyer. Thus, the classic case of buyer breach in a real estate transaction is where the buyer repudiates the contract after the parties sign the contract but before the sale closes. In most cases, the typical default remedy for the aggrieved seller in this situation is the seller's contractual right to keep the buyer's earnest money deposit. Some courts, however, are cautious about letting the seller keep the buyer's deposit, especially where the deposit is particularly large, where it is clear that the buyer breached for reasons beyond its control (such as inability to obtain financing), or where the seller is unable to show any actual damages sustained by the buyer's breach.

Depending on the terms of the particular sales contract, some states may allow the seller to recover contract-market damages against the buyer, but only where the seller can prove those damages (i.e., prove that the buyer overpaid) and where the seller first returns the buyer's deposit. Sellers are generally not entitled to contract-resale damages as such, but as the next case shows, an actual resale by the seller shortly following the buyer's breach will be persuasive evidence of the property's market value for the purpose of calculating contract-market damages.

Williams v. Ubaldo
670 A.2d 913 (Me. 1996)

Wathen, C.J.

Defendant John L. Ubaldo appeals from a judgment entered in the Superior Court (Oxford County, Alexander, J.) awarding damages to plaintiffs Roger and Cynthia Williams for breach of a real estate contract. Ubaldo, the purchaser under the contract, argues that the failure to consummate the sale resulted from his inability to secure financing, and the court erred in finding that he had breached the contract. He also challenges the elements of damage included in the judgment. We conclude that the court erred only in calculating the damage award. Thus, we modify the judgment and affirm.

The facts as developed in a jury-waived trial are as follows: In January 1993, Ubaldo entered into a written contract to purchase the Williamses' home in Oxford. The purchase price was $450,000. In preparation for closing, the property was appraised at $480,000. The terms called for a down payment of $10,000, the remainder to be paid at closing, scheduled for May, 1993. The contract contained a financing provision, stating that Ubaldo's obligation to purchase was contingent on his ability to secure adequate financing. He was required to seek and accept financing in good faith. In the event of a breach by Ubaldo, the contract provided that the Williamses would retain the earnest-money deposit, while still reserving all available legal and equitable remedies.

A few weeks prior to the closing, the parties amended the original contract, extending the time for Ubaldo's performance. The amendment resulted from the fact that he attempted to secure financing with a bank, but was unable to qualify for a mortgage loan. Ubaldo's mother agreed to co-sign the promissory note, and the bank then agreed to extend financing for the purchase. The loan was for $360,000; the remaining $90,000 was to be supplied by his mother on or before closing. The parties attended a closing, but the sale was not completed because the mother failed to provide the $90,000 cash payment. Ubaldo later applied for another mortgage loan without his mother, and was denied.

After a few months, the Williamses filed a complaint against Ubaldo seeking specific performance of the contract, and an award of the $10,000 deposit. Ubaldo then filed a complaint against the Williamses seeking a return of the deposit. The court consolidated the two cases. Before trial was held, the Williamses sold their home to another purchaser for $430,000.

At the trial, the court found that Ubaldo had breached the contract. In assessing damages, the court compared the contract price, $450,000, and the eventual selling price, $430,000, and awarded the $20,000 difference. In addition, the court assessed $3,500 for real estate taxes paid by the Williamses from the time of the breach to the time of sale, and $500 for expenses plaintiffs incurred in connection with snow removal. The court assessed damages in the total sum of $24,000; judgment was entered for $14,000 after offsetting the deposit. Ubaldo appeals. . . .

The court awarded plaintiffs the $20,000 difference between the contract price and the subsequent sales price as compensatory damages. "The overriding purpose of an award of compensatory damages for a breach of contract is to place the plaintiff in the same position as that enjoyed had there been no breach." Marchesseault v. Jackson, 611 A.2d 95, 98 (Me. 1992), citing Forbes v. Wells Beach Casino, Inc., 409 A.2d 646, 654 (Me. 1979). In an action for breach of contract for the sale of real property, the claimant is entitled to the "benefit of the bargain," which equals the difference between the contract price and the fair market value at the time of breach. The reports of professional appraisers have been accepted as evidence of the fair market value of real estate. Evidence of the price resulting from a subsequent sale is also probative of a property's fair market value.

Ubaldo argues incorrectly that the only evidence as to fair market value at time of breach is the testimony of the broker that the house had been appraised for

$480,000. In fact, no appraiser actually testified. The court had only the subsequent sale before it. There is no suggestion that that sale was unreasonable or made in bad faith. The court acted well within its discretion in finding that the subsequent sales price was an accurate measure of market value at the time the contract was breached.

Ubaldo argues that the court erred in granting $3,500 in damages for the property taxes paid by the Williamses for the period of time between the breach and sale. We agree. The Williamses retained ownership, use, and occupancy of a valuable asset during that time. There is no authority for the proposition that the avoidance of tax liability is part of the benefit of the bargain and may be included without considering corresponding financial benefits.

Finally, Ubaldo challenges the special damages awarded for the Williamses' costs in repurchasing winter-related equipment and the extra costs of snow removal. He argues that these special damages were not within the contemplation of the parties when they signed the contract. A claimant is entitled to "special damages" resulting from the unique needs and characteristics of the parties, if the parties were reasonably aware of those circumstances at the time the contract was created. . . .

It is not reasonable to conclude that the extra costs of snow removal and winter equipment are foreseeable consequences of a breach of a real estate contract in the ordinary case. People selling their homes in Maine are not necessarily in the process of moving to warmer climates: they could be staying in Maine, or moving to another northern state. There is no evidence in the record that Ubaldo was aware of the Williamses' plans after the sale. Neither is there any evidence that they communicated their intention to sell their winter equipment and move to a warmer climate.

The Superior Court did not err in finding that Ubaldo breached the sale contract, but it erred in awarding payment for taxes and snow removal.

The entry is: Judgment modified to $10,000, reflecting a total damage award of $20,000 minus the offset for the deposit. As so modified, judgment affirmed.

Some states, like Maine in the above case, will permit the aggrieved real estate seller to recover consequential damages in addition to contract-market damages. However, when consequential damages are recovered by sellers, the damages tend to be for costs associated with resale that the seller would not have incurred had the seller proceeded with the original sale: for example, if the original sale was to be "by owner" but the seller ended up having to use a real estate agent for the resale.

Note that in *Williams* the seller had apparently originally asked for specific performance from the buyer, although the seller eventually itself conducted a resale. For several reasons, a specific performance remedy for sellers in the real estate context would be extremely rare, but not out of the question. Because the most common reason for a buyer breach is lack of money, specific performance is ordinarily completely impractical: if Ubaldo, the buyer in the *Williams* case, had the $450,000 there never would have been a lawsuit, and a court order commanding him to pay the $450,000 doesn't do anything to remedy his lack of money.

Finally, note that the contractual remedies provision in *Williams* gave the seller the ability to retain the security deposit at the same time it was suing for other damages. That provision is rather unusual. Most residential form sales contracts force the seller to choose between retaining the security deposit or pursuing other remedies against the buyer. Consider the following:

REMEDIES UPON DEFAULT

If either party defaults in the performance of any obligation of this contract, the party claiming a default shall notify the other party in writing of the nature of the default and his election of remedy. The notifying party may, but is not required to, provide the defaulting party with a deadline for curing the default. If the default is by Buyer, Seller may either accept the earnest money as liquidated damages and release Buyer from the contract (in lieu of making any claim in court), or may pursue any remedy at law or in equity. If Seller accepts the earnest money, it shall be divided as follows: expenses of broker and seller in this transaction will be reimbursed, and balance to go one-half to Seller, and one-half divided equally between listing broker and selling broker (if working as subagent of Seller) in lieu of commission on this contract.... In the event of litigation between the parties, the prevailing party shall recover, in addition to damages or equitable relief, the cost of litigation including reasonable attorney's fees. This provision shall survive closing and delivery of Seller's deed to buyer.

Take a look at the last few sentences of this provision. Notice first the inclusion of a contractual reversal of the "American rule" on liability for attorney's fees. Second, note that this form contract allows the real estate brokers a right to a partial commission even in the absence of a consummated sale. These two special provisions on attorney's fees and broker commissions are probably understandable when you recall that the form in question (like most such forms) was promulgated by a brokers' association in conjunction with the local bar association.

Problem Set 18

18.1. Big Lou of Lou's Used Cars (from Problem 2.1) had not seen you for some time, but he just stopped by your office with a new problem. Lou's problem stemmed from an experience he had with a small fleet of used cars that he leased. A couple of years ago a new customer, Charlie Erker, had agreed to lease a '93 Cadillac for three years at $400 per month. Exactly one year into the lease, Charlie dropped the car off at Lou's and said, "I don't need it any-more." Even before dropping the car off, Charlie had missed the last two payments on the lease. At the point when Charlie repudiated his lease, Lou's lease fleet was all in use. Therefore, it took Lou three months and a $50 newspaper ad to re-lease the car to a different customer; the new lease was for two years at only $300 per month. Lou always uses the same standard lease form, which contains blanks for the length of the lease and the rental rate. Lou had, however, made a special allowance for Charlie only in which Lou agreed to have the car hand-washed every month for Charlie at Lou's expense (this had cost Lou $10 per month). Lou asks you what amount of damages he could claim against Charlie for Charlie's breach. What do you advise? U.C.C. §§2A-527, 2A-530, Official Comment 7 to §2A-527. (In calculating damages for this problem, don't bother actually discounting any of the payment streams to present value, but note to yourself where that would normally be done.)

18.2. Big Lou had one more problem that was lease-related, and this one, Lou said, was even worse than the first. Lou had leased a '94 Ford Taurus Wagon to Sam Miller, a single father with four children. That lease was for $250 per month for four years. One year into the lease, Sam missed two consecutive payments and Lou had the car repossessed. Much to Lou's horror, Sam's children had torn much of the upholstery off the seats inside the car. It cost Lou $800 to repair the upholstery damage, after which Lou sold the car for $14,000, since Lou had stopped leasing used cars the day after Sam had leased this one. Now Lou wants to sue Sam for his breach of the lease agreement. The $250-per-month lease payment was roughly equal to the market value of the lease at the time of the breach. For what amount of damages may Lou recover? U.C.C. §§2A-527, 2A-528, 2A-529, 2A-530, 2A-532. (In calculating damages for this problem, don't bother actually discounting any of the payment streams to present value, but note to yourself where that would normally be done.)

18.3. Steel Works, Inc., is a Des Moines, Iowa, manufacturer that contracts to sell to Canadian Brinks, a Toronto security firm, a set of 10 specially manufactured steel doors for $70,000. The delivery date is October 5, and the delivery term is "FOB Seller's Factory." Canadian Brinks was responsible for installing the doors. On October 1, Canadian Brinks calls Steel Works and repudiates the contract. In calling around to find other possible buyers, Steel Works gets two offers: the first is from an Iowa buyer that will pay $45,000 for the doors and will pick up and install the doors itself; the second is from a California buyer that will pay $60,000 for the doors if Steel Works ships them (at a cost of $3,000) and installs them (another $1,500). On October 1, the market price for these doors in Iowa is $45,000 and in Toronto it is $43,000. The president of Steel Works comes to you and asks what damage options are available to her company and which option would be the company's best alternative. What do you advise? C.I.S.G. Arts. 25, 64(1)(a), 74, 75, 76, 62, 77, 28.

18.4. Joe Thompson was a Portland, Maine, sportswriter who was tired of maintaining a single-family home and was looking to move into a condominium. He listed his house "For Sale by Owner" at $200,000, and he ultimately accepted Brad Pearson's offer of $190,000, in large part because it did not contain a financing contingency clause. Joe required that Brad put down a $5,000 earnest money deposit. Unfortunately for Joe, Brad ended up being unable to secure financing and Brad ultimately breached the sales contract for lack of a mortgage. Joe returned Brad's security deposit with a letter in which Joe retained his right to sue Brad for any and all remedies. When the house failed to sell after several more months, Joe relented and got a real estate agent. The agent convinced Joe to spend $10,000 for central air-conditioning, and finally the house sold almost exactly one year after Brad failed to close on his contract. The selling price was $170,000, but Joe owed his agent 6 percent of that. Besides the $10,000 Joe spent for central air-conditioning, he ended up paying $18,000 in mortgage payments and $1,500 in property taxes while he continued to occupy the house during the last year. Now that he finally has sold the house, Joe comes to you to ask for what amount he can recover from Brad for Brad's breach of the earlier contract. What do you advise?

Assignment 19: Buyer's Remedies with Sales of Goods

Just as with this book's coverage of seller's remedies, this assignment begins the subject of buyer's remedies by making the point that the vast majority of remedies exercised by aggrieved buyers are of the non-litigation variety. In many cases, buyers are even better situated than sellers to use non-judicial remedies since frequently buyers will not have paid all of the purchase price at the time they discover the seller's breach. In those situations, the buyer always has as a last resort simply withholding the price, which at a minimum puts the burden on the seller rather than the buyer to file a lawsuit. That simple act can be surprisingly effective in getting a seller's attention, particularly when the seller has borrowed money to fund its production or acquisition of the goods sold.

Typically when a buyer is dissatisfied with the seller's product, the first step that the buyer will take is to inform the seller and ask the seller to make things right. More often than not, the seller's response to the buyer's complaint will be to repair or replace the defective goods, unless the seller has some reason to believe that the buyer's complaint is unfounded.

In those unusual cases in which the seller does not or cannot fix the problem, the buyer will still retain some leverage if it has not yet paid the full purchase price. As noted above, this nonjudicial exercise of setoff can be a powerful tool for the aggrieved buyer. The in-house counsel for a Fortune 200 department store chain explains how the setoff right can be even more potent where the buyer has multiple accounts with the same seller: "The one remedies issue that we pay attention to in our standard forms is that we make sure the seller realizes that they are dealing with our larger company, not just the particular store that is making the purchase. In that way we can preserve our ability to set off if the same vendor has dealings with other of our stores."

If refusing to pay or delaying payment is inadequate to solve the problem, the buyer can turn to the more serious remedy of terminating its relationship with the seller. As the purchasing agent for a medium-sized plastics manufacturer put it: "We have never had to go to litigation in the 15 years that I've been here. Buyer remedies in practice are really pretty simple: if the material we get is not good, then the supplier fixes it for us or they don't get any more of our business. Think of it from the supplier's perspective: if we've got a $3,000 problem with one of their products and we do $400,000 worth of business with them in a year, doesn't it make sense for them to fix it for us?"

Just as with seller's remedies, it is a tribute to the UCC drafters that very few sales contracts spend a lot of space changing the Article 2 standard remedies for buyers. The one exception to this is consequential damages, which sellers are always eager to disclaim when they can. On the other hand, buyers will fight hard to retain their right to sue for consequential damages caused by the seller's breach.

The in-house counsel that advises the purchasing department of a Fortune 200 manufacturer explained it this way: "Our starting point is that a seller should be responsible for all damage that is caused by their breach. Depending on the seller and the leverage they have, they might be able to get us to make exceptions to that, like liquidated damages or limitation of consequential damages, but we fight hard to keep all of our remedies intact at the outset."

When informal negotiations fail and the buyer has not set off or used other nonjudicial leverage to satisfy itself, Article 2 provides a laundry list of possible litigation remedies for the aggrieved buyer. The potential UCC remedies available to the buyer will initially be a function of whether or not the buyer has accepted the goods. If the buyer has accepted the goods and it is too late to revoke acceptance, the buyer's remedies are limited to an action for breach of warranty, as outlined in §2-714. If the buyer has either failed to receive the goods or has justifiably rejected them or revoked acceptance of them, the buyer's remedies are more varied, as described in §2-711. Both categories of aggrieved buyers are eligible for incidental and consequential damages as defined in §2-715.

In all cases, the underlying idea of the buyer's remedies sections, as with seller's remedies, is to try to put the buyer in the position that the buyer would have been in had the seller performed. U.C.C. §1-106(1) (revised §1-305(a)). For the buyer that has accepted the goods and may no longer revoke its acceptance, the damages formula for seller's breach of warranty is found in §2-714: $VCG - VNCG + ID + CD$, where VCG = the Value of Conforming Goods, $VNCG$ = the Value of the Non-Conforming Goods that buyer in fact received, ID = Incidental Damages, and CD = Consequential Damages.

Oftentimes the difference between the value of what the buyer actually received and the value of what the buyer should have received can be as simple as whatever it costs the buyer to have the defect repaired. Although the cost of repair might in some cases exceed the $VCG - VNCG$ difference, it is normally viewed as an acceptable surrogate for this value difference because repair is often the practical way to provide the buyer with its expectation. Where repair is not possible, however, a court would be forced to assess in other ways the diminution in value that the seller's breach of warranty caused to the buyer's goods. In order for the aggrieved buyer to be eligible at all for breach of warranty damages, the buyer must give the seller notice of the breach "within a reasonable time after [the buyer] discovers or should have discovered any breach." U.C.C. §2-607(3)(a).

Although the buyer that has accepted the goods and can no longer revoke acceptance has lost its ability to dump the goods back to the seller, such a buyer is explicitly given the right in §2-717 to deduct from the price any damages that result from seller's breach. In order to exercise this right, the buyer must first notify seller of its intention to do so. The reason that this notice is important is that it gives the seller a chance to respond to the buyer's complaint and to assess its validity. More important as a practical matter, the right of the buyer to deduct damages from the purchase price is only as useful as the amount of the purchase price that yet remains unpaid.

As noted above, besides the buyer that is stuck with defective goods, the second category of aggrieved buyer is the one who will end up with no goods at all, either because the seller never delivered or because the buyer rightfully dumped defective goods back to the seller. This aggrieved buyer's options are set down in §2-711, and include (in addition to the buyer getting its money back) the right to "cover" and the right to contract-market damages. Such a buyer may, in certain circumstances, be entitled to specific performance.

In some cases the rightfully rejecting or revoking buyer will still have the goods in its hands. Where such a buyer has already paid all or part of the purchase price, §2-711(3) gives a special self-help remedy: the buyer may hold the goods as security for repayment of its purchase price as well as for any expenses the buyer incurs in holding or storing the goods. Ultimately, such a buyer can resell these goods "in like manner as an aggrieved seller" (under §2-706(1)) as a way to recover its damages.

The buyer's right to cover is described in §2-712. In order to cover, the aggrieved buyer must make "in good faith and without unreasonable delay any reasonable purchase of or contract to purchase goods in substitution for those due from the seller." U.C.C. §2-712(1). The covering buyer's damages are then measured as RBPP + CC − KP + ID + CD (ES, where RBPP = Return of any Purchase Price paid by Buyer, CC = Cost of Cover, KP = Contract Price, ID = Incidental Damages, CD = Consequential Damages, and ES = Expenses Saved as a result of seller's breach.

To the extent that there are disputes in cover situations, they tend to involve one of three issues: (1) Did the buyer wait too long to cover?; (2) Were the goods that the buyer purchased as a cover really the same as the contract goods?; and (3) Did the buyer pay too much for the cover goods?

Section 2-712 and its Official Comments are quite clear that buyer's cover is strictly an optional remedy for buyer. Section 2-712(3) says that "[f]ailure of the buyer to effect cover within this section does not bar him from any other remedy." Official Comment 3 (Official Comment 6 to §2-712 as amended) reinforces the optional nature of cover for the buyer by noting that "[t]he buyer is always free to choose between cover and damages for non-delivery under the next section."

The "next section" referred to in Comment 3 is §2-713, the aggrieved buyer's contract-market measure of damages. You might think of §2-713 as a kind of "hypothetical cover" for the buyer. The actual cover remedy of §2-712 does a great job of effectuating the "spirit of the remedies" policy of §1-106(1) (revised §1-305(a)), in that it almost always puts the buyer in exactly the same position that the buyer would have been in had the seller performed: the buyer ends up getting the goods, and the seller pays the buyer for any additional cost that the buyer incurred in order to get the substitute goods.

The contract-market measure of pre-amended §2-713 is less likely to put the buyer in exactly the same position that the buyer would have been in had the seller not breached. For one reason, its damage measure sets the market price as of the time that the buyer learns of the breach, U.C.C. §2-713(1), which may not end up being the market price of the goods as of the time of seller's originally promised performance. Amended §2-713 uses a two-pronged approach to the time for measuring the market price. In the case of non-delivery by the seller or proper rejection or revocation by the buyer, the market price is measured at the time for tender. If there is an anticipatory repudiation by the seller, then the market price is measured "at the expiration of a commercially reasonable time after the buyer learned of the repudiation," but no later than the time for tender. Under both pre-amended and amended §2-713, the place where the market price is measured is the place of tender, unless the buyer rejects or revokes acceptance of the goods after arrival, in which case the market price is measured as of the place of arrival. U.C.C. §2-713(2).

The §2-713(1) formula itself looks strikingly similar to the cover formula, with the only difference being that the market price number substitutes for the cost of cover: RBPP + MP − KP + ID + CD − ES, where RBPP = Return of any Purchase Price paid by Buyer, MP = Market Price, KP = Contract Price, ID = Incidental Damages, CD = Consequential Damages, and ES = Expenses Saved as a result of seller's breach.

One remedies-related set of issues that arises for both buyers and sellers is when one party gets information prior to the performance date that calls into question the other side's ability to perform the contract. At that point, the insecure party is entitled to demand adequate assurance of future performance. If such assurance is not forthcoming, then the insecure party can declare that the other side has committed an anticipatory repudiation of the contract, which is a form of breach that entitles the aggrieved party to all of the usual remedies. While the two sections governing this situation, 2-609 and 2-610, apply equally to buyers and sellers, buyers are more likely than sellers to utilize these sections. That may stem from the more complex nature of a seller's performance — manufacturing or procuring goods — than the buyer's, which is simply paying the price. A not uncommon situation that leads to a demand for adequate assurance is when one of the contracting parties becomes insolvent or files for bankruptcy.

In re Beeche Systems
164 B.R. 12 (N.D.N.Y. 1994)

SCULLIN, J.

In November 1990, appellant D.A. Elia Construction Corp. ("Elia") submitted a bid to the New York State Thruway Authority ("Thruway Authority") to provide materials and perform services in connection with a pier rehabilitation project at the Castleton Bridge (the "project"). As part of its bid, Elia allocated $62,000 as an estimate for its cost in obtaining scaffolding equipment necessary to access the bridge. Elia was awarded this contract in December 1990. Elia contracted with appellee Beeche Systems Corp. ("Beeche") to provide this scaffolding equipment (the "contract") because Beeche had provided a similar scaffolding system to another contractor who had performed work for the Thruway Authority on the same bridge one year earlier. The parties eventually agreed that Elia would purchase the scaffolding from Beeche at a cost approximately twice its rental value, and that Elia had the right to require Beeche to repurchase the scaffolding system at 50% of the contract cost.

On January 9, 1991, Elia executed a purchase order with Beeche regarding this equipment for a purchase price of $117,810.00. Under the terms of such agreement, 12 1/2% of this price was to be paid by Elia upon execution of the agreement, with the balance due 15 days after delivery of the system and acceptance of the equipment by the Thruway Authority.

On January 15, 1991, apparently unbeknownst to Elia, Beeche filed a voluntary petition for relief under Chapter 11 of the U.S. Bankruptcy Code (the "Code"). This filing for relief was allegedly precipitated by the Internal Revenue Service's commencement of enforcement proceedings against Beeche to recover purportedly delinquent taxes.

After several delays by Beeche in submitting design proposals to the Thruway Authority regarding the scaffolding equipment, Elia's project manager sent Beeche a letter dated February 28, 1991 that demanded that Beeche comply with the terms of the parties' agreement and advised Beeche that it may be liable for back-charges if it failed to perform in accordance with the agreement. Beeche in turn demanded a modification of the agreement. Under the terms of this modification, Beeche was entitled to accelerated payments regarding the scaffolding apparatus. Even though Elia allegedly viewed Beeche's proposal as "extortion," Elia agreed to these modifications and to accelerated payment under the contract. Thereafter, the value of this contract was subsequently increased to $138,518.22 in April 1991, reflecting change orders requested by Elia.

On April 2, 1991, Beeche provided Elia with the scaffolding equipment in accordance with the modified contract and as directed by Elia. On May 7, 1991, Elia acknowledged receipt of the equipment purchased and indicated that it would pay the balance due on the equipment in 15 days. Shortly after sending this letter, Elia claims that it became aware, for the first time, of Beeche's status as a party in bankruptcy.

Elia claims that on June 4, 1991, due to Beeche's failure to disclose the fact that it had filed for bankruptcy and Beeche's delays in submitting design proposals to the Thruway Authority, it determined that Beeche had acted in bad faith and that there were serious questions raised about Beeche's ability or willingness to comply with its contractual obligations. Therefore, rather than pay Beeche the $46,913.48 balance due under the contract, Elia sent Beeche a letter demanding that Beeche repurchase the scaffolding equipment for $69,259.11 — 50% of the purchase price. Elia also determined that it had the right to either set-off or recoup the $46,913.48 which it owed Beeche against Beeche's $69,259.11 obligation to repurchase the scaffolding system.

By letter dated July 22, 1991, Beeche demanded final payment from Elia under the contract and the return of the scaffolding equipment.

On March 27, 1992, Beeche commenced a suit to compel Elia to turn over the scaffolding equipment and pay the balance due under the contract, plus consequential damages. Elia's answer to such complaint contained a counterclaim which sought judgment in the sum of $69,259.11 against Beeche, with interest.

On September 3, 1992, this matter was tried before Chief Judge Mahoney of the U.S. Bankruptcy Court for the Northern District of New York. In his decision dated November 6, 1992, Judge Mahoney ordered Elia to turn the scaffolding equipment over to Beeche and denied Beeche's further claim for damages. That court also determined that Elia's claim with respect to the buy-back provision in the contract had been forfeited by Elia by its own actions....

. . . In its appeal, Elia argues that Beeche's insolvency and subsequent bankruptcy filing, as well as its failure to disclose such bankruptcy or to offer adequate assurance of performance constituted an anticipatory breach of the contract under the Uniform Commercial Code ("U.C.C.") as adopted by New York. It also argues that it was entitled to either offset or recoup the amount due Beeche under the contract with the amount Beeche owed Elia under the buy-back provision of the contract. It next contends that Beeche's failure to disclose its insolvency at the time of the contracting constituted fraud requiring rescission of the agreement. Elia further argues that the Bankruptcy Court improperly required Elia to turn over the scaffolding equipment without requiring Beeche to fully perform its repurchase obligation. Finally, Elia contends that Judge Mahoney "manifested a judicial intolerance and hostility towards Elia" which colored the lower court's decision against Elia.

Beeche argues that the Bankruptcy Court's decision should be affirmed, however it claims that it is entitled to the damages sought in its complaint, or that, at a minimum, Elia should be required to assure Beeche that the scaffolding equipment is in good working order at the time Elia turns over the equipment.

Under U.C.C. §2-610, Elia claims that Beeche's insolvency and subsequent bankruptcy constituted an anticipatory repudiation of the contract under U.C.C. §2-610. This statute provides, in part, that:

> When either party repudiates a contract with respect to a performance not yet due the loss of which will substantially impair the value of the contract to the other, the aggrieved party may:
>
> . . .
>
> b. resort to any remedy for breach even though he has notified the repudiating party that he would await the latter's performance and has urged retraction; and
>
> c. in either case *suspend his own performance* . . . (Emphasis added).

Elia argues that Beeche's acts and omissions regarding its filing of bankruptcy and failure to disclose same to Elia "reasonably indicated a rejection of the agreement to the extent of the repurchase obligation entitling Elia to withhold payment as contemplated within U.C.C. §2-610." Elia further contends that Beeche's failure to assume this contract under §365 of the Code constituted an "unequivocal rejection of the agreement."

However, pursuant to 11 U.S.C. §365, Beeche, as a debtor, had the authority to assume or reject its executory contract with Elia regarding the scaffolding. If the mere filing of bankruptcy constituted an anticipatory breach of contract, this decision by the trustee to assume or reject a contract could never be reached, thereby rendering meaningless this provision of the Bankruptcy Code. The mere fact that Beeche was in bankruptcy and failed to disclose this fact to Elia does not amount to an anticipatory repudiation of the contract. In fact, Elia's argument that such conduct amounted to an anticipatory repudiation in the present case is particularly puzzling since Beeche had already provided Elia with the scaffolding equipment and was not obligated to buy back this system until it had received final payment from Elia. . . .

Under U.C.C. §2-609, Elia alternatively argues that Beeches failure to disclose its bankruptcy, or to offer adequate assurances of performance, constituted an anticipatory breach of the contract under U.C.C. §2-609(1). This provision provides, in salient part, that:

> When reasonable grounds for insecurity arise with respect to the performance of either party the other may in writing demand adequate assurances of due performance and until he receives such assurance may, if commercially reasonable, suspend any performance for which he has not already received the agreed return.

This section continues by stating that:

> After receipt of a justified demand, failure to provide within a reasonable time not exceeding thirty days, such assurances of due performance as is adequate under the circumstances of the particular case is a repudiation of the contract.
> U.C.C. §2-609(4).

Elia contends that it had "reasonable grounds for insecurity" because Beeche had filed for bankruptcy within one week of executing the original agreement and had failed to disclose the existence of the bankruptcy filing to Elia. It claims that it was "gravely concerned" about this bankruptcy, especially in light of the modification of the agreement, which required accelerated payments to Beeche. It then contends that a letter it sent Beeche dated June 4, 1991 constituted the demand for adequate assurances required under U.C.C. §2-609(1).

However, Beeche had already designed, constructed and provided Elia with the scaffolding equipment (albeit with some delays regarding the submission of designs), all during a time when Beeche was in bankruptcy. Had Beeche failed to provide Elia with such equipment in time for the appellant to utilize same while working on its project with the Thruway Authority, then Elia may have had reasonable grounds for insecurity regarding Beeche's ability to continue its performance under the contract. However, since Beeche had already performed all that was required of it under the agreement until it had received final payment from Elia, and had never given any indication that it did not intend to honor the buy-back provision of the contract, this court finds that there were no reasonable grounds for insecurity sufficient to trigger the provisions of U.C.C. §2-609(1).

Moreover, the letter sent by Elia to Beeche dated June 4, 1991 that Elia claims constituted the demand for adequate assurances required under the U.C.C. does not appear to this court to be such a demand. This letter makes no reference to the U.C.C., does not track the language of U.C.C. §2-609(1), nor does it request that Beeche provide Elia with any assurance of performance. Rather, this letter reiterates that Elia wanted Beeche to repurchase the scaffolding equipment, states that Elia was "concerned" about Beeche's financial ability to do same, and that, in order to secure such performance, it had determined that it would set-off the amount it still owed Beeche under the agreement ($46,913.48) as a "prepayment of the aforementioned buy back." Rather than being a request for adequate assurances, this court finds that this letter constituted a statement of what Elia had determined it would do with respect to the balance due under the contract and the exercise of the buy-back provision.

In light of the foregoing, this court concludes that Elia could not reasonably conclude that Beeche had anticipatorily repudiated the contract under either U.C.C. §2-609 or §2-610. . . .

As noted earlier, the buyer in a sales of goods case can always recover, in addition to contract-market, contract-cover, or cost-of-the-defect damages, any incidental and consequential damages that it can show resulted from the seller's breach. We saw in Assignment 17 that for the first 40 years of Article 2 sellers could not recover consequential damages. It might seem odd at first blush that there should have been such a difference between the treatment of sellers and buyers on this score.

When you think about eligibility for consequential damages, think about the nature of the seller's and buyer's performance and the way in which either party can breach the contract. When the buyer breaches, the breach will almost always amount to the simple failure to pay the price. Failing to pay the price, however, will not cause someone to get physically injured, nor will it typically prevent a seller from fulfilling the seller's obligations to other parties. As Official Comment 2 to §2-710 as amended puts it: "In normal circumstances the disappointed seller will be able to sell to another, borrow to replace the breaching buyer's promised payment, or otherwise adjust its affairs to avoid consequential loss."

Consider, by contrast, the nature of a seller's breach. If the seller's goods are defective, lots of bad things can happen to the buyer as a direct consequence of that: the buyer might be injured, the buyer's property might be damaged, or third parties might be injured. In addition, there are all kinds of economic losses that a buyer is likely to suffer if the seller's goods fail to perform or if the seller fails to deliver the goods at all. If the buyer owns a business and buys a machine from the seller, the failure of the machine (or the seller's failure to deliver it) might impact on the buyer's ability to successfully carry out its business.

There is a special but not uncommon form of consequential damages that the buyer might suffer as a result of the seller's breach. In brief, that is the case in which the buyer is itself a seller and thus may suffer a lost profit in its contract with its own buyer. That will happen in any case where the original buyer is intending to resell the goods that it has contracted to buy from the initial seller.

Section 2-715(2) sets down two different categories of consequential damages available to Article 2 buyers. Oftentimes, a particular consequential damage that the buyer suffers will qualify for either category. Section 2-715(2)(a) allows as buyer's consequential damages those damages resulting from a seller's breach: (1) of any kind, including purely economic loss; (2) of which the seller had reason to know at the time of contracting (Hadley v. Baxendale foreseeability limit); (3) that were "caused in fact" (mere but-for cause, rather than "proximate cause") by seller's breach; and (4) that could not be prevented "by cover or otherwise" (basic mitigation principle).

The consequential damages that are allowed in the second category, §2-715(2)(b), are broader in some respects and narrower in others than the first category. For a buyer to show §2-715(2)(b) consequential damages, those damages must be (1) personal injury or property damage (economic loss does not qualify here); and (2) proximately caused by seller's breach (mere but-for cause is not enough). The way in which the second category of consequential damages is broader than the first is that there is no *Hadley* foreseeability limit to qualify for damages under the second category, nor is there the explicit language concerning buyer's need to mitigate.

Thus, suppose that the buyer purchases a machine from the seller for use in the buyer's factory. Imagine that the machine explodes because of a defect, injures the buyer, and causes the buyer's operation to shut down for two days. The buyer, unknown to the seller, purchased this machine to increase production for the benefit of a new client who would have given the seller enough business in the next year to produce $5 million in profits. Because of the delay occasioned by the explosion, the buyer's new client takes its business elsewhere.

For what consequential damages would this buyer be eligible? Certainly the buyer could recover for its personal injuries, under either §2-715(2)(a) or (2)(b). Under §2-715(2)(a), the personal injuries are "any loss," caused in fact, seller had reason to know (everyone knows that exploding machines can injure people), and buyer could not have prevented the loss "by cover or otherwise." Under §2-715(2)(b), this also qualifies because it was an injury to person proximately caused by the seller's breach.

The economic losses will be more difficult for the buyer to recover as consequential damages. They clearly will not fit under §2-715(2)(b), since that category is restricted to injuries to person or property. Even §2-715(2)(a) will be problematic, however, because of the *Hadley* foreseeability limit. It would be one thing if buyer were merely trying to recover "normal profits" in a case where seller knew that buyer was purchasing the machine for buyer's factory. But a $5 million profit that hinged on the performance of this machine seems to be a "particular" requirement or need of buyer's that seller had to have reason to know in order to be held responsible for it.

The buyer's incidental damages under §2-715(1) are a little more straightforward to deal with. Incidental damages for the aggrieved buyer are expenses that the buyer incurs in inspecting, transporting, storing, or reselling rejected goods, or in effecting cover as a result of the seller's breach, or "any other reasonable expense incident to the delay or other breach."

Despite their characterization as "incidental," §2-715(1) damages can sometimes be quite large for buyers. In one case, for example, a seller that disclaimed liability for consequential damages was nevertheless found liable for incidental damages of $293 million. These damages represented the buyer's storage costs for the radioactive nuclear fuel that was the subject of the breached contract. Commonwealth Edison Co. v. Allied Chemical Nuclear Products, Inc., 684 F. Supp. 1434 (N.D. Ill. 1988).

Problem Set 19

19.1.   Jack's Industrial Tile for Less does tile installation for schools, businesses, and other institutions with large buildings. Jack Kost, president of Jack's, has come to see you to discuss a couple of problem jobs that he has encountered during the last few weeks. The first involves Lakeside School, whose gymnasium Jack's had contracted to re-tile. The $40,000 contract called for a very hard grade of tile that would have cost Jack's $30,000 to obtain and install. Because of a mix-up at Jack's office, his workers installed a softer, but more expensive vinyl tile that cost Jack's $45,000 to obtain and install. Because of the various purposes for which the Lakeside School gym was used, the hard but cheaper tile was the only floor surface that would work for the school. The softer vinyl tile was essentially worthless for the school's purposes, at least in its original form. However, the vinyl could be treated with a special coating for $5,000 that would harden it and make it just as suitable for Lakeside's purposes as the tile that should have been installed. Removing the tile is not an attractive option, since it would cost Jack's more to remove the tile than the used tile could command in a resale. What would be the proper measure of Lakeside's damages if it chose to sue Jack's on a breach of warranty theory? U.C.C. §§2-714(2), 1-106(1) (revised §1-305(a)).

19.2. Another school that Jack's had a contract with, Beasley Prep, was a victim of the same mix-up as Jack's involving Lakeside's order. Beasley paid Jack's $55,000 to have the more expensive vinyl tile for its gym, which was the same size as Lakeside's. Instead, Beasley ended up getting the cheaper, hard tile that was intended for Lakeside. In fact, however, this foul-up on Jack's part turned out to be a blessing in disguise for Beasley. The Beasley principal had not realized at the time she ordered the softer tile that it would simply not work for the various purposes for which the Beasley gym was used. Indeed, the softer tile that Beasley had ordered would have proven worthless for that school's purposes. The cheaper, harder tile, by contrast, was in fact perfect for the several uses to which the Beasley gym was put. What would be the proper measure of Beasley's damages if it were to sue Jack's on a breach of warranty theory? U.C.C. §§2-714(2), 1-106(1) (revised §1-305(a)).

19.3. Joe Fortino owned a tennis specialty store. Two weeks ago he sold for $1,000 a custom-made, hand-strung racket to an up-and-coming pro player, Chrissie Austin. Chrissie had told Joe that she would be using this racket in an upcoming weekend tournament in Las Vegas that offered a $60,000 first prize. On that weekend, Chrissie cruised her way to the semifinal round of the tournament, at which point the frame cracked on her new racket while she was leading the match 6-2, 5-1. The cracked frame rendered the new racket worthless and clearly constituted a breach of the sales contract. Chrissie was able to borrow a racket from another player, but the new racket was a disaster for her. She ended up losing the next 12 games of the semifinal match, eventually dropping the match by scores of 2-6, 7-5, 6-0. The Vegas odds had made Chrissie a 4-1 favorite to win the tournament, and Chrissie can produce convincing evidence that she probably would have won the tournament if the racket had not cracked. Chrissie asks you for how much she can sue Joe Fortino. What do you advise? U.C.C. §§2-714(2) & (3), 2-715(2)(a), Official Comments 2 and 3 to §2-715.

19.4. Arlene Ledger, President of Heavy Metal, Inc. (from Problem 3.2) comes by your office looking glum. Today, she says, she is not here to ask you about problems she is having with a breaching customer. Rather, she says, this time her company is the breacher. A large retailer, Company Fitness, had contracted to purchase from Heavy Metal an industrial-sized multi-station weight machine for $35,000. Company Fitness was planning to display (but not sell) the machine at a major trade show in order to attract possible future customers in the burgeoning business of supplying on-site office exercise facilities. The week before the trade show, Arlene realized that her production department had dropped the ball on this order and there was no way that Heavy Metal could fill the order in time for Company Fitness' appearance at the trade show. When Arlene informed Company Fitness of this fact, Company Fitness sought to cover.

a. Suppose that Company Fitness could not find a precisely comparable machine on such short notice and instead paid $42,000 for a slightly better machine. What would its cover damages be against Heavy Metal? U.C.C. §2-712, Official Comment 2 to §2-712 (Official Comment 4 to §2-712 as amended).

b. Suppose that Company Fitness could have purchased for $40,000 a machine exactly comparable to the one Heavy Metal promised to make. Instead, it covered by purchasing a much better machine that happened to be on sale for $40,500 (this machine normally sold for $50,000). What would its damages be against Heavy Metal? U.C.C. §§2-712, 2-713.

c. Imagine under scenario a. above that Company Fitness was intending to sell rather than just display the machine. Suppose that Company Fitness expected to sell the original machine for $45,000, but thanks to the additional features in the machine it purchased, it was able to sell it for $48,000. What would Company Fitness' cover damages be then? U.C.C. §§2-712, 2-715(2)(a).

19.5. a. Henry Brock was a collector of sports memorabilia, including baseball cards. On September 1, Henry made a contract with a store called Sports Collectibles to purchase an original 1909 Ty Cobb baseball card for $1,700. The contract said that Henry could come in and pick up the card on November 11, at which point he would also pay the purchase price in full. On October 1, a different buyer offered Sports Collectibles $2,500 for the same card (on the theory that an upcoming ESPN special on Cobb would increase the value of Cobb cards), and the store sold it on the spot to the new buyer for that amount. That afternoon, the manager of Sports Collectibles called Henry to inform him that the Ty Cobb card deal was off. Stunned by this unexpected development, Henry replied, "Not so fast. I'm not going to let you off on this one. I think you'd better reconsider." Two weeks later, on October 15, Henry called Sports Collectibles to ask if his Ty Cobb card would be ready on November 11. The clerk who answered the phone politely explained to Henry that the Cobb card had been sold to someone else two weeks ago. "Well," said Henry, "you had better tell your boss to buy it back, because I will be there with my check on November 11." True to his word, Henry shows up with his check on November 11, but the store does not have the Cobb card to sell him. If the market price of the card was $2,500 on October 1, $2,700 on October 15, and $3,000 on November 11, to what amount is Henry entitled in damages from Sports Collectibles? U.C.C. §§2-713(1), 2-610, 2-609(4).

b. Same facts as part a., except suppose that Sports Collectibles did not sell the Ty Cobb card to a different buyer. However, one month after Henry purchased the card from the store, Shelly Lopez sues Henry to recover the card on the grounds that she was the true owner and the card was stolen from her last year. Henry spends $800 in attorney's fees defending the suit, but ultimately loses the suit (and the card) to Shelly. Even though the card had a market value of $3,000 on November 11, its value had increased to $4,000 by the time Henry lost the lawsuit. For what amount may Henry recover in a lawsuit against Sports Collectibles? U.C.C. §§2-312(1)(a), 2-714, 2-715(2), 1-106(1) (revised §1-305(a)).

19.6. a. Miles Gurney is a hog farmer, and for that reason he keeps a ready stock of hog feed in a warehouse on his farm. Miles had a contract with Mabel's Feed 'n Seed to purchase eight tons of hog feed for $6,400, which Mabel promised to deliver to Miles' farm on May 1. On May 1, Mabel fails to deliver the feed and announces to Miles that she is breaching the contract. On May 1, the market price for comparable hog feed is $1,000 per ton. Over the next month, as the market price for hog feed declines, Miles purchases three separate eight-ton loads of hog feed from other suppliers. The first load, purchased on May 20, costs Miles $7,000; the second, purchased on May 25, costs $6,500; and the third, purchased on May 30, costs $6,300. On June 15, Miles files suit against Mabel for breach of contract. To what amount is Miles entitled in damages? U.C.C. §§2-712, 2-713, Comment 3 to §2-712 (Official Comment 6 to §2-712 as amended), Official Comment 7 to §2-713 as amended.

b. Same facts as part a., except that the May 1 market price is $800 per ton, and Miles makes the same three purchases on the same dates at the same prices as part a. To what amount is Miles entitled in damages? U.C.C. §§2-712, 2-713, Comment 2 to §2-712 (Official Comment 5 to §2-712 as amended).

c. Same facts as part a., except Miles does not purchase any additional hog feed during the month following the breach. Instead, he takes eight tons from the stock of 20 tons in his warehouse. The average price of the 20 tons of hog feed, which Miles had purchased through several deals during the past year, was $1,200 per ton. To what amount is Miles entitled in damages? U.C.C. §§2-712, 2-713.

19.7. a. Rhonda Lewis, a traveling salesperson, buys a new Chevy Lumina for $22,000 from Jack Pollard's Chevy City, but the car's engine catches fire during the first week Rhonda drives it. Rhonda was not hurt, but she was so disgusted that she called Jack to revoke her acceptance and to get him to send out a tow truck to take the Lumina back to Chevy City. She then demanded her $22,000 back from Jack, who gave it to her. After getting her refund, Rhonda intended to search for another new Lumina at a different dealer. In the meantime, Rhonda rented a Lumina for $400 per month, plus 20 cents a mile for each mile over 1,000 per month. Because of her heavy travel schedule, Rhonda took four months to purchase a new Lumina, for which she ultimately paid $24,000. During the four months she used the rental Lumina, Rhonda put 2,500 miles on it per month, which added a total of $1,200 to her final rental bill. If Rhonda sues Jack Pollard's Chevy City for breach of contract, for what amount may she recover? U.C.C. §§2-712, 2-715, Comment 2 to §2-712 (Preliminary Comment 5 to §2-712 as amended), 1-106(1) (§1-305(a) as amended).

b. Same facts as part a., except that Rhonda had only paid $3,000 of the purchase price. Further, when Rhonda called to complain about the engine fire and give notice of her revocation, Jack Pollard failed to send out a tow truck and failed to tender a refund of Rhonda's $3,000. After a couple of days, Rhonda paid a towing firm $100 to take the car to a local storage company, which agreed to hold the car for Rhonda for $10 per day. Four months later, after Rhonda had rented the Lumina and then paid $24,000 for a different new Lumina, Jack Pollard called and said he wanted his car back and that he was willing to refund Rhonda's $3,000 in order to get it. To what extent may

Rhonda hold out for still more money from Jack as a condition to her return-ing the car to him? U.C.C. §2-711(3).

19.8. a.   Pro Roofing, Inc., an Atlanta residential roofing firm, made a contract with Industrial Shingles, a Nashville manufacturer, to purchase 20 tons of shingles for $50,000, "FOB Nashville." The stated delivery date was "on or before July 20," and the cost of delivering the shingles from Nashville to Atlanta was $1,500. On July 20, the shingles had not yet arrived to Pro Roofing, causing the president of Pro Roofing to call Industrial Shingles and learn that the seller was not going to perform. The market price of 20 tons of shingles on July 20 was $56,000 in Nashville, and $54,000 in Atlanta. Assum-ing that Pro Roofing does not cover, to what amount is it entitled in damages? U.C.C. §§2-713, 2-319(1), 2-509(1).

b.   Same facts as part a., except that the delivery term is "FOB Atlanta." Assuming that Pro Roofing does not cover, to what amount is it entitled in damages? U.C.C. §§2-713, 2-319(1), 2-509(1).

c.   Same facts as part a., except that the contract contains no delivery term whatsoever. Assuming that Pro Roofing does not cover, to what amount is it entitled in damages? U.C.C. §§2-713, 2-509(1), 2-308(a), Official Comment 5 to §2-503.

d.   Same facts as part a., except that the shingles arrive on July 20, prove to be obviously and horribly defective, and Pro Roofing immediately rejects the shingles. Assuming that Pro Roofing has already paid for the goods and does not cover, to what amount is it entitled in damages? U.C.C. §2-713.

e.   Same facts as part a., except that Pro Roofing learns on July 10 that Industrial Shingles filed Chapter 11 bankruptcy that day. In light of this news, what course of action should Pro Roofing pursue? U.C.C. §2-609, 2-610.

Assignment 20: Buyer's and Lessee's Remedies with Leases, International Sales, and Real Estate

A. Lessee's Remedies

The lessee's remedies under Article 2A track very closely the buyer's remedies that are outlined in Article 2. The translation is not perfect, of course, given the fundamental difference between a sale and a lease. Unlike a sale, the lease by definition will not give the lessee possession for the entire life of the goods. We saw with the lessor's remedies in Assignment 18 that this difference created some special obligations of care on the lessee's part as to the leased goods that the buyer does not have with respect to goods that it purchases.

The difference between a sale and a lease also creates some additional responsibilities for the lessor. Section 2A-508, which gives the laundry list of lessee's remedies, includes one remedy that has no counterpart in Article 2: the possibility that the lessor may be "otherwise in default under a lease contract." §2A-508(3) (amended §2A-508(2)). This is a reference, for example, to the not uncommon duty of a lessor in a lease agreement to keep the leased goods in good repair. When a lessor fails in this duty, the lessee may pursue remedies under the lease or may look to §2A-519(3), which would at a minimum give the lessee a right to recover from the lessor the cost of putting the leased goods back in working order.

The rest of the lessee's remedies more or less track those available to the aggrieved buyer. Section 2A-518 is the lessee's analogue to §2-712, the right to cover. The two differences between §2A-518 and §2-712 are ones that we have seen before in the context of a lessor's remedies: (1) §2A-518(2)'s formula speaks in terms of discounting future streams of rent to present value, a concept that we do not see in Article 2 damage sections; and (2) for a new lease to qualify as a valid cover under §2A-518, it must be "substantially similar" to the original lease.

While a valid sales cover must also be similar to the original goods, the "substantially similar" concept for lease covers is intended to encompass not just the leased goods themselves, but also the terms of the lease such as purchase option, lease covenants, and services to be provided by the lessor. Official Comment 5 to §2A-518. This is not to say that Article 2A denies damages to a lessee that covers with a new lease that is not substantially similar. Rather, as with Article 2, the statute merely remits such a lessee to its contract-market measure of damages. §2A-518(3).

Sections 2A-519(1) and (2) set out the lessee's contract-market damages, which are mostly analogous to §2-713 except again with the addition of the "present value" and "substantially similar" concepts. Sections 2A-519(3) and (4) provide a remedy for the lessee that does not reject or revoke acceptance, which is much like the position of the buyer stuck with a defective good in §2-714. Much like the sales counterpart provision, the lease remedy section here provides for the difference between the value of the use that the lessee was promised and the value of the use that the lessee actually got given the lessor's default. §2A-519(4).

Section 2A-520, defining the lessee's incidental and consequential damages, is almost an exact replica of §2-715. The final two lessee's remedies are specific performance (see §2A-521 and amended §2A-507)) and the right to recover goods on the lessor's insolvency (see §2A-522). These two lessee remedies also mimic closely the comparable Article 2 buyer's remedies.

B.   Buyer's Remedies with International Sales

There is a certain attractiveness to the simplicity of the damages provisions in the CISG. The CISG says all that it has to say about damages, for both aggrieved sellers and aggrieved buyers, in just four Articles. In the final analysis, these four articles end up coming to essentially the same results as Article 2 achieves with lots more than just four Article 2 sections on damages.

For the buyer's damages, the CISG once again relies (as it does with seller's damages) on a dichotomy between contracts that have been "avoided" by the buyer and those that have not. This is quite similar to the Article 2 dichotomy for buyer's damages between the buyer who has accepted the goods and can no longer reject or revoke acceptance of them, and the buyer who has never received the goods or who has rejected or revoked acceptance of them.

The buyer under the CISG may declare the contract "avoided" only if the seller's breach is "fundamental" or if the seller fails to deliver the goods on time or within any grace period that the buyer chooses to give the seller beyond the originally scheduled delivery date. C.I.S.G. Art. 49(1). Recall that the effect of a contract avoidance is that both sides are relieved of their contractual obligations, but the avoiding party retains its right to sue for damages. C.I.S.G. Art. 81(1).

Let us consider first under the CISG the plight of the aggrieved buyer that has not avoided the contract. If that buyer does not yet have the goods because of the seller's non-delivery, the buyer may have a right to specific performance. Article 46(1) gives the buyer who has not received the goods a right to specific performance "unless the buyer has resorted to a remedy which is inconsistent with this requirement." However, Article 28 allows a court to restrict any party's right to specific performance to whatever right would exist with the forum court's own sales law. Thus, in any case brought before a U.S. court, the buyer's right to specific performance might be no greater than that given in the UCC.

Alternatively, the non-avoiding buyer already might have the goods and be aggrieved because the goods are non-conforming. If the non-conformity amounts to a "fundamental breach," that buyer can ask for specific performance, C.I.S.G. Art. 46(2), subject again to the limitation in Article 28 about the forum court's law regarding specific performance. For a buyer that receives non-conforming goods and does not wish or is ineligible for specific performance, its damages are measured in much the same way as a similarly aggrieved buyer under the UCC: it is entitled to the "loss suffered . . . as a consequence of [seller's] breach." C.I.S.G. Art. 74. That would presumably amount to the difference between the value of the goods that were promised and the value that the goods actually had given the nonconformity, plus incidental and consequential damages.

Next let us consider the buyer in an international sale who avoids the contract, either because it got the goods and there was a nonconformity amounting to a fundamental breach, or because the goods were not delivered on time or within whatever grace period the buyer chose to give. This buyer, just like the Article 2 buyer, gets its choice between contract-cover damages (under Article 75) and contract-market damages (under Article 76). Both measures also include the broadly defined consequential damages of Article 74, which probably encompass what would be known as "incidental damages" under Article 2.

The buyer's cover rights under C.I.S.G. Article 75 track very closely the comparable rights of a buyer under U.C.C. Article 2. In order for the buyer's cover to be valid, it must be done "in a reasonable manner and within a reasonable time after avoidance." C.I.S.G. Art. 75. The properly covering buyer is also eligible for "further damages recoverable under Article 74 [consequential damages]." Id.

The buyer's contract-market damages under Article 76 also look very much like the U.C.C. Article 2 buyer's rights under §2-713. In order for a buyer to use the contract-market measure in the CISG, there must first be "a current [market] price for the goods." C.I.S.G. Art. 76(1). Under the CISG, the market price is measured at the time the buyer avoided the contract (unless the buyer avoided the contract after "taking over the goods," in which case the market price is measured at the time the buyer took over the goods rather than at the time of avoidance). C.I.S.G. Art. 76(1).

Under U.C.C. Article 2, the place for the market price to be measured is the place for tender, or if there is a rejection or revocation after arrival, then at the place of arrival. U.C.C. §2-713(2). Under the CISG, the market price is measured at the place "where delivery of the goods should have been made." C.I.S.G. Art. 76(2). Under both Codes, the idea of this remedy is to create a hypothetical cover. The CISG contract-market measure, just like the UCC version, also gives the buyer the right to recover consequential (and, effectively, incidental) damages.

The CISG provision that defines consequential damages, Article 74, defines those merely as "the loss, including loss of profit, suffered by the other party as a consequence of the breach." Article 74 then contains a sentence limiting such damages by the *Hadley* "reason to know" standard. Thus, even property damage must have been reasonably foreseeable for the buyer to claim them under the CISG, unlike the UCC, where only economic damages contain the foreseeability limit. This is perhaps not so surprising when one considers that the CISG expressly provides that it does not cover the sale of goods bought for consumer use. C.I.S.G. Art. 2(a). Further, the CISG expressly excludes from its coverage "liability of the seller for death or personal injury caused by the goods to any person." C.I.S.G. Art. 5.

The only other limit on the CISG's broad definition of consequential damages, besides the *Hadley* "reason to know" standard, is the CISG's general mitigation policy contained in Article 77. Article 77 says simply that if a party could have reasonably mitigated its damages but did not, then its damages must be reduced by the amount that they could have been mitigated. This is tantamount to the limit in U.C.C. §2-715(2)(a)'s category of consequential damages, which are not available to the Article 2 buyer to the extent that the damages could have been "reasonably . . . prevented by cover or otherwise."

C.   Buyer's Remedies with Real Estate

In discussing the remedies that are available to an aggrieved buyer in a real estate transaction, we must once again divide the world into the two common situations in which the buyer might be aggrieved: first, there is the classic case of the seller who simply refuses to deliver title to the buyer; and second, there is the case in which the buyer has possession of and title to the property but discovers some defect of which the buyer was unaware at the time of closing.

As to the first situation, where the seller simply refuses to close, the buyer's standard remedy is an action for specific performance. In order to obtain specific performance, the buyer must make a couple of different showings. First, the buyer must demonstrate that money damages are inadequate, but that is a typically easy showing with real estate since most courts presume land to be unique.

Second, the buyer must show that the buyer itself is fully capable of performing its side of the bargain. Because the buyer's main obligation in most cases is to pay for the real estate, this ordinarily requires nothing more than a showing that the buyer has adequate financing or assets to complete the transaction.

If the buyer does not want specific performance in the case of the seller's refusal to deliver title, the buyer can choose to sue for money damages instead. These will include at least the buyer's out-of-pocket damages. In about half of the states, the buyer can also ask for benefit-of-the-bargain damages if it can show that the price it agreed to pay was less than the market price for that property. One more twist normally bars benefit-of-the-bargain damages whenever the seller's breach is that the seller's own title is defective. Courts rationalize that rule as a limitation of the damages imposed on a seller whose breach is beyond its control.

All buyers that are aggrieved by a seller's refusal to close, even if they choose to demand specific performance, will also be eligible for consequential damages resulting from the delay in receiving title, as long as such damages were reasonably foreseeable. For example, if the seller wrongfully refused to close and the buyer ended up having to pay a higher mortgage rate when it finally forced the seller to close, the buyer could sue the seller for the difference between the buyer's original mortgage costs and the higher mortgage. Even if the higher rate was not necessarily predictable, it is nevertheless the sort of risk that a breaching seller must expect its buyers to face.

Unlike in the sales of goods context, it is not especially common in residential real estate transactions to have a buyer already in possession of the house suing the seller for some defect that the buyer discovers following the closing. The reason is that most standard residential real estate sales contracts have an "as is" clause that disclaims all warranties by the seller and also invites the buyer to have a professional inspection done as a condition to the effectiveness of the contract.

Thus, courts will not generally look favorably upon complaints by buyers that they discovered a material defect in the property following consummation of the sale. Generally, for a buyer to prevail in this situation the buyer will have to show fraud: not only that something ended up being wrong with the house, but that the seller affirmatively misrepresented a material fact that induced the buyer to purchase the house.

Jue v. Smiser

28 Cal. Rptr. 2d 242 (Cal. Ct. App. 1994)

ANDERSON, J.

The case at bench requires this court to resolve the following question: May a purchaser of real property who learns of potential material misrepresentations about the property after execution of a purchase agreement-but before consummation of the sale-close escrow and sue for damages? Our answer is, "yes."

On April 1, 1992, Kenn and Victoria Smiser (respondents) listed their home at 636 Hillgirt Circle in Oakland for sale with Tabaloff & Company, a realtor (Tabaloff). Tabaloff then began active marketing of the home. On April 22, 1992, an article about the home appeared in the San Francisco Chronicle. The article indicated that the home had been designed by Julia Morgan, a celebrated architect whose credits include Hearst Castle. Geoffrey and Charlene Jue (appellants) saw the article and called Tabaloff to make arrangements to see the home. When they toured it appellants were given a brochure which indicated that it was an "Authenticated, Julia Morgan Design, built 1917."

Appellants made a full price offer for the home, contingent on the sale of Geoffrey Jue's home. Respondents countered, requiring that the purchase agreement for their home not be contingent on the sale of Mr. Jue's home. Appellants accepted the counteroffer, and the parties agreed that the sale of respondents' home would close on June 11. Geoffrey Jue immediately listed his home for sale with Tabaloff, and he accepted an offer to sell it on May 5.

On June 8 appellants went to First American Title Company (apparently the escrow company for the sale) and signed the documents required for completion of the sale on June 11. After signing a note and deed of trust, as well as other closing documents, appellants were asked by Tabaloff to sign a contract supplement/addendum with two insignificant provisions and the following disclaimer: "BUYER AND SELLER ACKNOWLEDGE THAT THE RESIDENCE AT 636 HILLGIRT

CIRCLE IS COMMONLY KNOWN TO BE A JULIA MORGAN DESIGN AND THAT THERE ARE NO PLANS AVAILABLE AT THE OAKLAND CITY HALL VERIFYING SAME." Appellants signed off on (agreed to) the other two provisions in the supplement/addendum but did not sign off on the disclaimer.

Over the next two days appellants spoke to Sara Boutelle, the author of a book on Julia Morgan homes, who told appellants that she was convinced the home was designed by Morgan; they also spoke to Lynn Stone, Morgan's goddaughter, who indicated that she was unaware of any proof that the home was designed by Morgan.

On June 9 respondents signed the supplement/addendum, as modified by appellants. Escrow closed, and title to the home passed to appellants on June 11.

On November 24, 1992, appellants filed a complaint seeking damages from Tabaloff, two of Tabaloff's agents and respondents. The claims against respondents were based on a number of different theories: fraud, concealment, negligent misrepresentation, negligence, mutual mistake of fact, unilateral mistake of fact (on the part of appellants), intentional infliction of emotional distress, negligent infliction of emotional distress, and various common counts.

In February 1993 respondents filed a motion for summary judgment or, in the alternative, summary adjudication of each cause of action asserted against them. The motion was based on respondents' assertion that appellants' claims were barred as a matter of law because it was "undisputed that [appellants] had actual knowledge of all material facts before the close of escrow and nevertheless voluntarily elected to proceed with the purchase of the property in the face of such knowledge."

Respondents' motion for summary judgment was granted. In its written order of April 6, 1993, the trial court stated its reason for granting the motion: "The bottom line is that [appellants] knew, before the close of escrow, that there were no official records to authenticate 636 Hillgirt Circle as a Julia Morgan design. They chose to proceed anyway; thus they did not purchase the property in justifiable reliance on the alleged fraud. All [appellants'] causes of action fail for the same reason."

Thereafter, respondents moved for entry of judgment under Code of Civil Procedure §437c and for an award of attorney fees under the purchase agreement between the parties. Both motions were granted, and the court awarded respondents $43,118.59 in fees and costs. . . .

"When a party learns that he has been defrauded, he may, instead of rescinding, elect to stand on the contract and sue for damages, and, in such case his continued performance of the agreement does not constitute a waiver of his action for damages. [Citations.]" (Bagdasarian v. Gragnon (1948) 31 Cal. 2d 744, 750, 192 P.2d 935.)

Appellants urge us to follow *Bagdasarian* and our decision in Storage Services v. Oosterbaan (1989) 214 Cal. App. 3d 498, 262 Cal. Rptr. 689 and rule that the trial court erred in granting summary judgment predicated on appellants' supposed lack of "justifiable reliance" on respondents' fraud when appellants closed escrow. Respondents, in turn, argue (a) that reliance is an essential element in any fraud claim and (b) that California law does not permit a buyer who acquires knowledge of a seller's alleged fraud while the purchase agreement is executory to close escrow and sue for damages. . . .

In the case at bench respondents argue that our decision in *Storage Services* was "expressly limited" to the "specific facts" of that case. Respondents also argue that our decision should be read as "reconfirm[ing] the general rule [that] a party discovering fraud while the contract is still executory cannot complete performance and still sue for fraud." Respondents' reading of our decision in *Storage Services* is incorrect.

First, the only part of our opinion which could be construed as limiting its application to the facts of that case is our analysis of whether or not Storage Services should be deemed to have "purchase[d] or otherwise acquire[d]" the subject property so as to come within the provisions of Civil Code §3343, subdivision (a)(4). (*Storage Services, supra,* 214 Cal. App. 3d at p.510-511, 262 Cal. Rptr. 689.) Our analysis of whether or not Storage Services could maintain an action for fraud against the realtors, when Storage Services learned of the fraud after execution of the original purchase agreement and before escrow closed, was not so limited.

Respondents' second argument constitutes a distortion of our opinion in *Storage Services.* We specifically noted that any party who learns of a fraud before a contract has been completed will not complete it in "reliance" on the fraud. (*Storage Services,* supra, 214 Cal. App. 3d at p.511, 262 Cal. Rptr. 689.) However, we noted that under *Bagdasarian,* a party's continued performance of the agreement does not constitute a waiver of his action for damages. . . .

In sum, we see no reason to deviate from or limit our decision in *Storage Services* here. The trial court erred in determining that appellants' (apparent) knowledge that the home at 636 Hillgirt Circle could not be confirmed as a Julia Morgan design prior to the close of escrow precluded their advancement of claims against respondents. The relevant issue was (is) whether or not appellants relied on respondents' (alleged) misrepresentations when the purchase agreement was struck on April 27, 1992. No evidence was presented in support of respondents' motion for summary judgment which served to negate the appellants' claim that they did rely on those (alleged) misrepresentations at that time.

Sound public policy considerations support our decision. The Legislature has enacted a series of statutes designed to foster honesty and full disclosure in real estate transactions. Our decision should encourage sellers and their representatives to investigate and learn the "true facts" pertaining to real property before it is offered for sale. Possession and communication of such knowledge will be of benefit to all parties in the course of negotiations leading to execution of a sales agreement.

In addition, if we were to adopt the rule urged upon us by respondents, a buyer of real property who learns of a misrepresentation or a potential misrepresentation after a purchase contract is struck but before escrow closes would be faced with an extraordinarily difficult choice: (a) consummate the purchase and waive any claim for damages or (b) rescind and deal with the consequences of that choice. Among those consequences may be (1) problems in securing a return of moneys deposited with the escrow holder; (2) the loss of moneys spent to secure a loan and to meet other costs of acquisition, such as escrow fees; and (3) the risk of being sued by the seller and/or the seller's representatives. One who may be the victim of another's fraud should not be forced to make such a choice. That policy is especially strong where, as here, it is unclear whether or not a particular representation was (is), in fact, false at the time a choice is required, and the time period in which to choose is extraordinarily short.

The judgment is reversed. Respondents are to bear costs on appeal.

Another way to view the *Jue* case, besides as a decision that gave the buyers what they deserved, is as a precedent that would discourage sellers from relying on the time-honored "bait and switch" technique to lure potential buyers. After all, what the realtors in *Jue* appeared to be engaged in was a classic bait-and-switch: brag in advertisements and marketing literature that this was an "Authenticated Julia Morgan Design" as a way to get buyers in the door; then, once the buyers were in the door and it turned out they *really* cared a lot about this fact, just hem and haw and ultimately admit that you don't in fact know whether this is a true Julia Morgan.

Problem Set 20

20.1. a. Lou from Lou's Used Cars (from Problem 2.1) has recently gone back into the business of leasing used cars, and is he ever sorry about that. He has a number of problem leases that he needs to ask you about. The first problem lease was a four-year, $100-per-month lease of a 1989 Ford Taurus Wagon that Lou knew had an engine that suffered from hesitation problems. Lou had disclosed that fact to the lessee, and indeed the $100-per-month lease rate clearly reflected the car's shaky engine. Two months into the lease, however, the engine stopped working completely. When the lessee called Lou to complain, Lou told him to have the engine problem fixed and to send Lou the bill. Yesterday Lou got a bill for $2,500, which indicated that a brand-new engine had been installed to replace the dead one. "The lessee tells me the car works great now and the engine doesn't even hesitate," says Lou, "But what do you expect with a brand-new engine? I could probably lease that car for $150 per month with the new engine." Lou wants to know whether he must pay the entire $2,500 for the new engine or, alternatively, whether he can raise the lessee's monthly rate to reflect the addition of a new engine in the car. What do you advise Lou? U.C.C. §2A-519(4), 1-106(1) (revised §1-305(a)).

b. Lou's second problem arose when Lou made too many lease contracts with not enough cars to lease. Thus, he was forced to breach a lease that he had made on a '94 Honda Prelude. That was a three-year, $300-per-month lease with a purchase option at fair-market value at the end of the lease. This lease also provided that Lou's would give the car a complete tune-up every six months during the lease at no extra charge. The aggrieved lessee has gone out and leased a different '94 Honda Prelude from another dealer. The new lease was a four-year, $400-per-month lease with an end-of-the-lease purchase option at fair-market value minus 10 percent of the total lease payments made. The new lease required the lessee to have the car tuned up every six months at the lessee's expense, which Lou estimated would cost about $150 per tune-up. Both Lou's lease and the new lease could be terminated by the lessee at any time by paying a $500 liquidated damages fee. The aggrieved lessee had told Lou that she was planning to sue him for his breach of their lease contract. Assuming that the lessee seeks contract-cover damage, for what amount of damages may she recover from Lou? U.C.C. §2A-518, Official Comments 3 through 7 to §2A-518. (In calculating damages for this problem, don't bother actually discounting any of the payment streams to present value, but note to yourself where that normally would be done.)

c. Lou's third problem lease involved a '93 full-sized Dodge van that was leased to Larry Moppet, an unemployed cook who had just founded a new business that delivered food from popular local restaurants to people's homes. This van had given Larry so much trouble that he had been unable, due to the van's unreliability, to deliver meals on five evenings during the first two months on the job. Larry had brought the van in for repairs on three or four occasions during these first two months, but the van kept breaking down nevertheless. After revoking his acceptance of the van, Larry was suing Lou for the $300 that Larry was not paid for the delivery jobs he missed on those five evenings when the leased van failed to perform. Larry was also suing Lou for $100,000, representing what Larry claimed was the lost good will for his young business that was caused by the faulty van. Lou admits to you that Larry did tell Lou's salesperson about the intended use of the van. To what extent will Lou be liable to Larry? U.C.C. §2A-520(2)(a).

20.2. The Fun Factory was a Minneapolis-based toy manufacturer that had a contract to buy three tons of raw plastic from a Canadian plastics distributor, Toronto Works. The Fun Factory was going to use the plastic to make 5,000 figurines to fulfill a contract that it had with a major retailer, Statues 'R' Us. Fun Factory agreed to pay Toronto Works $36,000 for the three tons of plastic, "FOB Buyer's Factory." A week before delivery was due, Toronto Works repudiated the contract. If the Fun Factory had made reasonable cover efforts, it could have purchased substitute plastic from a Seattle distributor for $45,000, "FOB Seller's Plant." Delivery costs from Seattle to Minneapolis would have been $500. (Cover was not available at all in Minneapolis.) Because the Fun Factory did not cover, it was unable to perform its contract with Statues 'R' Us. Although Statues 'R' Us has indicated it will not sue the Fun Factory, the Fun Factory did lose an expected profit in its Statues 'R' Us deal of $14,000. For what amount may the Fun Factory recover from Toronto Works? C.I.S.G. Arts. 74, 75, 76, 77.

20.3. Last night you received a call from your cousin, Edgar, with whom you had not had contact since you were both children. It turns out Edgar heard that there was now a lawyer in the family, and you were it. Edgar's problem is that he was supposed to close on a house purchase deal four months ago, but he did not close until yesterday. The seller of the home had gotten "cold feet" the first time around, and only after much pleading from the seller's agent and many threats from Edgar's agent did the closing finally take place four months later. The four-month delay had a number of effects on Edgar's position, some negative and one positive: (1) He lost a $200 downpayment that he had given to the movers whose job he had to cancel at the last minute; (2) He had to continue renting his apartment on a month-to-month basis, which cost him $700 per month compared to the $500 per month he had been paying under his annual lease; and (3) He had originally locked in an 8.5 percent rate on a 30-year, $100,000 mortgage, which would have had monthly payments, including taxes and insurance, of $950. By the time of the closing, rates had gone down during the four-month delay so that he ended up getting a 7.75 percent rate on the same mortgage. On a $100,000 mortgage, Edgar's bank would generally charge a borrower $1,000 for every quarter of a point that the borrower wished to "buy down" the 30-year rate for its loan. Edgar wants to know for what amount he can sue the seller for damages due to the delay. (Assume that the sales contract simply says that an aggrieved buyer may pursue "any remedy at law or in equity.") What would you advise Edgar?

20.4. Mike and Carol Vilchuck were both big Frank Lloyd Wright fans, which is why they bothered to come look at an $800,000 house for sale in Palo Alto, California, that was advertised as a "Frank Lloyd Wright Original." Mike and Carol were both quite impressed in their walk-through of the house, and they began to talk seriously about making an offer on the house. Before making an offer, the couple called their friend, Barry Swedeen, who was the most knowledgeable Frank Lloyd Wright expert that the Vilchucks knew. Barry told them that there was a real question whether Frank Lloyd Wright himself ever designed any Palo Alto homes, even though it was generally accepted that several architects who were trained in Wright's studio had designed Palo Alto homes. Despite this uncertainty, the Vilchucks went forward and signed a sales contract to buy the house for $800,000. Three weeks after closing on this sale, the Vilchucks get a call from Barry, who managed through extensive research in the local real estate records to uncover definitive proof that their house was *not* designed by Frank Lloyd Wright. In light of this information, the Vilchucks come to you and tell you that they want to rescind this sales contract. What are the chances that they will be successful in a suit for rescission?

BOOK TWO
Financial Systems

Part One
Payment Systems

Introduction to Payment Systems

The three parts of this segment of the book discuss systems used to make, defer, and facilitate payment transactions. Those transactions occur in a wide variety of contexts, but for present purposes it is valuable to distinguish two broad classes of transactions. The first class is typical sales transactions, in which a seller receives payment at the time of the transaction. The second class is credit transactions, in which a lender (which could be either a seller or some entity in the business of making loans) agrees to accept deferred repayment of a financial obligation. Part One of this book generally focuses on the different systems for completing the first class of transactions, simple payments. Part Two generally focuses on the second class, credit transactions. Part Three discusses negotiability and securitization, two systems that facilitate both payment and credit transactions.

The first topic, then, is how purchasers pay for the things they wish to buy. When they use cash, payment is simple: The purchaser provides cash, with which the seller can buy whatever the seller wishes. For a variety of reasons, however, many transactions are not settled with cash. Although it is easy to imagine many reasons a person might not use cash in a particular situation, the most general reason is the practical difficulty of transporting and using cash securely. Most of us find it impractical or imprudent to carry a sufficient amount of cash to complete all of our payment transactions. Some think it inconvenient to go to a bank or an automatic teller machine to get the cash. Others worry that the cash might be stolen. Finally, a thoughtful purchaser might worry that a payment of cash would limit the leverage the purchaser has if it uses some other method of payment that is less final than cash (such as a credit card).

Those problems are particularly important in large transactions. For example, in the consumer context, few individuals ordinarily carry enough cash to complete purchases of major items such as furniture or stereo equipment. But the use of cash has steadily declined even in small, everyday transactions. As of 2003, cash was used in only 41 percent of consumer payment transactions, accounting for only 21 percent of dollars spent. And in commercial transactions, the use of cash is extraordinarily uncommon. Only the most unreasonable party would insist on a tender of cash to close a substantial commercial transaction: Imagine the spectacle of armored cars transporting the funds necessary to close a large commercial transaction.

The easiest way to satisfy a seller's desire to be paid without actually providing cash is to convince the seller that it can obtain payment from some financially reliable third party, usually a bank or other financial institution. Indeed, although we may not think of it when we make purchases, all of the most significant noncash payment systems used in this country—checks, credit cards, debit cards, wire transfers, and letters of credit—function by convincing the seller to rely on its ability to obtain prompt payment from a bank.

The substantive parts of this book differ from most law-school texts in placing great emphasis on the practical details of the various payment systems and relatively little emphasis on the abstract doctrinal rules that do not affect how the systems work in practice. Nevertheless, because the first part of the book discusses so many different payment systems, it is useful before discussing the details of any particular system to provide some relatively abstract generalizations about how payment systems work. If the next few pages seem a bit too removed from reality (or even hard to follow without some concrete system in mind), don't worry. The only purpose of this introductory section is to make it easier for you to discern the analogous problems that each system must face so that you can understand the different rules and practices the systems use to solve those problems. If this introductory section does not seem enlightening now, you might refer back to it from time to time when you start your study of the systems later in the first part of the book. Remember, what is important is that you understand how the systems work; the diagrams in this section are only aids to that goal.

Figure 21.1
Basic Payment Systems

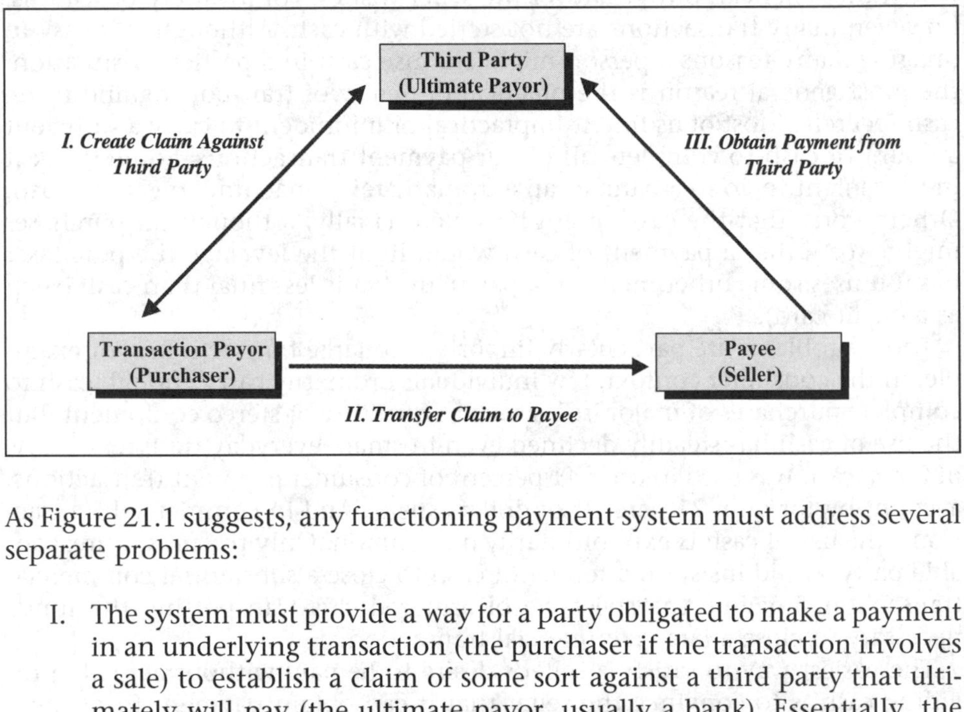

As Figure 21.1 suggests, any functioning payment system must address several separate problems:

I.   The system must provide a way for a party obligated to make a payment in an underlying transaction (the purchaser if the transaction involves a sale) to establish a claim of some sort against a third party that ultimately will pay (the ultimate payor, usually a bank). Essentially, the transaction payor gives some money to the third party based on the expectation (which might or might not be legally enforceable) that the third party will pay the money as directed in future transactions (Step I in Figure 21.1).

II. The transaction payor must be able to transfer the claim to the party entitled to payment (the seller if the transaction involves a sale) (Step II in Figure 21.1).

III. The seller must be able to obtain payment from the third party (Step III in Figure 21.1). That step requires a separate lower-tier payment transaction with all of the steps of the process repeated as between the seller and the third party (Figure 21.2).

IV. Although it is not a necessary part of each transaction (and thus does not appear in Figure 21.1), all systems must respond to the likelihood of mistake and wrongdoing and determine what to do about any losses that occur.

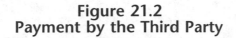

Figure 21.2
Payment by the Third Party

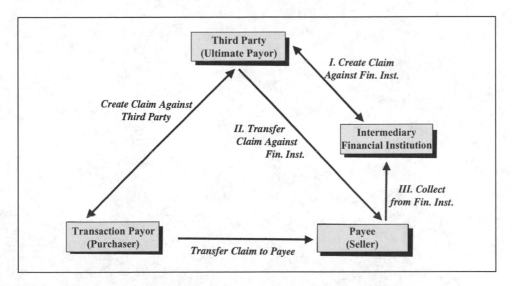

Although advances in information and electronic technology threaten to make the checking system obsolete, that system still has a dominant place in the current economy: As of 2003, Americans wrote about 37 billion checks worth $39 trillion (for an average value of $1,070). The long-standing importance of the checking system has led to a set of legal rules far more detailed than those that govern any of the other payment systems now in place. Accordingly, the best way to illustrate the general operation of payment systems is to examine the checking system, a task undertaken in Chapter 5 (Assignments 21 through 26). With that framework in place, Chapter 6 (Assignments 27 through 31) discusses electronic payments. Chapter 7 (Assignment 32) discusses developing payment systems, and Chapter 8 (Assignments and 34) closes this part of the book by discussing letters of credit.

Chapter 5.   Checking Accounts as the Paradigm Payment System

Assignment 21:   The Basic Checking Relationship and the Bank's Right to Pay Checks

A.   The Basic Relationship

To understand the checking system, it is best to start by identifying the parties that appear at the various steps of a checking transaction (as illustrated in Figure 21.3). If Cliff Janeway writes a check to Archie Moon to buy a book, that check is "drawn" on Cliff's account at Rocky Mountain Bank. That makes Rocky Mountain the "drawee" or the "payor bank." Uniform Commercial Code (UCC) §§3-103(a)(2), 4-104(a)(8), 4-105(3). Cliff, the person that directs the payment by writing the check, is called the "drawer" or "issuer." UCC §§3-103(a)(3), 3-105(c). Archie, the person to whom the check is written ("issue[d]," to use the statutory term, UCC §3-105(a)), is the "payee." Assuming that Archie does not have an account at Rocky Mountain Bank, the process of collecting on the check will involve one or more intermediaries between the payee and the payor bank. For example, Archie is most likely to deposit the check in his account, at Colorado National Bank. That makes Colorado National the "depositary bank." UCC §4-105(2). Finally, if other banks (such as the Federal Reserve Bank in Denver) handle the check before it gets from the depositary bank to the payor bank, all of those banks—intermediaries between the depositary bank and the payor bank—are "intermediary bank[s]." UCC §4-105(4). I discuss that process of collecting the check in detail in Assignment 23, but it is important even at this early stage to understand the identity and role of the various parties that handle a check as it passes from the drawer that writes the check to the bank on which it is drawn.

For a payment system to be available, the person that wants to make a payment (the "transaction payor" in Figure 21.1 or the drawer/issuer in Figure 21.3) must establish a claim against the third party that actually will pay the seller (the "ultimate payor" in Figure 21.1 or the payor bank/drawee in Figure 21.3). In the checking system, the transaction payor establishes that claim by opening a checking account (Step I in Figure 21.3). Notwithstanding the pervasive legal regulation discussed throughout the rest of this chapter, a checking account basically is a two-step arrangement between the bank and the customer, under which the customer deposits money with the bank and the bank then disposes of the money in accordance with the customer's directions. Many of the terms of that arrangement appear in the written contract between the customer and the bank, which typically consists of a brief signature card that incorporates by reference a relatively lengthy set of rules formulated by the bank to govern its accounts.

Figure 21.3
Payment by Check

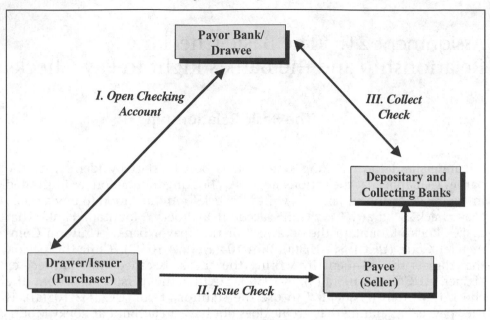

In addition to that contract, state and federal laws provide a variety of rules, many of which govern the rights of the parties even if they are contrary to the arrangements that the parties themselves select in their contract. The federal-law rules are in the form of federal statutes (principally the Expedited Funds Availability Act, discussed at length in Assignment 22) or rules promulgated by the Board of Governors of the Federal Reserve. Under general principles of preemption, those rules supersede not only the agreement of the parties, but also any inconsistent provisions of state law. See UCC §4-103(b) (acknowledging the preemptive effect of rules promulgated by the Federal Reserve).

The state-law rules generally appear in the Uniform Commercial Code (UCC). For purposes of this course, rules in the UCC fall into two different categories. First, Article 1 of the UCC sets forth general principles that apply to all substantive topics covered by the UCC, the most important of which are the lengthy set of definitions in UCC §1-201 and the general obligation of good faith set forth in UCC §1-201 (1a) (revised §1-203). Second, two of the eight substantive articles of the UCC (Articles 3 and 4) provide a variety of rules that affect checking accounts and check transactions. Later assignments discuss Articles 4A (related to wire transfers, Assignments 30 and 31), 5 (related to letters of credit, Assignments 33 and 34), and 8 (related to securities, Assignment 42).

The organization of those rules reflects the historical origins of the checking system. As a matter of history and legal contemplation, checks are negotiable instruments, governed (at least as a formal matter) by the rules set out in Article 3 of the UCC ("Negotiable Instruments"). Negotiability, however, is a system that developed centuries ago to accommodate transactions in a pre-industrial economy. Thus, it is not surprising that principles of negotiability have little to do with the day-to-day functioning of the checking system.

Responding to the checking system's deviation from traditional principles of negotiability, the UCC now includes a separate article directed at the checking system, Article 4 ("Bank Deposits and Collections"). Unfortunately for the student, however, some of the rules in Article 3 still apply to the checking system. Thus, although the most important (and difficult) UCC checking rules appear in Article 4, this chapter also refers occasionally to provisions of Article 3. For the most part, however, detailed discussion of Article 3 is deferred to the portion of the materials that covers negotiability itself (Chapter 11).

B.   The Bank's Right to Pay

From the perspective of the customer depositing its money with the bank, nothing is more central to the checking relationship than the rules that determine when the bank can give the customer's money to third parties and what happens if the bank does so improperly. I discuss those two issues separately.

1.   When Is It Proper for the Bank to Pay?

On the first point, the text of the UCC offers little guidance, stating only that it is proper for the bank to charge a customer's account for any "item that is properly payable." UCC §4-401(a). The comments to that section explain the concept more clearly, indicating that an item is properly payable "if the customer has authorized the payment." UCC §4-401 comment 1. In the checking context, the most common way for the customer to authorize payment (although not the only way) is by writing a check, which authorizes the bank to use funds in the customer's account to pay the amount of the check to the payee. Accordingly, if the payee presents the check to the customer's bank (the payor bank, as discussed above), it would be proper for the payor bank to "honor" the check. If the payor bank does honor the check, it gives funds in the amount of the check to the payee and charges the customer's account for the amount of the check. Thus, for example, if Archie presented Cliff's check to Rocky Mountain, it would be proper for Rocky Mountain to pay the check and charge Cliff's account.

In most cases, the payee does not take the check directly to the payor bank. Instead, the payee obtains payment from an intermediary, such as the payee's own bank or a check-cashing outlet. As long as the payee properly transfers the check to the intermediary (a topic discussed in detail in later assignments), the intermediary becomes, in the terms of UCC §3-301, a "person entitled to enforce" the check and thus is just as entitled to payment of the check as the original payee. See UCC §1-201(28), (30) (revised §1-201(b)(25), (27)) ("person" in the UCC includes not only natural individuals, but also organizations such as corporations, partnerships, trusts, and other legal or commercial entities). Thus, if Archie deposits the check into his account at Colorado National, Colorado National becomes, in the UCC's terminology, a person entitled to enforce the check. In that event, it is just as proper for Rocky Mountain to pay the amount of the check to Colorado National as it would have been for Rocky Mountain to pay the amount of the check to Archie directly.

Conversely, if the check is stolen through no fault of Archie's and presented by a party that does not have any right to enforce the check, it is not proper for Rocky Mountain to pay the check. See UCC §4-401 comment 1, sentences 5-7. The idea is simple: When a customer writes a check to a particular payee, it authorizes payment to that payee and to parties that acquire the check from the payee, but it does not authorize payment to thieves that do not properly acquire the check from the payee. Cliff's authorization to his bank to pay Archie may extend to Colorado National where Archie deposits the check, but it does not usually extend to thieves who steal the check from Archie. Assignments 25 and 26 discuss the rules about thieves in more detail.

(a) *Overdrafts.*   A variety of problems can complicate the bank's entitlement to pay a check even in cases in which the customer actually wrote the check and in which the party seeking payment is the proper holder of the check. The most common problem arises when the customer authorizes payment by writing a check, but the account does not have enough funds to cover the check when it arrives at the payor bank. The answer in that situation is simple, if not intuitively obvious: The payor bank is free to pay the check or dishonor it as the bank wishes. That is, the payor bank *can* charge the account, but (absent some specific agreement) it also is free to dishonor the check and refuse to pay it. UCC §§4-401(a), 4-402(a).

McGuire v. Bank One, Louisiana, N.A.
744 So. 2d 714 (La. App. 1999)

Before WILLIAMS, STEWART and DREW, JJ.
STEWART, J.
Lottie M. McGuire ("McGuire") filed suit against Bank One Louisiana ("Bank One") for damages after Bank One paid a check drawn by McGuire and thereby created an overdraft in the amount of $188,176.79. Bank One filed an exception of no cause of action which the trial court sustained. McGuire now appeals the dismissal of her suit for damages. We affirm.

FACTS

[O]n the morning of August 26, 1996, Timothy P. Looney ("Looney"), an acquaintance representing himself as an investment broker, approached [McGuire] with an offer to sell $200,000 in bonds due to mature on October 31, 1996 for $206,400. McGuire told Looney that she would think about it and let him know. Later that day, McGuire informed Looney that she would buy the bonds for $200,000. Looney agreed to come by later to pick up McGuire's check.

McGuire maintained both a checking account and an investment account with Bank One in Shreveport, Louisiana. Bank One's trust department administered McGuire's investment account. McGuire contacted Harvey Anne Leimbrook, an account officer in Bank One's trust department, and instructed her to [take the steps necessary to move funds from the investment account] to the checking account. Leimbrook informed McGuire that it would take two or three days for the money to be transferred.

Later that same day, Looney went to McGuire's house, and McGuire presented him with a check for $200,000 payable to his company, Paramount Financial Group. The check was dated August 26, 1996. McGuire gave Looney "strict instructions" not to present the check for payment until Wednesday, August 28, 1996, so as to insure that the transfer of funds would be complete. Looney did not heed McGuire's instructions, but instead he immediately deposited the check at Commercial National Bank ("CNB").

CNB then presented McGuire's check for payment to Bank One on August 27, 1996. Bank One, without notifying McGuire, honored the check even though the amount of money in McGuire's checking account was "grossly insufficient" to cover the check. Bank One did mail an overdraft notice to McGuire the next day informing her that her checking account was overdrawn in the amount of $188,198.79 and that an overdraft fee of $22 was charged to her account. McGuire received the overdraft notice on Friday, August 30, 1996.

Unfortunately, Looney did not purchase the bonds with McGuire's money. Instead, Looney converted the money for his own benefit. Looney subsequently pled guilty to mail fraud and was sentenced to serve time in a federal penitentiary. McGuire alleges that if Bank One had informed her on August 26 or 27 that her check had been prematurely presented for payment contrary to her explicit instructions to Looney, then she would have become suspicious of Looney and stopped payment on the check. McGuire seeks damages for Bank One's negligence in failing to exercise ordinary care in paying the check and creating the overdraft.

In response to McGuire's petition for damages, Bank One . . . asserted that McGuire's check was properly payable and that pursuant to [UCC §]4-401, it was authorized to honor the check even though an overdraft resulted. The trial court [ruled in favor of Bank One.]

DISCUSSION

. . . According to the facts alleged in her petition, McGuire seeks damages from Bank One because a substantial overdraft resulted when Bank One honored a check drawn by McGuire on her own checking account. . . . McGuire does not dispute that her check was properly payable. However, McGuire argues that the bank's authority to honor a check creating an overdraft is discretionary under [Section] 401(a) and that, as a matter of policy, this statutory right should be tempered by some standard of due care in compliance with the general usage and customs of the banking industry. As an alternative to reversal of the trial court, McGuire seeks leave to amend her petition to add additional pleadings regarding the duty of ordinary care owed by banks and the general banking customs and practices in this area. . . .

. . . The language of [Section] 4-401 permits a bank to charge a properly payable check against a customer's account even though an overdraft results. No showing of good faith is required to justify the bank's action. However, under the provisions of [UCC §]4-103, a bank is required to exercise ordinary care. Bank One asserts that it exercised ordinary care in paying McGuire's check and charging payment to her account. We agree. . . . Payment of a properly payable item creating an overdraft is an action approved by [Section] 4-401(a). Therefore, such action by a bank is the exercise of ordinary care. General banking usage, customs, or practices would have no bearing on whether Bank One did or did not exercise ordinary care since its payment of McGuire's check, even though an overdraft resulted, was expressly authorized by [Section] 4-401(a) and is *per se* the exercise of ordinary care under [Section] 4-103(c). Therefore, we find, as did the trial court, that McGuire's petition fails to state a cause of action against Bank One. . . .

In finding that McGuire's petition fails to state a cause of action against Bank One, we have reviewed similar cases from other jurisdictions interpreting [Section] 4-401(a) and have found no support for McGuire's position. In City Bank of Honolulu v. Tenn, 52 Haw. 51, 469 P.2d 816 (1970), the bank sued Tenn to collect $6,000 it paid out on an overdraft drawn by Tenn. Tenn had drawn the check as part of a business deal even though he knew that he did not have sufficient funds in his account, and he gave it to the payee with an express oral understanding that the payee would hold the check as evidence of his good faith. The payee, contrary to his understanding with Tenn, deposited the check.

The bank cashed the check after failing to reach Tenn by telephone. Thereafter, Tenn refused to reimburse the bank the amount of the overdraft. At issue was whether the bank had authority to cash Tenn's check without his express authorization. The court found that the bank had such authority and reasoned that the authority was impliedly given when Tenn drew the check and delivered it to the payee. The court based its reasoning on cases holding that payment of the check creating an overdraft constitutes a loan for which the bank customer is liable for repayment. Also, the court noted that once a depositor initiates circulation of an instrument, the depositor "must in conscience and law bear the ultimate consequences thereof." [469 P.2d at 818.] Although McGuire argues that the decision in *Tenn* was reached because the bank exercised ordinary care by attempting to first contact Tenn before paying the check, we find no support for this interpretation in the case. The court makes no reference to the bank's attempt to contact Tenn in holding that the bank had authority to pay the check.

In Pulaski State Bank v. Kalbe, 122 Wis. 2d 663, 364 N.W.2d 162 (App. 1985), *review denied,* 122 Wis. 2d 783, 367 N.W.2d 223 (1985), Kalbe drew a check that was later lost or stolen. The bank received the check and paid it. Payment of the check resulted in an overdraft of $6,542.12. The bank sued to recover the overdraft amount. The court determined that pursuant to [the Wisconsin version of UCC §4-401(a)], the bank could properly pay the check even though it created an overdraft. The court reasoned that such payment is treated as a loan that may be recovered from the depositor. Kalbe argued, just as McGuire argues in the instant case, that a check creating an unusually large overdraft is not properly payable. The court rejected this argument and stated that the applicable statute "places no limit on the size of the overdraft or the bank's reason for payment." [364 N.W.2d at 163.]

Just as in *Tenn* and *Pulaski,* Bank One had authority to pay McGuire's check even though it created an overdraft. The check was properly payable. The fact that a substantial overdraft resulted does not override the bank's authority under [UCC §]4-401(a). The allegations in McGuire's petition indicate that she drew the check knowing that she had insufficient funds in her checking account to cover the check. It is unfortunate that McGuire was the victim of fraud. However, her loss is not one for which Bank One can be found liable under the circumstances of this case.

CONCLUSION

For the reasons discussed, we affirm the trial court's judgment granting Bank One's exception of no cause of action. Costs of this appeal are assessed against McGuire.

At first glance, it might seem unduly deferential to give the payor bank unguided discretion to decide whether to pay the check, but it does make more sense than a mandatory legal rule that takes away that discretion and establishes a fixed course of action for such checks. Consider first a possible rule that would *require* banks to dishonor overdraft checks. That rule would be much worse for customers than the present discretionary rule. Most customers would prefer for their banks to honor their checks even if their accounts contain insufficient funds, if only to protect the customers from the difficulties they face when their checks bounce: monetary charges by those to whom they wrote the checks, possible criminal liability, and more general harm to the customers' reputations. Conversely, it would be unreasonable to require banks to honor checks even when accounts do not contain enough funds to cover the checks. That rule would expose banks to the risk of loss in any case in which the customer did not voluntarily reimburse the bank for the amount of the check.

As it happens, most banks are willing to agree to pay overdrafts for their customers (at least for some of their customers) by providing "overdraft protection." Thus, for a fee, banks agree in advance that they will honor checks up to a preset limit even if the checks are drawn against insufficient funds. That agreement overturns the standard Article 4 rule and leaves the bank obligated to pay the checks when they appear. See UCC §§4-402(a) (stating that "a bank may dishonor an item that would create an overdraft *unless it has agreed to pay the overdraft*" (emphasis added)), 4-103(a) (stating that "[t]he effect of the provisions of this Article may be varied by agreement").

A related issue is raised by the fees that banks charge when customers write checks against insufficient funds. The UCC itself does not generally regulate the fees that banks can charge their customers in connection with checking accounts. See UCC §§4-401 comment 3, 4-406 comment 3. In this particular area, however, there has been considerable activity limiting the charges that banks can impose. Specifically, a number of courts have suggested that high charges for processing bad checks could violate a bank's implied duty of good faith or could be unconscionable, at least if the charges substantially exceed the cost to the bank of processing the bad checks. The Oregon Supreme Court, for example, has suggested that such a charge would violate the bank's obligation of good faith if it was not in accordance with "the reasonable contractual expectations of the parties." The court remanded the case for a trial to determine whether fees of $3 to $5 per check were assessed in bad faith. Best v. United States Natl. Bank, 739 P.2d 554, 555, 559 (Or. 1987); see also Perdue v. Crocker Natl. Bank, 702 P.2d 503, 514 (Cal. 1985) (remanding for trial to determine whether a fee "far in excess of cost" was unconscionable). It is difficult to generalize, however, because other courts have rejected such claims out of hand. The highest court in the state of New York, for example, has concluded that such a claim of unconscionability could succeed only if the customers could "show that [because of a lack of competition] they were deprived of a meaningful choice of banks with which they could do business." Jacobs, P.C. v. Citibank N.A., 462 N.E.2d 1182, 1184 (N.Y. 1984). With such a conflict of result, the uncertainty seems to be sufficient that banks that do business throughout the country have to consider the issue in establishing their fee structures.

Another major topic of dispute relates to the order in which banks process checks for payment. Banks often pay the largest checks first and smaller checks later (that is, by descending order of amount). On a day when the account contains insufficient funds to pay all of the checks presented against it, that procedure can lead to a larger number of bounced checks (and thus a greater amount of bounced-check fees) than a policy that paid checks by increasing order of amount. Banks have defended those policies by pointing out that the largest checks often are items such as mortgage and car payments — for which consumers are most likely to suffer serious damage from payor-bank dishonor. Consumer advocates — skeptical of the sincerity of the bank's professed interest in customer welfare — have filed a number of suits challenging such policies, but those suits to date have foundered on the statement in UCC §4-303(b) that banks can pay items "in any order." E.g., Smith v. First Union Natl. Bank, 958 S.W.2d 113 (Tenn. App. 1997); Hill v. St. Paul Federal Bank, 768 N.E.2d 322, 325-327 (Ill. Ct. App. 2002). Similarly, efforts to revise the statute to provide a uniform policy failed because of the opposition of the banking industry.

(b) *Stopping Payment.*   A second problem regarding the bank's right to pay a check arises when a customer changes its mind after it has written a check and decides that it no longer wants the payor bank to pay the payee. That could happen for several reasons, ranging from dissatisfaction with the goods or services purchased with the check to completely unrelated financial distress (such as loss of a job) that alters the customer's willingness to pay. A notable feature of the checking system is that the customer's decision to pay does not become final at the time that the customer issues the check. Rather, Article 4 gives the customer that changes its mind the right to "stop" payment. Specifically, a check ceases to be properly payable if the customer gives the payor bank timely and adequate notice of the customer's desire that the payor bank refuse to pay the check. Hence, at least if the customer manages to send a timely and effective notice, the bank loses its right to charge the customer's account for the item even if the item initially was authorized by the customer. UCC §4-403 & comment 7.

Three major considerations, however, limit the practicality of the customer's right to stop payment. First, the customer must act promptly to exercise the right. UCC §4-403(a) provides that a stop-payment notice is effective only if it is "received at a time and in a manner that affords the bank a reasonable opportunity to act on it before any [final] action by the bank with respect to the item." As Assignment 23 explains, current check-collection systems usually result in final action on a check within one or two days after the check is deposited for collection. Accordingly, any attempt to stop payment that comes more than a few days after the underlying transaction is unlikely to be effective under UCC §4-403.

The second problem relates to the duration of the stop-payment order. Under UCC §4-403(b), a stop-payment order is valid only for six months. To be sure, the drawer can renew the stop-payment order every six months if it wishes to keep the check permanently unpayable, but as a practical matter few drawers remember to renew the stop-payment order every six months. Accordingly, it is easy enough for the savvy holder of a stopped check to wait out the six-month period and present it shortly after the termination of that period. Experience suggests that banks readily honor items presented shortly after the expiration of the statutory six-month period. The six-month limit is particularly odd because it is so obviously contrary to the typical intent of a customer seeking to stop payment—can you imagine wanting to stop payment on a check *now* but intending for your bank to pay the check *six months later*? Still, recent efforts to revise the statute to remove the six-month limit have failed because of opposition of the banking industry, which contends that it would be unduly difficult to design computer software that would treat stop-payment requests as permanently effective.

The third problem with a customer's effort to stop payment arises from the underlying obligation for which the check was written. When somebody satisfies a payment obligation with a check, the payee has two separate rights to payment: the right to enforce the check and the right to pursue the check writer on the underlying transaction. The right to enforce the check arises under Articles 3 and 4; the right on the underlying transaction arises under the law that governs that transaction, which might be the rules in Article 2 that govern sales, the terms of a lease if the check is issued to pay rent, or common-law rules governing promissory notes if the check is issued to make a payment on a note.

Section 3-310 of the UCC articulates a set of rules to govern the two rights of the payee, the general purpose of which is to enhance the likelihood that the payee will be paid once, but only once. For present purposes, two of those rules are crucial. First, to prevent the payee from obtaining double payment by collecting both on the check and on the underlying obligation, the UCC "suspend[s]" the payee's right to pursue the customer on the underlying transaction when the payee accepts the customer's check. See UCC §3-310(b). Second, to ensure that the payee is not prejudiced by its willingness to accept the check, the statute provides that the suspension ends if the check is dishonored. See UCC §3-310(b)(1). The termination of the suspension leaves the payee back where it started, with its right to pursue the check writer on the underlying transaction. Thus, even if a check writer succeeds in causing its bank to stop payment on a check, the check writer remains liable to the payee on the underlying obligation.

2. Remedies for Improper Payment

Sometimes a bank pays a check that was not, in the terms of UCC §4-401, properly payable. The most likely problem is (a) that the customer in fact did not write the check, (b) that payment was made after a forged indorsement (and thus was not made to the payee or some other person entitled to enforce the check), or (c) that the bank failed to comply with a valid order to stop payment. The basic remedy for an improper payment is simple and intuitively obvious. The bank must reverse the improper transaction. Specifically, because the item was not properly payable, the bank cannot sustain the charge on the customer's account based on that item. Accordingly, the bank must recredit the customer's account with the funds improperly paid out, so that the balance in the customer's account will be the same as it would have been if the bank had not made the improper payment. Moreover, as Assignment 22 discusses in more detail, the statute even provides a form of consequential damages in cases in which the charge to the account leads the bank to dishonor other checks. In that event, the bank not only must return any fees it charged in connection with those dishonored checks, but also must pay any damages to the customer that are proximately caused by the dishonor. See UCC §4-402(b).

However generous the obligation to recredit might appear at first glance, its practical import is limited sharply by UCC §4-407. That provision "subrogates" the bank to the rights of the payee of the check, so that the bank can assert the payee's rights against the drawer as a defense to the bank's obligation to recredit the account. Returning to the previous example, suppose that Cliff changed his mind about buying the books after he wrote the check to Archie and properly stopped payment before Archie presented the check to Rocky Mountain (the payor bank). If Rocky Mountain mistakenly paid Archie anyway, Rocky Mountain's right of subrogation would allow the bank to refuse to recredit Cliff's account *even though the check was not properly payable*. By subrogation to Archie's rights, the bank would be entitled to assert Archie's right to payment. Assuming that Cliff was obligated to pay for the books even though Cliff changed his mind (a plausible assumption), then the bank would be entitled to payment just as much as Archie was (because the bank already paid Archie on the check). Thus, the bank would not have to recredit the account. If that rule seems fundamentally unfair at first glance to the party that attempted to stop payment, it is worth considering matters from the perspective of the payee, a perspective well illuminated by the case that follows.

McIntyre v. Harris

709 N.E.2d 982 (Ill. App. 1999)

Justice LYTTON delivered the opinion of the court:

The plaintiff, Brian P. McIntyre, filed a complaint against the defendants, Twin Oaks Savings Bank (Bank) and Robert E. Harris (Harris), the Bank's executive vice-president. McIntyre alleged that the defendants coerced him into signing a $2,000 personal note made payable to the Bank after the Bank had erroneously paid out a check over McIntyre's valid stop payment order. The defendants counterclaimed, demanding payment on the overdue note. After a bench trial, the court found in favor of the defendants. . . . We affirm.

In mid-October 1996 McIntyre's company, Total Home, placed a telemarketing call to Sandra Bennett. As a result, Ray Archie visited Bennett's home and quoted her a price to repair her roof. McIntyre testified that since his company did not repair roofs, he referred the job to Archie. . . .

Around October 19, 1996, McIntyre visited Bennett and told her that in order to complete the job, it was necessary for her to give Archie $2,000 for the materials. Bennett wrote a check to Total Home for $2,000 that day. In return, McIntyre wrote Bennett a check for $2,000 and postdated it to October 28, 1996. Bennett said that McIntyre told her that she could cash his check if her roof was not repaired by October 28, 1996. McIntyre cashed Bennett's check and deposited it in his business account at the Bank. . . .

McIntyre admitted that Bennett's roof was not repaired by October 28, 1996. Nevertheless, on November 14, 1996, he ordered the Bank to stop payment on the check to Bennett.

Around November 27, 1996, the Bank erroneously paid out on McIntyre's check over his stop payment order. After McIntyre learned that the Bank had withdrawn the $2,000 from his business account, he spoke with Harris and told him that the withdrawal would cause his account to be overdrawn. He then went to the Bank and signed an agreement to pay the Bank $2,000 plus interest due by July 1, 1997. In return, the Bank agreed to leave the $2,000 in his account. McIntyre admitted that he never paid on the note and at the time of trial he was currently 2 ½ months overdue on it. . . .

The judge [concluded that] the Bank was subrogated to the rights of Sandra Bennett and could recover the money from McIntyre. The court then found in favor of the defendants. . . .

I

A. Unjust Enrichment

McIntyre first contends that the Bank is not entitled to a $2,000 reimbursement. In deciding this issue, we must determine. . . . whether the Bank properly paid out over a valid stop payment order to prevent unjust enrichment. . . . .

Section 4-407 of the UCC provides that if a payor bank has paid an item over the stop order of the drawer or maker, the bank may become subrogated to the rights of other parties in order to prevent unjust enrichment to the extent necessary to prevent loss to the bank by reason of its payment of the item. . . . When a bank pays out a check over a valid stop payment order, the ultimate burden of proof as to loss is on the customer [citing an out-of-state decision].

Since the Bank paid out over McIntyre's valid stop payment order, we must determine whether the Bank can become subrogated to the rights of another party to prevent unjust enrichment. McIntyre admitted that Bennett wrote a $2,000 check to Total Home and that he deposited it in his business account at the Bank. He did not dispute Bennett's testimony that he told Bennett she could cash his check to her if her roof was not completed by October 28, 1996. He agreed that the roof was never completed. Therefore, McIntyre deposited $2,000 of Bennett's money in his account for work that was never performed. Under these facts, the trial court properly...found that McIntyre was unjustly enriched. Thus, the Bank is entitled to repayment if it can subrogate itself to the rights of a proper party under the UCC.

[The court then considered whether Bennett was a proper party. Ultimately, it concluded that it did not matter whether Bennett was a holder in due course (a topic discussed in Chapter 11):] [U]nder 4-407(2), even if Bennett were not a holder in due course, the Bank would still be subrogated to her rights as a payee. Under subsection (2), Bennett, as the payee of the instrument, even as a mere holder, obtained the right to pursue McIntyre. A payor Bank is subrogated to the rights "of the payee or any other holder...against the drawer...on the item or under the transaction out of which the item arose." The Bank was properly subrogated to Bennett's interest as the holder of McIntyre's check. [ED.: Bennett plainly qualifies as a holder of the item under UCC §1-201(20) (revised §1-201(b)(21)).]...

The judgment of the circuit court of La Salle County is affirmed.

If the bank relied on subrogation to justify a refusal to recredit, the result doubtless would disappoint Cliff (who, after all, followed the correct steps to stop payment). It is justified, however, by the unfairness of allowing the drawer to have its account recredited when the drawer in fact is obligated to pay for the books. In the absence of subrogation (or some similarly equitable remedy such as restitution), the result would be that Cliff would get to keep the books without paying for them.

Whatever the theoretical propriety of the limits that subrogation places on a bank's obligation to remedy erroneous payments, the practical significance of the legal rule is debatable. In many cases, the costs to a bank of demonstrating the customer's continuing obligation are likely to dwarf the amount of the check. In those cases, the bank's statutory right to subrogation will go unasserted. Thus, in the end, the most common result in cases of wrongful honor is likely to be a windfall to the payment-stopping drawer: The payee keeps the payment it received from the payor bank, the payor's account is recredited, and the bank's failure to stop payment results in a loss by the bank in the amount of the check.

Problem Set 21

21.1.   Tertius Lydgate comes to you with a problem about a $1,500 check that his wife Rosamund wrote recently on their joint bank account. The account contained only $50 at the time, and Tertius had declined to purchase overdraft protection from the bank at which he maintained the account. Still, the bank honored the check and has now written Tertius a letter threatening unspecified "serious consequences" if he does not reimburse the bank for the amount of the check.

a.   Is Tertius liable for the check? UCC §§4-401(a) & 4-401 comment 1.
b.   Would your answer change if you learned that Rosamund and he are estranged and that she used the funds to purchase an airplane ticket for a trip that she took (by herself) to London? UCC §§4-401(b) & 4-401 comment 2.

21.2.   Your old college classmate Ben Darrow is a senior vice president at the First State Bank of Matacora (FSB), which is owned by his father-in-law. He calls you one Monday afternoon to ask you about a problem that has arisen at his bank. Darrow explains that his problem relates to a $900 check drawn by his customer Jasmine Ball, which Darrow's bank received for payment on Monday January 22. The check was payable to Matacora Realtors and dated February 1 of the current year. Because his bank's new automated check-processing system does not examine the dates on checks and because Ball's account at that time contained $1,000, the system paid the check and deducted $900 from Ball's account. Upon further examination, it appears that Ball sent the bank a letter in September of last year. The letter identified Ball's account by number and explained that she would be paying her rent for the next year by postdated checks payable to Matacora Realtors. The letter asked the bank not to cash any of the checks until the indicated dates. The bank never responded to the letter. Has Darrow's bank acted improperly? UCC §§3-113(a), 4-401(c), 4-401 comment 3, 4-403(b), 4-403 comment 6.

21.3.   Pleased with your advice in Problem 21.2, Darrow calls you again a few days later. Because of a clerical error, the bank paid a check in contravention of a written stop-payment order. The check was written by Albert "Bud" Lassen and payable to Carol Long in the amount of $1,500, apparently for some cooking equipment. Shortly after Bud got home with the equipment, he decided that he did not want it because it was slightly larger than he had understood. As a result, the equipment was too big for the space in his kitchen. Carol refused to take back the equipment. Bud immediately came to the bank and filled out the bank's stop-payment form, identifying the account number, as well as the number, amount, and date of the check. Unfortunately, a clerk incorrectly entered the information supplied by Bud. As a result, the system did not recognize the check to Carol when she came in and cashed it the next day. Bud is furious and insists that the bank recredit his account. Darrow wants to know if he must recredit Bud's account. If he does recredit Bud's account, will the bank lose the money? UCC §§4-401(a), 4-403(a) & (b), 4-407(2) & (3), 4-407 comments 2 & 3.

21.4.   What would have happened if the bank had complied with Bud's stop-payment order and had refused to honor Bud's check? Could Carol force Bud to pay for the equipment? UCC §3-310(b)(1), (3) & comment 3.

21.5.   You come in to work one morning to find a voice-mail message from Caleb Garth asking for an urgent appointment to discuss a problem with his bank. When you meet him later that morning, he explains that he is the president and sole shareholder of Garth Management, Inc. (GMI), a corporation that manages rural estates for absentee landowners. Caleb tells you that GMI has had its only bank account at Bulstrode Bank for the last three years. The signature card for GMI (executed at the time that the account was opened) listed as authorized signatories on the account Garth's daughter, Mary Garth, and his son-in-law, Fred Vincy, who took over operational control of GMI from Caleb about five years ago. Because GMI has been losing money ever since Mary and Fred took over, Caleb finally lost patience two weeks ago and decided to regain control of the corporation. He convened a shareholder's meeting at which he voted his shares to elect himself the sole director of the corporation. Acting in that capacity, he removed Mary and Fred as officers of the corporation and named himself as president.

His problem came when he went to the bank to remove Fred and Mary from the signature card. When he explained the situation to the bank, the account officer (Nicholas Bulstrode) told Caleb that the bank would freeze all funds in the account until Caleb presented the bank with a letter from Mary and Fred consenting to their removal from the account. The bank officer relied on the following provision in the account agreement:

> If another person or entity makes a claim against funds in your account, or if we have reason to believe there is or may be a dispute over matters such as the ownership of the account or the authority to withdraw funds, we may, in our sole discretion, (1) continue to rely on current signature cards, resolutions or other account documents, (2) freeze all or part of the funds until the dispute is resolved to our satisfaction, or (3) pay the funds into an appropriate court of law for resolution.

You are satisfied that Caleb has complied with all of the appropriate corporate formalities. His problem is that Mary and Fred are out of town (on a walking tour of old cathedrals). Can Caleb force the bank to release the funds without providing the letter from Mary and Fred? UCC §§4-103(a), 4-103 comments 1 & 2.

21.6. Your friend Jodi Kay is an executive at CountryBank. She comes to you to discuss a proposed restructuring of CountryBank's fee structure for checking accounts. CountryBank has been involved in an aggressive program to open branches of its bank in underserved areas of the community, where most of the customers have relatively modest incomes. Unfortunately, although the new branches have been doing well at getting accounts opened, several of them have been unprofitable. Because the bank's senior management is committed to keeping the branches open, it called Jodi in to investigate the situation. After studying the records of the branches, she attributed the lack of profitability to an unusually large number of overdrafts and stop-payment requests. Those items are consuming a larger amount of administrative time than is normal for branches of similar size.

Jodi has come up with two different ways to return the branches to profitability. First, she could increase the monthly account charges on low-balance accounts from $10 to $25. She is worried about that course because of the possibility that it will drive out the low-income customers she is trying to reach. Second, she could increase the fees on dishonored checks and stop-payment requests from $25 to $50. She asks you for your advice, specifically inquiring whether it would be lawful for her to impose the charges that she has proposed. UCC §§4-401 comment 3, 4-403 comment 1.

Assignment 22: The Bank's Obligation to Pay Checks

For the checking system to work, the payor bank's obligation to pay must be sufficiently certain to convince sellers to accept checks as a method of payment. Accordingly, the rules establishing when a bank must pay the customer's funds to another party are central to the success of the checking system. Those rules fall into two classes: rules obligating the bank to pay and rules establishing remedies for the bank's failure to pay as required.

A. When Are Funds Available for Payment?

As discussed in Assignment 21, a bank has the option to pay any item that is properly payable from the customer's account. When the account has funds "available" to cover the item, however, the bank has an affirmative obligation to pay the item. To be sure, as discussed in Assignment 23, that obligation runs only to the bank's customer (the drawer), *not* to the payee or any subsequent holder of the check. Thus, even if funds are available to pay the item at the time the item comes to the bank, the payee has no claim against the bank if the customer prevents the bank from paying the check by withdrawing those funds or otherwise stopping the bank from paying the check. But from the customer's perspective, the bank's obligation to pay is central because the reliability of that obligation is what makes it useful for the customer to make payments with checks.

Logically, the system must address two separate questions to establish a framework for determining whether sufficient funds are available to pay any particular item: When is the determination made, and what is the balance of funds available in the account at that time?

1. Time of Evaluation

First, at what point in time must the account contain enough funds to cover the check? It is easy to imagine a variety of points in time that could be determinative: (a) the moment that the check is written, (b) the moment that the payor bank receives the check, (c) the moment that the payor bank evaluates the check, or (d) the moment that the payor bank returns the check for lack of funds. The statute essentially chooses the third solution, which maximizes the bank's flexibility and minimizes the logistical difficulty of making the necessary determination. Thus, under UCC §4-402(c), the bank is free to determine whether the account has sufficient funds "at any time between the time the item is received by the payor bank and the time that the payor bank returns the item."

For example, consider a $350 check that Cliff Janeway writes on his account at Rocky Mountain Bank to buy a book from Archie Moon. Suppose that Cliff writes the check on Wednesday September 28 knowing that his salary will be deposited automatically into his account by Friday September 30. If Archie presents the check to Rocky Mountain Bank on Thursday September 29, the bank is free to evaluate the account at that time and decide not to pay the check (to dishonor it, in the terms of the UCC, see UCC §3-502) if the account contains only $200 of funds that are available. Then, if the amount of available funds in the account increases to $2,000 on the morning of September 30, the bank could dishonor the check later that day, even though the account at the time of dishonor contained funds sufficient to cover the check. See UCC §4-402(c) (explaining that "no more than one determination need be made") & comment 4 (explaining that dishonor remains appropriate notwithstanding new credits to the account after the bank has evaluated the sufficiency of the funds in the account).

2.   Availability of Funds

The second question is what balance of funds is in the account at the relevant time. Surprisingly, the question of how much money the customer has in its account to cover checks at any time is relatively complicated, with several sections of the United States Code and pages of Federal Reserve Board regulations providing a network of rules that limit the bank's discretion to decide that question for itself.

The complexity of those rules is an artifact of the modern checking system. In a simpler world, there would be no need for complicated rules about funds availability. For example, if all deposits to checking accounts were made in cash, there would be no need for disputes about the date when the deposited funds would be available for payment of checks written by the customer: As soon as the bank received the cash and noted the deposit on its records—probably by the next business day after the date of the deposit—the bank would be safe in disbursing the funds to pay checks written by the customer. See 12 C.F.R. §229.10(a) (requiring payor banks to make funds available by the next business day after the deposit if the funds are deposited in cash with a teller at the bank).

As it happens, however, many (if not most) of the deposits to checking accounts are made not in the form of cash or some other immediately verifiable means of payment (such as the wire transfers discussed in Assignments 30 and 31), but in the form of checks. Again, there would be no problem if all checks were deposited at the payor bank: Whenever a customer deposited a check to its account, the bank could refer to its records for the account on which the check was drawn to see if there was enough money to pay the check; if there was, the depositary bank safely could credit the customer's account and debit the drawer's account at the same time. See 12 C.F.R. §229.10(c)(1)(vi) (requiring payor banks to make funds available by the next business day after the deposit if the funds are deposited in the form of a check drawn on a local branch of the depositary bank).

In reality, of course, there are hundreds of different banks in this country, and thus banks receive deposits containing a prodigious number of checks that are drawn on other banks. Accordingly, a bank into which a check is deposited cannot tell from its own records whether it safely can allow the depositor to withdraw the funds represented by the check. Thus, if Bank A wants to be safe in deciding whether to honor a check based on funds that its customer has deposited in the form of a check drawn on an account at Bank B, Bank A will have to wait until it finds out whether Bank B will honor the deposited check. If Bank A grants immediate access to the funds, Bank A will have a problem if Bank B later dishonors the check after Bank A's customer already has withdrawn the money. Accordingly, depositary banks have an incentive to limit their customers' access to funds deposited by check until they can be certain that the deposited checks will be honored by the banks on which the checks are drawn. If Bank A does not limit that access, it exposes itself to fraud by a customer that might withdraw the funds even if the customer knows that the account at Bank B on which the deposited check was drawn does not contain sufficient funds to cover the deposited check.

For many years, the only legal rule governing the bank's evaluation of funds availability was the rule set forth in UCC §4-215(e) (and its predecessors). That statute grants the depositary bank unfettered discretion to protect itself by permitting the bank to limit the customer's access to funds deposited by check until the depositary bank can determine whether the check will be honored. The practices of banks under that rule eventually became intolerably onerous to consumers. As the Supreme Court has explained:

> [Under the UCC], the check-clearing process too often lagged, taking days or even weeks to complete. To protect themselves against the risk that a deposited check would be returned unpaid, banks typically placed lengthy "holds" on deposited funds. Bank customers, encountering long holds, complained that delayed access to deposited funds impeded the expeditious use of their checking accounts.
>
> In 1987, Congress responded by passing the Expedited Funds Availability Act, [which] requires banks to make deposited funds available for withdrawal within specified time periods, subject to stated exceptions.

Bank One Chicago, N.A. v. Midwest Bank & Trust Co., 516 U.S. 264, 266-67 (1996).

The Expedited Funds Availability Act (EFAA), 12 U.S.C. §§4001-4010, has been implemented by the Board of Governors of the Federal Reserve System. The Federal Reserve System is a quasi-governmental entity that is the principal entity in charge of controlling the growth of the American money supply (an important tool for economic policy). For purposes of this course, though, the Federal Reserve is important because it operates about a dozen banks spread throughout the United States — the Federal Reserve banks — that assist private banks in the process of clearing and collecting checks (the subject of Assignment 23). To implement the EFAA, the Federal Reserve has issued a detailed regulation codified as Part 229 of Title 12 of the Code of Federal Regulations. Federal Reserve regulations are codified in the "200" series of 12 C.F.R. and generally are referred to by shorthand alphabetic designations. Because "CC" is the twenty-ninth alphabetic designation, 12 C.F.R. Part 229 commonly is referred to as Regulation CC (just as other Federal Reserve regulations that you will study later commonly are referred to as Regulation E, Regulation J, and Regulation Z).

Regulation CC establishes a framework of deadlines within which a depositary bank must release funds that its customers deposit by check. Unlike UCC §4-215, those deadlines apply even if the depositary bank does not determine by the deadline if the payor bank will honor the check in question. The deadlines in Regulation CC mirror deadlines required in the text of the EFAA itself. To avoid duplication, this text discusses only the more detailed regulatory provisions.

Although the regulations contain plenty of special provisions and exceptions (several of which are discussed below), the general framework that they establish is not hard to follow. That framework is best understood as distinguishing transactions along two separate dimensions: (a) whether the customer deposited the funds in the form of a local check or a nonlocal check and (b) whether the customer wishes to use those funds indirectly (by writing checks against them) or directly (by withdrawing cash). On the first dimension, the regulations allow banks to impose a greater delay on the availability of funds from nonlocal checks (three extra business days) because it takes more time for them to learn whether nonlocal checks will be honored by the respective payor banks. For purposes of the regulation, a nonlocal check is any check drawn on a bank located outside the check-processing region of the bank at which the check is deposited. See Regulation CC, §229.2(m), (r), (s), (v) (defining nonlocal checks and describing the Federal Reserve's division of the nation into check-processing regions). On the second dimension, the regulations give banks more time before they must make funds available in cash, on the theory that individuals trying to defraud banks are more likely to withdraw funds in cash than by check.

The intersection of the local-nonlocal and noncash-cash dimensions produces a matrix of four separate rules for withdrawal (summarized in Figure 22.1):

Figure 22.1
Basic Funds Availability Rules

Type of Withdrawal		Type of Deposit	
		Local Check	Nonlocal Check
Noncash		Day 1: $100 Day 2: Remainder	Day 1: $100 Day 5: Remainder
Cash		Day 1: $100 Day 2: $400 Day 3: Remainder	Day 1: $100 Day 5: $400 Day 6: Remainder

- *Noncash withdrawals from local checks.*   This is the quickest way for funds to become available. In this situation, the bank must make $100 available on the first business day after the banking day on which the funds are deposited. Regulation CC, §229.10(c)(1)(vii). The rest of the funds must be available for withdrawal no later than the second business day. Regulation CC, §229.12(b).
- *Noncash withdrawals from nonlocal checks.*   The second situation is the same as the first, except that the checks are not local. In that situation, the bank still has to make $100 available on the first business day, but it can wait until the fifth business day (rather than the second) to make the remaining funds available. Regulation CC, §229.12(c)(1).
- *Cash withdrawals from local checks.*   The third and fourth rules apply if the customer wants to withdraw the funds by cash (rather than by check). In that event, the regulations permit the bank to defer for still another day the availability of all sums beyond the first $500. Regulation CC, §229.12(d). Thus, the third rule provides with respect to a local check that the bank still must make $100 available on the first business day and must make an additional $400 available on the second business day (for a total of $500), but allows the bank to defer the availability of any remaining amount until the third business day. Regulation CC, §229.12(b) & (d).
- *Cash withdrawals from nonlocal checks.*   The fourth rule provides for the longest deferral of availability. Like the third rule, the fourth rule starts from the noncash rule, but allows the bank to defer availability of sums in excess of $500 for an extra day. Thus, the bank still must make $100 available on the first business day and an additional $400 available on the fifth business day (for a total of $500), but the bank can defer the availability of any remaining amount until the sixth business day. Regulation CC, §§229.10(c)(1)(vii), 229.12(c)(1), (d).

It is important to examine one other introductory matter, Regulation CC's scheme for counting days. The Regulation CC deadlines employ distinct concepts of banking days and business days, with all of the deadlines running from the "banking day" on which an item is deposited, rather than the "business day" on which it is deposited. Under the regulation, banking days are a subset of business days, specifically those business days on which the bank is open "for carrying on substantially all of its banking functions." Regulation CC, §229.2(f). Business days, by contrast, are all calendar days other than Saturdays, Sundays, and federal holidays. Regulation CC, §229.2(g). The relevant point is that business days on which a bank is not open (perhaps as the day after Thanksgiving) are not banking days that start the running of the availability deadlines.

To complicate that basic framework, Regulation CC includes a set of special rules for a group of particularly low-risk items (see Figure 22.2). Instead of the $100 next-day availability discussed above, those rules generally require the bank to make the entire amount of funds from such items available on the first business day after the banking day on which the funds are deposited. Regulation CC, §229.10(c)(1). That group of special low-risk items includes seven different things. Two are items I already mentioned, which the bank should be able to evaluate overnight: cash deposits and deposits of checks drawn on a local branch of the bank where they are deposited. Regulation CC, §229.10(a)(1), (c)(1)(vi). The other five are instruments for which it is extremely unlikely that the party on which the instrument is drawn will refuse to pay the named payee: U.S. Treasury checks, U.S. Postal Service money orders, checks drawn on a Federal Reserve bank or Federal Home Loan bank, checks drawn on a local governmental entity, and cashier's checks or similar items drawn on banks. Because the likelihood of dishonor is so small for those instruments, a bank must make funds available on the next business day to a customer that is the original payee of one of those items if the customer personally deposits the item (that is, to a teller, rather than to an automatic teller machine or ATM). Regulation CC, §229.10(c) (1)(i)-(v).

The treatment of low-risk items that are not deposited with a teller in the payee's own account is more complicated. One set of rules defers availability for all low-risk items other than cash and checks drawn on the depositary bank if the item is deposited by somebody other than the original payee; the rationale for that set of rules is the higher risk of fraud when somebody other than the original payee claims to own the item. Under those rules, a Treasury check or Postal Service money order deposited by somebody other than the original payee is treated as if it were a typical local check. Regulation CC, §229.12(b)(2)-(3). If one of the remaining three low-risk items (Federal Reserve checks, local government checks, and cashier's checks) is deposited by somebody other than the original payee, the check is processed under the standard rules, with the availability of funds depending on whether the check is a local or a nonlocal check. Regulation CC, §229.12(b)(4), (c)(1)(ii).

Figure 22.2
Low-Risk Items Availability Rules

TYPE OF DEPOSIT	DATE OF AVAILABILITY	CITATIONS
In-Person, Own Account		
All low-risk items	1st business day	§229.10(c)(1)
ATM Deposits, Own Account		
On-us items, Treasury checks	1st business day	§229.10(c)(1)(i), (c)(1)(vi)
Cash, postal money orders, and Federal Reserve, local government, and cashier's checks	2d business day	§229.10(c)(2)
3d-Party Account		
On-us items	1st business day	§229.10(c)(1)(vi)
Treasury checks, postal money orders	Local check rules	§229.12(b)(2), (b)(3)
Federal Reserve, local government, and cashier's checks	Local or nonlocal check rules, depending on location of drawee	§229.12(b)(4), (c)(1)(ii)

Another set of rules defers availability of funds from low-risk items (other than Treasury checks or checks drawn on the depositary bank) when the items are deposited into ATMs. If cash is deposited at an ATM or if any of the remaining four low-risk items (Postal Service money orders, Federal Reserve checks, local government checks, and cashier's checks) are deposited at an ATM into an account owned by the payee of the check, the availability is deferred a single day, to the second business day. Regulation CC, §229.10(a)(2), (c)(2). Thus, for those items, the customer is entitled to nothing (not even $100) until the second business day.

Although the Regulation CC deadlines might seem unreasonably long to a customer waiting to use money that it gave to its bank several days earlier, they are short enough to put banks at some risk of loss, largely because of the possibility that the deadline will arrive — requiring the depositary bank to permit disbursement of the funds — before the depositary bank discovers whether a payor bank will honor a check. For example, a depositary bank must release funds represented by local checks on the second business day after deposit, even though banks frequently will not know by that time whether the check will be honored; 1996 Federal Reserve statistics indicate that only 48 percent of dishonored local checks are returned to the depositary bank before the applicable EFAA availability deadline. And that problem is not insignificant. The same survey suggests that about one-half of all industry losses from check fraud (amounting to about $300 million in 1995) are borne by depositary banks that release funds against checks that subsequently are dishonored.

To get a sense for the susceptibility of the system, consider a common scheme that takes advantage of the interplay between the funds availability rules and the mechanics of deposits at remote locations (usually ATMs). If a thief learns the hours at which a bank collects deposits from a remote location (often less frequently than once a day), the thief can go to the ATM and use an ATM card to feign a deposit transaction. The thief punches in the numbers for a deposit transaction and even deposits an envelope into the machine: The envelope, however, is empty. Because of the infrequency with which the deposit envelopes are collected, the funds from the deposit often become available before the envelope is collected and examined. For example, if the envelope is deposited at one o'clock Monday afternoon at a machine from which envelopes are collected at noon each day, some of the funds from the deposit often would become available for withdrawal on Tuesday morning. The knowledgeable thief could withdraw the (falsely deposited) funds the next morning and leave before the bank even retrieved the empty envelope from the machine!

Three general considerations, however, provide at least a partial justification for prompt funds-availability requirements notwithstanding the risk of loss that they impose. First, Regulation CC does not unconditionally obligate the bank to release funds immediately. It has a number of detailed exceptions describing circumstances in which a depositary bank can limit access even beyond the deadlines described above. For example, the bank can limit severely the availability of funds in a new account (which the regulation defines as any account less than 30 days old, see Regulation CC, §229.13(a)(2)). Among other things, new accounts are completely immune from the two-day and five-day rules related to standard checks. See Regulation CC,

§229.13(a)(1)(iii). Similarly, the two-day and five-day schedules do not apply to deposits made by checks that exceed $5,000 on any single banking day, even if the deposits include government-issued checks or other low-risk items. See Regulation CC, §229.13(b). The bank also can defer availability of funds if the funds are deposited in accounts that have had repeated overdrafts in the last six months, Regulation CC, §229.13(d) or, even more generally, if the bank "has reasonable cause to believe that the check is uncollectible," id. §229.13(e).

The second consideration is convenience. Many customers have important needs for their funds immediately at the time of deposit. It is plausible to argue that those needs, coupled with the fact that well over 99 percent of checks deposited in banks clear without incident, justify allowing prompt access to funds deposited by check, even if the check has not yet cleared. A rule making that money available might result in occasional losses that otherwise could be prevented, but it is arguable that the benefit to customers of that access exceeds the cost to the system of modest losses.

The third consideration is the most important: the likely long-term effects of giving banks the risk of loss that they face if the deadlines force them to release funds without determining whether a check will clear. By putting that risk on banks, the system gives banks the incentive to speed up the system to limit the frequency with which the deadlines arrive before information about the validity of the check. Thus, as new technology and systems develop to accelerate the check-clearance system, the risk of loss that the deadlines impose on the banks should decrease. As discussed above, banks in the pre-EFAA era tended to defer availability for long periods of time, often exceeding a week. As Assignment 23 discusses, the industry has developed systems for clearing checks that can provide certainty about clearing long before expiration of the Regulation CC deadlines. A 1996 Federal Reserve survey indicates that the average time for check processing has been reduced from 6.8 calendar days before Regulation CC was promulgated to only 5.5 calendar days in 1995. It is possible that competitive forces would have produced the same result without regulation, but it is hard to be sure of that.

One interesting twist about funds availability policies is evidenced by the extent to which banks have gone beyond their Regulation CC obligations. However much the deadlines might have spurred banks into action to develop faster procedures for clearing checks, the result is a process in which the regulatory deadlines have become irrelevant in many contexts. Presently, most banks offer availability much sooner than Regulation CC requires. One recent Federal Reserve study indicates that more than 40 percent of all banks offer same-day availability for local checks and that 56 percent offer second-day availability even for nonlocal checks; only about a quarter of all banks hold funds as long as the law permits. That same study concluded that even if the EFAA were amended to give banks an extra day before they had to make funds available, only about 40 percent of all banks would take advantage of that extension.

Moreover, it is not unusual for banks to make funds available even in advance of the waiting periods established under their normal policies. Here, as much as anyplace else in commercial law, the actors frequently are motivated not by legal commands, but by the desire to protect their reputations and augment the relationships that are crucial to their success. In this context, that desire causes banks to extend themselves in situations where the law does not require them to do so, by giving customers access to funds that have not yet been collected. That access, in turn, leaves banks exposed to schemes by which a customer can withdraw funds that it has deposited by check, even if the customer knows that the account on which the check was written does not have sufficient funds to cover the deposited check. To get a sense for how such a "check-kiting" scheme could succeed, consider the following case.

First National Bank v. Colonial Bank
898 F. Supp. 1220 (N.D. Ill. 1995)

GRADY, District Judge....
Check kiting is a form of bank fraud. The kiter opens accounts at two (or more) banks, writes checks on insufficient funds on one account, then covers the overdraft by depositing a check drawn on insufficient funds from the other account.

To illustrate the operation, suppose that the defrauder opens two accounts with a deposit of $500 each at the First National Bank and a distant Second National Bank. (A really successful defrauder will have numerous accounts in fictitious names at banks in widely separated states.) The defrauder then issues for goods or cash checks totaling $3000 against the First National Bank. But before they clear and overdraw the account, he covers the overdrafts with a check for $4,000 drawn on the Second National Bank. The Second National account will be overdrawn when the $4,000 check is presented; before that happens, however, the defrauder covers it with a check on the First National Bank. The process is repeated innumerable times until there is a constant float of worthless checks between the accounts and the defrauder has bilked the banks of a substantial sum of money. By timing the scheme correctly and repeating it over a period of time, the kiter can use the funds essentially as an interest-free loan....

A kite crashes when one of the banks dishonors checks drawn on it and returns them to the other banks involved in the kite. Usually, such a dishonor occurs when one bank suspects a kite. However, an individual bank may have trouble detecting a check kiting scheme. "Until one has devoted a substantial amount of time examining not only one's own account, but accounts at other banks, it may be impossible to know whether the customer is engaged in a legitimate movement of funds or illegitimate kiting." James J. White & Robert S. Summers, Uniform Commercial Code §17-1 (3d ed. 1988 & Supp. 1994). But each bank is usually able to monitor only its own account, and "[t]here is no certain test that distinguishes one who writes many checks on low balances from a check kiter." White & Summers, supra, §17-2. Even if a bank suspects a kite, it might decide not to take any action for a number of reasons. First, it may be liable to its customer for wrongfully dishonoring checks. [UCC §4-402.] Second, if it reports that a kite is operating and turns out to be wrong, it could find itself defending a defamation suit. Finally, if it errs in returning checks or reporting a kite, it may risk angering a large customer.

This case involves the fallout of a collapsed check kite. Two of the banks involved, First National Bank in Harvey ("First National") and Colonial Bank ("Colonial") are the parties to this litigation. The Federal Reserve Bank of Chicago (the "Reserve Bank"), through whose clearinghouse the relevant checks were processed, is also a party.

Shelly International Marketing ("Shelly") opened a checking account at First National in December 1989. . . . On December 31, 1991, the principals of Shelly opened a checking account at Colonial Bank in the name of World Commodities, Inc. Shelly and World Commodities were related companies, with the same or similar shareholders, officers, and directors. The principals of Shelly and World Commodities began operating a check kiting scheme among the accounts at the . . . banks in early 1992.

The main events at issue in this case took place in February 1992. The checks that form the basis of this suit are thirteen checks totaling $1,523,892.49 for which First National was the depositary bank and Colonial was the payor bank (the "Colonial checks"). Also relevant are seventeen checks totaling $1,518,642.86 for which Colonial was the depositary bank and First National was the payor bank (the "First National checks").

On Monday, February 10, Shelly deposited the thirteen Colonial checks to its First National account. First National then sent those checks through the check clearing system. That same day, World Commodities deposited the seventeen First National checks to its Colonial account.

The next day, Tuesday, February 11, the Colonial checks were presented to Colonial for payment, and the First National checks were presented to First National for payment. That day, David Spiewak, an officer with First National's holding company, Pinnacle, reviewed the bank's records to determine why there were large balance fluctuations in Shelly's First National account. Spiewak began to suspect that a kite might be operating. He did not know whether Colonial had enough funds to cover the Colonial checks that had been deposited on Monday, February 10, and forwarded to Colonial for payment. Later that day, First National froze the Shelly account to prevent any further activity in it.

On the morning of Wednesday, February 12, Spiewak met with First National president Dennis Irvin and Pinnacle's chief lending officer Mike Braun to discuss the Shelly account. Spiewak informed the others of what he knew, and the three agreed that there was a possible kite. They concluded that further investigation was needed. The First National officers decided to return the First National checks to Colonial. . . .

On Wednesday, First National returned the First National checks to Colonial. . . .

Colonial [learned of First National's decision to return the checks] at approximately 2:45 P.M. on Wednesday. . . . Randall Soderman, a Colonial loan officer, was informed of the large return, and immediately began an investigation. He realized that if the Colonial checks were not returned by midnight that same day, Colonial would be out the money. Returning the Colonial checks before midnight would protect Colonial from liability, but it would risk disappointing the customer. Anthony Schiller, the loan officer in charge of the World Commodities account, called World Commodities comptroller Charles Patterson and its attorney Jay Goldstein. Both assured Schiller that the First National checks were good and should be redeposited. Ultimately, Richard Vucich, Colonial's president, and Joanne Topham, Colonial's cashier, decided not to return the Colonial checks on Wednesday. They decided instead to meet on Thursday morning with Schiller to discuss the matter.

Schiller, Topham, and Vucich met on the morning of Thursday, February 13. At the conclusion of the meeting, they decided to return the thirteen Colonial checks to First National. At about 10:45 A.M., Colonial telephoned First National to say that it intended to return the Colonial checks. Colonial sent the Colonial checks back through the Reserve Bank. . . . . First National received the returned Colonial checks on Friday, February 14.

[First National eventually filed suit against Colonial, contending that Colonial was obligated to honor the checks drawn on the account at Colonial because of Colonial's failure to return the checks on Wednesday night. When the dust settled, Colonial was held liable for the full amount First National lost when Shelly absconded, plus interest, for a total of about $1,400,000.]

First National Bank is not unusual in involving a bank that lost not because of any legal rule that required it to release money, but because of its desire to accommodate its customer to an extent far beyond its legal obligations. For a more colorful example, consider United States v. Broumas, 69 F.3d 1178 (D.C. Cir. 1995), affirming the conviction for embezzlement of a director of a (now failed) Washington, D.C., bank. The embezzlement arose from the director's use of a "red star privilege" that granted him immediate access to all funds that he deposited by check at the bank. The fact is, bankers like to make their customers happy, and one easy way to make them happy is to let them withdraw money before the bank is obligated to make the funds available. To be sure, banks have made significant progress in the last few years in reducing losses from check kiting. They now use sophisticated software designed to detect patterns in deposits and withdrawals that are associated with check-kiting schemes. That software has made it significantly easier for banks to discover and prevent check-kiting schemes. But no matter how many times financial institutions lose from accommodating their customers, the importance of relationships and reputation suggests that those kinds of accommodations will continue to be a significant feature of the banking system. And as long as they are, banks will incur losses like those described in the *First National Bank* case.

B.   Wrongful Dishonor: What Happens If the Bank Refuses to Pay?

The reliability of the checking system is a function of the likelihood that banks will honor checks in accordance with their agreements with their customer. Unfortunately, banks, like all other actors in the economy, sometimes fail to perform as promised. When a bank violates its agreement with its customer by failing to pay a check that it was obligated to pay, it commits "wrongful dishonor." Recognizing the seriousness of that offense to the system, the UCC imposes a relatively onerous penalty. Specifically, the customer is entitled to all of the "damages proximately caused by the wrongful dishonor." UCC §4-402(b). That provision may not strike the first-time reader as notably generous to the customer. As it happens, though, UCC §4-402(b)'s remedy is considerably more generous than the remedy available in many contexts in the checking system, which frequently caps damages against a bank at the amount of the check. See UCC §4-103(e) (damages for failure to exercise ordinary care); Regulation CC, §229.38(a) (damages for failure to return dishonored checks within Regulation CC deadlines).

The generosity of the statute's damage formulation is particularly important because wrongful dishonor presents a context in which that formulation matters: The damages caused by wrongful dishonor often exceed the amount of the dishonored check. For example, when a bank dishonors a business's check, the bank's mistake might significantly harm the business's reputation with its suppliers: The suppliers might be reluctant to continue to ship goods to a customer on favorable credit terms if they believe that the customer is bouncing checks. Similarly, in the individual context, an individual who bounces a check might be subject to arrest or prosecution. Article 4 expressly states that the customer can recover consequential damages for those types of losses. It rejects prior judicial holdings that limited the damages available for wrongful dishonor. UCC §4-402(b); see UCC §4-402 comment 3. The case that follows is typical.

Maryott v. First National Bank

624 N.W.2d 96 (S.D. 2001)

GILBERTSON, Justice.

Ned Maryott (Maryott) sued First National Bank of Eden (Bank), its president and its branch manager under [UCC §]4-402 for the wrongful dishonor of three checks. A jury awarded Maryott $600,000 in damages for lost income, lost value of his business and emotional distress. On appeal, we affirm in part and reverse in part.

FACTS AND PROCEDURE

Maryott has owned and operated a cattle-dealing business known as Maryott Livestock Sales near Britton, South Dakota, since 1973. In the cattle industry, Maryott had a reputation for honesty and integrity. Because of his respected reputation, he was considered one of the best dealers in the business. Maryott earned a commission of $.50 per hundred weight on the cattle he sold. In an average year, he would sell approximately 50,000 head of cattle, generating revenues of $175,000.

Maryott began doing business with Bank in 1977. Over the years, Maryott had borrowed substantial amounts of money from Bank. During that time, Maryott had never written a bad check, had never incurred an overdraft, and had never been late on a loan payment. On December 29, 1993, Maryott and his wife signed a promissory note in favor of Bank for $176,171.60. That note served as a line of operating credit and was secured by mortgages on Maryott's real estate and security interests on most of his personal property and inventory. Bank valued the property mortgaged by Maryott at $663,861. The note was due on December 29, 1999. On March 13, 1996, the Bank loaned Maryott an additional $100,000, due on November 1, 1996. That note was secured by a security agreement and real estate mortgage.

One of Maryott's major customers was the Oconto Cattle Company (Oconto), located in Custer County, Nebraska. Oconto was owned by Warren Bierman, who Maryott had been doing business with for more than twenty years. In the normal course of business, Oconto paid Maryott within six to seven days after shipping the cattle. Between July 16 and August 29, 1996, Maryott shipped 887 head of cattle to Oconto. The value of those cattle was approximately $480,000. After repeated attempts to collect payment from Bierman were unsuccessful, Maryott ceased shipping cattle to Oconto. Maryott did receive two sight drafts from Oconto, drawn on its line of credit. However, these drafts were returned because Oconto's lender had revoked the line of credit. Despite repeated assurances from Bierman that he "was good for it," Maryott never received payment on the 887 head of cattle shipped to Oconto.

Bank first became aware of the Oconto situation when the two drafts were returned in mid-September. This situation caused concern to Tim Hofer, Bank's manager, and Peter Mehlhaff, its president. After visiting with Maryott regarding the situation on September 30, 1996, Mehlhaff and Hofer noticed that three large checks had been processed through Maryott's checking account. These checks were payable to Tri-County Livestock Auction for $30,544.38; to Tri-County Livestock (collectively "Tri-County") for $72,070.24; and to Schaffer Cattle Company (Schaffer) for $132,990. Each of these checks had been presented to Bank and paid in full on September 25, 1996. Maryott's checking account had been debited accordingly. In light of their concerns over the Oconto situation and after examining the physical checks, Hofer and Mehlhaff concluded Maryott was involved in or the victim of "suspicious activity." That afternoon, Bank decided to dishonor the three "suspicious" checks, even though Bank was aware such a dishonor was a potential violation of the "midnight deadline" rule found in [UCC §]4-302(1). Although Maryott had met with Hofer earlier in the day, he was not informed that Bank intended to dishonor his checks.

The next morning, October 1, 1996, Mehlhaff gave notice of dishonor for the three checks by filing a claim for late return with the Federal Reserve. Once the items were dishonored by the Federal Reserve, the funds were returned to Maryott's checking account. Bank immediately froze the assets in Maryott's checking account, meaning any additional checks drawn on his account would not be honored. That same day, Hofer received a call from Don Kampmeier, president of Central Livestock Company (Central). Kampmeier informed Hofer that Central was holding a check for $68,528 from Maryott. Hofer informed Kampmeier that the check would not be honored, despite the fact that Maryott's checking account contained nearly $300,000 at the time [including the amounts recredited for the dishonored items discussed above]. Later that same day, Bank deemed itself insecure and used the proceeds of the dishonored checks to pay down the balance of Maryott's loans, leaving $1 owing on each to maintain its superior priority date in the collateral.

Pursuant to the Packers and Stockyards Act, licensed livestock dealers must be bonded. Maryott was bonded in the amount of $70,000. After being informed that Bank would not honor the check it held from Maryott, Central made a claim against Maryott's bond on October 7, 1996. It submitted a claim for $247,030, which included the $68,538 check as well as Maryott's other outstanding debt owed to Central. On October 31, 1996, Schaffer, an intended payee on one of the dishonored checks, also submitted a claim against Maryott's bond. Because the claims exceeded the amount of the bond, Maryott was required to forfeit his dealer's license. Without a license, Maryott could not independently deal livestock, which effectively shut down his business.

... Maryott commenced this action against Bank on December 5, 1996, alleging ... wrongful dishonor. . . . A jury trial was commenced on March 27, 2000 on only the wrongful dishonor claim. On March 31, 2000, the jury returned a verdict in favor of Maryott in the amount of $250,000 for lost income, $200,000 for lost value of Maryott's business and $150,000 for emotional distress. With prejudgment interest, the total judgment came to $713,750. . . . Bank appeals the jury verdict. . . .

ANALYSIS AND DECISION

1. WHETHER THE WRONGFUL DISHONOR OF THE CHECKS PROXIMATELY CAUSED MARYOTT'S DAMAGES. . . .

[UCC §]4-402(b) provides that "[a] payor bank is liable to its customer for damages proximately caused by the wrongful dishonor of an item." Bank has not appealed the jury's determination that it wrongfully dishonored the three checks. Whether the wrongful dishonor proximately caused Maryott's damages is a question of fact for the jury to decide in all but the rarest of cases. Only when legal minds cannot differ as to the failure of proximate cause is judgment as a matter of law in favor of Bank appropriate. Bank claims this is one of those rarest cases. After reviewing the evidence in a light most favorable to the verdict, we cannot agree.

Bank's argument is based upon its claim that there is no connection between the three dishonored checks and the damage caused to Maryott, namely the loss of his dealer's license and the closing of his business after Central made a claim against his bond. Bank argues that Maryott had given Central the $68,543 check, knowing that he did not have sufficient funds in his account to cover the check. Therefore, according to Bank, the check would have bounced regardless of whether Bank had dishonored the checks and frozen his account. Hence, according to Bank, the wrongful dishonor did not proximately cause Maryott any damage.

Maryott points to testimony that he informed Central on the day he issued the check that he did not have enough funds to cover the check. Central personnel agreed to work with Maryott and hold the check until Maryott had sufficient funds. When Maryott discovered Bank had dishonored his checks and frozen his checking account, he informed Central of the situation. The president of Central, Kampmeier, then telephoned Hofer, who informed Kampmeier that Bank would not honor the check. Because of the freeze put on Maryott's account, he was essentially out of business at that time, as no future checks would be honored. In the words of Kampmeier, "I had no recourse. I had nothing else I could do, I had to go against his bond at that time." When asked if he would have moved against the bond if the check had been honored, Kampmeier replied, "[m]ore than likely not because he would have — that would have meant he was still in business and can continue in business and he could have probably worked out of his indebtedness to us."

In addition, Schaffer, one of the payees on the dishonored checks, also moved against Maryott's bond on October 31, 1996. At trial, the owner of Schaffer testified he would not have filed a claim against Maryott's bond if Bank had honored that check. Bank argues that Schaffer's claim on the bond is irrelevant, as the bond would have been lost because of the actions of Central. We have never endorsed such a restrictive view of proximate cause. Instead, we have stated that if the defendant's conduct was a substantial factor in causing the plaintiff's injury, it follows that he will not be absolved from liability merely because other causes have contributed to the result, since such causes, innumerable, are always present. The wrongful dishonor by Bank was clearly a substantial factor causing the actions taken by Schaffer. . . . Bank's actions clearly caused Schaffer to file a claim on the bond. In addition, Kampmeier testified that but for Bank's actions, Central would not have moved against Maryott's bond. After reviewing the evidence in a light most favorable to the verdict, there is sufficient evidence to support the jury's verdict. Bank has failed to carry its burden of showing that no reasonable minds could differ as to the existence of proximate cause.

2. WHETHER MARYOTT WAS ENTITLED TO EMOTIONAL DAMAGES.

Bank argues that the evidence fails to establish the necessary elements for recovery of damages for emotional distress. Bank notes that damages for emotional distress are recoverable in South Dakota only when the elements of either intentional or negligent infliction of emotional distress are proven. According to Bank, Maryott has failed to establish the elements of either cause of action. Maryott argues that his emotional damages are recoverable under [UCC §]4-402, which provides that a bank is liable for "actual damages proved and may include . . . other consequential damages." Maryott argues that damages for emotional distress are part of his consequential damages, and he is therefore not required to establish the elements of intentional or negligent infliction of emotional distress. In the alternative, Maryott claims he has nevertheless met those requirements.

Our initial inquiry must be whether [UCC §]4-402 has created a new breed of emotional damages or whether those damages are commensurate with theories of recovery already recognized under South Dakota law. This inquiry requires statutory interpretation, which is reviewed de novo as a question of law. The text of [UCC §]4-402 provides no assistance on this issue. Nor does the official comment to the U.C.C. offer guidance as to the requirements to establish emotional damages.

In support of his claim, Maryott directs us to Twin City Bank v. Isaacs, 283 Ark. 127, 672 S.W.2d 651 (1984). That case involved a wrongful dishonor under U.C.C. §4-402. The plaintiffs sued their bank and the jury awarded them damages for mental anguish. On appeal, the Supreme Court of Arkansas stated, "[i]n general, the type of mental anguish suffered under §4-402 does not need to rise to the higher standard of injury for intentional infliction of emotional distress." Id. at 654.

However, a number of courts have not interpreted §4-402 so broadly. In Farmers & Merchants State Bank of Krum v. Ferguson, 617 S.W.2d 918 (Tex. 1981), a bank froze its customer's checking account, without informing the customer, causing several checks to be wrongfully dishonored. The court stated that, in accordance with Texas law, "[d]amages for mental anguish [under §4-402] cannot be recovered absent a showing of an intentional tort, gross negligence, willful and wanton disregard, or accompanying physical injury." Id. at 921. Likewise, the court in First Nat'l Bank of New Castle v. Acra, 462 N.E.2d 1345 (Ind. Ct. App. 1984) examined a claim of emotional damages for wrongful dishonor in light of its state law requirements for intentional or negligent infliction of emotional distress. The *Acra* court noted that Indiana allowed recovery of damages for emotional distress only when intentionally inflicted or accompanied by a physical injury. Id. at 1350. In addition, the California courts require a plaintiff to prove either physical impact and resulting injury or intentional wrongdoing by the defendant before damages for emotional distress can be recovered under §4-402. Lee v. Bank of America, 218 Cal. App. 3d 914, 267 Cal. Rptr. 387, 390 (1990). Furthermore, the New Jersey Supreme Court applies a more stringent test, requiring proof of intentional infliction of emotional distress before emotional damages are recoverable under §4-402. Buckley v. Trenton Sav. Fund Soc., 111 N.J. 355, 544 A.2d 857, 864 (N.J. 1988).

Like those jurisdictions just discussed, South Dakota allows recovery of emotional damages only when intentionally inflicted or accompanied by actual physical injury. The U.C.C. provides that our common-law is effective in commercial transactions unless specifically displaced by a particular Code section. [UCC §]1-103. Because §4-402 does not define the consequential damages that may be recovered and does not clearly indicate an independent right of recovery of emotional damages, we must interpret that section in light of our precedent which requires a plaintiff to prove either intentional or negligent infliction of emotional distress to recover emotional damages. In Wright v. Coca Cola Bottling Co., 414 N.W.2d 608, 610 (S.D. 1987), we noted that:

> three principal concerns continue to foster judicial caution and doctrinal limitations on recovery for emotional distress: (1) the problem of permitting legal redress for harm that is often temporary and relatively trivial; (2) the danger that claims of mental harm will be falsified or imagined; and (3) the perceived unfairness of imposing heavy and disproportionate financial burdens upon a defendant, whose conduct was only negligent.

These concerns are equally applicable today. The best way to balance these concerns while still providing adequate relief for injured plaintiffs is to require plaintiffs to meet the standards already established in this state for the recovery of emotional damages. The simple statement that consequential damages are recoverable under §4-402 will not convince us otherwise. Therefore, while emotional damages may be recoverable under §4-402, they are not recoverable unless the plaintiff can establish the requirements of either intentional or negligent infliction of emotional distress.

We must now determine if the evidence introduced by Maryott is legally sufficient to satisfy the requirements of either of those causes of action. When reviewing the sufficiency of the evidence, we accept all evidence favorable to the verdict, and reasonable inferences therefrom, without weighing credibility or resolving conflicts. We will affirm the verdict if there is evidence, which if believed by the fact finder, could support the jury's verdict. Id.

To recover for intentional infliction of emotional distress, Maryott must show:

1) an act by defendant amounting to extreme and outrageous conduct;
2) intent on the part of the defendant to cause plaintiff severe emotional distress;
3) the defendant's conduct was the cause in-fact of plaintiff's distress;
4) the plaintiff suffered an extreme disabling emotional response to defendant's conduct.

For conduct to be deemed "outrageous," it must be so extreme in degree as to go beyond all possible bounds of decency, and to be regarded as atrocious, and utterly intolerable in a civilized community. 583 N.W.2d at 404. While Bank's actions were illegal and irresponsible, they do not rise to the level of outrageous conduct. Nor was any evidence introduced that Bank acted with the requisite intent. Indeed, Maryott did not even argue in his brief that he met the requirements of intentional infliction of emotional distress. . . .

We have repeatedly held that negligent infliction of emotional distress requires manifestation of physical symptoms. Maryott argues that his clinical depression and the symptoms thereof that resulted from Bank's wrongful dishonor are sufficient to establish "manifestation of physical symptoms." The physical symptoms of his depression included shame, interruption of sleep, and humiliation. . . .

. . . Maryott's claim that clinical depression satisfies the requirement of physical symptoms is inconsistent with our established law. Nor can shame and humiliation be classified as physical symptoms. Finally, interruption of sleep on its own cannot be considered a physical symptom that would allow for recovery of emotional damages. Because Maryott has failed to establish the elements of either intentional or negligent infliction of emotional distress, his claim for emotional damages under §4-402 must fail as a matter of law. . . .

CONCLUSION

We affirm the trial court's denial of Bank's motion for judgment notwithstanding the verdict on the issue of proximate cause. The jury's award of emotional damages is reversed as a matter of law. . . .

MILLER, Chief Justice, and AMUNDSON and KONENKAMP, Justices, concur.

SABERS, Justice (concurring in part and dissenting in part).
The citizens of South Dakota, represented by this Marshall County jury, found that the bank's wrongful dishonor was the cause of Maryott's mental anguish. The majority opinion jumps in the jury box and reverses the jury's award of $150,000 for Maryott's emotional damage which was clearly precipitated by the bank's wrongful conduct. In so holding, the majority opinion sidesteps the legislative pronouncement that when a bank chooses to wrongfully dishonor a properly payable item it is liable for any "actual damages." As the jury's determination is supported by law and fact, it should stand and not be overturned on a whim. . . .

The instructions to this jury properly stated that the Bank was liable for the foreseeable consequences proximately caused by its conduct. The jury was instructed that emotional distress "means mental suffering, mental distress or mental anguish. It includes all highly unpleasant mental reactions, such as fright, nervousness, horror, grief, shame, anxiety, humiliation, embarrassment, mortification, anger, worry and stress, as well as physical pain." Additionally, "the measure of damages is the amount which will compensate the party aggrieved for all detriment proximately caused thereby." The jury properly found that Maryott suffered emotional damages as a result of the Bank's wrongful conduct.

First National Bank of Eden and the majority opinion urge the view that emotional damages are never available unless the torts of negligent infliction of emotional distress or intentional infliction of emotional distress are independently asserted. Though this view is not without support in other forums, I concur with the commentators and courts that maintain that recovery for "actual damages proved" encompasses the mental suffering caused by a wrongful dishonor. The majority opinion's requirement for an independent tort theory of emotional distress to safeguard against baseless claims is an outdated approach supported only by jury distrust. I submit the juries of this state are capable of discerning when actual damages include mental anguish, as they did here.

. . . In addressing this issue, we are faced with the economic reality that embarrassment and humiliation suffered from the bank's wrongful acts are very real, though sometimes intangible harms. The damage to Maryott's reputation and the ensuing effect on his credit, a lifeline in his type of business, created very real and incredible damage. The jury recognized it based on proper instructions and so should we.

Leading commentators on the UCC have addressed the issue. "Might one argue that 'actual damages' excludes recovery for mental distress? We think not." White & Summers, Handbook of the Law Under the Uniform Commercial Code §17-4 p. 675 (2d Ed. 1980). Explaining further, White & Summers note: "It is inconsistent to allow recovery for embarrassment and mental distress deriving from arrest and prosecution and to deny similar recovery in other cases. Moreover, cases under the predecessor to 4-402, the American Banking Association Statute, held that 'actual damages' includes damages for mental distress." Id.

This rationale, coupled with the evidence adduced by Maryott and the jury's findings on proper instructions, demonstrate that the award was proper. Inability on the part of some members of this appellate court to appreciate or recognize these damages is no reason to vacate them. Therefore, I respectfully dissent.

Problem Set 22

22.1. One day a friend named Caleb Garth calls you with a question about his checking account. Upon examining one of his checks that the payor bank recently honored, Caleb noticed that the check was dated last summer (about seven months ago). Caleb thinks it ridiculous that the bank honored a check so stale. Can you do anything for Caleb? UCC §§4-404 & comment, 1-201(19), (revised §1-201(b)(20)), 3-103(a)(4), 3-103 comment 4, 4-103 comment 4, 4-104(c).

22.2. Your friend Jodi Kay (from Problem 21.6) has been asked to audit the bank's funds-availability policies to ensure that they comply with Regulation CC. She wants to know when that regulation requires the bank to release the funds from the following deposits made into accounts at a Houston branch of

CountryBank. For purposes of this problem, you should assume that each deposit was made on Monday March 1 and that CountryBank is open for substantially all of its operations six days a week (every day except Sundays). Finally, except as noted in question a, all of the withdrawals are to be made by check. (Although you need to understand how the statute justifies your answers, you may wish to refer to Figure 22.1 and Figure 22.2 to help you get started.)

a. Carl Eben wishes to withdraw cash against funds deposited with one of the bank's tellers in the form of a $7,000 check written by Archie Moon on Archie's Seattle bank account. UCC §4-215(e); Regulation CC, §§229.2(f), (g), (r), (s), (v), & (w), 229.10(c)(1)(vii), 229.12(c)(1) & (d), 229.13(b).

b. Carl Eben deposits a $1,000 cashier's check with one of the bank's tellers. The check was drawn on Rocky Mountain Bank in Seattle. The check originally was payable to Riverfront Tools, Inc. (to purchase some machine tools for Archie Moon's print shop), but was properly indorsed from that corporation to Carl. Regulation CC, §§229.10(c)(1)(v) & (vii), 229.12(b)(4) & (c)(1)(ii).

c. Carl Eben deposits a $1,000 check, payable to himself from the United States Treasury, at one of CountryBank's ATMs in Houston. Regulation CC, §§229.10(c)(1)(i) & (c)(2), 229.12(b)(2).

d. Carl Eben deposits a $1,000 check drawn on the State of Michigan with one of the bank's tellers. Regulation CC, §§229.10(c)(1)(iv) & (vii), 229.12(b)(4) & (c)(1)(ii).

22.3.   Recall the facts of Problem 21.2, in which the bank at which Ben Darrow works (FSB) honored a rent check that Jasmine Ball had written for $900 even though Ball had provided the bank a valid postdating notice. The day after those events (Tuesday January 23), another check drawn on Ball's account was presented, this one dated January 22, in the amount of $400, payable to Generic Motors Acceptance Corporation (GMAC), a finance company affiliated with Generic Motors (GM). Because the account at that time contained only $100 (as a result of the bank's decision to cash the $900 rent check the day before), FSB's system automatically dishonored the check and charged Ball a $25 fee for issuing a check against insufficient funds. Darrow started to worry about bouncing Ball's car payment when he read a notice in the paper this morning (January 29) that GMAC had repossessed Ball's brand-new GM pickup and when he arrived at the bank to find a $2,000 cash deposit to Ball's account. The funds from that deposit would have been available in time to cover the postdated rent check that raised the situation discussed in Problem 21.2. Does FSB have any significant liability? UCC §4-402(b) & comment 3.

22.4.   Darrow also wants to ask you about another problem he recently had with the bank's check-processing system. That software is designed to decide whether to honor a check by checking the balance in the account at the close of the banking day on the date that the check was presented. When Darrow saw a check written by Carol Long one morning included on a list of checks that were to be bounced because of insufficient funds in the account at the close of the previous banking day, he decided to recheck her account. Although he noticed a large cash deposit the previous day that had become available by the time he made the determination, he concluded that the software was working properly because the funds in the account at the close of the previous banking day were insufficient to cover the check. He wants to confirm with you that his current practices are satisfactory. Does he have a problem? UCC §4-402(c) & comment 4; Regulation CC, §229.10(a)(1).

22.5.   Early this week Jodi Kay called again, asking advice about her most recent job assignment. Several of the branches discussed in Problem 21.6 have received checks (often quite large) drawn on nonlocal banks that the payor banks eventually have refused to honor. Those branches have lost a substantial sum of money on those checks in cases in which the customers withdrew the funds and closed their accounts before CountryBank learned that the checks would not be honored. Jodi mentions that a large share of the problems occurred in cases that involved recently opened accounts or accounts on which overdrafts had been frequent past occurrences. Jodi wants to know if there is anything that she can do about that problem. In particular, she wants to extend to six business days the hold that the bank puts on all nonlocal checks deposited at the problem banks. What do you recommend? Regulation CC, §229.13(a), (b), (d), (e).

Assignment 23:   Collection of Checks

Once the payee has accepted a check from the drawer, the payee is left — like any party that accepts a noncash payment — with the task of converting the payment into cash or some other form of readily available funds. That task raises two separate questions, one legal and one practical. The legal question is whether the payee has a legal right to force the payor bank to pay the check. But whatever the answer to that question, a second, more practical question remains: How does the payee obtain payment?

A.   The Payor Bank's Obligation to the Payee

The checking system's approach to the payee's rights against the payor bank is simple. Although the UCC characterizes the payee (or any bank that acquires the check from the payee) as a "person entitled to enforce" an instrument, UCC §3-301, that designation does not say anything about the payee's rights to collect from the payor bank. On the contrary, in an ordinary check transaction, the payee has no rights whatsoever against the payor bank. First, for the reasons discussed in Assignment 22, even the drawer cannot complain if a payor bank dishonors a check because the account has insufficient funds to cover it. UCC §4-402(a). Perhaps more surprising, the payee cannot force the bank to pay even if the account does have sufficient funds. As explained in UCC §3-408, the check "does not of itself operate as an assignment of funds . . . available for its payment, and the drawee is not liable on the instrument until the drawee accepts it." Thus, although the payor bank might be liable to the drawer for wrongful dishonor, the payee itself ordinarily can do nothing to force the payor bank to pay the check. The following case aptly illustrates the principle in question.

Outdoor Technologies, Inc. v. Allfirst Financial, Inc.

2001 WL 541472 (Del. Super. 2001)

SLIGHTS, J.

I.   INTRODUCTION

My predecessor on the Court has stated that "[t]he facts of this case look like a payment systems hypothetical written by a law school professor." As usual, an apt observation from a wise jurist. Plaintiff, Outdoor Technologies, Inc. ("Outdoor"), presented a check for payment to defendants, Allfirst Financial Center, N.A. f/k/a

First Omni Bank, N.A. ("Omni"), Allfirst Financial, Inc. f/k/a Maryland Bankcorp ("Bancorp") and Allfirst Bank f/k/a First National Bank of Maryland ("FNB"). The defendant banks refused to cash the check. Because the drawer of the check, Hechinger, Inc., filed for bankruptcy protection before the check could be paid, leaving Outdoor without a remedy against Hechinger, Outdoor has determined to pursue its remedies against the banks in this Court.

At first glance, this controversy would appear to be subsumed within Delaware's Uniform Commercial Code ("UCC"). Article 3 of the UCC governs negotiable instruments; Article 4 governs bank deposits and collections. The parties agree, however, that statutory remedies under the UCC are not available to Outdoor in this case. Article 3 does not provide a basis for relief when the drawee bank has not accepted the negotiable instrument. [UCC §3-408.] And Article 4 limits the bank's statutory liability to its customer. [UCC §4-402.] In this case, the banks' customer was Hechinger as the drawer of the check, not Outdoor. Accordingly, left without a UCC remedy, Outdoor has raised common law claims against the banks for breach of a contract to which it was a third party beneficiary, fraud, negligent misrepresentation and civil conspiracy.

This Court has already dismissed Outdoor's breach of contract claim upon concluding that the claim is precluded by the UCC. Discovery has run its course and defendants have now moved for summary judgment on all remaining claims against them. For the reasons that follow, defendants' motion is GRANTED.

II.   FACTS

Outdoor is a Delaware corporation with its princip[al] place of business in Macon, Mississippi. Outdoor manufactures and distributes garden accessories and related goods such as vinyl fencing, decking and rail material. Outdoor enjoyed an ongoing business relationship with Hechinger, a retail supplier of garden, outdoor and hardware products. On June 2, 1999, Hechinger issued a check for $706,735.62 made payable to Outdoor as delayed payment for goods previously supplied by Outdoor. That check was drawn on Hechinger's account at Omni, although it mistakenly indicated on its face that it was drawn on a Hechinger account at FNB.[10] When Outdoor received Hechinger's check it was aware that Hechinger was on the verge of filing for bankruptcy protection. Outdoor's desire to expedite payment of the check, in advance of Hechinger's bankruptcy filing, animated the events which give rise to this litigation.

The Hechinger check was received by Outdoor at its Macon, Mississippi offices on June 4, 1999. Rather than deposit the check in the Outdoor corporate account, and face the delays of the Federal Reserve's inter-bank payment system, the corporate decision-makers at Outdoor determined that Outdoor's controller, John Hurt ("Hurt"), would travel personally to an FNB branch in Baltimore, Maryland to negotiate the check. Hurt's purpose was to secure immediate payment of the check through a wire transfer or receipt of certified funds.

On the morning of June 7, Hurt arrived at the Baltimore FNB branch to present the check for payment. The branch manager informed Hurt that the check was

---

10. Hechinger maintained accounts at each of the three defendant banks [which were at the time affiliated with each other]. Hechinger also printed its own checks. Apparently, Hechinger mistakenly identified FNB as the drawee bank on the printed check even though the check...identified the Omni account number.

drawn on an Omni account, not an FNB account as indicated on the check, and that FNB could not negotiate the check. The branch manager also provided Hurt with the name of FNB corporate attorney, William Thomas ("Thomas"), to whom Hurt's questions should be addressed. Hurt returned to his hotel room and placed a telephone call to Omni. During that call, Hurt was informed that Omni was owned by Bancorp.

Armed with this information, Hurt traveled to Bancorp's corporate headquarters in downtown Baltimore seeking guidance on the quickest means to get paid on the Hechinger check. Hurt ultimately was directed to Thomas.[11] Hurt and Thomas met for between five and fifteen minutes in the Bancorp legal department's lobby area. This brief conversation is the genesis of Outdoor's claims of fraud and misrepresentation.

The parties agree that during the course of the Hurt/Thomas conversation Thomas inspected the Hechinger check and confirmed that it was drawn on an Omni account. He then advised Hurt that neither FNB nor Bancorp were obligated to [accept] the check and that neither bank would do so. Thomas also generally discouraged Hurt from attempting to negotiate the check in person and, instead, prodded him to deposit the check in Outdoor's depository account and obtain payment of the check through customary channels. Undaunted, Hurt pressed Thomas to commit Omni to [accept] the check if he traveled to the closest Omni branch (located in Millsboro, Delaware). Thomas responded that if Hechinger maintained sufficient funds in the account, and if Hechinger had not yet filed for bankruptcy protection, Omni would negotiate the check upon presentation by Hurt of "proper authorization."[13] Aside from Hurt's mention that "proper authorization" would be required, Thomas and Hurt did not discuss what Omni would require as evidence of Hurt's "proper authorization" to negotiate the check. In his apparent haste to accomplish his mission, Hurt did not inquire what form of authorization would be required by Omni and Thomas did not volunteer this information.[14]

Hurt then contacted his superior, Ian Douglas, to discuss the next move. Hurt and Douglas decided that Hurt should attempt to negotiate the check at Omni's branch in Millsboro. They also decided that for "proper authorization" Hurt would present a letter from Peter Orebaugh ("Orebaugh"), Outdoor's President, indicating that Hurt was authorized to negotiate the check on behalf of Outdoor. That letter, printed on Outdoor station[e]ry, was faxed to Hurt on the morning of June 8, 1999. It read: "Please accept this letter as authorization for John Hurt, Controller of Outdoor Technologies Inc., to certify the check in the amount of $706,735.62 as payment from Hechingers [sic], Inc. Please release a certified check or wire transfer

---

11. As it turned out, Thomas served as corporate counsel to all three corporate affiliates named as defendants: Bancorp, Omni, and FNB.

13. Thomas' concession was contrary to Hechinger's account agreement with the defendant banks which provided that the banks were not obligated to cash a check made payable to a corporation. The banks' written policies also provided that the banks generally would not certify funds or initiate a wire transfer except at the request of a customer. The proffered reason for these policies is that the bank would bear the risk of loss if it provided immediate funds to the presenter of a check who, for whatever reason, was not authorized to negotiate the check. [UCC] §3-417.

14. The record reveals that Hurt was aware that banks generally required a board of directors' resolution as evidence of an individual's authorization to conduct banking business on behalf of the corporation. The record also reveals, however, that Hurt had never himself attempted to "cash" a check made payable to Outdoor and that he was aware that others had done so by simply presenting personal identification.

the amount according to the instructions John Hurt will provide." The letter is signed: "Peter Orebaugh, President."

Hurt entered the Omni branch in Millsboro at 9:00 A.M. on the morning of June 8 in possession of both the check and the faxed Orebaugh letter. After some delay, an Omni employee at the branch reported to Hurt that she had been speaking with Thomas on the telephone and that Thomas now wished to speak with Hurt. Thomas informed Hurt that the letter from Orebaugh was not "proper authorization" and that Omni would require a resolution from Outdoor's board of directors authorizing Hurt to negotiate the check. Unable to obtain a board resolution on such short notice, Hurt sent the check, via federal express, to a Detroit, Michigan bank where Outdoor maintained a depository account. As feared by Outdoor, Hechinger initiated its bankruptcy filing on June 11 before the check was paid. This filing froze Hechinger's accounts and prevented Omni from paying the check. Consequently, the check was returned to Outdoor unpaid. The $706,735.62 owed to Outdoor by Hechinger remains outstanding. . . .

III.   DISCUSSION

B.   COUNT II, FRAUD

In Delaware, the elements of fraud are: 1) a false representation, usually one of fact, made by the defendant; 2) the defendant's knowledge or belief that the representation was false, or was made with reckless indifference to the truth; 3) an intent to induce the plaintiff to act or to refrain from acting; 4) the plaintiff's action or inaction taken in justifiable reliance upon the representation; and 5) damage to the plaintiff as a result of such reliance. Delaware courts require proof of fraud to be made by a preponderance of the evidence.

The Court need not go beyond the first element of Outdoor's *prima facie* case for fraud to dispose of this claim. The evidence of record simply does not support the contention that Thomas made a false statement to Hurt or any other representative of Outdoor. Thomas advised Hurt that Omni would require the presentation of "proper authorization" before it would negotiate the Hechinger check. This statement was consistent with the direction Thomas provided to the Omni bank branch after Hurt left his office and consistent with banking industry practice. The fact that the conversation did not last long enough for either party to address what would or would not be deemed "proper authorization" is unfortunate but not a basis for actionable fraud.

Moreover, the statements made by Thomas clearly related to future events. Generally, statements which are merely promissory in nature and expressions as to what will happen in the future are not actionable as fraud. Only when such statements are made with the present intention not to perform will courts endorse a fraud claim. Defendants have presented evidence indicating that Thomas authorized Omni to negotiate the Hechinger check. Outdoor has failed in its burden to present evidence contradicting the banks' proffer. The only evidence of record that Thomas did not intend to negotiate the check is that he refused to do so when Hurt presented the check at Omni. Ordinarily, in the absence of additional circumstances, it will be found that a mere failure to perform is as consistent with an honest intent as with a dishonest one.

Finally, it is apparent from the record that Hurt made no effort during his discussions with Thomas to ascertain what would suffice as "proper authorization." Although the "deliberate concealment of material facts would qualify as a false representation," the Court cannot conclude on this record that a jury could find Thomas deliberately concealed anything from Hurt. In this regard, it is particularly probative that Hurt had absolutely no evidence of authorization from Outdoor to negotiate the check at the time he first discussed the issue with Thomas. It is also clear that Hurt had not yet received his "marching orders" to proceed to Omni when he discussed procedures with Thomas. It cannot be said, then, that Thomas even knew what Hurt was going to do next with the check when he discussed Omni's requirements with Thomas, much less what evidence of authorization Hurt might present to Omni if he attempted to negotiate the check. And, in light of these and the other circumstances of the conversation, it cannot be said that Thomas deliberately concealed either that the faxed letter would be insufficient evidence of authorization or that only a board resolution would be sufficient. . . .

C. COUNT III, NEGLIGENT MISREPRESENTATION

Under Delaware law, allegations of negligent [mis]representation require proof of the following elements: (1) a pecuniary duty to provide accurate information, (2) the supplying of false information, (3) failure to exercise reasonable care in obtaining or communicating information, and (4) a pecuniary loss caused by justifiable reliance upon the false information.

As was the case with Outdoor's claim of fraud, Outdoor cannot sustain a claim of negligent misrepresentation when it has failed to produce any evidence that the defendant banks supplied false information. Since the Court has already concluded that Thomas' statement incontrovertibly was not false or on its face misleading, the Court would be inclined to stop its analysis here and to enter summary judgment in favor of the defendants but for Outdoor's contention that Thomas negligently misrepresented facts by omission. Outdoor's presentation at oral argument suggested that this, in fact, is Outdoor's showcase argument. Accordingly, the Court will address this argument and the remaining elements of plaintiff's *prima facie* burden on this claim.

Section 551 provides: "One who fails to disclose to another a fact that he knows may justifiably induce the other to act or refrain from acting in a business transaction is subject to the same liability to the other as though he had represented the nonexistence of the matter that he has failed to disclose if, but only if, he is under a duty to the other to exercise reasonable care to disclose the matter in question." The question of whether a duty exists, while a mixed question of law and fact, is for the Court to decide as a matter of law.

Legal duties arise from relationships. At the heart of Section 551 is a recognition that certain "business" relationships which evolve in the context of "business transaction[s]" can give rise to a duty of complete disclosure. Restatement (Second) of Torts §552(1) speaks in terms of disclosures made in the context of a transaction in which the speaker has a "pecuniary interest." Delaware common law embraces a "pecuniary duty to provide accurate information." In each instance, the law contemplates that a duty of disclosure will arise when the parties are in the midst of a "business relationship" from which they expect to derive "pecuniary" benefits. Thus, while contractual privity may not be required to form a duty, something more than a casual business encounter must be demonstrated before a duty of care will be imposed.

Outdoor cannot establish the requisite relationship with the defendant banks to justify the duty of complete candor it urges the Court to impose here. Outdoor had no prior relationship with the defendant banks; prior to their meeting, Thomas had never met Hurt. During an unscheduled encounter in the lobby of defendants' legal offices, Hurt asked Thomas some questions and Thomas endeavored to respond. Outdoor has failed to identify what pecuniary interest Thomas or the banks he represented might have been protecting in the course of the discussions with Hurt and the Court cannot discern any such interest from the record *sub judice.* Consequently, the Court will not impose an affirmative duty of complete disclosure upon the defendants under these circumstances. . . .

IV.   CONCLUSION

Outdoor has failed to present any evidence that the defendant banks made a false statement or that they wrongfully withheld material information. This failure of proof in the record, in the face of evidence that the banks were truthful in their discussions with Outdoor, requires that summary judgment be entered on [Outdoor's] claims.

The rule in *Outdoor* does not impose any undue risk on the payee. If a payee is concerned about the possibility that the payor bank will decline to pay, it can protect itself in several ways. Most obviously, the payee could refuse to accept an ordinary check. The prudent payee instead might ask for a special check that offers an assurance that the payor bank will pay the check when presented. For example, the payee can require the drawer to obtain the payor bank's agreement to pay before the payee accepts the check; that "pre-accepted" check is called a certified check. UCC §3-409(d). Similarly, the payee can ask for a check drawn on a bank itself. That type of check would be a "cashier's check" or a "teller's check," depending on whether the drawer and drawee banks were the same or different institutions. UCC §3-104(g), (h). In the existing milieu, certified checks, cashier's checks, and teller's checks are not a large component of the system as a whole, largely because of the inconvenience they require: a special trip to the financial institution to produce the check. They are used most frequently to complete consumer transactions where certainty of payment is particularly important, such as purchases of automobiles or homes.

B.   The Process of Collection

Even though the payor bank is not legally obligated to pay the check, the practical reality is that payor banks pay more than 99 percent of the checks that are presented to them. Nevertheless, because the payee starts out not knowing whether any particular check will be paid, the collection process must complete two distinct functions: (1) The payee has to find out whether payment will be forthcoming, and (2) the payee has to obtain payment. The payee has two different ways to pursue collection. The payee can go directly to the payor bank and obtain payment itself (a relatively unusual course of action), or the payee can obtain payment indirectly by transferring the check to an intermediary (depositing the check in a bank); the intermediary, in turn (if all goes well), gives the payee funds in return for the check and then obtains payment from the payor bank itself.

1. Obtaining Payment Directly

The payee can obtain payment from the payor bank in two ways. The simplest is to cash the check, which the payee does by presenting the check "for immediate payment over the counter," in the phrasing of UCC §4-301(a). When the payor bank makes such a payment, the payment is final. UCC §§4-215(a)(2), 4-215 comment 4 (paragraph 5). Thus, if Archie cashed Cliff's check "over the counter" at Rocky Mountain Bank, Rocky Mountain could not recover the money from Archie even if Cliff's account did not have enough money to cover the check. That problem is not particularly significant, however, because the payor bank normally would refuse to cash the check if the drawer's account did not contain funds sufficient to cover the check.

The second way for the payee to obtain direct payment happens almost as a matter of coincidence, when the payee has an account at the same bank as the drawer. In that case, the payee gets the check to the payor bank when the payee deposits the check in its own account. From the perspective of the payor/depositary bank, that produces an "on-us" item: an item drawn "on us." Ordinarily, the payor bank gives the depositor credit (a "provisional settlement") for the item on the day that it receives the item. As long as the payor bank provides that provisional settlement on the day that it receives the item, the payor bank has until its "midnight deadline" — midnight of the next banking day, UCC §4-104(a)(10) — to decide whether it wishes to honor the check. UCC §4-301(a), (b). Figure 23.1 illustrates that process.

If the payor bank honors the check, it credits (increases) the payee's account by the amount of the check and deducts a corresponding sum from the drawer's account. For example, if Archie deposits Cliff's $1,000 check in Archie's account at Rocky Mountain Bank, the bank removes $1,000 from Cliff's account and adds the same amount to Archie's account. Because of the offsetting entries, the transaction has no net effect on Rocky Mountain Bank. Alternatively, if the payor bank decides not to honor the check, it sends a notice of dishonor to the payee/customer. Finally, if the payor bank does nothing — if it fails to send a notice of dishonor by the midnight deadline — it loses the right to dishonor the check. UCC §§4-214(c), 4-301(b). Here, as elsewhere, the system generally operates on the empirically reasonable assumption that each check will be honored. Thus, although payor banks do not start out with any obligation to pay checks drawn on them, the system imposes such an obligation if the payor bank fails to move swiftly to dishonor a check that comes to it.

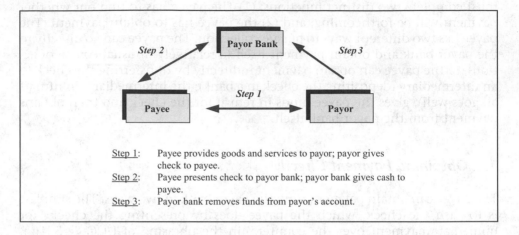

Figure 23.1
Direct Presentment

Step 1:   Payee provides goods and services to payor; payor gives
           check to payee.
Step 2:   Payee presents check to payor bank; payor bank gives cash to
           payee.
Step 3:   Payor bank removes funds from payor's account.

If the bank properly dishonors an on-us item, then it can "charge back" (that is, remove) the credit that it gave the payee's account when the payee deposited the check. Thus, if Rocky Mountain dishonored Cliff's check for lack of funds, Rocky Mountain would be entitled to take the $1,000 back out of Archie's account, which would leave the bank back where it started. If Archie already has withdrawn the money from his account, the payor/ depositary bank can sue him to recover the money. UCC §§4-214(c), 4-301(b). In that event, the check-collection part of the transaction has been completely nullified, without providing payment. At that point (as discussed in Assignment 21), the payee is left under UCC §3-310 with the check itself and the right to attempt to obtain payment from the purchaser on the underlying obligation. Finally, if Rocky Mountain is unable to recover from Archie, it should be able to recover from Cliff by pursuing him either as the drawer of the check under UCC §3-414(b) (discussed in Chapter 11) or under a general common-law restitutionary theory, see UCC §1-103.

2. Obtaining Payment Through Intermediaries

As we all know, in most cases it is not convenient for the payee to cash the check at the payor bank or to deposit the check into an account at the payor bank. Rather, the payee deposits the check into the payee's own account at its chosen depositary bank. The need to move the check from the depositary bank to the payor bank makes the process considerably more complicated. The simplest way to discuss the process is to break it down into two separate steps: what happens when the check goes from the payee to the depositary bank and what happens when the check goes from the depositary bank to the payor bank.

(a) *Payee/Customer to Depositary Bank.* When the customer deposits a check into its account, two things happen. The first is the creation of an agency relationship between the customer and the bank. Under UCC §4-201(a), the bank where the customer has deposited the check (the depositary bank) accepts a responsibility to act as the customer's agent in the process of obtaining payment from the payor bank. See UCC §4-201(a) (characterizing the depositary and intermediary banks as "agent[s]" of the customer). Charged with that responsibility, the depositary bank becomes a "collecting bank" in the UCC's terminology, see UCC §4-105(5), a status that carries with it a statutory duty to exercise ordinary care, UCC §4-202(a). Second, while it is attempting to obtain payment, the depositary bank ordinarily gives the customer a "provisional settlement" for the item. The settlement is a credit (addition) to the customer's account for the amount of the check. The settlement is called "provisional" because (as discussed above) the depositary bank retains the so-called charge-back right. That right allows the depositary bank to revoke the settlement and remove the funds from the customer's account if the payor bank does not honor the check. UCC §4-214.

(b) *Depositary Bank to Payor Bank.* Once the depositary bank has the check, the depositary bank is free to choose how it will go about attempting to collect from the payor bank, subject only to its obligation of ordinary care under UCC §4-202. See UCC §4-204 (giving collecting banks broad discretion about method of collection). Of course, the funds-availability rules discussed in Assignment 22 give the depositary bank an incentive to move as quickly as possible to find out if the payor bank will honor the check. As you should recall, the depositary bank will have to make the funds represented by the deposited item available to the depositor in just a few days, even if the depositary bank has not yet learned what the payor bank will do when it receives the check. Thus, banks have a considerable incentive to develop and use expeditious procedures for collection of checks they receive for deposit.

Current procedures for check collection focus on the physical object: the piece of paper written by the drawer and delivered to the payee. Thus, in most cases the depositary bank physically transmits the check to the payor bank, which then honors the check or returns it. In deciding how to transmit the check to the payor bank, the depositary bank chooses from among several different methods of transmission based on the relative cost and speed of the options available for each check. One of the most prominent options—clearance through the Federal Reserve process—is operated by the federal government. The other principal options—multilateral clearinghouses, bilateral correspondents, and direct-send arrangements—are established by private contracts among the banks involved. Most banks use some combination of all of those options, depending on the circumstances of each check.

When checks come into the bank (through either personal deposits to a teller or deposits at an ATM), the bank typically transports the checks to an operations center that serves all of the bank's branches in the area. Smaller banks might transport their checks to an operations center of a larger area bank, which processes the smaller bank's checks (for a fee, of course). At the operations center, the checks are placed in assembly-line feeders that carry each individual check to a keyboard operator. The keyboard operator determines the amount of each check and types it into a terminal; the terminal imprints a string of magnetic-ink characters normally referred to as a MICR (pronounced "miker" to rhyme with "biker") line, indicating that amount at the bottom right-hand corner of the check. A depositary bank normally charges commercial customers a fee for imprinting that amount on deposited checks. To save that expense, large commercial customers can imprint the MICR line themselves, either with smaller imprinting machines that they purchase or with cash registers that automatically imprint the MICR line at the point of sale. See UCC §4-209 comment 1. In the overwhelming majority of cases, that is the last time that human eyes examine the check.

From that machine, the check goes to a sophisticated high-speed sorter designed to read about 1,000 checks a minute, taking a microfilm photograph of the front and back of each check as it passes. That machine sorts the checks based on the MICR line at the bottom of the check, which by now includes not only the preprinted numbers at the bottom left of the check, but also the keyboard operator's indication of the amount of the check. The preprinted characters allow the sorter to determine how the check should be processed. The first string of characters is a standard routing number assigned by the American Bankers Association (ABA). The ABA routing number identifies the Federal Reserve district and bank on which the check is drawn. The machine is programmed to sort the checks based on that routing number. If the routing number reveals an on-us item, the check is directed to the depositary bank's payor-bank processing department. The remaining checks are sorted into separate batches for each of the possible clearing arrangements available to the bank. The following sections summarize the processes for the major clearing arrangements (clearinghouse clearing, direct-send and correspondent clearing, and Federal Reserve clearing).

(i) Multilateral arrangements (clearinghouses). Clearinghouses provide an efficient mechanism for clearing local checks. In most large metropolitan areas, banks clear checks drawn on other local banks through a multilateral clearinghouse system that nets out each bank's checks on a daily basis. Although it is difficult to generalize, clearinghouses often handle about a third of the transit items (that is, items other than on-us items) deposited at large metropolitan banks. That system is used for all checks that the bank receives for deposit that are drawn on other clearinghouse members. The operations center for the depositary bank sends a courier to carry all of those checks to the clearinghouse by a set time each day (usually late in the afternoon). The clearinghouse charges each depositary bank a fee that varies, depending on the number of checks that it submits for processing.

Like most aspects of the check-collection process, the clearinghouse starts from the assumption that payor banks eventually will honor all checks presented to them. Accordingly, the clearinghouse gives each bank a credit for the amount of each check that it sends to the clearinghouse each day. Conversely, each bank is debited the total amount of the checks drawn on it that are sent in by other clearinghouse members on each day. The clearinghouse aggregates all of those figures to compute a net position for each bank for each day and then applies that position to a designated account: usually the bank's account at the local Federal Reserve bank. If the bank has a net credit (the value of the checks deposited in its facilities that are drawn on other clearinghouse members is greater than the value of the checks drawn on it that are deposited with other clearinghouse members), it receives an addition to its account. If it has a net debit (the reverse situation), the bank pays the amount of the debit to the clearinghouse from the bank's Federal Reserve account.

For example, assume that Country Bank one morning receives deposits of $14,000,000 of checks drawn on other members of a local clearinghouse; other clearinghouse members receive $12,000,000 of checks drawn on Country Bank on that same day. The clearinghouse would distribute both sets of checks to the respective payor banks, give Country Bank a $2,000,000 credit to its Federal Reserve account, and withdraw a total of $2,000,000 from the Federal Reserve accounts of the other clearinghouse members. The funds deposited into the Federal Reserve accounts ordinarily would be available no later than the next day.

The clearinghouse then forwards all of the checks to the respective payor banks; in UCC terminology, it "presents" the checks for payment. UCC §3-501(a). For example, consider a check deposited at Country Bank, sent by Country Bank for collection through the clearinghouse, and forwarded by the clearinghouse to Hunt Bank. As discussed above, by the time that Hunt physically receives the check, it already will have been charged for the amount of the check (when the clearinghouse netted out Hunt's items for the day). To recover that money, Hunt then decides whether it wishes to honor the check (so that Hunt can remove the money from the drawer's account). If the clearinghouse did not impose any faster deadline, Hunt as payor bank would not have to decide until its midnight deadline, that is, midnight of the banking day following the banking day on which Hunt received the item. In most cases, however, the clearinghouse imposes a much faster deadline: perhaps late in the morning the day after the check was deposited. If the payor bank does not act by that time, the bank loses its right to dishonor. See UCC §4-215(a)(3) (bank makes final payment when it makes a provisional settlement "and fail[s] to revoke the settlement in the time and manner permitted by . . . clearing-house rule"). The speedy deadline accommodates the fact that the depositary bank ordinarily must release the funds under the EFAA the day after the check is deposited; a slower deadline would expose the depositary bank to the risk that the payor bank would dishonor the check after the depositary bank had released the funds.

Hunt (as payor bank) processes checks that it receives from the clearinghouse with the same sorters that it used to process checks deposited with it earlier in the day. When the checks come into the payor bank from the clearinghouse late each night, the sorters read each check and compare its amount to the funds available for withdrawal in each account. More sophisticated banks establish an on-line connection from the sorters to the bank's account records, so that the sorters post the checks to the accounts as the sorters process the checks. The sorters separate out checks that are questionable for one reason or another: The check might not have a readable MICR line (often an indication that the check is counterfeit), the account might not contain sufficient available funds to cover the check, or the account might be on a watch list based on a concern of the bank related to that account. The sorters also pull certain checks for examination of signatures. A typical arrangement for commercial accounts calls for the examination of the signatures on a random 1 percent sample of all checks, as well as all checks over a specific threshold in the range of $2,500; although that percentage is small, the total number of checks to be examined at a large metropolitan bank will be quite large, perhaps tens of thousands each day. Unless the check is rejected by the sorter for one of those reasons, the check is honored without any human examination whatsoever.

If the bank decides to honor the check, it deducts the funds from the draw-er's account. Because the clearinghouse operates by assuming in the first instance that all checks will be honored, the payor bank does not need to do anything to tell the clearinghouse or the depositary bank that it has decided to honor the check. The payment becomes final as to the payor bank when the deadline for dishonor under the clearinghouse rule expires. At that point, whether or not the drawer has sufficient funds to cover the check, the payor bank loses any right to recover from the clearinghouse, the depositary bank, or the payee. UCC §4-301. Similarly, the payment at that point becomes final as between the depositary bank and its customer. Thus, at the moment that the settlement becomes final between the depos-itary bank and the payor bank, the depositary bank loses the right to charge back any provisional credit that it gave to its customer when the check was deposited. UCC §4-214(a).

Kimberly A. Allen Trust v. FirstBank of Lakewood, N.A.

989 P.2d 203 (Colo. App. 1999)

Opinion by Judge KAPELKE.

In this action to recover funds charged back to its bank account, plaintiff, Kimberly A. Allen Trust (the Trust), appeals from the summary judgment entered in favor of defendant, FirstBank of Lakewood, N.A. (FirstBank). We reverse and remand with directions.

On March 14, 1997, the Trust deposited into its account with FirstBank a check drawn on Bank One (payor bank) in the amount of $110,737.50. A hold was placed on the account pending payment of the check. On March 17, 1997, the first business day after deposit, FirstBank presented the check to payor bank for collection and was given provisional credit.

On March 20, 1997, after payor bank advised FirstBank that the check had cleared, the Trust was informed that the hold on its account had been lifted. However, on March 25, 1997, payor bank notified FirstBank that it was returning the check for insufficient funds. After return of the check, FirstBank charged back the amount of the check, plus a return fee, to the Trust's account.

The Trust filed this action against FirstBank to recover the funds debited against its account, asserting that FirstBank was precluded from revoking the provisional credit and that the charge-back was therefore improper.

FirstBank filed a motion for summary judgment with supporting affidavits, and the Trust filed a cross-motion for summary judgment. The trial court granted First Bank's motion and denied that of the Trust.

I.

The Trust contends that FirstBank did not have a right of charge-back because the provisional payment it had received became final when the payor bank failed to return the check by its "midnight deadline." We . . . conclude that summary judgment should not have been entered and that further proceedings are necessary.

[UCC §]4-214(a), which defines a collecting bank's right of charge-back or refund, states:

> If a collecting bank has made provisional settlement with its customer for an item and fails by reason of dishonor, suspension or payments by a bank, or otherwise to receive a settlement for the item which is or becomes final, the bank may revoke the settlement given by it, charge-back the amount of any credit given for the item to its customer's account, or obtain refund from its customer, whether or not it is able to return the item, if by its midnight deadline or within a longer reasonable time after it learns the facts, it returns the item or sends notification of the facts. . . . *These rights to revoke, charge back, and obtain refund terminate if and when a settlement for the item received by the bank is or becomes final.* (emphasis added [by court])

If a collecting bank such as FirstBank here receives a settlement for an item which "is or becomes final," the bank is "accountable" to its customer for the amount of the item and any provisional credit given for the item in an account with its customer becomes final. [UCC §4-215(d).]

Pursuant to [UCC §]4-215(a), an item is "finally paid" by a payor bank when it has first done any of the following:

(1) Paid the item in cash;
(2) Settled for the item without having a right to revoke the settlement under statute, clearing-house rule, or agreement; or
(3) *Made a provisional settlement for the item and failed to revoke the settlement in the time and manner permitted by statute, clearing-house rule, or agreement.* (emphasis added [by court])

Pursuant to [UCC §4-302], if an item is presented to and received by a payor bank, that bank is "accountable" for the amount of the demand item if it "retains the item beyond midnight of the banking day of receipt without settling for it or, whether or not it is also the depositary bank, does not pay or return the item or send notice of dishonor until after its midnight deadline." The "midnight deadline" is midnight of the next banking day after the item is received by the payor bank. [UCC §4-104(a)(10).]

The Uniform Commercial Code requires strict compliance with the midnight deadline even if the item is not properly payable. This rule promotes efficiency, certainty, and finality in the national banking system. Moreover, the payor bank is in the best position to know the status of its depositor's account. Placing the loss on the payor bank will facilitate the use of the check as a medium of exchange and will force the one who can most cheaply avoid the loss to do so.

Here, it is uncontested that payor bank's deadline was midnight of March 18, 1997, and that the check was not returned until March 25, 1997. As noted above, under [UCC §4-215(a)(3)], if a collecting bank receives a settlement for an item which becomes final, any provisional credit given for the item in an account with its customer becomes final. Here, the payor bank failed to return the item before its midnight deadline and [thus] the provisional settlement became final.

We conclude that under the clear language of [UCC §4-215(a)(3)], final settlement occurs when an item is deemed "finally paid" as a result of the payor bank's failure to revoke a provisional settlement. Thus, when a payor bank becomes "accountable" on a check, the settlement becomes final and the collecting bank's right to charge-back against its depositor's account is terminated. See [UCC §4-214(a)].

The following pertinent analysis appears in 5 W. Hawkland, J.F. Leary & R. Alderman, Uniform Commercial Code Series §4-213:8 (1984):

> Section 4-201 states the general rule that a collecting bank is an agent or subagent of the owner of the item and any settlement given for the item is presumed to be provisional. Subsection [4-215(d)] . . . makes any provisional settlement given by the collecting bank final, and the collecting bank accountable, when the settlement received by the collecting bank is or becomes final. At that time, the relationship between the collecting bank and its customer changes from one of agent-principal to debtor-creditor. It should also be remembered that any right of charge-back or refund ceases upon receipt of final payment.
>
> For example, suppose customer deposits a check in depositary bank and receives a provisional credit in his checking account. Depositary bank then forwards the check to the presenting bank through the local clearinghouse and receives a provisional credit from presenting bank. Presenting bank presents the check through the clearinghouse and is given a provisional credit, which then becomes final through the payor bank's inaction pursuant to [UCC §4-215(a)(3)]. At that time all provisional credits down the line become final and the collecting banks are accountable to their customers. At the same time, the banks lose the right to charge back or obtain a refund under [UCC §4-214]. The depositary bank, no longer an agent for the depositor, is instead a creditor and therefore indebted to the depositor for the amount of the item.

Final payment "firms up all of the provisional credits made in the collection process and makes each collecting bank accountable to its customer for the amount of the item. The relationship between the depositary bank and its customer then changes, from one of agency-principal to debtor-creditor." 5 W. Hawkland, J.F. Leary & R. Alderman, *supra,* at §4-213:1.

Accordingly, the summary judgment in favor of FirstBank is not sustainable under the provisions of the Uniform Commercial Code.

The finality of payment completes the payment transaction, with a net effect of a transfer from the drawer's account at the payor bank to the payee's account at the depositary bank. The drawer has been charged the amount of the check. The payor bank is even: Its Federal Reserve account was charged for the check by the clearinghouse, and it has charged the drawer's account for the same amount. The clearinghouse is even: It has credited the depositary bank and charged the payor bank. The depositary bank is even: It gave a provisional (now final) settlement to the payee and received an equal credit from the clearinghouse. Finally, the payee has received the amount of the check through the now-final settlement from the depositary bank. (See Figure 23.2.)

Figure 23.2
Clearinghouse Collection

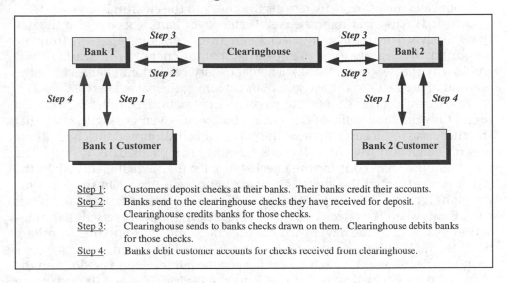

Step 1:   Customers deposit checks at their banks. Their banks credit their accounts.
Step 2:   Banks send to the clearinghouse checks they have received for deposit.
          Clearinghouse credits banks for those checks.
Step 3:   Clearinghouse sends to banks checks drawn on them. Clearinghouse debits banks
          for those checks.
Step 4:   Banks debit customer accounts for checks received from clearinghouse.

That description leaves untreated the checks that were pulled from the sorters for individual treatment. If the check is pulled for examination of the signature (or because of the absence of a MICR line), the check will be honored if no problem appears. If a problem does appear, though, the check might be dishonored (perhaps after telephone consultation with the drawer). If a check is drawn against insufficient funds or if the institution is monitoring the account for some other reason (usually because of concerns about fraud), the operations center forwards a computer message to an individual officer responsible for reviewing checks on that particular account. If the officer does not countermand the system by a set time (normally late in the morning of the day after the check was deposited), the bank dishonors the check.

Under UCC §4-301(a), the payor bank notifies the other parties to the transaction of its decision to dishonor by the relatively cumbersome act of returning the check. It is important to emphasize that the UCC deadline is satisfied if the payor bank simply "return[s]" the check, which requires nothing more than depositing the check in the mail. See UCC §§1-201(38) (revised §1-201((b) (36))) (defining "send" to include depositing in the mail), 4-301(d)(2) (explaining that the "return" requirement is satisfied if the check is "sent or delivered"). The UCC does not require the payor bank to give the depositary bank prompt notice of the payor bank's decision to dishonor. Given the expense and delay involved in a physical return, the effect of that rule is a perverse requirement of a notice that is at once unduly expensive and relatively slow.

The payor bank accomplishes the physical return by affixing a small strip of paper to the bottom of the check. The strip adds a new MICR line at the bottom of each dishonored check, indicating the routing number for the bank where the check originally was deposited. The sorters then sort the checks for return by the same transportation methods the payor bank would use to send deposited checks to those banks: Checks from direct-send banks are routed for direct return, checks that came through correspondents are routed for delivery back to the correspondents, checks from clearinghouses are routed back to the clearinghouse, and checks from the Federal Reserve are routed back to the Federal Reserve.

In our case, the payor bank returns the check to the clearinghouse. See UCC §4-301(d)(1). The clearinghouse credits the payor bank's account on the day that the payor bank returns the check, deducting a corresponding sum from the account of the clearinghouse member that sent the check to the clearinghouse (ordinarily the depositary bank). The depositary bank then charges back the amount of the check to the account of its customer, the payee. See UCC §4-214.

That return process leaves the payment transaction completely nullified (except for the time value of the credits that were given during the day that the check was in process). Because the payor bank dishonored the check, there was no deduction from the drawer's account. The payor bank is even: The clearinghouse charged it for the check, but gave it an equal credit when the payor bank returned the check. The clearinghouse is even: On the first time through, it credited the depositary bank for the check and charged the payor bank for it; when the check came back, the clearinghouse reversed that transaction by crediting the payor bank for the check and charging the depositary bank for it. The depositary bank is even: It gave its customer, the payee, a provisional settlement, which it now has revoked; it received a credit from the clearinghouse when it sent the check to the clearinghouse, but accepted a corresponding charge when the check was returned. Finally, the payee in the end has nothing: It initially received a provisional settlement, but that has been charged back, leaving the payee back where it started, as if it never had deposited the check. As always, the payee remains entitled to pursue the drawer on the check or on the underlying obligation, as provided in UCC §3-310(b).

(ii) Bilateral arrangements (direct-send and correspondent clearing). Because of the logistical difficulties of transporting checks, clearinghouses are not useful for clearing checks from different metropolitan areas. Many of those checks, however, can be cleared through individual bilateral arrangements between participating banks. Basically, a pair of banks that have a relationship — that have large numbers of checks drawn on each other each day — is likely to enter into a clearing arrangement that provides for "direct-send" clearing of checks without the use of the Federal Reserve or any other intermediary. That arrangement ordinarily would cover not only checks drawn on the two banks (the direct-send checks), but also checks drawn on small banks for which the two large banks have agreed to process checks. For those checks, the large bank is said to serve as a "correspondent" for the small bank.

A typical large metropolitan bank would establish direct-send arrangements with about 30 banks, covering about a third of the bank's total "transit" items (transit items being all items other than on-us items). For example, Bank of America in St. Louis and Bank One in Chicago might enter into a direct-send relationship. Because both Bank of America and Bank One also have extensive correspondent relationships with smaller banks in Missouri and Illinois, respectively, Bank of America would use its direct-send relationship with Bank One not only to clear checks drawn on Bank One, but also to clear checks drawn on smaller and rural Illinois banks for which Bank One serves as a correspondent.

The arrangement (a contract between Bank of America and Bank One) typically would provide that Bank of America would receive a provisional same-day credit for all checks that Bank of America delivers to Bank One by 2 P.M. on any banking day. The credit would be given to Bank of America's account at Bank One; the funds would be available for withdrawal by Bank of America on the next day. Late each morning Bank of America in St. Louis would collect all of the checks drawn on Bank One (or on other banks for which Bank One is a correspondent) and send them to Chicago by a bonded courier that would get them to Bank One's processing center before 2 P.M. The courier ordinarily carries the checks in large, waterproof cargo bags; in the rare event that the courier loses or damages the bags, the depositary bank reconstructs the lost items from the microfilm photographs of the checks that the depositary bank made when it sorted the checks. Bank One would take the same steps each day with checks drawn on Bank of America's St. Louis-based operations (or on banks for which Bank of America in St. Louis serves as a correspondent) that were deposited by Bank One customers.

Each bank would pay a fee to the other based generally on the number of checks that it submitted for processing. The relationship would be attractive to the two banks because it would be cheaper and faster than the Federal Reserve clearing process discussed below, the other option for clearing out-of-town checks. The per-check processing fee should be significantly lower than the comparable Federal Reserve fee, and the direct-send relationship ordinarily would make funds available much more quickly than the Federal Reserve process (discussed below).

Once the checks reach the payor bank's processing center, the process would proceed just as it would for checks received from a clearinghouse. The payor bank would sort the checks, decide whether to honor them, make the appropriate charges to its customers' accounts, and notify the depositary banks of any checks that it wished to dishonor. In the agreement establishing the relationship, the parties would address the timing of that notice and the mechanics of credits to the payor bank for the dishonored checks. Figure 23.3 illustrates that process.

(iii) Collection through the Federal Reserve system. The bank uses the Federal Reserve system for checks that it cannot process through a clearinghouse or through direct-send and correspondent arrangements. The Federal Reserve system (as illustrated in Figure 23.4) generally is the system of last resort because it is more expensive than the other systems and because it normally provides slower availability than the other systems. It retains its importance, however, because it provides a method for clearing checks on almost all of the banks in this country, wherever they are located. For small banks, for which direct-send, correspondent, and clearinghouse arrangements are less economical, the Federal Reserve handles close to half of the transit items; for large banks, the Federal Reserve share is somewhat less—about a third of all transit items.

The process works much like the clearinghouse process, except for its breadth of coverage. The process of Federal Reserve clearing starts with the depositary bank's decision to send a check to its local Federal Reserve bank. Under Regulation J, 12 C.F.R. §210.6, the Federal Reserve undertakes to collect

Figure 23.3
Direct-Send Collection

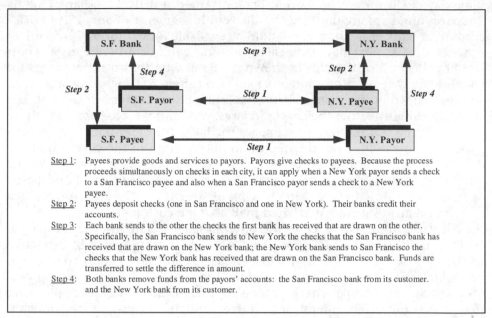

Step 1:   Payees provide goods and services to payors. Payors give checks to payees. Because the process proceeds simultaneously on checks in each city, it can apply when a New York payor sends a check to a San Francisco payee and also when a San Francisco payor sends a check to a New York payee.

Step 2:   Payees deposit checks (one in San Francisco and one in New York). Their banks credit their accounts.

Step 3:   Each bank sends to the other the checks the first bank has received that are drawn on the other. Specifically, the San Francisco bank sends to New York the checks that the San Francisco bank has received that are drawn on the New York bank; the New York bank sends to San Francisco the checks that the New York bank has received that are drawn on the San Francisco bank. Funds are transferred to settle the difference in amount.

Step 4:   Both banks remove funds from the payors' accounts: the San Francisco bank from its customer. and the New York bank from its customer.

the check as an agent for the depositary bank and then to forward any proceeds back to that bank. Operating on the assumption that the check will be honored, the local Federal Reserve bank gives the depositary bank's account with it a credit in the amount of the check. Using the same MICR line that the depositary bank used to route the check to the Federal Reserve, the Federal Reserve sorts each check for transmission to the Federal Reserve district in which the payor bank is located. The payor bank's Federal Reserve bank then charges the payor bank's account for the check and delivers it to the payor bank. Checks involving large banks often skip one step of the process: A large depositary bank might send checks directly to the payor bank's Federal Reserve bank (bypassing the depositary bank's Federal Reserve bank); checks drawn on a large payor bank might be sent directly to that bank by the depositary bank's Federal Reserve bank (bypassing the payor bank's Federal Reserve bank). In any event, the depositary bank's Federal Reserve bank makes the funds available to the depositary bank after one or two days, depending on the location of the payor bank and the availability policies adopted by that Federal Reserve bank.

The payor bank then has to decide whether to honor the check. If the payor bank honors the check, the process works much like it did above. It need send no notice of its decision because the system proceeds on the initial assumption that all checks will be honored. When the deadlines for dishonor pass — midnight at the close of the first banking day after the banking day on which the payor bank receives the check, UCC §§4-104(a)(10), 4-215(a)(3), 4-301(a) — the debit to the payor bank's account at the Federal Reserve becomes final, the Federal Reserve's credit to the depositary bank becomes final, and the provisional settlement that the depositary bank granted its customer, the payee, becomes final. UCC §§4-214(a), 4-215(a)(3).

Figure 23.4
Federal Reserve Collection

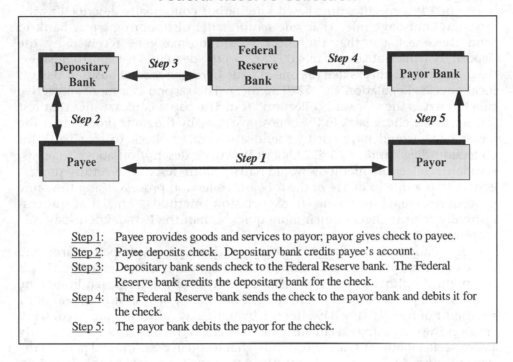

Step 1:   Payee provides goods and services to payor; payor gives check to payee.
Step 2:   Payee deposits check. Depositary bank credits payee's account.
Step 3:   Depositary bank sends check to the Federal Reserve bank. The Federal
Reserve bank credits the depositary bank for the check.
Step 4:   The Federal Reserve bank sends the check to the payor bank and debits it for
the check.
Step 5:   The payor bank debits the payor for the check.

If the payor bank wants to dishonor the check, however, the process is somewhat different. As the flip side of the EFAA requirement that depositary banks make funds available to their customers on a relatively short schedule (discussed in Assignment 22), the Federal Reserve has tried in Regulation CC to force payor banks to act quickly to advise depositary banks when they plan to dishonor a check. Because the Regulation CC obligations are imposed as part of the Federal Reserve's effort to speed check return under the Expedited Funds Availability Act, they apply whether the check is cleared through the Federal Reserve or not. As it happens, though, the most significant practical impact of the deadline is on checks cleared through the Federal Reserve because most direct-send and clearinghouse arrangements provide final settlement far in advance of the deadlines established by Regulation CC.

Regulation CC includes three significant provisions for the check-return process. First, it adds two new deadlines of its own, an accelerated return deadline and a notice-of-nonpayment deadline. Second, it significantly alters one of the UCC's rules, the standard UCC §4-301(a) midnight deadline for return described above.

• The Regulation CC return deadline. Although the UCC return obligation focuses only on the date that the payor bank puts the check in the mail, the Regulation CC deadline is more functional: It focuses on the speed with which the depositary bank actually receives the dishonored check. Specifically, Regulation CC requires the payor bank to return the check in an "expeditious" manner so as to satisfy one of two separate regulatory deadlines.

The first is a specific, time-based safe harbor colloquially described as the "two-day/four-day" rule. That rule requires the dishonoring payor bank to send the check so "that the check would normally be received by the depositary bank not later than 4:00 P.M." on the deadline: the fourth business day for nonlocal checks like the one at issue here; the second business day for local checks. Regulation CC, §229.30(a)(1). The second is a more subjective rule known as the "forward collection" test. The payor bank satisfies that test if it sends the check back to the depositary bank by the same process that the payor bank would have used to send a deposited check to that bank for collection. Regulation CC, §229.30(a)(2). As the description above suggests, standard collection methods would satisfy both tests. The return process generally is a mirror image of the forward collection process, using the same procedures, machines, and transportation methods, and that process normally returns checks much more quickly than the two-day/four-day rule requires.

- <u>Regulation CC and the UCC's midnight deadline.</u>   As a related part of the same effort to speed the return of checks, Regulation CC amends the UCC's midnight deadline. As described above, the text of the UCC standing alone requires the payor bank to return the check (that is, deposit it in the mail) by midnight of the banking day after the banking day on which the payor bank receives the check. In two circumstances in which the UCC rule is particularly perverse, Regulation CC alters (extends) that wooden deadline and permits the payor bank to defer "return" until the next day if the payor bank selects an appropriately expeditious mode of return that would result in a faster delivery than the UCC deadline. Regulation CC, §229.30(c)(1).

The first extension waives the midnight deadline as long as the payor bank delivers the check to its transferor (in this case, its Federal Reserve bank) by the first banking day after the deadline. For example, even if the Article 4 midnight deadline calls for action before the end of Wednesday, the payor bank acts properly if it sends the check to its Federal Reserve bank by messenger early Thursday morning (a process that would be much more expeditious than depositing the check in the mail on Wednesday evening).

The second extension waives the midnight deadline when the payor bank uses a "highly expeditious means of transportation, even if this means of transportation ordinarily would result in delivery after the receiving bank's next banking day." Regulation CC, §229.30(c)(1). Thus, assume now that because of the size of its operations in Southern California, a payor bank in New York deals directly with the Los Angeles Federal Reserve Bank and that the payor bank has decided to dishonor a check that it received directly from the Los Angeles Federal Reserve Bank. In that case (again assuming that the Article 4 midnight deadline calls for action by the end of Wednesday), Regulation CC permits the payor bank to forgo using the Wednesday night mail, wait until Thursday, and then send the check to the Los Angeles Federal Reserve Bank by an overnight delivery service for delivery Friday morning.

• The Regulation CC notice of nonpayment deadline. The final Regulation CC requirement is the most useful to the depositary bank: a notice of nonpayment required with respect to large nonlocal checks. Under Regulation CC, §229.33, a payor bank that decides to dishonor a check for $2,500 or more must get notice of its determination to the depositary bank by 4:00 P.M. on the second business day after the banking day on which the payor bank received the check. That requirement technically applies to both local checks and nonlocal checks, but it has little substantive impact with respect to local checks because the payor bank generally will have to return the check by the same time under Regulation CC, §229.30(a)(1). The return of the check will provide adequate notice to satisfy the Regulation CC notice requirement.

By requiring prompter notice with respect to large nonlocal checks, the regulation makes it safer for depositary banks to allow their customers faster access to funds that they deposit by means of large checks: The depositary bank safely can release the funds at the end of the second business day after the banking day on which the payor bank got the check.

It is important to distinguish between the effects of failure to meet the midnight deadline (as modified by Regulation CC, §229.30(c)(1)) and failure to satisfy the Regulation CC obligations to give notice and make an expeditious return. Failure to meet the midnight deadline directly affects the settlement process: The payor bank becomes "accountable" for the item under UCC §4-302, payment becomes final under UCC §4-215, and the depositary bank loses any right of charge-back under UCC §4-214. Failure to satisfy the Regulation CC requirements has much less dramatic consequences, generally limited to damages under Regulation CC, §229.38. To put it another way, a payor bank that meets the midnight deadline avoids responsibility for the item under the UCC even if it fails to satisfy its notice and return obligations under Regulation CC.

A common practice is to send a Regulation CC return notice over a standardized electronic-mail system known as the Electronic Advice of Return Notification System, colloquially referred to as EARNS. Figure 23.5 reproduces a typical EARNS notice generated during a visit by the author to a Chicago check-processing center. If you review that figure, you will see that it reflects a $5,442.90 check to General Electric Co., purporting to be drawn by North American Opertions [*sic*] General Motors on an account numbered 0952176. The depositary bank is identified only by its ABA routing number (061000104), which indicates a bank in Atlanta. The drawee bank is identified only by its MICR number (031100283), which identifies a bank in Chicago (the bank at which I saw the notice). The depositor account line is blank because the payor bank could not identify the depositor account from the check. The notice indicates that the payor bank bounced the check because it appeared to be "STOLEN/FORGED." In this particular case, the check was a photocopy of a real check. A forger successfully had deposited the photocopy — and this was not a high-quality color copy, but an obviously inauthentic black-and-white copy — in a bank in Atlanta. The false check managed to make its way to the payor bank because a keyboard operator at the depositary bank responded to the absence of a readable

Figure 23.5
Sample EARNS Notice

```
   03/14/96     E A R N S   I T E M S   S E N T   10:42:01 CENTRAL TIME


  MAKER NAME                          PAYEE NAME
  NORTH AMERICAN OPERTIONS GENERAL MOTORS GENERAL ELECTRIC CO. INC.

  DEPOSITOR NAME:GENERAL ELECTRIC CO. INC.

  DRAWEE BANK MICR:031100283          FIRST DEPOSIT ABA:      MICR:061000104

  MAKER ACCOUNT #:0952176             BRANCH NAME:????????????????????????

  CHECK NUMBER:001514347              DATE OF DEPOSIT:03/12/96

  CHECK AMOUNT:     $5,442.90          DEPOSITOR ACCOUNT #:????????????????????

  REASON:STOLEN/FORGED                TRACE/PROOF #:????????????????????????

  TRANSACTION NUMBER:104709           NOTIFY BANK ABA:      MICR:061000104

  REMARKS: QUEST. CALL 3127324691 IRENE
  ****************************************************************************



     1  ITEMS PRINTED  FOR A DOLLAR TOTAL OF          $5,442.90
```

MICR line on the photocopy by adding a completely new MICR line at the bottom of the check! The payor bank noticed the forgery only because the check was pulled from its sorters for signature examination (which the check failed).

To summarize, a successful return occurs only when the payor bank satisfies the requirements outlined in Figure 23.6. If the payor bank satisfies all of those requirements in a timely manner, the transaction is reversed all the way back to the depositary bank, just as it was in the clearinghouse situation. The Federal Reserve bank to which the payor bank returns the check gives the payor bank a credit for the check, leaving the payor bank back where it started. The depositary bank's Federal Reserve bank then charges the depositary bank for the check, leaving the Federal Reserve back where it started. Finally, the depositary bank attempts to charge back the account of its customer, the payee, leaving the depositary bank and the customer where they started, as if the customer never had deposited the check. If the depositary bank fails to obtain the money from its customer's account, it bears the loss unless it can recover from the original drawer of the check. In some cases (like the forgery case illustrated in Figure 23.5), that will not be plausible because the drawer will have no responsibility for the item. Moreover, even if a bounced check is genuine, it is not often worth the depositary bank's time and effort to try to recover its loss from the drawer. Thus, the depositary bank often bears the loss if it cannot recover from the customer that deposited the check.

Figure 23.6
Return Obligations

Obligation	Action Required	Citations
Midnight deadline	Send the item by midnight on the next banking day unless Regulation CC extends the deadline	UCC §§4-301(a), 4-104(a)(10), 1-201(38); Regulation CC, §229.30(c)(1)
Regulation CC return	Return the item to the depositary bank *either* by the two-day/four-day rule *or* by the forward collection rule	Regulation CC, §229.30(a)
Regulation CC notice	If the item is for $2,500 or more, give notice to the depositary bank by 4 P.M. on the second business day	Regulation CC, §229.33

The following case illustrates how those provisions operate in practice.

NBT Bank v. First National Community Bank

393 F.3d 404 (3d Cir. 2004)

Before RENDELL, FUENTES and SMITH, Circuit Judges.
Opinion of the Court
SMITH, Circuit Judge.

This is an appeal from an order of the District Court denying the motion of Appellant NBT Bank, N.A. ("NBT") for summary judgment, and granting summary judgment in favor of Appellee First National Community Bank ("FNCB"). At issue is a claim by NBT under Article 4 of Pennsylvania's Uniform Commercial Code ("UCC"), seeking to recover the face value of a $706,000 check (the "Disputed Check") that was drawn on an FNCB account and deposited at NBT by a participant in a check-kiting scheme.

In accordance with its established practice, NBT forwarded the Disputed Check to the Federal Reserve Bank of Philadelphia ("Reserve Bank"), which serves as a clearinghouse or transferor for checking transactions involving a number of banks, including both NBT and FNCB. When the Disputed Check was presented by the Reserve Bank to FNCB for payment, FNCB recognized that the drawer had overdrawn its account. Thus, FNCB sought to dishonor the Disputed Check and to return it to the Reserve Bank. Under the UCC, FNCB was required to return the Disputed Check to the Reserve Bank prior to the "midnight deadline," defined as midnight of the following banking day after the day the check was first presented to FNCB.

The parties agree that the Disputed Check was physically delivered to the Reserve Bank prior to the midnight deadline. The parties also agree that FNCB prepared the Disputed Check as a "qualified return check," meaning it was to be encoded with a magnetic strip containing information that would facilitate automated processing by the Reserve Bank. However, FNCB erroneously encoded the magnetic strip with the routing number for PNC Bank (which otherwise has no connection to this appeal), rather than NBT. The parties agree that NBT did not suffer damages as a result of this encoding error. Nonetheless, NBT seeks to hold FNCB accountable for the full amount of the Disputed Check, pursuant to the strict accountability provisions of [UCC §§4-301 and 4-302]. The key issue in this appeal is whether FNCB's violation of a Federal Reserve regulation requiring proper encoding provides a basis for imposing strict accountability on FNCB under §4-302 of the UCC, despite the fact that NBT incurred no actual loss as a result of FNCB's error.

Because we believe the District Court correctly concluded that NBT may not recover on the facts presented here, we will affirm the District Court's order granting summary judgment in favor of FNCB.

I.   FACTUAL BACKGROUND

A.   THE DISPUTED CHECK

. . . The dispute arises out of a check-kiting scheme under which a small group of Pennsylvania business entities arranged to write checks on one account, drawing on non-existent funds, and then cover these overdrafts with checks drawn on another account that also lacked sufficient funds. In this manner, the perpetrators of the scheme sought to obtain funds to which they were not entitled. The scheme collapsed when three checks initially deposited at NBT, and subsequently presented for payment to FNCB, were discovered by FNCB to have been drawn on an FNCB account that lacked sufficient funds. There is no dispute between the parties that two of these three checks were properly returned by FNCB to the Reserve Bank prior to the applicable midnight deadline.

The Disputed Check (i.e., the third check, for $706,000), was drawn on an FNCB account and drafted by an entity called Human Services Consultants, Inc. On March 8, 2001, the Disputed Check was proffered for deposit at NBT by an entity called Human Services Consultants Management, Inc., d/b/a "PA Health." Thus, in relation to the Disputed Check, NBT was the "depositary bank" (the first to receive the item), and FNCB was the "payor bank," meaning that the Disputed Check was drawn on an FNCB account held by a participant in the check-kiting scheme.

B.   THE PROVISIONAL SETTLEMENT

After the Disputed Check was presented for deposit at NBT, the bank gave provisional credit to the depositor, PA Health, for the amount of the Disputed Check. NBT also transmitted the Disputed Check to the Reserve Bank for presentment to FNCB. Upon transmission to the Reserve Bank, NBT was given a provisional credit from FNCB's Reserve Bank account for the face amount of the Disputed Check. The Reserve Bank then forwarded the Disputed Check to FNCB, and FNCB received it on March 12, 2001. Under the UCC, if FNCB wished to refuse payment on the

Disputed Check, FNCB was obligated to revoke the provisional settlement granted to NBT by 11:59 p.m. on March 13, 2001.

C. FNCB's Efforts to Return the Disputed Check

On March 13, 2001, FNCB determined it would not pay the Disputed Check because of the absence of sufficient funds in the account on which the check was drawn. That same day, FNCB sought to return the Disputed Check to NBT through the Reserve Bank. The parties agree that the Disputed Check was physically delivered to the Reserve Bank prior to 11:59 p.m. on March 13. In addition to sending the Disputed Check back to the Reserve Bank on March 13, FNCB also sent a notice of dishonor to NBT via the FedLine [a proprietary Federal Reserve communications system], in which FNCB indicated that it did not intend to pay the Disputed Check. NBT received this notice prior to the close of business on March 13. In addition, on the morning of March 14, 2001, FNCB executives telephoned NBT officials and telefaxed a letter to NBT, advising NBT that FNCB had decided to dishonor the Disputed Check.

D. FNCB's Encoding Error

When FNCB sent the Disputed Check to the Reserve Bank on March 13, 2001, FNCB included a letter designating it as a "Qualified Return Check" prepared for high speed processing. In so doing FNCB communicated to the Reserve Bank that it had attached to the Disputed Check a strip of paper encoded with magnetic ink that would permit the check to be processed through the Reserve Bank's automated processing system. However, FNCB erroneously encoded the strip with the routing number for PNC Bank instead of the routing number for NBT.

In sum, the Reserve Bank physically received the Disputed Check complete with the wrongly encoded strip prior to 11:59 p.m. on March 13, 2001. Because the Disputed Check was improperly encoded, NBT did not receive it back from the Reserve Bank until March 16, 2001. With proper encoding the Disputed Check likely would have been received on March 14, 2001. The parties have stipulated, however, that NBT suffered no damages or actual loss as a result of the encoding error, inasmuch as NBT had actual notice from FNCB on March 13 that the Disputed Check had been dishonored.

II. THE DISTRICT COURT PROCEEDINGS

NBT instituted this action against FNCB on May 25, 2001. The only claim before the District Court was a claim under the Pennsylvania UCC. NBT claimed that FNCB's encoding error meant FNCB had failed to return the Disputed Check prior to the midnight deadline as required by the UCC, and that FNCB was therefore accountable to NBT for the full amount of the Disputed Check. The parties stipulated to the facts and filed cross-motions for summary judgment.

The District Court granted FNCB's motion and denied NBT's motion. The District Court found that FNCB had returned the Disputed Check by the March 13 midnight deadline as required by [UCC §4-301], that FNCB's encoding error did not negate or nullify what otherwise constituted proper return as defined in §[4-301(d)], and that, in any event, NBT could not recover where it suffered no actual loss resulting from FNCB's conduct. The District Court reasoned that (1) the Reserve Bank was not a "clearinghouse" as that term is used in §[4-301(d)(1)], thus rendering that particular UCC provision inapplicable; (2) FNCB's encoding error did not negate FNCB's compliance with the UCC midnight deadline rule under §[4-301(d)(2)], which provides that an item is returned by a payor bank "when it is sent or delivered to the bank's customer or transferor [here, the Reserve Bank] or pursuant to his instructions"[;] and (3) NBT could not recover where it suffered no loss as a result of FNCB's conduct, and where, by operation of law, NBT and FNCB were parties to a binding agreement that incorporated federal regulations indicating that the measure of damages for a failure to exercise ordinary care in encoding was to be measured by the actual loss incurred. NBT appeals.

III.   DISCUSSION...

B.   PENNSYLVANIA UCC PROVISIONS GOVERNING CHECK-RETURN PROCEDURES

Article 4 of the UCC as adopted by Pennsylvania defines the rights between parties with respect to bank deposits and collections involving banks located in Pennsylvania. To the extent not preempted or superseded by federal law, Article 4 governs the process by which banks present checks for payment, settle on checks, and, if necessary, dishonor and return checks. NBT notes three interrelated UCC provisions that establish the circumstances under which a bank may return a dishonored check.

The first key provision is §[4-301]. Section [4-301(a)] provides that a bank may dishonor or return a check or other disputed item if, before the bank's midnight deadline, it either "(1) returns the item; or (2) sends written notice of dishonor or nonpayment if the item is unavailable for return." [UCC §4-301(a)(1)-(2)]. Section [4-301(d)] defines the ways in which a bank may "return" an item for purposes of compliance with §[4-301(a)(1)]. Section [4-301(d)] provides:

> **Acts constituting return of item.** — An item is returned:
> (1) as to an item presented through a clearinghouse, when it is delivered to the presenting or last collecting bank or to the clearinghouse or is sent or delivered in accordance with clearinghouse rules; or
> (2) in all other cases, when it is sent or delivered to the bank's customer or transferor or pursuant to his instructions.

[UCC §4-301(d)(1)-(2)]. . . .

The second key UCC provision with respect to a payor bank's attempt to dishonor a check is §[4-302]. . . . Section [4-302] . . . imposes strict accountability on a payor bank (subject to two enumerated defenses not relevant here) that fails to revoke its provisional settlement on a dishonored check prior to the midnight deadline.

The third UCC provision invoked by NBT is §[4-215], which addresses when a check is "finally paid." Upon "final payment" a provisional settlement by the payor bank becomes final, and the payor bank is accountable for the face amount of the check. Under §[4-215], a check "is finally paid by a payor bank when the bank has . . . made a provisional settlement for the item and fail[s] to revoke the settlement in the time and manner permitted by statute, clearinghouse rule or agreement." [UCC §4-214(a)(3)]. Official Comment 4 to §[4-215] states that "[a] primary example of a statutory right on the part of the payor bank to revoke a settlement is the right to revoke conferred by Section 4-301."

C. Regulation CC, Reserve Bank Operating Circulars, and Variation by Agreement

The Pennsylvania UCC provisions governing check-return procedures do not operate in a vacuum. Federal law forms part of the legal framework within which check-processing activities take place. Of particular relevance to this appeal are the 1988 regulations adopted by the Federal Reserve implementing the Expedited Funds Availability Act, 12 U.S.C. §§4001-4010. See 12 C.F.R. Pt. 229. These regulations, referred to collectively as "Regulation CC," complement but do not necessarily replace the requirements of Article 4 of the UCC. See 12 C.F.R. §229.41. . . . Regarding encoding, subpart C provides:

> A paying bank may convert a check to a qualified return check. A qualified returned check must be encoded in magnetic ink with the routing number of the depositary bank, the amount of the returned check, and a "2" in position 44 of the MICR [Magnetic Ink Character Recognition] line as a return identifier.

12 C.F.R. §229.30(a)(2)(iii).

Subpart C of Regulation CC also contains its own liability standard and its own remedy provision for a failure to comply with its requirements:

> A bank shall exercise ordinary care and act in good faith in complying with the requirements of this subpart [, which includes the encoding requirements referenced above]. A bank that fails to exercise ordinary care or act in good faith under this subpart may be liable to the depositary bank, the depositary bank's customer, the owner of a check, or another party to the check. The measure of damages for failure to exercise ordinary care is the amount of the loss incurred, up to the amount of the check, reduced by the amount of the loss that party would have incurred even if the bank had exercised ordinary care.

12 C.F.R. §229.38(a).

Along with Regulation CC, the Federal Reserve has adopted Operating Circulars utilized by Reserve Banks in connection with their check-processing services. Both Regulation CC and Federal Reserve Operating Circular No. 3 (which contains provisions relevant to this appeal), "apply to the handling of all cash items that [Reserve Banks] accept for collection and all returned checks that [Reserve Banks] accept for return." See Federal Reserve Op. Circ. No. 3 (Jan. 2, 1998), at 1, ¶ 1.1. . . .

Operating Circular No. 3 is not the original source of the encoding requirement at the center of this appeal, which instead is set forth in subpart C of Regulation CC, as noted above. However, Operating Circular No. 3 emphasizes that in handling a "qualified return check" the Reserve Bank may rely on the accuracy of "the identification of the depositary bank by routing number in magnetic ink." See Federal Reserve Op. Circ. No. 3, at 10, ¶ 15.6. Circular No. 3 further provides that the payor bank will indemnify the Reserve Bank for any loss or expense incurred by the Reserve Bank arising from an encoding error by the payor bank. *See id.* Circular No. 3 also notes that if for any reason a returned check is mistakenly forwarded by the Reserve Bank to the wrong depositary bank, the recipient should either send the returned check directly to the proper depositary bank or promptly return it to the Reserve Bank. See id. at 11, ¶ 15.12.

The Pennsylvania UCC also addresses the applicability of the federal regulatory provisions contained in Regulation CC and Operating Circular No. 3. Section [4-103(a)] of the UCC directs that the terms of the UCC may be varied by agreement, although parties cannot disclaim the duty to act in good faith and exercise ordinary care or limit the measure of damages for a failure to exercise ordinary care. Section [4-103(b)] states that "Federal Reserve regulations and operating circulars, clearinghouse rules and the like have the effect of agreements under subsection (a), whether or not specifically assented to by all parties interested in items handled." Section [4-103(c)] notes that a bank's compliance with Federal Reserve regulations and operating circulars constitutes prima facie evidence of the exercise of ordinary care.

In sum, under the UCC, the provisions of Regulation CC function as a binding agreement between the parties with respect to check-return transactions. This agreement supersedes any inconsistent provisions of the UCC itself, but only to the extent of the inconsistency. Similarly, the provisions of Operating Circular No. 3 are also binding on the parties in connection with the check-return activities at issue here. The rights and obligations granted and imposed by Operating Circular No. 3 overlap to a certain extent with the parties' rights and obligations under the UCC's statutory provisions and under Regulation CC. The provisions of Operating Circular No. 3 take precedence over any inconsistent portions of Regulation CC, but only to the extent of the inconsistency.

D.   Construing the UCC's Check-Return Provisions

NBT's claim raises a number of difficult questions of statutory construction under the UCC. An understanding of these issues aids in assessing the underlying theory of NBT's claim. Nonetheless, we ultimately conclude that even if these questions were to be resolved in NBT's favor, it would not change the outcome here. Thus, while our discussion may provide additional clarity concerning the issues implicated by NBT's appeal, we need not definitively resolve all the disputes between the parties concerning the construction of the UCC's check-return provisions.

As noted above, NBT invokes three interrelated UCC provisions governing the circumstances under which a bank may return a dishonored check. Section [4-301(d)] defines the acts that constitute "return" of an item. . . .

Under §[4-301(d)(1)], an item is deemed returned "when it is delivered . . . to the clearinghouse *or* is sent or delivered in accordance with clearinghouse rules." [UCC §4-301(d)(1)] (emphasis added). Under §[4-301(d)(2)], an item is returned "when it is sent or delivered to the bank's . . . transferor *or* pursuant to his instructions" (emphasis added). The phrasing of these sections is disjunctive, and here the parties agree that the Disputed Check was dispatched by FNCB on March 13, 2001, and was physically delivered to the Reserve Bank prior to the March 13 midnight deadline. Under one reading of §[4-301(d)], this would end the inquiry, because the Disputed Check was "delivered" to the clearinghouse or transferor prior to the midnight deadline. NBT challenges this reading, arguing that §[4-301(d)]'s references to simple delivery as constituting a valid "return" are relevant only where there are no applicable clearinghouse rules or transferor instructions that govern sending or delivery. NBT argues that only this construction gives effect to all the terms of §[4-301(d)], including the simple delivery option as well as delivery "in accordance with clearinghouse rules" or "pursuant to [transferor] instructions."

However, at least two other possible interpretations would give effect to §[4-301(d)]'s references to clearinghouse rules and transferor instructions while also maintaining the viability of the simple delivery option. First, the phrases "sent or delivered in accordance with clearinghouse rules" and "sent or delivered . . . pursuant to [transferor] instructions" could be read as referring to instances where a disputed item is to be returned to some address other than the clearinghouse or transferor from which it was initially received. Second, these phrases may also be meant to account for situations in which a payor bank attempts to deliver a disputed item to the clearinghouse or transferor, but through negligence of the clearinghouse or transferor the disputed item does not actually arrive at the proper location.

The multiple possible readings of §[4-301(d)] illustrate that even when the UCC's check-return provisions are considered in isolation from Regulation CC, NBT is not bound to recover on its claim for strict accountability. Similarly, even if NBT is correct in arguing that FNCB was obligated to comply with certain clearing house rules or transferor instructions in order to satisfy §[4-301(d)], it is not clear that the encoding requirement for returned checks is a rule that relates to "sending" or "delivery" under the UCC. . . . The UCC defines "delivery" as "voluntary transfer of possession." [UCC §1-201]. Even if the encoding requirement is a rule or instruction that FNCB was bound to follow, such a rule does not necessarily relate to the question of whether FNCB voluntarily transferred possession of the Disputed Check from itself to the Reserve Bank prior to the midnight deadline. Thus, FNCB's failure to comply with such a rule or instruction would not necessarily preclude a finding under §[4-301(d)] that FNCB returned the Disputed Check prior to the midnight deadline.

While the foregoing issues concerning the proper construction of the UCC's check-return provisions need not be definitively resolved, it is clear that NBT's interpretation poses numerous difficulties. We may nonetheless assume that if the UCC provisions are read in isolation from Regulation CC, FNCB was obligated to encode the Disputed Check correctly in order to effectively "return" it within the meaning of §[4-301(d)]. We may further assume that a failure to do so by FNCB would mean FNCB had not properly revoked its provisional settlement in a manner permitted under §[4-215]. This assumption would lead to the conclusion that under the UCC, the Disputed Check was "finally paid" by FNCB, thus rendering FNCB accountable to NBT for the full amount of the Disputed Check pursuant to §[4-302]. In the end, however, such assumptions do not change the result, because, as set forth in part III.E below, the UCC's check-return provisions do not operate in a vacuum. Even if NBT's interpretation of the UCC's check-return provisions is correct, Regulation CC and Operating Circular No. 3 preclude NBT from holding FNCB strictly accountable for the Disputed Check where NBT suffered no actual loss as a result of FNCB's encoding error.

E. THE DAMAGE LIMITATIONS INCLUDED IN REGULATION CC AND INCORPORATED IN OPERATING CIRCULAR NO. 3 PRECLUDE NBT FROM RECOVERING ON ITS UCC CLAIM

NBT argues that under §[4-301(d)] of the UCC, FNCB's encoding error effectively nullifies FNCB's efforts to "return" the Disputed Check. NBT contends that

Regulation CC's encoding requirement for qualified return checks is a clearinghouse rule or transferor instruction concerning the manner in which the Disputed Check was to be returned. NBT argues that FNCB's failure properly to comply with such a rule or instruction means that (1) FNCB did not revoke its provisional settlement in the "manner permitted by statute, clearinghouse rule or agreement[,]" as required by §[4-215]; and (2) the Disputed Check was not returned prior to the midnight deadline as required under §[4-301]. Thus, according to NBT, FNCB is strictly accountable for the full amount of the Disputed Check pursuant to §[4-302].

FNCB counters that, because *all* of Regulation CC is binding on the parties (pursuant to both Regulation CC's own terms, and as an "agreement" under §[4-103] of the UCC), NBT may not rely on FNCB's encoding error as a basis for recovering the amount of the Disputed Check. FNCB notes that Regulation CC specifies that damages for a bank's failure to exercise ordinary care in fulfilling its obligations under Regulation CC must be calculated based upon the actual loss caused by such failure. Implicit in FNCB's position is the concession that it failed to exercise ordinary care in encoding the Disputed Check. FNCB argues that, even if NBT's reading of the UCC is correct (a proposition FNCB disputes), Regulation CC has effectively amended §§[4-215], [4-301], and [4-302] of the UCC to preclude strict accountability where a payor bank's failure to return an item by the midnight deadline is based solely on the payor bank's noncompliance with an obligation imposed by Regulation CC. Instead, according to FNCB, where a payor bank's violation of a clearinghouse rule or transferor instruction arises solely from its failure to exercise ordinary care in executing its obligations under Regulation CC, Regulation CC's clause tying the measure of damages to a claimant's actual loss is incorporated into the UCC by operation of section [4-103]. FNCB contends this analysis precludes imposition of strict accountability in situations where, as here, the claimant seeking recovery concedes it suffered no loss as a result of the payor bank's actions.

We believe the District Court's analysis of this issue, which is largely consistent with FNCB's position, is correct. Regulation CC indisputably binds the parties, pursuant to both its own terms, see 12 C.F.R. §229.1(b)(3), as well as §[4-103] of the UCC, which indicates that "Federal Reserve regulations" are to be treated as agreements that may vary the terms of the UCC, see UCC §[4-103](a)-(b). Such agreements are binding "whether or not specifically assented to by all parties interested in items handled." UCC §[4-103](b). . . . .

Because Regulation CC *as a whole* is binding on the parties, and because Regulation CC is the source of the encoding requirement invoked by NBT, the extent of FNCB's liability for its encoding error must be measured by the standards set forth in Regulation CC. Regulation CC states that a bank that fails to exercise ordinary care in complying with the provisions of subpart C of Regulation CC (which includes the encoding requirement referenced above) "may be liable" to the depositary bank. Then, in broad, unrestricted language, Regulation CC states:

> The measure of damages for failure to exercise ordinary care is the amount of the loss incurred, up to the amount of the check, reduced by the amount of the loss that the [plaintiff bank] would have incurred even if the [defendant] bank had exercised ordinary care.

12 C.F.R. §229.38(a). This provision does not provide an exception to this standard for measuring damages in instances where noncompliance with Regulation CC is alleged to have resulted in noncompliance with the UCC's midnight deadline rule. Here, the parties have stipulated that NBT suffered no loss as a result of FNCB's encoding error. Thus, under the plain language of Regulation CC, NBT may not recover from FNCB for the amount of the Disputed Check.

This analysis is reinforced by Appendix E to Regulation CC, which contains the Federal Reserve Board's commentary interpreting the provisions of Regulation CC and providing examples "to aid in understanding how a particular requirement is to work." 12 C.F.R. Part 229, App. E, §I, A, 1. Appendix E states:

> Generally, under the standard of care imposed by §229.38, a paying or returning bank would be liable for *any damages incurred due to misencoding of the routing number*, the amount of the check, or return identifier on a qualified return check. . . . A qualified return check that contains an encoding error would still be a qualified return check for purposes of the regulation.

Id. at §II, BB, 2 (emphasis added). This Reserve Board commentary is significant, because as noted above, both Regulation CC and the UCC indicate that Regulation CC's provisions are binding on the parties, and that Regulation CC's provisions supersede any inconsistent provisions of the UCC. The fact that Appendix E specifically contemplates the possibility that a payor bank could encode a returned check with the wrong routing number, and yet states that the remedy for such an error is to be calculated based upon the damages caused by the error, strongly indicates that encoding errors do not give rise to strict accountability for a payor bank.

Notably, Appendix E also states that a wrongly encoded check is still considered a qualified return check. This statement illustrates that there is a distinction between whether a check has been properly encoded and whether a check has been properly returned. NBT's attempt to incorporate the proper encoding of a routing number as an essential element in determining whether a check has been "returned" under §[4-301] of the UCC is contrary to the approach required under Regulation CC. Thus, FNCB's encoding error, while constituting a violation of Regulation CC's encoding requirements, does not provide an adequate basis for imposing strict accountability on FNCB pursuant to the UCC's midnight deadline provisions.

NBT offers two reasons why it believes it should recover the full amount of the Disputed Check notwithstanding the measure of damages specified in Regulation CC. We find that these arguments lack merit. NBT's primary argument challenges the applicability of the Regulation CC provision concerning calculation of damages based upon actual loss. NBT believes this provision has no relevance because NBT's claim is brought under the UCC rather than under Regulation CC. NBT states, "[w]hether or not [FNCB] would have been liable on a claim under Regulation CC is wholly irrelevant to the issue presented here. The issue here is whether [FNCB] is accountable under the UCC[.]"

There are several problems with NBT's attempt to draw a sharp distinction between a claim "under the UCC" and a claim covered by Regulation CC. It is obvious that NBT's UCC claim is at least partially dependent on Regulation CC, in that Regulation CC is the source of the encoding requirement that directs a payor bank to include the routing number of the depositary bank in magnetic ink on all qualified return checks. Indeed, to the extent the UCC itself addresses encoding, it specifically provides that the measure of damages for an encoding error is the actual loss incurred by the claimant. See UCC §[4-209(a), (c)]. NBT's position also overlooks the fact that, pursuant to §[4-103] of the UCC, *all* of Regulation CC is binding on the parties. Moreover, to the extent there is a conflict between Regulation CC's broadly worded "actual loss" remedy and the provisions of the UCC that create a strict accountability regime with respect to the midnight deadline rule, such a conflict must be resolved in favor of Regulation CC. Support for this result flows from subpart C of Regulation CC itself, which states that "the provisions of this subpart supersede any inconsistent provisions of the UCC as adopted in any state. . . ." See 12 C.F.R. §229.41. This result is also supported by §[4-103] of the UCC, which, as set forth above, indicates that Federal Reserve regulations are binding on all parties operating under the UCC and that such regulations are considered "agreements" that may vary the effect of the UCC's provisions. In sum, where NBT's claim is dependent upon FNCB's noncompliance with the encoding requirements imposed by Regulation CC, NBT cannot render the Regulation CC damages clause inapplicable merely by characterizing its claim as an effort to hold FNCB accountable under the UCC.

NBT offers a second argument in support of its view that Regulation CC's ordinary care liability standard and "actual loss" remedy provision do not alter the UCC's regime of strict accountability for noncompliance with the midnight deadline rule in the circumstances presented here. NBT asserts that §[4-301](d) of the UCC requires a payor bank to comply with clearinghouse rules or transferor instructions in order effectively to return an item prior to the midnight deadline. NBT points out that the rules or instructions governing the Reserve Bank's check-processing services are contained in Federal Reserve Operating Circular No. 3. NBT argues that Operating Circular No. 3's references to encoding requirements, when read in conjunction with §[4-301] of the UCC, create an independent obligation on the part of FNCB to encode the Disputed Check with the correct routing number, and that FNCB's failure to do so means that the Disputed Check was not "returned" within the meaning of the midnight deadline rule.

While NBT correctly states that Operating Circular No. 3 binds the parties, NBT incorrectly asserts that the Circular's references to encoding requirements somehow negate Regulation CC's requirement that damages be measured with reference to actual loss. Operating Circular No. 3 does not contain an independent encoding requirement. Instead, it incorporates subpart C of Regulation CC *in its entirety*, including both the encoding requirement as well as ordinary care liability standard and the remedy provision stating that the measure of damages for failure to comply with subpart C of Regulation CC is to be measured by the claimant's actual loss. See Fed. Reserve Op. Circ. No. 3, at 1, ¶ 1.1. While Operating Circular No. 3 does state that its own provisions supersede any inconsistent provisions of the UCC and Regulation CC, nothing in Operating Circular No. 3 contradicts or is inconsistent with the Regulation CC provision calling for measurement of damages based upon actual loss. Nor does Operating Circular No. 3 impose an encoding requirement separate or apart from its incorporation of the encoding provisions of Regulation CC. The Circular's references to encoding simply emphasize that Reserve Banks retain the right to rely on the routing number encoded on a qualified return check, while stating that a payor bank that erroneously encodes a routing number agrees to indemnify the Reserve Bank for any loss suffered as a result of the error. See id. at 10, ¶ 15.6.

These encoding references in Operating Circular No. 3 do not impose a separate encoding obligation apart from the encoding requirement imposed by Regulation CC, and they in no way alter or conflict with Operating Circular No. 3's incorporation of the Regulation CC provision requiring that damages resulting from noncompliance be measured with reference to the claimant's actual loss. Thus, to the extent Regulation CC's encoding requirement is deemed a "clearinghouse rule" or "transferor instruction" by virtue of its incorporation into Operating Circular No. 3, it is a rule or instruction with a specific remedy attached. Moreover, to the extent that this remedy (damages based upon actual loss) conflicts with the strict accountability remedy available under the UCC's check-return provisions, the conflict must be resolved in favor of the former. As discussed above, this result is dictated by Operating Circular No. 3, which states that the Circular's provisions supersede any inconsistent provisions of the UCC. See id. at 1, ¶ 1.1. This result is also supported by the UCC itself, which provides that clearinghouse rules are binding on the parties involved in a checking transaction, and that such a binding agreement may vary the UCC so long as it does not purport to disclaim a bank's obligation to act in good faith and exercise ordinary care. See 13 Pa. Cons.Stat. Ann. §[4-103](a)-(b).

IV. CONCLUSION

NBT has consistently emphasized that it seeks recovery pursuant to §§[4-215], [4-301], and [4-302] of the UCC. The UCC itself directs that its provisions, including those that create a strict accountability regime in connection with the midnight deadline rule, may be altered by agreement. The UCC also provides that Federal Reserve regulations and operating circulars are by operation of law deemed binding agreements governing all parties subject to Article 4 of the UCC. The encoding requirements invoked by NBT are found in subpart C of Regulation CC. Subpart C indicates that compliance with its provisions is to be measured by a standard of ordinary care. Subpart C also states that the measure of damages for a failure to exercise ordinary care in complying with its requirements is the actual loss a claimant suffers as a result of such failure.

In the present case, the parties stipulated that NBT did not suffer any actual damages as a result of FNCB's encoding error. The parties are bound by Regulation CC in its entirety, including its remedy provision, which supersedes any inconsistent provisions of the UCC. NBT thus may not invoke §§[4-215], [4-301], and [4-302] of the UCC to require that FNCB be held strictly accountable for the Disputed Check based upon FNCB's failure to comply with Regulation CC's encoding requirement.

The fact that the parties are also bound by Federal Reserve Operating Circular No. 3 does not change the result. To the extent Operating Circular No. 3 incorporates the encoding requirement of Regulation CC, it also incorporates Regulation CC's liability standard and remedy provision. As with Regulation CC, the provisions of Operating Circular No. 3 by operation of law form an agreement that binds the parties and that varies any inconsistent UCC provisions. NBT's attempt to invoke UCC provisions that create strict accountability in connection with the midnight deadline rule fails to acknowledge that, in this case, these provisions have been effectively amended by Operating Circular No. 3's incorporation of Regulation CC's "actual loss" remedy provision.

Accordingly, because the facts are not in dispute, and because NBT's claim fails as a matter of law, we affirm the order of the District Court granting summary judgment in favor of FNCB.

Problem Set 23

23.1. One Tuesday morning Tertius Lydgate (from Problem Set 21) calls with a complaint about Bulstrode's treatment of a $1,000 check that Lydgate deposited into his bank account on the preceding Monday afternoon. The check was drawn on an account at a branch of Bulstrode located in New Haven, Connecticut. Lydgate deposited the check into a branch of Bulstrode in Boston, Massachusetts, at about 3 P.M. Lydgate tells you that a sign on the counter indicated that items received after 2 P.M. would be treated as received the next day, but doesn't see why that matters. "After all, either they got it Monday or they didn't, right?" The Boston branch apparently gave Lydgate a provisional settlement for the check immediately and forwarded the check to the New Haven branch on Wednesday morning. The New Haven branch dishonored the check on Thursday afternoon, returning the check to the Boston branch by a courier that arrived back at the Boston branch before midnight on Thursday. On Friday, the bank called Lydgate to advise him that it was revoking the provisional settlement and removing the funds from his account. Muttering something about "midnight deadlines," Lydgate wants to know if Bulstrode acted promptly enough for its dishonor to be effective. UCC §§4-104(a)(10) & comment 9, 4-107 & comment 4, 4-108 & comment 1, 4-215(a)(3) & comment 4, 4-301(a) & comment 2, 4-302(a); Regulation CC, §229.30(a).

23.2. Late one Thursday afternoon Ben Darrow (your friend from Problem Sets 21 and 22) calls you frantically and wants to know what he should do about a bad check his bank (FSB) received this morning. Bud Lassen came in first thing this morning and deposited a $10,000 check written by Carol Long. When Bud deposited the check, Carol's account contained only $100. Accordingly, the check was sent to Darrow for action. Darrow promptly placed a hold on the funds in Bud's account and placed a telephone call to Carol to see whether Carol would deposit funds to cover the check.

   a. Later in the morning, Bud came back down to the bank and attempted to cash a check for the total balance in his account ($12,000, including the funds from Carol's check). Because Darrow had placed a hold on the funds, the teller refused to cash the check. Early in the afternoon, Darrow learned that Carol had left town indefinitely to work on a construction project several hundred miles away. Accordingly, Darrow doubts that he will be able to get funds from Carol to cover the check. What should Darrow do? UCC §§4-214(c), 4-215(a), 4-301(a) & (b), 4-301 comment 4.

b. Assume instead that the bank allowed Bud to cash Carol's check when he first presented that check in the morning. Where would that leave the bank? UCC §§4-215(a)(1), 4-301(a).

c. Finally, assume that Darrow neglected to place a hold on the funds, perhaps because he thought that the bank's computerized check-processing system would do that automatically. As a result, the teller readily cashed Bud's check when Bud returned late in the morning. Now what is the bank's situation? UCC §§4-214(c), 4-301(a) & (b), 4-301 comment 4.

23.3. Recall the facts of *First National Bank v. Colonial Bank* case from Assignment 22: Shelly is running a check-kiting scheme through First National Bank (FNB) and Colonial Bank. On Tuesday February 11, First National presents $1.5 million of checks to Colonial for payment. The checks had been deposited at FNB and drawn on one of the accounts of a Shelly entity at Colonial. Although Colonial is concerned about the possibility that something is amiss, Colonial does not dishonor the checks on Tuesday or Wednesday, largely because an officer at Shelly's company assures the Colonial loan officer that everything is fine. Thursday morning, however, Colonial discovers the seriousness of Shelly's misconduct and attempts to dishonor the checks at that time.

Colonial lost the case because it had delayed its return of the checks past midnight Wednesday. If you had been called in by Colonial early Thursday morning, could you have suggested anything that might have helped its chances? UCC §§4-104(a)(10), 4-215(a)(3), 4-301(a), 4-302(a); Regulation CC, §229.30(c)(1).

23.4. The day after you handle Problem 23.2, Ben Darrow calls you back with another question, this one related to Carol's account. Carol deposited a $2,500 check from Jasmine Ball on Monday September 9. The check was drawn on Ball's account at TownBank in Los Angeles. FSB gave Carol a provisional credit for the Ball check on the date that Carol deposited that check and forwarded the check for collection through the Federal Reserve bank in Dallas. Under ordinary conditions, that would get the check to TownBank late Tuesday night (during Townbank's Wednesday banking day). At 3:00 P.M. on Friday afternoon, September 13, FSB received an electronic notice of nonpayment from TownBank, indicating that it was bouncing the check because Ball's account had insufficient funds to cover it. FSB responded by immediately charging the $2,500 back to Carol's account and mailing Carol a notice that it had removed the funds from Carol's account because Ball's check had bounced.

On Monday morning (September 16), a check in the amount of $2,000 was presented against Carol's account. Because of the charge-back on the Ball check Carol had deposited, FSB dishonored the $2,000 check. On the morning of September 18, FSB received the Ball check from TownBank by regular mail in an envelope bearing a Monday postmark. Reviewing Carol's account in connection with the Lassen transaction discussed in Problem 23.2, Darrow became concerned that the bank might have acted improperly in dishonoring Carol's $2,000 check. What do you say? Did TownBank meet the midnight deadline of Article 4? The return and notice requirements of Regulation CC?

Is there anything else you need to ask Darrow? UCC §§1-201(38) (revised §1-201(b) (36)), 4-214(a), 4-215(a), 4-215(d), 4-301(a), (d)(2); Regulation CC, §§229.30(a)(1), 229.33(a), 229.34(b) & (d), 229.38.

23.5.   Same facts as Problem 23.4, except that the postmark on the envelope with the Ball check was Friday rather than Monday.

23.6.   Having dealt with all of Ben Darrow's problems, you come back in the office on Friday morning to find an urgent phone message from Jodi Kay at CountryBank. When you call her back, Jodi tells you that she has a large problem with a long-time customer named Carl Eben. Carl wrote a check for $10.37 to purchase some materials at Deuce Hardware. Deuce's sales terminal mistakenly imprinted a MICR line indicating that the check was for $1,037,000.00. When Deuce deposited the check in its account at Hunt Bank, Hunt did not examine the check manually, but instead blindly deposited the million dollars to Deuce's account and forwarded the check to CountryBank. Because Jodi had authorized complete overdraft protection for Carl's account, CountryBank paid the million dollars to Hunt Bank and charged Carl's account; the computer generated and mailed an overdraft notice to Carl. Carl called Jodi to object this morning when he got the notice. When Jodi called Hunt to complain, Hunt pointed out that the mistake was made by Deuce, not Hunt. Jodi asks you what she should do. UCC §4-209(a), (c); Regulation CC, §229.34(c)(3).

23.7.   At the end of your conversation, Jodi mentions in passing a recent incident that caused a problem at the bank. The local clearinghouse has a rule that checks presented to a clearinghouse member by the clearinghouse before 11 P.M. become final at 12 noon the next banking day. A problem occurred because one of her bankers became stuck in traffic one morning. Unbeknownst to the banker, several notices were on his computer regarding checks written by his customers against insufficient funds. When he arrived at 12:30 in the afternoon, it was too late for him to act on the checks. The bank's system proceeded to honor the checks. The bank was unable to collect the funds from the drawers of the checks and thus took a loss on the incident. Jodi wants to know what you think about the rule. She knows that the bank has a representative on the drafting committee for clearinghouse rules and wants to send a memorandum to that representative proposing that the bank have the deadline pushed back until later in the afternoon. (Jodi proposes 6 P.M.) Can you think of any reason why such a change might trouble the bank? If that change won't work, can you think of anything else she could do to prevent that problem from occurring in the future? UCC §§4-104(a)(10), 4-215(a)(3) & comment 7, 4-301(a) & comment 2; Regulation CC, §§229.10(c)(vii), 229.12(b).

Assignment 24: Risk of Loss in the Checking System — The Basic Framework

Any functioning payment system will produce losses, either because of errors in the process of completing transactions or because of misconduct connected with the transactions. Although the first three assignments in this book have said little about those losses, the checking system is by no means immune from that problem. In fact, the checking system includes a detailed, two-tier framework that addresses those issues. The first tier (the topic of this assignment) is a basic framework that distributes losses based on generalized assumptions about the relative abilities of the parties to prevent certain types of losses. The second tier (discussed in Assignment 25) consists of several situation-specific exceptions to the general first-tier rules.

The first tier of the framework relies on two major legal theories to distribute losses, indorsement liability and warranty liability. This assignment uses those theories to describe the basic rules for distributing losses in three situations: nonpayment, forgery, and alteration.

A. Nonpayment

Losses from nonpayment are the simplest place to start. Two fundamental elements of the checking system make those losses relatively common: the payee's inability to know when it takes a check whether the payor bank will honor it, and the relatively long delay between the time that the payee accepts the check and the time that the payee finds out whether the check will be honored. Indorser liability under UCC §3-415 is the principal statutory mechanism for allocating these losses. To understand that concept, it is necessary to work through a few of the UCC's rules regarding indorsements.

The basic role of indorsement in the checking system is to provide a simple method for transferring checks. A check starts out being payable to the payee to whom the drawer issues it. If the payee wants to transfer the check (perhaps to the bank where it has a bank account, perhaps to a check-cashing business of some kind, perhaps to a friend), the simplest way to proceed is to indorse the check to the party acquiring it. The payee could sell the check without indorsing it (just as the payee could sell any other type of personal property), but under principles of negotiability discussed in Assignment 41 the transferee acquires greater rights in the check if the transferee acquires the check by indorsement. Thus, most transfers of checks are made with indorsements.

The indorsement itself need be nothing more than a signature by the person selling the check. UCC §3-204. That type of signature-only indorsement — a "blank" indorsement for purposes of Article 3 — has the legal effect of making the check "bearer paper," so that any party that subsequently is in possession of the check (even a thief) would be entitled to enforce it. UCC §3-205(b). If the indorser wants to make the paper payable to a particular person (such as the person cashing the check), it would add a statement identifying that person ("Pay to Otto's Check-Cashing Outlet") above the signature. That would be a "special" indorsement, which would make the check "order paper." Order paper, unlike bearer paper, can be enforced only by the identified party (Otto's Check-Cashing Outlet in the example). UCC §3-205(a). The payee also might wish to indorse the check "for deposit only" or "for collection." Those are "restrictive indorsements," which restrict the right of later parties to transfer the check except in accordance with the indorsement. UCC §3-206.

Indorsement, however, does more than confer a right to enforce an instrument. It is important in this assignment because it carries with it a form of liability that shifts the loss that arises when a payor bank refuses to pay a check. Under UCC §3-415, each party that indorses a check makes an implied contract with subsequent parties that acquire the check. [Technically, the warranty runs only to a "person entitled to enforce the instrument," a technical term discussed in detail in Chapter 11. For now, it is enough to know that it excludes parties that acquire the check by theft or similar misconduct.] That contract obligates the indorser to pay the check if the payor bank dishonors it. Because each party that indorses the check is liable on its indorsement and because each party's liability runs to all subsequent owners of the check, the rule results in a chain of liability under which each party can pass a dishonored check back up the chain to the last person in the chain (the earliest indorser) that is able to pay. Although the rule's chain of responsibility appears convoluted at first, the result is sensible: It leaves the loss with the party that made the imprudent decision to purchase the check from an insolvent entity (presumably the payee). The underlying principle is simple: Be careful when you purchase financial instruments from parties of questionable financial strength.

To see how the rule works, consider the following example. A drawer writes a hot check on an account at SecondBank and gives it to an insolvent payee. The payee then indorses the check and cashes it at Otto's, which in turn cashes the check at FirstBank. FirstBank presents the check to SecondBank without indorsing it. No indorsement is necessary for the transaction between FirstBank and SecondBank because that transaction does not involve a transfer of the instrument from one party to another; it is a request from one party (the owner of the check) for payment from another party (in this case the drawee or payor bank). Now suppose that SecondBank dishonors the check and returns it to FirstBank. As Figure 24.1 indicates, UCC §3-415's indorser-liability rule entitles FirstBank (the depositary bank) to pursue either Otto (the check casher) or the payee. If FirstBank chooses to pursue the check casher, the check casher would, in turn, be entitled to pursue the payee. Because the payee is insolvent, the loss eventually is borne by Otto (the one that dealt with the insolvent payee).

The fact that Otto is liable does not suggest that the drawer is free from responsibility. In addition to the indorser-liability rule in UCC §3-415, Article 3 also imposes liability on the drawer of the check. See UCC §3-414(b). If the check has been dishonored, however, there is a considerable likelihood that the check will not be paid: People whose checks are dishonored often are insolvent. Accordingly, in many cases, Otto's liability on the indorsement will result in Otto bearing the loss when a check is dishonored, in the sense

Figure 24.1
Indorser Liability

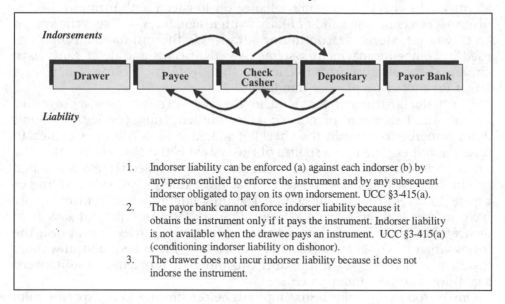

Indorsements

| Drawer | Payee | Check Casher | Depositary | Payor Bank |

Liability

1. Indorser liability can be enforced (a) against each indorser (b) by any person entitled to enforce the instrument and by any subsequent indorser obligated to pay on its own indorsement. UCC §3-415(a).
2. The payor bank cannot enforce indorser liability because it obtains the instrument only if it pays the instrument. Indorser liability is not available when the drawee pays an instrument. UCC §3-415(a) (conditioning indorser liability on dishonor).
3. The drawer does not incur indorser liability because it does not indorse the instrument.

that Otto pays the payee for the check but cannot recover from the drawer, the payee, or the payor bank.

Recognizing that an indorser's chances of collecting from a drawer diminish rapidly as time passes from the date that the drawer issued the check, the UCC includes two rules that protect the indorser from liability on stale obligations. First, the indorser's liability is conditioned on the check's being deposited or presented within 30 days of the indorsement. Thus, if the transferee does not process the check within 30 days, the indorser has no liability. UCC §3-415(e). Second, UCC §3-415(c) requires any person seeking to enforce a claim of liability on an indorsement to give prompt notice of dishonor to the indorser. If the person giving the notice is a collecting bank (which includes not only the depositary bank, but also any intermediary banks, see UCC §4-105(5)), it must give the notice by midnight of the banking day after it learns of the dishonor. In all other cases, the notice must come within 30 days. UCC §3-503(c).

The last important point about indorser liability is that it is not mandatory. Indorsement liability is only an implied contract. The UCC provides an easy mechanism for an indorser to disclaim indorser liability if the indorser does not wish to accept that responsibility. All the indorser must do to disclaim the liability is to add the phrase "without recourse" to the indorsement. If an indorsement is made "without recourse," subsequent owners of the check cannot sue the indorser even if the check is dishonored. UCC §3-415(b).

B. Forged Signatures

Another issue that all payment systems must confront is the problem of forgery. In the checking system, that problem has staggering proportions: An industry survey suggests that losses from fraud in 1997 amounted to more than $500 million. The reason for the high incidence of fraud is not hard to identify. The checking system's reliance on low-tech authorization mechanisms— pieces of paper and ordinary written signatures— leaves the system an easy target. Moreover, continuing advances in the anti-fraud mechanisms used in competing payment systems like credit cards and debit cards have enhanced the relative attractiveness of the low-tech checking system as a target for those who practice fraud.

The major instrument for fraud in the checking system is a forged or unauthorized signature of one kind or another. Thus, the legal system's main response to fraud in the checking system is to devise rules related to false signatures. The first response of the system is the obvious one that the unauthorized signer— the thief— should be responsible for all losses caused by the forgery. It is likely, however, that most thieves will be unwilling or unable to accept that responsibility: The thief might be insolvent or simply have moved without leaving a forwarding address. The difficult task is to devise rules to determine who among the innocent parties should bear the losses when the thief is unavailable. To see how the system allocates those losses, it is necessary to distinguish two different problems: false drawers' signatures and false indorsements.

One introductory point bears emphasis before turning to the specific rules for those problems. Much of the discussion for the rest of this assignment proceeds on the assumption that none of the parties is negligent and that no special circumstances justify a departure from the basic rules. As Assignment 25 explains, in many cases negligence or other circumstances *do* justify a departure from the basic rules set out in this assignment. Accordingly, while studying the materials in this assignment, you should consider the possibility that a result that appears inappropriate at first glance might be altered by one of the special rules discussed in Assignment 25.

1.   *Forged Drawers' Signatures and the Rule of* Price v. Neal

Turning to the specific rules, the first problem arises when a check is a complete forgery, not even signed by the purported drawer. For example, a thief might steal someone's checkbook and successfully purchase goods and services with checks written from the stolen checkbook. Alternatively, the forger might obtain a single valid check and use copying or printing equipment to fabricate a convincing duplicate check. In either case, the allocation of losses from that kind of forgery depends on whether the payor bank (a) is duped into paying the check or (b) notices the forgery and dishonors the check.

(a) *What If the Payor Bank Pays the Forged Check?*   A time-honored rule, dating to the famous eighteenth-century case of Price v. Neal, 97 Eng. Rep. 871 (K.B. 1762) (per Mansfield, C.J.), holds that a payor bank bears the loss if it fails to notice the forgery and honors the check. From the modern statutory perspective, the result follows from the idea that the check was not properly payable from the account of the purported drawer because that person did not authorize the check. Thus, the payor bank had no right to charge the drawer's account. UCC §4-401(a) & comment 1. The UCC does, though, set out two statutory exceptions that allow the payor bank in limited circumstances to shift that loss back to some earlier party in the collection process.

First, UCC §3-418(a)(ii) allows the payor bank to seek recovery from "the person to whom or for whose benefit payment was made." That provision does not apply, however, against a person that took the instrument "in good faith and for value." UCC §3-418(c). Thus, if the depositary bank (the person to whom the payor bank made payment) took the check from the forger knowing that the check was a forgery, the payor bank could recover from the depositary bank under UCC §3-418. But in the ordinary case the payor bank will not be able to prove bad faith or failure to pay value on the part of any of the parties involved in collection of the check. Accordingly, in that situation, the payor bank's remedy will be limited to the forger. Given the likelihood that the forger will be insolvent or unavailable, that framework tends to leave the loss on the payor bank.

The payor bank also could claim that some earlier party in the chain of collection breached a presentment warranty. UCC §4-208 creates a series of implied presentment warranties in favor of the payor bank. If any of those warranties is false, the payor bank (as illustrated in Figure 24.2) can recover from the party that presented the check to the payor bank or from any previous transferor in the chain of collection of the check. [I defer to Chapter 11, a more detailed discussion of what it means to be a "transferor" for purposes of those warranties.] The last of those warranties (set forth in UCC §4-208(a)(3)) imposes warranty liability if the transferor had "knowledge" that the signature of the drawer was unauthorized. Unfortunately for the payor bank, however, the statute requires "knowledge," rather than mere "notice." That means that the payor bank will be able to recover on this warranty only if some party took the check with actual knowledge that the check was unauthorized. See UCC §1-201(25) (revised §1-202) (distinguishing between "knowledge" and "notice"). Again, in the absence of some conspiracy between the forger and a solvent party, no solvent party will breach this warranty. Thus, like UCC §3-418, the presentment warranty ordinarily leaves that type of loss with the payor bank. The case that follows shows how those provisions work in practice.

Decibel Credit Union v. Pueblo Bank & Trust Company

996 P.2d 784 (Colo. App. 2000)

Opinion by Judge RULAND.

This case requires us to address which party must bear the loss for amounts paid on forged checks. Defendant, Pueblo Bank & Trust Company, appeals from the summary judgment awarded to plaintiff, Decibel Credit Union. We reverse and remand the case for further proceedings.

A thief stole blank checks furnished by Decibel to one of its checking account customers. During a period of approximately 40 days, the thief forged the signature of the customer on a series of 14 checks totaling $2,350. Each of the checks was cashed at Pueblo Bank where the thief had a bank account.

On some of the days during the 40-day period, the thief cashed more than one check per day. At no time during this period did either the thief's checking account

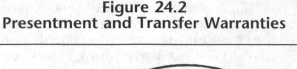

Figure 24.2
Presentment and Transfer Warranties

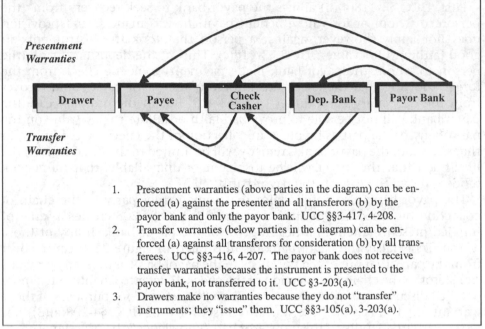

Presentment Warranties

| Drawer | Payee | Check Casher | Dep. Bank | Payor Bank |

Transfer Warranties

1. Presentment warranties (above parties in the diagram) can be enforced (a) against the presenter and all transferors (b) by the payor bank and only the payor bank. UCC §§3-417, 4-208.
2. Transfer warranties (below parties in the diagram) can be enforced (a) against all transferors for consideration (b) by all transferees. UCC §§3-416, 4-207. The payor bank does not receive transfer warranties because the instrument is presented to the payor bank, not transferred to it. UCC §3-203(a).
3. Drawers make no warranties because they do not "transfer" instruments; they "issue" them. UCC §§3-105(a), 3-203(a).

or his ready reserve account have sufficient funds to cover the checks that were being cashed.

Pueblo Bank processed all 14 checks through the Federal Reserve System to Decibel, and Decibel timely paid the checks. Decibel's customer discovered the forgeries when he received his bank statement. The customer immediately notified Decibel. Decibel then made demand upon Pueblo Bank for reimbursement. Pueblo Bank declined, and this litigation followed.

After the complaint was filed, both parties filed motions for summary judgment. Based upon those submissions, the trial court entered judgment for Decibel.

First, the trial court concluded that Decibel had given timely notice to Pueblo Bank as soon as the forgery was discovered by its account holder. Next, the trial court determined that in submitting the checks to Decibel for payment, Pueblo Bank had triggered its responsibility under the Colorado version of the Uniform Commercial Code for both presentment and transfer warranties. The court finally determined that a breach of these warranties had occurred and that Decibel was entitled to reimbursement. This appeal followed.

I.

For purposes of the Colorado Uniform Commercial Code, Decibel was the "drawee" bank in these transactions. See [UCC §3-103(2).] Pueblo Bank was the "presenting bank." See [UCC §4-105(6)]....

The parties also agree on most of the legal principles from the Uniform Commercial Code that apply. Generally, a drawee bank is liable to its checking account customer for payment of a check on which the customer's signature has been forged. Further, when the drawee bank honors the forged instrument, the payment is deemed final for a person who or an entity which takes the instrument in good faith and for value. . . .

II.

Pueblo Bank asserts that under the circumstances of this case, there were no presentment or transfer warranties made to Decibel and that the trial court erred in ruling to the contrary. We agree.

A.

Presentment warranties in the Colorado version of the Uniform Commercial Code appear in [UCC §4-208], as follows:

> (a) If an unaccepted draft is presented to the drawee for payment or acceptance and the drawee pays or accepts the draft, (i) the person obtaining payment or acceptance, at the time of presentment . . . warrant[s] to the drawee that pays or accepts the draft in good faith that:
>> (1) The warrantor is, or was, at the time the warrantor transferred the draft, a person entitled to enforce the draft . . . ;
>> (2) The draft has not been altered; and
>> (3) The warrantor has no knowledge that the signature of the purported drawer of the draft is unauthorized.

As noted in the Official Comment to a similar section, [UCC §3-417], the warranty in subsection (a)(1) is only a warranty that there are no unauthorized or missing *endorsements* on the checks. [ED.: See UCC §3-417 comment 2.] Further, subsection (a)(2) does not apply because there was no alteration to the checks. Finally, there is no claim that Pueblo Bank had actual knowledge of the forged signatures, and thus subsection (a)(3) does not apply.

Indeed, . . . if the warranty that all signatures were genuine applied to a bank in the position of Pueblo Bank, the final payment doctrine contained in [UCC §3-418] would be meaningless. [ED.: The court apparently refers to the rule in UCC §3-418(c), which prevents a payor bank from recovering under UCC §3-418 from parties that "took the instrument in good faith and for value."] This doctrine is of great importance in banking commerce because it creates certainty relative to which institution must bear the loss and thus avoids time consuming and expensive litigation.

Accordingly, we hold that Pueblo Bank did not extend any presentment warranty to Decibel by [processing] the checks . . . through the Federal Reserve System. Hence, the trial court erred in concluding that presentment warranties applied for the benefit of Decibel under the circumstances of this case.

B.

[The court summarily rejected Decibel's claim based on transfer warranties.]

III.

In support of the judgment, Decibel emphasizes the trial court's determination that Pueblo Bank acted without diligence in cashing the checks because the thief's accounts did not have sufficient funds to cover each of the items. Decibel views this determination as a finding that Pueblo Bank acted in bad faith, and it reasons that, therefore, Pueblo Bank may not rely upon the final payment rule [under UCC §3-418(c)]. We conclude that additional proceedings are required to resolve those issues.

Generally, a court may not resolve issues pertaining to a party's good faith or lack thereof on summary judgment because this decision requires an evaluation of a party's subjective intent.

Further, Decibel has failed to cite any legal authority, and we find none, for the proposition that cashing the checks under the circumstances here, standing alone, is sufficient to establish bad faith on the part of Pueblo Bank. Hence, we conclude that these issues must be resolved by a trial on the merits as disputed issues of fact.

[The court rejected Decibel's effort to raise a claim under UCC §3-406 for the first time on appeal. Assignment 25 discusses that issue in considerable detail.]

The judgment is reversed, and the cause is remanded for further proceedings consistent with the views expressed in this opinion.

Although those rules inevitably cause payor banks to lose money on transactions in which they were not involved in the fraud, it often makes some sense to allocate that risk to the payor bank because the payor bank's preexisting relationship with the drawer can give it a greater ability to prevent those losses than any other party in the collection chain.

To be sure, it is impractical for the payor bank to examine checks on a case-by-case basis to detect forgeries, which gives even the most primitive forgeries a substantial chance of success (recall the item at issue in Figure 23.5). Moreover, many forgeries would go undetected even if the payor bank did examine each check by hand. For example, one of the most common current methods of fraud develops utterly bogus checks from a single legitimate check. Consider a fraud-minded individual that receives a refund check from Sears. With existing desktop publishing software and color copiers, it would not be challenging for the individual to produce a replica of that check, including the facsimile signature, that would pass a cursory visual inspection. It is only marginally more difficult to encode the MICR line at the bottom of the check so that the check passes through the system and is honored without incident. If the checks are written in relatively small amounts, to a number of different payees, and deposited in differing accounts, visual inspection of the checks by Sears's bank is unlikely to catch the forgeries.

But visual inspection is not the only way to catch forgery. The payor bank's relationship with the drawer gives it considerable ability to prevent losses through the development of systems that recognize unauthorized withdrawals without visual inspection of the checks or of the signatures on them. One common approach relies on expert-system pattern-recognition software, which is designed to identify unusual transactions through algorithms analogous to those the IRS uses to identify tax returns suitable for auditing. Another common technique involves "positive-pay" systems. Those systems rely on software that the customer uses to provide an electronic record of all authorized checks. The customer transmits that record to its bank over a phone line each day. The bank's sorters are designed to recognize any check drawn on such a positive-pay account and to route each such check for comparison with the information provided by the customer in its previous daily transmissions. The bank honors checks only if those transmissions indicate that the check actually was issued by the purported drawer. Customers like those systems because they often provide faster access to more accurate information about disbursements. Although that system cannot prevent all forgeries (because the customer's positive-pay employees could forge checks and include them in the transmissions), it does appear to make considerable inroads on the problem. For example, check-processing personnel at one large bank told me that its positive-pay systems had caught 400 forgeries during the previous year.

Neither pattern-recognition software nor positive-pay systems are perfect solutions. But they do make it harder for forgers to succeed in getting unauthorized checks through the system. And a legal rule that puts the losses from forged checks on payor banks gives payor banks every incentive to work to develop institutions that limit losses from forged checks. The relatively rapid development and implementation of those systems make it plausible to believe that the incentive imposed by that legal rule is strong enough to have a beneficial effect on the system.

(b) *What If the Payor Bank Dishonors the Forged Check?* If the payor bank notices the forgery and dishonors the check, then the party that presented the check to the payor bank (usually a collecting bank) is left holding the uncollectible check. In that case, the presenting bank seeks to pass its loss (the sum that it paid for the check) on to some earlier party in the transaction. The UCC contains two legal rules on which the presenting bank can rely. The first is the indorser-liability rule discussed above. That rule allows the presenting bank faced with dishonor to pass the loss up the chain to the earliest solvent party that indorsed the check without disclaiming liability.

Although the preceding paragraph suggests a relatively simple legal distinction between the rights of the payor bank and the rights of other banks in the collection chain, the statute implements that distinction in an indirect way. Specifically, to ensure that the rights of the payor bank are less than the rights of other parties in the chain — to reflect the rule of *Price v. Neal* — the statute takes two steps: (1) it creates a special set of warranties that limit claims about forged drawer's signatures, and (2) it limits payor banks to pursuing that limited set of warranties. As the foregoing discussion suggests, step 1 (the limitation of the presentment warranty) appears in the qualification of the warranty regarding the drawer's signature that permits a payor bank to complain only if the warrantor had "knowledge" that the drawer's signature was unauthorized. UCC §§3-417(a)(3), 4-208(a)(3). The analogous transfer warranty (the warranty available to parties other than the payor bank) includes an absolute avowal of the authenticity of the drawer's signature. UCC §§3-416(a)(2), 4-207(a)(2). Step 2 (the limitation of the payor bank's recovery to presentment warranties) appears in the rule that the parties that can pursue transfer warranties must be parties to whom an instrument has been transferred. UCC §§3-416(a), 4-207(a). Because an instrument is presented to the payor bank, not transferred to it, the payor bank cannot pursue the broader transfer warranties. See generally Figure 24.2.

As with indorser liability, the presenting bank would have a number of potential defendants. Indeed, each party that transferred the check for consideration would be liable for a breach of warranty. But in the end, liability flows back to the earliest solvent party in the chain because any party that is liable to the presenting bank on its transfer warranty is entitled to sue earlier transferors on their transfer warranties.

One twist on the warranty rules is the interaction between Articles 3 and 4. The Article 4 transfer warranties provide liability only against banks and their customers (the parties that deposit the bogus checks). Accordingly, a party seeking to pass liability to a party that handled the check before it got to a bank (a party that transferred it, for example, to a check-cashier) would have to rely on the Article 3 transfer warranties (set forth in UCC §3-416); those warranties are substantively identical to the Article 4 transfer warranties. The only significant difference is the rule in UCC §3-416(a) that Article 3 transfer warranties can be enforced by remote transferees only against entities that indorsed the check.

The Special Case of Telephone Checks

The problems that make it difficult for the payor bank to identify forged checks have led to considerable discussion of the possibility of overruling *Price v. Neal* and allowing payor banks generally to shift losses from forged checks up the chain to depositary banks (and, in turn, to their depositors). Recent revisions to Articles 3 and 4 have taken that position for a narrow class of items described by the statute as "remotely-created consumer check[s]," but colloquially referred to as "telephone checks."

The situation arises when a payee obtains consent for a transaction completed over the telephone. If the payee wants to use a telephone check to obtain payment, it will induce the customer (the drawer of the check) to recite (from the bottom of one of the customer's conventional checks) the routing number for the customer's bank and the account number of the customer. The payee (typically a bill collection service or a telemarketer) then will use that information (together with software readily available on the Internet) to print a check drawn on the customer's account. The check, of course, will not include a manual signature by the customer but will suggest in some way that a signature is not required (for example, by a stamp that might say "AUTHO-RIZED BY DRAWER" or (with less sincerity) "SIGNATURE ON FILE").

Under applicable FTC regulations, the payee must retain a "verifiable authorization" of the transaction for 24 months. 16 C.F.R. §310.5(a)(5). That authorization could be in writing, or it could be a tape recording of an oral authorization. 16 C.F.R. §310.3(a)(3). Given the purpose of the system? to allow payees to obtain payment without waiting for the payor to transmit a written check? it is not surprising that the companies that have designed telephone-check software recommend that their customers rely on oral authorizations.

As the existence of the FTC regulation suggests, some of the businesses that use telephone checks have come under fire for processing checks that have not been authorized by their customers (or, in some cases, checks in amounts larger than the amounts authorized by their customers). Accordingly, several states (including California and Texas) have adopted nonuniform UCC provisions addressing the problem. Responding to those provisions, recently approved amendments to UCC Articles 3 and 4 have altered the warranty rules for such items. Specifically, those amendments add a new subsection to each of the warranty provisions under which each transferor makes a transfer warranty and a presentment warranty that the purported drawer has authorized the item in the amount in which the item has been issued. See UCC §§3-416(a)(6), 3-417(a)(4), 4-207(a)(6), 4-208(a)(4).

The premise of those provisions is that in that context at least the possibility of fraud is better policed by action on the part of the depositary bank. For example, depositary banks that accept deposits of telephone checks might be induced to monitor the activities of those customers or require them to provide financial assurances of the authenticity of the items, lest the depositary bank be left holding the bag on warranty claims for unauthorized items. It is too early to say whether those revisions will be an isolated change or the first step toward an eventual eradication of *Price v. Neal*.

2. Forged Indorsements

The second common type of forgery is a forged indorsement: The drawer actually signs the check in the first instance, but some other party subsequently forges an indorsement on the check. For example, an employee's paycheck might be stolen and cashed after the thief forged the employee's name to the check. The rules that apply in that situation are much more favorable to the payor bank than the rules related to forged drawers' signatures. Generally, they allow the payor bank—even if it mistakenly honors the check—to pass the loss back to the earliest solvent person in the chain after the forgery.

(a) *What If the Payor Bank Dishonors the Check Because of the Forged Indorsement?*   The situation is simple if the payor bank dishonors the check. In that case, the system works much the same as it does with a forged drawer's signature. The presenting bank is left with the dishonored check, but can recover its loss by pursuing transfer warranties. Because neither the forger nor any party after the forger in the process of collection is a person entitled to enforce the instrument, and because the indorsement itself is forged, each of those parties has breached its transfer warranty, either under UCC §4-207(a)(1) & (2) or under UCC §3-416(a)(1) & (2).

(b) *What If the Payor Bank Pays the Check Despite the Forged Indorsement?*   The worst case for the payor bank is the case in which the payor bank fails to notice the forged indorsement and thus pays the check. Unfortunately for the payor bank, it is no more proper to charge the drawer's account in that case than in the case of a forged drawer's signature. Because the check was presented at the instance of the forger, rather than by somebody claiming under the payee, it was not proper for the payor bank to pay the check. Accordingly, the payor bank is not entitled to charge the drawer's account. UCC §4-401(a) & comment 1. Also, for the reasons discussed above, the payor bank cannot recover under UCC §3-418 (payment by mistake) from the parties earlier in the chain of collection if those parties took the instrument "in good faith and for value," as they will have done in the typical case.

The payor bank, however, can recover for a breach of presentment warranty. Under UCC §4-208(a)(1), the presenting bank (and each of the earlier transferors of the check) warrants that it is "a person entitled to enforce the draft" or is collecting the check on behalf of a person entitled to enforce the draft. If the depositary bank took the check from someone that had forged the payee's indorsement of the check (or from someone that took from the forger), then the depositary bank was not a person entitled to enforce the draft. That is true because, absent a valid indorsement by the payee (or some other legitimate transfer of the check), nobody other than the payee can become a person entitled to enforce a check. UCC §3-301. Accordingly, a presenting bank that took a check from a forger would have breached its presentment warranty to the payor bank.

Thus, the payor bank would be entitled to recover its loss from the presenting bank. If the presenting bank did not deal directly with the forger, the presenting bank, in turn, would be entitled (as shown in Figure 24.2) to pass the loss to parties earlier in the chain of collection because those earlier parties would have breached the analogous transfer warranty set forth in UCC §4-207(a)(1) & (2). In the end, the loss generally should pass to the earliest solvent person after the forger (or the forger itself in the odd case in which the forger is solvent and available).

It is not an accident that the payor bank that mistakenly honors a check can recover its loss if the problem is a forged indorsement, although (as discussed above) the payor bank normally cannot recover its loss if the problem is a forged drawers' signature. As explained above, the payor bank's account relationship with the customer gives it the capability to develop systems for detecting forged drawers' signatures. There is not, however, any systematic reason to believe that the payor bank is better placed than anybody else to detect forged payees' signatures. Indeed, absent some special circumstances, the party best placed to detect a forged indorsement is the person that accepts the indorsement (ordinarily a depositary bank). For example, in response to persistent losses to check fraud, many banks have begun to institute biometric identification programs to deter fraud by their customers. The most common (and controversial) plan is a program that requires parties cashing checks to allow the bank to retain an electronic image of the check-casher's fingerprint. Although the program has been vilified in the popular press, early indications are that it reduces depositary bank losses from check fraud by 40 to 60 percent. As with the rules discussed above for forged drawers' signatures, the efforts of banks to develop mechanisms for limiting fraud suggest that the incentives that come from allocating losses can motivate financial institutions to expend the resources necessary to make the system function more safely.

(c) *Conversion.* A final problem to be dealt with in the forged-indorsement situation involves the rights of the party from whom the check has been stolen (ordinarily the payee). The rules discussed above are likely to lead to a situation in which the drawer's account has not been charged for the check and in which the payee has not been paid. Because the payee of a stolen instrument is barred from enforcing the underlying obligation under UCC §3-310(b)(4), the payee's loss of the check often deprives it of the ability to obtain the funds to which it was entitled. That leaves the payee looking for some recourse for the theft of the check.

The obvious remedy is that the payee/victim has a common-law right to pursue the thief for conversion. Recognizing that a right to pursue the thief might not provide a great deal of comfort, UCC §3-420(a) also grants the victim a statutory action for conversion against parties that purchase the check from the thief. Under that provision, the victim can pursue a bank that cashes the check for the thief (the depositary bank) or a payor bank that honors the check over the forged indorsement. UCC §3-420(a). A suit under UCC §3-420(a) is limited somewhat by the prohibition in UCC §3-420(c) on any action against nondepositary "representatives" in the collection process. Although the text of the statute is obscure, the comment explains that the statute is designed to bar a suit against an intermediary bank that does nothing but process the check for collection as a representative of the depositary bank's customer. UCC §3-420(c) & comment 3.

The payee's right to pursue a payor bank for conversion is in tension with the drawer's right to prevent the payor bank from deducting the funds from its account on the theory that the check was not properly payable. Exercise of both of those rights as to the same check would result in an unfair burden on the payor bank: The payor bank would pay the payee under UCC §3-420(a), but would not be able to charge the drawer's account under UCC §4-401(a). Indeed, the payor bank would have paid twice—once on the forged check and once to the payee—with no obvious recourse for either payment. In that case, however, the payor bank is protected by the subrogation provisions in UCC §4-407(2), which allow the payor bank that pays the payee under UCC §3-420(a) to charge the drawer's account just as if the item had been properly payable. In that case, the funds from the drawer's account compensate the payor bank for its payment to the payee in the conversion action. The payor bank can recover the funds that it paid on the check during the initial process of collection—that is, the funds that went to the thief—by suing down the chain for a breach of presentment warranty.

If the payee sues the depositary bank directly and recovers, a similar result would follow. If the payor bank already has used presentment warranties to pass the loss down to the depositary bank (based on the depositary bank's error in accepting the check with the forged indorsement), then the depositary bank should be able to recover the amount that it has paid through equitable (that is, nonstatutory) subrogation to the payor bank's right against the drawer. See UCC §1-103. Otherwise, the drawer would have a windfall, keeping whatever it purchased from the payee without having any obligation to pay for it. If the payor bank does not pay the item, the depositary bank should not be liable for conversion, because it has not obtained "payment" for the item (payment being obtained only if the item is honored). General Motors Acceptance Corp. v. Citizens Commercial & Savings Bank, 2001 WL 1657223 (Mich. Ct. App.).

C. Alteration

The last major type of misconduct with respect to a check is an unauthorized alteration of the check. The UCC recognizes two main types of alterations: a change in some relevant aspect of the check as originally written and an addition to an instrument that was incomplete when written.

Generally, UCC treatment of the first type of alteration is the same as for a forged indorsement. Thus, if the payor bank honors a check that has been altered to increase its amount, it cannot charge the drawer's account for the amount that it paid out on the check. Rather, it can enforce the check only "according to [the] original terms" of the check." UCC §3-407(c). The payor bank, however, can recover any loss by pursuing earlier parties in the chain of collection for a breach of a presentment warranty that the check had not been altered. UCC §4-208(a)(2). As illustrated in Figure 24.2, any party against whom the payor bank recovers is entitled, in turn, to pursue earlier parties based on a breach of a similar transfer warranty. UCC §§4-207(a)(3), 3-416(a)(3). Thus, as with a forged indorsement, the loss ultimately will rest with the earliest solvent party to handle the check after the alteration.

The rules are different if the alteration is the completion of a check that was incomplete at the time it was signed by the drawer. In that case, the payor bank can enforce the instrument as completed, even if "the instrument was stolen from the issuer and completed after the theft." UCC §3-407 comment 2. Thus, the bank is entitled to charge the drawer for such an item. UCC §4-401(d)(2). That rule reflects the notion that a party that signs an incomplete instrument bears a large portion of the responsibility for any loss that ensues when the instrument is completed fraudulently.

Problem Set 24

24.1. Impressed by the advice you've been giving his customers (most recently in Problem Set 23), Nicholas Bulstrode came in this morning to discuss a forgery incident that recently occurred with respect to a $300 check written by Dorothea Brooke. Dorothea wrote the check to Dr. Tertius Lydgate to pay for a recent visit to Dr. Lydgate. Bulstrode Bank honored the check, which now is in Nicholas's possession. The check bears what appears to be a blank indorsement by Lydgate, followed by indorsements by Edward Casaubon and Wessex Bank.

Lydgate, however, claims that he never received the check, and Bulstrode believes him (for reasons that should be clear from what ensues). Casaubon told Bulstrode on the phone yesterday that Casaubon got the check from Will Ladislaw (a somewhat disreputable relative of Casaubon's) as partial payment of some outstanding debts Ladislaw owed to Casaubon. Casaubon said that Lydgate's indorsement was on the check at the time that he got the check from Will. On inquiry to Lydgate, it appears that Will is a patient of Lydgate's who saw Lydgate the day before Will gave the check to Casaubon. Lydgate discovered Will's apparent theft of the check when he called Dorothea to ask her why she had not paid him. Bulstrode promptly agreed to recredit Dorothea's account. Bulstrode is galled at the prospect of taking a loss for the check and wants to know what he can do. What should he do? UCC §§3-203(a), 3-301, 3-415, 4-208.

24.2.   Referring to Problem 24.1, what could Wessex Bank have done if Bulstrode had noticed the forged indorsement and dishonored the check? UCC §§3-403(a), 3-415, 3-416, 4-207.

24.3   Before he leaves, Bulstrode asks about another problem arising out of a check written on an account that Dorothea Brooke has at another bank (Wessex Bank). It appears that some unknown person stole a check from Dorothea's checkbook and issued the check by forging her signature. Lydgate, tricked by the forger, agreed to cash the check for the forger. After Lydgate deposited the check in an account he has at Chettam Bank, Chettam forwarded the check for collection through its correspondent Bulstrode Bank. Chettam included the following legend as part of its indorsement: "Without Recourse and Without Any Warranty Whatsoever." Wessex Bank (the payor bank) dishonored the check and returned it to Bulstrode Bank. Recognizing that he has no right to pursue Dorothea, Bulstrode wants to know if he has any basis for recovering from Chettam Bank or the forger. See UCC §§3-403(a), 3-414(b), 3-415, 3-418(a), 4-207(a)(2), (d).

24.4.   Referring to Problem 24.3, what rights would Wessex Bank have had if it had honored the check, but then recredited Dorothea's account when the fraud was discovered? UCC §§3-415(a), 3-418(a) & (c), 4-207, 4-208(a).

24.5.   Ben Darrow asks you about another problem with Carol Long. Carol seems to have the habit of carrying signed checks in her wallet, completed except for the amount, date, and name of the payee. When Carol left her wallet in a diner last week, one of those checks was taken, completed for the amount of $1,000, cashed at Nazareth State Bank, and honored by Darrow's bank (FSB) without anybody noticing the problem. Carol has come to Darrow, claiming that the check should not have been honored. Darrow feels sorry for Carol, but does not want FSB to bear the loss. What are Darrow's options? UCC §§3-407(c) & comment 2, 4-208(a)(2) & (b), 4-401(d)(2) & comment 4.

24.6.   Before letting you off the phone, Darrow has one other question. In reviewing her statements in connection with the discussion in Problem 24.5, Carol noticed another check that she recalled writing to one of her suppliers for $1,000. At some point in the collection process, the check was altered to indicate an amount of $10,000. Darrow's bank did not notice the skillful alteration and honored the check for the full amount. Darrow tells you that he assumes that he can't charge Carol for anything but the $1,000 for which she wrote the check. What he wants to know is whether he can recover the extra $9,000 from anybody. What is your advice? UCC §§3-407(c), 4-208(a)(2), 4-401(d)(1).

24.7.   Dorothea Brooke receives a telephone call from a marketer selling encyclopedias. At first, she is quite attracted to the idea of buying a new encyclopedia. The marketer asks her for her checking account number so that he can collect payment. Dorothea then gives him the number. After further discussion, however, she decides not to go through with the transaction until she receives further details in the mail. To her surprise, the next month she finds that the telemarketer (EncarPedia.com) has created and processed a check charging her $1,800 for the encyclopedias. The check was deposited at Bulstrode Bank and paid by her bank, Wessex Bank. Assuming that EncarPedia.com is insolvent, who will bear the loss? UCC §§3-416, 3-417, 4-207, 4-208.

24.8.   For your last problem of the day, Darrow's bank recently honored a check, apparently created by a telemarketer, which shows a signature line for John Smith, with a stamp on the line indicating that "Drawer's Authorization Is On File With Payee." As it happens, however, John Smith does not have an account at Darrow's bank. The item was prepared (apparently by the payee) with MICR-line information for Stephanie Heller's account at Darrow's bank. As normal practice would make likely, the item was processed and paid from Heller's account without anybody noticing the discrepancy. Heller has now complained (justly) that the item should not have been charged to her account. Can Darrow recover from the bank from which he received the item? From the payee? UCC §§3-415, 3-416, 3-417, 4-207, 4-208.

Assignment 25: Risk of Loss in the Checking System — Special Rules

The framework outlined in Assignment 24 operates at a high level of generality, under rules that rest on generalized assumptions about the ability of the individual parties to prevent the losses in question. In many contexts, however, it is easy to see that one party might have prevented the loss much more easily than the party that would bear the liability under the general framework outlined above. Recognizing the variety of problems that can arise in different contexts, the UCC does not stick to a rigid "one-rule-fits-all" approach. Instead, it mitigates the force of the broad framework outlined above by including four more specific rules that enhance the general framework by shifting the risks in particular situations from the parties that normally bear them to other parties that more easily could have prevented losses in particular cases.

A. Negligence

Negligence is the basic theme of all the special provisions. If one of the innocent parties was negligent in a way that contributed substantially to the loss, it makes more sense to place the loss on that party than on an innocent party that was not negligent. As discussed in Assignment 24, a depositary bank that disburses funds to a customer that has forged an indorsement on the check ordinarily bears that loss if all of the other parties are innocent. But the UCC shifts that loss to the drawer if the drawer's negligence substantially contributes to the forgery. See UCC §3-406(a) (precluding a party "whose failure to exercise ordinary care substantially contributes to . . . the making of a forged signature . . . from asserting the . . . forgery against a person who, in good faith, pays the instrument"). For a typical example of how such a claim can be made, consider the following.

HSBC Bank USA v. F & M Bank Northern Virginia

246 F.3d 335 (4th Cir. 2001)

HAMILTON, Senior Circuit Judge:

On or about March 31, 1999, Donald Lynch purchased a check (the Check) from Allied Irish Bank (AIB) in Ireland. The Check was made payable to Advance Marketing and Investment Inc. (AMI) in the amount of US$250.00, which was hand written as "Two Hundred + Fifty" on the center line of the Check (with "US Dollars" hand written on the line below), (i.e., the written portion of the Check), and

"US$250.00" hand written on the upper right-hand side of the Check (i.e., the numerical portion of the Check). The manner in which AIB made out the Check left just less than one-half inch of open space in the numerical portion and one inch of open space in the written portion.

The drawee/payor on the Check was Marine Midland Bank, now known as HSBC Bank USA (HSBC). Prior to the Check's deposit into AMI's account at F & M Bank Northern Virginia (F & M), the amount of the Check was altered from $250.00 to $250,000.00 by adding three zeros and changing the period to a comma in the numerical portion of the check and adding the letters "Thoud" in the written portion. The alteration was unauthorized, and the Check was endorsed "A.M.I., Inc."

F & M presented the Check for payment to HSBC. In so doing, F & M warranted, pursuant to [UCC §]4-208(a)(2), that the Check "had not been altered." HSBC honored the Check as presented and paid $250,000.00 to F & M, and debited AIB's account for that amount.

HSBC was subsequently advised by AIB of the Check's unauthorized alteration. HSBC then recredited AIB's account for the amount of the unauthorized alteration and brought the present diversity action against F & M in the United States District Court for the Eastern District of Virginia. Among other claims not relevant to the present appeal, F & M alleged a claim for breach of presentment warranty. . . .

Using the Virginia Commercial Code as the substantive law governing HSBC's breach of presentment warranty claim, on July 12, 2000, the district court conducted a bench trial on the claim. F & M asserted as an affirmative defense that by leaving the open spaces as it did in the numerical and written portions of the Check, AIB failed to exercise ordinary care in preparing the Check, which failure substantially contributed to the unauthorized alteration of the Check. The only evidence F & M actually submitted in support of its affirmative defense was the Check itself. [ED.: The parties evidently assumed that any failure on the part of AIB would apply as well to bar any claim for relief by F & M. See UCC §4-208(b).]

The district court found that HSBC had established all elements of its breach of presentment warranty claim under [UCC §4-208]. The district court also found that AIB had exercised ordinary care in preparing the Check. In this last regard, the district court stated:

> I have examined this check. And, of course, there does have [sic] to be sufficient writing on a check that there is not an open space so someone can fill it in for additional amounts and alter the check.
>
> But regardless of what you do about writing in zero, zero over 100 and then put a line in, which is, I guess, the standard way to do it—I don't know that if I looked at all the checks in this country that I would know the standard. It is the way I have always done it. There is still some kind of an open space regardless of what you do.
>
> And so, the test has got to be is that line sufficiently filled so that someone cannot come along and add into that writing in a way that just alters the check so that it will go through unnoticed.
>
> That certainly wasn't done on this check. This check was substantially written across the line. As a matter of fact, it was written far enough along the line that you could not write the word "thousand" in. It had to be scrawled up in the manner in which it was.
>
> And I just[,] looking at this check[,] and the way it is made out, I can't find that the preparer was negligent or participated in the alteration of it.

There was sufficient writing there that any alteration that was made was obvious. And I can't find negligence in that regard.

Subsequently, on July 31, 2000, the district court entered an order stating that . . . judgment should be entered in favor of HSBC. . . . F & M noted a timely appeal.

On appeal, F & M contends the district court's factual finding that AIB exercised ordinary care in preparing the Check is clearly erroneous. F & M seeks reversal of the judgment in favor of HSBC solely upon this basis. For the reasons stated below, we affirm.

I.

F & M concedes that if the district court's factual finding that AIB exercised ordinary care in preparing the Check is not clearly erroneous, it cannot successfully rely upon its affirmative defense to HSBC's breach of presentment warranty claim and, therefore, the judgment in favor of HSBC should be affirmed. Fed. R. Civ. P. 52(a) (providing that a district court's finding of fact shall not be set aside unless clearly erroneous). We now turn to consider whether the district court's factual finding that AIB exercised ordinary care in preparing the Check is clearly erroneous. . . .

The only evidence submitted by F & M in support of its burden of proving that AIB failed to exercise ordinary care in making out the Check was the Check itself. The district court physically examined the Check, including the just less than one-half inch of open space in the numerical portion of the Check and the one inch of open space in the written portion of the Check. Based upon this physical examination, the district court found that AIB had filled in the open spaces in the numerical and written portions of the check sufficiently such that "any alteration that was made was obvious." Accordingly, the district court found that AIB had exercised ordinary care in making out the Check.

After reviewing a copy of the Check contained in the joint appendix (the sole evidence on this issue presented below), we are not left with a definite and firm conviction that the district court's finding that AIB exercised ordinary care in making out the Check is wrong, mistaken, or implausible. Indeed, we see sound logic in the district court's rationale that if the written portion of the Check contained enough writing such that the Check's alteration could only be accomplished with the "scrawled up," abbreviated form of the word "thousand," i.e. "Thoud," ordinary care was exercised in making out the Check. In short, we hold that the district court's factual finding that AIB exercised ordinary care in making out the check is not clearly erroneous.

We also note that F & M's reliance upon the following comment to Virginia Commercial Code §8.3A-406 is misplaced:

> 3. The following cases illustrate the kind of conduct that can be the basis of a preclusion under Section 3-406(a): . . . Case # 3. A company writes a check for $10. The figure "10" and the word "ten" are typewritten in the appropriate spaces on the check form. A large blank space is left after the figure and the word. The payee of the check, using a typewriter with a type face similar to that used on the check, writes the word "thousand" after the word "ten" and a comma and three zeros after the figure "10." The drawee bank in good faith pays $10,000 when the check is presented for payment and debits the account of the drawer in that amount. The trier of fact *could* find that the drawer failed to exercise ordinary care in writing the check and that the failure

> substantially contributed to the alteration. In that case the drawer is precluded from asserting the alteration against the drawee if the check was paid in good faith.

[UCC §3-406 comment 3 (emphasis added by court).] This illustration is easily distinguishable from the facts of the present case. First, the illustration involves typewritten preparation of a check. The small nature of typewritten characters obviously would take up much less space than the handwriting involved in the present case. Furthermore, the actual number of words and numbers typed on the check that is discussed in the commentary prior to alteration is significantly less than the number of words and numbers AIB hand wrote on the Check prior to its alteration.

Because the district court's finding that AIB exercised ordinary care in making out the Check is not clearly erroneous, we affirm the judgment in favor of HSBC.

You should note that Section 3-406 does not provide a general right to challenge negligence. It provides a defense only when the negligence leads to a "forged signature." Thus, for example, Section 3-406 provides no claim if a thief that is not the payee indorses the check in the thief's name rather than the payee's name. E.g., John Hancock Financial Services, Inc. v. Old Kent Bank, 185 F. Supp. 2d 771, 775-779 (E.D. Mich. 2002).

The UCC's imposition of a duty of ordinary care is not limited to customers. The UCC imposes a general duty on banks to exercise "ordinary care" in processing and paying checks. See, e.g., UCC §§4-103(a) (barring enforcement of agreements that waive a bank's responsibility for failure to exercise ordinary care), 4-202(a) (imposing a duty on collecting banks to "exercise ordinary care"), 4-406(e) (imposing liability on payor bank if "the bank failed to exercise ordinary care in [deciding to] pa[y an] item [if] the failure substantially contributed to loss"). The key question for the rules imposing a duty of ordinary care on banks is what constitutes "ordinary care." On that point, the UCC is remarkably deferential to general banking usage. Specifically, the bank establishes a prima facie case that it has exercised ordinary care if it can establish that its activities conform to "general banking usage." UCC §4-103(c); see also UCC §§3-103(a)(7) (defining ordinary care for businesses as the "observance of reasonable commercial standards, prevailing in the area in which the person is located"), 4-104(c) (incorporating the "ordinary care" definition from UCC §3-103(a)(7) into Article 4), 4-103 comment 4 (discussing a court's limited power to conclude that conduct conforming to general banking usage can fail to constitute ordinary care).

Establishing standards to govern bank conduct is a tricky issue. The comments to UCC §4-103 explain that the decision to govern banking operations with such an indeterminate standard rests on a concern that "it would be unwise to freeze present methods of operation by mandatory statutory rules." UCC §4-103 comment 1. Thus, the adoption of an indeterminate standard allows the banking industry to adopt new procedures that might prevent losses more effectively at lower costs for the system. On the other hand, the provisions that tie determinations regarding "ordinary care" to general banking usage limit the incentive of individual banks to experiment with new procedures to prevent losses, even when the procedures are likely to be cost effective. If a bank can show that most banks have not yet adopted a new procedure that would have prevented a loss, then the bank's potential liability if it keeps the old procedure is relatively small. Conversely, adoption of a new procedure that departs from general banking usage actually might enhance the likelihood that the bank would be held liable for any losses that ensue.

The bottom line, though, is that the UCC generally does not address such questions, trusting the market eventually to force banks to develop cost-effective procedures for preventing loss. Whether the market is forceful enough to serve that function is an empirical question that turns on considerations about which it is difficult to generalize. The size of the industry's losses from fraud (as of 2001 about $6 billion, 2 cents per $100 in volume) and the industry's continuing experimentation with more and more sophisticated systems for the detection and prevention of fraud do suggest, however, that the market provides a considerable incentive for banks to attend to the problem.

Finally, it is important to emphasize now that the framework specifically contemplates the possibility of negligence by both the customer and one of the relevant banks. To cover that circumstance, the modern UCC includes a regime of comparative negligence, under which each party should bear the portion of the loss attributable to its failure to exercise ordinary care. UCC §3-406(b).

B.   Bank Statements

The remaining three rules deal with specific types of losses that the drawer (or in some cases the payee) could have prevented. The first of those is the most general, the bank-statement rule. That rule rests on the general intuition that customers can stop extended forgery schemes by the simple expedient of promptly reviewing their bank statements. For example, in one recent case, an office manager embezzled about $1.5 million from a car dealer over a period of three years by (among other things) inserting his name as the payee on blank checks signed by the owner of the dealership. Globe Motor Car Co. v. First Fidelity Bank, N.A., 641 A.2d 1136 (N.J. Super. Ct. Law Div. 1993). The most cursory analysis by the dealer of its monthly bank statement and returned checks would have revealed the scheme and stopped it immediately. When a drawer fails to discover a forgery evident from its monthly bank statement, the UCC normally transfers ensuing losses from the payor bank to the drawer by precluding the drawer from challenging the payor bank's decision to honor future checks by the same forger. UCC §4-406(d)(2). Relying on that provision, the *Globe Motor* court concluded that the dealer's conduct precluded it from challenging the payor bank's erroneous payment of the checks.

Of course, the drawer is not the only person in a position to stop forgery schemes. Those schemes can succeed only if the payor bank continues to honor the checks even though they have not been authorized by its customer, the purported drawer. And a rule that made the drawer completely liable for forgeries that could have been stopped by a prompt review of bank statements would ignore the fact that the payor bank bears some responsibility for the success of the scheme. For example, in one recent case, the forger issued checks on a business account that called for two manual signatures to authorize each check. The forged checks did not satisfy that requirement because they had one manual signature and one facsimile signature. The court (applying an earlier version of Article 4) concluded that because the bank's conduct fell so far short of "reasonable commercial standards," the bank was responsible for the loss. Federal Insurance Co. v. NCNB National Bank, 958 F.2d 1544 (11th Cir. 1992). The current version of Article 4 would apply the same standard to the bank's conduct, but would take a slightly different approach to allocating the liability. The current statute would not make the bank wholly responsible, but would call for each party to bear a portion of the loss based on the extent to which its shortcomings contributed to the loss. UCC §4-406(e).

The bank-statement rule rests on an underlying norm that it is appropriate to cast losses on customers unless they take seriously their obligation to review their bank statements promptly and thoroughly. Given the inconsistency of that norm with the everyday conduct of a large portion of accountholders—how carefully and quickly do you review your bank statement?—it should be no surprise that the rule has been a particularly fertile source of litigation. And, as the following case suggests, the results of that litigation have not been forgiving of customer conduct.

Stowell v. Cloquet Co-op Credit Union
557 N.W.2d 567 (MINN. 1997)

STRINGER, Justice.

Plaintiff/respondent Randall Stowell ("Stowell") brought this action in Carlton County District Court seeking to recover approximately $22,000 that had been paid by the defendant/appellant Cloquet Co-op Credit Union ("Credit Union") over a ten-month period on checks forged on Stowell's account by Stowell's neighbor. . . .

The record indicates that the Credit Union uses an automated check processing system which reads the magnetically coded numbers printed across the bottom of each check. This system is used throughout the Federal Reserve System and by all banks and credit unions in the state of Minnesota. Because the Credit Union processes approximately one million transactions each day, it does not manually check individual signatures against signature cards to detect potential forgeries. Rather, the Credit Union provides its members with monthly account statements itemizing the transactions occurring in the previous calendar month, including the date of the transaction, the check number, the amount of the transaction, and the account balance before and after each transaction. Consistent with industry-wide practice, the Credit Union relies on the account holders to examine the statement each month and contact the Credit Union if they identify any unauthorized checks.

Stowell opened a savings account and a draft account at the Credit Union on May 29, 1984. In connection with the opening of the draft account, Stowell signed a "Draft Withdrawal Agreement" which contained the following provision:

> The statements of the Draft Account shall be the only official record of the transactions on this account. If items on the statements are not objected to within twenty (20) days from the mailing date of the statement, the accuracy of the items on the statement shall be considered final.

Stowell is a sophisticated businessman. Prior to signing the agreement, he read it, understood its terms, and recognized that he had a responsibility to review his account statements and notify the Credit Union of any errors. For the next eight years after opening the account, Stowell used the draft account for both personal and business purposes and maintained a running balance of his deposits and withdrawals in his checkbook. At the beginning of each month Stowell would receive in the mail an account statement from the Credit Union which he checked against his own records on a monthly or bi-monthly basis.

In the fall of 1992, Robert Nelson moved into a cabin located on the same country road as Stowell's house. Nelson's mailbox was next to Stowell's and both boxes were located approximately one-half mile from Stowell's house. Soon after he moved in, Nelson stole a number of Stowell's checks and, from November 1992 to September 1993, forged Stowell's signature on fifty of the stolen checks and cashed them at various banks and businesses in the Barnum/ Cloquet area. As a part of his fraudulent scheme, Nelson removed Stowell's Credit Union account statements out of Stowell's mail each month to prevent Stowell from discovering the forgeries.

In December 1992, Stowell realized that he had not received an account statement from the Credit Union for the previous month. After waiting a few more weeks for the statement to arrive, he informed an employee of the Credit Union's branch office that he had not received it. Although the Credit Union mailed a duplicate statement to Stowell's correct address, Stowell never received the duplicate either. In fact, due to Nelson's theft, Stowell did not receive any items of mail whatsoever from the Credit Union between December 1992 and September 1993.

During this period, Stowell periodically contacted the Credit Union and complained that his account statements had failed to arrive. On each occasion a Credit Union employee mailed Stowell duplicate statements. At no time did Stowell ask to have a statement printed as he waited or to look at copies of his canceled checks, nor did any Credit Union employee suggest such measures. Other than complaining that his statement had not arrived, Stowell did nothing to inform anyone at the Credit Union that he suspected anything was wrong with his draft account or his mail. Despite the fact that over $22,000 was eventually unlawfully withdrawn from his account by virtue of Nelson's forgeries, Stowell never expressed concern to any Credit Union employee regarding his diminishing account balance as disclosed in each transaction receipt. [ED.: The court refers apparently to receipts issued to Stowell for ATM transactions.]

In August 1993, Stowell called Credit Union vice president Terrance Kimber and informed him that he had not received any mail from the Credit Union for some time. Kimber replied that the Credit Union would again mail Stowell copies of his account statements and told him that he should contact the Credit Union if the statements did not arrive within a few days. Again, neither Stowell nor Kimber suggested taking further measures such as hand delivering to Stowell printed copies of the statement. Kimber mailed the statements to Stowell as promised but again, Stowell never received them; Stowell apparently ignored Kimber's directive to contact him if the statements were not received and did not contact Kimber until several weeks later.

Nelson's forgery scheme was finally discovered on September 15, 1993, when Stowell received a telephone call from the Finlayson State Bank at Barnum informing him that a check he had written to Robert Nelson had bounced. Because he had never written any checks to Nelson, Stowell became suspicious and notified the police and the Credit Union. Upon reviewing Stowell's account statements, Stowell and the Credit Union discovered that between November 13, 1992 and September 15, 1993 Nelson had forged fifty checks on Stowell's account in the total amount of $22,329.34. Stowell acknowledged at trial that he could identify the forged checks from his account statements.

When the Credit Union refused to reimburse Stowell for the full amount of the forged checks, Stowell brought suit against the Credit Union in district court. . . .

We first address the validity of the provision in the Draft Withdrawal Agreement, relating to Stowell's obligation to review and report inaccuracies in the monthly account statement. . . . [A]n account holder is generally barred from recovering from the bank the value of a series of forged checks written on the account by a single forger if the account holder does not exercise "reasonable promptness" in examining his or her account statements and notifying the bank of any forged checks. [UCC §4-406(c)]. While the statute does not define "reasonable promptness," [UCC §]4-103(a) states:

> The effect of the provisions of this article may be varied by agreement, but the parties to the agreement cannot disclaim a bank's responsibility for its lack of good faith or failure to exercise ordinary care or limit the measure of damages for the lack or failure. However, the parties may determine by agreement the standards by which the bank's responsibility is to be measured if those standards are not manifestly unreasonable.

. . . Here, the Draft Withdrawal Agreement signed by Stowell when he opened his accounts in effect defines the standard by which "reasonable promptness" will be measured by stating that "[i]f items on the statements are not objected to within twenty (20) days from the mailing date of the statement, the accuracy of the items on the statement shall be considered final." The issue then, is whether the provision requiring inspection of the statement within twenty days of mailing is manifestly unreasonable. . . .

The district court held that the provision of the Draft Withdrawal Agreement that mailing triggered the period to examine the statement was manifestly unreasonable because it did not allow the account holder a reasonable opportunity to examine bank statements and discover forged checks. The court of appeals agreed and added an additional concern — that "[t]he agreement alters the statutory standards [of §4-406(d)(2)] . . . by reducing the applicable time period from thirty days to twenty days. . . ."

Thus, our first concern in analyzing the validity of the Draft Withdrawal Agreement is whether Stowell's duty to inspect his account statements with reasonable promptness and notify the bank of any unauthorized checks could arise when the statements were mailed by the Credit Union, as the agreement provides, or can only be triggered by receipt of the statements by Stowell, as the lower courts have held. Put another way, the question is who, as between an account holder and a bank, bears the risk that account statements will be lost or intercepted in the mail. [UCC §]4-406(c) provides guidance: "If a bank sends or makes available a statement of account or items pursuant to subsection (a), the customer must exercise reasonable promptness in examining the statement...." The term "send" is defined as follows:

> "Send" in connection with any writing or notice means to deposit in the mail or deliver for transmission by any other usual means of communication with postage or cost of transmission provided for and properly addressed....

[UCC §]1-201(38).... The statutory language thus clearly indicates that the account holder's duty to inspect the account statements with reasonable promptness commences at the time the statements are mailed by the bank.

No Minnesota case has addressed the issue of when an account holder's duty to exercise reasonable promptness in examining account statements commences, but because one of the purposes of the UCC is to foster nationwide uniformity in the application of commercial law, [UCC §]1-102, cases from other jurisdictions interpreting the Code should be given substantial weight.... The modern UCC case law of other jurisdictions is virtually unanimous in holding that, once account statements are mailed to the account holder's proper address, the risk of non-receipt falls on the account holder and interception of the statements by a wrong-doer does not relieve the account holder of the duty to examine the statements and report unauthorized items to the bank....

The rationale for placing the risk of nonreceipt of the bank statements on the account holder is sound:

> [A]lthough the depositor [is] not better able than the bank to discover isolated forgeries, he [is] in a better position to uncover a pattern of forgery by a trusted employee, friend or relative.... To discharge [the duty imposed by section 4-406 to examine the bank statements] a depositor must necessarily obtain possession of the bank statements and scrutinize them or bear the losses which flow from his unreasonable lack of concern.

Mesnick v. Hempstead Bank, 434 N.Y.S.2d 579, 580 (Sup. Ct. 1980). Furthermore, allowing account holders to avoid their duty to inspect their account statements by denying receipt of the account statements would place unreasonable financial burdens on banks and other financial institutions by forcing them to prove receipt either through the use of certified mail or by individually contacting each account holder to confirm that they had, in fact, received their account statement. Such measures would often be prohibitively expensive, especially for nonprofit, member owned credit unions. Given that the statutory duty to make a reasonably prompt examination of the statements commences upon the mailing of the statements, an agreement as to the length of time an account holder has to inspect the items cannot be said to be manifestly unreasonable because it also frames the account holder's duty in relation to when the statements are mailed. We there-fore...conclude that the Draft Withdrawal Agreement commencing the account statement inspection time upon mailing of the statement was not manifestly unreasonable.

We turn next to whether the Draft Withdrawal Agreement unreasonably attempts to eliminate the Credit Union's duty to act in good faith and with ordinary care or whether the twenty-day time period constitutes an unreasonably short time period within which the account holder must examine the statements and notify the bank of unauthorized items.

... UCC commentators agree that, in order to avoid controversy over whether action is "prompt" under section 4-406(c), the account holder and the bank may determine by agreement the specific number of days within which the account holder must take action.

Stowell asserts that the Draft Withdrawal Agreement amounts to an attempt by the Credit Union to establish an absolute twenty-day limitation on bringing suit and therefore to disclaim its duty, under [UCC] §4-406(e), to exercise ordinary care in paying items presented to it.... If, in fact, the agreement did establish an absolute bar to suit after the passage of twenty days, even for a failure to exercise ordinary care in paying the checks, it would be manifestly unreasonable. But that is not what the agreement provides — there is no language in the agreement stating that the Credit Union will not be liable for breach of its duty to exercise ordinary care. Further, [UCC §]4-103 specifically states that the parties to an agreement "cannot disclaim a bank's responsibility for its lack of good faith or failure to exercise ordinary care...." Cases interpreting very similar agreements have held that "the fact that the resolution merely sets forth a condition precedent to liability does not ... disclaim the bank's responsibility for its own lack of good faith or failure to exercise ordinary care." J. Sussman, Inc. v. Manufacturers Hanover Trust Co., 2 UCC Rep. Serv. 2d 1605, 1608 (N.Y. Sup. Ct. 1986).

We also find unpersuasive Stowell's claim that, in this modern age of extended travel, twenty days is simply an unreasonably short period to which to limit an account holder's opportunity to discover and report unauthorized items in the account statements. In Brunswick [Corp. v. Northwestern National Bank & Trust Co., 8 N.W.2d 333, 336 (1943)], this court upheld a fifteen-day notice provision as "reasonable under the circumstances" and several post-UCC cases have held contractual provisions establishing notification periods shorter than twenty days to be valid. See J. Sussman, 2 UCC Rep. Serv. 2d at 1608 (14 days).

Finally, we turn to whether there was sufficient evidence to support the jury's determination that the Credit Union failed to exercise ordinary care in paying the checks forged in August 1993. [UCC §]4-406(e) provides:

> If subsection (d) applies and the customer proves that the bank failed to exercise ordinary care in paying the item and that the failure substantially contributed to the loss, the loss is allocated between the customer precluded and the bank asserting the preclusion according to the extent to which the failure of the customer to comply with subsection (c) and the failure of the bank to exercise ordinary care contributed to the loss.

In [UCC §]3-103(a)(7), "ordinary care" is defined in terms of reasonable commercial practice:

> "Ordinary care" in the case of a person engaged in business means observance of reasonable commercial standards, prevailing in the area in which the person is located, with respect to the business in which the person is engaged. In the case of a bank that

takes an instrument for processing for collection or payment by automated means, reasonable commercial standards do not require the bank to examine the instrument if the failure to examine does not violate the bank's prescribed procedures and the bank's procedures do not vary unreasonably from general banking usage not disapproved by this article or article 4.

[S]ee also [UCC §]4-104(c) (making Article 3 definition of ordinary care applicable to Article 4). Thus, the UCC establishes a "professional negligence" standard of care which focuses on the procedures utilized in the banking industry rather than what a reasonable person would have done under the same or similar circumstances.

Stowell's evidence on this issue was that Stowell contacted Credit Union Vice President Terrance Kimber in August 1993 and told him that he had not been receiving any mail from the Credit Union. Stowell argues that his conversations with Kimber regarding his lack of receipt of his account statements should have been sufficient to give the Credit Union notice of a problem and should have prompted the Credit Union to take some protective action. The Credit Union, on the other hand, provided testimony of its compliance with the standards of the banking industry through an expert witness who testified that the Credit Union's automated check processing procedures were the same as those used by all the banks and credit unions in Minnesota. The Credit Union is required to honor all checks presented for payment from the accounts of its members unless it receives a stop payment order from the account holder or there are insufficient funds in the account to cover the check. Stowell's failure to present any evidence that the Credit Union's course of conduct somehow fell short of the reasonable commercial standards defining ordinary care in [UCC §]3-103(a)(7) is fatal to his claims . . . , and in this evidentiary void, we conclude the jury could not reasonably have found that the Credit Union did not meet the statutory definition of "ordinary care." . . .

Reversed and remanded with instructions.

Although Section 4-406(e) exposes the bank to a risk of responsibility for comparative negligence much like Section 3-406, Section 4-406(f) removes that risk if the customer fails to examine the statement sent by the bank within a year. The one-year period, moreover, can be shortened by agreement. E.g., National Title Ins. Corp. Agency v. First Union Natl. Bank, 559 S.E.2d 668, 671-672 (Va. 2002) (upholding account agreement that shortens one-year period under §4-406(f) to 60 days).

C.   Theft by Employees

The next special loss-allocation rule deals with defalcation by employees, and specifically with an employee's forgery of a signature on a check related to its employer's business. The most common case for applying that rule occurs when an employee forges the employer's indorsement on a check payable to the employer. In many cases, either the general negligence rule or the bank-statement rule places such a loss on the employer. But when the loss is caused by a responsible employee, the UCC (specifically UCC §3-405) places the loss on the employer even if those more general rules do not apply. One complicating factor in such cases is that they often involve two counterarguments that the drawer/employer might use to shift the loss back to a bank: Not only the comparative negligence argument discussed above (codified in this context in UCC §3-405(b)), but also claims that a bank's willingness to allow an employee to obtain funds from the employer's account amounts to participation in the employee's breach of fiduciary duty (the topic of UCC §3-307). The following case is illustrative.

Cable Cast Magazine v. Premier Bank

729 So. 2d 1165 (La. App. 1999)

CARTER, C.J. Plaintiff, Telemedia Publications, Inc. (Telemedia), sued Premier Bank, National Association, now Bank One, Louisiana, National Association (Bank One) for the improper payment of a number of checks indorsed by one of its employees and deposited into her personal account. Bank One appeals the judgment of the trial court in favor of Telemedia in the amount of $7,913.04.

FACTS

Telemedia publishes Cablecast Magazine (Cablecast), a weekly guide for the listings of the cable television programming in Baton Rouge. In 1994, Cablecast hired Jennifer Pennington as a temporary employee to replace another employee who had taken maternity leave. Pennington had previously worked for Cablecast for a few months in 1992. According to John McGregor, the majority stockholder of Telemedia, and manager of Cablecast, he had not experienced any problems with Pennington's prior employment.

According to McGregor, he noticed sometime in 1994, after he hired Pennington, shortages in revenue coming into Cablecast. McGregor became aware that Pennington had taken checks payable to Cablecast and deposited these checks into her personal account at Bank One. When confronted about her activities, Pennington admitted to taking the checks. At trial, McGregor agreed the amount of money Cablecast had lost through Pennington's activities was $7,913.04.

Cablecast filed suit against Bank One alleging Bank One violated [UCC §3-]307 by allegedly accepting instruments with knowledge of Pennington's breach of her fiduciary duties to Cablecast. Bank One answered, denying liability and contending that Telemedia was solely responsible for losses caused by the fraudulent indorsements of its employees based on [UCC §§3-405 and 3-]406.

After a trial on the merits, in which only McGregor and Pennington testified, the trial court ruled in favor of Telemedia and awarded it $7,913.04. Bank One appeals the judgment.

DISCUSSION

The general rule established by long-standing jurisprudence is that when a depositary of money . . . pays on a forged check, it is liable for the amount of the checks. . . . However, [UCC §3]-405 applies to cases of fraudulent indorsements by employees. . . .

According to the 1990 Uniform Commercial Code Comments, this provision is addressed to fraudulent indorsements made by an employee with respect to instruments to which the employer has given responsibility to the employee. Among the categories of fraudulent indorsements this provision covers are indorsements made in the name of the employer to instruments payable to the employer. This provision adopts the principle that the risk of loss for fraudulent indorsements by employees who are entrusted with responsibility with respect to checks should fall on the employer rather than the bank that takes the check or pays it, if the bank was not negligent in the transaction. This provision is based on the belief that the employer is in a far better position to avoid the loss by using care in choosing employees, in supervising them, and in adopting other measures to prevent forged instruments in the name of the employer. See [UCC §3-405 comment 1.]

From a review of the record, we find [UCC §3]-405 applies to this case of fraudulent indorsements. The evidence clearly established Pennington was an employee of Cablecast. Pennington committed fraudulent indorsements on checks payable to Cablecast when she indorsed the checks in her own name d/b/a Cablecast, instead of using the Cablecast stamp that she was instructed to use. By doing so, Pennington clearly represented her signature as that of her employer.

Pennington was also entrusted with "responsibility" as defined by [UCC §3-405(a)(3).] The testimony at trial established that among Pennington's duties was the authority to use the Cablecast indorsement stamp and prepare incoming subscription checks for deposit into the Telemedia account used by Cablecast at City National Bank (CNB). The fact that Pennington was never authorized to manually indorse checks payable to Cablecast does not defeat the application of this provision because she was still vested with authority to process instruments received for deposit into the account used by her employer. According to McGregor, Pennington's duties at Cablecast included opening the mail, indorsing subscription checks received in the mail with the Cablecast deposit stamp, preparing the preprinted Cablecast deposit slip, and taking the checks to be deposited at CNB.

The employer must bear the loss under [UCC §]3-405 upon a showing that an employee such as Pennington commits a fraudulent indorsement. However, Cablecast seeks to defeat the application of [UCC §]3-405 by asserting that Bank One was not in good faith when it took the checks from Pennington. [UCC §] 1-201(19) defines good faith as honesty in fact in the conduct or transaction concerned, except as provided in [UCC §]1-203. According to Cablecast, because Bank One had notice of Pennington's breach of fiduciary duty to Cablecast [under UCC §3-307], this notice defeats the application of [UCC §] 3-405. . . .

Cablecast asserts that Bank One had notice of the breach of Pennington's fiduciary duty because Pennington deposited checks payable to Cablecast into her personal account at Bank One. Cablecast points to Pennington's testimony that a teller at Bank One instructed her how to indorse checks made payable to Cablecast so they could be deposited into Pennington's personal account. Pennington also testified that a branch manager at Bank One told her she would need a permit if she wanted to continue to deposit checks payable to Cablecast. However, no evidence was presented regarding what type of permit Pennington would have needed. Bank One argued in its brief to this court that there is no such requirement in existence for endorsing "d/b/a" checks.

In response, Bank One contends that Cablecast had not been reserved as a trade name by Telemedia with the Secretary of State, thus no inquiry would have revealed that Pennington was not Cablecast to trigger the notice provisions of [UCC §]3-307(b)(2) when Pennington deposited checks made payable to Cablecast into her personal account. Further, Bank One argues it did not have actual knowledge that Pennington was a fiduciary of Cablecast. Knowledge as defined in [UCC §]1-201(25)(c) constitutes actual knowledge of a fact. The record reflects the only actual knowledge Bank One had was that Pennington identified herself as doing business as Cablecast.

We find it was error to conclude Bank One was not in good faith. Pennington testified she represented to Bank One that she was Cablecast. Cablecast did not offer any evidence that Bank One knew that Pennington was not Cablecast. Telemedia had not reserved any rights to the Cablecast name, and Telemedia had its business accounts at a different bank. Moreover, Pennington testified she did not inform anyone at Bank One that Telemedia owned or had any relationship with Cablecast.

Having concluded that Bank One was in good faith, the next issue is whether Cablecast is able to shift the loss it suffered through Pennington's activities to Bank One under [UCC §]3-405 by proving Bank One did not exercise ordinary care in taking the checks payable to Cablecast and depositing them into Pennington's account. Even if Cablecast was negligent, Bank One could still be liable if it failed to exercise ordinary care. Stated another way, Cablecast is not prevented from shifting the loss to Bank One based on Bank One's failure to exercise ordinary care, regardless of whether Cablecast was negligent.

[UCC §]3-103(a)(7) defines ordinary care in the case of a person engaged in business as the observance of reasonable commercial standards, prevailing in the area in which the person is located, with respect to the business in which the person is engaged. The record does not contain any evidence regarding what reasonable commercial standards were in place with respect to Bank One's allowing Pennington to indorse checks payable to Cablecast by signing her own name and adding "d/b/a Cablecast." We cannot say Telemedia proved Bank One did not observe reasonable commercial standards.

CONCLUSION

For the above and foregoing reasons, we find the trial court erred in rendering judgment in favor of Telemedia and against Bank One for the forged indorsements. [UCC §]3-405 is applicable and Telemedia did not defeat that application by proving Bank One was not in good faith in the transaction. Particularly, Telemedia did not prove Bank One had notice that Pennington breached her fiduciary duty to Cablecast. Further, Telemedia did not prove Bank One failed to exercise ordinary care in taking checks payable to Cablecast and indorsed by

Pennington doing business as Cablecast, which would allow the loss to be shifted to Bank One.

The judgment of the trial court is reversed.

———————

Often in cases that involve employee fraud, the employer will have no substantial claim against the payor bank because the checks will not appear sufficiently unusual on their face to warrant a claim that the payor bank was negligent in paying the items. In such a case, the question arises whether the employer can pursue a claim directly against the depositary bank for losses that the employer sustained from the scheme. Because the UCC does not resolve that question directly, courts have struggled in deciding whether to permit such suits.

Halifax Corp. v. Wachovia Bank
604 S.E.2d 403 (2004)

Opinion by Senior Justice Harry L. CARRICO

INTRODUCTION

In the period from August 1995 to February 1999, Mary K. Adams embezzled approximately $15.4 million while serving as comptroller for companies that are now known as Halifax Corporation (Halifax). Adams accomplished the embezzlement by writing more than 300 checks on Halifax's account with Signet Bank and its successor, First Union National Bank (collectively, First Union). Adams used a stamp bearing the facsimile signature of Halifax's president and, in her own handwriting, made the checks payable to herself, to companies she had formed, or to cash. She deposited the checks in several accounts she maintained with Central Fidelity Bank and its successor, Wachovia Bank (collectively, Wachovia), receiving cash from some of the checks.

PROCEDURAL BACKGROUND

Upon discovery of the embezzlement, Halifax brought an action against First Union as the drawee bank and Wachovia as the depositary bank. (*Halifax I.*) The trial court granted summary judgment in favor of First Union. Halifax then took a nonsuit of the action against Wachovia and appealed to this Court from the order dismissing First Union. We affirmed the dismissal, holding that Halifax's claim was barred pursuant to [UCC §4-406(f)] for Halifax's failure to notify First Union of the unauthorized signatures within one year after the bank's statement covering the checks in question was made available to Halifax.

While the appeal to this Court was pending, Halifax filed in the court below a three-count motion for judgment asserting that Wachovia and First Union were liable to Halifax for the amounts embezzled by Adams. (*Halifax II.*) Count I alleged negligence, gross negligence, and bad faith on the part of Wachovia in violation of UCC §§3-404, -405, and -406. Count II alleged common law conversion by Wachovia and First Union. Count III alleged that Wachovia and First Union aided and abetted Adams' breach of fiduciary duty. . . .

Wachovia moved for summary judgment on Halifax's claims against it. The trial court granted the motion, holding, contrary to Halifax's contention, that [UCC §3-406] does not create an affirmative cause of action, that Halifax's common law claim for conversion had been displaced by [UCC §3-420(a)], and that Halifax had failed to allege sufficient facts to state a cause of action for aiding and abetting Adams' breach of fiduciary duty, assuming such an action exists. From the final order embodying these holdings and granting final judgment in favor of Wachovia, we awarded Halifax this appeal.

FACTUAL BACKGROUND

. . . The facts as alleged in Halifax's motion for judgment show that Mary Adams, also known as Mary Collins, became comptroller at Halifax's Richmond office in August 1995 and continued in that position until March 1999. She maintained four personal and two commercial accounts with Wachovia. One of the commercial accounts was styled "Collins Racing, Inc." and the other "Collins Ostrich Ranch."

When Adams first began embezzling money from Halifax in August 1995, she deposited in her personal accounts with Wachovia several checks each month for over $5,000.00. The amounts of the checks soon increased to between $10,000.00 and $15,000.00 each and before long to amounts ranging from $50,000.00 to $150,000.00 each, and deposits were made multiple times a day or week. For example, in July 1997, Adams deposited on July 9 a check for $95,550.00, on July 14, one check for $55,000.00 and another for $99,300.00, on July 16, a check for $93,500.00, on July 21, a check for $80,600.00, and, on July 30, a check for $149,305.00, totaling $573,255.00. In all, Adams drew 328 checks totaling $15,429,665.42 on Halifax's account with First Union.

Adams was "one of the best and largest individual customers" of Wachovia's branch where she did business. Managers and tellers saw Adams " 'a lot,' " and she stood out because of her large checks and banking activity." The entire branch was curious about her "because of her large checks," the likes of which "none of the tellers had ever seen ... before." Some tellers claimed "to have believed or assumed that Adams 'was at least part owner' of the corporate drawer."

Wachovia "repeatedly accepted such huge handwritten checks drawn on the account of Adams' employer despite the gross disparity with [Adams'] payroll amount [of about $1,000.00 per pay period] shown on each teller and manager screen." The tellers "had concerns about individual checks or the check activity, or both." Bank officials knew Adams was Halifax's comptroller and understood that "such transactions by a financial officer, or even a part owner, present[ed] a serious potential for fraud." Yet, branch "[m]anagers and supervisors told the tellers to do whatever Adams wanted."

DISCUSSION

NEGLIGENCE, GROSS NEGLIGENCE AND, BAD FAITH

Halifax contends that [UCC §3-406], when read in light of [UCC §§3-404 and -405], gives rise to an affirmative cause of action for the negligence of a depositary bank with respect to the alteration of an instrument or the making of a forged signature. These sections were part of the General Assembly's 1992 revision of the UCC....

In support of its contention that [UCC §3-406] creates an affirmative cause of action, Halifax cites our decision in Gina Chin & Assoc., Inc. v. First Union Bank, 256 Va. 59, 500 S.E.2d 516 (1998). That case involved both forged signatures of the drawer and forged indorsements of the payee. The drawer sought recovery from the depositary bank. The latter claimed it was liable under [UCC §§3-404 and -405] only for forged indorsements and not where both the payee's indorsements and the drawer's signatures are forged.

We disagreed. We stated that the depositary bank was erroneous in "its conclusion that [UCC §§3-404 and -405] cannot be utilized by a drawer against the depositary bank in a double forgery situation," and that the drawer "was not precluded from asserting a cause of action against [the depositary bank] pursuant to [UCC §§3-404 and -405]."...

It is plain, however, that the language quoted from *Gina Chin* has reference solely to [UCC §§3-404 and -405]. Indeed, the sentence immediately preceding the quotation states that "[t]he revisions to [UCC §§3-404 and -405] changed the previous law by allowing 'the person bearing the loss' to seek recovery for a loss caused by the negligence of any person paying the instrument or taking it for value based on comparative negligence principles." *Gina Chin,* 256 Va. at 62, 500 S.E.2d at 517. [UCC §3-406] simply was not an issue in the case in any manner. *Gina Chin,* therefore, does not serve as authority for Halifax's contention that [UCC §3-406] creates an affirmative cause of action....

We conclude that the trial court did not err in its holding that [UCC §3-406] does not create an affirmative cause of action and in awarding summary judgment to Wachovia with respect to that claim.

D. Impostors

The last of the UCC's special loss-allocation rules deals with checks procured by impostors or payable to fictitious persons. The general idea (reflected in UCC §3-404(a)) is that the loss should be allocated to the person that was victimized by the fraud. Although that might seem a little harsh to the victim of the trick, the idea is that it is better to place the loss on that party than on other parties that might have had no real opportunity to prevent the loss. The following case is slightly atypical in that it involves cashier's checks rather than conventional checks, but it does aptly illustrate both how UCC §3-404 applies and how a malefactor might construct a successful scheme to steal money through the use of a fictitious person.

Meng v. Maywood Proviso State Bank

702 N.E.2d 258 (Ill. App. 2001)

Justice GREIMAN delivered the opinion of the court. . . .

In 1995, plaintiffs wanted to purchase a building located at 712 West Diversey in Chicago, Illinois. The building was in foreclosure and a federal government agency (United States Department of Housing and Urban Development (HUD)) held the mortgage. To accomplish the purchase, plaintiffs retained John F. Parolin, an attorney who has since been disbarred. Parolin advised plaintiffs that, before HUD would consider plaintiffs as a potential purchaser, plaintiffs were required to establish a fund in the amount of the purchase price by obtaining cashier's checks. Parolin further advised plaintiffs that the cashier's checks must be made payable to himself and David L. Kelly, an alleged HUD employee who was authorized to make the sale. In fact, David L. Kelly does not, and never did, exist. David L. Kelly is a fictional person.

Plaintiffs purchased the following three cashier's checks from Albank, totaling $712,500: (1) $350,000; payable to Klaus Wieske; dated March 1, 1995; check no. 404885; (2) $125,000; payable to David L. Kelly and John Parolin; dated May 24, 1995; check no. 407067; and (3) $237,500; payable to David L. Kelly and John F. Parolin; dated June 26, 1995; check no. 410255. Plaintiffs delivered each check to Parolin.

The first check was specially indorsed by Klaus Wieske in the following manner:

EARNEST MONEY FOR 712 DIVERSEY
Pay to the order of:
John F. Parolin
David L. Kelly
 Klaus A. Wieske [signature]

All three cashier's checks were cashed by Parolin at defendants Maywood Proviso State Bank (check No. 1), First Security Trust & Savings Bank (check No. 2), and Greater Illinois Title Insurance Company (check No. 3), respectively. When cashed, each check bore the signatures of both Parolin and Kelly, the fictional person. Upon presentment, Albank made payment on the three checks.

Appeal No. 1-97-3289 (Albank)

On May 24, 1996, plaintiffs filed a complaint against Albank, alleging that Albank breached a contract with plaintiffs by making payment on the cashier's checks without the endorsement of David L. Kelly. . . .

On December 9, 1996, Albank filed a motion for summary judgment, asserting that it had paid the cashier's checks in the ordinary course of business, in good faith and without knowledge that Kelly was a fictitious payee. To its motion, Albank attached an affidavit from the personnel assistant at HUD in the Chicago regional office, who attested that no one by the name of David Kelly or David L. Kelly was employed by HUD in the entire United States during the time period 1994 through 1996. Albank contended, and the trial court agreed, that the fictitious payee rule completely absolves a bank from any liability for payment over a forged indorsement. . . .

Appeal No. 1-97-3288 (Maywood Bank)

On February 26, 1997, plaintiffs filed a complaint against the three defendant institutions that cashed the three cashier's checks, alleging that defendant institutions failed to exercise ordinary care in paying or taking the instrument under [UCC §]3-404(d). . . .

[The trial court in due course dismissed that complaint as well.]

The first issue on appeal is whether the fictitious payee provision in the Code bars plaintiffs' breach of contract claim against the bank (Albank) that issued and subsequently paid the cashier's checks upon presentment. . . .

We agree with plaintiffs that an enforceable contract arises when a cashier's check is purchased and the contract calls for the issuing bank to pay the instrument according to its terms. The implied contract is the issuing bank's promise to pay the cashier's check to the named payee only. . . .

Under the facts of the present case, however, we disagree with plaintiffs' contention that the Code does not deal with the relationship between the issuing bank and the remitter of a cashier's check. The dispositive fact in the present case is that the cashier's checks bore the forged signature of a fictitious payee, David Kelly. The Code specifically addresses the situation involving such a payee. . . .

As specifically stated in section 3-404(b)(ii) of the Code, where a named payee is a fictitious person, then the "indorsement by any person in the name of the payee . . . is effective as the indorsement of the payee." . . . A forged indorsement of a fictional payee is an exception to the general rule that places liability on a bank that pays over a forged endorsement.

The statutory fictitious payee rule relieves a bank from liability for honoring a check bearing the forged indorsement of a fictional payee by deeming the forged indorsement to be effective. The drawer of the checks in such a scenario suffers the loss because the drawer is in the best position to avoid the loss. . . .

Second, plaintiffs assert that there was no ambiguity to invoke the alternative payee method of payment in the cashier's check that was made payable to Klaus Wieske who, in turn, specially indorsed the back of the check as follows:

EARNEST MONEY FOR 712 DIVERSEY
Pay to the order of:
John F. Parolin
David L. Kelly
    Klaus A. Wieske [signature] . . .

Plaintiffs argue that the form of this indorsement is not ambiguous but rather requires that the cashier's check be paid jointly, not in the alternative, under [UCC §]3-110. We disagree.

Section 3-110(d) of the Code governs how to identify the person to whom an instrument is payable and provides for multiple payees as follows:

(d) If an instrument is payable to 2 or more persons alternatively, it is payable to any of them and may be negotiated, discharged, or enforced by any or all of them in possession of the instrument. If an instrument is payable to 2 or more persons not alternatively, it is payable to all of them and may be negotiated, discharged, or enforced only by all of them. If an instrument payable to 2 of more persons is ambiguous as to whether it is payable to the persons alternatively, the instrument is payable to the persons alternatively.

This multiple payee provision became effective in 1992 and replaced former section 3-116 of the Code. Under former section 3-116 of the Code, an instrument was presumed to be payable jointly where the instrument did not designate payment in the alternative. Contrary to the former provision, the current section shifts the presumption to pay on an instrument in the alternative rather than jointly.

We find, as a matter of law, that the designation of two payees on a cashier's check is ambiguous where no directives are stated on the checks to determine the manner of payment. In the present case, the cashier's check at issue names two payees but does not include any directions regarding whether the check is payable to the named persons alternatively or jointly. The subject cashier's check does not contain any language or markings to instruct the method of payment, such as the word "and" or the word "or." Accordingly, section 3-110 provides that the check is payable to the persons alternatively. Therefore, in the present case, one named payee was sufficient to negotiate the cashier's check at Maywood Proviso State Bank. . . .

Third, we consider whether plaintiffs stated a negligence claim against the institutions that paid the cashier's checks, relying on section 3-404(d) of the Code. . . .

Under the language of section 3-404(d) and the facts of the present case, we find that plaintiffs did not and, indeed, cannot demonstrate in their complaint any failure to exercise ordinary care on the part of the three institutions that accepted the cashier's checks. Plaintiffs, at oral arguments, suggested that banks should have a duty to question customers about the payees in transactions involving cashier's checks, but conceded that, even if such inquiries had been made in the present case, the outcome would not be affected. We believe that such a duty is not required under the Code and that imposing such a duty contravenes the very purpose of a cashier's check, which is meant to operate as cash. Furthermore, such a duty would infringe on the rights of a customer to access his or her own funds for the purpose of distributing them to his or her own designated payees.

The unfortunate facts of this case indisputably include a scam initiated by an attorney against his clients, a fictitious payee, forged check transactions, and the loss of hundreds of thousands of dollars. Although the fact that plaintiffs were duped by a scam is regrettable, their attempt to place blame on the institutions that actually followed and honored their orders is not supportable either under the Code or in common sense. . . .

For all of the foregoing reasons, we affirm both orders by the trial court.

Problem Set 25

25.1.   Late one afternoon you get a call from Cliff Janeway, a book-dealer friend of yours. He tells you that he is in Seattle and that yesterday he received a $200,000 check as a finder's fee for locating some rare books and manuscripts for an eccentric collector. He just got off the plane and has realized that he left the check on the seat of the airplane. Does he have anything to fear if a third party takes the check, forges his indorsement, and cashes it? UCC §§3-301, 3-310(b), 3-406, 3-420(a).

25.2. Sir Roderick Spode, a client that Bertie Wooster referred to you, operates a small women's clothing store on the west end of town. His business processes a large number of incoming checks (paying for items that he has shipped to customers all over the country) and outgoing checks (paying for supplies, materials, and payroll). He has never had any losses from theft, but is worried about the possibility. He tells you that he has a lot of customers and workers in and out of his shop all the time. Because he has only a single very large room for his business, it is hard to keep his checkbook and blank checks in a completely inaccessible location unless he removes all of those materials from the office entirely. Spode wants to know what he needs to do to be sure that he is not stuck with any losses if somebody steals some blank checks. Consider the following possible scenarios and decide whether Spode would have any liability in any of those scenarios. If so, what should he do to limit that liability? UCC §§3-404, 3-405, 3-406, 4-401(a), 4-406.

a. August ("Gussie") Fink-Nottle, an employee who packages outgoing shipments (but has no check-writing authority) picks up one of Spode's blank checks, makes it out to himself, and forges Spode's signature as drawer. Gussie then indorses the check and deposits it in his bank. After withdrawing the funds from his account, Gussie then disappears (ostensibly on some type of newt-hunting expedition). UCC §§3-406 & comment 3, 4-401.

b. Stephanie ("Stiffy") Byng comes to Spode's office and claims to be Madeline Bassett, a supplier to whom Spode owes money (whom Spode has not met). Spode issues a check to Madeline Bassett and gives it to Stiffy, who indorses the check in Madeline's name, cashes it, and then departs with the money for the Isle of Man. UCC §3-404(a).

c. Same facts as question a, but instead of writing the check to himself, Gussie writes a check to Madeline Bassett, intending to give the check to Gussie's friend Harold (the "Stinker") Pinker. After Gussie gives the check to Pinker, Pinker forges Bassett's indorsement and then cashes the check. UCC §§3-110(a), 3-404(b)(i), 3-406, 4-208(a)(1).

d. Same facts as question c, but Gussie makes the check out to Catsmeat Potter-Pirbright (a wholly fictitious character). Pinker indorses the check in Potter-Pirbright's name and deposits it in an account that Pinker maintains in Catsmeat's name. UCC §3-404(b)(ii), (d) & comment 2.

e. Same facts as question c, but Gussie is the person in Spode's office responsible for issuing checks. UCC §§3-402(a), 3-404(b)(i).

f. Same facts as question d, but Pinker stole the check and used Spode's facsimile signature machine to sign the check. Spode's account agreement stated that any signature using that machine would be treated as authorized by Spode. UCC §§3-404(b), 3-404 comments 1 & 2, 4-103(a).

g. Gussie also is responsible for depositing incoming checks. In that capacity, Gussie forges Spode's indorsement on an incoming check payable to Spode and deposits the check in Gussie's account. UCC §3-405.

h. Gussie's last task is to maintain a daily list of checks authorized to be written. The list is processed early in the afternoon each day to produce the checks indicated on the list. In an effort to defraud the bank, Gussie adds names to the list that reflect fictitious persons or close friends of Gussie willing to participate in the scheme. He then intercepts the checks after Spode writes them, indorses them in the name of the payees, and deposits them in his account. UCC §3-405.

25.3.   Jodi Kay wants to discuss another problem that CountryBank faces. Carl Eben (Jodi's long-time customer from Problem 23.6) has just been victimized by a lengthy forgery scheme by his accounts-payable clerk. The clerk forged checks on the account for 18 months before being caught, stealing a total of about $135,000. Because Carl never noticed any of the forgeries on his statement, Jodi is guessing (but is not sure) that the bank has no obligation to return the funds to Carl's account. Because of its long-standing (and highly profitable) relationship with Carl, however, the bank has decided that it is better to return the funds without getting into any messy arguments about who is responsible.

Jodi wants to know what the bank can do in the future to mitigate these problems. She wants both to mitigate the bank's exposure to legal liability and to mitigate the possibility that the losses will occur in the first place. But she has to be conscious of costs: "You can't ask me to do anything crazy like recommend that we actually look at the checks to identify forged signatures." Is the bank liable for losses like this? If so, what can Jodi do to limit that liability and the likelihood of future losses? UCC §§3-103(a)(7), 4-104(c), 4-208(b), 4-406.

Assignment 26:   Truncation and Check 21

A.   Payor-Bank Truncation

From the perspective of the banking industry, the process of transporting and sorting checks and delivering them to their customers each month is a wasteful expenditure of resources. Thus, the banking industry for decades has tried to develop procedures that limit its need to transport checks and return them to those who wrote them. Those procedures generally are designed to "truncate" the check-transportation process and thus customarily are referred to as check truncation.

The simplest way in which truncation can occur is at the payor bank: When the checks reach the payor bank, the bank does not sort the checks and return them to its customers. Instead, it retains the checks (or destroys them) and provides the customer a statement that either includes images of the items or describes the items in some detail. Unfortunately for banks, consumer advocates have interposed trenchant objections to all efforts by banks to implement check truncation. Those objections rest on the perception by consumer advocates that it is important to consumers that their checks are returned to them. The idea is that consumers need to receive the actual checks both to assess the propriety of charges to their accounts and to prove payment of the items for which the checks were written. That attitude is particularly ironic given the history of the process: Banks originally began returning checks to their customers to avoid the costs of internal storage of the items. Therefore, what started as a convenience to the banks has now become a burdensome obligation for banks and a coveted privilege of accountholders.

The legal status of payor-bank truncation differs from state to state and at the same time is in flux. Forty-eight states have adopted the version of UCC §4-406(a) included in the 1990 revisions to Article 4. That provision describes the items a bank must provide in periodic statements it sends to consumers:

> [The] bank...shall either return or make available to the customer the items paid or provide information in the statement of account sufficient to allow the customer reasonably to identify the items paid. The statement of account provides sufficient information if the item is described by item number, amount, and date of payment.

Because that provision permits the bank to provide *either* the items *or* the requisite information, it fully authorizes payor-bank truncation. Hence, that provision authorizes payor-bank truncation in all of the states except for New York and South Carolina (the two states that have not adopted the 1990 version of UCC Article 4), at least if the bank provides a statement that

Figure 26.1
MICR Line

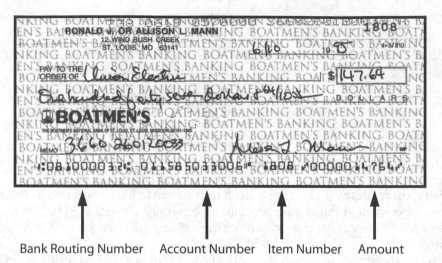

Bank Routing Number   Account Number   Item Number   Amount

includes the three items required by the safe harbor included in the last sentence of the provision.

As a practical matter, that provision has led to truncation for a large share of bank customers in this country. Consumer advocates have criticized not only the general process of truncation, but also the specific method permitted by the statute. For example, one complaint is that the information required by UCC §4-406 does not include the identity of the payee of the check (information that consumers ordinarily receive on credit-card statements). The reason for the limited information permitted by the safe harbor is that banks rely on the MICR line for the information they put in bank statements. The MICR line of a processed check—designed for easy reading by automated machines—includes all of the information required by the safe harbor. (See Figure 26.1.) Hence, banks can use automated processing to produce statements including the safe-harbor information. A requirement that payor banks include the name of the payee in statements sent to their customers would require a more costly process of item-by-item examination to determine the name of the payee from a line on the check that commonly is handwritten (perhaps illegibly).

As noted, New York and South Carolina have not adopted the 1990 version of Article 4. The dissatisfaction of consumer advocates with the limited-information statements that the provision permits is one of the principal reasons for New York's unwillingness to adopt that statute.

The banking industry has been critical of that argument, on the theory that the potential harm to consumers is quite limited and certainly insubstantial when compared to the cost of paper-based processing. For one thing, the absence of information from bank statements permitted by Section 4-406(a) is not likely to seriously prejudice consumers attempting to review their bank statements, at least with respect to their relationship with their bank. The main legal consequence to a consumer of receiving a bank statement is that Section 4-406(d) punishes consumers that fail to detect unauthorized charges to their accounts by limiting their ability to complain about those charges if they do not promptly notify their bank after the bank sends the relevant statement. But that provision applies only if the customer "should reasonably have discovered the unauthorized payment" based on the information that the bank chooses to include in the statement, Section 4-406(c).

If the unauthorized payment results from a wholly unauthorized check, consumers should be able to identify the unauthorized payment by noticing that a check was charged to their account that they had never written. Information identifying the payee ordinarily should not be necessary for a consumer to notice that type of problem. See UCC §4-406 comment 1 ("If the customer made a record of the issued checks on the check stub or carbonized copies furnished by the bank in the checkbook, the customer should usually be able to verify the paid items shown on the statement of account and discover any unauthorized . . . checks."). On the other hand, if the unauthorized payment resulted from the theft of a check the consumer wrote, the absence of payee information would make it difficult for the customer to discover the theft by review of the statement. Thus, a bank that sends a statement that does not include the items (or identify the payee) could not plausibly claim that the customer "should reasonably have discovered the unauthorized payment," Section 4-406(c). Hence, truncating payor banks often would end up bearing losses from such problems. See UCC §4-406 comment 1 ("[I]f a check is altered by changing the name of the payee, the customer could not normally detect the fraud unless the customer is given the paid check or the statement of account discloses the name of the payee of the altered check.").

Consumer advocates also express concerns about the ability of consumers that do not receive checks with their bank statements to prove that they have made the payments in question. That problem is difficult to resolve because it is more practical than legal. There is no general legal rule that requires a person to present an original check to prove that a payment has been made. There does, however, appear to be a cultural practice in some parts of our society (or, at least, a perception of such a practice) that treats the ability to display a cancelled check as the most persuasive method of proving that a payment has been made. To the extent such a practice exists, bank statements that do not return paid items to consumers cause problems for the consumers that receive them.

Because of the large cost savings available to banks that do not have to return paid items with the statements that they send to their customers, recent years have seen continuing efforts to reach a compromise acceptable to all parties that would allow banks to proceed with summary item-less statements. Those efforts include both continuing progress toward agreement on a revised version of Section 4-406 that could be adopted by New York and, more broadly, a failed attempt by NCCUSL and the ALI to produce a revised version of Section 4-406 that would respond to those concerns in a way that could be adopted uniformly throughout the country. Three types of provisions are typical of those efforts at compromise.

First, responding to the problems discussed above with statements that do not identify the payee, reformers in New York have proposed a rule to enhance the protection for consumers that receive safe-harbor statements without payee information. Under that rule, those consumers would be precluded from complaining about a payment based on the alteration of the payee's name only if the consumer had actual knowledge of the unauthorized payment. That knowledge could come, for example, from a complaint of the intended payee about the failure of payment. That rule differs from the current UCC rule discussed above, because under the current UCC rule customers are responsible if they reasonably should have discovered the unauthorized payment, even if they in fact did not discover it. Thus, the revision would help to diminish concerns that consumers receiving summary statements would be held responsible for losses related to stolen items.

The second set of provisions addresses the proof-of-payment concern directly, by adding specific statutory reassurance regarding the ability of consumers to prove payment. For example, the Drafting Committee that recently proposed amendments to Article 4 gave serious attention to a provision stating that any image a customer receives with its statement should have the same value in proving payment as the item itself. Because the need for the actual items comes not from any legal rule but rather from a practical view that the actual item is the most reliable form of proof, it was not clear that such a provision would have any significant effect on the problem. Indeed, the acceptance of such images is likely to turn less on any formal legal "blessing" of the validity of such images than on such practical considerations as whether banks deliver the images in a form that makes them appear more official—printing them on thicker document-style paper, for example. On that point, reports of a Federal Reserve truncation pilot project in Montana suggest that efforts to give the images a more official appearance substantially enhance customer satisfaction with the images as a substitute for the originals. Similarly, customers surely will be more receptive to images when it becomes common practice for the image to include both sides of the check (instead of the front only, as is the general practice currently). In any event, the drive to prepare a new version of Section 4-406 failed because of industry opposition to any alterations of Section 4-406.

Finally, various states (including California, Colorado, and Texas) have adopted statutes that obligate banks that do not provide items with the statements to provide a small number of items to their customers free of charge. Massachusetts goes even further, requiring the bank to return any original check on request without charge. Those provisions attempt to mitigate consumer concerns by making it practical for them to obtain copies when they want them.

B.   Depositary-Bank Truncation and the Check 21 Act

A more significant step toward truncation is the effort to develop systems for truncating check processing at the depositary bank. The depositary bank retains the check (or an image of the check) in storage and collects the check by sending (presenting) electronic information to the payor bank. Hence, the process often is called electronic check presentment (ECP). Because imaging technology remains relatively expensive, that process currently tends to rely on the information from the MICR line of the check, which depositary banks easily can capture and transmit to payor banks. In those systems as they currently operate, the depositary bank often must forward the actual check later by conventional methods; the principal benefit of ECP is that it gets the information to the payor bank sooner, which provides the depositary bank substantial protection against fraud losses.

To obtain the cost savings of truncation, banks must develop arrangements in which they do not forward the paper check, but instead send only the MICR-line information or an image of the check. In those more advanced arrangements, the check can be retained in storage at the depositary bank; the check itself is never sent to the payor bank and is destroyed in due course (usually in about 90 days). Then, the payor bank can rely on the MICR-line information or the image of the check itself to determine whether it will honor the check.

Although systems for ECP are growing rapidly, they still control a relatively small portion of the check market, perhaps one-tenth of the volume in the United States. The immense size of that market, however, makes even a small share quite significant (about 6 billion checks in 1999). And the share seems to be growing rapidly.

The biggest problem in getting check-truncation systems into place arises from this country's highly dispersed check-collection system. If our country had a single entity on which all checks were drawn, electronic processing could be implemented easily enough, whenever that bank chose to accept electronic information in lieu of the paper checks. As it happens, however, checks are drawn on literally thousands of banks. No single payor bank can implement a full system for electronic processing of checks that its customers deposit until each and every one of the thousands of payor banks is in a position to accept and process electronic information. In a country with so many payor banks, that cannot happen until there is considerable standardization of the technology for processing checks electronically.

Another problem is the continuing reluctance of the users of the system (those that write and receive checks) to rely on entirely electronic information. Thus, people who write checks still have a significant desire for a paper document to evidence the transaction. Similarly, people who receive checks that are dishonored will need some paper document to evidence the check that has failed to clear. Such documents are unlikely to be necessary in the great majority of cases; far more than 99 percent of checks clear when first presented, and it seems unlikely that creditors disavow their receipt of payment in any significant percentage of checking transactions. Thus, because one of the major goals of truncation is to eliminate the costs of transporting the original paper from place to place, it would be ideal if the users of the system would accept an image as a substitute for the original check.

One final complicating factor is the likelihood — at least in the short run — that despite the best efforts of system designers and statutory drafters, consumer advocates will be unsatisfied with substitute checks and will insist upon provisions for the return of the original checks. Obviously, it would be a relatively expensive proposition for banks to retain the original checks and to locate, retrieve, and deliver the original on demand. Still, at least in the short run there are plausible reasons why consumers might want the original checks. For example, in a dispute about the authenticity of a check, examination of the original might provide information about the signature (the traces

Figure 26.2
Check Processing Under Check 21

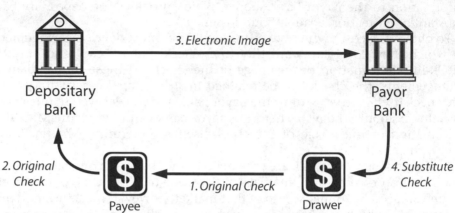

of the actual physical impression made at the time of signing) that currently is not included in the image or the substitute check.

In an attempt to facilitate check truncation, the Board of Governors of the Federal Reserve sponsored legislation that resulted in the Check Clearing in the 21st Century Act of 2003 (commonly known as Check 21), enacted in October of 2003 with an effective date of October 2004, 12 U.S.C. §§5001-5018. The most important thing to understand about Check 21 is its limited scope. The purpose of the statute is to make a "substitute check" the legal equivalent of the original check. Check 21 does not authorize electronic check processing: A bank can collect or present an electronic check only by means of a contractual agreement with the bank to which the check is being transferred or presented. Similarly, because Check 21 does not require banks to accept electronic images, it imposes no obligations on those that create them. Nor does Check 21 even alter whatever rights customers currently have to the return of their original checks. Rather, all of the provisions of the Act relate to the intermediate practical questions described above: facilitating truncation by depositary banks through the creation of reliable mechanisms for making an acceptable substitute of the original check in the few cases in which a substitute is necessary. Thus, the process contemplated by Check 21 is that banks will agree among themselves to present and accept electronic images of checks; the statute will facilitate the reconversion of those images to paper documents. Figure 26.2 illustrates that process.

The centerpiece of the statute is the concept of the substitute check, defined in §3(16) as follows:

The term "substitute check" means a paper reproduction of the original check that—

    (A) contains an image of the front and back of the original check;

    (B) bears a MICR line containing all the information appearing on the MICR line of the original check, except as provided under generally applicable industry standards for substitute checks to facilitate the processing of substitute checks;

Figure 26.3
Substitute Check

(C) conforms, in paper stock, dimension, and otherwise, with generally applicable industry standards for substitute checks; and

(D) is suitable for automated processing in the same manner as the original check.

Among other things, that provision makes it clear that a typical American-Express style "image statement"—reduced photocopies of checks sent perhaps six to the page—will **not** qualify as a substitute check. Rather, the document will need to include a MICR line and otherwise be of a size and texture suitable for automated processing. To give that definition some content, consider Figure 6.3, which shows the current ANSI standard for what such a document would look like.

To help foster public acceptance, the statute requires that banks provide customers with a plain-English statement—evident in Figure 26.3—that states: "This is a legal copy of your check. You can use it the same way you would use the original check." If a substitute check includes that legend and accurately represents the information on the original check, it is the legal equivalent of the check for all purposes. Check 21 §4(b). Similarly, although the statute does nothing directly to authorize the processing of electronic checks, it does provide that a person can deposit, present, or send a substitute check without consent of the party to whom it is sent. Check 21 §4(a).

To implement those rules, Check 21 creates a new series of warranties and indemnities. Those rules generally deal with three problems. The first is the problem that the image might not accurately reflect the original check. On that point, Section 5(1) obligates the reconverting bank to warrant that the substitute check meets the requirements for legal equivalence in Section 4(b) — which means, among other things, that the reconverting bank must warrant that the substitute check (made from an image that the reconverting bank has received from the converting bank) accurately represents the check still in the possession of the converting bank.

The second is the problem that despite the presentment of a check electronically the original paper check somehow might find its way into the check-collection process and be presented for payment in the future. To avoid losses from that scenario, the reconverting bank must warrant that no party will be called upon to pay either the original item or a subsequent substitute check made from that item. Check 21 §5(2).

The third problem is that the substitute check in some way might be an inadequate substitute for the original check. On that point, Section 6 obligates the reconverting bank and subsequent banks that process the substitute check to indemnify parties that suffer a loss because of the receipt of a substitute check instead of the original. If the substitute check complied with the statute, the indemnity is limited to the amount of the check, plus interest and expenses. Check 21 §6(b). If the check did *not* comply with the statute, the reconverting bank is liable for the entire loss proximately caused by the breach. Check 21 §6(b). To make it clear that banks can protect themselves by providing the original when it is necessary, liability on that indemnity is limited to losses that are incurred before the original check (or a copy that remedies a defect in the substitute check) is provided. Check 21 §6(d).

Finally, the most controversial provision of the statute is an expedited re-credit right for consumers, set forth in Check 21 §7. Under that provision, a consumer can claim a recredit if the consumer asserts that an item is not properly payable or that there has been a breach of one of the warranties in Section 5. Check 21 §7(1). The consumer must make the claim within 40 days of the date that the bank has delivered to the customer the substitute check and the relevant bank statement. Check 21 §7(2). The bank then must provide the recredit if it cannot "demonstrate[e] to the consumer that the substitute check was properly charged to the consumer account." Check 21 §7(c)(1). The recredit must be made no later than the end of the business day following the business day on which the bank determines the claim is valid. Check 21 §7(c)(2). Pending investigation, the recredit must be made before the end of the tenth business day after the submission of the claim. (If the item is for more than $2,500, the bank can delay recrediting the excess over $2,500 until the forty-fifth calendar day after the claim.) To protect the payor bank responding to such a claim, Section 8 includes a parallel expedited recredit right that permits the payor bank to recover funds from the bank from which it received the item in question.

Problem Set 26

26.1.   One Friday afternoon your client Bertie Wooster comes to see you. He tells you that he has a dispute with Roderick Spode regarding an antique silver cow creamer that Bertie recently purchased for $18,000. Bertie explains that he bought the item based on an Internet ad and mailed Spode a check as soon as he received the creamer. Spode has been hounding Bertie, claiming that Bertie has never paid for the item.

Bertie is certain that he did, both because he remembers mailing the check and, more importantly, because he received an image of the original check with his statement this month. (Bertie receives "image statements" that have a photocopy of the front of six checks on each page.) The image shows a signature on the back that appears to be the grandiose signature of Roderick Spode (with which Bertie is familiar). Bertie faxed the image to Spode, who claims that it is a forgery, that he never received the check, and that he will sue Bertie immediately if Bertie does not pay. "If you really paid, then you should be able to show me an original cancelled check," Spode says. At his wit's end, Bertie is worried that a suit against Spode would harm his reputation in the antiques industry, making it hard for him to acquire future items. But he can't believe he should have to pay twice. What do you advise?

26.2.   If the facts of Problem 26.1 eventually lead to a point where Bertie needs the original check, must his bank provide it to him? What if it is willing to provide the original check, but will charge $10 to do so? UCC §4-406(b) and comments 1 and 3.

26.3.   Same facts as in Problem 26.2, but now assume that the image was a substitute check that complied with Check 21.

(a)   Does that impose any new obligations on his bank? Check 21 §7.

(b)   What if Bertie claims that pen-impression data (expert evidence about the way in which the pen was pressed onto the paper) could have proven that Spode in fact signed the check, and that he cannot obtain that evidence because the substitute check does not include that data and the original has been destroyed? Check 21 §6.

26.4.   The next morning your old friend Carl Eben comes to see you. He has just discovered that a thief has been stealing money from him for several months. The thief has been stealing from Carl's mailbox on a regular basis and managed to steal an incoming package with some blank checks as well as several outgoing envelopes with payments to Carl's suppliers. The thief then wrote several checks payable to himself, which he cashed. On the checks to Carl's suppliers, he forged the name of the suppliers and then cashed the checks. Carl discovered the problem when a number of suppliers complained about his late payments.

When you asked Carl why he did not notice this on his bank statement, he admitted that he has been very busy lately and has simply failed to reconcile his bank statement for the last six months. Carl's bank admits that Carl ordinarily would not be responsible for any of the checks cashed by the thief. (Carl says that the officer said something about the checks not being "properly payable" under UCC §4-401.) The bank has, however, told Carl that Carl is liable for all of the unauthorized checks because of his failure to notify the bank about the problems when they sent him statements showing the charges for the forged checks. Carl has brought the statements with him. They are summary statements that show only the item number, amount, and date of payment. Is the bank right? UCC §4-406(a), (c), (d), and comment 1.

26.5.   Thursday morning you come into the office to find your old friend from college Mike McLaughlin waiting for you. Mike operates a computer services business. He wants to talk to you about a check for $20,000 that he recently received from one of his customers in payment of an invoice. When he deposited the check, it bounced. His bank did not, however, return the original check to him. Instead, it returned the image. He wants to know if this will hinder him in trying to collect the funds from the customer. (You should assume for purposes of the question that Mike would have been a person entitled to enforce the check if the check had been returned to him. The issue on which you should focus is whether he will be hindered by having an image of the check instead of the original.)

  a. What if the image is a simple photocopy? UCC §§1-201(20) (revised §1-201(b)(21)), 3-104(f), 3-301, 3-309, 3-310(b)(1), and 3-414(b).
  b. What if the image is a substitute check that complies with Check 21? Check 21 §4(b).
  c. What if the image is a substitute check that complies with Check 21 except that it omits the legend? In answering that question, assume that the check was reconverted by Mike's bank and that it inadvertently omitted the legend. Check 21 Act §§4(b), 5, and 7; Proposed Regulation CC 12 C.F.R. 229.2(bbb).

26.6. Stacy Vye (a longtime client and banker at Wessex Bank) comes to you for advice. She is about to enter into a major electronic-check presentation agreement with Wells Fargo, in which she agrees to accept electronic images from Wells Fargo in lieu of original checks. Can you think of any particular provisions she might need to include in such an agreement to protect herself from liability under Check 21? Check 21 §§5, 6, and 7.

26.7. A few months later, Stacy calls you back. She has had major difficulties with recredit claims under the statute. Apparently, a small but determined number of people are submitting large numbers of fraudulent claims. When she provides the recredited funds, the people remove it from their accounts. When Stacy is unable to recover the funds from the bank from which she received the item, she discovers that the customer and the funds are gone. Does Check 21 provide any help for her? Does it protect her adequately? Check 21 §7(d)(2).

Chapter 6. Electronic Payments

Assignment 27: The Credit-Card System

After cash and checks, credit cards clearly are the system of choice in the American economy; they currently are used to complete about 17 percent of direct payment transactions. To get a sense for the size of the system, at the end of 2004, Americans were charging more than $1.8 trillion worth of purchases a year. This assignment discusses the mechanics of how that system completes payment transactions. Assignment 28 discusses the losses that arise from error or fraud in those transactions.

A. The Issuer–Cardholder Relationship

The system involves four major participants: a purchaser that holds a credit card, the issuer that issues the credit card, a merchant that makes a sale, and an acquirer that collects payment for the merchant. (The acquirer is so named because it "acquires" the transaction from the merchant and then processes it to obtain payment from the issuer.) The credit card reflects a relationship between the cardholder and an issuing bank. The cardholder can make purchases on the account either by using the card directly or by using the number without the card. The issuing bank commits to pay for purchases that the cardholder makes in accordance with the agreement between the issuer and the cardholder. What that means, among other things, is that the merchant that accepts a credit card ordinarily gets paid even if the cardholder ultimately fails to pay its bills.

Although those four parties are the nominal parties to the transaction, lurking behind them in most cases is the network under which the card has been issued (usually Visa or MasterCard). Although credit cards originated in the 1920s as proprietary cards issued by department stores to save the time of evaluating the credit of purchasers on a purchase-by-purchase basis, they have gone far beyond that. By the 1950s, a few national organizations (entities like American Express, Diner's Club, and Carte Blanche) developed cards designed to allow travelers to pay for meals and lodging in remote locations without the uncertainty of writing a check. But more recently the market has come to be dominated by the familiar "universal" card, which aspires to universal acceptance for all purchases of any item anywhere. For those types of cards, Visa and MasterCard are the clear market leaders. As explained below, however, Visa and MasterCard do not participate directly in the transactions using the cards that bear their names and insignia. Rather, they operate more as facilitators, providing the technology and marketing to keep the system operating.

Because there is no UCC article generally applicable to credit-card transactions, state law has a much less pervasive influence on the credit-card system than it does on the checking system. Thus, the principal legal regulation of the credit-card system comes from the federal Truth-in-Lending Act (TILA) and from Regulation Z (12 C.F.R. Part 226), promulgated by the Federal Reserve under TILA. TILA is codified at 15 U.S.C. §§1601-1667e, as Title I of the Consumer Credit Protection Act, 15 U.S.C. §§1601-1693r. For clarity, citations in this book to TILA use the section numbers of the Consumer Credit Protection Act instead of the U.S. Code section numbers.

TILA and Regulation Z do not focus on the payment aspect of a credit card (the function that provides substantially immediate payment to sellers). Instead, they focus on the credit aspect (the function that allows a purchaser to pay a seller now in return for a commitment by the purchaser to repay the card issuer in the future). Specifically, TILA includes a series of rules that apply to any "credit card," which it defines in §103(k) as "any card . . . or other credit device existing for the purpose of obtaining money, property, labor, or services on credit." Thus, TILA applies not only to the most common credit cards issued by banks (Visa cards and MasterCards), but also to general-purpose cards issued by nonbank entities like American Express or Discover, and even to limited-purpose cards issued by department stores and gasoline retailers (among others).

Appearing as it does in the Consumer Credit Protection Act, it comes as no surprise that TILA for the most part is limited to consumer transactions. Specifically, with one minor exception discussed in Assignment 28, TILA is limited to credit extended to individuals, TILA §104(1), Regulation Z, §226.3(a)(2), and does not apply to credit extended "primarily for business, commercial, or agricultural purposes," TILA §104(1). It also does not apply to transactions involving more than $25,000. TILA §104(3).

The key to any credit-card arrangement is the relationship between the cardholder and the card issuer. Although the law leaves many of the aspects of the ongoing relationship to the parties, the legal regime does impose significant constraints on the practices that card issuers use to acquire customers, generally out of a concern that consumers will become overburdened with debt that they did not intentionally incur. Specifically, §132 of the Truth-in-Lending Act prohibits banks from issuing credit cards to consumers "except in response to a request or application." See Regulation Z, §226.12(a) (same). Similarly, Regulation Z requires that a bank issuing a credit card provide the consumer a "clea[r] and conspicuou[s]" written disclosure that summarizes the applicable legal rules. Regulation Z, §226.5(a)(1). The rules contemplate disclosures as complicated and unreadable as the disclosures discussed in Assignment 21 that are customary for checking accounts. Regulation Z, §§226.5, 226.6. In practice, the disclosures closely resemble model disclosures provided by the Federal Reserve in Appendix G to Regulation Z. Those rules are enforceable by a private right of action that the cardholder can bring in federal court.

The typical relationship between an issuer and a cardholder is a simple one. The issuer commits to pay for purchases made with the card, in return for the cardholder's promise to reimburse the issuer over time. That relationship is exactly the opposite of the common checking relationship, where the customer normally must deposit funds *before* the bank will pay checks. Of course that distinction is not universal, because some checking customers have overdraft arrangements with their banks under which their banks honor checks even if the checks exceed the amount of the funds that the customer previously has deposited. Conversely, some credit cards issued to persons of doubtful credit strength require the cardholders to limit their purchases to amounts the cardholder previously has deposited with the issuer. Even in those cases, however, the issuer cannot simply offset the charges against pre-deposited funds, as it does with checking accounts (or with debit cards that draw on those accounts). The credit-card issuer can periodically deduct an amount from the funds to pay a prearranged portion of the charges. TILA §169(a); Regulation Z, §226.12(d)(3). For example, a common arrangement grants the issuer an advance authorization to make a monthly ACH deduction from the customer's checking account equal to 3 percent of the customer's outstanding credit-card balance.

The buy-first, pay-later aspect of most credit-card relationships alters the underlying economics of the system. Banks that provide checking accounts can earn profits by investing the funds that customers have placed in their accounts. A credit-card issuer does not have that option because most card-holders do not deposit funds before they make purchases on their cards. The profit for the typical card issuer comes predominantly from the interest income that the issuer earns on the balances that its cardholders carry on their cards from month to month. Although issuers earn income from other charges (such as annual fees), interest and late charges typically account for about 80 percent of the income earned by a card issuer. And that dependence on interest income has been rising steadily over the last decade because the annual fees and other noninterest charges that used to be common features of credit cards have been declining steadily during that time.

The dependence on interest revenues produces an odd irony. The con-sumers that pay their credit-card balances every month — so-called conven-ience users — generally are the most creditworthy individuals in the system, but are definitely bad customers for the issuers, which depend on interest income to fund the system. Some issuers have responded to that problem by imposing annual fees limited to convenience users, but it seems unlikely that such a move will spread sufficiently to alter the basic economics of the system. As it happens, the problem of convenience users is not all that serious, mostly because of the surprisingly high number of cardholders that do not pay their balances every month. Indeed, less than 10 percent of credit-card balances are paid off before interest accrues. As a share of cardholders, the percentage of cardholders carrying balances is still about 60 percent (even though that percentage has declined substantially during the last few years). And those that do carry balances carry staggering amounts of debt. Outstanding credit-card balances at the end of 2004 on general-purpose credit cards in the United States totaled about $700 billion, almost $3,000 for each person in the entire population. That sum provides an ample base for interest and late charges sufficient to motivate issuers to par-ticipate in the credit-card system.

One last point about the relationship between the bank and the cardholder touches on the relation between the credit card and other products the bank might offer. For obvious reasons, cardholders sometimes have bank accounts at the banks that issue their credit cards. Among the reasons for that might be the ability of the bank where an individual has a bank account to acquire significant information about an individual's creditworthiness that gives that bank an advantage in assessing the individual as a credit-card customer. That relationship also could give the bank a fortuitous advantage when the cardholder fails to make payments required under the terms of its card agreement because the bank could obtain payment by offsetting its claim under the credit-card agreement against funds of the customer on deposit at the bank. TILA §169(a), however, strictly limits the issuer's right to obtain payment through an offset against the cardholder's bank account. First, an issuer can obtain payment through such an offset only if the cardholder consents in writing in connection with a plan for the bank to obtain automatic monthly payments on the card (a practice discussed above). TILA §169(a)(1). Second, even if the cardholder enters into such an agreement with the issuer, the issuer cannot deduct such a payment from the cardholder's bank account if the payment is for a charge that the cardholder disputes and if the cardholder requests the bank not to make such a deduction. TILA §169(a)(2).

B.   Using the Credit-Card Account

From the cardholder's perspective, payment with a credit card is simple. In a face-to-face transaction, the merchant normally swipes the card on a machine and produces a slip for the consumer to sign a few moments later, on which the cardholder promises to pay the transaction amount. In a transaction that is completed over the telephone (or the Internet) rather than face-to-face, the cardholder provides the card number to the merchant, and the transaction proceeds. The only difference is that the merchant does not have a signed slip as evidence that the cardholder in fact authorized the transaction.

Several significant things happen during the moments just after the cardholder provides its number to the merchant. First, the merchant's card terminal reads the magnetic strip on the back of the card. That strip ordinarily includes a magnetic description of the cardholder's issuing bank and account number, as well as a "card verification" value or code, which confirms that the card is not a counterfeit card.

Next, the merchant's terminal uses that information to conduct an authorization transaction. In that transaction, the terminal contacts the merchant's financial institution (usually by telephone) and sends an encrypted message identifying the card number, card verification value, expiration date, transaction amount, location, and Standard Industry Classification (SIC) code of the merchant. The acquirer then routes that message to processing computers at the card network (assume that it is Visa, for convenience). Visa then routes the message in accordance with the issuer's directions, either to the issuer itself or to a third party that processes credit-card authorizations on the issuer's behalf.

The recipient of the message (assume that it is the issuer, for convenience) then determines whether the account number reflects a valid card and whether the amount of the transaction is within the card's authorized credit limit. The issuer also compares the card verification value to its records (or to an algo-rithm for calculating that value) to determine whether the card is counterfeit. Finally, the issuer considers the overall package of information about the trans-action to determine whether there is an undue risk that the transaction is fraudulent. Large issuers use neural-network products designed to recognize out-of-pattern behavior that suggests a likelihood of fraud. The merchant's SIC code is crucial to the use of that software because it provides a general identi-fication of the type of item being purchased. For example, three separate trans-actions on the same day purchasing jewelry and stereo components in a city 800 miles from the billing address are much more likely to reflect fraud than three separate transactions purchasing meals in the same location. If the trans-action appears to be legitimate, the issuer (only seconds after receiving the incoming message) sends an encrypted message back to the merchant author-izing the transaction.

C.   Collection by the Payee

1.   The Mechanics of Collection

After the cardholder leaves the counter, the merchant is left with the author-ized credit-card "slip" (which might or might not be represented by a piece of paper). To turn that slip into money, the merchant must collect the slip through the network associated with the card that was used in the transaction. Visa and MasterCard are the largest networks; they each have more than 20,000 members and together cover more than three-fourths of the general-purpose credit-card market in this country. The Visa and MasterCard entities are not themselves financial institutions. Rather, they are loosely organized not-for-profit cooperative organizations composed of banks that participate in the industry. Their main purposes are to operate a clearance network and to coordinate advertising and research on technology and other issues important to the credit-card system.

To collect payments made by a credit card, a merchant must have an agree-ment with a member of the applicable network, normally referred to as the acquirer or acquiring bank. Thus, to collect a Visa receivable, a merchant must have an agreement with an acquirer that is a member of the Visa network. One of the principal topics of such an agreement is regulation of the merchant's relation with its customer, the cardholder. For example, the agreements es-tablish a tier of discount rates that give the merchant a strong incentive to act with care in deciding whether to accept a credit card. Among other things, those rates make the transaction cheaper for the merchant if the merchant obtains the appropriate authorization from the issuer *before* completing the transaction.

At one time, those agreements also included provisions that prevented mer-chants from offering discounts to customers that paid with cash. A merchant might have an incentive to offer a cash discount because cash sales would allow the merchant to obtain payment without losing the portion of the sales price that the merchant bank charges to process payment for the merchant (as discussed below). Given the tough competition in the credit-card market, it would be plausible to expect that the profits merchants could make by offering cash discounts eventually would induce acquirers to offer agreements that did not contain such restrictions. As it happens, however, it was positive law, not competition, that drove out those agreements. Specifically, §167 of TILA now prohibits those agreements and leaves merchants free to offer any cash discounts they find appropriate. Regulation Z, §226.12(f).

After completing the transaction with the cardholder, the merchant delivers the slips to the acquirer, usually on a daily basis. Ordinarily, the same terminal that conducted the authorization transaction stores information about all the merchant's transactions. At the end of the day, the terminal transmits a single mass ("batched") message to the acquirer that describes all of the day's transactions. It is possible for the process to be conducted based on the paper slips, rather than electronic messages, but that is less common (only about 5 percent of transactions in 1996) and tends to be significantly more expensive (about one-and-a-half times as costly per transaction from the merchant's perspective). Although the details depend on the particular agreement, the acquirer ordinarily gives a provisional credit to the acquirer's account for the charges processed that day. The funds become available a few days later, subject only to the acquirer's right (discussed below) to charge back funds if a cardholder declines to pay.

The amount of the credit that the acquirer provides the merchant is less than the gross amount of the slips because the acquirer deducts a small discount to cover the services that it is providing. The discount ordinarily has two components, a percentage of each transaction and a small per-item fee (in the range of 10 cents per transaction). In most contexts, the merchant receives a net credit in the range of 95-98 percent of the gross amount of the charges. The amount of the discount is negotiated as a key term of the agreement between the acquirer and the merchant, with the final amount depending on several factors. The most important factors are the volume and size of the transactions for which the merchant accepts credit cards. A local pharmacy with relatively few, relatively small transactions pays a much higher discount than a national department-store chain, with thousands of relatively large transactions each day.

Another important factor is whether the merchant sells face to face or over the telephone. Acquirers charge higher discounts for mail-order transactions because of the increased potential for fraud in transactions where the parties do not meet. Similarly, the agreements often include a separate (higher) charge that applies in "nonqualifying" transactions, those in which merchants type in a card number instead of swiping the whole strip. The failure to swipe the card deprives the network of the ability to use security features that appear only on the stripe (such as the card verification value). Accordingly, because there is a higher risk that such a transaction is fraudulent, the acquirer charges more to process payment for the merchant.

The acquirer promptly passes the slips along to obtain payment from the bank that issued the card. Ordinarily, it sorts all of the day's messages into on-us charges (credit-card charges for which it issued the credit card) and into separate piles for each network (Visa, MasterCard, and the like). It then sends a batched message describing all of its transactions to each network in which it participates. The network assesses an interchange fee on those transactions and then credits each acquirer for the difference: the face amount of the transactions (the amount the consumers promised to pay), reduced by the interchange fee. The amount of the interchange fee is slightly lower than the amount of the merchant discounts, so that the amount credited to the acquirer (gross amount, less interchange fee) is slightly higher than the amount the acquirer gave the merchant (gross amount, less the merchant discount). That relationship is not a coincidence; the business of acquiring credit card transactions would not be profitable unless the acquirer set its merchant discounts at a rate that exceeds its expenses. Ordinarily, the network credits the acquirer for 98-99 percent of the charges, depending on the type of transaction (card fully swiped; face to face, but card not swiped; remote telephone transaction). The credit is applied to a designated account of the acquirer, typically the acquirer's account at its Federal Reserve bank.

Finally, the network sorts the transactions by issuer and debits each issuer for the amounts credited to acquirers for transactions on that issuer's cards. Thus, the issuers are charged only the net amount of the charges (the face amount reduced by the interchange fees). The issuers, in turn, sort the transactions reported to them, post them to the separate accounts, and bill for them on a monthly basis. Figure 27.1 illustrates that process.

When the process is complete, the credit-card account of the purchaser/cardholder has been charged the face amount of the purchase. If all goes well, the issuer has a profit of 1-2 percent of the transaction: The issuer has been charged for 98-99 percent of the transaction and has obtained a right to collect 100 percent from its cardholder. Visa has not charged anything for its service in the particular transaction; it recoups its operating expenses by quarterly assessments of its members. The acquirer has a profit as well, although

Figure 27.1
Payment by Credit Card

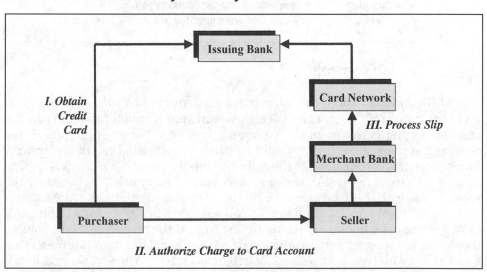

often much less than the issuing bank: It has received a credit for 98-99 percent of the transaction and passed on to its merchants some negotiated, but slightly smaller amount (usually between 95 and 98 percent). Finally, the merchant has received that 95-98 percent as payment for its transaction with the purchaser. Its profit (if it has one) has to come from its having sold the product for an amount that exceeds its costs by more than the 2-5 percent it expended in obtaining payment through the credit-card system. Figure 27.2 illustrates a typical allocation of the funds from such a transaction.

Figure 27.2
Dividing the Credit-Card Dollar

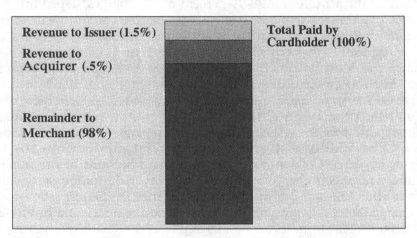

Revenue to Issuer (1.5%)

Revenue to Acquirer (.5%)

Remainder to Merchant (98%)

Total Paid by Cardholder (100%)

1. The Issuer's profit is the interchange fee (1.5 percent in this example).
2. The Merchant Bank's profit (2.5 percent in this example) is the difference between the discount (4 percent in this example) and the interchange fee (1.5 percent in this example).
3. The Merchant receives 96 percent (the difference between the face amount of the transaction and the interchange fee).
4. The Cardholder pays the face amount of the transaction, 100 percent.

2.   Finality of Payment

One of the most distinctive features of the current credit-card system is that it gives the consumer a right to cancel payment that is much broader than the consumer's rights in any of the competing systems. For example, under the checking system, a consumer's right to cancel payment is relatively limited. The consumer technically has the right to stop payment on a check, but that right is effective only if the consumer acts before the check is honored by the payor bank, which will be at most a matter of days and might be only a matter of hours on local checks. Similarly, as you will see when you study debit cards in Assignment 29, debit-card payments are final at the moment of sale, leaving the consumer no later opportunity to stop payment. That does not mean that a consumer who pays with a check or debit card has lost the ordinary contract-law right to rescind the transaction. But it does mean that the merchant already has the money while the cardholder is pursuing that right. As a result, it may be more difficult for the cardholder to challenge the transaction.

In the credit-card system, however, the issuing bank's obligation to pay does not become final at the time of the initial payment to the acquirer. Rather, TILA §170(a) grants a cardholder the right to withhold payment on the basis of any defense that it could assert against the original merchant. For example, suppose that Cliff Janeway uses a credit card to purchase some books as a gift for a friend, relying on the merchant's assurance that the books are rare first editions. If Cliff later discovers that the books in fact are not first editions, TILA §170(a) allows Cliff to refuse to pay the charge on his credit-card account. Specifically, he can assert against the issuer his ordinary contract-law defense that the goods fail to conform to the underlying sales contract.

Standing alone, that provision would wreak havoc with credit cards as a payment system. Issuers as a class would be in a difficult position if they could collect credit-card charges only when they could prove that the merchant had performed properly on the underlying sales contract. Furthermore, a system that allowed merchants to pass to the issuer any risk that the cardholder would refuse to pay because of nonperformance would leave merchants with an inadequate incentive to satisfy their customers. The card-issuing networks solve that problem by adopting rules that pass that risk back to the merchant. Thus, when a cardholder raises a defense against the issuer under TILA §170(a), the issuer can charge back the challenged slip to the acquirer. The charge-back is accomplished in the same way as the forward processing of the slip when the transaction first occurred: The issuing bank sends an item through the Visa network, seeking to recover the appropriate funds from the acquirer and, if all goes as it should, receives a credit from the Visa clearinghouse in the daily entry into the issuing bank's bank account at its Federal Reserve bank. Similarly, the acquirer's agreement with the merchant allows the acquirer to charge back the same transaction to the merchant. Thus, the acquirer removes the funds from the merchant's account (just as it would remove funds from a dishonored check that the merchant had deposited). In the end, the merchant bears the burden of obtaining payment from the disgruntled cardholder.

Several qualifications limit the cardholder's right to challenge payment. The first cuts off the right as the cardholder pays the bill. The cardholder's right under TILA §170(a) is only a right to withhold payment from the issuer; it does not include a right to seek a refund from the issuer or the merchant. Accordingly, the right dissipates as the cardholder pays off the credit-card balance generated by the transaction in question. See TILA §170(b) (limiting challenge right to "the amount of credit outstanding with respect to the transaction"); see also Regulation Z, §226.12(c) (same). That limitation should not trouble cardholders significantly because of the likelihood that defects in the purchased goods or services would be evident before the cardholder received the bill and paid it.

Another minor limitation is the requirement in TILA §170(a)(1) that the cardholder "ma[k]e a good faith attempt to obtain satisfactory resolution of [the] disagreement . . . from the [merchant] honoring the credit card." That also is not a significant problem. Few cardholders will challenge items on their credit-card bill if they easily can resolve the dispute directly with the merchant in question.

The most significant limitation relates to the location of the transaction. Specifically, TILA §170(a) prevents cardholders from withholding payment on transactions that occur outside the state where the cardholder resides and more than 100 miles from the cardholder's billing address. Under that rule, the only transactions that the cardholder can challenge are transactions that occur either in the state of the cardholder's residence or within 100 miles of the cardholder's billing address. As the following case suggests, the frequency with which consumers use credit cards while at locations remote from their homes brings that provision into play with some regularity.

Hyland v. First USA Bank

1995 WL 595861 (E.D. Pa. Sept. 28, 1995)

GILES, District Judge. . . .

In February, 1994, First USA Bank issued a Gold Visa Card to the Plaintiffs. In May, 1994, Plaintiffs traveled to Greece for a vacation, where they purchased an oriental carpet ("the carpet") from Aris Evangelinos, the owner of an antique store in Nauplia, Greece. Plaintiffs paid US $2,070.57 for the carpet with the Visa Card issued by the Bank.

Plaintiffs contend that in order to induce Plaintiffs to purchase the carpet, Evangelinos made express warranties that the carpet was an antique Kilim, circa 1930, that it was woven and embroidered with pure silk with a cotton warp, and that it had been colored with vegetable dyes. Upon inspection by a United States carpet expert, Plaintiffs discovered that these express warranties were false. The Plaintiffs contacted the Bank and the merchant to obtain a credit.

Plaintiffs allege that the Bank directed them to return the carpet to the merchant. They did so via Federal Express. However, the carpet was intercepted by Greek Customs, who informed Plaintiffs that a duty of approximately US $1,240 would have to be paid before the carpet could be released. Plaintiffs refused to pay the duty, and notified the Bank that they would hold the Bank responsible for the loss of the carpet. The carpet was ultimately confiscated by Greek Customs.

Plaintiffs maintain that the Bank repeatedly assured them that it would assist the Plaintiffs in resolving the matter if Plaintiffs (1) returned the carpet to Evangelinos; and (2) provided a return receipt to the Bank. Plaintiffs contend that they relied on the Bank's assurance of assistance, and ceased personal efforts to obtain a refund. The Bank later informed Plaintiffs that consumer protection does not exist for purchases made outside of the United States. Accordingly, the Bank refused to accept liability for the loss of the carpet. . . .

Plaintiffs allege that Evangelinos made certain express warranties regarding the authenticity of the carpet. The formation of an express warranty is governed by statute: Any affirmation of fact or promise made by the seller to the buyer which relates to the goods and becomes part of the basis of the bargain creates an express warranty that the goods shall conform to the affirmation or promise. [UCC §2-313(a)(1).] Breach of warranty claims serve to protect buyers from loss where the goods purchased do not meet commercial standards or affirmations. In the present case, Plaintiffs clearly allege that the carpet did not conform to the affirmations of authenticity made by Evangelinos.

However, Plaintiffs have chosen not to sue Evangelinos directly. Instead, Plaintiffs allege that under [TILA §170], and Regulation Z, 12 C.F.R. §226.12(c), Plaintiffs are permitted to assert against the Bank, as card issuer, the claim for breach of warranty that they are entitled to assert against Evangelinos. Plaintiffs further allege that the Bank has waived and is estopped from asserting any limitations or defenses to liability on the Truth in Lending Act claim. The Bank asserts that under §1666i(a)(3) of the Act, it cannot be held liable for the loss of the carpet because the transaction did not occur in the state of, or within 100 miles of, Plaintiffs' mailing address. In addition, the Bank contends that it has not waived its right to assert the geographic limitation as a defense.

As a general rule, the Truth in Lending Act provides that "a card issuer who has issued a credit card to a cardholder . . . shall be subject to all claims (other than tort claims) and defenses arising out of any transaction in which the credit card is used as a method of payment or extension of credit." 15 U.S.C. §1666i(a). However, a card issuer is liable for such claims only if "the place where the initial transaction occurred was in the same State as the mailing address previously provided by the cardholder or was within 100 miles from such address. . . ." 15 U.S.C. §1666i(a)(3). In the present case, Plaintiffs purchased the carpet in Greece, a foreign country that is neither in the same state nor within 100 miles of the Plaintiffs' mailing address. Therefore, the allegations in the Plaintiffs' complaint do not satisfy the geographical limitation provided by §1666i(a)(3). However, Plaintiffs also allege that the Bank waived the protection granted by this geographical limitation. Plaintiffs allege that by initially agreeing to assist Plaintiffs in an international dispute, the Bank knowingly waived its right to assert the geographical limitation as a defense.

A waiver is a voluntary and intentional relinquishment or abandonment of a known right. In the present case, Plaintiffs allege that they "specifically asked the BANK whether the BANK could assist them in obtaining reimbursement from a seller who was located not merely out of state but, in fact, abroad, in Greece." Plaintiffs contend that the Bank responded by assuring them that the Bank "could be of assistance." The complaint further alleges that Plaintiffs spoke frequently with the Bank by telephone, and referred the Bank's customer service representative to the charge statement which showed that the purchase had been made in Greece. According to Plaintiffs, the Bank repeatedly agreed to assist them.

Reading the complaint liberally, and viewing the allegations in the complaint in a light most favorable to Plaintiffs, we conclude that Plaintiffs have adequately alleged waiver of the geographic limitation by the Bank sufficient to survive a motion to dismiss.

It is difficult to assess the practical effects of the 100-mile limitation. On the one hand, the increasing nationalization of the economy and the rapid growth of mail-order businesses selling goods by credit cards have increased the share of nonlocal transactions. Furthermore, *Hyland* might give an exaggerated impression of the cardholder's rights. Many courts would not be as generous as the *Hyland* court, and many issuers would hesitate to offer assistance on transactions for which the 100-mile limit gives them immunity. On the other hand, it is not clear whether the 100-mile limitation applies to mail-order transactions; cases considering the location of a credit-card transaction made by telephone have reached conflicting results, with some concluding that the transaction takes place at the consumer's location and others concluding that the transaction takes place at the merchant's location. Moreover, a number of considerations can lead issuing banks to forgo a strict reliance on their rights under the 100-mile limitation. For example, as in most of the systems discussed in this chapter, the transaction costs to the bank of contesting the customer's claim readily could exceed the amount in dispute, especially on small charges. Finally, in an increasingly competitive market for credit-card business, issuers may be reluctant to alienate customers that are, after all, free to take their credit business to another issuer. In the end, though, even if the limitation is enforced strictly and applies to a significant portion of credit-card transactions, the right to withhold payment gives credit-card users an advantage much broader than anything they would have under the other payment systems readily available to consumers.

Problem Set 27

27.1. Ben Darrow (your client, a banker from FSB) stopped by late yesterday afternoon to show you a "bizarre" letter that he received in the mail yesterday. He mentions that because of a recent consolidation he now oversees his bank's credit-card issuing operations, even though he has little experience in the area. The letter is from one of FSB's cardholders and describes a $475 mountain bike that the cardholder recently purchased using an FSB Visa card. The letter explains that the bike's gear-shifting mechanism does not function properly and asks FSB to "refund" to the customer the amount shown on the customer's current Visa statement for the purchase of the bike. The letter encloses payment for $100 (the amount of the other charges shown on the statement).

Ben tells you that he is completely befuddled. "Why should I care whether the stupid bike works? If she doesn't like it, let her take it up with the merchant. My only job is to make sure I pay the merchant for her charges and then to make sure that she pays me. What does she think I am, some kind of traveling Better Business Bureau? Can you believe the nerve of some people?" Do you share Ben's assessment of the "nerve" of the letter writer? Is the writer entitled to a refund? To anything? Do you need to know anything about the charges on her statement to ascertain Ben's obligations to her? TILA §170; Regulation Z, §226.12(c).

27.2. After your discussion with Ben in Problem 27.1, Ben asks you how he would be able to respond to a cardholder's defenses in cases where the cardholder could assert those defenses. "How am I supposed to prove that her mountain bike works? I don't sell mountain bikes. I drive a car to work. I haven't ridden a bicycle since I was 15 years old. Do I just have to give her the money?" What do you tell Ben?

27.3. Jodi Kay from CountryBank calls to discuss a troubling article that she read in this morning's newspaper. The article reports that a client of hers named CompUPlus recently filed for bankruptcy in the face of rampant consumer complaints about CompUPlus's newest line of laptop computers. Jodi thinks that she is in good shape because (she says) she has never made any loans to the client. The only service that she has provided has been as a an acquirer processing CompUPlus's mail-order credit-card sales. Those sales recently have been substantial: $150,000 over the last three months. Does that relationship put her employer, CountryBank, at risk? TILA §170; Regulation Z, §226.12(c).

27.4. Your friend Willie McCarver runs a struggling computer-services company. Talking to you over dinner, Willie tells you that he has gotten into a tight spot with some of his most important suppliers. If he does not pay them $10,000 in the next week, they are going to stop shipping goods to him, which would finish his business in a matter of days. Willie thinks that some highly profitable orders are "just around the corner." In the meantime, he thinks that he has hit on a way to keep his suppliers satisfied and wants your advice. Specifically, he plans to use the MasterCard to pay the suppliers $10,000 to reduce the amount that he owes for past shipments; the card that he received in the mail conveniently has a $10,000 limit. Mindful of some advice you gave him several years ago about his rights on credit-card charges, he figures that he can dispute the charges (perhaps claiming that the goods were defective) and defer payment to the credit-card issuer indefinitely. He wants to know if you think the scheme will work and how he can design it to hold off the creditors as long as possible. TILA §§104(1), 170; Regulation Z, §§226.12(c).

27.5. Cliff Janeway drops in to discuss a difficulty he is having with Bulstrode Bank, the acquirer that clears credit-card transactions for him. Cliff found out this morning that Bulstrode has bounced several checks of Cliff's during the last week. Cliff is unhappy because the checks should have been covered easily by funds deposited into his account several days earlier in the form of credit-card receivables from his business. When Cliff called Bulstrode to complain, Bulstrode explained that it had adopted a new policy with respect to credit-card services. Under that policy, Bulstrode plans to place a hold on Cliff's credit-card deposits for 45 days after the date that Cliff deposited them to protect against the possibility that Bulstrode will be obligated to disgorge funds to card issuers if cardholders challenge any of the relevant transactions. Cliff wants to know if the bank can do this. "Isn't there some law requiring the bank to release the funds to me in just a few days?" UCC §§4-104(a)(9), 4-214(a), 4-215(e); Regulation CC, §§229.10-.12; TILA §170; Regulation Z, §226.12(c).

27.6. Your congressional representative, Pamela Herring, recently got involved in a credit-card dispute with a mail-order merchandiser and was outraged to discover that she could not cancel the transaction because of the 100-mile limit in TILA §170. She decided to look into introducing a bill to eliminate that limit. Shortly after she started investigating that problem, a similarly outraged constituent telecopied her the following excerpt from a recent Nevada Supreme Court decision:

[A]ppellants present policy arguments as to why they should be excused from th[e 100-mile] requirement. Appellants argue that the one hundred mile requirement is unrealistic because an explosion in credit card use has occurred since [TILA §170] was written. Appellants further complain that if the one hundred mile limit is enforced, an unscrupulous merchant could defraud travelers almost at will, secure in the knowledge that it is unlikely that the traveler would return to a remote location to press a claim against the merchant. Finally, appellants note that the credit card issuer, because of its regular contact with both the merchant and the cardholder, is in the best position to prevent problems such as those which occurred in this case.

Singer v. Chase Manhattan Bank, 890 P.2d 1305, 1306 (Nev. 1995). She wants to know two things: (a) Is there anything to be said for the 100-mile limit? (b) Who would be most seriously harmed by its removal?

Assignment 28:   Error and Fraud in Credit-Card Transactions

The credit-card system is as vulnerable to mistake and chicanery as any other payment system. Given its large place in the economy, though, it should come as no surprise that the system has well-developed institutions for dealing with those problems. This assignment discusses two general problems: erroneous charges and unauthorized charges.

A.   Erroneous Charges

The simplest problem is the erroneous charge: an item that appears on a credit-card statement that does not reflect an actual transaction on the account. In addition to the right to withhold payment set out in TILA §170 (described in Assignment 27), TILA §161 sets out detailed provisions for resolving alleged billing errors related to credit cards. See also Regulation Z, §226.13 (offering details on procedures for resolving billing errors). To challenge a billing error under TILA, the cardholder must provide written notice to the issuer within 60 days after the date on which the creditor sent the relevant statement to the cardholder. TILA §161(a).

The statute gives a broad meaning to the term "billing error," so that it includes not only claims that the cardholder did not make the charge in question, but also claims that the merchant failed to deliver the goods and services covered by the charge in question, and even requests for additional clarification about the charge. TILA §161(b); Regulation Z, §226.13(a). Thus, if Cliff's statement shows a charge for a purchase from Amazon.com, Cliff could use the billing-error procedures not only to press a claim that he never made the purchase, but also in cases where he did purchase the books so long as he can claim that the seller never delivered the books or that he wants further information justifying the charge.

If the cardholder sends the proper notice, the creditor must send a written acknowledgment of the notice within 30 days and must resolve the claim within two billing cycles. If the cardholder alleges that the merchant failed to deliver the goods or services covered by the charge, the issuer cannot reject the claim without first "conduct[ing] a reasonable investigation and determin[ing] that the property or services were actually delivered...as agreed." Regulation Z, §226.13(f) n.31; see TILA §161(a)(B)(ii). If the issuer does not accept the cardholder's allegation, the issuer must (within the two-billing-cycle period) give the cardholder a written explanation of the issuer's reason for not correcting the charge. TILA §161(a); Regulation Z, §226.13(c)(2), (f). Most important from the cardholder's perspective, the creditor is barred from closing or restricting the cardholder's account for failure to pay the disputed amount during the pendency of the dispute. TILA §161(d); Regulation Z, §226.13(d). The issuer can, however, accrue a finance charge against the disputed amount. The finance charge would be due only if the dispute is resolved against the cardholder. Regulation Z, §§226.13(d)(1) n.30, 226.13(g)(1). Finally, the statute provides a modest penalty for failure to follow the procedures, requiring the creditor to forfeit the first $50 of the charge in dispute. TILA §161(e).

The following case illustrates how those provisions operate in practice.

Belmont v. Associates National Bank (Delaware)

119 F. Supp. 2d 149 (E.D.N.Y. 2000)

TRAGER, District Judge.

Plaintiff Peter Belmont, an attorney licensed to practice in the State of New York, but acting pro se in this matter, brought this suit against Associates National Bank (Delaware) ("Associates") under the Truth in Lending Act ("TILA" or the "Act"), 15 U.S.C. §1601 et seq., and Regulation Z thereunder, 12 C.F.R. §226.13, for failure to properly respond to a notice of billing error and for having threatened to make adverse credit reports while the billing error remained unresolved.

Peter Belmont alleges that on a monthly statement dated May 5, 1998, he was improperly billed for charges made on his son's Associates MasterCard credit card account. While Associates maintained that Peter Belmont was a co-obligor on his son's account and was thus liable for charges on the account after his son filed for bankruptcy, Peter Belmont questioned whether he was an obligor and demanded documentary proof of his obligation. Peter Belmont claims that Associates failed to comply with the requirements of TILA in responding to his notice.

Associates has moved for dismissal of, or in the alternative, for summary judgment on, all claims brought by Peter Belmont. Peter Belmont filed a cross-motion for summary judgment in response.

BACKGROUND

Associates alleges that its records indicate that on September 21, 1987, Peter Belmont and his son, Jeremy Belmont, opened a Boatmen's Bank of St. Louis ("Boatmen's") MasterCard credit card account which was later purchased by Associates. Peter Belmont acknowledges that in September 1987 he did co-sign for a credit card account with his son, does not recall doing so with either Boatmen's or Associates and states that he no longer has a copy of the credit card application.

On April 6, 1992, Peter Belmont sent a letter entitled "NOTICE OF REVOCATION OF CO_SIGNER_SHIP" to Consumer Loan Center, P.O. Box 9101, Boston, MA 02209-9101, regarding a MasterCard account numbered 5417-6710-0001-9848, in which he stated that he wished to be removed as a co-signer on his son's account. In the letter, Peter Belmont noted that the account was "in arrears in the amount of $48.00 and going into a 30-day late status." Id. He further stated: "I no longer wish to guarantee borrowing against this account or to have my credit-worthiness affected by the failure of the account's holder, Mr. Jeremy Belmont, to pay his bills in timely fashion." Id. With the letter, Peter Belmont sent a check, dated April 5, 1992, for $48.00 to "The Massachusetts Co." with "Jeremy Belmont 5417 6710 0001 9848 M/C" specified on the check's memo line. See id. On the canceled check, cashed at the Texas Commerce Bank-Dallas on April 11, 1992, the account number was crossed-off on the memo line and replaced by the account number "5419312700002648," the Associates account number held by Jeremy Belmont from January 1993 until October 1995.

Associates denies ever having received Peter Belmont's April 1992 letter and avers that the Consumer Loan Center address specified in the letter was never an address used by Associates. Associates, however, offers no explanation of how its account number came to be placed on the check Peter Belmont enclosed with the letter.

At any rate, the Associates statements on the account sent to Jeremy Belmont at his addresses in Massachusetts and California from January 1993 through April 1998 continued to list Peter Belmont as an addressee. The elder Belmont, however, has resided at 166 Columbia Heights, Brooklyn, N.Y. 11201-2105 since September 1992. . . .

Then, on April 28, 1998, Associates removed Jeremy Belmont from the account when he filed for bankruptcy. Associates claims that his son's default made Peter Belmont the primary cardholder on the account and thus, solely responsible for payment of the debt. As a result, Associates sent the next monthly statement, dated May 5, 1998, to "Peter A Belmont, 166 Columbia Heights, Brooklyn, N.Y. 11201-2105." This statement showed that the account had been assessed finance charges and a late charge that brought the balance owed to $1,895.49 and stated that a minimum payment of $413.49 was due on May 30, 1998.

On May 15, 1998, Peter Belmont sent Associates a six-page letter (dated May 13, 1998) by certified mail, return receipt requested, with the caption "NOTICE OF BELIEVED BILLING ERROR AND REQUEST FOR DOCUMENTARY EVIDENCE OF CONSUMER INDEBTEDNESS." Associates received the letter on May 19, 1998. In the letter, Peter Belmont stated that he did not admit to being an obligor on the account and believed the bill for $1,898.49 was in error because he had no contractual obligation to pay any amount borrowed under the account. Specifically, Peter Belmont wrote: "The listing on this BILL of my name and address is, I believe, a computational or similar billing error of an accounting nature." Further, Peter Belmont stated that if he were proven to be obligated in some way, he would continue to challenge the amount due as a billing error, because he had never had prior correspondence from Associates, such as billing statements or other documents detailing the charges. Finally, Peter Belmont demanded that Associates provide him with documentary evidence, including contracts, agreements and applications executed by him for the account, as well as copies of any written communications sent to him by Associates or any other lender pertaining to the account.

On June 23, 1998, Peter Belmont sent by certified mail, return receipt requested, a second letter to Associates, that was "substantially identical" to his May 13, 1998 letter, Am. Compl. ¶8. Associates received this second letter on June 30, 1998.

On June 25, 1998 — thirty-seven days after Peter Belmont's first letter was received — Associates sent Peter Belmont a letter . . . , which stated:

> We have made several attempts to reach you [apparently not in writing] but have been unsuccessful. Our goal is to work out a solution for your delinquent balance and help bring your account to a current status. . . . Do not allow this situation to become more serious. Protecting your credit is important to you both today and in the future.

Enclosed with the letter was another billing statement showing that the account balance was now $1,959.88, with a total amount due of $266.00.

On July 20, 1998 — sixty-two days after Peter Belmont's first letter was received and twenty days after his second letter was received — Associates sent Peter Belmont a letter [that stated]: "We have received your recent correspondence regarding the above-referenced account. We have ordered additional information in order to respond to your correspondence properly."

Associates sent Peter Belmont a second letter . . . also dated July 20, 1998, stating that the account had been opened on September 21, 1987 in the names of Peter Belmont and Jeremy Belmont, and adding that plaintiff became the primary cardholder on the account when Jeremy Belmont filed for bankruptcy. The letter stated that Associates was unable to find a copy of the original application and further advised Peter Belmont that if he wanted a copy of the original application, he would have to contact Boatmen's.

On July 22, 1999, Associates sent Peter Belmont [yet] another letter . . . which was identical to its June 25th letter, except that the amount due was specified as $316.00 and the account balance had risen to $2,024.29. This letter also included the same warning regarding Peter Belmont's credit.

On July 29, 1998, Peter Belmont sent Associates a third letter bearing the caption "NOTICE OF BELIEVED BILLING ERROR AND REQUEST FOR DOCUMENTARY EVIDENCE OF CONSUMER INDEBTEDNESS." In the letter, Peter Belmont wrote that he believed the entire balance on the account — $1,959.88 (which included the $1,895.49 he had previously contested, as well as $29.00 in additional late charges and $35.39 in finance charges which were newly billed on the statement for the period ending June 5, 1998) — was erroneously billed. Peter Belmont referenced his previous letters to Associates and stated that the July 20, 1998 letter signed by Patrick Wilson "failed to satisfy [his] demand for documentation in any respect." Finally, Peter Belmont stated that he believed that his April 6, 1992 letter to Consumer Loan Center absolved him of responsibility for Jeremy Belmont's credit card debts.

On August 5, 1998, Associates sent Peter Belmont another monthly billing statement for the MasterCard account. The statement showed that no payment had been made, but a finance charge of $37.79 and a late charge of $18.00 had been assessed, raising the balance to $2,080.08, with a minimum payment of $748.08 due on August 30, 1998. Finally, this statement advised: "Your account is seriously past due. Send in the total amount due immediately."

On August 10, 1998, Associates sent Peter Belmont another letter . . . , which reiterated information from the second July 20th letter, and again asserted that Peter Belmont was the sole obligor on the account because of his son's bankruptcy filing. The letter also responded to Peter Belmont's belief that his 1992 request to be removed as a joint cardholder applied to the Associates account by stating:

> [O]ur records do not indicate that your name was ever removed as a primary cardholder on this account. Please forward supporting documentation from Boatmen's . . . confirming that your name was removed from this account . . . and we will adjust our records accordingly. Unfortunately, we are not legally obligated to provide you a copy of your original application. In order to obtain a copy of your original application, you will need to contact Boatmen's. . . .

[The record also indicates that a credit report issued in August 1988 for Peter Belmont by Trans Union, a national credit reporting firm, reported the delinquency in question.]

On June 18, 1999, Peter Belmont filed his original complaint in this action, seeking relief under 15 U.S.C. §§1640(a)(2)(A), 1640(a)(3) and 1666(e). On that same day, Associates sent Peter Belmont a letter, signed by Todd Mitchell, an Associates vice president, which advised that Associates had deleted the "trade-line from all credit reporting agencies. Nothing is due." ...

DISCUSSION ...

(1)

Peter Belmont brought this action under 15 U.S.C. §1640, alleging that Associates failed to comply with the billing-error correction provisions of TILA, 15 U.S.C. §§1666-1666a. Peter Belmont claims that defendant made a billing error when it sent him the May 5, 1998 billing statement for the MasterCard account numbered 5457-1500-5024-6016 because he had never borrowed on the account, and because he believed that his 1992 letter released him of responsibility for his son's debts. Peter Belmont further claims that Associates's response to his May 13, 1998 Notice of Billing Error did not comply with the provisions of TILA. ...

Associates argues that Peter Belmont's letter of May 13, 1998 is not a billing error notice within the meaning of §1666 — and hence did not trigger Associates's statutory obligation to respond — for two reasons. First, defendant contends that the "Wrong-Person Error" alleged by Peter Belmont does not constitute a "billing error" under §1666(b). Second, defendant argues that even if the error alleged by Peter Belmont does constitute a billing error, his Notice of Billing Error did not conform to the requirements of §1666(a). Each of defendant's arguments is considered in turn below.

a. Billing Error ...

Peter Belmont contends that a creditor's demand for payment on an account from someone who is (allegedly) not an obligor on the account, which he describes as a "Wrong-Person Error," qualifies as a billing error under paragraphs (1), (2), and (5) of §1666(b). In response, Associates argues that §1666 by the plain meaning of its language, simply does not cover alleged errors of personal identification. Associates characterizes §1666 as "a transaction dispute statute. It is not a statute that applies to questions of who is obligated to pay correct billing charges to the account." ...

[T]his case presents an issue which appears to be one of first impression in the federal courts, namely whether the "Wrong-Person Error" alleged by plaintiff is encompassed by §1666(b). It is necessary, therefore, to look first to the language of the statute. In doing so, it must be remembered that TILA is a remedial act intended to protect consumers, see 15 U.S.C. §1601(a) ... and, as such, its provisions are to be construed liberally in favor of consumers.

In this light, the "Wrong-Person Error" alleged by plaintiff can be deemed to fall under paragraphs (1) and (2) of §1666(b). Under paragraph (1) of §1666(b), a billing error includes "a statement of credit which was not made to the obligor or, if made, was not the amount reflected on such statement." 15 U.S.C. §1666(b)(1). Under TILA, "credit" simply refers to a right that a creditor grants a debtor to defer payments of debt, whereas an "extension of credit" occurs when an individual opens or renews an account that lets him do so. Here, although it appears that Peter Belmont opened a credit account and gained an "extension of credit" in 1987, he contended in his May 13, 1998 letter to Associates that he was not an obligor on the Associates account and, thus, implied that Associates never extended credit to him in the amount stated on the May 5, 1998 billing statement, viz., the entire amount of the statement, $1,898.49.[6] Nothing in paragraph (1) indicates that its scope is limited to particular charges to the account, as opposed to the entire account itself. Thus, plaintiff's "Wrong-Person Error" falls within the language of paragraph (1), liberally construed.

For similar reasons, plaintiff's "Wrong-Person Error" also qualifies as a billing error under §1666(b)(2). Peter Belmont's May 13, 1998 letter clearly requested clarification, including documentary evidence, regarding whether Associates had, in fact, extended him the credit reflected on the May 5, 1998 statement, viz., the entire balance of $1,898.49.

Whether, as argued by plaintiff, the "Wrong-Person Error" could also qualify as a "computation error or similar error of an accounting nature" under §1666(b)(5) presents a more difficult question of interpretation, which need not, and will not, be addressed given that the error alleged by Belmont clearly falls within the language of paragraphs (1) and (2), liberally construed.

b. Sufficiency of Plaintiff's Notice of Billing Error

Associates argues in the alternative that even if Peter Belmont's claims qualify as a billing error, it had no obligation to respond to his letters because Belmont did not comply with the notice requirements of §1666. . . .

Peter Belmont's May 13, 1998 "Notice of Billing Error" letter, which Associates received on May 19, 1998 — well within the sixty-day period following the May 5, 1998, statement — (1) repeatedly stated his name and account number, and (2) indicated the reason he believed a billing error occurred, as well as (3) the amount of such error. In point of fact, after examining Peter Belmont's letter (which is couched throughout in language mirroring that of §1666), it is doubtful that Associates has ever received a more perspicuous notice of billing error or one that adheres more closely to the requirements of §1666.

Associates's suggestion that plaintiff's letter was not recognizable as, and is not, a valid notice of billing error — despite the all-capitals heading on the first page which read "NOTICE OF BELIEVED BILLING ERROR AND REQUEST FOR DOCUMENTARY EVIDENCE OF CONSUMER INDEBTEDNESS" — appears to be simply a transparent, post-hoc excuse for its tardy and incomplete compliance with TILA. In

---

6. Although it remains an open issue whether plaintiff was in fact an obligor on the account after his 1992 letter, the disposition of that question has no bearing on the legal issue of whether a notice that alleges that the plaintiff is not an obligor qualifies as a notice of "billing error" under §1666(b). Section 1666's requirements that a creditor promptly respond to consumer inquiries is triggered upon receipt of a timely notice of "billing error" regardless of whether the consumer who sent the notice was correct in his belief that an error had been made. Simply put, the fact that a TILA plaintiff was incorrect in his belief that a billing error had occurred is not a defense to an action under §1640.

this regard, it should be noted that there is absolutely nothing in the correspondence between Associates and Peter Belmont that suggests that defendant did not recognize Peter Belmont's May 13, 1998 letter, or either of his two, equally meticulous subsequent letters, for what they manifestly were: notices of billing error under §1666.

Nonetheless, Associates contends that the plaintiff's May 13, 1998 letter did not indicate that he was disputing a particular charge or alleging a "particular billing error" and the amount of such error. However, Peter Belmont's letter clearly indicates at several different points that he believed the amount of the billing error to be $1,895.49; indeed, the heading of the letter's second paragraph reads "*The amount for which I was billed, and which ENTIRE AMOUNT I believe to be erroneously billed, as to me, is:* $1,895.49." . . .

(2) . . .

In this case, Associates received Peter Belmont's first Notice of Billing Error on May 19, 1998, but did not send any correspondence to Peter Belmont regarding the notice until July 20, 1998 — sixty-two days later. Associates's July 20, 1998 correspondence to Belmont consisted of two letters, the first of which appears to be a form response letter, while the second more directly responds to his notice(s) of billing error. On its face, defendant's response violates §1666(a)(3)(A), which requires a creditor to acknowledge the receipt of a notice of billing error within thirty days.

In its defense, Associates contends: "Both letters were mailed to the plaintiff within . . . [the] two complete billing cycle period allowed by 15 U.S.C. §1666(a)(B) [*sic*]. Indeed, at least one was mailed within the 30 days required by 15 U.S.C. §1666(a)(A) [*sic*]." However, Associates's argument is again based on an untenable interpretation of the statute. Although it is true that Associates's July 20th correspondence came within two complete billing cycles of the May 5, 1998 statement, §1666(a)(3)(B) states a requirement in addition to, not in lieu of, §1666(a)(3)(A), which sets forth the 30-day written acknowledgment requirement.

Finally, Associates's defense that at least one letter was sent within the thirty-day period of §1666(a)(3)(A) appears to be based on the fact that Associates's July 20th letters were sent within thirty days of Belmont's *second* Notice of Billing Error. However, the fact that Associates's response would have been timely as to Peter Belmont's second letter, does not excuse Associates for not responding to his initial notice until sixty-two days after it was received.

Moreover, even if the July 20th letters had been preceded by a timely acknowledgment of receipt of Peter Belmont's May 13th notice, they still would not have complied with §1666(a)(3)(B). Section 1666(a)(3)(B) is not satisfied simply by showing that the creditor sent any response at all to the notice of billing error; rather, it requires that the creditor either (1) make the appropriate corrections to the account, thereby remedying the billing error, or (2) send a written explanation or clarification, including copies of any documentary evidence requested. See 15 U.S.C. §1666(a)(3)(B). Associates's July 20th correspondence did neither.

On this point, Associates contends that "one of the [response] letters . . . provides a written explanation as to why defendant Associates believes the plaintiff was liable for the undisputed charges on the account. This is all that is required by

15 U.S.C. §1666(a)(B)(ii) [*sic*]." On the contrary, what is required by §1666(a)(3)(B)(ii) in this case is that "copies of documentary evidence of the obligor's indebtedness" be provided in accord with plaintiff's request. 15 U.S.C. §1666(a)(3)(B)(ii). No such documentation was provided with the July 20th letters, and while it may be that the pertinent documentary evidence rested with Boatmen's or some other prior holder of the account, even that would not release Associates of its statutory obligation. Therefore, Associates did not comply with the "procedure upon receipt of notice [of billing error] by creditor" prescribed by §1666(a)(3).

Nonetheless, Associates argues that even if their response letters were not sufficient for timely compliance with §1666, it still has established a good faith defense under 15 U.S.C. §1640(f). Section 1640(f) states that no liability under the Act shall apply "to any act done or omitted in good faith in conformity with any rule, regulation, or interpretation thereof by the [Federal Reserve] Board." 15 U.S.C. §1640(f). However, nowhere does Associates assert that it mistakenly relied on any rule, regulation or interpretation of the Federal Reserve Board in fashioning its response to plaintiff's Notice of Billing Error. Accordingly, Associates's argument under §1640(f) has no merit.

Because Associates manifestly did not comply with the 30-day written acknowledgment requirement of §1666(a)(3)(A) and because it has not established its entitlement to a good faith defense under §1640(f), its actions in failing to respond to Peter Belmont's May 13, 1998 letter until July 20, 1998, constitute a violation of §1666(a)(3).

(3)

Peter Belmont also claims that Associates violated 15 U.S.C. §1666a(a) and 12 C.F.R. §226.13(d)(2) when it made or threatened to make an adverse credit report while his Notice of Billing Error remained unresolved.

Peter Belmont alleges that Associates threatened his credit rating during the pendency of his billing error dispute in its letters dated June 25, 1998 and July 22, 1998. On June 25, 1998, Associates, despite having received Peter Belmont's Notice of Billing Error on May 19, 1998, wrote: "Do not allow this situation to become more serious. Protecting your credit is important to you both today and in the future." Then, on July 22, 1998, after having received two additional notices of billing error that reported the same believed billing error, but before it had complied with its obligations under §1666(a)(3)(B)(ii) to provide plaintiff with the documentary evidence he requested, Associates sent another letter to Peter Belmont that contained the same warning. Finally, while all three notices of billing error remained outstanding, Associates notified a credit agency, Trans Union, of Belmont's allegedly delinquent payments. It is, therefore, clear that Associates made an adverse credit report during Peter Belmont's pending billing error dispute.

Associates proffers no explanation or defense, other than those discussed and found unavailing above, for its actions with respect to Peter Belmont's credit rating. Because Associates's two letters constitute implicit threats to Belmont's credit rating, and the evidence indicates that Associates actually did make an adverse credit report to Trans Union after receipt of a valid notice of billing error, but before complying with its obligations under §1666(a)(3), Associates violated §1666a.

(4)

Finally, Associates argues that if Belmont was not obligated on the account (as he at one time claimed and possibly still does claim), then he is not eligible for the protections accorded to "obligor[s]" by 15 U.S.C. §§1666-1666a. Given the remedial nature of TILA, Congress's intent to protect consumers, and the courts' mandate that TILA be liberally construed, the term "obligor[s]" must necessarily be construed to include those whom the creditor claims are obligors, as well as individuals who are in fact obligors in the contract law sense. Otherwise, there would be a lacuna in the statute, and an important area in the statute's remedial scheme would be left unprotected. A consumer who believes that he is not obligated under a credit account, and promptly notifies the creditor of the mistake through a proper notice of billing error, deserves the broad protections that Congress intended under the Act.

The need for such protections [is] particularly illustrated by Associates's actions in this case and its ability to harm Peter Belmont's credit even if he is not an obligor and was not obligated to Associates at the time of the May 5, 1998 statement. Associates chose to treat Peter Belmont as if he were an obligor, threatened his credit and, indeed, was even able to carry out its threats, as evidenced by the Trans Union credit report which detailed adverse information about Peter Belmont. Thus, whether or not Peter Belmont is actually obligated on the account has no bearing on whether he has standing to bring this action under TILA. Accordingly, Peter Belmont does have standing to bring this suit under TILA to the extent that he is alleging a "Wrong-Person Error."

(5)

Having found that Associates violated TILA and that Peter Belmont has standing to invoke the Act's remedies, it is necessary to determine the appropriate TILA remedy.

Defendants argue that even if violations occurred, Peter Belmont should not be awarded penalties under the Act. Associates argues that the penalty provision applicable under the facts of this case is 15 U.S.C. §1666(e), which provides that a creditor who fails to comply with the requirements of §1666 forfeits any right to collect on the amount contested in the notice of billing error or any associated finance charges, except that the amount forfeited is not to exceed $50. See 15 U.S.C. §1666(e). As defendant would have it, if Peter Belmont's April 6, 1992 letter was insufficient to remove him from the account and he is deemed liable for the $1,895.49 or any other sum on the account, Associates, then, could collect whatever total sum was found due after $50 was subtracted in accord with §1666(e). Associates, however, contends that because it has "forgiven" the $1,895.49 debt owed by plaintiff, "the plaintiff has already recouped any amount he may have been entitled to under these provisions."

Associates's argument is flawed in two respects. First, it is not entirely clear whether Associates's letter of June 18, 1999 stating that "[n]othing is due," constitutes a binding forgiveness of debt. In light of defendant's argument, however, and to avoid unnecessarily reaching the question of whether Peter Belmont is still an obligor on the Associates account, Associates will be enjoined from collecting from Peter Belmont the first $50 on the account in accordance with §1666(e).

Second, the forfeiture provision of §1666(e) is not the sole remedy for Associates's violations in this case. Associates gives short shrift to the penalty provision of 15 U.S.C. §1640(a)(2)(A) which provides a penalty of "twice the amount of any finance charge in connection with the transaction...except that the liability...shall not be less than $100 nor greater than $1,000" for violations of §§1666 and 1666a." 15 U.S.C. §1640(a)(2)(A). Associates argues that Peter Belmont is not entitled to recoup a finance charge because he has not paid one.

The purpose of TILA, however, is not solely for plaintiffs to recoup finance charges wrongfully paid; rather, it is to assure that creditors comply with TILA's provisions, including those regarding the proper handling of billing errors. See 15 U.S.C. §1601(a). The goals of TILA—to provide for prompt disclosure of the basis for charges and to enable consumers to resolve disputes without fear that the creditor will make adverse credit reports during the pendency of such disputes—would not be served if the only protection offered to consumers was that they were forgiven finance charges that they were never obligated to pay, or refunded finance charges that they should not have paid because they were erroneously billed. Thus, even if a particular obligor is incorrect in his belief that a billing error has occurred, he is still entitled under the Act to a prompt response from the creditor disclosing the basis of his liability. Indeed, the irrelevance of actual damages is what makes §1640(a)(2)(A) a *penalty* provision. Therefore, regardless of what Peter Belmont's obligor status is and regardless of whether he actually paid any finance charges, Peter Belmont is entitled to recovery of twice the finance charge in the transaction under the penalty provision of §1640(a).[11]

In this case, when Associates erroneously billed Peter Belmont $1,895.49 on May 5, 1998, that amount included finance charges which had accrued over the history of the account for which it asserted Belmont was responsible as an obligor. The question thus becomes: What is the "finance charge in the transaction" under the facts of this case?...

Taking into consideration that the account was fully paid, i.e., had a zero balance and no finance charges, from January 1994 until April 1995, it seems most reasonable to consider the finance charges accumulated on the account from April 1995 until May 1998, when the alleged billing error occurred, in calculating the applicable penalty. The total accumulated finance charges from April 1995 to May 1998 amount to $769.13. This accumulated total finance charge on the account, when doubled, exceeds the maximum of $1,000 allowed by §1640(a). Therefore, the $1,000 maximum shall be granted to Peter Belmont as a penalty for Associates's failure to comply with §§1666 and 1666a.

(6)

Peter Belmont also seeks an award of reasonable attorney's fees pursuant to 15 U.S.C. §1640(a)(3)....

Although TILA is remedial legislation intended to protect consumers, its attorney's fee provision does not extend to attorneys who bring claims as pro se

---

11. Although Associates violated TILA on several occasions by continuing to send Peter Belmont billing statements after it received his notices of billing error and by threatening and then damaging his credit history, Peter Belmont is foreclosed by statute from recovering separate penalties for each violation. See 15 U.S.C. §1640(g).

litigants. While the issue of the availability of attorney's fees to a pro se attorney in TILA actions is another matter of first impression, Supreme Court and appeals court precedents on similar fee-shifting provisions of other federal remedial statutes compel this result. [I omit a lengthy discussion of that question.]

There is, however, no corresponding case law limiting the availability of an award of costs under §1640(a). Accordingly, Peter Belmont is entitled to an award of his costs in this action.

The provisions of TILA directly delay the issuer's right to collect from a cardholder that questions the correctness of the charge. As with the right to withhold payment discussed in Assignment 27, implementation of that provision standing alone would place a significant burden on the issuer because the issuer ordinarily is not in a position to demonstrate the correctness of the charge. The most that the issuer is likely to know is that the issuer received the charge from the acquirer acting on behalf of the merchant. The credit-card networks solve that problem just as they do the analogous problem arising from the right to withhold payment: They allow the issuer to pass the disputed charge back to the acquirer. The acquirer, in turn, has a right to pass the charge back to the merchant, putting the onus on the merchant to justify the charge.

B.   Unauthorized Charges

Erroneous charges may be irritating and occur with some regularity, but they do not present a serious problem for the system because they tend to reflect innocent errors, rather than the loss of money to parties outside the system. Unauthorized charges, on the other hand, are a more serious matter because they reflect attempts by interlopers to obtain goods and services without paying for them, leaving participants in the credit-card system to bear the cost of those purchases. Although they have declined in recent years, losses from unauthorized charges remain quite large: Industry fraud losses amount to more than a billion dollars a year in the United States alone.

The most significant feature of the system is the strong protection for cardholders on whose accounts unauthorized charges are made. Specifically, TILA §133(a)(1)(B) limits the cardholder's liability for unauthorized charges to a maximum of $50. Under TILA, that $50 limit is an absolute ceiling. Nothing in TILA contemplates a greater loss for the cardholder, even if the cardholder knows that its card has been stolen and never bothers to notify the issuer of the theft. See Regulation Z, §226.12(b)(1) (regulatory restatement of the same rule).

That is not to say that the cardholder has no incentive to give notice to the issuer when it loses its credit card. On the contrary, because the cardholder is absolutely immune from unauthorized charges that occur after the card issuer has been notified of a loss or theft of the card, the cardholder can cut off liability (even below the $50 threshold) by sending notice to the issuer. TILA §133(a)(1)(E). Moreover, at least as of the date that this assignment was written, that incentive is enhanced for cards issued by MasterCard and Visa by voluntary policies stating that the cardholder will be completely free from responsibility for unauthorized charges if it reports the lost card within two business days of the date that the card was lost, even if the unauthorized charges were made before the cardholder reported the loss of the card.

In addition to the incentive the cardholder has to keep its liability below the $50 limit and the ever-present incentive to avoid the hassle of dealing with unauthorized charges, a prudent cardholder also should worry—notwithstanding TILA—that a court will conclude that its conduct was so negligent that it should bear responsibility for charges beyond the $50 limit.

Minskoff v. American Express Travel Related Services Co.

98 F.3d 703 (2d Cir. 1996)

Before: VAN GRAAFEILAND, MAHONEY, and WALKER, Circuit Judges.
MAHONEY, Circuit Judge:
Plaintiffs-appellants Edward J. Minskoff and Edward J. Minskoff Equities, Inc. ("Equities") appeal from a final judgment entered September 15, 1995 in the United States District Court for the Southern District of New York, Robert P. Patterson, Jr., Judge, that granted the motion of defendant-appellee American Express Travel Related Services Company, Inc. ("American Express") for summary judgment dismissing plaintiffs-appellants' complaint. The complaint asserted claims under...the Truth in Lending Act, 15 U.S.C. §1601 et seq. (the "TILA")...for recovery of $276,334.06 paid to American Express through checks forged by an Equities employee to cover charges incurred by that employee on American Express credit cards that were fraudulently obtained and used by the employee. The complaint also sought a declaratory judgment that plaintiffs-appellants were not liable for the balance of the unpaid charges outstanding on those credit cards, but the district court granted American Express summary judgment in the amount of $51,657.71 on its counterclaim for that balance.

We vacate the judgment of the district court and remand for further proceedings.

BACKGROUND

Minskoff is the president and chief executive officer of Equities, a real estate holding and management firm. In 1988, Equities opened an American Express corporate card account (the "Corporate Account") for which one charge card was issued in Minskoff's name. Minskoff also maintained a personal American Express account, which was established in 1963.

In October 1991, Equities hired Susan Schrader Blumenfeld to serve as its assistant to the president/office manager. Blumenfeld was responsible for both the personal and business affairs of Minskoff, and her duties included screening Minskoff's mail, reviewing vendor invoices and credit card statements (including statements for the Corporate Account), and forwarding such invoices and statements to Equities' bookkeepers for payment. Prior to Blumenfeld's employment with Equities, Minskoff personally reviewed all Corporate Account statements; after hiring Blumenfeld, he no longer reviewed any of these statements.

In March 1992, defendant-appellee American Express received an application for an additional credit card to issue from the Corporate Account in Blumenfeld's name. The application had been pre-addressed by American Express and mailed to Minskoff at his business address. It had been completed and submitted by Blumenfeld without the knowledge or acquiescence of Equities or Minskoff. American Express issued the supplemental card and mailed it to Equities' business address. From April 1992 to March 1993, Blumenfeld charged a total of $28,213.88 on that card.

During this period, American Express sent twelve monthly billing statements for the Corporate Account to Equities' business address. Each statement listed both Blumenfeld and Minskoff as cardholders on the Corporate Account, and separately itemized Corporate Account charges for Minskoff and Blumenfeld. These twelve statements show a total of $28,213.88 in charges attributed to Blumenfeld and $23,099.37 in charges attributed to Minskoff, for a total of $51,313.25. Between April 1992 and March 1993, American Express received twelve checks, drawn on accounts maintained by Minskoff or Equities at Manufacturers Hanover Trust ("MHT"), in payment of these charges, with each check made payable to American Express and bearing Equities' Corporate Account number. Minskoff did not review any statements or cancelled checks received during 1992 and 1993 from either his personal account with MHT or the Equities account with MHT.

In July 1992, American Express sent Minskoff an unsolicited invitation to apply for a platinum card. Blumenfeld accepted the invitation on behalf of Minskoff, again without the knowledge or acquiescence of either Minskoff or Equities. Blumenfeld also submitted a request for a supplemental card to issue from this new account (the "Platinum Account") in her name. When platinum cards arrived in both Minskoff's and Blumenfeld's names, Blumenfeld gave Minskoff his card, claiming that it was an unsolicited upgrade of his American Express card privileges. Minskoff proceeded to use his platinum card for occasional purchases, and Blumenfeld charged approximately $300,000 to the Platinum Account between July 1992 and November 1993.

Between August 1992 and November 1993, American Express mailed sixteen Platinum Account monthly billing statements to Equities' business address. Each statement named Blumenfeld and Minskoff as cardholders and itemized charges for each separately. These statements attributed a total of $250,394.44 in charges to Blumenfeld and $10,497.31 to Minskoff, for a total of $260,891.75. These bills were paid in full with checks drawn on the MHT accounts, made payable to American Express, and bearing the Platinum Account number.

In November 1993, Equities' controller, Steven Marks, informed Minskoff that MHT had called to inquire about a check made payable to American Express for approximately $41,000 that had been written on Equities' MHT account. Minskoff stopped payment on the check, initiated an internal investigation of Equities' accounts that revealed the full extent of Blumenfeld's fraudulent activities, and gave notice to American Express of Blumenfeld's unauthorized charges to the Platinum and Corporate Accounts. Blumenfeld subsequently stated in an affidavit that she had forged approximately sixty checks drawn on Equities' MHT account and Minskoff's personal MHT account, including at least twenty payments to American Express for charges to the Platinum and Corporate Accounts. Although some of these checks were used to pay legitimate obligations of plaintiffs-appellants, an accounting analysis attributed losses totalling $412,684.06 to Blumenfeld's theft. In January 1994, Blumenfeld agreed to repay $250,000 to Minskoff and Equities in return for their promise not to institute legal action against her.

Plaintiffs-appellants initiated this action in the United States District Court for the Southern District of New York on February 15, 1994.... [T]hey sought (1) to recover $276,334.06 that had been paid to American Express in satisfaction of unauthorized charges by Blumenfeld, and (2) a declaration that they were not liable for the outstanding balances on the Platinum Account....

DISCUSSION

[The court of appeals first rejected the district court's conclusion that the cardholder's claim should fail because Blumenfeld had apparent authority to obtain and use the card. The court reasoned that a cardholder cannot be held to have authorized the fraudulent acquisition of a credit card by one of its employees, based on its conclusion that TILA reflects a policy that card issuers are in a better position than cardholders to prevent losses caused by fraudulent acquisition of a credit card.]

However, while we accept the proposition that the acquisition of a credit card through fraud or theft cannot be said to occur under the apparent authority of the cardholder, [that view] should not be interpreted to preclude a finding of apparent authority for the subsequent use of a credit card so obtained. Under the rule urged by plaintiffs-appellants, a cardholder could disregard both credit card and bank statements indefinitely, or even fail to act upon a discovery that an employee had fraudulently obtained and was fraudulently using a credit card, and still limit his liability for an employee's fraudulent purchases to $50. Nothing in the TILA suggests that Congress intended to sanction intentional or negligent conduct by the cardholder that furthers the fraud or theft of an unauthorized card user. We therefore agree with the district court to the extent that it decided that the negligent acts or omissions of a cardholder may create apparent authority to use the card in a person who obtained the card through theft or fraud. Apparent authority created through the cardholder's negligence does not, however, retroactively authorize charges incurred prior to the negligent acts that created the apparent authority of the user.

Applying these principles to the case at hand, we address the district court's conclusion that plaintiffs-appellants' failure to examine credit card and bank statements amounts to negligence which created an appearance of authority in Blumenfeld to use the card. Under New York law, consumers are obligated to "exercise reasonable care and promptness to examine [bank] statement[s]...to discover [any] unauthorized signature or any alteration." N.Y.U.C.C. §4-406(1). [ED.: New York has not yet adopted the Revised Article 4.]. This provision is derived from a common law obligation to examine bank statements and report forgeries or alterations, and it is based upon a determination that "the depositor [is] in the better position to discover an alteration of the check or forgery of his or her own signature." Woods v. MONY Legacy Life Ins. Co., 641 N.E.2d 1070, 1071 (1994) (extending application of N.Y.U.C.C. §4-406 to brokerage accounts).

This policy is no less applicable to credit card holders than it is to bank deposi-tors. Once a cardholder has established a credit card account, and provided that the card issuer is in compliance with the billing statement disclosure requirements of 15 U.S.C. §1637, the cardholder is in a superior position to determine whether the charges reflected on his regular billing statements are legitimate. A cardhol-der's failure to examine credit card statements that would reveal fraudulent use of the card constitutes a negligent omission that creates apparent authority for charges that would otherwise be considered unauthorized under the TILA.

It is undisputed that between April 1992 and November 1993, American Express mailed to Equities' business address at least twenty-eight monthly billing state-ments documenting charges made to the Platinum and Corporate Accounts. Each of those statements clearly lists Blumenfeld as a cardholder, and each specifically itemizes those charges attributable to her credit card. During that same period, MHT mailed to Equities' business address numerous bank statements showing that checks made payable to American Express had been drawn on Equities' business account and Minskoff's personal account to pay these American Express charges. Minskoff concedes that he failed to examine any of these statements until Novem-ber 1993, and no other employee or agent of Equities (other than Blumenfeld) became aware of the disputed monthly payments to American Express prior to the inquiry by Bankers Trust in November 1993. These omissions on the part of plain-tiffs-appellants created apparent authority for Blumenfeld's continuing use of the cards, especially because it enabled Blumenfeld to pay all of the American Express statements with forged checks, thereby fortifying American Express' continuing impression that nothing was amiss with the Corporate and Platinum Accounts.

Plaintiffs-appellants argue that summary judgment is inappropriate because they exercised reasonable care in the hiring and supervision of Blumenfeld and in the implementation and administration of internal accounting procedures de-signed to detect and prevent fraud. In this case, however, while American Express concedes that Equities employed bookkeepers who were responsible, inter alia, for reviewing credit card statements and arranging for their payment, as well as re-viewing bank statements and cancelled checks, the inadequate manner in which these procedures were performed from April 1992 to November 1993 enabled Blumenfeld to acquire unauthorized American Express credit cards, run up more than $300,000 in invalid American Express charges, and pay for them with ap-proximately twenty forged checks drawn on Equities' MHT account and Minskoff's personal MHT account, without detection.

A cursory review of any of the American Express statements would have dis-closed charges by Blumenfeld made with an unauthorized credit card. A review of any MHT statement would have disclosed one or more payments to American Express (or, if the cancelled checks had previously been removed by Blumenfeld, charges that could not be matched to cancelled checks) generally in amounts far exceeding Minskoff's habitual American Express charges. We are not dealing in this case with an occasional transgression buried in a welter of financial detail. In our view, once a cardholder receives a statement that reasonably puts him on notice that one or more fraudulent charges have been made, he cannot thereafter claim lack of knowledge. The district court was justified in determining that no reason-able jury could conclude that this standard had been satisfied as to plaintiffs-appellants on the record presented in this case, warranting summary judgment in favor of American Express to the extent that we have previously indicated.

In our view, the appropriate resolution in this case is provided by adapting the ruling [of the North Dakota Supreme Court] to provide that

> [American Express] is liable for [Blumenfeld's] fraudulent purchases [as to each credit card] from the time the credit card was issued until [plaintiffs-appellants] received the first statement from [American Express] containing [Blumenfeld's] fraudulent charges plus a reasonable time to examine that statement. After that time, [plaintiffs-appellants are] liable for the remaining fraudulent charges.

Transamerica Ins. Co. v. Standard Oil Co., 325 N.W.2d 210, 216 (N.D. 1982). We accordingly vacate the judgment of the district court and remand for further proceedings to make this determination. We leave it to the district court in the first instance to ascertain whether, as the record is developed on remand, any issues require submission to a jury.

The *Minskoff* case implicitly reflects one unusual aspect of the provisions of TILA that protect cardholders from paying unauthorized charges: They apply not only in consumer transactions, but also in business and commercial transactions. In the business context, however, the issuer and the cardholder can contract out of the statutory allocation of loss from unauthorized charges. Specifically, TILA §135 permits any business that issues credit cards to at least ten of its employees to accept liability for unauthorized charges without regard to the provisions of TILA §133, so long as the business does not attempt to pass on to the individual employees any liability greater than the liability permitted under TILA §133. See Regulation Z, §§226.3(a) n.4, 226.12(b)(5) (regulatory explanation of TILA §135).

The credit-card network rules treat claims that charges are unauthorized differently than they treat other cardholder claims. At least in face-to-face transactions, the issuer bears the loss from unauthorized charges as long as the merchant followed the requisite procedures (that is, verifying the signature and obtaining the appropriate authorization for the transaction). Thus, if the merchant incurs charges by accepting a card proffered by a thief, the network rules do not permit the issuer to pass those charges back to the acquirer or the merchant. In remote transactions (sales by telephone or, increasingly, over the Internet), however, the risk of loss is left with the merchant. Thus, a merchant that does not deal face to face has to accept the risk that its customers subsequently may disavow the transactions.

Moreover, several common situations remain in which true strangers execute transactions that plainly are not authorized by cardholders. For example, as recently as 1992, never-received cards—cards intercepted before they reached the cardholder—amounted for half of all losses to fraud in the credit-card system. Those losses have almost been eradicated in the last decade, in response to card-activation programs, under which cardholders must call the issuer to activate the card.

Losses from counterfeit cards have proved more intractable. Losses on counterfeit cards have risen significantly during the early 1990s, to a point where they exceed more than $100 million a year. The reason is easy to identify: The technology available to create false cards has improved significantly at a time when the major issuers have been slow to upgrade the security features of their cards that would make it harder to counterfeit cards. The main difficulty is that the most effective security features would require merchants to upgrade the terminals that they use to process credit cards. The desire to hold down the cost of credit-card transactions to the merchant has slowed the networks significantly in adopting more sophisticated security procedures. Although a few new card-based security features — holograms on the face and special printing on the signature strip — have limited counterfeit-card losses by increasing the costs of manufacturing plausible counterfeits, it is doubtful that those kinds of minor improvements can deter counterfeiters in the long run. The only plausible long-term deterrent is to increase the amount and sophistication of the encrypted data on the card. Significant advances on that front should come in the first decade of this century, when the industry finally adopts an advanced universal terminal that can process transactions from debit cards, credit cards, and stored-value cards.

In the last few years, identity theft has come on the scene as a significant mechanism for credit-card fraud. An identity thief takes over the credit identity of an affluent individual and then uses the financial strength associated with that identity to execute fraudulent financial transactions. For example, in a common scheme, the thief would start with the theft of a credit-card statement (or, even better, a preapproved credit-card application) from the victim's mailbox. With that statement, the identity thief could call the issuer and ask to have the mailing address and telephone number for the card changed so that the victim would not receive mail or telephone calls related to the card. If the issuer is vigilant, that step might require knowledge of the victim's mother's maiden name or some similar piece of information; but a talented thief would have acquired that information from the victim's publicly available birth certificate. At that point, the thief could use the card at will, without making any payments, until the point where the issuer cuts off the card for nonpayment. By that time, of course, the victim's credit-card accounts — accounts that the thief took over and new accounts that the thief opened while "in possession" of the victim's identity — are likely to have thousands of dollars of unauthorized charges for purchases made by the thief.

Although losses from identity theft have remained relatively modest to date, identity theft poses a serious threat to the system because of the identity thief's ability to operate on information (like credit-card numbers, Social Security numbers, and birth information) that is becoming readily available through electronic sources. Industry and legislative policymakers are considering a variety of reforms that would make it more difficult for identity thiefs to acquire the information necessary for them to succeed. None of those reforms, however, appears likely to respond to the central problem — the ease with which information alone can be used to fool the system into authorizing a credit-card transaction. Until the system adopts an authorization mechanism that requires more than information alone (most likely a biometric mechanism based on fingerprint or retinal characteristics), identity theft is likely to increase.

Problem Set 28

28.1.   When Cliff Janeway returned to his home in Denver this weekend, he called to tell you that he has discovered that at the same time he lost the check last week in Seattle (see Problem 25.1) he also lost his Iridium MasterCard, which has a $20,000 limit. It now has been more than a week since he lost it. Does that give him anything new to worry about? TILA §§133, 170(a); Regulation Z, §226.12(b), (c).

28.2.   While he has you on the phone, Cliff tells you that he is about to start selling books by mail-order, in an effort to build volume for his business. He is worried about accepting payment by credit cards because the cardholders won't be signing any slips. Does that mean the cardholders will have a greater right to get out of the transactions? TILA §§103(*o*), 133(a), 170; Regulation Z, §226.12(b), (c).

28.3.   Cliff's last question for you relates to a trip he had planned to take to London. Several weeks ago he bought tickets to fly to London on Great Atlantic Air. Yesterday Great Atlantic Air stopped flying. This morning's paper reports that the assets of Great Atlantic Air are being liquidated in bankruptcy. Cliff purchased his ticket on his MasterCard. Can he get the money back? What do you need to know to answer Cliff's question? TILA §§161, 170; Regulation Z, §§226.12(c), 226.13.

28.4.   Ben Darrow (your banker client from FSB) meets you for breakfast this morning to discuss a problem with some credit cards that FSB recently issued. As part of a general initiative to provide more services to small businesses, FSB has a program that provides credit cards for small businesses at low costs, with no annual fee and an interest rate that is two points lower than FSB's standard rate. As part of the program, however, the cardholding small business must sign an agreement accepting responsibility for any unauthorized charges that are made with a stolen card.

Ben got in a dispute this week with Carol Long (one of the first people to sign up for the program) after a thief came through her offices at lunch and stole three of the five credit cards she has issued to her employees. Although Carol called Ben to report the theft by the end of the day, the thief already had charged about $500 on each of the three cards. Based on Carol's agreement with Ben, Carol was not surprised to see the unauthorized charges on the statements for the employees. Because she had agreed to accept responsibility for those charges, she proposed to deduct them from the next paycheck due to each employee whose card was stolen. One of the employees, however, protested, arguing that Carol could not make him pay an unauthorized charge on the credit card. In response to that claim, Carol called Ben. She wants to know if the employee is right. Moreover, if the employee is right, she thinks that Ben should bear the charge, not her. What should Ben tell her? TILA §§133(a)(1), 135; Regulation Z, §226.12(b)(5).

28.5.   While you are having dinner at the Drones Club one evening, Jeeves (Bertie Wooster's valet) approaches your table to ask if you have time to talk to him about a problem that recently has come upon Bertie. The first problem involves Bertie's Diner's Club card. When Bertie tried to use the card to pay for lunch yesterday, the merchant refused to accept the card and asked Bertie if he would speak on the telephone to a representative of the issuer. The issuer advised Bertie that the card was not being honored because of Bertie's failure to pay any of the bills for the last three months; the total amount outstanding on the card currently is about $4,500.

Bertie was shocked to hear this because he only uses the card once or twice a month and can't imagine that he would have declined to pay the bill. On further examination, it appears that the problem arose from a $40 charge that the issuer erroneously entered on Bertie's statement as a charge for $4,000. Unfortunately, because Bertie neglected to send the credit-card issuer a notice of his new address when he moved three months ago, Bertie has not received the last three statements on that card (the first of which included the $4,000 entry).

When Bertie explained the problem to the issuer's service representative, the representative referred Bertie to a provision of his card agreement that states: "Except to the extent otherwise required by applicable federal law, all entries that appear on any account statement produced by Issuer shall be final and conclusive evidence of Cardholder's liability to pay Issuer, and Cardholder agrees to pay all such charges that Cardholder does not contest in accordance with the procedures established by applicable federal law." Bertie wants to get the $4,000 charge removed from his credit card. What can he do? TILA §161; Regulation Z, §226.13(b)(1).

28.6. Before you leave the club, Bertie's acquaintance Roderick Spode stops at your table to discuss a problem he has with his credit card. He asks if you recall an incident that happened a few weeks ago with Gussie Fink-Nottle (famed for his exploits in Problem 25.2), in which Spode's negligence permitted Fink-Nottle to obtain one of Spode's blank checks and issue the check fraudulently. As it happens, the checkbook from which Fink-Nottle took the blank check also contained one of Spode's credit cards. Fink-Nottle used the credit card to obtain a $1,000 cash advance from Bulstrode Bank (the bank that issued the card).

Spode did not mention that problem to you at the time he came to discuss Problem 25.2 because Spode assumed that he would be able to recover those funds by challenging the appropriate entry on his credit-card bill. As it happens, however, Spode's bank (Bulstrode) has not been successful at recovering the funds from Fink-Nottle (who appears to have left town indefinitely). Because Bulstrode cannot recover the funds from Fink-Nottle, Bulstrode is trying to obtain payment from Spode. Specifically, when Spode talked to Nicholas Bulstrode this morning, Bulstrode advised Spode that he planned to hold Spode responsible because (in Bulstrode's words) "the whole problem is your fault. After all, you're the one that was stupid enough to leave your credit card laying around where any buffoon could pick it up and make some false charges. There's nothing that I could have done to prevent this, so I think you should pay." Is Spode obligated to pay for the charge? What is Bulstrode's best argument? UCC §3-406(a); TILA §133.

Assignment 29: Debit Cards

A major theme of Chapter 5 was the continuing dependence of the checking system on cumbersome paper-based mechanisms to transfer, collect, and finalize rights of payment. The first two assignments of this chapter turned from the checking system to the dominant card-based system. This assignment discusses a system that combines those two systems to allow card-based access to a checking account: debit cards. Although debit cards are still a relatively small system — used for only about 7 percent of 2000 consumer payments (more than $300 billion) — the system is growing rapidly (more than doubling in use in the last few years) and by 2001, Visa already was processing more debit-card transactions per year (6.9 billion) than it was credit-card transactions (6.2 billion).

This assignment proceeds in two parts. The first part discusses the mechanics of making payment with a debit card. The second part discusses how the debit-card system deals with the inevitable problems of error and fraud.

A. Payment with a Debit Card

A debit card is physically almost indistinguishable from a credit card, with a magnetic stripe on the back that technologically is quite similar to the strip on a credit card. Sometimes a debit card may go by a different name — some banks call theirs ATM cards or banking cards — but whatever the name, the feature that distinguishes a debit card for purposes of this discussion is that a debit card always serves as an adjunct to a checking (or savings) account. Thus, unlike a credit card, a debit card does not reflect an independent source of funds. Rather, it is a device to facilitate the customer's ability to draw on funds that either are already in its account or are available through an overdraft feature of that account.

There is no reason why the credit and debit features cannot be combined on the same piece of plastic; indeed, such cards have become relatively common. See, e.g., Regulation E, 12 C.F.R. Part 205, specifically §205.12 (outlining regulatory requirements for dual-purpose cards). When cards combine the two features, the mechanisms for completing payment transactions made with the card depend on whether the customer pays with the debit feature or the credit feature. Thus, a transaction using the debit feature would be governed by the rules and practices discussed in this assignment, but a transaction using the credit feature would be completed as described in Assignment 27. See Regulation E, §205.12(a); Regulation Z, §226.12(g).

The key to the debit-card system is that it replaces the paper check with an electronic impulse that directs the bank to transfer funds to the customer (when the card is used to withdraw cash at an ATM) or to transfer funds to a third party (when the card is used in a sales transaction). The use of the electronic impulse removes the need for the check and thus many of the cumbersome problems raised by a paper-based checking system. Just as important for our purposes, the use of that impulse to obtain funds directly from an account causes the transaction to qualify as an electronic funds transfer regulated by the federal Electronic Funds Transfer Act (EFTA), 15 U.S.C. §§1693 et seq. The EFTA is Title IX, §§901-920, of the Consumer Credit Protection Act (the same statute in which TILA appears as Title I). As EFTA §903(6) states, the EFTA applies to any "transfer of funds . . . initiated through an electronic terminal so as to order . . . a financial institution to debit . . . an account." The term "account" is broadly defined to include not only checking accounts, but also savings accounts and even money-market or securities accounts held by broker-dealers. EFTA §903(2). Thus, the EFTA (and its regulatory counterpart, Regulation E, 12 C.F.R. Part 205) applies to all cards that can be used to make electronic withdrawals from any such account.

1. Establishing the Debit-Card Relationship

The law related to debit cards is pervaded with a deep-seated suspicion that consumers are not sophisticated enough to understand the nature of a debit card. For starters, although no law regulates the way in which a bank can initiate a checking-account relationship, the EFTA imposes two significant procedural requirements that complicate a bank's efforts to update its checking-account relationships to include debit cards. First, EFTA §911 generally allows a bank to send an unsolicited debit card to a customer only if the card is sent in an unvalidated condition. Hence, a bank cannot mail a debit card out to a customer hoping that the customer will begin to use it. Rather, it has to convince the customer either to request the card before the bank sends the card or cause the customer to validate the card when the customer receives it. Validation requires either a telephone call or a visit to the bank, depending on the issuer's technology. EFTA §911(b).

The second restriction is the disclosure requirement set forth in Regulation E. That regulation requires the bank to provide the consumer a detailed up-front disclosure of the terms and conditions that will govern use of the card. Regulation E, §205.7(a). To its credit, the regulation states that the disclosure must be "in a readily understandable written statement that the consumer may retain." Unfortunately, like the analogous regulations discussed in earlier assignments, the regulation reduces the likelihood that the disclosure will be "readily understandable" by imposing a requirement that the disclosure include 10 specified items, which require not only a summary of much of the EFTA and the substantive provisions of Regulation E, but also a detailed 300-word disclosure about the procedures for resolving disputes over transactions made with the card. The result should surprise nobody. The typical bank produces an attractive booklet — prominently displaying the bank's logo or trademark — for the bank officer to give the customer when it opens the account. The booklet usually contains about 30 to 40 pages setting forth the "agreement" of the parties related to the checking account. Toward the back of the booklet are three to five pages of single-spaced 10-point type setting forth the disclosures required by Regulation E, often in the form of model clauses set out in Appendix A to Regulation E. The typical large bank may promulgate aspirational procedures suggesting that the officer should go over the specific disclosures with the customer and even highlight important provisions. The reality, however, is that the busy consumer is unlikely ever to open the booklet, much less read (or understand) the dense legalese that describes the rules governing use of the debit card. As you consider the effect of the consumer-protection rules discussed later in this assignment, you should keep in mind the limited likelihood that the average consumer will be aware of those rules, much less understand how they differ from the analogous rules for credit cards or checks.

2.   Transferring Funds with a Debit Card

There are two basic uses of a debit card. The first use is where the cards initially became popular: depositing and withdrawing money from an account without the burden of going to the bank and waiting to see a teller during regular banking hours. In that use, a debit card allows a customer to go to an ATM and perform any of the transactions that the customer could perform directly with a teller at the bank: withdrawing funds, depositing funds, inquiring about balances, or transferring funds among different accounts. Those functions do not involve payments to third parties; rather, they are limited to adjustment of the relationship between the customer and the bank where the customer maintains its account. Thus, they are not the sort of substitute-check transactions that involve use of the debit card as a payment system.

For purposes of the payment system, the important function is a different one: the burgeoning use of debit cards in point-of-sale (POS) transactions. In those transactions, a customer can use the card at the point of sale as a substitute for a check. From the customer's perspective, payment with a debit card is simple. The customer or the merchant swipes the debit card through a machine that reads the magnetic stripe on the card to obtain data identifying the customer's bank and account. Depending on the type of card, the customer may be asked to type in a personal identification number (PIN) and verify the amount of the transaction. Finally, EFTA §906(a) requires that consumers be provided written documentation for each transaction that they initiate. Accordingly, if all goes well, a printer produces a paper record of the transaction 10-20 seconds later, and the customer is free to go.

3.   Collection by the Payee

As with a point-of-sale credit-card transaction, the apparently simple and straightforward swiping of the card hides a considerably more convoluted arrangement between the merchant/payee and the ultimate payor bank. In order to collect funds through debit-card transactions, a merchant must enter into a contract, either directly with the bank that issued the card or indirectly through a network that processes debit-card transactions for the card-issuing bank. There currently are two major types of networks: PIN-based (generally operated by independent regional networks) and PIN-less (operated by the Visa and MasterCard systems).

(a) *PIN-Based Debit Cards.* PIN-based debit cards generally are associated with regional or national networks of financial institutions established solely for the purpose of facilitating debit-card transactions. They were the first to make the debit card an operating reality and completed about 3 billion transactions in 2000 worth a total of about $100 billion. The role of the networks is to provide technical details regarding the types of machinery the merchant must use to read the magnetic stripes on the cards and how to send signals to the banks in connection with the transactions. Those systems — characterized by the requirement that a consumer identify itself with a PIN — use a pair of transmissions to complete the payment transaction at the moment of sale.

First, while the consumer is at the terminal, the terminal transmits an encrypted electronic signal (tagged with the customer's PIN) to the payor bank over a telephone line to which the terminal is connected. The signal includes a description of the requested transfer of funds from the customer's account to the credit of the merchant/payee. The payor bank's computer system examines the signal. If the PIN matches the PIN for the designated account and if the account contains available funds sufficient to cover the withdrawal, the payor bank ordinarily honors the request. The payor bank communicates that decision by a second electronic message sent back to the merchant over the same phone line. Under the typical network rules, the payor bank's obligation to pay becomes final at the moment that it transmits that message back to the merchant. The actual payment can be made in any number of ways, but it normally is made by a single daily deposit to an account designated by the merchant, giving it credit for all of that day's debit transactions. If that account is located at the payor bank (as it often is), the payor bank can make the deposit directly; if the account is at another bank, the payor bank can provide the credit by means of a wire transfer (the subject of the next two assignments).

The most notable thing about that arrangement is that it short-circuits one of the most cumbersome aspects of the paper-based checking system: the need for the payee that accepts a check to wait several days before finding out whether the payor bank will honor the check. With a debit card, the payor bank becomes obligated to honor the payment request before the customer leaves the counter. Thus, the payee's practical risk of nonpayment is limited to insolvency of the payor bank or failure in the processing system: During 2000, it was used for more than 4 billion transactions (worth about $160 billion).

(b) *PIN-Less Debit Cards.* In the mid-1990s, Visa and MasterCard introduced a new kind of debit-card system (operating under the trade names Visa CheckCard and MasterMoney, respectively) that has grown so rapidly that it now has far surpassed PIN-based systems in volume. Indeed, in the typical network, the bank can charge a transaction back to a merchant only if the merchant knew at the time of the authentication transaction that the system was not properly functioning. Like the PIN-based systems, the new system conducts an on-line authorization transaction while the consumer is at the terminal, but it does not clear and settle the transactions immediately. Rather, there is an authorization transaction while the cardholder is at the terminal, which confirms the availability of funds in the account to cover the requested transaction (and typically leads to a "hold" on those funds in the cardholder's bank account). Then, over the next few days, the merchant obtains funds for the transaction in the same way as it would obtain funds for a standard credit-card transaction. After that process, a few days later, the funds finally are removed from the cardholder's account: The comparatively casual method of these transactions is reflected in their general characterization as "offline" debit; the PIN-based transactions described above are described in contrast as "online" debit.

Because PIN-less debit-card transactions are collected through the regular credit-card collection networks, they cost the merchant about as much as standard credit-card transactions, something in the range between 1 and 2 percent of the transaction amount (depending on the type of merchant). That cost is quite high when compared to classic PIN-based debit-card transactions, which rarely exceed 20 cents. Because of their more modern technological infrastructure, the PIN-based debit-card networks ordinarily cost much less, something on the order of seven cents per transaction. Nevertheless, the widespread market penetration of Visa and MasterCard credit cards has provided an infrastructure and a base of consumer acceptance for Visa and MasterCard debit-card products that have given those products a significant market advantage over the cheaper PIN-based debit-card products.

The persistently high fees for PIN-less debit transactions, however, have caused considerable unrest in the merchant community, which has begun to develop programs to encourage consumers to use their PIN-based debit cards rather than the Visa and MasterCard products (whether debit *or* credit) that are so much more expensive to merchants. The hostility to MasterCard and Visa reached new heights in late 2001, when Visa tried to raise fees on Interlink (its own PIN-based debit-card network) substantially above the fees for other PIN-based debit-card networks, but was forced to back down when major retailers like Wal-Mart and Walgreen indicated that they no longer would accept the cards. Conversely, banks are trying hard to encourage their customers to sign for purchases instead of using the PIN-based debit feature of their cards, because it is difficult for banks to make ends meet given the low existing interchange rates on those products. Indeed, many banks have begun charging their customers fees for PIN-based debit-card transactions, hoping to push those customers to credit-card transactions instead.

Whatever system is used (PIN-based or PIN-less), the key difference between a credit-card transaction and a PIN-less debit-card transaction cleared through a credit-card network is finality. As a legal matter, debit-card transactions are electronic fund transfers; they are not credit-card transactions governed by Regulation Z and TILA. Accordingly, from the consumer's perspective, payment is as a practical matter final at the time of the transaction. The consumer has none of the TILA-based rights to challenge payment at a later time.

B. Error and Fraud in Debit-Card Transactions

Because the debit-card system allows the merchant/payee to determine at the time of the transaction that the payor bank will honor the transfer request and because the customer has no substantial right to stop payment, the risk of nonpayment is much less substantial in debit-card transactions than it is during traditional checking transactions. That leaves two other possible sources of loss for the system to address: erroneous transactions and fraudulent transactions.

1.   Erroneous Transactions

It is easy to see how the electronic portions of the debit-card processing system could make a variety of errors in handling payment transactions: The system could make an improper withdrawal (a withdrawal of the wrong amount or from the wrong account), or the system could fail to make a withdrawal that it should have made. Happily, those types of mistakes have not yet caused any significant losses. That is mostly because many of the common ways that the electronic system could fail ordinarily would not result in losses. In the debit-card context, the merchant is unlikely to allow the customer to complete the transaction unless the merchant's terminal receives the authorization from the payor bank agreeing to make the withdrawal. When the authorization system goes off-line, the merchant normally refuses to accept debit cards for transactions completed before the system appears to be functioning again. Similarly, at least in the absence of a serious processing failure, the payor bank is unlikely to send a signal committing to pay money to the merchant and then fail to charge some account for the funds it has agreed to pay.

Of course, that leaves the possibility that the system might fail in such a way that the merchant believes that it is receiving authorizations when it in fact is not communicating with the payor bank. In that situation, the POS network rules ordinarily protect the merchant and pass the loss back to the payor bank, on the theory that the network and the payor bank can mitigate losses from that problem much more readily than the merchant. If the customer's account happens to have insufficient funds to cover the transaction when the merchant presses for payment, the payor bank can pursue its customer for any deficiency just as it could on any overdraft transaction.

Similarly, it is possible that the payor bank could send a signal committing to make the payment, but then charge the wrong account. In that event, the payor bank would have to recredit the incorrectly charged account, but it then could charge the correct account and pursue the customer for any deficiency. That problem, however, is unlikely to leave the bank with any significant losses. In most cases, banks should find that the accounts contain funds sufficient to bear the correct charges. How many customers would try to use a debit card against insufficient funds on the negligible chance that the system would slip up and let them get away with it?

2.   Fraudulent Transactions

The most serious risk of loss in the debit-card context is the risk from false authorizations: debit-card transactions that the customer in fact has not authorized. For example, in one recent case, an aide to a District of Columbia

Council member made about $11,000 of unauthorized withdrawals on the council member's ATM card; the aide stole the card from the council member's office and guessed that the PIN would be the last four digits of the council member's home telephone number. See United States v. Miller, 70 F.3d 1353 (D.C. Cir. 1995) (affirming the thief's conviction for federal bank fraud). A more enterprising criminal recently used funds from fraudulent credit-card transactions to construct a false ATM (complete with a device to read and store the information on consumers' cards). He installed the ATM in a shopping mall, without any connection to a bank whatsoever. He then disabled the other ATM in the mall to increase usage of his false machine. Using that device, he created hundreds of counterfeit cards, with which he successfully stole more than $100,000. See United States v. Greenfield, 44 F.3d 1141 (2d Cir. 1995) (reviewing the sentence for Greenfield's conviction).

Several features of the debit-card system operate to minimize losses from fraud. First, the rules preventing unsolicited mailing of activated debit cards and the practice of mailing PINs separately from the cards should limit fraud from cards stolen without the customer's knowledge. Second, both the authorization request from the merchant to the bank and the bank's reply travel in an encrypted format that makes it relatively difficult to obtain funds through transmission of false messages: Even if an interloper intercepted and copied the message (an event usually described as a "man in the middle" attack), the encryption would make it difficult for the interloper to use the message to design its own forged messages or to alter the genuine message to call for payment to the interloper's account. Third, the PIN pads at the point of sale include software designed to prevent theft of the encryption protocol by destroying the encryption protocol if someone tampers with the pads.

The encryption technology used for debit cards is not at the highest level of sophistication. It is not, for example, nearly as secure as the technology used in the stored-value cards and electronic-money systems developed in recent years. Banks have resisted upgrading the technology for quite some time, based on concerns about the costs of requiring all merchants to purchase replacement terminals that would operate with more sophisticated encryption systems. Banks are particularly sensitive to those costs because merchants' concerns about high equipment costs have been one of the main obstacles to growth of debit-card networks. Whatever has been true in the past, however, that problem should pass in the near future, given the likelihood that the major payment-systems players will agree to adopt a single terminal format that can accept payments made not only with a "low-tech" debit card or credit card, but also with a "smart" stored-value card. At that point, a merchant could put itself in a position to accept payments under all three systems by purchasing a single universal terminal. Once a substantial share of merchants have such terminals, enhancements to the technological features of debit cards would be much more practical.

Although the relatively low level of technology in the current system has not been a major problem, it has not been impervious to attack. The rate of loss from unauthorized transactions on PIN-based debit cards, for example, is about 0.3 cent per $100, one-twentieth of the analogous rate on credit cards (6 cents per $100). For example, in one 1997 incident, hackers managed to access a computer program used to encode information on debit cards and succeeded in manufacturing and using a dozen false debit cards before the scheme was uncovered. Nevertheless, it is a testament to the clarity and effectiveness of the system that there is almost no reported litigation in this area. An overwhelming majority of the recent reported cases discussing debit cards involve criminal convictions of the malfeasors for various types of criminal conduct that are much more direct than attempts to compromise the technological protections of the system. See, e.g., Garner v. State, 1996 WL 9600 (Tex. Ct. App. — Houston (1st Dist.) 1996) (affirming a conviction for aggravated robbery after defendant forced the victim into a car at gunpoint and forced her to withdraw cash from an ATM); State v. Knight, 909 P.2d 1133 (Haw. 1996) (affirming a conviction for murder committed after defendant forced the victim at knifepoint to reveal his PIN); State v. Fortune, 909 P.2d 930 (Wash. 1996) (en banc) (affirming a conviction for murder after defendant beat the victim to death with a sledgehammer, stole his debit card, and then used the card to empty the victim's bank account).

In fact, statistics indicate that more than 99 percent of fraud on debit cards results from card usage by close acquaintances of the cardholder (relatives, friends, and the like). Although banks have difficulty documenting the identity of the user in POS transactions, they have been quite successful in using cameras at ATM locations to defeat these claims in the ATM context. These cameras photograph the person using the card at the instant that the ATM approves the PIN entered with the card. Most claims of unauthorized ATM usage are resolved when the customer, after reviewing the photograph of the allegedly unauthorized user, acknowledges that the user is not an unknown thief, but a close acquaintance of the customer.

Of course, the rapidly growing use of PIN-less debit cards issued through the major credit-card networks leaves the system much more exposed to fraud. Accordingly, although the credit-card networks can be expected to work to minimize losses, there is every reason to believe that the credit-card-related debit cards will become subject to fraudulent transactions much more frequently than debit cards have been. And that problem poses a serious threat to the success of the system because consumers react much more negatively to a surprise discovery that their bank account has been emptied (after a debit card has been stolen) than they do to a surprise discovery that their credit-card line has been exhausted (after a credit card has been used up). In the credit-card case, the consumer need only notify the issuer that the charges are unauthorized, pull a different card from its wallet, and go about its business. By contrast, when the consumer's bank account has been depleted upon a debit-card theft, the consumer faces a much more serious problem unless it can get the funds recredited immediately (something Regulation E does not require).

Turning to that problem, the system must resolve two questions when losses arise from false authorizations on debit cards. The first is deciding who bears a loss as between the merchant that accepts payment based on a stolen debit card and the bank on which the card draws. For example, if a merchant operating a POS system sells goods to somebody who pays with a stolen debit card, can the bank recover the funds that it paid to the merchant based on that sale? Because there is not yet any significant legal regulation of that issue, that question currently is answered by the contractual arrangements of the different systems.

Ordinarily, the network rules allocate that loss to the bank, relying on the notion that the bank is in a much better position to mitigate those losses than the merchant. It is the bank, after all, that maintains the system for authorizing withdrawals and has the ability to design the cards so as to limit the possibility of counterfeiting and incorrect identifications. To be sure, the system could rely on the merchant to limit losses through signature-verification or photograph requirements, but these devices are notoriously unsuccessful at limiting fraudulent authorizations. Thus, the merchant is entitled to payment from the bank even if the customer was not entitled to draw on the account.

The second problem for the legal system is deciding who bears the loss as between the bank on which the card draws and the customer whose card has been stolen. On that point, positive law provides an answer that protects the cardholder considerably even apart from the parties' own agreements. Specifically, federal law provides two separate protections related to unauthorized transactions, as well as a set of specified procedures for determining whether a particular transaction in fact was authorized.

The first set of rules establishes a threshold requirement that a card have some minimal security feature for confirming transactions, whether by PIN or by some other method (such as a photograph, signature, or fingerprint). EFTA §909(a). In the absence of such a feature, the EFTA bars any imposition on the consumer of liability for unauthorized use. That requirement has little operative significance because all of the significant current systems comply with that rule. The PIN-based systems use PINs, and the PIN-less systems rely on signatures and, in some cases, photographs.

The important part of the EFTA framework is its limitation of consumer liability even in cases in which the card does have a security feature. Those limitations appear in the complex and poorly drafted provisions of EFTA §909(a). Essentially, that section establishes three separate rules that a bank can use to impose liability on the consumer when the consumer's card is lost or stolen.

Although EFTA §909(a) seems to establish a rule limiting the customer's loss from each unauthorized transfer, the Federal Reserve has interpreted the rules in §909(a) to apply to any "series of related unauthorized transfers." Regulation E, §205.6(b). Thus, if a debit-card thief uses the card 10 times before it is caught, the dollar limits in §909(a) describe the consumer's exposure for the entire incident, not its exposure for each of the 10 unauthorized transactions.

The first rule appears in the second sentence of EFTA §909(a), which begins with "In no event." That rule allows the bank to hold the consumer responsible for up to $50 of unauthorized transfers that occur before the financial institution learns of the consumer's loss of the card. That rule applies without regard to fault or diligence on the part of the consumer. Thus, the consumer can be held responsible for losses under that rule even with respect to transactions made before the consumer knows that the card has been stolen.

The second rule appears in the fourth sentence of EFTA §909(a), which begins with "In addition." The second rule is a fault-based notice rule that allows the bank to charge the consumer for losses if the consumer does not promptly notify the bank after it discovers that the card has been lost. That rule operates on the assumption that the consumer should notify the bank within two business days after the time that the consumer learns of the theft and allows the bank to charge the consumer for all losses that occur more than two business days after the consumer learns of the theft, but before the financial institution learns of the loss of the card. The maximum amount that the consumer can be charged under the notice rule is $500. That $500 includes the $50 that could have been charged the consumer under the first rule. Thus, assuming that the consumer was aware of the theft from the moment that it occurred, the consumer would be responsible for a total of only $500 if $50 were charged on the first two days after a card was stolen and $500 on the third and fourth days.

The third rule is a bank-statement rule that appears in the third sentence of EFTA §909(a), which begins with "Notwithstanding the foregoing." Under that rule, the consumer must review its statements to identify unauthorized transactions that appear on the statements. Under the EFTA, the consumer has a (relatively generous) 60 days to review the statements (starting on the date they are sent). EFTA §909(a). If the consumer fails to report an unauthorized transaction within that 60-day period, the consumer bears responsibility for any subsequent unauthorized transactions that would have failed had the consumer identified the unauthorized transactions on the statement and advised its bank of the problem. EFTA §909(a); Regulation E, §205.6(b)(3). The consumer's liability under the bank-statement rule is entirely separate from its liability under the two previous rules and has no maximum dollar limit.

The federal rules described above establish a floor of risk that banks must accept, but they permit states to limit the consumer's share of the loss even more narrowly. See EFTA §919 (stating that the EFTA does not preempt state laws that "affor[d] any consumer [protection that] is greater than the protection afforded by [the EFTA]"). Some states have responded to that invitation by extending the EFTA deadlines. See Kan. Stat. Ann. §9-1111d (allowing four days rather than two to notify the bank of the loss). Others lower the amount of the consumer's exposure in cases in which the consumer fails to give the notice. See, e.g., Colo. Rev. Stat. §11-6.5-109(2) (absolute limitation of customer's responsibility to $50); Kan. Stat. Ann. §9-1111d ($300, rather than $500, exposure); Mass. Gen. L. ch. 167B, §18 (absolute limitation of customer's responsibility to $50).

Perhaps more surprisingly, a recent rash of publicity regarding the $500 potential loss rule under the EFTA has motivated the major PIN-less debit-card networks (MasterCard and Visa) to alter their network rules to limit the consumer's exposure to losses from unauthorized transactions. Specifically, both networks voluntarily have agreed that the banks issuing their cards will limit consumer liability for unauthorized transactions to $50, *even if* the consumer fails to notify the issuer of the theft of the debit card and fails to identify the fraudulent transaction within the 60-day EFTA period.

The EFTA also establishes a framework for resolving disputes about whether particular transactions were authorized. To invoke that framework, a customer must give its bank oral or written notice of transactions that it claims are unauthorized within 60 days after the bank mails documentation of the transaction to the customer. EFTA §908(a). When a bank receives such a notice, it must investigate the error and provide the customer a written explanation of its conclusion. The bank must respond within 10 business days or give the customer a provisional recredit for the disputed amount. Recognizing the importance to consumers of the date that funds return to a customer's account, Visa and MasterCard (in connection with their voluntary agreement to limit cardholder exposure to unauthorized losses to $50) have agreed that the recredit deadline for banks issuing their cards will expire after 5 days, instead of the 10 days permitted under the EFTA.

Even if the bank provides a provisional recredit, it still must proceed to investigate the customer's complaint. Under the EFTA, it must complete its investigation within 90 days after receiving the customer's 60-day notice. The statute backs up its procedural requirements by allowing a federal court to impose treble damages on any bank that (a) fails to recredit an account within the 10-day period when required to do so or (b) unreasonably rejects a customer's claim of error. EFTA §908; Regulation E, §205.11(c)(3).

In some cases, accountholders unable to recover under those provisions have sought relief under Article 4. As the case that follows illustrates, those efforts are unlikely to succeed. As you study the case, consider the reasons why the accountholder did not attempt to rely on the EFTA.

Hospicomm, Inc. v. Fleet Bank, N.A.

338 F. Supp. 2d 578 (E.D. Pa. 2004)

SURRICK, District Judge.

Presently before the Court is Defendant Fleet Bank, N.A.'s Motion to Dismiss Plaintiff's Complaint Pursuant to Rule 12(b)(6) (Doc. No. 2). For the following reasons we will grant Defendant's motion. . . .

BACKGROUND

Plaintiff Hospicomm, Inc. is a Pennsylvania corporation with its principal place of business in Philadelphia, Pennsylvania. Plaintiff provides data processing, marketing, operations management, and other services to healthcare providers. Defendant Fleet Bank, N.A., is a bank incorporated in Rhode Island with its principal place of business in Boston, Massachusetts.

Pursuant to an agreement reached on November 21, 2002, Plaintiff began performing all day-to-day management services for Hamilton Continuing Care Center ("Hamilton"). On behalf of Hamilton, Plaintiff established numerous bank accounts with Defendant. Access to these accounts was limited to authorized account signatories and authorized account managers. Defendant issued "transfer cards" to these authorized persons, to allow them to transfer funds between the accounts. . . .

On or about April 15, 2003, Plaintiff terminated an employee named Guillermo A. Martinez. Martinez had been employed as a financial analyst and his duties included bookkeeping for facilities managed by Plaintiff, including Hamilton. After terminating Martinez, Plaintiff discovered bank statements for one of the accounts held by Defendant that indicated that ATM withdrawal transactions had been processed through the account. Plaintiff determined that Martinez, an employee without access to the accounts, gained access when he requested and received a "VISA ATM" card. Over the course of an eight-month period, Martinez allegedly used the ATM card issued to him by Defendant to make more than 400 transactions and/or cash withdrawals from the accounts totaling in excess of $148,000.

After reimbursing Hamilton for the funds converted by Martinez, Plaintiff filed the instant action against Defendant. Plaintiff alleges that Defendant issued Martinez the ATM card without "prior notification, consultation, or approval" from Plaintiff or Hamilton; Defendant failed to detect these "highly suspect transactions and irregular withdrawals"; and Defendant failed to take any action or notify Plaintiff about the issuance of the ATM card or the suspicious activity connected to the account. On the basis of these allegations Plaintiff filed the instant Complaint, in the Court of Common Pleas in Philadelphia County, alleging [among other things, breach of the duty of] good faith in violation of Article 4 of the Uniform Commercial Code ("UCC"). Defendant removed the case pursuant to 28 U.S.C. §1441.

Defendant subsequently filed the instant motion to dismiss. Defendant contends that the entire Complaint should be dismissed because . . . Plaintiff's UCC Article 4 claim must be dismissed because Article 4 does not apply to ATM cards. . . .

DISCUSSION . . .

UCC ARTICLE 4

Plaintiff contends that Defendant violated various duties Defendant owed it under Article 4 of the UCC. Defendant contends that this claim should be dismissed because Article 4 does not apply to ATM transactions. . . .

. . . Defendant's sole argument is that Plaintiff's claim is insufficient because transactions related to the use of an ATM card are not covered by Article 4 of the UCC. Article 4 only applies to "items" as defined in [UCC §4-104]. Item is defined as "[a]n instrument or a promise or order to pay money handled by a bank for collection or payment. The term does not include a payment order governed by Division 4A (relating to funds transfers) or a credit or debit card slip." Id. Defendant argues that based on the definitions of "instrument," "promise," and "order" it is apparent that an ATM transaction is not contemplated by the definition of item. See [UCC §§3-103, 3-104]. Plaintiff contends that an ATM card replaces money, such that it can be considered an instrument as defined by the UCC.

There are no federal or state cases in Pennsylvania that address the extent to which Article 4 of the UCC covers electronic withdrawals of funds. Numerous cases in other jurisdictions have considered the question of whether Article 4 covers electronic fund transfers ("EFTs"). See, e.g. Bradford Trust Co. v. Tex.-American Bank-Houston, 790 F.2d 407, 409 (5th Cir. 1986); Evra Corp. v. Swiss Bank Corp., 673 F.2d 951, 955 (7th Cir. 1982); Security First Network Bank v. C.A.P.S., Inc., No. 01 C 342, 2002 WL 485352, *7 (N.D. Ill. Mar. 29, 2002); Fernandes v. First Bank & Trust Co., No. 93 C 2903, 1993 WL 339286 (N.D. Ill. Sept. 3, 1993). Each of the cases that have considered the issue have found that the UCC does not apply to EFTs. The issue presently before us — whether Article 4 applies to electronic withdrawals — has not been thoroughly analyzed. The Supreme Court of Kansas in the case of Sinclair Oil Corp. v. Sylvan State Bank, 254 Kan. 836, 869 P.2d 675 (1994), discussed an issue similar to the one currently before us. In Sinclair Oil, the plaintiff was paid for products it delivered by "making electronic debits" from its customer's bank account. On one such occasion, the defendant bank returned the debited funds to the customer's account because after the electronic debits the customer's account was left with insufficient funds. Plaintiff alleged that the return of the debited funds was late under the Article 4 of the Kansas Uniform Commercial Code. *Id.* at *677.* Ultimately, the court was forced to consider whether electronic debits are excluded from UCC coverage. The court initiated its analysis by noting that other courts had excluded EFTs from UCC coverage because: "(1) electronic debits are not 'items' within the meaning of Article 4; (2) the UCC 'does not specifically address the problems of electronic fund transfers'; and (3) the UCC drafters never contemplated electronic transactions when developing the Code." *Id.* at 680 (internal citations omitted).

The court first analyzed what "item" meant under Article 4. An item is an "instrument." An "instrument" under the UCC is defined as a "negotiable instrument." A "negotiable instrument," is defined as "'any writing' that was signed by the maker, containing an unconditional promise to pay a sum certain, payable on demand or at a definite time to order or to bearer." *Id.* at 680-81 (citing [UCC §3-104]). The court went on to recognize that the 1990 statute adopting that definition identified the writings that complied with the section to include drafts, checks, certificates of deposit, and notes. "An EFT is not a writing and is not within the specific list of writings that are 'instruments.'" *Id.*

The court moved on to consider the intent behind the adoption of Article 4. It noted numerous ways in which the concept of electronic transfers is not contemplated by the UCC. These reasons include: (1) Article 4A specifically excludes so called "debit transfers," where the order to pay is given by the person receiving payment; (2) electronic fund transfers were not in the contemplation of the Article 4 drafters, as Article 4 is "a direct outgrowth of the American Bankers Association Bank Collection Code, drafted in the early 1920s to govern check collection; and (3) the ideas in Articles 3 and 4 of the UCC . . . depend upon bankers looking at particular words and numerals on the face of a particular instrument. In the case of EFTs, the medium of communication is the computer. . . ." *Id.* at 681-82 (internal citations omitted).

Though the financial transactions at issue in this case are alleged unauthorized ATM withdrawals rather than electronic debits from one bank account sent to another, we are satisfied that the rationale of *Sinclair Oil* applies equally here. By its very definitions, Pennsylvania's adoption of Article 4 does not contemplate electronic withdrawals. The statute defines "item" as "[a]n instrument or a promise or order to pay money handled by a bank for collection or payment. The term does not include a payment order governed by Division 4A (relating to funds transfers) or a credit or debit card slip." [UCC §4-104]. In the instant case, Martinez allegedly withdrew funds using a Visa ATM card issued by Defendant. As in *Sinclair Oil,* Article 4 was meant to apply only to traditional written instruments, rather than electronic means of transferring and withdrawing funds. Nowhere in Article 4 are ATM withdrawals discussed. Rather, a review of the text supports the conclusion that Article 4 was meant to apply to checks and traditional, written, monetary instruments.

Our conclusion that Article 4 does not cover ATM withdrawals is buttressed by the federal law in this area. While focusing on Defendant's liability under Article 4 of the UCC, neither party addressed the fact that Congress enacted legislation covering ATM withdrawals when it enacted the Electronic Fund Transfer Act ("EFTA"), 15 U.S.C. §1693 *et seq.* The EFTA was enacted "to provide a basic framework establishing the rights, liabilities, and responsibilities of participants in electronic fund transfer systems." 15 U.S.C. §1693. The statute was designed to specifically cover withdrawals made from an ATM. See 15 U.S.C. §1693a (defining "electronic fund transfer" to mean "any transfer of funds . . . which is initiated through an electronic terminal, telephonic instrument, or computer or magnetic tape so as to order, instruct, or authorize a financial institution to debit or credit an account. Such term includes . . . automated teller machine transactions. . . ."). See also United States v. Goldblatt, 813 F.2d 619, 622 (3d Cir. 1987) (criminal case discussing applicability of EFTA to ATM withdrawals). Moreover, the EFTA enacted a defined process for a consumer to bring a claim against a bank for an alleged "unauthorized fund transfer." *See* 15 U.S.C. §§1693c-h.

The EFTA has an anti-preemption clause specifically allowing states to enforce consumer credit protections that go beyond the protections of the EFTA that are not inconsistent with EFTA. 15 U.S.C. §1693q; Metrobank v. Foster, 193 F. Supp. 2d 1156, 1159 (S.D. Iowa 2002). Article 4A of the UCC specifically states that "this division does not apply to a funds transfer any part of which is governed by the [EFTA]." [UCC §4A-108; see also UCC §4A-108 comment] ("The effect of section 4A-108 is to make Article 4A and EFTA mutually exclusive."). Though this text seems to suggest that in Pennsylvania the EFTA is the exclusive remedy for claims relating to ATM transactions, nowhere in the statute are ATM transactions explicitly removed from the application of Article 4. Even assuming, *arguendo,* that Article 4 of the UCC does in fact apply to ATM transactions, we believe it still would be preempted by the EFTA. The EFTA constructs a process for consumers wishing to contest unauthorized transfers, with clear burdens that must be satisfied in any suit. *See* 15 U.S.C. §§1693c-h. Under the circumstances, we conclude that in Pennsylvania, a cause of action for an unauthorized use of an ATM card should be brought under the EFTA, rather than Article 4 of the UCC.

Banks have not, of course, willingly accepted the idea that they are ultimately at fault for such transactions. As the following case shows, there often are creative ways in which such losses might be shifted to third parties.

Heritage Bank v. Lovett
613 N.W.2d 652 (Iowa 2000) (en banc)

CARTER, Justice.

Plaintiff, Heritage Bank (Heritage), appeals from an adverse summary judgment in an action seeking to recover funds obtained through the unauthorized use of an ATM card. The defendants, Terry Lovett, Robert Lovett, and Roma Lovett d/b/a Culligan Water Conditioning of Ida Grove, Iowa (Culligan), are the employers of Richard Bennett, the person who illegally obtained money from an ATM using an ATM card that Heritage had issued to Donald and Luella Buell. Heritage seeks to recover from Culligan on a theory of negligent hiring. After reviewing the record and considering the arguments presented, we agree with the conclusions of the district court that Culligan owed no duty to protect Heritage from Bennett's criminal action and that Heritage is not subrogated to any claim of the Buells against Culligan.

On December 5, 1995, Bennett, while working for Culligan, went to the residence of Donald and Luella Buell to perform services. While there he stole a wallet containing an ATM card issued in regard to the Buells' bank account with Heritage. Bennett subsequently used this card at various ATMs to misappropriate approximately $10,000. Heritage commenced this action based on two theories of recovery, *respondeat superior* and negligent hiring.

In ruling on successive motions for summary judgment filed by Culligan, the district court concluded that (1) Bennett's activities were not within the scope of his employment with Culligan so as to give rise to the doctrine of *respondeat superior*, (2) the loss for which Heritage seeks to recover was its own direct loss and not a loss suffered by the Buells to which Heritage is now subrogated, and (3) Culligan owed no duty to Heritage to protect it from Bennett's criminal acts. The legal consequence of these rulings was a total denial of Heritage's claims against Culligan.

I.   THE BANK'S COMMON-LAW SUBROGATION CLAIM

Heritage . . . posits its appeal on the claim that the loss occasioned by Bennett's use of the ATM card fell in the first instance on the Buells by way of diminution of their account and that Heritage became subrogated to the Buells' rights against Culligan by restoring all but fifty dollars of the Buells' loss. Heritage argues that because Culligan did owe a duty to protect the Buells from Bennett's actions it may assert the Buells' rights against Culligan in the role of a subrogee. We disagree with this contention.

As the district court correctly concluded, except for the sum of fifty dollars, the loss occasioned by Bennett's criminal acts was from its inception entirely that of the bank. The Buells never suffered any loss apart from the fifty dollars that was debited to their account. A subrogee may acquire no claim, security, or remedy that the subrogor does not have.

A bank deposit without reservation transfers the title of the funds from the depositor to the bank. The relationship that thereafter follows is one of debtor (the bank) and creditor (the depositor). . . .

A deposit agreement is subject to all applicable statutes that govern the relationship between the depositor and the bank to the same extent as if written in the agreement. Federal law sharply limits the extent to which a bank may debit a depositor's account as the result of an unauthorized electronic funds transfer. The applicable statute provides [that the consumer generally is liable only for $50 of unauthorized transfers. EFTA §909, 15 U.S.C. §1693g.] The foregoing rules may be altered if the bank can establish that the loss was increased as a result of a delay by the depositor in reporting either a stolen ATM card or an unauthorized entry on a statement that the bank has sent to the depositor. Even in such instances, however, the bank may not debit the depositor's account for more than $500.

In the present case, the Buells promptly reported the unauthorized transactions to the bank. Consequently, due to the proscriptions contained in this federal statute, Heritage, notwithstanding any contrary provision in its depositors agreement, could not debit the Buells' account for a sum greater than fifty dollars as a result of Bennett's unauthorized use of their ATM card.

We have recognized that subrogation may exist by agreement between the parties or may be based on equitable principles that permit one who has satisfied an obligation owed by another to a third party to be placed in the obligee's position vis-à-vis the primary obligor. The latter type of subrogation, which is the type involved in the present case, is granted to a person secondarily liable for a debt who has paid it and is designed to allow that party to enforce the creditor's right of exoneration against one that has been unjustly enriched. The need for the doctrine exists because ordinarily the subrogee does not possess a personal cause of action against the unjustly enriched party.

Heritage's attempt to claim against Culligan as a subrogee of the Buells must fail for two reasons. First, based upon the principles we have previously set forth, Heritage suffered the loss of the funds sought to be recovered in its own right and not as a result of satisfying any loss sustained by the Buells. Consequently, its entitlement to bring the present claim against Culligan should be based on its own relationship to that defendant rather than the Buells' relationship. In addition, and of equal significance, is the fact that the rights to which a subrogee succeeds are the same as and no greater than those of the person for whom the subrogee seeks to be substituted.

Prior to Bennett's criminal acts, the Buells' right to draw against their account at Heritage was measured by the balance of funds that they had on deposit at that time. Immediately following Bennett's criminal acts the Buells' rights vis-à-vis their bank account at Heritage were precisely the same except for the fifty-dollar debit transaction. The Buells sustained no injury for which they could maintain an action against either Bennett or Culligan apart from the fifty-dollar item, which is not an issue in the litigation.

We have considered Heritage's attempt to challenge our analysis based on language contained in 15 U.S.C. §1693g and conclude that its effort is flawed. The language upon which Heritage relies provides "reimbursement need not be made to the consumer for losses which the financial institution establishes would not have occurred but for the failure of the consumer to report [the unauthorized use or theft]." Heritage contends that this language is a recognition that the loss, in the first instance, falls on the depositor. This contention is inaccurate because the depositor's rights vis-à-vis the bank are at all times determined by the law governing the transaction. As a practical matter in automated transactions of this type the account will almost always be debited on the bank's electronic records when an unauthorized electronic transfer occurs, but this does not change the depositor's legal entitlement from the bank. If the depositor sued the bank for a declaratory judgment as to the status of the depositor's account, the result would be the same irrespective of whether the bank had restored an improperly debited item. Consequently, a statute requiring reimbursement has exactly the same legal significance as a statute that prohibits the debiting of the depositor's account.

II. THE BANK'S STATUTORY SUBROGATION CLAIM

As an alternative to its common-law subrogation claim, Heritage relies on the subrogation provisions contained in [UCC §4-407]....

It is at once apparent that this statute pertains to checks or other bills of exchange drawn on banks. It has no operative language governing electronic funds transfers. Nor may Heritage make a colorable argument involving this statute by way of analogy. Section [4-407(3)] only grants a right of subrogation against a payee or other holder of the check improperly paid by the bank. In framing an analogy that might be applied to the electronic transfer situation based on the statutory directive involving checks, the analogous persons to be claimed against would be those persons obtaining the cash or to whom the cash might be traced. Such an analogy would not permit a subrogation claim against an employer of one of those persons based on negligent hiring.

. . . Because there is no statute granting subrogation to a bank in Heritage's situation, it must depend on the common law, which grants it no rights as a subrogee.

We have considered all issues presented and conclude that the judgment of the district court should be affirmed.

Problem Set 29

29.1. The ever forgetful Cliff Janeway (your bookseller friend, most recently from Problem 28.1) calls you one afternoon from the airport in Albuquerque, where he just got off a plane to visit some local booksellers. He is frantic because he left his checkbook on the seat next to him when he left the plane. He is pretty sure that his debit card was stuffed inside the checkbook, and he is sure that his personal identification number is written on the inside cover of the checkbook. His account has about $12,000 in it because he planned to purchase several expensive books while in Albuquerque. He wants to know what he should do. Does he have anything to worry about? EFTA §§908, 909.

29.2. Joe Willie ("Bill") Robertson is a longtime friend of yours who operates a chain of independent grocery stores in Houston, Texas. His bank has just come to him with a proposal that he start accepting debit cards under a PIN-based system at his stores. The bank tells Bill that his account will be credited with funds much more rapidly on debit-card transactions than it is on traditional checking transactions, which should bring him additional interest income on an annual basis of about $160,000. Bill also hopes that it will save him a substantial amount on bad-check expenses; he currently has to write off about 1.5 percent of all receipts that come in the form of checks, either because the checks are uncollectible or because collecting them through litigation is too expensive. These cost savings far exceed the cost of the equipment that Bill would have to buy to implement the debit-card system, even taking account of the 15- to 35-cent discount Bill will have to pay his bank on each transaction.

Notwithstanding those possible benefits, Bill is skeptical about the bank's proposal for two reasons. He doubts the reliability of the computer technology, and he has a policy of always worrying when his banker claims to be doing something for his benefit. Bill asks you whether he faces any significant risks of loss if he starts accepting the cards. What if people present forged cards? What if they use stolen cards? What if the system malfunctions and lets him sell things to people whose accounts are empty? Can you think of anything else that he is missing?

29.3. Archie Moon comes by this morning and insists that he has to see you without an appointment. He tells you that about a month ago he purchased a new printing press. As it happens, he is completely dissatisfied with the printing press because it does not perform nearly as well as the salesperson promised him. Accordingly, he decided that he wanted to withhold payment. Remembering some advice you gave him several years ago, he did not write a check for the press; instead, he paid for it with his bank card. When Archie called his bank officer last week to tell her that he did not wish to pay for the press and identified the transaction, his bank officer told him that he could not challenge the transaction because he had purchased the press with a debit card.

Archie has looked at the card in his wallet and the information from his bank and tells you that the card contains two features, a conventional credit-card feature (a MasterCard, as it happens), and a debit-card feature. He believes that the clerk at the press shop erroneously processed the transaction as a debit-card transaction, rather than a credit-card transaction. Putting aside any right that Archie might have against the merchant and assuming that Archie is right about what happened (and that he can prove it), can Archie force the bank to refund the money to him? EFTA §§903(11), 909; TILA §170(a); Regulation E, §§205.2(m), 205.6(a); Regulation Z, §226.12(c)(1).

29.4. Luck being what it is, Archie calls you a few weeks later to report that in the course of reviewing his bank statements in connection with the transaction discussed in Problem 29.3, he noticed quite a number of unauthorized transactions. The transactions go back over a year and total $3,000. (The thief did not get greedy, but took only $250 each month.) Archie remembers ordering a new card about a year ago and has just remembered that the card was taken from him in a mugging about a year ago. Trying to put the mugging out of his mind, he entirely forgot to do anything about the lost card. For how much of the $3,000 is Archie responsible? (For purposes of the problem, assume that the theft occurred on March 1, that on the first day of each month the bank mails a statement that includes all of the previous transactions, and that the thefts occurred in individual $250 transactions on the fifteenth of each month.) EFTA §909(a); Regulation E, §§205.6(b), 205.12(a).

29.5. Just after you get off the phone with Archie, you discover that Cliff Janeway is waiting to see you. He explains that in response to the advice that you gave him in Problem 29.1, he promptly went to his bank to report the unauthorized transactions. That visit occurred on Monday March 1, the same day that he learned that the card had been lost. Based on a review of charges that had been posted to his account at that time, he reported a total of $1,000 of unauthorized charges, all of which apparently were used to purchase beer and wine at a nearby liquor store that accepts debit cards. Assuming that the problem had been dealt with, Cliff went about his business.

Much to his surprise, ten days later on March 11, Cliff got a telecopy from one of his suppliers advising Cliff that the supplier was canceling its contract with Cliff because Cliff's bank had bounced the check Cliff had written to that supplier on March 6. On inquiry, Cliff discovered that the bank bounced the check on the morning of March 9 because it had not yet determined how to respond to Cliff's claim that the beer-and-wine debit-card transactions were unauthorized. Does Cliff have a right to complain about the bank's dishonor of his check? UCC §4-402; EFTA §908(c); Regulation E, §205.11(c).

29.6. Would your answer to Problem 29.5 be different if Cliff's card was a MasterMoney debit card?

29.7. Jodi Kay calls you in response to a newspaper article that she just read about the staggering frequency with which criminal enterprises forge credit cards. Because she knows from prior conversations with you that her employer, CountryBank, bears most of the risk of loss from unauthorized debit-card transactions, Jodi is worried that her bank could lose a lot of money from transactions made with forged debit cards. Does the frequency of forged *credit* cards justify her in worrying about forged *debit* cards? What does she have to fear? Does it matter if she uses a PIN-based system or a PIN-less system? EFTA §909.

Assignment 30: The Wire-Transfer System

Measured by dollar volume alone, wire transfers are the dominant payment system in our country. Every day more than $2 trillion are transferred in the United States by wire. Although financial institutions make most of those transfers to settle transactions originally made by other payment systems, the use of wire transfers as a mechanism for payment in the first instance has increased considerably in recent years. The next two assignments address the latter topic, wire transfers as a payment system.

A. Introduction

Wire-transfer payments are attractive to businesses because they offer almost instantaneous payment at the time of the transaction. When a payee receives a payment by wire transfer, the payment normally reaches the payee in the form of immediately available funds in the payee's bank account. Immediate funds are much more satisfying to the payee than payment by check or credit card. When a payee accepts a check or credit card, the payee must deposit the check or credit-card slip with its own bank and hope that the stakeholder (the payor bank or the issuing bank, as the case may be) honors the transaction and remains solvent long enough to forward payment to the payee. In contrast, a payment received by wire transfer is much more like a payment by debit card, final for all practical purposes at the moment of receipt by the payee. The largest risk that the payee faces is that its own bank will become insolvent before the payee withdraws the funds.

Most wire-transfer transactions are made through networks of participating institutions. The three largest networks used by American banks are Fedwire, CHIPS, and SWIFT. Fedwire is a government institution operated by the Federal Reserve, which provides the predominant method for making domestic interbank wire transfers. CHIPS (the Clearing House Interbank Payment System) is a privately operated facility of the New York Clearing House (a group of Manhattan financial institutions). CHIPS is predominantly used to clear international transfers in dollars; it settles those transactions by transferring amounts in the accounts of participants at the Federal Reserve Bank of New York. SWIFT (the Society for Worldwide Interbank Financial Telecommunications) is an automated international system for sending funds-transfer messages that is the predominant method for completing international transfers that are not denominated in dollars. SWIFT transactions are settled by debits and credits on the books of the participating institutions.

The principal body of American law applicable to wire transfers is Article 4A of the Uniform Commercial Code. Article 4A applies only to "credit" transfers

(transfers initiated by the entity making payment). UCC §§4A-102, 4A-104 comment 4. A typical example would be a direction by Riverfront Tools, Inc. (RFT) to its bank to transfer $1,000,000 from RFT's account into a designated account of California Pneumatic Tools. Because the Federal Reserve's Regulation J, 12 C.F.R. Part 210, adopts Article 4A as the governing law for all transfers by Fedwire, Article 4A governs Fedwire transfers as a matter of federal law. Regulation J, §210.25(b). Article 4A does not, however, apply to debit transfers (transfers initiated by the entity being paid). UCC §4A-104 comment 4. For example, Article 4A would not apply to the monthly transfers that would occur if RFT authorized its mortgage lender to obtain RFT's monthly loan payment by means of an automatic debit from RFT's checking account. A simple way to put it is to think of Article 4A as applying to transfers that "push" money to another party, but not to transfers that "pull" money from the other party.

Another major exclusion from Article 4A governs systems normally used by individuals, such as the debit-card transfers described in Assignment 29. See UCC §4A-108 (excluding transfers covered by the EFTA); EFTA §903(6)(B) (limiting "electronic fund transfer[s]" covered by the EFTA to funds transfers made on systems "designed primarily to transfer funds on behalf of a [natural person]"). Although those exclusions from Article 4A are defined by consumer use, they do not reflect a desire to allow special rules to protect consumers in the other systems. Rather, the exclusions reflect a functional distinction between the types of systems used for consumer transfers and the highly developed and specialized systems that banks use for wire transfers. The purpose of Article 4A is to provide a consistent body of law for credit transfers made by businesses; it would make little sense to apply it to the wide variety of other systems for electronic funds transfers.

B.   How Does It Work?

1.   Initiating the Wire Transfer: From the Originator to the Originator's Bank

The process of initiating payment by wire transfer is not complicated. The party that wants to make the payment simply asks its bank to make the transfer (see Figure 30.1). The request could be made in person (if the customer is at the bank), by telecopy, by telex, by electronic mail, or even by telephone. In the terms of Article 4A, the customer is the "originator" of a "funds transfer," to be implemented by the "originator's bank," sent to the "beneficiary's bank," and there credited to the "beneficiary." See UCC §4A-105. In Article 4A's terminology, each step from the originator to the beneficiary's bank constitutes a separate "payment order"; the parties to each payment order are called a "sender" and a "receiving bank." UCC §§4A-103, 4A-104. The strange lack of parallelism — you would expect the statute to refer to a "sender" and a "receiver" — arises from the statute's definition in UCC §4A-103(a) of a payment order as an instruction to a bank to pay funds to a third party. That definition means that the receiving party always will be a bank (and thus

Figure 30.1
Payment by Wire Transfer

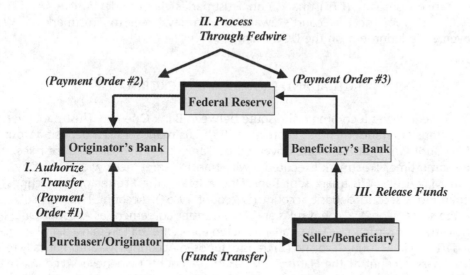

can be called the receiving bank), although the sending party need not be a bank (and thus could not be called the sending bank).

As the last part of this assignment explains, the originator's bank has no significant opportunity to avoid payment once it sends a payment order into the system. Accordingly, the originator's bank ordinarily obtains payment from the originator before taking action. The originator's bank typically obtains that payment by removing funds from the originator's account or, in some cases, by placing a hold on the funds (but leaving them in the account until the transfer is completed). If the originator's bank cannot obtain payment at the time of the transfer and is unwilling to rely on its ability to collect payment at a later time, it can reject the originator's payment order under UCC §4A-210(a).

Regardless of whether the originator's bank has obtained funds from the originator before sending the funds transfer, Article 4A (in its convoluted way) grants the originator's bank (as the receiving bank of the customer's payment order) a right to collect payment from the originator (as sender of that payment order) if the originator's bank executes the payment order as directed by the originator. See UCC §§4A-402(c) (receiving bank entitled to payment upon "acceptance" of the order), 4A-209(a) (receiving bank accepts an order when it "executes" it), 4A-301(a) (receiving bank "execute[s]" a payment order when it issues a new payment order carrying out the payment order that it received).

Trustmark Ins. Co. v. Bank One
48 P.3d 485 (Ariz. 2002)

GEMMILL, Judge.

If a banking customer sends a bank a letter of instructions requesting wire transfers of funds upon future occurrences of a specified balance condition in the customer's account, does the letter of instructions constitute a "payment order" under Article 4A of Arizona's Uniform Commercial Code ("UCC")? We address this question . . . in this decision.

Bank One, Arizona, NA ("Bank One") appeals from a jury verdict for Trustmark Insurance Company ("Trustmark") on Trustmark's claim under Article 4A of the UCC and from the trial court's award of attorneys' fees to Trustmark. . . . We reverse the judgment on the UCC claim. . . .

FACTUAL AND PROCEDURAL BACKGROUND

This case involves a commercial dispute between Bank One and Trustmark over a wire transfer arrangement. In February 1995, Trustmark set up a deposit account ("Account One") at Bank One governed by Bank One's deposit account rules. At the same time, Trustmark executed a wire transfer agreement with Bank One.

In May 1995, Trustmark sent Bank One a letter (the "Letter of Instructions") regarding a second deposit account ("Account Two"). Account Two was subject to the same deposit account rules and wire transfer agreement as Account One. In the Letter of Instructions, Trustmark instructed Bank One to (1) retain a daily balance of $10,000 in Account Two and (2) transfer funds in Account Two automatically to a Trustmark account at the Harris Bank ("Harris Account") whenever Account Two reached a balance of $110,000 or more. In September 1995, Trustmark's Arizona agent began depositing funds into Account Two. Bank One began transferring funds to the Harris Account whenever the Account Two balance rose above $110,000.

In August 1996, Bank One automated its wire transfer functions and consolidated its local departments into a central wire transfer department. Under the automated process, each account from which wire transfers were anticipated needed a new wire transfer agreement. In preparation, Bank One sent all of its wire transfer customers, including Trustmark, a letter dated July 1, 1996 informing the customers that Bank One required a new funds transfer agreement for each account from which wire transfers were anticipated. The letter stated that if a new funds transfer agreement was not in place by July 19, 1996, Bank One could not ensure uninterrupted wire transfer service from accounts lacking such agreements. Trustmark denies ever receiving this letter and never sent Bank One a new funds transfer agreement for Account Two.

In September 1996, the Account Two balance rose above $110,000 for the first time since the July 19, 1996 deadline. Bank One did not transfer funds from Account Two into the Harris Account. Bank One sent regular account statements to Trustmark showing the balances in Account Two, but received no further instructions from Trustmark. The Account Two balance continued to grow until December 1997, when Bank One brought the balance to the specific attention of Trustmark's Arizona agent, who contacted Trustmark's management. Bank One transferred $19,220,099.80 to the Harris Account, leaving $10,000 in Account Two. In early 1998, Trustmark instructed Bank One to transfer Account Two's remaining funds to the Harris Account and thereafter closed Account Two.

Trustmark then filed this action against Bank One, alleging a claim under Article 4A of the UCC, as well as claims for unjust enrichment and negligence. Trustmark alleged that Bank One failed to complete wire transfers from Trustmark's non-interest bearing account at Bank One (Account Two) to Trustmark's investment account at Harris Bank (Harris Account), contrary to the Letter of Instructions. Trustmark asserted a loss of more than $500,000 in interest on its funds as a result of Bank One's inaction, and that Bank One reaped a corresponding windfall profit through interest Bank One earned on Trustmark's money. Trustmark did not assert a breach of contract claim. According to Bank One, the contractual documents eliminated recovery or significantly limited the amount recoverable for breach of contract. However, Article 4A — if applicable — restricts the right of a bank to limit its liability regarding funds transfers. See [UCC §4A-305(f).]

Bank One filed motions to dismiss and for summary judgment on the UCC claim, arguing that the wire transfers at issue were not subject to Article 4A because the Letter of Instructions was not a "payment order" under Article 4A. The trial court denied Bank One's motions, and the case proceeded to a jury trial. At the close of evidence, the court granted Bank One's motion for judgment as a matter of law on the unjust enrichment claim, but continued to reject Bank One's argument that Article 4A of the UCC was not applicable. The court submitted Trustmark's UCC claim and its negligence claim to the jury.

The jury returned a verdict for Trustmark on the UCC claim and found damages of $573,197.02. . . . The trial court entered judgment for Trustmark with damages of $573,197.02, as well as pre-judgment interest, attorneys' fees, and taxable costs.

ISSUES ON APPEAL AND CROSS APPEAL

Bank One argues on appeal that Trustmark's judgment should be reversed as a matter of law because Article 4A of the UCC is not applicable. According to Bank One, the Letter of Instructions was not a "payment order" under Article 4A, and the trial court should not have sent this UCC claim to the jury.

BANK ONE'S APPEAL

Bank One challenges the trial court's submission of the UCC claim to the jury on the basis that the Letter of Instructions is not a "payment order" under Article 4A; therefore the UCC is not applicable, and this claim should have been dismissed as a matter of law. Whether the Letter of Instructions is a "payment order" is initially a question of law that we independently review.

AS A MATTER OF LAW, THE UCC DOES NOT APPLY BECAUSE THE LETTER OF INSTRUCTIONS WAS NOT A "PAYMENT ORDER" UNDER ARTICLE 4A

We begin our analysis of the applicability of Article 4A by noting its recent origin and its purpose. In 1989 the National Conference of Commissioners on Uniform State Laws and the American Law Institute promulgated Article 4A of the UCC, addressing funds transfers. Over the next several years, all fifty states and the District of Columbia enacted Article 4A as part of their existing UCC statutes. Arizona enacted Article 4A in 1991.

Technological developments in recent decades have enabled banks to transfer funds electronically, without physical delivery of paper instruments. Before Article 4A, no comprehensive body of law had defined the rights and obligations that arise from wire transfers. Article 4A was intended to provide a new and controlling body of law for those wire transfers within its scope. . . .

Because there are very few reported decisions—and none from Arizona—interpreting and applying the provisions of Article 4A defining its scope, we have considered primarily the language of the pertinent statutes, the purpose of Article 4A, and the comments of its drafters. In the Prefatory Note to Article 4A, the drafters discussed the funds transfers intended to be covered and several factors considered in the drafting process:

There are a number of characteristics of funds transfers covered by Article 4A that have influenced the drafting of the statute. The typical funds transfer involves a large amount of money. Multimillion dollar transactions are commonplace. The originator of the transfer and the beneficiary are typically sophisticated business or financial organizations. High speed is another predominant characteristic. Most funds transfers are completed on the same day, even in complex transactions in which there are several intermediary banks in the transmission chain. A funds transfer is a highly efficient substitute for payments made by the delivery of paper instruments. Another characteristic is extremely low cost. A transfer that involves many millions of dollars can be made for a price of a few dollars. Price does not normally vary very much or at all with the amount of the transfer. This system of pricing may not be feasible if the bank is exposed to very large liabilities in connection with the transaction.

Article 4A applies only to "funds transfers" as defined in the statute. [UCC §4A-102.] A "funds transfer" is "the series of transactions, beginning with the originator's *payment order*, made for the purpose of making payment to the beneficiary of the order." [UCC §4A-104(1) (emphasis added by court).] Accordingly, to fall within the scope of Article 4A, a transaction must begin with a "payment order."

A "payment order" is defined by the UCC, in pertinent part, as:

[A]n instruction of a sender to a receiving bank, transmitted orally, electronically, or in writing, to pay, or to cause another bank to pay, a *fixed or determinable amount of money* to a beneficiary if:

[i] *The instruction does not state a condition to payment* to the beneficiary *other than time of payment.*

[UCC §4A-103(a)(1) (emphasis added by court).]

Bank One argues that the Letter of Instructions was not a payment order, because the Letter was not for a "fixed or determinable amount of money" and imposed two conditions other than time of payment: that the account balance always remain $10,000 ("balance condition") and that transfers not occur until subsequent deposits have raised the balance to $110,000 or more ("deposit condition"). Trustmark argues that the conditions at issue were merely conditions regarding the time of payment—that the balance and deposit conditions essentially determined when transfers were to be made. Trustmark asserts that time of payment need not be set by a specific date, but may be set by events such as the bank's receipt of an incoming wire or deposit. However, the amounts to be transferred did not relate to incoming wires for the same amounts or even wires received on the same day of each month. Rather, Trustmark's agent made deposits sporadically and in varying amounts. Therefore, the conditions in the Letter of Instructions required Bank One to continuously monitor Trustmark's account balance to determine whether sufficient deposits had been made to enable the bank to make a transfer that satisfied both the deposit and balance conditions.

Neither party has cited, nor has our own research revealed, any reported decision addressing the precise issue presented: whether a letter of instructions from an account holder to its bank, requesting automatic wire transfers of funds in excess of a minimum balance whenever the total balance equals or exceeds a specified amount, constitutes a "payment order" governed by UCC Article 4A. We conclude that the Letter of Instructions was not a "payment order," because the Letter subjected Bank One to a condition to payment other than the time of payment.

Article 4A applies to discrete, mechanical transfers of funds. Comment 3 to UCC §4A-104 provides:

> The function of banks in a funds transfer under Article 4A is comparable to their role in the collection and payment of checks in that it is essentially mechanical in nature. The low price and high speed that characterize funds transfers reflect this fact. Conditions to payment . . . other than time of payment impose responsibilities on [the] bank that go beyond those in Article 4A funds transfers.

Bank One's obligation to make an ongoing inquiry as to Account Two's balance status removes the Letter of Instructions from the Article 4A definition of a "payment order." Conditions other than time of payment are anathema to Article 4A, which facilitates the low price, high speed, and mechanical nature of funds transfers. [Quotation marks, brackets, and citation omitted.] In their treatise on the UCC, James J. White and Robert S. Summers further explain:

> A payment order must not "state a condition to payment of the beneficiary other than time of payment." Few transactions will include such conditions. The exception for "time of payment" means that a payment order need not order immediate payment, though most do. For example, a payment order may specify that a certain amount of money must be paid on a certain date to a particular beneficiary.

3 James J. White & Robert S. Summers, *Uniform Commercial Code* §22-2 (4th ed. 1995) (citation omitted). White and Summers then quoted the same language from Comment 3 that we quote [above] to explain that "the drafters did not wish to involve banks in [inquiries] into whether other conditions have occurred." *Id.*

Based on the language defining "payment order," the purpose of Article 4A, and the drafters' intent that payment orders be virtually unconditional, we conclude that requiring the bank to continually examine the account balance is a condition to payment other than time of payment under [UCC §4A-103(a)(1)(i).] We perceive a qualitative difference between a condition requiring daily monitoring of the account balance and an instruction to wire funds on a specific day.

Trustmark also argues that the balance and deposit conditions were permissible conditions observed by Bank One in the past, and therefore Bank One cannot now argue that the conditions were impermissible under Article 4A. The fact that Bank One provided these services to Trustmark under the wire transfer agreement and the Letter of Instructions does not alter our analysis and is irrelevant to whether the Letter of Instructions falls within the definition of a "payment order." Bank One does not argue that such conditions are impermissible *per se;* Bank One simply argues that the Letter's conditions are beyond the permissible conditions for an Article 4A "payment order." Although parties may appropriately and legitimately make such a long-term arrangement for transfers to and from various accounts, their agreement does not automatically transform the arrangement into an Article 4A funds transfer. . . .

We conclude, as a matter of law, that Trustmark does not have a claim under UCC Article 4A, because the Letter of Instructions is not an Article 4A "payment order." Therefore, we reverse the judgment against Bank One on Trustmark's UCC claim.

Although the originator ordinarily pays the originator's bank for its payment order no later than the time at which the originator's bank executes the originator's payment order, it occasionally happens that the funds transfer cannot be completed for various reasons. For example, suppose that RFT's payment order instructed First Bank to send payment to a specified account of California Pneumatic Tools at Wells Fargo in San Francisco. If Wells Fargo could not locate an account with that number, Wells Fargo probably would reject the payment order. Wells Fargo's rejection of the payment order would leave the funds transfer incomplete, even if RFT already had paid First Bank for the transfer under UCC §4A-402(c). In that event, the last sentence of UCC §4A-402(c) excuses RFT's obligation to pay its payment order as sender. UCC §4A-402(d) then obligates First Bank to refund payment to RFT, including interest from the date that RFT paid First Bank for the order. The case that follows illustrates one such scenario.

Banco de la Provincia v. BayBank Boston, N.A.

985 F. Supp. 364 (S.D.N.Y. 1997)

Robert J. WARD, District Judge. Plaintiff Banco de la Provincia de Buenos Aires ("BPBA"), which filed this action seeking a declaratory judgment, now moves for summary judgment. . . . For the reasons that follow, plaintiff's motion is granted.

BACKGROUND

BPBA is a bank incorporated under the laws of the Province of Buenos Aires, Republic of Argentina. Defendant BayBank Boston, N.A. ("BayBank") is a federally chartered national banking association with its principal place of business in Boston, Massachusetts.

On January 11, 1995, BPBA extended a loan of $250,000 ("the loan") to Banco Feigin S.A. ("Banco Feigin"), an Argentine bank that is not a party to this action. BPBA disbursed the proceeds of the loan to a credit account maintained by Banco Feigin at the New York City branch office of BPBA. The term of the loan, which was to mature on July 10, 1995, was 180 days.

Between November 30, 1994 and March 14, 1995, Banco Feigin suffered a liquidity crisis, losing 49% of its deposits. In March 1995, the Central Bank of Argentina ("the Central Bank") commenced what is known under Argentine law as an Intervention ("the Intervention"), essentially an inquiry into the solvency of a bank. In the months that followed, the Central Bank issued a series of resolutions which suspended the operations of Banco Feigin and ultimately revoked Banco Feigin's authorization to operate as a bank under Argentine law. The assets of Banco Feigin were liquidated and sold for the benefit of Banco Feigin's depositors at an auction sponsored by the Central Bank in July 1995. . . .

In light of the Central Bank's suspension of Banco Feigin's operations on March 17, 1995, BPBA placed an administrative freeze on Banco Feigin's credit balance account on March 22, 1995. On that date, Banco Feigin's BPBA account contained $245,529.55, and consisted solely of proceeds from BPBA's January 1995 loan to Banco Feigin.

According to BPBA, . . . the Intervention by the Central Bank that began on March 17, 1995 gave BPBA the right, at any time after the Intervention, to a set-off against the money owed to BPBA by Banco Feigin. On April 19, 1995, BPBA exercised this statutory right of set-off by applying against the indebtedness of Banco Feigin to BPBA the funds contained in Banco Feigin's account. The amount of the set-off was $245,529.55, the remainder of Banco Feigin's BPBA account. BPBA notified Banco Feigin of the set-off by telex dated April 19, 1995. Banco Feigin's remaining indebtedness to BPBA as a result of the January 1995 loan was $12,637.12.

After the Central Bank began its Intervention, but before the April 19, 1995 set-off, Banco Feigin's Buenos Aires branch sent BPBA a request to transfer $245,000 from Banco Feigin's account with BPBA in New York to a Banco Feigin account at BayBank in Boston (the "wire transfer request"). According to BayBank, Banco Feigin intended to use the transferred funds to repay amounts it owed to BayBank. BPBA received the wire transfer request on March 24, 1995, but did not accept the payment order or transfer the funds because of the administrative freeze on Banco Feigin's account and BPBA's then existing but as yet unexercised right of set-off.

In a letter to BPBA dated August 4, 1995, BayBank demanded that BPBA pay it $245,000, plus interest, representing the monies not sent on March 24, 1995 to Banco Feigin's BayBank account. In its letter, BayBank stated its intent to initiate legal proceedings if the demand was not met in full by August 31, 1995.

BPBA commenced this action against BayBank in the Supreme Court of the State of New York, County of New York, on September 1, 1995. The case was subsequently removed to this Court based upon the parties' diversity of citizenship under 28 U.S.C. §§1332(a)(2) and 1348, and under 12 U.S.C. §632, since the defendant is a banking corporation organized under the laws of the United States and the lawsuit involves international banking transactions.

In its complaint, plaintiff seeks a declaratory judgment that on April 19, 1995, BPBA had the right to set-off against the funds in Banco Feigin's account at BPBA, and that this right to set-off was superior to any right BayBank may have had as the bank maintaining an account of Banco Feigin to which Banco Feigin had requested its funds be sent. BayBank counterclaims in the amount of $245,000 plus interest, alleging BPBA wrongfully converted its money when it refused to execute the wire transfer request. Claiming that the $245,000 became its property upon BPBA's receipt of Banco Feigin's wire transfer request, BayBank seeks a declaratory judgment that the set-off exercised by BPBA was unlawful and that BayBank's right to the funds which were the subject of the wire transfer request of Banco Feigin was superior to BPBA's right to such funds.

DISCUSSION . . .

II. N.Y. U.C.C. Article 4-A

Disputes arising from wire transfers are now governed by Article 4A of the Uniform Commercial Code. Article 4A was enacted in the wake of technological advances allowing the electronic transfer of funds, a means by which up to a trillion dollars is shifted daily. At the time Article 4A was drafted, "there was no comprehensive body of law—statutory or judicial—that defined the juridical nature of a funds transfer or the rights and obligations flowing from payment orders." N.Y. U.C.C. §4-A-102, Official Comment. The statute reflects "[a] deliberate decision . . . to use precise and detailed rules to assign responsibility, define behavioral norms, allocate risks and establish limits on liability, rather than to rely on broadly stated, flexible principles." Id.

The electronic transfer of funds is accomplished through the use of one or more payment orders. A payment order is sent by the "sender" to the "receiving bank," for ultimate payment to the "beneficiary" or the "beneficiary's bank." In the instant case, Banco Feigin is both the sender and the beneficiary, BPBA is the receiving bank, and BayBank is the beneficiary's bank. The first step in a funds transfer is the sender's transmission of a payment order to a receiving bank. Before the transfer proceeds, the receiving bank must accept the sender's payment order.

A. BPBA properly rejected the payment order under N.Y. U.C.C. §4-A-209(1)

Under §4-A-209(1), "a receiving bank other than the beneficiary's bank accepts a payment order when it executes the order." This provision has been interpreted to give receiving banks other than the beneficiary's bank general discretion in choosing whether to accept or reject payment orders. BPBA contends that its refusal to execute the payment order constituted a rejection of the payment order that was within its discretion.

According to BayBank, BPBA does not have absolute discretion in deciding whether to accept or reject payment orders. . . . This Court agrees that receiving banks' exercise of discretion in accepting or rejecting payment orders should not be above judicial scrutiny.

In examining the circumstances under which BPBA rejected the payment order, however, it becomes clear that BPBA's rejection was neither an abuse of discretion nor in bad faith. At the time BPBA rejected the payment order, Banco Feigin's BPBA account—which consisted solely of proceeds of BPBA's January 1995 loan to Banco Feigin—was under an administrative freeze, and Banco Feigin's banking activities had been suspended as part of an Intervention by the Central Bank of Argentina. . . . Moreover, Banco Feigin's debt to BPBA exceeded the balance in the account. Under those circumstances, it was not unreasonable for BPBA to refuse to wire the entire balance of the account to Banco Feigin's BayBank account. Therefore, BPBA's rejection of the payment order was a proper exercise of its discretion under §4A-209.

B. Since BPBA properly rejected the payment order, it incurred no duty to Banco Feigin or BayBank

Liability of receiving banks arises only if the receiving bank accepts a payment order, or if there is an express agreement between the sender and the receiving bank which requires the receiving bank to execute payment orders. BPBA incurred no liability since there was no acceptance under §4-A-209 and there was no agreement between BPBA and Banco Feigin requiring BPBA to accept the payment order.

III. BPBA's SET-OFF WAS LAWFUL UNDER N.Y.
DEBTOR AND CREDITOR LAW §151

[The court concluded that BPBA's set-off complied with applicable New York law.]

IV. BAYBANK'S CONVERSION CLAIM

For a conversion claim arising from a funds transfer to stand, it must not be inconsistent with Article 4A, which is

> intended to be the exclusive means of determining the rights, duties and liabilities of the affected parties in any situation covered by particular provisions of the Article. Consequently, resort to principles of law or equity outside of Article 4A is not appropriate to create rights, duties and liabilities inconsistent with those stated in this Article.

N.Y. U.C.C. Law §4-A-102, Off. Cmt. Plaintiff interprets the foregoing commentary as precluding an action for conversion arising from a funds transfer. This court adheres to the principle that Article 4A does not preclude common law claims. The question remains, however, whether defendant's conversion claim is inconsistent with Article 4A.

Under New York law, conversion is any act of dominion wrongfully exerted over the personal property of another inconsistent with that person's rights in the property. . . .

BayBank's conversion claim fails for several reasons. First, there is no support for BayBank's contention that the $245,000 that was the subject of the wire transfer request became the property of BayBank upon BPBA's receipt of the wire transfer request. To prevail on its claim for conversion, BayBank must prove that it had an ownership interest or an immediate superior right of possession to property. [Quotation marks and citations omitted.] BayBank has failed to do so, and thus has not established ownership, an essential element of conversion.

Second, there was no intent on the part of BPBA to ever deprive BayBank of the property. According to the wire transfer request, BPBA was to transfer the money to the account of Banco Feigin, not to BayBank. Banco Feigin was the beneficiary. BayBank was merely the beneficiary's bank. Finally, the question remains whether BayBank's conversion claim survives in light of the Court's determination that BPBA properly rejected the payment order and applied the funds in Banco Feigin's account as a set-off under N.Y. U.C.C. §4-A-209 and N.Y. Debt. and Cred. Law §151, respectively. [This Court previously has dismissed such claims.] The same is true here.

Finally, the Court notes that it has found no precedent allowing the intended beneficiary of a funds transfer to recover from a receiving bank. Any claim BayBank has is against Banco Feigin, not BPBA.

CONCLUSION

For the foregoing reasons, plaintiff's motion for summary judgment is granted and defendant's counterclaim is dismissed. The Court declares that on April 19, 1995, BPBA had the right to a set-off against the funds in Banco Feigin's account at BPBA, and that this right to a set-off was superior to any right BayBank may have had as the bank maintaining an account of Banco Feigin to which Banco Feigin had requested its funds be sent.

2. *Executing the Transfer: From the Originator's Bank to the Beneficiary's Bank*

As suggested above, the originator's bank has several choices in determining how to execute a funds transfer for its customer. In the absence of an instruction from the customer, the originator's bank ordinarily is free to "use any funds-transfer system [that it wishes] if use of that system is reasonable in the circumstances." UCC §4A-302(b)(i). The UCC's deference to the originator's bank allows the originator's bank to ignore its originator's instruction as to the method of sending the transfer if the bank, "in good faith, determines that it is not feasible to follow the instruction or that following the instruction would unduly delay completion of the funds transfer." UCC §4A-302(b).

In some cases, the originator's bank can complete the transfer by crediting an account of the beneficiary on its own books. See UCC §4A-104 comment 1 (Case #1). In most cases, however, wire transfers are used to transfer funds from one bank to another. To execute such a payment order, the originator's bank must find a way to do two things: notify the beneficiary's bank of the transfer and forward payment to the beneficiary's bank to cover the payment to the beneficiary. The following sections describe three systems for accomplishing those things, in increasing order of complexity.

(a)   *Bilateral Systems (Including SWIFT).*   The most direct process would be a simple bilateral arrangement: The originator's bank sends a message directly to the beneficiary's bank, asking the beneficiary's bank to complete the transfer. Theoretically, a bank could send such a message by telephone, telecopy, or even regular mail; in most cases, however, banks use more secure methods of transmission. For example, a common method would be to send a "tested" telex. The receiving bank can confirm the authenticity of such a message by applying a pre-agreed algorithm to the text of any message it receives. In international transactions, banks frequently send such messages through the SWIFT system, which transmits a mind-boggling 2 million messages each day for the more than 5,000 institutions that it serves, with an average daily payment value of about $2 trillion.

Devising a secure method for sending a payment order is insufficient without some method for sending payment from the sender/ originator's bank to the receiving/beneficiary's bank. If the sender and receiving bank have substantial relations between themselves, that can be done by arranging for orders to be paid by debits from accounts of the sender at the receiving bank. To continue with the example from above, First Bank could use SWIFT to execute RFT's requests by sending a payment order to Wells Fargo under an agreement that Wells Fargo would obtain payment by debiting First Bank's account at Wells Fargo. Under UCC §4A-403(a)(3), First Bank's obligation to pay Wells Fargo for the payment order would be satisfied by such a debit. See UCC §4A-403 comment 3.

A common enhancement of that process would provide for daily "netting" of the obligations of the parties. Because that arrangement is between only two parties, it is called bilateral netting. Under that arrangement, Wells Fargo and First Bank would not debit each other's accounts for each individual payment order sent between them each day. Instead, at the end of each day, they would add up all of the transfers sent between them that day, produce a single net figure for all of the transfers, and then "settle" for those transfers with a single debit covering that net figure. For example, assume that all of the payment orders First Bank sent to Wells Fargo on the date of RFT's order totaled $75,000,000 and that Wells Fargo sent $70,000,000 of payment orders to First Bank on the same day. Under a bilateral netting arrangement, the parties could pay for those orders by agreeing that Wells Fargo would make a single $5,000,000 debit from First Bank's account at Wells Fargo (or that First Bank would make a single $5,000,000 credit to Wells Fargo's account at First Bank).

Under UCC §4A-403(c), that single debit would satisfy both banks' obligations as senders of payment orders on that day. See UCC §4A-403 comment 4. Thus, once Wells Fargo made this $5,000,000 debit, the offset reflected in the bilateral netting arrangement would satisfy First Bank's obligation under UCC §4A-402 to pay Wells Fargo for its payment orders. The obligations would be satisfied even though First Bank would not have forwarded any funds to Wells Fargo for that day's payment orders.

(b) *CHIPS.* Bilateral systems can be costly and inconvenient because they require each bank to establish, maintain, and administer separate relations with each bank to which it sends wire transfers. Thus, it would be much cheaper for a bank to use a system that allows a large number of participants to send all messages through a central clearinghouse that can aggregate and net out all of the transfers for all participants at the end of each day. That process is described as multilateral netting.

The largest such system is CHIPS (the Clearinghouse Interbank Payment System) in New York City. (A similar system called CHAPS operates in London.) CHIPS clears transactions for about 60 entities, settling about 250,000 transfers a day totaling more than a trillion dollars. CHIPS uses a complicated array of netting mechanisms to transfer value as quickly as possible during the course of each day. At the beginning of each day, each participant funds a special CHIPS account at the Federal Reserve Bank of New York. As the day progresses, that participant's account decreases (to account for outgoing transfers charged to that participant) and increases (to account for incoming transfers charged to that participant). Because the overwhelming majority of CHIPS transfers are relatively small, 95 percent of all CHIPS transfers (amounting to about 30 percent of the value of all CHIPS transfers) can be settled immediately by deductions from those prefunded accounts; for those transactions, the receiving participant effectively receives final payment at that time.

In cases where adequate funds are in the prefunded accounts of the originator's banks of the relevant parties, the transactions are settled either by bilateral netting or by multilateral netting. Bilateral netting occurs when the CHIPS computer identifies transactions going in opposite directions between two financial institutions; the computer can settle the smaller of those transactions immediately. About 5 percent of CHIPS transfers are settled by bilateral netting (amounting to 15-20 percent of the value of all CHIPS transfers).

Finally, in cases where bilateral netting is not adequate, the parties rely on the CHIPS (patented) multilateral netting algorithm, in which transfers from three (or more) institutions are netted (as shown in Figure 30.2). For example, assume that Bank A, with $3M available in its account, needs to send $25M to Bank B; that Bank B, with $2.5M available in its account, needs to send $26M to Bank C; and that Bank C, with $2.6M available in its account, needs to send $22.5M to Bank A and $3M to Bank B. The CHIPS computer would resolve those transactions by reducing Bank A's account to $.5M, increasing Bank B's account to $4.5M, and increasing Bank C's account to $3.1M. Multilateral netting occurs in very large transfers: only about 1 percent of CHIPS transfers by number, but more than half of the value of all transactions.

(c) *Fedwire.* Notwithstanding the advantages of CHIPS, the Federal Reserve banks' Fedwire system remains the dominant system for transfers between United States banks: Fedwire transfers more than $1.5 trillion each day among the domestic institutions that it serves. One reason for Fedwire's

Figure 30.2
Multilateral Netting on CHIPS

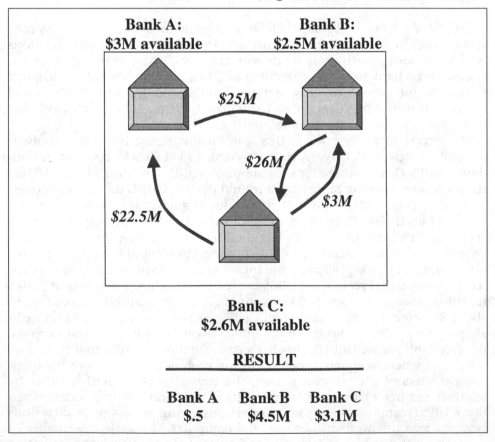

Bank A	Bank B	Bank C
$.5	$4.5M	$3.1M

domination is its ability to provide immediate settlement at the time of payment. (Until recently, CHIPS was able to provide settlement only at the close of the day.) Another reason is the inclusiveness of the Fedwire system: Fedwire serves more than 10,000 financial institutions. The cost of participating is remarkably modest: a monthly fee (depending on the type of connection the bank uses) of several hundred dollars, plus a per-transfer fee of about 50 cents. In addition to the fees, a bank that wants to use Fedwire must maintain an account at the Federal Reserve bank for its location. Although Fedwire does permit "off-line" transfers, almost all banks in the system also maintain an electronic communication link with their Federal Reserve bank (functionally equivalent to an e-mail system) over which Fedwire transactions proceed.

To initiate a transfer by Fedwire, the originating bank sends a funds-transfer message to its local Federal Reserve bank. In addition to a variety of technical details, that message must identify the beneficiary and the beneficiary's bank so that the Federal Reserve bank can determine how to carry out the request. To facilitate automated message processing, all messages must conform to a rigidly standardized format, which consists of a series of fields of information that occur in a specified sequence (see Figure 30.3). The message appears in the form of a standard four-digit identifier (field tag) for each of the given fields. After the message is typed into a terminal at the originating bank, software provided by the Federal Reserve encrypts the message and transmits it to the local Federal Reserve bank.

Figure 30.3
Sample Fedwire Message

```
### 02 ### FT PROD ### FT INCOMING          ### NORMAL MSG/ACCTG ENTRY ###
{3100} Sender: 029999999 FIRST BRONX NY   {2000} AMOUNT: $34,000.00
{3400} Receiver: 119999999 COWBOYBANK      {3600} Bus Function Code: CTR
{1510} Type Code:                          1000
{5000} Originator:                         DUNKNOWN
                                           FRANZ MO USS
                                           DBA STEAK PALACE
                                           MAXILLIANSTRASSE 38
                                           MUNICH, GERMANY
       {6000} Org to Bnf Info:             PAY T.EDWARDS $34,000 US
                                           $10,000 INV# TT3 2 CASES TEXAS T'S
                                           BAR-B-Q SAUCE, $24,000 FRANCHISE
                                           FEE FOR TEXAS T'S SECRET RECIPE
       {5100} Originators'FI:              BFBKDEZZ
                                           BLACKFOREST BK
                                           MUNICH,GERMANY
       {4200} Beneficiary:                 D123456
                                           T. EDWARDS
       {4000} Intermediary FI:             F028888888
                                           FIRST BANK XY2
       {4100} Beneficiary'FI:              F117777777
                                           BILLY BO BANK
                                           RODEO ROAD BRANCH
                                           AUSTIN, TX.
       {6100} Receiving FI Info:           PER BLACK FOREST BANK PAY
                                           IMMEDIATELY. DO NOT DEDUCT ANY
                                           RELATED FEES FROM THE TRANSFER
                                           AMOUNT-CHARGE FEE SEPARATELY
{1520} IMAD:                               19960105B1Q3947D001537
{3320} Sender Ref:                         13125
{1110} Timestamp:                          09141345FTIG
{1120} OMAD:                               19960105K1K1234001517
```

To aid understanding, the sample message includes descriptions of the different fields ("Originator," "Beneficiary," and the like) that do not appear in actual messages. If you study those descriptions and the sample message, you will see that it involves a single step of a transfer from Dunknown Franz in Munich (the originator) to T. Edwards in Austin, Texas (the beneficiary), paying for some barbecue sauce and a franchise fee. The transfer already has been routed from Blackforest Bank in Munich (the originator's bank; "FI" stands for financial institution) to First Bronx in New York. The message reflects a single payment order made in the course of the overall funds transfer. The payment order was sent by Fedwire from First Bronx in New York (as sender) to Cowboybank (as receiving bank). The wire also designates First Bank as another intermediary bank to which Cowboybank should send the money. First Bank, in turn, is directed to transfer the funds to a specified account of the beneficiary at Billy Bo Bank in Austin.

When the originator's bank sends a payment order to the Federal Reserve, it hopes that the Federal Reserve as receiving bank will execute the payment order it has received by sending a second payment order moving the funds toward the beneficiary. As sender of that second payment order, the Federal Reserve ordinarily will not have a later opportunity to avoid payment. Rather, when the receiving bank accepts the Federal Reserve's payment order, the Federal Reserve becomes directly obligated to pay that order, even if the bank that initially sent the message to the Federal Reserve fails to pay the Federal Reserve for its payment order. UCC §4A-402(b) & (c).

Accordingly, the first step a Federal Reserve bank takes when it receives an incoming Fedwire payment order is to determine whether the sender (for convenience assume that it is the originator's bank) has sufficient funds to cover the payment order. The Federal Reserve bank makes that determination by referring to a working balance that it maintains for each bank during the course of each business day. For example, First Bank's working balance starts with the balance in First Bank's Federal Reserve account at the beginning of the day, increases when First Bank receives incoming wire transfers or other credits, and decreases when First Bank executes outgoing wire transfers or when its account otherwise is debited. Because of the huge volume of transfers made by wire each day, it is common for a bank's working balance to go below zero. When that happens, the bank is said to have incurred a "daylight overdraft." Although it is common for banks to incur daylight overdrafts, Regulation J requires banks to cover those overdrafts by the end of each day. See Regulation J, §210.28(b)(1)(i) (requiring sender to cover overdrafts by the close of the day).

Modest daylight overdrafts cause no concern; they often result from the fact that most of a bank's outgoing wires on a given day are transmitted before the bulk of its incoming wires are received. The Federal Reserve, however, regulates the level of overdrafts closely, hoping to prevent any bank from getting so far out of balance during the course of a day that the bank will not be able to cover the overdrafts at the end of the day. The Federal Reserve's regulation takes two forms. First, since 1994, the Federal Reserve has discouraged daylight overdrafts by exacting a substantial fee for tolerating those overdrafts (currently 0.27 percent of the amount of the overdraft). That fee apparently has caused a significant flow of business away from Fedwire to CHIPS, although the loss of Fedwire business to date appears to have been less than the Federal Reserve expected when it first imposed the fee.

Second, the Federal Reserve limits overdrafts more directly by placing a bank-by-bank cap on daylight overdrafts. Banks cannot exceed the cap even if they are willing to pay the overdraft fee. The permitted overdraft level is determined through a process that allows each bank to choose its overdraft level based on how much scrutiny by the Federal Reserve the bank is willing to endure. Banks can make "de minimis" overdrafts (currently the greater of $10 million or 20 percent of the bank's capital) without any special regulatory supervision. Banks that wish to incur larger daylight overdrafts must agree to provide the Federal Reserve a variety of detailed information about their wire operations so that the Federal Reserve can determine appropriate permitted overdraft levels based on the Federal Reserve's assessment of the bank's solvency and liquidity. Once the permitted overdraft level has been chosen, the Federal Reserve can (and normally does) refuse to make any transfer that would cause the bank's overdrafts to exceed the predetermined level.

Most banks also internally manage the level of their daylight overdrafts, both as a matter of prudence and to avoid the daylight overdraft fee. Thus, a bank might establish a general policy that it will not incur a daylight overdraft exceeding $60 million, even if its Federal Reserve cap is $80 million. In that event, a central wire-transfer control office at the bank holds any outgoing wire-transfer requests that would cause the working balance to pass that level. If one of the bank's officers requested a $10 million transfer at a time when the bank's working balance was $55 million below zero, the central wire-transfer office would wait for an incoming transfer to offset the outgoing wire request. If a $5 million wire came in a few minutes later (increasing the bank's working balance to $50 million below zero), the bank then could release the $10 million outgoing wire without passing the $60 million internal overdraft limit. That practice is the reason why transactional lawyers so frequently sit around at closings waiting for the "wire to go through" hours after the bank officer has authorized transmission of the wire. It is not the wire-transfer system that takes so long; it is the bank's internal funding priorities that slow completion of the transaction.

If the payment order will cause the working balance of the originator's bank to sink below its permitted overdraft level, the transfer does not occur. If the payment order is consistent with the permitted overdraft level, the Federal Reserve bank obtains payment under UCC §4A-402(c) by removing the amount of the transfer from the working balance of the account of the originator's bank. See Regulation J, §210.28(a) (authorizing Federal Reserve to debit account of sender). The Federal Reserve bank then executes the originator's bank's payment order by sending a second payment order to the beneficiary's bank. If the beneficiary's bank has an account with that Federal Reserve bank, the Federal Reserve bank sends a message directly to the beneficiary's bank's Fedwire connection and simultaneously credits the account of the beneficiary's bank for the amount of the order. See Regulation J, §210.29(a) (authorizing Federal Reserve to execute payment orders by crediting the account of the receiving bank).

If the beneficiary's bank is located in a different Federal Reserve district, the originator's bank's Federal Reserve bank sends the message on to the beneficiary's bank's Federal Reserve bank, using an internal Federal Reserve encrypted e-mail system. See Regulation J, §210.30(b) (authorizing Federal Reserve to send Fedwire orders to the Federal Reserve bank of the beneficiary's bank). The beneficiary's bank's Federal Reserve bank then debits the account of the originator's bank's Federal Reserve bank on its books and credits the account of the beneficiary's bank. Finally, the beneficiary's bank's Federal Reserve bank sends the funds transfer message to the beneficiary's bank in the form of an encrypted signal to that bank's Fedwire connection.

3. Completing the Funds Transfer: From the Beneficiary's Bank to the Beneficiary

When a beneficiary's bank receives a payment order, it technically has a right to reject the payment order. UCC §§4A-210, 4A-209 comment 8. As discussed above, UCC §4A-210 grants that right of rejection to protect the receiving bank from the risk that the sender will not pay for the sender's payment order even if the receiving bank properly executes that order. That right is particularly important to the beneficiary's bank because a beneficiary's bank that accepts a payment order becomes obligated to pay the beneficiary even if the beneficiary's bank never obtains payment from the sender. UCC §4A-404(a).

As a practical matter, however, it is quite uncommon for a beneficiary's bank to reject a payment order because of a concern that the sender will not pay. In most (although certainly not all) cases, there is no doubt about payment because the parties have a regular arrangement that removes any concern of the receiving bank. Thus, just as the checking system operates on the assumption that checks will be honored unless the payor bank sends a prompt notice of dishonor, the wire-transfer system provides that the beneficiary's bank accepts a payment order if it does not act promptly to reject it. Generally, assuming that the receiving bank has been paid for the order or has access to adequate funds in the sender's account with the receiving bank, acceptance occurs at the beginning of the next business day after the date that the beneficiary's bank receives the order unless the receiving bank rejects the payment order within the first hour of that business day. UCC §4A-209(b)(3) (deemed acceptance on the day after the payment date); see UCC §4A-401 (absent special instructions, the payment date is the date that the order is received). Hence, when the receiving bank has funds on hand that it could take as payment for the order, the passage of the deadline automatically results in the beneficiary's bank's acceptance of the order, the beneficiary's entitlement to payment from the beneficiary's bank, and the beneficiary's bank's entitlement to payment from the sender. UCC §§4A-402(b), 4A-404(a). In the odd case where acceptance does not occur under that rule — usually because the sender has not paid for the order — the order is rejected by operation of law on the fifth business day after receipt at the receiving bank. UCC §4A-211(d); see UCC §4A-211 comment 7.

The rules related to rights of acceptance and rejection have no significance for payments transmitted by Fedwire. As explained above, Fedwire simultaneously provides final payment to the beneficiary's bank and transmission of the message to that bank by means of a credit to the Federal Reserve account of the beneficiary's bank. Thus, there is no reason to wait for the beneficiary's bank to decide whether to accept the order; the acceptance of the beneficiary's bank is implied at the instant that it receives a Fedwire message. UCC §§4A-209(b)(2), 4A-209 comment 6. As a result, the beneficiary's bank becomes directly obligated to pay the beneficiary the moment that it receives the Fedwire transfer. UCC §4A-404(a); Regulation J, §210.31(a) (bank receiving Fedwire payment is deemed paid when it receives the Fedwire message). In commercial payment transactions, the bank normally notifies the beneficiary in a matter of minutes, either by telephone or by some prearranged form of electronic communication. See also UCC §4A-404(b) (requiring notice by end of next day).

The rules treating Fedwire orders as automatically and immediately final reflect the willingness of the Federal Reserve to accept the risk that institutions using Fedwire will become insolvent during the course of the day. The Federal Reserve does its best to monitor that risk and to obtain compensation for it (through the daylight overdraft fees it assesses). But if it agrees to send the wire, it guarantees the beneficiary immediately available funds, backing that guarantee with the credit of our nation's central bank. The Federal Reserve's willingness to provide reliably immediate funds gives an important boost to the finalization of large commercial transactions. It is much easier to complete a transaction when irrevocable receipt of the appropriate sum can be verified at the closing table than it would be if the parties had to wait until banks settled their accounts after the close of business at the end of the day.

C.   Discharge of the Originator's Underlying Obligation

In most cases, the purpose of a wire-transfer payment is for the originator to discharge some underlying obligation that the originator owes to the beneficiary. Under UCC §4A-406(a), a payment made by wire transfer generally satisfies the underlying obligation of the originator as of the moment that the beneficiary's bank accepts a payment order for the benefit of the beneficiary. That rule reflects the perspective that in common contemplation an obligation is paid when the payor causes a bank to make a binding commitment to the payee. The same perspective underlies the rule in UCC §3-310(a), which discharges a payment obligation when the payee takes a cashier's check, even though acceptance of an ordinary check would only suspend the obligation under UCC §3-310(b)(1).

The cashier's check rule in UCC §3-310(a), however, is not absolute. It discharges the obligation only if the payee accepts the cashier's check for the obligation. Similarly, a wire transfer does not discharge the underlying obligation if the wire transfer is made in a manner that violates the underlying contract specifying the obligation to the beneficiary. UCC §4A-406(b). Of course, the beneficiary suffers no damages if the funds transfer is completed without incident. The point of UCC §4A-406(b), however, is the same as the point of UCC §3-310(a): to ensure that a payee cannot lose an underlying obligation through the failure of a bank to complete a payment transaction if the payee does not accept the bank's commitment to pay as satisfaction of the underlying obligation.

Another interesting problem in the use of wire transfers to satisfy obligations arises when one or more of the receiving banks in the course of a funds transfer deducts charges from the amount of the payment order before sending the order forward. If that occurs, the payment received by the beneficiary will be slightly less than the original amount of the originator's payment order. Given the trivial size of the typical charges in the system (in the tens of dollars) compared to the size of the typical transfer (in the millions of dollars), deductions for those charges are not likely to pose a significant problem for the beneficiary. An opportunistic beneficiary, however, might seize on the slight deficiency in the amount credited to its account as an excuse for claiming that the originator had failed to make payment in a timely manner. The UCC prevents that opportunistic response by providing that the original payment is deemed to discharge the entire obligation, even if deductions for bank charges reduce the actual payment slightly below the amount of the obligation, as long as the originator promptly forwards payment to the beneficiary for the charges. UCC §4A-406(c).

D. Finality of Payment

One feature of wire-transfer payment that makes it attractive to the beneficiary is the extremely limited right of the payor/originator to stop payment. Unlike the checking and credit-card systems, where the payor has days to change its mind, in most cases the time for the payor to cancel a payment authorized by wire transfer is measured in hours or even minutes.

Aleo International, Ltd. v. Citibank, N.A.
612 N.Y.S.2d 540 (Sup. Ct. N.Y. County 1994)

Herman CAHN, Justice: . . .

Plaintiff Aleo International, Ltd. ("Aleo") is a domestic corporation. On October 13, 1992, one of Aleo's vice-presidents, Vera Eyzerovich ("Ms. Eyzerovich"), entered her local Citibank branch and instructed Citibank to make an electronic transfer of $284,563 US dollars to the Dresdner Bank in Berlin, Germany, to the account of an individual named Behzad Hermatjou ("Hermatjou"). The documentary evidence submitted shows that at 5:27 P.M. on October 13, 1992, Citibank sent the payment order to the Dresdner Bank by electronic message. Dresdner Bank later sent Citibank an electronic message: "Regarding your payment for USD 284.563,00 DD 13.10.92 [indecipherable] f/o Behzad Hermatjou, Pls be advised that we have credited A.M. beneficiary DD 14.10.92 val 16.10.92 with the net amount of USD 284.136,16." This information was confirmed by the Dresdner Bank by fax to Citibank on July 29, 1993: "Please be advised that on 14.10.92 at 09:59 o'clock Berlin time Dresdner Bank credited the account of Behzad Hermatjou with USD 284.136,16 (USD 284.563,00 less our charges)." It is undisputed that Berlin time is six hours ahead of New York time, and that 9:59 A.M. Berlin time would be 3:59 A.M. New York time. At approximately 9 A.M. on October 14, 1992, Ms. Eyzerovich instructed Citibank to stop the transfer. When Citibank did not, this action ensued.

Article 4-A of the Uniform Commercial Code ("UCC") governs electronic "funds transfers." The Official Comment to UCC 4-A-102 states that the provisions of Article 4-A

> are intended to be the exclusive means of determining the rights, duties and liabilities of the affected parties in any situation covered by particular provisions of the Article. Consequently, resort to principles of law or equity outside of Article 4A is not appropriate to create rights, duties and liabilities inconsistent with those stated in this Article.

Article 4-A does not include any provision for a cause of action in negligence. Thus, unless Citibank's failure to cancel Ms. Eyzerovich's transfer order was not in conformity with Article 4-A, plaintiff Aleo has failed to state a cause of action, and this action must be dismissed.

UCC 4-A-211(2), which governs the cancellation and amendment of payment orders, provides that

> A communication by the sender cancelling or amending a payment order is effective to cancel or amend the order if notice of the communication is received at a time and in a manner affording the receiving bank a reasonable opportunity to act on the communication before the bank accepts the payment order.

"Acceptance of Payment Order" is defined by UCC 4-A-209(2), which provides that:

> a beneficiary's bank accepts a payment order at the earliest of the following times: (a) when the bank (i) pays the beneficiary . . . or (ii) notifies the beneficiary of receipt of the order or that the account of the beneficiary has been credited with respect to the order. . . .

The documentary evidence shows that Hermatjou's account was credited on October 14, 1992 at 9:59 A.M. Berlin time. Thus, as of 3:59 A.M. New York time, the Dresdner Bank "paid the beneficiary" and thereby accepted the payment order. Because this payment and acceptance occurred prior to Ms. Eyzerovich's stop transfer order at 9 A.M. on that day, according to UCC 4-A-211(2), Ms. Eyzerovich's attempt to cancel the payment order was ineffective, and Citibank may not be held liable for failing to honor it.

In a conversation with the author, counsel for Aleo explained that Ms. Eyzerovich tried to cancel the wire because she discovered that she had described the account incorrectly: The funds were sent to some random account holder at the Berlin bank. As discussed in Assignment 31, she theoretically should have been able to recover the money from the account holder, but that would have required a suit in the German courts, an expensive undertaking. The final-payment rule does not always lead to a "correct" result, but the certainty it provides is a benefit to commercial transactions that depend on irrevocable payments.

Problem Set 30

30.1. Your first appointment this week is with Nicholas Nickleby, who tells you he has a problem related to a payment from Walter Bray. Bray owed Nickleby $100,000 on a promissory note; the entire sum was due to Nickleby on April 1. Accordingly, on Monday March 30, Bray asked his bank (Gride National Bank) to send a wire transfer to Nickleby's account at Cheeryble State Bank. Gride sent a telex to Cheeryble executing Bray's request on the morning of Tuesday March 31, calling for payment to Nickleby on April 1. Pursuant to a preexisting agreement between Gride and Cheeryble, Cheeryble was entitled to obtain payment for that order from Gride's account at Cheeryble. At the time, that account contained more than enough funds to cover the Nickleby order.

Unfortunately, the Nickleby order was misplaced on the desk of the Cheeryble clerk (Timothy Linkinwater). Accordingly, Cheeryble did not accept or reject the order and did not notify Nickleby that the payment from Bray had come in by wire. On Friday April 3, the Comptroller of the Currency closed Gride and appointed the Federal Deposit Insurance Corporation receiver to supervise the winding up of Gride's affairs. Because Gride had withdrawn all of its funds late Thursday afternoon, no funds remained in the Gride account at Cheeryble.

    a. Nicholas is frustrated that he has not yet been paid. Given the fact that it is now April 6, five days late, can he pursue Bray for the $100,000? Alternatively, if he cannot sue Bray for the money, Nickleby wants to know if he is entitled to payment from Cheeryble. UCC §§4A-209(b), 4A-401, 4A-404(a), 4A-406.

    b. How would your answers to Nickleby differ if Linkinwater had rejected the order immediately after Cheeryble received it? (You should assume that Linkinwater's rejection of the Nickleby order was not a breach of Cheeryble's agreement with Gride.) UCC §4A-210(a).

    c. How would your answers to Nickleby differ if the payment to Cheeryble had been made by Fedwire instead of through an agreement that Cheeryble debit Gride's account with Cheeryble? UCC §§4A-209(b)(2), 4A-209 comment 6, 4A-403(a)(1); Regulation J, §210.29(a).

30.2. As you walk back into your office after your meeting with Nicholas Nickleby, your secretary tells you that Ben Darrow is holding on the telephone. When you pick up the telephone, he tells you that he is handling the bank's wire-transfer desk today while another officer is on vacation.

Because he has had only outgoing wires during the past hour, FSB's working balance at the Federal Reserve has been declining constantly. As Ben is speaking to you, the computer terminal that shows that balance indicates that the current balance is down to $3 million. The reason for Ben's call to you is that Ben has just received a request from another officer to send out a wire for $5 million. When Ben told the officer that FSB did not have enough money to send the wire right now, the officer told Ben that the bank regularly sends wires out for up to $20 million more than it has on deposit at the Federal Reserve. Ben is calling you because he wants to know how FSB possibly could send out a wire paying money that it does not yet have. Can the other officer be correct? Why would the Federal Reserve let FSB do this?

30.3.   Worn out from your hard morning, you decide to have lunch at the Drones Club. Unfortunately, you have not even reached your table when you see Jeeves approaching. Recalling your discussion with Jeeves in Problem 28.5, you resolve never to eat lunch at the Drones Club again. Nevertheless, you graciously agree to entertain Jeeves's explanation of Bertie Wooster's problem of the day. It appears that Bertie has continued his never-ending search for the perfect antique silver cow creamer, as well as his perennial indecisiveness. Today's problem arose yesterday at lunch when Bertie saw an advertisement in which one Galahad Threepwood offered a particularly elegant silver cow creamer for "only" $450,000. Having consumed a few more martinis than most would consider conducive to proper business judgment, Bertie immediately telephoned Threepwood and told him he wanted the creamer. He then called his banker and directed him to send a $450,000 wire to Threepwood for the purchase price (using his general business account).

When Bertie woke this morning, he learned from Jeeves that the Threepwood creamer could not possibly be worth more than $75,000. Accordingly, he wants you to "stop payment" on the wire. You agree to call Bertie's banker to inquire about the matter. When you do so, you learn that Bertie's bank sent the wire late last night (apparently by means of some bilateral arrangement between the banks) and that Threepwood's bank has received the wire, but not yet notified Threepwood or taken any other action. Can you cancel the wire for Bertie? UCC §4A-211 & comment 3.

30.4.   At the end of the day, Ben Darrow calls you back to ask your advice about two other mistakes that he fears he made during the course of the day. The first relates to a wire-transfer request that Carol Long submitted, asking the bank to transfer $750,000 from her checking account. She explained to Ben that she was transferring the funds out of her account at FSB (which does not bear interest) to an account at Wells Fargo that bears interest at 8 percent per annum. Although she submitted the request in time for it to be executed today and although the funds were in her account at the time, Ben nevertheless neglected to send out the wire. As he calls, it is too late to send the wire out until tomorrow morning. He is getting ready to call Carol and apologize, but before he calls her, he wants to know what damages she can seek from the bank. In particular, he wants to know if Carol's damages will be likely to exceed the interest that Ben's bank can earn by investing the funds until the time that it transfers them as Carol requested. Assuming that the bank's agreement with Carol does not address the issue of damages, what do you tell Ben? UCC §§4A-210(b), 4A-506(b), 4A-506 comment 2.

30.5. Ben Darrow's last problem relates to a payment order that he received by electronic mail this morning (April 6) from Matacora Realtors, an account holder at his bank. The message asked FSB to make a $500,000 payment to a designated account of Jasmine Ball that also is at FSB. Priding himself on his efficiency, Darrow immediately sent back a message accepting the order, deducted the funds from Matacora Realtors' account, and called Jasmine to tell Jasmine that the funds were available. Jasmine promptly came down to FSB and had the funds wired to an account in her name at a bank in Mexico. Darrow became worried a few minutes ago when he received a second message from Matacora Realtors, canceling the Ball payment order. On reviewing the file, Darrow noticed that the payment order that he received this morning stated at the top: "Transmission date: April 6; Payment date: April 8." Darrow is concerned because he is not sure that he can recover the funds from Ball. Does Darrow have to return the funds to the account of Matacora Realtors? UCC §§4A-209(b) & (d), 4A-211(b), 4A-401, 4A-402(c), (d).

30.6. Your last call of the day is from Carl Eben at Riverfront Tools, Inc. (RFT) (introduced in Problem Set 22). His problem arises out of a contract with California Pneumatic Tools (CPT). RFT sold CPT $450,000 worth of tools. The contract called for CPT to pay for the tools with a cashier's check from Wells Fargo. Notwithstanding that provision in the contract, CPT instead attempted to wire funds to an account of RFT at Texas American Bank (TAB). RFT had accepted payment by transfers into that account in several earlier contracts, but has not been using that account for several months because of Carl's decision to phase out RFT's relationship with TAB.

In any event, Wells Fargo (CPT's bank) accepted CPT's payment order, debited CPT's account, and executed the transfer to TAB. TAB, in turn, notified Carl that it had received the funds for RFT. Carl immediately called CPT to complain, but later that afternoon (before CPT could respond), the Comptroller of the Currency closed TAB and appointed the Federal Deposit Insurance Corporation receiver to supervise the winding up of TAB's affairs. The receiver informed Carl this morning that RFT probably would obtain very little from the account and certainly would be unable to obtain the entire $450,000. Carl wants to know if RFT still has a claim against CPT. What do you tell him? If he does have a claim against CPT, does CPT have any remedy? UCC §§4A-209(b)(1), 4A-402(c) & (d), 4A-404(a), 4A-406(b).

Assignment 31:   Error in Wire-Transfer Transactions

Because wire transfers are the most common choice for large transfers of funds, losses on wire-transfer systems are particularly serious. Thus, wire-transfer systems exhibit some of the most sophisticated mechanisms for limiting losses. As the *Aleo* case in Assignment 30 suggests, the wire-transfer system is just as vulnerable to mistaken payments as any other payment system. The mistake common to the wire-transfer system is a transfer that delivers funds to a beneficiary contrary to the subjective intent of the originator. Even without any fraudulent intent, that can happen for two general reasons: because of a mistaken description of the order by the originator or because of an inadvertent alteration of the order by the originator's bank or one of the other parties sending that order through the system. Whenever such an error occurs, the originator will want to recover the funds that it paid to the originator's bank. To see how the system responds to the originator's desire to recover those funds, it is useful to distinguish between claims against parties in the system (the originator's bank, some intermediary bank, or the beneficiary's bank) and claims against the party that received the funds (the de facto beneficiary).

A.   Recovering from Parties in the System

The wire-transfer system is not for the fainthearted or careless. For the most part, it assigns responsibility for errors based on the simple and unforgiving principle that each party bears responsibility for its own errors. That principle might seem common, but wire-transfer systems apply it more vigorously than most analogous areas of the law. Most important, in the wire-transfer system, that principle carries with it a strong corollary: Parties that participate in a transaction after the error have no obligation to discover or correct an error that one party made earlier in the transaction.

Thus, a party that makes a mistake in a payment order has little or no recourse against later parties in the system that faithfully execute the mistaken order. That is true however easy it might have been for them to detect the mistake, however obvious the mistake might have been. Instead, Article 4A obligates the sender to pay any payment order that the receiving bank executes as instructed. UCC §4A-402(b), (c). To understand how unusual that rule is, recall the discussion in Assignment 25 of the wide variety of contributory negligence rules in the checking system that give a bank potential exposure for failing to notice errors by a check writer. See, e.g., UCC §§3-404(d), 3-405(b), 3-406(b), 4-406(e). If the wire-transfer rule sounds harsh, it is worth recalling that Article 4A has no application to systems designed primarily for use by natural persons. UCC §4A-108; EFTA §§903(5), 903(6)(B).

1. Errors by the Originator

As the foregoing discussion suggests, wire-transfer systems generally hold an originator responsible for any mistakes that it makes in describing its order to the originator's bank. That rule applies even if the error is made not by the originator itself, but by some third-party communications network, on the theory that (at least as between the originator and the originator's bank) the originator is responsible for the communications network that it uses. Thus, if the originator transmits its payment orders to its bank over an Internet service and if the Internet service provider mistakenly duplicates the message, sending the bank messages for two orders, rather than a single order, the originator is liable for both orders. UCC §4A-206(a).

The system's firm commitment to hold originators to a high standard of care is not limited to rules that protect parties that comply with the literal terms of erroneous orders. In some cases, the originator also is burdened with losses that arise through execution of ambiguous orders. For example, a common payment-order error (apparently the problem in the *Aleo* case excerpted in Assignment 30) is to identify a beneficiary by name, but (because of an inadvertent typographical error) to call for payment to an account of some other (random) party. Ordinary rules of interpretation would give preference to the name of the payee over the numerical designation of the account. See, e.g., UCC §3-114 ("If an instrument contains contradictory terms, . . . words prevail over numbers."). The wire-transfer system, by contrast, allows the beneficiary's bank to rely on the number indicated in the order and deposit the money into that account, even if the identified beneficiary does not own the designated account. UCC §4A-207(b), (c); Regulation J, §210.27(b). The same rule applies to errors that the originator makes in describing the beneficiary's bank. See UCC §4A-208(b) (authorizing receiving bank to rely on routing number to identify beneficiary's bank, even if order also identifies beneficiary's bank by name); Regulation J, §210.27(a) (same rule for Federal Reserve).

Indeed, the case that follows suggests that the system affirmatively discourages any efforts to find such errors by people in the latter phase of wire-transfer transactions.

Corfan Banco Asuncion Paraguay v. Ocean Bank
715 So. 2d 967 (Fla. Dist. Ct. App. 1998)

SORONDO, Judge. Corfan Banco Asuncion Paraguay, a foreign banking corporation (Corfan Bank), appeals the lower court's entry of a Final Summary Judgment in favor of Ocean Bank, a Florida bank.

On March 22, 1995, Corfan Bank originated a wire transfer of $72,972.00 via its intermediary Swiss Bank to the account of its customer, Jorge Alberto Dos Santos

Silva (Silva), in Ocean Bank. The transfer order bore Silva's name as the recipient and indicated that his account number was 01007**0**21**0**40**0** (in fact, this was a nonexistent account). Upon receipt of the wire transfer, Ocean Bank noticed a discrepancy in this number and before depositing the money, confirmed with Silva that his correct account number was 01007**6**21**6**40**6**.[1] Ocean Bank did not, however, inform Corfan Bank or Swiss Bank of the error. Once the correct number was confirmed by Silva, Ocean Bank accepted the wire transfer and credited Silva's account.

The next day, Corfan Bank became aware of the account number discrepancy and, without first checking with either Silva or Ocean Bank, sent a second wire transfer of $72,972.00 to Silva's correct account number at Ocean Bank. The second transfer order did not indicate that it was a correction, replacement or amendment of the March 22nd transfer. Because the information of the transfer was correct, it was automatically processed at Ocean Bank and was credited to Silva's account. Several days later, Corfan Bank inquired of Ocean Bank regarding the two transfers, maintaining that only one transfer was intended. By that time, Silva had withdrawn the proceeds of both wire transfers.[2] When Ocean Bank refused to repay $72,972.00 to Corfan Bank, this litigation ensued. Corfan Bank proceeded on two claims, one based on [UCC §] 4A-207 . . . and one based on common law negligence. Ocean Bank answered denying liability under the statute and also contending that the negligence claim was precluded by the preemptive statutory scheme.

The trial court, emphasizing that Florida's adoption of the UCC sections concerning wire transfers did not abrogate the basic tenets of commercial law, found that Ocean Bank had not contravened [UCC §4A-207] by crediting the erroneous March 22nd wire transfer to Silva's account. Finding that Corfan Bank was the party best situated to have avoided this loss, the court held that Corfan Bank must bear that loss and, therefore, the court granted Ocean Bank's motion for summary judgment as to count one (the UCC count). Additionally, the court dismissed count two (the negligence count).

We begin with a review of the exact language of section 670.207(1), Florida Statutes:

> (1) Subject to subsection (2), if, in a payment order received by the beneficiary's bank, the name, bank account number, or other identification of the beneficiary refers to a nonexistent or unidentifiable person or account, no person has rights as a beneficiary of the order and acceptance of the order cannot occur.

Corfan Bank argues that this language is clear and unambiguous, where a name *or* bank account number, *or* other identification refers either to a nonexistent or unidentified person *or* a nonexistent account, the order *cannot* be accepted. Ocean Bank responds that such a "highly technical" reading of the statute is "contrary to commercial and practical considerations and common sense." It suggests that we look to the legislative intent and conclude that the "or" in the statute should be given conjunctive rather than disjunctive effect. We respectfully decline

---

1. As indicated by the bold, underlined numbers, the three sixes in the account number had been replaced with zeros on the transfer order.

2. Eventually, Silva acknowledged that he owed Corfan Bank $72,972.00 and gave Corfan a series of post-dated checks to repay that amount, plus interest. However, all the checks bounced.

Ocean Bank's invitation to look behind the plain language of the statute and conclude that given its clarity it must be read as written. . . .

. . . Although Ocean Bank's position has been noted in the legal literature,[4] unambiguous language is not subject to judicial construction, however wise it may seem to alter the plain language. [Quotation marks and citation omitted.] . . .

The Supreme Court of Florida has fashioned only one exception to this general rule: "[t]his Court will not go behind the plain and ordinary meaning of the words used in the statute unless an unreasonable or ridiculous conclusion would result from failure to do so." Holly v. Auld, 450 So. 2d 217, 219 (Fla. 1984). The plain and ordinary meaning of the words of the statute under review do not lead to either an unreasonable or ridiculous result. As discussed more thoroughly below, one of the critical considerations in the drafting of Article 4A was that parties to funds transfers should be able to "predict risk with certainty, to insure risk with certainty, to adjust operational and security procedures, and to price funds transfer services appropriately." [UCC §4A-102 comment.] All of these goals are reasonable and assured by the plain statutory language.

In the present case, although the payment order correctly identified the beneficiary, it referred to a nonexistent account number. Under the clear and unambiguous terms of the statute, acceptance of the order could not have occurred. . . . We trust that if the legislature did not intend the result mandated by the statute's plain language, the legislature itself will amend the statute at the next opportunity.

As indicated above, the trial court dismissed count two of the complaint which sounded in negligence. The court concluded that the statutory scheme preempts the common law remedy of negligence. It is not clear whether the adoption of Article 4A of the UCC abrogated the common law cause of action for negligence relating to a wire transfer, as raised in count two of the complaint. [The comment] following [UCC §4A-102] provides in part:

> In the drafting of Article 4A, a deliberate decision was made to write on a clean slate and to treat a funds transfer as a unique method of payment to be governed by unique rules that address the particular issues raised in this method of payment. A deliberate decision was also made to use precise and detailed rules to assign responsibility, define behavioral norms, allocate risks and establish limits on liability, rather than to rely on broadly stated, flexible principles. In the drafting of these rules, a critical consideration was that the various parties to funds transfers need to be able to predict risk with certainty, to insure against risk, to adjust operational and security procedures, and to price funds transfer services appropriately. This consideration is particularly important given the very large amounts of money that are involved in funds transfers.
>
> Funds transfers involve competing interests — those of the banks that provide funds transfer services and the commercial and financial organizations that use the services, as well as the public interest. These competing interests were represented in the drafting process and they were thoroughly considered. ***The rules that emerged represent a careful and delicate balancing of those interests and are intended to be the exclusive means of determining the rights, duties and liabilities of the affected parties in any situation covered by particular provisions of the Article.*** Consequently,

---

4. [The court refers to William D. Hawkland & Richard Moreno, Uniform Commercial Code Series §4A-207:01, which describes this aspect of UCC §4A-207 as an "anomaly" that was not "intended" by the drafters of the statute.]

resort to principles of law or equity outside of Article 4A is not appropriate to create rights, duties and liabilities inconsistent with those stated in this Article.

(Emphasis added by court). This comment suggests the exclusivity of Article 4A as a remedy. Although the commentary to the UCC is not controlling authority, we are persuaded by the expressed intent of the drafters.

In addressing this issue we restrict our analysis to the pleadings and facts of this case. In pertinent part, count two reads as follows:

> Ocean Bank owed Corfan Bank a duty of care to follow the accepted banking practice of the community, and to return the funds from the first transfer to Corfan Bank upon receipt due to the reference in the first transfer to a non-existent account number.

The duty claimed to have been breached by Ocean Bank in its negligence count is exactly the same duty established and now governed by the statute. Under such circumstances we agree with the trial judge that the statutory scheme preempts the negligence claim in this case and affirm the dismissal of count two.[5] We do not reach the issue of whether the adoption of Article 4A of the UCC preempts negligence claims in all cases.

We reverse the Final Summary Judgment entered by the trial court in favor of Ocean Bank as to count one of the complaint and affirm the dismissal of count two. We remand this case for further proceedings consistent with this opinion.

NESBITT, Judge, dissenting:

I respectfully dissent. I would affirm final summary judgment for Ocean Bank. In my view, the trial court's well-reasoned and pragmatic approach to the interpretation of [UCC §4A-207] was the best solution to the disagreement between these parties. Corfan Bank itself was negligent in handling the wire transfer in question. Corfan Bank incorrectly listed Silva's account number on the first wire transfer order and, compounding that error, Corfan sent the second wire transfer order with no indication that it was a correction of the first. These errors caused Corfan's loss.

More important, the language of [UCC §4A-207] does not proscribe the actions taken by Ocean Bank. [UCC §4A-207] precludes acceptance of a wire transfer order only if "the name, account number, or other identification of the beneficiary refers to a nonexistent or unidentifiable person or account." Considering this section in its entirety as statutory construction requires, it seems apparent that the part of the statute that permits the receiving bank to look to "other identification" surely allows more flexibility than the majority here would permit.

---

5. We note that allowing a negligence claim in this case would "create rights, duties and liabilities inconsistent" with those set forth in [UCC §4A-207]. In a negligence cause of action, Ocean Bank would be entitled to defend on a theory of comparative negligence because Corfan Bank provided the erroneous account number which created the problem at issue and then initiated the second transfer without communicating with Ocean Bank. [UCC §4A-207] does not contemplate such a defense. (Oddly enough, allowing Corfan Bank's negligence claim in this case might actually inure to Ocean Bank's benefit.) As explained in the comment, one of the primary purposes of the section is to enable the parties to wire funds transfers to predict risk with certainty and to insure against risk. The uniformity and certainty sought by the statute for these transactions could not possibly exist if parties could opt to sue by way of pre-Code remedies where the statute has specifically defined the duties, rights and liabilities of the parties.

In my view, the statute question should neither be construed in the disjunctive or the conjunctive. As stated above, the construction of a statute that will reject part of it should be avoided. . . . There are segments of this statute that plainly permit a receiving bank to look at other identification, thus affording the receiving bank more flexibility in making the correct identification than the court recognizes today.

Ocean Bank's actions seem to better comport with the overall statutory scheme relating to funds transfers than the avenue supported by the court. The primary purpose of using a wire transfer of funds is to enable the beneficiary to get the funds quickly. Indeed, commercial or contract deadlines may be adversely impacted if the wire transfer does not go through quickly, as anticipated. We should recognize that the importance of speed in a wire transfer becomes even more critical in transactions involving different countries with, perhaps, different time zones. For example, if transmitting bank Corfan was closed by the time the funds were received by Ocean Bank, Ocean Bank would not have been in a position to rectify the error until the next business day — which might well render the entire reason for the transfer moot.

Ocean Bank chose to use the beneficiary's name (which was properly included on the first wire transfer order) and "other identification of the beneficiary" — the fact that the account number given was similar to that of the beneficiary, as well as verification that the beneficiary was expecting the transfer — in order to accept the wire transfer and properly credit the beneficiary's account. Ocean Bank decided that there was enough information in the first wire transfer order for it, after verification, to credit the transfer to the beneficiary's account. The order contained the beneficiary's name and account number, with a few zeros replacing the correct "6"s. This information referred not to a "nonexistent or unidentifiable person or account" but rather to an existing customer — the intended beneficiary — and to an identifiable (through "other identification") account.

I can find no common sense reason to prohibit Ocean Bank or other banks from accepting the responsibility that goes with choosing to use "other identification" in order to deposit funds into a customer's account. Basically, by verifying with Silva that he was the intended beneficiary, Ocean Bank was correcting Corfan Bank's error. Ocean Bank was seeking to aid its customer, the intended beneficiary of the funds, in getting the funds in an expeditious manner. Had Ocean Bank erroneously deposited the funds into the wrong account, it would have to face the liability associated with that decision. However, it should not face liability because it deposited the funds into the correct account — the intended beneficiary's account. Indeed, it was only because of Ocean Bank's actions that the intended beneficiary, Mr. Silva, received the funds from the first transfer.

Moreover, as the trial court emphasized, Florida's enactment of the U.C.C. did not abrogate other common law principles applicable to commercial transactions. A longstanding equitable tenet of Florida law is that, as between two innocent parties, the party best suited to prevent the loss caused by a third party wrongdoer must bear that loss. . . .

Here, Corfan put in issue the question of the correlative negligence of its and Ocean's actions. It is undisputed that Corfan was initially negligent in transmittal of the first wire transfer. It realized its mistake the following business day, and sent a second wire transfer with no indication it was a correction of the former. It was entirely unnecessary to transmit additional funds merely to correct the previous day's error. If it had not sent the additional funds, it is unlikely there would ever have been a dispute bringing the matter before us. Simply, Corfan Bank was in a better position to prevent the loss and, indeed, Corfan's negligence played a "substantial role" in that loss. These facts should prevent its recovery from Ocean Bank.

For the above-mentioned reasons, I would affirm.

The court and the dissent both discuss the case entirely from a critical after-the-fact point of view — and from that perspective the dissent certainly scores some points. On the other hand, looking at the facts more broadly, it seems clear that the best approach here would have been for the beneficiary's bank to credit the funds (as it did) and promptly advise the originator's bank of the error. If Ocean had taken that course, the system would have worked to provide Ocean funding, as it should, and at the same time, the loss that occurred here would have been forestalled.

That broader perspective is important. In general, the simple per se rules that obviate any need for the receiving bank to exercise judgment in interpreting a poorly or erroneously crafted payment order do more than shift losses back to the originator. They also improve the efficiency of the system in two ways. First, they give originators (and the banks that want their business) a strong incentive to develop systems that eradicate errors before funds-transfer orders enter the wire-transfer system. Second, they limit the costs that a receiving bank needs to expend to operate a wire-transfer system. A system that does not require the exercise of judgment, but only rote mechanical responses, makes it safe for banks to hire employees (and program machines) that respond mechanically.

Article 4A does contain one exception to the rule absolving later parties in the system from noticing and correcting errors that an originator makes in formulating and transmitting payment orders. That exception, however, applies only when a bank has agreed that it will take specified steps to identify errors. UCC §4A-205 covers the common situation in which an originator and originator's bank have agreed on a security procedure for the detection of errors. When a bank has made such an agreement, UCC §4A-205 alters the standard "your error, your loss" rule in any case in which the bank fails to comply with the required procedure, if compliance with the procedure would have revealed the error. UCC §4A-205(a)(1). Indeed, at first glance, paragraphs (2) and (3) of UCC §4A-205(a) suggest that the originator is excused from paying all erroneous orders. The second paragraph of comment 1 makes it clear, however, that UCC §4A-205 provides an excuse for the originator only if the parties have agreed on an error-detection procedure and only if the bank's compliance with that procedure would have detected the error. UCC §4A-205 comment 1.

To get a sense for how that works in practice, consider the common procedure usually referred to as a "four-party callback" procedure. That procedure requires the involvement of four individuals: (1) the originator's employee that places a payment order; (2) the bank employee that receives the payment order from the originator's employee; (3) another bank employee, who places a call back to the originator, seeking an employee different from the one that placed the order in the first instance; and (4) that second employee of the originator. If the originator can show that such a telephone call would have caught the mistake — because the second originator employee would have noticed the error in the order — UCC §4A-205 shifts any loss from the originator to the receiving bank.

2.   Errors in the System

Originators are not the only parties that make mistakes in wire-transfer systems. On the contrary, several of the leading cases involve errors by banks that failed to comply with the instructions they received from the originator. As you would expect, Article 4A generally imposes the losses from those errors on the party that makes the error. But establishing rules to govern those errors is considerably more difficult than establishing rules for originator-error cases because providing a remedy requires at least partial reversal of the wire-transfer transaction. The emphasis on finality in the wire-transfer system complicates any effort to reverse transactions.

To understand how UCC Article 4A responds to those errors, it is useful to divide the potential errors into two classes: those that send the beneficiary excessive funds and those that send the beneficiary funds that are inadequate or untimely.

(a)   *Sending Excessive Funds.*   A bank could send excessive funds in a variety of ways. The most obvious is a simple mistake in the amount of the transfer; the bank could send the money at the correct time to the correct place, but set the amount of the transfer too high. The same problem, however, could arise for at least two other reasons. In one situation, the bank could respond to a payment order from its customer by sending two or more wires, thus sending two or more times the appropriate amount of money. Finally, the bank could respond to a payment order from its customer by sending the money to the wrong party.

The remedy for that type of error has two parts. First, because the originator's obligation under UCC §4A-402 is limited to the payment order that it sends, the originator is obligated to the originator's bank only for the correct amount of its order that the originator's bank has executed. UCC §4A-402(b), (c). Thus, in the excessive-amount and duplicate-order cases, the originator is obligated only for the amount designated in its payment order. UCC §4A-303(a). In the incorrect beneficiary case, the originator is obligated for nothing because it sent no payment order calling for payment to that beneficiary. UCC §4A-303(c).

The second part of the remedy recognizes the reality that the originator frequently (almost always) will pay for the payment order before the originator's bank executes it, through mechanisms that authorize the originator's bank to remove funds from the originator's account to pay for payment orders that the originator's bank sends on behalf of the originator. Accordingly, to remedy an excessive transfer, the system must require the originator's bank to refund to the originator the money that the originator's bank took as compensation for the order. UCC §4A-402(d) imposes that obligation on the originator's bank. As part of that obligation, the originator's bank also must pay interest on the funds from the date on which it initially paid the funds. UCC §4A-402(d); see UCC §4A-506 (describing rate at which interest accrues for purposes of UCC Article 4A). Finally, in some cases, the originator's bank might be able to recover its loss from the party to which it incorrectly sent the funds. That topic is addressed in the last section of this assignment.

(b) *Sending Inadequate Funds.* The converse problem occurs when the bank fails to send adequate funds to the beneficiary. Again, that problem could arise for several reasons, starting from a simple error in setting the amount of the payment order sent to the beneficiary. An inadequate-funds error also would occur in the incorrect-beneficiary scenario mentioned above. For example, if the bank mistakenly sends funds to Cliff Janeway when it was supposed to send them to Archie Moon, then it has the problem of an excessive transfer to Cliff at the same time that it has the problem of an inadequate transfer to Archie. Finally, the bank's error could be nothing more than delay: The bank sends the correct order, but fails to send it in a timely manner.

The response to inadequate-funds errors is analogous to the response to excessive-funds errors. First, the originator is obligated only for the amount of the transfer that the bank actually sends. Thus, even though UCC §4A-202 generally obligates an originator to pay the originator's bank the entire amount of its payment order, the originator is not obligated to the originator's bank beyond the amount that the originator's bank transmits. UCC §4A-303(b). The UCC does, however, permit the originator's bank to correct the error by sending a second wire that makes up the deficiency in the original wire. If the originator's bank sends a wire adequately supplementing the deficient wire, the originator remains obligated for the entire amount of its original order. UCC §4A-303(b).

As a corollary to the rule limiting the originator's obligation to funds actually sent by its bank, the originator's bank must return to the originator any funds that the originator's bank collected to reimburse itself for the payment order beyond the amount that it actually sent. UCC §4A-402(d). As with excessive-funds transfers, the originator's bank must pay interest on any funds that it improperly collected. UCC §4A-402(d).

One final problem, unique to the inadequate-funds error, arises from the originator's underlying obligation to the beneficiary. An error by the originator's bank that sends excessive funds to the beneficiary causes no difficulty for the originator as against the beneficiary because the excessive-funds transfer satisfies the obligation that motivated the originator to send the payment order. When the originator's bank sends funds that are too little or too late, however, the bank's error often will cause further damage to the originator. That damage can occur either because the bank has retained funds of the originator's longer than it should have or because the failure of the originator to make the payment to the beneficiary constitutes a default on the originator's obligation to the beneficiary.

The UCC includes three separate rules to deal with those damages. First, if the only problem is that the bank sent the funds later than it should have, then the bank must pay interest to compensate for its retention of the funds beyond the period during which it should have held them. UCC §4A-305(a). Second, if the bank fails to correct the error—the bank never completes the originator's payment order—then the bank must compensate the originator not only for interest losses, but also for the originator's expenses in the transaction. UCC §4A-305(b), (d).

The last rule deals with consequential damages, the most common of which would be the damages that the originator suffered from a default on its obligation to the beneficiary when that default was caused by the failure of the originator's bank to complete the wire transfer in a timely manner. For obvious reasons, the consequential damages for failure to make a wire-transfer payment in a timely manner could be quite large. Accordingly, they present an important issue for parties using wire-transfer systems. It is important for originators to protect themselves from the losses from mistakes by their bank. Conversely, it is important for banks to protect themselves from large and unforeseeable damage awards. The UCC adopts a default rule that bars consequential damages in the absence of an express written agreement. UCC §4A-305(c). Given the unforeseeable nature of possible damages, standard agreements ordinarily do not allow originators an unqualified right to consequential damages. Rather, they either bar such damages entirely or limit recoveries to some specified and foreseeable damage amount (such as the late charges imposed by the intended beneficiary).

(c)   *Bank-Statement Rule.*   The last important part of the rules governing the originator's recovery for errors in the transmission of its orders is a bank-statement rule analogous to the rule for the checking system in UCC §4-406. The wire-transfer bank-statement rule operates in two tiers. First, UCC §4A-304 generally imposes on the originator a duty of ordinary care to review statements regarding wire-transfer transactions. If the originator fails to use ordinary care to review those statements, then it cannot recover interest on any amounts that the bank is obligated to refund to it under UCC §4A-402(d). The UCC does not give the originator a specific amount of time within which it can act to preserve its rights. Instead, it gives the bank a safe harbor by stating that any originator challenge more than 90 days after receipt of the statement is too late. UCC §4A-304. Moreover, comment 2 to UCC §4A-204 makes it clear that a customer can lose its entitlement to interest earlier than 90 days if the circumstances indicate that the originator would have discovered the error sooner if it had reviewed the bank statements with ordinary care. Finally, for payment orders transmitted to Federal Reserve banks, the Federal Reserve has issued a regulation establishing 30 calendar days as a reasonable time. Regulation J, §210.28(c).

The second tier of the rule precludes the originator from challenging any debit from its account for a wire-transfer order unless the originator challenges the transaction within one year of the date that the originator received notice of the transaction from the originator's bank. UCC §4A-505. That rule is much more onerous than the 90-day rule discussed in the preceding paragraph because it bars the originator's claim to recover the principal amount of the transfer, a much more serious consequence than a bar on recovering interest losses.

B.   Recovering from the Mistaken Recipient

Most erroneous wire transfers, like the transfer at issue in the *Aleo* case, result in a transfer of money to a party that has no right to receive it. Although Article 4A limits the right of the party that makes the error to pass that loss on to other parties in the system, it does contemplate a recovery of the money from the unintended recipient under common-law principles of restitution. Thus, if the originator commits the error, the originator can pursue a restitution action against the incorrect beneficiary. See, e.g., UCC §§4A-207(d) (error in describing beneficiary), 4A-209(d) (error in date of execution), 4A-211(c)(2) (erroneous order canceled after acceptance by beneficiary). Similarly, when a bank makes a mistake that causes it to send excessive funds, the bank can pursue a restitution action against the party that received the funds. See, e.g., UCC §§4A-303(a), (c) (excessive-funds errors); Regulation J, §210.32(c) (error by Federal Reserve bank). Thus, although the originator in *Aleo* failed to recover her funds from the banks operating the wire-transfer system, Article 4A would permit her to pursue the party that received the unintended transmissions. Unfortunately, the boundaries of those rights to restitution are quite murky because the UCC does nothing to describe the circumstances in which restitution is available. Instead, in each case Article 4A simply states that the originators and receiving banks responsible for an error are "entitled to recover from the beneficiary of the erroneous order the excess payment received to the extent allowed by the law governing mistake and restitution." E.g., UCC §4A-303(a).

For reasons that are difficult to understand, the rules governing the availability of restitution from an incorrect beneficiary have been one of the most fertile grounds for high-stakes wire-transfer litigation. The most difficult issues have been raised in a series of cases in which the mistaken recipient of the transfer happened to have an independent right to payment from the originator. That situation is not nearly so farfetched as it sounds: It has produced two of the most celebrated wire-transfer cases of the 1990s, both of which involved mistakes by banks in processing transfer requests. In the first case, an Australian company named Spedley asked Security Pacific to wire about $2 million into an account at BankAmerica in the name of Banque Worms (a French bank to which Spedley owed money). Spedley canceled the wire-transfer request a few hours later, before Security Pacific made the transfer. Security Pacific nevertheless mistakenly proceeded with the transfer. Cf. UCC §4A-211(b) (cancellation of payment order is valid if received when the receiving bank has "a reasonable opportunity to act on the communication"). After protracted litigation, the New York Court of Appeals held that Banque Worms was entitled to retain the money because Banque Worms had applied the money to discharge a debt that Spedley owed to it (the debt that had been the basis for Spedley's original payment order). Banque Worms v. BankAmerica International, 570 N.E.2d 189 (N.Y. 1991).

The second case involved an attempt by a company named Duchow's Marine to defraud General Electric Capital Corporation (GECC). GECC financed Duchow's inventory of boats under an arrangement that required all proceeds from the sale of boats to be transferred into a special "blocked" account. Funds could not be removed from the blocked account without GECC's consent. The dispute arose when Duchow instructed one of its customers to wire its payment of the $200,000 purchase price into Duchow's regular (unrestricted) account. One of the banks processing the funds transfer, however, mistakenly dropped the number of the unrestricted account from the funds-transfer message. When the transfer reached Duchow's bank, that bank placed the funds in the blocked account. Showing considerable pluck, Duchow challenged the mistake and convinced its bank to reverse the transfer and move the funds into Duchow's unrestricted account. Judge Easterbrook, writing for the United States Court of Appeals for the Seventh Circuit, concluded that the beneficiary's bank should not have moved the money. Relying on *Banque Worms*, the court reasoned that GECC's entitlement to the funds barred the bank from moving the funds out of the blocked account. Once the beneficiary's bank properly executed the order that it received, the payment into the account was final. General Electric Capital Corp. v. Central Bank, 49 F.3d 280 (7th Cir. 1995).

It is easy to quarrel with the results of *Banque Worms* and *GECC*. First, those decisions interpret the bank's right of restitution more narrowly than traditional common-law principles, which would not allow a creditor in the position of Banque Worms or GECC to retain those funds unless the creditor could prove that it had detrimentally relied on the payment by changing its position toward the debtor. Nothing in Article 4A justifies a narrowing of the common-law restitution remedy in the wire-transfer context. Indeed, as explained above, the text of Article 4A is avowedly agnostic about the limits of that remedy.

Moreover, especially in the context of *GECC*, a rule protecting the improper transferee seems to forgive the transferee's failure to protect itself. As Professor Andrew Kull explains, Judge Easterbrook's decision in *GECC* effectively protects the secured creditor from the consequences of its own lax monitoring of its borrower:

> Denial of restitution shifts (to one of the banks) the consequences of a risk that GECC had agreed to bear: namely, the risk of the debtor's misconduct. GECC was paid to accept this risk; GECC negotiated the terms on which it would manage it (in its security agreement with the debtor); GECC was the only party in a position to police the debtor's behavior. The secured credit agreement, not the wire transfer, was the transaction that went seriously wrong in this case, yet to this transaction the banks were total strangers. Requiring them to bear a loss they could not control offends not only equity and good conscience but ordinary precepts of risk-spreading as well.

Andrew Kull, "Rationalizing Restitution", 83 Cal. L. Rev. 1191, 1241 n.143 (1995).

C. Fraud

Wire transfers are particularly attractive as a target for fraud both because they readily carry huge sums of money and because they are largely automated.

Banks have responded by implementing a variety of security procedures to enhance the difficulty of theft from the system. Those procedures take a variety of more or less sophisticated forms. For example, current Fedwire procedures for on-line transfers require an identification code and a confidential password to access the system, as well as encryption of the payment order during the transmission process. By contrast, off-line Fedwire transfers are confirmed through the more antiquated "four-party call-back" process described in the previous assignment. Many banks use a similar four-party procedure to confirm wire transfers requested by their customers. Some banks, however, use much less cautious procedures, such as a "listen-back" requirement, under which a second employee listens to a tape recording of the initial request. That procedure may limit the opportunity for theft by bank employees, but it does little or nothing to limit theft by outsiders.

Another common mechanism that indirectly limits fraud is a contractual overdraft limit. The bank and the customer commonly agree that the bank is *not* authorized to send any wire transfer that would create an overdraft in the customer's account (an agreement directly contrary to the overdraft protection a large customer generally would have on its checking account). See UCC §4A-203 comment 3. Then, if the bank receives a large wire-transfer order that exceeds the balance in the customer's account, the bank will not accept the payment order. Given the significant chance that the wire-transfer thief will not be sure exactly what the customer's balance is at any time, a wire-transfer thief frequently might try to send orders that would cause an overdraft. The agreement between the customer and the bank would keep such orders from being executed even if the thief managed to satisfy the security procedure. That approach would not catch a few small, incidental thefts, but it does limit the possibility of a really large theft in one transaction.

Presently, it is clear that even the most advanced available procedures are not entirely secure. For example, in one widely noted incident, a 34-year-old graduate student working from a computer terminal in St. Petersburg, Russia, gained access to the security procedures that CitiBank used to protect wire transfers from accounts of its large corporate clients. In about 40 separate incidents in late 1995, the student (acting with several accomplices) successfully made off with about $400,000 from accounts located in Finland, Germany, Israel, the Netherlands, Russia, Sweden, and the United States. Although he was arrested before the scheme went far, his success in breaking into accounts in so many countries highlighted the vulnerability of the system to sophisticated computer technology.

Because customers ordinarily are liable only for orders that they authorize, UCC §4A-202(a), the significant possibility of unauthorized orders gives banks a strong incentive to develop security procedures that prevent unauthorized orders. Article 4A buttresses that incentive with an unusual provision that rewards the bank for implementing security procedures by deeming customers to have authorized all orders made in conformity with preapproved security procedures even if the customer in fact did not authorize the orders. UCC §4A-202(b). For example, if a thief (like the student described above) with illicit access to the customer's computer uses the passwords from that computer to place unauthorized orders, the customer is fully responsible for those orders (subject only to a right to pursue restitution from the wrongdoer).

The statute imposes three significant restrictions on the bank's ability to use the security-procedure rule to charge its customer for orders that the customer in fact did not authorize. First, the security procedure must be commercially reasonable. UCC §4A-202(b)(i). That rule allows a customer charged for an unauthorized order to contend that the security procedure to which it agreed was so defective that it would be unreasonable to hold the customer to unauthorized orders sent pursuant to that procedure. Although the vagueness of that rule does limit the bank's ability to be sure that it is protected from responsibility for unauthorized orders, it does enhance even further the bank's incentive to develop the most sophisticated practicable procedures for preventing unauthorized wire-transfer orders. See UCC §4A-203 comment 4 (discussing the factors that determine the commercial reasonability of a security procedure).

One difficulty in imposing responsibility on the bank for unauthorized orders that go undiscovered by unreasonably lax security procedures is the possibility that the customer will prefer a less lax procedure because of the expense and inconvenience of more secure procedures. The statute deals with that problem by absolving the bank for responsibility for the customer's use of an unreasonably lax procedure if the bank previously offered the customer an appropriate procedure, but the customer selected the unreasonable procedure anyway. UCC §4A-202(c); see UCC §4A-203 comment 4.

The second restriction requires the bank to show that it processed the order in accordance with its agreement with the victimized customer. UCC §4A-202(b)(ii). Accordingly, the bank cannot charge its customer for an unauthorized order issued pursuant to a security procedure—even if the procedure is reasonable—if the bank failed to comply with the procedure or if the order violated some other provision of the bank's agreement with its customer (such as an overdraft limit). See UCC §4A-203 comment 3.

The third exception permits the customer to pass the liability back to the bank if the customer can identify the breach of the security procedure and demonstrate that the information that allowed the fraud was not obtained "from a source controlled by the customer." UCC §4A-203(a). Thus, where it is clear that the thief operated by compromising the bank's own computer system, the bank must accept responsibility for the unauthorized transactions. Notwithstanding the apparent generosity of that provision, two problems with the details of the provision make it likely that customers occasionally will bear responsibility for fraud committed by persons that do not obtain information from the customer.

First, the exception applies only in cases in which the customer can discover how the fraud was committed. See UCC §§4A-203(a)(2) (relief available only to customers that "prov[e]" that the malefactor did not obtain access through the customer); 4A-105(a)(7) (defining "[p]rove" to mean "meet the burden of establishing the fact"). If the customer cannot determine who committed the fraud or how it was done, the customer will remain responsible. The drafters of Article 4A apparently found that turn of events improbable; UCC §4A-203 comment 5 states that appropriate investigation ordinarily will discover the source of the fraud. The CitiBank incident discussed above, however, belies that suggestion. Despite a lengthy investigation and a number of convictions, there has been no public revelation of how the interloper obtained the passwords he used to gain access to the system. Accordingly, the victimized customers probably could not use UCC §4A-203(a)(2) to absolve themselves of responsibility. The lack of proof is particularly disquieting in light of the general opinion of industry sources to whom the author has spoken that the interloper was working with an employee of CitiBank to complete the unauthorized transactions.

Second, the statute's use of "contro[l] by the customer" as the key for allocating responsibility introduces substantial ambiguity into the system. For example, it is not clear how that test would treat one of the most likely types of theft: a man-in-the-middle attack that operates by interception of messages between the customer and the bank. Does the customer "contro[l]" the telephone line over which it sends a message to its bank? A sensible rule would place that loss on the bank—without regard to abstract concepts of "control" of the telephone line—because the bank is the only party realistically able to upgrade the security of the transmission. But UCC §4A-206 suggests that Article 4A would view the communications system as an agent of the customer and thus hold the customer liable for any malfeasance.

The last issue of the fraud topic is what happens when the system executes a fraudulent wire-transfer order. The rules closely resemble the rules for erroneous orders discussed earlier in this assignment. The simplest possibility is that the order is treated as authorized under the security procedure rules. In that case, the customer is treated as the sender of the order under UCC §4A-202(d) and accordingly is obligated to pay the order under UCC §4A-402(c). The customer's remedy is limited to a suit for conversion against the defrauder.

If the order cannot be treated as an authorized order under UCC §4A-202, then the bank must refund any sums that the customer already paid with respect to the order, with interest. UCC §4A-204(a). As with interest compensation for erroneous orders, the customer can lose its right to interest if it fails to complain within a reasonable time (not to exceed 90 days) of the time that the customer was notified of the unauthorized order. UCC §4A-204(a). For payment orders sent to Federal Reserve banks, the Federal Reserve has issued a regulation stating that 30 calendar days from the date that the sender receives notice is a reasonable time. Regulation J, §210.28(c).

In addition to the direct incentive to limit losses, banks have a powerful reputational incentive to convince their customers of the safety of the wire-transfer procedures that they offer. Commentators have noted how promptly CitiBank reimbursed all of its customers for the funds lost in the scheme described above, even though CitiBank's use of a security procedure might have given CitiBank the right to pass all or a portion of those losses on to its customers. The moral is apparent: To CitiBank at least, an appearance of security was more important than full pursuit of its legal rights with respect to the theft.

Problem Set 31

31.1. Your morning starts with a meeting with a new client, Josiah Bounderby. He is upset because of a number of problems that he has had recently with wire transfers. The first problem deals with a $500,000 payment that he asked his bank (Cheeryble Brothers) to send to James Harthouse. Bounderby provides you a printout from his computer of the payment order that he sent Cheeryble. That order identified Harthouse by name and indicated that the funds should be sent to Harthouse's account at Barclay's, identified in the order as account number 002131. Promptly upon receipt of the order, Cheeryble debited Bounderby's account for the amount of the order and executed the order by sending a payment order directly to Barclay's in Chicago. Barclay's, in turn, executed the order by depositing the funds in its account number 002131. Unfortunately, that account belonged not to James Harthouse, but to Thomas Gradgrind.

a. Can Bounderby recover the funds from Cheeryble? Do you need to know anything further to answer that question? UCC §§4A-207(c), 4A-207 comment 2.

b. If Bounderby cannot recover the funds from Cheeryble, does he have any way to recover the money? UCC §4A-207(d).

c. How would your answer change if you discovered that Barclay's recognized the discrepancy before it accepted the payment order from Cheeryble? UCC §§4A-207, 4A-207 comment 2, 4A-402.

31.2. Ben Darrow from FSB calls you to discuss a problem with a recent wire transfer the bank sent for one of Darrow's customers. Jasmine Ball sent FSB an e-mail message requesting a wire transfer for $100,000 to an account of Carol Long at the Second National Bank (SNB) of Muleshoe. The request was processed by a novice clerk at FSB, who accidentally duplicated the transaction and sent two identical $100,000 transfers, rather than one. FSB's processing system automatically deducted funds from Ball's account to cover both orders. Ball called to complain later that day when she happened to notice the unusually low balance in her account. As soon as Darrow discovered the problem, he called SNB. SNB told him that it had received the funds and notified Ms. Long, but that she had not yet removed the excess money. Darrow has several questions.

a. First, can Darrow force SNB to send the extra $100,000 back to FSB? UCC §§4A-209(b), 4A-209 comments 4 & 5, 4A-211(c), 4A-211 comments 3 & 4, 4A-402(b), 4A-404(a).

b. If not, can FSB recover the excess funds from Long? Do you need to know anything else about the relation between Ball and Long? What if Ball in fact owes Long $1,000,000? UCC §4A-303(a) & comment 3.

c. If FSB has no right to recover the excess funds from SNB or Long, can FSB retain all of the funds that it debited from Ball's account to pay for the orders? UCC §§4A-303(a), 4A-303 comments 2 & 3, 4A-402(c), (d).

31.3. Your old friend Jodi Kay calls to talk to you about a project she is supervising, which involves producing a new funds-transfer agreement form for CountryBank. CountryBank's new computer system has been plagued with operating shutdowns, so she is particularly concerned about CountryBank's liability in cases where it fails to execute a customer's order in a timely manner. She wants to have the customer waive any right to recover from the bank for such an occurrence: no interest, no incidental expenses, no consequential damages, no attorney's fees. After all, she says, computer failures are endemic and really beyond her control. Moreover, the customer hasn't really lost anything if the bank never sends the money to the wrong place and eventually sends it to the right place. She wants to know if such an agreement would be enforceable. If it would not be entirely enforceable, what things should she include that would be enforceable? UCC §4A-305.

31.4.   When you see Jeeves walking across the room toward you just as you start to enjoy your weekly lunch at the Drones Club, you think back to Problem Set 30 and groan inwardly at the prospect of facing another one of Bertie Wooster's problems. Thus, you are not the least bit surprised when Jeeves asks for a moment of your time to discuss a problem of Wooster's. The problem arises out of a wire transfer in the amount of $500,000 that was made from Wooster's account 13 months ago. Wooster's bank dutifully mailed a bank statement to Wooster reflecting that transfer the day after the transfer. Unfortunately, the notification was lost in the mail and received by Wooster only yesterday. When Jeeves looked at the notification for Wooster, Jeeves remembered immediately that Wooster had authorized a transfer for $50,000, not $500,000. Because the transfer had been shown on the lost statement, none of the intervening months' statements showed anything about the transfer.

If Jeeves is correct in his recollection (and he always is), can Wooster force the bank to recredit the funds from the transfer? If so, is Wooster entitled to interest as well? UCC §§1-201 (25) (revised §1-202), 4A-304, 4A-402(d), 4A-505.

31.5.   Before he leaves, Jeeves pauses to raise another problem with you. It appears that even Wooster's considerable bank balance was lessened substantially by the incorrect withdrawal of $450,000 discussed in Problem 31.4. As it happens, Jeeves discovered when he contacted the bank yesterday afternoon that the bank had dishonored several checks written by Wooster in the last few weeks. Jeeves has contacted just a few of the recipients and already has discovered that the bank's decision to bounce the checks has caused Wooster a variety of problems, ranging from bounced-check fees to more serious claims for default under agreements that Wooster had with the payees of the checks. Jeeves wants to know whether Wooster can pass the costs of solving those problems back to the bank as consequences of the bank's incorrect actions. UCC §§1-106(1), 4-402(b), 4-402 comment 2, 4A-305 & comment 2, 4A-402(d), 4A-402 comment 2.

31.6.   Your client Ben Darrow calls you to discuss a funds-transfer services agreement that he is negotiating with his customer Carol Long. FSB currently is marketing to its customers a newly developed AccuWire system that uses sophisticated encryption and multiple passwords to provide a high degree of security in wire transfers. When Ben started to describe the system to Carol, she said she was not interested (right after he told her that it would cost her "only" $3,500 to have the system installed). She says that she trusts her employees completely, believes that her workplace is totally secure, and has no interest in spending money on some expensive security procedure developed by an out-of-state bank that recently acquired FSB.

Carol tells Ben to draw up an agreement stating that FSB is authorized to act on any written instruction that it receives that appears to reflect a signature that matches the specimen signature she has provided the bank. Ben wants your help drafting the agreement. Does the agreement that Carol has proposed expose Ben or FSB to any significant risks? UCC §§4A-201, 4A-202, 4A-203, 4A-501(a).

Chapter 7.   Developing Payment Systems

Assignment 32:   Internet Payments

The Internet has provided an immense new market opportunity, with new retailers, new products, and new methods of delivering those products. The pages that follow discuss some of the important practical and legal developments in paying for products that are for sale on the Internet. In this discussion, you should think about the material in the two excerpts that follow, which underscore two fundamental problems for payments on the Internet. The first is a practical one: The markets began with strongly established networks for existing participants in the form of Visa and MasterCard. The second is a policy one: The legal distinctions developed for payment transactions in conventional face-to-face retailing do not apply coherently to the new payment transactions developing on the Internet.

A.   Background

Mark A. Lemley & David McGowan, Legal Implications of Network Economic Effects

86 Cal. L. Rev. 479 (1998)

Many things may increase in value as the number of users increases. The term network effects therefore must be used with great care, for it has been used to describe a number of distinct conditions in which value may increase with consumption. The state of both theoretical development and empirical research varies, and the confidence with which the law uses network theory as a basis for modifying or extending existing doctrine should be calibrated accordingly. Following Katz and Shapiro, we view network markets as falling on a continuum that may roughly be divided into actual networks, virtual networks, and simple positive feedback phenomena. The essential criterion for locating a good along this continuum is the degree to which the good provides inherent value to a consumer apart from any network characteristics. The greater the inherent value of the good relative to any value added by additional consumers, the less significant the network effect.

A.   ACTUAL NETWORKS

The archetypal examples of network markets involve products whose entire value lies in facilitating interactions between a consumer and others who own

507

the product. The benefit to a purchaser, in other words, is access to other purchasers. Telephones and fax machines are classic examples of actual network goods; owning the only telephone or fax machine in the world would be of little benefit because it could not be used to communicate with anyone. The value of the telephone or fax machine one has already purchased increases with each additional purchaser, so long as all machines operate on the same standards and the network infrastructure is capable of processing all member communications reliably. In this relatively strict sense, actual networks are effectively limited to communications markets. The principal characteristics distinguishing such products from others discussed below are the absence of material inherent value and the necessity for common standards among goods incorporated into the network....

Property rights (most importantly, the right to exclude others from a network) play a crucial role in network markets. In many potential networks, property rights created by legal rules, rather than physical laws, set the boundary conditions for the network. Actual networks such as telephone lines require capital investments in physical infrastructure. Such networks therefore may be owned: there are tangible assets to which property rights may be attached. Even where the capital investment in a network is negligible, the law can establish ownership rights by fiat (in this case by awarding exclusive rights in "intellectual property"). Where the law establishes a right to exclude others from the use of a thing — as with intellectual property — it constrains the ability of consumers to move between network standards, and it gives control over access and pricing to the owner of the intellectual property embodied in the standard....

B. VIRTUAL NETWORKS

Goods constitute virtual networks when they provide inherent value to consumers that increases with the number of additional users of identical and/or interoperable goods. Virtual network goods need not be linked to a common system as are the constituents of a communications network; very strong positive feedback effects tied to functional compatibility are sufficient. Computer software is the paradigm example. Unlike telephones and fax machines, an operating system or application program will allow even a single user to perform a variety of tasks regardless whether even a single other consumer owns the software. At the same time, the value of a given program grows considerably as the number of additional purchasers increases. As more consumers adopted WordPerfect, for example, it became easier for each previous user to share files without the need for a conversion program and easier for employees to switch jobs without retraining. And as Microsoft Word has replaced WordPerfect as the word processing program of choice, it in turn gained the benefits of widespread adoption. Data sharing in this sense requires direct horizontal technological compatibility akin to that required for telephones and fax machines to work together, but it does not require the actual connections that communications networks do. Further, the existence of conversion software may expand the network beyond a single, proprietary product.

In addition to horizontal technological compatibility, software may be subject to "increasing returns" based on positive feedback from the market in the form of complementary goods. Software developers will write more applications programs for an operating system with two-thirds of the market than for a system with one-third because the operating system with the larger share will provide the biggest market for applications programs. The availability of a broader array of application programs will reinforce the popularity of an operating system, which in turn will make investment in application programs compatible with that system more desirable than investment in programs compatible with less popular systems. Similarly, firms that adopt relatively popular software will likely incur lower costs to train employees and will find it easier to hire productive temporary help than will firms with unpopular software. Importantly, the strength of network effects will vary depending on the type of software in question. Network effects will be materially greater for operating systems software than for applications programs, for example, and a proper legal analysis of network effects in software markets must account for this difference.

Of course, technology comprises only one element of virtual networks. Like actual networks, virtual networks are likely to require intricate webs of both formal and informal contracts to create the value the network delivers. Bank-issued credit cards provide a good example. Although they might confer some utility on their own (particularly in their credit aspect), credit cards exhibit network effects because their utility increases dramatically as a network develops. As the number of merchants willing to accept a card grows, the utility of the card to consumers increases, thus likely increasing the number of consumers who will want to own the card, which in turn provides incentive for more merchants to accept the card, and so on. With innovation in computer and telephone technology yielding such benefits as real-time transaction processing, including such features as fraud detection and verification of available credit, transactions involving bank-issued credit cards have come to resemble interactions on an actual network.

But the technological links and potential for positive returns to scale in the credit card industry cannot themselves create value without a sophisticated system of contracts, including agreement on the compensation card issuers will receive and the rules governing their conduct relative to the network. Thus, merchants will have a contractual relationship with a bank, which will to some extent be subject to the bank's contractual relationship with the credit card entity. If the merchant's bank did not issue the consumer's credit card, it in turn will have a contractual relationship with the issuing bank pursuant to which transactions may be cleared. The issuing bank will of course have a contractual relationship with the consumer. These contracts are as vital to the functioning of the credit card network as are the electronic links that facilitate transactions.

Many of these contracts are standardized by the rules of the Visa and Master-Card joint ventures. Those rules govern general network membership, such as the manner in which member banks may use the Visa and MasterCard marks, communication among member banks, and fees charged by member banks for processing transactions with one another. The rules do not specify standard terms, however, for contracts between merchants and their banks or between consumers and their banks. Therefore, the degree to which network theory plays a role in the legal analysis of credit card networks depends in significant part upon the legal and economic analysis of contract law, including the relative efficiency of standard contract terms versus either a joint venture or horizontal integration, and limitations on the ability to contract (such as those imposed by antitrust law). . . .

C. POSITIVE FEEDBACK EFFECTS

Lastly, goods may increase in value as consumption increases even where the goods are not themselves connections to a network and do not interoperate with like (or "compatible") goods. Such goods reflect little more than the need for a given degree of demand to sustain production of the good and complementary goods and services. Where production of goods involves both fixed and marginal costs, the average fixed costs will decline as demand for the good increases, and the fixed costs are spread over a larger number of units. This is a common economic phenomenon — economies of scale. In some cases, a large population may be necessary to justify any production at all. We would intuitively expect exotic car repair shops to be more prevalent in large cities than rural towns because a minimum concentration of car owners is required to generate sufficient demand to sustain a shop.

Unlike actual or virtual networks, no technological compatibility, interoperability, or even contractual relationships are necessary to sustain this "network." Strictly speaking, it is not a network at all. Network effects are demand-side effects — they result from the value that consumers place on owning what other consumers already own. By contrast, economies of scale are supply-side effects — they are a function of the cost of making the goods and exist (at least conceptually) regardless of positive utility payoffs among consumers. Markets characterized by economies of scale are, of course, potentially subject to material diseconomies of scale as well. If too many consumers purchase the same exotic car, it may become difficult to schedule repairs, obtain parts, and the like. Similarly, once a steel plant is used to its full capacity, expanding supply will require building a whole new plant, raising the average cost. Thus, there are definite limits in most markets to the "value" to consumers of buying whatever other consumers want. By definition, those markets do not exhibit network effects.

D. WHY WE SHOULD CARE: THE POSSIBLE "EFFECTS" OF NETWORKS

... [M]any of the concerns surrounding network markets are based on the presumption that such markets offer increasing returns over a very large portion of the demand curve. Outside the realm of natural monopoly, by contrast, neo-classical economics generally posits declining returns to scale and thus offers few conceptual tools to address the problems that arise when returns increase over a very large portion or even all of the demand curve. Thus, arguments based on network effects may suggest that the law must rethink the rationality of behavior considered unlikely under neoclassical theory, such as predation in antitrust jurisprudence, and address new risks not considered under models based on declining returns.

With respect to the behavioral issues, network markets by definition offer potentially lucrative returns to firms that can establish their own products as standards on which competition in the market, or in aftermarkets for complementary goods, will be based. This fact presents the possibility of material first-mover advantages: being the first seller in a market may confer an important advantage over later entrants. Because the returns to the standards winner will be higher than in "normal" markets, relatively risky strategies, such as predation or, at a minimum, penetration pricing, might be rational in a networks market.

Increasing returns also raise questions about the possibility of effectively leveraging a monopoly from one market to another, an argument most commonly associated with antitrust tying claims. Chicago-school analysts have argued that leveraging is unlikely because a given amount of monopoly power can extract only a given amount of revenue from consumers, whether taken all in the monopolist's primary market or split between that market and some other. This view has been challenged even without regard to network theory, but the possibility of leveraging from a non-network market into a network market poses an important new challenge. Recent activity in the software industry also raises the possibility that markets for products that would be considered distinct under traditional antitrust analysis, such as Web browsers, might simply be absorbed into a network market through bundling with a strong network product, such as an operating system. One might also rethink unfair competition law in light of the arguably greater sensitivity of network markets to public pronouncements: in a market in which the standard product is preferred, statements about such products might carry greater weight than in other markets.

These arguments are closely related to the idea of "tipping," a concept Katz and Shapiro summarize as being based on

> [a] natural tendency toward de facto standardization, which means everyone using the same system. Because of the strong positive-feedback elements, systems markets are especially prone to 'tipping,' which is the tendency of one system to pull away from its rivals in popularity once it has gained an initial edge. Tipping is neither inherently good nor bad. If the economics of a particular market dictate that having one standard is more efficient than competition among standards, then "tipping" to one standard is in theory inevitable, absent significant transaction costs or some form of regulation. In such circumstances a "tipped" market would be efficient and therefore desirable; efforts to forestall tipping would result in suboptimal heterogeneity among systems and losses in terms of unrealized efficiencies. That a market is best served by a single standard, however, does not always imply that the standard should be owned by a single firm, or even that the standard should be owned at all.

Even in markets best served by a single standard or system, however, there is at least a theoretical risk that the "wrong" standard will be adopted or that a standard that was efficient when adopted will become relatively inefficient over time. The conclusion that a standard adopted by consumers is suboptimal should be approached with caution. Setting aside for the moment the very difficult question of deriving determinative criteria for defining "suboptimality," consumers might have difficulty moving to a new standard—even if they all agreed that the adopted standard was suboptimal—because of collective action problems. The value of any alternative system would depend on the number of users adopting it; the rational consumer might well choose to wait until an alternative had been adopted by others who incurred the costs of shifting to the new standard but reaped fewer benefits relative to later adopters.

From the standpoint of legal adaptation of network theory, each of these arguments is to some degree problematic. The presumed increasing returns of network markets are not guaranteed; networks will suffer net diseconomies of scale if the volume of interactions exceeds network capacity and causes delays or failure. Positive returns to some level of scale are in any event quite common, if not ubiquitous. Further, network effects might not be the only effects at work. A user might prefer Lexis to Westlaw, but only up to a certain point. If the information she needs is available only on Westlaw, she may start using that service, whatever the cost in terms of lost convenience. At a minimum, common sense tells us that there likely are differences material to most areas of the law between a network of telephones or fax machines and a "network" of Ferrari owners. It is thus important to analyze markets to determine the source of increasing returns—whether from actual or virtual networks—and to distinguish among markets displaying merely positive returns to scale, markets displaying network effects only up to a relatively low point on the demand curve, and markets displaying increasing returns over most or all of the demand curve. The ratio of inherent value to network value is of similar importance.

One final feature of network theory bears significant emphasis. Network effects tend to have conflicting implications that are very difficult to interpret. To take corporate governance as an example, some have argued that a given corporate governance term might display network effects by gaining greater clarity of meaning over time and through repeated interpretation by courts. If one observes that firms all use that term, however, does that reflect maximization of positive interpretive network effects or does it reflect suboptimal tipping? Or is the term inherently the best one? If firms use a variety of different terms on a given point, does that reflect the optimal convergence of heterogeneous firms with heterogeneous governance provisions or does it reflect opportunity costs of not using a standard term? In many cases, the observable data can lead to diametrically opposed conclusions, making the task of judicial adaptation extremely difficult.

Ronald J. Mann, Making Sense of Payments Policy in the Information Age

93 Geo. L.J. 633 (2005)

Two events at the close of the twentieth century have underscored the need to think more clearly about payments policy. The first is the proliferation of markets in which credit and debit cards are used. What once was a niche product designed for the payment of expenses by business travelers has now come into widespread use in a wide variety of contexts that raise differing policy concerns. The second, related to the first, is the substantial shift in the locus of retail payment transactions from retail, face-to-face payments in brick-and-mortar stores to remote payments for Internet purchases. Collectively, those changes have destabilized the system for which existing payments rules were designed.

... [I]t would be remiss to discuss harmonization of rules for payment cards without some general consideration of the propriety of uniformity in the law of payment systems. I am of course not the first to come upon that problem. The [Uniform New Payments Code], for example, rested on the basic premise that the law governing issues common to multiple payments should be as uniform as possible. As the Reporter explained in his memorandum justifying the project, the goal is "to arrive at a set of comprehensive rules applicable in some respects to all payment systems." Conversely, Peter Alces's perceptive analysis of that project argues that the UNPC goes too far by ignoring important differences between payment systems that justify differing rules for devices (primarily credit cards) that provide for the extension of credit. More recently, Clay Gillette has presented a particularizing argument about rules for unauthorized transactions, contending that those rules should turn on the relative ability of courts and legislatures to identify optimal risk-bearers.

Looking back from the vantage point of the 21st century, it seems clear that the basic problem with the earlier proposals is not that they are excessively uniform or excessively particularizing. The problem is that they have not undertaken to consider why it might be useful to have uniform or particularized rules on particular subjects. I attribute that blind spot in the existing literature to the historical accident of the structure of the modern commercial-law curriculum.

Even with the law of payments itself, work that attempts to address broader policy concerns is hampered by the balkanized nature of the existing regulatory apparatus. The UCC itself is promulgated by the ALI and NCCUSL for adoption by the various state legislatures. The Federal Reserve—motivated primarily by concerns about stability and to a lesser degree by concerns about cost-effectiveness—implements most of the relevant provisions of the EFAA, TILA, and the EFTA. Even the Federal Trade Commission has a minor role, with some frankly protective regulations related to holder-in-due-course status.

The basic problem is that payments policy needs to attend more consciously to the contexts of the transactions in which payments are made. Existing law articulates rules that are bounded almost entirely by the nature of the technology with which the payment is made. Thus, we have separate rules for wire transfers, letters of credit, checks, electronic transfers, and the like. That type of boundary makes sense only for issues driven by the nature of the technology. It makes no sense, however, for issues that should be resolved by reference to the nature of the underlying transaction in which the payment is made.

At its heart, payments law must resolve four fundamental questions: who bears the risk of unauthorized payments, what must be done about claims of error, when are payments completed (so that they discharge the underlying liability), and when can they be reversed. The first three questions are categorically different from the last, because they often should be resolved based on the nature of the underlying technology. Thus, for example, with respect to the risk of unauthorized payments, the fundamental question is how to design a system that gives adequate incentive to the user to avoid and mitigate losses from unauthorized transactions, while giving adequate incentive to the system operator to make advances in technology and system design that can avoid and mitigate those losses. In our legal system, we have taken the view for most high-technology payments that an almost complete allocation of the risk of those losses to the system operator is appropriate.

The premise of those rules (admittedly unspoken) is that even a complete allocation of loss to the network operator will leave the consumer a sufficient incentive to attend to these problems. That could be true because of the hassle of reversing unauthorized charges, because of doubts that financial institutions readily will fulfill their obligations in such a situation, or even because of ignorance of the legal protections for unauthorized transactions. At the same time, the rules reflect the implicit premise that losses in technology-driven systems are most effectively reduced by technological and system-design initiatives that are exclusively within the control of the system operator. Thus, we are not surprised to see major investments in fraud-prevention technology in the credit-card and debit-card sectors. Because the justifications for those rules relate to the nature of the technology, it is plausible for federal law to prescribe such a rule for all electronic transfers from consumer accounts. It is less plausible to include a similar rule for credit card transactions based on the availability of credit in the transaction. It would be more sensible, surely, for that rule to be justified by the fact that the transactions are processed and cleared in an electronic way, which justifies rules like those discussed above.

Rules related to error are similar. The types of events that are likely to lead to an error, as well as the mechanisms for detecting, confirming, and responding to an error are likely to depend on the technology that is used to clear and process payments. Thus, it makes some sense that the rule for transactions processed electronically (covered by the EFTA) would differ from the rule for transactions processed entirely by paper (conventional check transactions governed by Article 4). At the same time, the continuing shift of check transactions from paper to electronic processing (probably to be accelerated by the Check 21 Act) might undermine that distinction.

Rules that determine when a payment is made are similar, in that they are for the most part made based on the practicalities of a particular system. Thus, in the wire-transfer system, we say that the payment is complete when the beneficiary's bank becomes obligated to pay the beneficiary. In the checking system, we say that the payment is not complete with respect to an ordinary check until the check is paid, but that it occurs with respect to a cashier's check when the payee accepts the instrument.

Rules related to reversibility however, are completely different. Rules related to reversibility should depend on the dynamics of the underlying transaction in which the payment is made. In the simplest cases, payment systems are specialized for use in particular situations. Thus, for example, in business transactions, parties often choose to make payments with letters of credit or wire transfers. Those systems include particular rules designed for the particular transactions in which they are used, which determine the timing and circumstances in which payments can be recovered or stopped once the process has been initiated. Because those systems are quite specialized, the system-specific rules work well for them.

It is important to see that the rules make sense because of the underlying transaction, not because of anything about the payment instrument itself. For example, there is nothing inherent in the use of a bank's written commitment to pay that calls for the formalistic emphasis on both an absolute obligation of payment upon presentation of conforming documents and at the same time an utterly unconstrained right to refuse payment upon presentation of nonconforming documents. On the contrary, that structure has grown up solely as an adjunct to the particular sales transaction for which the instrument is commonly used. If the law of letters of credit makes sense — and for the most part I think it does — it makes sense only in the light of a practical assessment of the realities of the sales transactions in which that law is brought to bear.

The law of wire transfers is animated by an even more conclusive rejection of reversibility. From the perspective articulated here, that emphasis reflects a desire to create an entirely "pure" payment system, entirely divorced from any transaction: the wire transfer is suitable for cases in which the party making the payment is willing to forgo any payment-related right of recovery at all. Once the payment is made by wire transfer, there is no substantial recourse inside the system. That makes sense in context, because wire transfers are used typically by reasonably informed businesses that select such a pure system in contexts in which the most important aspect of the transaction is to provide reliably final payment as promptly as possible.

When we turn to less specialized payment systems, however, the issues become considerably more difficult. Historically (if not in current practice), the most prominent is the negotiable instrument. The most distinctive feature of the negotiable instrument is the ability of those that acquire the instrument to obtain holder-in-due-course status. As a practical matter, that status involves an ability to separate the instrument from the transaction as much as possible and thus make the obligation to pay irreversible at an early point, at least as regards claims related to the underlying transaction.

The complicating features of negotiable instruments law, however, largely operate to render that separation irrevocably permeable. For present purposes, what is most important is that the policy justifications for those complicating features uniformly relate to concerns about the balance of power in the underlying transaction for which the instrument was issued. For example, a series of arbitrary formalities limit the use of the negotiable instrument to cases in which the parties are sufficiently sophisticated and focused to ensure that the payment instrument is drafted in a stripped-down form that includes the requisite formal language and omits any substantial discussion of the underlying transaction. Similarly, even if the instrument is issued in a proper form and transferred in the appropriate way, certain defenses will remain valid against the purchaser. These defenses — the so-called real defenses — address such matters as contracts with minors or contracts procured by fraud; they plainly are designed to protect fundamental concerns about fairness in the underlying transaction. Finally, in nonmortgage credit transactions that involve consumers, holder-in-due-course status is generally prohibited as a matter of supervening federal law.

The negotiable instrument, of course, has been superseded for the most part by its main surviving descendant, the check, an instrument for which the classic rules of negotiability have little continuing significance. Because the check is less specialized than the letter of credit or the wire transfer (or the negotiable instrument in its heyday), its rules do not reflect the close accommodation to the balance of the underlying transaction that typifies the law of those earlier, primarily business-related payment systems. Thus, many of the most important rules in the checking system reflect issues discussed above, allocating losses from unauthorized transactions and risks of errors related to the payment device that have little or nothing to do with problems in any underlying transaction. Of course, the focus of modern check law on such questions, to the exclusion of any substantial concern for the consumers that use them, is the basis of much of the most forceful criticisms of Articles 3 and 4 as they now appear in the UCC. But even the checking system includes rules that address the basic problem at the intersection of every payment system and the transactions for which it is used: the consequences of the payee's failure to perform. On that point, the UCC frankly grants the check-writer a right to stop payment, without any assessment of the validity of the claim.

The check, however, is now outdated. As we now know, it has been declining in use for some time. The pressure to revise rules related to the check thus will continue to decrease. At the same time, consumer use of credit and debit cards is increasing rapidly. Moreover, of importance for our purposes, credit and debit cards over the last decade have come into dominance in areas in which they were not frequently used. Thus, credit cards have come to dominate payments in remote purchase transactions, especially on the Internet. Debit cards, reaching broad use in this country only in the last decade, are now commonly used in face-to-face transactions and perhaps soon will be a major option for remote transactions as well.

Thus, if there is an area of payments law that is both important and currently contestable, it is the law that addresses card-based payment transactions.

B. Credit Cards on the Internet

With the rise of Internet retailing, the advantages of the credit card as a payment system are obvious. The preexisting Visa and MasterCard networks, and the widespread distribution of cards to consumers in the United States, gave credit-card issuers a built-in nationwide payment network available when Internet commerce began. Other payment systems that existed at the time were not as easily transferred to the Internet setting. For example, cash is entirely impractical in a remote transaction unless the consumer has some reliable way to send the cash to the merchant; and even if some hypothetical consumer were willing to mail cash for an Internet purchase, the merchant would not receive the cash for several days until it came in the mail. Similarly, a commitment to pay by check gives the merchant nothing for several days while the merchant waits for the check (except a promise that "the check is in the mail"). Finally, when commerce on the Internet began, there was no system by which online retailers could accept ACH transfers. That is changing — as you will see in the discussion below — but the change is slow and is happening only after the system is to some degree "locked in" to reliance on credit-card payments.

1. Processing the Transactions

Although some merchants (and third-party security providers) are developing creative ways to enhance the authenticity of their online credit-card transactions, the typical process requires nothing more than that the consumer enter a credit-card number and billing address on the merchant's checkout page. Indeed, if the consumer uses an electronic-wallet product, the information might be entered automatically (a possibility that would be more likely if those products become more functional and less cumbersome). As discussed below, a merchant concerned about fraud might request some additional information, but the need for that information is unlikely to delay the completion of the transaction more than a few seconds beyond the time necessary to provide the information to the merchant's checkout software.

With respect to unauthorized transactions, the cardholder that purchases on the Internet often is not responsible even for $50. The relevant provision of TILA conditions the cardholder's responsibility for $50 on the issuer's having provided some method for the cardholder to identify itself as the authorized user of the card (such as a signature, photograph on the card, or the like). TILA

§133(a)(1)(F); Regulation Z, §226.12(b)(3). At least in the view of the Federal Reserve staff, an Internet transaction that verifies the customer's identity solely by asking for the card number and billing address has not identified the customer adequately. Accordingly, the Federal Reserve has concluded in its commentary to Regulation Z, cardholders have no responsibility at all in unauthorized transactions that are conducted based solely on card numbers. Regulation Z Official Staff Commentary to §226.12(b)(2)(iii). In any event, the ability to impose the $50 on cardholders has diminishing practical relevance, because both Visa and MasterCard generally waive the $50 of liability that the statute permits, at least if the cardholder notifies the issuer promptly after discovering the loss of control of the card (or its number).

2. Problems

Despite its current dominance, the credit card faces a number of problems as a long-term vehicle for Internet purchases. Thus, it remains to be seen whether it can retain its first-mover advantage in the long run. The following sections discuss the three most salient obstacles to continued use of credit cards as the dominant Internet payment system: fraud, privacy, and the need to facilitate micropayments.

(a) *Fraud* The most obvious problem is the astonishing rate of fraud perpetrated through the relatively insecure system of credit-card authorization as it currently exists for Internet transactions. In a face-to-face credit-card transaction, the merchant can swipe the card. When that is done, the terminal on which the card is swiped transmits to the card issuer (or its agent) data on the back of the card (unknown to the cardholder) that allows the issuer to verify that the card in fact is physically present. Although it is possible to forge a card, it is relatively difficult. Thus, because of the costs of the technology necessary to collect that data and apply it to forged cards, only sophisticated and professional criminals will be able to produce such cards.

By contrast, in an Internet transaction (included in the industry within the category known as card-not-present transactions), the merchant often will proceed with no information other than the card number and the billing address (the idea being that it is harder for a malefactor to obtain a billing address than it is to obtain a card number). As it happens, it is not difficult for malefactors to obtain the credit-card number, either from a credit-card slip used in a face-to-face transaction or by hacking into the records of Internet merchants from whom cardholders have made purchases. The billing address of course ordinarily can be obtained from public records (such as a telephone book or Internet database). The ease of obtaining that information has led to a rash of so-called identity thefts, in which malefactors masquerade for a considerable period of time as another individual, often even obtaining new credit cards in the name of other individuals. Those thefts have been a particular problem on the Internet (where, of course, the risk of being caught is relatively small); they were one of the main causes of the failure in late 2001 of NextBank.

The problem is exacerbated by the ease with which a cardholder can disavow an Internet transaction in which it in fact did participate. That seems to be particularly common for merchants that sell information that is delivered over the Internet. (It is harder for cardholders to disavow transactions in which tangible goods were delivered to their home or office.) Online merchants try to counter that activity through a variety of responses, which collectively consume 1 to 2 percent of their revenues. About half of online merchants now require the "card verification code," a three-digit code that is not part of the card number and not embossed on the card, but included in the string of digits encoded on the magnetic stripe and visible on the signature strip on the back of the card. About 45 percent of merchants currently use some form of a "hot list," which identifies card numbers known to be stolen. Others use sophisticated analysis of transaction information to identify transactions that match profiles of fraudulent behavior. Finally, the newest response is geolocation technology, which examines the ISP through which the purchaser is connecting to assess the likelihood that the purchaser would be contacting the merchant from that location. But even with those products, the costs of fraud are high. Fraud in the early days of the commercial Internet ranged as high as 5 to 15 percent of all transactions, but persistent technological advances have brought the rate down to about 33 basis points (one-third of 1 percent), about five times the rate for face-to-face transactions.

For legal and historical reasons, losses from unauthorized transactions on the Internet are not treated the same way as losses from unauthorized transactions in conventional face-to-face retail transactions. As discussed above, issuers absorb losses from unauthorized transactions in the conventional face-to-face setting. Because the risk of fraud in transactions where the card is not present is so high, for many years the major credit-card networks excluded mail-order and telephone-order (MOTO) transactions from their networks. With the rise of the credit card as a major payment device of the American consumer, it became increasingly important to mail-order and telephone-order merchants that they be permitted to accept credit cards. So, after discussions with the credit-card networks, MOTO merchants began conducting card-not-present transactions, but they agreed to accept the risk that those transactions would be unauthorized. When Internet merchants began accepting credit cards, they became subject to the same card-not-present rules developed for MOTO transactions.

Still, even though Internet merchants bear the losses from fraud, credit-card issuers have a strong incentive to respond to fraud losses: If fraud losses remain as high as they have been to date, Internet merchants will have a powerful incentive to encourage their customers to use other payment systems that are more secure. The simplest possibility for the credit-card issuers would be to disseminate some PIN-like password authentication system. This is an almost revolutionary step, because for years only the debit-card system has relied on personal identification numbers (PINs); the credit-card system (as well as the debit-card systems promulgated by Visa and MasterCard) have stubbornly relied on the signature and account number alone as adequate for authentication. Finally, though, Visa and MasterCard introduced such products in the fall of 2001. The first step in getting those products deployed was to persuade individual issuing banks to implement systems to issue and check passwords. That process has been successful; more than 90 percent of Visa issuers, for example, participate in the "Verified by Visa" program. MasterCard's parallel program is called SecureCode.

The second step is to persuade merchants to modify their check-out software to require the consumer to enter the password. Merchants obviously have an incentive to keep their check-out procedures as simple as possible — data indicate that a substantial number of Internet purchases are lost from consumer frustration caused by lengthy check-out procedures. Nevertheless, to date merchants have been cooperative, at least in making the systems available to their customers. The incentive has been the willingness of the major networks to consider transactions authorized through the new PIN systems as card-present transactions: The issuers of the cards accept the risk of loss on those transactions. (The experience with debit-card transactions in the offline world suggests that fraud in those transactions will be quite low. Retail fraud on PIN-based cards is about one-twentieth the rate of fraud on signature-authorized cards.)

The problem, however, has been to persuade customers to sign on to those systems. The consumer is not liable in either event, so the consumer has little incentive to go to the trouble of collecting a PIN from the consumer's issuer for credit-card transactions. Thus, unless the issuer or the merchant *forbid* Internet transactions without a PIN (which no merchant or issuer has done to date), it is not at all obvious why any consumer would use the system.

A more dramatic possibility is that credit-card issuers could deploy "smart" cards. In this context, "smart" cards or "chip" cards refer to credit cards enhanced with an integrated-circuit chip. That chip includes a microprocessor and storage device which allows the card to perform a variety of functions, including — crucially for security reasons — a card-authentication function. When the cardholder first received the card, it would insert the card into a card-reader attached to a personal computer and enter a PIN.

Thereafter, to use the card in a card-not-present credit-card transaction, the cardholder would have to enter the card in the reader and enter the correct PIN. If the card and PIN are entered properly, the issuer can verify with considerable certainty that the card in fact is present and that the proper PIN has been entered. If the card and PIN were not properly entered, the issuer would decline the transaction. It is expected that those precautions would lower the fraud rate to something approaching the rate for PIN-protected transactions in the current environment.

The biggest obstacle to that solution is in getting the cards and readers disseminated to cardholders. Credit-card issuers have been looking for ways to use smart-card technology for years, without success. Several times in the last decade major American issuers have initiated widely advertised programs to issue general-purpose credit cards enhanced with such a chip; American Express's Blue card being the most prominent. No issuer, however, has yet succeeded in shifting a substantial portion of its Internet purchases to that technology.

Deployment of smart cards has been much more successful in other countries, but the driving force in most cases (as in the UK "Chip-and-PIN" program) has been brick-and-mortar fraud, not Internet transactions, which are much less important to overseas issuers than they are to American issuers. Thus, even in those countries in which consumers have chip-enhanced smart cards, they do not appear to use them commonly to make Internet purchases.

Looking even farther ahead, the "holy grail" of fraud prevention would be some form of "biometric" identification, which would authenticate transactions based on verification that certain physical characteristics (retina, fingerprint, or the like) of the individual presenting the card match the previously recorded physical characteristics of the person to whom the card was issued. For example, a smart card might store a record of the cardholder's fingerprint and prevent use of the card without entry of a matching fingerprint into a fingerprint pad connected to the computer through which the card was being used. Biometric technology has struggled for a variety of reasons, including not only technical difficulties but also consumer resistance. That technology has received a big boost in recent years from government initiatives that have forced the development of technology for use in, among other things, passports of foreign nationals entering this country. There is some possibility that the improvement in that technology might lead to its use in the credit-card market in the coming decade, but it remains quite a speculative subject.

(b) Privacy Even if the fraud problems are resolved, credit cards still face other serious issues, which continue to undermine the use of credit cards for Internet purchases. The most important of those issues surely is the privacy problem. For this context, the privacy problem has two manifestations. The first is the prospect, mentioned above, that interlopers will steal data from Internet merchants. In several widely publicized incidents, malefactors have succeeded in stealing large volumes of consumer data from prominent Internet merchants. The prospect that their transaction data will be compromised is likely to trouble some consumers even apart from the burden they will face in convincing their issuers to credit them for any unauthorized transactions that may result.

A more serious problem for consumers is the likelihood that the merchants and issuers themselves will make use of the data for reasons that trouble consumers. As a greater share of consumer purchases drift into online venues, the possibility continuously grows of aggregating individual consumer profiles at greater levels of detail. Consumers find it chilling to contemplate a database in the hands of direct marketers (or investigative reporters) that describes in detail the kinds of books, music, videotapes, clothes, and information they tend to purchase.

It is difficult to assess the seriousness of that problem. For many years, privacy concerns were thought to be a substantial obstacle that would keep consumers from using credit cards on the Internet and foster the development of more anonymous payment systems, such as so-called electronic-money systems. But the rapid growth of Internet retail transactions and the dominance of credit cards in those transactions suggest that the privacy issue may trouble consumers less than many observers expected.

The industry also has developed a technological response in the form of disposable credit-card numbers that inhibit the aggregation of payment information. Those systems (pioneered by Orbiscom, but now widely available) provide software to the purchaser's personal computer. The software generates a new credit-card number for each transaction. When the merchant sends the number through to the issuer, the number is valid only for that transaction. Thus, the merchant is no longer in a position to aggregate information based on the credit-card number (which will differ in each transaction). The only party in a position to aggregate information is the issuer (or, depending on the structure of the system, a third party generating the disposable numbers).

Thus, at least for the time being, it seems unlikely that privacy concerns will pose a substantial obstacle to the continued primacy of credit cards as a vehicle for Internet retail payments. However serious the concerns might be, the available technological solutions should solve the problem without significant disruption.

(c)   Micropayments   Another problem that confronts credit cards is that of micropayments. Because of their relatively high fixed costs, merchants generally have found credit cards unsuitable for transactions much below $10 in amount. In the early days of the Internet, it was expected that much of Internet commerce would involve information merchants selling information piece by piece for very small amounts—twenty-five cents or less in the near future, perhaps even fractions of a cent in decades to come. Those transactions could not occur, however, unless merchants could find a practical way to obtain payment. If credit cards could not provide that, then some other alternative would be necessary. As with the privacy issue, observers thought that the natural solution was a purely electronic payment system.

As it happens, however, the market has developed quite robustly without such a system, relying for payment on a variety of relatively conventional devices, most but not all of which rely on credit cards or checks in some way. First, most existing information merchants (primarily newspapers and sports-information sources) do not charge piece-by-piece, but instead charge a monthly subscription fee in an amount adequate to justify conventional credit-card payment. Economists studying the issue suggest that the piece-by-piece pricing model will be useful in many fewer contexts than observers originally had expected. Generally, they reason that the development of sophisticated bundling techniques by merchants, together with customer aversion to piece-by-piece pricing plans, has lessened the importance of the issue. Of course, it is entirely possible that customer aversion was caused not by piece-by-piece pricing models, but by the "clunky" software available for such programs several years ago. Software programs available now, not surprisingly, work much more smoothly and simply, and thus might be more acceptable to consumers.

Moreover, even when merchants do charge piece-by-piece, the problem has been resolved by one of a variety of payment aggregators that have arisen. Those aggregators provide software that gathers up a large number of a consumer's small transactions and then uses a conventional payment system to charge the consumer for the transactions periodically (normally once a month). For example, a consumer might receive a single monthly bill for all Internet information purchases, which the consumer could pay with a conventional check or credit card. In other systems, such as the highly touted Bitpass system that went online in late 2003, the consumer deposits money in advance (perhaps $20) through some conventional payment system and then replenishes the funds whenever they are consumed. The provider typically provides the consumer a PIN to help ensure authenticity of the transactions. Yet another model (used most prominently by MicroCreditCard) aggregates a number of charges and then when the aggregate amount reaches a certain point (perhaps $8 to $10), charges the aggregate amount to the customer's credit card.

A variation on that model (used by companies like NTT DoCoMo in Japan, and by iPin and Trivnet in this country and in Europe) works through an Internet or wireless service provider to obtain a reliable identification of the payor from the payor's point of access to the Internet or wireless network: The Internet service provider and wireless service provider invariably are able to identify in a reliable way the account of the person accessing their systems. (At least theoretically, that person might not be the accountholder, but that seems to be a relatively small problem under current conditions.) Relying on that identification, those systems can dispense with the PIN requirement, which makes the transactions simpler to execute. Those systems then charge for the transactions by adding the appropriate charges to the monthly bill for Internet or wireless access. Because those payments come much later (perhaps 45 days after the transaction by the time the bills are sent and collected), merchants often must wait a considerable amount of time to obtain payment. But the charges merchants incur to obtain payment through those systems are so much lower than those associated with traditional credit cards that the systems are relatively attractive.

In sum, although it is much too early to identify what response will resolve the problem definitively in the long run, the technological responses discussed above seem to have solved the micropayment problem quite adequately for the time being. They might result in the insertion of an intermediary between credit-card issuers and merchants, but it is not clear that they will result in a major shift of Internet payments away from the credit card.

C.   Debit Cards on the Internet

In the early days of the Internet, credit cards had an appreciable advantage over debit cards largely because debit cards were relatively uncommon at the time. Debit cards, however, have made major advances in the United States since 1999, so that they now are used almost as frequently as credit cards. Moreover, because about 20 percent of American consumers do not have a credit card (including many teens and elderly persons that might be ideal customers for Internet retailers), Internet retailers that accept both credit cards and debit cards have access to a broader customer base than those that accept only credit cards. Moreover, acceptance of PIN-less debit cards is easy, because those transactions can be processed with precisely the same interface as Visa and MasterCard credit transactions.

Several other reasons apparent from the discussion above also motivate Internet merchants to accept debit cards. First, Internet merchants also prefer debit cards because of the smaller interchange fee they pay. Second, Internet merchants should prefer the finality of debit cards. As discussed above, credit-card transactions have been plagued with chargebacks. The more limited chargeback rights of debit cards should be particularly attractive to merchants. Third, the security of the debit card makes it a good substitute for the credit card. As discussed above, many Internet merchants are losing substantial revenues to claims of unauthorized transactions. If a product based on the PIN-based debit card could provide payment with the success rate that PIN-based debit cards enjoy in the offline environment, merchants would eradicate more than 99 percent of those fraud losses.

Given those advantages, it is not surprising that online retailers prefer debit-card transactions. For example, one recent survey of the top 25 online merchants suggested that they actually receive about 5 percent of their online payments by debit card, but that they would prefer to be paid by debit card in 25 percent of their transactions.

To date debit-card transactions on the Internet overwhelmingly are conducted with signature-based debit cards (VisaCheck and MasterMoney cards). Because those cards do not require a PIN, they can be used at most major online retailers in precisely the same way consumers use credit cards. Merchants would prefer that their customers be able to use PIN-based cards, both because of the diminished risks of fraud and because the charges they would pay for the transactions would be smaller as well. As it happens, however, it has been harder than expected to develop an Internet version of the debit card that would allow consumers to make PIN-protected debit transactions from the personal computer. The most likely significant advance in the next few years will be widespread deployment of such a product. Unlike the parallel credit-card programs, banking experts expect it to be quite easy to get customers to use PINs with those cards, because customers are accustomed to using PINs with those cards at ATMs and at retail locations

D. ACH Transfers (WEB Entries)

The last advance in Internet payments has been the development of an ACH transfer that can be used to make retail Internet purchases. Those transactions have grown exponentially in the years since the promulgation in early 2001 of new NACHA Rules governing "Internet-Initiated Entries"—WEB entries in the NACHA terminology. In 2003, customers initiated almost 700 million of those transactions, with an average amount of $291. NACHA reports that 80 percent of the payments have been to pay bills, 18 percent to transfer funds, and about 1 percent to make purchases.

The NACHA Rules make WEB systems generally available to all banks that participate in the ACH system, which in turn should facilitate merchants in incorporating those systems into their Web sites so that consumers can use them. Because about one in five consumers in the United States lacks a credit card, the availability of this system offers merchants a way to serve those customers. Thus, although retail Internet use has a relatively small market share (about 6 percent of payments in 2003), it is expected to grow rapidly, as major merchants like Wal-Mart have recently started accepting such payments at their sites.

Those systems start with a software program that a buyer and a seller place on their respective computers. If the buyer wishes to purchase an item using one of the ACH-check systems, a check-like form appears on the buyer's screen. The buyer fills out the form, except for the signature line (which typically is marked "No Signature Required"). When the buyer confirms the information on the form, the software encrypts the information and transmits it to the service provider. The service provider then generates a WEB ACH debit entry based on the information and clears that information through the normal ACH system discussed above. That entry is processed and cleared in much the same way a typical ACH transaction is cleared. Thus, the buyer's account is debited one or two business days later, and the merchant receives the funds at that time (or perhaps a few days later, depending on the system's specific features). Figure 32.1 illustrates that process.

Those transactions functionally are quite similar to debit-card transactions: They result in a contemporaneous transfer of funds from the purchaser's bank account to the seller, and the EFTA and Regulation E govern them. The principal difference is the information that the purchaser must provide: normally information that identifies the customer's bank account. Industry officials expect considerable consumer resistance to providing that information to a retailer; although the legal and practical risks are not in fact very different, consumers are much more willing to provide their credit- or debit-card number to an Internet merchant than the information from the bottom of a check that identifies their bank account.

As with all ACH transactions, the system places fraud risks on the party that sends the entry to the system. Thus, if a transaction is fraudulent, the provider that is a member of the ACH system and entered the entry will bear the loss: It will have to return the funds to the account from which they were taken and will be left with a right to pursue the malefactor. Again, NACHA strongly urges those providers to use robust methods of identifying parties that enter transactions.

When the buyers are consumers (rather than businesses), those transactions are subject to all of the protections of the EFTA. Thus, as discussed above, the consumer ordinarily will have the right to disavow any transaction that is unauthorized. The consumer also will have the benefit of the EFTA dispute-resolution mechanism and will be able to see the identity of the payee on its monthly bank statement.

E. Foreign and Cross-Border Payments

Because consumers in countries other than the United States use credit cards much less frequently, credit cards are not as dominant for Internet retail purchases in other countries. They are, however, the leading method of paying for Internet retail purchases. Interestingly, jurisdictions outside the United States generally have statutory protections for the users of those cards that are much less protective than those in the TILA/Z regime discussed

Figure 32.1
ACH "Checks"

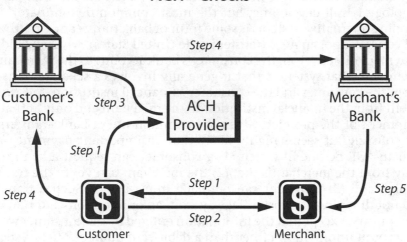

Step 1   The Customer sends payment information to the ACH Provider
         (probably through a link at the Merchant's Web site). The
         information should include the information from the MICR line
         of the Customer's check (the ABA routing number of the Customer's
         Bank and the Customer's account number at the bank).

Step 2   Based on the commitment to pay represented by that
         information, the Merchant completes the transaction. It might
         ship the goods at that time, or it might wait a few days to
         receive payment.

Step 3   The ACH Provider sends the ACH debit entry to the Customer's
         Bank.

Step 4   The Customer's Bank responds to that entry by removing funds
         from the Customer's account and sending them to the
         Merchant's Bank (through ACH network).

above. There is a great deal of variety among the specific protections, but often
there are no protections at all, and where protections exist, they often have
more exceptions than the rules in TILA and Regulation Z. Thus, disputes about
payments in those countries are much more likely to be resolved under the
contracts between the issuer and the cardholder or between the issuer, the
merchant, and the merchant's financial institution.

In the absence of a substitute for the credit card, one consequence has been
to make it more common in other countries to pay for an Internet purchase
with an offline payment method—a check sent through the mail or cash on
delivery. In Japan, for example, a common model involves the retailer mailing
the goods to a convenience store near the purchaser's home. The purchaser
can obtain the goods by going to the convenience store and paying for them
at that location. Similarly, statistics indicate that as of 2002 almost two-thirds
of German online shoppers regularly used cash on delivery as a payment
method. Few U.S. online shoppers have ever used that method.

In the absence of credit cards, retailers that wish to establish a presence in foreign markets have strong incentives to accept alternate forms of payment. Technology is still developing, but the most common denominator among developing alternative systems is some form of bank transfer or giro (the functional equivalent of an ACH transfer in the United States), which would result in a payment directly from the consumer's bank account to the merchant. The problem with that system is that it generally involves a separate transaction between the consumer and the consumer's financial institution, followed by a payment from the financial institution to the merchant and only at that point by shipment of the product. Given the common use of bank transfers in so many countries, it seems highly likely that an important payment product eventually will be one in which (1) a consumer can request a bank transfer directly from the merchant's site, (2) the merchant can verify the transfer in real time, and (3) shipment can be made immediately. Such a transaction would not differ in any substantial way from an online debit-card transaction in this country, except that the information entered by the consumer would be bank account information rather than a debit-card number. Such systems are not, however, widely deployed at this time.

At this time, cross-border payments are an even smaller market than foreign payments. Because most of the major retailers operate a number of country-specific sites, the great majority of Internet retailing occurs on a "national" basis. To date, transactions that occur across borders are predominantly settled by Visa, MasterCard, American Express, or JCB, because those are the only major card brands with substantial cross-border clearance networks. The law that applies to domestic purchases by the cardholder usually would govern payments in those transactions. The agreement between a card issuer and cardholder establishes the cardholder's obligations, and TILA and the EFTA limit those obligations, regardless of whether the card is used to buy something from Amazon.co.uk, from a brick-and-mortar retailer in London or Tokyo, or a restaurant in the United States. The principal difference is that the right to withhold payment under TILA §170 does not technically apply to transactions overseas. (Indeed, strictly speaking it does not apply to transactions more than 100 miles from, or outside the state of, the cardholder's residence. In practice, most issuers do not enforce any geographical limitation on rights under that section.)

The credit card is likely to face serious competition for cross-border payment systems that can affect transfers directly from bank accounts. In the absence of international bank-clearance systems—something that the industry is only beginning to develop—those payments are not likely to be generally available for some time. They do, however, have considerable potential within closely integrated economies like the member states of the European Union or NAFTA, where those kinds of clearing networks already are developing.

F.   A Note on Mobile Payments

Although Internet retail transactions have been growing steadily over the last few years, the most rapid growth has been in mobile transactions—transactions where the purchase is made over a cellphone or other mobile electronic device. M-commerce transactions in the United States are expected to amount to $600 million in 2005. Those transactions are much more common overseas, largely because of the greater penetration of the mobile phone: estimates are for $1.7 billion in Europe and $3.5 billion in Japan. For example, one recent press report contends that 40 percent of parking meter charges in Estonia are currently paid by use of a mobile phone with a proximity-pay-ment feature (discussed in more detail below).

Because the market is developing so rapidly, it is difficult to generalize, but a few points warrant attention. Security is the most serious issue that network operators confront. Because mobile-phone calls are notoriously insecure, it is important for payment information to be encrypted in some way that prevents it from being intercepted between the holder of the phone and the other party to the communication.

Generally, there are three main categories of payments. The first are so-called "in-band" or content payments, normally payments for information or content delivered directly to the telephone. For example, the most successful m-commerce application to date is the I-mode service provided by Japan's DoCoMo, which is used primarily to download "character" information. Other promising applications would deliver driving instructions, weather information, or the like. A second category is "out-of-band" payments — purchases in which a telephone is used to purchase something that cannot be delivered to the telephone. For example, industry officials hope to design systems in which pay-per-view television events can be purchased by mobile phone and charged directly to the telephone. The final category is proximity payments — when the telephone is used to make a payment by communication with a local device such as a parking meter or vending machine.

The methods of collecting for those payments are likely to develop over time, but presently two methods dominate. The first is the aggregation method discussed above for micropayments. For example, charges for i-Mode usage are simply added to the monthly mobile-phone bill; payments can be forwarded from the telephone company to the appropriate content provider. The second is for the merchant to use information sent from the telephone to conduct a contemporaneous credit- or debit-card transaction. That method makes much more sense for larger transactions, especially the out-of-band transactions discussed above. It functions in practice in just the same way as a conventional retail Internet purchase.

Problem Set 32

32.1. Cliff Janeway (your book-dealer client) comes to see you to talk about developments in his industry. He finds that many of the people from whom he buys books now have many of the items he needs available for sale over the Internet. The three sites that he has examined so far accept both credit cards and debit cards. He has heard a lot about fraudulent transactions on the Internet, and he particularly remembers the press coverage when credit-card numbers were stolen in 2000 from CD Universe. As a result, he is worried that if he starts making such purchases he will expose himself to a significant risk. What do you tell him about his risks of being charged for unauthorized transactions on his credit card? Would it matter if the retailer from whom he made the purchase forced him to enter a PIN or the CVV from the back of his card? Would your advice be any different for his debit card? What if he made the purchase with a WEB entry? Does it make sense that those things should change the outcome? TILA §133; EFTA §§903(5), 909; Regulation E, §205.6; Regulation Z, §226.12.

32.2. Shortly after Cliff leaves, you get a call from your old friend Don Branson, who recently opened a Web site selling a variety of content useful for philosophy professors and graduate students, ranging from analytical outlines of major works, to translations of works in other languages, to sample questions for use in undergraduate philosophy courses. He had a major sale last week of $4,400 to one Quentin Lathrop (or, at least, to someone sending e-mail from quentin.lathrop@hotmail.com). As required by his bank, Don's Web page collected Lathrop's credit-card number, billing address, and telephone number. All of those items appear to match information for the holder of the card that was used for the transaction. Also as required by his bank, Don transmitted that information to the bank before completing the transaction, and waited to be sure that the bank had authorized the transaction. Don then sent the purchased information to Lathrop electronically. Don was happy to receive the money from that sale a few days later, because it was by far the largest sale he ever had done.

Things got worse after that. About three weeks later, Don got a call from the bank saying that Lathrop had repudiated the transaction, claiming that he never visited Don's Web site or purchased anything there. Don's banker called this morning to tell Don that Don had to return the money from the transaction. Don (a philosopher by trade) is most puzzled. He feels that he did everything he was supposed to do, and has already sent the purchased information to Lathrop. He does not understand what the purpose of having the bank authorize the transaction is if he's still liable if something goes wrong. What do you tell him? Would your answers differ if the purchase had been made with a PIN-based debit card? A signature-based debit card? A WEB entry?

32.3. Would your answers to the previous questions be different if the purchaser used a cellphone to communicate with and received information from the merchant instead of an Internet connection? Would the EFTA apply? TILA? (Consider both the case where the charges are added to the cellphone bill and the case where the charges are posted to a credit-card or debit-card account.)

32.4. Your congressional representative, Pamela Herring, asks for your help on a new bill she is developing. She has been trying to update the protections Congress has provided for consumer payment systems. Her perception is that debit cards and credit cards are more or less substitutes for each other. Thus, she wonders whether you think it would be a good idea, at least in the Internet context, to extend the right to withhold payment from TILA §170(a) to the EFTA, so that debit-card Internet purchasers would have the same right to withhold payment as credit-card purchasers do. What do you think?

Chapter 8.   Letters of Credit

Assignment 33:   Letters of Credit —
The Basics

In form, the letter of credit is nothing more than a letter from a financial institution promising to pay a stated sum of money upon the receipt of specified documents. The basic concept is that the prospective payor goes to a bank and asks it to issue a letter of credit to the prospective payee.

As you will see later in this assignment, the letter of credit is attractive to the payee because issuance of a letter of credit provides an assurance of payment that has two particularly favorable aspects: The stakeholder (almost always a bank or similar financial institution) provides an advance commitment that it will make payment when the actual date for payment arrives, and the transaction payor has no right to cancel payment at any point after the institution makes that commitment. Thus, a payee that receives a letter of credit before performing faces a relatively small risk of nonpayment after it performs. Those features distinguish letters of credit from all the payment systems discussed in the previous assignments of this book because none of those payment systems provides an advance assurance of payment as firm as letter-of-credit transactions.

Although letters of credit have been common for centuries, the growth of other modern payment systems has limited the types of transactions in which they are useful. They continue to be widely used, however, to provide payment in international transactions for the sale of goods, a usage that has important implications for the continuing development of the applicable legal rules. The only major domestic context involves the "standby" letter of credit. Because standby letters of credit serve a credit function quite different from the function that letters of credit serve as a payment system, discussion of standby letters of credit is deferred to Chapter 10 (Assignment 38). Hence, this assignment and the next are devoted exclusively to the "commercial" letter of credit, a letter of credit used as a payment mechanism in sale-of-goods transactions.

Among other things, the increasingly international use of letters of credit has enhanced the importance of reliably uniform international legal principles. For decades, banks have responded to that concern by providing in most of their letters of credit for the application of the rules set forth in the Uniform Customs and Practice for Documentary Credits, a publication of the International Chamber of Commerce commonly referred to as the UCP. The current version is ICC Publication No. 500 (1993). Unfortunately, the rules established for letters of credit in the original version of Article 5 of the Uniform Commercial Code were not entirely consistent with the UCP. In response to that concern (among others), in 1995 the American Law Institute and the National Conference of Commissioners on Uniform State Laws adopted a revised version of Article 5 of the UCC, designed to bring American law into closer conformity with the UCP. See, e.g., UCC §5-116(c) (stating a general rule that in the event of a conflict between the UCP and Article 5, a letter of credit that incorporates the UCP should be interpreted in accordance with

529

the UCP). Thus, widespread adoption of the new Article 5 should bring international uniformity considerably closer than it has been.

A.   The Underlying Transaction

To understand the letter of credit as a payment system, it is necessary to examine it in the context of the transaction in which it commonly is used. For illustrative purposes, assume that a company in Missouri (the Toy Importing Company) has contracted to buy certain toys from a company in Hong Kong (the Toy Manufacturing Company) for a price of $250,000. The task of providing payment presents something of a "chicken-and-egg" problem. The Hong Kong company is reluctant to ship the goods overseas until it has been paid, but the American company is reluctant to send money to Hong Kong until it has received the goods. The letter of credit provides a compromise solution that addresses the concerns of both of the companies. The American company (as "applicant," see UCC §5-102(a)(2)) can ask its bank (Boatmen's National Bank of St. Louis, the "issuer," see UCC §5-102(a)(9)) to issue a letter of credit in favor of the Hong Kong company (as "beneficiary," see UCC §5-102(a)(3)), in which the issuing bank commits to pay $250,000 upon proof that the goods have been shipped. The charges for letters of credit vary considerably in different markets, but the major fees for issuing and providing payment on a typical letter of credit ordinarily come to about ¼ of 1 percent of the amount of the letter of credit ($625 in this case); for particularly good customers, the fees might drop by as much as 50 percent.

One problem with that arrangement is that the Hong Kong company may have neither a close relationship with Boatmen's in St. Louis nor a desire to travel to Missouri to obtain payment or resolve any disputes about its entitlement to payment. To solve that problem, Boatmen's can nominate a bank — a "nominated person" for purposes of UCC §5-102(a)(11) — with an office at the location of the beneficiary to process payment for the beneficiary. The nominated person proceeds on the implicit understanding that Boatmen's will reimburse the nominated person if it makes a payment under the letter of credit. Similarly, Boatmen's also might use a bank in the beneficiary's location to provide more expeditious notification of Boatmen's issuance of the letter of credit. A bank that plays the latter role — advising the beneficiary of the terms of the letter of credit that Boatmen's has issued — is known as an adviser or advising bank. UCC §5-102(a)(1). As you will see, the nature of a bank's role is important because Article 5 and the UCP impose different types of liability on nominated persons, advising banks, and issuers of letters of credit.

The most common practice in the transaction described above would be for Boatmen's to send the letter of credit to a Hong Kong bank (Hang Seng Bank in our example) that would assist the beneficiary at both stages of the transaction, as an adviser (when the credit is issued) and as a nominated person (when the beneficiary seeks payment). Thus, Hang Seng Bank would deliver the letter of credit to the Toy Manufacturing Company in Hong Kong and formally "advise" the Toy Manufacturing Company that the credit has been issued. The use of the adviser expedites the notification of the issuance of the letter of credit because Boatmen's usually can send the letter of credit to Hang Seng in Hong Kong by a secure electronic transmission that would be much faster and more secure than conventional delivery services. See UCP art. 11(a) (permitting issuance of a credit by "authorized teletransmission"); UCC §5-104 comment 3. Unlike the checking system, Article 5 can accommodate fully electronic letters of credit because it requires only a "record" of the letter of credit, see UCC §§5-102(a)(14), 5-104, not the writing required by UCC §3-104(a) for items in the checking system.

When Hang Seng receives that transmission, it prints out a hard copy of the letter of credit and authenticates a single original for delivery to the Toy Manufacturing Company (the beneficiary). Different banks have different ways of authenticating original letters of credit. Most use some combination of special secure paper (paper that is not easily photocopied) or a special colored-ink stamp, together with a manual signature by a responsible officer of the bank. Figure 33.1 sets out a typical letter of credit that would be used in such a transaction.

Figure 33.1
IRREVOCABLE COMMERCIAL LETTER OF CREDIT

DATE:

IRREVOCABLE LETTER OF CREDIT NO.

ADVISING BANK: APPLICANT:

HANG SENG BANK   TOY IMPORTING COMPANY

(ADDRESS)   (ADDRESS)

BENEFICIARY:

TOY MANUFACTURING COMPANY

(ADDRESS)

AMOUNT: $250,000.00

WE HEREBY ESTABLISH OUR IRREVOCABLE DOCUMENTARY LETTER OF CREDIT IN YOUR FAVOR.

DATE AND PLACE OF EXPIRY: SEPTEMBER 22, 1996 IN THE COUNTRY OF THE BENEFICIARY

CREDIT AVAILABLE WITH: ANY BANK

BY: NEGOTIATION OF YOUR DRAFT(S) AT SIGHT DRAWN ON THE BOATMEN'S NATIONAL BANK OF ST. LOUIS BEARING THE CLAUSE "DRAWN UNDER THE BOATMEN'S NATIONAL BANK OF ST. LOUIS LETTER OF CREDIT NO. _____" ACCOMPANIED BY THE DOCUMENTS INDICATED HEREIN.

1. COMMERCIAL INVOICE IN TRIPLICATE
2. PACKING LIST IN TRIPLICATE
3. CERTIFICATE OF ORIGIN IN TRIPLICATE
4. CERTIFICATE OF INSPECTION IN TRIPLICATE
5. FULL SET OF CLEAN ON BOARD OCEAN BILLS OF LADING CONSIGNED TO
    APPLICANT (AS SHOWN ABOVE) MARKED NOTIFY APPLICANT (AS SHOWN
    ABOVE) AND "BROKER" AND FREIGHT COLLECT

MERCHANDISE DESCRIPTION — MUST BE DESCRIBED IN INVOICE AS: TOYS PER
P.O. 1234

SHIPPING TERM: FOB HONG KONG

SHIPMENT FROM: HONG KONG TO ANY U.S. PORT

LATEST SHIPMENT DATE: SEPTEMBER 1, 1996

PARTIAL SHIPMENTS PERMITTED

TRANSSHIPMENTS PERMITTED

INSURANCE IS COVERED BY APPLICANT

DOCUMENTS MUST BE PRESENTED WITHIN 21 DAYS AFTER DATE OF SHIPMENT
BUT WITHIN THE VALIDITY OF THE CREDIT.

NEGOTIATING BANK IS REQUESTED TO FORWARD ONE SET OF ORIGINAL
DOCUMENTS BY COURIER TO (BROKER) AND THEIR STATEMENT TO THIS EFFECT
MUST ACCOMPANY THE REMAINING DOCUMENTS WHICH ARE TO BE SENT TO
US. ALL BANKING CHARGES, EXCEPT THOSE OF THE ISSUING BANK, ARE FOR
THE ACCOUNT OF THE BENEFICIARY.

UPON RECEIVING DOCUMENTS IN COMPLIANCE, WE WILL REMIT THE PRO-
CEEDS AS PER THE NEGOTIATING BANK'S INSTRUCTIONS.

THE AMOUNT OF EACH DRAFT MUST BE ENDORSED ON THE REVERSE OF THIS
CREDIT BY THE NEGOTIATING BANK. WE HEREBY ENGAGE WITH DRAWERS AND/
OR BONA FIDE HOLDERS THAT DRAFTS DRAWN AND NEGOTIATED IN CONFOR-
MITY WITH THE TERMS OF THIS CREDIT WILL BE DULY HONORED ON PRESENTA-
TION AND THAT DRAFTS ACCEPTED WITHIN THE TERMS OF THIS CREDIT WILL BE
DULY HONORED AT MATURITY. DRAFTS MUST BE MARKED AS DRAWN UNDER
THIS CREDIT.
THIS CREDIT IS SUBJECT TO THE UNIFORM CUSTOMS AND PRACTICE FOR DOC-
UMENTARY CREDITS (1993 REVISION) INTERNATIONAL CHAMBER OF COM-
MERCE PUBLICATION 500.

AUTHORIZED SIGNATURE

B. Advising and Confirming Banks

If the Hang Seng Bank does nothing more than advise of the issuance of the credit and agree to serve as a nominated person to process payment, the Hang Seng Bank has no independent liability on the letter of credit. Accordingly, it normally would charge only a nominal fee (such as $75) for that service. Neither status — as an adviser or as a nominated person — creates any obligation to honor requests for payment under the letter of credit. UCC §5-107(b), (c); UCP art. 7(a). Rather, those roles are purely procedural: providing the original credit, on the one hand, and receiving and forwarding requests for payment, on the other.

In most transactions involving imports into the United States, the foreign seller is satisfied with the credit of the American bank issuing the credit and thus is satisfied to obtain the procedural assistance from its local advising bank that is described above. Hence, in the letter of credit reproduced in Figure 33.1, the beneficiary was content with advice from Hang Seng Bank. By contrast, in a significant number of transactions involving exports from the United States, the American beneficiary is not satisfied with the credit of the foreign bank (something that might be rendered doubtful by, among other things, concerns about the stability of the country in which the foreign bank is located). To protect itself from the risk of relying on the foreign bank's credit, the American beneficiary frequently seeks a direct commitment of payment from its local bank. If the nominated person wishes to accommodate that concern, it will not stop at advising the credit, but will proceed to "confirm" the credit as well (see Figure 33.2). If Hang Seng Bank confirmed the credit, it implicitly would have accepted direct liability on the credit, just as if it had issued the credit itself. UCC §5-107(a); UCP art. 9(b). The fees for that service vary considerably based on the stability of the country in which the underlying letter of credit is issued and the reputation of the bank that issues it. Generally, though, an American bank confirming a letter issued in a solid country by a bank of ordinary reputation would charge something

Figure 33.2
Issuing the Letter of Credit

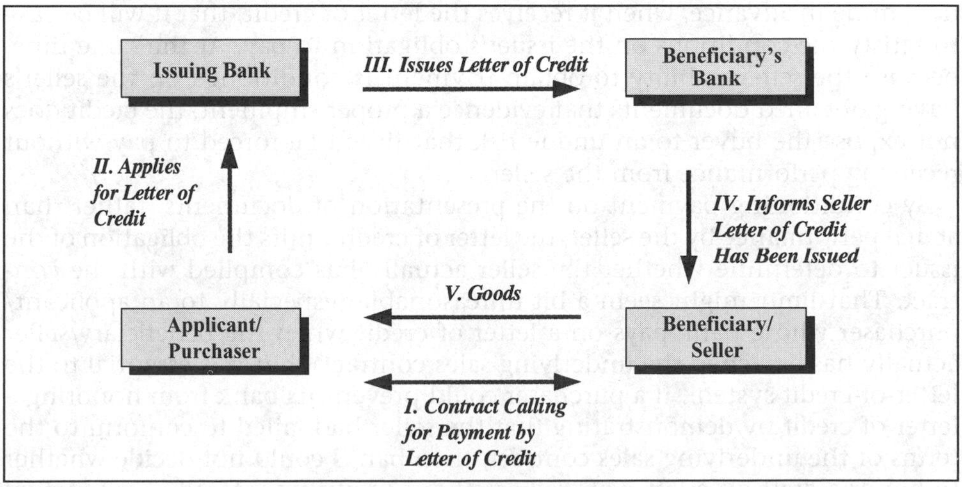

in the range of $\frac{1}{20}$ to $\frac{1}{10}$ of 1 percent per calendar quarter that the confirmation was outstanding. In our example of a $250,000 letter of credit, those fees would range from $125 to $250 if the confirmation was outstanding less than one quarter.

C.   The Terms of the Credit

As the opening paragraphs of this assignment explained, the principal reason that a seller seeks a letter of credit is to obtain a particularly firm assurance that payment will be forthcoming if the seller in fact ships the goods called for by the seller's contract with the purchaser. For the letter of credit to give the seller a satisfactory assurance of payment, the conditions on the obligation of the issuer need to be as objective as possible. Thus, payment ordinarily is not directly conditioned on the seller's satisfaction of the terms of the contract (a condition that frequently would be subject to good-faith dispute), but is conditioned instead on the seller's presentation of a request for payment (usually called a "draft"), together with specified documents that ordinarily would be available only if the seller in fact had satisfied the contract. See UCP art. 4 ("In Credit operations all parties deal with documents, and not with goods, services and/or other performances to which the documents may relate.").

For example, the letter of credit set forth in Figure 33.1 requires the seller to present five documents to obtain payment: an invoice and a packing list (items that the seller itself can prepare), a certificate of origin (satisfying customs regulations), a certificate of inspection (evidence of the quality of the goods that would be readily available at the point of shipment), and a set of bills of lading (evidencing receipt of the goods by a common carrier). If the seller actually has shipped the goods as required by the contract, it should be easy for the seller to provide those documents. Conversely, if the seller in fact has failed to ship the goods, it will be unable to obtain those documents (at least in the absence of some relatively bald-faced fraud). Thus, the letter of credit gives the seller satisfactory assurance of payment because the seller can determine in advance, when it receives the letter of credit, that it will be easy to satisfy the conditions on the issuer's obligation to pay. At the same time, because the seller's ability to obtain payment is conditioned on the seller's having obtained documents that evidence a proper shipment, the credit does not expose the buyer to an undue risk that it will be forced to pay without receiving performance from the seller.

By conditioning payment on the presentation of documents, rather than actual performance by the seller, the letter of credit limits the obligation of the issuer to determine whether the seller actually has complied with the contract. That limit might seem a bit unreasonable (especially to an applicant/purchaser whose bank pays on a letter of credit when the beneficiary/seller actually has breached the underlying sales contract), but it is essential to the letter-of-credit system. If a purchaser could prevent its bank from honoring a letter of credit by demonstrating that the seller had failed to conform to the terms of the underlying sales contract, then banks could not decide whether to honor a draft on a letter of credit without inquiring into all of the factual issues that would be relevant in a suit for breach of contract between the beneficiary/seller and the applicant/purchaser.

For the letter of credit to provide a reliable assurance of payment, it must create an entirely independent obligation between the issuer and the beneficiary so that the issuer is obligated to pay upon satisfaction of the specified documentary conditions, whether or not the beneficiary has complied with the beneficiary's underlying contract with the applicant. As the UCC puts it: "Rights and obligations of an issuer to a beneficiary... under a letter of credit are independent of the existence, performance, or nonperformance of a contract or arrangement out of which the letter of credit arises..., including contracts or arrangements between the... applicant and the beneficiary." UCC §5-103(d). Article 3(a) of the UCP sets out the same principle in more emphatic terms:

> Credits, by their nature, are separate transactions from the sales or other contract(s) on which they may be based and banks are in no way concerned with or bound by such contract(s), even if any reference whatsoever to such contract(s) is included in the Credit. Consequently, the undertaking of a bank to pay, accept and pay Draft(s)...or to fulfil any other obligation under the Credit, is not subject to claims or defences by the Applicant resulting from his relationships with the Issuing Bank or the Beneficiary.

As you will see in Assignment 34, the UCC does recognize a narrow exception to the independence principle, but it applies only in cases of egregious fraud by the beneficiary; it requires misconduct much more serious than a garden-variety contract dispute. Moreover, even the most egregious fraud does not undermine the issuer's *right* to honor the letter of credit in good faith.

That separation of the issuer's obligation on the letter of credit from the applicant's obligation on the underlying contract—often called the "independence" principle—has important implications for the solidity of the assurance of payment provided by the letter of credit. To pick one of the most common implications, the independence principle means that a bank is obligated to honor a proper draft on a letter of credit even if the applicant has gone into bankruptcy. Thus, although bankruptcy's automatic stay generally bars actions to collect debts of the applicant (11 U.S.C. §362(a)), the issuer's obligation to honor a letter of credit should continue in full force even during the applicant's bankruptcy.

The UCP includes a wide variety of rules designed to enhance the objectivity of the requirements that the parties set forth in a letter of credit. Those provisions not only provide guidance as to how issuers should draft letters of credit to limit ambiguity, but also frequently provide rules of interpretation that produce a meaning much more objective than the literal terms of the credit. For example, the UCP urges issuers to refrain from using vague "[t]erms such as 'first class', 'well known', 'qualified', 'independent', 'official', 'competent', 'local' and the like" to describe the parties issuing documents to be presented under a letter of credit. UCP art. 20(a). But if an issuer ignores that advice—for example, by issuing a letter of credit calling for a bill of lading issued by a "first-class" shipping company—the UCP directs the issuer to ignore that term in determining whether to honor a request for payment under the credit. Specifically, Article 20(a) calls for the issuer to honor a request for payment if the document in question "appears on its face to be in compliance with the other terms and conditions of the Credit and not to have been issued by the Beneficiary."

Similarly, as discussed above, Articles 3 and 4 of the UCP state that the parties to credits should deal only with documents, not with the underlying contract. If an issuer ignores that advice and issues a credit that contains conditions that cannot be satisfied by the presentation of documents, the UCP provides that the nondocumentary conditions should be ignored: "If a Credit contains conditions without stating the document(s) to be presented in compliance therewith, banks will deem such conditions as not stated and will disregard them." UCP art. 13(c); see UCC §5-108(g) (adopting the same rule).

The UCP's focus on objectivity also manifests itself in a number of interpretive rules that provide uniform answers to questions that frequently arise in the course of administration of letters of credit. By providing that definitional background, the UCP obviates the need for the parties to address those questions in the terms of each individual letter of credit. Article 39 of the UCP provides a good example, a three-tiered rule to address variations in price and quantity. First, if a letter of credit describes a quantity or price term as "about," "approximately," or "circa" some numerical figure, the UCP provides that the credit permits a 10 percent variance. UCP art. 39(a). Second, if the credit calls for shipment of a quantity of goods without any qualification, the UCP permits a 5 percent variance from the stated quantity. UCP art. 39(b). Finally, the credit requires precise adherence to a stated quantity term if the credit "stipulates that the quantity of the goods specified must not be exceeded or reduced" or if the credit "stipulates the quantity in terms of a stated number of packing units or individual items." UCP art. 39(b).

D. Drawing on the Credit

Once the seller/beneficiary has performed its obligations on the underlying contract, obtaining payment under the credit is a simple process. The seller collects the documents called for by the credit and then prepares a "draft" under the credit. The "draft" is nothing more than a letter written to the issuer, from the beneficiary, identifying the credit and seeking to "draw" on the credit.

When the issuer receives the draft and the accompanying documents, the issuer compares the draft and the documents with the letter of credit to determine whether the draft satisfies the letter of credit. The goal of the system is for that task of comparison to be as ministerial as possible: If the documents themselves conform to the terms of the letter of credit, the issuer should honor the draft and pay the sum called for by the letter of credit; if they do not, the issuer should dishonor the draft and refuse to pay. To emphasize the ministerial nature of the task, the UCC adopts a "strict compliance" standard and rejects the "substantial compliance" standard that had been adopted in some earlier American cases: "[A]n issuer shall honor a presentation that...appears on its face strictly to comply with the terms and conditions of the letter of credit." UCC §5-108(a); see UCC §5-108 comment 1 (discussing rejection of "substantial compliance" standard).

The ministerial task envisioned by the strict compliance standard is closely related to the independence principle discussed above. By requiring strict compliance with the terms of the letter of credit and ignoring circumstances not evident from the face of the documents submitted with the draft, the system helps to insulate the issuer's obligation on the letter of credit from disputes about the quality of the beneficiary's performance on the underlying contract.

As the following case suggests, the strict compliance rule is designed to facilitate an almost shamelessly literal interpretation of letters of credit. It is only a slight exaggeration to state that the issuer must dishonor a presentation that is inconsistent with the terms of the letter of credit, no matter how clear it might be that the beneficiary is entitled to payment under the beneficiary's underlying contract with the applicant. A right to payment on the underlying contract is a matter for resolution under ordinary contract principles in litigation between the parties to that contract. It is completely independent from the issuer's obligation, which depends entirely on the terms of the letter of credit itself.

Samuel Rappaport Family Partnership
v. Meridian Bank

657 A.2d 17 (Pa. Super. Ct. 1995)

HESTER, Judge.

. . . On May 7, 1985, McKlan, Inc., apparently seeking to take over the operation of a Philadelphia restaurant, agreed to lease from several individuals and entities property housing both the restaurant and a delicatessen. . . . Although the lease's effectiveness was contingent upon the Pennsylvania Liquor Control Board approving the transfer of the landlords' liquor license, it required McKlan to post a substantial cash security deposit with a named escrow agent pending the Board's decision. In addition, the lease obliged McKlan to substitute an irrevocable $100,000 letter of credit for the cash security deposit upon approval of the liquor license transfer. The terms of the lease required the letter of credit to be drawn on a reputable bank and made payable to the escrow agent upon the presentation of his sight draft[1] and certain other documentation. That documentation was to consist of the escrow agent's certification that McKlan had been given ten days notice of the sight draft's presentment and the landlords' certification regarding the existence of an uncured default.

In August, 1985, Marvin Orleans purchased the property, and the original landlords assigned their interest in the lease to him. I. David Pincus, Esquire, was named the new escrow agent. On October 2, 1985, at McKlan's behest, Central Penn National Bank issued the letter of credit required by the lease. The letter of credit provided that it would remain effective for a period of one year and that payment was contingent upon the bank's receipt of certain documentation. Specifically, it required the presentation of Mr. Pincus's sight draft along with his certification that McKlan had received ten days notice of the presentment. The letter of credit also required the

---

1. A sight draft may be defined as an instrument payable upon presentment.

submission of a certificate signed by Mr. Orleans indicating that an event of default had occurred under the terms of the lease, that McKlan was notified of the default's existence, and that McKlan failed to cure it in a timely fashion.

[Mr. Orleans subsequently died. After his death, Mr. Pincus submitted a draft on the credit to Meridian (successor by merger to the original issuer). That draft complied with the letter of credit in all respects except that the certificate was signed not by the deceased Mr. Orleans, but instead by Samuel Rappaport, the sole general partner of the entity that purchased the property from the estate of Mr. Orleans.]

Michael Bohley, one of Meridian's employees, examined both the letter of credit and the documentation supporting the sight draft's presentment. He noticed that Mr. Pincus failed to include in his presentment the required certificate signed by Mr. Orleans. Consequently, Mr. Bohley contacted McKlan to see if it would waive that requirement and permit payment. McKlan's representatives informed him that it would not consent to payment. Accordingly, Meridian refused to honor Mr. Pincus's sight draft.

On October 28, 1988, shortly after Meridian dishonored the sight draft, appellant filed a complaint against it. In that complaint, appellant asserted causes of action for both breach of contract and breach of the implied warranty of good faith. In addition, it requested a declaration of the parties' rights and obligations with respect to the letter of credit....

[The trial court] concluded that Meridian properly dishonored the sight draft due to the presentment's failure to comply with the strict terms of the letter of credit....

[A] transaction involving a letter of credit encompasses at least three distinct agreements: 1) the underlying contract between the customer and the beneficiary, the person entitled to demand payment; 2) the contract between the bank and its customer relating to both the issuance of the letter of credit and the reimbursement of the bank upon honoring a demand for payment; and 3) the letter of credit obligating the bank to pay the beneficiary.

Moreover, the primary purpose of a letter of credit is to provide the assurance of prompt payment upon the presentation of documents. The issuing bank's obligation under the letter of credit is independent from the other agreements and arises *only* upon the presentation of documents which conform to the requirements of the letter of credit.

In the present case, appellant attempts to overcome the necessity of presenting documents which conform strictly to the requirements of the letter of credit. Specifically, appellant asserts that the death of Mr. Orleans rendered ambiguous the question of the continuing vitality of the requirement of the letter of credit regarding the presentation of a certificate signed by him.... We reject this claim.

Generally, under the U.C.C., the law of contracts may be utilized to supplement the law relating to letters of credit as long as it does not interfere with the unique nature of letters of credit. Consequently, rules of contract interpretation which are not inconsistent with the nature of letters of credit may be utilized to examine the terms of a letter of credit, determine whether they are ambiguous, and resolve any perceived ambiguity. In this regard, we note: It is firmly settled that the intent of the parties to a written contract is contained in the writing itself. When the words of a contract are clear and unambiguous, the intent is to be found only in the express language of the agreement. Clear contractual terms that are capable of one reasonable interpretation must be given effect without reference to matters outside the contract....

It is undisputed that the requirement in the letter of credit relating to the presentation of a certificate signed by Mr. Orleans facially is unambiguous. Consequently, the question becomes whether that requirement latently was ambiguous. Appellant claims that extrinsic evidence establishing Mr. Orleans's death rendered the question of the requirement's continuing vitality latently ambiguous. . . .

The death of Mr. Orleans did not render the provisions of the letter of credit ambiguous regarding the continuing necessity of submitting a certificate signed by him in order to obtain payment. Rather, it rendered performance on the requirement impossible. Although appellant characterizes this conclusion as "ludicrous," we believe that it conforms with both the nature and purpose of letters of credit. As mentioned previously, the purpose of letters of credit is to assure prompt payment upon the presentation of documents. Moreover, the issuer's payment obligation comes into play *only* upon the presentation of conforming documents. Finding an ambiguity due to the death of a person mentioned in a letter of credit would have the practical effect of requiring banks and other issuers to go beyond the mere examination of documents to determine whether they facially comply with the terms of the letter of credit. Specifically, issuers would have to determine whether all such people are living and adjust the requirements of the letter of credit accordingly. Such a result would destroy the assurance of prompt payment and lead to uncertainty regarding the requirements necessary to obtain payment. Consequently, it would impair the basic utility of letters of credit.

Our resolution affects only Meridian's payment obligation under the letter of credit. It has no impact upon appellant's rights, if any, against McKlan. In addition, we note that had appellant's agents examined the terms of the letter of credit prior to completing the purchase of the leasehold premises, this entire litigation might have been avoided. Had appellant's agents examined the letter of credit's terms prior to the purchase, appellant could have declined to complete the transaction or made the purchase contingent upon Mr. Pincus and McKlan agreeing to modify the requirement at issue. In the event that appellant chose to exercise neither of those options and completed the purchase, it promptly could have attempted to invoke a lease provision requiring McKlan to take all action necessary to cause the letter of credit to remain in full force and effect during the term of the lease. Appellant's agents, however, did not examine the terms of the letter of credit until after McKlan had declared bankruptcy and defaulted and thus, could not exercise any of the described options. Accordingly, appellant must bear the burden of the impossibility of performance occasioned by Mr. Orleans's death. . . .

OLSZEWSKI, Judge, concurring:

We are constrained to concur with the majority that Mr. Rappaport cannot avail himself of the letter of credit. The letter required that Mr. Orleans, as landlord, sign a certificate that his tenants had defaulted on their rent payments. Orleans died and Rappaport bought the property, assuming all of Orleans's rights. When the same tenants defaulted, Rappaport signed the certification of default as landlord, explaining that he was Orleans's lawful assignee under the lease.

While common sense would dictate that Rappaport stood in Orleans's shoes as landlord, the law of letters of credit does not follow the dictates of common sense. Rather, it follows a rule of strict compliance. The letter required Orleans's signature, and once he died, the letter of credit became worthless. It was Rappaport's burden to discover this, and because he did not, he cannot blame the Bank for refusing to honor the letter. Such a departure from reasonable expectations might be unconscionable in the realm of consumer transactions. In the sophisticated area of high finance, it is a valid risk shifting device.

We therefore concur in the result reached, despite its harsh and counter-intuitive appearance.

An unfortunate side effect of the strict-compliance rule is its potential to allow issuers to seize on obviously irrelevant mistakes as a pretext for dishonoring drafts drawn on their letters of credit. The UCC and UCP respond to that problem in two ways. First, they provide that even the strict compliance standard can accept some minimal defects that would be condemned under an absolute compliance standard. Thus, the UCC calls for the question of strict compliance to be determined in accordance with "standard practice of financial institutions that regularly issue letters of credit" and makes it clear that "oppressive perfectionism" and "slavish conformity" to the literal terms of the credit are neither required nor appropriate. UCC §5-108(e) & comment 1. The UCP adopts a similar standard, calling for compliance to be determined in accordance with "international standard banking practice as reflected in these Articles." UCP art. 13(a).

Comment 1 to UCC §5-108 walks a fine line, trying to confirm the vigor of the strict compliance standard and, at the same time, to give a sense for the types of drafts that should be honored despite some type of noncompliance. Not surprisingly, the examples all involve cases of trivial and plainly nonsubstantive typographical errors. For example, in one case, a letter of credit called for "drafts Drawn under Bank of Clarksville Letter of Credit Number 105," but the draft referred to "Bank of Clarksville, Clarksville, Tennessee letter of Credit No. 105." Comment 1 states that the draft should have been honored even though it failed to conform to the letter of credit in three respects: the superfluous reference to Clarksville, Tennessee; the lower-case "l" in the word "Letter"; and the abbreviation of the word "Number." UCC §5-108 comment 1. Similarly, an authoritative interpretation of the UCP (from the ICC) holds that a bank should ignore an obvious typographical error, even if the error prevents the submitted documents from complying precisely with the requirements of the letter of credit. The interpretation offers the example of an address that refers to a location in an "Industrial Parl" rather than an "Industrial Park." ICC Opinions, Response No. 209. For a good example of mistakes that a court might forgive as substantial compliance, consider the case that follows.

Carter Petroleum Products, Inc. v.
Brotherhood Bank & Trust Co.

97 P.3d 505 (Kan. Ct. App. 2004)

GREEN, P.J.

This action involves a bank's wrongful refusal to honor a letter of credit. Carter Petroleum Products, Inc. (Carter) sued Brotherhood Bank & Trust Company (Bank) for its failure to honor a letter of credit. The Bank appeals from a judgment of the trial court granting summary judgment in favor of Carter on the letter of credit. On appeal, the Bank contends that the untimely presentment of the letter of credit and the noncompliance of the submitted documents with the letter of credit relieved the Bank of its duty to honor the letter of credit. We disagree and affirm.

Carter is in the petroleum business and sells fuel products to Highway 210, LLC (Highway 210), which operates a gas station. Highway 210 is also a customer of the Bank. On October 19, 2001, the Bank issued a letter of credit, No. 2001-270, in the aggregate amount of $175,000, for the benefit of Carter on the account of Highway 210.

By its terms, the letter of credit authorized Carter to draw on the Bank on the account of Highway 210, to the aggregate amount of $175,000 available by Carter's draft at sight accompanied by the following document: "STATEMENT SIGNED BY CARTER PETROLEUM PRODUCTS STATING THAT HIGHWAY 210, LLC HAS FAILED TO PAY OUTSTANDING INVOICES IN ACCORDANCE WITH TERMS OF PAYMENT."

The letter of credit further provided that "[e]ach draft must state that it is 'Drawn under Brotherhood Bank & Trust Company's Letter of Credit #2001-270 dated July 26, 2001.' This credit must accompany the draft(s)." The date of "July 26, 2001" in the aforementioned quotation was a typographical error because the letter of credit at issue was dated October 19, 2001. This letter of credit was a renewal of one of a series of previous letters of credit which were referenced in the lower margin of the letter of credit. The October letter of credit replaced the letter of credit dated July 26, 2001, in the amount of $125,000.

Additionally, the letter of credit stated "that all draft(s) drawn under and in compliance with the terms of this credit will be duly honored on delivery of documents as specified if presented at this office in Shawnee, KS no later than June 26, 2002." The letter of credit was also subject to the Uniform Customs and Practice for Documentary Credits, International Chamber of Commerce Publication No. 500 (1993 Revision) (UCP).

Hal O'Donnell, Carter's credit manager, delivered a draft request to the Bank for payment on June 26, 2002. Carter's draft request contained the following statement:

> Pursuant to the terms stated in the Letter of Credit #2001-270 dated October 19, 2001 (copy attached), Carter Petroleum Products, Inc., hereby exercises its option to draw against said Brotherhood Bank and Trust Company's Letter of Credit in the amount of $175,000 due to non-payment of invoices in accordance with terms of payment (copies also attached).

The account name listed on the draft request was Highway 210 Texaco Travel Plaza, LLC, not Highway 210, LLC, as listed on the letter of credit. In addition, the draft request contained a statement that Highway 210 had failed to pay outstanding invoices and contained a statement that Carter was exercising its rights under the letter of credit. Carter's draft request was accompanied by the letter of credit and copies of Carter's outstanding invoices to Highway 210.

O'Donnell arrived at the Bank at approximately 5 p.m. on June 26, 2002, to present the draft request. When O'Donnell arrived at the Bank, the lobby doors were locked, but after O'Donnell knocked on the door, an employee of the Bank admitted O'Donnell into the lobby. O'Donnell indicated he was there to see Ward

Kerby, the assistant vice president of the Bank. Upon meeting Kerby, O'Donnell handed him the draft request accompanied by the letter of credit and unpaid Carter invoices of Highway 210. The draft request was then stamped received on June 26, 2002, and was signed by Kerby with a notation that it was received at 5:05 p.m.

When O'Donnell delivered Carter's draft request to the Bank, the drive-through window was still open for business. O'Donnell maintained that had the employee of the Bank not opened the lobby, he would have delivered the draft request along with the attachments to the drive-through window attendant.

June 26, 2002, was a Wednesday. There is no dispute that the lobby of the Bank closed at 5 p.m. on Wednesdays. Similarly, there is no dispute that the drive-through lane at the Bank was open until 7 p.m. on Wednesdays. Additionally, inside the Bank there were several signs which alerted customers that any transactions occurring after 2 p.m. would be posted on the next business day.

The Bank dishonored Carter's draft request on the letter of credit on June 28, 2002. The Bank's dishonor notice stated two reasons: (1) The draft request was presented to the Bank after regular banking hours of the Bank on the date the letter of credit expired, and (2) the request failed to contain the specific language required by the letter of credit: "Drawn under Brotherhood Bank & Trust Company's Letter of Credit #2001-270 dated July 26, 2001."

Carter sued the Bank for its failure to honor the letter of credit. Both parties moved for summary judgment. The trial court ruled in favor of Carter and granted its motion for summary judgment. The Bank requested time to conduct further discovery concerning Highway 210's current debt to Carter. Carter furnished the Bank's counsel with copies of documents including an acknowledgment by Highway 210 that its debt to Carter exceeded the $175,000 face amount of the letter of credit. Later, the trial court entered its judgment in favor of Carter in the amount of $175,000, plus interest, costs, and attorney fees. . . .

On appeal, the Bank relies on two theories. First, the Bank contends that the attempted presentment of the draft request was untimely. The Bank makes two separate arguments. It argues that the presentment was untimely either because it occurred past 2 p.m. and, thus, should be considered on the next day's business or because the presentment occurred past 5 p.m., after the regular banking hours of the Bank. Second, the Bank argues that the draft request did not strictly comply with the terms of the letter of credit. . . .

Turning first to the issue of timeliness, we notice that there is no dispute that the letter of credit was subject to the UCP. Both parties agree that Article 45 of the UCP provides that "[b]anks are under no obligation to accept presentation of documents outside their banking hours." . . .

The letter of credit first stated that $175,000 was available by Carter's draft at "sight" accompanied by certain documents. It then stated that the letter of credit would be honored "if presented at this office in Shawnee, KS no later than June 26, 2002." The only office referred to in the letter of credit is the Bank's office at 7499 Quivira, Shawnee, Kansas.

O'Donnell arrived at the Bank just after 5 p.m., and the lobby was closed. The drive-through window at the Bank, located at 7499 Quivira, was still open. The letter of credit made no reference that the sight draft must be presented before the lobby closed on June 26, 2002. Similarly, it did not state that the draft needed to be presented before 2 p.m. or before 5 p.m. The letter of credit did not state that the draft needed to be presented to a loan officer, a vice president, or any particular person. The letter of credit simply stated that the money was available by draft at "sight" and would be honored "if presented at this office in Shawnee, KS no later than June 26, 2002."

Under the rules of construction, the presentment of the draft did comply with the requirements set forth for the time and place of presentment. The draft was presented at the Bank on June 26, 2002, at a time when the Bank was still open for business. Although the lobby was closed, by the terms of the letter of credit, anyone working at the Bank was authorized and could have accepted the draft, including the drive-through teller who was open for business.

Although the Bank may have intended to limit the presentment of a sight draft to either before 2 p.m. or 5 p.m. on June 26, 2002, the Bank did not specify in the letter of credit that presentment was to be conducted in this way. This was the source of the confusion; other than the date, no specific time of day was mentioned as to when it must be presented. For example, the letter of credit could have stated that it must be presented "no later than 5 p.m., June 26, 2002, at which date and time the letter of credit expires." The letter of credit failed to contain such language or any similar language to that effect. "Any ambiguity in a letter of credit must be resolved against the party drafting it." East Girard Sav. Ass'n v. Citizens Nat. Bank & Trust Co. of Baytown, 593 F.2d 598, 602 (5th Cir. 1979). The Bank was the sole drafter of the letter of credit. Accordingly, if the Bank wanted more specificity as to when and where Carter had to make presentment, the Bank could have included such provisions in its letter of credit. The ambiguities or lack of explicitness in the letter of credit stemmed from the Bank's own pen. As a result, the Bank's argument fails.

Next, we must consider whether the draft request strictly complied with the terms of the letter of credit. When do documents comply with the terms of the letter of credit so that a bank is forced to pay the draft is a difficult legal question. The UCC furnishes no easy answer to this question.

The Bank was to make funds available to Carter under its sight draft when it was accompanied by a "statement signed by Carter Petroleum Products stating that Highway 210, LLC has failed to pay outstanding invoices in accordance with terms of payment."

Additionally, the letter of credit required that "[e]ach draft must state that it is 'Drawn under Brotherhood Bank & Trust Company's Letter of Credit #2001-270 dated July 26, 2001.' This credit must accompany the draft(s)."

On June 26, 2002, Carter presented to the Bank a sight draft in the amount of $175,000. The account name on the draft was Highway 210 Texaco Travel Plaza, LLC. The draft contained the following statement:

> Pursuant to the terms stated in the Letter of Credit #2001-270 dated October 19, 2001 (copy attached), Carter Petroleum Products, Inc., hereby exercises its option to draw against said Brotherhood Bank and Trust Company's Letter of Credit in the amount of $175,000 due to non-payment of invoices in accordance with terms of payment (copies also attached).

The draft was accompanied by the letter of credit and Carter's outstanding invoices to Highway 210.

On appeal, the Bank contends that the demand was not in strict compliance because (1) the draft request stated the account name as "Highway 210 Texaco

Travel Plaza, LLC," not "Highway 210, LLC," and (2) the draft request did not contain the exact language from the letter of credit....

In the instant case, although the draft request submitted by Carter was not in complete conformity with the letter of credit issued by the Bank, it did contain all the necessary information requested by the letter of credit. Moreover, the Bank could not have been misled by the nonconformity.

Although the draft request listed the account name as "Highway 210 Texaco Travel Plaza, LLC," not "Highway 210, LLC" as requested in the letter of credit, the draw request was accompanied by the letter of credit which properly named the account. Obviously, there was no confusion caused by the different name referred to in the draft request because the Bank did not rely on this ground in rejecting the letter of credit. Moreover, the Bank failed to raise this particular argument before the trial court. Issues not raised before the trial court cannot be raised on appeal.

The draft request also contained all of the other pertinent information requested in the letter of credit. The letter of credit accompanied the draft, the draft stated it was drawn under Brotherhood Bank and Trust Company's letter of credit, and the draft contained the correct letter of credit number: #2001-270. Additionally, as required by the letter of credit, the draft stated that Carter was exercising its option to draw against the Bank due to nonpayment of invoices in accordance with the terms of payment.

The draft request differed from the requirements stated in the letter of credit in that the letter of credit mistakenly referred to the letter of credit dated July 26, 2001. In its draft request, Carter properly referred to the letter of credit dated October 19, 2001. Had Carter referred to the incorrect date as specified in the letter of credit, it would have been likely to cause confusion on the part of the Bank because the October 19, 2001, letter of credit was for a different amount and superceded the July 26, 2001, letter of credit. As a result, the Bank's argument fails.

The second response is more interesting: rules that require banks to give prompt notice of defects they perceive in drafts. A bank is precluded from justifying a decision to dishonor a draft by reference to any defect of which the bank did not promptly advise the beneficiary. UCP art. 14(e); UCC §§5-108(c), 5-108 comment 3. The idea is that if a defect is substantial enough to justify a dishonor, the bank will notice the defect when the bank first examines the draft and supporting documents. It would undermine the reliability of letters of credit to permit issuers to dishonor for illegitimate reasons (such as the bank's desire to accommodate the applicant or the bank's inability to obtain reimbursement from the applicant) and then prevail in subsequent litigation by identifying a defect that the bank failed to notice at the time of the dishonor and first noticed only in the harsh light of litigation.

The pretextual-dishonor problem is complicated by the fact that most drafts on commercial letters of credit do not satisfy the strict compliance standard. Although the rate of compliance surely differs from place to place, empirical research in the files of American issuers suggests that less than 25 percent of the drafts presented against commercial letters of credit comply with the letters of credit. The normal course of events is for the issuer to seek a waiver from the applicant of the identifiable defects. See UCP art. 14(c) (allowing issuer to seek such a waiver); UCC §5-108(a) (permitting an issuer to honor a nonconforming presentation when it has "agreed with the applicant" to do so). In the overwhelming majority of cases, the applicant grants the waiver because waiving the defect ordinarily is the simplest way for the applicant to provide payment to the beneficiary and thus to fulfill the applicant's obligation under its contract with the beneficiary. If the applicant declines to grant the waiver, the issuer sends a notice to the beneficiary specifying the defects identified by the issuer. That notice gives the beneficiary an opportunity to cure the defects.

E. Reimbursement

If the beneficiary makes an appropriate draft on the letter of credit and the confirming bank honors the draft and pays, the confirming bank has a statutory right to immediate reimbursement from the issuing bank. UCP art. 14(a); UCC §§5-107(a), 5-108(i)(1). The confirming bank ordinarily obtains that reimbursement by forwarding to the issuing bank the documents on which the confirming bank paid. If the issuing bank agrees that the draft was proper, the issuing bank reimburses the confirming bank. The issuing bank then has a right to reimbursement from the applicant. UCC §5-108(i)(1). In most cases, though, that right to reimbursement is not significant because the issuer ordinarily will have obtained payment from the applicant in advance or, at a minimum, will have required the applicant to maintain a deposit account balance with the issuer adequate to cover the amount of the credit.

Figure 33.3
Payment with a Letter of Credit

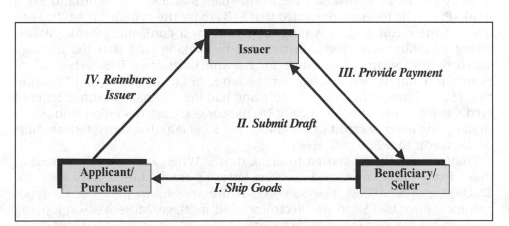

Problem Set 33

33.1. Jodi Kay at CountryBank calls first thing this morning to ask you about a minor letter-of-credit problem. Her problem arises from a letter of credit that her bank has issued, which states that it will provide payment for goods shipped "from the end of February 1998." She received a draft this morning including an invoice for goods shipped on February 21, 1998. She tells you that the letter of credit incorporates the UCP by reference. Can it be possible that the draft complies? UCP art. 47(a), (d).

33.2. Right after you get off the phone with Jodi, your assistant tells you that you have a call holding from Cliff Janeway (your book-dealer friend). Cliff is frustrated because he is having trouble collecting on a letter of credit for a large shipment of books that he just sent overseas. When he submitted a draft on the letter of credit, the confirming bank (SecondBank) told him that it was not obligated to pay Cliff because the issuing bank (FirstBank) had closed. Thus, the officer explained to Cliff, SecondBank would not be able to obtain any reimbursement if it paid Cliff. Accordingly, the officer argued, Second-Bank's confirmation of Cliff's letter of credit was unenforceable for lack of consideration. Cliff wants to know what he can do to obtain payment. UCC §5-105 & comment.

33.3. Ben Darrow (your banker client from FSB) has an appointment this morning to discuss two letter-of-credit problems with you. The first arises from a situation where FSB misfiled a draft presented on a letter of credit and thus failed to respond to it. In the case in question, the beneficiary presented a draft on January 5, 1998. Ben's bank did absolutely nothing until the beneficiary wrote in early February and repeated its demand for payment. Upon review of the letter of credit, Ben saw that the letter of credit called for payment based on documents covering a shipment of 100 cases of Llano Estacado wine at a price of "around $140 per case." The draft seeks payment of $120 per case. Ben wants to know if he is obligated to pay on the credit. What do you say? UCP arts. 13(b), 14(d) & (e), 39(a); UCC §§5-108(c), 5-108 comment 3.

33.4. Ben's second question involves a letter of credit that FSB received initially by an authenticated electronic-mail message from Portland State Bank (PSB). The message requested that FSB advise the beneficiary of the issuance of the credit and, if willing, also serve as a confirming bank. Always trying to follow procedures, Ben started by making sure that the message satisfied FSB's security procedure for transmissions from PSB. When it appeared to comply, Ben printed out the letter of credit, added an indication that FSB confirmed the letter of credit, and had the original confirmed letter of credit delivered to the beneficiary by messenger. Last week Ben honored a draft on the letter of credit in the amount of $500,000 (the stated face amount of the credit that Ben delivered).

That's where things started to break down. When Ben sought reimbursement from PSB, Ben learned that the letter of credit should have been for $50,000, not $500,000. The $500,000 figure appears to have been a typographical error by PSB in the electronic-mail message. Moreover, on looking through his file, Ben sees that he received a written copy of the letter of credit with the correct $50,000 amount in the mail the day after Ben delivered the letter of credit to the beneficiary. Does PSB have to reimburse FSB for the funds that FSB disbursed on PSB's letter of credit? UCP art. 11(a)(i); UCC §§5-107(a), 5-108(a), (i)(1).

33.5.   You return from lunch to an appointment with Jane Halley from Boatmen's Bank. She has a customer, Toy Importing Company (TIC), for whom she has issued a letter of credit in the form set forth in Figure 33.1. The letter of credit was to pay for a shipment of toys from Toy Manufacturing Company (TMC) in Hong Kong. Because TIC is dissatisfied with the toys, TIC wants Boatmen's to reject the draft that has been presented to Boatmen's under the letter of credit. Jane wants to be as accommodating as possible, but does not want the bank to dishonor a proper draft.

Acting under that letter of credit, TMC on September 21, 1996, submitted a draft with the appropriate documents to its main bank, Bank of Hong Kong. Bank of Hong Kong processed those documents, paid TMC on the letter of credit, and submitted the draft to Boatmen's on September 24, 1996. Jane wants to know if she can reject the draft because it was presented to her after the letter of credit had expired. She says she could understand if she was obligated to accept a draft presented to Hang Seng Bank (the advising bank) in a timely manner, but how can she possibly be obligated to respect a draft presented to some bank with which she has not had any prior dealings? What do you tell her? UCC §§5-102(a)(11), 5-102 comment 7, 5-108 comment 1; UCP art. 10(b)(i), (d).

33.6.   Before Jane leaves your office, she raises one other situation with you. One of her department's largest customers is the April Company, a department store that has a large volume of imported shipments. As part of a master letter-of-credit agreement with Boatmen's, the April Company and Boatmen's established special procedures for drafts submitted under letters of credit issued to some of April's regular suppliers. April and Boatmen's agreed that Boatmen's would provide same-day service on drafts for less than $25,000 submitted on designated "Express Draft" letters of credit. As part of that arrangement, April agreed that Boatmen's would not be obligated to review any of the documents submitted with such drafts, and Boatmen's agreed to reduce its normal processing fees by 50 percent for those drafts.

Jane's problem comes from a $20,000 draft submitted last week on one of the "Express Draft" letters of credit. Following its normal practice, Jane's department honored the draft in a few hours, without even looking at the underlying documents. When the documents got to April, April noticed that the documents did not include the bill of lading called for by the letter of credit. On further inquiry, April has discovered that the supplier/beneficiary (a small Indonesian company) in fact did not ship the goods in question; indeed, that company has become insolvent and stopped operations. April's shipping clerk called Jane yesterday and said that under the circumstances April did not want to reimburse Boatmen's for that draft. Jane tells you that she is not sure she wants to make an issue of the matter, but she wants to know whether she has a right to payment from April. What do you say? UCC §§4-103(a), 5-103(c), 5-103 comment 2, 5-108(a) & (i)(1), 5-108 comment 1 paragraph 6.

Assignment 34: Letters of Credit — Advanced Topics

Letter-of-credit transactions are not always as simple as the picture set out in Assignment 33. This assignment discusses three of the most significant complicating problems: error and fraud, assignment by the beneficiary of its rights under the letter of credit, and choice-of-law problems in transnational transactions.

A. Error and Fraud in Letter-of-Credit Transactions

Assuming that a letter of credit has been issued and delivered to the beneficiary without incident, the transaction can go awry in four major ways. First, the beneficiary can fail to perform, and the issuer can rely on that failure to justify its refusal to pay. That problem poses no difficulty for the payment system because it matches nonperformance by the beneficiary with nonpayment by the applicant. The other three problems, however, are more tricky: wrongful honor (the issuer honors a draft on the letter of credit despite the beneficiary's failure to present the required documents), wrongful dishonor (the issuer dishonors a draft on the letter of credit even though the beneficiary presented the required documents), and fraud (the beneficiary presents fraudulent documents that comply with the letter of credit even though the beneficiary did not in fact perform its underlying obligations to the applicant). The following sections discuss these three topics.

1. Wrongful Honor

A wrongful honor occurs if a bank honors a letter of credit even though the beneficiary fails to present the appropriate documents. The rules for responding to that problem are straightforward, much like the rules applicable to a bank's decision to honor a check that is not properly payable. First, because the honor was not a proper use of the applicant's funds, the issuer has no right to reimbursement. Interestingly, like the rule in UCC §4-401(a) that a bank cannot charge a checking account for a check that is not properly payable, the no-reimbursement rule does not appear explicitly in the statute. Instead, it must be implied from the direct statement that a bank is entitled to reimbursement when it honors a presentation "as permitted or required by [Article 5]." UCC §5-108(i).

The same analysis applies when a confirming bank honors a letter of credit improperly and seeks reimbursement from the issuer. As Assignment 33 notes, the confirming bank's right to seek reimbursement from the issuer for a proper honor derives from the statement in UCC §5-107(a) that a confirmer "has rights against . . . the issuer as if the issuer were an applicant and the confirmer had issued the letter of credit": The confirming bank (a quasi-issuer) seeks reimbursement from the issuer (a quasi-applicant) under the same rule that the issuer would use to seek reimbursement from the applicant. UCC §5-108(i)(1). Thus, the confirming bank's right to reimbursement from the issuer, like the issuer's right to seek reimbursement from the applicant, is implicitly limited to cases of proper honor. See also UCP art. 10(d) (obligating issuer to reimburse confirming bank that pays "against documents which appear on their face to be in compliance with the terms and conditions of the Credit").

It is rare for an applicant successfully to sue an issuer for wrongful honor, mostly because it is relatively uncommon for a bank to honor a draft that has significant defects without first obtaining a waiver from the applicant of any defects in the draft. That is true for several reasons. First, the bank is the party skilled in evaluating drafts; the bank is much more likely to find trivial defects that would justify dishonor (and much less likely to miss them) than the applicant. Second, by the nature of the transaction, the issuer is much more likely to have ongoing relations with the applicant than with the beneficiary. Accordingly, if anything, the issuer is more likely to err on the side of dishonoring a questionable presentation than honoring it.

It is easy to make too much of the last point because the issuer that decides to dishonor a draft on a letter of credit must consider not only the reaction of the applicant, but also the adverse effects on the issuer's reputation that flow from an insufficient readiness to honor its letters of credit. Financial institutions prize the solidity of letters of credit, and they prize their reputations as solid issuers of them. They do not lightly dishonor letters of credit just to accommodate their customer/applicants that become involved in commercial disputes with beneficiaries.

In the rare event that an applicant successfully establishes that the issuer has acted wrongfully in honoring a draft on a letter of credit, Article 5 limits the applicant's right to recover its funds from the issuer in just the same way that Article 4 limits the rights of the bank customer to recover funds from the payor bank that honors a check that was not properly payable. Specifically, UCC §5-117(a) recognizes a right of subrogation that permits the issuer to assert whatever rights the beneficiary has against the applicant on the underlying transaction. For example, suppose that an issuer honored a draft on a letter of credit even though the draft was not accompanied by the invoice required by the terms of the letter of credit. If the omission of the invoice was an inadvertent mistake and if the beneficiary in fact had performed all of its obligations to the applicant, the applicant would remain obligated to the beneficiary on the underlying sales contract even if it was improper for the issuer to honor the draft on the letter of credit. In that event, the issuer's right of subrogation under UCC §5-117(a) to the beneficiary's right to seek payment from the applicant would bar the applicant from any recovery from the issuer for the wrongful honor. That right of subrogation is particularly important in the standby letter-of-credit context, discussed in Assignment 38.

The same perspective informs the UCC's rules regarding damages for wrongful honor. Under UCC §5-111(c), an issuer that wrongfully honors a draft on a letter of credit is responsible to the applicant for "damages resulting from the breach, including incidental but not consequential damages, less any amount saved as a result of the breach." Comment 2 explains that when the beneficiary properly performs the underlying contract, the applicant frequently will suffer no harm because the issuer's breach will not affect the applicant's obligation on that underlying contract. Essentially, the funds paid out in the wrongful honor by the issuer are "a[n] amount saved as a result of the breach" for purposes of UCC §5-111(c) in the sense that the applicant would have been forced to pay the beneficiary for the properly delivered goods even if the issuer had dishonored the improper draft on the letter of credit.

The remedies for wrongful honor by a confirming bank operate in precisely the same way. First, the confirming bank is subrogated to the rights of the beneficiary against the applicant in the same way that the original issuer would be. UCC §5-117(c)(2). Second, the confirming bank's responsibility for damages for wrongful honor is limited in the same way as the responsibility of the issuer is limited under UCC §5-111(c). See UCC §5-111(c) ("To the extent of the confirmation, a confirmer has the liability of an issuer specified in this subsection.").

2. *Wrongful Dishonor*

Wrongful dishonor is the opposite problem from wrongful honor: A beneficiary presents documents that in fact comply, but the issuer nevertheless refuses to pay. Two features of the letter-of-credit system suggest that a generous measure of damages is appropriate here. The first, mentioned above, is the possibility that the issuer's relation with the applicant will influence the issuer's evaluation of a draft on the letter of credit; the issuer might try to curry favor with its customer (the applicant) by dishonoring a proper draft. The second is more fundamental, the emphasis that the letter-of-credit system places on certainty of payment. Unlike any of the payment systems discussed in the preceding assignments, the letter-of-credit system is designed to provide an up-front commitment that the issuer will pay. That commitment is designed to induce the seller to part with value by performing its obligations (shipping its goods) even before it receives payment from the purchaser — the shipment comes *before* payment, not at the same time as the payment. As part of that arrangement, it is important that the applicant have no right to stop payment. Thus, as discussed below, the only thing that can justify an issuer's refusal to pay a proper draft is egregious fraud.

For that system to work, the issuer must have a significant incentive to honor a proper draft. Given the importance of reputation in the commercial banking industry, the reputational harms from wrongful dishonor probably provide a more significant remedy than anything that the legal system can impose. But that is no reason for the legal system to refrain from providing relief. And so it is no surprise that Article 5 includes a strong remedial frame-work for the beneficiary faced with wrongful dishonor by the issuer.

The most important rule limits the excuses that the issuer can use to justify its decision to dishonor. Under the independence principle, the only proper justification for dishonor is a failure of the documents to comply with the terms and conditions of the letter of credit. Failure of the beneficiary to com-ply with the underlying contract with the applicant is not relevant (except for occasions of egregious fraud, discussed below). In this context, the UCC relies on this principle to bar the issuer from defending its decision to dishonor by reference to the beneficiary's failure to perform on the underlying contract. Thus, although UCC §5-117 generally grants the issuer broad rights of subro-gation (frequently broader than those recognized under prior law), UCC §5-117(d) specifically bars the assertion of subrogation by an issuer that does not honor a letter of credit. Thus, the issuer that dishonors generally cannot rely on defects in the beneficiary's performance on the contract to offset the issuer's obligation to the beneficiary on the letter of credit. See UCC §5-117 comment 2 ("[A]n issuer may not dishonor and then defend its dishonor or assert a setoff on the ground that it is subrogated to another person's rights.").

Article 5 also provides a relatively generous remedy for wrongful dishonor. First, the beneficiary can sue the issuer for specific performance and also recover any incidental damages that result from the breach, together with a mandatory award of attorney's fees and other litigation expenses. UCC §5-111(a), (d), (e). Furthermore, recognizing the likelihood that a delayed payment will cause significant harm, Article 5 includes an express right to interest as compensation for the delay. UCC §5-111(d). Moreover, in a depar-ture from the general trend in modern commercial transactions, Article 5 provides that the beneficiary has no obligation to mitigate damages. As com-ment 1 to UCC §5-111 explains, the drafters of the revised Article 5 concluded that it would not be sufficiently painful for the issuer to dishonor if the issuer could rely on the beneficiary to mitigate any losses flowing from the issuer's wrongful refusal to honor.

Nevertheless, the UCC stops short of allowing the beneficiary to receive fully compensatory damages. In particular, the UCC expressly bars the bene-ficiary from recovering consequential damages. UCC §5-111(a). As comment 4 to UCC §5-111 explains, that rule rests on "the fear that imposing consequen-tial damages on issuers would raise the cost of the letter of credit to a level that might render it uneconomic." That rationale is difficult to evaluate because it depends on assumptions about the extent to which the system otherwise provides issuers an adequate motivation to honor proper drafts. Several con-siderations, however, suggest that the issuer is adequately motivated even without potential liability for consequential damages. First, by including lia-bility for incidental damages, costs of litigation, and attorney's fees, the UCC remedy for wrongful dishonor already exposes the bank to damages that easily could exceed the amount of the letter of credit. Additional motivation is generated by the reputational harm discussed above, the problems a bank would suffer if it became known as a bank that was willing to bow to improper influence from its customer and dishonor proper drafts on its letters of credit. In context, it is implausible to suggest that issuers take lightly their obligation to honor proper drafts on their letters of credit.

3. *Fraud*

As with all payment systems, the most difficult problems are not those that arise from simple mistakes by the parties in the system, but those that arise from fraud. In the letter-of-credit system, two kinds of fraud warrant discussion: forged drafts on letters of credit submitted by a party other than the beneficiary and drafts that the beneficiary submits even though the beneficiary knows that it is not entitled to payment on the underlying contract.

(a) Forged Drafts. One type of fraud that can disrupt a letter-of-credit transaction occurs if an interloper — a party not acting on behalf of the beneficiary — submits a draft on the letter of credit. If the interloper deceives the issuer into honoring the forged draft, the issuer then will have expended the funds it was obligated to expend on the letter of credit, but will not yet have paid the beneficiary. That occurrence would pose a significant problem if the beneficiary subsequently submitted an authentic draft on the letter of credit.

UCC §5-108(i)(5) addresses that situation by stating that the issuer's obligation to honor a draft on a letter of credit is not discharged if it honors a presentation that bears a forged signature of the beneficiary. Thus, when the beneficiary submits an authentic presentation after a forged presentation that the issuer previously has honored, the issuer still must pay the beneficiary even though the issuer already has paid the forger. See UCC §5-108 comment 13 ("If the issuer pays against documents on which a required signature of the beneficiary is forged, it remains liable to the true beneficiary.").

Provided it did not know that the draft included a forgery, the issuer that honors a forged draft is entitled to reimbursement from the applicant. UCC §5-109(a) states that an "issuer, acting in good faith, may honor or dishonor" a presentation in which "a required document is forged." UCC §5-108 comment 12 states, in turn, that "[a]n issuer is entitled to reimbursement from the applicant after honor of a forged . . . drawing if honor was permitted under Section 5-109(a)." See also UCP art. 10(d) (issuer's obligation to reimburse confirming bank extends to presentations in which "documents . . . appear on their face to be in compliance with the terms and conditions of the Credit").

At first glance, a rule permitting the issuer to obtain reimbursement when it honors a forged draft appears difficult to reconcile with the principles discussed in the earlier payment systems. After all, a rule casting those losses on the issuer (like the analogous rules in the checking and credit-card systems) would enhance the issuer's incentive to scrutinize presentations carefully for authenticity and would motivate the issuer to develop mechanisms for issuing and designing letters of credit that make it more difficult for forgers to submit forged drafts. As it happens, however, the absence of any legal responsibility by issuers in those cases does not appear to be a significant problem. The relative rarity of such schemes — I am not aware of any case involving such a draft — suggests that issuers have not been unduly lax in examining presentations for forged signatures.

(b) Fraudulent Submissions by the Beneficiary. The hardest case for the letter-of-credit system involves not a forged draft submitted by a stranger to

the transaction, but a draft submitted by the beneficiary itself. The problem arises when the beneficiary does not perform its underlying obligations, but nevertheless presents documents that comply on their face with the terms of the credit. The focus of the letter-of-credit system on the documents that actually are presented to the issuer makes that case particularly difficult. A rule that broadly permitted issuers to dishonor based on uncertainty about the beneficiary's performance in the underlying transaction would remove the reliability that is the most attractive feature of the system. On the other hand, courts and legislators have been unwilling to accept a rule that unequivocally requires the issuer to honor the draft in that situation: That rule would leave beneficiaries an opportunity for fraud that almost everybody finds unacceptable.

In response to those directly conflicting concerns, the current version of the UCC articulates a compromise solution to that situation. The heart of that solution is a rule—the same rule that protects the issuer that honors a forged draft—that gives broad discretion to the issuer to decide whether it wishes to honor or dishonor the presentation. If the issuer is skeptical of the applicant's claim of fraud, the issuer is almost completely free to ignore the claim and honor the presentation. UCC §5-109 comment 2. The sole limitation on the issuer's right to honor is that the issuer act in good faith. UCC §5-109(a)(2). Because good faith in Article 5 requires nothing more than "honesty in fact," UCC §5-102(a)(7), the issuer ordinarily would be safe to reject any claim of fraud unless the applicant actually could convince the issuer that the claim was true.

The rule does not, however, *require* the issuer to honor fraudulent presentations solely because they are facially compliant. Rather, the rule gives the issuer latitude to dishonor a facially compliant presentation based on a claim of fraud, but only if the fraud satisfies the rigorous standard set forth in the opening clause of UCC §5-109(a): "[A] required document is forged or materially fraudulent, or honor of the presentation would facilitate a material fraud by the beneficiary on the issuer or applicant." As comment 1 to UCC §5-109 emphasizes, the drafters intended the "material fraud" standard to be a rigorous one. Even a willful default by the beneficiary on the underlying contract is likely to fall far short of material fraud. To justify dishonor, the fraud must be so severe that "the beneficiary has *no* colorable right to expect honor" and "there is *no* basis in fact to support . . . a right to honor." UCC §5-109 comment 1 (emphasis added).

The drafters of the UCC expected that issuers faced with the foregoing rules generally would reject claims of fraud and proceed to honor drafts on letters of credit even when applicants presented plausible arguments that beneficiaries had committed the kind of material fraud that would permit dishonor under UCC §5-109. The drafters went further in cases where the issuer receives a draft from a confirming bank or other party that properly has honored a draft in good faith. In that case, the issuer *must* honor the draft, even if the issuer believes that the draft is materially fraudulent. UCC §5-109(a)(1). In either case, honor would be proper under Article 5. Hence, the applicant would be obligated to reimburse the issuer even if the presentation had been totally fraudulent. The applicant then would be entitled to sue the beneficiary for making the fraudulent presentation. UCC §5-110(a)(2).

That framework presents a serious problem for the applicant in situations in which the applicant has no effective remedy against the beneficiary. For example, the beneficiary might be judgment-proof or otherwise inaccessible (in a foreign country, for instance). One response, of course, is that the applicant should have thought about the responsibility and trustworthiness of the beneficiary before obtaining a letter of credit in the beneficiary's favor, and the statutory framework certainly rests in part on that sentiment. But Article 5 does provide one narrow mechanism by which the applicant can protect itself. Specifically, UCC §5-109(b) authorizes the applicant to obtain an injunction against honor if it can convince a court that the presentation satisfies the material fraud standard set forth in UCC §5-109. That rule does not impose undue uncertainty on the issuer because Article 5 authorizes the issuer to dishonor a draft in response to a judicial injunction issued under UCC §5-109(b). Thus, the issuer safely can obey that injunction with no risk that it will be held liable to the beneficiary for wrongful dishonor.

B.   Assigning Letters of Credit

Letter-of-credit practice traditionally has been hostile to efforts by beneficiaries to transfer letters of credit after they have been issued. The most common justification for that hostility is the implicit trust that a letter of credit requires an applicant to bestow on its beneficiary. As the discussion of fraud in the previous section should make clear, a purchaser/applicant's willingness to obtain a letter of credit in favor of a seller/beneficiary with whom it is doing business leaves the applicant exposed to a considerable risk of loss if the beneficiary is not trustworthy. Article 5 follows the UCP's lead on that point by adopting a default rule that letters of credit are not transferable. UCC §5-112(a); UCP art. 48(b); see UCC §5-112 comment 1. Thus, a beneficiary that plans to transfer a letter of credit before performance needs to obtain a letter of credit that states expressly that it is transferable.

Article 5 articulates two significant exceptions to that rule. First, UCC §5-113 provides rules for transfers by operation of law. Those transfers occur in the context of corporate mergers, as well as on the occasion of the appointment of a receiver or trustee to deal with insolvency. When such a transaction occurs, the issuer must recognize the successor as the beneficiary of the letter of credit and thus must honor a presentation from the successor. The only limitation is that the successor must comply with reasonable requirements imposed by the issuer to ensure that the successor is authentic. UCC §5-113(b).

Given the limited likelihood that a party will submit a presentation fraudulently claiming to be the successor of the beneficiary, the UCC absolves the issuer of any obligation to "determine whether a purported successor is a successor of a beneficiary or whether the signature of a purported successor is genuine or authorized." UCC §5-113(c). Instead, the UCC states that payment of a presentation submitted in support of such a scheme—a presentation that purports to be from a successor, but, in fact, is from a fraudulent interloper — is treated as a proper payment under UCC §5-108(i). UCC §5-113(d). The forged documents are treated under the standard fraud rule in UCC §5-109, so that the issuer is entitled to honor the draft from the purported successor so long as the issuer proceeds in good faith. UCC §5-113(d).

The second exception to the default rule against transferability draws a distinction between an assignment of the letter of credit per se and an assignment of the beneficiary's right to receive proceeds under the letter of credit. Although hostile to the former, both the UCC and the UCP permit the latter. See UCC §5-114(b) (permitting such an assignment); UCP art. 49 (same). That type of transfer does not raise the concerns that motivate the general rule against an assignment by a beneficiary of a letter of credit because it continues to condition the issuer's obligation to pay on performance by the original stated beneficiary. The only thing that is assigned is the beneficiary's right to receive proceeds in the event that the beneficiary performs. Thus, if the beneficiary in fact performs after such an assignment, the issuer will pay the funds from the transaction to the assignee, not the named beneficiary. If the beneficiary fails to perform, the issuer will not be obligated to disburse funds under the letter of credit, even if the assignee attempts to perform.

Perhaps the most common use of an assignment of a beneficiary's right to receive proceeds of a letter of credit is to enhance the ability of the beneficiary to obtain funds to finance the beneficiary's purchase or production of the goods that it is selling. For example, in the typical letter-of-credit transaction in which the beneficiary is a seller of goods, the beneficiary might have an arrangement with a lender under which the lender advances funds to the beneficiary that the beneficiary uses to support its manufacturing operations or to purchase inventory from some other party that manufactures the goods in question. In either case, the lender funding the beneficiary's operations will want its loan to be repaid when the beneficiary sells the goods in question (or at least the portion of the loan attributable to those goods). If the beneficiary is being paid by means of a letter of credit, the lender commonly will prefer for the proceeds of the letter of credit to be paid directly to the lender because direct payment to the lender will limit the ability of the beneficiary to abscond with the funds instead of repaying the loan.

As the preceding paragraph suggests, it is not enough from the perspective of the lender/assignee for the statute to make an assignment of the right to receive proceeds from a letter of credit effective as against the beneficiary. The assignee wants more than a right to force the beneficiary to pay; the loan agreement undoubtedly already contains that right. What the assignee really wants is a way to force the issuer to pay the letter-of-credit proceeds directly to the assignee. The issuer, however, would be reluctant to accept that arrangement unless it could be sure that it could avoid the risk of duplicate presentations under the letter of credit: The issuer wants to know at all times the identity of a single party to whom it is obligated to make payments under its letter. To accommodate that concern, the UCC states that an issuer generally has no obligation to recognize an assignment of proceeds of a letter of credit. UCC §5-114(c). Thus, absent some action by the issuer, the assignee will not be able to force the issuer to pay the proceeds directly to it.

The assignee can solve that problem, however, by taking a few simple steps to limit the possibility of duplicate presentations. Specifically, if the letter of credit requires presentation of the original letter as a condition to honor and if the assignee obtains that original from the beneficiary, then the assignee can satisfy the issuer that only the assignee will be in a position to present proper drafts under the letter of credit. See UCC §5-114 comment 3 (stating that "the risk to the issuer...of having to pay twice is minimized" in those circumstances). In that case, the UCC states that the issuer cannot unreasonably withhold its consent to the assignment. UCC §5-114(d). The drafters obviously expect issuers to consent to an assignment that involves those characteristics. After such a consent, the assignee is protected because "the issuer...becomes bound...to pay to the assignee the assigned letter of credit proceeds that the issuer or nominated person otherwise would pay to the beneficiary." UCC §5-114 comment 3.

C. Choice-of-Law Rules

At first glance, the frequently transnational character of letter-of-credit transactions suggests that choice-of-law rules would be crucial to letter-of-credit transactions because of the need to determine what body of law specifies the rights and obligations of each party to such a transaction. Responding to that likelihood, Article 5 includes a choice-of-law provision (UCC §5-116). The first and last subsections of UCC §5-116 set out a broad and absolute deference to choice-of-law and choice-of-forum clauses, including a statement that the chosen jurisdiction "need not bear any relation to the transaction." UCC §5-116(a), (e). If the letter of credit does not include a choice-of-law clause, the liability of a party obligated on the letter of credit is governed by the law where that party is located. UCC §5-116(b). Article 5 does not include a choice-of-law rule governing the liability of the applicant, apparently because of a perception that there is no need for such a rule. See UCC §5-116 comment 1.

Choice-of-law rules have practical significance only in cases in which different legal systems resolve the same dispute in different ways. As the drafters of Article 5 recognized, that is not likely to occur frequently in the letter-of-credit system. Indeed, even before the revised version of Article 5 was adopted, the general consistency of letter-of-credit law in different nations made such disputes uncommon. See UCC §5-116 comment 2. And the revised version of Article 5 should make those disputes even less common, both because Article 5 now adopts rules that follow as closely as practicable the rules articulated in the UCP, UCC §5-101 comment, and because Article 5 generally allows application of the UCP in cases where those rules conflict with rules set out in Article 5, see UCC §5-116(c). Thus, future choice-of-law conflicts should be relatively rare in transactions involving letters of credit. See UCC §5-116 comment 2.

Problem Set 34

34.1. Consider anew the facts of Problem 33.3, in which FSB failed to make a timely response to a draft on a $12,000 letter of credit issued by FSB. As the facts of that problem indicate, the draft did not comply with the requirements of the letter of credit.

    a.   Assume that FSB received a $12,000 deposit from the applicant at the time that FSB issued the letter of credit. If FSB is forced to pay $12,000 to the beneficiary, can FSB keep the $12,000 to reimburse itself? UCC §§4-407, 5-108(i)(1), 5-117(a), 5-117 comment 1.

    b.   Same facts as question a, but FSB did not take a deposit from the applicant. Can FSB recover the $12,000 from the applicant? UCC §5-117(a).

34.2.   Jane Halley from Boatmen's Bank (introduced in Problem Set 33) calls first thing one morning with another letter-of-credit problem for you. This one involves a letter of credit that Boatmen's issued for $1 million to Riverfront Tools (RFT). Early last week (10 days ago) she received a draft on the letter of credit, which appeared to contain all of the requisite documents. For reasons that are not clear, her office failed to process the draft in a timely manner. When she found out about the problem this morning, she immediately contacted the applicant to tell it that she had found the draft and was about to process it. The applicant told her that the draft must be forged because the applicant had talked that morning to Carl Eben (the president of RFT), who had told the applicant that RFT would be submitting a draft tomorrow. Given Jane's delay, must Boatmen's honor the draft? UCC §5-108(b), (c), (d); UCP art. 14(d), (e). Would your answer be different if the letter of credit were issued by a Boatmen's branch located outside the United States? UCC §5-116(b).

34.3.   At a meeting with Jodi Kay (back from Problem Set 33), Jodi asks your advice about some of the risks she faces in letter-of-credit transactions. Specifically, she wants to know what her responsibility will be if she receives a presentation drawing on one of her letters of credit that is totally forged, fails to understand that the presentation is forged, and consequently honors it. Specifically, she wants to know if she will be able to obtain reimbursement from her customer and if she will still be obligated to honor a later legitimate draft. (She wants to know whether she can be forced to pay twice.) What do you tell her? UCC §§5-108(a), 5-108(i)(1), 5-108(i)(5), 5-108 comment 12, 5-109(a)(2).

34.4.   As you leave the office for the weekend, you get a desperate call from Archie Moon. He tells you that he has just received a shipment from Malay Ink Company of what should have been four barrels of expensive indigo ink. Unfortunately, the barrels appear to contain ordinary black printer's ink, which has only one-fourth the value of the ink that he ordered. Archie is concerned because he obtained a $75,000 letter of credit to pay the shipper and is worried that his bank will proceed to pay a draft on the letter of credit. He called his bank this morning. The banker told Archie that she had received a draft on the letter of credit and that the draft appeared to be in order. The banker declined to defer her consideration of the draft and told Archie that in the ordinary course of business the bank would honor the draft Monday morning. What do you advise? UCC §§2-601, 2-711, 5-108(a) & (i)(1), 5-109(b), 5-109 comment 1, 5-111.

34.5.   Same facts as Problem 34.4, but assume now that the draft and supporting documents were presented to the issuer by the Bank of Hong Kong and that nobody at that bank had any reason to doubt the legitimacy of those documents or the underlying transaction. Does your answer change? UCC §§5-108(i)(1), 5-109(a)(2), 5-109(b)(2).

34.6.   When Jane Halley comes in at the end of the day to finish up some paperwork associated with Problem 34.2, she mentions another problem related to a letter of credit that she has issued with Toy Manufacturing Company as the beneficiary. The letter of credit is in the form set forth in Figure 33.1. Today she received a draft drawn on that letter of credit by Hong Kong Toys. The draft included all the documents specified by the letter of credit. Attached to the draft was the original letter of credit, to which a single piece of paper was stapled. The piece of paper appears to be signed by Sun Yat Toy as president of Toy Manufacturing Company and reads as follows: "The undersigned Toy Manufacturing Company hereby transfers the attached letter of credit and all rights under that letter of credit to Hong Kong Toys."

a. Is Jane obligated to honor the draft? Should she honor the draft? UCC §§5-112(a), 5-114(d).

b. Would your answer change if the draft also included a cover letter explaining that Hong Kong Toys had acquired the letter of credit in connection with a transaction in which it merged with Toy Manufacturing Company? UCC §5-113.

Part Two
Credit Systems

Introduction to Credit Systems

The payment systems described in Part One of this book provide mechanisms by which a person can make a payment that is for all practical purposes immediate. In many circumstances, however, parties enter into credit transactions, in which payment is not intended to be immediate. For example, it is common for a seller to agree that it will accept payment from a purchaser over time. Alternatively, using a credit card, a purchaser might pay a seller immediately, using money that the purchaser must repay to the credit-card issuer over time. More generally, even without any specific sales transaction, business enterprises go to financial institutions to borrow the money that they need to operate, with the understanding that the borrowers will repay the money to the financial institutions at specified times in the future.

This part of the book discusses the systems that individuals and businesses use to facilitate those transactions. It is divided into two chapters, reflecting the two central issues in any credit transaction. Chapter 9 discusses contractual and legal rules regarding the amount of compensation the payor will provide to the payee for the time-value of the deferral of payment. Chapter 10 discusses credit-enhancement mechanisms that allow the payee to pursue the assets of third parties if the payor fails to make payments as agreed.

Chapter 9. The Borrower's Obligation

Assignment 35: Promissory Notes and Interest Rates

The central issue in any credit transaction is how the payor will compensate the payee for the delay in payment. Because of the time value of money, a payee makes a significant concession when it agrees to forgo receiving immediate payment and instead to accept payment at some future date: We all would rather have $1,000 today than $1,000 next spring. Accordingly, the key terms of any transaction involving deferred payment are (a) the time when payment must be made and (b) the way in which the payor will compensate the payee for the delay. This chapter focuses solely on the manner of compensation. For simplicity, this chapter discusses only transactions in which the parties agree on a relatively lengthy deferral because those are the transactions in which the most is likely to be at stake. For example, §3 of the note set forth below calls for repayment through a series of monthly payments over 20 years.

A. Promissory Notes

The law does not require any particular form for a transaction in which the parties agree to defer payment. When the transaction involves modest sums and the period of deferral is short, the parties might rely on a simple oral agreement that payment will be forthcoming by a specified time. In most contexts, however, the parties have some written agreement describing the time when payment is due and the amount of compensation that the payee will receive for the delay. In minor transactions, that agreement can be a simple statement on the bottom of an invoice that payment is due in 30 days. In the consumer context, it also might take the form of a credit-card agreement, in which the issuer describes the terms under which the cardholder will be required to repay funds that the cardholder might borrow in the future. In cases that involve large sums of money and significant deferrals of payment, it is customary for the payor to execute a promissory note detailing the terms under which the payment will be made. That is especially true in cases where the payment obligation previously has been in dispute, as in the following case.

Schillace v. Channell Shopping Partnership

623 So. 2d 45 (La. Ct. App. 1993)

Before EDWARDS, SHORTESS and WHIPPLE, JJ.

SHORTESS, Judge. . . .

On June 23, 1988, plaintiff's late husband, Joe Schillace, III, entered into a commercial lease agreement with Channell Shopping Center, a partnership, for the lease of certain space located within the shopping center. The primary term of the lease was two years commencing September 1, 1988, and terminating August 31, 1990, at a monthly rental of $2,500.00. On May 9, 1989, plaintiff's husband died. Thereafter, she was appointed administratrix of his succession and continued to operate the business located in the shopping center for approximately two and one-half months following his death. Plaintiff failed to make rental payments on the lease during this period, and some time in early August 1989 she removed the merchandise and other movables from the leased premises and brought them to a store operated by her son. Defendants subsequently filed suit on the lease and obtained a writ of sequestration ordering the seizure of all goods, wares, and merchandise located in plaintiff's son's store.

To avoid seizure of the merchandise, plaintiff and defendants entered into an agreement whereby plaintiff paid defendants $15,000.00 in cash and executed a promissory note in the amount of $27,150.00, which represented the remaining balance due under the lease. Following this agreement, the sequestration was recalled by defendants' attorney and no further action was taken in the suit. Plaintiff subsequently defaulted on the note, and defendants filed a new suit on May 9, 1990. A judgment was ultimately rendered in defendants' favor on December 5, 1990. Thereafter, defendants . . . filed garnishment proceedings resulting in the seizure of certain certificates of deposit belonging to plaintiff.

Plaintiff then filed the instant suit against defendants, seeking to dissolve the seizure of the certificates of deposit on the ground that the funds seized were derivative proceeds of the life insurance policy on her late husband, and as such were exempt from seizure under the provisions of Louisiana Revised Statute 22:647(A)(1). . . .

. . . That statute provides:

> The lawful beneficiary, assignee, or payee, including the insured's estate, of a life insurance policy or endowment policy, heretofore or hereafter effected shall be entitled to the proceeds and avails of the policy against the creditors and representatives of the insured and of the person effecting the policy or the estate of either, and against the heirs and legatees of either such person, and such proceeds and avails shall also be exempt from all liability for any debt of such beneficiary, payee, or assignee or estate, existing at the time the proceeds or avails are made available for his own use. For purposes of this Subsection, the proceeds and avails of the policy include the cash surrender value of the policy.

Plaintiff argues the debt sued upon existed at the time the insurance proceeds were made available to her and, therefore, such proceeds are exempt from seizure. More specifically, plaintiff argues the note which she executed in favor of defendants was merely a continuance of the prior obligation on the lease, and, therefore, the certificates of deposit purchased with the proceeds are not subject to seizure in satisfaction of defendants' judgment. Defendants, on the other hand, contend the debt sued upon arose after payment of the life insurance proceeds to plaintiff, and therefore such proceeds are not exempt from seizure. They argue the execution of the note was in full settlement of the prior sequestration suit and thus amounted to a novation. Accordingly, defendants claim the note represents a new debt which arose only after the insurance proceeds were paid to plaintiff. . . .

Novation is the extinguishment of an obligation by the substitution of a new one. Novation takes place when, by agreement of the parties, a new performance is substituted for that previously owed, or a new cause is substituted for that of the original obligation. Novation may not be presumed. The determining factor is the intention of the parties. The intention to novate may be shown by the character of the transaction, the facts and circumstances surrounding it, as well as by the terms of the agreement itself.

After a thorough review of the facts and evidence presented, and in light of the law regarding novation, we are convinced that the prior obligation under the lease was novated by the execution of the August 15, 1989 promissory note. Clearly, the existing obligation, i.e., the debt under the lease, was extinguished by the substitution of a new one, i.e., the promissory note. The respective obligations were different in date, amount, method of payment, date of payment, and signatories. Furthermore, it is apparent the parties intended for a novation to take place when they settled the sequestration suit. Indeed, both plaintiff's and defendants' attorneys agreed on the record during plaintiff's deposition that the $15,000.00 cash payment and execution of the promissory note were in full settlement of defendants' suit and, necessarily, the underlying obligation on the lease. Accordingly, the debt sued upon arose only after the date the life insurance proceeds were made available to plaintiff, and [those proceeds] therefore were not exempt from seizure under Revised Statute 22:647(A)(1).

Schillace illustrates the significance that execution of a promissory note can have in resolving a preexisting payment dispute. In most commercial transactions, a party does not issue a promissory note to resolve a prior dispute. Instead, a borrower issues the note as part of a lending transaction that establishes a new obligation to pay. The following document is an example based on the standard promissory note used by the investment arm of a major Houston-based life insurance company for its long-term lending transactions.

PROMISSORY NOTE

$2,300,000.00   Houston, Texas   June _____, 1996

1. **For Value Received,** and as hereinafter specified, **LA DOMAIN, LTD.** ("Maker"), a Texas limited partnership, by and through its duly authorized general partner, promises to pay to the order of **COUNTRYBANK OF TEXAS, N.A.,** a national banking association ("Payee", which term shall in every instance refer to any owner or holder of this Note), at its office at 2521 Westheimer, Suite 600, Houston, Harris County, Texas 77854, or at such other address as Payee may request from time to time in writing to Maker, in lawful money of the United States of America, which shall be legal tender for the payment of all debts, public and private, in immediately available funds, (i) the principal sum of Two Million Three Hundred Thousand and No/100 Dollars ($2,300,000.00); (ii) interest from date of advancement until maturity (unless sooner paid in accordance herewith) upon the balance of the principal sum remaining unpaid from time to time at a rate equal to the lesser of (a) the Maximum Lawful Rate (defined herein) or (b) the Stated Rate; and (iii) interest upon past due principal and, to the extent permitted by Applicable Law, on past due interest, from maturity (whether by acceleration or otherwise) until paid at the Maximum Lawful Rate; provided, however, that for purposes of

determining the Maximum Lawful Rate in subparts (ii) and (iii) above, any commitment, extension, brokerage, or other fees that are considered interest shall be treated as interest and taken into account in calculating the Maximum Lawful Rate and all such fees (and other sums deemed interest) shall be amortized, prorated, allocated, and spread in equal parts over the full stated term of the loan hereby evidenced. Interest owed under this Note shall be calculated based on a 360-day year and the actual number of days elapsed; provided, however, if such calculation would cause interest on the loan evidenced by this Note to exceed the Maximum Lawful Rate, that to the extent necessary (and only to such extent), interest shall be calculated on a 365-day year (or 366-day year, if applicable), basis.

2. In this Promissory Note ("Note"), the following terms have the following meanings:

a. **Applicable Law:** that law, regulation, or judicial determination in effect from time to time and applicable to this Note, which lawfully permits the contracting for, charging, and collecting of the highest permissible lawful nonusurious rate of interest on this Note, including laws, regulations, and judicial interpretations of the State of Texas and laws of the United States of America.

b. **Business Day:** any day that Payee is open for business.

c. **Loan Year:** a period of twelve consecutive calendar months commencing on the first day of the second month following the date hereof, or any anniversary of that date.

d. **Maximum Lawful Rate:** a rate of interest:

(a) that, when multiplied by the true principal balance of this Note outstanding from time to time, and the product of which is then added to

(b) all commitment, extension, brokerage, or other fees or sums paid on the loan evidenced by this Note that under Applicable Law are deemed to constitute interest;

will equal (but will not exceed) the maximum nonusurious rate of interest that may be contracted for, charged or received under Applicable Law. For the purposes of this Note, "true principal" means all sums advanced pursuant to this Note less (i) all payments made on the principal of this Note; (ii) any credits to the principal of this Note; and (iii) any other sums that Applicable Law would require to be deducted from the stated outstanding principal balance of this Note in any calculation to determine the maximum nonusurious amount of interest that may be contracted for, charged, or received on this Note. If there is no Maximum Lawful Rate under Applicable Law, the Maximum Lawful Rate shall be a per annum interest rate equal to the greater of (i) the Prime Rate, plus three percent (3%) per annum, or (ii) eighteen percent (18%) per annum. The parties specifically agree that the monthly ceiling described in Tex. Finance Code §303.204 applies to the preceding provisions of this Note calling for calculation of an interest rate on a monthly basis.

e. **Prime Rate:** the per annum rate of interest that Texas Commerce Bank, National Association ("TCB") announces from time to time as its prime lending rate, which rate may be set by TCB as a general reference rate of interest and may not necessarily represent the lowest prime rate or best rate actually charged to any customer, in that TCB may make commercial loans or other loans at rates of interest at, above, or below the Prime Rate. If there exists any dispute or uncertainty with respect to the Prime Rate, the rate certified in writing by the president or any vice president or cashier of TCB shall be conclusive evidence of such fact, absent manifest error. Should TCB, during the term of this Note, for whatever reason, abolish or abandon the practice of announcing or publishing a general reference rate, then the Prime Rate used during the remaining term of this Note shall be that interest rate then in effect that from time to time, in the good-faith judgment of the Payee, most effectively approximates the initial definition of Prime Rate.

f. **Stated Rate:** a per annum rate of interest equal to 10% per annum.

3. Subject to the conditions set forth in this Note, principal and interest installments shall be payable as follows:

(a) A payment of interest only shall be due and payable July 1, 1996.

(b) Commencing on August 1, 1996, this Note shall be payable in two hundred and thirty-nine (239) consecutive equal monthly installments of $22,195.50 each, the first of said monthly installments shall be due and payable on August 1, 1996, and a like installment shall be due and payable on the first day of each and every month thereafter through and including June 30, 2016.

(c) On July 1, 2016, the entire unpaid principal of this Note, together with all unpaid accrued interest thereon, shall be due and payable.

4. This Note may not be prepaid in whole or in part at any time prior to the fifth anniversary of the date hereof. Thereafter, Maker shall have the right to prepay the entire amount of the outstanding principal balance and accrued interest of this Note, upon payment of a prepayment premium that shall equal five percent of the amounts prepaid in the sixth Loan Year and that shall decline from five percent by one percent in each successive Loan Year but that in no event shall be less than one percent. The foregoing provisions shall apply to any payment or other reduction of the balance due under this Note, regardless of whether such payment or other reduction, (a) is voluntary or involuntary; (b) is occasioned by Payee's acceleration of this Note or demand hereunder; (c) is made by Maker or a third party; or (d) is made during a bankruptcy, reorganization or other proceeding or pursuant to any plan of reorganization or liquidation. If any such involuntary payment is made before the end of the fifth Loan Year, the prepayment premium shall be ten percent of the amount so prepaid.

5. Each payment shall be credited first to fees or other charges hereunder (other than interest), next to interest then due, and the remainder to principal, and interest thereupon shall cease upon the principal so credited. All payments of principal shall be applied in the inverse order of maturity.

6. If any payment required hereunder shall not be made within ten (10) days after the due date, Payee may charge a late charge equal to the lesser of (i) the greatest amount that, when added to all other amounts constituting "interest" under applicable state or federal law, does not produce a rate of interest that exceeds the Maximum Lawful Rate, or (ii) four percent (4%) of the amount of any such delinquent payment so overdue, for the purpose of defraying the expense incident to handling such delinquent payments. Such late charge represents the reasonable estimate of Payee and Maker of a fair average compensation for the loss that may be sustained by Payee due to the failure of Maker to make timely payments. Such late charge shall be paid without prejudice to the right of Payee to collect any other amounts provided to be paid or to declare a default hereunder.

7. Notwithstanding any provision to the apparent contrary herein contained, it is expressly provided that in no case or event shall the aggregate of (i) all "interest" on the unpaid balance of this Note, accrued or paid from the date hereof through the date of such calculation, and (ii) the aggregate of any other amounts accrued

or paid pursuant to this Note that under Applicable Law are or may be deemed to constitute interest upon the debt evidenced hereby from the date hereof through the date of such calculation, ever exceed the Maximum Lawful Rate on the true principal balance of the debt evidenced by this Note from time to time remaining unpaid. In furtherance thereof, none of the terms of this Note shall ever be construed to create a contract to pay, as consideration for use, forbearance or detention of money, interest at a rate in excess of the Maximum Lawful Rate. The Maker or any endorsers or other parties now or hereafter becoming liable for the payment of this Note or any other indebtedness incurred incident to this debt shall never be liable for interest in excess of the Maximum Lawful Rate, and the provisions of this paragraph shall control over any other provisions of this Note. If under any circumstances the aggregate amounts paid on this Note prior to and incident to the final maturity include amounts that by law are interest and that would exceed the Maximum Lawful Rate of interest that lawfully could have been collected on this debt, Maker stipulates that such amounts collected would have been and will be deemed to have been the results of a mathematical error on the part of both the Maker and holder of the Note, and that the party receiving such excess payment promptly shall refund the amount of such excess (to the extent only of the excess of such interest payments above the maximum amount that lawfully could have been collected and retained) upon discovery of such error by the party receiving such payment or upon notice thereof from the party making such payment.

8. This Note shall become immediately due and payable, at the option of the Payee or other holder hereof, without presentment or demand or any notice of intent to accelerate, notice of acceleration or any other notices to the Maker or any other person obligated or to become obligated hereon, upon default in the payment of any sum hereon when due.

9. If this Note is collected by suit, through probate, or bankruptcy court, or by any other judicial proceedings, or if this Note is not paid at maturity, howsoever such maturity may be brought about, and is placed in the hands of an attorney for collection, then the Maker promises to pay reasonable attorney's fees in addition to all other amounts owing hereunder at the time this Note is placed in the hands of such attorney.

10. Except as expressly provided herein, the Maker and all sureties, endorsers, and guarantors of this Note, (i) waive demand, presentment for payment, notice of nonpayment, protest, notice of protest, notice of intent to accelerate, notice of acceleration, and all other notice, filing of suit, and diligence in collecting this Note or enforcing any of the security therefor; (ii) agree to any substitution, exchange or release of any party primarily or secondarily liable hereon; (iii) agree that the Payee or other holder hereof shall not be required first to institute suit or exhaust its remedies hereon against Maker or others liable or to become liable hereon or to enforce its rights against any security herein in order to enforce payment of this Note by them; (iv) consent to any extension or postponement of time of payment of this Note and to any other indulgence with respect hereto without notice thereof to any of them; and (v) agree that the failure to exercise any option or election herein upon the occurrence of any event of default shall not be construed as a waiver of the right to exercise such option or election at any later date or upon the occurrence of a subsequent event of default.

11. This Note has been executed and delivered and shall be construed in accordance with and governed by the laws of the State of Texas and of the United States of America, where applicable.

12. Maker warrants and represents to Payee that all loans evidenced by this Note are for business, commercial, investment or other similar purposes and not primarily for personal, family, household or agricultural use, as such terms are used in Tex. Finance Code §§303.204 and 303.305.

13. This promissory note represents the final agreement between the parties and may not be contradicted by evidence of prior, contemporaneous, or subsequent oral or written agreements of the parties.

> LA DOMAIN, LTD., a Texas limited
> partnership, by its sole general partner LA
> DOMAIN, INC., a Texas corporation
>
> By: _____
>
> Jean La Domain, President

B. Determining the Amount of Compensation

1. Fixed and Variable Interest Rates

Interest on promissory notes can be calculated as a fixed rate or as a variable rate. In a fixed-rate note (like the note set forth above, henceforth referred to as the Promissory Note), the parties agree to a specific interest rate at the time of the borrowing transaction (in that case 10 percent per annum). The principal balance of the note accrues interest at that fixed rate as long as any portion of the principal remains unpaid. In a variable-rate note, by contrast, the parties do not agree up front to a fixed rate. Instead, they agree that the principal of the note will bear interest at a "floating" rate that changes from time to time, depending on market conditions. Ordinarily, the variable rate is described as a certain number of percentage points per year above an objectively determinable reference rate, often the prime rate of a major bank in the area. For example, the note set forth above refers to the prime lending rate of Texas Commerce Bank (which was the largest Houston-based bank at the time that the form was developed). To change the note set forth above to a variable-rate note, the definition of Stated Rate in §2(f) might be revised to call for "a per annum rate of interest one and one-half percent (1.50%) per annum above the Prime Rate." The variable rate then could be adjusted with each monthly payment, so that each monthly payment would include the interest that accrued during the preceding month at the interest rate in effect for that month.

The mechanics of allocating monthly payments are an important aspect of the standard commercial promissory note. Ordinarily, the monthly payment includes all of the interest that accrued during the preceding month. If the note is an "interest-only" note, then the interest that accrued during the preceding month is the only amount due on the note each month. If the note "amortizes," like the note set forth above, then the payment also will include an additional amount that will be applied to reduce the outstanding principal balance of the note. See Promissory Note §5 (stating that payments are applied first to outstanding fees, then to interest, and then to principal). Because a portion of each amortizing note payment is applied to reduce the principal balance of the note, the outstanding principal declines slightly each month. Accordingly, the interest that is due each month declines commensurately. Thus, in the standard amortizing arrangement in which the amounts of the monthly payments are constant through the term of the note the amount of each payment that is applied to principal increases each month as the amount applied to interest decreases.

The choice between fixed-rate notes and variable-rate notes determines which party bears what risks from changing interest rates. A fixed-rate note places the risk that interest rates will rise on the lender and the risk that interest rates will fall on the borrower. Thus, if market interest rates rise by 5 percent during the term of the note set forth above, the borrower continues to make interest payments at the rate agreed on up front even though the note will be much less profitable for the lender than it was when it was issued: If the lender made a new loan after the rates have risen by five points, it could (presumably) earn 15 percent interest, rather than the 10 percent the borrower is paying. Conversely, if interest rates fall by 5 percent, the borrower (unless it can "prepay" the note) still has to make the payments at the stated rate even though the borrower otherwise might be able to borrow money at a much lower rate in a falling market.

A variable-rate note, on the other hand, reverses the risks, so that the borrower loses if interest rates rise and the lender loses if interest rates fall. In that case, an increase in interest rates will increase the borrower's interest costs even though the borrower's income might remain unchanged. Conversely, if interest rates fall, the lender's income falls, without regard to the lender's expenses or other aspects of its affairs.

Because different kinds of notes present different risk profiles to the parties that use them, specialized players in the economy tend to prefer specific kinds of notes. For example, consider the position of the life-insurance companies, one of the most important types of lenders in our economy (holding about $200 billion of loans at any given time). The primary business of life-insurance companies is to sell life-insurance policies, annuities, and similar financial products. The primary obligation of those companies thus is relatively easy to predict and relatively insensitive to changes in future interest rates. Thus, life-insurance companies traditionally have preferred to invest the proceeds that they receive from policyholders in obligations with fixed interest rates. Thus, although the insurance companies abandon the opportunity to profit from rising interest rates, they are protected from much of the risk of loss from falling interest rates. Even if interest rates fall, the insurance companies will be entitled to payments on their fixed-rate notes adequate to support their obligations to their policyholders. To put it simply, because insurance companies typically pay fixed rates to obtain the funds that they have available for investment, they prefer to receive fixed rates of interest from the parties to whom they lend those funds. By limiting their risk of loss (or profit) from changes in interest rates, the insurance companies leave themselves free to make (or lose) money in their core businesses without regard to shifts in interest-rate markets in which they have less expertise.

The other major type of institutional lender in this country is the depositary institution (banks, savings and loan associations, and credit unions). Unlike insurance companies, the principal cost that depositary institutions pay for the funds that they lend is one that varies with market interest rates (the interest rates that depositary institutions pay on the accounts of their depositors and on certificates of deposit (CDs)). Because those rates are immediately sensitive to changes in broader market rates of interest, it is extraordinarily risky for a depositary institution to commit large portions of its assets in debts that pay interest at a fixed rate. The reason is simple: If interest rates rise while an institution's assets are invested at a fixed rate of interest, the institution's obligations on its deposits will rise rapidly, while the institution's income remains stagnant. One of the key causes of the savings-and-loan crisis of the 1980s was the failure of savings-and-loan associations to account for that risk. Many of those institutions failed because they held large portfolios of long-term fixed-rate home mortgages at a time when market interest rates for deposits rose rapidly.

2.   Interest-Rate Swaps

Because of the variances in risk preferences, it is common for two parties to a financial transaction to have inconsistent preferences about the type of interest rate that should apply to the note. A borrower might want to make fixed-rate payments (to protect itself from future increases in interest rates), while its bank lender might prefer to receive variable-rate payments (to protect itself from those same increases). The textual discussion above suggests one simple solution: that the borrower should borrow the money from a different kind of lender (such as an insurance company).

A more sophisticated response, however, would be for the lender to enter into an interest-rate swap with a third party (the swap partner). In that kind of interest-rate swap (illustrated in Figure 35.1), the lender would "swap" the fixed-rate payments its borrower had contracted to pay for variable-rate payments that a third-party swap partner would agree to pay. The basic terms of such a contract include a "notional amount," on which the parties agree to trade interest rates, as well as the two rates that the parties are trading. For example, a lender receiving fixed-rate payments from a borrower on an obligation of $2 million might enter into a swap allowing it to pay a fixed rate of interest on a notional amount of $2 million. The swap partner then might agree to pay interest at the rate of LIBOR plus 2 percent per annum on the same notional amount. "LIBOR" is the London Inter-Bank Offered Rate, the rate at which money is offered for investment with banks in a specialized money market in London. For ease of comparison, variable rates in interest-rate swaps normally are stated in terms of LIBOR rates.

Figure 35.1 shows how that arrangement would remedy the inconsistent payment preferences of the parties. The borrower pays the fixed rate that it prefers, but the lender does not have to accept that fixed rate. Instead, the lender obtains a net variable-rate payment by using the swap to pass on the fixed-rate payment from the borrower and receive in its stead a variable-rate payment from its swap partner.

Figure 35.1
Interest-Rate Swap

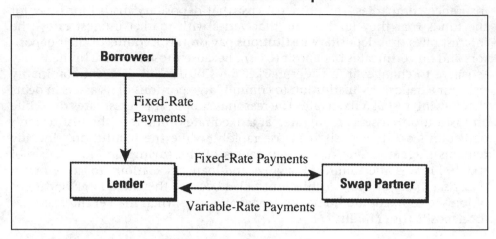

3.   The Enforceability of Interest-Rate Agreements

It is appropriate to add a final cautionary word about the intricate mechanisms parties use to obtain the particular interest-rate risk profiles that they desire; those mechanisms do not ensure that the promised payments actually will be made. Their role is limited to calculating the amount of payment that is due. Payees still bear a variety of risks related to interest rates. The most obvious problem is that an insolvent obligor or swap partner might not pay at all.

That problem is particularly serious because swap transactions can involve sums of money that are large even by the standards of commercial enterprises. Accordingly, the entities that provide swap services (like the swap partner in the transaction described above) tend to be extraordinarily well capitalized, often with AAA credit ratings. Conversely, those entities are reluctant to provide swap services to entities that are not themselves creditworthy.

One common device for mitigating potential losses from the insolvency of a party to a swap transaction is a close-out netting provision in the swap contract. Under such a provision, either party can "close out" its relationship with the other upon a default on any contract between the parties. Those provisions permit the nondefaulting party to close out the relationship by making a single payment to the defaulting party. That single payment is a net sum that reflects the value of all of the outstanding contracts between the two parties at that time. Some of the contracts would have a positive value to the defaulting party (contracts entered into at interest rates more favorable to the defaulting party than interest rates at the time of default), and some would have a negative value (contracts entered into at interest rates less favorable to the defaulting party than interest rates at the time of default). The close-out netting provision, however, allows the terminating party to add the values of all the contracts and terminate all the contracts with a single payment reflecting the net value.

Bankruptcy procedures pose a special problem for netting provisions, however, because bankruptcy typically allows a trustee to "cherry pick" among the contracts of the bankrupt and enforce only the ones with a positive value to the insolvent firm. To solve that problem, Congress passed a series of statutes that make such netting provisions enforceable even in bankruptcy, at least when the counterparty is a United States financial institution. See Roberta Romano, A Thumbnail Sketch of Derivative Securities and Their Regulation, 55 Md. L. Rev. 1, 54 (1996).

Another difficulty for the lender, even if the obligor survives bankruptcy with an obligation to pay, is that the bankruptcy court might alter a fixed-rate obligation to bear interest at a variable rate or vice versa. That alteration might seem relatively minor, given the likelihood in many cases that a bankruptcy will result in complete termination of the bankrupt's obligation. In some cases, however, a borrower cannot use bankruptcy to terminate its obligation. In those cases, the ability of a bankruptcy court to alter the terms of obligations is important. In this context, the ability to alter the type of rate comes from the Bankruptcy Code provisions that allow bankruptcy courts to confirm reorganization plans that alter the debtors' prebankruptcy obligations. Among other things, those provisions permit a bankruptcy court to confirm a plan that limits a debtor's interest obligation to the market rate at the time of the bankruptcy, even if that rate is lower than the rate that the debtor agreed to pay before bankruptcy. 11 U.S.C. §1129(b)(2). In the course of selecting the market rate that the debtor would have to pay, the court not only could change the amount of the rate to reflect current conditions, but also could change the character of the rate, altering a fixed rate to a variable rate or vice versa.

In most cases, however, the power to alter a rate from fixed to variable or variable to fixed would not harm the lender significantly. The statute obligates the court to impose a rate based on market conditions at the time. Thus, the most that the court could do if prime had fallen to 5 percent would be to change a prime-plus-two loan to a fixed 7 percent loan. The court ordinarily could not change the prime-plus-two loan to a fixed 4 percent loan.

Problem Set 35

35.1.   Jude Fawley (a friend of yours who is a stonemason) calls you to help finalize the settlement of a dispute that he has with one of his customers. He recently completed a custom headstone for a customer that had promised to pay $8,000 for the headstone. When the customer received the headstone, though, the customer insisted that the headstone should have been made from green serpentine marble, rather than white marble. Feigning dissatisfaction, the customer refuses to pay. Jude privately believes the customer simply doesn't have the money. In any event, the customer has offered to settle the dispute by signing a promissory note for $6,000, payable with 10 percent interest in 12 equal monthly installments. Jude wants to know whether the customer's agreement to sign a note for the $6,000 will eliminate any of the customer's defenses to payment. How would you advise him? In evaluating Jude's question, consider §13 of the Promissory Note.

35.2.   Jodi Kay comes to you with a question about a variable-rate promissory note held by CountryBank. The note calls for interest at the rate of "the Prime Rate plus two percent per annum." The Prime Rate is defined as it is in

§2(e) of the Promissory Note. She read in the newspaper that the Federal Reserve raised its interest rates yesterday, and she knows that the interest that CountryBank pays on its funds will rise over the next few days. She is concerned because she also knows that Texas Commerce Bank has been merged into Chase Bank and thus no longer announces a prime rate. She wants to know whether the interest payments due under the variable-rate note will remain constant now that Texas Commerce Bank no longer announces its own prime rate. What do you tell her? If the amounts of the payments will not remain constant, how can she determine how much the payments will be?

35.3. Bill Robertson (your friend that operates and develops grocery stores) comes in to discuss a problem he has in obtaining financing for a new shopping center that he is in the process of constructing. When Bill finishes the shopping center, the income will come from long-term leases with rents that should provide a fixed return to Bill above the expenses of operating the shopping center. Bill tells you that he does not wish to try to make a profit on the financing. He just wants to make sure that once he obtains a loan, future fluctuations in the interest markets do not put him in a position where payments on the loan exceed the amount he is receiving from the leases that he already has in place.

After Bill leaves, you ask your associate Tom McCaffrey to draft a promissory note for the transaction. Tom — always careful — comes back a few minutes later and points out that Bill never said specifically whether the note should have a fixed interest rate or a variable interest rate. Tom wants to know which type of note he should use. What do you tell him?

35.4. As it turns out, the lender from whom Bill obtains his loan (Town-Bank) uses a five-year interest-rate swap to facilitate the transaction. The notional amount of the swap is $2 million. TownBank agrees to pay a fixed rate of 9 percent against a return from the swap dealer (Cheeryble Bros.) of LIBOR plus 3 percent. (LIBOR is 6 percent at the time of the swap.) Bill's loan for $2 million is at a fixed rate of 10 percent per annum, with interest-only payments for a term of five years. Answer the following questions about the transaction:

a. If interest rates do not change during the first year, what net payment will be due under the swap during that year?

b. If LIBOR increases to 7 percent during the second year, what net payment will be due under the swap during that year?

c. If LIBOR falls to 5 percent during the third year, what net payment will be due under the swap during that year?

d. For each year, what will the net rate of return be for TownBank, taking account of its outstanding loan to Bill, the interest that Bill pays to TownBank, and the payment made on the swap?

35.5. Your last task of the week is to write a policy memorandum for a bar committee advising the Board of Governors of the Federal Reserve. The memorandum relates to unsolicited loan checks (ULCs). ULCs are a device through which lenders make low-cost preapproved consumer loans. Lenders use publicly available credit information to identify consumers to whom they would be willing to make loans and then mail checks in the amount of the loan directly to the consumers. The consumer need not come to the bank office to fill out an application. The consumer need only cash the check. The amount of the check is less than the face amount of the loan because it reflects a deduction for the costs of the loan that the bank wishes the consumer to pay. If the consumer does not wish to accept the loan, the consumer need only discard the check.

Congress is considering a bill that would ban ULCs. Representatives opposed to the bill have asked the Federal Reserve for its perspective. Do you think the bill is a good idea? In evaluating that question, consider the policies reflected in TILA §132 and EFTA §911.

Chapter 10.   Credit Enhancement

Assignment 36:   Credit Enhancement by Guaranty

A.   The Role of Guaranties

When the parties to a transaction decide that payment will be deferred, the risk that the party that promises to pay (the borrower) will not pay as promised is a key factor in determining how much compensation is necessary to make deferred payment acceptable to the party to whom payment is due (the lender). If the lender thinks that the borrower is financially unsound, the lender might insist on a great deal of compensation for deferral to offset the possibility that the borrower ultimately will not pay the debt.

Alternatively (and probably more commonly), a lender might be altogether unwilling to enter into a transaction unless the borrower can convince the lender that the borrower is sufficiently creditworthy to satisfy the lender's concerns. In that event, the borrower might go to another type of lender to obtain the money that it wishes to borrow. For example, if a bank refuses to provide the desired funding, perhaps an asset financier or some other lender that specializes in more risky projects might be willing to provide the necessary financing (albeit at interest rates significantly higher than those ordinarily charged by banks). If those avenues fail as well, the business owner may simply be unable to obtain the money that it wants.

Organizational structure is one of the main reasons that many small businesses have particularly questionable credit. It is common for a small business to be organized as a separate entity (often a corporation) distinct from the entrepreneur that owns and operates the business. Although courts in some cases look through the entity to the individual or company behind the corporation—pierce the corporate veil, to use the common phrase—the organization of a separate corporation creates a strong presumption that the individual behind the corporation is not liable for the debts of the corporation. Accordingly, if the corporation borrows money and fails to repay it, ordinarily the creditor cannot pursue the owner of the corporation to obtain repayment. To overturn the presumption that the owner is not liable, a plaintiff must establish some substantial wrongdoing or misuse of the corporate entity. The mere existence of unpaid corporate creditors is not an adequate justification for allowing recourse against the owner.

That common organizational structure suggests an easy way to satisfy some of a lender's concerns about the creditworthiness of the small business. The business can offer a guaranty from its owner that allows the lender to pursue not just the business entity, but also the individual owner (who may have assets other than the business). For example, suppose that a wealthy individual named Carl Eben is the founder, president, and sole owner of a small industrial tooling company named Riverfront Tools, Inc. (RFT). RFT needs about $500,000 to finance its development of some new tool designs. If

RFT is a relatively small company or does not have a lengthy track record in its industry, a lender advancing the $500,000 to RFT probably would worry that RFT might fail to repay the loan. The risks to the lender are easy to see: RFT might have a poor business plan that produces insufficient operating revenue to repay its creditors, RFT might be subjected to a large tort judgment if one of its tools fails to work properly, or (sorry to say) Carl might abscond with RFT's funds. In many (if not most) cases, those risks would convince institutional lenders that it would not be profitable to make a loan to RFT standing alone. Instead, an institutional lender ordinarily would insist on a guaranty from Carl Eben personally.

By executing a guaranty, Carl would agree to provide a backup source of payment for the lender, from which the lender could obtain payment even if RFT was unable (or unwilling) to repay its debt voluntarily. In legal parlance, Carl would become a guarantor, a surety, or (more formally) a secondary obligor. The party that owes the money directly (RFT) would be known as the principal obligor or just as the principal. Finally, the party to whom the money is owed (the lender) would be referred to as the creditor or the obligee (the person to whom the obligor is obliged).

One of the most important considerations to a lender in evaluating the value of a guaranty is the creditworthiness of the guarantor. The general idea is that a guaranty from a strong and creditworthy guarantor provides a firm enhancement of the credit of the borrower because of the strong likelihood that the guarantor will repay the loan even if the borrower fails to do so. Conversely, a guarantor of undistinguished financial strength provides little or no assurance of payment beyond the assurance that would come from the borrower's direct promise to pay.

Creditworthiness is a relatively subjective concept. For starters, the fact that a company has valuable assets or significant operating revenues says little about its creditworthiness. An airline with a troubled operating history that recently went through bankruptcy would not generally be considered creditworthy even if the company had a large fleet of valuable airplanes and a relatively small level of existing debt. Conversely, a single individual with a lengthy and impeccable business record might be considered an excellent credit risk even if his tangible assets were relatively modest. The size of the guaranteed debt also is crucial to the concept of creditworthiness: Carl might be thought to be very creditworthy in the context of providing a guaranty for a $500,000 loan, but not at all consequential in the context of a $50 million transaction.

Another significant factor in evaluating the usefulness of a proposed guaranty is the relation of the guarantor to the borrower. In many cases (especially those that involve small businesses), the status of the guarantor is just as important as (or even more important than) the creditworthiness of the guarantor standing alone. To continue with our example, Carl's relation to RFT would make a lender considering a loan to RFT particularly interested in obtaining a guaranty from Carl. When the lender obtains a guaranty from Carl, the lender forces Carl to commit his personal assets to repaying the loan and thus ties Carl to the company. If Carl does not guarantee the loan, he always has the option of walking away from the company, letting it fail, and using his resources to start another company. Alternatively, he might engage in conduct that harms the business more subtly. For example, Carl might lose interest in RFT and start devoting his interests to a new project. A guaranty mitigates the lender's concern about those problems. When Carl has guaranteed the loan, he has a direct interest in RFT's success because RFT's success is necessary to Carl's ability to protect Carl's personal assets from the lender. That interest gives Carl's guaranty a unique value that the lender could not obtain from another source, even if the alternate source has a balance sheet more impressive than Carl's.

The guaranty relationship occurs (under a variety of different names) in a wide variety of contexts. For example, in a simple lending transaction like a car loan, a lender might ask a relative of the borrower to be a cosigner on the note. Although the status would depend on the terms of the note, the relative ordinarily would become a guarantor (rather than a primary obligor). Similarly, Article 3 of the Uniform Commercial Code (which deals with negotiable instruments) creates a set of implied guaranty obligations to deal with the rights of accommodation parties and accommodated parties. An accommodation party is any party that signs a negotiable instrument for the purpose of incurring liability without directly benefiting from the value that the creditor gives for the instrument. UCC §3-419(a). The accommodated party is the party for whose benefit the value was given, generally the principal borrower or issuer of the instrument. Under Article 3, an accommodation party is treated as a guarantor; the accommodated party is treated as the primary obligor. UCC §§3-419, 3-605.

Moving further afield, the surety and insurance industries are founded on such transactions. If an insurance company issued an insurance policy for RFT, the insurance company would be the surety, RFT would be the principal, and the party with a claim against RFT (hoping to be paid by the insurer) would be the creditor or obligee. Similarly, if RFT obtained a bond to back up its performance on a construction contract, the issuer of the bond would be a surety, RFT would be the principal, and the beneficiary of the bond would be the obligee or creditor.

There is no single "standard" form for a guaranty, and insurance policies and surety bonds obviously have provisions called for by particularities of the industries in which they are used. Most forms for guaranty transactions, however, contain relatively standard terms. The following pages set forth a relatively simple form that is representative of the forms that would be used for a guaranty in a substantial commercial lending transaction. (Later references to this document describe it as the Continuing Guaranty.)

Thomas S. Hemmendinger, Hillman on
Commercial Loan Documentation 373-377
(PLI 4th ed. 1994)*

CONTINUING GUARANTY

1. For valuable consideration, the undersigned ("Guarantors") jointly and severally unconditionally guarantee the payment when due, upon maturity,

---

*I have added the section numbers to the guaranty for ease of reference. They do not appear in the original.

acceleration, or otherwise, of any and all indebtedness of [*insert name of Borrower*] ("Borrower") to [*insert name of Lender*] ("Lender"), with an office at [*insert Lender's address*]. If any or all indebtedness of Borrower to Lender becomes due and payable hereunder, Guarantors jointly and severally unconditionally promise to pay such indebtedness to Lender or order, on demand, in lawful money of the United States.

2. The word "indebtedness" is used herein in its most comprehensive sense and includes any and all advances, debts, obligations, and liabilities of Borrower heretofore, now, or hereafter made, incurred, or created, whether voluntary or involuntary and however arising, absolute or contingent, liquidated or unliquidated, determined or undetermined, whether or not such indebtedness is from time to time reduced or extinguished and thereafter increased or incurred, whether Borrower may be liable individually or jointly with others, whether or not recovery upon such indebtedness may be or hereafter become barred by any statute of limitations, and whether or not such indebtedness may be or hereafter become otherwise unenforceable, and including all principal, interest, fees, charges, costs and expense (including reasonable attorneys' fees).

3. Guarantors jointly and severally unconditionally guarantee the payment of any and all indebtedness of Borrower to Lender whether or not due or payable by Borrower upon (a) death, dissolution, insolvency, or business failure of, or any assignment for benefit of creditors by, or commencement of any bankruptcy, reorganization, arrangement, moratorium, or other debtor-relief proceedings by or against, Borrower or any of the Guarantors; or (b) the appointment of a receiver for, or the attachment, restraint of, or making or levying of any order or legal process affecting the property of, Borrower or any of the Guarantors, and jointly and severally unconditionally promise to pay such indebtedness to Lender or order on demand, in lawful money of the United States.

4. This guaranty may be terminated only as to future transactions and only as to such Guarantors as give written notice thereof to Lender, and such notice shall be deemed to be effective as of noon of the next succeeding business day following actual receipt thereof by Lender at its address above. No such notice shall release Guarantors, whether or not giving such notice, from any liability as to (a) any indebtedness that may be owing to or held by Lender or in which Lender may have an interest or for which Lender may be obligated at the time of receiving such notice, (b) all extensions and renewals thereof, (c) all interest thereon, and (d) all collection expenses therefor (including reasonable attorneys' fees).

5. The liability of Guarantors hereunder is exclusive and independent of any security for or other guaranty of the indebtedness of Borrower, whether executed by Guarantors or by any other party, and the liability of Guarantors hereunder is not affected or impaired by (a) any direction of application of payment by Borrower or by any other party; (b) any other continuing or other guaranty, undertaking, or liability of Guarantors or of any other party as to the indebtedness of Borrower; (c) any payment on or in reduction of any such other guaranty or undertaking; (d) any notice of termination hereof as to future transactions given by, or by the death of, or the termination, revocation, or release of any obligations hereunder of, any other of Guarantors; (e) any dissolution, termination, or increase, decrease, or change in personnel of any of Guarantors; (f) any payment made to Lender on the indebtedness that Lender repays pursuant to court order in any bankruptcy, reorganization, arrangement, moratorium, or other debtor relief

or other judicial proceeding; or (g) merger of another entity into Borrower or merger of Borrower into another entity.

6. The obligations of Guarantors hereunder are joint and several, and independent of the obligations of Borrower, and a separate action or actions may be brought and prosecuted against Guarantors whether or not action be brought against Borrower and whether or not Borrower be joined in any such action or actions. Guarantors waive, to the fullest extent permitted by law, the benefit of any statute of limitations affecting their liability hereunder or the enforcement thereof. Any payment by Borrower or other circumstance that operates to toll any statute of limitations as to Borrower shall operate to toll the statute of limitations as to Guarantors.

7. Guarantors authorize Lender (whether or not after revocation or termination of this guaranty), without notice or demand, and without affecting or impairing their liability hereunder, from time to time to (a) renew, compromise, extend, increase, accelerate, or otherwise change the time for payment of, or otherwise change the terms of, the indebtedness or any part thereof, including increase or decrease of the rate of interest thereon; (b) take and hold security for the payment of this guaranty or the indebtedness and exchange, enforce, waive, and release any such security; (c) apply such security and direct the order or manner of sale thereof as Lender in its discretion may determine; and (d) release or substitute any one or more endorsers, Guarantors, Borrower, or other obligors. Lender may without notice assign this guaranty in whole or in part.

8. It is not necessary for Lender to inquire into the capacity or powers of Borrower or the officers, directors, partners, or agents acting or purporting to act on Borrower's behalf, and any indebtedness made or created in reliance upon the professed exercise of such powers shall be guaranteed hereunder. If Borrower is a partnership, the words "Borrower" and "indebtedness" as used herein include all successor partnerships and liabilities thereof to Lender.

9. Any indebtedness of Borrower now or hereafter held by Guarantors is hereby subordinated to the indebtedness of Borrower to Lender; and such indebtedness of Borrower to Guarantors, if Lender so requests, shall be collected, enforced, and received by Guarantors as trustees for Lender and be paid over to Lender on account of the indebtedness of Borrower to Lender, but without affecting or impairing in any manner the liability of Guarantors under the other provisions of this guaranty. Any instruments now or hereafter evidencing any indebtedness of Borrower to the undersigned shall be marked with a legend that the same are subject to this guaranty and, if Lender so requests, shall be delivered to Lender.

10. Guarantors waive any right to require Lender (a) to proceed against Borrower or any other party, (b) to proceed against or exhaust any security held from Borrower or any other party, or (c) to pursue any other remedy in Lender's power whatsoever. Guarantors waive any defense based on or arising out of any defense of Borrower other than payment in full of the indebtedness, including without limitation any defense based on or arising out of any disability of Borrower, or the unenforceability of the indebtedness or any part thereof from any cause, including any impairment of any security by Lender or Borrower or any other party, or the cessation from any cause of the liability of Borrower or any other party other than payment in full of the indebtedness. Lender may at its election foreclose on any security held by Lender by one or more judicial or nonjudicial sales, whether or

not every aspect of any such sale is commercially reasonable, or exercise any other right or remedy Lender may have against Borrower, or any security, without affecting or impairing in any way the liability of Guarantors hereunder except to the extent the indebtedness has been paid. Guarantors waive any defense arising out of any such election by Lender, even though such election operates to impair any security or to impair or extinguish any right of reimbursement or subrogation or other right or remedy of Guarantors against Borrower or any security.

11. Guarantors shall have no right of subrogation, and waive any right to enforce any remedy that Lender now has or may hereafter have against Borrower, and waive any benefit of, and any right of reimbursement, indemnity, or contribution or to participate in any security now or hereafter held by Lender. Guarantors waive all presentments, demands for performance, protests, and notices, including without limitation notices of acceptance of this guaranty, and notices of the existence, creation, or incurring of new or additional indebtedness.

12. Guarantors assume all responsibility for being and keeping themselves informed of Borrower's financial condition and assets, and of all other circumstances bearing upon the risk of nonpayment of the indebtedness and the nature, scope, and extent of the risks that Guarantors assume and incur hereunder, and agree that Lender shall have no duty to advise Guarantors of information known to it regarding such circumstances or risks.

13. In addition to the amounts guaranteed hereunder, Guarantors jointly and severally agree to pay reasonable attorneys' fees and all other costs and expenses incurred by Lender in enforcing this guaranty or in any action or proceeding arising out of, or relating to, this guaranty, including but not limited to cases or proceedings under Chapters 7, 11, 12, or 13 of the Bankruptcy Code, or under any successor statute thereto.

14. In all cases where there is but a single Guarantor, then all words used herein in the plural shall be deemed to have been used in the singular where the context and construction so require; and when this guaranty is executed by more than one Guarantor, the word "Guarantors" shall mean all and any one or more of them. This guaranty and the liability and obligations of Guarantors hereunder are binding upon Guarantors and their respective heirs, executors, administrators, successors, and assigns, and inures to the benefit of and is enforceable by Lender and its successors, transferees, and assigns.

15. In addition to all liens upon, and rights of setoff against the moneys, securities, or other property of Guarantors given to Lender by law, Lender shall have a lien upon and a right of setoff against all moneys, securities, and other property of Guarantors now or hereafter in the possession of or on deposit with Lender, whether held in a general or special account or deposit, or for safekeeping or otherwise; and every such lien and right of setoff may be exercised without demand upon or notice to Guarantors.

16. No right or power of Lender hereunder shall be deemed to have been waived by any act or conduct on the part of Lender, or by any neglect of such right or power, or by any delay in so doing; and the terms and provisions hereof may not be waived, altered, modified, or amended except in a writing duly signed by an authorized officer of Lender and by Guarantors.

17. This guaranty shall be deemed to be made under and shall be governed by the laws of the State of Rhode Island in all respects, including matters of construction, validity and performance.

18. If any of the provisions of this guaranty shall contravene or be held invalid under the laws of any jurisdiction, this guaranty shall be construed as if not containing those provisions and the rights and obligations of the parties hereto shall be construed and enforced accordingly.

19. This guaranty, together with [*describe mortgage or other agreement or instrument securing Guarantors' obligations*], constitutes the entire agreement and understanding between Guarantors and Lender relating to the subject matter hereof and supersedes all prior proposals, negotiations, agreements and understandings relating to such subject matter. In entering into this guaranty, Guarantors acknowledge that Guarantors are relying on no statement, representation, warranty, covenant or agreement of any kind made by Lender or any employees or agents of Lender, except as set forth herein.

20. Guarantors absolutely, irrevocably and unconditionally waive any and all right to assert any defense, setoff, counterclaim or cross claim of any nature with respect to this guaranty, any agreement or instrument securing this guaranty, or any obligations of any other person or party (including Borrower) relating to this guaranty, in any action, suit or proceeding Lender may bring to collect any of Borrower's indebtedness or to enforce any of Guarantors' obligations hereunder or under any agreement or instrument securing this guaranty.

21. Guarantors consent to the in personam jurisdiction of any State or Federal court located in the State of Rhode Island. Each Guarantor agrees that service of process may be made by mailing a copy of the summons to such Guarantor at Guarantor's address as set forth in the records of Lender.

To make any sense out of a guaranty transaction, it is necessary to understand the legal relations that arise when a party executes a guaranty. The rules establishing those relations usually are referred to as the law of suretyship (because surety bonds are one of the oldest and most important areas in which those rules apply). The remainder of this assignment focuses on the first set of relations: the rights of the creditor against the guarantor. Assignment 37 continues that discussion by discussing the rights of the guarantor against the principal and the creditor.

B.   Rights of the Creditor Against the Guarantor

Although the guarantor or surety is called a "secondary" obligor, there is little that is secondary about the guarantor's obligation to the creditor. In the absence of some special language in the guaranty, the guarantor is liable to pay the obligation in question immediately upon the default of the principal. Restatement of Suretyship §15(a). Thus, the lender can sue Carl the instant that RFT defaults. The lender does not have to seek payment first from RFT, and the lender certainly does not have to sue RFT or otherwise consider whether it would be able to force RFT to pay. Rather, the lender is free to proceed as it deems appropriate: suing the principal first or suing the guarantor first.

Although it may seem surprising to allow the lender to proceed directly against the *secondary* obligor without first trying to extract payment from the *principal* obligor, a little thought shows the sense of the rule. A contrary rule would limit the value of a guaranty considerably because in many cases it would obligate a lender to pursue recovery against an insolvent principal, even though the lender might be able to recover the money immediately by suing the guarantor directly. Almost invariably the reason that a principal has failed to pay as promised is that the principal is unable to pay. In those cases, it is pointless to construct a legal rule that requires the lender to sue the principal before proceeding to collect from the solvent guarantor.

That is not to say that the parties cannot create an arrangement in which the creditor has to pursue the principal first and can sue the guarantor only after its efforts to collect from the principal are unsuccessful. Such an arrangement is called a guaranty of collection. To create that arrangement, the parties need only describe Carl in the guaranty as a "guarantor of collection" or title the document a "guaranty of collection." If the parties use those terms, then the lender ordinarily cannot pursue the guarantor unless (1) it is unable to locate and serve the principal, (2) the principal is insolvent, or (3) the lender is unsuccessful in obtaining payment even after it obtains a judgment against the principal. UCC §3-419(d); Restatement of Suretyship §15(b).

Given the impracticality of forcing a lender to satisfy those requirements before obtaining payment, it is not surprising that the guaranty of collection is relatively rare. Indeed, the lender's desire to avoid any obligation to sue the principal ordinarily is underscored by a lengthy and specific statement in the guaranty in which the lender requires the guarantor to acknowledge with considerable repetitiveness that the document creates a conventional guaranty obligation rather than a guaranty of collection. See, e.g., Continuing Guaranty §§6, 10.

Notwithstanding the rarity with which lenders accept guaranties of collection, the bankruptcy process provides a ready mechanism by which a guarantor that controls its principal can produce a similar roadblock for the creditor seeking to collect on a guaranty. However clear the law regarding the independence of the guarantor's obligation to the creditor and however clear the terms of a particular guaranty, it is not unusual for bankruptcy courts faced with a bankruptcy by the principal to enjoin the creditor from attempting to collect from the surety. The following case is a representative example.

F.T.L., Inc. v. Crestar Bank (In re F.T.L., Inc.)
152 B.R. 61 (Bankr. E.D. Va. 1993)

Douglas O. Tice, Jr., Bankruptcy Judge...

Debtor ("FTL") operates a car wash under the trade name Car-Robics Brushless Auto Wash in Newport News, Virginia. On July 31, 1991, debtor filed a voluntary bankruptcy petition under chapter 11. Frank Lash, Jr., and Robyn Lash ("Lashes") are officers and directors of FTL, and together they hold 60 percent of the stock in FTL....

Crestar Bank is the primary secured creditor of FTL, holding secured debt of approximately $785,000.00. Frank Lash, Jr., and Robyn Lash personally guaranteed this debt. In January 1992 Crestar secured a judgment lien against the Lashes and subsequently perfected its lien against the Lashes' personal residence. A foreclosure sale on the residence was scheduled for January 28, 1993. Crestar also issued suggestions in garnishment on the Lashes' personal bank accounts. . . .

FTL filed its amended plan of reorganization in December 1992. The plan calls for the Lashes to contribute all the equity in their home to the reorganization. The Lashes are prepared to accomplish this through a home equity loan, and they have already obtained a $115,000.00 written loan commitment from First Fidelity Mortgage to be secured by a second deed of trust on their residence. In addition, FTL is conceivably 30-45 days away from a commitment on a SBA loan through NationsBank. However, this loan is conditioned upon the continued ownership and management of FTL by the Lash family and the personal guarantee of the Lashes. Frank Lash, III, and Tom Lash have been able to secure new financing commitments of approximately $41,000.00, and a personal friend of the Lashes, Don Sweeney, has expressed interest in investing up to $30,000.00 in FTL if a plan is eventually confirmed.

DISCUSSION AND CONCLUSIONS OF LAW

The plain language of 11 U.S.C. §362 provides only for the automatic stay of judicial proceedings and enforcement of judgments against the debtor or the property of the estate. This court has previously held that in the absence of compelling unusual circumstances, guarantors of a debtor must file their own bankruptcy petition to receive the benefits of bankruptcy law. Nothing in §362 suggests Congress intended to strip from creditors of a bankrupt debtor the protection they sought and received when they required a third party to guaranty the debt.[2] The very purpose of a guarantee is to assure a creditor that in the event the debtor defaults, the creditor will have someone to look to for reimbursement.

While the automatic stay provisions are generally said to be available only to the debtor and not to third party guarantors, . . . in unusual circumstances the bankruptcy court can enjoin proceedings against non-debtor third parties pursuant to 11 U.S.C. §105(a). Where the identity of the debtor and the third party are inexorably interwoven so that the debtor may be said to be the real party against whom the creditor is proceeding a bankruptcy court may exercise equitable jurisdiction to enjoin proceedings against non-debtor third parties. 11 U.S.C. §105(a). For example, a situation may exist where proceeding against the third party would actually reduce or diminish property the debtor could otherwise make available to the creditors as a whole. Allowing such action would undermine two basic principles of chapter 11: to provide creditors with a compulsory and collective forum to sort out their relative entitlement to a debtor's assets and to provide the debtor with a realistic opportunity to formulate a plan of reorganization.

---

2. Congress knew how to extend the automatic stay to nonbankrupt parties when it intended to do so. Chapter 13, for example, contains a narrowly drawn provision to stay proceedings against a limited category of individual cosigners of consumer debts. See 11 U.S.C. §1301(a).

I believe . . . that this case presents the kind of "unusual circumstances" . . . that warrant a temporary injunction against Crestar to cease collection activities against the Lashes.

First, the evidence establishes that the collection activities against the Lashes arise from FTL debt to Crestar, not direct personal obligations of the Lashes to Crestar. The evidence also establishes that FTL is currently operating at a profit with several promising avenues of new financing on the horizon. With a brief respite from protracted litigation the Lash family may be able to successfully reorganize this debtor. Accordingly, the court believes the debtor is likely to succeed on the merits by proposing a confirmable chapter 11 plan.

Second, the facts establish that proposing a confirmable plan will be virtually impossible without the active involvement of Frank Lash, Jr., in pursuing new financing arrangements. If Frank Lash, Jr., filed his own bankruptcy petition he probably would not be able to contribute the equity in his residence to the debtor's plan of reorganization as proposed, and his ability to secure new financing for the debtor would be foiled. Accordingly, the court must conclude that irreparable harm will occur to the debtor's realistic opportunity to reorganize if collection activities against the Lashes are allowed to continue.

Third, the evidence establishes that little or no harm will be caused to Crestar if it is temporarily enjoined from collection activities against the Lashes.[3] What Crestar seeks through foreclosure on the Lashes' residence is effectively being proposed under the plan of reorganization by the Lashes contributing all the equity in their home to the plan; as the primary secured creditor Crestar will be the beneficiary of these funds. The Lashes are not holding back any substantial asset that would otherwise be available to Crestar via the Lashes' guarantor liability. Moreover, since the commencement of this case Crestar has received and will continue to receive monthly adequate protection payments equivalent to the monthly payments of principal and interest due prepetition. Given its predominant secured creditor position it is unlikely that a plan can be confirmed over Crestar's objection. Accordingly, the court must find that issuing a temporary injunction will not substantially harm Crestar or any other interested party.

Fourth, the court believes the creditors as a whole are best served by giving this debtor an opportunity to propose a plan of reorganization. By seeking to foreclose on the Lashes' residence Crestar is attempting to opt-out of chapter 11's compulsory and collective forum of sorting out the creditors' relative entitlement to the debtor's assets. The creditors as a whole deserve the opportunity to evaluate and vote on a plan of reorganization in this case. Accordingly, the court concludes that the "public interest is best served by maintaining the status quo" and enjoining Crestar's collection activities against the Lashes for a period of 90 days or until the merits of the debtor's plan can be promptly and fully considered at a confirmation hearing.

---

3. This injunction is temporary only, and issued to assist the debtor through a crucial point in the reorganization proceedings; the injunction will expire in 90 days or upon confirmation of a plan. The need for permanent injunctive relief in this case is remote because any confirmed plan would likely render unavailable the Lashes' main asset, the equity in their home. Moreover, this court is disinclined to permanently enjoin collection activities against a non-debtor because 11 U.S.C. §524(e) arguably prevents what would in effect be granting a discharge to a non-debtor. This type of extraordinary relief may be appropriate in rare circumstances . . . but should not be liberally granted.

Accordingly, the court will enjoin Crestar's collection activities against the Lashes for a period of 90 days.

The inquiry into whether a debtor's bankruptcy presents sufficiently "unusual" circumstances to justify an injunction preventing a lender from pursuing a guarantor is so imprecise that a guarantor will rarely be confident that initiating a bankruptcy proceeding for its principal will allow it to defer payment. Thus, the guarantor cannot use bankruptcy as a reliable mechanism for holding off the lender. But the converse is just as true: The vagueness of the legal rule means that a lender rarely can be sure that it will be able to enforce the guaranty against a guarantor if (as is frequently the case) the guarantor is one of the prime movers of the borrower. Accordingly, the threat of a bankruptcy filing by the borrower makes the lender concerned about the possibility that the borrower's bankruptcy will defer the lender's ability to pursue the nonbankrupt guarantor.

Problem Set 36

36.1. Your friend Tertius Lydgate comes by this morning to discuss another round of financial difficulties. He says that he has found one bright spot in one of his transactions and wants to tell you about it. Lydgate is the guarantor of a large loan from Bulstrode Bank to Middlemarch Medical Clinics, Inc. (MMC). MMC has just closed its doors after protracted litigation with Bulstrode. Although Lydgate is depressed at the failure of MMC—MMC has no remaining assets to pay Bulstrode or any of its other creditors—Lydgate tells you that he gets some satisfaction out of the knowledge that Bulstrode spent $400,000 in legal fees pursuing MMC. Lydgate said that he was reading the terms of his guaranty agreement last night (which is identical to the Continuing Guaranty in the assignment) and figured out that Bulstrode cannot collect those legal fees from Lydgate under his guaranty. Lydgate explains that he has read §13 of the Continuing Guaranty carefully and understands that it allows Bulstrode to recover the litigation expenses of a suit against Lydgate, but not the expenses of a suit against MMC. Is Lydgate correct? Continuing Guaranty §§1, 2, 13; Promissory Note §9.

36.2. California Fidelity Bank (CFB) has issued a $20 million line of credit to Jaffe Investments, Inc., a business operated by Wendell Jaffe and Carl Eckert. Although Jaffe runs the day-to-day affairs, Eckert provides most of the capital for the business. Accordingly, CFB took a continuing guaranty from Eckert in the terms set forth in the assignment. Yesterday morning a grand jury indicted Jaffe on charges of embezzling funds from the company's clients. Yesterday afternoon Jaffe's sailboat was found floating off the Santa Barbara coast. There was a suicide note, but police suspect that Jaffe fled to avoid his legal problems. This morning Mac Voorhies (the loan officer at CFB) received a hand-delivered letter from Eckert, stating: "I hereby terminate the Continuing Guaranty that I have signed with respect to your loan to Jaffe Investments,

Inc., and abjure any further liability whatsoever with respect to any future advances under that loan."

Voorhies is concerned about the effects of the notice, mostly because he doubts that Jaffe left any assets in the company and because Eckert is his only likely source of payment. CFB currently has $2 million outstanding on the line of credit, which is accruing interest at about 13 percent per annum. More seriously, CFB has another important transaction pending under the Jaffe line of credit: CFB issued letters of credit backing up $10 million of short-term commercial paper that Jaffe Investments, Inc., issued almost two months ago. The paper matures next week. If Jaffe Investments fails to pay the holders of the paper the $10 million that they are owed at that time (and Voorhies has no reason to think that Jaffe will make that payment), the holders of the paper will be entitled to payment from CFB.

Voorhies says that Eckert easily has the assets to pay the entire amount. Voorhies wants to know if the notice will limit Voorhies's ability to pursue Eckert for the amounts CFB might have to pay on the commercial paper or subsequently accruing interest. What do you tell him? Continuing Guaranty §4.

36.3.   Jude Fawley (your wealthy stonemason friend) comes to consult you about some serious problems with his business, Obscure Wessex Headstones (OWH). Several years ago you organized Jude's business as a corporation, with Jude as the sole shareholder. Jude has guaranteed OWH's $1.2 million line of credit with Wessex Bank (which contains a provision similar to §8 in the Promissory Note in Assignment 35). Over the last six months, OWH's net monthly income has decreased from $20,000 to only $2,000. At the same time, operating expenses have caused OWH to draw down its entire line of credit, so that it now owes Wessex the entire $1.2 million. OWH has only $10,000 cash on hand right now. Its current obligations include a $10,000 monthly payment due to Wessex on the first of the month and $8,000 in overdue bills from suppliers.

Jude tells you that he would feel terrible if he did not pay his suppliers, many of whom have been doing business with him for decades, but that he doesn't want to do anything that would worsen his personal financial situation. He also tells you that he doesn't mind all that much if he loses the stonemason business as long as he can keep the rest of his assets (which include a multimillion-dollar business syndicating walking tours of rural Britain). What should he do?

36.4.   Ben Darrow (your friend from the early days of the book) calls you in distress. He read in the paper this morning that one of his borrowers, Matacora Pipelines, Inc., was hit yesterday with a $1 million tort judgment. The judgment resulted from a tragic accident in which a Matacora employee working on the construction of a new pipeline was killed by an exploding dynamite charge. Ben knows that Matacora does not have enough assets to pay the judgment and is worried about his bank's $250,000 loan to Matacora (for which Ben has no collateral). On further questioning, Ben tells you that he has a personal guaranty from Bud Lassen, the independently wealthy owner and operator of Matacora. Ben also tells you that he believes the entry of the tort judgment is a default on the loan to Matacora because it constitutes a "material adverse change" in Matacora's financial condition. What is your assessment of Ben's situation? Will the situation change if Matacora files for bankruptcy?

36.5. Impressed with your work on the Jude Fawley matter (in Problem 36.3), Wessex Bank retains you to handle a proposed restructuring of one of its loans. For several years, Wessex has been lending to a growing chain of specialty stores called We-R-Red, which specialize in bright red clothing and accessories. Until now the business has been operated as a sole proprietorship owned by Diggory Venn. Because of Venn's considerable wealth, Wessex traditionally has considered the relationship a safe one even though the loan is unsecured.

Venn recently learned that the Environmental Protection Agency has decided to list as a toxic substance the chemical that Venn uses to makes his products (reddelic acid). Venn believes that the resultant dye (ordinary "reddle") is completely safe, but is worried about the possibility of some accident that would result in environmental liability that would wipe out all of his assets. In response, Venn has decided to incorporate the business under the name of We-R-Red, Inc. Venn will remain the controlling shareholder and chief executive officer. Venn would like to transfer the loan to the new entity, but is willing to issue a guaranty of the loan himself. The loan officer at Wessex, Eustacia ("Stacy") Vye, wants to know what you think about Venn's proposal. What do you say?

Assignment 37:   Protections for Guarantors

A.   Rights of the Guarantor Against the Principal

As Assignment 36 suggests, in most cases a guarantor is closely affiliated with the principal whose debt it guarantees. Accordingly, it is relatively uncommon for a guarantor and a principal to execute a written agreement memorializing the terms of their relationship. As a result, their relations generally are governed by a set of obligations that are implied as a matter of common law (supplemented in some contexts by statute). Specifically, the law grants the guarantor three major rights against the principal: the rights of performance, reimbursement, and subrogation (see Figure 37.1). Although those rights overlap in many circumstances, it is useful to analyze the substance of each of them separately.

1.   Performance

The right of performance (or exoneration) allows the guarantor to sue the principal in order to force the principal to perform the guaranteed obligation. Restatement of Suretyship §21. The idea behind the right of performance is that the guarantor should not have to go to the trouble of performing and then seeking reimbursement from the principal when the principal can perform in the first instance. The right of performance rarely is significant because in most cases the principal would be performing if it could. Thus, an injunction formally commanding performance ordinarily does not alter the difficulties that keep the principal from performing in the first place. Moreover, in the typical case where the guarantor is a controlling officer or owner of the principal, a guarantor usually will have more direct ways to induce the principal to perform than filing a lawsuit seeking an injunction.

2.   Reimbursement

The right of reimbursement entitles the guarantor to recover from the principal any sums that the guarantor pays to the creditor under the guaranty. Again, it exists entirely apart from any specific contractual agreement, being implied as a matter of law. Restatement of Suretyship §22; UCC §3-419(e) (applying that rule to payments by an accommodation party to a negotiable instrument).

Figure 37.1
Rights of the Guarantor

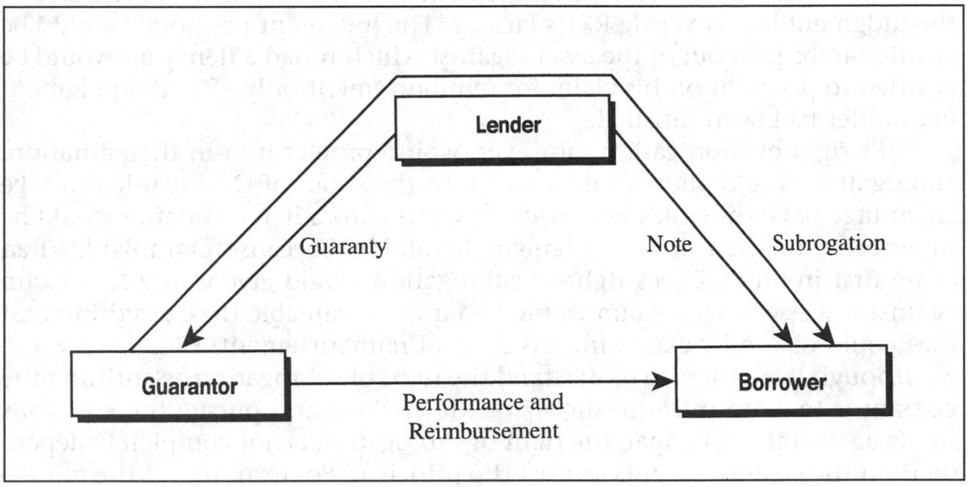

3. Subrogation

The third of the guarantor's rights, subrogation, is the most difficult to understand. Generally, subrogation allows a guarantor forced to pay on its guaranty to recover that payment by stepping into the shoes of the creditor and asserting against the principal all of the rights that the creditor could have asserted against the principal. Restatement of Suretyship §§27-28. As a practical matter, subrogation ordinarily works as if the rights of the creditor had been assigned to the guarantor in return for the guarantor's payment on the underlying debt. For that reason, older decisions describe subrogation as "equitable assignment" or "assignment by operation of law." For example, if Carl paid the lender $500,000 on Carl's guaranty of a debt owed by RFT, Carl would be subrogated to the lender's rights against RFT. Thus, Carl could sue RFT to collect that $500,000 just as the lender could have sued RFT on the note for the $500,000.

In a simple transaction where the lender's only right against RFT is to sue RFT to collect the debt, the right of subrogation has no independent significance because it duplicates Carl's right of reimbursement. But in more complex transactions the lender will have rights beyond a simple right to sue, such as a lien or security interest, or perhaps an Article 2 right of reclamation (see UCC §2-702). The guarantor's ability to obtain those rights makes subrogation an important tool for the guarantor.

To see how that might occur, suppose that OmniBank loaned RFT $500,000, taking back both a lien on RFT's factory (RFT's only significant asset) and a guaranty from Carl. Now suppose that one of RFT's tools causes a catastrophic accident, resulting in a $2 million judgment lien against RFT's factory. When RFT fails to pay OmniBank in a timely manner, RFT's lender calls on Carl's guaranty. If Carl has substantial assets outside of his interest in RFT, he might proceed to pay OmniBank on the guaranty. Carl's right of reimbursement would provide Carl little solace in this situation. Carl's claim for reimbursement would be an unsecured claim, which would go nowhere in the face of the judgment lien covering RFT's factory. The judgment lienholder would be entitled to be paid out of the assets against which it had a lien; Carl would be entitled to payment on his claim for reimbursement only after the judgment lienholder had been satisfied.

Carl's right of subrogation, however, would protect him in that situation. Subrogation would allow Carl to step into the shoes of OmniBank and take advantage of OmniBank's lien. Because OmniBank's lien ordinarily would be superior to the lien of the judgment lienholder (because OmniBank's lien came first in time), Carl's right of subrogation would give Carl a first claim against the assets. That claim would be far more valuable than anything that Carl could obtain by exercising his right of reimbursement.

Although it is easiest to understand the right of subrogation as entitling the guarantor to "step into the shoes" of the creditor and pursue the creditor's rights against the principal, the right of subrogation is not completely dependent on the creditor's rights against the principal. For example, as the following case shows, in some situations a guarantor can retain its right of subrogation even if the creditor grants the principal a complete release from liability.

Corporate Buying Service v. Lenox Hill Radiology Associates
1995 WL 608288 (S.D.N.Y. Oct. 17, 1995)

SCHEINDLIN, District Judge . . .

This dispute has its origin in three loan agreements ("Loans") totaling $5.5 million between Citytrust, a Connecticut bank and trust, and the Lenox Hill defendants, three affiliated entities, the combined assets of which comprised a radiology practice. On October 14, 1987, Diasonics guaranteed payment on the Loans to the extent of $725,000.00 as an inducement to Citytrust to make loans to the Lenox Hill defendants, who were planning to use a portion of the proceeds to purchase equipment from Diasonics.

By 1991, [Toshiba assumed Diasonics's obligation on the guaranty,] and the Federal Deposit Insurance Corporation ("FDIC") was appointed receiver for Citytrust.

On May 8, 1992, the FDIC sued the Lenox Hill defendants under the Loans and Toshiba under the Guaranty after the Lenox Hill defendants defaulted. [Eventually, the FDIC and the Lenox Hill defendants agreed on a settlement that] called for a one-time settlement payment in an amount less than the aggregate principal amount on the Loans in return for an agreement to settle any claims against one another arising from the Loans ("Mutual Release"). The Mutual Release specifically reserved the FDIC's right to pursue both Diasonics and Toshiba on the Guaranty. The total amount paid by the Lenox Hill defendants on the Loans was $2.53 million.

[Toshiba then filed a motion for summary judgment, claiming that the Mutual Release discharged its obligation on the guaranty. Alternatively, Toshiba sought a declaration that, if the Mutual Release did not release Toshiba on the guaranty, Toshiba was subrogated to the rights of the FDIC and Citytrust against the Lenox Hill defendants. Subsequently, the FDIC's rights on the Loans and Guaranty were assigned to Corporate Buying Service ("CBS").] . . .

A guarantor who becomes liable for the debt of a principal has [the] optio[n] to . . . pay the debt in full and thereby become subrogated to the rights of the creditor.

Subrogation is an equitable remedy, the purpose of which is to compel the ultimate discharge of a debt or obligation by one who in good conscience ought to pay. Accordingly, subrogation is intended to be used as a remedy in order to aid the enforcement of a legal right. The existence of the duty to pay the principal's debt gives the [guarantor], who is required to pay, the right to be subrogated to the creditor's claims against the principal. The right of subrogation is a creature of equity, and is enforced solely for the purpose of accomplishing the ends of substantial justice.

Lenox Hill argues that if the creditor has no remaining rights at the time of payment, then the guarantor obtains no right by way of subrogation. Lenox Hill further asserts that because the Release completely extinguished any claims the creditor had against the principal, the guarantor cannot recover from the principal.

When a creditor releases a principal debtor but reserves its rights against a guarantor, the question remains whether the guarantor retains its right to subrogation as against the principal debtor. This appears to be a question of first impression in this circuit, although it has been addressed by some state courts. [As one of those courts has explained:]

> [W]hen a creditor clearly reserves his rights against [a] surety, [the] debtor is notified that [the] release is no more than [a] covenant not to sue, despite words such as "full satisfaction" and "final release" in [the] compromise agreement between creditor and debtor; consequently, [the] principal debt remains alive, [the] surety's rights to reimbursement and subrogation are unimpaired, and [the] surety is not discharged.

This Court agrees that fundamental fairness and principles of equity require that the guarantors be reimbursed for any amount they pay on behalf of the principal. CBS expressly reserved the right to pursue the guarantors on their $725,000.00 Guaranty despite its settlement with the Lenox Hill defendants. This reservation preserved Toshiba and/or Diasonics' right to subrogation and reimbursement. Any other conclusion would be contrary to the fundamental principles underlying the concept of subrogation.

Although it may be simplest to understand the rights that come with subrogation by visualizing the guarantor stepping into the shoes of the creditor, too much attention to that concept produces improper results. As the court explains, it makes sense (absent a contrary contractual provision) to allow a guarantor to recover from the principal even though the creditor has released its own right to recover.

The most important limitation on the right of subrogation is that the guarantor normally has no right of subrogation until the entire guaranteed debt has been paid. Restatement of Suretyship §27(1). Allowing a guarantor to acquire a right of subrogation by repaying only a portion of the debt would have a number of odd consequences. For example, as one court explained:

> [I]f the surety upon making a partial payment became entitled to subrogation pro tanto, ... it would operate to place such surety upon a footing of equality with the holders of the unpaid part of the debt, and, in case the property was insufficient to pay the remainder of the debt for which the guarantor was bound, the loss would logically fall proportionately upon the creditor and upon the surety. Such a result would be grossly inequitable.

Jessee v. First Natl. Bank, 267 S.E.2d 803, 805 (Ga. App. 1979).

Perhaps more serious is the possibility that the guarantor's "pro tanto" right of subrogation might hinder the creditor's attempt to collect from the borrower. If pro tanto subrogation were available, a borrower in difficulty could derail its creditor's collection efforts by causing its guarantor to make a partial payment of the debt. Asserting its rights of subrogation, the guarantor then could argue that its pro tanto share of the claim against the borrower entitled it to participate in the litigation pursuing the borrower. The guarantor's ability to impair the creditor's pursuit of the principal usually would not be catastrophic, however, because the creditor would retain the ability to go directly against the guarantor for debt unpaid by the principal. Moreover, the right of subrogation would not be the only way that the guarantor could obtain a right to sue the borrower; even the right of reimbursement would give the guarantor a right to sue the borrower (albeit not a right to pursue the creditor's collateral) without repaying the debt in full.

In any event, the possibility that the guarantor would interfere with the creditor's attempts to collect is sufficiently frustrating to justify steps to prevent it. Accordingly, even though the common-law rule bars pro tanto subrogation, creditors ordinarily buttress their position by exacting from guarantors a complete or partial waiver of their rights of subrogation. See, e.g., Continuing Guaranty §11.

The situation is complicated by a separate concern that formerly justified creditors in seeking waivers of subrogation. Before the Bankruptcy Reform Act of 1994, lenders almost universally insisted on complete waivers of subrogation to circumvent the odd treatment of payments on guaranteed loans as improper "preferences" under 11 U.S.C. §547(b). That section of the Bankruptcy Code allows a bankrupt debtor to recover certain payments (called "preferences") that a debtor made shortly before it filed for bankruptcy, but only if these payments are made "for the benefit of" a "creditor." Under a somewhat counterintuitive reading of the statute, courts concluded that payments made by a borrower to a lender on guaranteed loans satisfied both of those requirements and thus were preferences. On the "benefit" question, a borrower that makes a payment on a guaranteed loan benefits the guarantor (albeit indirectly) by reducing the guarantor's potential liability to the creditor on the guaranty. Accordingly, courts treated a payment by a borrower on a guaranteed loan as a payment "for the benefit of" the guarantor for purposes of §547(b). On the "creditor" question, courts concluded that the guarantor's rights of subrogation and reimbursement were sufficient to make a guarantor a "creditor" of the borrower. Accordingly, bankruptcy courts frequently treated payments on guaranteed loans as preferences and allowed bankrupt debtors to recover those loan payments from their creditors as long as the payments were made within the statute of limitations for actions relying on §547(b) (up to one year before the bankruptcy). Figure 37.2 illustrates the problem.

Figure 37.2
Guarantor Preferences

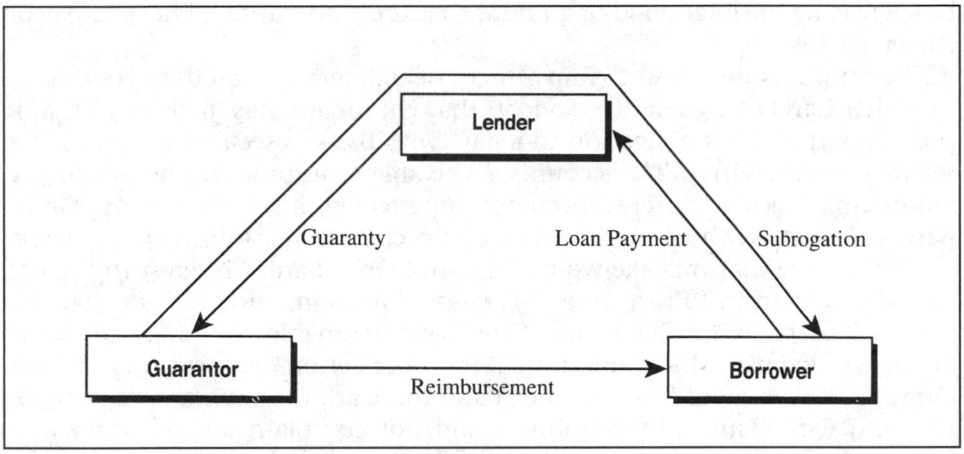

- The loan payment "benefit[s]" the Guarantor by reducing the Guarantor's obligation on the guaranty.
- The Guarantor's rights of reimbursement and subrogation make the Guarantor a "creditor" of the Borrower.
- Before 1994, a bankrupt Borrower could recover the loan payment as a "preference" from the Lender under 11 U.S.C. §547. Since 1994, 11 U.S.C. §550(c) bars that recovery.

Lenders tried to solve this problem by obtaining an absolute waiver of the guarantor's rights against the borrower. If a waiver meant that the guarantor had no claim against the borrower, then (lenders argued) the payment to the lender could not be a payment for the benefit of a "creditor" because the guarantor sans subrogation and reimbursement would not be a creditor of the debtor. The guarantor-preference problem was for the most part solved by the enactment in 1994 of 11 U.S.C. §550(c). That provision prevents borrowers from relying on the guarantor's status as a creditor to justify recovery of such payments from third-party creditors. Regardless of that statutory fix, however, the problem has continuing significance because the same waiver provisions continue to appear in standard guaranty forms.

B.   Rights of the Guarantor Against the Creditor

1.   Suretyship Defenses

Assignment 36 explained that the guarantor's "secondary" status does not ordinarily limit the creditor's right to proceed directly against the guarantor in response to a default by the principal obligor. That is not to say, however, that the secondary nature of the guarantor's obligation has no effect on the rights of the creditor. To the contrary, the secondary nature of the obligation drives a series of rules that release the guarantor from its obligation. Those rules serve as a remedy for creditor misconduct that might harm the guarantor by increasing the likelihood or amount that the guarantor will have to pay on the guaranty.

The simplest rule relates to impairment of collateral. Recall the hypothetical in which Carl Eben guaranteed a loan that OmniBank has made to RFT. Suppose now that RFT's obligation to repay OmniBank is secured by a perfected security interest in RFT's accounts receivable, equipment, and inventory. OmniBank's security interest becomes unperfected, however, because Omni-Bank fails to make the filings required by Article 9 of the Uniform Commercial Code. Because that mistake would "impair" OmniBank's interest in the collateral it took from RFT, it usually is referred to as impairment of collateral.

If RFT becomes insolvent and OmniBank is unable to collect from RFT because of OmniBank's failure to maintain perfection of its security interest, OmniBank then would look to the guarantor, Carl, for payment. As between RFT and OmniBank, RFT certainly could not complain about OmniBank's failure to maintain perfection. Rather, RFT is directly liable on the debt whether or not OmniBank takes care to protect OmniBank's interest in the assets that RFT offered as collateral. Carl, however, would have some justification for a complaint because OmniBank's actions lessened OmniBank's ability to recover from RFT and thus increased Carl's likely obligation to OmniBank. In fact (absent some contrary agreement), Carl would have a defense to a suit on his guaranty to the extent that OmniBank's mistake harmed Carl. The harm would be the amount that OmniBank would have recovered from RFT if OmniBank had maintained perfection, reduced by the amount that OmniBank actually recovered from RFT notwithstanding OmniBank's mistake. Restatement of Suretyship §36(1), (2)(a); UCC §3-605(e),(g).

Impairing collateral is not the only thing a creditor can do that might increase the exposure of the guarantor. Another common possibility is for the creditor to grant the principal an extension of time to pay. Suppose that RFT's loan from OmniBank is due on July 1, 1999. On the due date, RFT is still solvent, but experiencing financial difficulties. OmniBank does not force RFT to pay at that time, but instead grants a one-year extension. By the time the extension expires, RFT is insolvent. OmniBank collects nothing and sues Carl on his guaranty. In that event, Carl would argue that Omni-Bank's grant of an extension to RFT caused Carl a loss by decreasing the amount that OmniBank was able to recover from RFT. The merits of that claim, however, are not as clear as those of the impairment-of-collateral claim because there is no obvious reason why the extension would be more likely to harm Carl than to help him. From the point of view of the creditor at the time that it grants the extension, it is hard to predict whether it would be better to pursue RFT vigorously on the original due date or instead to grant the extension. A premature suit might destroy RFT unnecessarily, but an extension might defer collection efforts until all of RFT's assets have been dissipated. Notwithstanding the dilemma that the creditor faces, the law generally offers Carl a discharge on his guaranty to the extent that he can prove that the extension decreased OmniBank's ability to recover from RFT. Restatement of Suretyship §40(b); UCC §3-605(c).

A third common situation occurs when the creditor grants some modification of the indebtedness other than an extension of the due date. For example, suppose that RFT defaults on its loan and that the creditor chooses not to enforce its remedies against RFT immediately; instead, the creditor allows RFT to reinstate the loan, conditioned on an increase in the interest rate of 1 percent per annum. If RFT eventually fails to repay the loan and OmniBank pursues Carl, Carl could defend against OmniBank's claim by arguing that the amendment of the loan caused Carl's exposure on the guaranty to be more than it otherwise would have been. For example, Carl might try to prove that OmniBank would have been paid in full if it had exercised its rights against RFT on the first default or that the outstanding balance would have been smaller if OmniBank and RFT had not raised the interest rate. If either of those things was true, Carl would have at least a partial defense to OmniBank's claim. Restatement of Suretyship §41(b); UCC §3-605(d).

A more extreme situation occurs when the creditor completely releases the principal from liability and then proceeds to sue the guarantor, as in the *Corporate Buying Service* case excerpted above. The intuitive response to this situation would be that a complete release of the principal should most clearly justify release of the guarantor because a complete release of the principal is the most serious possible modification of the principal obligation. The law has not, however, taken that course.

Instead, the traditional approach to a release of the principal obligor focuses on the question whether the creditor intended for its release of the principal also to release the guarantor. If the terms of the release indicate that the creditor intended to retain its right to pursue the guarantor (usually referred to as a "reservation of rights"), then the creditor retains its right to pursue the guarantor. A typical provision would state: "Nothing in this Release shall be construed to release any right of Lender to recover the Debt from Guarantor or any party other than Borrower that is primarily or secondarily liable for all or any portion of the debt."

As the *Corporate Buying Service* case shows, the law justifies the rule allowing the creditor to pursue the guarantor after granting a release to the principal by also allowing the guarantor to retain its right to pursue the principal (via reimbursement or subrogation), even though the creditor has released the principal. See Restatement of Suretyship §39. From the borrower's perspective, however, that result is highly counterintuitive. The borrower, having negotiated a release of its liability to the creditor in return for a partial payment, discovers that the release granted by the creditor is meaningless because the guarantor still can pursue the borrower for any amount of the debt that the borrower failed to pay.

2. Waiver of Suretyship Defenses

The complicated rules discussed above rest on a desire to protect the guarantor from the corrosive prejudice of agreements between the principal and the creditor. Those rules take on a surreal aspect in a world in which the majority of guaranties are issued by guarantors that are closely related to the principals. Because those rules threaten the lender with a loss of its rights against the guarantor as a result of the lender's dealings with the principal, they severely limit the lender's ability to respond flexibly to a default by its borrower. Moreover, it is unreasonable to release Carl from liability because of OmniBank's willingness to accommodate the company that Carl owns and operates.

Fortunately, the legal system provides a solution to that problem, permitting the guarantor to waive the suretyship defenses. Both common-law rules and the UCC treat those waivers as enforceable. Restatement of Suretyship §48(1); UCC §3-605(*i*)(ii). As a result, it is rare for a commercial guaranty to omit a thorough waiver of suretyship defenses. See Continuing Guaranty §§7, 10, 20.

Courts reviewing clauses waiving suretyship defenses traditionally construed those clauses quite narrowly, often to the point of ignoring their plain intent. These courts usually referred to the antiquated principle of *strictissimi juris*, under which creditors must conform their dealings with guarantors to standards of the "utmost equity." Not surprisingly, guarantors have not been above invoking that doctrine to seek a release of their liability even when it is absolutely clear that the guarantor controlled the borrower and participated directly in the lender's decision to grant the accommodation on which the guarantor bases its claim for a release. As the following case shows, recent decisions have been less sympathetic to such claims, reflecting a growing willingness to enforce the plain intent of provisions waiving suretyship defenses.

Modern Photo Offset Supply v. The Woodfield Group
663 N.E.2d 547 (Ind. App. 1996)

DARDEN, Judge.

The Woodfield Group, Inc. was a printing company, with Richard C. MacGill as its president and sole shareholder. Modern Photo Offset Supply was a supplier of photographic and printing products. In September 1988, Woodfield applied to Modern Photo for credit to purchase various supplies, and credit was extended to Woodfield by Modern Photo.

In May 1993, a series of credit purchases by Woodfield began to cumulate with no corresponding payments. Modern Photo responded to Woodfield's increasing debt by seeking a personal guaranty from MacGill. On July 22, 1993, Modern Photo obtained from MacGill a "Personal Guarantee of Payment" on Woodfield's indebtedness of $150,473.18; in return, Modern Photo agreed to continue extending credit to Woodfield.

Also in July 1993, MacGill began negotiating on behalf of Woodfield with James B. Harmon of Chromagraphics, Inc. to sell Woodfield assets to a limited partnership which would be . . . called Repro Image, Ltd.[1] These negotiations culminated in an asset purchase agreement on November 19, 1993, which provided for the sale of substantially all of Woodfield's assets to Repro and [that] MacGill would become a 15% limited partner in Repro and a Repro employee.

[After Modern Photo learned of the pending sale to Repro], Don Meek, chairman of Modern Photo, met with Harmon to discuss the outstanding Woodfield account. On . . . November 30th, MacGill and Harmon signed an [agreement] providing that Repro "assume[d]" Woodfield's debt to Modern Photo (calculated on that date to have a balance of $206,694.26). On December 1st, an agreement was signed by Meek for Modern Photo and Harmon for Repro, whereby Modern Photo "agree[d] to accept payment from Repro . . . in connection with monies owed to Modern Photo" by Woodfield. MacGill began his employment with Repro on December 1st. Modern Photo extended credit for sales to Repro on a new account. Very quickly the business relationship of MacGill and Repro began to unravel, completely disintegrating within a few months.

On March 11, 1994, Modern Photo filed a complaint against both Repro and Woodfield on the account debt and against MacGill on his personal guaranty. . . .

MacGill argued to the trial court that (1) "Modern Photo took actions which materially changed and altered the nature of the obligation underlying MacGill's" guaranty, and (2) "Modern Photo accepted Repro Image, Ltd.'s assumption" of the Woodfield debt to Modern Photo "and agreed that payment 'shall be made by Repro Image, Ltd.;'" both of which "discharged" MacGill from any responsibility under the guaranty. The trial court agreed, holding that the Modern Photo–Repro agreement ("the Agreement") "changed the legal identity of the principal's contract" and was a "material alteration" made without MacGill's "knowing consent," thereby effecting a discharge of MacGill's guaranty obligation.

Our determination as to whether as a matter of law MacGill was discharged from his liability pursuant to his personal guaranty turns upon the terms of the guaranty and the Agreement.

The guaranty agreement (wherein Woodfield is "Buyer," Modern Photo is "Seller," and MacGill is "Guarantor") states that "in consideration of the past and future sale . . . of goods and merchandise by Seller to Buyer and the extension of credit by Seller to Buyer in connection with such sales," MacGill "does hereby UNCONDITIONALLY AND ABSOLUTELY GUARANTEE to Seller payment of the purchase price of such goods." Further, the personal guaranty contained the following "Waivers Regarding the Guaranteed Debt:"

> The guarantor expressly waives the following: notice of the incurring of debt by the Buyer; notice of default on the debt; the acceptance of this guaranty by the Seller; presentment and demand for payment, protest, notice of protest and notice of dishonor or nonpayment of any instrument evidencing debt of the Buyer; any right to require the pursuit of any remedies against the Buyer, including

---

1. Chromagraphics would become the general partner of Repro Image, Ltd.

commencement of suit, before enforcing this guaranty (this is a guaranty of payment, not a guaranty of collection); any right to have security or the right of setoff applied before enforcing this guaranty; and any right of subrogation to the Seller's rights against the Buyer.

The guarantor hereby consents and agrees that renewals and extensions of time of payment (including interest rate adjustments), surrender, release, exchange, substitution, dealing with or taking of additional collateral, taking or release of other guarantors, abstaining from taking advantage of or realizing upon any collateral security or other guaranty, and any and all other forbearances or indulgences granted by the Seller to the Buyer or any other party may be made, granted or effected by the Seller without notice to the guarantor and without in any manner affecting his liability hereunder. The guarantor hereby expressly consents to any impairment of collateral including, but not limited to, failure to perfect a security interest and release of collateral.

The complete terms of the Agreement between Modern Photo and Repro provide that Modern Photo

does hereby agree to accept payments from Repro Image, Ltd. . . . in connection with monies owed to Modern Photo Offset Supply by The Woodfield Group, Inc. This amendment shall not release The Woodfield Group, Inc. and/or Richard C. MacGill from liability, but is merely intended to be an acknowledgment that the payments shall be made by Repro Image, Ltd., pursuant to Repro Image, Ltd.'s assumption of said debt. . . .

Indiana law has long agreed that words used in a contract are to be given their usual and common meaning unless, from the entire contract and the subject-matter thereof, it is clear that some other meaning was intended. Moreover, all of the words in the contract must be considered in determining its meaning. According to the guaranty, MacGill agreed to unconditionally and absolutely guarantee payment to Modern Photo for goods purchased by Woodfield.

Even if we were to assume that Repro was an additional guarantor, MacGill expressly consented to Modern Photo's taking of other guarantors without notice to him and without affecting his liability under the guaranty. The term giving MacGill's consent to the taking of other guarantors is specific. Woodfield and MacGill argue that the later phrase consenting to "any and all other forbearances or indulgences" is too ambiguous to constitute MacGill's consent to the Agreement. However, the phrase is general and unspecific with respect to MacGill's consent. Therefore, the specific provision consenting to the taking of other guarantors controls.

Likewise, the terms of the Agreement expressly provide that it does not release Woodfield or MacGill from liability for the debt of Woodfield to Modern Photo. The subsequent reference to Repro's "assumption" of the Woodfield debt is general and unspecific in context; thus, the specific provision denying any release supersedes such a general, unspecific reference. . . .

We reverse the summary judgment for MacGill and direct the trial court to enter summary judgment on behalf of Modern Photo on MacGill's liability as guarantor on the Woodfield account.

Waivers of suretyship defenses may be quite common, but they are still problematic. The biggest difficulty with those provisions is the difficulty that they can cause the guarantor if the guarantor loses control of the principal. For example, suppose that Carl sold RFT to Rick Compo at a time when RFT's obligation to OmniBank remained outstanding, still guaranteed by Carl. Suppose then that OmniBank and Compo subsequently agreed to a sale of RFT's assets at a price of $250,000 when Carl believed that a fair price would be $500,000. If Carl had signed a guaranty in a customary form (like the form at issue in *Modern Photo Offset Supply* or in Assignment 36), Carl's rights to challenge the sale would be quite limited. OmniBank could collect the proceeds of the sale and then sue Carl for the amount that remained unpaid on RFT's obligation. If Carl complained that OmniBank's actions had harmed Carl by impairing the collateral, OmniBank could point to the provisions in the guaranty in which Carl authorized OmniBank to "waive, and release" any collateral or to "direct the order or manner of sale thereof as Lender in its discretion may determine," and in which Carl "waive[d] any defense based on or arising out of . . . any impairment of any security by Lender or Borrower or any other party." Continuing Guaranty §§7, 10. If a court enforced those provisions as written, Carl would have no defense to the suit by OmniBank, even if OmniBank's action in agreeing to the sale did cause harm to Carl.

The most common way for commercial parties to resolve that dilemma is to include in the guaranty a "defeasance" provision, which gives the guarantor an absolute right to terminate its liability under the guaranty by purchasing the debt from the creditor. A typical, relatively simple provision might read as follows:

> Notwithstanding anything to the contrary elsewhere in this Guaranty, Guarantor's liability on the Debt shall terminate entirely upon Guarantor's payment to Lender of the entire amount of principal and interest due on the Debt. Upon payment by Guarantor of that amount, the Debt and all of Lender's rights related to the Debt shall be assigned to Guarantor, and Lender agrees to execute an instrument in a form satisfactory to Lender reflecting that assignment. Lender also agrees to provide Guarantor a written statement of that amount (including a method for calculating daily accruals of interest) on five (5) business days' notice; Lender shall warrant to Guarantor the accuracy of that statement. If Guarantor in good faith disagrees with Lender as to the amount due, Guarantor shall be entitled to terminate its liability on the Debt by (a) paying to Lender unconditionally the amount that Guarantor acknowledges to be due; and (b) depositing into the registry of a court of competent jurisdiction the additional amount claimed by Lender, the deposited funds to be disbursed by the court in accordance with the court's resolution of the disagreement. In connection with any such purchase, Guarantor must provide Lender with a release by Borrower of all claims Borrower might have against Lender arising out of or related to the Debt or Lender's administration of it.

A defeasance provision solves the concerns that make the creditor wary of suretyship defenses: The creditor retains free discretion to deal with the borrower until the creditor has received full payment. Conversely, it mitigates the guarantor's concerns about inappropriate leniency by the creditor by allowing the guarantor to take over the creditor's position and deal with the principal as the guarantor wishes.

Of course, a defeasance provision does little for the guarantor that is not in a position to pay off the underlying obligation. But the guarantor's risk is considerably diminished when the guarantor's own financial status is precarious. If the guarantor's ability to perform is in doubt, the creditor is unlikely to behave recklessly in its dealings with the principal. For example, in the hypothetical sale to Rick Compo discussed above, OmniBank would be much less inclined to agree to a fire-sale price for RFT's assets if it knew that the guarantor would be unable to pay any balance of the debt that remained after the sale. The cases where the guarantor is most worried about the creditor behaving recklessly are the opposite cases, in which the creditor does not care what it gets from the principal because it knows that it easily can obtain full payment from the guarantor. If OmniBank is sure that it can collect its debt from Carl, then it has little reason to quibble with Compo about anything.

C.   Bankruptcy of the Guarantor

The last topic on traditional guaranties is the effect of the bankruptcy of the guarantor. The normal expectation might be that such cases would be rare: If the guarantor was selected to enhance the credit of the principal, we should not expect to see the guarantor failing nearly so often as the principal. In any event, when a guarantor does become bankrupt, that bankruptcy can have the same effect as the bankruptcy of a principal (discussed in the *FTL* case in Assignment 36). Thus, where the *FTL* court delayed the creditor's right to proceed against the guarantor, the following case delays the creditor's right to proceed against the principal.

Trimec, Inc. v. Zale Corporation

150 B.R. 685 (N.D. Ill. 1993)

Ann Claire WILLIAMS, District Judge.

In June 1984, Aeroplex O'Hare, a joint venture between Aeroplex Stores, Inc. ("Aeroplex")[1] and Trimec, Inc. ("Trimec"), contracted with the City of Chicago (the "City") to operate three drug store concessions at O'Hare International Airport. The agreement required Aeroplex O'Hare to operate the concessions for five years and pay the City a license fee of approximately $14 million during that time. Zale guaranteed Aeroplex O'Hare's obligations under the contract and Aeroplex O'Hare also posted a $1 million performance bond guaranteed by the Federal Insurance Company (FIC). The concessions were not successful and, after approximately two years and with several million dollars of rent past due, Aeroplex O'Hare abandoned its operations at O'Hare International Airport.

---

1. At the time, Aeroplex was a wholly-owned subsidiary of Zale Corporation ("Zale"). In June 1986, Zale sold all of its interest in Aeroplex.

In 1986, Trimec brought suit against Aeroplex and Zale to recover its lost capitalization funds and profits. Aeroplex and Zale then filed a third-party complaint against the City and three former officials of the City's Department of Aviation, alleging [various causes of action not relevant to this opinion]. The City filed a counterclaim against Aeroplex O'Hare, Trimec, Aeroplex, Zale in its capacity as guarantor of Aeroplex O'Hare, and FIC as the surety of Aeroplex O'Hare's performance bond. Trimec has settled its lawsuit with Aeroplex and Zale. The litigation involving the City remains.

In January 1992, Zale went into bankruptcy and the automatic stay provision of the Bankruptcy Code, 11 U.S.C. §362, stayed all further proceedings against Zale, including those in this case. On November 3, 1992, the City moved to have the automatic stay lifted to permit this case to proceed. Zale objected to this motion and moved to extend the stay to cover all parties to this action. . . .

Zale, Aeroplex, and Trimec (the "parties") move to stay this proceeding pending resolution of the claim submitted by the City in Zale's bankruptcy case. The parties argue that proceeding in this case without Zale would be inequitable because Zale would be bound by a judgment in favor of the City since it is Aeroplex O'Hare's guarantor under the contract and has agreed to indemnify the other defendants. . . .

The City counters that it is inappropriate to stay this proceeding merely because one party has filed for bankruptcy. According to the City, a stay which protects solvent parties is inconsistent with the statutory scheme established in the federal bankruptcy code which limits the protection of the automatic stay to bankrupt parties. Moreover, the City argues that discovery has been completed and this case is ready to go to trial. The City claims that staying the proceeding at this late date would deny the City its right to vigorously pursue its action against the solvent defendants.

As the City suggests, the automatic stay is generally only available to the debtor, and not related third-party defendants or solvent co-defendants. However, there is a limited exception to this rule in "unusual circumstances" where the relief sought against the third party would result in harm to the debtor. As the Fourth Circuit explained in [A.H. Robins Co. Inc. v. Piccinin, 788 F.2d 994, 999 (4th Cir. 1986), a predecessor to the *FTL* case in Assignment 36], a stay is appropriate where "there is such identity between the debtor and the third-party defendant that the debtor may be said to be the real party defendant and that the judgment against the third-party defendant will in effect be a judgment or finding against the debtor."

This court finds that a judgment in favor of the City in the instant action would serve as a judgment against Zale, thus improperly defeating the purpose of the automatic stay invoked in Zale's bankruptcy proceeding. As explained above, Zale would be bound by a judgment in this case regardless of whether it was involved in the litigation because Zale is Aeroplex O'Hare's guarantor under the contract and agreed to indemnify the other defendants. Permitting such a judgment to be entered against Zale would be inequitable since Zale would not have had the opportunity to defend itself and a judgment in favor of the City could have a significant impact on Zale's estate in its bankruptcy proceeding. Given the identity of the parties and the effect of this proceeding on the debtor's estate, an extension of the stay to the solvent parties in this action is clearly warranted as the parties suggest.

Again, as with the *FTL* case, it is difficult to see anything unusual about the circumstances of the *Trimec* guaranty. Thus, *Trimec* presents a strategic opportunity for the borrower with a related guarantor that has significant financial problems. At the same time, it poses a corresponding strategic hazard to the lender considering whether to take a guaranty from a party of questionable financial strength. Of course, the lender ordinarily could solve the problem by waiving its rights against the guarantor. In *Trimec*, however, and probably in other large-firm bankruptcies as well, the likelihood that the guarantor would emerge from bankruptcy with significant assets makes that alternative unpalatable.

Problem Set 37

37.1. Jude Fawley is back to see you again, following up on the issues that you discussed with him in Problem 36.3. Shortly after the events at issue in that problem, Jude managed to sell his company OWH to a new investor (a Canadian named Rick Compo), who planned to put up the additional funds necessary to keep the business running. Unfortunately, the headstone business was not as profitable as Compo anticipated. Compo called Jude this morning to advise him that OWH will not make a loan payment that is due from OWH to Wessex next week. OWH is primarily obligated on that loan, with a guaranty by Jude individually. Jude thinks that OWH's assets still have considerable value and thus has determined that the best approach is to pay off the loan with his personal assets and then try to recover from the business. Assuming that Jude's guaranty was in the form set forth in Assignment 36, will that plan work? Continuing Guaranty §11.

37.2. Your regular client Jodi Kay from CountryBank has a question about a guaranty that she is negotiating. She sent the potential guarantor her standard-form guaranty (identical to the form in Assignment 36). The guarantor responded by asking her to delete the first sentence of §11. The provision currently states:

> Guarantors shall have no right of subrogation, and waive any right to enforce any remedy that Lender now has or may hereafter have against Borrower, and waive any benefit of, and any right of reimbursement, indemnity, or contribution or to participate in any security now or hereafter held by Lender.)

The guarantor proposes replacing it with the following: "Guarantors shall be entitled to rights of reimbursement and subrogation, but only to the extent of payments actually made to Lender under this Guaranty." The guarantor explained to Jodi that a recent amendment of the Bankruptcy Code (adding 11 U.S.C. §550(c)) had made the old provision unnecessary. Jodi wants to know how you would respond to the request. What do you say?

37.3. Stacy Vye extends a loan to We-R-Red, Inc. (WRRI). She also obtains a guaranty from Diggory Venn, the sole shareholder of WRRI. Later, Stacy, concerned about the solvency of WRRI, settles with WRRI for 60 cents on the dollar and releases WRRI from any further liability. Consider the following hypotheticals:

a. Both the note and the guaranty are on the lender's standard forms, resembling the forms in Assignments 35 and 36. To what extent does UCC §3-605 apply to determine the rights of WRRI and Venn? UCC §§3-103(a)(17), 3-605 & comment 2.

b. The original transaction is effectuated with a negotiable promissory note, on which Venn signs as a cosigner. The relevant settlement agreement does not include any terms that address the effect of the release on the rights of Stacy against Venn or the rights of Venn against WRRI. What effect does the release have on those rights? UCC §3-605 & comment 4.

c. Same facts as item b, except that the settlement agreement states that Stacy retains the right to enforce the note against Venn on its original terms. UCC §3-605 & comment 4.

d. Same facts as item b, except that the settlement agreement states that Stacy retains the right to enforce the note against Venn on the original terms and that Venn retains its rights against WRRI. UCC §3-605 & comment 4.

37.4. Cynthia Sharples has been referred to you by a friend of yours that practices family law. It appears that Cynthia and her former husband, Ernest, owned a framing business, for which Ernest obtained a loan that Cynthia guaranteed. In their divorce last year, the business was assigned to Ernest, along with full responsibility for the loan (the balance of which at the time was about $220,000). Cynthia knew that the business was not doing well, but learned yesterday that it has gotten worse than she had known. Specifically, Cynthia received a letter from the lender advising her that the lender graciously has accepted her ex-husband's request to modify the terms of the loan to increase the stated interest rate from 8 percent to a floating rate of prime plus 3 percent. (Prime currently is 7.5 percent.) In return, the lender also has agreed to forgo taking action in response to Ernest's failure to make a number of past-due payments that total about $32,000; the lender proposes to add those payments to the current principal balance, together with fees for this transaction. At the end of the day, the total principal balance would be about $265,000. The lender is seeking Cynthia's consent and a reaffirmation that her guaranty continues to apply to the debt as modified.

The letter is courteous and respectful, but closes by expressing an intention to pursue its remedies as aggressively as possible if Cynthia does not agree to the proposal by the end of the week. What do you recommend to Cynthia?

Assignment 38: Third-Party Credit Enhancement — Standby Letters of Credit

A. The Standby Letter-of-Credit Transaction

Many borrowers cannot solve their credit problems with the kind of related-party guaranty discussed in Assignments 36 and 37. In some cases, no party related to the borrower has enough financial strength to satisfy the creditor's concerns. In other cases, even if some party related to the borrower has considerable wealth, the potential creditor has doubts about the reputation or the credibility of the related party that undermine the creditor's willingness to rely on a commitment by the related party to back up the obligation in question. In still other cases (particularly international transactions), the parties are so geographically separated that the creditor prefers a right to proceed against a party located nearby (at least in the creditor's home country).

The most common way to solve those problems is for the borrower to obtain a backup promise from a third party whose financial strength, credibility, and location are satisfactory to the creditor. In this country, that promise usually comes from a bank. Although such a transaction closely resembles a guaranty in substance, historical concerns cause United States banks to provide that service with a document styled "letter of credit," rather than "guaranty." To distinguish it from the letter of credit used in a simple payment transaction (the subject of Assignments 33 and 34), this type of letter of credit is called a "standby" letter of credit. Antiquated limitations on the power of state and national banks in this country often prohibit those institutions from doing business as a "guarantor" or a "surety." Because overseas banks commonly engage in that business — through the issuance of what are called "bank guaranties" or "demand guaranties" — competitive pressures have driven United States banks to use the standby letter of credit to provide a similar service. Thus, although the standby letter-of-credit transaction has the substance of a conventional guaranty, the common use of the practice has motivated federal regulatory authorities to confirm the legitimacy of the standby letter of credit. Accordingly, however much the standby letter of credit looks like a guaranty, it is now well settled that domestic banks can issue standby letters of credit even if they cannot issue ordinary guaranties. See, e.g., Citizens State Bank v. FDIC, 946 F.2d 408, 414 (5th Cir. 1991) (discussing Federal Reserve regulations governing standby letters of credit issued by national banks); American Insurance Assn. v. Clarke, 865 F.2d 278, 281-282 (D.C. Cir. 1988) (discussing regulations issued by the Comptroller of the Currency governing standby letters of credit issued by national banks).

Like the conventional letters of credit discussed in Assignments 33 and 34, the standby letter of credit (or demand guaranty) is frequently used in international business transactions. The last decade has seen several efforts to standardize the law in that area. One project by the United Nations Commission on International Trade Law produced the UNCITRAL Convention on Independent Guarantees and Stand-by Letters of Credit. That document, however, has not yet been adopted by any of the important commercial countries. A more successful project is the International Standby Practices promulgated by the International Chamber of Commerce in 1998 (ISP98). Like the Uniform Customs and Practice for Documentary Credits, banks frequently incorporate ISP98 by reference into international letters of credit to which it would be relevant. Because ISP98 is similar to the rules that American courts apply under Article 5 of the Uniform Commercial Code, the result is a substantially uniform body of law that applies regardless of the location of the parties to the standby letter-of-credit transaction.

To see how parties would use a standby letter of credit, consider again the transaction between RFT and OmniBank, used as an example in Assignments 36 and 37. Suppose that OmniBank is unwilling to provide a $4 million loan that RFT needs to fund construction of a new factory even if Carl guarantees the loan. OmniBank might be willing to make the loan, however, if RFT provides a $500,000 letter of credit from CountryBank. That letter of credit would provide that OmniBank could draw $500,000 from CountryBank upon any default by RFT under the construction loan. The letter of credit thus would reduce considerably the risk that OmniBank's construction loan would go unpaid: OmniBank would have the letter of credit from CountryBank, *in addition to* its normal rights to pursue RFT, Carl (if Carl guarantees the loan), and any collateral that OmniBank might obtain from RFT or Carl. Moreover, CountryBank's obligation on the letter of credit (unlike Carl's obligation on the guaranty) would be unconditional; because of the independence principle, CountryBank would not be entitled to assert defenses to RFT's underlying obligation that might allow Carl as a guarantor to withhold payment. ISP98 Rule 1.06(c). CountryBank, in turn, should be willing to issue that letter of credit only if it is confident that it could obtain reimbursement from Carl (or RFT) if CountryBank was called on to pay on the standby letter of credit.

Relational considerations are almost as important in the standby letter-of-credit transaction as they are in the standard guaranty transaction. In the abstract, it might seem puzzling that Carl and RFT can persuade CountryBank to issue a letter of credit that exposes CountryBank to the same risk of nonpayment that makes OmniBank unwilling to accept Carl and RFT's credit in the same transaction. But CountryBank's willingness to accept that risk does not necessarily suggest that CountryBank is less prudent than OmniBank. On the contrary, it probably indicates that CountryBank is more familiar than OmniBank with the credit and reputation of Carl and RFT. The ordinary practice would be for Carl and RFT to obtain a standby letter of credit from the institution with which Carl and RFT do their regular business banking. For example, if CountryBank has a long business relationship with Carl and RFT, CountryBank should be more comfortable with the financial strength and commitment of Carl and RFT than a lender engaged in a first-time transaction with Carl and RFT. From that perspective, the standby letter of credit provides a relatively inexpensive and effective mechanism by which Carl and RFT can convince third parties of the reliability that Carl and RFT already have demonstrated to their principal lender. For that service, CountryBank typically would charge Carl a fee equal to the return over its cost of funds that CountryBank would expect on a typical loan to Carl. For a typical customer, that fee might be 1 percent per annum; for a high-quality customer, the fee might drop as low as one-tenth of that amount.

As illustrated in Figure 38.1, the resulting transaction is functionally identical to a conventional guaranty transaction, but has the issuing bank playing the role of the guarantor, the applicant as the borrower or principal obligor, and the beneficiary as the creditor. When the creditor believes that the applicant/borrower has committed a default on the underlying obligation, it simply submits a draft on the letter of credit to the issuer. At that point, the issuer is obligated to pay the creditor much as a conventional guarantor would. The only difference is that the rules governing that obligation are the (somewhat different) rules in Article 5 of the Uniform Commercial Code, rather than the common-law rules of traditional guaranties.

Figure 38.1
Standby Letters of Credit

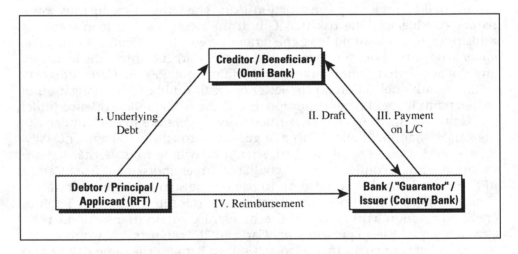

The dynamics of the standby letter-of-credit transaction differ in important respects from those of the conventional letter-of-credit transaction discussed in Assignments 33 and 34. The letter of credit issued in that conventional transaction normally is referred to as a "payment" or "commercial" letter of credit. In the commercial letter-of-credit transaction, where the letter of credit is a simple payment device, the parties anticipate a draw on the letter of credit in the ordinary course of business. The key condition for payment is the beneficiary's production of documents suggesting that the beneficiary has complied with the obligations imposed on it by its contract with the applicant. In a standby letter-of-credit transaction, by contrast, a draft on the letter of credit is the unusual, unhoped-for event. It should occur only if the applicant defaults. Thus, a typical banker would receive drafts on only 5-10 percent of its standby letters of credit, where it would receive drafts on almost all of the commercial letters of credit that it issues.

The following case is a good example of the transactions that give rise to standby letters of credit.

Nobel Insurance Co. v. First Nat'l. Bank
821 So. 2d 210 (Ala. 2001)

HARWOOD, Justice.

Nobel Insurance Company (hereinafter referred to as "Nobel") appeals the summary judgment for The First National Bank of Brundidge (hereinafter referred to as "the Bank"), J.T. Ramage III, Henry T. Strother, Jr., William F. Hamrick, and Palomar Insurance Corporation (hereinafter referred to as "Palomar"). . . . We reverse and remand.

Nobel first sued the Bank in the United States District Court for the Middle District of Alabama to enforce certain letters of credit issued by the Bank. The letters of credit were issued by order of the Bank's customers, Strother and Hamrick, both of whom were insurance brokers for Palomar. The letters of credit were signed by Ramage, the Bank's president, and issued in favor of Western American Specialized Transportation Service, Inc. (hereinafter referred to as "Western American"), one of Hamrick's clients who sought insurance coverage from Nobel. . . .

[Nobel issued various insurance policies to Western American, which had large deductible amounts. The policies required that Nobel hold collateral to secure the obligation of Western American to pay those amounts. Western American satisfied that requirement by causing the Bank to issue the three letters of credit in issue. When Western American became indebted to Nobel for uncollected deductibles, Nobel drew on the letters of credit, but the Bank refused to pay.]

[The district court ruled in favor of the Bank, relying on general principles of suretyship law, including [an Alabama statute that] provides]:

> A surety upon any contract for the payment of money or for the delivery or payment of personal property may require the creditor or anyone having the beneficial interest in the contract, by notice in writing, to bring an action thereon against the principal debtor or against any cosurety to such contract.
>
> (b) If an action is not brought thereon in three months after the receipt of such notice and prosecuted with diligence according to the ordinary course of law, the surety giving such notice is discharged from all liability as surety or his aliquot proportion of the debt, as the case may be.
>
> (c) One surety may give notice in behalf of his cosureties.

[Ala. Code §8-3-13.]

[The court noted that the applicants for the letters of credit sent such a notice and that Nobel did not dispute the receipt or the sufficiency of the notice.] . . .

Nobel argues that the trial court erred in applying suretyship law to the transaction underlying this lawsuit because, it argues, letters of credit are subject to a separate body of law. Under the law governing letters of credit, Nobel argues, the letters of credit in this case cannot be extinguished by application of §8-3-13 even though they were arguably posted as collateral by Strother and Hamrick, as sureties, to answer for the debt of Western American.

The letters of credit at issue all state, in pertinent part:

> We hereby agree with the drawers, endorsers and bona fide holders of drafts drawn under and in compliance with the terms of this credit that such drafts will be duly honored upon presentation to the drawee. *The obligation of The First National Bank of Brundidge, under this Letter of Credit is the individual obligation of The First National Bank of Brundidge and is in no way contingent upon reimbursement with respect thereto.*
>
> Except as otherwise stated herein, this credit is subject to the Uniform Customs and Practice for Commercial Documentary Credits (1983 Revision) I.C.C. Publication No. 400. Notwithstanding Article 19 of said publication, if this credit expires during an interruption of business as described in Article 19, we agree to effect payment if the credit is drawn against within thirty (30) days after resumption of business.

(Emphasis added [by court].) . . .

[The court relied heavily on its explanation of the function of standby letters of credit in an earlier decision:]

> Parties that enter into a credit arrangement do so to avail themselves of the benefits of that arrangement. Shifting litigation costs is one of the functions of a standby credit. In this situation, the parties negotiate their relationship while bearing in mind that litigation may occur. This cost-shifting function gives one party the benefit of the money in hand pending the outcome of any litigation. It is important to understand the functions of letters of credit in order to fully understand the consequences the fraud exception has on this commercial device. A demand for payment made upon a standby credit usually indicates that something has gone wrong in the contract. Indeed, this is the nature of the standby letter of credit. In contrast to the commercial credit, non-performance that triggers payment in a standby credit situation usually indicates some form of financial weakness by the applicant. For this reason, parties choose this security arrangement over another so that they may have the benefit of prompt payment before any litigation occurs. We recognize that, as a general rule, letters of credit cannot exist without independence from the underlying transaction. Thus, when courts begin delving into the underlying contract, they are impeding the swift completion of the credit transaction. The certainty of payment is the most important aspect of a letter of credit transaction, and this certainty encourages hesitant parties to enter into transactions, by providing them with a secure source of credit. [Citations and quotation marks omitted.]
>
> The extensive use of the fraud exception may operate to transform the credit transaction into a surety contract. A standby credit is essentially equivalent to a loan made by the issuing bank to the applicant. *Like a surety contract, the standby credit ensures against the applicant's nonperformance of an obligation. Unlike a surety contract, however, the beneficiary of the standby credit may receive its money first, regardless of pending litigation with the applicant.* The applicant may then sue the beneficiary for breach of contract or breach of warranty, or may sue in tort, but without the money. *Parties to standby credit transactions have bargained for a distinct and less expensive kind of credit transaction.*

In light of the analysis above, we agree that the letters of credit issued by the Bank to Nobel are properly characterized as "standby" letters of credit. Because we also conclude that the letters of credit are properly viewed as distinct from the parties' surety arrangements, we must also conclude that the trial court erred in applying the law of suretyship to extinguish the Bank's responsibility to honor the letters of credit. The letters of credit are independent of the underlying transaction between Nobel and Western American.

[W]e reverse the trial court's summary judgment in favor of the Bank, Ramage, Strother, Hamrick, and Palomar, and we remand the cause for further proceedings consistent with this opinion.

Accordingly, the documentary conditions for a draw on a standby letter of credit normally focus on establishing that the applicant has defaulted, rather than establishing that the beneficiary has performed. For example, Figure 38.2 sets forth the standard form that a large regional American bank uses for standby letters of credit. That form contemplates payment based on an invoice and a certification by the beneficiary that the invoice remains unpaid. It differs from the typical commercial letter of credit (like the one in Assignment 33) in that it does not require the beneficiary to provide nearly the level of detailed objective proof that the beneficiary has complied with its obligations (such as a bill of lading or some type of transport document). The result is that it tends to be much easier for the beneficiary to comply with the requirements of the letter of credit. As Assignment 34 explained, bankers report that most presentations on commercial letters of credit do not comply with the letter of credit; the same bankers report that the overwhelming majority of presentations on standby letters of credit do comply and thus are honored by the issuing bank.

Figure 38.2
Form Standby Letter of Credit

ISSUE DATE: XX/XX/XX

L/C NO.: X-XXXXXX

ADVISING BANK:

APPLICANT:

DIRECT APPLICANT NAME

APPLICANT ADDRESS

CITY, STATE ZIP

BENEFICIARY:

BENEFICIARY NAME   AMOUNT:

USD XX, XXX.XX

BENEFICIARY ADDRESS

CITY, STATE ZIP

WE HEREBY ESTABLISH OUR IRREVOCABLE STANDBY LETTER OF CREDIT NO. X-XXXXXX EXPIRING XX/XX/XX AT OUR COUNTERS WHICH IS AVAILABLE UPON PRESENTATION TO US OF YOUR SIGHT DRAFT(S) DRAWN ON THE BOATMEN'S NATIONAL BANK OF ST. LOUIS, ST. LOUIS, MISSOURI, ACCOMPANIED BY:

BENEFICIARY'S SIGNED STATEMENT THAT:

"OUR DRAFT REPRESENTS AN AMOUNT DUE US AS [APPLICANT] HAS FAILED TO PAY OUR INVOICE(S) WITHIN AGREED UPON TERMS AND SUCH INVOICE(S) REMAIN UNPAID, ALTHOUGH JUSTLY DUE AND OWING."

COPY OF INVOICE(S) DEEMED UNPAID.

THE ORIGINAL LETTER OF CREDIT AND AMENDMENT(S), IF ANY, MUST BE PRESENTED FOR ENDORSEMENT AT TIME OF DRAWING.

WE HEREBY ENGAGE WITH DRAWERS THAT DRAFT(S) DRAWN AND NEGOTIATED IN CONFORMITY WITH THE TERMS OF THIS CREDIT WILL BE DULY HONORED ON PRESENTATION. DRAFT(S) MUST BE MARKED AS DRAWN UNDER THIS CREDIT.

THIS LETTER OF CREDIT IS SUBJECT TO THE UNIFORM CUSTOMS AND PRACTICES FOR DOCUMENTARY CREDITS, 1993 REVISION, INTERNATIONAL CHAMBER OF COMMERCE PUBLICATION 500.

AUTHORIZED SIGNATURE

Because the standby letter-of-credit transaction contemplates that the beneficiary will draw on the letter of credit only if the applicant defaults on its contract with the beneficiary, the conditions on the beneficiary's right to draw on the letter of credit are crucial to the success of the beneficiary in obtaining payment. A failure by the beneficiary to comply with the conditions of a commercial letter of credit normally has little consequence because the applicant has received the goods and thus has to pay for them if it wishes to keep them. In that context, insistence by the applicant on strict compliance with the letter of credit only increases the procedural obstacles to payment, and thus the cost of payment; it does not avoid payment. By contrast, a beneficiary will not present a draft on a standby letter of credit until a serious dispute arises. In that context, the beneficiary frequently will be unable to obtain payment through any avenue other than the letter of credit. Thus, failure of the beneficiary to comply with the requirements for a draft on a standby letter of credit normally is a much more serious problem.

The key point of demarcation in the conditions under which a beneficiary can draw on a standby letter of credit is whether the letter of credit is "clean." If the letter of credit is clean, the beneficiary need present nothing more than a draft demanding payment (and perhaps the letter of credit itself); no additional documentation is necessary. Thus, for example, the form set forth in Figure 38.2 is not technically a clean standby letter of credit because it requires the beneficiary to include a signed statement that some specified invoice is due, but unpaid. The difference between a clean and an "unclean" standby letter of credit may be unimportant in cases where the applicant's default is clear, but the following case shows how certification requirements like those required in Figure 38.2 can make the difference between a successful and an unsuccessful attempt to draw on the letter of credit.

Wood v. State Bank

609 N.Y.S.2d 665 (App. Div. 1994)

Before THOMPSON, J.P., and PIZZUTO, SANTUCCI and GOLDSTEIN, JJ....

On January 29, 1987, the plaintiffs and Jacklyn Construction Corp. (hereinafter Jacklyn) entered into a contract for Jacklyn to buy the plaintiffs' real property. Under clauses 5 and 6 of the rider to the contract of sale, the parties agreed that certain moneys "shall be a non-refundable payment to the [plaintiffs] for allowing [Jacklyn] to obtain the zoning approvals and for agreeing to sell said property and making said property subject to the change of zone". As part of the contemplated payment, Jacklyn caused the State Bank of Long Island (hereinafter the State Bank) to open a clean irrevocable letter of credit in favor of "Thomas F. Wood Esq., as attorney for [the plaintiffs]". The letter of credit provided for payment on or before the close of business on January 16, 1988, against a sight draft making reference to credit number 1147 and a sworn statement by the plaintiffs' attorney "certifying that: Jacklyn...or its assigns, has willfully failed to close title in accordance with the provisions of a certain contract, dated on or about January 29, 1987 between [the plaintiffs] and Jacklyn". On or about January 12, 1988, State Bank received a sight draft that made no reference to State Bank's credit number and an affidavit of the plaintiffs' attorney that mentioned the credit number and read: "1. That he is the attorney for [the plaintiffs], and makes this affidavit pursuant to the terms and conditions of a Letter of Credit No. 1147.... 2. That pursuant to a contract dated January 29, 1987 . . . the sum of FORTY THOUSAND ($40,000.00) DOLLARS was to be deposited with him on or before January 1, 1988. 3. That pursuant to said contract of sale, your affiant makes demand upon the State Bank of Long Island for the sum of FORTY THOUSAND ($40,000.00) DOLLARS pursuant to Letter of Credit No. 1147". The Supreme Court found that the plaintiffs complied in all respects with the letter of credit and granted summary judgment in their favor. We disagree.

New York requires strict compliance with the terms of a letter of credit, rather than the more relaxed standard of substantial compliance. The documents presented against the letter of credit must comply precisely with the requirements of the letter of credit. The New York Court of Appeals thus stated the rule: "We have heretofore held that these letters of credit are to be strictly complied with, which means that the papers, documents and shipping descriptions must be followed as stated in the letter. There is no discretion in the bank or trust company to waive any of these requirements" (Anglo-South American Trust Co. v. Uhe, 261 N.Y. 150, 156-157, 184 N.E. 741). The letter of credit is not tied to or dependent upon the underlying commercial transaction.

In the case at bar, the plaintiffs' counsel was required under the terms of the letter of credit to present a sight draft mentioning credit number 1147, accompanied by a certification that Jacklyn "has willfully failed to close title in accordance with the provisions of [the contract]". He failed to comply precisely with the terms of the letter of credit. Therefore, State Bank properly refused to honor the letter of credit. Accordingly, we deny the plaintiffs' motion for summary judgment and grant summary judgment in State Bank's favor.

Although the court could describe the letter of credit in this case as clean in the sense that it did not require any ancillary documentation regarding the beneficiary's performance, it was not entirely clean because it did require a certification that the applicant "willfully failed" to perform. In considering the transaction that led to the litigation, consider whether it is more likely that the attorney's failure to present a draft that complied was an unfortunate oversight or instead reflected a conscious unwillingness to provide the appropriate certification. Is it really plausible that the attorney could have been so incompetent as to fail to understand how to prepare a proper draft? It is more likely (although admittedly impossible to tell from the published opinion) that the attorney acted with full knowledge of the detailed certification called for by the letter of credit, but was unwilling to provide it.

When a letter of credit is completely clean, a beneficiary can draw on the letter of credit without any significant difficulty even when the beneficiary has no right to the money. And the high standard for fraud set forth in UCC §5-109 (discussed in Assignment 34) will make it quite difficult for the issuer to avoid payment even if the beneficiary has no right to the money. The beneficiary might submit such a draft because of frustration over unrelated disagreements with the applicant or even because of completely unrelated financial difficulties. But even the simplest certification requirements can make it considerably more hazardous for a beneficiary to present an unjustified draft on a letter of credit. Among other things, a draft that includes a false statement of fact would expose the party signing the draft to a federal felony conviction under 18 U.S.C. §1344 (criminalizing any knowing scheme to obtain moneys of a federally insured financial institution by means of false representations). Thus, a requirement that a beneficiary describe the basis for the draft with some particularity (like the requirement in *Wood*) might deter beneficiaries from submitting false drafts.

It is worth noting that the form of draft submitted in *Wood* could have been factually accurate even if the beneficiary was not entitled to draw on the letter of credit. The fact that the draft was found inadequate rested entirely on the "unclean" aspects of the letter of credit. Absent those departures from "cleanness," the beneficiary in *Wood* could have succeeded in obtaining funds from the bank even if the beneficiary's draft was completely unjustified.

B.   Problems in Standby
Letter-of-Credit Transactions

Standby letter-of-credit transactions can raise many of the same issues as commercial letter-of-credit transactions, but the differences in context cause certain issues to be more important for standby letters of credit than they are for commercial letters of credit. For example, the likelihood that a draft will be presented against a standby letter of credit only when the beneficiary and applicant are at odds about the applicant's performance enhances the importance of the rules that obligate the issuer to pay when the applicant's performance is in doubt. The issuer's obligation to pay absent material fraud covered by UCC §5-109 leads to frequent litigation over application of the "material fraud" standard in the standby context. The nature of that standard, however, is no different here than it is in the commercial letter-of-credit context, discussed in Assignment 34.

In some areas, however, standby letters of credit present issues qualitatively different from the issues presented by commercial letters of credit. Generally, those issues arise from the difficulty of accommodating the form that the parties have selected (a letter of credit) to the substance of the underlying transaction (a guaranty). The remainder of this assignment discusses two of the most troubling problems: bankruptcy of the applicant and subrogation rights of the issuer.

1.   Bankruptcy of the Applicant

The creditor that receives a standby letter of credit must take the possibility of bankruptcy by the applicant just as seriously as the creditor that receives a conventional guaranty must take the risk of bankruptcy by the principal obligor. As Assignment 36 explains, bankruptcy courts in recent years have shown a growing tendency to rely on bankruptcy of an obligor to justify deferring a creditor's right to pursue a guarantor. Accordingly, it should come as no surprise that in the early years of the Bankruptcy Code some bankruptcy judges concluded that they had a similar power to enjoin a creditor from collecting on a standby letter of credit after the applicant (the principal obligor) had filed for bankruptcy.

Those concerns were crystallized by the notorious decision in Twist Cap, Inc. v. Southeast Bank (In re Twist Cap, Inc.), 1 B.R. 284 (Bankr. D. Fla. 1979), handed down shortly after the 1978 enactment of the Bankruptcy Code. That case involved a typical standby letter-of-credit transaction. Two parties selling goods to Twist Cap obtained standby letters of credit to ensure that they would be paid for goods that they regularly shipped to Twist Cap. When Twist Cap filed for bankruptcy, the sellers predictably attempted to obtain payment from the still-solvent bank that had issued the letters of credit. The bankruptcy court enjoined the sellers from drawing on the letter of credit, vitiating the protection the sellers thought that they had obtained when they received the letters of credit.

Given the ready analogy of the standby letter of credit to a guaranty, the result in *Twist Cap* should not seem terribly surprising. The decision was, however, widely condemned in the financial and scholarly communities. The dominant perspective contended that the decision ignored the strong tradition in merchant circles that the bank's obligation on a letter of credit is entirely independent of the underlying obligation. As Douglas Baird states: "Parties that bargain for a letter of credit assume that regardless of war, revolution, or other catastrophe, the letter will be honored when the documents specified in the letter are presented." Douglas G. Baird, "Standby Letters of Credit in Bankruptcy," 49 U. Chi. L. Rev. 130, 145 (1982). The willingness of the *Twist Cap* court to enjoin the sellers' attempts to draw on the letters of credit defied that tradition.

Also, the difference between this situation and the conventional guaranty situation (discussed in the preceding assignments) undermines the result in *Twist Cap*. As you should recall, in the conventional guaranty context, the intertwined relationship between a guarantor and a borrower is the principal justification for allowing the insolvency of a borrower to prevent a creditor from collecting on a relational guaranty. In the standby context, the creditor's decision to insist on an enhancement of the borrower's credit from a third-party bank makes it difficult to justify the rule in *Twist Cap*. Among other things, it ordinarily will be impossible to suggest that obtaining payment on the standby letter of credit will undermine the solvency of the borrower or its principal because the issuer of the letter of credit (ordinarily) is an independent party.

Thus, the principal legal argument available to debtors is that a draw on the letter of credit acts against "property of the debtor's estate." Using that approach, debtors argue that a draw on the letter of credit violates the automatic stay that bankruptcy imposes on all actions against property of a debtor's estate. 11 U.S.C. §362(a)(3). As the following decision suggests, those arguments have not been well received in recent years.

In re Ocana
151 B.R. 670 (S.D.N.Y. 1993)

LEVAL, District Judge.

[Latino Americano de Reaseguros, S.A. ("LARSA") entered into a series of reinsurance agreements pursuant to which it agreed to pay money to Hannover if Hannover experienced heavy losses on certain insurance policies. A Panamanian bank named Banco Cafetero issued a standby letter of credit backing up LARSA's obligations. In 1990, LARSA filed for statutory reorganization, a Panamanian procedure roughly equivalent to bankruptcy. Hannover brought suit against Banco Cafetero in the United States District Court for the Central District of California, arguing that Banco Cafetero was liable to Hannover on the letter of credit because LARSA had failed to pay Hannover about $1,700,000 that LARSA owed Hannover on the reinsurance agreements.

LARSA responded by filing a proceeding in the bankruptcy court in the United States District Court for the Southern District of New York, seeking to enjoin

Hannover from collecting on Banco Cafetero's letter of credit. The bankruptcy court issued a stay of Hannover's action. Hannover appealed to the district court.]

The stay of Hannover's action against Banco Cafetero is based on an incorrect theory of law. Hannover's action against Banco Cafetero is not brought against the debtor (LARSA) nor against the debtor's property. The letter of credit is an irrevocable and unconditional promise on the part of Banco Cafetero to pay the beneficiary upon the presentation of specified documents. The beneficiary's action is against the bank, not the account party, and the money to be used in making the payment is the bank's money. The fact that the issuing bank holds collateral of the debtor to secure the bank's extension of credit to LARSA has no bearing on the beneficiary's right to receive payment from the bank on the bank's contract. . . .

Moreover, allowing the debtor's bankruptcy to interfere with payment on clean, irrevocable letters of credit would vitiate the purpose of such letters. Letters of credit are an ingenious device of international commerce. By interposing the bank between buyer and seller, as an independent party, they permit a seller to ship merchandise abroad with confidence that payment is guaranteed by a bank; and permit the purchaser to pay with assurance that the payment will not be released to the seller unless the seller delivers proof of the shipment of the goods. One of the principal purposes of letters of credit is to relieve the seller-shipper from worry as to the purchaser's solvency, for the seller looks not to the purchaser, but to the bank, for payment. If the payment of letters of credit could be stayed, as here, merely because the account party had obtained the protection of a bankruptcy court, this would do incalculable harm to international commerce. Letters of credit would no longer reliably perform the function they were designed for.

Judge Leval's reference to the collateral held by Banco Cafetero points to the true significance of the controversy. If the seller cannot collect on the letter of credit, the seller ordinarily will have an unsecured claim for payment of the purchase price for the goods that it has sold to the debtor. Unless the seller can establish some Article 2 right of reclamation, that claim will not succeed in the bankruptcy, where all or almost all of the debtor's assets usually are distributed to pay secured creditors and the administrative costs of the bankruptcy. The seller's unsecured claim is limited to a pro rata share of any remaining assets, which will bring little or nothing in most cases. On the other hand, if the seller does collect on the letter of credit, the issuing bank then will have a claim for reimbursement. As in *Ocana*, the issuing bank frequently will have collateral that secures its claim for reimbursement. That collateral will enable the issuing bank to obtain full payment on its claim, even though the seller's pre-letter-of-credit claim would have received marginal payment at best. Thus, the decision in *Ocana* essentially transforms an unsecured claim with little chance of payment into a secured claim that is highly likely to be paid. As a practical matter, that transformation redistributes money away from creditors with general unsecured claims (by removing from the estate the funds that are used to pay the bank that issued the letter of credit). That redistribution does not directly benefit the party paid on the letter of credit, but by ensuring that the bank that pays the claim is paid in full, it certainly enhances the willingness of banks to pay such claims.

In the end, those rules largely insulate the beneficiary from the risk of insolvency by the applicant. They do not, however, protect the beneficiary from the risk of insolvency by the issuer. Indeed, upon the insolvency of a bank that has issued a standby letter of credit, the beneficiary's claim on the letter of credit is not even entitled to a payment of $100,000 from the Federal Deposit Insurance Corporation's insurance fund. Rather, the beneficiary loses its claim entirely upon the failure of the bank that issued the letter of credit. See FDIC v. Philadelphia Gear Corp., 476 U.S. 426, 430-440 (1986) (holding that a beneficiary's claim on a standby letter of credit is not a "deposit" entitled to recovery from the FDIC insurance fund).

2. The Issuer's Right of Subrogation

Another situation that frequently leads to litigation arises when an issuer that has honored a draft on a standby letter of credit attempts to use subrogation to recover the funds that it has paid on that draft. As Assignment 36 explains, a guarantor that pays a creditor on behalf of the obligor ordinarily is subrogated to any rights that the creditor had against the obligor. Treatment of the standby letter of credit as analogous to a guaranty would recognize a right of subrogation for the issuer. Notwithstanding that functional similarity, many courts have focused on technicalities of the letter-of-credit form to deny that right of subrogation. The following case provides a cogent explanation of the problem.

CCF, Inc. v. First National Bank (In re Slamans)
175 B.R. 762 (N.D. Okla. 1994)

ELLISON, Chief Judge.

Debtor Thomas William Slamans operated gas stations. On December 4, 1990, Slamans gave First Capital Corporation a revolving credit note for $750,000. Appellant CCF, Inc. ("CCF") is the successor-in-interest to First Capital Corporation.

On December 20, 1994, Slamans entered into a distribution agreement with Sun Company ("Sun") for the purchase of oil products. Under the agreement, Slamans purchased the oil products from Sun on credit and then sold the products either for cash or by credit-card purchase. [When Slamans sold the products by means of a credit card, he sent the proceeds of the credit-card sales directly to Sun, without regard to the current status of his account. If Sun determined that Slamans's account was current, Sun returned the appropriate portion of those proceeds to Slamans.] The agreement [also] required Slamans to obtain a letter of credit.

On February 6, 1991, Appellee First National Bank [FNB] issued a standby letter of credit to Slamans in favor of Sun. The letter provided that FNB agreed to pay Sun up to $200,000 if Slamans defaulted under the distributor agreement. The letter of credit was secured by a note, mortgage and security agreement covering Slamans's accounts receivable [that is, sums that Slamans's customers owed to him].

On February 28, 1992, Slamans filed bankruptcy. On March 9, 1992, Sun — because Slamans had not paid them — requested $192,433.15 from FNB pursuant to the letter of credit. On March 11, 1992, FNB paid Sun the money. Also, at that time, FNB demanded the $111,053.41 in proceeds from credit card sales in Sun's possession. [Sun held those proceeds pursuant to the distribution agreement discussed above. If it had not been paid on the letter of credit, Sun could have asserted a right in Slamans's bankruptcy proceeding to keep those funds pursuant to the distribution agreement. In any event,] Sun did not turn the money over to FNB; instead it filed an interpleader complaint with the Bankruptcy Court....

The dispute itself is straight-forward: Should FNB have received the $111,053.41 from Sun pursuant to 11 U.S.C. §509 of the Bankruptcy Code? Section 509 states: "Except as provided in subsection (b) or (c) of this section, an entity that is liable with the debtor on, or that has secured, a claim of a creditor against the debtor, and that pays such claim, is subrogated to the rights of such creditor to the extent of such payment."

The initial issue is whether FNB was "liable with" Slamans on the debt to Sun. Two divergent lines of authority address this issue. The first line, and what appears to be the majority position, is that only a party that is "secondarily liable", such as a guarantor, can be "liable with" the debtor under §509. Issuers of letters of credit, such as FNB, do not fit into the Section 509 "liable with" language because they are primarily liable, according to this reasoning. The distinctions between a guarantor and letters of credit issuers are based, in part, on the legal characteristics of each. One court explains:

> The key distinction between letters of credit and guarantees is that the issuer's obligation under a letter of credit is primary whereas a guarantor's obligation is secondary — the guarantor is only obligated to pay if the principal defaults on the debt the principal owes. In contrast, while the issuing bank in the letter of credit situation may be secondarily liable in the temporal sense, since its obligation to pay does not arise until after its customer fails to satisfy some obligation, it is satisfying its own absolute and primary obligation to make payment rather than satisfying an obligation of its customer. Having paid its own debt, as it has contractually undertaken to do, the issuer cannot then step into the shoes of the creditor to seek subrogation, reimbursement or contribution.... The only exception would be where the parties reach an agreement. Tudor Development Group, Inc. v. United States Fidelity & Guaranty Co. 968 F.2d 357, 362 (3rd Cir. 1992).

Tudor is a non-bankruptcy case, but several bankruptcy courts have applied the same reasoning. These courts, in effect, conclude that a letter of credit issuer has a separate legal obligation (and remedy) than the debtor. This means they have a primary liability — not a secondary one. Guarantors, on the other hand, are only secondarily liable and, as a result, can obtain Section 509 subrogation. In re Kaiser Steel Corporation, 89 B.R. 150 (Bankr. D. Colo. 1988).

A second group of cases spurn the foregoing reasoning. They conclude that, for the purposes of Section 509 subrogation, issuers of letters of credit and guarantors should both be eligible for subrogation. For example, [one] court states: "While a letter of credit may require conformity with certain obligations and formalities which are not required of a guarantee . . . , precluding the assertion of subrogation rights to issuers of standby letters of credit while allowing guarantors to assert them would be no more than an exercise in honoring form over substance." [In re Minnesota Kicks, 48 B.R. 93, 104 (Bankr. D. Minn. 1985).]...

[T]he undersigned rejects a rule that, in effect, states that, absent an agreement by the parties, an issuer of a letter of credit can never be eligible for Section 509 subrogation....

Slamans obtained a letter of credit, at Sun's request, from FNB. Slamans filed bankruptcy, owing Sun $192,433.15. Sun drew upon the letter of credit for that amount, which FNB paid. FNB then requested that Sun turn over $111,053.41, which was owed to Slamans. The Bankruptcy Court subrogated FNB into Slamans' shoes, awarding the $111,053.41 under Section 509. That ruling was both equitably and legally well-founded, and, as a result, the Bankruptcy Court's decision is AFFIRMED.

The conclusion of the *Slamans* court did not survive an appeal to the United States Court of Appeals for the Tenth Circuit. Still, the *Slamans* rule is the rule reflected in current law. The revised version of Article 5 states in UCC §5-117(a) that an issuer of a letter of credit "is subrogated to the rights of the beneficiary to the same extent as if the issuer were a secondary obligor of the underlying obligation owed to the beneficiary." Comment 2 goes so far as to state that the statute is designed (like *Slamans*) to reject the reasoning of the Third Circuit in *Tudor Development*. Accordingly, assuming that the revised Article 5 is adopted widely, it will be clear in the future that issuers of letters of credit are entitled to subrogation under Article 5 of the UCC.

In light of that result, it would be appropriate for bankruptcy courts to follow the same rule in bankruptcy. Such a holding would rest on the idea that banks issuing letters of credit on behalf of applicants that subsequently become bankrupt are "liable with" the applicant on the underlying obligation for purposes of 11 U.S.C. §509(a). Accordingly, they should be entitled to use §509(a) to assert subrogation in the bankruptcy to the same extent that they would be entitled to assert subrogation under Article 5 outside the bankruptcy.

Problem Set 38

38.1. Archie Moon (a printer friend that you've been representing for some time) sends you a telecopy one morning that includes a proposed agreement with one of his major suppliers. The agreement states that Archie "at all times will maintain a clean standby letter of credit from a bank reasonably satisfactory to Seller." Archie has called his banker at Safety Central Bank, who has agreed to issue a letter of credit in the appropriate amount if Archie allows the bank to maintain possession of some certificates of deposit that Archie owns. Archie has no problem with that arrangement and wants to know if you have any concerns about the letter-of-credit provision quoted above.

38.2. Jodi Kay is working on a possible construction loan to Chancellor Investments, a longtime developer in her area that has suffered some hard times recently. Because Jodi has never done any business with Chancellor before, she is highly motivated to get the transaction for her bank. Jodi's bank ordinarily insists on a personal guaranty for at least one-quarter of the construction-loan amount, even for the most attractive projects from the most reputable developers.

Jodi's concern is that the principal of Chancellor Investments (Olive Chancellor) has suffered some financial reverses during the last several years that make Jodi doubt Olive's ability to cover the $500,000 guaranty that would be standard in this transaction. When Jodi raised that concern with Olive, Olive responded that she understood Jodi's concern. Olive asked if Jodi would be willing, in lieu of the guaranty, to accept a $500,000 letter of credit from SecondCity Bank, Chancellor's principal bank. Olive faxed SecondCity's letter-of-credit form to Jodi, who says it is identical to a form that you have approved in the past. Jodi is completely satisfied with SecondCity's financial strength. Is there any other reason that you can see why Jodi should be concerned about accepting a standby letter of credit as a substitute for a guaranty?

38.3. Jodi followed your advice in Problem 38.2, and the loan transaction went forward without incident. Several months later, however, you read in the newspaper one morning of a bankruptcy filing by Chancellor Investments. Accordingly, you are not surprised later that afternoon to receive a phone call from Jodi. She tells you that she has just spoken with the general contractor on the project, who tells her that he could finish the project for $300,000. Jodi started by calling Olive to tell her that she plans to pursue her remedies as forcefully as possible to get the $300,000. Jodi became concerned when she received a telecopied letter from Olive's attorney, advising her that any action against Olive or the SecondCity letter of credit would violate the Bankruptcy Code's automatic stay. What do you advise? 11 U.S.C. §§105, 362(a)(3).

38.4. Stacy Vye (the Wessex Bank loan officer) calls you about a $40,000 standby letter of credit that one of her less experienced loan officers issued several weeks ago. The letter of credit was issued for the benefit of Timothy Fairway at the behest of Stacy's customer Damon Wildeve. Fairway had agreed to build some customized cabinetry for Wildeve's office. This morning Fairway called Stacy to tell her that Fairway would be drawing on the letter of credit because Wildeve refused to pay when Fairway went by yesterday to collect payment. When Stacy called Wildeve, Wildeve told Stacy that he was sorry, but that his business had done so poorly that he had no money to pay Fairway. A few minutes ago Fairway appeared at Stacy's office with a draft on the letter of credit. Because the draft appeared to be in order, Stacy paid it.

Stacy is concerned because the loan officer that issued the letter of credit (Clym Yeobright) arranged for reimbursement by having Wildeve pledge $50,000 of Wildeve's stock in Tram Whirl Airlines (TWA). Because of TWA's bankruptcy last week, that stock is now completely worthless. Stacy wants to know what she can do to get paid if, as appears likely, Wildeve has no money to pay her. UCC §§2-702(2), 5-117(a); 11 U.S.C. §§509(a), 546(c).

38.5. Before she leaves, Stacy asks about a problem that she has on another one of her letters of credit. Wessex Bank issued a standby letter of credit for the benefit of Bulstrode Bank. Stacy issued the letter of credit to back up the obligation of Tertius Lydgate to repay a construction loan for a new medical office building that Lydgate has under construction, but neglected to take any collateral securing Lydgate's obligation to reimburse Wessex if it should be forced to pay on the letter of credit. In addition to the letter of credit from Stacy, Bulstrode took a lien on the office building to secure Lydgate's obligation to repay the loan. Because Lydgate's financial affairs have collapsed, Lydgate has fallen into default on the loan from Bulstrode. Accordingly, Bulstrode last week presented a draft on the letter of credit to Stacy. In response to the draft, she issued a check to Bulstrode in the full amount of the loan from Lydgate.

Thinking it was a routine matter, Stacy hired one of your associates to attempt to obtain reimbursement from Lydgate. Stacy assumed that Wessex would be subrogated to Bulstrode's lien against Lydgate's office building and that Wessex could use that lien to take the office building from Lydgate. It turns out, however, that a state statute requires mortgage creditors to release liens whenever they receive full payment of their loans. Hence, Bulstrode released the lien on the building the day after Bulstrode received payment of the loan from Wessex.

a. Does that release by Bulstrode mean that Wessex has lost its right to use that lien to pursue Lydgate? UCC §5-117 & comment 2.

b. Would the same thing be true if Stacy had acted as a guarantor instead of having Wessex issue a letter of credit? In pondering that question, assume that the guaranty would have been in the form set out in Assignment 36, except that it also would have included a defeasance provision like the one set out in Assignment 37. Continuing Guaranty §10.

38.6. Bulstrode issues a standby letter of credit related to an issue of bonds by General Motors. The letter of credit incorporates ISP98 by reference. The letter of credit conditions payment on presentation of a draft described as follows: "The draft must include the exact wording that follows: 'Jeneral Motors has failed to make a payment on its Series C 20-year bonds maturing January 1, 2006.'"

General Motors defaults on the bonds. Subsequently, the beneficiary of the letter of credit submits a draft that states: "General Motors has failed to make a payment on its Series C 20-year bonds maturing January 1, 2006." Is Bulstrode obligated to pay? UCC §5-108(a) & comment 1; UCP art. 13(a); ISP98 Rule 4.09.

38.7. In a weak moment last summer, you agreed to serve on a committee considering revisions to the ICC Uniform Customs and Practice for Documentary Credits. (One of your partners suggested that it might be a good way to attract some new clients.) Your first task on the committee is to consider differences between that document and the ICC ISP98. You have been asked to write an analysis of two of the ISP provisions. The first of the provisions is ISP Rule 4.09, at issue in the previous problem. The second is Rule 4.08, which provides that a standby letter of credit is presumed to require a demand for payment even if the letter of credit does not call for it. As you know, those rules differ from the rules set out in UCP art. 13, which include no analogous requirement for specific documents and contemplate examination under "international standard banking practice."

Do you see any basis for either of the two distinctions? Would you recommend revising the UCP to bring it into conformity with ISP98?

Part Three
Systems for Enhancing Liquidity

Chapter 11.   Negotiability

Assignment 39:   Negotiable Instruments

A.   Negotiability and Liquidity

The concept of liquidity is central to the "big picture" of financial transactions. Generally, liquidity refers to the ease with which an asset can be sold at a price that reflects the asset's economic value. For example, a certificate for 100 shares of stock traded on the New York Stock Exchange is one of the most liquid of all assets: Under normal conditions, a call to a stockbroker can produce a sale in a matter of minutes. Conversely, a partnership interest in a two-person general partnership is very illiquid: The uniqueness of that kind of asset precludes the establishment of any organized market for its sale. The lack of a market makes a sale difficult because it forces a prospective seller to expend considerable effort to locate a buyer and educate the buyer about the value of the asset.

Liquidity is as useful for payment obligations as it is for other assets. If a payment obligation is highly liquid, the payee easily can sell the obligation and thus convert it to cash. By providing a ready source of cash, an active market for payment obligations aids the financial position of operating businesses that generate payment obligations when they sell things to their customers. Many businesses (especially small ones) prefer to have immediate cash rather than waiting for payment from their customers. Indeed, many businesses prefer immediate cash even if they have to sell their payment obligations at a discount. To put it in economic terms, liquidity allows those businesses to shift financial risks to third parties.

That process also enhances the general efficiency of financial markets by making it easier to form financial businesses that specialize in bearing the financial risks that operating businesses want to trade for cash. In turn, a system that encourages the formation of those financial enterprises allows specialization in evaluating, monitoring, and collecting those obligations. Specialization can lead to administration of those obligations that is cheaper and more effective than administration under a system in which each business holds and monitors all of the payment obligations that its sales generate.

Putting aside money, the negotiable instrument is the oldest device for enhancing liquidity with any role in modern commerce. Rules related to negotiability enhance liquidity in two distinct ways. First, negotiable instruments offer an easy way for verifying a party's power to transfer an enforceable interest in the instrument. As you will see in the assignments to come, all the relevant information appears on the two sides of the instrument. That means (at least in theory) that the only thing that a purchaser of a negotiable instrument needs to do to determine that the purported seller can transfer a right to enforce the instrument is look at the instrument and verify the identity of the party with whom it is dealing. The prospective purchaser's title search need not include inquiries to the payor or to any public or private records. Indeed, if the instrument is "bearer" paper (discussed below), the purchaser acquires a right to enforce the instrument even if it buys the instrument from a thief!

The second liquidity-enhancing feature of negotiable instruments arises from a defense-stripping rule that makes a negotiable instrument more valuable in the hands of a purchaser than it was in the hands of the payee that sold it. Upon compliance with that rule, a transfer of a negotiable instrument strips away most of the defenses to payment that the payor could have asserted against the original payee. In the common terminology, a purchaser that becomes a "holder in due course" takes the instrument free from all "personal" defenses. Thus, a holder in due course could force Carl to repay a negotiable instrument that he issued even if Carl had a defense to payment against the original payee. By stripping away the payor's defenses to payment, that rule enhances the likelihood that the purchaser will be entitled to payment from the payor. Accordingly (at least theoretically), those rules make the purchase of a negotiable instrument a more attractive investment, which in turn makes such instruments more liquid.

As the previous paragraphs suggest, the subject of the negotiability system is a piece of paper, a physical writing that evidences the payment obligation. That piece of paper is central to both of the rules mentioned above. The evidence of transfer takes the form of physical signatures (indorsements) on the instrument. Similarly, holder-in-due-course status can be attained only by a person that has possession of the instrument. Every student who has worked through the first part of this book should understand that no system that requires manipulation and transmission of physical documents can survive undiminished in the computer age. As systems for electronic transmission of information become less expensive and more reliable, the increasing relative expense of systems that rely on physical documents generates pressures that diminish wide use of any document-based system. Indeed, the pressures of a modernizing economy began to limit the use of negotiable instruments even before the computer age. Thus, as this chapter explains, a variety of practical considerations already have made negotiable instruments considerably less common than they were even a generation ago.

That is not to say that the negotiability system is a useless relic. Negotiable instruments still play some role in commerce, especially in the banking system. Furthermore, newer and more sophisticated systems for enhancing liquidity (such as securitization) are likely to draw heavily on the concepts developed in the negotiability system. Thus, an understanding of negotiability and how it works will be helpful in keeping pace with the changing mechanisms of commerce in the decades to come.

The remainder of this assignment discusses the basic framework of the negotiability system: the rules that determine whether any particular payment obligation constitutes a negotiable instrument. The next two assignments (Assignments 40 and 41) discuss other aspects of the system, including the two liquidity-enhancing features of negotiable instruments described above (free transferability and holder-in-due-course status), explaining how they work and discussing the concerns that have begun to limit their role in modern commerce.

B.   A Typical Transaction

To get a feel for how a negotiable instrument could be used in commerce, consider the following transaction. It is a simple international sale-of-goods transaction, both because it is easy to understand and because this context is one common use of negotiable instruments in commerce today. The parties to the transaction are B.K. Werner, a St. Louis businessman, and Neville Russell, a London bookseller.* Werner has purchased some engineering textbooks from Russell at an agreed price of 1,500 British pounds. Werner could pay by mailing a check on his account, but it would take several weeks for Russell to obtain payment for that check if he deposited it with his bank in Britain. Furthermore, unless Werner is a man of impressive solvency, Russell might doubt the value of Werner's check and thus refuse to ship the books until the check has cleared. Werner also could pay by means of a wire transfer or letter of credit, which would satisfy Russell with prompt and sure funding. Wire transfers and letters of credit, however, tend to be too expensive for small transactions like the one in question. Accordingly, unless Russell is in such a rush that he needs to provide payment on a same-day basis, it would be plausible for him to select a draft as the best mechanism for payment (see Figure 39.1).

Figure 39.1
Sample Negotiable Draft

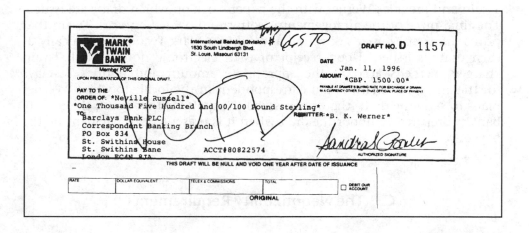

---

* The names identify real individuals, taken from a sample draft kindly provided to me by Mercantile Bank (then Mark Twain Bank). The remainder of the example is fictional, based on interviews with several bankers about common uses of drafts.

To pay with a draft, Werner goes to his bank (in this instance, Mark Twain Bank) to purchase the draft. Although the stylized form of the draft obscures the substance of what it says, careful study reveals something like a letter addressed to Barclays Bank (in London), asking Barclays to pay Neville Russell the agreed upon sum:

> January 11, 1996. Upon presentation of this original draft, pay to the order of Neville Russell One Thousand Five Hundred and 00/100 Pound Sterling. To Barclays Bank PLC.
>
> [Authorized Signature for Mark Twain Bank.]

If all goes as planned, Werner transmits the draft to Russell in the ordinary course of business. Russell, in turn, could present the draft directly to Barclays or sell it to his own bank in London (in which case Russell's bank would present the draft to Barclays). Meanwhile, Mark Twain notifies Barclays by telex that it has issued the draft so that Barclays recognizes the draft as valid when it is presented. When Barclays receives the draft, Barclays pays the money to Russell (or Russell's bank, as the case may be) and deducts the money from an account that Mark Twain maintains with Barclays for the purpose of handling such transactions. The result is the same as if Werner had paid Russell directly, except that the bank draft expedited the payment transaction.

If Werner is a large customer that engages in numerous draft transactions, Mark Twain could expedite the process further by allowing Werner to issue drafts directly, which would eliminate the need for Werner to come to the bank to purchase drafts. In that arrangement, Mark Twain authorizes specified officers of Werner's company to sign drafts that would be binding on Mark Twain and provides Werner with the paper stock on which drafts are issued. The final piece of the arrangement is software provided by Mark Twain that prints drafts at Werner's direction and notifies Mark Twain electronically as each draft is issued. Upon receipt of each electronic notice, Mark Twain charges Werner's account the appropriate amount and notifies Barclays (or the analogous Mark Twain correspondent in the locale to which Werner plans to send the draft) that it has issued the draft. At that point, the remote bank is prepared to honor the draft when it is presented for payment by the payee.

C.   The Negotiability Requirements

Although rules about negotiability originally developed through judicial decisions, they now have been codified into a formal and rigid statutory framework that appears in Article 3 of the Uniform Commercial Code.

Because of the formality of the rules set forth in Article 3, it is important to start with some basic terms used by Article 3 to identify the various parties to a transaction involving an instrument. Referring back to the Russell-Werner example, Article 3 calls the party that directs the payment (Mark Twain in this case) the "drawer" (UCC §3-103(a)(3)) or the "issuer" (UCC §3-105(c)). Werner, the person who caused the draft to be issued, is called the "remitter" (UCC §3-103(a)(11)) because of the understanding that Werner will remit the draft to the payee Russell. Neville Russell, to whom the payment is to be made, is the payee. Barclays, the person directed to make payment (the person on whom the draft is drawn, as it were), is the "drawee" (UCC §3-103(a)(2)) (see Figure 39.2).

Figure 39.2
The Players in a Negotiable Draft Transaction

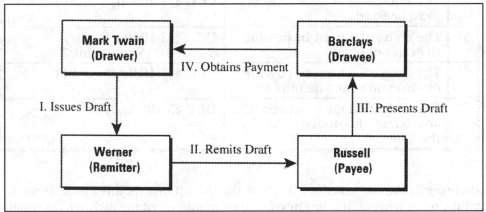

As explained above, the foundation of negotiability is a physical object: the negotiable instrument. The text of Article 3 uses a two-stage framework to set out the rules for determining whether any particular obligation is negotiable. The first stage is a general definition of a negotiable instrument, which appears in UCC §3-104(a). The second stage is contained in an array of provisions scattered throughout Article 1 and other provisions in Part 1 of Article 3, which provide detailed definitions of many of the terms that appear in UCC §3-104.

UCC §3-104 sets forth seven requirements for negotiability. An obligation that satisfies all seven requirements is a negotiable instrument, or simply an "instrument." See UCC §3-104(b) ("'Instrument' means a negotiable instrument."). If an obligation fails to meet any of the seven requirements, then (with one minor exception discussed below) none of the substantive rules set forth in Article 3 applies. Figure 39.3 summarizes those requirements and the UCC provisions that relate to them. The paragraphs that follow the table then discuss each of those seven requirements in turn.

1. The Promise or Order Requirement

The introductory paragraph of UCC §3-104(a) limits negotiability to obligations that are either a "promise" or an "order." Those terms are defined and .distinguished in UCC §§3-103(a)(6) (defining "order") and 3-103(a)(9)

Figure 39.3
The Negotiability Requirements

	REQUIREMENT	STATUTORY REFERENCES
1.	The obligation must be a written promise or order.	UCC §§3-104(a),1-201(43), 3-103(a)(2), (3), (5), (6), & (9), 3-104(e), (f), (g) & (h)
2.	The obligation must be unconditional.	UCC §§3-104(a), 3-106
3.	The obligation must require payment of money.	UCC §§3-104(a), 1-201(24), 3-107
4.	The amount of the obligation must be fixed.	UCC §§3-104(a), 3-112(b)
5.	The obligation must be payable to bearer or order.	UCC §§3-104(a)(1) & (c), 3-109, 3-115 comment 2
6.	The obligation must be payable on demand or at a definite time.	UCC §§3-104(a)(2), 3-108
7.	The obligation must not contain any extraneous undertakings by the issuer.	UCC §3-104(a)(3)

(defining "promise"). Because each of the definitions requires that the obligation be in writing, the promise or order requirement implicitly requires all negotiable instruments to be in writing. Although the UCC includes a broad definition of "writing," it still requires an "intentional reduction to tangible form." UCC §1-201(46)(revised UCC §1-201(b)(43)). Accordingly, obligations reflected only in electronic form cannot be negotiable. However much that "tangible-form" requirement may limit use of the system in the future, it would be hard to dispense with it and maintain anything like the current system, which relies on physical signatures as a means for transfer and physical possession as the touchstone for enforcement. A future system might recognize indorsements made by electronic signatures attached to payment messages, but implementing such a system would require a significant conceptual reworking of Articles 3 and 4 of the UCC.

In addition to the writing requirement, the promise or order requirement limits the scope of Article 3 by limiting the types of obligations that it covers: If the obligation is not a "promise" or an "order," it cannot qualify. A "promise" is a direct commitment to pay. UCC §3-103(a)(9). The party that makes a promise is called a "maker," UCC §3-103(a)(5); the instrument that contains a promise is called a "note," UCC §3-104(e). An "order," by contrast, does not contain a direct promise to pay. Rather, an order is an instruction by one person (the "drawer," as described above, see UCC §3-103(a)(3)) directing some other party to pay (the "drawee," as described above, see UCC §3-103(a)(2)). An instrument that contains an order is called a "draft," UCC §3-104(e), the type of negotiable instrument illustrated by the Werner draft in Figures 39.1 and 39.2.

UCC §3-104(f), (g), (h) defines three of the most common types of drafts. The first is a check, which is simply a draft drawn on a bank. UCC §3-104(f); see UCC §1-201(4)(revised §1-201(b)(4)) (defining a "bank" as "any person engaged in the business of banking"). Thus, the Werner draft could be characterized as a check (although the transnational relationship would make that characterization unusual). The second is a cashier's check, a type of check in which the drawer and drawee are the same bank. UCC §3-104(g). For example, if Mark Twain had given Werner a draft drawn on itself, rather than on Barclays, the draft would have been a cashier's check. The third is a teller's check, a draft drawn by one bank on another bank. UCC §3-104(h). Because the Werner draft was issued by Mark Twain and drawn on Barclays, it technically would be correct (albeit unusual, as mentioned above) to describe that instrument as a teller's check.

2.   The Unconditional Requirement

The introductory paragraph of UCC §3-104(a) also requires negotiable instruments to be "unconditional," a term that UCC §3-106 defines in detail. That requirement generally limits negotiability to instruments that are absolute and include on their face all of the terms of payment. Thus, if a document includes a promise to pay that is subject to a condition, the instrument cannot be negotiable. UCC §3-106(a)(i). For example, the draft in Figure 39.1 would not be negotiable if it included a notation stating that it was "valid only upon remitter's receipt of the agreed-upon merchandise." That notation would make the obligation conditional because the drawer's instruction would be ineffective if Werner did not receive the promised books.

By excluding conditional promises, that provision obviates the need for potential purchasers of instruments to evaluate the likelihood that the issuer will become obligated to pay; if the issuer is unwilling to create an unconditional obligation to pay, the document is not negotiable. At the same time, that provision significantly limits the utility of the negotiability system because it excludes from the system any transaction that calls for a conditional payment obligation. The following case illustrates such a transaction.

DBA Enterprises, Inc. v. Findlay
28 U.C.C. Rep. Serv. 2d 1297 (Colo. App. 1996)

Opinion by Judge ROY.

In this action relating to the sale of a business, defendants, Lauretta and James Findlay (Sellers), appeal . . . the denial of their counterclaim to enforce a promissory note given by Purchasers in partial payment for the business. . . .

In March 1992, Sellers sold their franchise in Lawn Doctor, Inc. (Lawn Doctor), a lawn fertilization business, to Purchasers. The business sold and applied fertilizer, pesticides, and herbicides under the franchise and provided core aeration services in Littleton and Englewood, Colorado. The sale included all the assets of the business, including the customer list. The total purchase price was $72,500, part of which was paid by a promissory note in the amount of $53,750, payable with interest to Sellers in specified installments. . . .

The assets were transferred by means of a bill of sale that included a covenant not to compete by which Sellers agreed that, until December 31, 1997, they would not provide, directly or indirectly, fertilizers, herbicides, pesticides, or core aeration to lawns within the geographic area described in the Lawn Doctor franchise agreement. . . .

After the sale, and as permitted by the bill of sale, Sellers continued to operate a lawn maintenance business, Acres Green Maintenance (Acres Green), which had been owned and operated separately from the Lawn Doctor franchise. Acres Green provided lawn mowing and trimming services and had many of the same customers served by Lawn Doctor.

. . . Later, on two occasions, Sellers provided services prohibited by the covenant as an accommodation to two of their Acres Green customers without charge. They also "contracted out" on a pass-through basis such services for two commercial accounts of Acres Green that insisted upon paying one vendor for all lawn care services. . . .

In February 1993, Sellers wrote a letter to their Acres Green customers recommending the services of The Greenery, a business owned by an acquaintance, for fertilization or aeration services. The letter, in part, stated: "ACRES GREEN MAINTENANCE AND THE GREENERY will work together to provide you with a healthy green lawn." Both Sellers and the owner of The Greenery signed the letter and participated in the cost of its preparation and mailing. Sellers did not participate in any revenues or profits from the services rendered by The Greenery, and the letter generated only two or three inquiries.

In March 1993, Purchasers discontinued payments on the promissory note, and in May 1993, Sellers resumed the services prohibited by the covenant not to compete and earned approximately $22,000 in gross revenues from such services during the balance of the 1993 season. In August 1993, Sellers sold Acres Green and moved to Florida.

Purchasers commenced this action, alleging among other things breach of contract, tortious interference with contract, and civil conspiracy, and requesting both damages and the cancellation of the promissory note. Sellers counterclaimed on the promissory note, which had an outstanding principal balance of $46,400 as of March 1, 1993, accrued interest, and a provision for attorney fees.

The trial court found that Sellers had materially breached the covenant not to compete, awarded damages equal to the amount due on the promissory note plus $1,000, [and] denied Sellers' counterclaim with respect to the promissory note. . . .

III.

Sellers brought three counterclaims, the first of which related to a promissory note representing a portion of the purchase price payable to them in the initial principal amount of $53,750. . . .

In its oral findings, the trial court found that Sellers had failed to establish the promissory note claim by a preponderance of the evidence. However, with the exception of the allegations concerning a default and amount owing, Purchasers admitted the allegations in the promissory note counterclaim in their reply. Further, Sellers introduced unchallenged evidence that Purchasers did not pay the March 1993 and subsequent payments, [and] that the principal balance due as of

March 1, 1993, was $46,300. . . . Moreover, the original promissory note was admitted into evidence without objection.

Under this state of the record, we conclude that Sellers, as a matter of law, presented an unchallenged prima facie case with respect to the promissory note. However, additional language in the note precludes disposition of the counterclaim on the basis of the prima facie case alone.

The promissory note in question here contains the following statement: "Maker's obligation under this note is subject to the conditions recited in that Bill of Sale and Covenants not to Compete between the parties of even date." To be a negotiable instrument a promissory note must be an unconditional promise to pay a sum certain. Section 4-3-104, C.R.S. (1995 Cum. Supp.). The quoted statement in the note renders it conditional and, therefore, nonnegotiable. But, the language does not make the note unenforceable. See §4-3-106, C.R.S. (1995 Cum. Supp.).

The bill of sale to which the promissory note refers, while calling for a promissory note as a portion of the purchase price, is silent as to the terms of the promissory note. The evidence at trial made no reference to the intention of the parties in including the conditional language in the promissory note. Therefore, although Sellers have otherwise demonstrated a right to recover under the note the matter must be remanded to the trial court for a determination as to the intent of the parties, if any, concerning the effect of the conditional language contained in the promissory note. . . .

The trial court, in addition, may separately consider whether the breach of the covenant not to compete constitutes such a failure of consideration as to excuse payment of the promissory note. In determining whether there has been a complete failure of consideration, the trial court may consider, inter alia, that the parties allocated only $29,000 to the customer list in the first instance and that Purchasers lost a substantial number of the customers prior to any breach. Further, the parties allocated $22,000 to the franchise and $2,250 to the equipment, both of which items have been retained by Purchasers.

The unconditional requirement also addresses the related concern that the terms of payment be evident from the face of the document itself. Thus, under clauses (ii) and (iii) of UCC §3-106(a), a document is not negotiable if it states that it "is subject to or governed by" another writing or if it states "that rights or obligations with respect to [the document] are stated in another writing." Thus, the Werner draft would not be negotiable if it included the notation that it was "to be paid as stated in remitter's agreement with payee." A document that required potential purchasers to search other documents to discover the terms of payments would be too cumbersome for the negotiability system.

UCC §3-106(b) sets forth two important exceptions to the unconditional requirement. The first recognizes the reality that a note for which the maker gives collateral often includes references to other writings (such as a loan agreement, security agreement, or mortgage) describing rights related to the collateral and to the payee's remedies upon default. Those types of terms ordinarily do not limit the rights of the payee as a condition would. Rather, they tend to enhance the rights of the payee by giving the payee a greater ability to enforce payment than the payee would have without collateral or without the remedies stated in the ancillary documents. Accordingly, a strong case could be made that inclusion of those terms would not make a document conditional in the first instance. In any event, UCC §3-106(b)(i) resolves any concern by stating expressly that inclusion of such terms does not undermine negotiability.

The second provision is qualitatively different because it permits terms that directly limit the enforceability of the instrument. Specifically, UCC §3-106(b)(ii) extends negotiability to documents in which "payment is limited to resort to a particular fund or source." The most common example would be a "nonrecourse" real-estate note, which limits the payee's remedies to the mortgaged real estate and bars any suit directly against the maker of the note. Under UCC §3-106(b)(ii), that nonrecourse provision would not preclude negotiability.

The last paragraph of UCC §3-106 comment 1 states that particular-fund provisions should not undermine negotiability because the market can evaluate the effect those terms have on the value of the underlying obligation. That explanation, however, would justify a complete abandonment of the unconditional requirement. As explained above, the basic rationale for the unconditional requirement is the idea that purchasers of instruments should not have to evaluate the effect of conditions on the value of obligations. There is no logical reason why a condition permitted by the "particular fund" exception (like the common "nonrecourse" requirement) is any easier to evaluate than other possible conditions (such as a condition that payment be made only if the stock market rises a specified amount). A more plausible explanation is that particular-fund conditions are so common that a rule excluding them would exclude a large class of potentially negotiable instruments for which conditions do not pose a serious problem. By allowing inclusion of those instruments, UCC §3-106(b)(ii) permits some broadening of the use of negotiable instruments without unduly compromising the streamlining that characterizes the system.

3. The Money Requirement

The third requirement contained in the introductory paragraph of UCC §3-104(a) requires the promise or order to be for the payment of money. That requirement excludes obligations to deliver commodities other than money. For example: "The undersigned promises to deliver 100 tons of wheat on June 1, 1997." The UCC's concept of "money," however, is a broad one, which includes both domestic and foreign currency. UCC §1-201(24)(revised §1-201(b)(24)); see UCC §3-107 comment (stating that an instrument can be payable in foreign currency). Thus, there is nothing unusual or disqualifying about the provision in the Werner draft calling for payment in pounds sterling rather than dollars.

4. The Fixed-Amount Requirement

The fourth (and last) requirement embedded in the introductory paragraph of UCC §3-104(a) requires the amount of the obligation to be fixed. That rule excludes promises to pay unspecified sums of money ("I promise to pay to payee one-half of the 2002 profits from sales of my casebooks."). In commercial transactions, an instrument that includes a promise to pay a fixed sum often also includes a promise to pay interest and other charges that accrue on a debt. Like provisions related to collateral, provisions obligating the maker to pay interest or other charges only enhance the value of the instrument. Accordingly, a rule excluding documents with such provisions from the system would exclude a large class of obligations in which there is little doubt as to the amount due. UCC §3-104(a) expressly includes them by stating that the fixed amount can be "with or without interest or other charges described in the [instrument]."

The principal topic of litigation about interest provisions has been whether a provision providing for a variable rate of interest violates the fixed-amount-of-money requirement. There was considerable litigation of that point in the 1980s, resulting in a number of decisions holding that variable-rate notes could not be negotiable instruments. The revised Article 3 rejects those decisions in UCC §3-112(b). This section states that interest "may be stated in an instrument as a fixed or variable amount of money or it may be expressed as a fixed or variable rate or rates." Those provisions may impose some doubt on the purchaser (by requiring it to ascertain the rate at which interest accrues), but their wide use in financial markets convinced the revisers of Article 3 to include them as instruments.

As demonstrated by the case that follows, that requirement still causes difficulties in cases when the principal amount is not fixed. That is particularly true when documents are not drafted by attorneys versed in the rules of Article 3.

Nagel v. Cronebaugh

782 So. 2d 436 (Fla. Dist. Ct. App. 2001)

ORFINGER, R.B., J.

Richard Nagel (Nagel), as Personal Representative of the Estate of Marjorie E. Peirce (Mrs. Peirce), appeals a final judgment denying foreclosure of a mortgage. . . .

Mrs. Peirce and Mrs. Cronebaugh met in Virginia in 1958. Mrs. Cronebaugh moved to Florida in 1962 and married Mr. Cronebaugh in 1965. While there was sporadic contact between them over the years, that contact increased in 1993 when Mrs. Cronebaugh advised Mrs. Peirce that they wished to purchase a lakefront home but could not do so until they sold their existing residence. According to Mrs. Cronebaugh, "one thing led to another," and Mrs. Peirce agreed to give the Cronebaughs $50,000.00 and loan them an additional $50,000.00 so they could purchase the lakefront home. The $50,000.00 loan was to be secured by a mortgage.

The Cronebaughs' attorney drafted the note and mortgage. The note provided as follows:

FOR VALUE RECEIVED, the undersigned, (jointly or severally, if more than one) promises to pay to MARJORIE H. [sic] PEIRCE, or order in the manner hereinafter specified, the principal sum of To be determined at the time of contengencies [sic] below /100 DOLLARS ($ unknown) with interest from date of -0-percent, per annum on the balance from time to time remaining unpaid. The said principal and interest shall be payable in lawful money of the United State of America at 3720 East Old Gun Rd, Midlothian, VA or at such other place as may be designated by written notice from the holder to the maker hereof, on the date and in the following manner:

1. This is a demand note, due on October 1, 2018,

OR

2. Upon sale of the house by makers of this note, located at 7230 Lake Ola Dr., Tangerine, Orange County, Florida, Marjorie B. [sic] Peirce will get 1/3 of net proceeds from sale of the house to be determined by amount of sale of the house, minus any liens on the property at the time of signing this note, plus expenses of the sale,

OR

3. Upon the death of the makers, within 90 days of death, the heirs of makers of this note will have the option of (A) # 1 above or (B) 1/3 of equity in the house, to be determined at the time of death and to be determined as follows (1) by agreement between the parties; (2) if no agreement can be reached, each party will get an appraisal by separate MIA appraisers, and the mean average of the appraisals will be the value of the house, from which the liens on the house shall be subtracted. All liens on the house shall be only as of the date of signing of this agreement,

WHICHEVER OCCURS FIRST.

This note with interest is secured by a mortgage on real estate o[f] even date here-with, made by the maker hereof in favor of the said payee, and shall be construed and enforced according to the laws of Florida.

If default be made in the payment of any of the sums or interest mentioned herein or in said mortgage, or in the performance of any of the agreements contained herein or in said mortgage, then the entire principal sum and accrued interest shall at the option of the holder hereof become at once due and collectible without notice, time being of the essence; and said principal sum and accrued interest shall both bear interest from such time until paid at the highest rate allowable under the laws of the State of Florida. Failure to exercise this option shall not constitute a waiver of the right to exercise the same in the even of any subsequent default. . . .

. . . The Cronebaughs obtained a bank mortgage for the remainder of the purchase price and, with the money provided by Mrs. Peirce, closed on the home. . . . After Mrs. Peirce died, Nagel demanded payment in full on the note based on his belief that paragraph 1 of the note created an obligation due on demand. The Cronebaughs contended that paragraph 1 did not require payment until October 1, 2018. The trial court found that paragraph 1 was unambiguous and created an obligation due on October 1, 2018, unless one of the conditions specified in paragraph 2 or 3 of the note occurred first. . . .

THE PROMISSORY NOTE

Nagel argues that paragraph 1 of the promissory note is controlled by [UCC §3-108(c), which] provides, "If an instrument, payable at a fixed date, is also payable upon demand made before the fixed date, the instrument is payable on demand until the fixed date and, if demand for payment is not made before that date, becomes payable at a definite time on the fixed date." Thus, Nagel asserts that the language in paragraph 1 of the promissory note created a demand note payable at any time on demand by the payee and if no demand had been made, would become due on its own on October 1, 2018, or upon the earlier occurrence of the conditions in paragraph 2 or 3 of the note.

. . . In order for an instrument to be negotiable under the UCC, it must contain an unconditional promise to pay a sum certain. [UCC §3-104(a).] Here the note does not provide a fixed principal amount. Hence, the note is not a negotiable instrument and [Section 3-108] does not apply.

We turn, therefore, to general contract principles to interpret the note. The interpretation of a contract is an issue of law. As a result, this court is not bound by the trial court's conclusions regarding construction of the contract.

While the trial judge found that paragraph 1 of the note unambiguously created an obligation due October 1, 2018, we disagree. A phrase in a contract is ambiguous when it is of uncertain meaning and may be fairly understood in more ways than one. Insofar as the language contained in paragraph 1 of the note is ambiguous as to the ability of the holder to demand payment prior to 2018, the ambiguity must be interpreted against the party who selected that language — in this case, the Cronebaughs. Because we conclude the note is ambiguous, we construe it against the Cronebaughs and find that the trial judge erred in determining that the note did not create a demand obligation. . . .

REVERSED AND REMANDED.

COBB, J., concurring specially.

I concur in the result reached by the majority. As I see it, the note is *not* ambiguous and it is a demand note, the same as it would be if it had been negotiable and construed pursuant to [UCC §3-108(c).] The statute is merely a codification of common sense, which should control the construction of any contract, negotiable or not. The trial court simply deleted the word "demand" from the mortgage note.

5.   The Payable-to-Bearer-or-Order Requirement

In addition to the four requirements set forth in the introductory paragraph to UCC §3-104(a), three more requirements appear in the three numbered subparagraphs of UCC §3-104(a). The first of those three (the fifth requirement overall) appears in UCC §3-104(a)(1): The document must be payable to "bearer" or "order." That provision refers to hoary terms of art detailed in UCC §3-109, an area where the formalism of Article 3 reaches its height. If an instrument does not contain the precise words required to satisfy the tests set forth in UCC §3-109, it is not an instrument. Accordingly, it is important to look carefully at the precise words authorized by the statute.

An instrument can be made payable to bearer in two general ways. The first way is the obvious one: The instrument can state that it is "payable to bearer" or "payable to the order of bearer." The closing phrase of UCC §3-109(a)(1) states that an instrument also can be payable to bearer if it "otherwise indicates that the person in possession of the promise or order is entitled to payment," but it seems unlikely that an instrument would satisfy that test if it did not contain the word "bearer" or some other phrase quite close to the words of the statute.

The second type of bearer paper is paper that is not payable to any particular identifiable person, which is covered in the second and third subsections of UCC §3-109(a). Subsection (a)(2) covers the simplest case, an instrument that does not state a payee. Imagine an instrument where the maker fails to fill in the name of the payee: "Pay to the order of _____." Article 3 treats that instrument as payable to bearer. UCC §§3-109(a)(2), 3-109 comment 2, 3-115 comment 2. Subsection (a)(3) offers the same rule for instruments made payable "to cash." UCC §3-109(a)(3) & comment 2.

If an instrument is not payable to bearer, it can be made payable to order in one of two ways. First, under UCC §3-109(b)(i), the document can state that it is payable to the order of an identified person: "Pay to the order of Dan Keating." Second, under UCC §3-109(b)(ii), it can state that it is payable to an identified person or order: "Pay to Dan Keating or order."

The reference in UCC §3-109(b)(ii) to an "identified person or order" contains an unfortunate ambiguity. As written, it could be construed to include two types of instruments: instruments payable "to an identified person" and instruments payable "to order." That reading is incorrect. The statute should be read as if there were quotation marks around the entire phrase: A promise or order is payable to order if it is payable "to an identified person or order." An instrument satisfies that provision only if it includes the entire phrase, both the name of the identified person and the "order" language. An instrument that is payable "to Dan Keating" is not payable to order. Indeed, it is not an instrument at all because it fails the bearer-or-order requirement. Nor does order paper include an instrument made payable simply "to order." That instrument's failure to identify the payee would make it bearer paper under UCC §3-109(a)(2).

Finally, the practicalities of the checking system call for an exception to the bearer-or-order requirement for checks. Specifically, a check that fails the bearer-or-order requirement, but satisfies all of the remaining negotiability requirements, qualifies as an instrument despite that failure. UCC §3-104(c). Comment 2 succinctly explains the motivation for that exception:

> [I]t is good policy to treat checks, which are payment instruments, as negotiable instruments whether or not they contain the words "to the order of." These words are almost always pre-printed on the check form. Occasionally the drawer of a check may strike out these words before issuing the check.... Absence of the quoted words can easily be overlooked and should not affect the rights of holders who may pay money or give credit for a check without being aware that it is not in the conventional form.

6.   *The Demand or Definite-Time Requirement*

The sixth requirement appears in UCC §3-104(a)(2): The obligation must be payable on demand or at a definite time. UCC §3-108 defines those terms so broadly that they include all significant payment obligations. First, a demand obligation includes not only an obligation that is payable "on demand" (or "at sight," which is the same thing), but also an obligation that states no time for payment. UCC §3-108(a). The "no-time" provision allows the system to cover checks (which typically prescribe no specific time for payment). Second, the "definite time" category includes not only the conventional obligation that is due on a particular date or particular schedule of dates (like the promissory note in Assignment 35), but also documents that allow the holder a right to extend the date of payment, UCC §3-108(b)(iii). As the comment to UCC §3-108 explains, the rationale for that rule is that a provision giving the holder the option to extend should not undermine negotiability because the holder always could extend the time for payment even if the document did not include such a provision.

UCC §3-108(b) also permits provisions that alter the time of payment to permit acceleration and prepayment. Indeed, the statute even permits extensions at the option of the maker (if the instrument limits extension "to a further definite time") or "automatically upon or after a specified act or event." Apparently, the only obligation that would fail that rule would be a document giving the issuer either a completely unqualified option to extend or a qualified option to extend that did not state a date to which the extension would run.

7.   The No-Extraneous-Undertakings Requirement

The last requirement for negotiability is the requirement in UCC §3-104(a)(3) that forbids inclusion of a promise calling for something other than the payment of money. For historical reasons (that do not seem to have much explanatory value), that requirement typically is referred to as the "courier without luggage" requirement. The general concept is that a document cannot be negotiable if it includes any nonmonetary promises. Thus, a document cannot be an instrument if it includes provisions in which the maker not only promises to pay $100,000, but also promises to deliver 100 tons of wheat by a specified date.

The three numbered clauses at the end of UCC §3-104(a)(3) articulate three exceptions to the no-extraneous-undertakings requirement, identifying provisions that are so customary that the statute permits their inclusion even if they are not, strictly speaking, monetary promises. The first, which resonates with the provisions related to collateral in UCC §3-106(b)(i), permits "an undertaking or power to give, maintain, or protect collateral to secure payment." UCC §3-104(a)(3)(i). Thus, an instrument can be negotiable even if it includes provisions in which the maker promises to provide collateral to secure the debt evidenced by the instrument. Second, UCC §3-104(a)(3)(ii) permits "an authorization or power to the holder to confess judgment or realize on or dispose of collateral." That provision is intended to validate the provisions common in older promissory notes in some jurisdictions in which a maker authorizes the holder to obtain a default judgment on the note; in some cases, such a provision gives the holder procedural advantages that expedite enforcement of the instrument. Finally, UCC §3-104(a)(3)(iii) permits conditions in which the borrower waives laws intended for the benefit or protection of the borrower or obligor. That clause validates a group of common provisions in which borrowers waive various common-law protections — requirements of presentment, dishonor, notice of dishonor, and the like — that would hinder the holder's collection of the instrument.

Problem Set 39

39.1.   Jodi Kay (your long-standing client from CountryBank) has started work on a project to sell a number of the bank's less desirable miscellaneous assets. The first item that comes to hand is a corporate bond issued by HAL Corp., in the following (standard) form:

HAL Corp.
Albany, New York
8 percent Bond
Due January 1, 2020

For value received, HAL Corp., a New York corporation (the "Corporation"), promises to pay to Mark Henry, or registered assigns, on January 1, 2020, the principal sum of $1,000 in lawful money of the United States of America. The Corporation further promises to pay interest on the principal sum from January 1, 1990, at the rate of 8 percent per annum in lawful money of the United States of America. Interest will be paid semiannually on July 1 and January 1 of each year after January 1, 1990, until the principal sum hereof has been paid or provision for its payment has been made.

The principal of this Bond will be payable at the principal office of the Corporation (or at whatever other place may be designated in writing by the Corporation from time to time) upon the presentation and surrender hereof. The semiannual interest payments will be mailed to the registered holder hereof at the address last furnished in writing to the Corporation.

This bond is registered both as to principal and interest and is transferable only on the books of the Corporation by the presentation and surrender hereof accompanied by an assignment form duly completed and executed by the registered holder hereof or a duly authorized attorney.

IN WITNESS WHEREOF, the Corporation has caused this Bond to be signed by its duly authorized officers on January 1, 1990.

Trying to determine exactly what she can say about it, she faxes you a copy of the bond with a cover sheet asking you to get back to her as soon as possible. She is trying to fill out a form that requires her to state whether each asset is a negotiable instrument. Does the bond qualify? UCC §§3-104(a), 3-109.

39.2.   Pleased with your thoughtful advice in Problem 39.1, Jodi faxes you another one. This time it's the Promissory Note set out in Assignment 35. What is your opinion? UCC §§3-103(a)(9), 3-104(a), 3-106(a), 3-108, 3-109, 3-112(b).

39.3.   Late in the evening, Jodi calls to tell you that she has "just one more" for you to look at. She tells you that she has a cache of several hundred home-mortgage notes, all of which are on identical forms. She faxes you the form, which appears to be the standard form promulgated by the Federal National

Mortgage Association and the Federal Home Loan Mortgage Corp. It includes the following provisions:

> 4. *Borrower's Right To Prepay* I have the right to make payments of principal at any time before they are due. A payment of principal only is known as a "prepayment." When I make a prepayment, I will tell the Note Holder in writing that I am doing so. . . .

> 10. *Uniform Secured Note* ...In addition to the protections given to the Note Holder under this Note, a Mortgage, Deed of Trust or Security Deed (the "Security Instrument"), dated the same date as this Note, protects the Note Holder from possible losses which might result if I do not keep the promises which I make in this Note. That Security Instrument describes how and under what conditions I may be required to make immediate payment in full of all amounts I owe under this Note.

Do those provisions prevent the home-mortgage notes from being negotiable? UCC §§3-104(a), 3-106, 3-108.

39.4. Ben Darrow (your rural banker friend) calls you to ask about an unusual item that has landed on his desk. This morning's ATM deposits included a $12,000 check where the drawer (Carol Long) had crossed out the printed words "to order of" and written in pen "only to." The result is that the check states: "Pay only to Jasmine Ball." It appears from the back of the check that Ball cashed the check at Ovco Drugs in downtown Matacora. Ovco Drugs, in turn, deposited the check into its account at First State Bank of Matacora (Darrow's bank). Darrow wants to know if the check is valid and what advice you have as to what he should do. He tells you that Long is a valued customer, so he does not want to do anything wrong. UCC §§3-104(c), 4-301(a).

39.5. An old law-school classmate of yours named Doug Kahan works for the Internal Revenue Service (IRS). While you are reminiscing with him one afternoon, he asks you about a funny incident that came up the preceding week. He tells you that he's always heard stories about taxpayers mailing in their payments written on shirts, the "shirt off their back," as it were. Because he had never seen such a thing in all his years at the IRS, he had dismissed those tales as nothing but a common urban myth. This week, however, he received just such a package: a box including a (somewhat worn) white dress shirt, with the following written in black ink across the back of the shirt: "Pay to the order of the Internal Revenue Service $150,000." The taxpayer had scrawled its signature below that sentence and written "SecondBank" and a series of numbers to the left of the signature. Those numbers appear to identify the taxpayer's account at SecondBank.

Doug's assistant took the shirt to a branch of SecondBank a few blocks away. SecondBank, however, refused to honor the shirt-check. It acknowledged that the taxpayer had an account at SecondBank, that the shirt properly identified the taxpayer's account number, and that the account contained funds adequate to cover the specified payment. The bank explained, however, that it had a policy of honoring checks only if they were written on forms supplied by the bank.

Doug is frustrated because he has been attempting to collect payment from that particular taxpayer for several years. He tells you that the shirt-check story he's heard always ended with the statement that the shirt is a valid instrument. Is that right? If so, doesn't the bank have to pay it? What do you tell him? UCC §§3-103(a)(6), 3-104(a), 3-104(e), 3-104(f), 3-108(a), 3-408.

Assignment 40: Transfer and Enforcement of Negotiable Instruments

A. Transferring a Negotiable Instrument

One of the advantages of negotiable instruments is the ease with which an owner of a negotiable instrument can transfer clean and verifiable title: A transfer of a negotiable instrument never requires anything more than delivery of the instrument and a signature by the transferor. Furthermore, by examining the chain of signatures on the instrument (a topic discussed below), the purchaser generally can verify that the transfer is effective, in the sense that it will give the purchaser the ability to enforce the instrument. The ability to make a clean, complete, and verifiable transfer without the aid of any public official or recording of notice in a centralized record system substantially enhances the liquidity of negotiable instruments.

1. Negotiation and Status as a Holder

Two concepts are central to the rules for transferring negotiable instruments: the "holder" that possesses the instrument and has a right to enforce it (UCC §3-301(i)) and the act of "negotiation" by which it is transferred to a new holder. The UCC's definition of "negotiation" is not enlightening: It defines negotiation as any transfer of possession (even an involuntary transfer) by a person other than the original issuer that causes the transferee to become a holder. UCC §3-201(a). To make any sense out of that definition, you have to consider the UCC's definition of the "holder" in §1-201(20)(revised §1-201(b)(21)).

One aspect of the document-centered focus of the negotiability system is the importance of possession of the physical document. Possession is the sine qua non of holder status: No person can be a holder without possession of the instrument. Thus, if an owner loses possession of an instrument (whether through inadvertence or theft), it loses its status as a holder at the same time. If an instrument is bearer paper (as defined in UCC §3-109), then possession is determinative. Any person in possession of bearer paper is a holder, however tenuous (or nonexistent) that person's claim to ownership of the instrument. UCC §1-201(20). That rule is absolute: A thief that steals a piece of bearer paper becomes the holder of that instrument even though it is not the rightful owner. See UCC §3-203 comment 1 ("A thief who steals a check payable to bearer becomes the holder of the check and a person entitled to enforce it."). Accordingly, a prospective purchaser that examines an instrument and determines that it is bearer paper can purchase the instrument safe in the knowledge that it will be entitled to enforce the instrument as soon as it obtains possession.

Determining whether someone holds a piece of order paper is only slightly more complicated. As defined in UCC §3-109, order paper always must be payable to some particular, identified person. That identified person is the only person that can be a holder. UCC §1-201(20). Thus, order paper in the possession of that identified person will have a holder (the identified person), but order paper in the possession of any other person will not have a holder. To put it another way, order paper has a holder only when the person in possession and the identified person "match up."

A variety of complications can arise in determining the precise party that is the identified person for a particular instrument. For example, checks frequently are payable to more than one person (such as a husband and wife). Article 3 relies on the precise words used on the instrument to decide whether one or both of the two is the holder. If the instrument is payable to "Husband or Wife," then it is treated as payable to them "alternatively," so that either of them that had possession would be a holder. UCC §3-110(d) & comment 4. The opposite rule applies if an instrument is payable to "Husband and Wife." In that case, the instrument is payable to them "not alternatively," so that "[n]either person, acting alone, can be the holder of the instrument." UCC §3-310(d) & comment 4.

Another common problem arises when the instrument is made payable to an account identified by number. That would happen if, for example, a person indorsed a check by writing an account number on the back and signing the check. In that case, the UCC treats the owner of the account as the identified person. UCC §3-110(c)(1). As you should recall from Assignment 31's discussion of wire-transfer errors, a likely problem in that area would be for the indorsement to identify an account both by name and by number, but for the account to be owned by somebody other than the named individual. In that case, Article 3 recognizes the named individual as the identified person, even if the named individual does not own the identified account. UCC §3-110(c)(1).

2. Special and Blank Indorsements

The requirement that a holder of order paper be the identified person to whom that paper is payable means that a transfer of possession standing alone is not sufficient to make the purchaser a holder of order paper. If the seller is the identified person, then a transfer of possession with nothing more destroys the seller's holder status (because the seller no longer has possession) without giving the purchaser holder status (because the seller is still the "identified person").

To make the purchaser the identified person (and thus the holder), the seller must indorse the instrument. An indorsement can be as simple as a signature on an instrument. Indeed, the UCC presumes that any signature that appears on an instrument is an indorsement unless the circumstances "unambiguously indicate that the signature was made for a purpose other than indorsement." UCC §3-204(a). The most common contrary indication is the location of a signature in the lower right-hand corner of the face of an instrument. (Think of the place where you sign a check.) Courts recognize a signature in that location as the signature of an issuer (the maker of a note or the drawer of a draft), even without any specific written indication of purpose. UCC §3-204 comment 1 paragraph 2 sentence 14. Absent some specific written indication of contrary intent, a signature in any other place (even on the front) ordinarily will be treated as an indorsement.

A holder transferring an instrument can use two different types of indorsements to make the purchaser the holder of the instrument. The first is a special indorsement, which identifies a person to whom the instrument is to be paid. If Carl Eben had a check that he wished to transfer to Jodi Kay, he could indorse it by writing: "Pay to Jodi Kay, /s/ Carl Eben." If Carl held the instrument as the identified person at the time he made that indorsement, the indorsement would make Jodi the identified person. UCC §3-205(a). Thus, the instrument would remain order paper, but now the identified person would have changed to Jodi, so that a transfer of possession to Jodi would make Jodi the holder. If Carl held the instrument as bearer paper, the special indorsement would change the instrument to order paper, again with Jodi as the identified person, and thus the holder. UCC §§3-109(c), 3-205(a).

The second main type of indorsement is a blank indorsement. A blank indorsement is any indorsement made by a holder that does not indicate an identified person. For example, if Carl Eben had signed his name to the instrument, without more, he would have made a blank indorsement. A blank indorsement transforms order paper to bearer paper, so that any person in possession is a holder. UCC §§3-109(c), 3-205(b). Hence, if Carl made a blank indorsement and gave the instrument to Jodi, Jodi would be the holder solely because of her possession of the instrument. A blank indorsement on bearer paper has no effect on the character of the instrument, although (as discussed in Assignment 39 and later in this assignment) it does create liability for the indorser under UCC §3-415.

To accommodate the automated procedures used for processing the large volume of checks transferred to banks, the system includes a variety of special rules for checks that depart from the rules outlined above. First, Article 4 generally dispenses with the requirement of indorsements for transfers of checks in the check-collection system. Thus, a depositary bank automatically becomes a holder of a check deposited by its customer, even if the check was order paper and the customer failed to indorse it to the bank at the time of deposit. UCC §4-205(1). Similarly, a bank need not indorse the check when it transfers it to any other bank. Instead, "[a]ny agreed method that identifies the transferor bank is sufficient." UCC §4-206. See also 12 C.F.R. 229.35(a) (setting federal standards for indorsement under Regulation CC).

Similarly, to limit the potential for fraudulent enforcement of checks stolen during the course of collection, Regulation CC provides that no party other than a bank can become the holder of a check once it has been indorsed by a bank. Thus, even if a bank indorsed a check in blank (so that it was bearer paper), an employee that stole the check from a check-sorting machine could not become the holder of the check. The only way that a party other than a bank can become a holder of such a check is for the bank to specially indorse the check to a nonbank party or for the bank to return the check to the person that deposited it (presumably because the check was dishonored). Regulation CC, 12 C.F.R. §229.35(c); see also UCC §4-201(b) (articulating a similar rule that applies when a check is indorsed "pay any bank").

3. Restrictive and Anomalous Indorsements

Article 3 also discusses two other kinds of indorsements. The first is a restrictive indorsement, an indorsement that purports to limit the indorsee's ability to deal with the instrument: "Pay to Jodi Kay, but only if Cal Ripken plays every game in 1998. /s/ Carl Eben." Article 3 invalidates most types of restrictive indorsements. UCC §3-206(a), (b). It does, however, respect the common restrictive indorsements of an instrument "for deposit only" or "for collection." If an instrument bears one of those indorsements, a party that pays or purchases the instrument commits conversion unless the proceeds of the instrument are received by the indorser or applied consistently with the indorsement. UCC §3-206(c). Thus, a bank can give a payee cash for a check, even if the payee mistakenly indorsed the check "for deposit only," but the bank would commit conversion if it deposited the funds in somebody else's account or cashed the check for a third party.

The last type of indorsement discussed in Article 3 is an anomalous indorsement. An indorsement is anomalous when it is made by a person that was not a holder at the time it made the indorsement. UCC §3-205(d). For example, if Kay Eben signed the back of a check payable to Carl Eben and Carl then negotiated the instrument to Jodi Kay, the signature by Kay Eben would be an anomalous indorsement. An indorsement by a party that is not a holder plays no role in negotiation of the instrument because only a holder can make a blank indorsement or a special indorsement. For example, if Kay Eben signed the back of the check "Pay to Jodi Kay," the instrument would remain order paper payable to Carl. Because anomalous indorsements play no role in negotiation, Article 3 gives them another purpose. It presumes that they were made for "accommodation," so that the anomalous indorser becomes a guarantor of the instrument. UCC §3-419. In Article 3 terminology, the anomalous indorser becomes an "accommodation" party. The rules governing that status are similar to the standard guaranty rules discussed in Chapter 10. See UCC §§3-419, 3-605.

B. Enforcement and Collection of Instruments

1. The Right to Enforce an Instrument

The principal legal attribute of status as a holder is the right to enforce the instrument. Thus, any person that holds an instrument is a "[p]erson entitled to enforce the instrument" under UCC §3-301(i). What that means is that the holder has the legal right to call for payment from any party obligated to pay the instrument. Because a party can become a holder without actually owning the instrument (consider a thief in possession of bearer paper), the holder's absolute right to enforce the instrument means that Article 3 permits a party to enforce an instrument even if the party has no lawful right to payment. The system accepts that occasional injustice because of the benefits that the absolute rule brings in streamlining the process for determining whether a party has a right to enforce the instrument. A lawsuit to enforce a negotiable instrument requires proof of only the simple facts necessary to establish holder status; the holder need not establish the facts necessary to prove the underlying right to payment.

To be sure, it is not necessary to be a holder to become a person entitled to enforce an instrument. For example, one party that is a holder can transfer its rights to enforce an instrument to another party by selling the instrument to the second party. Under ordinary property rules, the transferee acquires whatever rights in the instrument the transferor had before the sale, whether or not the parties complied with the special Article 3 rules for making the transferee a holder. UCC §3-203(b). Thus, if Carl Eben sold a check to Jodi Kay without indorsing it, Jodi Kay would not become a holder herself, but she would obtain Carl's rights to enforce the instrument and thus would become a person entitled to enforce the instrument. UCC §3-301(ii). Moreover, because that circumstance generally would arise only because of the seller's inadvertent failure to indorse the instrument at the time of the sale, UCC §3-203(c) grants the purchaser a right to force the seller to indorse the instrument at any time after the sale. That indorsement, in turn, would make the purchaser a holder as of the time of the indorsement.

2. Presentment and Dishonor

Article 3 codifies a formalistic two-step process for the collection of instruments established under common-law divisions that predate the UCC. The first step, presentment, is taken by the holder. Presentment is nothing more than a demand for payment made by a person entitled to enforce an instrument. UCC §3-501(a). If the instrument is a note, the demand ordinarily is made to the maker of the note. If the instrument is a draft, the demand ordinarily is made to the drawee. UCC §3-501(a). The demand is called "presentment" because the party to whom the demand is made is entitled to insist that the holder exhibit the instrument—"present" it, in the language of bills and notes. UCC §3-501(b)(2).

The second step in the collection process is the response of the party to whom presentment is made. It has a choice of honoring the instrument or dishonoring it. In most cases, the system assumes that a party intends to dishonor an instrument if it does not take an affirmative action to honor it. Thus, if the instrument is payable at the time of presentment, in most cases it is dishonored if it is not paid on the date of presentment. UCC §3-502(a)(1), (b)(2). If it is a check, however, the opposite rule applies: The drawee is assumed to honor the check unless it acts promptly to dishonor it. UCC §3-502(b)(1). Although dishonor usually has no immediate consequences as between the holder and the dishonoring party (because dishonor does not alter the dishonoring party's liability on the instrument), you will see later in the assignment that dishonor has a number of important consequences for the liability of indorsers of the instrument and the enforceability of the obligation for which the instrument was given.

3. Defenses to Enforcement

Although Article 3 includes detailed rules regarding the steps that a party must take to become a person entitled to enforce an instrument, it is completely agnostic about that person's success in enforcing that instrument. As long as the person entitled to enforce the instrument is not a holder in due course (a status discussed in Assignment 41), Article 3 allows the obligor to interpose a wide variety of defenses, which includes not only any defense created by Article 3, but also any claim that the obligor has against the payee with respect to the original transaction. UCC §§3-305(a)(2), (3). The following case illustrates what probably is the most common defense interposed by parties seeking to withhold payment of an instrument: failure of the payee to provide the goods and services for which the instrument was given.

Turman v. Ward's Home Improvement, Inc.

26 U.C.C. Rep. Serv. 2d 175 (Va. Cir. Ct. 1995)

HALEY, J.

I.

The question here for resolution is whether an assignee of the payee of a negotiable instrument is a holder in due course, and as such immune to the defenses that the makers might raise against the payee of the negotiable instrument.

II.

The pertinent facts can be concisely stated.

G. Michael Turman and Carolyn May Cash Turman (hereafter "Turman") executed a deed of trust note dated February 23, 1993 for $107,500.00 payable to Ward's Home Improvement, Inc. (hereafter "Ward"). The note was consideration for a contract by which Ward was to construct a home on property [owned] by Turman. . . . On that same date, Ward executed a separate written assignment of that note to Robert L. Pomerantz (herafter "Pomerantz"). This document specifically uses the word "assigns." Ward did not endorse the note to Pomerantz or otherwise write upon the note. Ward apparently received $95,000.00 for the assignment from Pomerantz. Ward failed to complete the house and to do so will require the expenditure of an additional $42,000.00. Pomerantz maintains that he is a holder in due course of the $107,500.00 note and has demanded payment. . . .

IV.

[UCC §3-201(b)] states that ". . . if an instrument is payable to an identified person, negotiation requires its indorsement by the holder." An assignment is not an endorsement. Accordingly, such a transfer is not a negotiation. And the transferee is not a holder. Official Comment 2 to Code §[3-]203(b).

An assignment does, however, vest ". . . in the transferee any right of the transferor to enforce the instrument . . . (under Code §[3]-301)." Code §[3]-203(b). The transferee's rights are derivative of the transferor's. Accordingly, and pursuant to Code §[3]-305(a)(2), a maker may assert a defense ". . . that would be available if the person entitled to enforce the instrument were enforcing a right to payment under a simple contract." In short, the assignee of a negotiable instrument is subject to defenses the maker can raise against the original payee/assignor. And such a defense is failure of consideration. See Code §[3]-303(b) ". . . If an instrument is issued for a promise of performance, the issuer has a defense to the extent performance of the promise is due and the promise has not been performed."

In light of the foregoing . . . the court holds Pomerantz is not a holder in due course and is subject to the defenses to payment of the $107,500.00 note that Turman could raise against Ward.

C.   Liability on an Instrument

A key part of a system for the enforcement of instruments is a set of rules deciding which parties are liable on any particular instrument. Part 4 of Article 3 sets out a series of rules on that point, which are relatively straightforward. First, UCC §3-401 articulates a general rule of exclusion. Except for the transfer and presentment warranty liability discussed in Chapter 5, no party is liable on an instrument unless it has signed the instrument. Two major difficulties arise in applying that rule. The first occurs when a party has applied some authenticating mark to a document that does not include a formal written signature. On that point, Article 3 follows general UCC principles by applying a broad definition of signature that includes "any name, including a trade or assumed name," as well as "a word, mark, or symbol executed or adopted by a person with present intention to authenticate a writing." UCC §3-401(b); see UCC §1-201(39)(revised §1-201(b)(37)) (similar definition of "signed").

The more challenging issues arise in cases where an individual signing an instrument arguably is acting as an agent or representative of another individual. For example, Carl Eben might sign a note for Riverfront Tools, Inc. Two sets of issues arise: whether the signing individual (Carl) is liable and whether the nonsigning individual or entity (Riverfront Tools, Inc.) is liable. UCC §3-402 includes a series of rules to resolve those questions. In reading these rules, you should note that the UCC describes the signing party (Carl) as the "representative" and the nonsigning party (Riverfront Tools, Inc.) as the "represented person."

To decide whether the represented person is liable, Article 3 defers to customary principles of agency law: The UCC itself does not undertake to define these principles; it simply states that when "a representative signs an instrument . . ., the represented person is bound by the signature to the same extent the represented person would be bound if the signature were on a simple contract." UCC §3-402(a). To see how that would work, assume that Carl signed an instrument as "Carl Eben, President, Riverfront Tools, Inc." and that Carl had sufficient authority under ordinary principles of agency law to bind Riverfront Tools, Inc., to the contract. In that event, Riverfront Tools, Inc., would be just as liable on the instrument as an ordinary individual that had signed the instrument directly.

To decide whether the representative that signs is liable, Article 3 looks to the form of the signature. Generally, Carl is not liable if (a) the signature shows unambiguously that he is signing on behalf of the represented person *and* (b) the instrument identifies the represented person. Thus, Carl would not be liable on the signature set out in the preceding paragraph. UCC §3-402(b)(1). Conversely, if the signature fails either one of those tests, then Carl will be personally liable on the instrument unless he can prove that the original parties did not intend for him to be bound. UCC §3-402(b)(2).

To determine the liability of the parties that have signed the instrument, Article 3 includes a series of four separate rules to cover each of the capacities in which a party can sign an instrument. The first type of liability is absolute. The party that issues a note is directly and unconditionally liable on the instrument. UCC §3-412. That rule makes sense because the party issuing a note has agreed by issuing the note to accept liability; that is the purpose of the note.

The other three types of liability all depend on some occurrence after the issuance of the draft. The first of those three deals with the liability of the drawee of a draft. As you should recall from your study of the checking system, a drawee of a draft has no liability on a draft at the time it is issued. UCC §3-408. If it accepts the draft (which requires nothing but a signature, UCC §3-409(a)), however, the drawee at that point becomes directly liable on the draft. UCC §3-413(a).

The last two types of liability are conditioned on dishonor. Thus, except for drafts on which the drawer and the drawee are the same person (cashier's checks and the like), the drawer of a draft is not liable on the draft unless it is dishonored. UCC §3-414(b). Moreover, the drawer's liability is discharged if a bank accepts the draft (because the holder of the draft then can look to the bank for payment). UCC §3-414(c). The rules for indorser liability are quite similar. First, the indorser is liable only if the instrument is dishonored. UCC §3-415(a). Second, the indorser's liability is discharged if a bank accepts the instrument after it has been indorsed. UCC §3-415(d). Finally, an indorser (or a drawer of any type of draft other than a check) can limit its liability by indicating that it is signing the instrument "without recourse." UCC §§3-414(e), 3-415(b).

Figure 40.1 summarizes those provisions.

Figure 40.1
Liability on an Instrument

PARTY	NATURE OF LIABILITY	STATUTORY REFERENCES
Issuer	Absolute	UCC §3-412
Drawee	Conditioned on acceptance	UCC §§3-408, 3-413(a)
Drawer	Conditioned on dishonor, discharged upon bank acceptance	UCC §3-414
Indorser	Conditioned on dishonor, discharged upon bank acceptance	UCC §3-415

D. The Effect of the Instrument on the Underlying Obligation

The last topic related to liability on an instrument is the relation between the liability parties have on an instrument and the underlying obligation for which the instrument is given. Outside the loan context, payment obligations ordinarily are given in satisfaction of some underlying obligation. For example, if a tenant writes a check for rent, the tenant offers the check to satisfy the tenant's obligation to pay rent under its lease. As discussed above, the issuer of a negotiable instrument incurs liability on the instrument without regard to the terms of the underlying transaction. Accordingly, when a party issues a negotiable instrument, it incurs liability that is completely separate from its liability on any underlying obligation. If that liability is conditional, it is conditional only as indicated by the Article 3 rules discussed above.

The first problem in this area is the effect of the instrument on the ability of the payee to enforce the underlying obligation. If the issuer or drawer issues an instrument offering full payment of an obligation, it seems somehow unfair to allow the payee to continue to enforce the underlying obligation: It would be nonsensical to allow a landlord to sue for rent the day after the landlord accepts a check for the rent. On the other hand, it is not clear that issuance of the instrument should discharge the underlying obligation. If the check bounces, shouldn't the landlord then be able to sue for the rent?

UCC §3-310 sets out the rules governing the relation between liability on the instrument and liability on the underlying obligation. Those rules divide instruments into two classes: near-cash instruments (governed by UCC §3-310(a), (c)) and ordinary instruments (governed by UCC §3-310(b)).

The near-cash instruments governed by UCC §3-310(a) are certified checks, cashier's checks, and teller's checks. Each of those instruments is an instrument on which a bank has incurred liability. Cashier's checks and teller's checks are checks on which a bank is the drawer, so the bank has liability under UCC §3-412 (for cashier's checks) and UCC §3-414(b) (for teller's checks). A certified check is a check that a bank otherwise has agreed to pay. UCC §3-409(d). UCC §3-310(c)(i) provides that the near-cash rules set out in UCC §3-310(a) also apply to any other instrument on which a bank is liable as maker or acceptor.

Because of the bank's obligation to pay, most parties that accept such an instrument view themselves as having received final payment; the principal risk of nonpayment is the risk that the bank will become insolvent. Reflecting that perception, UCC §3-310(a) and (c) provides (absent a contrary agreement) that the underlying obligation is discharged when the obligee takes one of those near-cash instruments. That rule imposes no substantial burden on the obligee because the obligee that doubts the solvency of the relevant bank could protect itself by refusing to accept the instrument or agreeing with the payor that the underlying obligation will remain in effect. Absent such an action, though, it makes good sense to treat the underlying obligation as discharged when the obligee accepts the instrument.

UCC §3-310(b) sets out the rules for ordinary instruments such as notes and uncertified checks. Because a bank has not agreed to pay those instruments, the likelihood of nonpayment is considerably higher. Accordingly, UCC §3-310(b), unlike UCC §3-310(a), does not immediately discharge the underlying obligation. Instead, when an obligee takes an ordinary instrument, the underlying obligation is suspended. UCC §§3-310(b)(1), (2). That suspension continues until the instrument is dishonored or paid. If the instrument is paid, the underlying obligation is discharged. UCC §3-310(b)(1),(2). If the instrument is dishonored, the suspension terminates, and the obligee has the option to enforce either the instrument or the underlying obligation. UCC §3-310(b)(3). Thus, if a tenant's rent check bounces, the landlord can sue the tenant either on the check (for which the tenant would be liable as a drawer under UCC §3-414(b)) or on the underlying rent obligation (taking advantage of any remedies available under the lease).

A discharge of the underlying obligation under UCC §3-310 is effective only to the extent of the amount of the instrument. UCC §3-310(a),(b). In some cases, however, a party will try to use an instrument to pay an obligation for which the parties dispute the amount. For example, if Lydgate and Bulstrode disagree regarding the amount that Lydgate owes on a promissory note, Lydgate might write a check for half of the disputed amount, mark the check "PAID IN FULL," and tender the check to Bulstrode, hoping that Bulstrode's acceptance of the check will satisfy the entire amount of the disputed obligation. UCC §3-311 generally supports that use of instruments to resolve disputes. Specifically, such a "paid in full" check will discharge Lydgate's entire obligation (even if the obligation is for more than the instrument) if (a) the instrument is tendered as full satisfaction of a disputed claim, (b) the payor conspicuously notifies the payee that it intends the instrument to constitute full satisfaction of the claim, and (c) the payee successfully obtains payment of the instrument. UCC §3-311(a), (b). To get a richer sense for how that process would work, consider the following case.

McMahon Food Corp. v. Burger Dairy Co.

103 F.3d 1307 (7th Cir. 1996)

Before CUDAHY, COFFEY, and FLAUM, Circuit Judges.

COFFEY, Circuit Judge.

Burger Dairy Company ("Burger") and McMahon Food Corporation ("MFC") were involved in a contract dispute over milk products that Burger sold to MFC, as well as credits for empty milk cases that MFC returned. MFC brought a declaratory judgment action against Burger, asserting that it effected an accord and satisfaction of its debt by tendering two checks with attached vouchers, one marked "payment in full through 6/6/92," the other marked, "paid in full thru 8/8/92," to Burger. Burger countersued, seeking $58,518.41 from MFC. The trial court denied MFC relief, ruling that the accord which the first check purported to satisfy was obtained by deceit, while the second check was a unilateral action by MFC, on which the parties reached no accord. . . . [W]e affirm.

I.   BACKGROUND

Burger Dairy Company, an Indiana vendor of dairy products, regularly sold milk products to McMahon Food Corporation, a Chicago distributor of dairy products, from October, 1991, until August 15, 1992. [Burger charged MFC a deposit of $1.00/case for each milk case in which it delivered milk to MFC.]

In addition to buying dairy products, MFC had a side-business selling used plastic milk cases to Burger. . . . Burger agreed that when MFC returned a truckload of cases to its plant, it could add some of its "stockpiled" cases to the shipment, and Burger would credit MFC $1.00/case. . . .

[Discrepancies in credits for milk cases delivered to MFC and returned to Burger] became a major source of friction between the two companies throughout the period of their business relationship. Burger's records indicated that by mid-February of 1992, MFC was in arrears $58,518.41 ("the February debt"). About half of this total was for unauthorized credits for returned milk-cases.

Bylsma, on behalf of Burger, met with Frank McMahon on February 27, 1992, to discuss MFC's account with Burger, including the February debt. The parties dispute the results of that meeting. Both parties agree that they examined the invoices in question, and ultimately agreed that Burger would no longer charge MFC a deposit for milk cases — according to Bylsma, in exchange for MFC's agreement to pay the invoices as they became due. Bylsma testified that he and McMahon did not otherwise resolve the amounts past due, nor did they agree upon the amount of credit due for the empty milk cases allegedly returned.

Bylsma further claimed that he never agreed to excuse MFC from making payment in full for the past due accounts. Instead, he claims he made clear during their conversation, when he and McMahon were unable to reach an agreement, that they would simply table further discussion of the February debt at that time. Upon returning to Burger's plant and checking the records, Bylsma satisfied himself that the company had been giving MFC proper credit for the cases returned. . . .

After the February meeting, MFC made full payments for three weeks of current purchases (nothing was done to pay off the February debt), but then made no further payments until May 13, 1992, when it remitted a $100,000 check to Burger with an accompanying voucher stating "on account detail to follow." Burger's records, however, reflected that the $100,000 covered less than half the debt that MFC had amassed by that time, including the $58,518.41 February debt which was the subject of McMahon's meeting with Bylsma.

II.   THE JUNE 17TH CHECK

A.   BACKGROUND

Larry Carter, who replaced Bylsma as Burger's general sales manager about the first of May, 1992, met with McMahon on June 17, 1992, to review MFC's account. McMahon asserts that at the beginning of the meeting he told Carter that if they could agree on the amount that MFC owed, he would pay it on the spot. According to Carter's notes, made contemporaneously during the June 17th meeting, McMahon assured Carter that he had settled the February debt with Bylsma. Carter's notes included both a reminder to himself to call Bylsma to confirm McMahon's assertion, and a statement that McMahon "want[ed] a new statement of account reflecting these events." Accordingly, Carter and McMahon went through only the invoices dated February 15 through June 6, 1992. They determined that MFC still owed a balance of $51,812.98. McMahon promptly made out a check to Burger for that amount. He attached a voucher to the check on which was typed, "payment in full thru 6/6/92 . . . $51,812.98." Below the typed language McMahon added a handwritten note stating, "Clear statement of account thru 6/6/92 to follow," followed by his signature. . . . McMahon also asked Carter to sign the voucher as a condition of receiving the check, which Carter did without protest. At the end of his notes, Carter wrote, "current to 6-6-92."

After returning to Burger, Carter contacted Bylsma, who told Carter that he had never reached an agreement with McMahon about the February debt. Thereafter, sometime before the end of June, Carter called McMahon and told him that it was Burger's position that the February debt had not been settled. When McMahon replied that he refused to pay the February debt, and continued to insist that he had settled it with Bylsma, Carter held McMahon's June 17th check throughout the summer of 1992.

On September 24, Edward J. Geoghan, Burger's accounting manager and comptroller of Burger's parent company, negotiated the June 17th check. Before doing so, and without consulting with Carter, Geoghan crossed out MFC's restrictive endorsement "payment in full" and "full statement of account to follow" from the voucher, and added the notation "without prejudice," followed by his own signature. Geoghan later testified that he struck out the language on the voucher because he knew it was insufficient to make MFC's account current. The next day, Geoghan wrote to McMahon, informing him that the check had been cashed, the restrictive endorsement stricken, and that MFC still owed Burger over $64,000. . . .

B. ANALYSIS

1. Uniform Commercial Code §3-311

Initially, MFC argues that Burger's negotiation of the check which McMahon tendered to Carter at their June 17th meeting constituted an accord and satisfaction. An accord and satisfaction is a contractual method of discharging a debt: the "accord" is the agreement between the parties, while the "satisfaction" is the execution of the agreement. The parties accept that Illinois law, including Illinois' enactment of the Uniform Commercial Code, governs the case at bar.

Shortly before this dispute arose, Illinois adopted a revised version of Article Three of the Uniform Commercial Code, including a new section [§3-311] specifically addressing the creation of an accord and satisfaction by use of a negotiable instrument. . . . The purpose of §3-311 is to encourage "informal dispute resolution by full satisfaction checks." U.C.C. §3-311, comment 3. Its drafters intended to codify the common law of accord and satisfaction "with some minor variations to reflect modern business conditions." Id.

In the case at bar, Burger does not dispute that the voucher attached to MFC's June 17th check contained a conspicuous notation that it was tendered as full satisfaction of MFC's entire debt, thus satisfying the prerequisites of §3-311(b) for discharging the claim. Neither did Burger follow the procedures which §3-311(c) establishes to keep a claim from being discharged: it neither instructed MFC to send any full satisfaction checks to a specific person or office, nor sought to repay MFC after it deposited the check. Furthermore, Geoghan's attempt to cash MFC's check without jeopardizing Burger's claim against MFC was improper under the U.C.C. Assuming there was an accord, Geoghan's bid to prevent a satisfaction by accepting the check but scratching out the restrictive endorsement and adding the words "without prejudice" before he cashed the check was to no avail, for under the revised version of the U.C.C., words of protest cannot change the legal effect of an accord and satisfaction. [UCC §1-207(2) (revised §1-308)]. Accordingly, MFC argues, because the voucher clearly stated that the instrument was a full satisfaction check, and because Geoghan clearly understood that the check was tendered in full satisfaction of MFC's claim before he deposited it, Burger's acceptance and negotiation of the check completed the accord and satisfaction.

We disagree. Initially, under the plain language of the statute, in order to establish an accord and satisfaction, MFC bore the burden of establishing that it met the criteria of §3-311(a) before the other subsections establishing the discharge of a claim come into play. To meet the criteria of §3-311(a) . . . under Illinois law, "a party must ordinarily prove that he or she acted in good faith *in tendering* an instrument as full satisfaction of a claim[.]" [Fremarek v. John Hancock Mutual Life Ins. Co., 651 N.E.2d 601, 605 (Ill. App. 1995)]. Thus, Illinois courts interpreting §3-311 follow the common law of accord and satisfaction in holding that "there must be an honest dispute between the parties as to the amount due *at the time payment was tendered.*" A.F.P. Enterprises, Inc. v. Crescent Pork, Inc., 611 N.E.2d 619, 623 (Ill. App. 1993) (emphasis added). Consequently, under Illinois law, there can be no accord and satisfaction unless there was an "honest dispute" between MFC and Burger at the time McMahon tendered the $51,812.98 check to Carter on June 17th. No such "honest dispute" existed.

The trial court found that McMahon deliberately misled Carter, who had but recently been appointed to his position of general manager and did not know the specifics of his predecessor's dealings with MFC. McMahon did so, according to the court, by assuring Carter from the outset of their June 17th meeting that he had settled with Bylsma, the former general manager, all accounts prior to mid-February, 1992. The court found that McMahon was acting dishonestly and taking advantage of Carter at the time he tendered payment, and therefore MFC failed to meet the good faith requirement of §3-311(a). A trial court's conclusion that a party failed to act in good faith is a finding of fact which we reverse only for clear error. We find no such error in the case before us. . . .

[The court's discussion of the second check is omitted.]

AFFIRMED.

Problem Set 40

40.1.   This morning you meet with a new client named Tom Mae. Tom has operated billiard halls on the west side of town for several years and recently started to operate a check-cashing business, with counters in each of his billiard halls. The check-cashing business operates as Tom's Kash Outlet (TKO). The business has been successful; Tom is cashing about 150 checks a day. A long-time regular at one of the locations suggested to Tom that he see a lawyer to make sure that Tom was handling his checks properly.

Tom tells you that his normal practice requires the customers to sign the top end of the reverse of the check. Like most check-cashing services, Tom's business has a policy against cashing checks for parties other than the named payee. Accordingly, his clerks always check to make sure that the name with which the customer signs matches the name of the payee on the front of the check. The clerks then examine a driver's license to ensure that the signer is in fact the payee. Finally, his clerks stamp the top end of the reverse of each check, just below the signature by the customer. The clerks use a rubber stamp that reads "Tom's Kash Outlet." The result is something like Figure 40.2.

Figure 40.2
Reverse of Sample TKO Check

S/ PAUL PAYEE

TOM'S KASH OUTLET

a. Tom first wants to know if his procedures expose him to any undue risks. What do you think? UCC §§1-201(20)(revised §1-201(b)(21)), 1-201(39)(revised §1-201(b)(37)), §3-109(c), 3-204(a), 3-205(b) & (c), 3-206(c), 3-401(b), 3-401 comment 2, 3-402(a).

b. Tom also wants to know what additional risks he would face if he began accepting third-party checks. He says that customers frequently try to cash checks that have been indorsed to them by the named payee. If the check appears to have been specially indorsed by the named payee and is submitted for cashing by the person to whom the named payee indorsed the check, what risk does Tom face in cashing the check? UCC §§1-201 (20)(revised §1-201(b)(21)), 3-415(a), 3-416(a)(1), 3-417(a)(1), 3-420(a).

c. What advantages would TKO gain if it altered the stamp with a line above its name that said either "Pay to TKO" or "For Deposit Only"?

40.2. While Tom is in your office, you get a call from Doug Kahan, who wants to follow up on your analysis of Problem 39.5 (the problem where Doug could not get a taxpayer's bank to honor a check written on the back of the taxpayer's shirt). What Doug wants to know is this: If the IRS can't make the bank pay the check, can the IRS at least sue the taxpayer on the shirt-check? UCC §§1-201(20)(revised §1-201(b)(21)), 3-301(i), 3-310(b)(1) & (3), 3-414(b).

40.3. While having lunch with your friend Bill Robertson (a grocery-store operator and real-estate developer that you've represented on a variety of matters), Bill's assistant Jan Brown asks you about a problem she has. She has a particularly difficult tenant that has been complaining constantly about problems with the space it leases from Bill. Finally, Jan received from the tenant this morning a check for exactly half of what she believes the tenant owes, including a notation on the check that it constitutes "Full Payment for All Past-Due Rent." In the past, Jan has had a practice of drawing a line through such a notation and depositing the check. Her view is that the tenant cannot unilaterally decide that the check constitutes full payment and that drawing a line through the full-payment notation is adequate evidence of her rejection of the tenant's position. Jan wants to know what you think of her practice. What do you say? UCC §3-311.

40.4. Pleased with the thoughtful advice that you provided in Problem 40.1, Tom calls you back a few weeks later to ask whether you would be interested in doing some work for him collecting checks that payor banks dishonor after he cashes them. For the first installment of the project, Tom wants to know whom he could sue on each of the following three checks:

a. The first check was written by Dorothea Drawer and payable to Paul Payee. Tom's employee took the check in accordance with Tom's procedures. Thus, the check bears an indorsement that purports to be the signature of Paul Payee. It turns out, though, that the person that cashed the check actually was Ingrid Interloper. Ingrid had mugged Paul and stolen his wallet, including Paul's driver's license and the check. Ingrid indorsed the check as requested by Tom's clerk. Tom's clerk did not understand that Ingrid in fact was not Paul.

When Dorothea heard of the attack on Paul, she stopped payment on the check. Dorothea's bank dishonored the check, so it eventually was returned to Tom. Can Tom sue Dorothea on the check? Paul? Ingrid? UCC §§1-201(20)(revised §1-201(b)(21)), 3-205(a), 3-301(i), 3-401(a), 3-403(a), 3-414(b), 3-415(a), 3-416(a)(1).

b. The second item is a check that was written by Dorothea as "Pay to the order of bearer." Paul brought the check into one of Tom's facilities. Because Tom's clerk could not figure out whose signature to get, the clerk simply paid Paul cash for the check and took possession of it without obtaining any indorsement at all. The bank dishonored the check and returned it to Tom. Can Tom sue Dorothea? Paul? UCC §§1-201(20)(revised §1-201(b)(21)), 3-109, 3-301(i), 3-401(a), 3-414(b), 3-416(a)(1).

c. The third check was written by Dorothea to Paul. Two signatures appear on the back of the check. The first (at the top) is by Paul and states "Pay to Tom Mae, /s/ Paul Payee." Below that appears a signature by Martin Chuzzlewit. Tom is not sure what happened, but when he tried to deposit the check, it was dishonored, apparently because Dorothea has closed her account and left town. Can Tom sue Paul? Martin? If Tom successfully sues Martin, can Martin recover from anybody else? UCC §§1-201(20)(revised §1-201(b)(21)), 3-205(b), 3-205(d), 3-301(i), 3-414(b), 3-415(a), 3-416(a), 3-419.

40.5.   One Friday morning you get a call from Jodi Kay (your friend and longtime client from CountryBank). She has a question from an irate customer named Ishmael Chambers. Chambers wrote a $3,400 check to purchase a new stereo system from Alan's Stereo Service. When Chambers put the stereo together the next day, the stereo would not work. Chambers called Alan's and asked if Chambers could return the stereo, but could not get an answer on the phone. Chambers then drove by the store and observed prominent "going out of business" signs. Chambers promptly called the bank and asked Jodi to stop payment on the check. Jodi told Chambers that Jodi could not stop payment because she already had paid the check. Chambers asked Jodi if he could come in and look at the check.

When Chambers came in, he looked at the back of the check and saw that there was no indorsement by Alan's, only a stamp by BigTown Bank (which appeared to be Alan's depositary bank). Bragging of his undergraduate business-law class, Chambers told Jodi that Jodi had acted improperly in paying the check. He insisted that BigTown Bank was not the holder of the check because of Alan's failure to indorse the check. Accordingly, he said that Jodi has to give him back the money. Jodi wants to know if Chambers is correct. What do you say? UCC §§1-201(20)(revised §1-201(b)(21)), 4-205(1), 4-401, 4-401 comment 1.

40.6.   Cliff Janeway (your book-dealer client dating back to Assignment 25) calls you with a question about a payment he just received from one of his large customers named Clydell Slater. Janeway's normal arrangement with Slater requires Slater to pay him once a month for all of the books that Slater bought during the preceding month. Slater's recent purchases, however, have been much larger than usual: They totaled $12,000 during the last two weeks. Accordingly, Janeway called Slater last week and asked Slater to forward payment immediately. Today in the mail Janeway received an odd-looking check for $12,000: It appears to be drawn on the Third State Bank of Yakima, but also is signed by that bank in the lower right-hand corner. In the lower left-hand corner, it lists Clydell Slater as "remitter." Cliff thinks he recently heard some negative news about that bank and worries that Slater might be trying to pull something on him. Cliff asks you what he should do. What do you say? UCC §§3-104(g), 3-310, 3-412, 3-414(a).

Assignment 41:   Holders in Due Course

A.   Holder-in-Due-Course Status

The most distinctive feature of negotiable instruments is the concept of the holder in due course, a specially favored type of transferee that is immune from most defenses that the issuer of an instrument could raise against the original payee. As discussed in Assignment 39, holder-in-due-course status implements the idea — dating to common-law decisions that predate the American Revolution — that enhancing the ability of transferees to enforce instruments increases the liquidity of negotiable instruments by making negotiable instruments more attractive investments.

1.   The Requirements for Holder-in-Due-Course Status

To become a holder in due course, the purchaser of an instrument must satisfy two sets of rules. First, it must obtain the instrument through the process of negotiation described in Assignment 40 so that it becomes a holder. A person that acquires an instrument through some other process (such as a simple sale without negotiation) will not become a holder and thus cannot become a holder in due course.

The second set of rules is the special qualifications that must be satisfied to elevate an ordinary holder to the favored status of a holder in due course. Like the definition of instrument in Part 1 of Article 3, the definition of holder in due course in Part 3 of Article 3 is set out in two stages, a general definition (in UCC §3-302(a)), followed by a series of sections with definitions of the terms that appear in the basic definition in UCC §3-302(a). Generally, the holder must satisfy three tests to become a holder in due course: It must take the instrument for value, in good faith, and without notice of certain problems with the instrument.

The "value" requirement appears in UCC §3-302(a)(2)(i) and is defined in UCC §3-303(a). That requirement generally excludes transfers that are made as a gift or for some other insignificant reason. The value requirement is closely related to, but slightly more strict than, the classic concept of consideration: An instrument can be transferred for consideration and still fail the value requirement. The statute distinguishes Article 3's definition of value from the standard definition of "value" in Article 1, which states that value includes "any consideration sufficient to support a simple contract." UCC §1-201(44) (revised §1-204(4)). The Article 1 definition does not apply in Article 3.

Ordinary payment easily qualifies as value, as does the release by the purchaser of a preexisting claim against the seller. UCC §3-303(a)(3). On the other hand, a promise of future performance ordinarily will constitute consideration, but it will not constitute value until performance has occurred. UCC §3-303(a)(1). Thus, if Carl Eben transfers an instrument to Jodi Kay in return for Jodi's offer to provide consulting services to Carl's business, Jodi does not give value until she performs the services.

The "good faith" requirement appears in UCC §3-302(a)(2)(ii). The key point here is that, at least since its revision in 1990, Article 3 has used the modern UCC definition of good faith, which requires not only "honesty in fact," but also "the observance of reasonable commercial standards of fair dealing." See UCC §1-201(20) (revised §1-201(b)(21)); UCC §3-103(a)(4) (1990 version). Thus, a plaintiff challenging a claim of holder-in-due-course status need not establish that the potential holder in due course acquired the instrument dishonestly. It is enough to establish that the actions of the claimed holder in due course failed to conform to reasonable commercial standards of fair dealing.

The most common claims regarding the good-faith requirement have challenged long-term relationships between lenders purchasing negotiable instruments, on the one hand, and their clients (operating businesses that sell the instruments), on the other hand. Essentially, those lenders are funding the operations of their clients by financing the sales that the clients make to retail purchasers. The issuers of those instruments (typically the retail purchasers from the operating businesses) have had considerable success arguing that those lender-client relationships can become so close that the lender acts in bad faith when it tries to use holder-in-due-course status to insulate itself from defenses that would have been valid against its longtime client. E.g., General Investment Corp. v. Angelini, 278 A.2d 193 (N.J. 1971) (denying holder-in-due-course status to a financier of home improvement contracts on a loan purchased from an aluminum siding contractor that provided 10 percent of the financier's business).

In a related line of cases, courts do not rely explicitly on the good-faith provision, but simply say that there is such a "close connection" between the purchaser and the seller of the note that there has been no cognizable sale at all, leaving the purported purchaser subject to all defenses that could have been asserted against the seller. E.g., St. James v. Diversified Commercial Finance Corp., 714 P.2d 179 (Nev. 1986) (denying holder-in-due-course status to a financier that supplied preprinted forms for the customers of its client the originating lender). Collectively, those cases have made it difficult for lenders to rely on holder-in-due-course status for instruments that they acquire from entities with whom they deal regularly.

The last requirement for holder-in-due-course status is the notice requirement, which appears in clauses (iii) through (vi) of UCC §3-302(a)(2). That requirement reflects the notion that a person that purchases an instrument with notice of a problem cannot use holder-in-due-course status to protect itself from that problem. Holder-in-due-course status rests on the paradigm of an anonymous unknowing purchaser that knows nothing about the underlying transaction and thus cannot fairly be charged with problems in that transaction. When that paradigm collapses because the transferee had notice of a problem when it purchased the instrument, holder-in-due-course status collapses as well.

The first salient point about the notice requirement is the distinction that the UCC draws between "notice" and "knowledge." As defined in Article 1, a person has "notice" of a fact not only when it has actual knowledge of the fact, but also when it "has reason to know" of the fact based on "all the facts and circumstances known to [it] at the time." UCC §1-201(25) (revised §1-202(a)). Thus, a plaintiff can defeat holder-in-due-course status without proving that the purported holder in due course actually knew about the problem; it is enough to prove that the purported holder in due course had reason to know about the problem.

The second salient point about the notice requirement is that it is not enough to prove that the holder generally had notice that something was wrong in the abstract with the instrument, the maker, or the payee. Rather, the maker must prove notice of one of the four problems listed in the clauses that close UCC §3-302(a)(2): The instrument is overdue, has been dishonored, or is in default (UCC §3-302(a)(2)(iii)); the instrument has a forgery or an alteration (UCC §§3-302(a)(1), 3-302(a)(2)(iv)); a third party claims to own all or part of the instrument (UCC §3-302(a)(2)(v)); or one of the obligors has a defense or claim that would limit or bar enforcement of the instrument by the original payee (UCC §3-302(a)(2)(vi)). If the notice does not fall within one of those four classes, the notice is relevant only if it is sufficiently damaging to undermine the holder's good faith in acquiring the instrument.

The most intricate interpretive question about those notice requirements is whether an instrument is overdue or has been dishonored. UCC §3-304 explains the circumstances that make an instrument overdue. For demand instruments, an instrument becomes overdue if it is not paid on the day after demand is made; checks automatically become overdue 90 days after their date. Instruments payable at a definite time become overdue upon any failure to make a scheduled payment of principal or upon any other event that results in acceleration of the date of maturity of the instrument. As explained in Assignment 40, dishonor generally occurs under UCC §3-502 when an instrument is presented to a party obligated to pay and that party fails to pay the instrument in accordance with its obligation.

2. Rights of Holders in Due Course

Unlike a simple holder, a holder in due course takes the instrument free of all of the most significant defenses to payment. Most importantly, a holder in due course is immune from most ordinary contract claims or defenses (described by the UCC as claims "in recoupment"). Thus, if Carl Eben gave Jodi Kay an instrument as payment for consulting services that Jodi had agreed to provide Carl, and if Jodi had sold the instrument to Bulstrode Bank, so that Bulstrode became a holder in due course, Bulstrode could force Carl to pay even if Jodi never provided the agreed-on services. UCC §3-305(b). Carl's sole remedy for Jodi's failure to perform would be a suit against Jodi; Carl would have no defense against the bank. Similarly, if a thief that stole a piece of bearer paper from Carl sold the instrument to Bulstrode, Bulstrode as a holder in due course would be immune from any attempt by Carl to recover the note. UCC §3-306. Carl's only remedy would be a suit against the thief.

The only defenses that bind a holder in due course are the four "real" defenses described in UCC §3-305(a)(1). The inclusion of those defenses reflects a pragmatic recognition of strong public policies that in a few unusual circumstances can override the concerns about free transferability that justify holder-in-due-course status. The first is infancy: Even a holder in due course cannot enforce an instrument issued by a minor that has no capacity under state law to bind itself to a simple contract. UCC §§3-305(a)(1)(i), 3-305 comment 1.

The second real defense encompasses duress, lack of legal capacity, and illegality. UCC §3-305(a)(1)(ii). Again, the holder in due course cannot enforce an instrument if the underlying transaction in which the instrument was issued occurred under circumstances that would make the original obligation completely void. Courts traditionally have interpreted that exception narrowly. For example, one notable case upheld holder-in-due-course status with respect to an instrument allegedly induced by bribery, relying on the theory that the crime of bribery only rendered the instrument voidable, not void. Bankers Trust Co. v. Litton Systems, Inc., 599 F.2d 488 (2d Cir. 1979); see UCC §3-305 comment 1 paragraph 4 (stating that laws vitiate holder-in-due-course status only if they render obligations "entirely null and void").

The third real defense is fraud that induced issuance of the instrument "with neither knowledge nor reasonable opportunity to learn of its character or essential terms." UCC §3-305(a)(1)(iii). As with the previous exceptions, courts have interpreted that exception quite narrowly. For example, in one leading case that predates the UCC, a farmer who signed an instrument while working in his field claimed that he should not be bound by the instrument because he did not have his glasses when he signed the instrument and also because he barely could read even with his glasses. In an opinion by future United States Supreme Court Justice David Brewer, the Kansas Supreme Court rejected the farmer's claim that he did not understand that he was signing a promissory note. The court placed the blame squarely on the farmer: "If he has eyes, and can see, he ought to examine; if he can read, he ought to read. . . . If he relies upon the word of a stranger he makes that stranger his agent . . . and . . . cannot disaffirm the acts of that agent." Ort v. Fowler, 2 P. 580, 583 (Kan. 1884).

The final real defense is discharge of the obligor in insolvency proceedings. UCC §3-305(a)(1)(iv). That defense accepts the reality of the supremacy of federal law. Whatever state law might say, a discharge of liability under the federal bankruptcy laws bars enforcement of that same liability under Article 3 (or any other state law).

Because the real defenses are so limited, the ability of a holder to claim holder-in-due-course status significantly limits the ability of a party liable on an instrument to interpose a defense to enforcement of an instrument. The following case is illustrative.

State Street Bank & Trust Co. v. Strawser

908 F. Supp. 249 (M.D. Pa. 1995)

CALDWELL, District Judge. . . .

I. BACKGROUND

On December 19, 1986, the Defendants, Chester L. and Connie M. Strawser, executed an Adjustable Rate Note ("the Note") in favor of Homestead Savings Association ("Homestead"), in consideration of and as security for a loan in the amount of $350,000.00. Pursuant to a Security Agreement executed at the same time, the Note was secured by a mortgage on four parcels of real property, and by farming and industrial equipment. The Note is payable in monthly installments with the balance, if any, due January 1, 1997. On March 22, 1993, the Note and Mortgage were assigned to Plaintiff, State Street Bank & Trust Company ("State Street"). . . .

. . . In paragraph 7(C), the Note provides that "[i]f I am in default, the Note Holder may send me a written notice telling me that if I do not pay the overdue amount by a certain date, the Note Holder may require me to pay immediately the full amount of principal which has not been paid and all the interest that I owe on that amount."

On October 17, 1994, State Street sent a Notice of Default to Defendants, indicating that if Defendants did not pay the past due principal and interest within thirty days, State Street would exercise the acceleration clause in paragraph 7(C), causing the entire balance and per diem interest to become due immediately. State Street asserts that it received no response from Defendants as a result of this demand.

On January 23, 1995, State Street instituted this action for breach of contract, alleging that the Strawsers have not made monthly payments since April 1, 1993, and are thus in default under . . . the Note. State Street seeks the balance due on the Note, per diem interest, late charges, and attorneys' fees pursuant to paragraph 7(E) of the Note. In their answer, Defendants deny that they are in default and assert an affirmative defense that State Street's claim is barred by the doctrine of illegality because the Note and Mortgage were obtained in violation of 7 P.S. §311(e). . . .

II. LAW AND DISCUSSION . . .

B. BREACH OF CONTRACT

Because our jurisdiction is premised on diversity of citizenship, we apply the substantive law of Pennsylvania. In this case, we look to the Pennsylvania Commercial Code ("the Code"), which provides that the holder of an instrument has a right to enforce that instrument, subject to certain enumerated exceptions. 13 Pa. C.S.A. §§3104, 3301, 3305. Here, the Note is an instrument, as that term is defined in the Code, State Street is a holder of the Note, and, as such, has a right to enforce the Note subject to the limitations of section 3305 of the Code. 13 Pa. C.S.A. §3301.

Additionally, State Street asserts that it is a "holder in due course," and is therefore entitled to enforce the Note free from all defenses that the Strawsers may assert. 13 Pa. C.S.A. §3302. . . .

The Defendants contend that Plaintiff is not a holder in due course because it had notice of a potential defense under section 3305(a). . . . The potential defense raised by the Strawsers is the alleged violation of 7 P.S. §311(e) by Homestead and its president, Gary Holman.[4] Plaintiff had notice of this potential violation, Defendants argue, as a result of a letter from Defendants' former counsel to Homestead. However, even assuming that section 311(e) was violated and is a defense under section 3305 of the Code, Plaintiff is a holder in due course and therefore entitled to enforce the Note.[5]

Admittedly, if State Street had notice of a potential defense, it could not assert the rights of a holder in due course. 13 Pa. C.S.A. §3302(a)(2)(vi). However, there is no evidence in the record to indicate that State Street had notice of the letter relied on by the Defendants when the assignment occurred on March 22, 1993. The Code provides that

> A person has "notice" of a fact when: (1) he has actual knowledge of it; (2) he has received a notice or notification of it; or (3) from all the facts and circumstances known to him at the time in question he has reason to know that it exists.

13 Pa. C.S.A. §1201[(25)].

Here, the letter is addressed to Homestead. Defendants submitted no evidence that could establish that Plaintiff had actual knowledge of the letter, or that it received timely notification of the contents. Further, there is nothing in the record to support a finding that State Street had reason to know of a potential violation of 7 P.S. §311(e), particularly since the Letter of Commitment, Note, Security Agreement, and Appraisals indicate that the appraised value of the collateral exceeded

---

4. Defendants' brief is, at best, fragmented. Thus, while we assume that this is the basis of their argument, Defendants could be advancing two other defenses that limit a holder in due course's right to enforcement. However, neither of those defenses is applicable.

In using the term "illegality" to describe the execution of the Note and Mortgage, Defendants may be attempting to assert a defense under section 3305(a)(1)(ii), which provides a defense for an illegal transaction that nullifies the obligor's promises. However, an agreement between parties which violates a statute is illegal, unenforceable and void ab initio only if the subject of the agreement is specifically proscribed by statute. Here, the subject of the agreement between Defendants and Homestead was not prohibited by statute. Thus, even assuming the Note and Mortgage were obtained in violation of 7 P.S. §311(e), the agreement was not "illegal", as that term is used in section 3305(a)(1)(ii). In any event, as set forth infra, section 311(e) was not violated.

Defendants also contend that Holman induced them into purchasing bank stock with funds from the executed Note and Mortgage through "fraudulent conduct." Thus, Defendants could be attempting to assert a defense under section 3305(a)(1)(iii), which permits an obligor to avoid enforcement if fraud "induced the obligor to sign the instrument with neither knowledge nor reasonable opportunity to learn of its character or its essential terms." However, that exception applies only to fraud in the factum, as opposed to fraud in the inducement, and here there is no allegation of fraud in the factum.

5. Section 311(e) provides that

> An institution shall not extend credit, directly or indirectly, for the purpose of enabling a customer to acquire or hold shares of stock or capital securities issued by the institution unless all indebtedness incurred for that purpose is secured by other readily marketable collateral with a value not less than one hundred twenty percent of the indebtedness.

7 P.S. §311(e). Defendants, allegedly at Holman's urging, used some of the proceeds from the loan to purchase shares of stock in Homestead. Apparently, Defendants contend that the market value of the property securing the loan was not one hundred twenty percent of the total indebtedness.

one hundred twenty percent of the indebtedness. We conclude that State Street is a holder in due course.[6]

The evidence produced by Plaintiff establishes that Defendants have not made monthly payments since April, 1993. Although Defendants deny that they are in default, they have failed to submit any evidence of payment to State Street since that time. Defendants have breached their contract and Plaintiff is entitled to summary judgment.

The *Strawser* case is illustrative not only because it provides a rare modern example of a case explaining the benefits of holder-in-due-course status, but also because it helps to show why holder-in-due-course status has so little continuing relevance. Here, as in most cases involving litigation to enforce instruments, there is no reason to believe that the court would have found for the defendants even in the absence of holder-in-due-course status. The crux of the case is the defendants' failure to articulate any substantial defense. Without any substantial defense, the makers of the note would have lost whether or not the plaintiff was a holder in due course.

3.   *Payment and Discharge*

The defenses of payment and discharge require special rules because an instrument can be paid in part, or a party can be discharged, even without any default or other problem with the instrument. For example, the fact that a party has partially paid an instrument by making scheduled monthly payments does not suggest a problem that should bar holder-in-due-course status. Similarly, the fact that one party has been discharged from liability does not indicate a problem with enforcing the note against remaining parties. Thus, as you should recall from Assignment 37, an accommodation party might be discharged under UCC §3-605 when a holder grants the borrower an extension of the due date. There is no reason that a subsequent purchaser with knowledge of that fact should not become a holder in due course able to enforce the instrument against the principal obligor.

Article 3 offers a two-step solution to that problem. First, UCC §3-302(b) states that holder-in-due-course status is not precluded by notice of payment or discharge (other than the real defense of discharge in insolvency proceedings mentioned above). Second, any whole or partial discharge is effective against a person that takes with notice of the discharge. UCC §3-302(b). Returning to the examples of the preceding paragraph, consider a party that purchases an installment note, knowing that the maker has made the first two years' worth of payments. The purchaser could become a holder in due

---

6. In any event, we reject Defendants' argument that the Note and Mortgage were obtained in violation of 7 P.S. §311(e) and that such violation is a defense under §3305(a)(2). The record is replete with evidence that the market value of the collateral that secured the Note was "not less than one hundred twenty percent of the indebtedness" as required by Section 311(e), and Defendants have not submitted evidence to contradict those values. Thus, even assuming Plaintiff was not a holder in due course, Defendants have not set forth any grounds to deny Plaintiff's right to enforce the Note.

course free from personal defenses of the maker, but the purchaser would be bound to recognize the decrease in the amount owed on the note caused by the payments of which the purchaser had notice. Similarly, assume that a financier purchases a note from which an accommodation party has been released under the guarantor-protective rules of UCC §3-605. If the financier was on notice of that discharge (perhaps because the documents included an amendment extending the due date, but did not indicate that the accommodation party had consented to the extension), the discharge of the accommodation party would be binding on the holder in due course. UCC §3-302(b).

Conversely, a discharge would not be binding on a holder in due course that took without notice of the discharge. UCC §3-601(b). For example, if a party selling an instrument misled a purchaser into believing that an accommodation party had consented to an extension (and thus had not been discharged by it), the purchaser would take free of the discharge. UCC §3-601(b). Thus, in that case, the holder in due course could enforce an instrument against an accommodation party even if the accommodation party would not have been liable to the prior holder of the instrument. A fortiori, a party that purchased an instrument would take free of a payment that a borrower made to the transferor after the date of the transfer (even if the borrower had no idea that the instrument had been transferred): How could the transferee take with knowledge of a payment that had not been made at the time of the transfer?

Those rules pose significant difficulties for parties that want to make sure that their payments and discharges are effective to bind subsequent holders of an instrument. Article 3 offers several ways in which obligors can protect themselves, but none of them is particularly practical. The simplest applies to a party that obtains a discharge. As the preceding paragraphs suggest, the discharged party can make the discharge effective only if the discharged party takes steps to make sure that subsequent parties cannot acquire the instrument without notice of the discharge. The most obvious device would be to obtain possession of the note and destroy it at the time of payment. By forcing the lender to produce the instrument, the borrower could ensure that the lender was still the holder. By destroying the instrument, the borrower could ensure that no subsequent party could become a holder of the note (because no subsequent party could obtain possession of the destroyed instrument). The UCC does obligate a holder to surrender an instrument when it receives full payment (UCC §3-501(b)(2)(iii)), but in practice a modern institutional lender with thousands of borrowers spread around the country may not locate the original instrument until weeks (if not months) after the borrower makes the final payment.

If a discharge is only partial (such as the partial discharge based on a monthly payment), the borrower obviously is not entitled to destroy the instrument. In that case, however, the statute offers the maker the ability to protect itself by forcing the holder to indicate on the instrument that the payment has been made. UCC §3-501(b)(2)(iii). That procedure would protect the maker because it would allow the maker to verify that the lender still was the holder, limiting the risk of making a payment to the wrong person. Also, no subsequent party could take without notice of the payment because subsequent parties would be on notice of the facts indicated by notations on the face of the instrument. See UCC §1-201(25)(c) (revised §1-202(a)(3)).

The problem with that solution is that it contemplates the borrower requiring the lender to produce the promissory note for examination by the borrower each month as a payment is due. The practical reality is that borrowers make their payments every month without insisting that lenders produce the original notes. Imagine the chaos of a system in which every homeowner went to the lender's office to view the promissory note before making each monthly mortgage payment!

The practical difficulties summarized in the foregoing paragraphs have motivated strong criticism of the traditional rules set out in Article 3. In the real-estate area, for example, the recently approved Restatement of Mortgages rejects those rules and provides instead that a payment by a borrower to a party that the borrower believes to be the holder is valid even if the supposed holder already has transferred the note to a third party. Restatement of Mortgages §5.5. Article 3, however, does not adopt that rule, but instead retains the traditional rule under which a payment is valid only if it is made to a person entitled to enforce the instrument at the time of the payment. UCC §3-602(a)(ii). Pending revisions to Section 3-602 would reverse the rule of the 1990 version of Article 3 and bring Article 3 into conformity with the conventional rule articulated in the Restatement of Mortgages.

4. Transferees Without Holder-in-Due-Course Status

For the reasons explained in the preceding section, it frequently happens that a party acquires a negotiable instrument without becoming a holder in due course. As Assignment 40 suggests, the position of a purchaser without holder-in-due-course status is not so bad: The worst problem the purchaser faces from the absence of holder-in-due-course status is its exposure to defenses that would have been effective against the original payee of the instrument. Frequently, as in *Strawser*, the issuer will have no such defense. Nevertheless, Article 3 includes two rules that make the position of the purchaser that is not a holder in due course even better than that of the purchaser of a non-negotiable obligation.

The first rule applies when the only problem is the purchaser's failure to obtain an indorsement from the seller. As discussed in Assignment 40, a purchaser of order paper cannot become a holder of the instrument unless it obtains an indorsement from the previous holder. Thus, a purchaser that gave value for order paper and purchased it in good faith and without notice of any problems would not become a holder in due course unless it also obtained the requisite indorsement. You learned in Assignment 40 that UCC §3-203(c) protects that purchaser by obligating the seller to provide the indorsement upon request, which elevates the purchaser to the status of a holder. If the purchaser satisfies the value, good faith, and notice requirements, that same rule makes the purchaser a holder in due course as well.

The second rule is the "shelter rule." That rule implements the basic property principle that a purchaser of property obtains all of the rights that its seller had in the purchased property. That is the same rule that applied in

Assignment 40 to allow a party that purchased an instrument without negotiation to obtain all of the rights that the seller had to enforce the instrument.
In this context, that rule allows a purchaser that fails to obtain its own holder-
in-due course status to assert any holder-in-due-course rights that the seller
had before the sale. UCC §3-203(b). For example, going back to Carl's note to
Jodi, assume that Jodi negotiated that note to Bulstrode Bank, which became a
holder in due course. If Bulstrode donated the note as a charitable contribution to Wessex College, the college's failure to give value would prevent
the college from obtaining its own holder-in-due-course status. The shelter
rule, however, would allow the college to assert Bulstrode's rights as a holder
in due course. The result grants the college protection that is nearly the same
as the protection the college would have had if it had purchased the note and
attained its own holder-in-due-course status.

B.   The Fading Role of Negotiability

No picture of negotiability is complete without a comment on its current
significance. Although it might be unfair to declare negotiability dead, it is
clear that a combination of consumer-protective regulation and the pressures
of the modern commercial world have limited substantially the areas where
negotiability has any real importance. The decline has two facets: the declining use of negotiable instruments and the declining significance of negotiability concepts in the processing of the negotiable instruments that remain.

1.   The Declining Use of Negotiable Instruments

For several reasons, the sphere within which negotiable instruments are used
has contracted significantly during the last few decades. Two of the most
significant reasons rest directly on legal reforms. The first of those involves
credit for consumer sales transactions. To protect consumers from being
forced to pay for goods and services that they do not actually receive, the
Federal Trade Commission (FTC) has promulgated a regulation that absolutely
bars holder-in-due-course status for consumer credit transactions. That rule
operates by declaring it an unfair trade practice to receive a promissory note in
a consumer credit sale transaction unless the note includes the following
legend:

> Any holder of this consumer credit contract is subject to all claims and defenses which
> the debtor could assert against the seller of goods and services obtained pursuant
> hereto or with the proceeds hereof. Recovery hereunder by the debtor shall not exceed
> amounts paid by the debtor hereunder.

16 C.F.R. §433.2(a). If a lender violates that rule, the FTC is authorized to
impose a penalty of up to $10,000 for each violation. 15 U.S.C. §45(*l*).
    Because that requirement conditions the maker's obligation to pay on the
absence of defenses against the seller, it places consumer credit contracts

outside the normal scope of negotiability. UCC §3-106(d) does provide that such a note still can be characterized as an instrument even though it is, strictly speaking, conditional. See UCC §3-106 comment 3. Article 3 makes it clear, however, that the note's status as an instrument is merely technical because "there cannot be a holder in due course of the instrument." UCC §3-106(d). Thus, holder-in-due-course status has no role in the financing of credit for consumer sales transactions. To make that point even clearer, recent amendments to UCC §3-405 specify that a note that should contain the FTC statement will be construed as if it had the statement even when it is omitted! See UCC §3-405(e).

Commercial pressures also have hampered the use of negotiable instruments. If negotiability was an important feature of commercial lending transactions, you would expect that the notes in question would use provisions that left no doubt regarding negotiability. As you saw in Problem Set 39, however, many common commercial payment obligations include provisions that cast considerable doubt on their negotiability. There are two general reasons for this. The first is the increasing complexity of modern commercial transactions. That complexity makes it difficult for commercial parties to stick to the simple and absolute terminology for which the law of negotiable instruments is framed. As a practical matter, most commercial entities are much more interested in producing documents that accurately reflect their agreement than they are in ensuring that the documents satisfy the technical rules for negotiability.

The second reason for the declining importance of negotiable instruments is the ease with which parties can protect themselves from surprise defenses even without negotiable instruments. If the purchaser of a commercial payment obligation perceives a significant risk that the maker will assert defenses to payment, the purchaser can insist that the seller retain the risk that the maker will interpose any such defense. For example, the seller of the note might agree to indemnify the purchaser from any such defenses or, alternatively, to repurchase the note if the maker refuses to pay as required by the terms of the note. A less accommodating seller could provide the purchaser a statement from the maker (often called an estoppel certificate) in which the maker waives any defenses based on events that occurred before the sale. Any of those approaches provides a close substitute for the benefits of holder-in-due-course status because each protects the purchaser from defenses related to events that took place before the purchaser's acquisition of the instrument. Indeed, given the difficulties a purchaser faces in being sure that it will attain holder-in-due-course status, it is plausible to say that those approaches give the purchaser a position superior to the position in which the purchaser would be if the purchaser attempted to rely on holder-in-due-course status alone.

2. The Decreasing Relevance of Negotiability to Negotiable Instruments

Practical constraints also have limited the role of negotiability even in cases in which the documents are negotiable. For example, the check certainly is the dominant form of negotiable instrument in our economy. Yet neither of the key negotiability concepts—negotiation by indorsement and holder-in-due-course status—plays any significant role in the processing and enforcement of checks. First, as Assignment 40 explained, the checking system includes a series of special rules that allow the processing and collection of checks to proceed without indorsement. Thus, when a customer deposits a check in its account, the bank becomes a holder whether or not the customer indorses the check. UCC §4-205(1). Similarly, at least as far as Article 4 is concerned, the bank need not indorse the check to transfer it in the check-collection process; any method of identification is adequate. UCC §4-206. See also 12 C.F.R. 229.35(a) (setting federal standards for indorsement under Regulation CC). Moreover, given the huge volume of checks that banks must process in the modern checking system, it is no longer practical for banks to examine indorsements to ensure that their customers have complied with the technical transfer rules contemplated by the rules of Article 3. In sum, indorsements play no significant role in the modern check-processing system.

Nor does holder-in-due-course status play a significant role in the checking system. Consider the ordinary transaction in which a payee deposits a check into its bank account. In that case, the depositary bank becomes a holder in due course of the check when it allows the customer access to the funds represented by the check. UCC §4-210. If the payor bank refuses to pay the check, the depositary bank's status as a holder in due course gives the depositary bank the legal right to proceed directly against the issuer of the check without fearing the issuer's ability to assert defenses arising out of the issuer's transaction with the customer. In practice, however, that almost never happens. Instead, it is much more likely that the depositary bank will charge the check back to the account of the customer that deposited it. UCC §4-214. The ease and simplicity of the charge-back make the lawsuit against the (often insolvent) issuer a relatively impractical remedy. That impractical and uncommon remedy, however, provides the principal opportunity for using holder-in-due-course status in the checking system.

Consider also the Werner draft transaction outlined at the introduction to this chapter. The decision of the drawee (Barclays) to pay the draft did not depend at all on the proper appearance of the indorsements on the instrument; its decision to pay rested on a direct message from the drawer advising it of the draft. Similarly, holder-in-due-course rules have little significance to the successful functioning of those drafts. The ability of the payee and its depositary bank to obtain holder-in-due-course status against the issuer of a draft has no relevance to the transaction because there is no significant chance that Mark Twain will use some personal defense as a basis for denying payment. Mark Twain made the payment decision when its customer purchased the draft. The only thing likely to hinder Mark Twain's payment would be its insolvency, a real defense against which holder-in-due-course status would offer no protection.

The rise of a public secondary market for payment obligations has presented yet another obstacle to continued reliance on negotiability concepts. For example, consider the home-mortgage note. Most home-mortgage lenders do not retain ownership of the notes generated by their businesses. Instead, as you will see in Chapter 12, those lenders commonly sell those notes to other institutions, which package large groups of the notes for resale on public securities markets. Although that transaction involves the repeated transfers that once would have been the classic case for the use of negotiability, the size of the transactions makes it impractical for the parties to use the document-based transfer system offered by Article 3. To use the system as it was designed, the originating lender would have to indorse each of its notes separately and then deliver the notes to the purchasing institution; that institution, in turn, would have to indorse each note and deliver it to the (usually numerous) parties purchasing interests in the note. Then, whenever the maker of the note repaid the note, those parties would have to return the note to the maker to surrender it.

Not surprisingly, the industry has abandoned the cumbersome transfers contemplated by a pure negotiability system, moving instead to a much more streamlined system in which the actual documents remain in a single place, "warehoused" with a servicer (often the original lender) or some other custodian. The system facially addresses Article 3's requirement that a holder take possession by providing a complicated network of custody agreements under which the party that has physical possession agrees that it is holding the instrument as agent for the actual holder (or holders). The need to maintain those cumbersome devices illustrates just how outmoded the negotiability system's focus on possession of a physical document has become.

Finally, advances in electronic and computer technology can only accelerate the obsolescence of the negotiability system. As the checking system illustrates, advances in technology are continuously making it cheaper, easier, and more reliable to transmit information electronically than on paper. Those advances inevitably force a contraction in the use of systems that rely on the physical transmission of paper objects. Thus, just as the checking system already is moving to electronic presentment and truncated nondocumentary processing, there is every reason to believe that any other areas that still use negotiable instruments will make similar advances. Accordingly, even if parties continue to execute documents that are negotiable on their face, the processes for their transfer and collection will take less and less account of the "advantages" afforded by the document- and possession-based negotiability system.

Problem Set 41

41.1.   When you come into the office Monday morning, you find a telephone message from Stacy Vye (from Wessex Bank), asking you to call her about a package of promissory notes that she wants to acquire. None of the notes matures during the next five years, but in each of them the borrower has missed one or more of the recent scheduled monthly payments. The seller of the notes has not yet accelerated the dates of maturity of the notes or otherwise responded to the defaults. Wessex Bank plans to acquire a package of the notes at a deeply discounted purchase price, reflecting the fact that the notes currently are in default. Stacy says that she does not need you to examine the notes to determine whether they are negotiable in form. Instead, assuming that they are negotiable in form, that the seller of the notes is the current holder of the notes, and that Stacy obtains proper indorsements in connection with the purchase, she wants you to tell her whether her knowledge that the borrowers have missed payments will prevent her from becoming a holder in due course of the notes.

She tells you that the notes have two different types of payment schedules. Some call for a series of amortizing monthly payments (part interest and part principal), while others call for monthly payments of interest only, with the entire principal due in a single "balloon" payment on the date of maturity. What do you tell her? UCC §§3-302(a)(2)(iii), 3-304, 3-304 comment 2.

41.2. You have lunch today with Bill Robertson, the grocery-store operator whom you have represented on a variety of matters. He tells you that he has gotten into a dispute with Bulstrode Bank over a $2,000,000 promissory note that Bill issued to Texas American Bank (TAB) in connection with a mortgage of his recent project "Shops at Four Corners." Bill tells you that he paid off the TAB note last month with a lump-sum payment of $2,000,000, made by a wire transfer directly to TAB. Accordingly, Bill was surprised yesterday to receive a telephone call from Bulstrode Bank informing Bill of the address to which Bill should send this month's payment. When Bill told the officer from Bulstrode (Nicholas Bulstrode) that Bill already had paid off the TAB note last month, Bulstrode laughed and said that wasn't his problem because Bulstrode purchased the TAB note from TAB six weeks ago (two weeks before Bill made the $2,000,000 payment). Bill can't believe that he might be liable to Bulstrode for a note that Bill already has paid. What do you tell him? UCC §§3-302(b), 3-601(b), 3-602(a).

41.3. Following up on your successful work in Problem Set 40, you take an afternoon field trip to visit your client Tom Mae at his pool-hall check-cashing service. While there, he asks you about a traveler's check that he recently cashed for a customer. The check was issued by Hunt Bank and payable to "bearer," but required a countersignature from Jane Kingsley as a condition to payment. It turns out that the customer for whom he cashed the check had stolen the check from Kingsley. The customer forged the Jane Kingsley countersignature. Because Kingsley had notified Hunt Bank of the theft before the check was processed, Hunt Bank refused to honor the check. Accordingly, Tom is stuck with the check. Not surprisingly, Tom cannot locate the customer for whom his employee cashed the check. Tom points out to you that he did not really do anything wrong. Because the forgery was quite good, he could not plausibly have known that there was a problem. Why can't he rely on holder-in-due-course status to enforce the check against Hunt Bank? UCC §§1-201(25) (revised §1-202), 3-104(a), 3-106(c), 3-106 comment 2, 3-305(a)(2).

41.4. Jodi Kay (from CountryBank) calls with a problem about a cashier's check that her bank has issued. It appears that one of her customers (Fluffy Feed Corporation) issued a check for $10,000 payable to Flatiron Linen. Because Fluffy Feed's account did not have $10,000 on the day that the check was presented for payment, Jodi's bank dishonored the Fluffy Feed check. A few days later Fluffy Feed sent Jodi a stop-payment order covering the check. Three months later the president of Flatiron walked into a branch of CountryBank and asked the teller if the teller would exchange the Fluffy Feed check for a cashier's check payable to Flatiron. Because Fluffy Feed's account at that time had a balance of far more than $10,000, the teller happily complied.

Minutes later the teller's supervisor noticed that payment had been stopped for the check the teller had taken in exchange for the cashier's check. The supervisor immediately called Flatiron and told the president that Country-Bank would dishonor the check. Flatiron insists that the bank must honor its cashier's check. The matter is now on Jodi's desk and seems headed for litigation. What do you tell her? UCC §§3-302, 3-303, 3-305, 3-412 & comment 2, 3-418 & comment 2.

41.5.   Your friends at the World Wilderness Fund (WWF) call you for some advice about a gift that they recently received. They explain that the problem arises out of a transaction between Diggory Venn and Clym Yeobright. Venn operates a dyeing business, under which he dyes clothes a bright red that (he claims) is permanent and impervious to extremes of heat and cold. Clym Yeobright asked Venn to dye for him a set of 20 uniforms that Yeobright planned to sell to the local fire department. Yeobright agreed to pay for the work with a negotiable promissory note in the amount of $3,000, payable to the order of Venn in equal monthly installments over two years. When Venn finished the uniforms, Yeobright delivered the note. Venn promptly took the note to Stacy Vye at Wessex Bank. She agreed to purchase the note from Venn for $2,800. Venn added a special indorsement, as follows:

Pay to Wessex Bank
/s/ Diggory Venn

Venn then gave the note to Stacy. A few weeks later Stacy called your friends at WWF and told them that Wessex wanted to donate the note to WWF. She delivered the note to them, with a special qualified indorsement, as follows:

Pay to WWF, Without Recourse
Wessex Bank,
by /s/ Eustacia Vye
Vice President

It turns out that Venn did a poor job of the dyeing. The dye washed out of the uniforms the first time that they got wet. Accordingly, Yeobright refuses to pay the note. WWF got a letter today from Yeobright's lawyer, asserting that WWF could not force Yeobright to pay because WWF is not a holder in due course. WWF wants to know your opinion. What do you say? UCC §§3-203(b), 3-204, 3-205, 3-302(a)(2), 3-303(a), 3-305(a)(3), 3-305(b), 3-412.

41.6.   Consider again the facts of Problem 21.3, in which Bud Lassen wrote Carol Long a $1,500 check for some kitchen equipment that was too large for his kitchen and then stopped payment on the check in an effort to avoid payment. Suppose that instead of cashing the check at the First State Bank of Matacora (as Carol did in Problem 21.3), Carol properly indorsed the check and deposited it into an account at her own bank (the Nazareth National Bank). Now suppose that the Matacora bank (on which the check was drawn) dishonored the check the next day based on the stop-payment request and returned it to Nazareth before the funds were available to Carol under Nazareth's customary funds availability policies. What can Nazareth do to recover the funds that it has credited to Carol's account? UCC §§1-201(20) (revised §1-201(b)(2)), 3-302, 3-303(a)(2), 3-305(b), 4-105(5), 4-210, 4-211, 4-214.

Chapter 12. Securitization

Assignment 42: Securitization

A. Securitization and Liquidity

Negotiability is not the only system for making commercial assets liquid. Indeed, it is not even the most common system. The most important group of liquid assets (aside from cash itself) in the modern economy is securities.

Although it might not be obvious at first glance, the process of turning assets into securities—securitization—rests on many of the same premises as negotiability. Specifically, securitization is a process for enhancing the value of assets by increasing their liquidity. Essentially, securitization takes a single asset (or pool of similar assets), divides it into a large number of identical shares, and then sells those individual shares; each individual share is a security.

Securitization enhances liquidity in two related ways. The simplest rests on the relation between the size of an asset and its liquidity. On the one hand, all other things being equal, smaller assets tend to be more liquid than larger assets because the universe of potential purchasers for small assets is larger than the universe of potential purchasers for large assets. For example, compare the number of people that you know that could consider investing $1,000 in a company with the number that could consider investing $10,000,000. And the difference does not rest simply on the smaller number of people that have $10,000,000 to invest. It also rests on the notion of portfolio diversification. Most people prefer to limit risk by investing in a wide variety of assets so that a misfortune on one investment will not have a serious impact on the entire portfolio. The desire of investors to diversify their portfolios significantly limits the willingness of even large investors to purchase assets that have very high prices. On the other hand, the larger the asset, the easier it is for businesses like stockbrokers and investment banks to profit by acquiring, analyzing, and promulgating the kind of information that makes it easier for investors to make an informed assessment of the value of an investment in the asset.

Securitization responds to that dichotomy by taking very large assets (large enough to reward investigation into their value) and dividing them up into very small pieces (small enough to be suitable purchases for investors). Because securitization divides the single asset into a large number of small pieces, each of the smaller pieces has a much lower purchase price than the entire asset, yet each of the smaller pieces retains the financial characteristics (the same risk, return, maturity date, and the like) of the asset out of which the securities have been carved.

Securitization also enhances liquidity by enhancing the potential for an organized market in which assets can be bought and sold. If a potential purchaser must purchase an entire company (or an entire building or an entire loan), then sales of interests in the company will be relatively infrequent because they will occur only when that single purchaser wishes to make a sale. Accordingly, it is unlikely that there will be any organized market for making such a sale. Thus, the seller will incur substantial time, effort, and cost in locating and reaching an agreement with a purchaser.

By contrast, if the ownership of the company is divided into a large number of small interests (securities), sales will occur more frequently because they will occur whenever any one of the many owners wishes to sell some portion of its interest. Because sales are more frequent, it is easier for a regular market to develop, which will display a market price around which potential sellers and purchasers can focus their discussions. The result of the process is a market in which the transaction costs of a sale (essentially a broker's commission) are much smaller than in a conventional market without securities. Indeed, in many cases, the securities seller can complete a sale within minutes (or seconds) with nothing more than a simple telephone call or a few keystrokes at a computer terminal.

B.   The Rise of Securitization

Although securitization probably is not as ancient as negotiability, it is certainly not novel. Organized securities markets have existed for at least three centuries, dating to the late seventeenth century in England. But for almost all of that time, securitization has been limited to a narrow range of assets: debt and equity interests in the largest and most creditworthy businesses and governmental entities. Thus, until the 1960s, there were really only two major types of securities, which can be referred to loosely as stocks and bonds. If a large company wished to securitize its equity ownership interests, it could issue stock in the company, so that the individual shareholders would own the company. Similarly, if an entity (like the United States government) wished to securitize a portion of its debt, it could issue the debt in the form of securities, distributing a large number of relatively small but identical debt instruments (bonds) rather than a single large promissory note that would be purchased by a single investor. Thus, as a tool to provide liquidity to debt obligations, securitization is a direct alternative to negotiability.

On that point, it is important to distinguish between a securitized debt and a secured debt. Although the terms sound similar, they have quite different implications. A securitized debt is a debt (like an issue of bonds) that has been divided up into a large number of identical pieces. A secured debt is a debt for which the borrower has given collateral, like a home mortgage or a car loan; the collateral is said to "secure" the borrower's obligation to repay the debt.

Since the 1960s the use of securitization has spread into many contexts other than the traditional issues of stocks and bonds by large creditworthy companies. Many of the newer uses involve relatively small payment obligations, for which negotiability once would have played an important role. The first significant advance (and still the most important one) occurred in the market for home-mortgage notes. Starting with the 1970 creation of the Federal Home Loan Mortgage Corporation (colloquially referred to as Freddie

Mac), the federal government has supervised the creation of a variety of quasi-governmental entities that have succeeded in securitizing hundreds of billions of dollars of home-mortgage notes. By the late 1990s, those entities (which now include not only Freddie Mac, but also the Federal National Mortgage Association (Fannie Mae) and the Government National Mortgage Association (Ginnie Mae)) had securitized almost half of all of the outstanding home-mortgage debt in this country.

The key concept necessary to extend securitization to home-mortgage notes was asset pooling. Taken one by one, home-mortgage notes are not at all liquid because a careful assessment of the value of an individual note would require evaluation of not only the home for which the money was used, but also the credit characteristics of the borrower. Given the relatively small size of the typical home-mortgage note, it is relatively expensive to perform that assessment on a case-by-case basis. The law of large numbers, however, suggests that a large pool of home mortgages can be evaluated quite accurately at a relatively low cost. That is true because the total return for a large pool of mortgages will not be affected significantly by a small number of unusual unfortunate occurrences.

To implement that insight, Freddie Mac, Fannie Mae, and Ginnie Mae (joined now by a number of large banks and other investors) purchase huge numbers of home-mortgage notes as soon as borrowers sign them, collect similar notes into large pools, and then issue massive numbers of securities reflecting minuscule interests in each of those pools. A large and thriving market for those securities makes them an asset that is in practice not significantly less liquid than a stock traded on the New York Stock Exchange.

That same pooling concept has been applied in a variety of other areas, the most notable of which involves credit-card receivables. In that context, major credit-card issuers collect pools of their outstanding credit-card receivables and securitize them. Just as with home-mortgage notes, an individual credit-card receivable is not at all liquid; its value depends on the vagaries of the individual cardholder's repayment patterns. But the repayment pattern of a large pool of credit-card receivables is sufficiently predictable to make it easy to find investors willing to invest in small shares of such a pool. Hundreds of billions of dollars of those securities have been sold in the 1990s alone.

C. Investment Securities and Article 8

The average student (or lawyer) thinking of legal rules for securities thinks immediately of the extensive federal regime of securities regulation reflected in the Securities Act, the Securities Exchange Act, and the voluminous regulations issued by the Securities and Exchange Commission (SEC). Although those rules obviously are crucial to a complete picture of the market for securities, they are not directly relevant here. For the most part, they respond to the potential for fraud or sharp dealing in the issuance and sale of securities. Thus, they require a large variety of registrations and disclosures as a condition to the issuance of certain types of securities. Similarly, they closely regulate securities exchanges to ensure that those exchanges provide fair venues for the purchase and sale of securities.

The concern here, however, is not with the fairness of the market in which securities are sold, but with the way in which the mechanisms for effecting their issuance and sale can enhance their liquidity. The primary legal rules relevant to that topic appear in the revised version of Article 8 of the Uniform Commercial Code. Adopted by the American Law Institute in 1994, that statute has been enacted in all 50 states. Moreover, pursuant to regulations issued by the United States Treasury Department, the rules in Article 8 apply directly to all United States Treasury securities.

The best way to provide a general picture of the system is to summarize the basic coverage and terminology of Article 8. After that introduction, the assignment closes by discussing the obligations of the issuer and the two separate systems for holding and transferring securities: the traditional direct holding system (in which each investor deals directly with the issuer) and the modern indirect holding system (in which a few intermediaries hold each issuer's shares on behalf of investors at large).

1. The Subject Matter: What Is a Security?

The basic subject matter of Article 8 is the "security," a term defined in UCC §§8-102(a)(15) and 8-103. The most important thing to remember about that definition is that it has nothing to do with the federal securities laws or the relatively vague definition of "security" found there. Although most assets that are securities under Article 8 will be securities under the federal securities laws, and vice versa, the Article 8 definition is distinct.

The Article 8 definition includes four separate requirements. The first three requirements are simple descriptive requirements that implement the concept of a security described in the opening pages of the assignment. First, under the introductory clause to UCC §8-102(a)(15), the item must be either an obligation of an issuer (such as a bond) or a share or other interest in the issuer (such as a share of stock). Second, under UCC §8-102(a)(15)(ii), the item must be divided or divisible into a class or series of shares. Thus, Article 8 applies to a series of bonds, but it does not apply to a single undivided promissory note.

Third, under UCC §8-102(a)(15)(iii), the item either must be of a type that is traded on securities exchanges or markets or must expressly provide that it is governed by Article 8. To limit the ambiguity in the question whether assets satisfy that test, UCC §8-103 includes several bright-line rules that govern the most common types of investment assets. For example, any "share or similar equity interest issued by a corporation, business trust, joint stock company, or similar entity is a security." UCC §8-103(a). Conversely, except for a special rule related to federally regulated investment companies, "[a]n interest in a partnership or limited liability company is not a security unless it is dealt in or traded on securities exchanges or in securities markets [or] its terms expressly provide that it is a security governed by this Article." UCC §8-103(c).

The fourth requirement (UCC §8-102(a)(15)(i)) is the only one that presents any significant complexity. That requirement governs the form in which the security exists. Specifically, Article 8 applies only if the security appears in one of three forms. The first two forms involve certificated securities, that is, securities represented by a physical piece of paper, a certificate. UCC §8-102(a)(4). Certificated securities can appear in either bearer form or registered form. To be in bearer form, the certificate must provide that the security is payable to the bearer of the certificate. UCC §8-102(a)(2). For reasons explained in Assignment 41, bearer securities are no longer common; this assignment will not discuss them further. To be in registered form, the certificate must specify a person entitled to the security and provide that the security can be transferred on books maintained by (or on behalf of) the issuer. The corporate bond in Problem 39.1 is a registered certificated security.

The third permissible form is the uncertificated security, a security for which there is no physical certificate. UCC §8-102(a)(18). Because there is no certificate to reflect the ownership interest, those securities necessarily must be transferred by entries on books maintained by (or on behalf of) the issuer. UCC §8-102(a)(15)(i).

The last significant point about the definition of the Article 8 security applies to documents that qualify as both a security under Article 8 and an instrument under Article 3. Under UCC §8-103(d), such documents are treated as securities, not instruments.

2. The Obligation of the Issuer

Investors ordinarily do not purchase securities because of their interest in the form of the certificate. Rather, they are interested in the monetary return that will come from the security. Accordingly, the nature of the obligation that the security represents is central to the system.

Unlike Article 3's treatment of instruments, Article 8 does not itself impose an obligation to pay a security. Instead, it accepts the obligation imposed by the laws governing contracts and business associations and uses the term "issuer" to describe the entity obligated under those laws. If the security is a bond or some other debt instrument, the issuer is the party obligated to pay the debt. If the security is stock or some other ownership interest, the issuer is the party in which the security creates an interest. UCC §8-201.

Article 8 does, however, have much to say about enforcement of that obligation. Most important, Article 8 includes a series of rules (parallel to the rules that govern holder-in-due-course status) that limit the defenses an issuer can impose to the obligation created by the security. Following the reasoning of the negotiability system, Article 8 accepts the premise that strict limitation of the defenses that an issuer can interpose enhances the value of securities by improving their liquidity. Thus, with only two exceptions discussed below, Article 8 generally bars issuers from asserting defenses against any party that purchases a security for value and without notice of the defense. UCC §8-202(d).

The "notice" that is adequate to allow interposition of a defense is the standard UCC concept of notice set forth in UCC §1-201(26) (revised §1-202(a)), which extends to all facts of which a person "has reason to know" based on "all the facts and circumstances known to [it]." Thus, a person might have notice under UCC §1-201(26), and thus be subject to a defense on a security, even if the person had no actual knowledge of the defense, so long as the person had reason to know of the defense. UCC §8-202 amplifies that point by stating expressly that a purchaser (even if it technically does not have "notice") is bound by terms stated on a certificated security, by terms incorporated into the security by reference, and by terms stated in any applicable legal rule governing the issuance of the security. UCC §8-202(a).

The "value" that a purchaser must give to take advantage of that rule also refers to the standard UCC definition, which includes "any consideration sufficient to support a simple contract." UCC §1-201(44) (revised §1-204 (4)). That concept is conspicuously broader—easier to satisfy—than the concept of value that must be given for a party to become a holder in due course of a negotiable instrument under Article 3. As Assignment 41 explains, the value that a purchaser must give to become a holder in due course of a negotiable instrument excludes a variety of things that would constitute consideration (and thus value under Article 8), the most important of which probably is a commitment to provide future services. See UCC §3-303(a)(1).

The first of the two defenses valid against a purchaser for value without notice is a claim that the security is counterfeit. UCC §8-202(c). The second exception is more complicated. It relates to defenses that go to the validity of the initial issuance of the security. If the security is issued by a person that is not a governmental entity, Article 8 allows a defense of invalidity to be asserted against purchasers for value without notice only if the defense arises from constitutional provisions. Even then, the defense can be asserted only against a party that purchased the security at its original issuance. UCC §8-202(b)(1).

Governmental issuers are permitted considerably more leeway. Thus, to defeat a defense of invalidity interposed by a governmental issuer, a purchaser must not only overcome the private-issuer standard articulated in UCC §8-202(b)(1), but also demonstrate one of two things: that the security was issued in "substantial compliance" with the applicable legal requirements, or that the issuer received a substantial consideration for the securities and that the "stated purpose of the issue is one for which the issuer has power to borrow money or issue the security." UCC §8-202(b)(2). Although those rules do give governmental issuers a greater opportunity to disavow their securities than private issuers, they are not exceptionally onerous. After all, a purchaser can be safe in purchasing a security without examining every aspect of the issuer's conduct in issuing the securities. It is enough to determine that the issuer "substantial[ly] compli[ed]" with the applicable laws. Similarly, even if it is not practical for the purchaser to evaluate the issuer's compliance with applicable rules governing the issue, it ordinarily would not be difficult for a purchaser (or, more likely, a broker marketing the securities to the purchaser) to determine that the issuer actually received funds from the issue and that the stated purpose of the issue is a legitimate one.

Although the special rules for governmental issuers are not particularly onerous, and admittedly have a long history, they are difficult to justify as a policy matter. The premise of Article 8 is that general rules barring issuers from interposing defenses enhance the liquidity of all securities by enhancing the reliability of the obligation that they present. If that premise is correct, then special rules giving governmental issuers a greater right to disavow their securities should diminish the liquidity of the securities that they issue, thus lowering the price that purchasers will pay for those securities.

That problem is particularly troubling, given this country's long and sordid record of local disavowal of securitized obligations. Orange County's willingness to file for bankruptcy in 1994, rather than raise tax revenues to pay its debts, may be the most recent instance in which a major governmental entity chose not to meet its financial obligations, but other jurisdictions frequently have used the less direct tactic of interposing technical claims of invalidity, to which state courts on occasion have been receptive. Thus, Article 8's willingness to give governmental issuers broader leeway to interpose such defenses only diminishes the value of their securities.

3. The Two Holding Systems

Just as the Article 8 rules limiting the defenses of the issuer are analogous to the holder-in-due-course provisions in the negotiability system, the Article 8 rules regarding systems for holding and transferring securities are analogous to the mechanisms by which the negotiability system facilitates the easy transfer of negotiable instruments and documents. Article 8 recognizes the same underlying premise regarding transferability as the negotiability system: A cheap and reliable system for transferring assets enhances their liquidity. Indeed, although it is not technically accurate, people often refer to securities as "negotiable" to describe the freedom with which they can be transferred.

The revised version of Article 8 deals with the transferability issue by recognizing two separate systems for holding and transferring securities. The first is the direct holding system, a traditional system in which the issuer deals directly with the purchaser of the security. The second is the more modern indirect holding system, in which the purchaser holds the security through an intermediary.

(a) *The Direct Holding System.* The best place to start in understanding the way in which securities are held and sold is with the traditional direct holding system. To see how that system works, you should consider three issues: what it takes for a transfer to be effective between a seller and a purchaser, what it takes for a transfer to be effective against the issuer of the security, and what it takes for a transfer to cut off the claims that third parties might have to the security.

(i) *Making the transfer effective as between seller and purchaser.* Article 8 uses the term "delivery" to describe the point at which a transfer of a security becomes effective between the parties to the transaction. UCC §8-302(a). Thus, whether the transaction is an original issuance (from the issuer to the original purchaser), a sale of a previously issued security, or a pledge of a security to a lender, "delivery" of the security gives the transferee all of the transferor's rights in the security. UCC §§8-302(a), 8-301 comment 1.

The mechanism for delivery depends on the type of security. If the security is represented by a certificate, the security is delivered when the purchaser acquires possession of the certificate. UCC §8-301(a)(1). If the security is not represented by a certificate (an uncertificated security in Article 8 terminology), then the purchaser cannot obtain physical possession of the security because there is nothing to possess. Accordingly, in that case, the security is delivered through registration of the purchaser as the owner on the books of the issuer (the process of registration is discussed below). UCC §8-301(b)(1).

UCC §8-301 also recognizes the possibility of delivering a security to an agent that either would take possession (of a certificated security) or obtain registration (of an uncertificated security). UCC §§8-301(a)(2) & (3), 8-301(b)(2). If that agent is a broker or some other securities intermediary, the transfer ordinarily will be governed by the indirect holding system discussed below. Accordingly, it is best to ignore that possibility for the time being.

(ii) Making the transfer effective against the issuer. Although delivery is sufficient to make a transfer effective between the transferor and the transferee, an issuer generally is free to ignore the transfer of a security until the transfer is registered on the books of the issuer. To put it another way, the issuer of a security has a broad right to treat the registered owner as the true owner of a security, even if the registered owner no longer has possession of or actual title to the security. UCC §8-207(a). Accordingly, a party that purchases a security has a powerful incentive not only to take delivery of the security, but also to have itself registered as the owner of the security on the books of the issuer.

To obtain registration as the owner of a security, the purchaser must notify the issuer (or a designated transfer agent that acts for the issuer) that it has purchased the security and provide adequate evidence of the purchase. Ordinarily, this is done by obtaining an indorsement of the security from the seller. See UCC §§8-401(a)(2) (allowing issuer to condition registration on an indorsement or instruction from the "appropriate person"), 8-107(a)(1) (specifying the "appropriate person" as the currently registered owner). Even if the purchaser neglects to obtain that indorsement at the time of the transaction, Article 8 grants it a right to obtain the indorsement later upon demand. UCC §8-304(d); see UCC §8-307 (obligating the seller to provide "proof of authority or any other requisite necessary to obtain registration of the transfer").

Although UCC §8-401 offers a long list of potential problems that could allow the issuer to refuse to register a security, the presentation of a security that bears a signature purporting to be the signature of the previously registered owner ordinarily is sufficient to induce the issuer to register the security in the name of the purchaser. If the security is uncertificated, the issuer's notation of the transfer on its books finishes the registration. If the security is certificated, the issuer completes the registration by issuing a new certificate in the name of the purchaser.

(iii) The effect of a transfer on third parties. Under UCC §8-302(a), a purchaser of a security obtains all of the rights that its transferor had to the security. But the desire for clean and irrevocable transfers is as powerful for securities as it is for negotiable instruments. Accordingly, Article 8 includes rules analogous to Article 3's holder-in-due-course rules, which allow certain parties to take free of claims that third parties might have to a security. As you

know from the earlier sections of the assignment, Article 8 imposes strict limits on defenses that issuers can interpose against all purchasers (even those that dealt directly with the issuer). Thus, the main concern is not the ability of a transferee to take free of a defense to enforcement of the security (because Article 8 already has removed most of those defenses); the main concern is the ability of the purchaser to cut off adverse claims to the security. The classic problem is a sale of a stolen security: When does a party that buys a security from a thief take free of the claim of the (previously) true owner?

The Article 8 answer is that the purchaser takes free of the adverse claim if the purchaser qualifies as a "protected purchaser." UCC §8-303(b). The rules for protected purchaser status are considerably simpler than the Article 3 holder-in-due-course rules; Article 8 requires only that the purchaser give value without notice of the claim and obtain control of the security. As mentioned above, the Article 8 concept of value is much broader than the Article 3 definition, extending to any consideration sufficient to support a simple contract. UCC §§8-303 comment 2, 1-201(44). The notice requirement incorporates the familiar standard from UCC §1-201(26), which includes not only claims of which the purchaser has actual knowledge, but also claims of which the purchaser has reason to know from all the facts and circumstances. The only new requirement is the control requirement. The purchaser can satisfy that requirement if it both obtains possession of the security (which constitutes delivery under UCC §8-301) and obtains either an indorsement of the security or a registration in its own name. UCC §8-106(b), (c).

The last component of the system is a shelter rule that mirrors the shelter rule in UCC §3-203(b) (which should be familiar to you from Assignment 41). Under basic property principles, a transferee of a security acquires all of the rights of its transferor. Accordingly, if one protected purchaser (insulated from an adverse claim to a security) delivers the security to another purchaser, the second purchaser is as insulated from the claim as the previous owner would have been, even if the second purchaser fails to obtain protected-purchaser status in its own right. UCC §8-302(a) & comment 1. For example, assume that a thief sells a security to a person that becomes a protected purchaser. If the protected purchaser contributes the security to a charity, the charity's failure to give value would deprive it of protected-purchaser status. The shelter rule nevertheless would let the charity take free of the claim of the (previously) true owner.

(b)   The Indirect Holding System.

(i)   The basic framework.   For a variety of reasons, the direct holding system described above is no longer the principal method for holding securities. Among other things, that system was doomed by its requirement that each sale of a security be registered on the books of the issuer. It is not practical for each sale of a security to be completed by transportation of a paper certificate to the issuer, registration of the transfer by the issuer, and issuance of a new certificate to the purchaser. Indeed, during the 1960s (when that system still was widely used), the major securities exchanges frequently experienced considerable disruptions of trading because of backlogs in the process of delivering certificates to settle previous trades.

To be sure, that problem could have been solved to some extent by the issuance of uncertificated securities. By abandoning the paper certificate, an issuer of uncertificated securities saves the bulk of the transaction costs contemplated by the classic paper-based system. But abandonment of certificates—dematerialization of securities—would have required each separate issuer (or some agent on its behalf) to maintain procedures for processing transfers of securities on a daily basis. And so the issuance of uncertificated securities has not been the dominant response to the inconveniences of the paper-based system. The most common response has been a system of indirect holding of securities—immobilization—in which the overwhelming majority of securities that are in circulation are immobilized in the custody of a small number of intermediaries. Trades among the vast number of retail purchasers of securities are consummated by entries on the books of these intermediaries. The following explanation by the Reporter for the revised Article 8 is illuminating:

> If one examined the shareholder records of large corporations whose shares are publicly traded on the exchanges or in the over-the-counter market, one would find that one entity—Cede & Co.—is listed as the shareholder of record of somewhere in the range of sixty to eighty per cent of the outstanding shares of all publicly traded companies. Cede & Co. is the nominee used by The Depository Trust Company ("DTC"), a limited purpose trust company organized under New York law for the purpose of acting as a depository to hold securities for the benefit of its participants, some six hundred or so broker-dealers and banks. Essentially all the trading in publicly held companies is executed through the broker-dealers who are participants in DTC, and the great bulk of public securities—the sixty to eighty per cent figure noted above—is held by these broker-dealers and banks on behalf of their customers. If all of these broker-dealers and banks held physical certificates, then as trades were executed each day it would be necessary to deliver the certificates back and forth among these broker-dealers and banks. By handing all of their securities over to a common depository, all of these deliveries can be eliminated. Transfers can be accomplished by adjustments to the participants' DTC accounts. . . .
>
> The development of the book-entry system of settlement seems to have accomplished the objective of ensuring that the settlement system has adequate operational capacity to process current trading volumes. At the time of the "paperwork crunch" in the late 1960s, the trading volume on the New York Stock Exchange that so seriously strained the capacities of the clearance and settlement system was in the range of ten million shares per day. Today, the system can easily handle trading volume on routine days of hundreds of millions of shares. Even during the October 1987 market break, when daily trading volume reached the current record level of six hundred eight million shares, the clearance and settlement system functioned relatively smoothly.

James Steven Rogers, "Policy Perspectives on Revised U.C.C. Article 8," 43 UCLA L. Rev. 1431, 1443-1445 (1996).

In the indirect holding system, transfers of securities rarely require either physical delivery of a certificate or registration on the books of the issuer. On the contrary, most transfers can be made by the book-entry method, which requires nothing more than entries on the accounts of the various intermediaries at a central depository. For example, assume that Edward Casaubon has purchased 100 shares of stock in ABC Corp. Like most investors, Casaubon never received a stock certificate. He purchased the stock through his broker Bullish Broker and monitors the transaction (and the securities that he "owns") only through the statements that Bullish periodically sends to him. In fact, it may be that Bullish also has no certificates, but instead has an account at DTC that contains 100,000 shares in ABC Corp. DTC, in turn, has certificates representing 3,000,000 shares in ABC Corp. If Casaubon sells his stock to Dorothea Brooke, nothing will happen to any of the certificates. Instead, Bullish will simply transfer some shares from its DTC account to the DTC account of Dorothea's broker, which will hold those shares in Dorothea's account. Alternatively, if Bullish also is Dorothea's broker, then Bullish need only transfer the shares from Dorothea's account to Casaubon's account. DTC need take no action. Most important, the issuer takes no action in either case.

The revised Article 8 expressly recognizes the indirect holding system and includes a variety of rules to facilitate transactions using that system. Working from the classic holding system, it would be possible to construct rules that would treat the retail purchasers as owning individual stock certificates, based on the intermediaries' status as agents for the retail purchasers. And Article 8 still permits that result, but only if the intermediaries register their individual purchasers' transactions with the issuer. UCC §§8-301(a)(3), 8-301(b)(2).

For the most part, however, Article 8 dispenses with such a cumbersome framework and instead attempts to articulate functional rules that more directly reflect the true relationships of the parties. These rules reflect the absence of any direct relationship between Casaubon and Brooke, on the one hand, and the issuer, on the other. Instead, the only relationship that has any substance is the relationship between the retail purchaser and the intermediary with which it deals. Part 5 of Article 8 establishes a legal framework to govern that relationship. In that framework, Casaubon's right to the securities makes him an "entitlement holder" (defined in UCC §8-102(a)(7)). His right to the shares of ABC Corp. is a "security entitlement" (defined in UCC §8-102(a)(17)). Bullish, the party against which Casaubon holds this entitlement, is a "securities intermediary" (defined in UCC §8-102(a)(14)). The same rules apply at each tier of the holding system, so that Bullish also is an entitlement holder with a security entitlement against DTC based on the shares in Bullish's account at DTC. To illustrate the basic features of that framework, the remainder of the assignment discusses two topics: the rights of the entitlement holder against its securities intermediary and the rights of the entitlement holder against third parties.

(ii) Rights against the intermediary. The best place to start in examining the relationship between the entitlement holder and its securities intermediary is to see how an entitlement holder can obtain an entitlement that is valid against its securities intermediary: How does Casaubon get the stock into his account at Bullish in the first place? Article 8 uses two separate, overlapping functional tests. The first test focuses on Bullish's conduct and recognizes that Casaubon has a security entitlement if Bullish agrees that Casaubon has one, that is, if Bullish "indicates by book entry that a financial asset has been credited to the person's securities account." UCC §8-501(b)(1). The second test focuses on actions that other parties take that should lead to the same result. If Bullish receives securities on Casaubon's behalf, Casaubon has a security entitlement to the extent of those securities. UCC §8-501(b)(2).

Once Casaubon obtains a security entitlement, Article 8 imposes a variety of duties on Bullish with respect to the entitlement. The most important duty is a duty to maintain assets sufficient to cover the entitlement. Because Article 8 recognizes an entitlement for Casaubon immediately upon Bullish's crediting Casaubon's account, it is entirely possible for Casaubon to acquire an entitlement against Bullish to stock of ABC Corp. without Bullish obtaining a corresponding amount of ABC Corp. stock. UCC §8-504(a) obligates Bullish to "promptly obtain and thereafter maintain a financial asset in a quantity corresponding to the aggregate of all security entitlements it has established in favor of its entitlement holders with respect to that financial asset." Thus, when Casaubon acquired the stock, Bullish was obligated to make sure that it had enough ABC Corp. stock in its portfolio to cover that purchase. If it did not, it would have to acquire more shares of that stock to bring its balance of that stock up to the level of the entitlements of its customers. As the discussion above suggests, Bullish ordinarily would satisfy that duty by increasing the amount of stock in its account at DTC (which it would do by purchasing stock from some other securities intermediary), not by obtaining additional physical certificates.

The second major duty of the securities intermediary relates to administration of the security. Generally, the securities intermediary is obligated to take all steps necessary to protect the rights of the entitlement holder with respect to the security so that the entitlement holder will be in the same position as if it held the security directly. Among other things, the securities intermediary is obligated to "take action to obtain" all payments that the issuer of the security makes with respect to the security. UCC §8-505(a). Thus, if ABC Corp. issues a dividend (or makes a payment on its bonds), Bullish has to take steps to obtain that payment. Then Bullish must forward to Casaubon all of the payments that it receives with respect to Casaubon's security entitlements. UCC §8-505(b).

In the same way, Bullish is obligated to act for Casaubon with respect to voting rights and other rights related to the securities (such as rights to redeem securities). UCC §8-506. With respect to those matters, Bullish can either take the steps necessary to allow Casaubon to vote on his own behalf (to "exercise the rights directly," UCC §8-506(1)) or act for Casaubon, provided that it "exercises due care in accordance with reasonable commercial standards to follow the direction of the entitlement holder," UCC §8-506(2).

Finally, the securities intermediary is obligated to follow the instructions of the entitlement holder regarding sale or other disposition of the security entitlement. UCC §§8-507(a) (obligating securities intermediary to comply with an "entitlement order"), 8-102(a)(8) (defining "entitlement order"). A common problem arises when a third party asserts a claim to the securities reflected by the security entitlement. If the securities intermediary proceeded to sell the securities pursuant to the instructions of its customer (the entitlement holder), the third party would be likely to assert a claim against the securities intermediary, contending that the intermediary should not have allowed the entitlement holder to sell the securities. To ensure liquidity of securities, UCC §8-115 bars any such claim against the securities intermediary except in three narrow cases: where the creditor obtains an injunction barring transfer of the securities (UCC §8-115(1)), where the intermediary "acted in collusion with the wrongdoer" (UCC §8-115(2)), or where the securities intermediary has notice of a claim that the applicable security certificate constitutes stolen property (UCC §8-115(3)). The last exception obviously could arise only in the relatively unusual case in which the securities intermediary received a stock certificate as the basis for the entitlement instead of an entry in the securities intermediary's account at a higher-level securities intermediary.

(iii)   Rights against third parties.   The indirect holding system must deal with two logically distinct claims that third parties can interpose against an entitlement holder: claims that third parties assert against a particular security and claims that third parties assert against the securities intermediary.

The first topic is a simple one, as to which the indirect holding system uses rules much like those of the direct holding system. Specifically, an entitlement holder that acquires a security entitlement for value and without notice of an adverse claim takes free of the claim, just as a protected purchaser would in the direct holding system. UCC §§8-502, 8-503(e). That is true even though the entitlement holder does not obtain "control" of any particular certificate representing the security in question. It is enough for the entitlement holder to obtain a security entitlement that is valid under UCC §8-501.

The second topic is considerably more difficult. Because Article 8 recognizes security entitlements that are not necessarily backed by specific stock certificates, it is possible for a securities intermediary to incur obligations that exceed the amount of the securities that it owns. Of course, the system includes a wide variety of safeguards designed to limit the possibility of such losses. For one thing, most securities intermediaries are subject to considerable regulatory oversight, which substantially diminishes the risk of malfeasance that would result in such a shortage. Moreover, all brokers and dealers in securities are required to join the Securities Investor Protection Corporation (SIPC). The SIPC provides retail purchasers insurance analogous to the deposit insurance provided by the FDIC. That insurance currently covers up to a $500,000 shortfall that a customer experiences upon a liquidation of the assets of a securities intermediary. For example, if a customer had $1,500,000 in its account, but received only $900,000 upon liquidation of the intermediary, the SIPC insurance would provide $500,000, leaving the customer short "only" $100,000.

Nevertheless, the possibility of shortages remains, and a functioning system must devise rules to deal with those situations. Hence, the inevitable question remains: If the securities that the intermediary owns are inadequate to satisfy all of the claims against the intermediary, which creditors are entitled to the securities that are on hand? Essentially, Article 8 resolves the problem by recognizing three different types of claims a creditor might have against a securities intermediary: an ordinary creditor's claim, a security entitlement, and a controlling security interest in the intermediary's security entitlements.

The first category of claimants includes most creditors of the securities intermediary. These could be employees of the intermediary, suppliers of services or equipment, or financial institutions that have loaned money to the intermediary. Because those entities hold no security entitlements, their claims against the securities held by the securities intermediary are subordinate to the claims of customers that hold security entitlements against the securities intermediary. UCC §8-503(a). Thus, if a shortage of securities held by the securities intermediary means that there are not enough securities to satisfy all of the entitlement holders, the general unsecured creditors will have no claim against any of the securities that the intermediary does have. The same rule would apply even to creditors that had a security interest in the securities, except in the situation (discussed below) in which the creditors took control of the securities. UCC §8-511(a) (entitlement holders have priority over secured creditors that do not have control of securities).

The second category of claimants is entitlement holders. In the event of a shortage, Article 8 puts all entitlement holders on an equal footing, without regard to the time that they acquired their individual entitlements. UCC §8-503(b). Thus, all entitlement holders would receive pro rata shares of whatever securities were available to satisfy their claims. If the securities intermediary held 70 percent of the ABC Corp. securities for which its customers held security entitlements, then liquidation of the assets of the securities intermediary would give each of the entitlement holders 70 percent of its security entitlements to shares of ABC Corp.

The only claimants that can defeat claims of the entitlement holders are secured creditors that hold liens against the securities in question. For a variety of reasons, that situation should be unusual, even in the context of insolvent securities intermediaries. Among other things, UCC §8-504(b) expressly prohibits an intermediary from "grant[ing] any security interests in a financial asset it is obligated to maintain [to cover the security entitlements of its entitlement holders]." Accordingly, creditors will not have such interests in the ordinary course of financing the operations of a securities intermediary. Those interests should arise only through the coincidence of a shortage that occurs for other reasons with the existence of a creditor that has a security interest in securities of the securities intermediary.

Nevertheless, if that situation occurs and if the holder of the security interest has control of the securities in question, the holder of the security interest prevails over the customer of the entitlement holder. UCC §8-511(b). Although that result might seem counterintuitive from the perspective of the customer, it was one of the most thoroughly debated issues in the revision of Article 8. In the end, the drafters decided that traditional practices related to the purchase of securities required recognition of the rights of secured creditors in that limited circumstance. The key to that outcome is the part of the rule stating that a creditor can prevail only if it has "control" of the security. To have control of the security under UCC §8-106, the creditor would have to have a directly held security indorsed over to it or registered in its name. If the securities intermediary itself held the security indirectly (as it usually would, through an account at DTC), the creditor would have to obtain control by having the securities transferred to it, so that the creditor would become the entitlement holder. Thus, for CountryBank to obtain control of securities held by Bullish in the form of a security entitlement at DTC, CountryBank would have to cause DTC to transfer the entitlement to CountryBank.

At that point, Bullish technically would remain the owner of the securities as against CountryBank, in the sense that CountryBank would return the entitlement to Bullish if Bullish repaid the loan. But there is no real sense in which Bullish still retains the securities: No stock certificates show Bullish's ownership, and Bullish has no entitlements against any securities

intermediary. Because the securities industry operates on the practical understanding that acquisition of control of a security cuts off adverse claims to the
security (a rule that receives broad application throughout Article 8), the
drafters concluded that it would be too disruptive to adopt a rule allowing
Bullish's customers to recover securities from creditors in that situation.

Problem Set 42

42.1. Pleased with your fine analysis in the matter of Problem 41.2, Bill
Robertson comes to you this Monday morning with a similar problem. This
one involves one of a series of bonds issued by Bill's company, Pearland Holdings, Inc. Each of the bonds states that it is payable to the order of the initial
purchaser (identified by name on each bond). The bonds also state that transfers of the bonds can be registered on Pearland's books. This particular bond
was issued to Texas American Bank. Like the note in Problem 41.2, the bond
was acquired from Texas American Bank by Bulstrode with an appropriate
indorsement from Texas American Bank. Bulstrode did not, however, register
its acquisition with Pearland or otherwise notify Pearland of its ownership of
the bond. Accordingly, Pearland has made the last two payments on the bond
to Texas American Bank, rather than Bulstrode.

Bulstrode has written Pearland demanding the two payments that Pearland
has made to Texas American Bank that were due after the date on which
Bulstrode acquired the bond. Is Pearland obligated to Bulstrode for those
payments? UCC §§3-302(b), 3-601(b), 3-602(a), 8-102(a)(13), 8-102(a)(15),
8-103(d), 8-207(a).

42.2. Following up on the advice that you rendered in Problem Set 39,
Jodi Kay calls you to ask about a few problems with some securities that
CountryBank has purchased. On the first one, she sends you a telecopy of
a bond issued by Chiripada Investment Trust (CIT). The bond states on its
face that the entire series of bonds is governed by Article 8, includes standard
provisions for registering transfers on CIT's books, and recites that it was
issued pursuant to and in accordance with the provisions of the New Mexico
Investment Trust Company Act. Jodi received a letter last week from CIT,
stating that CIT intends to stop making payments on the bonds. The letter
states that the bonds are invalid because they were issued without a
unanimous vote of the trust managers of CIT. The letter asserts that the
New Mexico Investment Trust Company Act requires such a vote for a
trust validly to issue securities and that all purchasers of the securities are
on notice of that requirement because of the reference to that statute on
the face of the securities.

Jodi tells you that she was personally responsible for CountryBank's investment in the CIT securities, so she is directly interested in establishing their
validity. Assuming that the letter from CIT accurately describes the provisions
of the New Mexico statute, does CIT's letter establish a defense that is valid
against CountryBank? UCC §§1-201(26) (revised §1-202), 8-102(a)(13),
8-102(a) (15), 8-202.

42.3. Jodi's other question relates to a bond that she purchased about a
month ago from one of her customers (Harlan Smythe). Because the bond is

in a registered form, she tried last week to register her purchase with the issuer, but failed when she discovered that she had neglected to obtain an indorsement from Smythe at the time that she purchased the bond. She became concerned when yesterday's newspaper included a detailed article describing a federal indictment alleging that one J.R. McDonald has engaged in a wide-ranging scheme to defraud his creditors by selling securities that he already has pledged to his lenders. Under the scheme, McDonald would obtain possession of a security from his lender on the pretext of using it for internal auditing purposes. Instead of returning the security to the lender, however, he would sell it to a third party, hoping to purchase a substitute security to return to the creditor within a few days.

Because Jodi could tell from a McDonald indorsement on the bond that Smythe had purchased the bond from McDonald the day before Smythe sold the bond to CountryBank, Jodi was concerned that one of McDonald's creditors might assert a claim against CountryBank. Accordingly, she went down to Smythe's office yesterday and obtained his indorsement on the bond. Does that indorsement protect her from the claims of McDonald's creditors? If not, does Jodi have any other way to defeat that claim? UCC §§8-102(a)(4), 8-106, 8-301(a), 8-302(a), 8-303, 8-304(d).

42.4.   Edward Casaubon comes to you to ask you a question about a potential problem that he has with his broker (Bullish Broker). Casaubon tells you that he asked his contact at Bullish last week to purchase 10,000 shares of stock in Advanced Tactical Devices, Inc. (ATDI). The contact advised Casaubon that the purchase had been completed. Furthermore, Casaubon has ascertained by examining his account record from his home computer that Bullish credited Casaubon's account with the ATDI stock on the date of the purchase.

While talking to his broker this morning, Casaubon was upset by a comment to the effect that the broker had not yet been able to obtain the ATDI securities that Casaubon thought he had purchased last week. Casaubon wants to know if he has anything to be worried about. Does Casaubon own the securities or not? Does Bullish have any obligation to remedy the situation? UCC §§8-102(a)(7), 8-102(a)(14), 8-102(a)(17), 8-501(b), 8-503(a), 8-503(b), 8-504(a).

42.5.   A few weeks later Casaubon calls you back to tell you that the situation has deteriorated at Bullish Broker. Apparently because of large investments in Southeast Asian municipal bonds, Bullish has become insolvent. This morning it was closed for liquidation. Casaubon's broker tells him that Bullish's portfolio will be inadequate to cover the accounts of many of its customers. Among other things, Bullish owns only 180,000 shares of ATDI stock, although its customers have accounts for 200,000 shares. Also, the broker has told Casaubon that 120,000 of the 200,000 shares in the accounts were acquired by the entitlement holders before Casaubon acquired his entitlement. Finally, the broker has told Casaubon that Bullish in the aggregate has only 75 percent of the securities that would be necessary to cover all of the various types of securities in all of its customers' accounts.

   a.   Assuming that the broker's statements are accurate, what will Casaubon receive upon liquidation of Bullish? UCC §8-503(b) & comment 1.

b. How would your answer change if 80,000 of the ATDI shares were pledged to ThirdBank? What further information would be helpful in answering that question? UCC §§8-106, 8-503(a), 8-511(a), (b).

42.6.   Jude Fawley is a stonemason and tour guide whom you have represented on a variety of matters. He has decided that he wants to raise more money to expand his tour-guide business (Wessex Tours, Inc.). Based on some reading that he has been doing, he wants to know whether he should propose to issue negotiable instruments for the debt or securities. He wants your advice as to the relative merits of the two possible approaches. He tells you that his conversations with potential lenders have convinced him that Wessex Tours, Inc., is sufficiently large and creditworthy to accomplish the proposed borrowing in either format, and he will be able to determine for himself whether one transaction would cost more to perform than the other. He wants your advice on something that is not strictly a legal question, but (he hopes) still within your expertise. What he is trying to determine is which approach would be likely to produce a more marketable obligation. Essentially, he wants to know which approach would be more liquid. What do you say?

BOOK THREE
Secured Credit

Part One
The Creditor-Debtor Relationship

Chapter 13.   Creditors' Remedies Under State Law

Assignment 43:   Remedies of Unsecured Creditors Under State Law

Much of law is about liability and the determination of damages. But winning a money judgment for a breach of contract, a tort, a treble damage antitrust suit, or some other kind of case may be only the beginning of the story. One of the authors of this book worked hard on the liability issues of her first trial (a rousing traffic accident in Rockaway, New Jersey, in 1977). At the conclusion of the trial, the judge awarded her client full damages — $147.58. The defendants left the courtroom sullen and unhappy. The plaintiffs were ebullient. But once the courtroom had cleared and smiles and handshakes had been exchanged all around, the client paused and, with evident embarrassment, asked the truly critical question: "Uh, how do we get paid?" A long, painful silence followed. The clever coauthor-to-be did not have the faintest idea. Because the defendants did not whip out their checkbooks and pay up, it seemed that still more legal process might be required.

Liability may be hotly disputed and parties may litigate vigorously, as they did in the Rockaway car accident. Or liability may be undisputed, as often happens when a debtor borrows money and is simply unable to repay. Either way, if no payment follows, the party owed an obligation may find that even after judgment has become "final," there can be a long and sometimes tortuous process ahead before any money changes hands.

A.   Who Is an Unsecured Creditor?

The legal concepts of *debtor* and *creditor* apply to a wide variety of human relationships. Perhaps the archetypical debtor-creditor relationship is that between lender and borrower of money. But the legal categories of debtor and creditor are much broader. Anyone owed a legal obligation that can be reduced to a money judgment is a creditor of the party owing the obligation. At the instant one car slid into another, the victim of the Rockaway car accident became a creditor. Similarly, the company with a valid patent infringement claim, the consumer with a defective product still covered by a warranty, and the child who is the beneficiary of a noncustodial parent's court-imposed support obligation are all creditors. The obligations owed to them can be reduced to money obligations of the company that infringed the patent, the manufacturer or seller of the goods, or the noncustodial parent. "Creditor" embraces a variety of characters in a multitude of circumstances.

Many debtor-creditor relationships are entered into voluntarily, as when a creditor has lent money to a debtor. But many are involuntary. The soon-to-be debtor's first contact with the soon-to-be creditor may be when their cars occupy the same space in the road simultaneously, as in the Rockaway dispute. The parties may meet on a happy occasion, such as the cash purchase of a product covered by a warranty; until the product fails they may not even realize that they are not just buyer and seller, but also debtor and creditor. Or a party may be wary about the credit relationship — a child's representative may be acutely aware of the depressing statistics on support compliance — but the party may have neither the knowledge nor the leverage to negotiate in advance for the collection rights the party will need for swift collection in the event of default.

Unless a creditor contracts with the debtor for secured status or is granted it by statute, the creditor will be *unsecured*. Unsecured creditors are the *general creditors* or *ordinary creditors* that populate state collection proceedings. They include creditors who contracted for unsecured status, but also creditors such as the tort victims mentioned above, who got their creditor status in circumstances that do not permit prior negotiations. They also include incautious creditors, uninformed creditors, and creditors who were unable for any number of reasons to negotiate for security. If the unsecured creditor has already obtained a court judgment to establish liability, the creditor is a *judgment creditor*, but the mere grant of a judgment does not alter the creditor's unsecured status.

In this assignment, we examine the legal remedies available to unsecured creditors. These remedies are available to all creditors. They are the minimum collection rights guaranteed to anyone owed an obligation that can be reduced to a money judgment. In later assignments, we will use these remedies as a baseline for comparing and understanding the enhanced collection rights that secured creditors enjoy.

Nothing in this discussion should be taken to imply that debtors seldom pay their unsecured debts. How often debtors actually repay is an empirical question. In fact, evidence suggests that voluntary payment occurs in the overwhelming majority of cases. Even when debtors would like to escape their obligations, their unsecured creditors typically can muster enough leverage, legal and otherwise, to compel repayment. But these are not the situations most attorneys are likely to encounter in their practices. Unsecured creditors bring lawyers into the tough cases, when the debtors are likely to be resistant and the availability of assets is uncertain. The lawyer who seeks to collect on a judgment on an unsecured debt usually faces a stiff challenge.

B.   How Do Unsecured Creditors Compel Payment?

The unsecured creditor's path to payment is narrow. Not only does the law provide procedures for the collection of unsecured debts, it regulates or bars outright many alternatives. Among the remedies prohibited to unsecured creditors is self-help seizure of the debtor's property. (This rule does not prevent the creditor from "setting off" a debt owing to its debtor against a debt owing from its debtor; it merely prohibits the creditor from seizing property for the purpose of creating such a setoff.) In most instances, a prohibited seizure of a debtor's property will constitute the tort of conversion.

> Conversion is the wrongful exercise of dominion and control over another's property in denial of or inconsistent with his rights. Exercising dominion or control over another's property in denial of, or inconsistent with, his rights constitutes conversion. A plaintiff need not establish that the defendant acted with a wrongful intent. The intent required is not necessarily a matter of conscious wrongdoing. It is rather an intent to exercise a dominion or control over the goods which is in fact inconsistent with the plaintiff's rights. Winkle Chevy-Olds-Pontiac, Inc. v. Condon, 830 S.W.2d 740 (Tex. App. 1992).

Additionally, the creditor that wrongfully takes possession of property of the debtor may be charged with larceny, even though the value of the property taken is less than the amount owed. Finally, though the creditor has the right to demand payment from the debtor, if it does so in an unreasonable manner, it may incur liability for wrongful collection practices. The creditor is entitled to coerce payment of the debt only through the judicial processes specified by the state. Although these processes are fundamentally the same in all states, there are differences in the language used to describe the processes and the myriad ways they are implemented. These differences in language and method of implementation can make it difficult to see the common system structure. In this assignment we try to focus on that common system structure.

The following case tells a story of a person who never intended a debtor-creditor relationship, but was pulled into one anyway. His attorney obtained a court judgment establishing liability, and then spent countless hours trying to collect. We include the case not so much for its exposition of the law governing execution, levy, and the obscure remedy of amercement as for what it shows about the system by which execution is made. The story of Jeffrey Israelow's tenacious pursuit of $6,317 conveys something of the enormity of the unsecured creditor's task when facing a recalcitrant debtor.

The basis for the plaintiff's judgment against Hotel California is briefly alluded to in the first footnote of the case. The judgment was only a milestone on a long, torturous route to collection. The opinion is something of a catalog of the kinds of problems that plaintiffs encounter in attempting to collect an unsecured judgment against a recalcitrant debtor. What is extraordinary about this case is that the court did something about these problems and published a lengthy opinion. Read it for what it tells you about the collection process, not for legal or procedural detail.

Vitale v. Hotel California, Inc.
446 A.2d 880 (N.J. Super. Ct. Law 1982)

STALLER, J.S.C.

Plaintiff David J. Vitale, Jr. brings this motion pursuant to N.J.S.A. 40A:9-109 to amerce, that is, hold liable the Sheriff of Monmouth County, William Lanzaro, for failing to execute a writ based on a judgment against defendant Hotel California, Inc. (California). [A]mercement of a sheriff has not been the topic of any reported decision in New Jersey since 1907, and [has been] infrequently reported elsewhere.

The chronology of events is as follows: Vitale obtained a final judgment against California in the amount of $6,317 plus costs on August 12, 1980,[2] and thereafter learned that California held the liquor license for "The Fast Lane," a bar featuring "punk rock" entertainers, located in Asbury Park, New Jersey. A writ of execution issued on June 23, 1981, and on July 9 the sheriff received the writ along with a cover letter from plaintiff instructing him to levy upon all monies and personal property at The Fast Lane. A check to cover the sheriff's costs up to $50 was enclosed.

Then began plaintiff's travail with the sheriff's office which gave rise to this proceeding. On July 27 the office indicated to plaintiff's attorney, Jeffrey K. Israelow, that a levy was not possible since the bar was only open late in the evening, from about 10 P.M. to 2 A.M., and that the writ would be returned unsatisfied. Israelow thereupon advised a deputy sheriff that it was absolutely necessary to proceed to make the levy during the open hours.

The writ was turned over to a deputy sheriff by the name of Guinan whom Israelow persuaded to make the levy during those late weekend hours when the bar was primarily open for business. Guinan reported to Israelow that he went to The Fast Lane on July 31 accompanied by an Asbury Park police officer, identified himself and announced his purpose at the door, but was denied access by the bar's "bouncers." Fearing that violence might ensue, the officers left. Lanzaro confirmed this fact by a letter dated August 3 in which he asked plaintiff for further instructions. Israelow then advised Guinan to make the levy and arrest anyone interfering with execution, pursuant to the officer's authority under N.J.S.A. 2C:29-1 and other statutes. After conferring with his superiors, Guinan informed Israelow that a court order would be necessary to gain access to the establishment!

On August 5, on plaintiff's application reciting the above facts, this court ordered that the sheriff be permitted access to the bar and to arrest anyone who interfered with the levy to show cause before the court why such person should not be held in contempt of the order. Israelow immediately transmitted the order to the sheriff's office with a letter instructing him to levy first upon the cash registers or places where cash might be held and advising him to be accompanied by sufficient personnel to effectuate any arrests that might become necessary. Guinan then went to the bar on the weekend of August 8, but found it had closed early. After speaking with Israelow he again went on the morning of August 15 and was able to seize $714 in cash and other personal property. Guinan reported back to Israelow the same day and indicated his belief that additional money may have been secreted before he was able to levy upon it. When Israelow instructed Guinan to make further levies until the writ was satisfied, Guinan told Israelow that he would have to consult with his superiors before taking further action.

On or about August 17 or 18 Israelow again instructed the sheriff's office to make successive levies and then was informed of the sheriff's contention that only

---

2. In the principal action, Vitale v. Hotel California, Inc., plaintiff obtained a default judgment based on the claim that defendant's wrongful refusal to verify that plaintiff was an employee of defendant at the time of an automobile accident deprived him of income continuation benefits under an insurance policy.

one levy need be made under a writ of execution. After telephoning but not getting through to Lanzaro, Israelow forwarded him a letter dated August 19 and a mailgram dated August 20, again requesting the additional levies. Lanzaro telephoned Israelow on August 21 to tell him that he would consult with Monmouth County counsel, Richard O'Connor. Later that day, O'Connor's office informed Israelow that the sheriff had been instructed not to make any additional levies under the writ.

Unable to reach O'Connor by phone, Israelow wrote a letter to him on August 24 detailing plaintiff's position and threatening to seek amercement. On August 31 Israelow made good the threat by filing this motion. The hearing on the motion was continued several times until January 14, 1982 at the request of the parties who were trying to negotiate a solution.

The sheriff does not refute the facts outlined above but maintains that it is unreasonable to expect any sheriff to command his officers or deputies "to go forth on an unknown number of occasions, at an unreasonable hour, to seize proceeds of an establishment such as The Fast Lane." The sheriff suggests that plaintiff pursue other "reasonable, speedy and inexpensive measures" to satisfy the judgment, to wit, obtaining an order that defendant pay over proceeds of the operation, conducting proceedings to determine where the proceeds are deposited, or locating and seizing other assets of the judgment debtor.

At argument Israelow described his difficulty in collecting the judgment debt: The personal property levied on at The Fast Lane on August 15 was verified as belonging to the landlord of the establishment. Upon this discovery, that California was only a tenant, a scheduled sheriff's sale was necessarily canceled. Also, California's president made a complete disclosure of assets after she had been arrested on an order to show cause, but an attempted levy on the corporate bank account was unsuccessful because the account was overdrawn.

The sheriff further argues that upon seizure of money on August 15 the writ of execution was satisfied and should have been returned, although no return in fact was ever made within the three-month life of the writ. Lack of proof as to loss or damage to plaintiff resulting from the sheriff's [in]action is also raised as a defense. Lastly, the sheriff maintains that the pleading is deficient for failure to specifically state the basis for amercement.

Three basic, interrelated questions are presented for resolution. (1) Are successive levies possible under one writ of execution? (2) When may a sheriff refuse to levy as instructed by a plaintiff, on the basis that the request is unreasonable or onerous? (3) Was the conduct of Sheriff Lanzaro and his office in respect to the writ such as to subject him to amercement?

Before proceeding to answer the first question, a brief overview of execution procedure would be beneficial. A successful plaintiff who obtains a judgment against a defendant may cause the personal property of the defendant/judgment debtor to be seized and sold and the proceeds applied to the judgment and costs by way of execution. N.J.S.A. 2A:17-1 et seq. To do this, plaintiff obtains a writ of execution, directing the sheriff to levy and make a return within three months after the date of issuance. A "return" is the physical return of the original writ to the court clerk, indorsed with the executing officer's brief description of what was done. In addition, the officer must file a verified statement of when and how much money was collected and the balance due on execution fees or costs. N.J.S.A. 2A:17-9.

The writ must be promptly executed upon and returned, N.J.S.A. 2A:15-20. The writ may be returned before the return date if, notwithstanding diligent effort, the judgment cannot be satisfied any further. Once an execution has been returned, a sheriff cannot thereafter levy upon any property under the writ. Nor can a valid levy be made after the return date. Successive executions upon the same judgment are possible. N.J.S.A. 2A:17-3. Therefore, if the first seizure is insufficient, the creditor may seek an alias writ for levy upon other goods. Thereafter, the plaintiff may seek an unlimited number of pluries writs until the judgment is satisfied. The proceeds from the sheriff's sale of seized property are paid to the judgment creditor or to his or her attorney or to the court clerk. N.J.S.A. 2A:18-26.

Throughout the process plaintiff plays a crucial role. Plaintiff must prepare the writ, have it entered by the court clerk and see that it is delivered to the sheriff with instructions as to levying. If necessary, plaintiff should conduct discovery to locate and identify property to be levied upon. Complementary to plaintiff's responsibility is the sheriff's duty to execute the writ according to the plaintiff's instructions. The writ is in the "exclusive control" of the judgment creditor; the sheriff must follow the creditor's reasonable instructions regarding the time and manner of making the levy and must abide by special instructions to make an immediate levy, if practicable, when plaintiff demonstrates necessity.

I.   SUCCESSIVE LEVIES UNDER ONE WRIT

The first question presented, whether successive levies can be made under one writ, can be simply answered — "yes." The rule that further levies under one writ are authorized under the same writ before the return day if the initial levy does not satisfy the judgment is recognized universally. . . .

If property levied on is not sufficient to satisfy the execution, a return should not be made without a showing that attempting another levy would be fruitless. That is not to say that Sheriff Lanzaro would have been exposed to potential liability for returning the writ after seizure of money on August 15. Arguably, the sheriff might have returned the execution with "so much money as collected." N.J.S.A. 2A:17-15. Had the sheriff in fact returned the writ, plaintiff could then have obtained an alias writ, expecting that more money would be available to be seized at The Fast Lane during the remainder of the summer season. Since an alias writ should not issue before the original execution is returned, and may be voidable as irregular if prematurely issued, plaintiff was under no duty to seek an alias writ, the original writ not having been returned.

[T]he clear import of the communications from Lanzaro's office to Israelow was that plaintiff's request was unreasonable despite plaintiff's preparedness to pay any associated costs or pursue any necessary procedural course. That objection remained, notwithstanding any possible issuance of an alias writ, which properly could not have issued while the original writ was outstanding.

II.   REASONABLENESS OF REQUESTED LEVIES

That brings us to the second question, whether the sheriff rightly refused to honor an unreasonable request to levy. The particular elements of the request perceived as unreasonable must be reviewed.

The sheriff first objects to the "unknown number of occasions" that he and his deputies would have to go forth to attempt levy in order to comply with plaintiff's wishes. Since there is no limit to the number of executions that conceivably could issue within 20 years after a judgment was entered until the judgment is satisfied, there is technically no limit to the number of times that a sheriff might be required to levy. Nevertheless, practical, operational considerations of a sheriff's office impose an obligation on a plaintiff not to request inordinately frequent and numerous levies. The one successful levy netting $714 on August 15 can be used to project what was entailed by plaintiff's request for levies on successive weekend nights. By extrapolation, the sheriff might have had to levy approximately nine times in the space of one to two months to comply with the request. This many potential levies under one judgment may be unusual but is not in itself unreasonable and, under the circumstances, was not excessive since the bar was basically a summer operation. Furthermore, seizure of several hundred dollars at one time demonstrated the effectiveness of this mode of levying.

There was also some indication of irregularity in the days of the week that The Fast Lane was open for business. Sheriff's counsel acknowledged, however, that local newspaper advertisements for The Fast Lane could be consulted to remove uncertainty about operating hours. Plaintiff, moreover, expressed a willingness to facilitate the execution in any way, and no doubt would have relayed the necessary information if lack thereof had actually presented a stumbling block.

The objection as to the unreasonably late hour requested for the levy cannot be sustained either. The bar was open for business, mostly on weekends, from about 10 P.M. to 2 A.M. Israelow directed that service be made during those hours; the sheriff avers that the instruction was to levy at 2 A.M. Whatever the precise instruction was, levy was to be made at some time during those night-time hours — levying at 2 A.M. would probably find the cash registers near their fullest and thus minimize the number of additional levies required. Levy under a writ of execution may be made at any hour of the day; there is no issue of privacy here that might dictate otherwise. The Fast Lane's late open hours impelled the late-at-night levy. Like police officers, sheriffs and their deputies may be obliged to work at times of the day and week when the rest of the populace sleep or recreate.

The threat of violence engendered by attempting the levy goes to the heart of the sheriff's objections. "[T]o seize proceeds of an establishment *such as The Fast Lane*" uncamouflages what may have been the most unappetizing aspect of the requested levy. (Emphasis supplied.) On July 31, fearing violence, the deputy sheriff and an Asbury Park police officer allowed themselves to be turned away by bouncers at the door. At that juncture, at the sheriff's instigation and upon plaintiff's application, this court ordered, under what it considered as its inherent powers, that anyone interfering with the execution be arrested and brought before the court to show good cause. Armed with the order, the sheriff successfully levied on August 15. Nevertheless, the refusal to make further levies implies that a conscious decision may have been made to risk amercement rather than further confrontations at the bar.

When is physical force appropriate in making a levy? The general rule is that:

[an] officer may force an entry into any enclosure except the dwelling house of the judgment debtor in order to levy a fieri facias on the debtor's goods and even in the case

of the debtor's home, when the officer is once inside, he may break open inner doors or trunks to come at the goods. . . .

[A]ccording to Lanzaro's recital, on July 31 The Fast Lane bouncers did in fact obstruct the officer from "performing an official function by means of intimidation," N.J.S.A. 2C:29-1, giving the officers probable cause to arrest them. Their resistance to the lawful process might have been a basis for criminal conviction. Although the officers did not believe themselves to be in a position to use physical force, they apparently did not summon back-up help to effectuate the levy or make arrests incidental thereto.

   Are sheriffs' deputies to be faulted for not using physical force in a nonemergency situation? The nature of law is to physically force people, if need be, to do things or refrain from doing things that they would be free to do or not do in the "natural state"; the hope is that the benefit to society will more than compensate for the loss of individual freedom. Sheriff's officers act as the physical extension of the power of the court, and thus, of the law and the will of the people. Necessarily, then, the privilege of such civil service occasionally demands risking bodily harm to oneself. Only in this way will the lawless be kept from becoming the de facto law makers. Philosophy aside, the record is barren of facts showing any imminent harm to the sheriff's officers on July 31 other than the vague averment that attempting to carry out the levy may have triggered a violent reaction. I find this unembellished defense insufficient to justify not making the levy.

III.   AMERCEMENT

Consequently, by concluding that the sheriff failed to abide by plaintiff's proper requests to levy, I reach the question of amercement.

   By proceeding in amercement, a judgment creditor may hold a sheriff liable for failing to properly execute against a judgment debtor.

   If a sheriff or acting sheriff fails to perform any duty imposed upon him by law in respect to writs of execution resulting in loss or damage to the judgment creditor, he shall be subject to amercement in the amount of such loss and damage to and for the use of the judgment creditor. Such amercement may be made by the court having jurisdiction of the judgment and proceedings for the enforcement thereof in an action or proceeding for amercement or in the nature of an amercement brought for the purpose. The court may proceed in a summary manner or otherwise. The delinquent sheriff or acting sheriff shall also be subject to attachment or punishment for contempt. . . .

   Amercement has been defined as "a pecuniary penalty in the nature of a fine, imposed upon a person for some fault or misconduct, he being 'in mercy' for his offense," Black's Law Dictionary 107 (4th ed. 1957), and is derived from the Anglo-French "amercier." Webster's Third New International Dictionary 68 (1971). Traditionally, "amercement" has been used to describe a fine imposed on officers of the court for failing to turn over money or, more particularly, for a sheriff's neglect to levy upon or turn over proceeds of an execution. . . .

   Whether or not statutory interpretation favors a liberalized remedy, plaintiff still bears the burden of proof on this motion. Since a public officer such as a sheriff is presumed to have acted properly, plaintiff must clearly establish some default of duty. . . .

The sheriff suggests that plaintiff should have pursued other more reasonable means to satisfy the judgment but points to no failure of plaintiff to satisfy any statutory prerequisites to the requested levies. By comparison, had plaintiff sought to execute against real property, he would have had to first attempt, in good faith, to locate personal property of the debtor and levy upon it. N.J.S.A. 2A:17-1. Discovery proceedings to ascertain personal assets should be conducted before real estate is levied upon. In Spiegel, Inc. v. Taylor, 148 N.J. Super, 79, 84 (Cty. D. Ct. 1977), plaintiff sought an order to allow a constable to enter the debtors' homes for the purpose of making an inventory and levy. The court, referring to the First Amendment right of privacy, citing Griswold v. Connecticut, 381 U.S. 479 (1968), was unwilling to permit "fishing expeditions" which could frighten the inhabitants of the home and possibly endanger the constable where less drastic means such as discovery proceedings or an investigation would suffice.

Plaintiff Vitale has done all that was necessary with respect to the execution herein. . . . The money in The Fast Lane cash registers was subject to levy, N.J.S.A. 2A:17-15, and plaintiff could properly ask the sheriff to enter the bar to seize it. In light of the plaintiff's persistent efforts to negotiate a solution with both the sheriff and judgment debtor, and the unsuccessful levy on the bank account after discovery was conducted of the debtor-corporation's president, the demand upon the sheriff appears all the more reasonable.

The final issue is whether plaintiff has demonstrated a loss. Plaintiff must show that the officer's conduct has deprived him of a "substantial benefit to which he was entitled" under the writ, that but for the officer's conduct, he would have received such benefit through the execution. Plaintiff is not bound to prove the value of the property subject to levy because "[i]t would be highly inconvenient and unjust to require an innocent plaintiff to prove the value of the goods which had been in the sheriff's power but which, through his neglect, may have been eloigned beyond the reach of plaintiff's investigation." White v. Rockafellar, 45 N.J.L. 299 (Sup. Ct. 1833). Based on the findings that the execution was in the hands of the sheriff on July 9, 1981 and that only one levy was actually made on August 15 although the bar was open most weekend nights through the summer and is now closed for the winter, I conclude that plaintiff was denied the benefit of the writ and that the consequential loss amounts to the judgment debt of $6,317 less any amounts heretofore collected. The speculation that The Fast Lane will operate again this summer is not cognizable in mitigation of the amercement but would suggest that the sheriff pursue whatever civil remedy may be available against the judgment debtor for indemnification.

The difficult, distasteful aspects of executing writs demand that sheriffs be dealt with fairly, with an eye to the practicalities of their job. My reluctance to amerce a sheriff beset with such unpleasant tasks is only overcome by the convincing proof that Sheriff Lanzaro owed and breached a duty to plaintiff to make the successive levies as requested. In short, by invoking the remedy of amercement, I choose to satisfy plaintiff's debt where the sheriff has not.

In describing its ruling as a choice to "satisfy" plaintiff's debt, the court exaggerates only slightly. The sheriff will almost certainly write a check to Mr. Vitale. (If you have considered the possibility that the sheriff might not do so, you already have caught the spirit of our subject.) If the sheriff chooses to return to The Fast Lane, the next time it will be to collect for the sheriff's own account.

Vitale shows the highly technical nature of the legal process for collection of a judgment. The steps may be many. At any one of them, the judgment creditor may make a mistake or be frustrated by the mistakes of others. Even the creditor who makes no mistakes, encounters no legal anomalies, and enjoys the full cooperation of officials, may find the path difficult. Mr. Vitale was an employee at The Fast Lane before he became its creditor. He may have known its legal structure (a corporation named Hotel California, Inc. doing business under the trade name "The Fast Lane") and probably had some idea what assets the corporation had. Many creditors will start with far less information.

Even the information known to Mr. Vitale proved inadequate at several points. Recall that earlier in Mr. Vitale's collection efforts, California's president had been arrested on an order to show cause. She was apparently released only after she had made a complete disclosure of assets, including the existence of a bank account. But before Mr. Vitale could get the sheriff to levy on the bank account, the debtor evidently withdrew the money. Also recall that Vitale levied on the personal property in The Fast Lane, probably assuming the property (tables, chairs, and sound equipment) belonged to the judgment debtor. Vitale began the steps necessary to schedule a sheriff's sale, only to discover that the property belonged to the landlord. If the landlord and the judgment debtor were corporate cousins, kissing cousins, or some other kin or conspirators, Vitale *may* have had legal grounds to challenge the separate ownership. But that challenge itself would have increased the expense of collection and perhaps also slowed collection. Notice also that the court's opinion mentions earlier collection attempts only incidentally to the decision at hand; Vitale may have made other efforts to collect this debt. Moreover, note that while The Fast Lane was no ordinary business, it at least had a regular trade in a stable location and generated hard cash on a daily basis. Had the debtor been mobile or able to hide its assets the plaintiff's task might have been much harder.

The *Vitale* case illustrates the power of the judgment creditor ultimately to coerce payment. In *Vitale*, the coercion was through the remedy of levy under writ of execution. Other remedies are available as well. For example, if a third party is in possession of property of the debtor or owes money to the debtor, the creditor can cause the sheriff to serve a writ of garnishment on the third party. The effect of the writ is to require the third party to pay the judgment creditor rather than the debtor. Garnishment and other remedies of unsecured creditors are covered in more detail in the debtor-creditor course.

One side note on the *Vitale* case: We find ourselves speculating on how many attorney hours (and consequent fees) went into this little collection story to net $6,317. Law is not free — a point that may be driven home with more force in collection law than almost anywhere else.

C.   Limitations on Compelling Payment

Vitale also illustrates a number of procedural and practical limitations on the exercise of the judgment creditor's power. For example, the court notes the obligation of the judgment creditor to use discovery to locate assets, which serves as a reminder both of the creditor's right to demand information (backed up by the threat of civil contempt charges and jail) and that the sheriff will only act on clear directions about what to get and where to get it. The sheriff says, in effect, "Figure it out and tell me; then I'll get on out there and do something." The risk of error is even greater than is apparent from the court's opinion in *Vitale*. If the property seized turns out to be that of a third party, the judgment creditor may be liable for any damages caused to the third party. Worse yet, the wrongful exercise of dominion and control over the property of another constitutes the tort of conversion. The third party can refuse to accept return of the property and instead recover its value from the judgment creditor. Even if the judgment creditor is willing to take the risk of a wrongful execution, the *Vitale* court points out creditors have no right to conduct "fishing expeditions" simply by showing up at the debtor's place of business with a cooperative law enforcement officer.

While a judgment creditor has the right to obtain information about the judgment debtor's assets through discovery, the process can be long and painful. The judgment creditor must find the judgment debtor and force him or her to sit for examination. The judgment debtor may be less than forthcoming in discovery. Debtors may not keep their assets in predictable forms. As a result, questions about assets must be carefully framed. Any attorney more than a few years in practice can tell stories about carefully caged answers and tiny verbal loopholes that permitted determined debtors to continue to conceal their assets without crossing the line to criminal fraud or provable perjury. Our favorite story is of a defendant who was asked about cash assets in his bank account (none), his stock market accounts (none), his home (none), his car (none), his office (none), and so on. After the plaintiff had given up on discovering cash, the defendant revealed to a friend that he sat through the entire deposition with more than $10,000 in cash in his pocket. While we can think of a number of ways to frame the question to reveal that fact, we note that the attorney conducting the deposition was a good attorney who was not quite as careful as the defendant.

Even if the judgment creditor discovers the location of the assets, the assets may not remain stationary. The debtor compelled to reveal their location may move them before the judgment creditor can get the sheriff to respond. Recall that the money in The Fast Lane's checking account disappeared just one step ahead of the sheriff. Debtors who plan a little more in advance can transfer title to others, move assets out of the jurisdiction, or consume them. All states have adopted laws authorizing the courts to void debtors' "fraudulent transfers" in actions brought by creditors. The study of these laws is beyond the scope of this book. For now it is enough to know that use of these laws is expensive and the laws themselves are relatively ineffective. If, for example, a debtor sells its property to a bona fide purchaser for value and disperses the proceeds in numerous transactions, that value is probably beyond the creditor's reach.

A creditor who has filed suit against the debtor to collect an unsecured debt may be eligible for a "provisional remedy" even before obtaining a judgment. If, for example, the debtor is fraudulently disposing of its property during the lawsuit, the creditor may have the right to an immediate "attachment" of whatever property the debtor still has. But access to this remedy is sharply limited by the constitutional requirements of due process and, in most states, by statutory prerequisites to issuance of a prejudgment writ of attachment.

When debtors refuse to answer questions during discovery, they can be subject to contempt sanctions. If they lie, they can be charged with perjury. But, in fact, few creditors consider it worth it to pursue these remedies and many prosecutors are reluctant to employ them against debtors anyway.

To employ any of the remedies discussed here, creditors typically face many of the information and control problems previously discussed. And the practical problems of finding the debtor or the debtor's property can be overwhelming. When the debtor disappears and the creditor discovers that the assets it has been chasing were the subject of a wire transfer of money to a corporation in the Bahamas, that is probably the end of the game.

Even if the debtor does not deliberately attempt to defeat the creditor's collection effort, the creditor's task may be complex. The creditor may obtain a judgment and begin enforcement procedures only to discover that the debtor has moved to another state. Because a money judgment can be enforced only in the state where rendered, the creditor must establish the judgment in the destination state before invoking the enforcement procedures of that state. If the debtor moves out of the United States, the creditor's task may be even more difficult.

Until the sheriff arrives to levy on a debtor's assets, the debtor can continue to transact business. Without violating any law, the debtor may lose the assets in business operations, exchange them for other assets of reasonably equivalent value, or apply them to the payment of other bona fide debts. It is not fraudulent for a debtor to pay one of its creditors, even if the effect is to leave nothing for others, so long as the debtor does not make the payment for the purpose of defrauding the others. Such a payment is referred to as a *preference*. Absent the filing of a bankruptcy case, once such a payment is made, it is irreversible.

Exemption statutes may provide yet another impediment to collection of the judgment debt. These statutes, which exist in all 50 states, prevent the sheriff from seizing certain property under a writ of execution. The property is said to be *exempt* from the remedies available to unsecured creditors.

The content of the statutes vary from state to state, but many of the recurring themes are present in the Wisconsin statutes that follow.

Wisconsin Statutes Annotated

(2005)

§815.18   PROPERTY EXEMPT FROM EXECUTION

(1) This section shall be construed to secure its full benefit to debtors and to advance the humane purpose of preserving to debtors and their dependents the

means of obtaining a livelihood, the enjoyment of property necessary to sustain life and the opportunity to avoid becoming public charges.

(2) In this section:

(c) "Debtor" means an individual. "Debtor" does not include an association, corporation, partnership, cooperative or political body. . . .

(e) "Depository account" means [an] account maintained with a bank, credit union, insurance company, savings bank, . . . or like organization.

(f) "Equipment" means goods used or bought for use primarily in a business, including farming and a profession. . . .

(h) "Exempt" means free from any lien obtained by judicial proceedings and is not liable to seizure or sale on execution or on any provisional or final process issued from any court, or any proceedings in aid of court process. . . .

(3) The debtor's interest in or right to receive the following property is exempt. . . .

(a) *Provisions for burial.* Cemetery lots, aboveground burial facilities, burial monuments, tombstones, coffins or other articles for the burial of the dead owned by the debtor and intended for the burial of the debtor or the debtor's family.

(b) *Business and farm property.* Equipment, inventory, farm products and professional books used in the business of the debtor or the business of a dependent of the debtor, not to exceed $7,500 in aggregate value. . . .

(d) *Consumer goods.* Household goods and furnishings, wearing apparel, keepsakes, jewelry and other articles of personal adornment, appliances, books, musical instruments, firearms, sporting goods, animals or other tangible personal property held primarily for the personal, family or household use of the debtor or a dependent of the debtor, not to exceed $5,000 in aggregate value. . . .

(g) *Motor vehicles.* Motor vehicles not to exceed $1,200 in aggregate value. Any unused amount of the aggregate value from paragraph (d) may be added to this exemption to increase the aggregate exempt value of motor vehicles under this paragraph.

(h) *Net income.* Seventy-five percent of the debtor's net income for each one week pay period. The benefits of this exemption are limited to the extent reasonably necessary for the support of the debtor and the debtor's dependents, but to not less than 30 times the greater of the state or federal minimum wage. . . .

(k) *Depository accounts.* Depository accounts in the aggregate value of $1,000. . . .

(6)(a) A debtor shall affirmatively claim an exemption or select specific property in which to claim an exemption. The debtor may make the claim at the time of seizure of property or within a reasonable time after the seizure, but shall make the claim prior to the disposition of the property by sale or by court order. . . . The debtor or a person acting on the debtor's behalf shall make any required affirmative claim, either orally or in writing, to the creditor, the creditor's attorney or the officer seeking to impose a lien by court action upon the property in which the exemption is claimed. A debtor waives his or her exemption rights by failing to follow the procedure under this paragraph. A contractual waiver of exemption rights by any debtor before judgment on the claim is void. . . .

(9) In the case of property that is partially exempt, the debtor or any person acting on the debtor's behalf is entitled to claim the exempt portion of property. The exempt portion claimed shall be set apart for the debtor . . . and the nonex-

empt portion shall be subject to a creditor's claim. If partially exempt property is indivisible, the property may be sold and the exempt value of the property paid to the debtor....

(12) No property otherwise exempt may be claimed as exempt in any proceeding brought by any person to recover the whole or part of the purchase price of the property or against the claim or interest of a holder of a security interest ... mortgage or any consensual or statutory lien.

§815.20 HOMESTEAD EXEMPTION DEFINITION

(1) An exempt homestead as defined in §990.01(14) selected by a resident owner and occupied by him or her shall be exempt from execution, from the lien of every judgment and from liability for the debts of the owner to the amount of $40,000, except mortgages, laborers', mechanics' and purchase money liens and taxes and except as otherwise provided.

§990.01

(14) "Exempt homestead" means the dwelling, including a building, condominium, mobile home, house trailer or cooperative, and so much of the land surrounding it as is reasonably necessary for its use as a home, but not less than 0.25 acre, if available, and not exceeding 40 acres, within the limitation as to value under §815.20....

A few states recognize homestead exemptions without dollar limitation, with the result that houses and the surrounding real estate worth millions of dollars can qualify. Some recognize no homestead exemption at all. Most, like Wisconsin, recognize a homestead exemption, but impose a dollar limit.

Both state and federal law protect debtors' wages. Federal statutes provide that a minimum of 75 percent of debtors' earnings from personal services will generally be exempt in all states. 15 U.S.C.A. §1671. Some states exempt a greater percentage of earnings from personal services, and a few, including Florida (for the head of a household only), Texas, and Pennsylvania, exempt all earnings from personal services. State and federal laws exempt most pensions and retirement accounts.

In short, exemption laws prevent creditors from taking many of the most valuable and easy-to-locate assets that debtors own. Such laws also protect individual debtors, in part by keeping households intact and preventing some debtors from becoming charges of the state. The course on debtors' and creditors' rights examines exemption laws in more detail.

D. Is the Law Serious About Collecting Unsecured Debts?

The law governing the enforcement of unsecured legal obligations affects a wide spectrum of rights. In contract law, tort law, antitrust law, and a long list of other areas, rights and liabilities are enforced only through the imposition of civil liability in the form of unsecured money judgments. Yet, as we have seen in this assignment, the mechanisms for the enforcement of civil judgments for money damages are often ineffective.

Legal mechanisms are available for the enforcement of obligations that the law takes seriously. Courts can order those subject to their jurisdiction to meet their legal obligations and imprison them if they refuse to comply. The law authorizes courts to do so in regard to many obligations, including the obligation to pay alimony or child support, the obligation to respect the property of others by not trespassing or stealing, and the obligation to perform under a contract to sell real property. But they do not include judgments for personal injuries, the wages of working people, or the breaches of most kinds of contracts. The availability of effective remedies to enforce particular rights reflects to some degree the relative values society places on those rights. Whether enforcement of a particular right is civil or criminal, monetary or equitable, summary or with great delay, is an important measure of the right itself. It is not surprising to observe that criminal remedies are reserved for violation of rights we hold more dear than mere money obligations. It may be somewhat more surprising, however, to discover that some civil creditors have collection rights superior to those of others. Thus, the study of the mechanisms for the enforcement of debt, both unsecured and secured, can provide insight into the social values reflected in law.

Problem Set 43

43.1. A year ago, the local Fun Furniture Outlet was having a liquidation sale. Lisa Charney wanted to buy some redwood lawn furniture but didn't have the cash. Her friend and neighbor, Jeffrey Reed, lent $1,000 to Lisa. Jeff and Lisa were good friends, and Lisa said she would pay him back in a couple of months. When she did not, Jeff's reminders became increasingly acrimonious. Now Lisa and Jeff haven't spoken for two months, and she still hasn't paid anything.

Jeff is a journeyman electrician whose union has legal insurance entitling Jeff to four hours of consultation a year with your firm. Jeff came in today, showed you Lisa's signed "I.O.U." for the loan, and asked if he could just go over and take the lawn furniture Lisa had purchased with his money. The furniture is out in the backyard, and he says it looks really nice. Jeff is sure it is worth less than the amount Lisa owes him, but he says he'd be satisfied if he got it. What do you tell him?

43.2.   The following debt collection story appeared in David Margolick's *New York Times* column, "At the Bar":

> Jonesport, Me. . . .
>
> Earlier this sumer Bert S. Look, whose family has been catching crustaceans out of this sleepy fishing village on the eastern end of the Maine coast since 1910, was the picture of frustration. For months, he has since explained, a local seafood wholesaler named John Kostandin had owed him nearly $30,000, and he was powerless to make him pay. The usual legal remedies, he believed, were worthless.
>
> "I could have gone through nine million district attorneys and nine million lawyers and I wouldn't have gotten anything," Mr. Look said. "I was willing to try anything nonviolent." So, in the best tradition of Maine lobstermen, who cut the lines on the traps of their disreputable competitors, he resorted to self-help. Actually, he had one helper: a self-styled professional prankster known only as "Deep Homard." (Homard is French for lobster.)
>
> In June, Homard, posing as a friend of [horror novelist Stephen King], called Mr. Kostandin. He said that the novelist, who lives nearby in Bangor, needed three-and-a-half tons of lobsters for his annual lobster bake. Of course, the lobsters would end up with Mr. Look rather than Mr. King; at slightly more than $4 a pound, they would neatly cover Mr. Kostandin's tab to Mr. Look. . . .
>
> Apparently enticed by meeting Mr. King — and the prospect of catering future King shindigs — Mr. Kostandin, accompanied by his wife and 78 crates of live lobsters, drove to Dysert's Truck Stop in Hermon, where they were told, Mr. King would meet them. Told there that the novelist had been detained, Mr. Kostandin left the lobsters behind and headed, via a limousine provided by Mr. Look, for a purported rendezvous with the author at the Panda Garden, a Chinese restaurant in Bangor. By the time he deduced that he had been had, Mr. Look had the lobsters, which he promptly sold.

David Margolick, At the Bar, N.Y. Times, Sept. 17, 1993, at B8 col. 1. Mr. Look got only $19,000 for the lobsters. He comes to you for legal representation in collecting the rest. Your first call was to Stephen King. Although the conversation was very scary, it is clear that King doesn't want to be involved. What do we do next?

43.3.   Karen Benning is a successful dentist who was approached last year to lend money to a day care center that wanted to expand. She checked into the center thoroughly and saw that they had a good location, a friendly staff, few outstanding debts, and reasonable profit projections. They had substantial capital assets, including an elaborate network of teaching computers and child-sized exercise equipment. She made a $10,000 loan to the owner, Ted Knopf, repayable in quarterly installments over five years, at prime plus five points.

The center has not missed a quarterly payment. But Benning has heard some very bad reports from a friend who used to have a child in the center, so she renewed her investigations. Benning sees that the center has moved to a new, more "upscale" location that is far more expensive. Their prices are higher, forcing out more than a third of their old customers. Because the new location is farther away from public transportation, many of their old employees have left. Many of the new employees are temps, resulting in high turnover rates and low employee morale. The person now in charge is the brother of the owner, a foul-tempered man who barks orders and frightens the children. Knopf sold the best of the computers and exercise equipment to finance the move and to pay himself and his brother during the start-up phase at the new location. The business is much deeper in debt and is behind on rent and utility payments. Benning is unsure whether the business will even survive, much less whether it will pay her.

Benning consults you for help. She feels sure the business could make a profit if it were properly run. She has heard that the old manager Knopf fired to make room for the brother would be pleased to return. Benning wants to be repaid in full and she is worried. What do you advise?

43.4. Six months have passed since the preceding problem. The day care center has folded and you have obtained a default judgment against its owner, Ted Knopf, for more than $12,000 in past due interest and principal on Benning's loan. Benning wants to know when she will be paid. What do *you* need to know to answer her question? What are the possible sources of that information? If Knopf doesn't pay the judgment, how will you collect it? What do you think of Benning's suggestion that you send the sheriff to levy on the day care center equipment?

43.5. Assume now that Knopf is living in Wisconsin. During his deposition, Knopf testifies that he owns the following property, all free and clear of any liens or security interests:

a. A four-year-old Toyota automobile worth $6,000

b. A house that he recently inherited from his mother, estimated to be worth about $35,000

c. The equipment from the day care center, which has a resale value of about $10,000

d. A bank account with a current balance of $2,265.92

What can the sheriff take from him to satisfy your judgment? Is there any hurry in getting the sheriff to do that? Can you move fast enough?

43.6. During a deposition in aid of execution, you, as Benning's lawyer, asked Knopf whether anyone owed him (Knopf) any money. Knopf hesitated briefly in a way that made you suspicious, and then answered "Not that I can remember." You'd like to jog his memory, or maybe even set up a perjury charge, by following up with some questions that suggest specific kinds of debts that might be owing to him. What questions might you ask? If he does remember a debt, such as a bank account, how and when will you pursue that asset further?

Assignment 44: Security and Foreclosure

A. The Nature of Security

The law provides for enforcement of money obligations. But, as should be apparent from Assignment 43, the legal remedies of unsecured creditors are cumbersome, expensive, and problematic in terms of what they will yield. The financial institutions that make car loans, home loans, and most business loans can and do insist on having a set of collection rights considerably more effective than the baseline set of collection rights discussed in the preceding assignment.

This more effective set of collection rights is known as a *lien*. The Bankruptcy Code, which is the ultimate arbiter of the rights of debtors and creditors when one of the parties petitions for bankruptcy, accurately describes a lien as "a charge against or an interest in property to secure payment of a debt or performance of an obligation." Bankr. Code §101 (definition of "lien"). Thus, a lien is a relationship between particular property (the *collateral*) and a particular debt or obligation. The general nature of the relationship is that if the debt is not paid when due, the creditor can compel the application of the value of the collateral to payment of the debt. The process by which the creditor does this is called *foreclosure*.

The most common form of lien is the *security interest*. Used in its broadest sense, that term encompasses any lien created by contract between debtor and creditor. It includes real estate mortgages and deeds of trust as well as the security interests in personal property created under Article 9 of the Uniform Commercial Code. See Bankr. Code §101 (definitions of "security agreement," "security interest," and "lien"; Internal Revenue Code §6323(h)(1)).

Although security interests will be our primary focus in the remainder of this book, you will also encounter two types of nonconsensual liens: (1) liens granted by statute, such as mechanic's liens (*statutory liens*) and (2) liens obtained by unsecured creditors through judicial process (*judicial liens*).

In Part One of this book, we discuss security interests in the simplest situations — that is, where only the interests of a debtor and a single creditor are involved. We look first at the remedies available to a secured creditor, and then we turn to what a creditor must do to become secured. Later, in Part Two, we will take up the question of priorities — the relative rights of creditors competing for the same collateral.

What property will serve as collateral for a security interest depends on custom and the needs of the particular parties. When a car dealer lends the money to purchase a car, the car will usually be the collateral. When a business borrows, it might grant a security interest in its equipment, its inventory, its accounts receivable or any or all other property it may own. Virtually anything recognized as property can serve as collateral. (Spouses and children won't work, but your dog or your parakeet will.) The usefulness of property as collateral will ultimately depend on (1) how much value the creditor can extract from it after default (will it bring anything at resale?), and (2) how much leverage the creditor can derive from the creditor's ability to deprive the debtor of the property (how much will the debtor be willing and able to pay to keep it?).

The agreement that creates the security interest may impose obligations on the debtor that apply even in the absence of default. (For the curious, there is an example of a security agreement in Assignment 56 of this book. Peek now or save it for later.) The security interest itself has effect only in the event of the debtor's default. The default may be a failure to pay the debt or a failure to comply with some other provision of the security agreement. Because the rights of the holder of a security interest are principally rights that take effect after default, a security interest can be described as a right in property that is contingent on nonpayment of a debt. That is, the right to enforce the debt against the property that serves as collateral is contingent upon the occurrence of a default. The typical methods of enforcement lead to a sale of the collateral and payment of as much of the debt as possible from the proceeds of sale.

The recognition of enhanced collection rights for secured creditors necessarily diminishes the effectiveness of the collection rights of general unsecured creditors. For example, if Creditor *A* has a security interest in the debtor's car that exceeds the entire value of the car, the value of the car will not be available to satisfy unsecured Creditor *B*'s execution. The ease with which a debtor can grant security interests virtually assures that by the time a debtor is in serious financial difficulty, an unsecured creditor will have difficulty finding property to sell to satisfy its debt. In essence, unsecured creditors get only what is left after provisions have been made for secured creditors. In contested cases, that is usually nothing. Having security, or lacking it, is a key attribute of the relationship between debtors and their creditors.

Considering the disadvantages inherent in being an unsecured creditor, one might wonder why anyone assumes that role. Some creditors may prefer unsecured status because they are compensated by receiving a higher rate of interest. (This is the standard explanation given by economists who study credit.) Others, such as the victim of a car accident or an employee with an action for wrongful discharge, do not choose the role of unsecured creditor; they are thrown into it without the opportunity to negotiate. Some unsecured creditors agree to a contract that leaves them unsecured without realizing that fact or without recognizing its importance. For example, if you have ever prepaid rent on an apartment or paid for an airline ticket (even if you charged it to your credit card), you agreed to accept unsecured status in the event the landlord did not provide the apartment or the airline did not provide the flight. More than a few people have discovered their unsecured status when an airline stopped flying or a landlord went broke.

Others may understand the implications of assuming unsecured status, but be constrained by business custom and practice from seeking secured status. Consider, for example, the law student who accepts a job with a large law firm. Along with the job, the student accepts the status of an unsecured creditor for wages, accrued benefits, and other obligations. To request security for those obligations would be an egregious social error. The problem is not just that the law student lacks bargaining leverage; the inability to negotiate for security applies even to the law student who is in great demand, and the inability persists even if the student were willing to accept a much lower salary. In fact, even if the law firm *wanted* to accede to a job applicant's demand for security, to do so probably would breach the firm's contracts with its bank lenders. Who gets security is as much a matter of established custom as of economics.

Why does the law permit a debtor to grant one creditor collection rights superior to those of another? There are a number of competing economic explanations for this harsh economic inequality, as well as some explanations rooted in custom and long-standing business practice. We think the principal reason is the tremendous complexity the law would have encountered if it had attempted to ban security. Were security banned, debtors temporarily short of cash still would have been able to sell their property to get the cash they needed. They still would have been able to buy it back later when they had the cash. At the same time, debtors would have been unable to grant a lesser right — a right in the buyer/secured creditor to keep the property contingent on the debtor's nonpayment of a debt. The following story is just for fun, but it illustrates that there is little difference between failing to buy back property one previously sold and failure to pay a secured debt. As you read the story, think about how the chancellor should have decided the cases brought before him if he had wished to prohibit the use of property as security and how future lenders and borrowers might have reacted to those decisions.

The Invention of Security: A Pseudo History

The place is England. The time is the Middle Ages. Existing legal concepts include the ownership of property, the ability to transfer it, and the ability to contract for such transfers.

Debord is the owner of Blackacre and is in need of a loan. His neighbor, Creech, is willing to make the $100 loan, but wants to be *certain* he* will be repaid. Debord and Creech intend to create what we today call a security interest, but our story opens long before the courts recognized such a device.

To maximize the likelihood that the courts would give effect to their intention without a recognized legal device, Creech and Debord expressed their deal using legal concepts that were familiar to the courts. Their deal had three parts:

True intent of Debord and Creech	*Legal form they adopted*
1. Debord grants Creech a security interest in Blackacre	1. Debord sells and deeds Blackacre to Creech
2. Creech lends $100 to Debord	2. Creech pays $100 purchase price for Blackacre
3. Debord agrees to repay the loan with $10 interest, on March 1	3. Creech grants Debord an option to purchase Blackacre from Creech on March 1 for $110

*At that time in history, only men were allowed to engage in these transactions.

Because Blackacre was worth $500, once this transaction was in place Creech could be "secure" in the knowledge that the loan would almost certainly be repaid. Even if it were not, he would have something even more valuable, the ownership of Blackacre. Assuming he repaid the loan on time, it cost Debord nothing to provide Creech with this security. The result was to enable the two of them to get together on a loan that might otherwise not have been made.

The first time they made this deal, matters went smoothly. Debord repaid the loan on time and Creech reconveyed Blackacre. But the second time they did it, Debord was late with the payment. When he tendered the money on March 15, Creech refused to take it and refused to reconvey Blackacre. "You breached the deal, and I'm keeping the land," he said with some delight. The law governing the form in which they had put their transaction was on Creech's side. "Time was of the essence" in an option contract, and if the buyer did not pay the purchase price at the agreed time, the buyer lost the right to purchase.

With no remedy at law, Debord went to the chancellor for "equity." He explained the true intention of the deal he had made with Creech and the position Creech was now taking. He emphasized that unless the chancellor granted relief, his $500 property would be forfeited for failure to repay a $100 loan. Although the documents supported Creech's position, the chancellor granted relief. Reciting the maxims (maxims were very big in the Middle Ages) that "Equity abhors a forfeiture" and "Equity looks to substance over form," he ordered that Debord could "redeem" Blackacre by repaying the loan with interest and compensating Creech for any damages sustained by the delay. Debord did so, and never did business with Creech again.

Despite Creech's loss before the chancellor, his experience with secured lending to this point had not been all that bad. True, the Chancellor had dashed his dream of picking up Blackacre for $100. In Debord v. Creech the chancellor had established that even slow-paying debtors had an equitable right to redeem their property. But the chancellor had conditioned this "equity of redemption" on payment in full, including Creech's attorneys' fees. Security worked.

Creech continued to make loans and continued to put them in the form of a "deed absolute" combined with an option to purchase. Inevitably, he ran into a problem. Davenport, another of Creech's borrowers, failed to repay a loan secured by Greenacre. Months passed. Creech had possession of Greenacre and wanted to spruce it up and sell it to another buyer. But what if Davenport later exercised his equity of redemption? How long did Creech have to wait for his title to Greenacre to be clear of the equity of redemption? Creech asked his lawyer. "No way to know," the lawyer said, "short of asking the chancellor." The lawyer prepared a petition asking the chancellor to "foreclose" Davenport's equity of redemption. That petition was the first mortgage foreclosure.

When Creech and his lawyer went before the chancellor, Davenport was there. Davenport made the usual arguments about forfeiture and told the same old stories about how he was just about to come up with the money to redeem. By today's standards, the chancellor was a bleeding-heart liberal. He gave Davenport a continuance, reset the hearing for a date two months away, and expressed his hope that Davenport would redeem before then. Knowing the chancellor, Creech's lawyer feared a string of continuances unless he could persuade the chancellor that Creech's interests were in greater jeopardy than Davenport's.

At the continued hearing, Creech's lawyer presented expert testimony that the value of Greenacre was no greater than the amount of the loan. Even if the chancellor cut off the equity of redemption today, Creech would take a loss. Davenport had no "equity" in Greenacre to protect, said Creech's lawyer, picking up the language the court of equity used to refer to the amount by which the value of the property exceeded the amount of the loans against it. Because of the accruing interest, the lawyer continued, Creech's potential loss grew greater with every passing day. After Creech's lawyer had finished his presentation, Davenport, in a voice choked with emotion, spoke of his many happy years on Greenacre, the little knoll where his dog was buried, and his expert appraisals showing that Greenacre was worth "at least five times" the amount owing on the loan.

The chancellor reflected on the issues and concluded that where the equities now lay depended on the value of Greenacre. Despite his generally liberal beliefs, the chancellor, a very early Renaissance man, was also a staunch believer in the marketplace. Based on that belief, he devised what he considered a very clever, "market-based" solution. The issue of value would be resolved by offering Greenacre for sale. To assure that the sale was fair and open, the chancellor would have a notice posted in the town square, and the sheriff would conduct a sale of Greenacre on the courthouse steps. The highest bidder would get the land free of Davenport's right to redeem. As the chancellor put it, the sale would "cut off the equitable right of redemption." The proceeds from the sale would be used first to repay Creech's loan, thus assuring that Creech would recover whatever value there was in the property, up to the amount of the loan. If the property brought less than the amount owing to Creech, Creech would have to bring his action for the *deficiency* on the law side. If the property brought more, the *surplus* would go to Davenport on the equity side. Because Davenport would get the market value of the property less the amount he owed on the debt, he would suffer no forfeiture.

The sale was held, and Creech v. Davenport was entered in the Year Book. Unfortunately, the amount of the sale price was not recorded. The entries were, however, sufficient to show that the remedies of the parties to a secured transaction had assumed the form they would retain for a millennium.

This story makes several important points about security and foreclosure. First, it illustrates that parties who wish to do so can easily construct the security relationship using the everyday conventions of sale and option to purchase. (Indeed, it might be difficult to permit a debtor like Debord to transfer ownership of property yet prohibit him from transferring mere collection rights relating to the same property.) If the chancellor had refused to recognize the special nature of the sale from Debord to Creech, the sale and option to repurchase would have been valid. Debord could still have entered into this "secured" transaction, but he would not have been protected against forfeiture. To *prevent* these transactions would have required both the chancellor's recognition of the special nature of this sale and some more aggressive action such as, for example, forfeiting the *creditor's* interest.

Second, the story shows that in the hands of clever parties, or their clever lawyers, existing legal forms can be employed in ways unanticipated by the lawmakers. Using nothing but existing concepts of sale and option, Creech and Debord invented security. Such resourcefulness in structuring transactions is common in commercial law. As the lawyers invent new devices, the courts must consider whether to recognize and give effect to them, or whether to deny recognition and wrestle with the consequences. In making their decisions about whether to recognize new devices, courts are often constrained by the practicalities of enforcing the rules they think most desirable from a policy standpoint. Thus the judges are not entirely in control; lawyers play an active role in shaping the law.

Third, in determining which transactions are in the nature of security and must be foreclosed, one cannot rely on the documents. A transaction is in the nature of security if the intent is to provide one party with an interest in the property of another, which interest is contingent upon the nonpayment of a debt. Even if the only document in existence is a deed absolute, the relationship created may be a mortgage. It is truly the substance of what is going on that matters, not the form.

The lesson to be learned from Creech v. Debord is subtle and complex. Real estate foreclosure is time-consuming and expensive. Lawyers and their clients naturally wish to avoid it when possible. The irony is that if the intent of the contract between the parties is to relieve a secured creditor of the necessity to foreclose, the attempt will fail. Regardless of the form in which the parties choose to cast their deal, the law will recast it as a mortgage. The concept is not an easy one to grasp. As is illustrated in the following case, commercial lawyers frequently embarrass themselves by making deals that run afoul of the "intended as security" doctrine.

Basile v. Erhal Holding Corporation

538 N.Y.S.2d 831 (N.Y. App. Div. 1989)

JUDGES: MOLLEN, P.J., THOMPSON, RUBIN and SPATT, JJ., concur. . . .

In 1982, the plaintiff, the owner of property located at 244 Morris Avenue in Peekskill, mortgaged the property to the Erhal Holding Corp. (hereinafter Erhal) in return for a loan at an alleged usurious rate. The plaintiff instituted this action, inter alia, to declare the mortgage null and void on the ground of usury. On June 2, 1986, and June 6, 1986, while the matter was awaiting trial, the parties entered into a stipulation of settlement in open court whereby the plaintiff agreed to execute a mortgage to Erhal in the sum of $101,303.59 together with a deed "in lieu of foreclosure" which would not be recorded by Erhal as long as the plaintiff fulfilled her obligations under the terms and conditions of the mortgage. The mortgage provided, inter alia, that the plaintiff would pay monthly interest payments on the mortgage amount at a rate of 12% per annum for a one-year period; at the end of that period, the entire balance was to become due. The mortgage agreement also included the following provision; "The mortgagor herein has simultaneously executed a deed in lieu of foreclosure which may be recorded by the mortgagee for any default herein."

During the settlement colloquy, the trial court questioned the plaintiff regarding her understanding of the terms of the settlement. At that time, the plaintiff indicated that she understood that if she violated the terms of the mortgage agreement, Erhal could record the deed and become the owner of the subject premises.

The plaintiff subsequently defaulted in several mortgage payments and failed to pay the real estate taxes and fire insurance premiums for the demised premises as provided for in the mortgage agreement. As a result of the plaintiff's default, Erhal recorded the deed in lieu of foreclosure in December 1986. Thereafter, Erhal moved, by order to show cause, for an order declaring that the plaintiff's right of redemption with respect to the property was waived when the mortgage and deed in lieu of foreclosure were executed in June 1986. The plaintiff cross-moved, inter alia, for an order directing Erhal to accept a check in the sum of $101,303.59 plus interest tendered by the plaintiff and to deliver to the plaintiff a satisfaction of mortgage and a deed for the premises, free and clear of all encumbrances.

The Supreme Court granted Erhal's motion and declared that "the plaintiff no longer has any right of redemption of the subject property." The plaintiff's cross motion was denied.

We conclude that the Supreme Court erred in declaring that the plaintiff waived her right of redemption in the demised premises. A deed conveying real property, although absolute on its face, will be considered to be a mortgage when the instrument is executed as security for a debt. The purpose behind this rule was explained in Peugh v. Davis (96 U.S. 332, 336-337):

> It is an established doctrine that a court of equity will treat a deed, absolute in form, as a mortgage, when it is executed as a security for a loan of money. That court looks beyond the terms of the instrument to the real transaction; and when that is shown to be one of security, and not of sale, it will give effect to the actual contract of the parties.... It is also an established doctrine that an equity of redemption is inseparably connected with a mortgage; that is to say, so long as the instrument is one of security, the borrower has in a court of equity a right to redeem the property upon payment of the loan. This right cannot be waived or abandoned by any stipulation of the parties made at the time, even if embodied in the mortgage. This is a doctrine from which a court of equity never deviates (see also Maher v. Alma Realty Co., 70 A.D.2d 931 ["plaintiffs cannot waive their right of redemption even by stipulation in open court"]).

In this case, it is clear that the deed in lieu of foreclosure executed by the plaintiff with the $101,303.59 mortgage was not intended as an absolute conveyance or sale of the property by the plaintiff but rather was intended to be security for the plaintiff's $101,303.59 debt to Erhal. As such, the deed constituted a mortgage and the attempted waiver of the plaintiff's right of redemption in the property in the in-court stipulation of settlement as well as the mortgage agreement was ineffective. Erhal's sole remedy is to institute an action in foreclosure. The plaintiff will have a right to redeem the property at any time prior to the actual sale of the premises by tendering to Erhal the principal and interest due on the mortgage.

The "intended as security" doctrine applies to personal property transactions as well as those involving real property. U.C.C. §9-109(a)(1) provides that Article 9 applies to "any transaction, regardless of its form, that creates a security interest in personal property. . . . " Comment 2 to that section elaborates: "When a security interest is created, this Article applies regardless of the form of the transaction or the name that parties have given to it." For example, assume that Smyrna wants to sell her Buick Skylark to Brodsky. Brodsky wants to take delivery of the car now and pay for it in monthly payments over the course of a year. Smyrna doesn't mind receiving her payments over the course of the year, but neither does she want to be troubled with the formalities of secured credit. Smyrna and Brodsky strike the following deal: Smyrna agrees to sell her car to Brodsky one year from today. The agreement is contingent on Brodsky's paying the purchase price in equal monthly payments over the year. Until Brodsky has finished paying, Smyrna will remain the owner of the Skylark and keep the title in her name. So long as he is current on his payments, Brodsky will have the right to use it. Once he finishes paying, Smyrna will transfer title to him.

Smyrna and Brodsky may think they have invented an ingenious substitute for security. They have not. What they have done is to reinvent security — just as the lawyers and parties in *Basile* did. Article 9 will apply to the transaction. U.C.C. §9-109(a)(1). For the purpose of applying the rules in Article 9, Brodsky is the owner of the Skylark, Smyrna is a secured party, and the contract they have entered into is a security agreement. If Brodsky and Smyrna fail to comply with the Article 9 rules governing their transaction, they will suffer the consequences.

B. Foreclosure Procedure

The procedures for real estate foreclosure differ widely from state to state and with the type of collateral involved. Article 9 provides a uniform procedure for personal property foreclosure that can be very quick and easy, but it also permits secured parties to use judicial foreclosure methods if they prefer.

As you read the following material, be sure to distinguish the foreclosure of a security interest from the taking of possession of collateral. Foreclosure is a process that operates on the ownership of collateral. It transfers ownership from the debtor to the purchaser at the foreclosure sale and cuts off the debtor's right to redeem the collateral. This change in ownership is typically accompanied by a transfer of possession. But the transfer of possession can occur before, during, or after foreclosure. In some cases, it may not occur at all. For example, the secured creditor may foreclose against collateral, purchase it at the foreclosure sale, and lease it back to the debtor who has been in possession all along. Assignment 45 of this book discusses the secured creditor's right to possession and the means by which the secured creditor can get it. Foreclosure operates on ownership, not possession.

1. Judicial Foreclosure

A foreclosure process is referred to as *judicial* if it is accomplished by the entry of a court order. Procedures by which secured creditors can sue for such orders are available in every state. In a judicial foreclosure, a creditor holding a mortgage or security interest typically files a civil action against the debtor. In the complaint, the creditor details the terms of the loan and the nature of the default, and requests that the equity of redemption be "foreclosed." The complaint is served on the debtor and any subordinate lien holders, who then have a period of time (usually 20 days) in which to raise defenses.

Only in rare cases will the debtor have a defense that would preclude foreclosure altogether. But a debtor who seeks a delay can often find some technical defect in the complaint (such as an erroneous calculation of interest) that will at least require amendment and at most require that the case be placed on a trial calendar that is months or years long. Only when such issues have been resolved and the plaintiff has established that it is entitled to foreclose will the court enter a *final judgment of foreclosure.*

Typically, as part of the judgment, the court will set a date for the foreclosure sale. In the large majority of jurisdictions, the method of sale is specified by statute. The statute usually requires that the county sheriff or the clerk of the court conduct the sale. The procedures specified in the statute may be supplemented by the terms of the final judgment. In most jurisdictions, the sales are held at a particular time of day (usually around mid-day) in a particular place (often immediately outside the main door of the courthouse).

The statute typically requires that the sale be advertised beforehand by the person who will conduct it. The advertising may be by posting notices in some public place or by placing one or more advertisements in a newspaper of general circulation. The period for advertising ranges from as little as a week in some jurisdictions to six weeks or more in others. Because the advertising cannot commence until the final judgment has been entered, the advertising period adds to the minimum time in which foreclosure can be accomplished.

On the date fixed for the sale, the sheriff or clerk conducts an auction. Bids are usually announced orally. In most procedures, the highest bidder must immediately pay the entire purchase price to the sheriff or clerk. In some states, the creditor can pay a part of the bid and return with the remainder of the money in an agreed upon time (typically a day or two). Upon receipt of the money, the sheriff or clerk certifies that person to be the highest bidder.

Under the procedures of most jurisdictions, a foreclosure sale must be *confirmed* by the court. That is, after the auction is held, parties to the mortgage foreclosure case have some period of time in which they can object to the manner in which it was actually conducted. Typical objections are that the sale was not advertised strictly in accord with the final judgment and the applicable statutes, the auction was not held in precisely the location advertised, someone (real or hypothetical) was prevented from attending the sale or bidding, some arrangement between interested parties "chilled" the bidding, or the highest bid was grossly inadequate. In some jurisdictions there will be a confirmation hearing even if no objections have been filed; in others, the court will enter the order after the time for filing objections has expired. The process of confirming the sale also adds to the minimum time in which foreclosure can be accomplished.

After the confirmation order has been entered and the time for appeal has expired, the sheriff or clerk disburses the sale proceeds. If the amount is greater than that owed to the foreclosing creditor, the *surplus* is distributed first to the holders of junior liens or mortgages and then to the debtor. If, as is far more common, the amount realized from the sale is less than the amount owed the foreclosing creditor, the foreclosing creditor can request a judgment for the *deficiency*. If, for example, the property sold for $25,000 but the creditor was owed $40,000, the creditor could sue for a $15,000 deficiency. In many jurisdictions, antideficiency laws prohibit the granting of deficiency judgments in particular kinds of cases or give the court discretion to deny them. (Discussed in Assignment 46.)

Ordinarily, the debtor will remain in possession of the mortgaged premises until the sale has been confirmed by the court. The purchaser is then entitled to possession. If the debtor will not surrender the premises, the purchaser is entitled to a *writ of assistance*, which in some states is known as a *writ of possession*. The writ of assistance directs the sheriff to remove the debtor from the premises and put the purchaser in possession. The process is much like that for a levy under a writ of execution.

The large majority of foreclosures are unopposed, and the debtors often abandon the premises before the sheriff comes to remove them. But a substantial minority of debtors resist at some or all stages of the proceedings. To avoid the foreclosure, they may raise a number of defenses. They may object to the sale, sometimes on the basis of irregularities they themselves played a part in causing. They may appeal the courts' rulings. They may refuse to surrender the premises after they are sold. Usually, their purpose is to delay the proceedings until they can get the money necessary to redeem the property or reinstate the mortgage. Sometimes they simply try to stay in the property as long as they can, with no further plan in mind.

Farm Credit of St. Paul v. Stedman, 449 N.W.2d 562 (N.D. 1989), illustrates both the determination and the effectiveness with which debtors may resist foreclosure. The Stedmans mortgaged their 2,500-acre farm in Foster County to Federal Land Bank of Saint Paul for a $525,000 loan. After the Stedmans defaulted on their loan payments, the Federal Land Bank foreclosed the mortgage. The foreclosure judgment was entered in June 1984. Through the filing of bankruptcy cases, the Stedmans delayed the sheriff's sale until some time in 1988. At that time, the sheriff sold the farm to the Farm Credit Bank of St. Paul. The Stedmans refused to vacate the farm, forcing the Bank to sue to evict them. The Stedmans did not defend the eviction case and the court entered a default judgment of eviction on December 15, 1988. After the default judgment was entered, the Stedmans swung back into action. Representing themselves after the resignation of their attorney, they raised several frivolous defenses to the eviction. The judgment was amended slightly on January 17, 1989. On March 8, the Bank moved for a writ of assistance to get possession, and the trial court set a hearing on the motion for March 28. Before the hearing could be held, the Stedmans appealed from the amended judgment of eviction.

Following their appeal, the Stedmans filed a flurry of documents seeking to stay the judgment of eviction. When both the trial court and the Supreme Court of North Dakota denied relief, the Stedmans obtained further delay by filing another bankruptcy case.

With the bankruptcy case disposed of, the Stedmans argued four issues before the Supreme Court of North Dakota. Among them was the claim that the writ of assistance issued by the trial court to enforce the eviction judgment violated the Fourth Amendment to the U.S. Constitution, which prohibits unreasonable searches and seizures. In its opinion, the Supreme Court of North Dakota pointed out that the writ of assistance used for searches in colonial days and which were outlawed by the Fourth Amendment had nothing in common with the writs of assistance used to enforce judgments of eviction except the name.

On December 20, 1989, five years and six months after the trial court entered judgment of foreclosure and five days before Christmas, the Supreme Court of North Dakota affirmed the judgment of eviction. That would seem to exhaust the Stedmans' defenses and pave the way for the sheriff to physically remove them from the farm property, but with debtors as determined as the Stedmans, we wonder even about that.

Statutes in some states mandate delays or waiting periods in addition to those the debtor can gain by defending the action. Consider, for example, the following Wisconsin statutes:

Wisconsin Statutes Annotated

(2005)

§846.10 FORECLOSURE....

(2) No sale involving a one- to four-family residence that is owner-occupied at the commencement of the foreclosure action, a farm, a church or a tax-exempt nonprofit charitable organization may be held until the expiration of 12 months from the date when judgment is entered, except a sale under §846.101.... Sales under foreclosure of mortgages given by any railroad corporation may be made immediately after the rendition of the judgment.

§846.101 FORECLOSURE WITHOUT DEFICIENCY; 20-ACRE PARCELS

(1) If the mortgagor has agreed in writing at the time of the execution of the mortgage to the provisions of this section, and the foreclosure action involves a one- to four-family residence that is owner-occupied at the commencement of the action, a farm, a church or a tax-exempt charitable organization, the plaintiff in a foreclosure action of a mortgage on real estate of 20 acres or less ... may elect by express allegation in the complaint to waive judgment for any deficiency which may remain due to the plaintiff after sale of the mortgaged premises against every party who is personally liable for the debt secured by the mortgage, and to consent that the mortgagor, unless he or she abandons the property, may remain in possession of the mortgaged property and be entitled to all rents, issues and profits therefrom to the date of confirmation of the sale by the court.

(2) When plaintiff so elects, judgment shall be entered as provided in this chapter, except that no judgment for deficiency may be ordered therein nor separately rendered against any party who is personally liable for the debt secured by the

mortgage and the sale of such mortgaged premises shall be made upon the expiration of 6 months from the date when such judgment is entered. . . .

The existence of statutes such as these demonstrates that the delay in the procedure for judicial foreclosure is not entirely inadvertent. Particularly in farming regions of the United States, there is a strong populist tradition in which the image of the foreclosing lender is that of the cold, calculating bank seeking a windfall through the debtor's default, while the image of the defending debtor is that of the victim struggling to keep a home and often a means of livelihood. Although it would be easy to make mortgage foreclosure more efficient, for those who make the laws in many states, the perceived fairness of the system is of greater concern.

With the cooperation of the debtor after default, a secured creditor may be able to avoid the necessity to foreclose. If there are no other liens or interests in the collateral, the debtor can simply transfer the property to the creditor by means of a *deed in lieu of foreclosure*. Such a deed does not "clog the equity of redemption" if it immediately extinguishes the mortgage and the underlying mortgage debt. Creditors sometimes persuade the debtor to grant a deed in lieu of foreclosure by persuading the debtor that it is better to lose the house now and have no further liability than to lose the house later and be liable for a deficiency. In some cases, creditors persuade debtors to surrender the property by paying the debtors an additional sum of money — in effect, purchasing the debtors' equity of redemption.

2.   Power of Sale Foreclosure

About 25 states permit the mortgage lender and borrower to opt for a quicker, simpler method of foreclosure against real property. They do so by including in the security agreement a *power of sale*. In some of these states, the security agreement will be in the traditional form of a *mortgage*; in others, including California, it will be in the form of a *deed of trust*. The deed of trust states in essence that the collateral will be held in trust by the creditor or a third party such as a bank or title company. The borrower agrees that in the event of default, the trustee can sell the property and pay the loan from the proceeds of sale. Because the purpose of this arrangement is to secure payment of the loan, the law regards it not as an actual trust but as simply another form of security interest.

Foreclosure is still necessary when the creditor has a power of sale, but it can be accomplished through a procedure that does not include filing a lawsuit. For example, under California law, upon default under a mortgage or deed of trust containing a power of sale, the creditor can record in the public records a notice setting forth the nature of the debtor's default and the creditor's election to sell the property. If the debtor does not cure the default within 90 days, the creditor can set a time and place for sale, advertise it for 20 days, and then sell the property at auction. Pursuant to the power of sale contained in the deed of trust, the trustee conveys title to the purchaser at auction. The sale forecloses the debtor's right to redeem.

The primary purpose for permitting power of sale as an alternative means of foreclosure is to avoid the expense and delay of litigation. But even a power-of-sale foreclosure may end up in court. If the debtor refuses to surrender possession after the sale, the purchaser must sue for it. The cause of action may be for unlawful detainer, ejectment, or eviction. The debtor who has defenses to the foreclosure can defend that action or bring the debtor's own action to enjoin the sale or, if it has already been held, to set it aside. In some states the debtor can also bring a tort action for *wrongful sale*. In some states the secured creditor can sue for a deficiency judgment after the sale has been held, but others prohibit deficiency judgments when the foreclosure is by power of sale.

3. U.C.C. Foreclosure by Sale

The process by which a secured creditor forecloses a security interest in personal property is much simpler than the corresponding process for real property. The difference results largely from historical accident. The law and traditions of real estate foreclosure developed at an earlier time, when the lending of money was considered not quite so respectable as it is today. Restrictions placed on real estate foreclosure during that era have survived, but those restrictions were not extended to the later-developing process of personal property foreclosure.

The differences in procedures for real and personal property foreclosure may also reflect underlying assumptions about what really hurts: Some may feel that the loss of a home or family farm tears the social fabric in a way that repossession of a car does not. The law may reflect an assumption that greater value, social stability, and future wealth are tied up in the ownership of real property. Whether those assumptions are true today is questionable, but the legal differences persist.

Article 9 of the Uniform Commercial Code governs the foreclosure of security interests in personal property. It provides that after default, the secured party may sell, lease, license, or otherwise dispose of any or all of the collateral. U.C.C. §9-610(a). That sale or disposition itself forecloses the debtor's right to redeem the property. U.C.C. §9-623. It extinguishes the creditor's security interest in the collateral and transfers to the purchaser all of the debtor's rights in the collateral. U.C.C. §9-617(a). Alternatively, if the creditor so chooses, it may foreclose by any available judicial procedure. U.C.C. §9-601(a).

Problem Set 44

44.1. In a parallel universe, you are again pursuing Ted Knopf from Problem 43.5 in Wisconsin to recover Karen Benning's $10,000. This time, however, Benning had the foresight to get Knopf to sign a security agreement taking the following property as security. As in Problem 43.5, Knopf owns the property free and clear of any liens or security interests other than

Benning's. Which of the following items can Benning reach through foreclosure of her security interest?

    a.   A four-year-old Toyota automobile worth $6,000.

    b.   A house that Knopf recently inherited from his mother, estimated to be worth about $35,000.

    c.   Knopf still owns the equipment from the day care center, which has a resale value of about $10,000.

    d.   A bank account containing $2,265.92.

See Wisconsin Statutes §815.18, §815.20, and §990.01(14), reproduced in Assignment 43.

    44.2.   Bonnie Brezhnev runs a used-car lot in a low-income neighborhood. Even with cheap prices and low payments, she ends up repossessing a lot of cars. To ease the administrative burden, Bonnie plans to begin leasing the cars rather than selling them. That is, on a car she currently would sell for $5,000, no money down, with interest at 18 percent per annum, the payments would be $180.77 for three years. Instead, Bonnie proposes to lease the same car for $180.77 per month and offer the lessee an option to buy the car at the end of that period for $10. The lease will provide that, on default, Bonnie has the right to terminate the lease and the option to buy. "If a lessee defaults, I'll just repossess the car and put it back on the lot instead of having to go through all that Article 9 rigamarole," Bonnie says. What advice do you give Bonnie about this plan? U.C.C. §9-109(a)(1), Comment 2 to §9-109, and U.C.C. §1-201(37) (Rev. §§1-201(b)(35), 1-203).

    44.3.   The statutes of the state in which you are practicing authorize foreclosure against real property only by judicial process. Your firm is on retainer for the asset recovery department of Enterprise State Bank, and your case load includes more than a dozen foreclosures that are now in process for ESB. The cases are averaging about a year in the courts, producing substantial fees for the firm and good billables for you. Last week, Hiri Mashimoto, your contact at the bank, sent you yet another file, a residential foreclosure against John and Linda O'Hurley. You wrote the usual letter detailing the defaults under the mortgage documents and exercising the bank's right to accelerate.

    a.   Much to your surprise, Linda O'Hurley came to see you today. She explained that about a year ago her husband was diagnosed as having cancer, and that he has been undergoing both chemical and radiation therapy. Given the level of the family's noninsured medical expenses and his reduced workload, the O'Hurleys realize that they can no longer afford the house. She says the house is still worth more than the balance owing on the loan, but her efforts to sell it in a slow market have been unsuccessful. She and her husband are willing to turn the house over to the bank, but they don't want to be sued or to have "a foreclosure on their record." O'Hurley said she is not represented by an attorney, but she would like you to draw up the necessary papers.

    The O'Hurley offer sounds fine to Mashimoto, but he wants to know if there are any "legal problems." Are there? Rule 4.3 of the ABA Model Rules of Professional Conduct provides:

> In dealing on behalf of a client with a person who is not represented by counsel, a lawyer shall not state or imply that the lawyer is disinterested. When the lawyer

knows or reasonably should know that the unrepresented person misunderstands the lawyer's role in the matter, the lawyer shall make reasonable efforts to correct the misunderstanding.

b. What if the O'Hurleys execute the deed today, with an understanding that you will give it back to them if they make up the back payments within 60 days, but that otherwise you will record it?

44.4. Your discussions of the O'Hurley plans got Mr. Mashimoto thinking about other ways to escape the delay and expense of foreclosure. He is back in your office today with an idea for "getting around this foreclosure thing." He proposes that when the bank makes a real estate loan, the bank will require that the borrower sign an irrevocable power of attorney authorizing another bank (the borrower can select the "trustee bank" from an approved list) to execute and deliver a deed in lieu of foreclosure in the event that (1) the debtor is in default under the mortgage and (2) the default continues for a period of 90 days. Mr. Mashimoto realizes that the trustee bank won't sign the deed if the debtor contests the default in any way, and he would still have to foreclose in such case. But he hopes that "at least this will eliminate the expense and delay in the clear cases." Will it?

44.5. Mr. Mashimoto has yet another idea. Many of the bank's commercial loans are made to corporate debtors. He proposes that at the time such a loan is made, in addition to the mortgage against the real estate owned by the corporation, the bank take a security interest in the stock of the corporation and take possession of the share certificates. If there is a default, the bank will foreclose on the stock by conducting a sale pursuant to U.C.C. §§9-610(a), (b), and (c), and 9-604(a)(1). In that sale, the bank can buy the stock for a modest price. The bank will then elect its own employees as directors of the corporation, and the employees as directors will cause the corporation to execute a deed in lieu of foreclosure on the defaulted mortgage. You know that all of this can be done under the corporation law of the state, and someone else in your firm will tend to the securities law issues, but will it work from the debtor-creditor angle? U.C.C. §§9-610(a), (b), and (c), 9-623.

44.6. You are on the staff of state Senator Candy Rowsey. Rowsey sees herself as an activist reformer, and she is concerned about the high cost and excessive litigation involved in mortgage foreclosure. The state currently permits only judicial foreclosure, and the statute has no mandatory waiting periods. But debtors struggling to save their homes or businesses often raise petty issues in the hopes of obtaining delays, much like what happened in the *Stedman* case. Because Rowsey gets her campaign money from the banks and her votes from the farmers, she doesn't want to do anything that will harm either interest, but she is appalled at the waste of money and judicial effort as the parties fight over issues of no real importance. She wants you to come up with something that will be neutral in its effect but more efficient. Any ideas?

Assignment 45: Repossession of Collateral

A. The Importance of Possession Pending Foreclosure

As we discussed in Assignment 44, the period of time from the debtor's default until the debtor's equity of redemption has been irrevocably foreclosed may be as little as a few days or as much as several years. Who will have possession of the property during that time? The answer is complex.

The secured creditor has a number of reasons to want possession pending foreclosure. First, a debtor whose rights in the property are about to be extinguished through foreclosure may have little incentive to preserve and maintain the property. An angry, frustrated debtor who will be judgment-proof after the foreclosure may even decide to destroy it. Collateral is often in poor condition by the time it is repossessed. A quicker recovery will tend to preserve its value. Second, the use of the collateral between the time the right to foreclose accrues and the time it becomes final may have substantial economic value. If the debtor can continue to live in the mortgaged house without making the mortgage payments, for example, the secured creditor will likely lose that value forever. A fight over possession may be a fight over the economic use of the property during the interim period. Third, if the debtor is in possession of the property in the period leading up to the sale, it may be difficult or impossible for prospective purchasers to evaluate the property, thereby depressing the resale price. This problem may be exacerbated if the debtor is uncooperative.

Debtors have a very different view of the equities. They are, after all, being ousted from possession of property they own. They may not yet have had their day in court. Foreclosure is a legal safeguard that exists in part to protect debtors from wrongful repossession. Even though the vast majority of debtors are in default when foreclosure proceedings are filed against them, some are not. If the latter are ousted from possession during the case, a very real loss is imposed on them. Imagine the plight of a family that is evicted from its home or a business that loses the use of its production machinery. The losses may be significant and sometimes irreparable.

Moreover, the creditor who can make a credible threat to dispossess the debtor — even if only temporarily — has extraordinary leverage over the debtor. The creditor can use that leverage to force other changes in the debtor-creditor relationship, to raise the rate of interest, demand additional collateral, or even to require waiver of a cause of action against the creditor for its breach of the loan agreement.

This kind of leverage can flow in the other direction as well. The debtor who can credibly threaten to retain possession of the collateral for a long time, to run up the cost of repossession, or to reduce the value of the collateral before the creditor can gain possession, may be able to take advantage of the creditor in post-default negotiations.

The ability to gain or retain possession during foreclosure can have a value far in excess of the use value of the property during the period in question. The holder of the enforceable right to possession pending foreclosure can terminate the debtor's business or permit it to continue, can control access to the property while bidders are preparing for the foreclosure sale, or can cut off the cash flow that enables the debtor to continue to resist foreclosure.

Many security agreements provide that the creditor has the right to possession immediately upon default, but such a provision is only the starting point for legal analysis. Whether courts will enforce such a provision depends on the circumstances. Even if the secured creditor obtains the *right* to possession from such a provision, the jurisdiction may require that the secured creditor follow particular procedures to obtain that possession. Because the rules for possession of real estate and personal property differ sharply, we discuss them separately.

B.   The Right to Possession Pending Foreclosure — Real Property

1.   The Debtor's Right to Possession During Foreclosure

The general rule is that mortgagees never become entitled to possession of mortgaged real property in their capacity as mortgagees. The debtor remains owner of the property and is entitled to possession of it until the court forecloses the debtor's equity of redemption and the sale is held. Only the purchaser at the foreclosure sale (who may, of course, be the mortgagee) is entitled to dispossess the debtor.

The remedies by which purchasers at foreclosure sales obtain possession vary from state to state. In some jurisdictions, the purchaser must file an action for eviction or ejectment and obtain a court order for removal. In others, the court can issue a writ of possession or writ of assistance on motion by the purchaser. In either event, the purchaser can probably have the sheriff on the scene with uniform and gun in no more than 10 to 20 days after the purchase.

2.   Appointment of a Receiver

While a foreclosure case is pending, any interested party can apply for the appointment of a *receiver* to preserve the value of the collateral. To illustrate, assume that the collateral is an apartment building. Although some of the apartments are occupied by rent-paying tenants, the total rents have been insufficient to enable the debtor to make its mortgage payment. The debtor-landlord has fallen behind in its mortgage payments, and the mortgagee has filed a complaint for foreclosure. The debtor currently sees no way it can redeem the property, but also knows that foreclosure will take several months. The debtor continues to collect the rents from the existing tenants, but does not pay anything to the mortgagee. It spends no money on necessary maintenance for the apartment building. Tenants begin to complain about the appearance of the property and its poor state of repair. Some move out, further reducing the flow of rents and impairing the value of the collateral. In circumstances such as these, the court may grant temporary relief to the mortgagee in the form of the appointment of a receiver.

The receiver will be an officer of the court with fiduciary obligations to all who have an interest in the property. He or she will have the right to collect the rents and use the money to maintain the building, as well as the authority to rent them out as necessary. Typically, the receiver will retain any rents collected in excess of the amounts necessary to maintain the property, pending the outcome of the mortgage foreclosure action.

On the facts of this illustration, appointment of the receiver will cut off temporarily the debtor's cash flow from the collateral until the judgment of foreclosure cuts it off permanently. The mortgagee does not get access to the cash flow directly, but the cash flow will be used in part to maintain the value of the collateral — in effect giving the mortgagee the benefit of it.

A foreclosing mortgagee does not always succeed in winning the appointment of a receiver. Courts rarely appoint receivers unless the terms of the mortgages provide for such appointments. Even when the mortgages so provide, appointment is an equitable remedy that remains in the sound discretion of the court. The creditor must show that under the circumstances of the particular case its remedy at law (foreclosure alone) is inadequate. That usually will be true only when the value of the property is inadequate to satisfy the mortgage debt and the mortgagor is insolvent so that any deficiency judgment will be uncollectible. Only in rare and extreme circumstances do the courts appoint receivers to take possession of owner-occupied residential real estate; a defaulting debtor can nearly always count on retaining possession of the family homestead while the debtor struggles to save it from foreclosure. Receivers are appointed to take possession of owner-occupied commercial real estate somewhat more often, but the courts are understandably reluctant to dispossess a debtor who is operating its business from the mortgaged premises.

As the *Stedman* case in Assignment 44 illustrated, entry of judgment in favor of the mortgagee is not necessarily the end of a mortgage foreclosure case. After entry of the judgment, debtors may appeal, challenge the procedure by which the property was sold, or exercise their rights to redeem. But during this period, the court is likely to be more receptive to the mortgagee's request for the appointment of a receiver. For example, in Norwest Bank of Des Moines, N.A. v. Bruett, 432 N.W.2d 711 (Iowa Ct. App. 1988), the court took the unusual step of appointing a receiver to take possession of the farm that served as collateral from the debtors who personally occupied it. The court made the appointment after it entered judgment, but during the one-year redemption period provided under Iowa law. The applicable statute provided that "The debtor may redeem real property at any time within one year from the day of sale, and will, in the meantime, be entitled to the possession thereof. . . ." The court determined, however, that debtors could waive this right to possession and that the Bruetts had done so by a provision in the mortgage. The effect was that the Bruetts retained their right to redeem their farm, but lost possession of the farm in the meantime.

Many states have statutes governing the appointment of receivers in mortgage foreclosure cases. Typically these statutes mention a few of the factors of concern to the courts in determining whether to appoint a receiver, but do not prohibit consideration of other factors. The factors mentioned in these two statutes are typical of the statutes generally.

California Code of Civil Procedure

Cal. Civ. Proc. Code §564(b) (2005)

[A] receiver may be appointed by the court in which an action or proceeding is pending, or by a judge thereof, in the following cases:...

    2. In an action by a secured lender for the foreclosure of the deed of trust or mortgage and sale of the property...where it appears that the property is in danger of being lost, removed, or materially injured, or that the condition of the mortgage has not been performed, and that the property is probably insufficient to discharge the deed of trust or mortgage debt.

Illinois Mortgage Foreclosure Law

Ill. Rev. Stat. ch. 110, para. 15-1701(b)(2) (2005)

[In cases involving nonresidential real property,] if (i) the mortgagee is so authorized by the terms of the mortgage or other written instrument, and (ii) the court is satisfied that there is a reasonable probability that the mortgagee will prevail on a final hearing of the cause, the mortgagee shall upon request be placed in possession of the real estate, except that if the mortgagor shall object and show good cause, the court shall allow the mortgagor to remain in possession.

The receiver typically takes possession of the collateral during the foreclosure case and delivers possession directly to the purchaser at the foreclosure sale.

3. Assignments of Rents

If the parties contemplate that the debtor will rent the collateral to others during the term of the mortgage, the mortgage is likely to include a provision by which the debtor assigns the rents from the property to the mortgagee as additional security. The provision gives the mortgagee the right to collect the rents directly from the tenants in the event of default under the mortgage. Because collecting the rents from mortgaged property that has been rented to third parties, like appointing a receiver, is functionally the equivalent of taking possession, some courts are reluctant to give effect to the assignment of rents clause. But other courts hold that a mortgagee who declares a default, notifies the tenants to pay the rent to it, and proceeds to collect the rent without foreclosing, acts within its rights.

C.   The Right to Possession Pending Foreclosure — Personal Property

Article 9 of the Uniform Commercial Code governs nearly all security interests in personal property. On the issue of possession pending foreclosure, it favors the secured creditor in the strongest terms. Unless otherwise agreed, U.C.C. §9-609 gives the secured party the right to take possession immediately on default. The secured party need not involve courts or public officials if the secured party can get possession without a breach of the peace. But if the debtor resists repossession, the secured party must obtain a court order for possession and have the sheriff take possession from the debtor. The easiest way to obtain such an order is by filing an action for replevin.

The replevin action is a direct descendant of the common law "writ of replevin" commonly used to recover possession of wandering cattle and other tangible personal property. Generally speaking, any party entitled to possession of tangible personal property is entitled to the writ. The writ directs the sheriff to take possession of the property from the defendant and give it to the plaintiff. By far the most common users of replevin today are secured creditors entitled to possession of collateral pursuant to U.C.C. §9-609.

To obtain the remedy, the secured creditor files a civil action against the debtor. Immediately upon filing, the creditor can move for an order granting immediate possession pending the outcome of the case. Typically, the plaintiff can obtain a hearing on the motion in no more than about 10 to 20 days. In most states, the plaintiff must give notice of the hearing to the debtor, but in some, the hearing can be held and the writ of replevin issued before the debtor is even aware that the case has been filed. If the secured creditor establishes at the hearing that it is likely to prevail in the action, the court issues the writ of replevin. Issuance of the writ is usually conditioned on the creditor's posting a bond to protect the debtor in the event that the debtor ultimately prevails in the replevin action. The debtor can regain possession by posting a similar bond, but if the debtor is in financial difficulty (as is usually the case in a replevin action), the debtor will probably be unable to do so. Once the writ has been issued and possession of the collateral transferred to the secured creditor, most debtors have no reason to defend the replevin action. Judgment is entered by default. The effect is that after default, a secured creditor usually can obtain possession of collateral that is tangible personal property through judicial procedure within two or three weeks. The creditor can then complete the foreclosure by selling the collateral in a commercially reasonable manner. U.C.C. §9-610.

In the following case, the secured creditor, with the help of the Wisconsin legislature and the state court trial judge, explored the limits of this powerful remedy.

Del's Big Saver Foods, Inc. v.
Carpenter Cook, Inc.

603 F. Supp. 1071 (W.D. Wis. 1985)

CRABB, CHIEF JUDGE. . . .

FACTS

Before December of 1983, plaintiffs Burdell and Janice Robish owned and operated Del's Big Saver Foods, Inc., a retail grocery store. In July of 1983, in order to finance their business, the plaintiffs individually and as officers of their incorporated store, signed a note and security agreement, giving defendant Carpenter Cook Company, a subsidiary of defendant Farm House Foods Corporation, a security interest in "[a]ll furniture, equipment, now owned or hereafter acquired by the [b]orrower, together with all inventory [and] the proceeds from the sale thereof."

On December 6, 1983, the defendant law firm of Doyle, Ladd & Philips, P.C. filed a complaint in the Circuit Court of Vilas County, Wisconsin on behalf of defendant Carpenter Cook, alleging among other things that Burdell and Janis Robish had repeatedly defaulted on their note, that Carpenter Cook had a security interest in some of the Robishes' property, and that pursuant to [UCC §9-609], Carpenter Cook was entitled to possession of the property. Along with the complaint, defendant Carpenter Cook submitted an affidavit in support of its motion for possession of the secured property. In the affidavit, Philip Strohl, an officer of Carpenter Cook, stated that the Robishes had defaulted repeatedly on their loan and had breached other covenants of the security agreement. Strohl asserted that the collateral would deteriorate in the hands of the Robishes. Also, Strohl stated the value of the collateral and its location. Defendant Cook submitted to the court a $100,000 indemnity bond issued by defendant United States Fidelity & Guaranty Company.

On December 6, 1983, the day the complaint was filed in the Vilas County court, the state trial judge issued an order granting defendant Carpenter Cook immediate possession of the collateral, the right to operate the Robishes' store as a going concern, and the right to use the proceeds from the sale of the collateral "in the operation of the store." That same day, defendant Strohl, as agent for defendant Carpenter Cook, with the aid of the defendant law firm, obtained certification of the order from the deputy clerk of the Circuit Court of Vilas County. Members of the defendant law firm then proceeded to plaintiffs' store claiming that if plaintiffs did not turn over possession of the store, the county sheriff would be summoned pursuant to the court order to serve the documents and remove the plaintiffs bodily. In response to these demands, plaintiffs turned over the premises to defendant Carpenter Cook.

Plaintiffs had no notice of defendant Carpenter Cook's intent to take possession of the store, or of the court proceedings to gain possession, until the order was presented to them on December 6, 1983. Plaintiffs would not have relinquished possession of the store but for the court order signed by the circuit judge.

OPINION...

[I]n creditor repossession or garnishment cases, the due process clause requires either (1) that the debtor be provided a hearing before his property is taken, or (2) that the debtor be provided certain preseizure procedural safeguards, coupled with a prompt post-deprivation hearing before final judgment. Those preseizure safeguards need not include a hearing, but must include a deprivation order issuable only by a judicial officer based upon detailed factual allegations provided by the party seeking possession.

In this case, since I must accept as true plaintiffs' allegation that they did not receive a hearing prior to the seizure of their property, I can grant defendants' motion for summary judgment only if I am satisfied that plaintiffs had the benefit of the requisite predeprivation procedures and the right to a post-deprivation hearing pending final judgment.

2.   Wisconsin Procedures

The plaintiffs base their claim on what they contend is the state judge's unconstitutional application of [UCC §9-609]. That section, ... gives a secured creditor the right to take possession of a defaulting debtor's secured property. It provides that "[i]n taking possession a secured party may proceed without judicial process if this can be done without breach of the peace or may proceed *by action*." (Emphasis added.) Since the defendants Carpenter Cook, Philip Strohl, and Doyle, Ladd & Philips resorted to the courts to seize plaintiffs' property, they proceeded "by action." Plaintiffs' claim is that the state judge misapplied the "by action" method of repossession by permitting a deprivation which fell short of plaintiffs' right to due process.

The text of the UCC and the Official Comments to [§9-609] fail to provide any guidance to the meaning of "by action." However, the courts and commentators agree that "by action" refers to the applicable state's replevin procedures.

It appears that the 1977 revisions of the Wisconsin replevin procedures were drafted specifically in response to the Supreme Court's holdings in *Mitchell* and *North Georgia Finishing*. The preseizure requirements set out in those cases are satisfied by the provision in the Wisconsin replevin procedures that an order directing a return of the property may be issued only by a judge or other judicial officer and only after the creditor has submitted a verified complaint or affidavit containing several detailed allegations specified in the statute. Also, the replevin statutes provide that at any time the debtor may request a hearing before the judge for vacation or modification of the possession order "for any sufficient cause." Wis. Stat. §810.05. Moreover, the statutes make it clear that the ex parte seizures merely provide for delivery before final judgment.[3]

3.   Application of [UCC §9-609] and Chapter 810

The undisputed facts of the seizure in this case reveal that the state court judge did not deprive plaintiffs of their constitutional rights. Carpenter Cook's state court affidavit and complaint incorporated by exhibit into the Robishes' complaint in this case establish that defendants complied with Wis. Stats. §810.02. Thus plaintiffs cannot contend that the judge abridged their preseizure rights. Also, because the judge merely granted an order for possession, rather than entering a final judgment, plaintiffs had an opportunity to seek an immediate post-seizure hearing. Whether plaintiffs exercised their right to a hearing is irrelevant to this discussion. The due process clause guarantees only the "right to an *opportunity* to be heard [and thus] no hearing need be held unless the [debtor], having received notice of his opportunity, takes advantage of it." Fuentes v. Shevin, 407 U.S. at 92 n.29 (emphasis in original). Because the judge complied with the plaintiffs' preseizure procedural rights and did not deny them a post-seizure hearing, plaintiffs cannot prevail on their claim that their due process rights were violated.

ORDER

IT IS ORDERED that defendants' motion to dismiss this case is GRANTED.

In the constitutional rhetoric of this opinion it is easy to miss the harsh reality of what the courts did to the Robishes. Creditor Carpenter Cook filed a replevin action alleging that the Robishes were behind on their payments. The complaint contained no allegations of fraud or special circumstances to warrant what then occurred. No one notified the Robishes of the filing of the case, and they had no opportunity to respond to the allegations made against them. Instead, the court discussed the matter with Carpenter Cook's lawyers and then ordered the sheriff to take the Robishes' business from them and give it to Carpenter Cook. The Robishes learned what was happening only when Carpenter Cook's lawyers arrived and presented them with the order. The entire proceeding occurred in a single day. The court nevertheless held that the Robishes had been afforded due process. *Del's Big Saver Foods* is not a bizarre aberration; it is merely the logical extension of what occurs in routine replevin cases every day.

----

3. The plaintiff in a replevin action may claim the delivery of the property *prior to final judgment* in a manner provided in this chapter. (Emphasis added.)

D. The Article 9 Right to Self-Help Repossession

The creditors discussed in the preceding sections of this assignment probably would have liked to avoid the hassle and expense of working through courts and sheriffs to obtain possession of their collateral. But they probably had no choice. Use of available judicial procedures is often mandatory.

The principal exception is that a creditor with an Article 9 security interest in tangible, personal property can bypass the courts and the sheriff and do its own work. The creditor's reason for doing so is usually to save time, effort, and money. The right to "self-help repossession" is derived from U.C.C. §9-609. That section provides that after default a secured party may take possession of the collateral.

Security agreements typically require that the debtor surrender possession upon default, and some debtors actually do just that. A debtor who is behind on payments on his car loan may simply drive the car to the bank and hand over the keys. But most debtors do not surrender so easily. They ignore the bank's demands for possession and keep on driving. Some try to get together enough money to make up the back payments in the hope that they can renew their relationship with the bank. Others plan to deal with the problem when necessary by filing bankruptcy. Still others simply try to get as much use out of the car as they can before it is taken from them. Probably most debtors have no plan at all — they just wait to see what tomorrow brings. The secured creditor who wants the car from any of these debtors must take the initiative.

The secured creditor can file a lawsuit against the debtor, obtain judicial recognition of its right to possession, and send the sheriff out to take the car. But the secured creditor can move even faster without judicial process. For example, if the car buyer is behind on the payments and the car is parked in a public place, unlocked, with the keys in it, the secured creditor is in business. The agent of the secured creditor, unlike the agent of its unsecured counterpart, is entitled to hop in and drive the car away.

Finding the car with the keys is a neat story, but repossession is seldom so easy. In many cases, the secured creditor will have difficulty locating its collateral. The car may be kept on private property, inside a fence, or in a locked garage. The car itself may be locked or inoperable. And the neighbors may want to know what somebody skulking in the back lot with a picklock is up to.

A small, somewhat disreputable industry specializes in solving these kinds of problems for secured lenders. For a few hundred dollars, these collection or repossession agencies will find an item of collateral, take it from the debtor, and turn it over to the secured creditor. Much can go wrong in the process. Repossessors may invade the property of third parties in search of their collateral or they may repossess the wrong goods. Debtors may defend their possession with harsh words, fists, or guns. The courts generally hold the duty to refrain from breach of the peace during repossession nondelegable, making the secured creditors liable for the consequences of illegal repossessions by their independent contractors. E.g., Robinson v. Citicorp National Services, Inc., 921 S.W.2d 52 (Mo. App. 1996) (holding secured creditor potentially liable for debtor's death by heart attack during a wrongful repossession).

738 Chapter 13. Creditors' Remedies Under State Law

U.C.C. §9-609(a)(2) gives the creditor the option to leave "equipment" temporarily in the possession of the debtor but render it unusable. In the ordinary application of that provision, the collateral is a large piece of equipment, such as a combine or threshing machine, for which removal to a warehouse would be slow and costly. The creditor might remove key parts from the engine so that the equipment could not be used pending sale.

E. The Limits of Self-Help: Breach of the Peace

A secured creditor is entitled to repossess collateral. This is not a license to engage in any behavior necessary to get it. The U.C.C. permits self-help repossession only if the secured creditor can repossess without breach of the peace. U.C.C. §9-609(b)(2). Not surprisingly, most lawsuits involving a creditor's self-help repossession — and much planning advice about self-help — turn on what constitutes a breach of the peace.

Salisbury Livestock Co. v. Colorado Central Credit Union

793 P.2d 470 (Wyo. 1990)

GOLDEN, J.

[Colorado Central Credit Union (Colorado Central) loaned money to George Salisbury III (young Salisbury). The loans were secured by young Salisbury's motor vehicles. Young Salisbury defaulted and Colorado Central sent a team of repossessors after the motor vehicles. The repossessors took some of the motor vehicles from a ranch owned by Salisbury Livestock Company (Salisbury Livestock), a family corporation run by young Salisbury's father, George Salisbury, Jr. The repossessors took the vehicles from an outdoor area adjacent to the ranch house, just after dawn. They gave no advance notice to Salisbury Livestock and encountered no opposition to the repossession. When Salisbury Livestock discovered what had happened, it sued Colorado Central for wrongful repossession and trespass.]

Our review convinces us that Salisbury Livestock is entitled to have a jury decide the merits of its argument. There is no real disagreement as to whether a trespass occurred.[1] The crux of this dispute is whether the entry to repossess was privileged either by the self-help statute or by consent. From our review of the evidence in a light favorable to Salisbury Livestock, we conclude that a reasonable jury could find that it was not. . . .

---

1. A trespass against real property is simply defined as, "consist[ing] of an interference with the possessor's interest in excluding others from the land." Restatement (Second) of Torts §163 (1965). In its ruling on the motion for a directed verdict the district court said, "I don't think that there's any doubt under any law that [the entry to repossess] was a trespass, because there was an intentional entering of the land of another."

[U.C.C. §9-609] does not define breach of the peace, and there is no definition offered elsewhere in the Wyoming statutes that address rights of secured parties.[3] In our review of decisions from other jurisdictions we find no consistently applied definition, but agree with the analysis of the Utah Supreme Court in Cottam v. Heppner, 777 P.2d 468, 472 (Utah 1989), that, "[c]ourts have struggled in determining when a creditor's trespass onto a debtor's property rises to the level of a breach of the peace. The two primary factors considered in making this determination are the potential for immediate violence and the nature of the premises intruded upon." These factors are interrelated in that the potential for violence increases as the creditor's trespass comes closer to a dwelling,[4] and we will focus our analysis on them. It is necessary to evaluate the facts of each case to determine whether a breach of the peace has occurred.

We agree with the trial court that the Restatement (Second) of Torts §198 reasonableness requirement provides appropriate criteria for evaluating whether a creditor's entry has breached the peace. If, as here, there was no confrontation and the timing and manner, including notice or lack of notice, are found reasonable, the entry is privileged. If the jury should find that the manner or timing of this entry was unreasonable because it may have triggered a breach of the peace, it in effect finds the entry a breach of the peace and unprivileged. We foresee the possibility that a rational jury could reach the conclusion that this entry was unreasonable.

As asserted by Salisbury Livestock, one specific inquiry is whether, as discussed in Comment d, §198, a demand for the property is required. [Demand is unnecessary] if such demand would be futile, but there must be a determination whether demand would have been futile in these circumstances. Young Salisbury had not responded to Colorado Central's demands for payment, but Salisbury Livestock, on whose property the vehicles were found, was not given an opportunity to deliver the pledged vehicles to Colorado Central or its representatives. Notice is not an express requirement of the statute, but is a common law element which helps to determine the reasonableness of the repossessors' actions. . . .

Neither of the Cottam factors, nor the Restatement reasonableness analysis, requires or suggests that a trespass is necessarily a breach of the peace. Property owners may be entirely unaware of a trespass, so that there is no potential for immediate violence. Likewise, a peaceful, inadvertent trespass on lands remote from any home or improvements is unlikely to provoke violence. Therefore, we do not agree with Salisbury Livestock's contention that a trespass without more is a breach of the peace. A trespass breaches the peace only if certain types of premises are invaded, or immediate violence is likely.

---

3. Wyoming's criminal breach of the peace statute, W.S. 6-6-102(a) (June 1988 Repl.), reads, "[a] person commits breach of the peace if he disturbs the peace of a community or its inhabitants by using threatening, abusive or obscene language or violent actions with knowledge or probable cause to believe he will disturb the peace." Restatement (Second) of Torts §116 is more useful in arriving at what constitutes a civil breach of the peace: "A breach of the peace is a public offense done by violence, or one causing or likely to cause an immediate disturbance of public order." We note that, although actual violence is not required to find a breach of the peace, a disturbance or violence must be reasonably likely, and not merely a remote possibility.

4. Decisions elsewhere have established a general rule that a creditor's entry into a residence without permission is a breach of the peace. J. White & R. Summers, Handbook of the Law Under the Uniform Commercial Code 26-6 (2d ed. 1980).

However, we cannot agree with Colorado Central's assertion that there can be no finding of a breach of the peace because there was no confrontation. Confrontation or violence is not necessary to finding a breach of the peace. The possibility of immediate violence is sufficient. Two elements of this case create questions which we believe might lead reasonable jurors to a conclusion at odds with the trial court's directed verdict. First, this was an entry onto the premises of a third party not privy to the loan agreement. Particularly if there was no knowledge of young Salisbury's consent to repossession, this could trigger a breach of the peace. The few reported cases involving repossession from third party properties suggest that such entry is acceptable. However, these cases do not address third party residential property. When entry onto third party property is coupled with the second unusual element, the location and the setting of this repossession, the possibility of a different verdict becomes more apparent.

We have not located any cases addressing a creditor's entry into the secluded ranchyard of an isolated ranch where the vehicles sought are not even visible from a public place. The few cases involve urban or suburban driveways, urban parking lots, or business premises. We believe that the location and setting of this entry to repossess is sufficiently distinct, and the privacy expectations of rural residents sufficiently different, that a jury should weigh the reasonableness of this entry, or whether the peace may have been breached by a real possibility of imminent violence, or even by mere entry into these premises: the area next to the residence in a secluded ranchyard.

Not surprisingly, there is considerable dispute over precisely what kind of facts constitute a breach of the peace. Here is a sampling of cases holding there was a breach of the peace:

1. The creditor took a uniformed police officer to the debtor's home on a repossession attempt. With the police officer present, the debtor verbally consented to the repossession. The police officer was there to prevent anticipated violence. The court concluded that a breach of the peace had occurred, stating that "the fact that the deputy did not say anything is not significant. [To hold otherwise] would set a precedent by involving local law enforcement in self-help repossessions, and would create the very volatile situations the statute was designed to prevent." In re Walker v. Walthall, 588 P.2d 863 (Ariz. Ct. App. 1978).

2. The first time the repossessor attempted to take a heavy duty rotary mower from the debtor's home, the debtor ordered him off the premises. Almost a month later, the repossessor came back with two more men. The debtor was not home, but the debtor's son told the men they should not take the mower and "protested" its removal. But "surrounded" by the three, he did nothing further to stop them because he "was afraid of being beaten." The court held that "when [the secured creditor's] agents were physically confronted by [the debtor's] representative, disregarded his request to desist their efforts at

repossession and refused to depart from the private premises upon which the collateral was kept, they committed a breach of the peace within the meaning of [U.C.C. §9-609], lost the protective application of that section, and thereafter stood as would any other person who unlawfully refuses to depart from the land of another." Morris v. First National Bank & Trust Co. of Ravenna, Ohio, 7 U.C.C. 131 (Ohio 1970).

3. During the repossession of a car, the Marcuses "argued loudly" with the repossessor. The repossessor beckoned a nearby police officer to the scene. Both sides argued with the officer and the Marcuses tried to unhook the car from the repossessor's wrecker. When the officer told the Marcuses to "keep [their] mouths shut, go back in the house, or [they] would indeed go to jail that day," the Marcuses let the repossession occur. The appeals court said

> officers are not state actors during a private repossession if they act only to keep the peace, but they cross the line if they affirmatively intervene to aid the repossessor.... The plaintiff's resistance to the taking of his property need not be strong. The general rule is that a debtor's request for the financer to leave the car alone must be obeyed. Even polite repossessors breach the peace if they meet resistance from the debtor. If a breach of peace occurs, self-help repossession is statutorily precluded.

Marcus v. McCollum, 394 F.3d 813 (10th Cir. 2004).

4. To repossess a bulldozer, the repossessors cut a chain used to lock a fence. Because that was done after the end of the work day, it left plaintiff's heavy equipment storage area containing approximately $350,000 worth of equipment unsecured and unprotected. Citing a case in which the repossessor's having broken a window to unlock a door to a debtor's residence and repossess a piano was a breach of the peace, the court held that cutting the chain was improper. Laurel Coal Co. v. Walter E. Heller & Co., Inc., 539 F. Supp. 1006 (W.D. Pa. 1982).

Cases holding there was not a breach of the peace:

5. The debtor's complaint for wrongful repossession alleged that the repossessor followed him to Big Stone Gap, Virginia, where he was staying with his daughter. About 2:00 A.M., the repossessor entered plaintiff's truck, started it, raced the engine, and "barrel[ed] out of the lot and down the street." The debtor said he and his daughter "did not know what was happening and were in fear." The court held that the complaint failed to state a cause of action. The court considered the "stealthy manner" in which the repossession was effected as "calculated to avoid a breach of the peace because the prospect of a confrontation with the plaintiff was less at 2 A.M. than it would have been in the daylight hours or in the early evening." Even though the repossession may have violated some traffic ordinance, it was not "an incitement to violence or to break the peace." That the repossessor was an off-duty deputy sheriff also did not matter, because the plaintiff did not know that while the repossession was in

progress. Wallace v. Chrysler Credit Corp., 743 F. Supp. 1228 (W.D. Va. 1990).

6. Two repossessors used a wrecker to repossess a woman's automobile from her driveway. Awakened by the noise, she ran outside to stop them and "hollered at them" as they were driving away. The two men stopped. They told her they were repossessing the car. She explained that she had been attempting to bring the past payments up to date and informed the men that the car contained personal items belonging to a third person. The men "stepped between her and the car" when she attempted to retrieve them, gave her the personal items, and drove off with her car "without further complaint from [her]." She admitted that the men were polite throughout the encounter and did not make any threats toward her or do anything that caused her to fear any physical harm. The dissent noted that plaintiff was a single parent living with her two small children and observed that "facing the wrecking crew in the dead of night, [plaintiff] did everything she could to stop them short of introducing physical force," but the majority said the repossession was proper. Williams v. Ford Motor Credit Co., 674 F.2d 717 (8th Cir. 1982).

7. On the secured creditor's first attempt to repossess her car, the debtor successfully ordered the repossessor off the premises. The debtor claimed that she had a gun in the house and would use it if he came back. She later called the repossessor's office and threatened that "if she caught anyone on her property again trying to take her car, [she] would leave him laying right where [she] saw him." Thirty days later, the intrepid repossessor took the car from the debtor's driveway, awakening her with the sound of "burning rubber." No confrontation occurred. The debtor did not know the car was being taken until the repossessor had safely departed with it. The court held that despite the "potential for violence" the debtor had previously communicated, the repossession had not breached the peace. Wade v. Ford Motor Credit Co., 668 P.2d 183 (Kan. Ct. App. 1983).

8. The collateral was a bus located in the debtor's business premises. The repossessor cut a lock to enter property marked "No Trespassing" to get the bus. The court held this repossession not to be a breach of the peace because the security agreement signed by the debtor permitted the creditor to "enter any premises . . . without liability for trespass." Wombles Charters, Inc. v. Orix Credit Alliance, Inc., 39 U.C.C. Rep. Serv. 2d 599 (S.D.N.Y. 1999).

9. The two truck rigs that served as collateral were in the possession of a truck equipment dealer. The repossessor obtained possession of the rigs by fraudulently misrepresenting to the truck equipment dealer that the debtor had given him permission to repossess. The court ruled that the misrepresentation was not a breach of the peace because it did not "support a potential for immediate violence." K.B. Oil Co. v. Ford Motor Credit Co., Inc., 811 F.2d 310 (6th Cir. 1987).

10. The repossessing team had hooked the plaintiff's car to the tow truck and had started driving away when the plaintiff voiced an objection to the repossession and started moving toward the car. The car had

already been moved from its parking spot when the plaintiff began objecting to the repossession. A third person restrained the plaintiff, and the car was successfully repossessed. The court said "once a repossession agent has gained sufficient dominion over collateral to control it, the repossession has been completed." Clark v. Auto Recovery Bureau Conn., Inc., 889 F. Supp. 543 (D. Conn. 1994).

F.   Self-Help Against Accounts as Collateral

Many businesses sell their products or services on unsecured credit. For example, it is common for manufacturers of home audio equipment to give their dealers 30 days to pay for merchandise shipped to them. While the debt is outstanding, it is an "account payable" of the dealer-debtor and an "account receivable" of the creditor-manufacturer (APs and ARs, in the accounting lingo). Article 9 refers to an account receivable as simply an "account." U.C.C. §9-102(a)(2). Although each separate account may be small and remain outstanding for only a short period of time, a business that sells on credit will typically have many of them. In the aggregate, the accounts of such a business may have substantial value over a long time. At any given time, a manufacturer of audio equipment, for example, might be owed tens of thousands of dollars by its dealers. When the manufacturer wants to borrow money for its operations, a creditor looking for security might see the accounts as adequate collateral — if it could find a way to reach those accounts cheaply and quickly in the event of default.

One of the objectives of the drafters of Article 9 was to facilitate secured transactions in which the debtors' accounts could serve as collateral. Today, debtors routinely borrow against their accounts. Several arrangements are common, depending on the amount of control that the secured creditor is willing to cede to the debtor while the debtor is not in default. Here are some frequently used alternatives:

1. The secured creditor may give the debtor virtually complete freedom to collect the accounts and to use the proceeds in its business.
2. The secured creditor may agree to let the debtor collect the accounts, but require the debtor immediately to apply a specified portion of them to the loan. Under this kind of arrangement the debtor will expect the lender to make additional loans, usually referred to as "future advances," secured by new accounts as they arise. The result may be a rapid cycle of borrowing, repaying, and reborrowing.
3. The secured creditor may arrange with the debtor that the account debtors will pay directly to the secured creditor. With the permission of the debtor, the secured creditor will notify the account debtors to pay directly to it. This procedure may also involve a rapid cycle of borrowing, repaying, and reborrowing to keep the debtor in business.
4. The secured creditor may vary the arrangements described in the preceding paragraph by requiring the debtor to direct its account debtors to make their payments to a post office box that is under the control of the

secured creditor. This arrangement is sometimes referred to as a *lockbox* to signify that the debtor cannot reach the money coming in from its own accounts. The principal reason for using a lockbox rather than direct payment to the secured creditor is to avoid letting the account debtors know that the accounts have been used as collateral.

The bank in our example that lends money to an audio manufacturer secured by an interest in the manufacturer's accounts might use any of these arrangements.

In the event of default, U.C.C. §§9-607 and 9-406(a) provide a self-help remedy to the party holding a security interest in accounts. Under §9-607, the secured creditor who knows the identity of the account debtors can simply send them written notices to pay directly to the secured creditor. Although the express provisions of Article 9 stop short of saying that the account debtor must follow the instructions of the creditor, that is the practical effect.

For example, in Marine National Bank v. Airco, Inc., 389 F. Supp. 231 (W.D. Pa. 1975), Midland National Bank made loans to Craneways that were secured by various collateral of Craneways, including its accounts receivable. In June of 1971, Craneways' president notified the Bank that it had a contract with Airco to reconstruct a crane. Once the work was complete, Airco owed Craneways $23,000.

On July 19, 1971, the Bank sent, and Airco acknowledged receiving, a registered letter notifying Airco that the Bank held a security agreement covering all of Craneways' accounts receivable. The letter demanded that Airco pay any sums due Craneways to the Bank.

In August 1971, Craneways delivered the crane. Airco then paid $18,000 of the balance owing to Craneways. Craneways endorsed the check to the IRS to pay its taxes. In the Bank's lawsuit against Airco, the court entered judgment in favor of the Bank for $13,000, the remaining amount Craneways owed to the Bank.

Marine National demonstrates how powerful the self-help remedy against accounts can be. The Bank was able to recover its collateral — the account — even though that required the account debtor, Airco, to pay more than it owed. Airco theoretically had the right to recover its first payment from Craneways, but by the time Marine National sued Airco, Craneways was out of business and the debt was uncollectible.

In some respects, accounts make good collateral. The self-help remedy is easy to employ and accounts are by their nature readily converted to cash. But there are serious practical problems that render them less than ideal as collateral. A secured creditor's exercise of its right to notify account debtors can have devastating effects. Account debtors are motivated to pay their debts in part by their desire to keep doing business with the debtor and in part by the fear of legal action. To continue our earlier example, absent notice from the bank, the audio dealers generally continue to pay the manufacturer because they know that if they don't, the manufacturer will stop shipping audio equipment to them and may bring suit against them.

If, however, the manufacturer's bank has taken over the account, both motives may be undermined. The takeover signals to the dealers that the bank has lost confidence in the manufacturer's ability to meet its obligations and may suggest that the manufacturer will soon be out of business. The dealers may decide to withhold payment of the accounts in order to protect themselves against the manufacturer's future failure to provide service or honor warranties. Knowing that debtors in financial difficulty lack credibility, dealers may be more likely to complain about the manufacturer's products or to question the manufacturer's accounting. Worse yet, the dealers may realize that if the manufacturer's business fails, it may be difficult for either the manufacturer or the bank to sue them on the unpaid account. The bank financing the manufacturer may not have the information necessary to prove the account obligation to a judge or jury and the failed debtor may be unwilling to assist. As a result, the accounts can be expensive to collect or may become completely uncollectible.

Problem Set 45

45.1. Look back at Problem 43.1. Now assume that Jeffrey produced a second paper at your meeting with him. He explained that he had gone to an office supply store and picked up a form titled "Personal Property Security Agreement" and he had Lisa sign it. You look it over and decide it is a perfectly enforceable security agreement designating the lawn furniture as collateral. Does your advice change? U.C.C. §§9-102(a)(72) and (73), 9-609.

45.2. Faye Maretka is the head of the collections department at Commercial Finance, a valued, long-time client of your firm. CF frequently has occasion to repossess equipment from building construction sites in several states. CF's usual practice is to obtain judicial process and then have the sheriff do the actual repossession. When the judicial process is too slow or the sheriff too inflexible, Maretka hires local repo people to effect a self-help repossession. To make sure they act responsibly and effectively, she personally goes with them and "calls the shots." CF can't afford to bring counsel along every time they repossess property, so Maretka has asked you to work out some guidelines on "how far she can go" in attempting a repossession.

Maretka explains the circumstances she usually encounters: The borrower typically is a general contractor or a subcontractor who is responsible for some specific aspect of construction, such as excavation or the concrete work. The general contractor deals with the owner and provides safety and security for the site. Larger sites are fenced; some, but not all, have guards on the premises during the night. Some equipment is left on the construction site overnight, while the rest is typically under heavier security at the debtor's place of business. Some of the repossession targets are motor vehicles, but most are heavy equipment such as bulldozers or power generators that must be carried by truck.

Outline your advice to Maretka. Focus on the situation where the collateral is a bulldozer owned by a subcontractor, the site is owned by a developer, and fences and security are provided by the general contractor. Consider each of these three situations:

a. Sites where there is neither a guard nor a fence,
b. Sites where there is a fence but no guard, and

c. Sites where there is a guard.

d. The debtor keeps the bulldozer in a locked, steel building on the debtor's own property.

e. As CF's regular counsel, you should also consider whether there is anything that should be in CF's security agreements about repossession that might make Maretka's job easier.

See U.C.C. §§9-609, 9-201, 9-602(6), 9-603.

45.3. Salvatore Ferragamo is the sole owner of Ferragamo Construction Company. Your firm has worked with Sal for 16 years, doing all the legal work for his company from incorporation through the negotiation of its insurance contracts. Terrible weather and late deliveries by suppliers have put the company behind in its work schedule and consequently in what it can collect from its customers. The company has missed its third monthly payment to ITT Finance, which provides financing secured by Ferragamo's equipment. Sal says he needs just a week or two of uninterrupted operations to turn the corner financially.

This morning Sal received a letter by registered mail from ITT declaring the loan in default and directing him to assemble the collateral and make it available to ITT for repossession. Even though his security agreement with ITT provides that he will do precisely that, Sal has decided not to. Instead, he wants to know what he can do, short of bankruptcy, to resist repossession. If the ITT people come for the equipment, how should he handle the situation? What if they bring the sheriff with them? If the ITT people don't bring the sheriff, should Sal call the sheriff? Can he hide the equipment where the repo people won't be able to find it? U.C.C. §9-609. Assume that the state has a statute identical to Wisconsin Statute §943.25: "Whoever . . . conceals any personal property in which he knows another has a security interest . . . is guilty of a Class E felony."

Rule 1.2 of the ABA Model Rules of Professional Conduct provides in part:

> (d) A lawyer shall not counsel a client to engage, or assist a client, in conduct that the lawyer knows is criminal or fraudulent, but a lawyer may discuss the legal consequences of any proposed course of conduct with a client and may counsel or assist a client to make a good faith effort to determine the validity, scope, meaning or application of the law.

45.4. If ITT's lawyers gave ITT the same advice you gave Commercial Finance in Problem 45.2, would they be able to repossess Sal's equipment through self-help? In other words, if both the debtor and the creditor have the best legal advice regarding self-help repossession and follow it carefully, who "wins"?

45.5. Deare Distributors sells farming equipment to retail farming supply stores. Firstbank and Deare have a working arrangement under which Firstbank lends an amount equal to 60 percent of Deare's accounts receivable. When Deare makes a sale, it sends a copy of the invoice to Firstbank. The bank deposits an amount equal to 60 percent of the invoice to Deare's bank account. When the supply store pays the invoice, Deare is required to apply 60 percent of the proceeds to repay the loan immediately.

Deare has requested that Firstbank's interest in the accounts not be made known to the account debtors "because it might make them nervous." First-bank is considering honoring that request in the absence of default, but it consults with you to ask about the risks of this arrangement. You want to consider why Deare might cheat and how it could do so. Is there any way to discover such cheating without contacting Deare's customers?

45.6.   A year after the preceding problem, Firstbank is back with additional questions. Deare ultimately defaulted on the loan, and four months ago First-bank notified the account debtors to pay Firstbank directly.

a.   Horne's Feed and Seed, one of Deare's account debtors, claims that it paid Deare in full last month and refuses to pay Firstbank. Can Firstbank collect from Horne's? U.C.C. §§9-406(a), 9-607(a).

b.   Another account debtor, Wilson's Farming Goods, has refused to pay anything, claiming that although they received $42,000 in equipment, they have untended warranty claims amounting to $19,000. What can Firstbank collect from Wilson's? U.C.C. §9-404(a).

45.7.   You have been counsel for Ronald Silber, the owner of Sound Em-porium, for several years. Silber tells you that the business is experiencing some temporary cash-flow problems and he would like your advice on how to deal with them. You elicit the following list of problems:

a.   The business owes Southern Savings about $260,000 against the business premises, which are worth about $300,000. The mortgage is at 9 percent, and payments are $2,091 a month. Silber is two payments in ar-rears, and a third one is due next week. He received a notice from Southern's lawyers stating that if the payments are not brought up to date within ten days, Southern will foreclose.

b.   The business owes about $90,000 to Citizen's Bank. The loan is secured by the trade fixtures and equipment of the business. The loan is at 11 percent per year and the quarterly interest payment in the amount of $2,575 is 45 days past due. The loan officer says it must be brought current or "legal action will be taken."

c.   The utility bill is almost two months past due. The total amount owing for the two-month period is about $1,200. Silber has received the standard form notice that unless payment has been made within ten days, utility ser-vice will be cut off.

d.   Two suppliers are hounding Silber to pay invoices that are now more than 120 days old. Silber owes each about $20,000. One supplier has a security interest in the inventory it sold to Sound Emporium; the other does not. Both suppliers have hired local attorneys and are threatening immediate legal action. Silber says he can purchase similar inventory else-where for cash.

There are several other creditors, but none are really pushing for immediate payment. Silber wants desperately to keep the doors open because he thinks that in four to six months he can turn the business around. But over the next two or three months, he will have only about $4,000 a month to devote to the payments listed above. Silber says bankruptcy is "absolutely out of the ques-tion," and, from the way he says it, you know he means it (at least for now). Instead, he wants your opinion on how to allocate the money among these creditors and he also wants to know "what they can do if they don't get paid."

What are your questions for Silber? What do you need to know about the law of your state? Based on what you now know and assuming your state's law is in accord with the majority, what's your advice? See U.C.C. §9-609.

> Model Rules of Professional Conduct, Rule 3.2: Expediting Litigation — A Lawyer shall make reasonable efforts to expedite litigation consistent with the interest of the client.
>
> Official Comment: Dilatory practices bring the administration of justice into disrepute. Nor will a failure to expedite be reasonable if done for the purpose of frustrating an opposing party's attempt to obtain rightful redress or repose. It is not a justification that similar conduct is often tolerated by the bench and bar. The question is whether a competent lawyer acting in good faith would regard the course of action as having *some substantial purpose other than delay*. Realizing financial or other benefit from otherwise improper delay in litigation is not a legitimate interest of the client.

In light of these provisions, can you counsel Silber at all?

45.8. Your firm represents Stanley Zabriskie and Zabriskie Autos. When Zabriskie sells a car, he arranges financing. The loans are made by a separate financing company. When the buyer defaults, Zabriskie usually has to buy the loan back from the finance company and enforce it himself. (This procedure is known as *recourse financing*.) After a default and repurchase, Zabriskie typically refers the matter to Auto Repossessors (AR). If AR can get possession of the car peacefully, Zabriskie pays them $300; if not, Zabriskie refers the matter to Tyler & Yin (T & Y), a law firm that specializes in small collection cases. T & Y will file an action for replevin and, as permitted under local law, obtain the writ of possession without prior notice to the debtor. Provided that the debtor does not defend the replevin action, they charge a flat $600 for the case; otherwise they charge on an hourly basis.

Five months ago, Zabriskie Autos sold a car to Sandra Evans. Evans made the first two payments, then missed the next three. On the few occasions that Stanley Zabriskie has been able to contact her, she has complained about the quality of the car, the representations the salesperson made to her, and the financing Zabriskie obtained for her. Stanley Zabriskie thinks her complaints are just an excuse to keep him from repossessing, but when you press him, he admits there may be some truth to her claims. He'd like to "run this one through the regular procedure." As corporate counsel, what's your advice? U.C.C. §9-609.

45.9. Your client, Mel Farr, sells used cars to customers with bad credit. After encountering all kinds of problems with repossessions he thinks he has found a technical solution to the problem. He plans to equip each automobile with a computerized device that will allow the car to start only if the driver correctly enters a new code each week. Farr will give each driver the code only upon receipt of the driver's weekly payment. Is this device legal? U.C.C. §§9-102(a)(33), 9-201, 9-602, 9-609(a)(2). Should it be?

Assignment 46: Judicial Sale and Deficiency

After a judgment has been entered in a judicial foreclosure, the collateral is sold in a public sale. As we suggested in the Pseudo History in Assignment 44, the purpose of the sale was, at least initially, to determine the value of the property. Like some law and economics professors today, the Ancients believed that the price a thing could bring at a public sale was the best measure of its value. If that value was in excess of the lien against the collateral, the surplus could be returned to the debtor after payment of the secured debt. If the value was less than the secured debt, the value could be applied against the debt and the debtor could be held liable for the resulting deficiency.

As we also suggested in the Pseudo History, the requirement that collateral be exposed to public sale as part of the foreclosure process generally cannot be varied by contract. Even if the mortgage specifically provides for the secured creditor to become the owner of the collateral in the event of default and foreclosure, the public sale must still be held. Without the sale, the possibility always remains that the creditor has picked up the property at too great a bargain, or, to reverse the focus and put it in the language of the courts, the debtor has suffered a forfeiture. Recall that foreclosures are in equity, and "equity," the maxim goes, "abhors a forfeiture."

As you read this assignment, keep in mind that Article 9 security interests can be foreclosed judicially, see U.C.C. §9-601(a)(1), but seldom are. Assignment 47 discusses the sale procedure commonly employed in nonjudicial foreclosure under U.C.C. §§9-610(a), (b).

A. Strict Foreclosure

Notwithstanding the tradition of a foreclosure sale, some foreclosure procedures or situations do not require a sale of the collateral. They are typically referred to as *strict foreclosures*. Probably the most common is the foreclosure of a *contract for deed*, or *installment land contract*, which is a contract for the sale of real property that provides for the payment of the purchase price in installments over many years, with the deed to be delivered only after the last installment has been paid. A contract for deed has long been recognized as a security device. If the purchaser does not make timely payments, the seller must foreclose through court process. But the large majority of states do not require that the foreclosure conclude with a sale of the property. Instead, if the debtor does not pay the full purchase price in accord with the contract or at least by the end of a statutory *grace period*, the debtor's interest in the property is forfeited and the court confirms that title remains with the seller.

Contracts for deed are used primarily in sales of real estate of relatively small value on small down payments. Their strict foreclosure occasionally forfeits a substantial equity that a buyer has built up over several years, a result that has prompted serious policy concerns and some protective litigation. However, the level of their use is not sufficient to warrant detailed coverage in this book. Throughout the remainder of this assignment, we focus on the typical foreclosure procedures that require public sale of the collateral.

B. Foreclosure Sale Procedure

In most states, statutes specify the manner in which a foreclosure sale must be held. A typical statute might provide that all foreclosure sales within the county are to be held by auction sale on the steps of the court-house between the hours of 10:00 A.M. and 2:00 P.M. on the first and third Tuesdays of the month, with the property going to the highest bidder for cash. Judicial foreclosure sales are nearly always conducted by a public official, usually the sheriff, the clerk of the court, or a court commissioner. Anyone may bid at the sale. For reasons that will become apparent in the next section, the creditor who brings the foreclosure case is typically the highest bidder at the sale.

The court that orders a foreclosure sale may have discretion to determine some aspects of the manner in which the sale is held, such as the period of advertising, the manner in which bidders identify themselves, and the min-imum increments for bidding. When the last bid is made, the officer conduct-ing the sale identifies the highest bidder. Typically, that bidder must immediately make a deposit of a portion of the purchase price in cash or by cashier's check. Under most procedures the balance of the purchase price must be paid within a few hours or days. If the high bidder does not make good on its bid, the applicable procedure may require either that the property then be sold to the second highest bidder or that a new sale be scheduled. The high bidder who did not perform may forfeit its deposit and may also be liable in contract for damages.

In most foreclosure procedures, the court must review the circumstances under which the sale was held and *confirm* the sale before the sale can be consummated. The debtor, or other parties in interest, may object to the sale on the grounds that the officer did not conduct the sale in accord with the law or the judgment of foreclosure, or that the sale price was inadequate. If the court does not confirm the sale, it will schedule a resale. If it confirms the sale, the officer who conducted the sale will execute a deed conveying the property to the purchaser.

Once a sale has been confirmed, the official disburses the sale proceeds. The money goes first to reimburse the foreclosing creditor for the expenses of sale. Next, the proceeds are distributed to the foreclosing creditor up to the amount of the debt secured by the foreclosed lien. Assuming there are no other liens, any remaining surplus goes to the debtor. If the proceeds of sale are insufficient to pay the full amount of the debt secured by the foreclosed lien, the foreclosing creditor may ask the court to enter a judgment for the deficiency. The circumstances under which courts grant deficiency judgments are discussed in section D, below. If the deficiency judgment is granted, the foreclosing creditor can collect it in the same manner as any other judgment on an unsecured debt.

While the foreclosure is in progress, the mortgage debtor has the right to redeem the property from the mortgage by paying the full amount due under the mortgage, including interest and attorneys' fees. This *common law* right to redeem is typically cut off (*foreclosed*, in the legal parlance) as of the time of the sale. In more than half the states, the debtor also has a *statutory* right to redeem the collateral from the buyer after the sale. Statutory rights to redeem range in length from about six months to three years, with one year being the most common period. Except when the court appoints a receiver, the debtor usually remains in possession during the statutory period for redemption. Redemption is accomplished by paying the purchaser the amount the purchaser paid at the sale. Under some procedures, the redemption price will also include interest on the sale price and other expenses incurred by the purchaser in connection with the sale. But the redemption price typically does not include the purchaser's costs of maintaining or improving the property during the period, if any, it was in the purchaser's possession.

Statutory rights of redemption are freely transferrable. As a consequence, debtors who cannot afford to exercise their rights of redemption can sell those rights to others who can exercise them. The greater the discount at which a debtor's property is sold in the judicial sale, the greater is the value of the right to redeem it. The debtor can recapture some of that discount by selling the right to redeem. When the buyer of a statutory right to redeem exercises it after the sale, the auction purchaser loses both the property and the benefit of the purchase. Some courts hold that the redeeming assignee takes the property free and clear of the lien causing the sale and all subordinate liens. The rule makes the price of statutory redemption the price paid at the sale. Others hold that the redeeming assignee takes the property subject to the lien causing the sale, and all subordinate liens. The latter rule makes the price of statutory redemption the same as the price of common law redemption. The redeemer must pay the entire debt.

C.   Problems with Foreclosure Sale Procedure

When property is sold at a foreclosure sale, the debtor is often shocked by how little it brings. Sometimes the debtor is sufficiently outraged to bring a lawsuit asking the court to set aside the sale because of the inadequate sale price. In the following case, the debtors asked the court to set aside a foreclosure sale that left them with a large deficiency judgment. The court recognized that the debtors' property was sold for less than its fair market value, but also recognized that usually happens in foreclosure sales.

Armstrong v. Csurilla

817 P.2d 1221 (N.M. 1991)

MONTGOMERY, J.

When property subject to a mortgage or other lien is sold in foreclosure proceedings, the buyer is usually the mortgagee or other lien creditor and the price for which the property is "bought in" is sometimes significantly less than the property's fair market value. This can result in considerable unfairness to the debtor, the owner of the property, who may wind up both losing the property (and any attendant equity) and becoming subject to an onerous deficiency judgment, while the creditor may realize a substantial profit on ultimate disposition of the property and collect the deficiency from the debtor's other assets, if any. This problem can lead to abuse, an abuse which has been well documented and the subject of various attempts at legislative or judicial correction or amelioration.[1]

In this case the debtors, whose property became subject to a judgment lien after their default under two contracts by which they had purchased the property, . . . seek to set aside the foreclosure sale by relying on the equitable doctrine that permits a court to invalidate a judicial sale when the price is so low as to "shock the conscience" of the court. We hold that . . . the debtors, having been afforded opportunities to protect themselves from the consequences of an inadequate price and to provide evidence that the price was inadequate, cannot now avail themselves of that equitable doctrine. . . . We hold that the trial court did not err in the proceedings that led ultimately to confirmation of the sale of the debtors' property, and we affirm its judgment.

I

The case has a simple factual history and a more complicated procedural one. The debtors, William and Josephine Csurilla, entered into two contracts to purchase the real property at issue from Calvin and Dorothy Armstrong on April 5, 1987. The contracts were more or less standard, long-term real estate contracts, prepared by the Csurillas' attorney. The two contracts covered adjacent parcels of land and improvements in Quemado, New Mexico. One covered a gasoline service station, with associated pumps, inventory, and a storage building (the "station contract"); the other covered an adjoining residential dwelling and garage-carport (the "house contract"). One well serves both the house and the service station; electrical, sewer and plumbing lines run through one property to the other; and the garage-carport and storage building share a common wall. The trial court found that the parties used two separate contracts for tax purposes and the convenience of the Csurillas and for no other reason.

---

1. See . . . Washburn, The Judicial and Legislative Response to Price Inadequacy in Mortgage Foreclosure Sales, 53 S. Cal. L. Rev. 843 (1980). The Uniform Land Transactions Act (ULTA) — which, however, has not yet been adopted by any state — contains several provisions designed to prevent double recovery by creditors, protect debtors from the hardships of deficiency judgments and inadequately priced sales, and bring judicial sales into closer conformity with commercially reasonable, free-market transactions. See U.L.T.A. §§3-501 to 3-513, 13 U.L.A. 599-622 (1977).

The purchase price under the station contract was $156,594, with $1,000 paid down and the balance payable in monthly installments of $1,122.31 commencing April 1, 1987. The station property included approximately $28,600 in inventory. The purchase price for the house property was $75,000, on which $1,000 was paid down, another $52,000 credited by virtue of an exchange of property owned by the Csurillas in Lake Havasu, Arizona, and the deferred balance of $22,000 payable $194.42 per month. Thus, the total purchase price for the two properties was $231,594, and the total monthly debt service was $1,316.73.

Three months after signing the contracts, the Csurillas defaulted under the station contract. They continued making payments on the house contract and did not relinquish possession of either property. They continued to operate the station for a few months but closed it in November 1987. Mr. Armstrong retook possession of the station in September 1988, when the court appointed him as receiver to protect the property. By that time, the property had deteriorated significantly in value; much of the inventory was depleted, and the station was in generally poor condition. It never reopened as a service station.

[The court held that default under the service station contract constituted a default under both contracts and entered a judgment of foreclosure against both properties.] The... judicial sale then took place in December 1989, with the Armstrongs buying in both properties for [a total of] $90,000.... The Csurillas objected to confirmation of the sale.... The court conducted a hearing, received opinion testimony (but no appraisal) as to the value of the property, found that the sale was fair and regular in all respects, and entered an order confirming it. The order also granted the Csurillas a one-month period in which to redeem the property... and awarded the Armstrongs a deficiency judgment of $125,037. The Csurillas then... took the present appeal to this Court....

V

What protection, then, does a judgment debtor have from the potentially abusive practice described at the beginning of this opinion — sale for an inadequate price, followed by imposition of an onerous deficiency judgment? To answer this question we turn to the Csurillas' final contention — that the price bid by the Armstrongs for the combined house and station property, $90,000, was so low that it should "shock the conscience of the court."

In Las Vegas Railway & Power Co. v. Trust Co. of St. Louis County, 15 N.M. 634, 110 P. 856 (1910), we said:

> It is perfectly well settled that a judicial sale will not be set aside for inadequacy of price unless it be so gross as to shock the conscience, or unless there be additional circumstances which would make it inequitable to allow the sale to stand....
>
> While mere inadequacy of price has rarely been held sufficient in itself to justify setting aside a judicial sale of property, courts are not slow to seize upon other circumstances impeaching the fairness of the transaction, as a cause for vacating it....

From these various formulations, we discern two instances in which equity will intervene to set aside a judicial sale where the price, compared with the value of the property sold, is inadequate. The first is when the disparity is so great as to shock the court's conscience. While "mere inadequacy" will seldom be sufficient to justify vacating the sale, simply stating that rule obviously connotes some situations in which mere inadequacy, if sufficiently gross, will warrant the court's intervention.

The second instance in which the sale may be vacated on the ground of price inadequacy is when, in addition to the inadequate price, there are circumstances which would make it inequitable to allow the sale to stand. We need not attempt to catalogue the kinds of "additional circumstances" contemplated by this branch of the rule, because the Csurillas do not invoke it and contend only that the price for their property was so grossly inadequate that the court's conscience should have been shocked and the sale set aside on that ground alone.

When will the disparity between price and value be so great that a court will be justified in setting aside a judicial sale, either because the inadequate price, by itself, is so low as to shock the court's conscience or because the inadequacy, while not so great, is combined with other circumstances resulting in unfairness to the debtor? Obviously, if only the inadequate price is relied on to invoke the court's equitable discretion, the inadequacy must be very great — gross — as compared with the inadequacy that will be sufficient when other, unfairness-producing circumstances are present. In *Las Vegas Railway*, the purchase price amounted to between 54% and 65% of the property's value and was held so inadequate as to warrant setting the sale aside, but other circumstances — two parties interested in the sale were prevented from bidding — were present. Other cases provide examples of situations in which courts have found prices bid at judicial sales inadequate under various circumstances. See, e.g., Chew v. Acacia Mut. Life Ins. Co., 165 Colo. 43, 437 P.2d 339 (1968) (en banc) (69% of appraised value shocked the court's conscience); Straus v. Anderson, 366 Ill. 426, 9 N.E.2d 205 (1937) (sale for 23% of value would shock average individual); Home Owners' Loan Corp. v. Braxtan, 220 Ind. 587, 44 N.E.2d 989 (1942) (17% of value set aside); Suring State Bank v. Giese, 210 Wis. 489, 246 N.W. 556 (1933) (bid of 20%-60% of property's value set aside). Professor Washburn, in Washburn, supra note 1, at 866, observes: "There is general agreement at the extremes as to what constitutes gross inadequacy. Sale prices less than ten percent of value are generally held grossly inadequate, whereas those above forty percent are held not grossly inadequate."[15]

The midpoint of Professor Washburn's range is 25%. We decline to adopt any fixed numerical percentage as establishing a price-value disparity that in every case will be so great as to shock the court's conscience. The answer to the question necessarily resides in the sound discretion of the trial court, and there are too many subtle variations in the facts of this kind of case to make it feasible to lay down a fixed rule as to when a court's conscience should or should not be shocked.

The policy . . . reflected in Section 39-5-5 — that sheriff's execution sales for less than two-thirds of the appraised value of the property should not be permitted — is perhaps instructive here. However, . . . there are significant differences between a sheriff's sale under a writ of execution and a judicially supervised sale under a court-ordered foreclosure. Where the inadequate price does not fall into the

---

15. Professor Washburn also notes that the debtor faces a heavy task in convincing a court that a foreclosure sale price is inadequate, since "the court's inquiry into the adequacy of the foreclosure sale price is limited by two well-established principles: valuation of foreclosed property occurs at the date of the foreclosure sale, and the sale price is conclusive of the property's value." Id. at 858.

"shock the conscience" range (25% plus or minus 15%, for example), it may still be so inadequate (if less than two-thirds of the appraised value, for example) as to call for judicial invalidation of the sale if other circumstances, leading to unfairness, are present. We do not hold that in every case where the price falls below two-thirds of the fair market value, that price should be held inadequate as a matter of law, or that in every case where the price falls into the 10-40% range (or, conceivably, less) the inadequacy should shock the judicial conscience. We hold only that prices in these ranges call for special scrutiny by the court to be sure that, in the first case, additional circumstances do not produce an inequitable result and, in the second case, the grossly inadequate price is not confirmed absent good reasons why it should be.

In the present case, the purchase price for the combined properties was $90,000. The Csurillas complain that this was only about 39% of the property's value — assuming that its value was the amount they paid for it. There, however, is a major problem for the Csurillas' position in this case. They do not know; the court below did not know; we do not know — no one knows what the actual value of the property was at the time of the judicial sale.

We do know that included with the station property under the station contract was approximately $28,600 in inventory, much of which had been dissipated at the time of the sale. We also know that when the station contract was executed, the service station was operating and apparently making money; by the time of the sale, it had long since been closed and, according to the trial court, some or all of its "going concern" value was gone. In addition, as the court also found when the partial summary judgment was entered in September 1988, the station property had a fair market value "far less" than the amount of that judgment, the property having deteriorated significantly during the Csurillas' ownership. For all of these reasons, it seems likely (although we cannot be sure — no one can) that the sale price approached or exceeded 50% of the property's value. . . .

While the Csurillas claimed that the price was inadequate and now complain generally that consummation of the sale results in great unfairness to them, they do not contend that there was any impropriety in the conduct of the sale itself.[16] And they did not prove, or offer to prove, the extent, if any, to which the price fell short of the property's value. They did not, in other words, meet their burden to give the trial court sufficient information to enable it to exercise its discretion in passing upon the adequacy or inadequacy of the price and, if inadequate, whether the price was so low as to shock the court's conscience. They did not, despite the court's observation in September 1988 that they had not provided evidence of value and despite their own stipulation (when the first sale was set aside by agreement) that they could have the property appraised before the next sale, proceed with an appraisal or otherwise adduce evidence as to the fair market value of the property at the time of the sale. . . .

The order confirming the sale and granting a deficiency judgment is accordingly affirmed.

IT IS SO ORDERED.

---

16. Any such impropriety would be the kind of "additional circumstance" that, in combination with an inadequate price, might result in unfairness and so warrant setting the sale aside.

A number of aspects of foreclosure sale procedure contribute to its failure to bring reasonable prices for the property that is sold. (1) The sales are poorly advertised. (2) Prospective buyers are given little opportunity to inspect the property before the bidding, but they must accept the property "as is." (3) The rule of caveat emptor applies with regard to the state of the title. (4) The sale often takes place in a hostile environment making it difficult for the prospective bidder to get information about the property. (5) The buyer may be unable to use the property until the statutory redemption period expires.

1. Advertising

An owner who wants to sell property usually advertises for buyers. If the property is a house, for example, the owner may hire a real estate broker to find buyers or will, at the very least, run an ad in a newspaper. The owner will try to describe the house in a way that will both encourage readers to respond and help them decide whether the house is suitable to their needs. Owners who want to sell their property advertise in a manner calculated to attract potential buyers.

The way a foreclosure sale is advertised may be fixed by statute or the judgment of foreclosure. The following procedure is typical:

Wisconsin Statutes Annotated
(2005)

§815.31 NOTICE OF SALE OF REALTY; MANNER; ADJOURNMENT

(1) The time and place of holding any sale of real estate on execution shall be publicly advertised by posting a written notice describing the real estate to be sold with reasonable certainty in 3 public places in the town or municipality where such real estate is to be sold at least 3 weeks prior to the date of sale; and also in 3 public places of the town or municipality in which the real estate is situated, if it is not in the town or municipality where the sale is to be held.

(2) A copy of the notice of sale shall be printed each week for 6 successive weeks in a newspaper of the county prior to the date of sale.

The officer conducting the sale is rarely concerned with the price the sale will bring. Because debtors sometimes attempt to have sales set aside on the basis that they were not conducted strictly in accord with formal legal requirements, the officer's primary concern is usually to comply with those requirements. The result is sale notices like those in Figure 46.1, which were published in a Milwaukee legal newspaper.

The sheriffs, lawyers, or parties who place legal notices often select newspapers of limited circulation because the cost of running the ad is lower. Major newspapers segregate legal notices from the advertisements placed by owners and realtors. Either way, the legal notices rarely attract buyers interested in owning the property. To the extent they bring in bidders at all, the bidders are usually professional bargain hunters who plan to resell the property at a profit.

FIGURE 46.1.
Notice of a Foreclosure Sale

LEGAL NOTICES

SC-832738#

NOTICE OF TRUSTEE'S SALE TS No. 05-05695 Doc ID #000609411112005N Title Order No. 05-8-025953 Investor/Insurer No. 060941111 APN No. 068-0493-020-0000 YOU ARE IN DEFAULT UNDER A DEED OF TRUST, DATED 07/15/2004. UNLESS YOU TAKE ACTION TO PROTECT YOUR PROPERTY, IT MAY BE SOLD AT A PUBLIC SALE. IF YOU NEED AN EXPLANATION OF THE NATURE OF THE PROCEEDING AGAINST YOU, YOU SHOULD CONTACT A LAWYER." Notice is hereby given that ReconTrust Company, N.A., as duly appointed trustee pursuant to the Deed of Trust executed by LATIFU MUNIRAH, AN UNMARRIED WOMAN, dated 07/15/2004 and recorded 07/30/04, as Instrument No. , in Book 20040730, Page 4051), of Official Records in the office of the County Recorder of Sacramento County, State of California, will sell on 07/20/2005 at 9:30AM. At the East main entrance to the County Courthouse, 720 9th Street, Sacramento, CA at public auction, to the highest bidder for cash or check as described below, payable in full at time of sale, all right, title, and interest conveyed to and now held by it under said Deed of Trust, in the property situated in said County and State and as more fully described in the above referenced Deed of Trust. The street address and other common designation, if any, of the real property described above is purported to be: 3632 SUNRISE PINES DRIVE, SACRAMENTO, CA, 95827. The undersigned Trustee disclaims any liability for any incorrectness of the street address and other common designation, if any,

shown herein. The total amount of the unpaid balance with interest thereon of the obligation secured by the property to be sold plus reasonable estimated costs, expenses and advances at the time of the initial publication of the Notice of Sale is $228,466.79. It is possible that at the time of sale the opening bid may be less than the total indebtedness due. In addition to cash, the Trustee will accept cashier's checks drawn on a state or national bank, a check drawn by a state or federal credit union, or a check drawn by a state or federal savings and loan association, savings association, or savings bank specified in Section 5102 of the Financial Code and authorized to do business in this state. Said sale will be made, in an "AS IS" condition, but without covenant or warranty, express or implied, regarding title, possession or encumbrances, to satisfy the indebtedness secured by said Deed of Trust, advances thereunder, with interest as provided, and the unpaid principal of the Note secured by said Deed of Trust with interest thereon as provided in said Note, plus fees, charges and expenses of the Trustee and of the trusts created by said Deed of Trust. DATED: 06/29/2005 ReconTrust Company, N.A. 5898 CONDOR DRIVE, MP-88 MOORPARK, CA 93021 Phone: (800) 281 8219, Sale Information (805) 578-6618 By: Trustee's Sale Officer ReconTrust Company, N.A. is a debt collector attempting to collect a debt. Any information obtained will be used for that purpose. SACA708726 06/29, 07/06, 07/13 06/29/2005, 07/06/2005, 07/13/2005

SC-832731#

NOTICE OF TRUSTEE'S SALE TS No. 05-05173 Doc ID #00020886442005N Title Order No. 05-8-023626 Investor/Insurer No. 4343201008447 APN No. 243-0332-010-0000 YOU ARE IN DEFAULT UNDER A DEED OF TRUST, DATED 07/14/1987. UNLESS YOU TAKE ACTION TO PROTECT YOUR PROPERTY, IT MAY BE SOLD AT A PUBLIC SALE. IF YOU NEED AN EXPLANATION OF THE NATURE OF THE PROCEEDING AGAINST YOU, YOU SHOULD CONTACT A LAWYER." Notice is hereby given that ReconTrust Company, N.A., as duly appointed trustee pursuant to the Deed of Trust executed by RODERICK L. ROGERS, AN UNMARRIED MAN, dated 07/14/1987 and recorded 07/17/87, as Instrument No. 201258, in Book 87 07 17, Page 2424), of Official Records in the office of the County Recorder of Sacramento County, State of California, will sell on 07/13/2005 at 9:30AM, At the East main entrance to the County Courthouse, 720 9th Street, Sacramento, CA at public auction, to the highest bidder for cash or check as described below, payable in full at time of sale, all right, title, and interest conveyed to and now held by it under said Deed of Trust, in the property situated in said County and State and as more fully described in the above referenced Deed of Trust. The street address and other common designation, if any, of the real property described above is purported to be: 6045 MERLINDALE DRIVE, CITRUS HEIGHTS, CA, 95610. The undersigned Trustee disclaims any liability for any incorrectness of the street address and other common designation, if any, shown herein. The total amount of the unpaid

2. Inspection

As we discussed in Assignment 45, under most foreclosure sale procedures the debtor is entitled to remain in possession of the property until after the sale is held. The mortgage contract usually grants the foreclosing creditor the right to inspect the collateral in preparation for bidding at the sale. Such a provision ordinarily will be specifically enforced. Others who wish to bid at the sale can observe the property from adjacent public places, but they have no right to enter in order to inspect.

Homebuyer Finds Remains of Owner
Associated Press, November 21, 2000

TOLEDO, Ohio (AP) — A man making his first visit to a house he bought at a sheriff's auction found skeletal remains believed to be those of the former owner. Police said there was no evidence of foul play, but the county coroner was to examine the remains. Authorities said the man may have been dead more than two years. Police said the remains apparently were those of Eugene Bearringer, who would have been 50. The skeleton was found on the living room floor Monday by William Houttekier of Temperance, Mich.

The house was sold last week at auction because taxes weren't paid on the property for several years. County authorities had tried to contact Bearringer and out-of-state relatives through mailings. County Auditor Larry Kaczala said that when the property is foreclosed and goes up for sale, no one from the county ever sets foot in it. "The government would have no right to go onto that property, because we don't own it. We just sell it for the back taxes," he said.

Dean Nowakowski, 33, who lives two houses away, said the last time he saw Bearringer was more than two years ago. "I always wondered what happened to that dude," he said. "It got awful quiet over there."

Buyers who want the property for their own use are unlikely to be willing to purchase without looking inside the building. What prospective home buyer would like to purchase a house without knowing the floor plan, the condition of the walls and floors, or the functioning of the heating and plumbing? Only professionals who plan to find a bargain and resell for a large profit are likely to be interested.

3.   Title and Condition

Judicial sales are one of the few situations in which the rule of caveat emptor still applies. As the case that follows illustrates, buyers take subject to any defects in the title that they could have discovered through a search of the public records or an inspection of the property. Mr. Marino might have had a reasonable chance in an action against the seller in an ordinary private sale, but he discovered that in a judicial foreclosure sale he was without remedy.

Marino v. United Bank of Illinois, N.A.
484 N.E.2d 935 (Ill. App. Ct. 1985)

SCHNAKE, J.

Lawrence Marino, plaintiff, successfully bid at a sheriff's sale which took place on November 22, 1983. The property was being sold after United Bank of Illinois filed a complaint to foreclose a mortgage executed by Kenneth and Elizabeth Vosberg on January 9, 1981. After purchasing the property plaintiff attempted, in the instant action, to vacate the sale and to have his purchase money returned, on the basis of misrepresentations alleged to have been made by Linda Kream, an attorney who was sent to bid at the sale as representative of Theodore Liebovich, the attorney for the mortgagee. On May 30, 1984, the trial court ordered the sale vacated. However, on defendant's motion to reconsider, the trial court reversed its earlier order and confirmed the sale. Plaintiff Marino appeals from that order.

On November 22, 1983, the sheriff's sale of the property was held. According to plaintiff, Lawrence Marino, he intended to find out about the property and then make a decision as to whether to bid. He did not examine the records of the Winnebago County recorder's office to check the title, nor did he consult an attorney prior to submitting a bid. He attempted to obtain information through talking with Deputy Sheriff Claytor before the sale. Plaintiff asked Claytor about liens and encumbrances on the property, and Claytor told him that there was a mortgage of $8,800, $2,000 in attorney fees, $2,100 in taxes owed, and other miscellaneous liens, the total of which amounted to $14,327. Claytor told plaintiff to check with Liebovich, the attorney who was handling the case. Plaintiff then talked with attorney Linda Kream, who told him that she was attending the sale in place of Liebovich. According to plaintiff, he asked Linda Kream whether there were any encumbrances on the property. Before replying, Kream looked through a file and replied, "Well there's none that I can see," and then said, "This isn't my case, so I wouldn't know." Kream indicated to Marino that it was Liebovich's case, but that he was not available that day.

Linda Kream testified that she was an associate attorney with the firm of Liebovich and Gaziano and that Liebovich had asked her to appear at the sale and bid on behalf of the United Bank of Illinois. She had a foreclosure file and a cashier's check in an amount over $13,000. Kream testified that she was unfamiliar with the file as she had not been handling the case. Before the sale, plaintiff approached her and asked her how much she was going to bid. After telling him, plaintiff indicated that he would bid $1 more. Kream testified that plaintiff then asked her if there were any liens ahead of the bank's, and that she replied that it was not her case, so she would only know what was contained in the file. Plaintiff asked if she would look through the file, and she did. She then told plaintiff that there did not appear to be any other liens, but that she was not sure and she would not want him to rely on that. On cross-examination, Kream indicated that there was a title policy on file, but that she did not examine it.

Plaintiff successfully bid $13,541 for the property and the court approved the sale on December 12, 1983. On April 6, 1984, plaintiff sought to vacate the sale, alleging that Kream had informed him that no other liens or encumbrances existed on the property, and that he relied on her statement and thereafter purchased the property. He further asserted that he had since been joined as a defendant in an action by First Federal Savings and Loan of Rockford, and that it was at that time that he first became aware of liens and encumbrances superior to his interest. Marino's complaint alleged that United Bank of Illinois had a duty to join all parties with liens on the property, and asked that the sale be vacated and his money returned.

In response, United Bank of Illinois contended that plaintiff was not entitled to set aside the sale unless he could show fraud or misrepresentation, there were no statements made to induce plaintiff to purchase the property, and that plaintiff could not reasonably have relied on any statements that were made. In an affidavit,

Kream stated that at the time of the sheriff's sale, she did not have knowledge of the liens which were listed in plaintiff's motion to vacate.

The court found no fraud, but ordered the sale vacated because of Marino's reliance on Kream's unintentional misrepresentation. The court ordered United Bank of Illinois to reimburse Marino for the amount of money it received from the sale. United Bank of Illinois moved for reconsideration, alleging that Marino failed to prove that an assertion of fact was made to him on which he was entitled to reply, that plaintiff failed to prove the existence of the liens, and that there was no cause of action for an unintentional misrepresentation. The court granted defendant's motion to reconsider, vacated its prior order, and confirmed the sheriff's sale of November 22, 1983. Notice of appeal was timely filed.

Generally the doctrine of caveat emptor applies to judicial sales, and the risk of a mistake or defect of title is to be borne by the purchaser unless there is fraud, misrepresentation, or mistake of fact. In this case, plaintiff Marino alleges that because there was a misrepresentation by Kream, equity requires that the sale be vacated.

To establish fraudulent misrepresentation, plaintiff must show a false statement of material fact made by defendant, defendant's knowledge or belief that the statement was false, defendant's intent to induce plaintiff to act, an action by plaintiff in justifiable reliance on that statement, and damage to plaintiff resulting from such reliance. These elements must be proved for a charge of fraud, whether in a suit at law or in equity.

Examining these elements, it is clear that plaintiff failed to prove a fraudulent misrepresentation by attorney Kream. To begin with, plaintiff failed to prove a false statement of material fact. Matters of fact are to be distinguished from expressions of opinion, which cannot form the basis of an action of fraud. A representation is one of opinion rather than fact if it only expresses the speaker's belief, without certainty, as to the existence of a fact. By both plaintiff's and Kream's account, Kream indicated that from the information in the file there did not appear to be any liens or encumbrances, but she expressly told plaintiff that she was not sure of that fact because it was not her case. Her statement would appear to be an opinion since it was only her belief, stated without certainty, as to the existence of a fact. In his brief, plaintiff argues that due to Kream's status as an attorney, she can be said to have held herself out to have "special knowledge" such that there was an implied assertion of fact. In view of her expressed disclaimer of knowledge of any facts of the case, plaintiff's argument is not persuasive.

There was also no evidence that the statement made was known to be false, and the lack of certainty expressed by Kream would not support a finding that she made the statement with the intent to induce plaintiff to act. In determining whether there was justified reliance, it is necessary to consider all of the facts in plaintiff's actual knowledge as well as those which he could have discovered by the exercise of ordinary prudence. While a person may rely on a statement without investigation if the party making the statement creates a false sense of security or blocks further inquiry, it must be determined whether the facts were such as to put a reasonable man on inquiry. In this case, the lack of certainty of Kream's statement was sufficient to put a reasonable person on inquiry, and plaintiff was not justified in relying on that statement without taking appropriate steps to check the title. . . .

Plaintiff contends that it was incumbent upon defendant to search for liens and encumbrances and join all parties having subsequent liens, and that, in foreclosure, the mortgagee should search for intervening transfers or liens and should join record owners as parties defendant. However, in Baldi v. Chicago Title & Trust Co. (1983), 13 Ill. App. 3d 29, 31-33, 446 N.E.2d 1205, 1207-1208, the court rejected an argument that a junior mortgagee should be a necessary party to a foreclosure of a senior encumbrance. While defendant could have joined those parties with subsequent liens on the property, it had no duty to do so.

The judgment of the circuit court of Winnebago County is therefore affirmed.

The court notes that there are "liens and encumbrances" on the property that the bank's foreclosure did not extinguish. Neither their nature, nor the precise reason that the foreclosure did not extinguish them, matters. Whatever the liens are, Marino takes subject to them because he is a purchaser at a foreclosure sale. As the court makes clear, finding out what liens survive foreclosure is the responsibility of the foreclosure sale bidder. Caveat emptor!

The risks to a bidder at a judicial sale extend beyond the state of the title. In Horicon State Bank v. Kant Lumber Co., Inc., 478 N.W.2d 26 (Wis. Ct. App. 1991), the bank foreclosed its mortgage against property owned by the lumber company. In preparation for the sale, the bank hired an appraiser who examined the property and appraised it as worth $6,000. The bank was the only bidder at the sale. It bid $10,000 to be sure the court would confirm the sale. When the bank attempted to resell the property, it discovered that the property was environmentally contaminated and that cleanup costs would be from $5,000 to $13,500 and perhaps more. On the bank's application, the court refused to set aside the sale, saying that the bank's appraiser should have seen evidence of the pollution when the appraiser inspected the property and "the bank should have had the [environmental] evaluation made before the sale." The court concluded "[We] will not intervene if an overbid at a sheriff's sale results from the bidder's ignorance."

As Marino and Horicon illustrate, a person who would like to bid at a sale may have to incur substantial expense in preparation. Yet many of the judicial sales that are advertised never take place. The debtor finds the money to redeem the property, makes peace with the foreclosing creditor, or files bankruptcy. Persons who have spent time and money preparing to bid at those sales simply lose their investments.

4. Hostile Situation

To make an intelligent purchase of a parcel of real estate, particularly if it includes a building, the buyer must know a good deal about it. Most sales of real property occur between willing buyers and sellers. The buyers get most of the information they need by refusing to purchase unless the seller furnishes it. Because sellers want to sell, they are usually willing to furnish the needed information, as well as to cooperate in providing access to the property, past records, and so on.

Many foreclosure sales, on the other hand, take place in a hostile environment. Often there is no one with either a motive or an obligation to furnish information to prospective purchasers. In fact, a debtor's strategy for retaining its property often calls for preventing third parties from obtaining the information they need to bid. Foreclosing creditors may not be able to furnish information because they do not themselves have access to it. In many cases, the creditors prefer to purchase the property themselves at the judicial sale, evaluate it, and then resell it. As a result, the price at the first sale is of little consequence to them. They are satisfied with a low-price sale, followed by another sale for an amount approaching a market price.

The officer who conducts the sale is rarely a good source of information, either. Typically the officer has no obligation or incentive to furnish information, but the officer may have liability for furnishing incorrect information. As a result, it is not surprising that most have little to say about the condition of the property or the terms of the sale.

Often the debtor's best strategy is to provoke some procedural irregularity in the sale and litigate over it as a means of obtaining delay. For example, the debtor may encourage judgment-proof friends or relatives to make the highest bid at the sale and then not pay the purchase price. The high bidder at a judicial sale must consider the possibility that it will become entangled in litigation over the validity of the sale. Finally, there is always the possibility that after the bidding is concluded, but before the buyer can be put into possession, the debtor will destroy the property.

5. The Statutory Right to Redeem

As we noted above, a debtor who has the right to redeem the property after sale usually also remains entitled to possession. The high bidder at the sale may have to wait months or even years for possession. Even if the bidder can obtain possession, if the right to redeem is later exercised, the bidder may be unable to recover money spent to preserve or improve the property during the bidder's time of possession. That may discourage the successful bidder from making improvements necessary to return the property to productive use until the statutory redemption period runs. That in turn may reduce the amounts that bidders are willing to pay for property at a judicial sale.

With all these problems, it is hardly surprising that there are few bidders at most judicial sales and that, except for credit bids by foreclosing creditors, the bidding usually stops far short of the market value of the property.

D. Antideficiency Statutes

Foreclosure sales rarely yield the "market value" of the property — the amount it would bring in a sale by a willing buyer to a willing seller, neither of whom was under compulsion. Instead, they yield prices that reflect the adverse conditions under which they are held.

Legislatures have responded to the problem by enacting *antideficiency statutes*. These statutes either prohibit the court from granting deficiency judgments in particular circumstances, give the court the discretion to refuse to grant them, or limit the amount of the deficiencies to be granted. Notice that this approach addresses only one aspect of the problem created by inadequate sale prices: the possibility of a deficiency judgment. It does not address the plight of the debtor who has a substantial equity in property but loses it through a forced sale of the property for an inadequate price.

The most common type of antideficiency statute credits the debtor for the fair market value of the property even if the property brings a lower price at the foreclosure sale. For example, assume that the debtor owed $100,000 on the mortgage, the market value of the property was $80,000, but the sheriff sold it for $45,000 at the foreclosure sale. Without an antideficiency statute, the deficiency judgment would be for $55,000. With the type of antideficiency statute discussed here, the deficiency judgment would be for only $20,000. Other common types of antideficiency statutes prohibit deficiency judgments on purchase money mortgages or vest the court with discretion to deny deficiency judgments where they would be inequitable.

California has a particularly rich scheme of antideficiency statutes. The following provisions of the California Code of Civil Procedure are just a few of them, but they illustrate the variety of approaches that are possible.

California Code of Civil Procedure

Cal. Civ. Proc. Code (2005)

§580A.   DEFICIENCY JUDGMENTS

[The statute applies whenever a money judgment is sought for the balance due upon an obligation for the payment of which a deed of trust or mortgage with power of sale upon real property or any interest therein was given as security, following the exercise of the power of sale in such deed of trust or mortgage.] . . . Before rendering any judgment the court shall find the fair market value of the real property, or interest therein sold, at the time of sale. The court may render judgment for not more than the amount by which the entire amount of the indebtedness due at the time of sale exceeded the fair market value of the real property or interest therein sold at the time of sale with interest thereon from the date of the sale; provided, however, that in no event shall the amount of the judgment, exclusive of interest after the date of sale, exceed the difference between the amount for which the property was sold and the entire amount of the indebtedness secured by the deed of trust or mortgage. . . .

§580B.   CONDITIONS UNDER WHICH DEFICIENCY JUDGMENT FORBIDDEN

No deficiency judgment shall lie in any event after a sale of real property . . . under a deed of trust or mortgage given to the vendor to secure payment of the balance of the purchase price of that real property . . . or under a deed of trust or mortgage on a dwelling for not more than four families given to a lender to secure repayment of a loan which was in fact used to pay all or part of the purchase price of that dwelling occupied, entirely or in part, by the purchaser. . . .

§580D.   DEFICIENCY JUDGMENT AFTER FORECLOSURE UNDER POWER OF SALE FORBIDDEN; EXCEPTIONS

No judgment shall be rendered for any deficiency upon a note secured by a deed of trust or mortgage upon real property or an estate for years therein hereafter executed in any case in which the real property or estate for years therein has been sold by the mortgagee or trustee under power of sale contained in the mortgage or deed of trust. . . .

E.   Credit Bidding at Judicial Sales

The creditor who forces the sale is permitted to bid at it and will usually do so. The procedural shortcomings that discourage strangers from bidding at judicial sales have considerably less effect on a secured creditor who forces the sale. That creditor will know of the sale even though it is poorly advertised, may be familiar with the title and condition of the property already, and may have an enforceable contractual right to inspect it.

The creditor who forces the sale has yet another important advantage. Recall that whatever is paid for the property over and above the expenses of sale, up to the amount of the secured debt, goes to the creditor who forced the sale. Whatever that creditor pays the sheriff for the property, up to the amount of the secured debt, the sheriff will pay back to the creditor as soon as the sale is confirmed. In recognition of this fact, foreclosure sale procedures generally allow the creditor a shortcut. The creditor need not pay the money to the sheriff, merely to get it back a few days later. Instead, the creditor can bid on credit up to the amount of the debt. Such a bid is referred to as a *credit bid*. Recall also that the amount paid for the property at the judicial sale is credited against the debt. When the secured creditor buys the collateral by a credit bid, an equal amount of the debt is canceled. In effect, the creditor buys the collateral for all or part of the secured debt. The creditor is then free to resell the collateral. If the resale is for more than the secured creditor paid at the judicial sale, the creditor earns a profit (or obtains a windfall, depending on how you choose to look at it).

Once the creditor's collateral has been sold at a judicial sale, the balance of the debt is often uncollectible. An antideficiency statute may bar the creditor from obtaining a deficiency. Even if the creditor gets a judgment, the creditor may be unable to collect because the debtor is bankrupt or judgment-proof. In such cases, the creditor loses nothing by bidding the full amount of its debt at the foreclosure sale, even if the bid is far in excess of the value of the collateral.

Assume that a creditor has forced a sale of collateral and knows that it will not be able to collect a deficiency. Such a creditor has little reason not to bid the full amount of its debt. The reason may be clearer from an example. Assume that the debtor owes the creditor $1 million, secured by collateral worth $200,000. If the creditor buys the property for $200,000 at the foreclosure sale, its total recovery on the debt will be the $200,000 it obtains from resale of the property. If, instead, the creditor bids $1 million at the sale, the outcome would be the same. The creditor need not pay the $1 million purchase price to the sheriff; the creditor is entitled to a credit for the amount of its bid. In this scenario too, the creditor's total recovery on the debt is the $200,000 it obtains from resale.

The creditor who makes a high credit bid gains several advantages. The creditor minimizes the likelihood that the sale will be set aside for inadequacy of price. The creditor also minimizes the likelihood that the debtor will exercise its statutory right to redeem the property. Most statutory redemption is for the amount of the sale price. If the debtor in our example wanted to redeem its $200,000 property, the debtor would have to pay $1 million — a highly unlikely event. The foreclosing creditor who is willing to credit bid the entire amount of its secured debt need not incur the expense of evaluating the collateral prior to the sale. If the creditor is outbid, the creditor will recover the full amount of the secured debt; if it is not outbid, it will have the property to inspect, evaluate, improve, and resell at its leisure.

A creditor who buys its collateral at the sale always runs some risk that the sale will be set aside or the property redeemed. Notwithstanding that risk, the creditor-purchaser is completely free to seek a profit on resale. That profit on resale will belong to the creditor, not the debtor.

In fact, purchase by the foreclosing creditor for later resale is by far the dominant pattern in mortgage foreclosures. A recent study of mortgage foreclosures in one county in New York revealed that the mortgagee purchased the property by credit bid in 77 percent of all cases. Eighty-five percent of the creditor-purchasers resold the property within four to five years, and a large majority of the resales took place in the first two years. Of the third parties who purchased at foreclosure sales, about two-thirds resold the property within four to five years. Wechsler, Through the Looking Glass: Foreclosure by Sale as De Facto Strict Foreclosure — An Empirical Study of Mortgage Foreclosure and Subsequent Resale, 70 Cornell L. Rev. 850 (1985).

In effect, this means that the mortgage foreclosure process, in its most common manifestation, is a two-sale process: The first sale, the judicial one, is not so much a real exposure of the collateral to the market as a symbolic formality that cuts off the debtor's right to redeem or at least starts the redemption period running. The resale for market price that will return the property to productive use occurs some time later. Notice what happens to the debtor's equity in the property when the first sale is for only the amount of the foreclosed lien. The buyer at the first sale (usually the lien holder) gets the property for the amount of the lien and resells it for a price approaching market value, thereby capturing the debtor's equity.

F.   Judicial Sale Procedure: A Functional Analysis

As we noted at the beginning of this assignment, some commentators see the judicial sale process as intended to value the collateral. By fixing a value for the collateral, the process determines the amount of the deficiency judgment or, if the debtor has an equity in the property, it insures that the equity will not be forfeited. But if that is the intent, the process does not accomplish it. Except in those cases in which foreclosing creditors credit bid the amounts of their debts, the bids at foreclosure and other judicial sales bring only a fraction of the value of the property sold. While credit bids are often near or even in excess of the market value of the property sold, they are hardly a sign that the process is working. To the contrary, the purpose of a credit bid is usually to avoid reliance on the judicial sale process.

Although the judicial sale process does a poor job of valuing the collateral, it has important side effects that some see as its virtue. If the debtor has an equity in the property, a judicial sale threatens to forfeit it. Some commentators suggest that this motivates knowledgeable debtors to liquidate their property before that occurs. If the debtor owes more than the property is likely to bring at the sale, forced sale at an inadequate price may threaten to result in a deficiency judgment in an excessive amount. That in turn motivates knowledgeable debtors to attempt to come to terms with the foreclosing creditor. It would be wrong, however, to conclude that these side effects render the grossly inefficient procedures for foreclosure sale either elegant or efficient. Threatening to blow the property to bits would accomplish as much, and the explosives might be less expensive.

Problem Set 46

46.1.   You represent Commercial Bank with regard to an upcoming judicial foreclosure sale. The balance owing on the mortgage is $53,231. Commercial estimates that the house is worth between $40,000 and $45,000. Under the law of your state, Commercial will not be able to obtain a judgment for any deficiency remaining after the sale. Commercial wants to know how much they should bid at the sale. Consider these possibilities as you map out your strategy:

a.   Commercial is the only bidder present at the sale. For what amount should they buy the property?

b.   A third party has bid $53,232. Should Commercial go higher?

c.   A third party has bid $44,000. Should Commercial go higher?

46.2.   As part of your firm's pro bono program, you represent Sallie Hudson. Sallie fell three payments behind on her mortgage. First Savings, the mortgage lender, accelerated, filed for foreclosure, and obtained a judgment. The foreclosure sale is set for a date four weeks from now. The judgment is for $53,231. Sallie would like to keep the house, but her finances are generally shaky, and she doesn't have the money to redeem it. She is wondering whether she should be doing anything in preparation for the sale? Assume you are in a jurisdiction where the grant of a deficiency is within the discretion of the court, based on the equities of the case. In this situation, the practical effect is that neither you nor First Savings can be certain whether the court will grant a deficiency judgment.

a.   If the house has a fair market value of $40,000 to $45,000, what is your answer?

b.   If the house has a fair market value of $70,000, what is your answer?

c.   Sallie's brother-in-law deals in real estate and has the financial ability to buy this house. He is willing to do so and let Sallie keep living in it. How does that change your answers to a and b?

46.3. In a parallel universe in which you've never met Sallie Hudson, you are interested in buying a house. The neighborhood you like best is Spring Green. In scanning the legal notices this morning, you saw that a house in Spring Green is scheduled for a judicial foreclosure sale in four weeks. The notice shows that First Savings and Loan is plaintiff in the foreclosure case, Sallie Hudson is the defendant, and the case number is 96-263. The notice does not indicate the balance owing on the mortgage. It does give the address and legal description of the property and the name of the creditor's attorney, Jason Kovan. You'd like to try to buy this house, particularly if you can get a bargain on it. What information will you need to formulate a bid? Where will you get it? Will Hudson be willing to help? Kovan? First Savings? The sheriff who will conduct the sale?

46.4. You represent American Insurance Company. They have asked you to prepare a "bidding strategy" for an upcoming foreclosure sale. American holds the first mortgage, in the amount of $20 million, against an apartment building that is under construction and unoccupied. They estimate that the building is worth about $18 million as is. The debtor is a corporation that owns no other assets, but payment of the loan has been guaranteed by four wealthy individuals who are the owners of the corporation. So long as there are no problems with the foreclosure sale, American anticipates that they probably will be able to recover any deficiency from the four guarantors. The law of your state provides for no statutory right to redeem. In planning your strategy, consider the following possibilities:

a.   American is the only bidder present at the sale. For what amount should they buy the property?

b.   A lawyer representing a corporation you have never heard of appears at the sale and bids $20 million. You doubt that the mysterious bidder actually has $20 million, but under the law of your state, the successful bidder who makes a $1,000 deposit will have four hours to increase the deposit to one-third of the bid price. The officer conducting the sale tells you that if the bidder does not increase the deposit within that time, the court probably will reschedule the sale for a date about a month from now. Should American bid higher?

c.   Under the law of your state, if the high bidder at a public sale fails to purchase the property, the officer conducting the sale must sell to the second highest bidder. Does this change your initial bidding strategy? What if there are two strangers at your sale, and one bids $12 million and the second immediately bids $25 million. What should you do?

46.5. You received a call from Paul Tosci, a senior lending officer for Seal Rock Bank. The Bank has been approached by a shopping center developer,

Margo Marshak, who would like a $2.5 million standby commitment to enable her to bid on a shopping center that is to be sold at a judicial foreclosure sale. On the basis of recent sales of roughly comparable shopping centers, Tosci estimates the value of this one to be $5.1 million. He explains that Marshak will pay a $25,000 nonrefundable fee for the Bank's legally binding commitment to lend $2.5 million against the shopping center in the event that the developer wins the bid. The Bank will also earn the market rate of interest on the loan if the Bank is called on to make it. Marshak will provide title insurance at her own expense and invest at least $500,000 of her own money in the shopping center. What advice do you give Tosci? Is this likely to be good business for Seal Rock? What problems do you foresee? Would you feel better about the deal if (1) Marshak was the one who originally developed the shopping center and her brother-in-law is the debtor being foreclosed against, or (2) Marshak is an outsider with no prior ties to the shopping center?

46.6.   You continue in your job as chief legislative aide to state representative Candy Rowsey. A recent state supreme court decision has ruled that creditors can recover deficiency judgments from their debtors following any kind of foreclosure sale. Several newspaper editorials have decried this result, focusing on hapless homeowners caught in a real estate market downturn. Representative Rowsey chairs the judiciary committee, and she wants a recommendation from you on whether she should propose legislation to restrict deficiency judgments. Give her an outline of your point of view, including the kinds of restrictions you would choose if some proposal to limit deficiency judgments went forward.

Assignment 47: Article 9 Sale and Deficiency

Sales under Article 9 of the Uniform Commercial Code serve essentially the same purposes as judicial sales. They determine the value of the collateral and convert that value into cash. If the debtor has equity in the collateral, conversion to cash makes it possible for the secured creditor to deduct the amount owing from the proceeds of sale and send the remainder to the debtor. If the sale is for less than the amount of the debt, that determination of value provides the basis for a court to later decide what portion of the debt has been paid and what portion remains owing.

As with real property foreclosures, the requirement that the collateral be offered for sale as part of the personal property foreclosure process cannot be waived or varied in the initial lending contract. U.C.C. §§9-602(10), 9-620. For example, a provision in a car loan agreement that, in the event of default and repossession, the secured creditor can retain the car in satisfaction of the debt is unenforceable. The sale is an essential feature of the foreclosure process, and the debtor has a right to have the collateral sold regardless of the contractual language.

A. Strict Foreclosure Under Article 9

After a default has occurred, the debtor can consent to the secured party retaining the collateral in full or in *partial satisfaction* of the obligation it secures. "Partial satisfaction" means that the debtor receives credit against the debt in some amount but continues to owe the remainder. While a right to consent probably sounds harmless enough, in most instances the consent will not be real. U.C.C. §9-620(c)(2) implies consent if the secured party sends the debtor a proposal for retention of the collateral in full satisfaction of the debt and does not receive a notification of objection to the proposal within 20 days. An oral objection is insufficient. Debtors who do nothing, perhaps because they are confused by the procedures, are deemed to have consented.

This right to consent is subject to three conditions. First, there must be no objection from others holding liens against the collateral. See U.C.C. §9-620(a)(2). Second, if the collateral is consumer goods, the debtor can consent, in writing or by silence, to strict foreclosure only after repossession. U.C.C. §9-620(a). Third, strict foreclosure is not permitted if the debtor has paid 60 percent of the cash price of consumer goods purchased on credit or 60 percent of the loan against other consumer goods. Once again, the debtor may waive this right after default, but this kind of waiver requires a writing. U.C.C. §§9-620(a)(4) and (e), 9-624(b).

The third condition is directed against the unscrupulous practice of forfeiting debtors' equities in property when the debtors have nearly completed payment. If the debtor has paid 60 percent of the cash price or original loan amount, the likelihood that the debtor has an equity in the property is high. U.C.C. §9-620(e) was drafted to protect debtors against loss of such equities. What is perhaps more remarkable about the provision is its narrowness: It provides no protection to consumers who have paid less than 60 percent and no protection to nonconsumers, regardless of how much the nonconsumers have paid. The implicit assumptions seem to be that consumers who have paid less than 60 percent don't have an equity, and anyone other than a consumer will be sophisticated enough to protect its equity by making the objection described in U.C.C. §9-620(c).

B.   Sale Procedure Under Article 9

When Article 9 applies, U.C.C. §9-610 governs the procedure for sale of the collateral. The most important difference from the judicial sale procedure studied in the previous assignment is that the secured creditor, not a public official, conducts the sale and distributes the sale proceeds. U.C.C. §9-610 gives the creditor broad latitude to determine the method and timing of the sale. Depending on the circumstances, the creditor may be able to sell the property by auction, by setting a fixed price and finding a buyer who will pay that price, or by negotiating with interested parties.

This does not mean a foreclosing creditor can sell the collateral however it pleases. The foreclosing creditor has a duty to the debtor to choose a procedure for sale that is commercially reasonable. In fact, "every aspect of the disposition, including the method, manner, time, place and terms must be commercially reasonable." U.C.C. §9-610(b). To a much greater degree than most judicial sale procedures, the U.C.C. sale procedure is directed at getting a good price for the collateral. Under many judicial sale procedures, for example, shares of stock in Microsoft would have to be sold at a sheriff's sale after foreclosure; under the provisions of Article 9, they can be sold cheaply and quickly through NASDAQ.

Section 9-611(c)(1) also requires that the creditor give the debtor prior notice of the sale. The purpose of notice is to enable the debtor to observe the sale, participate in it, or otherwise protect its rights. One thing the debtor might do, if it learns of the sale in time, is seek out additional persons to bid.

U.C.C. §9-623 incorporates the common law right to redeem. Under its provisions, redemption is accomplished by paying the full amount of the debt, including the secured creditors' attorneys' fees and expenses of sale. As we explored in Assignment 46, judicial sales are often subject to an additional, statutory right to redeem that continues after the sale. No additional statutory right to redeem exists after an Article 9 sale. At the moment the creditor enters into a contract for disposition of the collateral, it is too late for the debtor to redeem it.

The debtor's right to set aside a defective or irregular sale is more constricted under the U.C.C. than under most judicial sale procedures. If the only defect in the sale is that it was commercially unreasonable, the debtor is likely to be left with merely the right to sue the creditor for damages. (If, however, the collateral is consumer goods, the debtor has the right to recover a statutory penalty. U.C.C. §9-625(c)(2).) But the dispute remains between the debtor and the creditor. The good faith purchaser at a U.C.C. sale can buy with confidence that it will not lose its bargain because the sale is set aside. See U.C.C. §9-617(b).

Sales under Article 9 are governed by these procedures even if the creditor obtained possession of the collateral by filing a replevin case rather than using a U.C.C. self-help remedy. The court that granted the judgment of replevin does not supervise the sale process or confirm the sale after it has occurred. Again, the U.C.C. provisions simplify the sale procedure by eliminating protections for the dispossessed debtor.

When collateral is sold for an insufficient price, the injury to the debtor may come in either of two forms. Where the debtor has an equity in the collateral, the insufficient price may forfeit all or part of this equity. In fact, few debtors sue for such a loss. First, many debtors have no equity to lose. For example, the balance owing on a car loan often exceeds the resale value of the car during the early part of the loan repayment period (when debtors are most likely to default). Second, the debtor who has lost an equity may not have the financial resources necessary to bring suit. Third, even if the debtor can afford to bring suit, it may not be worth it. The cost of the suit may exceed the amount that could be recovered.

The second type of injury to debtors from an insufficient sale price is the entry of a deficiency judgment in an amount larger than is appropriate. Litigation over deficiencies is more common than litigation over a debtor's loss of equity. One reason is that the deficiency litigation is initiated by the creditors, who can usually better afford it, both because they are in better financial condition and because they tend to be repeat players who can make this kind of litigation part of their business routine. Nonetheless, important disincentives to suing for deficiencies exist, especially against debtors who resist. The U.C.C. standard of a "commercially reasonable sale" is so vague that such a debtor can nearly always find something to complain about. By investing a relatively small amount to defend the creditor's action for a deficiency, the debtor can put the creditor to substantial legal expense. If the debtor shows any inclination to resist, the creditor will find it difficult to justify the expense of continuing. Even creditors who win deficiency judgments seldom collect them.

Debtors commonly defend actions for deficiency judgments by asserting that the creditor retained the collateral instead of conducting a sale, that the creditor did not give proper notice of the sale, or that the creditor conducted the sale in a manner that was not commercially reasonable. Each of these defenses is considered below.

C.   Problems with Article 9 Sale Procedure

1.   *Failure to Sell the Collateral*

U.C.C. §9-610(a) provides that a secured party *may* sell the collateral after default. But there is no specific provision that the secured party *must* sell the collateral after default and, aside from the narrow exception for some consumer goods in §9-620(f), no time fixed within which any sale must occur. A secured party who obtains possession of the collateral after default may prefer to keep it and use it. For example, suppose a farmer sold equipment to a neighbor and then had to repossess it. The farmer may then prefer to keep it and use it rather than sell it again. A secured creditor who plans to sell the collateral if necessary may want to keep it temporarily while waiting to see if the repossession itself spurs the debtor or a guarantor to come up with the money. In some cases a secured party might be unable to sell the collateral because a law or regulation prohibits resale or because the collateral has been destroyed or become worthless (for example, a secured party might repossess alcoholic beverages but not have a license to sell them). Finally, a secured party who intends to sell repossessed collateral may simply procrastinate.

While the secured party has possession of the collateral, it may decline in value. That alone entitles the debtor to no remedy. But if the secured creditor's delay in selling is commercially unreasonable, the secured creditor's deficiency will be limited to the amount that would have been left owing if the sale had been commercially reasonable. See U.C.C. §9-626(a).

2. The Requirement of Notice of Sale

U.C.C. §9-611 requires that the secured party send notice to the debtor, guarantors, and some lienors. To identify the lienors, the secured party may have to conduct a search of the public records. The failure to give this notice does not invalidate the sale, U.C.C. §9-617, but it is a defect that can have the effect of reducing the amount of the deficiency the secured party can recover or, as the following case illustrates, eliminating the deficiency altogether.

In re Downing
286 B.R. 900 (Bankr. W.D. Mo. 2002)

ARTHUR B. FEDERMAN, CHIEF BANKRUPTCY JUDGE.

FACTUAL BACKGROUND

On September 25, 2000, Mr. Downing purchased a 1999 BMW 528i from BMW, and granted BMW a lien on the car. . . . On March 27, 2002 . . . Mr. Downing surrendered the vehicle to BMW. On April 4, 2002, BMW notified Mr. Downing that it intended to sell the car, as allowed under state law, no sooner than 10 days after the date of the notice. On August 1, 2002, BMW sold the car at a commercial auction in Milwaukee, Wisconsin. After the sale, BMW filed an unsecured deficiency claim in this case in the amount of $18,517.24. Mr. Downing objected to the claim, on the grounds that BMW did not provide him with proper notice of the sale as required by Missouri's version of Revised Article 9 of the Uniform Commercial Code (the UCC). . . .

DISCUSSION

In Missouri, compliance with the notice provisions of Article 9 is a prerequisite to the recovery of a deficiency following the sale of repossessed collateral. As the court in *McKesson Corporation* stated, "strict compliance is required because deficiency judgments after repossession of collateral are in derogation of common law...in other words, since deficiency judgments were unheard of in common law, the right to a deficiency judgment accrues only after strict compliance with a relevant statute."[1] The party seeking the deficiency judgment has the burden of proving the sufficiency of the notice. Any doubt as to what constitutes strict compliance with the statutory requirements must be resolved in favor of the debtor.

The parties agree that the adequacy of the notice is governed by [U.C.C. §§9-613 and 9-614]. [U.C.C. §9-613] provides the contents and form of notification prior to the disposition of non-consumer goods.

Except in a consumer-goods transaction, the following rules apply:
(1) The contents of a notification of disposition are sufficient if the notification:
    (A) Describes the debtor and the secured party;
    (B) Describes the collateral that is the subject of the intended disposition;
    (C) States the method of intended disposition;
    (D) States that the debtor is entitled to an accounting of the unpaid indebtedness and states the charge, if any, for an accounting; and
    (E) States the time and place of a public sale or the time after which any other disposition is to be made.

[U.C.C. §9-614] applies those same requirements to consumer-goods dispositions. In addition, when disposing of consumer goods, the creditor must provide a "description of any liability for a deficiency of the person to which the notification is sent," and a "telephone number from which the amount that must be paid to the secured party to redeem the collateral under [U.C.C. §9-623] is available." The pertinent distinction between the two provisions is that in nonconsumer-goods dispositions, the question of whether the contents of a notification that lacks any of the required information are nevertheless sufficient is a question of fact. Since an automobile is a consumer good, however, the sufficiency of the notice sent by BMW must be evaluated pursuant to both [U.C.C. §§9-613 and 9-614].

The notice sent by BMW was in the form of a letter dated April 4, 2002. The letter identified the debtor as Steven L. Downing, the creditor as BMW, and the collateral as a 1999 BMW 528i, WBADP5340XBR95304. It then stated as follows:

This letter confirms you have rejected and/or terminated your loan due to the filing of bankruptcy. BMW Financial Services NA, LLC has taken possession of the Vehicle.

You are notified that BMW Financial Services NA, LLC intends to sell the vehicle as allowed under state law, but no sooner than 10 days after the date of this letter.

This letter is not being sent in violation of the discharge injunction of 11 U.S.C. §727 and/ or 1328(e), if any, but is merely an attempt to comply with requisite notice requirements under the contract/lease and applicable law. If you have received a discharge in bankruptcy, this letter is an attempt to collect a debt solely from the vehicle

---

1. McKesson Corp. v. Colman's Grant Village, Inc., 938 S.W.2d 631, 633 (Mo. Ct. App. 1997) (citations omitted).

pledged to secure payment of the contract/lease and not from you personally and any information obtained will be used for that purpose.

Should you have any questions, call us at the number referenced below, Monday through Friday, 9:00 A.M. to 5:00 P.M. ET or at either address listed below.

At the hearing, BMW represented that it sold the 1999 BMW at a commercial auction in Milwaukee, Wisconsin attended only by automobile dealers. As such, BMW argues that the sale was a private sale to commercial buyers, therefore, it was not required to provide Mr. Downing with the exact time and place of the auction. While BMW offered no support for this contention, in fact, other courts have held that a dealers-only auction is not public in character. Professor Barkley Clark, likewise, posits that where a sale is open only to automobile dealers, it is closed to some aspect of the market; therefore, it is a private sale. Nonetheless, the UCC clearly required BMW to inform Mr. Downing as to whether it would sell the car at either a private sale or public sale. Mr. Downing rightly points out in his brief that the notice sent by BMW did not inform him of the type of sale contemplated, or that he would be responsible for any deficiency. It also failed to inform Mr. Downing of his right to an accounting of the exact amount of his indebtedness, or what BMW claimed the indebtedness to be at the time of the sale. The burden of proof is on BMW to demonstrate that it has in all respects complied with the notice provisions of the UCC. By the express terms of the statute, that includes the method of disposition. BMW did not specify the nature of the sale, it did not inform Mr. Downing of his potential liability, and it did not inform him of his right to an accounting. For all of these reasons, I find that the notice did not strictly comply with the requirements of [U.C.C. §613] as made applicable to consumer-goods transactions by [U.C.C. §9-614].

BMW also argues that since the Downings' plan provided that Mr. Downing intended to surrender the vehicle, Missouri law does not require it to advise him of his right to redeem the vehicle. But that is not the sole purpose served by the notice. If a debtor is given the terms of the private sale, he has the opportunity to offer better terms. If a debtor is told the time and place of a public sale, he has an opportunity to appear at the sale, or have someone appear on his behalf, and bid. In any event, Missouri has long held that the right to a deficiency exists only if the creditor strictly complies with the statutory requirements of the UCC, regardless of whether there was any resulting harm to the debtor from the failed notice.

The notification was not sufficient, therefore, under Missouri law, BMW loses its right to a deficiency judgment. Debtors' objection to the claim of BMW will be sustained.

---

3.   The Requirement of a Commercially Reasonable Sale

The provision of U.C.C. §9-610(b) requiring that "[e]very aspect of a disposition of collateral, including the method, manner, time, place, and other terms, must be commercially reasonable" is deliberately vague. The purpose is to bring the knowledge and ingenuity of the secured party to bear in determining a reasonable way to dispose of the particular kind of collateral. The underlying assumption is that what methods, manners, times, or places are reasonable will differ with the type of collateral, and perhaps with other circumstances. Procedures that are reasonable to dispose of a few hundred dollars worth of office furniture may not be reasonable for disposing of millions of dollars worth of laboratory equipment. In each case, the secured creditor should discover a reasonable method of disposition and use it. Ordinarily that will be a method that reasonable owners of the particular type of property would use when their own money is at stake.

In most cases in which the commercial reasonableness of a sale is challenged, a close factual inquiry is required. In the following case the debtor had filed for bankruptcy, so the bankruptcy court heard the case without a jury, according to bankruptcy procedures. But the applicable law was the Tennessee version of the U.C.C.

Chavers v. Frazier

93 B.R. 366 (Bankr. M.D. Tenn. 1989)

HONORABLE GEORGE C. PAINE, II, BANKRUPTCY JUDGE.

[Mr. and Mrs. Chavers repossessed a Lear jet from the Frazier group and sold it. When the Chavers sought a deficiency judgment in an amount in excess of $400,000, the Frazier group defended on the ground that the sale had not been held in a commercially reasonable manner.]

In order to make the determination of commercial reasonableness, we must look to the facts and circumstances of the sale. Following repossession of the aircraft and the transfer of rights to the Chavers, the Lear jet was sold at a public sale. The aircraft, which sold to Frank Frazier's group for $850,000.00 in March, 1985, was sold in April, 1986 for $415,000.00. Although failure to procure the best price for collateral does not in and of itself make a sale commercially unreasonable, [U.C.C. §9-627(a)], and reasonableness is primarily assessed by the procedures employed, "a sufficient resale price is the logical focus of the protection given debtors...." Smith v. Daniels, 634 S.W.2d 276, 278 (Tenn.App. 1982). The great disparity between the purchase price and the sale price of the collateral approximately one (1) year later raises the issue of whether the total circumstances demonstrate that the Chavers took all steps considered reasonable by prevailing practices to insure that the sale of the Lear jet would bring a fair price. After reviewing the circumstances of the sale and the relevant legal factors, the Court determines that the Chavers have not met their burden for the following reasons.

Procedures employed to sell small jet aircraft are matters particularly within the knowledge of a small group of persons who are experts in the highly technical endeavor. The Chavers offered the testimony of two (2) experts, and [the Frazier group] offered a third expert, Mr. Charles Mulle. After considering both the demeanor and the relative qualifications of these experts, the Court finds that Mr. Mulle was by far the pre-eminent expert. Mr. Mulle was a graduate of Riddle Aeronautic Institute where he received a Bachelor of Science Degree in Aeronautic sciences with a minor in aviation management. Prior to attending Riddle Aeronautic Institute, he served in Army aviation for four (4) years and assisted in the testing projects for certain military aircraft. He has served as a Canadian bush pilot, a corporate pilot, and since 1975 has been employed full time in the commercial aircraft leasing sales and management area. Since 1981 he has been the principal owner of Business Aircraft Leasing, Inc., a company which is solely involved in the buying, selling and leasing of corporate and commercial aircraft. In addition, Mr. Mulle had specific knowledge of the aircraft at issue in this case from the date it was initially ordered from the manufacturer. He had been responsible for leasing the aircraft and had subsequently sold the aircraft to [the Frazier group]. One of the Chavers' expert witnesses agreed that Mr. Mulle was a competent and knowledgeable person in the field of aircraft sales and procedures. The other expert witness offered by the Chavers advised the Court that he respected Mr. Mulle's opinion and looked to him for information and advice. Mr. Mulle's experience was far in excess of that of the Chavers' experts. Based on his experience, candor and qualifications, the Court finds Mr. Mulle highly credible and uniquely qualified to assist the Court in its determination. The Chavers' expert, who actually assisted them in devising a plan for the sale, testified that he had never conducted a retail sale of jet aircraft prior to the transaction in question.

The value of the aircraft at the time of its sale to [the Frazier group] was approximately $825,000.00 to $850,000.00, as established by the testimony of the banker who initially granted the loan to [the Frazier group]. Mr. Mulle testified that the value was in that range and may have contained a premium of approximately $25,000.00 to $50,000.00 because the initial sale was one hundred percent (100%) financed.

1. THE HASTY SALE WAS NOT REASONABLE

The plaintiffs gained possession of the aircraft on May 2, 1986 and sold it at public auction on June 3, 1986. The Court finds the plaintiffs acted with unreasonable haste in their efforts to sell the aircraft. . . .

The collateral at issue is a jet aircraft with a highly specialized and limited market. Under the circumstances of this case, the Court finds that the time permitted to advertise and market the plane to this select group of potential buyers was grossly inadequate. The Chavers could not satisfactorily explain their actions in April and May of 1986, but the following is clear from the record. First, the Chavers['] . . . principal advisor, who also testified at trial, was extremely inexperienced in the commercial sale of jet aircraft. The plaintiffs were aware that Mr. Mulle had worked on the aircraft previously and that he was available to assist them in the sale of the aircraft, yet neither the Chavers nor their advisors sought Mr. Mulle out for advice or aid. The plaintiffs' advisor knew of the proposed repossession on April 23, 1986 and that the custody of the aircraft would pass to the Chavers on May 2, 1986, but made no immediate recommendations as to the means of disposing of the aircraft. After "investigating options" for at least two (2) weeks, he and the Chavers made the initial decision to sell the aircraft at auction approximately three (3) weeks prior to the actual sale. All advertising for the sale was done from May 20, 1986 to May 29, 1986 and terminated within five (5) days of the sale.

The other expert witnesses, including the Chavers' own expert, believed greater time was needed to explore and reach the potential market. The Chavers' other expert witness testified that six (6) months to one (1) year was needed for the fair and proper sale of such an aircraft. Mr. Mulle considered ninety (90) days to be an appropriate, although minimum, time frame to judge the market and to make commercially reasonable efforts.

Regardless of the specific time requirements, which this Court does not determine, it is clear to the Court that the time requirement...agreed to between the Bank and the Chavers was, in itself, unreasonable. The Court further finds that the Chavers sold an expensive and sophisticated jet aircraft in [an] unreasonably brief time...and that this hasty sale was a significant cause of the low sale price....

2.   THE ADVERTISING WAS NOT ADEQUATE

The Court considered substantial testimony concerning the adequacy of the advertising and further determines that the advertising was wholly inadequate for a commercially reasonable sale. Advertisements ran briefly in the *Wall Street Journal* and a trade publication known as *Trade-A-Plane*. The advertisements were described by Mr. Mulle as telegraphing a distress sale during "a brief flurry of advertising." Even one of the Chavers' experts felt that the use of the "as-is" phrase in the text of the advertising suggested a distress sale.

Mr. Mulle described a reasonable advertising protocol as follows. He testified first that advertisements in the *Wall Street Journal* and *Trade-A-Plane* should be positive and run for an appropriate length of time. The Chavers' advertisements ran briefly and suggested a distress sale. He also testified that the potential market for jet aircraft was concentrated in corporations and professional aircraft brokers throughout the country. From this pool of qualified buyers the most likely prospects should have been determined; the particular needs of a buyer should have been addressed in a formal sales effort, including if necessary, taking the aircraft for a buyer to view. While the Chavers provided some information to those who responded to their advertisements, such information was described by Mr. Mulle as "laughable" and indicative of an amateur effort to sell the aircraft. The sales packet provided by the Chavers' advisor to potential buyers did not include a log book summary or copy of the log book, which even the Chavers' advisor admitted was important information to a potential buyer and would reflect the high degree of maintenance required by the Federal Aviation Authority for commercial and charter work.

3.   A "DISTRESS SALE" AUCTION WAS
NOT REASONABLE

The method of sale is also an important factor. Under these circumstances, the Court finds that an initial effort to contact the fairly limited pool of qualified commercial buyers would have been in keeping with prevailing responsible practice, and not immediate resort to the public sale option, which in the words of even the Chavers' experts, is ordinarily a "last resort" method of sale. The Court finds the use of a public auction, under these circumstances, was not reasonable. It could be expected to draw only those it did — experienced wholesale aircraft dealers in an already small potential market looking for a distress type "deal." Potential retail buyers who would normally have concerns about the aircraft that could be addressed in the normal course of business were not identified and could not be reasonably presumed to attend an auction advertised in this manner within this time frame. This method of sale, while always a possibility, under these facts immediately telegraphed the message that this was a "fire sale." Under these circumstances, there was no reason initially to conduct such a distress disposal of the aircraft, and the Court finds it commercially unreasonable to have done so.

4.   AIRCRAFT MAINTENANCE WAS NOT PROPERLY ADDRESSED PRIOR TO THE SALE

A great deal of attention focused on the need for a "hot section inspection" on the aircraft. According to the rules and regulations of the Federal Aviation Authority, jet engines have to be inspected and, if necessary, overhauled. Estimates of the cost of performing this service were varied. From the testimony, it appears to the Court that the Chavers did not even consider whether this work should be accomplished and borne as a cost prior to sale, and if so, what effect it would have on resale value. The Court finds that under the circumstances, and in light of the condition of this particular airplane, a hot section inspection was an important and necessary step to prepare the plane for sale and failure of the Chavers to undertake the inspection seriously lessened their ability to obtain a fair price for the aircraft. The Chavers also failed to investigate paint options, possible financing options and a procedure for either undertaking or "capping" the hot section charges, which process likely would have allowed for recoupment of these charges upon sale. The failure to reasonably prepare the aircraft for sale, in the determination of this Court, constitutes a commercially unreasonable manner of sale.

5.   THE PURCHASE PRICE WAS NOT REASONABLE

The final factor is the purchase price obtained at the sale. Although this factor is not, by itself, determinative, it is a factor to consider. The proof in this case showed that even though the plane sold for $415,000.00, it was insured at that time for $700,000.00, as testified to by the bank officers. Even the Chavers' expert, Mr. Bunyan, was "surprised" that the plane sold for $415,000.00. Mr. Chavers testified that he thought the value of the plane was in the neighborhood of $700,000.00 when it was returned to him. Mr. Mulle testified that it was ludicrous to think that the fair market value of the plane could decrease by approximately one-half of its sale value a year earlier.... [Because the Chavers had not introduced evidence from which the court could determine the fair market value of the Lear jet at the time of the sale, the court declined to enter a deficiency judgment.]

Article 9 cases like *Chavers* show the stark contrast to judicial sale cases. The *Chavers* court says that 60 days was a grossly inadequate time for advertising and marketing the aircraft, but judicial sale procedures rarely allow that much time, even for complex collateral worth millions of dollars. The *Chavers* court is disappointed in advertising that ran only briefly in the *Wall Street Journal* and *Trade-A-Plane*, but under judicial sale procedures, the ads for this aircraft might have run in the legal notices column of a local newspaper. The *Chavers* court says that a "distress auction" was not reasonable, yet nearly every judicial sale is precisely that. The *Chavers* court complains about the maintenance of the aircraft, but in a judicial sale, the aircraft could have been sold in exactly the condition in which it was repossessed. Last, notice that the *Chavers* court declined to enter a deficiency judgment after a sale for almost 60 percent of the fair market value of the collateral, a price that would easily have passed muster in most judicial sale procedures.

If the secured party fails to give notice of sale or to conduct the sale in a commercially reasonable manner, there is a rebuttable presumption that the value of the collateral was at least equal to the amount of the debt. U.C.C. §9-626(a)(4). As a result, the secured creditor can recover a deficiency only by rebutting the presumption. It does that by proving that the collateral was worth some amount less than the amount of the debt. In that event, the secured creditor is entitled to a deficiency in an amount equal to the amount by which the debt exceeds the value of the collateral. Notice that the overall effect is that the court must determine the value of the collateral. See U.C.C. §§9-626(a)(3) and (4).

To illustrate, assume that Paul owes Carson $25,000, and that when Paul defaults, Carson repossesses the fixtures that were subject to Carson's security agreement. The fixtures were worth $12,000, but Carson sells them in a commercially unreasonable manner and receives only $8,000. Carson sues for the deficiency. Provided that Carson carries his burden of proving that the collateral was worth only $12,000, Carson can recover a $13,000 deficiency judgment.

This approach represents a change in revised Article 9 from earlier law, which left the question of a deficiency solely to the courts. But revised Article 9 carves out an exception for consumer contracts, leaving the case law to resolve the consequences of a failure to abide by the requirements imposed on an Article 9 sale. U.C.C. §9-626(b). Interestingly, the jurisdictions are split as to the appropriate remedy for failure to give notice of sale or failure to conduct the sale in a commercially reasonable manner. The majority hold that there is a rebuttable presumption that the value of the collateral was at least equal to the amount of the debt, with the consequence that, if the consumer debtor objects, the court ends up determining what the sale price should have been. A substantial minority hold that any significant irregularity in the sale procedure is sufficient to deny the deficiency altogether — a view that relieves the court of the necessity to guess what the price would have been absent the defect. This means, of course, that the treatment of consumer cases will vary from jurisdiction to jurisdiction.

To illustrate the difference between these views, assume that Consumer Paul owes Carson $25,000, and that when Paul defaults, Carson repossesses the fixtures that were subject to Carson's security agreement. The fixtures were worth $12,000, but Carson sells them in a commercially unreasonable manner and recovers only $8,000. Carson then sues Paul for the $17,000 deficiency. In a jurisdiction that followed the minority rule, the court would not grant a deficiency judgment. In a court that followed the rebuttable presumption rule, the court would begin with a presumption that the collateral was worth the full amount of the debt, $25,000, and no deficiency judgment should be granted. But if Carson proved that the value of the collateral was in fact $12,000, Carson still could recover a $13,000 deficiency judgment.

D.   Article 9 Sale Procedure:
A Functional Analysis

The Article 9 sale procedure may seem like a case of the vampire guarding the blood bank. It is the debtor's property that is being sold. Because Article 9 preserves both the debtor's right to the surplus and the creditor's right to a deficiency, it is the debtor who directly suffers the effects of a poorly conducted sale that brings a low price. The secured creditor may seem to have no incentive to seek a fair price for the collateral. Yet the secured creditor is given virtually complete control over the manner of sale.

Proponents of the Article 9 sale procedure argue that the requirement of a "commercially reasonable sale," backed by the threat to deny some portion of the deficiency, gives incentives to repossessing secured creditors to encourage bidding and seek a market price for the goods. We doubt it.

The threat to deny a deficiency could be a powerful motivator, at least where the expected deficiency was substantial and the likelihood of collecting it from the debtor high. But the threat in revised Article 9 is only to reduce the amount of the deficiency to what it would have been had the secured creditor complied with Article 9.

The secured creditor that knows it won't be able to collect any deficiency because its debtor is insolvent or bankrupt will want to sell the collateral for the highest net price it can get, because that may be all it collects on the loan. But the secured creditor that expects to collect the deficiency from the debtor or the guarantor has little or no incentive to get a good price at the sale. It expects to get its money either way.

In fact, revised Article 9 seems to give secured creditors the incentive to shoot for a double recovery by purchasing the collateral at sale for less than its value, collecting the deficiency from the debtor or guarantor, and then re-selling the collateral in a commercially reasonable sale — for its own account. If the debtor understands what is happening and defends the action for deficiency, the court is supposed to limit the deficiency to what the creditor would have lost in a commercially reasonable sale. U.C.C. §9-615(f). That will thwart the secured creditor's attempt to overreach. But in many cases, the debtor won't figure it out and defend. Given that the secured creditor loses nothing in the former cases and gains something in the latter cases by trying, it seems to make sense for secured creditors to try.

The secured creditor will have similarly little incentive to preserve a relatively small equity the debtor may have in the collateral. If the creditor is successful in preserving it, the creditor must pay the surplus over to the debtor anyway. If the creditor is unsuccessful in preserving it, it is unlikely the debtor will be able to bring and win a lawsuit for the damages. Again, the creditor may choose to bid in at a poorly advertised sale and take its chances.

Ultimately, these kinds of speculations are incapable of discovering the true level of effectiveness of the Article 9 sale system. What is needed is empirical evidence on the frequency with which the different fact patterns present themselves. How often do debtors have equity in repossessed collateral? How common is it for creditors to buy at Article 9 sales? How likely are debtors to defend against the entry of deficiency judgments? Unfortunately, little of this kind of evidence is available.

Problem Set 47

47.1. The bank repossessed Maxwell's silver Mercedes and sent him notification that the bank would sell it in a private sale "after ten days from this notice." The balance owing on the loan, including principal, interest, attorneys' fees, and expenses of sale is $10,000.

a. If the fair market value of the car is $8,000, but it sells for $7,000 in a commercially reasonable sale, what is the proper amount for the court to award as a deficiency? U.C.C. §§9-615(d) and 9-626(a)(3) and (b).

b. How much would Maxwell have to pay to redeem the car? U.C.C. §9-623.

c. If Maxwell has enough money to redeem the car, would you recommend that he do so or that he purchase another car just like it for $8,000?

d. At Maxwell's prompting, a friend of his offers $8,000 for the car. The bank refuses the offer because they follow a policy of selling all the cars they repossess through auto auctions. The friend can't go to the auction, because it is only open to dealers. At the auction, the car sells for $7,000. Now how much should the deficiency be? U.C.C. §§9-626, 9-627.

47.2. Your firm represents Wewoka State Bank, which recently repossessed and sold the inventory and equipment of an auto parts store. The debt secured by the collateral was in the principal amount of $57,345, plus interest to the date of the sale in the amount of $3,541. The security agreement provides that in the event of default, the debtor will pay the bank's reasonable attorneys' fees incurred in collecting the debt. Your fees are in the amount of $3,000 for replevy of the collateral and $650 for preparing for sale; you intend to charge an additional $350 for your opinion on distribution of the proceeds of sale. The bank also spent $1,500 preserving the collateral while it was in their possession and an additional $750 advertising the sale. The debtor has numerous other creditors, none of whom has a lien or security interest against the inventory and equipment. One of those creditors, Auto Parts Depot, heard about the auction and sent the bank a letter demanding that the $4,200 owing to them be paid out of the proceeds of sale. (If you need to know what the security agreement says to answer these questions, use the security agreement in Assignment 56, below.)

a. The highest bid at the auction was $47,136. That money is now in your possession. To whom should you pay it? (That is, indicate to whom you would make the checks out, and in what amounts.) How much is the deficiency? See U.C.C. §§9-615(a), 9-203(b).

b. If the highest bid at the auction had been $75,000, to whom should you pay the money? Is the bank either required or permitted to pay Auto Parts Depot from the proceeds?

47.3. East Bank does a steady business in the repossession of automobiles. They sell the automobiles through a "dealers-only" auction. Over the years they have had numerous problems with the sending of notice of sale to the debtors whose cars are being sold. Notices have been sent in improper form or with typographical errors or have been returned because the debtor has changed addresses. Debtors have occasionally challenged the length of notice (East Bank gives five days' notice, but tries to send it at least ten days before the sale). The ten-day delay runs up the storage costs on the automobiles and the bank gets stuck for most of them in the end. The people at the bank think the notice requirement is rather silly anyway, given that the debtors can't get into the auto auction.

East Bank would like you to look into whether there is any way to dispense with the notice requirement. They are sure that none of their borrowers would object to a waiver contained in the security agreement, even if it were specifically pointed out to them. Does East Bank have to send these notices? See U.C.C. §§9-602(7), 9-603(a), 9-611, 9-612, 9-613, 9-614, and 9-624(a); Comment 4 to §9-610.

47.4. Your client, Grizzly Bear Bank, is on a run of bad luck. The Bank recently repossessed what should have been a $345,000 helicopter, only to find that the engine and all of the electronics had been removed by the debtor (in violation of the security agreement), leaving a hull with no resale value. The amount of the debt is currently $345,000. Fortunately, the debt is personally guaranteed by four wealthy individuals.

a.   Grizzly would like to know if it is all right to throw the hull away. If not, what is the Bank supposed to do with it? See U.C.C. §§9-610(a), 9-620, 9-626, and Comment 4 to §9-610.

b.   Assume that Grizzly throws the hull away and the guarantors later prove that if Grizzly had spent $245,000 to install electronics in the hull it would have been able to sell the helicopter for $345,000. To what deficiency judgment is Grizzly entitled? U.C.C. §§9-102(64), 9-626(a)(3).

47.5. Your client, Pedro Perez-Ortiz, bought a retail store from Lamp Fair, Inc. for $50,000 down and a promissory note in the amount of $277,000. The note was secured by a security interest in the store. Pedro couldn't make the payments on the debt, so he gave Lamp Fair the keys. Lamp Fair resumed operation of the store and sent Pedro a bill for $131,000, which the company said was the excess of what Pedro owed after crediting him for the value of the store. Pedro refused to pay, and Lamp Fair has now sued him for the $131,000. When you told Lamp Fair's lawyer that Lamp Fair couldn't sue for a deficiency without selling the store first, she snapped "where does it say that in Article 9?" U.C.C. §§9-610(a), 9-620, 9-626.

47.6. You represent the Chavers, who have repossessed another Lear jet similar to the one they previously repossessed from the Frazier group. In this case, however, the debtor is insolvent; even if a deficiency judgment is entered, it will be uncollectible. The Chavers estimate that the jet is worth about $800,000. The debt is about $850,000. The Chavers would like to avoid the expenses of sale (after the opinion in *Chavers*, Mr. Mulle has raised his rates) and just keep the jet for their personal use.

a.   What should they do? U.C.C. §§9-610, 9-611, 9-620, 9-621.

b.   What if the debtor objects to their retention of the collateral and they simply ignore the objection? See U.C.C. §§9-619, 9-622. Will they have a title problem if they later decide to sell or encumber the plane? Uniform Motor Vehicle Certificate of Title Act §16(b). Model Rules of Professional

Conduct Rule 1.16 provides: "[A] lawyer shall not represent a client or, where representation has commenced, shall withdraw from the representation of a client if: (1) the representation will result in violation of the rules of professional conduct or other law."

c. What if the Chavers simply announce that they have sold the jet to themselves for $800,000? U.C.C. §§9-610(c), 9-617.

Chapter 14.   Creditors' Remedies in Bankruptcy

Assignment 48:   Bankruptcy and the Automatic Stay

A.   The Federal Bankruptcy System

The preceding assignments focused on the rights of debtors and creditors in the state law collection system. In those assignments we explored the limited rights of ordinary creditors to force their debtors to repay and the enhanced rights of secured creditors in that regard. We also probed the strategic advantages of both debtors and creditors in any struggle over the payment of outstanding obligations. That would have concluded the story, but for the fact that there is a federal collection system.

Because there is, state courts sometimes are not the final arbiters of the rights of parties. If a debtor is in financial difficulty, either the debtor or the creditors may be able to move the matter to a federal bankruptcy forum. Only a small fraction of all debtors fail to pay their debts and thereby become vulnerable to the state collection system. But of those who do, a substantial portion consider bankruptcy the preferable means of dealing with their unpaid obligations.

The bankruptcy system differs from the state collection system in many respects. The state collection system permits creditors to pursue collection over very long periods of time, while the bankruptcy system imposes a relatively quick, efficient resolution of the debtor's financial problems. In order to achieve that faster resolution, the bankruptcy system offers permanent forgiveness of debt (referred to as *discharge*) or rescheduling of repayment (referred to as *extension* or *debt adjustment*). The laws permitting debts to be discharged or extended are complex, and generalizations are difficult. However, when the bankruptcy system works as intended, debtors who qualify for bankruptcy relief emerge with less debt or with debts due on different repayment schedules and their creditors as a group collect at least as much as they could have in the absence of bankruptcy if the debtor had been uncooperative.

The Constitution gives Congress the power to establish "uniform laws on the subject of Bankruptcies throughout the United States." U.S. Const. art. I, §8. Most of the bankruptcy laws currently in force are collected in Title 11 of the U.S. Code and referred to as the Bankruptcy Reform Act of 1978, or, for the bankruptcy cognoscenti, simply as "the Code."[*]

---

[*] Reference to "the Code" sometimes offers an opportunity for friendly competition among commercial lawyers as to the identity of the true bearer of the title "the Code." Tax mavens refer to the Internal Revenue Code as "the Code," commercial law generalists refer to the U.C.C. as "the Code," and debtor-creditor specialists refer to the federal bankruptcy statute as "the Code." The whole area is such barren ground for jokes that no one seems inclined to fix the problem and remove this tiny source of humor.

Under the supremacy doctrine, federal bankruptcy law supersedes state collection law. This means that when a debtor is in bankruptcy, a new set of collection laws govern. In fact, bankruptcy law incorporates many aspects of state collection law and allows them to continue to apply. Nonetheless, it is critical to understand that once a bankruptcy process has begun, federal law — not state law — is the ultimate arbiter of the rights of the parties.

While only a small percentage of all debt is ultimately resolved in bankruptcy, the bankruptcy system has an important impact on debtor-creditor relationships. Three decades ago debtors and creditors bargained in the shadow of their collection rights under state law, including the Uniform Commercial Code. Bankruptcy law had little influence because the likelihood either party would resort to it was vanishingly small. Today, a sufficiently large number of debtors find their way into the bankruptcy courts so that sophisticated lenders bargain with their borrowers primarily in the shadow of bankruptcy law instead. While it would be an exaggeration to say that they expect their debtors to file for bankruptcy, they realize that if a debt is not paid on time, bankruptcy is a real possibility. They may plan to pursue their remedies under state law if their debtors should default, but they understand that their right to do so can be preempted at any time if the debtor files for bankruptcy. For that reason, they structure their relationships with the possibility of bankruptcy in mind. Through their impact on business planning, bankruptcy laws affect the collection system even more than the number of actual bankruptcy filings would suggest.

It is not possible to teach the entire bankruptcy system in a course on secured credit, and we do not attempt to do so here. Nonetheless, it is not possible to understand the secured credit system without understanding the role that bankruptcy plays in it. In this assignment we give a brief overview of bankruptcy and discuss how a bankruptcy filing can stop all the collection actions you studied in prior assignments. In Assignment 49 we explore how creditors collect on a claim in bankruptcy and how much they can expect to receive. In both assignments, pay close attention to the sharp differences in the rights of secured and unsecured creditors.

B.   Filing a Bankruptcy Case

A bankruptcy case can be initiated by either a debtor or its creditors, but statistics published by the Administrative Office of the U.S. Courts show that well over 99 percent are initiated by the debtor. The proportion of filings initiated by creditors is considerably higher in business cases, but may be declining in recent years. In a 1983 study, Professor Lynn LoPucki found that 6 percent of a group of small business reorganization cases were initiated by creditors; in a 1994 study, Professors Warren and Westbrook found that only about 3 percent were. Professors LoPucki and Whitford found that 14 percent of the largest bankruptcy reorganization cases (publicly traded companies with more than $100 million in assets) were initiated by creditors in the early 1980s. Professor LoPucki's Bankruptcy Research Database shows that the involuntary rate for such cases has been only 3 percent since 1994. The "voluntary-ness" of a voluntary petition may also vary dramatically: Many debtors walk the plank to the bankruptcy clerk's office with the creditors' swords at their backs, with the creditors having made clear what they will do unless the debtor files. In this assignment we focus on the typical debtor who files a petition with the bankruptcy court — even if that debtor is only a few steps ahead of the creditors.

The debtor may be a business or an individual, and the debtor may choose to file under Chapter 7 (liquidation), Chapter 11 (reorganization, typically for businesses), Chapter 12 (reorganization only for owners of family farms), or Chapter 13 (reorganization only for individuals). The debtor fills out a number of forms, usually with the assistance of an attorney, disclosing a great deal about the debtor's assets, income, debts, and financial history. The debtor pays a filing fee ($220 in Chapter 7, $150 in Chapter 13, $200 in Chapter 12, and $1,000 in Chapter 11), and the forms are filed (usually by a runner from the attorney's office) with the clerk of the bankruptcy court.

Upon receiving the forms, the bankruptcy clerk stamps the front page with the date and time of filing. At that instant, two things happen: A bankruptcy estate, which consists of all the property of the debtor, is automatically created; and a stay against any collection activities is automatically imposed. Bankr. Code §§362(a), 541(a)(1). Both events occur by operation of law without any additional action by the court.

Because the debtor's property is now a part of a bankruptcy estate, the debtor is not supposed to pay prepetition debts, nor is any prepetition creditor supposed to collect anything from this estate until the case is resolved. From this moment forward, the payments and collections are to be handled according to the procedures imposed by bankruptcy law.

Who is in control after the bankruptcy is filed? In the liquidation cases filed under Chapter 7, the U.S. Trustee appoints (or, in a few cases, the creditors elect) a trustee to administer the estate. In the reorganization and debt adjustment cases filed under Chapters 11, 12, and 13, the debtors are left in control of their own estates, to administer them in accord with bankruptcy law. Trustees are appointed in cases under Chapters 12 and 13, but they do not take possession of the property of the estate. Instead, they examine the debtors, review their repayment plans, receive payments from the debtors after their plans are confirmed by the court, distribute the money they receive to the appropriate creditors, and collect their fees. The debtor continues to work and manage the property much as before the filing. In a Chapter 11 case the debtor's management usually remains in possession of the property of the estate as "debtor in possession" (DIP) and operates the business. If, however, the court determines that the DIP is not running the estate effectively, it may order the appointment or election of a trustee to replace current management. Bankr. Code §1104(a). Such appointments or elections rarely occur before the court has decided to convert the case to Chapter 7.

The bankruptcy case may be resolved through liquidation, reorganization, or some combination of the two. In a Chapter 7 liquidation case, the Chapter 7 trustee liquidates all of the property of the estate. To liquidate property is to convert it into cash — usually by selling it. The trustee makes distributions to unsecured creditors only in money.

The property available for liquidation differs depending on whether the debtor is an individual or a corporation. If the debtor in Chapter 7 is an individual (bankruptcy parlance for a human being), the debtor will be entitled to exempt certain property from the estate. Every Chapter 7 debtor is entitled to keep the property of the bankruptcy estate that would have been exempt from creditors' remedies on a judgment under state law. Bankr. Code §522(b)(1) and (3). Thus, the debtor living in a state that would not permit a judgment creditor to claim the debtor's household goods can keep those same household goods if the debtor declares bankruptcy. In addition, in some states, debtors have the option to exempt the property listed in Bankruptcy Code §522(d) instead of the property exempt from execution under state law. Bankr. Code §522(b)(1) and (2). Debtors in a low exemption state, such as Pennsylvania, can usually exempt more property under Bankruptcy Code §522(d) than they can under the state exemption laws. Corporations are not entitled to exemptions under either state or bankruptcy law. In a Chapter 7 case all corporate assets are either abandoned or liquidated.

Following liquidation of the nonexempt property of a Chapter 7 estate, the trustee distributes the money pro rata to the general creditors. Bankr. Code §704. If the debtor is an individual, the debtor is then discharged from all remaining debts. If the debtor is a corporation, it has been stripped of all assets. At the end of the liquidation case, the corporate Chapter 7 debtor is a corporate shell that has no assets but still owes all its debts. Bankr. Code §727(a)(1).

Reorganization cases proceed differently. The debtor proposes a plan to pay its creditors all or part of the debts owing to them from currently available assets or future income. If the case is under Chapter 13, the debtor files a proposed budget, with a plan to devote all "disposable income" to the repayment of debt for a period of three or five years, depending on whether the debtor's income is below or above the median of incomes in the debtor's state. Bankr. Code §1325(b). The plan must also promise to pay creditors at least as much as they would have received in a Chapter 7 liquidation. Bankr. Code §1325(a)(4). The Chapter 13 trustee examines the budget and appears at the court hearing to consider the confirmation of the debtor's plan. Bankr. Code §1302(b)(2). If the plan is confirmed, the trustee receives the payments from the debtor and distributes them pro rata to the general creditors over the life of the plan. The plan lasts from three to five years, and the debtor is discharged from most kinds of remaining debt when the last payment is made. Bankr. Code §1328(a). A Chapter 12 bankruptcy follows the same basic pattern for cases involving family farms.

The Chapter 11 reorganization is similar to a Chapter 13 debt adjustment, with some key differences. The plan that a debtor in possession proposes in a case under Chapter 11 can provide for payments over any length of time. Some extend for 20 or 30 years, but most plans pay unsecured creditors over a period of about 5 to 7 years. As with a Chapter 13 plan, a Chapter 11 plan must promise creditors at least as much as they would have received in a Chapter 7 liquidation. Bankr. Code §1129(a)(7).

In some respects, the role of the trustee in a liquidating bankruptcy is similar to the role of the sheriff in a state collection action. The trustee finds property, sells it for cash, and distributes the cash to creditors. The difference, of course, is that the trustee has broad control over all the debtor's property and acts on behalf of all the creditors.

Reorganization bankruptcy performs a very different role. In essence, the law encourages and sometimes compels the creditors to accept a modification of the debtor's obligations to them. The purpose is to reduce those obligations sufficiently so that the debtor can meet them, thereby encouraging the debtor to pay what it can rather than nothing at all. For individuals, this means retaining their property and paying from future income. For corporations and other artificial entities, this means continuing operations and paying surviving obligations over time.

All bankruptcies, whether liquidation, reorganization, or some combination of the two, are designed to resolve the claims against the debtor, make some provision for repayment, and discharge the debts that will not be paid.

C. Stopping Creditors' Collection Activities

Once the debtor has filed for bankruptcy, unsecured creditors (*general creditors*, in bankruptcy parlance) can file their claims and have disputes regarding them resolved in the bankruptcy case, but they have few other specific rights as the case moves toward resolution. If the debtor violates the provisions of the Bankruptcy Code, the creditor or the trustee may complain in court. Barring that, there is little that an individual unsecured creditor can do. For unsecured creditors, bankruptcy is a collective — and largely passive — proceeding.

Creditors benefit from some aspects of this collective action. They reduce their costs of collection, confident both that the trustee will act on their behalf and that no other creditors will move ahead of them by seizing the debtor's assets. They can also count on a streamlined process to liquidate the debtor's assets or to collect from the debtor's future income with costs minimized and shared among all the creditors. The creditor who would do little at state law may be better off participating in an automatic collection device for a relatively low cost.

Aggressive creditors, on the other hand, are generally worse off in bankruptcy than they would have been under state collection law. Bankruptcy dissipates the individual creditor's leverage because, to the extent unsecured creditors are permitted to act during the bankruptcy case, it is for the collective gain. The aggressive creditor can no longer enjoy the exclusive benefits of its own diligence in pursuit of assets or its cleverness in seizing property others might have overlooked. Benefits are shared pro rata with all other unsecured creditors.

In the absence of bankruptcy, an aggressive unsecured creditor can disrupt the debtor's business, employment, and financial affairs by seizing assets. The leverage generated by these activities can sometimes be so great that the debtor will do whatever is necessary to pay the debt, even if sale of its assets would yield nothing for the aggressive creditor. Once bankruptcy is filed, the unsecured creditor cannot generate much leverage at all. And at the end of the bankruptcy process, the creditor's claims may be discharged entirely, eliminating any right to collect from the debtor.

Bankruptcy courts take stay violations seriously. They usually hold deliberate violators in contempt of court and impose a fine sufficient to make them regret their transgressions. In some circumstances, an individual injured by the stay violation can sue for damages. See Bankr. Code §362(k). Actions taken in violation of the stay are either void or voidable, and many courts impose on even the innocent violator of the stay the obligation to undo the violation by returning property or correcting public records. As a result, few lawyers or parties deliberately violate the automatic stay.

The reasons for the creation of the estate and imposition of the automatic stay are both practical and theoretical. By stopping all payments and collections, bankruptcy provides an opportunity to account for all the assets in the estate and all the charges against the estate. In a sense, the automatic stay locks up the estate temporarily so that an accurate count and an orderly distribution can be made. The stay also gives the debtor breathing room either to make an orderly liquidation of assets or to construct a plan of reorganization. Imposing a stay halts ongoing litigation in the state system and substitutes what is often a more abbreviated and efficient set of bankruptcy procedures for resolving disputes over outstanding debts. Perhaps most critical from the point of view of the general creditor, the stay freezes the relative rights of creditors as of the moment of the bankruptcy filing. The race of diligence fostered by state procedures is over; creditors can take no additional action to improve their own chances of recovery at the expense of others. Instead, all further actions by unsecured creditors against the debtor must be collective actions taken on behalf of *all* the creditors. The stay illustrates, and other Code provisions reinforce, that for general, unsecured creditors, bankruptcy is a collective proceeding.

The language of the Bankruptcy Code fixing the scope of the automatic stay is broad. It provides a stay "applicable to all entities" against "any act" to collect a prepetition debt. Bankr. Code §362(a). The stay protects the debtor personally as well as the property of the estate. The stay applies both to direct collection attempts (e.g., levying against the debtor's property), as well as more indirect attempts (e.g., initiating a lawsuit to establish the debtor's liability on a debt as a prerequisite to eventual collection).

While the stay is broad, it is not unlimited. Only actions to collect prefiling obligations are stayed. The Bankruptcy Code does not halt criminal proceedings against the debtor. If the debtor is under criminal indictment, for example, filing a bankruptcy petition will not stay the trial. Bankr. Code §362(b)(1). (This is not a surprising provision, lest every criminal defendant make a quick stop at the bankruptcy desk on the way to trial.) Similarly, a debtor might file for bankruptcy and receive immediate relief from the government's attempts to collect fines and penalties for past violations of government regulations, but the debtor will still be subject to actions to abate continuing violations. Bankr. Code §362(b)(4). (Again, it is not a big surprise that airlines must follow FAA safety restrictions and oil drillers must comply with pollution regulations, even if they are flying or drilling after they have filed for Chapter 11.)

With regard to unsecured creditors, the automatic stay generally remains in effect until the conclusion of the bankruptcy case. See Bankr. Code §362(c). Unsecured creditors rarely have grounds to lift the stay; they must rely on the operation of the bankruptcy process to collect the debts owed to them. In effect, unsecured creditors are on board for the ride through bankruptcy. They can monitor the process to make certain the rules are followed, or they can rely on the bankruptcy trustee or debtor in possession, but they have only collective rights and they must await disposition of the case to get any money. An unsecured creditor's best course is usually to file a proof of claim, hope for the best, and expect the worst.

D.   Lifting the Stay for Secured Creditors

For secured creditors the consequences of bankruptcy are significantly different. While bankruptcy alters the secured creditors' rights in many respects, the bankruptcy system recognizes their most important state-created rights and gives these creditors much better treatment. Bankruptcy may delay enforcement of some of those rights and certain collection actions are prohibited even to secured creditors, but bankruptcy still promises secured creditors eventual access to either their collateral or to property or money of equivalent value. In most cases bankruptcy gives neither the secured creditor nor the unsecured creditor the right to full payment of the outstanding debt, but in all cases bankruptcy gives the secured creditor the right to be paid at least the value of its collateral.

Because each secured creditor is usually secured by different collateral, the interests of two secured creditors are not likely to be precisely the same. For example, the holder of an over secured first mortgage on the debtor's home may suffer only minor inconvenience from the automatic stay, while the holder of a second security interest in accounts receivable may stand to lose everything unless automatic stay issues are dealt with promptly and skillfully. To assure that their individual rights are protected, bankruptcy procedure permits each secured creditor the right to participate individually in the bankruptcy case rather than forcing on them the collective treatment forced on the unsecured creditors. Secured creditors, each claiming different collateral or different priority in the same collateral, stand in sharp contrast to unsecured creditors who share pro rata in whatever is available after provisions have been made for the payment to secured creditors of the value of their collateral.

Bankruptcy procedure affords secured creditors a number of ways in which they can monitor their collateral and participate individually in the bankruptcy case. Both their greater substantive rights and the fact of their participation give them greater ability to influence the course of the bankruptcy case.

When a bankruptcy case is filed, the collection actions of a secured creditor, like those of an unsecured creditor, are immediately interrupted. But for the secured creditor, imposition of the automatic stay is often only the beginning of a new game. The secured creditor retains its lien and may be able to get the stay lifted and continue with its nonbankruptcy collection efforts.

The grounds for lifting the stay are set forth in Bankruptcy Code §362(d). To summarize, the court must always lift the stay if the trustee or debtor does not provide the creditor with adequate protection. But even if the trustee or debtor provides adequate protection, the court must nevertheless lift the stay if (1) there is no equity in the collateral that the trustee or debtor might realize for unsecured creditors and (2) the collateral is not necessary to an effective reorganization. (Two other bases for lifting the stay are not discussed here. The first applies only to a narrow range of "single asset real estate" cases; the second applies only if the petition was part of a scheme to delay, hinder, and defraud a real property secured creditor.) This complex combination of requirements may seem a jumble at first, but it sorts out rather sensibly once one understands two reasons why the bankruptcy system might want to commandeer a secured creditor's collateral against the secured creditor's will.

The first is that the collateral may be worth more than the debt secured by it and the estate's equity in it may be available to the debtor and other creditors only through bankruptcy procedure. For example, if Dubchek files under Chapter 7 owing $3,000 to Cicero and the debt is secured by a nonexempt Buick Skylark worth $4,000, the estate has a $1,000 equity in it. If the stay is left in place, the trustee can sell the Skylark for $4,000 and pay the secured creditor $3,000, leaving $1,000 (less the expenses of sale) to pay unsecured creditors. The fear apparently motivating bankruptcy policy in this regard is that if the stay is lifted, Cicero will foreclose and the Skylark will be sold for less than its value, leaving little or nothing for the unsecured creditors. That is, bankruptcy policy is based on the realization that state sale procedures often are ineffective. Even if the Skylark were sold for its full value under non-bankruptcy law, the net proceeds after payment of the secured creditor and the expenses of sale would have been turned over to the debtor, not the unsecured creditors. The unsecured creditors might have had a difficult time reaching the proceeds through garnishment or execution.

The second reason for commandeering a secured creditor's collateral is to enable the debtor to reorganize — that is, to remain in business or keep a job, make money, and pay some of the debts. For example, if Dubchek had no equity in the Skylark, but could not continue her profitable Donut Delivery Service without it, the Skylark might be "necessary to an effective reorganization." Bankr. Code §362(b)(2). Without it, Dubchek might have no income and be unable to pay anything to unsecured creditors. (On the other hand, if Dubchek had two cars and the Donut Delivery Service could carry on just as well with either one, retention of the Skylark would not be necessary for an effective reorganization.) In the remainder of our discussion of the stay, we will refer to these two reasons for retaining collateral — that the debtor has an equity in it or that it is necessary to an effective reorganization — as *bankruptcy purposes*. To be entitled to retain the secured creditor's collateral, the debtor or trustee must show at a minimum that its retention of the collateral serves a bankruptcy purpose. In the absence of such justification, the secured creditor can demand that the stay be lifted.

To appreciate fully the importance of these bankruptcy purposes, it is critical to realize how much more effective the bankruptcy system can sometimes be in realizing the full value of the debtor's assets or income earning potential. In re 26 Trumbull Street, 77 B.R. 374 (Bankr. D. Conn. 1987), provides an excellent example. Before bankruptcy, the debtor closed the restaurant it had been operating in leased premises. The bankruptcy estate contained two items of property: the restaurant equipment and the restaurant's interest in its lease. The parties agreed that if the restaurant equipment were removed from the leased premises, the equipment would have been worth only $21,500, but sold together with the lease, it was worth $90,000. The case did not explain why the difference was so great. Most likely, it was because the equipment was suited for use with the leased premises. It fit the space and might even have been damaged through removal. In place, the equipment and lease constituted a restaurant; removed, the equipment was a difficult marketing problem. Nevertheless, if a creditor with a debt of $21,500 (or less) that was secured by the equipment could have repossessed the equipment and sold it separate from the lease for $21,500, the secured creditor would have had little reason not to do so immediately. The estate — and the other creditors — would have lost the additional $68,500 value. Only by leaving the stay in effect could the bankruptcy court assure that would not happen.

Even if the estate's retention of the collateral would serve a bankruptcy purpose, that alone is not sufficient to defeat a secured creditor's motion to lift the stay. The debtor also must protect the secured creditor against loss as a result of the delay in foreclosure that is caused by the stay. Bankr. Code §362(d)(1). The debtor must furnish *adequate protection*, a term of art defined only by example in Bankruptcy Code §361. Generally speaking, a secured creditor's interest is adequately protected when provisions that the court considers adequate have been made to protect the secured creditor from loss as a result of a decline in the value of the secured creditor's collateral during the time the creditor is immobilized by the automatic stay. If the debtor cannot provide what the court considers adequate protection, the court must lift the stay and allow the creditor to foreclose.

To continue with our earlier example, assume that Dubchek owes $5,000 to Cicero and that the Skylark is worth $4,000 when the automatic stay is imposed. Based on these numbers, Dubchek has no equity in the Skylark. But assume further that retention of the Skylark is necessary to Dubchek's reorganization. The court should not lift the stay pursuant to Bankruptcy Code §362(d)(2) because the property is necessary for an effective reorganization. But Cicero is not through. Cicero can move to lift the stay for lack of adequate protection pursuant to Bankruptcy Code §362(d)(1). Under these circumstances, Dubchek must furnish adequate protection against postfiling decline in the value of the car or lose it.

The bankruptcy court decides what constitutes adequate protection. Based on experience with the depreciation of similar automobiles, the parties may show that the decline in the value of the Skylark will be about $1,200 during the year Dubchek will be in bankruptcy, so the value of the car will go from $4,000 to $2,800. If this $1,200 decline in fact occurs, the resulting loss imposed on Cicero would be a result of the delay imposed by the automatic stay. That is, were it not for the automatic stay, Cicero could foreclose now and recover $4,000. If the stay prevents Cicero from foreclosing for a year and the value of the collateral drops to $2,800, Cicero might recover only $2,800, losing the additional $1,200 he would have enjoyed in an early foreclosure. The bankruptcy court will require Dubchek to protect Cicero against this anticipated $1,200 loss.

Cicero's adequate protection may come in any of several forms. Dubchek might pay Cicero $100 each month as the car declines in value. Or Dubchek might grant Cicero an additional lien against property worth at least $1,200. There are few limits on the form the protection must take, so long as it is "adequate" in the eyes of the bankruptcy judge. But if Dubchek does not furnish adequate protection to Cicero, Cicero will be entitled to have the stay lifted and Dubchek's potentially profitable Donut Delivery Service will be history.

Notice that if the car in the preceding example had been worth $10,000, Cicero would have been in no real danger of loss from ordinary depreciation. Even if the value of the car had fallen to $7,000 during bankruptcy, it would have remained easily sufficient to cover the balance on the loan, plus accruing interest and attorneys' fees. Such an excess of collateral value over loan amount is referred to in bankruptcy parlance as a *cushion of equity*. The bankruptcy courts recognize that a cushion of equity of sufficient size may alone adequately protect a secured creditor against loss. If such a cushion already provides adequate protection to the secured creditor, the secured creditor has no right to additional protection in the form of periodic payments or additional collateral.

Exactly how large the cushion of equity must be to provide protection depends on the circumstances. Key circumstances include (1) the nature of the factors that might change the value of the collateral, (2) the volatility of the market in which the creditor might have to sell it, and (3) the rate at which the secured debt is likely to increase in amount. Of course, the apparent size of the cushion of equity depends on the value the court assigns to the collateral. The question of how large a cushion exists often becomes intertwined with the question of how large a cushion is necessary, giving the court considerable flexibility to do what it thinks best.

While secured creditors are entitled to adequate protection against loss from a decline in the value of their collateral, they are not entitled to protection against other losses resulting from imposition of the automatic stay. To illustrate, assume that the Skylark is worth $4,000, Cicero's lien against it is in the same amount, and that the value of the Skylark is not expected to decline during the one-year bankruptcy. On these facts, Dubchek need do nothing to provide adequate protection even though Cicero will lose the time value of his $4,000 in this scenario. But for the stay, Cicero could have invested his $4,000 and earned interest during the year. With the money stuck in a bankruptcy case, he could not.

In the following case, the Craddock-Terry Shoe Corporation was attempting to reorganize in Chapter 11. Two of its secured creditors, Lincoln and Westinghouse, sought to lift the stay, raising issues under both prongs of Bankruptcy Code §362(d). The court addressed whether the stay should be lifted under either, providing us with a look at how the two sections are used in tandem by many undersecured creditors. In order to decide any of the legal issues, however, the court first had to resolve the threshold question of the value of the property. If the court had assigned the property a different value, the outcome might have been different as well.

In re Craddock-Terry Shoe Corporation
98 B.R. 250 (Bankr. W.D. Va. 1988)

WILLIAM E. ANDERSON, UNITED STATES BANKRUPTCY JUDGE

The plaintiffs, Lincoln National Life Insurance Company ("Lincoln") and Westinghouse Credit Corporation ("Westinghouse"), have moved the Court to lift the automatic stay imposed by section 362(a) of the Bankruptcy Code, 11 U.S.C. §362(a), or in the alternative, to provide Lincoln and Westinghouse adequate protection for certain collateral in which they have a security interest. The collateral at issue is the customer mailing lists, catalogues, and certain trademarks of Hill Brothers, a division of Craddock-Terry Shoe Corporation ("Craddock-Terry"), the debtor.

BACKGROUND FACTS

On April 30, 1986, the plaintiffs, Lincoln and Westinghouse, loaned the debtor, Craddock-Terry, $9,000,000. As security for that loan, Lincoln and Westinghouse obtained a security interest in the mailing list, customer list, catalogues and four trademarks ("the collateral") of Hill Brothers, a mail-order division of Craddock-Terry. Debtor's Chapter 11 petition was filed on October 21, 1987. Craddock-Terry has shut down all its operations, except for Hill Brothers.

As of the petition date, debtor owed Lincoln and Westinghouse $9,587,812.50. The debtor does not dispute that Lincoln and Westinghouse have a valid and perfected lien on the mailing list, customer list, catalogues and trademarks of Hill Brothers. The collateral is worth less than the amount owed Lincoln and Westinghouse. In fact, the debtor had on the petition date, and still has, no equity in the collateral.

On January 5, 1988, Lincoln and Westinghouse obtained a court order authorizing a Bankruptcy Rule 2004 examination of the debtor. The examination and document production was conducted during January. Concerned that the value of their collateral appeared to be seriously declining, Lincoln and Westinghouse originally filed their motion for relief from stay on March 1, 1988. The hearing on the motion, originally scheduled for April 21, 1988, was continued to May 4, 1988, and final arguments were heard on May 10, 1988.

The evidence introduced at the hearing indicates that, during the Chapter 11 case, Hill Brothers has experienced a serious cash flow problem which has reduced the number of orders which can be filled (the fill rate), cut in half the number of spring catalogues planned to be mailed, and reduced the rate at which new names are added to the Hill Brothers mailing list. In addition, returns of merchandise have increased. These factors have resulted in a serious decline in the value of the collateral.

The plaintiffs presented evidence that on the date debtor's petition was filed, before the adverse impact of the cash flow problems and the list management problems, the value of the mailing list in place and in use at Hill Brothers was $8.7 million, but that its value on April 30, 1988 was $5.7 million. Their expert at trial had used the same valuation method as that used by an accounting firm whose earlier appraisal the debtor had used to obtain the loans. He testified that he had used a method appropriate for valuing a mailing list in use by a company, known as the discounted cash flow method. The resulting value is the value to the business which is using the list. A mailing list is carefully built up over the years, by adding names each year, and developing an active list of persons who like and buy the particular product of the company. Its value in place to the company using it is necessarily much greater than to an outside buyer or renter.

The debtor presented its own expert testimony from an individual heavily involved in the direct marketing industry. The debtor's expert stated that the fair market value of the list, if sold to other companies, was $700,000 on the petition date and $330,000 as of the hearing date. He utilized a model containing twelve factors from which he calculated the value of the list. These factors included expected revenues and expenses, customer attrition, rental income, comparison to outside lists, and customer affinity for the debtor's product....

DISCUSSION

Bankruptcy Code section 362(d) provides relief from the stay imposed by section 362(a) in either of two circumstances. The stay will be lifted "for cause, including the lack of adequate protection of an interest in property of [a] party in interest." 11 U.S.C. §362(d)(1). The stay will also be lifted "with respect to a stay of an act against property under subsection (a) of this section, if (A) the debtor does not have an equity in such property; and (B) such property is not necessary to an effective reorganization." 11 U.S.C. §362(d)(2). Lincoln and Westinghouse have asserted that they are entitled to relief under either part of section 362(d). The debtor claims to the contrary that its mailing list is vital to its reorganization and that it has offered adequate protection for any decline in the collateral's value. The court will consider sections 362(d)(1) and 362(d)(2) in reverse order.

I. SECTION 362(D)(2)

Neither party disputes that Craddock-Terry has no equity in the collateral. The debt secured by the collateral is greater than $9,000,000, and although the parties have widely divergent views of the value of the collateral for purposes of this motion, each places a lower value on it than the amount of the debt. "Equity" is defined as the amount by which the value of the collateral exceeds the debt it secures. Thus, the debtor has no equity in the collateral and the first requirement of section 362(d)(2) is met.

Each party also agrees that if the debtor can possibly reorganize, this collateral is essential to its survival. Lincoln and Westinghouse claim, however, that even if the debtor retains and uses the collateral, no effective reorganization is possible. In short, Lincoln and Westinghouse have no faith in the debtor's proposed plan for reorganization or its proposed business plan. They point to reduced catalog mailings and the reduced fill rate for customers' orders since the initiation of bankruptcy proceedings, both of which have caused the decline in value of the mailing list and, therefore, of the business itself.

The debtor, on the other hand, while admitting that its fill rate and catalog mailings have decreased, introduced evidence that the intrinsic value of the mailing list has not been irreparably harmed. The debtor's expert testified that an infusion of capital appropriately applied to the mailing list could revive the list's value, and that he had in fact seen this occur in a similar situation. The debtor's own representative testified that approximately $4,000,000 would be available to the debtor from the recent sale of the bulk of the company's assets to The Old Time Gospel Hour and to T/W Properties. He further testified that $900,000 of this influx of cash was designated for revitalization of the mailing list, and thereby, the company.

Since the filing of the debtor's petition the general theme of this reorganization has been to sell most of the company's assets and use the proceeds to reorganize the company's Hill Brothers division into a viable entity. The debtor has finally reached the point where it will have capital with which to effect those plans. The law is clear that a court "should not precipitously sound the death knell for a debtor by prematurely determining that the debtor's prospects for economic revival are poor." In re Shockley Forest Indus., Inc., 5 B.R. 160 (Bankr. M.D. Tenn. 1980). The evidence before the court as yet gives no basis for a conclusion that this reorganization is no longer in prospect, and therefore the court finds that the collateral at issue here is necessary to an effective reorganization. Consequently, the automatic stay will not be lifted pursuant to section 362(d)(2).

II. SECTION 362(D)(1)

Lincoln and Westinghouse are entitled to relief from the stay, however, if the debtor cannot satisfy section 362(d)(1) by providing adequate protection for the interest of Lincoln and Westinghouse in the collateral. The debtor has offered replacement liens in all its assets, which it claims will provide adequate protection either from the date of the motion or, if necessary, from the date of the petition. The parties agree that the value of the collateral has declined since the date the petition was filed and also since the date the motion was filed. They disagree as to the amount of decline in value and as to the date from which adequate protection is necessary.

The major focus of the parties during the hearing on this motion and in their final arguments was on the proper value to assign to the collateral at the various stages herein. The Bankruptcy Code provides no specific guidance as to the standard to be used to value property for purposes of providing creditors adequate protection with respect to section 362(d). Section 361 establishes three non-exclusive methods of providing adequate protection of a creditor's interest in property, but specifies no means for valuing that interest. Section 506(a) states that the value of a creditor's interest in the estate's interest in property "shall be determined in light of the purpose of the valuation and of the proposed disposition or use of such property, and in conjunction with any hearing on such disposition or use or on a plan affecting such creditor's interest," 11 U.S.C. §506(a), but gives no other insight into how such value should be determined.

Consequently courts have looked to the legislative history behind these two sections to find reasonable and proper methods of valuation. The legislative history of section 506(a) establishes that valuation methods should not be rigid:

> "value" does not necessarily contemplate forced sale or liquidation value of collateral; nor does it always imply a full going concern value. Courts will have to determine value on a case-by-case basis, taking into account the facts of each case and the competing interests in the case.

H.R.Rep. No. 95-595, 95th Cong., 1st Sess. 356 (1977)....

In order to determine the most commercially reasonable disposition practicable, the court must follow the directive of section 506 and consider the purpose of the valuation. The purpose of adequate protection "as stated in the legislative history [of section 361] is to insure that the secured creditor receives in value essentially what he bargained for." In re Ram Mfg., Inc., 32 B.R. 969, 971 (Bankr. E.D. Pa. 1983). Therefore "adequate protection for a secured creditor means that the creditor must receive the same *measure* of protection in bankruptcy that he could have had outside of bankruptcy although the *type* of protection may differ from the bargain initially struck between the parties." Id. at 972. (quoting In re Winslow Center Assoc., 32 B.R. 685, 688 (Bankr. E.D. Pa. 1983)) (emphasis in original). In other words, the value of the interest of Lincoln and Westinghouse in the collateral is equivalent to what they could have recovered through foreclosure, had the debtor defaulted but not filed its petition for Chapter 11 relief. The benefit initially bargained for, and to be protected under sections 361 and 362, was the value obtainable from the most commercially reasonable disposition of the collateral within the context of foreclosure proceedings....

A customer list, as an asset, is a strange hybrid. Although actually represented by a physical asset (the list), its worth is basically as an intangible. The utility of the list results both from Craddock-Terry's established reputation and service, and from the inclination of the particular consumers on the list to purchase shoes, of the kind and quality which Craddock-Terry sells, from Craddock-Terry. The testimony indicated that the value of the list is far greater to Craddock-Terry than to anyone else. The debtor's expert testified that even competitors in the shoe business would not value the list as highly as Craddock-Terry for various reasons, including the fact that crossover with their own lists could be as high as fifty percent.

The debtor did introduce evidence of the value of the list if sold through an arms length transaction. The debtor's expert testified that this was not a "fire-sale" value, but indeed the fair market value. He used a model which is widely used in the direct marketing industry to determine mailing list values for third parties. His analysis took into account a variety of factors including not only list maintenance expenses and revenues, but also customer attrition, customer affinity for Craddock-Terry, and replacement cost, among others. His appraisal indicated that the collateral had a fair market value of not more than $700,000 as of the petition date, not more than $500,000 as of February 1988, and not more than $330,000 as of the hearing date. The Court finds this evidence to be credible and, as to the value of the collateral, the only evidence of the most commercially reasonable disposition practicable in these circumstances.

Since there is no dispute that the debtor has no equity in the collateral or that its value has declined during these proceedings, the debtor must provide adequate protection to Lincoln and Westinghouse. The final question presented in this case is the date from which adequate protection is required. Lincoln and Westinghouse argue that they should be protected from the decrease in value of the property resulting from the stay in its entirety, and therefore from the date of the petition. The debtor contends that relief should only cover the period of decline following the date these creditors filed their motion for relief.

The debtor, citing In re Grieves, 81 B.R. 912 (Bankr. N.D. Ind. 1987), contends that to allow a creditor adequate protection from the commencement of the case, even though the creditor does not formally request such protection until some months later, would place an undue burden on the debtor by forcing it to make back payments for an arrearage which the debtor didn't know was accruing. The debtor also claims that such a rule would encourage secured creditors to "sit on their rights" rather than acting to preserve their security. These arguments are not persuasive.

To the contrary, to adopt the rule which the debtor suggests would be even more harmful to the purposes of bankruptcy law. Such a requirement would force creditors to rush to the courthouse as soon as they learn of a debtor's petition in order to ensure that they obtain adequate protection from as early a date as possible. The resulting litigation would likely be prodigious, and certainly would interrupt the expected "breathing space" which debtors normally enjoy after a petition is filed. Surely a debtor in possession will do all it can to preserve the value of all property of the estate whether encumbered or not. Such a requirement, even absent a formal motion by a secured creditor, and even from the commencement of the case, is consonant with bankruptcy policies. . . .

The Court finds that Lincoln and Westinghouse are entitled to adequate protection for all decline in the value of the collateral since the petition date. The value of the collateral on that date, for the purposes of this motion, was $700,000. The debtor has offered replacement liens in all its remaining assets, which its representative testified are worth in excess of $2,000,000 (not including $7,000,000 in accounts receivable). Therefore the automatic stay imposed by 11 U.S.C. §362(a) will remain in effect, and this court will enter an order directing the debtor to execute a security agreement, all necessary financing statements, and any other supporting documents necessary to perfect a valid security interest in remaining assets in which the estate has an aggregate equity of no less than $700,000, in favor of Lincoln and Westinghouse, to secure the same indebtedness secured by the collateral at issue here.

On the face of this opinion, it appears that Lincoln and Westinghouse lost. They moved to lift the stay, and the court refused. But lifting the stay may not have been their real objective. Before the hearing Lincoln and Westinghouse had a security interest in a customer list that was admittedly declining in value. By persuading the court that they were not adequately protected by their existing collateral, they forced the debtor to a choice — let the stay be lifted or provide additional protection. Predictably, Craddock-Terry came up with additional protection. After the hearing, Lincoln and Westinghouse still had the customer list as collateral, but they also had a security interest in other estate assets. The additional collateral satisfied the court that the total value of Lincoln and Westinghouse's collateral would not fall below the $700,000 value it had at the time Craddock-Terry filed bankruptcy.

It is also instructive to notice the effect of the court's decision on unsecured creditors. If the court had simply lifted the stay, without making an award of adequate protection, Lincoln and Westinghouse would have had the customer list and sold it for what they could. The additional $700,000 of assets would have remained unencumbered. If the business had then liquidated, as it most likely would without its customer list, the $700,000 would have been among the assets available to unsecured creditors. Once the award was made, however, those assets became the collateral of Lincoln and Westinghouse. If the reorganization later failed, Lincoln and Westinghouse would be satisfied first from that collateral, perhaps leaving considerably less for the unsecured creditors.

Because the value of the secured creditor's collateral may be in jeopardy, motions to lift the stay receive high priority on the bankruptcy court's calendar. Bankruptcy Code §362(e) provides that the stay is automatically terminated unless, within 30 days after a secured creditor moves to lift it, the court enters an order continuing it in effect. In addition, if the debtor is an individual the stay terminates 60 days after the secured creditor moves to lift it unless the court renders a final decision on the motion by that time or extends the 60-day period for good cause. Thus, while the stay is imposed automatically, its continuation is not automatic. More important, this provision demonstrates Congress's intent that stalling tactics on the part of the debtor should not cause the secured creditor to lose value.

Notice that the protection awarded by the court in *Craddock-Terry* was retroactive to the date of the filing of the petition. Most courts make the protection retroactive only to the date of the filing of the motion for adequate protection; a few refuse to make it retroactive at all. Under the latter two views it will be particularly important for a secured creditor who needs adequate protection against ongoing depreciation to make the motion as early as possible.

Not surprisingly, motions to lift the automatic stay constitute a substantial part of the work of the bankruptcy court, particularly in reorganization cases. In an empirical study of Chapter 11 cases, Professor Charles Shafer found that the single most-frequently instituted motion in reorganization cases was a motion to lift the stay. Professor Shafer found, however, that most of the motions did not result in a contested hearing; 87 percent were settled before the court rendered its decision. Charles Shafer, Determining Whether Property Is Necessary for an Effective Reorganization: A Proposal for the Use of Empirical Research, 1990 Ann. Surv. Bankr. L. 79 (Callahan 1990). In liquidation cases there is somewhat less emphasis on getting the stay lifted, because the process is usually much quicker and the secured creditor is about to reach the property anyway. But even in liquidation cases, the traffic is substantial.

Secured creditors can move to lift the stay at any time. Even if a prior motion to lift the stay in the same case was denied, the secured creditor can try again if the circumstances have changed. Secured creditors are most likely to try again when it appears the debtor is settling in for a long stay in bankruptcy.

E. Strategic Uses of Stay Litigation

The effect of an order lifting or modifying the automatic stay differs greatly depending on the nature of the collateral and importance of the collateral to the debtor's business or life. An order lifting the stay to permit repossession of a speedboat the debtor rarely uses may do nothing more than help the debtor get its financial affairs in order. But an order lifting the stay to permit repossession of assets necessary to the operation of the debtor's business may signal the end of that business. For example, had the stay been lifted in the *Craddock-Terry* case, Lincoln and Westinghouse could have repossessed and sold the customer lists. Without its customer lists, Craddock-Terry probably would have been unable to continue its mail-order shoe business. In opposing the motion to lift the stay, Craddock-Terry probably was fighting for its survival.

Yet it does not necessarily follow that if Lincoln and Westinghouse had won the motion they would have taken the lists. Negotiation and negotiated solutions permeate the American legal system, particularly in the commercial law area. One can do more with legal rights than simply enforce them. They constitute the working capital for playing in the great American game of "let's make a deal."

The reorganization of McLouth Steel Company, one of the cases studied by Professors LoPucki and Whitford in their empirical study of large Chapter 11 cases, offers an illustration. McLouth's financing was provided by a group of six banks and four insurance companies. Their $166 million loan was secured by all of the company's assets, primarily steel plants located in Michigan. When McLouth filed for bankruptcy reorganization in the mid-1980s, the secured creditors quickly moved to lift the automatic stay. The cash flow from the steel plants was insufficient to provide adequate protection through periodic payments, and McLouth had no equity in the collateral. The parties realized that if the motion were heard by the court, relief from the stay almost certainly would be granted.

Before the hearing, the parties reached a settlement. The secured creditors agreed not to press their motion or to take possession of the steel mills. McLouth could continue to operate. In return, McLouth agreed to seek buyers for its assets and apply the proceeds of sale to pay down the secured debt. If the assets were not sold by a fixed date, which was then only a few months away, the "drop-dead" provision of the settlement agreement would take effect. Under that provision, the mills would be closed, the stay would be lifted, and the secured creditors would take possession. Probably neither the debtor nor the secured creditors believed that a sale could be completed before the drop-dead date.

As the drop-dead date approached, McLouth had not yet found a buyer for the mills. The creditors expressed their lack of confidence in McLouth's chief executive officer and he obliged by promptly resigning. The creditors extended the drop-dead date for 90 days. When the new drop-dead date arrived, McLouth was in negotiations with a potential buyer, Tang Industries. Again, the secured creditors forbore their right to take possession of the mills, and instead gave McLouth additional time to pursue the possibility of sale. About a year after the filing of the reorganization case, McLouth concluded a sale to Tang and the automatic stay became moot.

What was going on? The secured creditors' acknowledged ability to lift the stay gave them tremendous leverage over the debtor — enough that the secured creditors were virtually in control of the company. At the same time, the secured creditors realized that it was not in their interest to take possession of the mills. Closing the mills would have greatly reduced their sale value. Continuing to operate the mills after foreclosure would potentially have exposed the creditors to a variety of regulatory problems, the most important of which were probably banking and environmental regulations. So long as McLouth did what it was told, there was little to gain by taking possession and much potential trouble to be avoided by not doing so. As a result of this delicate balance of considerations, McLouth's formal legal structure (secured creditors holding claims against a debtor protected by the automatic stay) did not match the true business relationship (secured creditors virtually in control of the company).

McLouth is a good illustration of the strategic use of stay litigation because it is such an extreme example. In most cases, the degree of control a creditor can achieve by means of a threat to lift the stay and repossess the assets is considerably less. But to realize that secured creditors have such means to influence reorganizing debtors is important to understanding the full extent of the enhanced collection rights that secured creditors have in, as well as out, of bankruptcy.

Problem Set 48

48.1. You have been counsel to CompuSoft, a computer software and servicing company, for over six years. As you were reviewing other legal matters with the CFO, Mandy Elkins, she mentioned that client bankruptcies were costing them a lot of money. She said that 12 of their clients were currently in bankruptcy and that none of these clients were making any payments on their outstanding accounts, even though CompuSoft billed them each month. She said they were not accepting any new orders from the nonpayers, but she thought maybe they should do some "serious collection efforts with these guys." What do you tell her? See Bankr. Code §§362(a), 501(a), 502(b) (disregarding the exceptions in §502(b)).

48.2. You have been working for Kansas Savings to collect a $1.2 million loan from Jayhawk Enterprises. The defaulted loan is secured by grain-processing equipment worth $1.5 million, so you haven't been worried about collection. Your attempts at self-help repossession have been stymied, however, so you have obtained a judgment. You and the sheriff are off this morning to seize the collateral. When you arrive at Jayhawk, the sheriff shows the appropriate writ and announces that he is here to take the grain-processing equipment. Jayhawk's president says you are too late; Jayhawk filed for bankruptcy earlier this morning. Can you go forward with the repo? Bankr. Code §§362(a), 541(a)(1). Can the sheriff? Bankr. Code §101 (definition of "entity").

48.3. You are the senior in-house counsel for BankWest, a commercial bank in northern California. This morning you received a file referred by a loan officer in one of the Sacramento branches. The case involves the bankruptcy of Prime Cuts, a small restaurant chain that filed for Chapter 11 last week owing BankWest $250,000. According to the file, the loan is secured by the property of one of the restaurants. That restaurant is worth no more than $250,000 and probably less. While some of the other Prime Cuts locations have been profitable, this one was in a weaker location and had few customers. Prime Cuts had closed it just before they filed the bankruptcy petition. The loan officer recommends "we foreclose as soon as possible and take our hit on this one." Can we do that? See Bankr. Code §§362(a), (c), and (e).

48.4.   Another of the BankWest files you received is that of Sprouts Up, a Riverside chain of fast-food health-food stores. They too have filed under Chapter 11. Sprouts Up owes $210,000 and has missed four payments. BankWest has begun foreclosure proceedings on the mortgage it holds on the building where the corporate headquarters are located. The building is in a good area, and it is appraised at about $600,000 fair market value. Even at a sheriff's sale you are confident that there would be bidding in excess of your outstanding mortgage. The loan officer anticipates an "agonizingly long reorganization while the corporate officers fight among themselves." She wants the bank to get out as quickly as possible so the bank can loan this money elsewhere. What is your advice? See Bankr. Code §§362(a), (d).

48.5.   The same afternoon that you received the Sprouts Up case, you also get the file for Paradise Boat Leasing. Three years ago, BankWest financed Paradise's purchase of a 65-foot yacht. The yacht rents with crew by the day or the week from a port in the Virgin Islands. Although Paradise is in financial trouble, the yacht loan seems generally in pretty good shape. The value of the yacht is about $350,000, the amount of BankWest's loan is $175,000, and Paradise is current on its payments. Just before Paradise filed under Chapter 11 of the Bankruptcy Code, BankWest got notice that the insurance had been canceled. Under the security agreement it is Paradise's responsibility to keep the yacht insured and its failure to do so constitutes a default. The security agreement further provides that in the event of default, BankWest can purchase insurance and add the cost to the secured debt and/or take possession of the yacht. BankWest tried to get another policy, but nobody seems to want to insure a boat that belongs to a bankrupt. What do you do now? See 11 U.S.C. §§362(a), (d).

48.6.   Your firm does some debtor's work as well, and you are working on Hill Farms Industries, a food processing company that filed for Chapter 11 three months ago. When you arrived at work this morning your secretary gave you phone messages from two irate creditors of the company. How do you plan to deal with each? Bankr. Code §§361, 362(a), (c), and (e).

a.   The first caller was the attorney for Watson Investment, a company from which Hill Farms borrowed $126,000 unsecured. He was upset that Hill Farms is now six months behind on the loan with no plans to make any payments until it gets a plan confirmed.

b.   The second call was from the attorney for Macklin Mortgage. Macklin has a security interest in Hill Farms sterilization equipment to secure a $50,000 debt Hill Farms owes Macklin. She is upset because she just received an appraisal showing the equipment, which was appraised at $50,000 as of the commencement of the case, is now worth only about $40,000.

Assignment 49: The Treatment of Secured Creditors in Bankruptcy

Bankruptcy not only stops collecting creditors in their tracks, it may also change the amount of money those creditors are entitled to collect. In this assignment we explore how a creditor collects from a bankrupt debtor, focusing once again on important differences between the treatment of unsecured and secured creditors.

A. The Vocabulary of Bankruptcy Claims

To understand the treatment of secured creditors in bankruptcy, it helps to begin with a clear understanding of the terms used and the concepts to which they refer. Unfortunately, nonbankruptcy law uses some of the same terms to describe concepts that are similar but nonetheless different. To minimize confusion, we point out the differences where they are important.

Under both bankruptcy and nonbankruptcy law, a *debt* is a sum of money owing. The amount owing typically fluctuates as interest accrues, attorneys' fees and other collection expenses are incurred, and payments are made. The amount of a debt is determined under nonbankruptcy law, typically by application of contract law, tort law, antitrust law, or some other substantive law that determines the rights and liabilities of disputing parties. When the word "debt" is used in bankruptcy, the reference is nearly always to the debt, in whatever amount, as it exists under nonbankruptcy law.

Debts can be *discharged* in bankruptcy. A discharged debt still exists, but the discharge permanently enjoins the creditor from attempting to collect it. See Bankr. Code §524(a)(2). For all practical purposes, once a debt is discharged, the debtor does not owe it.

Both secured and unsecured debts can be discharged. In either case, the discharged debt would be described as *nonrecourse*, meaning that it cannot be enforced against the debtor. A nonrecourse unsecured debt is merely an artifact of legal metaphysics: It is not connected to anything and has no known consequence. The same is not true for a nonrecourse secured debt.

Although no one owes the nonrecourse secured debt, the failure to pay such a debt can have important consequences. If the lien has not been removed during the bankruptcy case, it continues to encumber the collateral afterward. If the underlying debt is not paid, the creditor can foreclose on the property after bankruptcy. The foreclosure sale will transfer ownership of the collateral to the purchaser, and the proceeds of sale will be applied to pay the nonrecourse debt. If those proceeds are sufficient to satisfy the nonrecourse debt, the debt will be paid in full and any excess will be distributed to junior lien holders or the owner; if they are insufficient to satisfy the discharged nonrecourse debt, the secured creditor cannot obtain a deficiency judgment against the debtor because the debtor no longer owes the debt.

Under Article 9 of the Uniform Commercial Code, the special collection rights of a personal property secured creditor are referred to as a *security interest*. The special collection rights of a previously unsecured creditor who has levied against property of the debtor are referred to as a *lien*. See, e.g., U.C.C. §9-102(a)(52), defining *lien creditor*. The special collection rights of a creditor consensually secured by an interest in real estate are typically referred to as a *mortgage*. U.C.C. §9-102(a)(55). In some states, those rights might be in the form of a *deed of trust*, a device that, despite its difference in form, has much the same effect as a mortgage.

The Bankruptcy Code, §101(51), like the Internal Revenue Code, §6323(h)(1), groups Article 9 security interests together with real estate mortgages and deeds of trust under the term *security interest*. The Bankruptcy Code then lumps security interests together with all other secured statuses, including judicial and statutory liens, under the term *lien*. Bankr. Code §101(37). Thus, an Article 9 security interest, a real estate mortgage, a deed of trust, and the rights of a lien creditor are all liens within the contemplation of the Bankruptcy Code.

A creditor's *claim* in bankruptcy is, in essence, the amount of the debt owed to the creditor under nonbankruptcy law at the time the bankruptcy case is filed. Bankr. Code §§101(5) and (12). Notice that the amount of the claim is the amount actually owed. In this respect, the word *claim* does not have its ordinary meaning when used in bankruptcy. Absent bankruptcy, to say that a party "claims" something implies that the claim may not be correct; the same implication does not inhere in the use of "claim" in bankruptcy.

Only claims that are *allowed* are eligible to share in the distributions made in the bankruptcy case. Bankruptcy Code §502(b) contains a list of the kinds of claims that are not allowed, but the exceptions are not relevant for our purposes. Because the difference between a claim and an allowed claim is so slight, bankruptcy lawyers often speak of "claims" when they mean "allowed claims." We often do the same.

Because the amount of the debt and the amount of the corresponding claim are determined under different rules, they can diverge as the bankruptcy case continues. In determining the creditor's rights in the bankruptcy case, it is usually the amount of the *claim* that is important. In determining the creditor's rights in a nonbankruptcy forum after the stay has been lifted or the bankruptcy case dismissed, it is usually the amount of the *debt* that is important. So, for example, a secured creditor may not be able to expand its *claim* as time passes while the debtor is in bankruptcy, but the amount of the *debt* may continue to climb as a result of the accrual of interest. If the case should be dismissed from bankruptcy without a discharge for the debtor, the creditor might reassert its collection rights at state law. In such a case, the creditor would seek payment of the debt, including all the interest due from the inception of the loan, rather than simply the claim that would have been allowed in the bankruptcy case.

B.   The Claims Process

How much creditors are paid from a bankruptcy estate depends on how much the various creditors are owed, the creditors' relative priorities in the estate, and the value available with which to pay them. How the bankruptcy system determines these three variables and combines them to yield a set of distributions for a particular case is the subject of the remainder of this assignment.

To guide you through it, we provide this quick overview. Through a claims process, the bankruptcy system determines the Bankruptcy Code §502 amounts of all creditors' claims — that is, the amounts those creditors were owed under nonbankruptcy law as of the date of bankruptcy. Some claims are permitted to grow through the accrual of interest and collection costs during the bankruptcy case while others are not. The system separates the claims into classes based on the priorities to which they are entitled and other factors. In a Chapter 7 case, the amounts available for distribution are determined by actually selling the assets. In a Chapter 11 case, the value of property that will be distributed under the plan is determined through negotiations or by the court. The proceeds are then matched to the amounts of the claims and their relative priorities to determine the distributions that will be made to each claimant.

Absent bankruptcy, in order to establish the amount owed to it an unsecured creditor has to bring a lawsuit, usually in state court, alleging the facts that establish the underlying liability as well as the amount owed. Even a secured creditor that is unable to gain possession by self-help must bring an action in court. If the debtor contests the action, the secured creditor must prove the existence of the debt and the amount owing.

Once a bankruptcy has been filed, the automatic stay bars creditors from taking those steps. Bankruptcy substitutes a much cheaper, easier system for a creditor to establish its claim. The creditor simply files a one-page form called a *proof of claim*, describing the debt and stating that it remains outstanding. Bankr. Code §501(a). If the claim is based on a written contract or other document, the contract or document must be attached. If no one objects to the claim, the claim is deemed "allowed" in the bankruptcy process. Bankr. Code §502(a). In Chapter 11 cases, the process is even easier. The debtor must file a list of its creditors with the amounts owing to each. If the debtor schedules the debt correctly and does not dispute it, the creditor need not even file a proof of claim. Bankr. Code §1111(a).

Under nonbankruptcy procedures, debtors often have a substantial incentive to dispute collection claims. Absent a dispute, a creditor can obtain a quick judgment and enforce it by seizing the debtor's assets. If the debtor disputes all or part of the debt, the creditor typically has no remedy until the dispute is resolved. In the meantime, the debtor can remain in business and continue to use its assets. It should not be surprising that in the absence of bankruptcy, many debts are disputed on the flimsiest of grounds.

In bankruptcy, however, a determination that the debt is owed does not lead to seizure of the debtor's assets. Whether the debtor retains possession of the property does not turn on whether the money is owed. Thus the principal incentive for the debtor to raise disputes is eliminated. In addition, most of the disputes that are raised in a bankruptcy proceeding are easier to resolve because the parties realize that the estate will pay only a small percentage of whatever is ultimately determined to be owed. If the debtor will pay only ten cents on the dollar of allowed claims, a dispute over whether the debtor owed the creditor $10,000 at the time the petition was filed is actually a dispute over $1,000. Neither side will be as inclined to fight it. For both these reasons, objections to claims in bankruptcy cases are relatively rare. Most claims are simply filed by the creditors and deemed allowed by operation of law.

Claims against the estate are accelerated as a consequence of the bankruptcy filing. Bankr. Code §502(b)(1). If, for example, the debtor owes the creditor $10,000 payable in monthly installments of $1,000 each month over the next ten months and only one payment is currently due, the claim in bankruptcy is the total amount owed, not just the current payment. The creditor will file a claim for $10,000, the full, accelerated debt. And the whole debt, not just the payments currently due, will be resolved during the bankruptcy case.

If a claim is disputed, bankruptcy law provides for a quicker resolution of the dispute than is generally available under state law. While complex disputes may be subject to a full-scale trial after both sides have had an opportunity for discovery, probably most objections to claims are resolved in a single evidentiary hearing. If the ultimate resolution of a claim threatens to delay the bankruptcy case or distribution, the bankruptcy court can estimate the amount of a claim, allow it in the estimated amount, and proceed. Bankr. Code §502(c). In either a hearing on an objection to a claim or in a claims estimation proceeding, a creditor might show, for example, that it had sold the debtor equipment, the agreed price of the equipment, and the payments received by the time of the filing. The debtor might then bring in evidence that the equipment had failed to operate as promised, giving the debtor a contract law right to set off damages against the amount owed. The debtor might claim that nothing is owed or that a reduced sum is appropriate. If the debtor outside bankruptcy had a legal defense to payment, the bankruptcy estate will have the same defense. Bankr. Code §558. But if the bankruptcy court determines that the full amount is owed, the claim will be allowed in full. The court would typically consider the evidence proffered (often by affidavit) and rule on the amount of the claim.

Different creditors may have different bases for their claims. A department store, for example, might have a claim for the charges made by a debtor and not yet paid. An employee might have a claim for past wages. A tort victim might have a claim for injuries. Taxing authorities might have claims for back taxes due. Utilities may have claims for unpaid services. Landlords may have claims for unpaid rents, and hospitals may have claims for services provided that were never paid. Sellers of goods may have claims for the purchase price of goods sold to the debtor. Buyers of goods may have warranty claims against their sellers. Some creditors may even have claims for events that have not yet occurred (e.g., a potential claim against a debtor's guarantor when the debtor is not yet in default), or claims that are not yet fixed in amount (e.g., claims for personal injuries that have not yet been heard by a jury). The list is as long and varied as the number of ways one can become obligated to pay money. Unless the holders of these claims had obtained liens before the filing of the bankruptcy case, their claims will all be unsecured in the bankruptcy case and the amounts owed will be determined through the routine claims procedure.

Bankruptcy law gives some groups of unsecured creditors priority over others, see Bankr. Code §507(a), but of the unsecured creditors listed in this paragraph, all but the taxing authorities and the employee would share pro rata with each other.

The procedure for claims estimation is itself remarkable. In re Apex Oil Co., 92 B.R. 843 (Bankr. E.D. Mo. 1988), illustrates the point: A $1.4 billion dispute between the debtor oil company and the U.S. Department of Energy had gone on for years, with no resolution in sight. Within a short time after the debtor filed bankruptcy, the bankruptcy court established procedures for resolving the dispute and scheduled two days of court hearings on the amount of the claim. The parties quickly settled the claim, and the company, which had been spending enormous resources on trying to resolve this dispute, returned to its primary business functions. Such accelerated procedures are necessary for achieving the rapid resolution of financial problems that bankruptcy contemplates. Of course, it should also be apparent that as procedures are abbreviated and parties are hurried toward a compromise, some rough justice may be dispensed along the way.

C.   Calculating the Amount of an Unsecured Claim

Most debts listed (*scheduled*, in the parlance of bankruptcy) in a bankruptcy case are undisputed. The debtor owes the money and has no defense. Even so, calculating the amounts in which the various claims should be allowed and from that the amounts appropriate for distribution on each can require considerable knowledge of bankruptcy law.

The amount of an unsecured claim in bankruptcy is essentially the amount owed on the debt under nonbankruptcy law as of the moment the bankruptcy petition is filed. Bankr. Code §502(b). If the creditor's contract with the debtor provides for the debtor to pay the attorneys' fees of the creditor or to reimburse the creditor for other fees, those amounts are included in the Bankruptcy Code §502(b) amount of the claim, provided that they were incurred prior to the time the bankruptcy case was filed. Bankr. Code §502(b)(1).

The amount of the unsecured claim does not grow with the accrual of interest during the bankruptcy case. This conclusion is derived from the restriction that an unsecured creditor's claim may not include "unmatured interest." Bankr. Code §502(b)(2). The reason for disallowing postpetition interest lies in the collective nature of bankruptcy. To understand it, consider that in the vast majority of bankruptcy cases, estate assets will be sufficient to pay only a portion of the claims. As of the moment of the filing of the petition, each unsecured creditor is entitled to a pro rata share of a fixed pool of assets. To allow interest to accrue on the claims between the filing of the case and the ultimate distribution would not increase the value of the pool. If unsecured creditors were allowed to accrue interest on their claims at the rates specified in their contracts, the only effect would be to shift some of the recovery from low interest creditors to high interest creditors. While some might argue that is the bargain initially struck among the creditors, that is not the policy reflected in the Bankruptcy Code. Instead, for the purposes of accruing post-petition interest, all the unsecured creditors are equal, even if their initial contracts were different. In addition to principled reasons such as preservation of equality among creditors, there are more practical reasons to insist on similar postpetition treatment among the creditors. To give creditors differential rates of interest after the bankruptcy filing would create differences among them that might even undermine the collective proceeding. For example, a creditor who was accruing interest at 21 percent, while another was accruing no interest, might not work nearly so hard nor compromise nearly so readily to conclude the bankruptcy case.

Traditionally, the courts have declined to permit unsecured creditors to include postpetition attorneys' fees in the amounts of their claims. Some recent cases, however, have permitted inclusion of postpetition attorneys' fees in cases where the contract between creditor and debtor provided for their payment.

To illustrate the calculation of the amount of an unsecured claim, assume that Maggie purchased computer paper from John on June 1 at an agreed price of $5,000 payable in three months at 12 percent interest, and that Maggie filed for bankruptcy on September 1. John would file a claim for $5,150 ($5,000 principal and $150 accrued interest). If Maggie filed bankruptcy on July 15 instead, the claim would be for $5,075 ($5,000 plus $75 accrued interest). If Maggie made no payments but delayed filing until the following June 1, John would have to consult the contract and applicable contract law to determine the amount of his claim: If his contract entitled him to accrue interest after default at the same contract rate, he would have a claim for $5,600; if the contract provided for a higher rate of interest after the default (sometimes referred to as a *default rate*) on September 1, as many contracts do, he could claim that higher amount. In addition, if John spent $1,000 in collection costs before the bankruptcy filing, and the contract provided for reimbursement of these costs, he could add that amount to his claim. But John could not claim any amount he would not be entitled to under nonbankruptcy law as of the moment of filing, with the possible exception for attorneys' fees mentioned in the preceding paragraph.

If the estate had sufficient assets to pay 10 percent of the claims against it, John's claim of $5,600 (June 1 filing) would yield a check for $560. The remaining $5,040 would be uncollectible. Absent extraordinary circumstances, the bankruptcy court would discharge Maggie from liability for it. If the claim were larger, including $1,000 in prefiling collection costs and another $500 in default interest, John's claim would grow to $7,100, and his actual recovery would rise to $710.

D.   Payments on Unsecured Claims

How much do unsecured creditors typically receive in a bankruptcy? There have been only a handful of careful empirical studies of the bankruptcy system. In one of the most detailed studies focusing on repayments to creditors in consumer bankruptcies in a single district, Professor Michael J. Herbert and Mr. Dominic E. Pacitti documented repayments to general, unsecured creditors. Their conclusion paints a grim picture for the general creditors listed in Chapter 7 cases:

> During the study period, a total of 4,892 cases were closed in the bankruptcy court. Of these, 4,723 were closed under Chapter 7, 167 under Chapter 13 and 2 under Chapter 11. In percentage terms, 96.55% of the cases were closed under Chapter 7, 3.41% under Chapter 13 and .04% under Chapter 11.
>
> Of the 4,723 Chapter 7 cases, there were 4,515 in which no assets were distributed, and, as noted above, there were 208 cases in which at least some assets were distributed. In percentage terms, 95.6% of the Chapter 7 cases were cases in which nothing was distributed. Of all the cases closed during the study period, 92.3% were no asset Chapter 7 proceedings and 4.25% were Chapter 7 proceedings in which some assets were distributed.

Herbert & Pacitti, Down and Out in Richmond, Virginia: The Distribution of Assets in Chapter 7 Bankruptcy Proceedings Closed During 1984-87, 22 U. Rich. L. Rev. 303, 311 (1988). Persistence of these low payouts was more recently confirmed in a study by the U.S. General Accounting Office of distributions in the 1.2 million Chapter 7 bankruptcy cases closed in statistical years 1991 and 1992. The GAO found that about 5 percent (56,994) of those cases generated some receipts for distribution to professionals and creditors, a total of about $2 billion. Money reached the hands of unsecured creditors in only about 3 percent of the Chapter 7 cases.

Not all bankruptcies yield so little. Debtors in Chapter 13 cases frequently promise to repay 100 percent of their outstanding debts. In a multidistrict study of debtors in bankruptcy, the researchers discovered great variation by district, but, overall, 41 percent of the Chapter 13 debtors promised full repayment, and another 21 percent promised to repay more than half their outstanding debts. Teresa Sullivan, Elizabeth Warren, & Jay Lawrence Westbrook, The Persistence of Local Legal Culture: Twenty Years of Evidence from the Federal Bankruptcy Courts, 17 Harv. J.L. & Pub. Poly. 801 (1994). Of course, this means only that the debtors promised to pay, not that the creditors actually got the money — an important distinction in the debtor-creditor biz. In a recent study of the largest Chapter 11 cases, promised payments were also high. Professor LoPucki found that plans provided 100 percent repayment of allowed claims to general unsecured creditors in 44 of 78 reorganization cases completed during the period 1991-1996 (56 percent). The Myth of the Residual Owner, 82 Wash. U. L.Q. 1341 (2004). (His preliminary study of more recent cases suggests that the current proportion of 100 percent repayment plans is lower.) In most instances these were not just paper recoveries. The distributions were made in stocks, bonds, and promissory notes that the creditors could immediately sell for cash.

The data from these studies lead to two conclusions, both of which must be kept in mind when evaluating the prospects for recovery in a particular case. First, the fate of most unsecured creditors in bankruptcy is not a happy one. The vast majority face discharge of all or a substantial portion of their outstanding debt with no payment or, at best, nominal payment. Second, there are many cases in which unsecured creditors manage a substantial or even a full recovery. Sophisticated unsecured creditors know that the average recoveries from bankruptcy cases are minuscule because the value of the debtors' assets are small. But they also know that in the cases of debtors with substantial assets, an allowed claim can sometimes yield substantial dividends.

E.   Calculating the Amount of a Secured Claim

Calculating the amount of a creditor's secured claim begins with a determination of the amount owing under nonbankruptcy law, as indicated in Bankruptcy Code §502. This step is the same for a claim secured by a lien as for an unsecured claim.

The next step is to bifurcate the claim as required under Bankruptcy Code §506(a)(1). That section provides that the claim of a secured creditor can be a *secured claim* only to the extent of the value of the collateral. The remainder of the creditor's claim is an *unsecured claim*. Bankr. Code §506(a)(1). If the value of the collateral is less than the Bankruptcy Code §502 amount of the secured creditor's claim, the effect will be to divide the secured creditor's claim into two claims: One will be a secured claim in an amount equal to the value of the collateral, and the other will be an unsecured claim for the deficiency.

To illustrate this bifurcation of claims, consider an example. If Bonnie Kraemer owes First National Bank $40,000 secured by a boat worth $50,000, First National has a $40,000 allowed secured claim. If the boat were worth only $35,000, First National would have a $35,000 secured claim and a $5,000 unsecured claim. Kraemer's unsecured claim would be treated just like any other unsecured claim. The treatment of her secured claim is the primary subject of the remainder of this chapter.

The next step in determining the amount of the secured claim is to determine whether the creditor is entitled to accrue postpetition interest, attorneys' fees, or costs on its claim. As we saw in section C, unsecured creditors cannot accrue such postpetition charges, even if they were entitled to these charges under their contract and under nonbankruptcy law. Bankruptcy Code §506(b) entitles the holder of a secured claim to accrue postfiling interest, attorneys' fees, and costs on its claim when three conditions are met: (1) attorneys' fees and costs must be "reasonable"; (2) payment of the attorneys' fees and costs by the debtor must be "provided for under the agreement or state statute under which [the] claim arose"; (3) interest, attorneys' fees, and costs can be accrued only to the extent that the value of the collateral exceeds the amount of the claim secured by it. (Bankruptcy lawyers and judges refer to such a claim as being *over secured*.)

Therefore, to continue with the example, if Bonnie Kraemer's debt of $40,000 is secured by a boat worth $50,000 at the time the bankruptcy case is filed, the claim could grow as interest, attorneys' fees, and other costs accrue during the bankruptcy case, up to an additional $10,000. The entire secured claim could not exceed the value of the collateral, $50,000. If, on the other hand, the collateral were worth only $35,000, First National's $40,000 claim would be bifurcated into a secured claim of $35,000 and an unsecured claim of $5,000, and neither claim would be permitted to grow. (Bankruptcy lawyers and judges would refer to the $40,000 claim as *undersecured*.) Keep in mind that these rules that prevent interest, attorneys' fees, and costs from accruing on a *claim* do not prevent them from accruing on the underlying *debt*.

The ability of over secured creditors to recover interest, attorneys' fees, and costs accrued during bankruptcy as part of their claims minimizes the injury bankruptcy inflicts on them. The data collected in Teresa Sullivan, Elizabeth Warren, & Jay Lawrence Westbrook, As We Forgive Our Debtors 306-311 (1989), documents that in consumer bankruptcies the secured creditors' claims were often fully secured. Secured creditors may be unable to repossess their collateral or terminate their relationship with the debtor, as we saw in the last assignment, and they may have new payment terms imposed on them, as we will see below. Unlike their unsecured counterparts, however, they can typically look forward to substantial repayment.

F. Selling the Collateral

As we discussed in the preceding assignment, a primary purpose of Chapter 7 of the Bankruptcy Code is to maximize the creditors' recovery by maximizing the sale price of the debtors' property. As we saw in Assignment 46, judicial sale procedures are often grossly ineffective in that regard. Chapter 7 provides a sale procedure that is generally much more effective. Under the supervision of the bankruptcy court, the Chapter 7 trustee sells the property in whatever manner the trustee thinks will maximize the net proceeds. The broader leeway given to the trustee permits alternative forms of sale, such as going-out-of-business sales at the business sites, sales in already established markets, or sales through brokers, to name just a few.

When the trustee liquidates the property of the estate, the trustee ordinarily sells only the debtor's equity in property subject to a security interest, because that is all the estate has succeeded to under Bankruptcy Code §541(a). The trustee does that by making the sale "subject to" the secured creditor's lien. For example, if Bonnie Kraemer's boat were worth $50,000 and the only lien against it was the $40,000 security interest of First National Bank, the trustee would sell the estate's interest for $10,000. The buyer would take the boat subject to the bank's $40,000 lien and the trustee would distribute the $10,000 purchase price to the unsecured creditors, as set forth in Bankruptcy Code §726(a).

The sale in this example would terminate the automatic stay with regard to the boat. Bankr. Code §362(c)(1). The bankruptcy case might continue, but the boat would no longer be part of it. First National Bank would be free to foreclose its lien, just as if there had not been a bankruptcy. As a practical matter, foreclosure probably would not be necessary. The buyer probably bought with full knowledge of First National's lien and its ability to foreclose it, and had already set aside $40,000 to pay First National.

If the boat were worth $35,000 instead of $50,000, the debtor's interest (bare ownership) would have become property of the estate. But that interest would have been of inconsequential value to the estate: The trustee would have a difficult time finding a responsible buyer for a $35,000 boat that was subject to a $40,000 lien. In fact, ownership of such a boat probably would have been a financial burden on the trustee, for to fulfill its minimal obligation to the secured creditor it would have had to incur storage expenses. Section 554(a) of the Bankruptcy Code authorizes the trustee to *abandon* property of the estate that is burdensome or of inconsequential value to the estate. When a trustee abandons property, it ceases to be property of the estate and ownership reverts to the debtor. Because the automatic stay protects the debtor as well as the estate, Bankr. Code §362(a)(5), the secured creditor must still move to lift it before continuing with foreclosure.

One other disposition of collateral is common in Chapter 7. Under some circumstances, the trustee can sell the collateral "free and clear of liens." Bankr. Code §363(f). For example, assume again that Bonnie Kraemer's boat was worth only $35,000, but the circumstances were such that the trustee was entitled to sell it free and clear of liens. The trustee presumably would sell it for $35,000 in cash. The sale would transfer First National's lien from the boat to the proceeds of sale. The amount of First National's secured claim would then be limited not by the value of the boat, *approximately* $35,000, but by the value of the proceeds, *exactly* $35,000. A secured creditor may also see a trustee's greater flexibility in conducting a sale as likely to yield more money on liquidation and may ask the trustee to conduct the sale.

If the sale of the boat free and clear of liens brought $50,000 instead, First National's entire claim would be secured. The trustee would pay $40,000 to First National and $10,000 would remain in the estate. In some limited circumstances, a trustee can sell collateral free and clear of liens and then make appropriate distributions to secured parties.

G. Who Pays the Expenses of Sale by the Trustee?

The preceding example makes little mention of the expenses that would have been incurred by the trustee in storing or selling the boat. Yet some expenses will be incurred almost any time a trustee sells property. Initially, the trustee will incur them, by, for example, contracting for the services of a real estate broker. When the trustee sells property subject to a security interest, can these expenses be passed along to the secured creditor by deducting them from the secured creditor's proceeds of sale? Or must the estate bear the expenses? In some situations, the resolution of this issue will be critical. Consider, for example, a house that probably can be sold for $100,000, but only through a real estate broker who will charge a $6,000 fee. If the mortgage against this house is $92,000, the estate's interest might be worth $2,000 or $8,000, depending on who must bear the expenses of sale.

Resolution of this issue is found in Bankruptcy Code §506(c), which authorizes a trustee who has incurred "reasonable, necessary costs and expenses of preserving, or disposing of" property securing an allowed secured claim to recover them from the property. That language is ambiguous, however, as to whether the trustee deducts the costs and expenses from the secured creditor's share of the proceeds, from the debtor's share of the proceeds, or from some combination of the two. The ambiguity is at least partially resolved by the language limiting the trustee's right to deduct from the proceeds "to the extent of any benefit to [the secured creditor.]" That is, absent benefit to the secured creditor from the trustee's expenditures, the trustee cannot deduct anything from the proceeds of sale.

Some ambiguity remains: "benefit" in comparison to what? Selling through a broker instead of selling without a broker? Paying for a security service instead of letting the property be destroyed by vandals? If this were the comparison, trustees would virtually always be able to charge their costs and expenses to the collateral. In In re The Wine Boutique, Inc., the court answered the "In comparison to what?" question in a manner that cost the secured creditor in that case but would favor the secured creditors in many other cases. In that case, the debtor in possession hired a real estate broker to sell its liquor store. The agent sold the store for $338,000, which all agreed was a fair price. Twin City State Bank held a lien against the store for an amount in excess of $338,000. The trustee nevertheless sought to deduct the $21,000 fee it paid the broker from the proceeds of sale before turning them over to Twin City. Having identified the issue as whether Twin City "benefitted from the sale," the Court answered the question in the affirmative — and stuck Twin City with the costs:

> [In bankruptcy] Twin City did not have to foreclose on the property and incur the financial burdens, and time burdens, that are usually associated with such action. Instead, Twin City was freed from these problems by virtue of the broker's prompt disposition of the property. Further, had *Twin City lifted the stay and taken possession of the realty and the personalty, it would have had to sell same and pay its broker a commission also.* [Emphasis added.] 117 B.R. 506 (Bankr. W.D. Mo. 1990)

Notice the comparison employed by the court to answer the "benefit" question. The court compares what actually happened with what would have happened if the stay had been lifted and the secured creditor had dealt with the problem on its own.

Apply this reasoning to the hypothetical in which the trustee incurs $6,000 of selling expense to sell property subject to a $92,000 lien for a gross price of $100,000. Can the trustee recover the $6,000 expenditure from the $92,000 of proceeds otherwise destined for the secured creditor? Applying the analysis from *Wine Boutique*, the answer is probably no, because the secured creditor probably did not benefit from the trustee's expenditure of the brokerage fee. Had the secured creditor lifted the stay and taken possession of the realty in this example, it would most likely have had to sell same and pay its broker a commission as well. But unlike *Wine Boutique*, the loss here would not have come to rest on the secured creditor: The secured creditor almost certainly would have had the contract right to add the amount of the commission to the amount of the secured debt. In contrast to *Wine Boutique*, there is an equity in the property in this hypothetical. As a result, the secured creditor will be able to recover the commission, along with any other expenditures it may have to make in connection with the property, from the property. The secured creditor does not "benefit" from the trustee's costs and expenses because even if the secured creditor incurred those expenses itself, it would have been reimbursed for them in the foreclosure process.

The result is that a trustee's sale of an *undersecured* creditor's collateral will ordinarily benefit that creditor and be deducted from its recovery. But the trustee's sale of property when the debt is sufficiently *over secured* will not. The actual outcome often depends on a complex analysis of what would have happened if the stay had been lifted and the secured creditor had been permitted to liquidate the collateral.

H.   Chapters 11 and 13 Reorganizations

In reorganization cases, the debtor typically seeks to keep the property that is subject to a security interest and to continue using it. The property may be anything from a car or boat in a Chapter 13 to millions of dollars' worth of factory equipment or a hotel or office building in a Chapter 11. In many of these cases, the debtor also seeks to reduce the amount of the secured debt and accompanying lien, to reschedule payment over a longer period of time, or to do both. These things can be accomplished over the objection of the secured creditor, if at all, only through confirmation of a Chapter 11 plan or a Chapter 13 plan by the bankruptcy court.

The confirmation of a Chapter 11 plan discharges the old secured debts and payment schedules and substitutes new ones. Bankr. Code §1141(d)(1)(A). The plan must specify that the creditor retain its lien under Bankruptcy Code §1129(b)(2)(A)(i)(I), but after confirmation, the lien secures only the new debt. The confirmation of a plan to which the creditor has not agreed is graphically referred to by bankruptcy lawyers and judges as a *cramdown*. Chapter 13 also authorizes cramdown. Procedure under Chapter 13 is materially different in that the discharge occurs only after the debtor completes all the payments under the plan. Bankr. Code §1328(a). But once the debtor completes the plan payments, the secured debts will be similarly stripped down to the value of the collateral by entry of the discharge.

Debtors and their secured creditors often agree on the treatment to be accorded the secured creditors under plans, but the negotiations take place in the shadow of what the court would do in the absence of agreement. The terms agreed upon are usually just the parties' best estimate of what the court would impose. For that reason, we examine the statutory standards for cramdown with an eye to determining the minimum repayment the court will consider "fair and equitable," which is the amount the plan proponent will therefore be entitled to cram down. The minimums are basically the same under both Chapter 11 and Chapter 13. Compare Bankruptcy Code

§1129(b)(2)(A) with Bankruptcy Code §1325(a)(5). They are most clearly stated in the latter section. Under that section, unless the secured creditor accepts (agrees to its treatment under) the plan, the debtor must either:

1. surrender the collateral to the secured creditor in satisfaction of the secured claim or
2. distribute to the creditor, on account of the secured claim, property with a value as of the effective date of the plan that is not less than the amount of the allowed secured claim.

The first alternative is pretty clear and is one most debtors want to avoid. The second requires some explanation. It essentially establishes a three-step process for testing the adequacy of the proposed distribution to a secured creditor. The first step is to determine the amount of the allowed secured claim. The second is to determine the value of the proposed distribution. The final step is to determine that the latter is at least as great as the former.

Although the secured claim must be paid in full, the payment promised under the plan need not be immediate or in cash. The debtor need only promise the creditor property that has a value at least as great as the amount of the secured claim. Theoretically, the property handed over might be an automobile or an elephant. But nearly always the property is a promise of future payments. The payments are usually regular monthly, quarterly, or annual payments (although an occasional case may provide for a balloon payment at some specified time in the future). A Chapter 13 debtor, for example, might propose to pay $100 per month for three years on her car loan. Alternatively, a debtor might propose irregular payments that reflect the odd times when the debtor expects to have cash available. A farmer, for example, might propose to pay $3,000 of the secured claim on the effective date of the plan and the balance in a lump sum when the debtor sells the wheat crop next August.

I. Valuing Future Payments

It is not sufficient that the payments total the *amount* of the allowed secured claim. They must have a *value* as of the effective date of the plan of that amount. (The "effective date of the plan" is nowhere defined in the Bankruptcy Code, but it is generally understood to be a date, specified in the plan, about 10 to 30 days after confirmation.) Of course, a payment of $1,000 made on the effective date of the plan has a value of $1,000 as of that date. But a promissory note, delivered on the effective date of the plan, promising to pay $1,000, without interest, one year after the effective date, will have a value lower than $1,000.

This concept is generally known as the *time value of money*. To illustrate the concept, assume that the market rate of interest is 10 percent. In the market in which that rate was fixed, some parties (lenders) are agreeing to pay $100 now in return for the agreement of other parties (borrowers) to pay back $110 one year later. If both lenders and borrowers are acting voluntarily (in some sense at least), this market is telling us that $100 now is the equivalent in value of $110 a year from now.

It follows that the amount of money that must be paid at some later time to have a present value of $X as of the effective date of the plan is $X plus interest at the market rate from the effective date of the plan to the date of payment. So, for example, if a creditor's allowed secured claim is $100, any plan that proposes to pay the creditor at least $100 plus interest at the market rate from the effective date of the plan to the date of payment will meet the "value" requirement. The promise of future payments will have a *present value*, as of the effective date of the plan, of at least $100.

In establishing a market rate of interest, the participants in a market consider a number of factors. They estimate the effects of inflation and the likelihood that $100 paid back in a year will not purchase as much as would $100 today. They also consider the risk that this particular borrower or borrowers of this type will not repay the loan or will not repay it in full. The greater the parties' assessments of both inflation and risk, the higher the charge for the use of the creditor's money and the higher the interest rate for the loan.

The term *market rate of interest* is necessarily ambiguous. At any given time, money is being borrowed and lent at many different rates of interest in many different "markets." For example, a bank may be borrowing money from the Federal Reserve at 6.5 percent and paying interest on short-term deposits at 7 percent and long-term deposits at 8 percent, while at the same time it is lending money on home loans at 8.5 percent, on commercial loans at rates from 9 percent to 12 percent, and charging 19% on outstanding credit card balances. If there is such a thing as a market rate of interest, each of these rates must represent a different market. To which market should the court look to fulfill the objectives of the Bankruptcy Code provisions regarding cramdown? In the following case, the Supreme Court faced precisely that question.

Till v. SCS Credit Corporation
541 U.S. 465 (2004)

STEVENS, J., announced the judgment of the Court and delivered an opinion, in which SOUTER, GINSBURG, and BREYER, JJ., joined. THOMAS, J., filed an opinion concurring in the judgment. SCALIA, J., filed a dissenting opinion, in which REHNQUIST, C.J., and O'CONNOR and KENNEDY, JJ., joined.

STEVENS, J.

To qualify for court approval under Chapter 13 of the Bankruptcy Code, an individual debtor's proposed debt adjustment plan must accommodate each allowed, secured creditor in one of three ways: (1) by obtaining the creditor's acceptance of the plan; (2) by surrendering the property securing the claim; or (3) by providing the creditor both a lien securing the claim and a promise of future property distributions (such as deferred cash payments) whose total "value, as of the effective date of the plan, . . . is not less than the allowed amount of such claim." 11 U.S.C. §1325(a)(5). The third alternative is commonly known as the "cram down option" because it may be enforced over a claim holder's objection.

Plans that invoke the cram down power often provide for installment payments over a period of years rather than a single payment. In such circumstances, the amount of each installment must be calibrated to ensure that, over time, the creditor receives disbursements whose total present value equals or exceeds that of the allowed claim. The proceedings in this case that led to our grant of certiorari identified four different methods of determining the appropriate method with which to perform that calibration. Indeed, the Bankruptcy Judge, the District Court, the Court of Appeals majority, and the dissenting Judge each endorsed a different approach....

I

On October 2, 1998, petitioners Lee and Amy Till, residents of Kokomo, Indiana, purchased a used truck from Instant Auto Finance for $6,395 plus $330.75 in fees and taxes. They made a $300 down payment and financed the balance of the purchase price by entering into a retail installment contract that Instant Auto immediately assigned to respondent, SCS Credit Corporation. Petitioners' initial indebtedness amounted to $8,285.24 — the $6,425.75 balance of the truck purchase plus a finance charge of 21% per year for 136 weeks, or $1,859.49. Under the contract, petitioners agreed to make 68 biweekly payments to cover this debt; Instant Auto — and subsequently respondent — retained a purchase money security interest that gave it the right to repossess the truck if petitioners defaulted under the contract.

On October 25, 1999, petitioners, by then in default on their payments to respondent, filed a joint petition for relief under Chapter 13 of the Bankruptcy Code. At the time of the filing, respondent's outstanding claim amounted to $4,894.89, but the parties agreed that the truck securing the claim was worth only $4,000. In accordance with the Bankruptcy Code, therefore, respondent's secured claim was limited to $4,000, and the $894.89 balance was unsecured....

Petitioners' proposed debt adjustment plan called for them to submit their future earnings to the supervision and control of the Bankruptcy Court for three years, and to assign $740 of their wages to the trustee each month. The plan charged the trustee with distributing these monthly wage assignments to pay, in order of priority: (1) administrative costs; (2) the IRS's priority tax claim; (3) secured creditors' claims; and finally, (4) unsecured creditors' claims.

The proposed plan also provided that petitioners would pay interest on the secured portion of respondent's claim at a rate of 9.5% per year. Petitioners arrived at this "prime-plus" or "formula rate" by augmenting the national prime rate of approximately 8% (applied by banks when making low-risk loans) to account for the risk of nonpayment posed by borrowers in their financial position.... Accepting petitioners' evidence, the Bankruptcy Court overruled respondent's objection and confirmed the proposed plan.... We granted certiorari and now reverse.

II

The Bankruptcy Code provides little guidance as to which of the rates of interest advocated by the four opinions in this case — the formula rate, the coerced loan rate, the presumptive contract rate, or the cost of funds rate — Congress had in mind when it adopted the cram down provision. That provision, 11 U.S.C. §1325(a)(5)(B), does not mention the term "discount rate" or the word "interest." Rather, it simply requires bankruptcy courts to ensure that the property to be distributed to a particular secured creditor over the life of a bankruptcy plan has a total "value, as of the effective date of the plan," that equals or exceeds the value of the creditor's allowed secured claim — in this case, $4,000.

That command is easily satisfied when the plan provides for a lump-sum payment to the creditor. Matters are not so simple, however, when the debt is to be discharged by a series of payments over time. A debtor's promise of future payments is worth less than an immediate payment of the same total amount because the creditor cannot use the money right away, inflation may cause the value of the dollar to decline before the debtor pays, and there is always some risk of nonpayment. The challenge for bankruptcy courts reviewing such repayment schemes, therefore, is to choose an interest rate sufficient to compensate the creditor for these concerns.

... [T]he Bankruptcy Code includes numerous provisions that, like the cram down provision, require a court to "discoun[t] ... [a] stream of deferred payments back to the[ir] present dollar value," Rake v. Wade, 508 U.S. 464, 472 (1993), to ensure that a creditor receives at least the value of its claim.[2] We think it likely that Congress intended bankruptcy judges and trustees to follow essentially the same approach when choosing an appropriate interest rate under any of these provisions. ...

... [A]lthough §1325(a)(5)(B) entitles the creditor to property whose present value objectively equals or exceeds the value of the collateral, it does not require that the terms of the cram down loan match the terms to which the debtor and creditor agreed prebankruptcy, nor does it require that the cram down terms make the creditor subjectively indifferent between present foreclosure and future payment. Indeed, the very idea of a "cram down" loan precludes the latter result: By definition, a creditor forced to accept such a loan would prefer instead to foreclose. Thus, a court choosing a cram down interest rate need not consider the creditor's individual circumstances, such as its prebankruptcy dealings with the debtor or the alternative loans it could make if permitted to foreclose. Rather, the court should aim to treat similarly situated creditors similarly, and to ensure that an objective economic analysis would suggest the debtor's interest payments will adequately compensate all such creditors for the time value of their money and the risk of default. ...

IV

... Taking its cue from ordinary lending practices, the approach begins by looking to the national prime rate, reported daily in the press, which reflects the financial market's estimate of the amount a commercial bank should charge a

---

2. See 11 U.S.C. §1129(a)(7)(A)(ii) (requiring payment of property whose "value, as of the effective date of the plan" equals or exceeds the value of the creditor's claim); §§1129(a)(7)(B), 1129(a)(9)(B)(i), 1129(a)(9)(C), 1129(b)(2)(A)(ii), 1129(b)(2)(B)(i), 1129(b)(2)(C)(i), 1173(a)(2), 1225(a)(4), 1225(a)(5)(B)(ii), 1228(b)(2), 1325(a)(4), 1228(b)(2) (same).

creditworthy commercial borrower to compensate for the opportunity costs of the loan, the risk of inflation, and the relatively slight risk of default. Because bankrupt debtors typically pose a greater risk of nonpayment than solvent commercial borrowers, the approach then requires a bankruptcy court to adjust the prime rate accordingly. The appropriate size of that risk adjustment depends, of course, on such factors as the circumstances of the estate, the nature of the security, and the duration and feasibility of the reorganization plan. The court must therefore hold a hearing at which the debtor and any creditors may present evidence about the appropriate risk adjustment. Some of this evidence will be included in the debtor's bankruptcy filings, however, so the debtor and creditors may not incur significant additional expense. Moreover, starting from a concededly low estimate and adjusting upward places the evidentiary burden squarely on the creditors, who are likely to have readier access to any information absent from the debtor's filing (such as evidence about the "liquidity of the collateral market"). Finally, many of the factors relevant to the adjustment fall squarely within the bankruptcy court's area of expertise.

Thus, unlike the coerced loan, presumptive contract rate, and cost of funds approaches, the formula approach entails a straightforward, familiar, and objective inquiry, and minimizes the need for potentially costly additional evidentiary proceedings. Moreover, the resulting "prime-plus" rate of interest depends only on the state of financial markets, the circumstances of the bankruptcy estate, and the characteristics of the loan, not on the creditor's circumstances or its prior interactions with the debtor. For these reasons, the prime-plus or formula rate best comports with the purposes of the Bankruptcy Code.

We do not decide the proper scale for the risk adjustment, as the issue is not before us. The Bankruptcy Court in this case approved a risk adjustment of 1.5%, and other courts have generally approved adjustments of 1% to 3%. Respondent's core argument is that a risk adjustment in this range is entirely inadequate to compensate a creditor for the real risk that the plan will fail. There is some dispute about the true scale of that risk — respondent claims that more than 60% of Chapter 13 plans fail, but petitioners argue that the failure rate for approved Chapter 13 plans is much lower. We need not resolve that dispute. It is sufficient for our purposes to note that, under 11 U.S.C. §1325(a)(6), a court may not approve a plan unless, after considering all creditors' objections and receiving the advice of the trustee, the judge is persuaded that "the debtor will be able to make all payments under the plan and to comply with the plan." Together with the cram down provision, this requirement obligates the court to select a rate high enough to compensate the creditor for its risk but not so high as to doom the plan. If the court determines that the likelihood of default is so high as to necessitate an "eye-popping" interest rate, 301 F.3d at 593 (Rovner, J., dissenting), the plan probably should not be confirmed.

Problem Set 49

49.1. You are still counsel to CompuSoft (see Problem 48.1). CFO Mandy Elkins wants you to go over the calculation of a claim so that they can file one correctly when a debtor files for bankruptcy. Mandy has picked out one of the outstanding debts — $30,000 worth of repair work done for Argossy, Inc. The contract provides for interest at 18 percent for all accounts, beginning at billing. The market rate of interest is 12 percent. The work was done on February 15 and the bill was sent to Argossy on March 15. Argossy never paid, and it filed for bankruptcy on September 15. The bankruptcy case is still pending on December 15, when you consult with Elkins. You also note that you spent two hours working on the case in August, for which you billed CompuSoft $400, but the contract between Argossy and CompuSoft says nothing about who will pay collection costs. How much is the claim in the Argossy case? Explain to Elkins how you arrived at the calculation. Bankr. Code §502(b).

49.2. Several months after the meeting in Problem 49.1, Elkins called you to say that she just received the trustee's Final Report and Account showing that after payment of the expenses of administration and the other priority debt, there will be $59,575 available for distribution to general unsecured creditors in the Chapter 7 case. Unsecured claims (including CompuSoft's) total $1,191,500. She wants to know what that means for CompuSoft.

49.3. Another of your firm's most active clients is Commercial Investors, a consortium of private investors that places high-risk loans with small businesses. Today Andrea Wu, the Vice-President for the Workouts department, asks you to file a proof of claim against Speedo Printing, a small company that filed for Chapter 11 three months ago. According to CI's records, at the time Speedo filed it owed CI $340,000 plus six months of interest at 12 percent per year. The loan was secured by an interest in Speedo's printing equipment, which was appraised a couple of months ago at $400,000.

a. Assuming that collateral value holds up in bankruptcy court, how much is CI's claim? Bankr. Code §§502, 506.

b. If the court also used a 12 percent interest rate for the pending bankruptcy, how much should CI expect to be paid under a plan of reorganization that is confirmed today? Bankr. Code §1129(b)(2)(A)(i)(II).

c. How much should CI expect to be paid if the reorganization plan is not confirmed for another year?

49.4. Wu is back in your office about a week later. She had the property reappraised, and it seems that the fair market value is more like $325,000. (The earlier appraisal was wrong.) She has also learned that the debtor estimates that there will be sufficient assets to pay the unsecured creditors about 10 percent of their outstanding claims.

a. Describe CI's claim now. Bankr. Code §§502, 506.

b. What should CI expect to be paid under a plan of reorganization?

c. Does it matter to CI whether the plan is confirmed today or a year from today?

49.5. Another week passes and Wu is back again. At your request, she had been searching her records for a copy of the security agreement. She has finally come to the conclusion that no security agreement was ever signed.

a. Now what is the nature of CI's claim? Bankr. Code §§502, 506.

b. If the 10 percent payout for unsecured creditors persists, what should CI expect under a plan of reorganization? See Bankr. Code §726(a).

49.6. As a member of the U.S. Panel of Trustees, you have been appointed to serve as trustee in a number of Chapter 7 cases. One of them is the case of Tonia Perez, whose summer house is in the estate. The summer house is encumbered by a mortgage to First Capital. The amount currently owing on the mortgage is $85,000, which includes interest accrued to date at the contract rate of 10 percent per annum. You talked with the real estate broker you ordinarily use in such cases. She told you that she thought she could get $100,000 for the summer house. But the market is slow, and she estimates that there is only about a 50 percent chance that the sale would take place in the next six months. As usual, she would discount her commission from the 7 percent that most brokers charge to the 6 percent she charges you. She estimates your share of the other costs of sale and the prorations, including $700 in property taxes, at $1,000.

a.   If you are able to sell this house in exactly six months, how much money will the sale produce for the estate? Bankr. Code §541(a)(1).

b.   How does that amount vary if you sell at an earlier or later time? Is trying to sell the house the right thing to do? See §§506(b) and (c).

c.   Can First Capital prevent you from trying to sell? Bankr. Code §554(b).

49.7.   Martin O'Keefe recently filed under Chapter 7, and you were appointed trustee. After you approved O'Keefe's exemptions, abandoned property that would be worthless to the estate, gathered and liquidated the remaining nonexempt property, and made allowance for payment of your own fees, you have the following:

Proceeds from sale of Piper aircraft	$214,000
Proceeds from sale of coin collection	26,000
Proceeds from turnover of cash in bank account	2,200
Total	$242,200

O'Keefe has only one secured creditor, Friendly Credit, who is owed $150,000 against the Piper aircraft.

a.   If O'Keefe owes $300,000 to other creditors, all unsecured, what distributions do you make? What is the percentage paid to the unsecured creditors?

b.   If Friendly Credit's security interest had been in the coin collection instead of the Piper aircraft, what would your distributions have been? What would the percentage paid to the unsecured creditors have been?

Chapter 15.   Creation of
Security Interests

Assignment 50:   Formalities for Attachment

In Part One of this book, we focus on the relationship between the debtor and the creditor. In earlier assignments we compared the collection rights of secured creditors with their unsecured counterparts, both under state law rules and in federal bankruptcy. We observed the limited collection rights available to unsecured creditors and the more expansive rights given to secured creditors. In all these assignments we observed that a secured creditor is usually in a better position to collect than an unsecured creditor, although either creditor may face substantial uncertainty if the debtor resists.

In this assignment we turn to the question of how someone becomes a secured creditor. As in earlier assignments, our focus continues to be on security interests created under Article 9 and, for comparison purposes, on mortgages and deeds of trust created under real estate law.

Creditors taking a security interest either under Article 9 or real estate law have one key feature in common: They obtain their status by contract with the debtor. Article 9 secured creditors or real estate mortgagees are, by definition, consensual creditors. That is, they have enhanced collection rights because, at an earlier time in the relationship, their debtors consented to them. In this assignment we explore that agreement between debtor and creditor and how it is regulated by the Uniform Commercial Code or state mortgage laws.

A.   A Prototypical Secured Transaction

Most security interests are created as part of a transaction in which money is lent or property is sold. When a bank lends money to a corporation, for example, it may insist, as a condition of the loan, that the corporation grant it a security interest in some or all of the corporation's assets. Similarly, an automobile dealer who sells on credit will nearly always require the buyer to give a security interest in the automobile purchased.

The law governing security interests is easier to understand when it is placed in the context of the business transactions in which security interests are created. The story that follows describes an ordinary secured transaction: a debtor who borrows money from a bank to start a business.

Fisherman's Pier: A Prototypical Secured Transaction

Pablo Escobar has been in the restaurant management business for several years. Among the eating places he has managed is Fisherman's Pier, which is owned by Stella Parker. Stella recently decided to sell Fisherman's Pier and retire. When Pablo heard the news, he went to talk to her about buying the place. In a series of meetings, Pablo and Stella worked out the terms of sale. Stella would sell Fisherman's Pier, including the kitchen equipment, furniture, fixtures, furnishings, building lease, and goodwill to Pablo for $100,000 in cash.

Pablo did not have $100,000, but he had family and friends lined up to invest in his venture. He could raise enough money to provide working capital for the business, of which about $40,000 could be applied toward the purchase price. The rest would have to be borrowed. Pablo retained attorney Ellen Bartell to draft an "Agreement for Purchase and Sale," which he and Stella signed. The agreement was contingent on Pablo's getting a $60,000 bank loan to complete the purchase. That is, if Pablo could not get the loan, neither party would be bound by the contract.

Pablo made an appointment to see Mark Sun in the Commercial Loan Department of First National Bank. In their first meeting, they talked about the weather, the restaurant business, Pablo's experience, the Agreement for Purchase and Sale, and some of the key terms on which First National makes commercial loans. Before Pablo left, Sun gave him a copy of the bank's Loan Application form.

The application form asked for essentially four kinds of information. The first was personal information about Pablo. What was his date of birth? His social security number? Where had he lived during what periods of time? Was he married? The second was information about his financial condition. What did he own? What debts did he owe? What had his income been over the past several years? The form required that he attach copies of his income tax returns for the past two years. The third was information about his credit history. From whom had he borrowed money in the past? What credit cards did he have? Had he ever filed for bankruptcy? Been foreclosed against? The last part of the form was a description of the collateral he could offer for the loan. Pablo completed the application in a couple of days and returned it to Sun. Sun told Pablo that it "looked like everything was in order" and he thought there would be no problems with the loan. Sun said he would get back to Pablo within about a week.

Sun ordered a credit check on Pablo from a credit reporting agency, personally called three of Pablo's credit references, and scheduled Pablo's application for a meeting of the bank's loan committee. Both the report and the references were good. Sun presented the loan application to the committee and it was approved, contingent on an appraisal of the restaurant at a value of at least $100,000. The bank's appraiser visited the restaurant, looked at the equipment, measured the square footage of the building, checked the business receipts for the past year, collected information on some comparable sales, and appraised the restaurant as having a "market value" of $100,000.

Sun then called Pablo and told him the good news. The loan had been approved and Morton Friedman, the bank's lawyer, would "handle the closing." The lawyers scheduled the loan closing for a date about three weeks away and began preparing the documents and gathering the information they would need.

At the bank's request, Pablo signed a financing statement on the form set forth in U.C.C. §9-521. (The signature was not required by Article 9, but for reasons that will be explained later in this book, the bank had adopted a policy of obtaining prospective debtors' signatures on financing statements.) Friedman sent the financing statement to the Secretary of State for filing in the U.C.C. filing system. The financing statement would provide public notice of the bank's security interest in Fisherman's Pier. Friedman also ordered a search of the U.C.C. filing system for other financing statements filed against Stella Parker or Fisherman's Pier and a search of the county real estate records for mortgages filed against them. The bank wanted a security interest in the assets prior to all others; only through such a search would Friedman know whether there were already other security interests against those assets. The search results showed no mortgages and only one financing statement other than First National's. It was in favor of Valley State Bank, who had lent money to Stella using the restaurant as collateral. Friedman wrote to Valley State Bank, advising Valley State that Stella was selling the restaurant and requesting that Valley State advise him of the exact amount necessary to pay off the loan. He also asked that Valley State prepare a security interest "termination statement" for filing in the U.C.C. records.

The closing was held as scheduled at Ellen Bartell's office. Pablo signed a promissory note for $60,000 and the preprinted form Security Agreement used by First National for most of their small commercial loans (a copy of a security agreement appears in Assignment 56). Stella delivered a bill of sale for the restaurant property, an assignment of her rights under the lease, and the keys to the restaurant. Friedman delivered First National Bank's check to an employee from Valley State Bank. The check was for $38,839, the exact balance outstanding on the Valley State loan, with interest computed up to the day of the closing. The Valley State employee gave Friedman the signed Authorization to File Termination Statement. Then he delivered a check for the balance of the $60,000 loan (after deducting the expenses, including Friedman's attorneys' fees) to Stella. Pablo paid the balance of the purchase price with a cashier's check he obtained that morning with money from his investors and from his own savings. At that point Stella had her $100,000 sale price, less the amount paid Valley State. Pablo had his restaurant, subject to a $60,000 security interest in favor of First National. First National had Pablo's promissory note for $60,000, secured by a first security interest in the assets of the restaurant. First National could be reasonably confident that if the loan was not paid when due, it would have the right to take possession of the restaurant and sell it to satisfy the outstanding debt. The parties all shook hands and agreed among themselves that the closing was complete.

———————

Secured transactions vary in detail and complexity. As the hundreds of published cases each year attest, some are less than orderly. Nonetheless, the transaction described here is typical of many commercial credit transactions.

Two aspects of the Fisherman's Pier story require some additional explanation. First, as you were reading the story you may have wondered what would have happened if one of the checks or documents had been missing. Most closings are conducted on the implicit understanding that unless all of the contemplated checks and documents are exchanged, none that are exchanged should be taken from the room or be of any effect. If one or more are missing, the parties will select one member of the group to hold the checks and documents currently available until all the contemplated checks and documents are available. Only then is the escrow agent authorized to deliver any of them and only then do they take effect.

Second, while the bank in this story obtained and filed a financing statement, it is important to realize that this step was not necessary to create a security interest enforceable against Pablo in the absence of bankruptcy. U.C.C. §9-203(b). That a security interest is *enforceable* against the debtor Pablo means that, in the event of default, the secured party can foreclose on the collateral. By contrast, for a security interest to have priority over some other creditors, such as another secured party who lends against the same collateral, the creditor must *perfect* the interest by having the debtor authorize a financing statement and filing that statement in the public records. (The subject of priority is reserved for Part Two of this book. We mention the financing statement here only because nearly all creditors who create a security interest choose to take the additional step of perfecting it against third parties. Not to mention it would have made the story unrealistic.)

As parties create security interests, they themselves sometimes confuse the formalities necessary to create a security interest with those necessary to perfect it. As you read the following section about the formalities necessary to create a security interest, the reasons for this confusion should become clearer.

B.   Formalities for Article 9 Security Interests

U.C.C. §9-203(b) lists three formalities required for the creation of a security interest enforceable against the debtor: (1) Either the collateral must be in the possession of the secured creditor or the debtor must have "authenticated a security agreement which contains a description of the collateral"; (2) value must have been given; (3) the debtor must have rights in the collateral. Only when all three of these requirements have been met does the security interest *attach* to the collateral and become enforceable against the debtor. U.C.C. §§9-203(a) and (b).

1.   Possession or Authenticated Security Agreement

Article 9 ratifies two different kinds of security agreements. Most agreements are authenticated records (usually, but not necessarily, a signed writing), but the secured creditor may create a security agreement without a record if the creditor takes possession of the goods pursuant to an oral agreement to create a security interest.

Perhaps the most familiar example of a security agreement made effective by possession occurs in pawnshops. In a typical pawn, the debtor comes in with an item of some value. (In B-movies of the 1930s and 1940s, a down-and-out musician brings in his instrument to signify that he has reached the end of the line both financially and spiritually. This usually happens in the opening scene, before he meets the woman who saves his life, and so on. It is usually drizzling rain when he approaches the pawnshop.) The pawnshop offers to lend some amount against the goods, typically for 30 days. It holds the goods for the agreed period, during which time the debtor (if fortunes reverse quickly) can come in to pay off the loan and reclaim the collateral. If the debtor does not redeem the property by paying the loan, the pawnbroker sells the collateral and — pursuant to pawn broker statutes that supersede Article 9 — keeps the proceeds of sale.

While pawnshops and pawnbrokers have a long and colorful history, most commercial finance is not based on a creditor's possession of the collateral. Most debtors who borrow against their property want to keep the property while they repay the loan. Those who incur debt to buy a home, an automobile, or production machinery typically are unwilling to defer possession until the debt is paid. Most of the time their creditors really don't want possession anyway. Although commercial financiers realize that they would be more secure if they took possession of the pigs or packing emulsion against which they lend, the added safety is in most cases insufficient to justify the added expense. Even more important, in a commercial context most debtors use the collateral to produce the income to pay the loan. To accommodate them, lenders have devised methods (referred to as *field warehousing*) for taking possession of collateral while at the same time allowing debtors to use it. But even these methods add expense and complexity that most lenders consider unwarranted in most situations. Hence, the most common arrangement is to rely on a written security arrangement and leave the debtor in possession of the collateral.

The prototypical secured transaction is based on a writing. The debtor signs a document called a *security agreement*, which contains a description of the collateral, a description of the obligations secured, and provisions defining default, specifying the rights of the secured creditor on default, requiring that the debtor care for the collateral and keep it insured, and imposing other obligations on the debtor. (Recall that an example of such agreement appears in Assignment 56.) When the debtor has signed such an agreement, the U.C.C. §9-203(b)(3)(A) requirement of an authenticated security agreement is fulfilled. See U.C.C. §9-102(a)(7).

A third kind of security agreement that is neither oral nor written can also fulfill the requirement of U.C.C. §9-203(b)(3). This third kind must be inscribed on some "tangible medium" in which it can be stored and from which it can be retrieved. An example would be a security agreement typed on a computer and saved to disk, but never printed or signed. Information so inscribed is referred to as a "record." See U.C.C. §9-102(a)(69). To constitute a security agreement of the third kind, that record must be "authenticated" by "processing it" with the intention to identify the authenticator and "adopt or accept" the record. U.C.C. §9-102(a)(7)(B). The language is sufficiently obscure to provide little clue as to the boundaries of the doctrine, but the intent to validate entirely electronic security agreements is clear. If Pablo Escobar borrows money from First National Bank, and in the course of that transaction the bank sends Pablo an e-mail containing an offer of security agreement terms and Pablo sends an e-mail reply accepting those terms, Pablo and First National have a security agreement of the third kind — without a writing or a signature.

Although the authenticated security agreement requirement is easy to comply with, in a surprising number of cases the parties fail to do it. Either no security agreement is authenticated by the debtor or the one that is authenticated has no description of the collateral. When that occurs, the secured creditor often attempts to rely on other documents that, although not intended as a security agreement, nevertheless meet the skeletal requirements of U.C.C. §9-203(b)(3). In these cases, the courts are often asked to decide what is the minimum record that will suffice.

In re Thompson (Wieberg v. Thompson)

315 B.R. 94 (Bankr. W.D. Mo. 2004)

Count III contends . . . that the Thompsons disposed of livestock in which Wieberg held a valid security interest, that such action constitutes conversion of Wieberg's property, and that such conversion constitutes willful and malicious injury to his property. The Thompsons asserted, as an affirmative defense, that Wieberg failed to state a claim for which relief can be granted because he did not have a valid security interest, thus a property interest, in the cattle he sold to the Thompsons. I, therefore, begin with that issue.

A. Security Interest

Article 9 of the Uniform Commercial Code (the UCC) applies to "any transaction, regardless of its form, that creates a security interest in personal property or fixtures by contract." [U.C.C. §9-109(a)(1).] A security interest is "an interest in personal property or fixtures which secures payment or performance of an obligation." [U.C.C. §1-201(37) (Rev. §1-201(b)(35)).] The Agreement does not specifically state that the Thompsons grant Wieberg a security interest in 365 head of cattle. The Agreement does, however, refer to Wieberg as the "Seller" and the Thompsons as the "Buyers." Pursuant to the Agreement, possession of the cattle was transferred to the Thompsons, and Wieberg held the Note from the Thompsons with their promise to pay the sum of $233,000.

The true nature of a secured transaction is often found by looking beyond the words used in the documents, to the intent of the parties. There is undisputed evidence that the Thompsons intended to grant Wieberg a security interest in the cattle. . . .

The question before me, however, is whether the Agreement granted a valid security interest in the collateral. There is no dispute that the Agreement satisfies the first two requirements of [U.C.C. §9-203(b)]. Value was given when Wieberg sold the Thompsons 365 heard of cattle, and the Thompsons promised to pay

$259,150 over a two-year period.... And the Thompsons had rights in the cattle and the power to transfer same, hence the reason for this litigation. The only issue is whether the Thompsons authenticated a security agreement.

There is no magic language to create or provide for a security agreement, but in the Eighth Circuit there must be some language in the agreement itself that can be construed to convey a security interest.... The intent of the parties only becomes relevant if there is language in the agreement that can be construed as granting a security interest. As other courts have stated, there must be some language in the document that "'leads to the logical conclusion that it was the intention of the parties that a security interest be created.'" [citations omitted] As one treatise states, the essence of a security agreement is to inform "an objective observer that the debtor intended to transfer an interest in personal property as security to a creditor." James J. White and Robert S. Summers, 4 White & Summers, Uniform Commercial Code §31-3 (5th Ed. 2004).

... In the official comments to revised Article I, the authors state that the definition of a security interest is substantially the same in the revised version. Whether an agreement creates a security interest, however, under the revised version "depends not on whether the parties intend that the law *characterize* the transaction as a security interest but rather on whether the transaction falls within the definition of 'security interest' in Section 1-201." [U.C.C. §9-102, Official Comment.]

Within this legal framework, I go to the language in the Agreement. Paragraph nine provides:

> (9) That if any payment is ten days late, all cattle here mentioned, any and all other cattle, personal property, vehicles, farm equipment, hay, real-estate, notes receivable, accounts receivable, owned by "Buyer" or any partnership, corporation, company or like business entity that "Buyer" has ownership in; becomes property of "Seller" until the full debt plus any incurred expenses and interest are paid-in-full; Unless agreed to in writing and signed by "Seller."

Paragraph 13 provides that "this agreement is the only encumbrance that will be placed upon said cattle. (The cattle and their calves may not be used as collateral on any other indebtedness)." These two paragraphs, taken together, lead to the logical conclusion that Wieberg held an interest in the cattle to secure payment of the Thompsons' obligation.

The Thompsons argue that the term "encumbrance" is a term of art defined by the UCC, and applicable only to real estate transactions:

> [U.C.C. §9-102(a)(32)] "Encumbrance" means a right, other than an ownership interest, in real property. The term includes mortgages and other liens on real property.

Wieberg, on the other hand relies on a broader definition of encumbrance:

> A claim or liability that is attached to property and that may lessen its value, such as a lien or mortgage; an encumbrance cannot defeat the transfer of possession, but it remains after the property is transferred. Black's Law Dictionary 223 (Bryan A. Garner, ed. 1996).

The gravamen of the Thompsons' argument seems to be that the parties could not have intended to create a security interest in the cattle because they used an inappropriate term to indicate that Wieberg held an interest in the cattle. Other courts, however, do not make this semantic distinction.

I find, therefore, that the language in paragraphs nine and thirteen, taken as a whole, leads to the logical conclusion that it was the intention of the parties that a security interest be created. I further find that that obvious intention, coupled with the parties' testimony, and their actions following execution of the Agreement, did provide for and create a valid, enforceable security interest.

In *Thompson*, the court found all of the elements of a security agreement in a single document. In others, the courts have found those elements spread through two or more documents.

In re Ace Lumber Supply, Inc.

105 B.R. 964 (Bankr. D. Mont. 1989)

JOHN L. PETERSON, UNITED STATES BANKRUPTCY JUDGE.

In this Chapter 7 case, the Trustee has filed objections to the motion of Minot Builders Supply for relief from the automatic stay under §362 of the Code. The basis for the objections is that Minot is not a secured creditor as alleged in the motion. The issue raised by the parties involves whether the Debtor executed a security agreement in favor of Minot to entitle Minot to perfect a security interest in Debtor's inventory, accounts receivable and equipment....

The facts show the Debtor pre-petition operated a retail building supply business and purchased a number of products at wholesale from Minot. By April, 1988, the Debtor's account with Minot was about $160,000.00 and was in default. On April 26, 1988, a telephone conversation took place between two representatives of Minot and Debtor's president, which discussed the delinquent account and future credit purchases between the parties. A copy of the financial statement of the Debtor was reviewed by the parties and Richard Winje, vice president of Minot, took notes of the telephone conversation which reflect a series of numbers about Debtor's financial affairs. The parties decided the Debtor would pay cash on delivery for all future purchases and attempt to pay on the delinquent account in the ensuing two to three weeks.

On May 25, 1988, another three-way conversation between representatives of both companies took place. Taylor, the Debtor's president, was in the office of Minot's credit manager, who arranged a telephone call with Winje in Minot, North Dakota. Again, Winje took personal notes about the delinquent obligation. Taylor agreed, and the notes of Winje reflect, that the Debtor would pay $35,000.00 per month, with interest at 1% over prime, on the delinquent balance, a cash discount would be granted on new purchases if payment was timely made, the current purchases would be limited to $10,000.00 per month, and both the delinquent account and current purchases would be secured by Debtor's inventory, accounts receivable and equipment.... Minot's credit manager prepared a U.C.C.-1 financing statement, which was signed by Taylor. A copy was sent to Winje, who signed on behalf of Minot and the U.C.C.-1 financing statement was then sent to the Montana Secretary of State office, where it was filed on June 2, 1988. Subsequent to the agreement, one payment of $35,000.00 was made on the account by the Debtor, but no other payments were made.... By the date of the bankruptcy petition on May 1, 1989, the Debtor was indebted to Minot in the sum of $162,031.00. Minot was scheduled as a secured creditor in the Debtor's Schedules. Other than the U.C.C.-1 financing statement, no other documents have been signed by the Debtor. All parties believed the execution of the U.C.C.-1 financing statement was sufficient to satisfy the Montana Uniform Commercial Code in order to create a valid security interest by Minot in Debtor's assets.

Based on these facts, Minot asserts in its Motion for Relief from the Automatic Stay that it has a valid security interest in the Debtor's assets described in the U.C.C.-1 financing statement. The Trustee contests such assertion on the basis that [U.C.C. §9-203(b)] requires a security agreement authenticated by the Debtor, and that execution of the U.C.C.-1 financing statement does not satisfy the requirement of [U.C.C. §9-203(b)].

Montana has adopted the provisions of the Uniform Commercial Code regarding perfection of security interests in property. As is pertinent to the present case, [U.C.C. §9-203(b)] states:

> ..., a security agreement is not enforceable against the debtor or third parties with respect to the collateral and does not attach unless:
> (a) ... the debtor has [authenticated] a security agreement [that provides] a description of the collateral....

In order to perfect the security agreement and interest in the collateral against the Debtor and third parties, such as the Trustee in this case, [U.C.C. §9-310(a)] requires in most instances, a financing statement to be filed with the Secretary of State. [U.C.C. §9-501]. The formal requisites of a financing statement are detailed in [U.C.C. §9-502]....

Anderson, supra, §9-203:18, p.670 ... states:

> When the secured transaction is nonpossessory, the security agreement must be in writing ... The requirement of a written security agreement is in the nature of a statute of frauds ... When a written security agreement is required but there is none, the creditor does not have a security interest in the collateral and can not enforce an oral agreement that he have such an interest as against the debtor or third parties.

The facts here show no formal security agreement was signed by the Debtor. What was signed by the Debtor was a standard U.C.C.-1 financing statement, attached to this Order. The creditor contends such suffices as a security agreement, citing In re Amex-Protein Development Corporation, 504 F.2d 1056 (9th Cir. 1974). In that case, a promissory note was signed by the debtor which included language that the note "is secured by a security interest in subject personal property as per invoices." A financing statement signed by the debtor was also filed on record describing items of personal property. There was no issue in the case that the parties intended, as they did in the present case, to create a security interest in the property described in the financing statement. Thus, two documents were signed, a promissory note and a financing statement. Under these facts, the Ninth Circuit Court of Appeals [concluded]

> the promissory note herein qualifies as a security agreement which by its terms "creates or provides for" a security interest.

[In] Matter of Bollinger Corp., 614 F.2d 924, 927 (3d Cir. 1980)... the Third Circuit adopted the so-called "composite document" rule by reading the promissory note, financing statement and correspondence between the parties together.

> When the parties have neglected to sign a separate security agreement, it would appear that the better and more practiced view is to look at the transaction as a whole in order to determine if there is a writing, or writings, signed by the debtor describing the collateral which demonstrates an intent to create a security interest in collateral. [Id. at 928.]

The Court concluded the "minimum formal requirements of Section [9-203(b)(3)(A)] were met by the financing statement and the promissory note, and the course of dealings between the parties indicates the intent to create a security interest." ...

I conclude that under Montana law the composite document rule is available to provide evidentiary support to create a security interest in collateral. That rule, however, does not allow only a financing statement signed by the debtor to satisfy [U.C.C. §9-203(b)(3)(A)]. In this regard, I find a major distinction between *Amex-Protein* and the facts in the case sub judice. Other than the financing statement signed by the Debtor, the only other writing presented by the creditor were hand-written telephone notes attached to this Order. The combination of the financing agreement and the telephone notes do not satisfy the requirements of Article 9 in that none of them contain any language creating a security interest in the collateral. As *Amex-Protein* states:

> While there are no magic words which create a security interest there *must be language in the instrument* which "leads to the logical conclusion that it was the intention of the parties that a security interest be created." [Id. at 1059. (Emphasis supplied.)]

Further, In re Owensboro Canning Co., Inc., 82 B.R. 450, 453-454 (W.D. Ky. 1988), interpreting identical Uniform Commercial Code sections under §9-203(b)(3)(A) and §9-102(73) holds:

> Giving due consideration in tandem to [§§9-203(b)(3)(A) and 9-102(73)] of the Code, White and Summers contend that the question of whether a security agreement is established calls for two independent inquiries which may be stated as follows: The court must first resolve, as a question of law, whether the language embodied in the writing objectively indicates that the parties may have intended to create or provide for a security agreement. [citations omitted]. If the language crosses this objective threshold [citations omitted], that is, if the writing evidences a possible secured transaction and thus satisfies the statute of frauds requirement, then the factfinder must inquire whether the parties actually intended to create a security interest. [citations omitted]. Parol evidence is admissible to inform the latter [citations omitted], but not the former, inquiry.

White & Summers, supra.

Other courts have followed the same test. In re Zurliene, 97 B.R. 460, 464 (Bankr. S.D. Ill. 1989), states:

> While this court agrees with Community [creditor] that no specific words of grant are necessary in order to create a security agreement, it also believes that, in the absence of a separate written security agreement there must be some language to reflect the parties' desire to grant a security interest, in the documents surrounding the transaction, in order to establish the existence of a security agreement under UCC §9-203....

Applying the above law, I conclude there simply is no language in the only written instrument signed by the Debtor in this case (the financing statement) which embodies any intent to create a security agreement. There are no promissory notes, invoices or written correspondence which grant, create or "objectively indicates the parties intended to create a security interest." I hold as a matter of law the U.C.C.-1 financing statement standing alone is insufficient under [U.C.C. §9-203(b)(3)(A)] to create a security interest in the Debtor's assets.

In *Ace Lumber Supply*, the court recognized the composite document rule, but still refused to read Winje's notes together with the financing statement, presumably because those notes were not authenticated by the debtor. In a later case, Longtree, Ltd. v. Resource Control Intl., 755 P.2d 195 (Wyo. 1988), the court applied the composite document rule to include a document that not only was not authenticated by the debtor, but was not even in existence at the time the security agreement was signed. In *Longtree*, debtor RCI agreed to purchase logs and granted a security interest in the logs to the seller, Pacific Star. The purchase agreement described certain logs as the subject of the agreement, but expressly recognized that the agreement was "subject to revision from time to time." Later, the parties revised the agreement to include other logs, but the revision was not authenticated by the debtor. The court nevertheless employed the composite document rule to read the original agreement together with the revision. The court quoted from 8 Hawkland, Uniform Commercial Code Series §9-110:04 (1986):

> One question that has arisen is the extent to which more than one document may qualify as a security agreement, when one document contains the debtor's signature (and perhaps a description of some collateral) and another document contains a description of additional collateral. The majority rule appears to be that so long as the documents express some internal connection with one another, they may be read together for purposes of including the collateral described in the second document within the security agreement's umbrella. This, or even a more liberal application of the statute of frauds function of the security agreement is certainly in keeping with the liberality evidenced by section [9-108(a)]. Some courts, however, would probably require more than mere internal consistency or connection, instead demanding that there be a reference within one document to the other.

As for the Statute of Frauds function to be served by the writing, the court said that the language of the original agreement indicated that it did not purport to be a complete expression of the parties' agreement, but expressly contemplated future revisions. The revisions were consistent additional terms to the agreement and were therefore admissible. Some might conclude that *Longtree* is inconsistent with *Ace Lumber Supply*, while others might find a way to reconcile the two. In any case, it should be clear that, although the requirement is simple, case outcomes are not readily predictable at the margins.

Ace Lumber Supply illustrates the consequence of failing to obtain an authenticated security agreement: The creditor has no security interest and is therefore an unsecured creditor. When the parties intended to create a security agreement and thought they had succeeded, as they did in *Ace Lumber Supply*, the remedy is surprisingly harsh. Of course, for those who remember covering the Statute of Frauds in first-year contract law, the remedy of non-enforcement even in the face of clear intent of the parties should be familiar.

A number of justifications have been put forward for the requirement of an authenticated security agreement — so many and from so many different directions, in fact, as to cast doubt on whether the requirement can be justified. Not surprisingly, the rationales closely track those offered for the Statute of Frauds, and they raise many of the same issues.

1. *Preventing fraud.*   Comment 3 to U.C.C. §9-203 explains that the requirement of a writing in Article 9 is "in the nature of a Statute of Frauds." That, however, hardly adds to its luster. As some leading commentators once put it, "[t]he statute of frauds is a much despised statute that has fallen into disrepute in the United States, is the laughing stock of Article 2 and has been repealed in England." Speidel, White & Summers, Secured Transactions 89 (West 1987).

   The modern theory is that courts should be skeptical about agreements that are not in writing. If the parties are engaged in an honest transaction, they can memorialize their transaction with at least a minimal writing. On the other hand, to refuse flatly to enforce unwritten agreements, particularly when their existence is not even in dispute, may facilitate more fraud than it prevents.

   The applicability of the Statute of Frauds in the Article 9 context raises an interesting conceptual problem. In the Article 2 context, the fraud supposedly to be prevented is by one party to the contract against the other. In the Article 9 context, however, the fraud to be prevented might be either (1) a creditor falsely claiming the debtor granted it a security interest orally, or (2) the debtor and creditor together falsely claiming that they orally agreed to create a security interest in a situation where a third party will be the only one injured. The debtor, for example, may have filed for bankruptcy by the time the dispute arises (as was the case in *Ace Lumber*) and the secured creditor may be battling the trustee for the collateral, while the debtor sits out the argument. Some courts think that it makes more sense to require documentary evidence in the latter context than in the former, because in the former case, the person defrauded was a party to the alleged agreement and so would know whether it was made at the time or invented afterward. If a third party stood to end up with the collateral in the absence of a valid security interest, that party probably would have no direct knowledge of the transaction and no source of information about it except the writing. If the law did not even require that a writing be created, the defrauded person would be at the mercy of the supposedly contracting parties.

2. *Minimizing litigation.* If the security agreement and the description of collateral are in writing, there will be less chance that the debtor and the creditor will differ as to whether a security interest was granted and, if so, what property was to serve as collateral. That in turn will reduce the number of litigated cases. It also assures that the only agreements enforced will be those intended by the parties, thus minimizing the possibility that a party who did not grant security will be held to have done so.

3. *Cautioning debtors.* The theory here is that many people make oral promises without reflecting on their consequences, but do not make written commitments so lightly. Requiring that the promise of security be in writing to be enforceable will result in debtors making better decisions about whether security agreements are in their interest.

4. *Channeling transactions.* By refusing to enforce oral security agreements, the law encourages the parties to put them in writing. Subscribers to this "channeling" justification usually believe that the parties ought to do that anyway because it is sound business practice, and that the law ought to reinforce such good business practices. (No, this view is not related to the channeling work done by Shirley MacLaine.)

These last three justifications focus on the good that might come from requiring a writing generally. The cases also reveal many situations in which the requirement of a writing seems to have caused considerable harm. Not everyone is aware that a written security agreement is necessary. Among those who do know of the requirement, some will attempt to comply with it and fail. In both situations, creditors will lose valuable property interests, perhaps even where no one was harmed by the lack of a writing. Sophisticated creditors have no difficulty complying with the requirement, while occasional creditors fall victim to it. A writing requirement produces some neat, satisfying uniformity, but it may come at a high price in particular cases.

5. *Discouraging secured credit.* Secured creditors are typically banks and insurance companies, the most sophisticated financial institutions in the economy. As secured creditors they invoke a legal device that gives them collection advantages not universally shared. When they do so imperfectly, by failing to obtain a security agreement in writing, for example, some observers believe it is fair to pull them down to the level of the unsecured folks they were trying to best.

The argument has emotional appeal, relying as it does on a kind of populist, David-against-the-corporate-Goliath ethos. But it is seldom the sophisticated creditor that forfeits an interest in collateral by failing to document it. More commonly, it is the unsophisticated trade creditors and other commercial equivalents of widows and orphans who make the mistakes. Finally, it is worth noting that for every commentator who asserts that "public policy" seeks to discourage secured credit, there are at least two who assert that public policy seeks to encourage it.

The competing policy — that written security agreements should *not* be required in every case — is expressed in the doctrine of equitable mortgages. Under that doctrine, the courts can enforce oral security agreements where to do so would be "equitable." The doctrine is impliedly repudiated in the text of U.C.C. §9-203(b)(3). Widows and orphans who want the special collection rights of the Article 9 secured creditor must jump through the hoops like everyone else.

Cases in which the security agreement did not contain a description of the collateral at the time it was authenticated by the debtor have divided the courts. For example, in In re Hewn, 20 U.C.C. 2d 745 (Bankr. W.D. Wis. 1976), the debtors signed the security agreement while it was blank and contained no description of the collateral. The secured creditor filled in the description of collateral and sent it to the debtors. The debtors received it without comment. Later, the debtors filed bankruptcy. At the request of the trustee, the court held the security interest unenforceable. The court concluded that the U.C.C., as "adopted by Wisconsin, does not allow a secured creditor to complete the security agreement or the financing statement, whether authorized or not, after the debtor has signed the instruments." In re Couch, 5 U.C.C. 255 (M.D. Ga. 1968), comes to a similar conclusion.

In two similar cases, however, the security agreements also contained no description of collateral when they were authenticated by the debtors, but the courts reached the opposite result. In re Blundell, 25 U.C.C. 571 (D. Kan. 1978); In re Allen, 395 F. Supp. 150 (E.D. Ill. 1975). The secured creditors in both cases filled in the descriptions afterwards, in accordance with the intention of the debtors. The courts in *Blundell* and *Allen* upheld the security agreements, commenting that the "sequence of events is immaterial" so long as the resulting document meets the statutory requirements.

It is useful to look closely at U.C.C. §9-203(b)(3)(A) to see what it says about the fill-in-the-blanks-later problem. Does that provision require that the description of collateral be in the agreement at the time the agreement is authenticated? Statutory interpretation often requires close reading.

2. *Value Has Been Given*

A security interest is not enforceable until "value has been given." The drafters of the U.C.C. defined "value" in §1-201(44) so broadly that the requirement is virtually always met in a commercial transaction. As a result, it is difficult to discern any policy reason for the inclusion of the *value* requirement in U.C.C. §9-203(b)(1). Although the section does not say who must give value, the assumption seems to be that it is the creditor.

In most security agreements the debtors assume numerous obligations (pay the debt, keep the collateral insured, notify the creditor of any change of address, etc.), raising no question about whether the debtor's promises constitute value. But the secured creditor may assume few or no obligations. In fact, some forms of security agreements do not even have a place for the secured party's signature. Nevertheless, the creditor typically will have lent money, sold property to the debtor on credit, or promised to do one or the other in reliance on the debtor's grant or promise of a security interest. After all, that's usually why the debtor signed the agreement. It is true that a debtor might sign a security agreement with neither a loan nor the promise of a loan. But in that case, the debtor does not need a "no value given" defense. If the creditor hasn't made a loan, the debtor's defense to any collection effort — whether or not a security interest exists — is that the debtor doesn't owe anything to the creditor.

The definition of "value" used in Article 9 not only encompasses all forms of consideration that would support an ordinary contract, it even includes one form of consideration that does not pass muster in common law contracts: past consideration. U.C.C. §1-201(44)(b) provides that "a person gives value for rights (the security interest) if he acquires them...(b) as security for...a pre-existing debt." This means that even in situations where the debtor grants a security interest to secure an already outstanding debt and the creditor neither gives nor promises anything new in return, the creditor has given value under the Code definitions.

It is worth noting the ease with which an unsecured debt can become a secured debt at any time in the debtor-creditor relationship. While the typical transaction includes the grant of security at the time the debt is incurred, a significant portion of commercial transactions involve credit relationships that start out unsecured and become secured at some time during the course of the business dealings. Some trade creditors ordinarily extend credit on an unsecured basis, as Minot Builders Supply was doing in *Ace Lumber Supply*, but insist on a security agreement if the debtor does not pay within a reasonable time. Or a creditor may have a judgment stemming from a tort action or contract breach, but recognize that the pursuit of state collection remedies might be expensive. The creditor might agree to take payment of the outstanding obligation over time, secured by an interest in some property of the debtor. The Code provides the parties with an easy, enforceable mechanism to change the debtor-creditor relationship to include a security interest.

A situation in which the secured creditor did not give value at all is unlikely to lead to litigation for the simple reason that the secured creditor won't be injured by whatever happened. Nonetheless, the value requirement has not become entirely irrelevant to commercial transactions. For reasons we explain in later chapters, it may matter *when* the secured creditor gave value because only then did the security interest attach. A delay in giving value can sometimes lead to surprising results.

3. The Debtor Has Rights in the Collateral

It may seem to go without saying that a person cannot grant a security interest in someone else's property. Despite that, and the fact that the drafters of Article 9 were not getting paid by the word, they chose to address the matter anyway, in U.C.C. §9-203(b)(2).

The courts have read at least three significant subtexts into this rule. First, they read it to mean that if the debtor owns a limited interest in property and grants a security interest in the property, the security interest will generally attach to only that limited interest. See Comment 6 to U.C.C. §9-203. For example, Wilson Leasing owns machinery and leases it to Darby Construction. Darby grants a security interest in the machinery to CreditLine Investors. CreditLine will have a security interest only in what Darby owns, which is a leasehold. CreditLine will not have a security interest in the machinery. (Of course, CreditLine may have a cause of action against Darby for breach of covenants in the security agreement, and Darby may also have violated its agreement with Wilson Leasing as well.) To lend more dignity to this simple rule that a debtor can't grant a security interest in someone else's property, lawyers sometimes translate it into Latin (*nemo dat non habet*) and then back into old English (He who hath not, cannot give). In oral argument or negotiations, the effect is much more powerful than saying it in ordinary English.

Parties sometimes deliberately create security interests in property in which the debtor has something less than outright ownership. The debtor may, for example, be the lessee under a favorable long-term lease of real property. The right to occupy an apartment that today would rent for $1,000 a month, but to pay only the $440-a-month rent specified in the lease you signed five years ago, before the neighborhood was "hot," may be a valuable right indeed, particularly if many years remain on the lease term. The lessee's rights under such a lease may be a valuable asset. The lessee can grant a security interest in the lease, and if the debtor-lessee defaults under the secured loan, the secured creditor can foreclose on the lessee's rights under the lease. Similarly, a debtor may have no more than a contract to purchase property, but if the contract is favorable and enforceable, the debtor may have significant value. If it does, someone may be willing to lend against it. Once again, Article 9 is written expansively to encompass the creation of security interests in nearly anything that has value, if the parties choose to create them.

The second subtext the courts read into the rule may seem virtually a contradiction of the first. Some "owners" who acquired their rights in property by fraud have the power to transfer to bona fide purchasers ownership rights they themselves do not have. See U.C.C. §2-403. In the same analytic vein, such "owners" can also grant security interests in the rights they do not have. The subject is subtle, complex, and peripheral to an understanding of the basic concepts of security, so we do not address it until nearly the end of this book. For now, it is safe to ignore it.

The third subtext the courts read into the rule relates to the *time* at which the security interest becomes enforceable. For example, assume that Alice owns Blackwidget. The debtor, Harris, grants to Credit Corporation a security interest in Blackwidget. At this instant, CC's security interest is not enforceable because Harris has no rights in the collateral. If Harris later purchases Blackwidget from Alice, CC's security interest becomes enforceable at the precise instant Harris first acquires rights in the property. In later assignments, it will become clear why parties want their security interests to arise at the instant their debtors acquire the collateral. For now, we note that this provision makes that possible.

C. Formalities for Real Estate Mortgages

Like virtually every other aspect of real estate law, the formalities for the creation of real estate mortgages enforceable against the debtor differ from state to state. Most states require that the mortgage be in writing and signed by the debtor in the presence of one or more witnesses. Some, as in the Ohio statute that follows, require acknowledgment — essentially notarization — as well, although most require that step only as a prerequisite to recording the mortgage.

Ohio Revised Code Ann.

(2005)

§5301.01 ACKNOWLEDGMENT OF DEEDS, MORTGAGES, LAND CONTRACTS, AND LEASES

A deed, mortgage, land contract . . . or lease of any interest in real property . . . shall be signed by the grantor, mortgagor, vendor, or lessor. . . . The signing must be acknowledged by the grantor, mortgagor, vendor, or lessor in the presence of two witnesses, who shall attest the signing and subscribe their names to the attestation. The signing shall be acknowledged by the grantor, mortgagor, vendor, or lessor before a judge of a court of record in this state or a clerk thereof, a county auditor, county engineer, notary public, mayor, or county court judge, who shall certify the acknowledgment and subscribe the official's name to the certificate of the acknowledgment.

While real estate law generally requires more formality to create an enforceable security interest than does Article 9, real estate law is probably also more flexible in dealing with extreme cases. For example, in Wolf v. Schumacher, 477 N.W.2d 827 (N.D. 1991), the court found that an oral mortgage was excepted from the Statute of Frauds on the basis of partial performance. Had the case been governed by the U.C.C., it is unlikely that the security agreement would have been upheld. Notwithstanding an occasional case that saves a careless creditor, real estate practice is known for its obsessive adherence to the details of conveyancing, and the field abounds with stories of millions of dollars that were lost because someone failed to execute some particular paper in the agreed ritualized form. This part of law practice is not a good place for free spirits who are happier working out approaches that are "probably just as good."

Problem Set 50

50.1. You are working as a law clerk for Judge Heather Clifford. Judge Clifford has given you the exhibits from a recently completed bench trial and asked you "whether they meet the authenticated security agreement requirement of U.C.C. §9-203(b)(3)(A)." The first is a promissory note for $50,000 that was signed by the debtor but not the secured party. The note recites that it is "secured by collateral described in a security agreement bearing the same date as this note." The second is a financing statement that describes the collateral as "all of the inventory and equipment of [the debtor's] business." Although the financing statement was not signed, it was accompanied by another writing that was signed by the debtor: an authorization for the secured party to file such financing statements and amendments as the secured party may deem necessary or expedient to protect its existing and future rights in collateral. The third is a letter from the debtor's attorney to the creditor that states, "Enclosed are the promissory note and financing statement which give you a security interest in my client's inventory and equipment." No other writings were introduced. What do you tell the judge? Is this a question that can be answered from the documents alone, or do you need to read the testimony? U.C.C. §9-102(a)(7).

50.2. You recently joined the legal department at First National Bank and work under the direct supervision of Morton Friedman. To begin your training, Friedman takes you to the Pablo Escobar closing described in the first few pages of this assignment. While you are driving back to the bank from the closing, Friedman asks you at precisely what point in time First National Bank's security interest attached to the Fisherman's Pier restaurant. What do you tell him? See U.C.C. §§1-201(44) (Rev. §1-204), 9-203(b)(3)(A), 2-501(1).

50.3. When you arrived at the Pablo Escobar closing, you pulled from your file the security agreement you had prepared. The description of collateral read: "The restaurant equipment described on the attached list." No list was attached. Ellen Bartell had promised to bring the list of equipment to the closing so it could be attached, but by the time you arrived at the closing, both of you had forgotten. Without realizing the error, the parties signed the security agreement without the list attached. The closing was completed and the loan proceeds were disbursed.

a. Did the bank, at that moment, have a security interest enforceable against Pablo?

b. Two weeks later, Ellen Bartell remembered the list. She mailed it to Friedman with a letter of apology. When he received it, he immediately stapled it to the security agreement. He then asked you whether you thought the agreement was enforceable. What should your reply have been?

c. Would it have made any difference if Bartell had discovered the omission two years later and the parties did the same thing?

d. What if she discovered it after Pablo filed for bankruptcy and the parties did the same thing? See Bankr. Code §362(a)(4) and (5).

50.4. Early in your second year of solo practice, things seem to have gotten out of control. Although the work is incredibly interesting and you're making really good money, there never seems to be enough time to get everything done. Several months ago, you represented Mestre Equipment on a deal for Mestre to sell earthmoving equipment (essentially, a bulldozer) to Winfield Construction Company. At the closing, Mestre took $80,000 of the purchase price in the form of a promissory note secured by an interest in the bulldozer. A few weeks ago, Winfield filed for bankruptcy. Today, the trustee called and asked that you forward a copy of the security agreement.

When you checked the file, you noted that the financing statement on file with the Secretary of State describes the collateral as a "bulldozer," but the description of the collateral in the security agreement is simply blank. You noted the sick, breathless feeling that seemed to come from the pit of your stomach, but, since you began practicing law, you had learned to recognize as an adrenaline-induced palpitation of the heart. By rummaging around in the file you were able to jog your memory as to what had happened. Ed Mestre had promised you a description of the bulldozer a few days before the closing, but he hadn't sent it. At the closing, you had explained to the president of Winfield that the description of the bulldozer was forthcoming. He signed the security agreement with the description blank and orally authorized you to fill it in when you got the description. Mestre sent you the description a few weeks later when you were especially busy. The cover letter said "Here is the description I promised." You stuck the description in the file, meaning to come back to it later, but it slipped your mind.

Your first thought was self-loathing. How could *you*, who always had it together better than your law school classmates, have committed malpractice? Your thoughts turned darker yet when you realized that even if Mestre got most of his $80,000 out of your tight-fisted malpractice carrier (more likely, he'd net about $30,000 to $40,000 after his attorneys' fees — after all, he too was negligent, right?), you were going to be humiliated in the process, he was never going to trust you again, and you would probably never be able to pay even the balance of his loss. Eventually, you settle down to think about what really mattered. What do you do now?

Assume that your state has adopted the Model Rules of Professional Conduct. Those rules provide in relevant part:

Rule 1.4
(b) A lawyer shall explain a matter to the extent reasonably necessary to permit the client to make informed decisions regarding the representation.
Rule 1.6
(a) A lawyer shall not reveal information relating to the representation of a client unless the client gives informed consent, the disclosure is impliedly authorized in order to carry out the representation or the disclosure is permitted by paragraph (b).
(b) A lawyer may reveal information relating to the representation of a client to the extent the lawyer reasonably believes necessary: . . .
    (2) to prevent the client from committing a crime or fraud that is reasonably certain to result in substantial injury to the financial interests or property of another and in furtherance of which the client has used or is using the lawyer's services;
    (3) to prevent, mitigate or rectify substantial injury to the financial interests or property of another that is reasonably certain to result or has resulted from the client's commission of a crime or fraud in furtherance of which the client has used the lawyer's services. . . .
Rule 1.16
(b) . . . [A] lawyer may withdraw from representing a client if:
    (1) withdrawal can be accomplished without material adverse effect on the interests of the client;
    (2) the client persists in a course of action involving the lawyer's services that the lawyer reasonably believes is criminal or fraudulent; [or]
    (4) the client insists upon taking action that the lawyer considers repugnant or with which the lawyer has a fundamental disagreement . . .

Rule 1.9

(c) A lawyer who has formerly represented a client in a matter or whose present or former firm has formerly represented a client in a matter shall not thereafter:

(1) use information relating to the representation to the disadvantage of the former client except as these Rules would permit or require with respect to a client, or when the information has become generally known; or

(2) reveal information relating to the representation except as these Rules would permit or require with respect to a client.

Rule 3.3

(a) A lawyer shall not knowingly:

(1) make a false statement of fact or law to a tribunal or fail to correct a false statement of material fact or law previously made to the tribunal by the lawyer;

(3) offer evidence that the lawyer knows to be false. If a lawyer, the lawyer's client, or a witness called by the lawyer, has offered material evidence and the lawyer comes to know of its falsity, the lawyer shall take reasonable remedial measures, including, if necessary, disclosure to the tribunal....

Rule 4.1

...[A] lawyer shall not knowingly make a false statement of material fact...to a third person.[*]

Rule 8.4

It is professional misconduct for a lawyer to... engage in conduct involving dishonesty, fraud, deceit or misrepresentation.

Terminology

"Fraud" or "fraudulent" denotes conduct having a purpose to deceive and not merely negligent misrepresentation or failure to apprise another of relevant information.

So what do you do?

50.5. Assume that in the previous problem you finally turned the matter over to the client and withdrew. About five months later, you arrived at the bankruptcy court early for a scheduled hearing in another case and decided to listen in on the case then before the court. By coincidence, it was the trustee's case against Mestre Equipment. Mestre's new lawyer, Harold Silver, was examining Ed Mestre, the company president, on direct. Mestre testified that the signature on the security agreement was his own, that the agreement was "genuine" and that it expressed the agreement between the parties. Mestre was not asked, and did not say, when the description of collateral was filled in. Silver offered the agreement in evidence. The trustee did not object and the court admitted it. What do you do now?

---

[*]The comment to Rule 4.1 provides that a lawyer generally has no affirmative duty to inform an opposing party of relevant facts. — EDS.

Assignment 51: What Collateral and Obligations Are Covered?

A security interest is, in essence, the right to apply the value of the collateral to the holder's debt. It follows that the value of a security interest can be no greater than the value of the collateral covered by it. Legally, a security interest in a toothpick is very much the same thing as a security interest in a cruise ship, but the former is unlikely to be worth as much as the latter.

In this assignment, we begin with the legal principles that govern the interpretation of security agreements generally. Next we apply those principles to the interpretation of the security agreement description of the collateral. From the previous assignment, you know that every security agreement contains a description of the collateral. Each also contains a description of the obligations secured. These descriptions determine what will be covered (unless they conflict with some specific provision of law). In this assignment we will consider the possibility that a description will be so vague or indefinite that it will be legally insufficient. We discuss the circumstances that determine whether property acquired after the agreement is signed is included in descriptions and briefly describe the law governing descriptions of collateral in real estate mortgages. We close with a brief discussion of the law governing what obligations are secured.

As you read, keep in mind that in most secured transactions there will be at least two descriptions of collateral: one in the security agreement that is the contract between the parties and one in the financing statement that will be filed in the public records. In keeping with our focus in Part One of this book on the relationship between the debtor and the creditor, we examine only the security agreement description here. The financing statement description serves different functions. These are addressed in Assignment 59.

A. Interpreting Security Agreements

1. Debtor Against Creditor

A security agreement is, among other things, a contract between debtor and creditor. U.C.C. §9-102(a)(73). The rules that govern the interpretation of contracts generally apply to security agreements as well. See U.C.C. §§9-201(a), 1-201(3) (Rev. §1-201(b)(3)), and 1-205 (Rev. §1-303). Generally, the court will try to determine the intention of the parties as objectively expressed in the written security agreement. Where the agreement is ambiguous, parol evidence may be introduced; where the writing results from mutual mistake, the security agreement can be reformed. For example, in State Bank of La Crosse v. Elsen, 421 N.W.2d 116 (Wis. Ct. App. 1988), the bank agreed to lend the debtors $15,000, secured by a mortgage against their house. The bank sent the mortgage to the debtors for their signatures along with a cover letter indicating that the mortgage would secure only the $15,000 loan. But the mortgage itself, which both debtors signed, provided clearly that it secured *all* obligations the debtors owed to the bank. One such obligation was the debtors' previously unsecured guarantee of a $44,000 loan the bank had made to the debtors' son. When the debtors' son defaulted on the $44,000 loan, the bank attempted to foreclose against the debtors' house. The court denied foreclosure and instead reformed the mortgage so that it secured only the $15,000 loan. The guarantee remained unsecured, in accord with the agreement of the parties.

2. Creditor Against Third Party

Although a security agreement is a contract between the debtor and creditor, in most circumstances, it binds third parties as well. See U.C.C. §9-201(a). This should strike you as remarkable. We know of no other law that gives A and B the right to enter into an agreement that is binding on C. The effect of this provision is often that the secured party takes collateral that the other creditors were counting on for collection. Not surprisingly, when the courts are called upon to construe the meaning of security agreements in cases involving such a third party, the courts are likely to interpret them more literally than in accord with the intention of the debtor and secured party. That applies also to the provisions of a security agreement that state what collateral is covered by the agreement.

3. Interpreting Descriptions of Collateral

Article 9 defines many types of collateral, including "accounts" (U.C.C. §9-102(a)(2)), "equipment" (U.C.C. §9-102(a)(33)), "inventory" (U.C.C. §9-102(a)(48)), "instruments" (U.C.C. §9-102(a)(47)), "consumer goods" (U.C.C. §9-102(a)(23)), and "general intangibles" (U.C.C. §9-102(a)(42)). Some of the definitions are not in accord with the common meanings of the defined terms. When parties use one of these terms in a security agreement, the courts usually (but not always) give the term its Article 9 rather than its common meaning. We think the courts are often wrong in doing so; the results can easily be contrary to the intention of parties who were not even aware of the Article 9 definitions of the words they were using. For example, the grant of a security interest in all of the debtor's *accounts* might be intended to include bank accounts, but U.C.C. §9-102(a)(2) defines "accounts" in such a manner that bank accounts are not included. Similarly, U.C.C. §9-102(a)(33) defines "equipment" much more broadly than does the common usage of that term. Only a person who has read the definition would be likely to guess that racehorses might be included in the term. See In re Bob Schwermer & Assoc., Inc., 27 B.R. 304 (Bankr. N.D. Ill. 1983). The owner of a restaurant could easily sign a security agreement with boilerplate language granting a security interest in its "general intangibles" without realizing that its liquor license would be included. See, e.g., In re Genuario, 10 U.C.C.2d 978 (Bankr. R.I. 1989) (grant of a security interest in debtor's "general intangibles" includes liquor license). We believe the better view is that words used in a security agreement, like words used in any other agreement, should be assigned the meaning that the parties intended in using them. The definitions of those same words under Article 9 are only one indication of what the parties might have intended by using them.

B.   Sufficiency of Description: Article 9 Security Agreements

The primary function of the description of collateral in a security agreement is to enable interested parties to identify the collateral. Those parties certainly include the debtor and creditor. They may also include other creditors disadvantaged by the grant of security, trustees in bankruptcy, or courts that must decide cases brought by any of them. To identify the collateral means to determine that a particular item of property is or is not included. In the following case, the court required a relatively high level of precision in describing collateral.

In re Shirel

251 B.R. 157 (Bankr. W.D. Okla. 2000)

RICHARD L. BOHANON, UNITED STATES BANKRUPTCY JUDGE.

The central issue raised by this motion to avoid a lien is whether or not the respondent has a security interest in property of the debtors.

Kevin Shirel applied for a credit card from Sight 'N Sound Appliance Centers, Inc., ("Sight and Sound" or "respondent"). The credit application purports to become the agreement of the parties and is a barely legible, seven page, single spaced, small print document. Shirel signed it on the first page.

The form contains a statement that the respondent will have a security interest in all "merchandise" purchased with the credit card. This statement is located approximately four pages into the application. Shirel's credit was approved and he purchased a new refrigerator using the credit card.

Several months later the debtors filed their bankruptcy petition listing the remaining credit card debt as unsecured and claiming the refrigerator exempt under Oklahoma law. No timely objections were made to the claim of exemption. . . .

I.   DISCUSSION. . . .

B.   Contract of Adhesion

It must be noted from the outset that this agreement is one of adhesion. The Oklahoma Supreme Court, in Max True Plastering Company v. United States

Fidelity and Guaranty Company, et al., 912 P.2d 861 (Okla. 1996), stated that "an adhesion contract is a standardized contract prepared entirely by one party to the transaction for the acceptance of the other. These contracts, because of the disparity in bargaining power between the draftsman and the second party, must be accepted or rejected on a 'take it or leave it' basis without opportunity for bargaining."

In this state, such "contracts are interpreted most strongly against the party preparing the form." Grimes v. Swaim, 971 F.2d 622 (10th Cir. 1992). Therefore, the agreement here must be interpreted using this rule of construction.

Any inferences drawn from contractual ambiguity must be interpreted against the drafter. In other words, if there are two or more possible interpretations as to whether a valid security agreement exists, the one most favorable to the debtor will be adopted.

C.   Language Does Not Sufficiently Identify the Collateral

The central issue . . . is whether or not the agreement is legally sufficient to grant a security interest at all. In that connection I must decide whether the language included in the credit application is sufficient to grant a security interest under the Oklahoma Uniform Commercial Code. . . .

Neither the Oklahoma Supreme Court, nor the Court of Appeals for this Circuit has indicated what precise language is required to create a security interest in goods purchased with a credit card. Therefore, I will evaluate the plain language of the Uniform Commercial Code and determine whether or not this credit card application is a security agreement.

Oklahoma has adopted Article 9 of the Uniform Commercial Code. This statute defines a security agreement as "an agreement which creates or provides for a security interest." [U.C.C. §9-102(a)(73).]

The formal requirements are set forth in section 9-203. The relevant provision states that, "a security interest is not enforceable against the debtor or third parties . . . unless . . . the debtor has signed a security agreement which contains a description of the collateral."

Section [9-108] of the UCC clarifies how the word "description" should be interpreted. It states that, "for the purposes of this Article any description of personal property . . . is sufficient whether or not it is specific if it reasonably identifies what is described."

While the UCC encourages courts to interpret "description" liberally so as to avoid requiring a precise detailed description, such as a serial number, the agreement must at minimum "do the job assigned." That job is to sufficiently describe the collateral so that a third party could reasonably identify the items which are subject to the security interest.[1]

The credit application here states that the card issuer, "will have a purchase money security interest in all merchandise purchased on [the] account until such merchandise is paid in full." The description "all merchandise" is vague, broad, and fails to sufficiently identify a refrigerator.[2]

Since there are several interpretations of what "all merchandise" could mean, I must seek to find the interpretation which is most favorable to the debtor. There is a need, however, to balance the UCC's policy of moving away from the rigid requirements of a description of the collateral, with the need to interpret an adhesion contract in a way favorable to the debtor.

Although the UCC encourages a liberal view concerning the description of collateral, the phrase "all merchandise" is, quite simply, too liberal, too imprecise and is not a description. This court is not implying that the security agreement for a refrigerator be elaborately detailed, such as, e.g., "the almond, 18 cubic foot, side-by-side, refrigerator with ice maker serial #1234." However, it must at least identify the type or class of collateral. Thus, a sufficient description might have been merely "a refrigerator."

This is in accord with the dictionary definition of "description" which is "[a] statement which describes, sets forth, or portrays; a graphic or detailed account of a person, thing, scene, etc." The verb "describe" means "to set forth in words, written or spoken, by reference to qualities, recognizable features, or characteristic marks; to give a detailed or graphic account of." THE OXFORD ENGLISH DICTIO-NARY VOL. IV, 511-512 (2d ed. 1998). It is plain to see that the noun "merchandise" is not a "description" within the common usage of the term for it does not set forth a graphic or detailed account of the purported collateral.

It is understandable for a creditor to desire one catchall phrase which creates a security agreement in every possible situation. However, in doing so, it may not ignore one of the primary reasons for creating a security agreement, which is to give notice to a third party. This can only be achieved by describing what property is subject to the security interest.

Oklahoma courts have held that the following were sufficient descriptions for section 9-110 purposes: "laundry equipment" when referring to a washing-machine; "all machinery" and "paving equipment" to describe a wheel loader; and the words "pickup truck" were held sufficient even though the borrower owned two pickup trucks.

A reasonable third party would understand those descriptions alone, with no need to inquire further. One could be reasonably certain, based on those descriptions, of what collateral is secured. This is not so with the description "all merchandise." This description could conceivably cover any type of item.

II. CONCLUSION

In conclusion, no reasonable third party would understand that a security interest was created in the refrigerator by merely looking to the description itself. By examining this adhesion contract and construing it strongly against Sight and Sound, this court can only conclude that the word "merchandise" does not "sufficiently identify" the collateral at issue here. Thus, the purported security agreement is void as a matter of law.

Accordingly, it is determined that respondent does not have a security interest in the refrigerator.

Whether a description enables "third parties" to identify collateral depends on who the third parties are, what information they start with, and what obligations can be placed on them to gather additional information. Outside the consumer context, courts have generally construed the description requirement more liberally. Descriptions such as "all inventory, equipment, and accounts of the debtor" are routinely held effective, even though a third party looking at the security agreement alone would have no idea what was included. The same is true of descriptions that use terms of art that would have no meaning to most third parties. For example, in In re Schmidt, 1987 U.S. Dist. LEXIS (W.D. Okla. 1987), the security agreement described the collateral as "crops . . . growing on the real estate described by ASCS Farm Serial Numbers . . . J-528, J-552, J-557 & J-572." People dealing in agricultural finance would generally know what these numbers mean and how they could use them to look up the descriptions of the land in other records. The parcels described by the ASCS numbers included both land not farmed by the Schmidts and land farmed by them. The court held the description adequate.

U.C.C. §9-108(c) provides that "A description of collateral as 'all the debtor's assets' or 'all the debtor's personal property' or using words of similar import does not reasonably identify collateral." The drafters chose not to state their reasons for adopting this provision. Based on prior case law, the probable reason was that the drafters feared that use of such descriptions would make it too easy to grant a security interest in all of one's property without realizing one was doing so. There is no indication that the provision was intended or will be interpreted to prevent a debtor from giving a security interest in all of the debtor's assets by describing them individually or by categories.

C.   Describing After-Acquired Property

After-acquired property is a term used to refer to property that a debtor acquires after the security agreement is authenticated or the security interest is otherwise created. Recall our discussion back in Assignment 45 about accounts as possible collateral. We talked about how an audio home equipment manufacturer might give its dealers 30 days to pay, and that the "accounts receivable" might be valuable to a creditor of the manufacturer as collateral. But there is an interesting hitch in using the accounts as collateral: The accounts that exist on any given day will disappear as they are paid off. The collateral existing on the day of the loan transaction may shrink considerably in 30 days and nearly disappear in 60 or 90. If the manufacturer remains in the same business and operates on the same terms, more accounts will be generated during that time. The overall value of the debtor's accounts may remain steady. The accounts that are generated after the security agreement is signed are "after-acquired property" — that is, they are acquired by the debtor after the debtor signed the security agreement. Having them as collateral is crucial to the position of the accounts-secured lender. Both debtors and secured creditors may want them to serve as collateral.

Under some of the laws that preceded Article 9, it was impossible to grant a security interest in after-acquired property. If the parties wanted after-acquired property to secure an obligation between them, they had to execute a security agreement each time the debtor acquired additional property. At the time, that was a staggering inconvenience with collateral such as accounts. The drafters of Article 9 addressed the problem by validating provisions in security agreements that extend the description of collateral to after-acquired property. U.C.C. §9-204(a). Such descriptions commonly include the words "after-acquired property," but descriptions can use other words and, as is discussed in the case below, the inclusion of after-acquired property can even be implied in compelling circumstances.

After-acquired property clauses remain in common use, but with computerization of the American economy, the necessity for them is declining. A computer can be programmed to grant a security interest in each account as it is created. Some department stores include a security agreement on the receipt for each credit purchase. Similarly, there is no reason why the record of the sale of a case of toothpaste from a distributor to a retail drugstore cannot contain the grant of a security interest. But in the latter illustration, the individual grant of a security interest offers no obvious advantage over an after-acquired property clause and so seems unlikely to replace it.

In the following case, the court discusses the differing views on the necessity for a specific provision in the secured agreement as a prerequisite to claiming after-acquired collateral as security.

Stoumbos v. Kilimnik

988 F.2d 949 (9th Cir. 1993)

FLETCHER, CIRCUIT JUDGE:

[On May 1, 1982, Kilimnik sold a business to AAM, retaining a security interest. The description of collateral was obscure and scattered through several documents, but the court held it to be the equivalent of "inventory and equipment." The security agreement did use "after acquired" language with respect to accounts receivable. When the buyer defaulted in October 1985, Kilimnik seized all of the inventory and equipment then in the possession of the buyer, including inventory and equipment acquired by the buyer after May 1, 1982. The buyer filed bankruptcy and the trustee, Stoumbos, sued Kilimnik for return of the after-acquired inventory and equipment.]

Kilimnik, however, argues that, where a creditor acquires a security interest in equipment and inventory, the court should find that this interest automatically extends to after-acquired inventory and equipment. There is substantial support for the proposition that, where a financing statement or security agreement provides for a security interest in "all inventory" (or uses similar broad language), the document incorporates after-acquired inventory. The rationale is that inventory is constantly turning over, and no creditor could reasonably agree to be secured by an asset that would vanish in a short time in the normal course of business. The position that no express language is required is described as the "majority" view, American Family Marketing, 92 Bankr. at 953, or the "modern trend." Sims Office Supply, 83 Bankr. at 72. There is, however, contrary authority, which reasons that "the [U.C.C.] contemplates that a security agreement should clearly spell out any claims to after acquired collateral." Covey v. First Nat'l Bank (In re Balcain Equip. Co., Inc.), 80 Bankr. 461, 462 (Bankr. C.D. Ill. 1987).

No Washington or Ninth Circuit cases appear to be directly on point. We conclude that we need not decide whether to adopt the "majority" view in this case since the Purchase Agreement does not contain the usual language granting a security interest in "all inventory" or "inventory," but only in the items specifically described in paragraph 1 as "inventory . . . on hand at May 1, 1982."

In addition, the rationale of the "automatic" security interest cases does not apply to after-acquired equipment. Those cases discuss cyclically depleted and replenished assets such as inventory or accounts receivable. Unlike inventory, equipment is not normally subject to frequent turnover.

We are aware that the financing statement mentions after-acquired equipment, suggesting that the parties intended Kilimnik's security interest would extend this far. Yet we must look to the entire circumstances under which the purchase agreement was made to ascertain its meaning. Under Washington law, a contract is interpreted by reference to many contextual factors, including the subject matter of the transaction, the subsequent conduct of the parties and the reasonableness of their interpretations.

The trustee here advances the more reasonable interpretation: Kilimnik took a kind of "purchase money" interest in the equipment he sold to AAM, but he did not get the additional security of a blanket interest in all equipment the company ever acquired after the sale. The subject matter of the transaction also supports this conclusion.

Kilimnik would not have had a clear reason to want after-acquired equipment covered by the purchase agreement. As we have seen, equipment, unlike inventory, is not normally subject to frequent turnover. Even if limited to the equipment on hand at the time of the sale, his interest would have been secure.

In summary, we conclude that Kilimnik's security interest was limited to equipment and inventory owned by AAM on May 1, 1982. . . .

The preceding case illustrates the typical use of after-acquired property clauses: to enable the security interest to "float" on collateral, the precise components of which are constantly changing but which as a whole remains relatively stable in identity and value, much like the accounts example we used to introduce this idea.

While after-acquired property clauses are most frequently used with regard to inventory and accounts receivable, they are also employed in other contexts. After-acquired property clauses are not unusual when creditors take interests in broad categories of collateral such as equipment, farm products, or general intangibles. With regard to each, a particular debtor is likely to be disposing of some items and acquiring others over time, so that it makes more sense to think of the collateral as the category rather than as the individual items within it at any given time. After-acquired property clauses make it possible for the parties to a long-term financing relationship to do that. Such a security interest is also sometimes referred to as a *floating lien*.

Lending contracts often link the total value of the collateral, including after-acquired collateral, to the total amount of the loan. A bank, for example, may agree to lend 65 percent of the purchase price of all inventory owned by the debtor. When inventory is sold, the debtor must pay down the loan; when new inventory arrives, the bank advances a portion of the purchase price. But after-acquired property clauses are not always linked to agreements to make additional loans. Under some arrangements, additional acquisitions of collateral covered by the after-acquired property clause are simply a windfall to the creditor. Perhaps for this reason, after-acquired property clauses become ineffective upon the filing of a bankruptcy case. Bankr. Code §552(a). We explore this subject in more detail in Assignment 53.

D. Sufficiency of Description: Real Estate Mortgages

While the rules regarding descriptions of collateral in real estate mortgages are controlled by a separate body of law, they are remarkably similar to the rules under Article 9. The description in a mortgage must describe the land sufficiently to identify it. But the description may refer to separate documents, such as maps or plats for that purpose. A description may be so vague as to render the mortgage void. But if the description is merely ambiguous, parol evidence may be used to explain its meaning. Broad descriptions such as "all grantor's property in the county" are generally good as between the mortgagor and mortgagee. (Real estate lawyers refer to these as "Mother Hubbard clauses," presumably because the cupboard will be bare when the next creditor arrives.)

The physical nature of real estate makes it easier to identify than many kinds of personal property. While older descriptions of land, particularly in the northeastern United States, may describe it by reference to "monuments" such as trees, rocks, and streams that are later difficult to identify or less than permanent, in most parts of the United States, descriptions are by reference to maps or plats that are ultimately located by reference to monuments (iron stakes) placed by government survey. The stakes are carefully maintained as reference points for surveyors. As a result, a well-written description of real property can identify it with virtually no uncertainty.

In real estate practice, the debtor executes a separate mortgage document each time the debtor adds land to the secured creditor's collateral. Real estate law recognizes a doctrine of *after-acquired title* that applies to mortgages and permits an earlier mortgage document to convey a security interest in land later acquired by the mortgagor. See United Oklahoma Bank v. Moss, 793 P.2d 1359 (Okla. 1990). But, in contrast to the situation with respect to personal property, where after-acquired property clauses are common, there seems to be little need for the doctrine with respect to real estate transactions and correspondingly little use.

Permanent buildings and other structures permanently affixed to land (known as *fixtures*) become part of the real estate. They are automatically included in a description that refers only to the land. The rule applies whether they are affixed to the real estate before or after the mortgage is executed. Thus, in a sense, every real estate mortgage automatically reaches "after affixed" property. In later assignments we will discuss property affixed to real estate in greater detail.

E.   What Obligations Are Secured?

The general rules regarding interpretation of security agreements apply to provisions specifying what obligations are secured. Virtually any obligation can be secured if the parties make their intention clear. In Pawtucket Institution for Savings v. Gagnon, 475 A.2d 1028 (R.I. 1984), the mortgage secured a promise by the debtor to build a building. That is, if the debtor did not build the building, the debtor would owe a debt for the resulting damages and the mortgage against already existing real property would secure it. In indicating what obligations are secured, no particular form is required. If the security agreement states that it secures a certain debt in the amount of $25,000 and such a debt exists, it is secured. A security interest can also secure a debt that does not yet exist but which the parties contemplate will come into existence in the future. If the future obligation will come in to existence as the result of an additional extension of credit by the secured creditor, it is referred to as a *future advance*. U.C.C. §9-204(c) provides that "A security agreement may provide that collateral secures . . . future advances. . . ."

Debtors often execute agreements that purport to secure every obligation to the secured creditor of any kind that may come into existence in the future. If the creditor later lends additional money, a security agreement with such a future-advance clause will assure that the subsequent loan is secured from its inception. Such provisions are often referred to as dragnet clauses. They are valid when contained in Article 9 security agreements. The comment to U.C.C. §9-204 states that "the parties are free to agree that a security interest secures any obligation whatsoever. Determining the obligations secured by collateral is solely a matter of construing the parties' agreement under applicable law. This Article rejects the holdings of cases decided under former Article 9 that applied other tests. . . ." For an example of a very simple, straightforward dragnet clause, see paragraph 3 of the Deutsche Financial Services "Agreement for Wholesale Financing" in Assignment 56.

Future-advance clauses can be included in real estate mortgages. The typical construction mortgage, under which the lender agrees to make advances each time construction reaches designated stages of completion, is an example. There are, however, some limitations on the use of future-advance clauses in real estate mortgages. First, some states "disfavor" the use of dragnet clauses by demanding strict proof that the later advance is one that was in the contemplation of the parties at the time they executed the real estate mortgage. In those states the mortgagee will want to describe the future debt as specifically as possible at the time the mortgage is granted and refer to the mortgage in the documentation for the future debt when it is incurred. Second, some states require that a recorded mortgage indicate a maximum amount of indebtedness to be secured; the mortgage cannot effectively secure more than the amount indicated in it. For example, a $75,000 home mortgage in such a state might recite that it secures a loan in the initial amount of $75,000, that future advances are contemplated, but the mortgage will not secure obligations exceeding $90,000. See, e.g., Fla. stat. ch. 697.04 (1994). Finally, in some states real property cannot secure obligations not reducible to money. Fluctuating accounts, contingent debts, or promises to build a building as referred to above do not fall into that category. Any of them could be reduced to a specific dollar amount at the time of foreclosure. But an obligation to provide future support for a living person might be much more difficult to value and as a result not considered a proper subject of security.

Security agreements and mortgages usually provide that, in the event of default, the debtor will pay the creditor's attorneys' fees and other expenses of collection. They authorize the creditor to add these amounts to the secured indebtedness. These provisions are considered valid and effective in both personal property and real estate security agreements, and, as you have already seen in Assignment 49, in bankruptcy. In recent years, courts have begun to refer to them as "nonadvance" provisions, because the creditor does not advance the amount secured by them to the debtor. Interest that accrues on a secured obligation is also included in the nonadvance category. Between debtor and secured creditor, provisions securing nonadvances are of equal validity and effect with those securing advances.

Problem Set 51

51.1.   Robert and Mary Gillam have come to see you about their financial problems. For the past seven years, they have made their living farming. When they started, they borrowed $35,000 from the First National Bank of Frenville and granted a security interest in "crops growing on the debtor's farm in Osprey County, about 14 miles from Tilanook" and most of their farm equipment. (The location information is correct and the debtors own only a single farm.) The Gillams have paid that loan down to $19,000. It is now the middle of the growing season and the Gillams don't have enough cash to get them through the harvest. They would like to borrow against their current crop, but First National won't lend them any more money. The second lender they approached, Production Credit Association (PCA), told them that the current crop was unacceptable as collateral because "First National already has it, and we don't make crop loans in second position." This upset the Gillams, because they had assumed that their current crop was not covered by First National's security interest.

a.   Who is right on the point of law?

b.   What should the Gillams do? U.C.C. §§9-108(a), (b), 9-203(b)(3)(A), 9-204.

51.2. The Gillams are also raising sheep on the property. They sell the wool and sometimes the cuddly little lambs themselves. (You've heard of lamb chops, right?) They would like your written opinion that the sheep are not covered by First Bank's security interest. With the opinion letter, they say that PCA will make a loan against the sheep. Can you give it? U.C.C. §9-102(a)(34).

51.3. Richard Cohen, a client of your firm, asked Sandra Bernhard, the partner for whom you work, for an opinion on a "situation" in which he is involved. Because it is a very small matter, Bernhard has asked you to look into it, tell her what the arguments will be on each side, and evaluate them. You have learned that Cohen lent $30,000 to Aircraft Video Marketing, Inc. (AVMI) four years ago and entered into a security agreement that listed the collateral as "All of Debtor's equipment, including replacement parts, additions, repairs, and accessories incorporated therein or affixed thereto. Without limitation the term 'equipment' includes all items used in recording, processing, playing back, or broadcasting moving or still pictures, by whatever process." AVMI owned certain video equipment at the time the security agreement was signed and acquired additional video equipment of a similar nature later. Like the original equipment, the additional equipment was used in AVMI's business for playing back motion pictures. When AVMI defaulted, another creditor of AVMI's, First National Bank of Omaha, claimed the equipment. After Cohen established that his security interest predated First National's, they dropped their claim to the original equipment. But they continue to claim the equipment AVMI bought later, saying that it is not covered by the terms of Cohen's security agreement. What's your assessment?

51.4. You are practicing with a small firm in Oklahoma that does all the legal work for Walter's Department Store (Walter's). Walter's practice has been to take a security interest in everything that a credit card holder purchases on his or her account. While they do not repossess clothing or other items without resale value, they do repossess many kinds of appliances and household goods. They make the decision after default. Prior to Judge Bohanon's opinion in *Shirel*, they thought they obtained the right to do such repossessions by the following language in the application for a Walter's credit card: "...and cardholder grants Walter's a security interest in all items purchased on the account." Can you think of a way for Walter's to take security interests that would be good even under Judge Bohanon's reasoning? U.C.C. §§9-203(b)(3)(A), 9-102(a)(23), 9-108(e).

51.5. This morning you met with Sharon Hammacher, general counsel for the Sun Bank chain. Sharon, a close friend from law school, has been considerably more successful than you, and tries to steer business your way when she can. Sharon is redrafting the standard documents the bank uses in routine commercial lending. After several cases in which loan officers have failed at the simple task of checking a few boxes on the security agreement to indicate the collateral covered, Sharon has an idea: The Bank's form security agreement should provide that the Bank takes a security interest in absolutely everything the debtor has, and then the loan officer and the debtor should check boxes to indicate what is *not* included. That way, any omissions will cut against the debtor, not the Bank. Sharon wants to know what you think of her idea. She would also like your suggestions on how to word the omnibus clause. What do you tell her? U.C.C. §9-108(c).

51.6.   As a matter of policy, why should a description that says "all the debtor's property" be invalid?

51.7.   a. In 1997, your firm represented Ed Mestre in the closing of a working capital loan from Firstbank. In that transaction, Ed gave Firstbank a security interest in his "accounts." When Ed recently sold a piece of real estate, the buyer refused to pay Ed the proceeds of sale without a release from Firstbank. Ed doesn't want to go to Firstbank for this release because the relationship is bad, so he has come to you. "I had no idea that the proceeds owing from a sale of real estate were an account," Ed tells you.

Having done your research, you realize that proceeds from the sale of real property were not "accounts" when the agreement was signed in 1997; they only became accounts upon the adoption of revised Article 9. Did the expansion in the Article 9 definition of "accounts" expand the scope of Firstbank's security interest? U.C.C. §9-102(a)(2).

b.   If so, does your firm need to do anything about the hundreds of security agreements covering "accounts" it prepared while former Article 9 was in force?

c.   If not, how do you handle this problem with Firstbank?

Assignment 52: Proceeds, Products, and Other Value-Tracing Concepts

In the previous assignment, you learned that when a debtor and creditor contract for a security interest, they must describe the collateral. Once they have done so, they typically put the documents away. They are likely to refer to the documents again only when some difficulty arises in their relationship, by which time it is often too late to make changes.

In the meantime, items of collateral may go through transformations that take them outside the description of collateral in the security agreement. Oil may become plastic, and then plastic shipping containers. Individual cattle in a herd may die, but only after they have produced an even larger number of offspring. Inventory that serves as collateral may be sold on credit. The account debtors who purchased the inventory may pay their accounts with checks, and the debtor may deposit those checks into a bank account.

When a debtor and creditor anticipate such transformations, they usually choose to have the security interest continue in the collateral as it changes form or, if the debtor disposes of it to a third party, to have the security interest attach to whatever the debtor receives in return.

The source of this preference lies in the nature of the secured creditor's relationship to the collateral. Secured creditors look to collateral for repayment. Although they care about the form their collateral takes, they care more about what it is worth. When the debtor transforms the value of an item of collateral to some other type of asset, the secured creditor usually wants and expects the security interest to follow. Were it otherwise, a debtor could unilaterally deprive the creditor of the value of its security interest.

At the time the parties negotiate the security agreement, the debtor generally is willing to permit the security interest to follow the value because the debtor too is typically thinking in terms of value. By giving its secured creditor an interest that "floats" from one item to another as the value is transferred, transformations in value become less threatening to the secured creditor. Where security interests follow value, secured creditors have less reason to object to such transformations. As a result, debtors find it easier to persuade creditors to grant them freedom to make transformations when necessary.

One way to assure that a security interest will follow the value is to include express language in the description of the collateral in the security agreement that covers all forms the value is likely to take. For example, a bank that lends against inventory can easily anticipate that the inventory will be sold, resulting in accounts, negotiable instruments, or money. If the description of collateral is "inventory, accounts, instruments, money, and bank accounts," transformation of the value from one of these forms of collateral to another will not reduce the value of the bank's security. Similarly, if the parties contemplate the possibility that the collateral will be destroyed by accident but the loss will be insured, they can provide that any payment from an insurance company for loss of the inventory also will serve as collateral.

As you might imagine, secured creditors cannot always anticipate the transformations their collateral might undergo or the nature of the property for which it may be exchanged. An alternative might be to encumber all of the debtor's property. But that may unduly restrict a debtor. Consider, for example, the debtor who is financing not the entire business, but only a single piece of equipment. If that debtor grants a security interest in the equipment and every other form that value might later take, the debtor might not be able to obtain inventory financing or other equipment financing. And all the secured creditors would want a first claim on the debtor's accounts, instruments, money, and bank accounts.

A more practical solution is to employ what we call *value-tracing concepts* — terms of art that indicate that in certain kinds of transformations of the collateral the security interest should follow the value in prescribed ways.

The value-tracing concepts most commonly employed are *proceeds, products, rents, profits,* and *offspring.* Debtors and creditors use these terms of art in security agreements and legislatures use them in statutes. In theory, each of these terms identifies a particular set of tracing rules, although, as is usual in law, neither the parties that use the terms, nor the courts that interpret them, always agree on what the rules are. We begin with the most important of these concepts.

A.   Proceeds

1.   Definition

Read the definition of "proceeds" in U.C.C. §9-102(a)(64). Under this definition, a security interest will follow the value of collateral through some transformations but not others. If the debtor sells the collateral, the security interest will attach to the price paid, whether it is in the form of an account, a promissory note, or cash. If the debtor leases the collateral, the security interest will attach to the rents received.

U.C.C. §9-102(a)(64)(C), providing that "rights arising out of the collateral" are proceeds, is new. The drafters of Revised Article 9 — great champions of the secured creditor — inserted it without explanation. The provision can be used to argue that virtually any property linked to the collateral in any way is "proceeds."

In re Wiersma, 283 B.R. 294 (Bankr. D. Idaho 2002), was the first case to interpret the new provision. Through the negligence of an electrician, the debtors' dairy cows were subjected to electrical shocks and became sick or died. When the debtors settled their $6 million lawsuit for $2.5 million, their secured creditor bank claimed the settlement as "proceeds" of the herd and the milk it produced. The court said

> Debtors argue that some of the components of their damages do not represent proceeds of cows and milk serving as collateral and should not, therefore, be

subject to UCB's security interest. For example, their complaint includes a reservation of a right to amend the complaint to request punitive damages. Because
Gietzens' insurer is offering to settle all claims, including potential punitive damage
claims which are not attributable to any particular item of UCB's collateral, Debtors
contend the settlement represents some damages not directly related to the loss of
collateral.

   In this instance, though, the legislature has spoken. The UCC definition of "proceeds" includes within its scope whatever is acquired upon disposition of collateral,
all rights arising out of collateral, and includes all claims arising out of the loss of, or
damage to, collateral. [U.C.C. §9-102(64).] All of the categories listed in Debtors'
damage analysis stem from either damage to Debtors' cows or from the loss of milk
and cows. Even the "miscellaneous" and "labor" categories arise from damage to or
loss of cows and milk because they represent expenses such as veterinarian bills and
the Debtors' extra labor costs associated with dealing with the electrical problem
affecting the cows. The same is true with respect to Debtors' claim for punitive
damages. Thus, given these facts, the Court concludes Debtors' claims against
Gietzen arose out of the loss of, and damage to, UCB's collateral, the cows and milk.

In other words, it doesn't matter whether the settlement paid was for the
collateral or for other damages. It is all proceeds because it "arose out of"
the collateral.

   Note that the specific rules governing what is proceeds also give secured
creditors more than they would be entitled to under a strict value-tracing
analysis. For example, the secured creditor is able to claim all of the proceeds
of a sale or rental, even though a substantial part of that value does not flow
from the collateral, but is instead contributed by the debtor. Consider the
specific case of a bank that finances the inventory of a furniture store. The
store buys an item of furniture wholesale for $500 and sells it retail for $1,000.
To generate the $1,000 in proceeds the bank will claim when the item is sold,
the debtor store must maintain a place of business, advertise, provide a salesperson to assist the customer, and make delivery. In the typical case, the value
of proceeds exceeds the value of the collateral that can be traced into them.

   Perhaps because the consequence of finding that collateral has been disposed of is so severe, some courts are reluctant to make that finding. In cases
where the value of the collateral disposed of is small in relation to what is
received, these courts ignore the disposition of collateral and hold that none
of the property received is proceeds. For example, if you buy food and drink in
a hotel and charge it to your room, the obligation to pay for it is not considered proceeds of the food and drink even if the secured creditor has a security
interest in the food and drink inventory. The reasoning is that most of the
food and drink account is not for the food and drink but for the service of
preparing and serving them. The rest, these courts assume, should be ignored.

   When the parties have done a poor job of expressing their desire that the
security interest follow the value of the collateral, some courts are quick to
infer it, even if the inference does violence to the definition of the terms used.
For example, in McLemore, Trustee v. Mid-South Agri-Chemical Corp., 41 B.R.
369 (Bankr. M.D. Tenn. 1984), one creditor's security agreement provided an
interest in the debtor's "corn crop" and "proceeds" of the corn crop and
another's provided an interest in "all crops, annual and perennial, and
other plant products now planted, growing or grown, or which are hereafter

planted or otherwise become growing crops or other plan products" and "proceeds" from these crops. Later, the debtor joined the PIK Diversion Program, a government subsidy program in which the debtor contracted with the U.S. government not to grow crops on the property. The debtor received a substantial cash payment for *not* growing crops on the land identified. The court held that the PIK payments were proceeds of the crops that were never planted. The court reconciled its decision with the definition in U.C.C. §9-102(a)(64) by stating that "Participation in the PIK program 'disposes' of the debtor's corn crops by precluding their cultivation." But to talk of disposing of something that never came into existence is to engage in a legal fiction. The *McLemore* court focused on the economic equivalence of the crops and the payments; the existence of one precluded the existence of the other. While the court did not talk of value tracing, that is what it was doing. We should note that not all courts have taken this route with regard to PIK payments. Some have stuck with the plain meaning of U.C.C. §9-102(a)(64) and found the payments not to be proceeds of the crop. But the *McLemore* case is important as an illustration of the impetus in some courts to translate "proceeds" into a concept of economic equivalence.

"Proceeds" are "collateral" within the definition of the latter term in U.C.C. §9-102(a)(12). As a result, when proceeds are disposed of or rights arise out of them, whatever is received is "proceeds." Thus the proceeds of proceeds are proceeds. To illustrate, assume ZBank has a security interest in the inventory of Billie's Toy Shop. Billie's Toy Shop sells some toys to Marjorie Venutti and Venutti writes a check for the $250 purchase price. We already know that the check is proceeds. Now assume that Billie's Toy Shop deposits the check to its bank account and the check is collected. The money in the account is now proceeds of the toys because it was received in exchange for proceeds of the toys. If Billie's Toy Shop uses the money to buy more toys, the new toys will be the proceeds of the old toys.

Even without using the concept of proceeds or tracing the value from the old toys into the new ones, the new toys would be subject to ZBank's security interest as "after-acquired property." See *Stoumbos v. Kilimnik*, in Assignment 51. The concepts of proceeds and after acquired property frequently overlap, but the former is a value-tracing concept, while the latter is not. We will say more about this later.

Even if the security agreement makes no mention of proceeds, a security interest automatically covers them. The rule derives from U.C.C. §§9-203(f) and 9-315(a). To illustrate, assume the ZBank's security agreement with Billie's Toy Shop describes the collateral as "inventory," but does not mention the proceeds of inventory. ZBank's security interest nevertheless extends to the proceeds of sales of inventory.

2. Termination of Security Interest in the Collateral After Authorized Disposition

Secured creditors sometimes authorize their debtors to dispose of the collateral free of the security interest. This authorization might be contained in the security agreement, as when the inventory lender to a department store agrees that the store can sell inventory to customers free of the security interest. Alternatively, this authorization might be expressed by the secured creditor at some later time, as when the bank that financed an automobile approves the owner's plan to sell it free of the security interest. Finally, this authorization might be implied from the circumstances or conduct of the parties, as when the security agreement between an inventory lender and a department store is silent on the matter of sale of collateral or where the bank that financed a herd of cattle knows that the debtor has been selling cattle from the herd to buyers who do not think they are taking subject to a security interest and the bank has not objected to the sales. In any of these instances, U.C.C. §9-315(a)(1) gives effect to the authorization: The buyer takes free of the security interest and the secured creditor can look only to the debtor and the proceeds.

3. Continuation of Security Interest in the Collateral After Unauthorized Disposition

In some secured financing arrangements, the parties contemplate that the debtor will sell the collateral only pursuant to further arrangements. For example, the security agreement may require that the secured creditor authorize sales to particular customers. This arrangement is often used in the financing of expensive items of collateral. For example, the bank that finances an airplane dealer may require that the dealer obtain authorization each time it sells an airplane. When the dealer finds a buyer for one of its planes, it makes the contract contingent on the approval of its financing bank and forwards the contract to the bank. One reason for such an arrangement is to allow the bank to pass on the nature and adequacy of the consideration the dealer will receive from the sale. Another is to alert the bank that the consideration is about to be paid, so the bank can be involved in determining what portion should be applied to the secured debt and what portion should remain with the dealer.

The language of many security agreements prohibits sale of the collateral. For example, the following provision appears in the Wisconsin Bankers Association standard form for a Motor Vehicle Consumer Security Agreement: "[The debtor] shall . . . not sell, lease or otherwise dispose of [the automobile] except as specifically authorized in this Agreement or in writing by the Seller." The Agreement does not authorize any sales by the debtor. Of course, such a clause does not mean that the buyer cannot sell the car at all. A security interest is only a contingent right to the collateral in the event that the debtor does not pay the secured obligation. When the debtor pays, the security interest terminates and the debtor is free to sell. The true meaning of such a clause is that the debtor must pay the debt in full to have the right to sell the collateral.

To understand how this might work in practice, assume that Arthur Dent purchased a Ford Prefect with financing from ZBank, under a security agreement that contained the provision set forth in the preceding paragraph and did not otherwise authorize sale. Arthur owes $12,000 against the car, and wants to sell it to Trillian McWilliams for $10,000. If Arthur has $12,000 in cash, he can pay ZBank, terminate its lien, and then sell the car.

Similarly, if Arthur has $2,000 and Trillian is willing to pay in advance, Arthur can do the same. But it would be foolish for a person in Trillian's position to do so. If Arthur got Trillian's money, but for some reason could not (or did not) deliver the car, Trillian might be only an unsecured creditor of Arthur's. Just as ZBank won't give up its security interest until it gets its money, Trillian should not give up her money until she gets clear title to the car.

The solution is to arrange for a simultaneous exchange of the security interest, the car, and the money. Arthur, Trillian, and ZBank will agree that someone will be escrowee or trustee for the transaction. In this example, the parties are likely to select ZBank. (Even with the nasty things some banks have done in recent decades, most people still trust banks more than they trust each other.) ZBank will wear two hats in the transaction: that of secured party and that of trustee or escrowee. Arthur and Trillian will pay their money to ZBank in trust, Arthur will authorize transfer of title to Trillian, and ZBank will execute the document terminating its lien. The terms of the trust are that if ZBank receives all the money, the transfer authorization, and the termination statement by an agreed date, ZBank can "close" the transaction by filing the termination statement and the transfer authorization with the Department of Motor Vehicles and disbursing the $12,000 from its trust account to its operating account. If ZBank does not receive the money and the documents, ZBank must return what it did receive and the nonbreaching party may then seek appropriate legal remedies against the breaching party.

If Arthur doesn't have $2,000, he cannot close. He may then be in a position where he can neither make his payments on the car, nor sell it without ZBank's consent. If ZBank does not give consent, Arthur might need to seek relief in bankruptcy.

Of course, if Arthur owed less than the sale price of the car, he could have closed and walked away with some cash. For example, if he owed $12,000 and Trillian were buying for $14,000, the parties would still need the escrow arrangement to protect themselves, but the sale would go through and Arthur could get the $2,000 difference between the loan amount and the contract price.

Despite their contracts not to sell collateral without their secured party's consent, debtors often do so. Some even go a step further by collecting the purchase price and spending it without paying the secured loan. Many states have enacted statutes making such conduct criminal. For example, Illinois adds the section set forth below to its version of U.C.C. §9-315. Notice that this statute does not make every unauthorized sale a crime — only those in which the debtor willfully and wrongfully fails to pay the proceeds to the secured party.

Illinois Revised Statutes

ch. 26, para. 9-315.01 (2005)

It is unlawful for a debtor under the terms of a security agreement (a) who has no right of sale or other disposition of the collateral or (b) who has a right of sale or other disposition of the collateral and is to account to the secured party for the proceeds of any sale or other disposition of the collateral, to sell or otherwise dispose of the collateral and willfully and wrongfully to fail to pay the secured party the amount of said proceeds due under the security agreement. Failure to pay such proceeds to the secured party within 10 days after the sale or other disposition of the collateral is prima facie evidence of a willful and wanton failure to pay. [Such conduct is a Class 3 felony.]

New York goes a step further, making it a crime merely to sell collateral in violation of a security agreement that prohibits sale.

New York Penal Law

§185.05 (2005)

A person is guilty of fraud involving a security interest when, having executed a security agreement creating a security interest in personal property securing a monetary obligation owed to a secured party, and . . . [h]aving under the security agreement no right of sale or other disposition of the property, he knowingly secretes, withholds or disposes of such property in violation of the security agreement. Fraud involving a security interest is a Class A misdemeanor.

Even if the security agreement expressly prohibits sale of the collateral, the debtor has the power under U.C.C. §9-401 to transfer ownership to a buyer. (The transfer will be a breach of the security agreement and perhaps even a crime.) To understand the effect of U.C.C. §9-401, you must read it together with U.C.C. §9-315(a)(1), which provides that a security interest "continues in collateral notwithstanding sale." The result is that after a sale that the secured party has not authorized to be free of the security interest, the buyer will own the collateral subject to the security interest. The buyer may or may not know of that interest. (In Assignment 69, we will examine U.C.C. §9-320(a), which protects buyers in the ordinary course of business against security interests created by their sellers, but for now you should assume that the sales we talk about are not in the ordinary course of business.)

Unless the secured party has authorized the debtor to sell the collateral free of the security interest, the security interest continues in the original collateral and also in the proceeds. U.C.C. §9-315(a). This is no mere tracing of the value of the collateral; it is potentially a multiplication of the value in favor of the secured creditor. Probably the rationale is that when the debtor sells without authorization, the secured creditor needs additional protection. The original collateral, the proceeds, or both are likely to be in jeopardy. Indeed, a common scenario is that the debtor sells the collateral to obtain cash, which it desperately needs to meet other obligations. By the time the secured party learns of the sale, the debtor has spent the money and the collateral itself is in the hands of a bona fide purchaser or somewhere the secured creditor cannot find it.

Nevertheless, the multiplication of collateral that can result from the rules of U.C.C. §§9-102(a)(12) and (64) and 9-315(a) is striking. Assume, for example, that ZBank has a security interest in Jack's cow. Without authorization from ZBank, Jack sells the cow to Barbara for $2,000. Zbank's security interest continues in the collateral (the cow) and also in the identifiable proceeds of that sale (the $2,000). If Jack then uses the $2,000 of proceeds to buy some beans, the beans will also be proceeds under U.C.C. §9-102(a)(64) (recall that the proceeds of proceeds are proceeds) and ZBank's security interest will continue in the beans under U.C.C. §9-315(a). ZBank can foreclose against the cow and the beans, and collect its money where it can. Whether Zbank can also collect from the cash in the hands of the bean seller is considered in the next section.

Now assume that before ZBank forecloses, Barbara resells the cow for $2,500. Under U.C.C. §9-315(a), ZBank's security interest continues in the cow despite the resale. (Notice that U.C.C. §9-315(a) does not say that the sale must be by the debtor.) The $2,500 Barbara received for the cow is also proceeds of ZBank's collateral because it was acquired upon disposition of the cow that was collateral. This example illustrates that unauthorized sales of collateral can cause it to multiply dramatically. Just as the monster in the old B-movie, *The Blob*, absorbed everything it came in contact with and grew constantly larger, the secured creditor's collateral absorbs everything for which it is exchanged and grows larger also. (If you decide to do outside research on this one, be sure to see the original film, starring Steve McQueen. The concept was entirely botched in the remake.)

Associated Industries v. Keystone General Inc. (In re Keystone General Inc.), 135 B.R. 275 (Bankr. S.D. Ohio 1991), gives an example of how collateral can proliferate through unauthorized disposition. Star Bank financed Keystone General's inventory under a security agreement that extended to after-acquired property. Keystone General bought $1.9 million dollars of inventory from Associated. Even though Keystone General never paid for the inventory, Star Bank's security interest attached to it. When Keystone General returned the inventory to Associated in exchange for a credit to Keystone's account, Star Bank's security interest continued in the inventory pursuant to U.C.C. §9-315(a). Star Bank ended up with a security interest in electronic components that the debtor hadn't paid for, no longer owned, and didn't even possess. This result startles even jaded commercial law types.

Secured creditors who insist on security agreement provisions restricting the sale of their collateral often intend to enforce the restriction only if their relationship with the debtor sours. So long as the relationship remains good, they allow the debtor to sell portions of the collateral and ignore the restrictions. When the relationship later sours, these creditors often find that the courts will not enforce the restrictions. Instead, the courts may hold that the creditor waived the conditions on sale by its course of dealing with the debtor and that the sale to the third party was therefore impliedly authorized.

These waiver cases usually seem to arise in the context of sales of livestock, where sales by debtors are pretty much continuous and the buyers are not protected by U.C.C. §9-320(a). For example, in Gretna State Bank v. Cornbelt Livestock Co., 463 N.W.2d 975 (Neb. 1990), the security agreement prohibited sale of the dairy cows that served as collateral except with the express written permission of the Bank. The Bank knew, however, that the debtor had been selling cows without the Bank's express written permission in violation of the security agreement and had not objected. Later, when the Bank sued a livestock market that had participated in the sales, the Court directed a verdict against the Bank on the ground the Bank had waived the prohibition on sales.

4. Limitations on the Secured Creditor's Ability to Trace Collateral

In *The Blob* it quickly became apparent to Steve McQueen that if his proceeds-like adversary went unchecked, it would eventually absorb everything. What keeps a secured creditor's collateral from doing the same? To answer this question completely, you will need some concepts that we do not discuss until Part Two of this book. But you should know that the protection is far from complete. The cereal you ate for breakfast this morning was probably covered with security interests. Yuck!

One limitation we can discuss here is that a security interest continues to encumber proceeds only so long as they remain "identifiable." See U.C.C. §9-315(a)(2). To figure out what this means, begin by distinguishing the concepts of *commingling* and *identifiability*. To commingle collateral is to put it together in one mass with identical noncollateral so that no one can tell which is *actually* which. When Farmer Brown puts her wheat in a storage silo in Oklahoma, the grain will become commingled with that of lots of other Okie farmers. No one could pick out which grains were Brown's. Nevertheless, such commingled grain may be legally identifiable: that is, the law may provide a rule that arbitrarily designates a particular part of the mass as the collateral. Such a tracing rule enables the court to tell which grain is *legally* which.

Tracing is most often required when the debtor commingles cash proceeds with other money in a bank account. The secured creditor may be quick on the debtor's heels but fail to arrive until after the debtor has written checks on the account disbursing some of the money to payees from whom it cannot be recovered. The secured creditor, of course, would like to claim that the money remaining in the account is its collateral and, if necessary, that the money paid out was someone else's. Other parties (typically other creditors and the bank in which the funds were deposited) will probably want to make the opposite claim: The secured creditor's collateral was used to make payments and the money remaining in the account is theirs. U.C.C. §9-315(b) provides that the secured party can prevail by identifying the funds remaining in the bank account as its collateral by "a method of tracing, including application of equitable principles" that is permitted under non-U.C.C. law with respect to the type of collateral. Comment 3 to that section refers to the "equitable principle" most commonly employed: the *lowest intermediate balance rule*. That rule provides that the amount of the secured creditor's collateral remaining in a bank account is equal to the lowest balance of all funds in the account between the time the collateral was deposited to the account and the time the rule is applied.

To return to an earlier example, assume that Arthur Dent sells his encumbered Ford Prefect for $12,000 and deposits the proceeds in his bank account, which already contains $3,000. At the end of the month, Arthur's bank statement reveals the following transactions:

Description	Deposits	Withdrawals	Balance
Opening balance			$ 3,000
Sale of Ford Prefect	$12,000		15,000
Tuition payment		$11,000	4,000
Student loan	6,000		10,000
Books		5,000	5,000

The amount of identifiable proceeds remaining in the account at the end of this sequence is the lowest intermediate balance between the deposit of $12,000 and the present balance of $5,000. The correct number? The $4,000 balance remaining after the tuition payment.

What about money emerging from the bank account? U.C.C. §9-332(b) provides that "a transferee of funds from a deposit account takes the funds free of a security interest in the deposit account unless the transferee acts in collusion with the debtor in violating the rights of the secured party." Even though the cash proceeds that the debtor transfers from the bank account are free of the security interest, anything the debtor purchased with that cash may nevertheless still be proceeds. Recall the example in which Jack sold the cow that served as collateral for $2,000, and used the $2,000 to buy beans. Provided the seller of the beans did not know that the cash it received was encumbered, ZBank could not recover the cash from the seller. But the beans are collateral as proceeds of the cash.

One limit on the ability of the security interest to follow the value of its collateral is that the secured creditor must be able to trace that value with specificity. The following case illustrates.

In re Oriental Rug Warehouse Club, Inc.

205 Bankr. 407 (Bankr. D. Minn. 1997)

NANCY C. DREHER, UNITED STATES BANKRUPTCY JUDGE.

1. The Debtor is a Minnesota corporation engaged in the business of selling oriental rugs and carpets at retail. On April 29, 1993, the Debtor and Yashar entered into a "consignment agreement," whereby Debtor took possession of several of Yashar's rugs for the purpose of reselling them in its business. Debtor agreed to pay Yashar a total consignment price of $106,073.00 for the rugs, and agreed to apply the proceeds received from resale to the outstanding amount owed to Yashar.

2. On May 7, 1993, Yashar filed a UCC-1 financing statement with the Secretary of State for the state of Minnesota to perfect its interest in the consigned rugs possessed by the Debtor.

3. Debtor sold a portion of the consigned rugs but failed to remit the proceeds from the sales to Yashar as provided by their agreement. Instead, the Debtor

invested the proceeds from the sale of Yashar's rugs into the purchase of replacement rug inventory or otherwise retained the proceeds. On or around May of 1995, the brother of the president of Yashar went to the Debtor's place of business and repossessed all of the consigned rugs which were still in the Debtor's possession and which had not yet been sold. Although the Debtor currently has rugs in its inventory, the Debtor no longer possesses rugs that were supplied by Yashar.

4. On April 15, 1996, Debtor filed a petition for relief under Chapter 11 of the United States Bankruptcy Code. On August 20, 1996, Yashar filed a proof of secured claim in the amount of $64,243.00, representing the outstanding amount still owed to Yashar for the rugs which had been sold by the Debtor without remitting the proceeds. Pursuant to 11 U.S.C. §502, the Debtor has objected to Yashar's secured claim.

CONCLUSIONS OF LAW

In this case, the objective characteristics of the agreement between the Debtor and Yashar indicate that the parties did not intend to create a true consignment, but instead intended to grant Yashar a security interest in the consigned rugs. . . . Therefore, instead of creating a true consignment relationship whereby the consignee acts as agent to sell the property of the consignor, the parties to the present case created a standard "floor plan" arrangement whereby Yashar agreed to finance the Debtor's inventory in exchange for a security interest in the consigned rugs. As a secured financing arrangement, therefore, the transaction between the Debtor and Yashar is governed by the provisions of Article 9 of the UCC.

II.   SECURITY INTERESTS IN PROCEEDS UNDER [U.C.C. §9-315(A)]

Although the originally consigned rugs no longer remain in the Debtor's possession, Yashar argues that the Debtor's current inventory constitutes "proceeds" from the Debtor's sale of the consigned rugs, and that Yashar is therefore entitled to a security interest in the Debtor's remaining inventory. Section [9-315] of the Uniform Commercial Code governs the continuation and perfection of a security interest in proceeds. Therefore, before addressing the merits of the arguments of counsel, it is appropriate to address the provisions of [§9-315] in some detail.

A.   Continuation of a Security Interest in Proceeds: §9-315(a)

Section [9-102(a)(64)] of the UCC defines the term "proceeds" to include "whatever is received upon the sale, exchange, collection or other disposition of collateral or proceeds." [U.C.C. §9-102(a)(64)]. Section [9-315(a)], in turn, provides that, upon the sale of collateral, a security interest in that collateral "continues in any *identifiable proceeds* including collections received by the debtor." [U.C.C. §9-315(a)] (emphasis added). The secured party has the burden of establishing that something constitutes identifiable proceeds from the sale or disposition of the secured party's collateral. To do this, the secured party must "trace" the claimed proceeds back to the original collateral; in other words, the secured party must establish that the alleged proceeds "arose directly from the sale or other disposition of the collateral and that these alleged proceeds cannot have arisen from any other source." [C.O. Funk & Son v. Sullivan Equipment], 415 N.E.2d at 1313.

Special tracing problems arise where cash proceeds are commingled with other deposits in a single bank account. Because of the fungible nature of cash proceeds, there is some authority that cash proceeds are no longer identifiable once they are commingled with other funds. The majority of courts, however, have utilized equitable principles borrowed from the law of trusts to identify whether commingled funds constitute proceeds received from an earlier disposition of collateral. In particular, these courts have utilized the "intermediate balance rule," which creates a presumption that the proceeds of the disposition of collateral remain in a commingled account as long as the account balance is equal to or exceeds the amounts of the proceeds. Therefore, the intermediate balance rule presumes that a debtor who spends money from a commingled account spends first from his own funds. Once the balance of the commingled account drops below the amount of the deposited proceeds, then the secured creditor's interest in the proceeds abates accordingly. . . .

III. YASHAR'S CLAIM

In this case, Yashar alleges that the Debtor sold its collateral in exchange for cash proceeds, deposited the cash proceeds into the Debtor's general checking account, and then reinvested the cash proceeds to buy more rug inventory. Therefore, to succeed in its claim under the UCC, Yashar must show that: 1) the Debtor's current assets constitute "identifiable proceeds" arising from the disposition of its original collateral under [§9-315(a)]; and 2) the proceeds were properly perfected under [§§9-315(c) and(d)]. Yashar has not argued that it can trace the Debtor's current rug inventory to the sale of its collateral, however. In fact, Yashar has conceded that "it is impossible to reconstruct exactly what the Debtor did with the proceeds of the sale of Yashar's consigned inventory." Instead, Yashar argues that, although a secured creditor claiming an interest in proceeds has the burden of tracing proceeds when it litigates against other secured creditors, a secured creditor should not bear the burden of tracing when it litigates against the debtor. In suits between a debtor and a secured creditor, Yashar asserts, it is unfair to place the burden of tracing proceeds on the secured creditor, who has no ability to control the debtor's books and record keeping procedures.

Yashar's argument simply has no support in either the case law or in the UCC. Although Yashar may think it unfair to place the burden of tracing proceeds squarely on the shoulders of the party claiming the security interest, both the case law and the leading commentaries are clear in this regard. Where a creditor wishes to claim a security interest in proceeds under [§9-315], the burden is on the party claiming the security interest to identify the proceeds. . . . In this situation, Yashar should have protected itself by carefully monitoring the Debtor's inventory and by requiring the Debtor to maintain segregated accounts for the deposit of proceeds. The Court declines to disregard the clear provisions of the UCC and holds that Yashar's argument is without merit. . . .

Accordingly, and for the reasons stated, it is hereby ordered that the secured claim of Yashar Rug Co., Inc. is disallowed in its entirety. Yashar has an unsecured, nonpriority claim in the amount of $64,243.00.

B. Other Value-Tracing Concepts

As we noted in our discussion of the U.C.C. §9-102(a)(64) definition of "proceeds," that term may not encompass all of the states the value of a secured creditor's collateral can assume. A secured party who wants to contract as nearly as possible for the value of its collateral, in whatever form it may take, will want to employ some additional value-tracing concepts.

The *product* of collateral is something the collateral produces. The term is most commonly used in the context of agriculture. It has been held that wool is the product of sheep, milk the product of cows (although, as you will see in the next assignment, not everyone agrees), and maple syrup the product of trees. These "products" may also be "proceeds" of the collateral named because they "aris[e] out of collateral," U.C.C. §9-102(a)(64), but that is unclear.

Another value the secured creditor may take as collateral is the *profit* from other collateral. "Profit" is another term of art, but with more than one meaning. In a general sense, the word can be used to describe the excess of revenues of a business over the expenses where the business itself is the collateral. In the context of real property, "profit" may be short for *profit a prendre*: "a right exercised by one man in the soil of another, accompanied with participation in the profits of the soil thereof. A right to take a part of the soil or produce of the land. A right to take from the soil, such as by logging, mining, drilling, etc. The taking (profit) is the distinguishing characteristic from an easement." Black's Law Dictionary 1211 (6th ed. 1990). Note that even if U.C.C. §9-315 applied to real estate, a "profit" might not be "proceeds." The former is a right to remove; the latter typically is a thing received in exchange.

Two other value-tracing concepts are worthy of mention. *Rents* are money paid for the temporary use of collateral. The offspring of collateral is a term most often used with regard to animals. A calf is the offspring of a cow, although it may also be considered the product of a cow.

The concept described by each of these terms is to some degree a value-tracing concept, in that the value of the collateral and the value of the product, profit, rent, or offspring are the same value. For example, if the owner of property rents it, the value of the owner's remaining interest in the property will be approximately the value it had before it was rented, less the value of the rent to be paid. A portion of the value of a breeding animal is the offspring it is expected to produce. By including the rents or offspring as collateral, the secured creditor is, to some degree, not adding to the value of the collateral but merely anticipating a transformation of existing value.

Products, profits, rents, and offspring of collateral are all arguably "rights arising out of collateral." Thus they are arguably all proceeds. Assuming they are, adding these terms to a description of collateral in a security agreement adds nothing, at least according to Article 9. Even if a description of collateral does not mention proceeds, their inclusion is implied. See U.C.C. §9-203(f). But, as we shall see in the next assignment, bankruptcy law arguably employs a narrower definition of "proceeds" that leaves room for the concepts of products, profits, rents, and offspring to operate.

C. Non-Value-Tracing Concepts

Concepts such as "after-acquired property," "replacements," "additions," and "substitutions" in a description of collateral are non-value-tracing in that they can pick up property acquired by the debtor with value not derived from the previously existing collateral. The value in proceeds, product, offspring, rents, or profits arguably comes in whole or in part from previously existing collateral. The value in after-acquired property, replacements, additions, and substitutions can come entirely from some other source, such as unencumbered property of the debtor, a new loan, or a capital contribution by the debtors' owners.

To illustrate the difference between value-tracing concepts and non-value-tracing concepts, assume that Billie's Toy Shop has $100,000 worth of display equipment and that ZBank has a security interest in its "equipment, including after-acquired equipment." Billie's Toy Shop spends $6,000 to buy additional display cases. To know that ZBank's after-acquired property clause will reach the additional cases, we need only know that the cases are equipment and that Billie's owns them. We do not need to know the source of the $6,000.

Now assume instead that ZBank's security interest was in "equipment, not including after-acquired equipment, but including the proceeds of equipment." If Billie's spends $6,000 to buy the additional display cases, we can know if ZBank's security interest attaches to it only by knowing the source of the $6,000. If Billie's obtained the $6,000 by selling equipment that was already collateral, the $6,000 was proceeds, and the new equipment will be proceeds. If the $6,000 was neither collateral nor the proceeds of collateral, the new equipment will not be collateral either.

In the illustration where the $6,000 did not come from existing collateral, application of the after-acquired property clause increased the total value of ZBank's collateral. ZBank had $100,000 of collateral before the purchase and $106,000 afterward. In the illustration where the $6,000 did come from existing collateral, application of the proceeds doctrine did not change the total value of ZBank's collateral. ZBank had $100,000 of collateral in the debtor's possession before the purchase and $100,000 afterward.

The distinction between after-acquired property and proceeds is a fine one. In practice, the security agreement usually provides that the collateral includes both. In such cases, it may not matter which is being applied and it may be unnecessary to distinguish between the two.

Problem Set 52

52.1. Firstbank has a perfected security interest in all of the "equipment, inventory, and accounts" of Polly Arthur, who is doing business as Polly's Plumbing. The contract makes no mention of proceeds, products, offspring, substitutions, additions, or replacements. Are they included? U.C.C. §§9-102(a)(64), 9-201(a), 9-203(f), 9-204(a).

52.2.   Which of the following are collateral of Firstbank under the security agreement described in Problem 52.1 and why? U.C.C. §§9-102(a)(2) and (64), 9-315(a).

a.   The money now in Polly's bank account.

b.   A parrot that Polly took in payment of an overdue account.

c.   A new computer that Polly bought to replace the computer she owned at the time she granted the security interest to Firstbank.

d.   A Myna bird that Polly took from Robin Watts in payment for some plumbing work (Watts didn't have the money to pay for the plumbing work and arranged in advance to trade the bird for the work; Polly did the plumbing while Watts was at her own job; Watts gave Polly the Myna bird the following day and Polly kept it as a pet).

52.3.   A few months ago, Equipment Leasing Partners (ELP) financed the Lucky Partners Syndicate's acquisition of a thoroughbred race horse named Horace. ELP took a security interest in Horace and "all proceeds, products, and profits therefrom." Lucky Partners defaulted on the $750,000 loan. ELP repossessed Horace and sold him for $275,000. Shortly before the repossession, Horace won $50,000 in a race. Lucky Partners has demanded the purse, but the track has not yet paid it. ELP asks you whether they have a valid claim to the purse. What do you tell them? U.C.C. §9-102(a)(64).

52.4.   Joey Teigh contracted to buy Billie's Toy Shop, including the leasehold, furniture, fixtures, equipment, goodwill, accounts receivable, and trademarks. Joey hired you to represent her in the closing. In preparing for the closing, you learned that Joey and Billie omitted the inventory from the sale because Firstbank had a security interest in it. You've looked at Firstbank's security agreement and the description of collateral is just "inventory." Is it possible that the security interest encumbers some of the accounts receivable? The other property Joey is buying? (For now, don't worry about whether the security interest could be perfected; confine your inquiry to whether it could attach.)

52.5.   a. ELP consults you about a $35,000 loan to Golan Industries that was made for the express purpose of purchasing an XT-100 copier. Golan signed a security agreement granting ELP a security interest in the copier. (The entire description of collateral reads "XT-100 copier, serial number XEX3088372.") The copier was destroyed in a fire six months ago. Fortunately, the loss was insured. At this point, what is ELP's collateral? U.C.C. §§9-102(a)(12)(A) and (64), 9-203(f).

b.   Unfortunately, ELP was not named as a loss payee on the policy, so the insurance company paid the $35,000 in insurance proceeds to Golan. Golan deposited the check to a little-used bank account that contained $5,000 at the time. At this point, what is ELP's collateral?

c.   From the account Golan wrote a check for $2,000 to rent another copier for the month it would take to replace the XT-100, leaving $38,000 in the account. At this point, what is ELP's collateral?

d.   Golan then wrote a check from the account for $32,000 to pay the IRS, leaving only $6,000 in the account. At this point, what is ELP's collateral? U.C.C. §§9-315, 9-332.

52.6.   Your investigation of the Golan account indicates that the $32,000 check that cleared the account was not to the IRS. Golan used the $32,000 to buy another XT-100 to replace the one that had been destroyed. (It seems the price of XT-100s had fallen a bit since the initial purchase.) The new XT-100 was delivered immediately and the debtor is operating it now. If this new information is correct, what is ELP's collateral?

Assignment 53: Tracing Collateral Value During Bankruptcy

Transformations of a debtor's property can continue to occur after the debtor is in bankruptcy. If the debtor or a trustee operates the business, inventory may be sold, accounts may be collected, and cows may produce calves or milk. These changes may result in increases or decreases in the categories of property originally described as collateral in the security agreement. In addition, the bankruptcy court may authorize the consumption of a secured creditor's collateral during bankruptcy, but, generally speaking, only if equal value is substituted for it.

A. Distinguishing Proceeds from After-Acquired Property

Article 9 permits a secured creditor to trace the value of its collateral through concepts such as proceeds or products and also to pick up additional collateral by means of an after-acquired property clause. It often makes no difference whether a creditor obtained its security interest in property acquired after the security agreement as proceeds or by operation of an after-acquired property clause, so long as it is clear that at least one of the concepts would cover the property in question.

Once the debtor files for bankruptcy, however, the distinction becomes critical. Bankruptcy Code §552 permits the secured creditor to trace the value of its collateral, but the rules on picking up additional collateral are narrower than those under Article 9 in two respects. First, once the debtor is in bankruptcy, the secured creditor can no longer pick up additional collateral by means of an after-acquired property clause. Bankr. Code §552(a). Second, Bankruptcy Code §552(b) limits value-tracing to five concepts: proceeds, product, offspring, rents, or profits.

The result is that the secured creditor generally can keep what collateral value it has as of the filing of the bankruptcy case, even if that collateral value is transformed, but cannot acquire additional collateral value during bankruptcy. The policy rationale is in keeping with general bankruptcy policies regarding the protection of secured creditors. Once bankruptcy stays creditors from exercising their state remedies, it must safeguard their entitlements. Bankruptcy law prohibits the debtor or trustee from favoring one creditor over another in its postpetition dealings. For example, the debtor cannot use property of the estate to pay one prepetition unsecured claim without paying other claims of the same kind pro rata. To permit an after-acquired property clause to operate postpetition would violate this basic principle of bankruptcy.

Consider this example. Tonia Wellfoot operates Wellfoot Electrical Service. She owes Sunshine Bank $10,000 on a loan giving the Bank a security interest in "all of Wellfoot Electrical's equipment, current and after acquired." At the time of the filing, the business owns only some power tools valued at $7,000. While she is in bankruptcy, Tonia has the opportunity to trade her collection of power tools for a compressor and several fittings that will permit her to do her work more easily. She makes the trade, and Sunshine's security interest attaches to the new tools as proceeds. U.C.C. §9-315(a); Bankr. Code §552(b). A little later, Tonia decides to use some of her income from the business to buy a computer system worth $3,000 to handle the billing and paperwork. In the absence of bankruptcy, Article 9 would have permitted the security interest to extend to the newly acquired computer, but bankruptcy law does not. Bankr. Code §552(a). Because Tonia is in bankruptcy, all her unencumbered assets, including the business's income, are property of the estate, equally available to all her creditors even though none of them can reach the assets while the automatic stay remains in place.

In effect, Bankruptcy Code §552 permits a secured creditor to trace collateral value from one form to another, but does not permit the secured creditor to enhance its position by claiming assets that would have been available equally to all the creditors. Without the security interest, Sunshine Bank had an allowed secured claim for $7,000 and an unsecured claim for $3,000. Assuming that Tonia's trade was for equal dollar value, Sunshine still had only a $7,000 secured claim afterward. The same is not true of the computer purchase. If Sunshine's security interest could attach to the computer, Sunshine's allowed secured claim would grow to $10,000, and Sunshine would receive payment in full on the underlying loan. The other unsecured creditors would get nothing in return for the $3,000 spent to enhance Sunshine's collateral.

To repeat: To permit debtors to use unencumbered property of the estate to buy property that would then be collateral for preexisting debts would enable debtors to apply the unencumbered values of their estates for the benefit of particular secured creditors and to thereby deprive their unsecured creditors of their expectancies in those unencumbered values. To prevent such applications, the Bankruptcy Code protects proceeds, products, offspring, rents, and profits for the secured creditors, but does not honor after-acquired property clauses.

In the following case, the court carries the value-tracing concept even further. Interpreting a provision in Bankruptcy Code §552 that permits orders based on the "equities of the case," the court holds that the equities require a tracing not in broad legal concepts, but with whatever mathematical precision can be brought to bear in the circumstances.

In re Delbridge

61 B.R. 484 (Bankr. E.D. Mich. 1986)

ARTHUR J. SPECTOR, U.S. BANKRUPTCY JUDGE

Question: Is the cup half full or half empty? Answer: yes.

The debtor in possession in this dairy farm Chapter 11 case strenuously argues that milk is not the product of a cow. Since about half of the published court opinions dealing with this logically preposterous proposition have adopted it, it must be conceded that the argument passes the straight-face test.[1] Of course, when this question is put to a lay-person, that is, someone not blinded or befuddled by excessive legal training, the response is blunt and distinctly to the contrary.

What has the learned folk so confounded — has, so to speak, caused them to throw up their hands in "udder" frustration — is the application of a federal statute to a common fact of economic life down on the dairy farm. Most dairy farmers who find their unfortunate way into the bankruptcy court come encumbered by liens on all bovine animals, their proceeds and their products (which, I suspect, even they would have conceded — until their first meeting with their bankruptcy lawyer — includes milk). . . .

[Production Credit Association of Mid-Michigan (P.C.A.)] is conceded to have a perfected prepetition lien on the debtor's cows and their milk. The debtor argues, however, that §552(a) limits that lien to the milk in being at the time the bankruptcy was filed, citing [five bankruptcy court cases]. P.C.A. counters by citing [five bankruptcy court cases] which hold to the contrary.

Since none of the relevant terms in §552(b) are defined in the Bankruptcy Code, reference should be made to state law or at least to a legal dictionary. In fact, §552(b) explicitly requires the court to look to "applicable non-bankruptcy law." Clearly, milk produced postpetition is neither a "rent," a "profit" nor an "offspring"[2] of cow or of milk in being prepetition. U.C.C. [§9-102(a)(64)] states: "'Proceeds' includes whatever is received upon the sale, exchange, collection or other disposition of collateral or proceeds." A "proceed" of milk or of a cow, is the cash or the account one receives after its disposition by sale or otherwise. The issue is thus whether milk which comes into existence postpetition is a "product" of a cow.

Most courts that have held that milk is indeed a product of a cow actually felt compelled to seek legal support for the proposition . . . and found it in U.C.C. §9-102(a)(34)(D), which defines farm products to include "products of livestock in their unmanufactured states (such as . . . milk)." Moreover, [Official Comment 4.a. to U.C.C. §9-102] states that:

> Products of crops or livestock, even though they remain in the possession of a person engaged in farming operation, lose their status as farm products if they are subjected to a manufacturing process. What is and what is not a manufacturing operation is not determined by this Article. At one end of the scale, some processes are so closely connected with farming — such as pasteurizing milk or boiling sap to produce maple syrup or maple sugar — that they would not rank as manufacturing. On the other hand an extensive canning operation would be manufacturing. The line is one for the courts to draw. After farm products have been subjected to a manufacturing operation, they become inventory if held for sale.

From this it is clear that the drafters intended that milk not lose its status as a farm product at least through delivery of the raw milk to the dairy, as is the case here. As Michigan has adopted that section of the UCC, one can confidently pronounce that, at least under Michigan law, milk is a farm product.

Some courts have taken the position that notwithstanding the UCC definition of farm products, something is a product of collateral "for purposes of §552(b)" only when the collateral is necessarily consumed or has its existence essentially and irrevocably altered during the manufacturing process. Thus they held that since a cow is neither consumed nor materially altered during the milking process, the milk is not a product. Some debtors take this hypothesis to its logical conclusion. In essence, this theory holds that a cow is a milk machine: the farmer puts feed in one end, waits awhile, and milk comes out the other. This process is no different, they argue, from the concept of work-in-process in fabricating plants. There, the lender typically has a security interest in equipment and inventory which consists of both raw material, such as steel, and work-in-process. If the debtor obtains new steel postpetition and shapes it into a product by use of its machinery, the lender's prepetition lien on this new work-in-process is cut off by §552(a) and not saved by §552(b). In the case of a dairy farmer, the feed is the steel and the cow is the machinery. They argue that milk is the product not of a cow — but of a farmer. Though this is an ingenious argument, it is its very genius which is its fatal flaw.

Courts ought not to use sophistry to turn what appears plain on its face into a conundrum. The argument that milk is a farm product for purposes of the UCC but is not a product for purposes of §552(b) is reminiscent of Humpty Dumpty's statement to Alice: "When [I] use a word . . . it means just what I choose it to mean — neither more nor less." L. Carroll, Through the Looking Glass, Chapter 6 (1872). "Definitions should not be too artificial. For example — 'dog' includes a cat is asking too much of the reader; 'animal' means a dog or a cat would be better." Memorandum on Drafting of Acts of Parliament and Subordinate Legislation (1951), Department of Justice, Ottawa, Canada, quoted in Ritchie, Alice Through the Statutes, 21 McGill L.J. 685 (1975). A common sense reading of the plain word "product" is all that ought to be necessary when applying a statute that simply is not ambiguous. Any ambiguity found by others is created only by going outside the statutory language for a peek at legislative history. But "[w]hen confronted with a statute which is plain and unambiguous on its face, we ordinarily do not look to legislative history as a guide to its meaning." Tennessee Valley Authority v. Hill, 437 U.S. 153, 184 n.29 (1978). The flaw in this theory, then, is that there is no need to consider the "purposes" of §552(b): courts need only read it and apply it.

I surmise that the real reason certain courts agonized over the meaning of this section is that they didn't like the result that would have occurred had they played the music the way it read. In their view, if the postpetition milk were indeed encumbered by the lender's prepetition lien, the farmer would be considerably less likely to successfully reorganize. However, policy-based decision making, if defensible at all, is even less so where it is unnecessary. In this context, policy ought to be irrelevant, since §552(b) itself contains ample room for the exercise of policy-anchored discretion.

Just as the answer to the question of whether the cup is half empty or half full is yes, the question of whether milk is produced by the cow or the farmer is yes. Neither is wrong. The cow can't make milk without being fed, cared for and milked. The farmer alone can't turn feed into milk any more than he can spin straw into gold. What any school child can see is that you need all of the above to produce milk for sale. That is not reason to say that milk is not a product of the cow; it's simply a reason to apply the "equities of the case" language found in §552(b). While I share the concern expressed by those courts which felt that it is unfair to let the creditor with a prepetition lien on milk walk away with the entire cash proceeds of milk produced largely as a result of the farmer's postpetition time, labor, and inputs, §552(b) allows the court leeway to fashion an appropriate equitable remedy, without the need to mangle the English language or cause judicial decision-making to become the object of derisive laughter. Indeed, legislative history is emphatic on this point:

> The provision allows the court to consider the equities in each case. In the course of such consideration the court may evaluate any expenditures by the estate relating to proceeds and any related improvement in position of the secured party. Although this section grants a secured party a security interest in proceeds, products, offspring, rents, or profits, the section is explicitly subject to other sections of title 11. For example, the trustee or debtor in possession may use, sell, or lease proceeds, products, offspring, rents, or profits under section 363.

124 Cong. Rec. H11,097-98 (daily ed. Sept. 28, 1978); S17,414 (daily ed. Oct. 6, 1978).

Although it has been stated, and I agree, that courts should not establish a hard and fast rule or formula when exercising their equitable powers under §552(b) it is often helpful if an easy-to-state and easy-to-apply rule can be formulated. The concepts of equity and mathematics are not necessarily mutually exclusive.... [A] rule based on sound economics is more desirable than one founded on nothing more than the judge's own policy predilections. With all due humility, I hereby announce what I hope is such a rule for application in this case and others like it.

"The purpose behind the 'equities of the case' rule of 11 U.S.C. §552(b) is, in a proper case, to enable those who contribute to the production of proceeds during Chapter 11 to share jointly with prepetition creditors secured by proceeds." In re Crouch, 51 B.R. 331, 332 (Bankr. D. Ore. 1985). Since it is established that the farmer's labor, postpetition raw materials and the cow are all integral components of a commercial dairy farming operation, the owners of those commodities, are, in essence, joint venturers in the process of the commercial production and sale of milk. The mathematical equation which follows is intended to yield an equitable division of the products of that joint venture. The formula is as follows:

$$CC = \frac{D}{D+E+L} \times P$$

where: CC = "cash collateral," i.e.: the amount of the milk check which is encumbered by the lender's lien;

D = the average depreciation of the capital, i.e.: the cow;

E = the farmer's average direct expenses such as for feed, supplement, and veterinary services;

L = the average market value of the farmer's or his employees' labor (excluding labor in the production of feed); and

P = the average dollar proceeds of the milk sold.

The rule is easy to state. The lender is entitled to the same percentage of the proceeds of the postpetition milk as its capital contribution to the production of the milk bears to the total of the capital and direct operating expenses incurred in producing the milk. Because the parties are in a direct mathematical relationship, the rule should be easy to apply. Very simply, the larger is the lender's capital contribution to the venture, the larger its share of the proceeds ought to be. Conversely, if the farmer's input in the venture is great, the "equities of the case" compel that his share of the proceeds likewise be great.

Delbridge is an example of value-tracing made painfully explicit. Not all courts conduct their value-tracing so explicitly. In the following case, the court sets out a different formula for taking account of the debtor's and the secured creditor's respective contributions to postpetition revenues: First, the debtor is reimbursed for expenditures made to generate the postpetition revenue and whatever remains is collateral.

To understand the case, you must know a little history. Prior to the 1994 Amendments to the Bankruptcy Code referred to in the case, several courts had reached the somewhat surprising conclusion that the bill paid by customers of a hotel when they checked out was an "account" arising out of a sale of services, rather than "rent" for the use of a hotel room. These courts reasoned that (1) most of what the customer got was in fact services, such as check-in, check-out, room cleaning, bell-hop, food, telephone, ice-making, etc., and (2) rather than attempting to allocate the payment between services (earned by the debtor's expenditures of postpetition dollars) and rent (earned by use of the secured creditor's collateral), the courts should treat it as entirely what it was mostly: a payment for postpetition services. As such, it was not the proceeds of the secured creditor's collateral. Bankruptcy Code §552(a) prevented the secured creditor from claiming the postpetition revenues under the after-acquired property provision in its security agreement, leaving the revenues unencumbered.

Why this tortured reasoning? If secured creditors had been able to enforce their claims that postpetition revenues were proceeds and therefore cash collateral, debtors attempting reorganization would have been able to use them only by providing adequate protection. But where would debtors get the resources to provide adequate protection against loss of the revenues if all their revenues were collateral the moment they generated them? Had the secured creditors prevailed in their claims, bankruptcy reorganizations would have been impossible — not just in the hotel industry, but in other industries as well. Without the reorganizations that provide half the business of the bankruptcy courts, the jobs of the bankruptcy judges would have been in jeopardy. Hence the decisions. (The courts that made these decisions seemed not to notice their authority under §552(b) to except postpetition revenues from the secured creditors' collateral "based on the equities of the case.")

In 1994, Congress responded by amending Bankruptcy Code §552(b) to make clear that a security interest could extend to room revenues. In the following case, the Ninth Circuit casually sidesteps the amendment by interpreting it to mean only the *net* room revenues, after allowing the debtor to pay the expenses necessary to stay in business and complete the reorganization.

In re Hotel Sierra Vista Limited Partnership

112 F.3d 429 (9th Cir. 1997)

BEEZER, CIRCUIT JUDGE:

Hotel Sierra Vista Limited Partnership (HSVLP) built a 151-room hotel in Sierra Vista, Arizona, that opened for business in 1986 as a Ramada Inn franchise. Additional hotel facilities include a lounge, a restaurant, a ballroom, banquet rooms and meeting rooms.

HSVLP financed the hotel's construction by borrowing a total of $6,196,000 in two secured loans from [Chequers, a Texas-based investment group]. HSVLP defaulted on its loans in 1990. Chequers demanded payment in full from HSVLP and commenced foreclosure proceedings. HSVLP sought Chapter 11 protection in June 1993.

In August 1993, Chequers moved to sequester the hotel's post-petition room revenues. Chequers maintained that these revenues were "cash collateral" within the meaning of 11 U.S.C. §363(a). The bankruptcy court heard Chequers's motion in September 1993, but explicitly deferred deciding whether the room revenues were cash collateral. The court ordered HSVLP to sequester the room revenues and meet its operating expenses from those funds.

At the time of its initial filing, HSVLP's principal assets were the hotel itself, whose value the parties estimated and stipulated to be $2,200,000, together with $625,844 evidencing accumulated pre-petition revenues. Between the time HSVLP filed its petition and the December 1994 plan confirmation, the hotel received an additional $812,425 in net revenues.

The bankruptcy court confirmed the plan over Chequers's objections by using the "cramdown" alternative of 11 U.S.C. §1129(b). In its order confirming the plan, the bankruptcy court concluded that the post-petition room revenues were cash collateral. The bankruptcy court nevertheless denied Chequers a secured interest in the post-petition hotel revenues. The bankruptcy court determined that Chequers had not met the burden of proving the "extent" of its interest as required by 11 U.S.C. §363(o)(2).

III

Sometimes yesterday's confusion resolves itself into today's easily-applied rule of law. Between the June 1994 confirmation hearing and the bankruptcy court's December 1994 order, Congress amended the statutory definition of cash collateral to clarify that the term "rents" included hotel room revenues. On this basis, the bankruptcy court concluded that the hotel's post-petition room revenues were cash collateral. This development places us in an unusual position, however, one where we must assess the actions undertaken by the parties and the bankruptcy court in this case in light of yesterday's confusion.

After its Chapter 11 filing and through the time of the bankruptcy court's order confirming its plan, HSVLP deposited all revenues received from the hotel, including those attributable to room occupancy, in a single money market account. Chequers contends that HSVLP's trustee violated 11 U.S.C. §363(c)(4) by so doing. That section provides that "...the trustee shall segregate and account for any cash collateral in the trustee's possession, custody, or control." 11 U.S.C. §363(c)(4).

IV

A party seeking to prove the "extent" of its interest under §363(p)(2) must do two things. First, as a preliminary matter, the party must prove that it holds a perfected security interest in post-petition revenues to which its liens still rightly attach. See Financial Security Assurance, Inc. v. Days California Limited Partnership, 27 F.3d 374, 377 (9th Cir. 1994) ("Days California"). Second, a party must prove the amount of money to which its liens attach. See 11 U.S.C. §363(o)(2). Our decision in *Days California* provides the formula for determining the amount of revenues to which liens may survive post-petition. In *Days California* we stated that

> Hotel methods of accounting will permit the identification of the revenues generated by the rooms and those generated by services. Determination of the net revenues will require allocation of direct and indirect expenses in proportion to each category of revenue.

Id. at 377. Thus, proving the extent of one's interest involves submitting evidence that enables the bankruptcy court to determine the sum to which the party asserting the security interest is entitled. See id.

Documentary evidence introduced at the confirmation hearing with respect to the extent of Chequers's post-petition security interest included both a copy of a valid security instrument and accounting statements reflecting post-petition gross room revenues. Because of the unusual timing of events in this case, neither the parties nor the bankruptcy court attempted to apply the *Days California* formula to the hotel's revenues and expenses. Equity requires that the court and the parties have the opportunity to allocate direct and indirect expenses to each category of revenues listed on the trustee's reports. This will result in a net diminution of gross room revenues to which Chequers's liens attach after petition, but will be consistent with effectuating the burden structure of 11 U.S.C. §363(p)(2) and our decision in *Days California*.

V

Days California requires Chequers to prove the exact amount of its interest in HSVLP's post-petition room revenues through application of the *Days California* formula. A new hearing in this case shall be conducted to apply that formula. We remand this case to the district court for proceedings consistent with this opinion.
Reversed and remanded.

If property is "proceeds" under Article 9 definition of that term, does that mean it is "proceeds" within the meaning of Bankruptcy Code §552(b)? The question is important because §9-102(a)(64)(C) arguably makes a dramatic expansion of the concept from what it was when Congress enacted Bankruptcy Code §552. In Financial Security Assurance, Inc. v. Tollman-Hundley Dalton, L.P., 74 F.3d 1120 (11th Cir. 1996), the court answered the question in the negative, noting that a positive answer would give state lawmakers control of the meaning of a word used in a federal statute:

> Contrary to the district court's determination, nothing in [the Supreme Court's opinion in] *Butner* suggests that state [law] defines the language of the federal Bankruptcy Code in general, or of §552 in particular. Neither does §552 dictate such a result. Section 552(b) provides that a prepetition security interest in derivative property may extend to post petition derivative property "to the extent provided by [the] security agreement and by applicable nonbankruptcy law." This reference to "nonbankruptcy law," or state law, is consistent with *Butner*: it prevents a creditor from using a debtor's bankruptcy to acquire rights to which he would not otherwise be entitled under state law. The reference to "nonbankruptcy law" does not suggest that state law defines the language of §552.
>
>   Thus, we hold that the district court erred in looking to Georgia law to define the language of §552, specifically, to define the term "rents" as used in §552(b). To construe this term, we look to the plain meaning of the statute.

The court noted that two other Circuits, the Fifth and the Ninth, had held to the contrary, but declined to follow them. The issue will almost certainly make its way to the Supreme Court.

Assuming that the Eleventh Circuit view prevails, what is the definition of "proceeds" as used in Bankruptcy Code §552? Probably most believe that, with regard to personal property, it is the definition of "proceeds" contained in the Official Text of Article 9 when the Bankruptcy Code was adopted in 1978:

> U.C.C. §9-306(1) (1978). Proceeds includes whatever is received upon the sale, exchange, collection or other disposition of collateral or proceeds. Insurance payable by reason of loss or damage to the collateral is proceeds, except to the extent that it is payable to a person other than a party to the security agreement.

Thus, four views of the scope of the secured creditor's right to proceeds under Bankruptcy Code §552(b) are plausible. The secured creditor may be entitled to (1) "proceeds" as defined in U.C.C. §9-102(a)(64), (2) "proceeds" as defined under the 1978 Official Text of Article 9, (3) only that portion of proceeds that are collateral under the *Delbridge* test, or (4) only the net proceeds derived from use of the collateral as specified in *Hotel Sierra Vista*.

B.   "Cash Collateral" in Bankruptcy

As you have seen in earlier chapters, the debtor or trustee in a bankruptcy case is generally permitted to use the secured creditor's collateral. Bankr. Code

§§363(c)(1) and (b)(1). Thus, if the secured creditor's collateral is a factory, the bankruptcy estate can operate the factory while it remains in bankruptcy. The debtor or trustee may also use highly liquid collateral, such as the money in a bank account or the rents that are paid by tenants of an apartment building. Such highly liquid collateral is referred to as *cash collateral*. Bankr. Code §363(a).

Regardless of whether collateral is cash collateral, the debtor or trustee who uses it must provide adequate protection to the secured creditor against its loss or decline in value. The debtor's or trustee's use of collateral such as a factory or apartment building ordinarily presents no immediate threat to the interests of the secured creditor. Significant decline in the value of the collateral is likely to occur only over a period of months or years; in the meantime, the secured creditor has access to the bankruptcy court to seek appropriate orders for adequate protection. Bankr. Code §361.

The debtor's or trustee's use of cash collateral presents a more immediate threat to the secured creditor. The typical use of cash collateral will be to pay expenses incurred by the estate during the bankruptcy case. This may be the wages and salaries of employees who operate the business, the utility bills, or the cost of other supplies. Once the cash collateral is used for such purposes, it may be permanently lost to the secured creditor. The typical solution in such a case is for the trustee or debtor to provide adequate protection in the form of a lien on other property of the estate. Often, that lien is against property which, although not "proceeds" under the definition of U.C.C. §9-102(a)(64), will come into existence only as a result of the cash expenditures. For example, when cash collateral is used to pay employees and for utilities and supplies, the ultimate result may be to produce factory inventory for sale. The value of such cash collateral becomes the inventory, but the relationship between the two is not tight enough for the inventory to qualify as proceeds of the cash within the definition in U.C.C. §9-102(a)(64). Because the inventory is not proceeds under U.C.C. §9-102(a)(64), the secured creditor is not entitled to it under Bankruptcy Code §552.

An order of the bankruptcy court permitting the use of cash collateral and granting a lien in the resulting inventory as adequate protection can bridge the gap left by U.C.C. §9-102(a)(64). In the example used here, it assures preservation of the value of the secured creditor's collateral as that value changes form. You should keep in mind, however, that adequate protection orders are not limited by the concept of value-tracing; the court can grant a substitute or replacement lien against property completely unrelated to the collateral the debtor or trustee uses. Recall from Assignment 48 that when Craddock-Terry Shoe Corporation had to provide adequate protection against the declining value of its $700,000 customer list, it did so by granting the creditor a security interest in all of its property, which was valued at $2,000,000.

Because a debtor or trustee can dissipate cash collateral almost instantly by using it, the Bankruptcy Code requires notice to the secured creditor and the opportunity for a hearing *before* the debtor or trustee can use cash collateral. Bankr. Code §363(c)(2). Nearly all assets of most debtors are fully encumbered by the time they file bankruptcy. Any expenditure of funds by such a debtor is an expenditure of cash collateral. It is a rare business that can go more than a few days without paying anyone for anything. Thus, within a few days of the filing of most bankruptcy reorganization cases, the debtor has to obtain an order from the Bankruptcy Court authorizing the use of cash collateral on an emergency basis. It is not unusual for such hearings to be held by telephone, at the homes of judges, during court recesses, or at uncivilized hours of the morning. Such hearings are life-and-death matters for most debtors. If the debtor cannot find a way to provide adequate protection so that it can use its cash collateral, it may also be unable to find a way to stay in business.

Problem Set 53

53.1. On the facts of Problem 52.3, assume that some uncertainty existed as to whether the $50,000 purse was ELP's collateral. Before the matter could be resolved, Lucky Partners filed bankruptcy. Not knowing of the filing, the track paid the purse to Lucky Partners a few days later. The money is now in a trust account, awaiting the court's decision. Is your claim to the purse stronger, weaker, or unchanged? Bankr. Code §552.

53.2. Polly Arthur, from Problem 52.1, filed bankruptcy but continued to run her business. A few days later, she worked for 28 straight hours repairing a dangerous leak at Golan Industries' power plant and billed Golan at $65 an hour for a total of $1,820. When Polly receives that money, will it be subject to Firstbank's security interest? U.C.C. §9-102(a)(64); Bankr. Code §552.

53.3. You are still representing ELP against Golan Industries. After the fire that destroyed the copier in Problem 52.5, but before the insurance company paid the claim, Golan filed for bankruptcy under Chapter 11. (The information ELP gave you earlier to the contrary was wrong.) When Golan got the $35,000 in insurance proceeds, it deposited them in its bank account and wrote the $2,000 and $32,000 checks. Those checks have cleared the bank account, leaving only $6,000 in the account. Today ELP got a call from Golan's attorneys notifying it of an emergency cash collateral hearing to be held later this afternoon. What is ELP's collateral in the bankruptcy case? U.C.C. §§9-315(a) and (b); Bankr. Code §§362(d), 552, 549(a), 363(c)(2) and (e).

53.4. Your client, Globus Real Estate Investment Trust (Globus) holds a security interest against Hotel Sierra Vista. The description of collateral includes the real property, equipment, inventory, and "all income, rents, royalties, revenues, issues, profits, fees, accounts, and other proceeds (including without limitation, room sales and revenues from sales of services, food and drink)." Hotel Sierra Vista filed for bankruptcy on October 14 and on that same day the court entered an order that the hotel segregate and account for any cash collateral in the hotel's possession, but also permitting the hotel to "meet its operating expenses from those funds." The value of all collateral for the loan is substantially less than the amount owing to Globus. In accord with the order, the hotel opened a new bank account, deposited all receipts in it, and paid all expenses from it. The hotel's attorney sent you the following list of revenues and expenses for the first 17 days after bankruptcy. Globus wants to know how much money you think should be segregated as cash collateral under Bankruptcy Code §363(c)(4) and why:

	Type	Amount
Revenues	Room charges	$510,000
	Food and drink	121,000
	Total	631,000
Expenses	Room-related	520,000
	Food and drink	100,000
	Total	620,000
Profit		11,000

Some of the food and drink is served in the bar and restaurant, some of it is served in the room.

a. If the court follows *Hotel Sierra Vista*, what is your answer?

b. If the court follows *Delbridge*, what is your answer? (Assume that the value of the hotel neither increased nor decreased during the 17-day period since the filing of bankruptcy.)

c. If the court applies Bankruptcy Code §552(b)(2) literally to the room revenues and declines to make an exception based on the equities of the case, what is your answer?

53.5.   You also represent Globus in the reorganization of Pine Manor, a 360-unit apartment building that was in foreclosure for more than a year before it filed Chapter 11 yesterday. The apartment building is Pine Manor's only asset, Globus's mortgage is for $900,000, and the apartment building is worth only $700,000. The parties have no reason to believe that value will change during the bankruptcy case. Meredith Johnson, Pine Manor's attorney, filed a motion to use cash collateral along with the petition. The motion seeks use of whatever portion of the rents collected during the Chapter 11 case is necessary to pay the management company that will operate the building during the case and the other postpetition expenses of operation, such as maintenance, repairs, insurance, etc. The hearing is set for 7 A.M. tomorrow morning. Globus's mortgage extends to "rents and proceeds" of the apartment building and clearly was perfected prior to the filing of the petition. The parties expect $10,000 in rents each month. Globus wants you to get aggressive with Pine Manor because "it's our property and we are the ones losing money. Pine Manor doesn't even have an equity." Meredith wants you to sign a consent to the cash collateral order. "Every dime we propose to spend is going to benefit your collateral," she says. "There's no point in going to a 7 A.M. hearing when you don't even have an argument." Bankr. Code §§363(a), (c), and (e), 552(b). Working through the following may help you assess the situation.

a.   What was the amount of Globus's secured claim at the time the petition was filed?

b.   Was Globus entitled to accrue interest on that amount?

c.   Will the $10,000 in rent received in the first month after filing be Globus's collateral?

d.   If the court permits Pine Manor to use that $10,000, to what protection is Globus entitled? How will Pine Manor provide it?

Chapter 16.   Default: The Gateway to Remedies

Assignment 54:   Default, Acceleration, and Cure Under State Law

A.   Default

In the first five assignments of this book, we discussed the remedies available to creditors under state law. Creditors have access to those remedies if, and only if, the debtor is "in default." U.C.C. §9-601(a). Article 9 of the U.C.C. does not define default or make any effort to say when a debtor is in it. Defined most simply, *default* is the debtor's failure to pay the debt when due or otherwise perform the agreement between debtor and creditor.

Secured creditors may need to exercise their remedies as soon as a debtor goes into default. Yet, if they exercise their remedies under state law before the debtor goes into default, they act wrongfully and are liable for any damage they inflict. To clear the way for a speedy exercise of remedies, secured creditors generally prefer that the security agreement define precisely what acts or failures constitute default. Secured creditors also prefer that those acts or failures be expansively defined so that in any circumstance in which they may want remedies, remedies will be available to them.

Debtors typically share the secured creditors' preference for precise definition of the terms of default. Debtors, of course, want default defined narrowly and precisely so they can avoid it. The result is that most security agreements contain extensive definitions of default. As to the substance of the definition, the interests of secured creditors and their debtors are in conflict — it is in precisely those situations where secured creditors want to exercise remedies that debtors want contract protection against them. The conflict usually is resolved in favor of the secured creditor: Security agreements nearly always define default expansively. The reason may be that secured creditors are more concerned than debtors about default and more ready to contemplate it, or it may be that such terms merely reflect the relative bargaining power of the parties.

The default provisions that follow are typical of those included in well-drafted security agreements.

Standard Default Provisions

Howard Ruda, Asset Based Financing,
A Transactional Guide 3-285-86 (1997)

11.   EVENTS OF DEFAULT; ACCELERATION

... The following are events of default under this agreement ... :

(a)   Any of Debtor's obligations to Secured Party under any agreement with Secured Party is not paid promptly when due;

(b) Debtor breaches any warranty or provision hereof, or of any note or of any other instrument or agreement delivered by Debtor to Secured Party in connection with this or any other transaction;

(c) Debtor dies, becomes insolvent or ceases to do business as a going concern;

(d) it is determined that Debtor has given Secured Party materially misleading information regarding its financial condition;

(e) any of the collateral is lost or destroyed;

(f) a petition in bankruptcy or for arrangement or reorganization be filed by or against Debtor or Debtor admits its inability to pay its debts as they mature;

(g) property of Debtor be attached or a receiver be appointed for Debtor;

(h) Whenever Secured Party in good faith believes the prospect of payment or performance is impaired or in good faith believes the collateral is insecure;

(i) any guarantor, surety or endorser for Debtor defaults in any obligation or liability to Secured Party or any guaranty obtained in connection with this transaction is terminated or breached.

If debtor shall be in default hereunder, the indebtedness herein described and all other debts then owing by Debtor to Secured Party under this or any other present or future agreement shall, if Secured Party shall so elect, become immediately due and payable....

13. WAIVER OF DEFAULTS; AGREEMENT INCLUSIVE

Secured Party may in its sole discretion waive a default, or cure, at Debtor's expense, a default. Any such waiver in a particular instance or of a particular default shall not be a waiver of other defaults or the same kind of default at another time. No modification or change in this Security Agreement or any related note, instrument or agreement shall bind Secured Party unless in writing signed by Secured Party. No oral agreement shall be binding.

―――――――

Under an agreement such as this, virtually any breach of contract by the debtor puts the debtor in default. In fact, the debtor may be in default even if the debtor has performed every obligation under its contract and done everything in its power to placate the secured creditor. In section D of this assignment, we explore the limits of the secured creditor's power under such expansive definitions of default. First, more basic matters beckon.

B. When Is Payment Due?

Most defaults actually acted upon by secured creditors include defaults in payment. That is, the debtor failed to pay all or part of the loan by the deadline specified in the contract between the parties. To predict the likely legal consequences of failures in payment, it is helpful to understand the commercial contexts in which the particular failures occur. For that reason, we describe some of the more common arrangements for repayment. Keep in mind as you read about them that these arrangements are fixed by contract at the time the loans are made and are therefore subject to almost infinite variation.

1. Installment Loans

A loan is an *installment loan* if the parties contemplate that the debtor will repay in a series of payments. Ordinarily, these payments will be at regular intervals. They may be due monthly, quarterly, or annually. The payments may vary in amount, but more often all the payments in the series are equal. Probably the most common kinds of installment loans are real estate mortgages and car loans, which usually specify repayment in equal monthly installments over a specified number of years. Installments are the typical form for repayment of a seller or lender who finances the debtor's purchase of a particular item of business equipment, such as an aircraft, a computer, or a drill press, or even an entire business. Even unsecured loans are often made on an installment basis. From the debtor's point of view, repayment in installments is preferable to many of the other repayment contracts discussed here, because it provides the debtor with maximum legal protection against arbitrary action by the lender. The debtor knows that if it makes each payment by the due date and otherwise complies with the loan agreement, it will not be in default or subject to creditor remedies. Installment payments also provide a form of enforced budgeting that is absent in single payment loans.

2. Single-Payment Loans

Many secured loans are made payable on a particular day. Often this is because the parties expect that the debtor will have the money to pay on that date. For example, a loan secured by a large account receivable of the debtor may be payable on the date the account is due. In other instances, loans are made payable on a particular date, perhaps 60 days, 90 days, or a year later, with no expectation that the debtor will have the money to pay on that date. In such cases, the understanding is usually that if the debtor's financial circumstances remain satisfactory, the bank will renew the note for an additional period, without requiring actual payment. (This is referred to as *rolling the note* or a *rollover*.) The usual understanding is that the bank has no legally binding obligation to roll a note.

This combination of a legally binding document that says one thing and a nonlegally binding understanding that the document won't be strictly or arbitrarily enforced is even more apparent in the case of loans payable "on demand." The literal meaning of this term is that the debtor will pay the loan whenever the bank demands the money. (The making of such a demand is referred to as "calling" the loan.) Yet in most situations in which loans are made payable on demand, the parties know full well that if the bank called the loan without warning, the debtor would not be able to pay and would go into default. One study found, for example, that only 16 to 23 of 72 debtors (22 percent to 32 percent) found new financing after their initial lender terminated them. Ronald J. Mann, Strategy and Force in the Liquidation of Secured Debt, 96 Mich. L. Rev. 159, 215 (1997). One might expect that debtors would be reluctant to agree to repayment terms they know they cannot meet. That appears, however, not to be the case. Statistics issued by the Federal Reserve show that over 30 percent of the dollar amount of all loans by commercial banks is payable on demand. Whether the courts should give literal effect to repayment contracts such as these is considered in section D of this assignment.

3. Lines of Credit

A business's need for capital may vary widely over time. For example, a manufacturer of toys may need substantial amounts of capital to pay suppliers and payroll as it builds inventory in anticipation of the Christmas season. As it receives payment from sales of the Christmas inventory, its need for capital may decline. One way for this toy manufacturer to assure that it will have sufficient capital for the Christmas season would be to capitalize the business at its peak need and keep the money in a bank account or other liquid investment during the rest of the year. To illustrate, if the debtor assessed its peak capital need at $1 million, the debtor might attempt to raise about $1.1 million through the sale of stock in the company. Debtor would deposit the $1.1 million in a bank account and draw on those funds to meet its peak needs at Christmas. This way of dealing with the problem is rarely practical, because the toy manufacturer would have to pay a high rate of return for the stock investments, while for much of the year the funds would be in a bank account earning a much lower rate of return.

Probably most toy manufacturers prefer to borrow the money they need for the Christmas season and pay it back when the season is over. Our toy manufacturer could accomplish this in a crude fashion by estimating how much extra cash it will need at the peak of the season and borrowing a little more than that amount (in case the estimate is low) at the beginning of the season under a contract that calls for repayment on a date safely after the end of the season. By that means, the toy manufacturer could make sure it would have enough money to repay the loan when it was due and that it would not go into default. The problem with this approach is essentially the same as with the first. The toy manufacturer would be paying high interest rates to have money during times when it didn't need it and would be reinvesting the same money at much lower rates.

A *line of credit* is a more sophisticated application of the second approach. The bank contracts to lend up to a fixed amount of money (the line "limit") as the debtor needs it. Under most line arrangements, the debtor "borrows" the money simply by writing a check on its bank account. The bank covers all overdrafts up to the limit of the line of credit by drawing against the line, and charges the debtor interest on the money only from the time it pays the money out. As the debtor receives revenues from its operations, it uses the money to pay down on the line of credit obligation, thereby stopping the accrual of interest. A debtor operating under a line of credit may have no cash of its own; all payments may be made from the line and all revenues applied to the line. In some line of credit arrangements, the debtor does not even have a bank account. It pays bills by sending instruction to the bank; the bank writes and mails the checks, charging them to the debtor's loan account. When the debtor receives payments from customers, it forwards the payments to the bank, which logs them in as loan payments.

As we have described the line of credit thus far, the debtor is in the happy position of having to pay its debts only when it has the money to do so. Banks cannot be quite so accommodating. They must know there is some due date, so they can get out of the arrangement if they want. To make that possible, some require that the line debt fall due at a particular date during the debtor's off season. In the case of our toy manufacturer, that might be in January, when all of its Christmas revenues will be in and its cash needs will be at their lowest. A debtor who can pay the line to zero each year will not mind doing so. Many debtors, however, expect to have an outstanding balance on their line of credit during the entire year. Such a debtor's cash needs are for an indefinite time; yet banks do not make indefinite loans. Here again, the likely solution will be to set a date for repayment with the expectation of a rollover or to make the loan payable on demand with the expectation that the bank will be reasonable about calling it.

C.   Acceleration and Cure

1.   Acceleration

Assume that Debtor agrees to repay an interest-free loan in ten monthly installments of $10,000 each. Debtor makes the first payment when due and then misses the next two. Creditor sues. But for how much? Absent a contract provision to the contrary, the ten installments are treated as ten separate obligations. Debtor is in default only with regard to two payments, and Creditor is entitled to sue only for those two. Creditor will sue for $20,000.

From the creditor's point of view, this must seem entirely unreasonable. The creditor is put to a choice. It can sue now for only two payments and bring additional lawsuits when, as the creditor expects, the debtor misses more payments, or it can wait seven more months and then sue for all nine payments at the same time. (In the meantime, the debtor might dissipate its remaining assets or disappear altogether.)

Not surprisingly, most creditors require a provision in an installment loan agreement that opts out of the common law rule. Such provisions are referred to as *acceleration clauses*. Typically, they state that in the event of default by the debtor in any obligation under the repayment contract, the Creditor may, at its option, declare all of the payments immediately due and payable. (Such a provision appears at the end of the Standard Default Provisions in section A of this assignment.) The creditor can then enforce the entire obligation in a single lawsuit.

The practical effect of acceleration is often to eliminate the debtor's ability to cure its default. Assume, for example, the typical case in which George finances the purchase of a $100,000 house by executing an $80,000 mortgage, payable in equal monthly installments, with interest at 8 percent per year. The monthly payments on this mortgage are $587.02. George encounters temporary financial difficulties and falls three payments behind, for a total of $1,761.06. The creditor, Federal Savings, sends George a letter stating that George is in default and that if George does not "cure" the default by paying $1,761.06 within ten days, it will exercise its right to accelerate. If George pays the $1,761.06 arrearage before Federal Savings accelerates, the installment payment schedule continues in force and George can continue to pay $587.02 each month. If, however, George does not pay the arrearage within the ten-day period and Federal Savings sends George another letter electing to accelerate, the entire mortgage balance of approximately $80,000 becomes due and payable. George can no longer cure the default by paying $1,761.06. Of course, George still has the common law right to redeem the house by paying the entire balance of approximately $80,000. But it is a rare debtor who can't cure by paying the arrearage before acceleration, but can redeem by paying the entire balance after acceleration. So as a practical matter, acceleration usually ends the installment debtor's ability to retain the collateral and permits the creditor to get out of the installment lending arrangement.

2. Limits on the Enforceability of Acceleration Clauses

A secured creditor can exercise its right to accelerate for even a tiny or fleeting default in payment, as the following case makes clear. But if the grounds for acceleration are merely that the secured creditor "deems itself insecure" (often called an *insecurity clause*), the creditor has the right to accelerate only if it in good faith believes the prospect of payment or performance is impaired. U.C.C. §1-208 (Rev. §1-309).

J.R. Hale Contracting Co. v. United New Mexico Bank at Albuquerque

799 P.2d 581 (N.M. 1990)

RANSOM, JUSTICE . . . .

The company had been a customer of the bank for about eleven years prior to the circumstances that gave rise to this suit. During this period of time the company entered into numerous revolving credit notes with the bank in gradually increasing amounts. These notes routinely were renewed on or about the due date despite the fact that the company frequently was late a number of days or even weeks in making its payments. The bank seems not to have been troubled by the payments being past due and took no action in each instance other than possibly contacting the company to request that the payments be brought up to date. The company would send a check or the bank simply would deduct the payment from one of the company's accounts at the bank and send a notice of advice regarding the transaction.

The note at issue in this case was executed in November 1982 in the amount of $400,000. This was double the amount of any previous note. The first and only interest payment on the note was due March 1, 1983, and the note itself was due on July 31, 1983. The note provided that:

> If ANY installment of principal and/or interest on this note is not paid when due . . . or if Bank in good faith deems itself insecure or believes that the prospect of receiving payment required by this note is impaired; thereupon, at the option of Bank, this note and any and all other indebtedness of Maker to Bank shall become and be due and payable forthwith without demand, notice of nonpayment, presentment, protest or notice of dishonor, all of which are hereby expressly waived by Maker. . . .

Toward the end of February 1983, J.R. and Bruce Hale, on behalf of the company, approached the bank to borrow additional funds to cover contracting expenses associated with construction at the Double Eagle II Airport in Albuquerque. The existing $400,000 line of credit was fully drawn. Beginning in the first week in March, the Hales met with the bankers several times a week hoping to arrange for additional financing. The company had not made the March 1 interest payment on the existing loan. J.R. and Bruce Hale stated that no one ever contacted them concerning the delinquent payment and the matter never came up during the March meetings. J.R. Hale carried a blank check to these meetings for the purpose of making the interest payment but stated that he forgot to do so. He stated that on one occasion he called the bank officer assigned to his account and asked the officer to remind him at the next meeting and he would make the payment, but the officer had not done so. Apparently, it was necessary for the bank to calculate the interest payment in order to know the specific amount to be paid.

At the same time that the company was seeking to secure additional financing, the bankers had become concerned about the existing $400,000 loan. The financial statements that the company periodically supplied the bank indicated that the company had lost approximately $800,000 during the last six to seven months. While the Hales were under the impression that additional financing was in the works (a loan application to this effect had been prepared and had been taken to the loan committee for discussion), the bank seriously was considering calling in the company's existing obligations. This possibility never was communicated to the Hales as the bank wished them to remain cooperative. After a meeting on March 22 the bank requested and received from the Hales a list of customers for the undisclosed purpose of using it to collect directly the company's accounts.

The bank called a meeting on March 24 and presented the Hales with a letter stating that all amounts due on the $400,000 revolving line of credit were due and payable immediately. The grounds for the acceleration were stated to be that "The promissory note is in default due to your failure to pay the March 1, 1983 interest payment when due, and also due to the Bank's review of your financial situation which causes the Bank to believe that its prospect for receiving payment of the note is impaired." J.R. Hale produced a blank check and offered to pay the delinquent interest charges but the bank would not reconsider. The bank was able to collect the balance of the note with interest, $418,801.86, in about two weeks after exercising its right to set off the company's accounts at the bank and after receiving payments from the company's customers on their outstanding accounts....

WAIVER, MODIFICATION, AND ESTOPPEL DISTINGUISHED

The company's arguments regarding waiver, modification, and estoppel are intertwined and rely upon the same root proposition: that the conduct of the bank negated the express default provision in the note. The distinctions to be made in the application of these concepts, especially in that of waiver and estoppel, have not always been clear in our cases and some discussion on the point is warranted....

Generally, New Mexico cases have defined waiver as the intentional relinquishment or abandonment of a known right. Our decisions recognize that the intent to waive contractual obligations or conditions may be implied from a party's representations that fall short of an express declaration of waiver, or from his conduct. While not express, these types of "implied in fact" waivers still represent a voluntary act whose effect is intended.

In Ed Black's Chevrolet Center, Inc. v. Melichar, 81 N.M. 602, 471 P.2d 172 (1970), we stated that, based upon the honest belief of the other party that a waiver was intended, a waiver might be presumed or implied contrary to the intention of the party waiving certain rights. Following that decision a number of our opinions discussed a waiver "implied" from a course of conduct in terms of estoppel. These cases represent what we would term here as *waiver by estoppel*. To prove waiver by estoppel the party need only show that he was misled to his prejudice by the conduct of the other party into the honest and reasonable belief that such waiver was intended. The estoppel is justified because the estopped party reasonably could expect that his actions would induce the reliance of the other party. However, unlike the case of a voluntary waiver, either express or implied in fact, the waiver of the contractual obligation or condition and the effect of the conduct upon the opposite party may have been unintentional....

NO ACTUAL WAIVER, EXPRESS OR IMPLIED IN FACT

...We believe that the postagreement conduct of the bank does not suggest that the bank actually intended to waive its rights under the contract. When a party accepts a late payment on a contract without comment he waives the default that existed. With repetition his actions may suggest an intention to accept late payments generally. In this case, the overdue interest payment was the first payment due under the contract; the bank had not accepted any earlier late payments on that contract. The payment was overdue, the company did not request an extension, and after twenty-three days the bank declared a default. The parties agree that the matter of the overdue interest payment was not discussed during the series of meetings when the company sought to obtain additional financing. For good reasons, the fact that the bank would declare a default based upon the unpaid interest payment may have come as a surprise to the Hales, the bank's silence may have been misleading in the light of the earlier commercial behavior of the parties, but we do not believe that the bank's conduct during the month of March gives rise to a factual question that it was the bank's actual intention to relinquish any contractual rights. At most, the bank's conduct indicated an intention simply to ignore the delinquency for about three weeks.

NO MODIFICATION

Likewise, we agree with the trial court that the facts of this case do not raise an issue of contract modification. We have concluded in our discussion of the waiver issue that no factual question exists on whether the bank for its part actually intended to waive its right to declare a default based upon the past due interest payment. It follows that there can be no issue of whether the parties intended to substitute a new agreement for their earlier one, or whether the parties mutually agreed to amend the contractual provision concerning default and acceleration, and whether this agreement was supported by consideration . . . .

"WAIVER BY ESTOPPEL" PRESENTED AN
ISSUE OF FACT

The company's estoppel argument rests upon an important distinction from actual waiver. Here the previous course of dealings between the parties is relevant to show the meaning that the company reasonably might attribute to the bank's conduct in not mentioning the overdue interest payment. Implicit in [U.C.C. §1-205(1) (Rev. §1-303)] is the recognition that, as a practical matter, one party to a contract will use his past commercial dealings with another party as a basis for the interpretation of the other party's conduct. Thus it is to be expected that the company would interpret the bank's behavior during the month of March in light of their earlier dealings and we believe the bank should have been aware of this consideration . . . .

Some of the facts to which we refer can be regarded as silence on the bank's part in the face of an apparent false sense of security of the company. Silence may form the basis for estoppel if a party stands mute when he has a duty to speak. As we have discussed, the circumstances here suggest that the bank reasonably could expect that the company would rely on the bank's failure to request the interest payment. Under these circumstances we believe the bank had a duty to inform the company that the bank would enforce performance under the contract according to the letter of their agreement.

On the question of detrimental reliance we note that the company cannot be said to have been lulled by the postagreement conduct into missing the payment when it was first due on March 1. However, we believe the company reasonably might have been induced into not taking the initiative to correct the delinquency and waiting instead for the bank to request the payment or in some fashion draw the matter to the company's attention. Certainly to have the bank declare a default without warning and then accelerate all payments can be considered the detrimental result of the reliance on the impression that the bank's conduct reasonably might have conveyed.

"LACK OF GOOD FAITH" PRESENTED AN ISSUE OF FACT UNDER CLAUSE PROVIDING FOR ACCELERATION BECAUSE OF INSECURITY

At trial the bank moved for a directed verdict on a second ground, that the company failed to introduce sufficient evidence showing the bank lacked a good faith belief that its prospect for repayment was impaired. The company had the burden of proof on that issue. [U.C.C. §1-208 (Rev. §1-309)]. The trial judge denied the bank's motion, stating that he believed there were facts in the record from which a jury could conclude that the bank lacked good faith. The bank asserts that the judge applied the wrong standard regarding "good faith" as used in an insecurity clause giving a secured party the power to accelerate payments.

[U.C.C. §1-208 (Rev. §1-309)] governs the acceleration of notes. It provides that a party may accelerate payment or performance "only if he in good faith believes that the prospect of payment or performance is impaired." "Good faith" is defined by [U.C.C. §1-201(19) (Rev. §1-201(b)(20))] as "honesty in fact in the conduct or transaction concerned." . . .

In essence, the requirement of honesty in fact is subjective and is concerned with the actual state of mind of the creditor. Nevertheless, the determination of ultimate fact, whether or not the bank lacked a good faith belief in the impairment of its prospect for repayment, should be based on the facts and circumstances surrounding the acceleration and not solely on the bank's testimony concerning its state of mind. Even under a subjective test of good faith the trier of fact may evaluate the credibility of a creditor's claim and in doing so may take into account the reasonableness of that claim. Thus, the conduct and credibility of the creditor may be tested by objective standards subject to proof and conducive to the application of reasonable expectations in commercial affairs.

We do not mean to suggest that dual elements of reasonableness and good faith are required. Put simply, in the absence of an objective basis upon which a reasonable person would have accelerated the note, the fact finder could infer that the creditor really did not perceive his prospect for repayment to be impaired. This inquiry necessarily will focus on the facts and circumstances that were known to the creditor. As Judge Sutin noted in [McKay v. Farmers & Stockmens Bank of Clayton, 585 P.2d 325, 329 (N.M. 1978)], expert testimony may be necessary to assist the trier of fact. 92 N.M. at 185, 585 P.2d at 329. . . .

CONCLUSION

For the reasons stated above, we reverse the district court's grant of a directed verdict in favor of the bank based on the interest default clause and hold that an issue of waiver by estoppel exists to be resolved by the jury. In addition, the company also must prove that the bank lacked a good faith belief that its prospect for repayment was impaired.

It is so ordered.

To most people, calling a loan when the debtor is current on the payments probably seems pretty outrageous. But the vast majority of security agreements contain laundry lists of provisions under which debtors can be in default even while current on the payments. The typical agreement permits the creditor to accelerate for any default, however small.

3. The Debtor's Right to Cure

As we noted above, a debtor has the right to cure a default by paying the amounts then due. If the debtor cures before the creditor accelerates, the necessary sum may be small. Some debtors, particularly those who get reminders from their creditors, make up the payments in time and get out of jeopardy. The following case illustrates the general rule that once acceleration has occurred, a debtor can cure, or, more accurately, redeem, only by paying the entire amount of the accelerated debt.

Old Republic Insurance Co. v. Lee

507 So. 2d 754 (Fla. Dist. Ct. App. 1987)

UPCHURCH, C.J.

Appellant, Old Republic Insurance Co., appeals an order granting a motion to reinstate a mortgage.

The promissory note that the second mortgage at issue secured provided for monthly payments of $387.85 each. On April 29, 1986, Old Republic declared the note in default because appellees, the Lees, had not made the payments due March and April 19th. The Lees were notified that the mortgage was being declared in default and the unpaid principal balance was being accelerated. On May 16, William Lee sent Old Republic a certified check for the payments due March, April and May 19. Old Republic returned the check and filed suit to foreclose. Lee filed an answer and a motion to reinstate the mortgage on the basis that the Lees had tendered payment and that the property was now for sale and Old Republic would be paid from the proceeds.

The court granted the motion to reinstate finding that there was substantial equity in the real estate subject to the mortgage, that the first mortgage, having a principal balance of approximately $47,000.00 was current, and that the second mortgage of Old Republic was to be paid out of the proceeds of a proposed sale.

We find that the reinstatement of the mortgage and the refusal of the court to order foreclosure was error and reverse. As a general rule of law, a mortgagor, prior to the election of a right to accelerate by the mortgage holder upon the occurrence of a default, may tender the arrears due and thereby prevent the mortgage holder from exercising his option to accelerate. However, once the mortgage holder has exercised his option to accelerate, the right of the mortgagor to tender only the arrears is terminated....

REVERSED and REMANDED for further proceedings consistent with this opinion.

Statutes in some states permit cure and reinstatement of the original loan terms by payment of only the arrearages even after the secured creditor has exercised its contract right to accelerate.

Reinstatement

Ill. Rev. Stat. ch. 110, ¶5-1602 (2005)

In any foreclosure of a mortgage . . . which has become due prior to the maturity date fixed in the mortgage, or in any instrument or obligation secured by the mortgage, through acceleration because of a default under the mortgage, a mortgagor may reinstate the mortgage as provided herein. Reinstatement is effected by curing all defaults then existing, other than payment of such portion of the principal which would not have been due had no acceleration occurred, and by paying all costs and expenses required by the mortgage to be paid in the event of such defaults, provided that such cure and payment are made prior to the expiration of 90 days from the date the mortgagor [is served with summons or by publication in the foreclosure case or submits to the jurisdiction of the court]. . . . Upon such reinstatement of the mortgage, the foreclosure and any other proceedings for the collection or enforcement of the obligation secured by the mortgage shall be dismissed and the mortgage documents shall remain in full force and effect as if no acceleration or default had occurred. . . .

The state legislatures that enact provisions such as these usually limit their application to home mortgages, to consumer borrowers, or to some other circumstances that the legislators believe most require this form of regulation.

D.   The Enforceability of Payment Terms

As we described in section B of this assignment, debtors and creditors often agree to payment terms the debtors have no real hope of satisfying. Given the severe consequences of a default, some courts have sought ways of softening those terms. If the facts of a particular case are capable of supporting a defense of waiver or estoppel, these courts may be amenable. (Recall the efforts of the court in J.R. Hale Contracting v. United New Mexico Bank.) But when lending institutions are careful in their administration of the loan, the courts are eventually forced to deal with the ultimate issues: Are harsh payment terms enforceable? Can debtors contract to be at the mercy of their secured creditors?

In a landmark case that helped establish the doctrine of "lender liability," the Sixth Circuit declined to enforce literally the contract between a bank and a borrower engaged in the wholesale and retail grocery business. KMC Co. v. Irving Trust Co., 757 F.2d 752 (6th Cir. 1985). In 1979, Irving and KMC entered into an agreement for a $3.5 million line of credit, secured by an interest in all of KMC's assets. The promissory note was payable on demand. In 1982, KMC sought to draw $800,000 on the line of credit, which would have increased the loan balance to just under the $3.5 million limit. Without prior notice, Irving refused to make the advance. At the time it sought the advance, KMC was attempting to sell its business. Irving's refusal of the advance killed the possibility of a sale and assured the collapse of KMC's business. Irving's defenses were that (1) KMC was already collapsing anyway, and (2) refusing to honor KMC's draw was no different from honoring the draw and immediately making a demand for the entire $3.5 million, which Irving had the right to do under the demand promissory note.

KMC sued Irving for breach of contract, arguing in part that Irving called the loan based on a "personality conflict" between a bank officer and KMC's president. The court instructed the jury that

> there is implied in every contract an obligation of good faith, that this obligation may have imposed on Irving a duty to give notice to KMC before refusing to advance funds under the agreement up to the $3.5 million limit; and that such notice would be required if necessary to the proper execution of the contract, unless Irving's decision to refuse to advance funds without prior notice was made in good faith and in the reasonable exercise of its discretion.

The jury found Irving liable and fixed damages at $7,500,000, the entire value of KMC's business. Irving appealed.

The Sixth Circuit upheld the verdict, saying:

> As part of the procedure established for the operation of the financing agreement, the parties agreed in a supplementary letter that all receipts of KMC would be deposited into a "blocked account" to which Irving would have sole access. Consequently, unless KMC obtained alternative financing, a refusal by Irving to advance funds would leave KMC without operating capital until it had paid down its loan. The record clearly established that a medium-sized company in the wholesale grocery business, such as KMC, could not operate without outside financing. Thus, the literal interpretation of the financing agreement urged upon us by Irving, as supplemented by the "blocked account" mechanism, would leave KMC's continued existence entirely at the whim or mercy of Irving, absent an obligation of good faith performance. Logically, at such time as Irving might wish to curtail financing KMC, as was its right under the agreement, this obligation to act in good faith would require a period of notice to KMC to allow it a reasonable opportunity to seek alternate financing, absent valid business reasons precluding Irving from doing so. . . .
>
> Nor are we persuaded by Irving's reasoning with respect to the effect of the demand provision in the agreement. We agree with the Magistrate that just as Irving's discretion whether or not to advance funds is limited by an obligation of good faith performance, so too would be its power to demand repayment. The demand provision is a kind of acceleration clause, upon which the Uniform Commercial Code and the courts have imposed limitations of reasonableness and fairness. See U.C.C. §1-208 (Rev. §1-309). . . .

In the case that follows, the Seventh Circuit rejected the holding in *KMC*. While the case applies the equitable subordination doctrine from bankruptcy law, the case ultimately turns on the U.C.C. issue of good faith.

Kham & Nate's Shoes No. 2, Inc. v. First Bank of Whiting

908 F.2d 1351 (7th Cir. 1990)

EASTERBROOK, CIRCUIT JUDGE.

Kham & Nate's Shoes No. 2, Inc., ran four retail shoe stores in Chicago. . . . The Bank first extended credit to the Debtor in July 1981. This $50,000 loan was renewed in December 1981 and repaid in part in July 1982. The balance was rolled over until late 1983, when with interest it came to $42,000. . . . In late 1983 Debtor, experiencing serious cash-flow problems, asked for additional capital, which Bank agreed to provide if the loan could be made secure. . . . Debtor and Bank then signed their loan agreement, which opens a $300,000 line of credit. The contract provides for cancellation on five days' notice and adds for good measure that "nothing provided herein shall constitute a waiver of the right of the Bank to terminate financing at any time."

The parties signed the contract on January 23, 1984, and Debtor quickly took about $75,000. . . . On February 29 Bank mailed Debtor a letter stating that it would make no additional advances after March 7. Although the note underlying the line of credit required payment on demand, Bank did not make the demand. It continued honoring . . . draws. Debtor's ultimate indebtedness to Bank was approximately $164,000. . . .

Bankruptcy Judge Coar held an evidentiary hearing and concluded that Bank had behaved inequitably in terminating the line of credit. . . . [The remedy imposed by Judge Coar was to subordinate the bank's security interest to the interests of other creditors, essentially rendering it uncollectible.]

Cases subordinating the claims of creditors that dealt at arm's length with the debtor are few and far between. Benjamin v. Diamond, 563 F.2d 692 (5th Cir. 1977) (*Mobile Steel Co.*), suggests that subordination depends on a combination of inequitable conduct, unfair advantage to the creditor, and injury to other creditors. Debtor submits that conduct may be "unfair" and "inequitable" for this purpose even though the creditor complies with all contractual requirements, but we are not willing to embrace a rule that requires participants in commercial transactions not only to keep their contracts but also do "more" — just how much more resting in the discretion of a bankruptcy judge assessing the situation years later. Contracts specify the duties of the parties to each other, and each may exercise the privileges it obtained. Banks sometimes bind themselves to make loans (commitment letters and letters of credit have this effect) and sometimes reserve the right to terminate further advances. Courts may not convert one form of contract into the other after the fact, without raising the cost of credit or jeopardizing its availability. Unless pacts are enforced according to their terms, the institution of contract, with all the advantages private negotiation and agreement brings, is jeopardized.

"Inequitable conduct" in commercial life means breach plus some advantage-taking, such as the star who agrees to act in a motion picture and then, after

$20 million has been spent, sulks in his dressing room until the contract has been renegotiated. Firms that have negotiated contracts are entitled to enforce them to the letter, even to the great discomfort of their trading partners, without being mulcted for lack of "good faith." Although courts often refer to the obligation of good faith that exists in every contractual relation, this is not an invitation to the court to decide whether one party ought to have exercised privileges expressly reserved in the document. "Good faith" is a compact reference to an implied undertaking not to take opportunistic advantage in a way that could not have been contemplated at the time of drafting, and which therefore was not resolved explicitly by the parties. When the contract is silent, principles of good faith — such as the UCC's standard of honesty in fact, U.C.C. §1-201(19) (Rev. §1-201(b)(20)), and the reasonable expectations of the trade, U.C.C. §2-103(b) (a principle applicable, however, only to "merchants", which Bank is not) — fill the gap. They do not block use of terms that actually appear in the contract.

We do not doubt the force of the proverb that the letter killeth, while the spirit giveth life. Literal implementation of unadorned language may destroy the essence of the venture. Few people pass out of childhood without learning fables about genies, whose wickedly literal interpretation of their "masters' " wishes always leads to calamity. Yet knowledge that literal enforcement means some mismatch between the parties' expectation and the outcome does not imply a general duty of "kindness" in performance, or of judicial oversight into whether a party had "good cause" to act as it did. Parties to a contract are not each others' fiduciaries; they are not bound to treat customers with the same consideration reserved for their families. Any attempt to add an overlay of "just cause" — as the bankruptcy judge effectively did — to the exercise of contractual privileges would reduce commercial certainty and breed costly litigation. The UCC's requirement of "honesty in fact" stops well short of the requirements the bankruptcy judge thought incident to contractual performance. "In commercial transactions it does not in the end promote justice to seek strained interpretations in aid of those who do not protect themselves." James Baird Co. v. Gimbel Bros., Inc., 64 F.2d 344, 346 (2d Cir. 1933) (L. Hand, J.).

Bank did not break a promise at a time Debtor was especially vulnerable, then use the costs and delay of obtaining legal enforcement of the contract as levers to a better deal. Debtor and Bank signed a contract expressly allowing the Bank to cease making further advances. The $300,000 was the maximum loan, not a guarantee. The Bank exercised its contractual privilege after loaning Debtor $75,000; it made a clean break and did not demand improved terms. It had the right to do this for any reason satisfactory to itself. See also U.C.C. §1-208 (Rev. §1-309)(official comment stating that the statutory obligation of good faith in accelerating a term note does not apply to a bank's decision to call demand notes). The principle is identical to that governing a contract for employment at will: the employer may sack its employee for any reason except one forbidden by law, and it need not show "good cause."

Although Bank's decision left Debtor scratching for other sources of credit, Bank did not create Debtor's need for funds, and it was not contractually obliged to satisfy its customer's desires. The Bank was entitled to advance its own interests, and it did not need to put the interests of Debtor and Debtor's other creditors first. To the extent KMC, Inc. v. Irving Trust Co., 757 F.2d 752, 759-763 (6th Cir. 1986), holds that a bank must loan more money or give more advance notice of termination than its contract requires, we respectfully disagree. First Bank of Whiting is not an eleemosynary institution. It need not throw good money after bad, even if other persons would catch the lucre.

Debtor stresses, and the bankruptcy judge found, that Bank would have been secure in making additional advances. Perhaps so, but the contract did not oblige Bank to make all advances for which it could be assured of payment. Ex post assessments of a lender's security are no basis on which to deny it the negotiated place in the queue. Risk must be assessed ex ante by lenders, rather than ex post by judges. If a loan seems secure at the time, lenders will put up the money; their own interests are served by making loans bound to be repaid. What is more, the bankruptcy judge's finding that Bank would have been secure in making additional advances is highly questionable. The judgment of the market vindicates Bank. If more credit would have enabled Debtor to flourish, then other lenders should have been willing to supply it. Yet no one else, not even the SBA, would advance additional money to Debtor. . . .

Although Debtor contends, and the bankruptcy judge found, that Bank's termination of advances frustrated Debtor's efforts to secure credit from other sources, and so propelled it down hill, this is legally irrelevant so long as Bank kept its promises. . . .

––––––––––––

If there remained any doubt, Judge Easterbrook made clear his views about lender liability suits. When asked to comment on their rise, he said, "I have a five-word comment. Not in the Seventh Circuit." Speeches from the Federalist Society Fifth Annual Lawyers Convention: Individual Responsibility and the Law, 77 Cornell L. Rev. 955, 1111 (1992).

Ordinarily, contract law strives to fulfill the expectations of the parties. Easterbrook's rule would fit the law of contracts in a world where everyone expected it. But in the world we live in, expectations are far less clear. Undoubtedly, many debtors are willing to sign harsh contracts because they don't think the courts will enforce them. It is interesting to speculate on what the long-run effect of the absence of lender liability would be. Will the debtors who sign security agreements some day all realize that "what you contract for is what you get"? Or will some debtors continue to sign the kinds of agreements they sign today, on the assumption that if lenders act outrageously, equity will come to their rescue?

Article 9 defines "good faith" as "honesty in fact and the observance of reasonable commercial standards of fair dealing." On its face, it seems to be taking the Sixth Circuit's side against the Seventh Circuit. But the Article 9 definition applies to "good faith" only when the term is used in Article 9. See U.C.C. §9-102(a)(43). *KMC* and *Kham & Nate's Shoes* are both cases construing the term "good faith" as used in Article 1. Revised Article 1 changes the definition of "good faith" in Article 1 to conform to Article 9. That change undermines the reasoning of *Kham & Nate's Shoes,* and buttresses the reasoning of *KMC.* But, as of this writing, revised Article 1 has been adopted in only 13 jurisdictions and more than half of those adoptions retain the "honesty in fact" language of good faith from the current Article 9.

E.   Procedures After Default

Once the debtor is in default, the secured creditor usually has a choice of remedies. As you saw in earlier assignments of this book, those remedies fall in two basic categories: (1) judicial remedies such as foreclosure and replevin, which are administered by the courts, and (2) self-help remedies such as repossession without judicial process, the notification of account debtors, or the refusal to make further advances to the debtor under a line of credit.

The creditor's choice among these remedies is often based on the creditor's assessment of the likelihood that the debtor will resist, the creditor's appraisal of the strength of the debtor's defenses, if any, and the manner in which the sufficiency of those defenses will be determined in each remedial procedure. To illustrate the importance of the differences in procedures, consider the case of a bank that decides to call a loan secured by all the assets of a restaurant supply company, including equipment, inventory, and accounts receivable. Calling such a loan is almost certain to lead to the closing of the business. Probably the most aggressive approach the bank could take would be to notify the restaurant supply company's account debtors to make their payments directly to the bank. U.C.C. §9-607. The combination of the loss of the account revenues and the reputational damage to the debtor from the giving of notice are likely to destroy the restaurant supply company's business. If the bank has doubts about whether the debtor is really in default, or whether it (the bank) has the right to call the loan, it may be reluctant to employ so harsh a remedy. The bank could wind up on the wrong end of a lender liability action.

Judicial foreclosure would be a more cautious way to proceed. After declaring the debtor in default, the bank would file the foreclosure case. The bank's complaint would set forth the alleged nature of the default and the basis of its right to foreclose. To preserve its defenses — perhaps it wasn't in default, or, if it was, the default resulted from wrongful action by the bank — the restaurant supply company might have to raise them in its answer to the complaint or in a counterclaim. By pressing the foreclosure action to a conclusion, the bank could get a final judicial determination of the respective rights of itself and its debtor before taking irreversible action.

The weakness of foreclosure as a remedy is that it is slow. While the case makes its way through the courts, the debtor may be collecting the accounts, selling the inventory, and allowing the equipment to deteriorate. Replevin offers something of an intermediate course. Recall that in a replevin action the secured creditor can move for an order granting it temporary possession of the collateral. In most jurisdictions, the motion will be heard in the first month of the case. While the debtor is not under compulsion to raise its defenses in response to the motion or lose them, the debtor may choose to do so in an effort to retain possession of the collateral. That may give the secured creditor a basis for assessing the strength of the debtor's defenses.

FIGURE 54.1.
The Spider Ad.

Shortly after mating, the black widow spider eats her mate.

Sadly, many business banking relationships don't last much longer.

Business banking, it seems, has long taken its cues from nature. You know, survival of the fittest. Natural selection. Cannibalism.

Okay, wait a second. That last thing may occur in nature, but at Continental Bank, we prefer to share the future with our partners for a period of time that's just a wee bit shy of forever.

You see, more and more businesses are finding themselves caught in tangled webs of quick-fix financial quick fixes.

Which all too often leads to a string of somewhat confusing, short-term, transaction-oriented acquaintances. The financial equal of a love-'em-and-leave-'em attitude.

So, to untangle the complexity of business banking, we encourage our customers to feed off us. (A sort of financial symbiosis, if you will.) And with all we have to offer, they're in for a long, satisfying feast.

Through extensive consultation, our customers benefit from Continental's expertise in all aspects of financial risk management, corporate finance and treasury management. Through custom-designed solutions, our customers' problems meet with a quick, clean kill. Through it all, our customers deal with relationship managers who are above reacting on instincts alone. Instead, they study, analyze and view each problem from every conceivable angle before using the tools needed to get the job done.

Perhaps that's why Continental can boast of so many steady client relationships that span not years, but decades. Chances are, the life span of your business banking relationships can last as long, too. Just call Continental Bank at (312) 828-5799. Who knows, to start things off, maybe we could have you...uh... that is...join you for lunch.

Burp.

Continental Bank
A new approach to business.

This ad ran full page in the *Wall Street Journal* just a few years after the bank was hit with a $105 million verdict for knocking off one of its customers, Port Bougainville of Key Largo, Florida. Should its implication that the bank will not act in an arbitrary manner in calling loans be considered part of the contract of a debtor who signs a demand note? Or should debtors know better than to believe this stuff?

Problem Set 54

54.1.   Pat Roskoi, a plumbing subcontractor, consults you about a problem she is having with Lincoln State Bank. Pat accidentally missed two $434 payments on her truck loan. Her contract with the bank says that missing two payments is a default and that "upon default, at the secured party's option, the entire balance of the loan shall become due and payable." She noticed her omission before she received any kind of notice from the bank and promptly sent a check for the two overdue payments.

a.   The bank mailed her check back to her with a note stating that the entire loan balance of $16,701 is due and payable. She called the Bank, but the person she talked with told her that there was no mistake, and she simply has to pay the entire balance of the loan. Pat says she doesn't have the money and that the loss of the truck would make it impossible for her to continue her business. Pat asks you, "can they get away with this?" What do you tell her? See U.C.C. §9-623, including the Comment.

b.   What would have been the effect if the Bank had accelerated the loan on their books before receiving the check? Instead of returning it, the bank deposited the check to the Bank's account, and promptly sent Pat a statement showing the entire balance, less the amount of the check, as due and payable. U.C.C. §9-601(a).

54.2.   Your friend, Art Leff, is experiencing what he calls "a temporary cash flow problem." He owes Lincoln State Savings a balance of about $127,000 on his house; his monthly payment is $860. He did not make his mortgage payment on the due date last week (October 1) and he is worried about what happens next. Of course, you refused to give any advice without first reading the agreement. The relevant provisions were as follows:

Default. Upon the occurrence of any of the following events of default . . . (1) the Debtor shall have outstanding an amount exceeding one full payment which has remained unpaid for more than 10 days after the due dates . . . mortgagee shall have all of the rights and remedies for default provided by applicable law and this Agreement, including the right to declare the entire outstanding balance immediately due and payable.

Art wants to delay making his house payments as long as he can and would like you to tell him how long that will be.

a. Is Art in default?

b. If Art makes no payments, when will he go into default?

c. If Art makes no payments, what will be the order of events? When is the last time he can make this and subsequent payments without serious repercussions? What are those repercussions?

d. What difference would it make if Art's case were governed by the Illinois reinstatement statute?

54.3.   You represent Harvey Macklin and his company, Macklin Mortgage. Two years ago, Macklin lent $60,000 to Lance's Landscaping, Inc. (LLI), repayable in equal monthly payments over seven years. The loan is secured by an interest in all of LLI's equipment; the default provisions of the agreement are those set forth in the standard default provisions in section A of this assignment. Harvey has come to see you today because he wants to call the LLI loan. When you asked why, Harvey told you it was because LLI had failed for two consecutive years to provide Macklin with proof of liability insurance, as required by the terms of the security agreement. But in response to your questions, Harvey admitted that LLI is a strong debtor that has made every payment on time and that the real reason he wants to call the loan is that Macklin itself is in financial difficulty and desperately needs the cash. ("When you need cash," Harvey explains, "you don't get it by calling your *bad* loans.") Harvey can't get his cash out by selling the loan, because the loan carries such a low rate of interest.

The last due date for proof of insurance was 23 days ago. Macklin doesn't know if LLI has the insurance or not. There has never been any discussion of the contract provision requiring it. "Do I or don't I have the right to call this loan?" Harvey asks.

a.   What is the answer to Harvey's question? U.C.C. §§1-201(19) (Rev. §1-201(b)(20)), 1-203 (Rev. §1-304), 1-208 (Rev. §1-309), 9-102(a)(43), and 9-601(a).

b.   Are you willing to continue representing Harvey?

c.   If you had to continue, what would you advise?

54.4.   Teresa Revez, a personal friend of yours, recently resigned her position in a software development firm in order to start her own golf course supply business. She seeks your advice regarding a number of start-up concerns, including the acquisition of financing. She estimates her capital need (beyond the amount she can invest) at about $150,000 at the peak of the season in May and at about $75,000 at the minimum point in January. To hold her capital needs to that level, she will need to make extensive use of unsecured credit from suppliers, buy her inventory on credit, and perhaps pay the inventory suppliers a little slower than the 60 to 90 days the suppliers want. Teresa has tentatively arranged for a $150,000 line of credit loan from the Bank of Orange, through David Walker, another friend of hers who is a loan officer at the Bank.

a.   Teresa was surprised to learn from David that the proposed line of credit would be payable "on demand." Once she is in business, she will have every dime of her money tied up in this business; if the Bank called the loan, she would have no way to meet the call. When she raised this point with David, he told her that line loans are all on demand and it was not something she should worry about. "Bank of Orange has been serving the community for 75 years and has a reputation to protect," he said. "We're not going to do anything unfair or unreasonable." Teresa believes that David is 100 percent sincere, but still wants your opinion as to whether she should enter into this arrangement. What do you advise? Are there any terms that might alleviate Teresa's concerns and be acceptable to the Bank?

b.   Teresa was also bothered by David's statement that she would be signing a note for $150,000, but drawing only half that much money initially. David said that the Bank always has customers sign a note for the line limit, as a matter of convenience. "You don't want to be coming into the Bank every time you want a draw," he said. Should Teresa sign a note for $150,000 when she is only drawing $75,000? Would you in such circumstances?

54.5. Arthur Oman, a loan officer at Second National Bank, has been given the unpleasant task of "pulling the plug" on one of the Bank's customers, Rebel Discount Drugs. Rebel owes $150,000 on a loan against inventory, equipment, and the debtor's interest under its lease. Rebel's note is payable "on demand." Arthur has come to see you, the Bank's lawyer, to discuss the possibility of giving 30 days' notice to Rebel before making the demand. "They won't find another lender in this market," he says, "but I feel like I owe it to Walt Rebel to let him try." In response to your questions, Arthur tells you that Rebel buys its inventory on credit from suppliers, floats them for about 90 to 120 days, and then pays them out of the $1,000 to $2,000 a day that comes in through the cash registers. (Arthur knows this because the agreement between Rebel and the Bank requires that Rebel keep its account at the Bank and deposit its cash register receipts to the account daily.) Once the Bank forecloses, the equipment is probably worth about $20,000 on the resale market and the inventory would probably bring in another $60,000. The lease might bring another $10,000 to $20,000 — if the Bank can find anyone who wants it. Arthur expects that the Bank will simply take a $50,000 loss on the balance. The Bank has always in the past met its obligations to Rebel and Walt Rebel has never had any complaints about the Bank's practices. Will you approve Arthur's proposal to give notice? If so, how much notice should the Bank give? If not, how should the Bank proceed?

54.6. Assume that the facts are the same as in Problem 54.5, except that Arthur relates these additional facts: Six months ago Walt asked for an increase in his line of credit, and Arthur told him he "thought there would be no problem." The loan committee saw it differently and refused the increase. Walt then wrote an angry letter to the Bank, asserting that the Bank had "reneged on their commitment" and had also "given false information [about Rebel] on a credit reference." Arthur thinks the "false information" reference is to a conversation Arthur had with a loan officer from First National Bank shortly after the loan committee refused the increase. Rebel applied to First National for a line of credit and First National had, naturally, called Second National. "I didn't tell her anything that wasn't true," Arthur says. Would these facts change your advice?

Assignment 55: Default, Acceleration, and Cure Under Bankruptcy Law

As we saw in Assignment 54, state law generally enforces the contract between debtor and secured creditor regarding default, acceleration, and the possibility of cure. A contract for repayment of debt in installments usually gives the creditor, upon default, the option to accelerate the due dates of future payments. In some states, statutes intervene, permitting at least some debtors to cure their defaults and thereby reinstate their contracts for payment in installments. Generally speaking, however, once acceleration has occurred, it is irreversible. Without the ability to decelerate, most debtors in most situations cannot recover from their defaults.

To look at acceleration and cure only under state law, however, gives a false impression. To see the relationship between default, acceleration, and cure requires consideration of state and bankruptcy law together. Most of the creditor's rights are found in state law; most of the debtor's rights are found in bankruptcy law. The following case explains how these two sets of laws combine to create a system in which the debtor who has the ability to cure a default and make the installment payments generally will have the opportunity to do so. There is a catch: To get that opportunity, the debtor must go into bankruptcy.

In re Moffett (Tidewater Finance Co. v. Moffett)
356 F.3d 518 (4th Cir. 2004)

WILKINSON, CIRCUIT JUDGE:

I.

On January 22, 2001, Marlene Moffett purchased a used 1998 Honda Accord from Hendrick Honda in Woodbridge, Virginia. Moffett agreed to pay $20,024.25 with interest in 60 monthly installments, and Hendrick Honda retained a security interest in the vehicle. Under the purchase contract and Virginia state law, Hendrick Honda had the right to repossess the vehicle in the event of default, subject to Moffett's right to redeem it. See [U.C.C. §§9-609, 623]. Hendrick Honda assigned its rights under the purchase agreement to Tidewater Finance Company, which subsequently perfected its security interest. According to the bankruptcy court, the automobile was Moffett's only means of traveling the forty miles from her home to her workplace at the Federal Emergency Management Agency.

Moffett made her payments in timely fashion for approximately one year. Because Moffett failed to make her monthly payments in March and April 2002, however, Tidewater Finance lawfully repossessed the vehicle on the morning of April 25, 2002. Later that day, Moffett filed for voluntary Chapter 13 reorganization. On May 1, 2002, Moffett's attorney notified Tidewater Finance of Moffett's bankruptcy filing and demanded return of the vehicle, according to the Bankruptcy Code's automatic stay and turnover provisions. See 11 U.S.C. §§362(a), 542(a).

II.

Once a debtor files for Chapter 13 bankruptcy, the Bankruptcy Code automatically stays any act by parties to exercise control over, or to enforce a pre-petition or post-petition lien against, property of the bankruptcy estate. 11 U.S.C. §§362(a)(3)-(5) (2003). Any entity that possesses property that the bankruptcy trustee may use, sell, or lease under the Bankruptcy Code is required to turn over or account for the property. *Id.* §542(a). Before requiring a party to turn over property, however, courts must ensure that the party's interest in the property is adequately protected. *Id.* §§362(d)(1), 363(e). The central question here is whether Tidewater Finance and the repossessed vehicle are subject to these automatic stay and turnover provisions of the Bankruptcy Code.

A.

We must first determine the nature of Moffett's property interests in the repossessed vehicle, and whether those interests became part of her bankruptcy estate. A debtor's bankruptcy "estate" is automatically created at the time she files for bankruptcy. It broadly includes, among other things, "all legal or equitable interests of the debtor in property as of the commencement of the case." *Id.* §541(a)(1). The inclusive scope of the bankruptcy estate reflects the desire of Congress to facilitate the financial rehabilitation of debtors. Yet, while federal law defines in broad fashion what property interests are included within the bankruptcy estate, state law determines the nature and existence of a debtor's rights. We therefore must look to Virginia law in determining the nature of Moffett's interests in the vehicle upon repossession.

Because we deal here with a debtor's default on a purchase agreement with a secured creditor, Virginia's Uniform Commercial Code-Secured Transactions ("UCC") controls our analysis. [U.C.C. §9-609] expressly permits a secured creditor to repossess the collateral protecting its security interest after default by the debtor. Upon repossession, Virginia's UCC grants the secured creditor a number of important rights. Here, for example, once Tidewater Finance repossessed Moffett's vehicle, it was permitted to dispose of the vehicle under certain conditions. See [U.C.C. §9-610].

At the same time, however, the UCC grants certain rights to the debtor upon repossession and otherwise imposes duties on a secured creditor in possession of collateral. Most importantly for purposes of this case, [U.C.C. §9-623(c)(2)] granted Moffett the right to redeem the vehicle at any time before Tidewater Finance disposed of it. This right of redemption was further protected by a duty imposed on Tidewater Finance to notify Moffett of any planned disposition, at least ten days prior to disposing of the vehicle. See [U.C.C. §§9-611, 9-612]. Indeed, Tidewater Finance was even required to advise Moffett of her right of redemption. See [U.C.C.

§9-614]. Moffett was also entitled to any surplus amount that the secured creditor made in excess of its interest in the collateral. See [U.C.C. §9-615(d)]. Furthermore, the UCC makes clear that Moffett's rights of redemption, notification, and surplus — among other rights — are not extinguished until Tidewater Finance disposes of the repossessed vehicle under [U.C.C. §9-610] or itself accepts the collateral under [U.C.C. §9-620]. See [U.C.C. §9-617]. Since Tidewater Finance has not taken any steps to dispose of the vehicle, Moffett still possessed these rights when she filed for bankruptcy.

These interests, and particularly the statutory right of redemption, are unquestionably "legal or equitable interests" of Moffett's that are included within her bankruptcy estate. See 11 U.S.C. §541(a)(1). As the Supreme Court observed in United States v. Whiting Pools, Inc., 462 U.S. 198 (1983), Congress broadly defined the property of the estate in §541(a)(1) to include all tangible and intangible property interests of the debtor. Indeed, the *Whiting Pools* Court expressly stated that "interests in [repossessed] property that could have been exercised by the debtor — in this case, the rights to notice and the surplus from a tax sale — are already part of the estate by virtue of §541(a)(1)."

Consequently, Moffett's statutory right to redeem the vehicle was properly made part of her bankruptcy estate under 11 U.S.C. §541(a)(1).

B.

We consider next whether Moffett's right to redeem the repossessed vehicle was sufficient to subject Tidewater Finance to the automatic stay and turnover provisions of the Bankruptcy Code. The bankruptcy court found that Moffett's reorganization plan proposes to exercise her right of redemption. Consequently, the court held that Tidewater Finance's security interest was adequately protected and that it must return the vehicle to Moffett.

We agree. [U.C.C. §9-623(b)] permits a debtor to redeem collateral by tendering fulfillment of all obligations secured by the collateral, as well as reasonable expenses from repossessing and holding the collateral. As the bankruptcy court found, Moffett's modified reorganization plan facilitates the exercise of this right of redemption by tendering to Tidewater Finance the full amount due under the contract.

Specifically, the modified plan requires Moffett to make the same monthly installment payments contemplated in the purchase agreement directly to Tidewater Finance, and it provides for the trustee to cure the existing delinquency with payments made over the course of the plan. The estate must pay all applicable interest from the delinquent payments. Moreover, the vehicle is insured. Moffett has now begun to make payments pursuant to the reorganization plan.

It is true that Moffett's reorganization plan does not provide for a lump sum payment of all outstanding debts. However, even if the purchase agreement and [U.C.C. §9-623] require such acceleration of her debts upon default, the Bankruptcy Code entitles Moffett to restructure the timing of her payments in order to facilitate the exercise of her right of redemption. Section 1322(b)(2) of the Bankruptcy Code permits debtors to modify the rights of holders of secured claims. Section 1322(b)(3) also allows debtors to cure their defaults. Courts have recognized that the Bankruptcy Code permits debtors to restructure the timing of payments to secured creditors by de-accelerating debts, in order to allow debtors to regain collateral necessary to their financial recuperation. Pursuant to these powers, the bankruptcy plan here provided for the payment of all future installments, the curing of all delinquent payments, and the payment of all applicable interest, over the course of the plan. Such a flexible approach to repaying claims is precisely what the Bankruptcy Code allows in order to facilitate a debtor's successful rehabilitation.

Moffett's right to redeem the vehicle is being exercised in the bankruptcy estate, and Tidewater Finance's security interest is thus adequately protected. For these reasons, we find that the bankruptcy court was correct in ordering Tidewater Finance to turn over the vehicle to Moffett.

Bankruptcy protection of the debtor who has suffered an acceleration of installment debt occurs in two stages. In the first stage, which extends from the filing of the bankruptcy case until confirmation, the automatic stay protects the debtor from foreclosure while the debtor attempts to formulate a plan. In the second stage, confirmation of the debtor's plan reverses the acceleration, the debtor cures its default, and the installment payment contract between the debtor and creditor is reinstated.

A.   Stage 1: Protection of the Defaulting Debtor Pending Reorganization

As we saw in Assignment 48, when a debtor files a bankruptcy petition an automatic stay against collection and foreclosure is instantly imposed by operation of law. Unless lifted pursuant to Bankruptcy Code §362(d), the stay of an act against property (e.g., foreclosure) continues until the property is no longer in the bankruptcy estate. The stay of any other act continues until the case is closed or dismissed, or the debtor is granted or denied discharge. Bankr. Code §362(c). Thus, in a successful case under either Chapter 11 or Chapter 13, the stay will remain in effect at least until a plan is confirmed.

A debtor who provides adequate protection to its secured creditor typically will be permitted to use the collateral while the case remains pending. Bankr. Code §§363(b)(2) and 363(c)(2). Thus, if the collateral is a house, the debtor can continue to live in it while seeking to cure and reinstate; if the collateral is a hotel, the debtor can continue to operate it. Keep in mind that the "adequate protection" the debtor is required to provide is only protection against decline in the value of the secured creditor's interest in the collateral. Use of the collateral does not itself trigger an obligation on the part of the debtor to make the installment payments that fall due during the bankruptcy case.

Whether the debtor will be required to make installment payments pending confirmation of a plan depends on the chapter under which the case is pending. Bankruptcy Rule 3015 requires Chapter 13 debtors to file plans within 15 days after the filing of the petition, a limit that the court can extend only for "cause shown." Bankruptcy Code §1326 requires that the debtor "commence making payments not later than 30 days after the filing of the Chapter 13 case." If the plan proposes to reinstate a schedule for installment payments, the Chapter 13 debtor probably will have to resume making the installment payments no later than 30 days after filing the petition.

Chapter 11 is considerably more generous to debtors. Debtors need not begin making payments under the plan until the plan has been confirmed by the court. Empirical studies of Chapter 11 cases indicate that the median time to confirmation is about a year. In the interim, the debtor typically has the best of both worlds: It has the use of the collateral, but need not make the installment payments. (The Chapter 11 debtor may end up having to make some interim payments to the secured creditor if necessary to provide adequate protection. Such payments will be necessary only if the collateral is declining in value and the debtor cannot or does not want to furnish adequate protection in the form of additional collateral. The payments required to provide adequate protection may be more or less than the installment payments.)

B.   Stage 2: Reinstatement and Cure

Reinstatement and cure is a process accomplished through the confirmation of a plan of reorganization in either Chapter 13 or Chapter 11. To understand the legal requirements for accomplishing it, reinstatement and cure must be distinguished from *modification* of the rights of the secured creditor.

1.   Modification Distinguished from Reinstatement and Cure

Modification is sometimes referred to as "rewriting the loan." You saw this technique used in *Till v. SCS* in Assignment 49. Like reinstatement and cure, modification is accomplished through confirmation of a plan that provides for it. The minimum amount the debtor must pay on a modified secured claim is determined in two steps: (1) Determine the amount of the allowed secured claim; and (2) formulate a schedule for payments that will have a value, as of the effective date of the plan, not less than the amount of the allowed secured claim. As shown in *Till v. SCS*, the accepted method for meeting that test is that the payments must be at least equal to the amount of the claim plus interest at the "market rate" from the effective date of the plan until the payments are made. In effect, when the debtor proposes to modify the rights of the holder of a secured claim, the debtor must propose to pay the full amount of the secured claim together with interest at the market rate. In cases under Chapter 11, payments can extend over any period of time that is "fair and equitable." Bankr. Code §1129(b)(1). It is not uncommon in cases involving real property for courts to approve periods as long as 20 or 30 years.

In cases under Chapter 13, payments can extend only over the period of the plan. For debtors with below-median incomes that period is usually three years, but the court can approve a period of up to five years for "cause" if the debtor proposes it. For debtors with above-median incomes the plan period is five years unless the debtor can pay all allowed unsecured claims in full over a shorter period. Bankr. Code §1325(b)(4). Chapter 13 plans often provide for modification of loans against cars and other personal property, but few debtors can afford to pay their real estate loans over so short a period of time. Aside from the exception in Bankruptcy Code §1322(c)(2) for home mortgages with only a few years left to run, the Bankruptcy Code prohibits modification of principal-home mortgages altogether. Debtors are limited to modifying their car loans, mortgages on second homes, and similar kinds of obligations. Bankr. Code §1322(b)(2).

By contrast, reinstatement and cure is always a return to the repayment terms agreed to between the debtor and creditor. When a default is "cured" and terms for payment are "reinstated" the debtor takes on two obligations: Any payment that, by the contract between the parties, was due on a date after the reinstatement date remains payable on its original due date; any payment that, by the contract between the parties, is overdue as of the reinstatement date is part of the obligation to cure. As the requirements for cure differ from Chapter 11 to Chapter 13, we discuss them separately.

2.   Reinstatement and Cure Under Chapter 11

The Chapter 11 debtor's right to cure and reinstate is described in Bankruptcy Code §1124(2). That section provides that a class of claims (recall that each class of secured claims ordinarily contains only a single secured claim) is *unimpaired* if the debtor's proposed treatment of the class under its plan complies with four requirements:

(1) The debtor must cure any default that occurred before or after the commencement of the bankruptcy case. This provision does not state when the cure must be made, but the courts have generally held that cure must be in a lump sum at the effective date of the plan.

(2) The plan must reinstate the maturity of that part of the claim that remains outstanding after cure, as such maturity existed before such default. That is, future payments remain due at the times specified in the original contract.

(3) The debtor must compensate the holder of the secured claim for any damages incurred through reasonable reliance on the breached repayment contract.

(4) The plan must not otherwise alter the legal, equitable, or contractual rights to which the claim entitles its holder. For example, if the original contract between the parties provided that the debtor would pay the creditor's reasonable attorneys' fees for collection in the event of default, that term must continue to be applicable to the debtor's post-reinstatement obligations.

If a class of claims is unimpaired under a Chapter 11 plan, the holder of the claim in the class is conclusively presumed to have accepted the plan and is not entitled to vote on it. Bankr. Code §1126(f). If the plan meets the other requirements for confirmation, it can be imposed on the holder of the unimpaired claim over the holder's objection.

To illustrate the operation of these provisions, assume that Debtor borrowed $100,000 from Firstbank. By the terms of the agreement between them, the loan was repayable with interest at 8 percent per year in equal monthly installments over 25 years. The payment on such a loan is $771.82. The agreement provided that payments were due on the 26th day of each month. Debtor made the first 12 payments when due, missed the next three payments, and then filed under Chapter 11. After filing, Debtor continued to miss payments. Debtor then proposed a plan that specified an effective date ten days after confirmation, obligated Debtor to cure the default and to compensate Firstbank for resulting damages on the effective date of the plan, and thereupon reinstated the contract for repayment. Such a plan would meet the requirements of Bankruptcy Code §1124(2) and the court would impose it on Firstbank over Firstbank's objection. Bankr. Code §1129(a)(8).

Assuming that a year passed between the filing of the Chapter 11 case and confirmation of Debtor's plan on March 4, Debtor's payment obligations under the plan would be as follows. First, on March 14, Debtor would have to make up the 15 missed payments in a single payment of $11,577.30. As damages for its breach, Debtor probably would have to pay interest on the overdue sums and any attorneys' fees and expenses of collection provided for under the contract and incurred by Firstbank as a result of the breach. On March 26, and the 26th day of each month thereafter, Debtor would be required to make the originally scheduled payment of $771.82.

Why would Debtor have chosen to cure and reinstate this loan rather than modify the repayment schedule through cramdown under Bankruptcy Code §1129(b)(2)(A)(i)? If the loan was secured only by a mortgage against the principal residence of the debtor, modification was prohibited. See Bankr. Code §1123(b)(5). Otherwise, the likely answer is that Debtor wished to preserve some favorable term of the original contract for repayment that Debtor could not preserve in a cramdown. For example, assume that by the time Debtor proposed its plan, the market rate of interest on this kind of loan had increased to 12 percent per year. If Debtor had modified the secured claim through cramdown, Debtor would not have had to make a lump sum cure, but Debtor would have had to pay interest at 12 percent. See *Till v. SCS*, supra. By curing and reinstating the original terms of the loan, Debtor preserved the 8 percent interest rate specified in the original loan contract.

3.   Reinstatement and Cure Under Chapter 13

The Chapter 13 debtor's right to cure and reinstate is described in Bankruptcy Code §1322(b)(5). That section provides that a Chapter 13 plan may "provide for the curing of any default within a reasonable time and maintenance of payments while the case is pending on any . . . secured claim on which the last payment is due after the date on which the final payment under the plan is due." Although this provision is considerably shorter than §1124(2), its effect is to impose much the same four requirements:

(1)   The debtor must cure any default that occurred before or after the commencement of the bankruptcy case. But under Bankruptcy Code §1322(b)(5), the debtor need only cure "within a reasonable time." The courts have given a flexible meaning to this phrase and approved cures over periods of months or years. All seem to agree that the cure need not be in a lump sum at the effective date of the plan. But all seem also to agree that cure cannot extend beyond the period of the plan. Within that range, the courts consider the size of the arrearage and the debtor's ability to pay in determining whether a particular proposal is reasonable.

(2)   Like a Chapter 11 plan, a Chapter 13 plan must reinstate the maturity of the claim as such maturity existed before such default. That is, future payments remain due at the times specified in the original contract.

(3)   Chapter 13 does not expressly require compensation for damages incurred by the creditor as a result of the breach, but instead directs the courts to look to applicable nonbankruptcy law to determine the amount necessary to cure. Bankr. Code §1322(e). In some states, that law requires payment of interest on the overdue arrearages; in others it does not.

(4)   Like a Chapter 11 plan, a Chapter 13 plan cannot otherwise alter the legal, equitable, or contractual rights to which the holder is entitled.

Debtors who file under Chapter 13 are far more likely to use reinstatement and cure than modification to deal with a long-term secured obligation because, as noted above, Chapter 13 requires full payment of modified claims within the period of the plan; most debtors cannot pay their long-term obligations in such a short time. Bankruptcy Code §1322(b)(2), like Bankruptcy Code §1123(b)(5), prohibits modification of the rights of the holder of a claim secured only by a security interest in real property that is the debtor's principal residence. Under either chapter, reinstatement is the only means available to save the family home once the lender has accelerated the debt. In Nobelman v. American Savings Bank, 508 U.S. 324 (1993), the Supreme Court gave this mortgagee protection provision an expansive reading. In that case, American Savings held a $71,000 purchase money mortgage against the Nobelmans' condominium, which was worth only $23,500. The Court held that the Nobelmans could not, in their Chapter 13 plan, modify even the unsecured portion of American Savings' claim. To save their $23,500 home, the Court ruled, the Nobelmans had to pay $71,000. Justice Thomas, writing for the Court, based his explanation solely on the language of Bankruptcy Code §1322(b)(2). Justice Stevens, concurring, explained the somewhat surprising result as follows:

At first blush it seems somewhat strange that the Bankruptcy Code should provide less protection to an individual's interest in retaining possession of his or her home than of other assets. The anomaly is, however, explained by the legislative history indicating that favorable treatment of residential mortgages was intended to encourage the flow of capital into the home lending market. It therefore seems quite clear that the Court's literal reading of the text of the statute is faithful to the intent of Congress.

508 U.S. 332.

Every secured debt other than a home mortgage can be modified. Evidently, either Congress was not so worried about the flow of capital into car loan markets or furniture loan markets or the lobbies for these consumer lenders were not so well organized.

4. When Is It Too Late to File Bankruptcy to Reinstate and Cure?

A debtor can reinstate and cure a default and acceleration even though the deadline for doing so under state law has passed before the debtor invokes bankruptcy procedure. Bankruptcy does not just preserve rights existing under state law, it recognizes rights that state law does not. But how far is bankruptcy willing to go in reversing what has already taken place under nonbankruptcy law? This case gives one view. It happens to involve a home mortgage, but that fact has no significant bearing on the portions of the opinion included here.

In re DeSeno

17 F.3d 642 (3d Cir. 1994)

ROTH, CIRCUIT JUDGE:

This appeal requires us to determine whether Chapter 11 of the Bankruptcy Code authorizes a debtor to cure or modify a foreclosure judgment obtained under New Jersey law. The bankruptcy court concluded that it does and thereby denied appellee Midlantic National Bank's motion requesting relief from the automatic stay. Midlantic appealed to the district court, which reversed the decision of the bankruptcy court. We will affirm the district court's decision insofar as it holds that a Chapter 11 debtor may not cure a default . . . following a foreclosure judgment in New Jersey. Because we agree with the bankruptcy court that Chapter 11 allows a debtor to modify such a foreclosure judgment, however, we will reverse the decision of the district court on that issue.

I

Midlantic holds a first purchase money mortgage, executed by the debtor Jean R. DeSeno and her ex-husband Stefano T. DeSeno and dated November 19, 1979, on property owned by Ms. DeSeno. . . . On August 20, 1991, Midlantic obtained a foreclosure judgment in the Superior Court of New Jersey on the mortgage. Pursuant to the judgment, the court issued a writ of execution directing the Sheriff of Monmouth County to sell the property in order to satisfy the judgment. The Sheriff scheduled the sale for March 2, 1992; however, at the request of Ms. DeSeno the sale was postponed until March 30. On March 25, 1992, prior to the foreclosure sale, Ms. DeSeno filed her petition for protection under Chapter 11 of the Bankruptcy Code.

On September 9, 1992, Midlantic filed a motion for relief from the automatic stay, arguing, inter alia, that it was entitled to relief from the stay under this court's decisions in In re Roach, 824 F.2d 1370 (3d Cir. 1987), and First Natl. Fidelity Corp. v. Perry, 945 F.2d 61 (3d Cir. 1991). On October 19, 1992, the bankruptcy court entered an order denying Midlantic's motion on the basis of its conclusion that *Roach* and *Perry* do not apply in Chapter 11 cases.

Midlantic appealed this order to the district court. On April 5, 1993, the district court vacated the bankruptcy court's order, reasoning that *Roach* and *Perry* do apply in Chapter 11 cases, and remanded the case to that court. On May 3, 1993, Ms. DeSeno filed a timely appeal. The bankruptcy court has stayed all proceedings in the case pending the outcome of this appeal. . . .

III

Both Chapter 11 and Chapter 13 authorize a debtor's bankruptcy plan to provide for the "curing or waiving of any default." 11 U.S.C. §§1123(a)(5)(G) & 1322(b)(3). See also 11 U.S.C. §1322(b)(5). In *Roach*, 824 F.2d at 1376, this court observed that "[§]1123 of Chapter 11 and §1322 of Chapter 13 are parallel provisions, and we believe it very likely that Congress' understanding of the authorization to cure defaults in each was identical." Based on this understanding, we looked to the text and legislative history of 11 U.S.C. §§1123 & 1124 to guide our interpretation of the scope of the authorization to cure defaults in Chapter 13. . . . The Second Circuit has also concluded that the concept of "curing a default" has the same meaning in Chapters 7, 11, and 13. In re Taddeo, 685 F.2d 24, 28-29 (2d Cir. 1982).

In *Roach*, we held that "§1322(b) must be read in the context of state law and . . . its right to cure a default on a mortgage on a home located in New Jersey terminates upon entry of a foreclosure judgment." 824 F.2d at 1373. We reasoned that §1322(b)(5) authorized the curing of a default only in a contractual relationship, which, under New Jersey law, ceases to exist following a foreclosure judgment. Since the mortgage no longer exists, its default can no longer be cured, and the mortgagee's rights arise solely from the judgment. Moreover, we noted that the rights in the property created by a foreclosure judgment are of a different nature than those established by the mortgage in that the foreclosure judgment makes the entire amount of the debt immediately due and payable out of the proceeds of the sale of the property. Because we could find no "statutory language, legislative history, or a significant federal interest mandating federal interference with state foreclosure judgments," id. at 1378-1379, we held "that in New Jersey the right to cure a default on a home mortgage under §1322(b) does not extend beyond the entry of a foreclosure judgment." Id. at 1379.

We decline to reconsider our conclusions in *Roach* and we will specifically extend our holding in that case to Chapter 11. Neither the text of the statute, the legislative history, nor the policies animating the Bankruptcy Code suggest that the concept of "curing a default" should be ascribed any more than a single, consistent meaning throughout the Code. Thus, absent a change in New Jersey's law concerning foreclosure judgments, we will not reexamine our holding that entry of a foreclosure judgment on a New Jersey home mortgage terminates a debtor's right to cure a default on that mortgage. In this case, Midlantic has obtained a foreclosure judgment on Ms. DeSeno's mortgage. As a result, her right to cure her default on the mortgage has terminated, and Midlantic cannot be prevented from lifting the stay on this basis.

IV

We must next consider whether a Chapter 11 debtor has the authority to provide for modification of a foreclosure judgment as part of a plan of reorganization. The modification power is found in §1123(a), which provides in relevant part:

> Notwithstanding any otherwise applicable nonbankruptcy law, a plan shall . . .
>> (5) provide adequate means for the plan's implementation, such as . . .
>>> (E) satisfaction or modification of any lien;
>>> (F) cancellation or modification of any indenture or similar instrument. . . .

The district court concluded that this provision does not give a debtor the authority to modify a foreclosure judgment created under New Jersey law. . . .

We believe the district court erred in reaching this conclusion. . . . The district court incorrectly characterized the foreclosure judgment as a judicial lien. In *Perry*, 945 F.2d at 64-65, we concluded that "a New Jersey home mortgage lender retains a security interest for the purposes of §1322(b)(2) following the entry of a foreclosure judgment." Id. at 65. We reasoned that a foreclosure judgment, since it is the product of the mortgage agreement, is created by this agreement, and thus is a "security interest" within the definition provided in 11 U.S.C. §101 [definition of "security interest"]. As such, it cannot also be a judicial lien.

Nevertheless, our analysis remains the same under the assumption that a foreclosure judgment is a security interest rather than a judicial lien. The Code's definition provides that a security interest is a "lien created by an agreement." 11 U.S.C. §101(51). Here again, the internal reference to the concept of "lien" compels the conclusion that the reference in §1123(a)(5)(E) to "any lien" includes rather than excludes security interests. . . .

V

For the foregoing reasons, the decision of the district court will be affirmed to the extent of its ruling that Ms. DeSeno is not authorized to cure her default on her home mortgage but will be reversed to the extent that it held that Ms. DeSeno may not modify Midlantic's foreclosure judgment in her Chapter 11 plan. The case will be remanded to the district court, for remand by it to the bankruptcy court, for further proceedings consistent with this opinion.

———————————

After *DeSeno* was decided, Congress adopted the Bankruptcy Reform Act of 1994 and in so doing amended Bankruptcy Code §1322 to add subsection (c). That subsection provides:

> Notwithstanding applicable nonbankruptcy law...a default with respect to, or that gave rise to, a lien on the debtor's principal residence may be cured...until such residence is sold at a foreclosure sale....

This amendment would have no direct effect on *DeSeno*, because *DeSeno* was a case under Chapter 11. But it does cut away the logical roots of *DeSeno*: The court in *DeSeno* decided that entry of the final judgment of foreclosure should cut off the right to reinstate and cure in Chapter 11 because that was the rule in Chapter 13. Now the rule in Chapter 13 is that the debtor has until foreclosure to file and reinstate.

The fact that Congress amended Chapter 13 to deal with this problem but made no change in Chapter 11 is ambiguous. Perhaps Congress meant to give Chapter 13 debtors longer to file and for that reason amended only Chapter 13. Perhaps Congress thought that Chapter 11 debtors already had until the foreclosure sale to file, and therefore needed no change. It seems more plausible to us that Congress was lobbied for the change in Chapter 13 and restricted its attention to that chapter for that reason alone. In any event, we expect that the courts soon will be called upon to explain.

Ms. DeSeno apparently filed under Chapter 11 to save her home because, at the time of her case, debtors could modify mortgages against their principal residences in Chapter 11 but not in Chapter 13. The Bankruptcy Reform Act of 1994 amended Bankruptcy Code §1123(b)(5) to conform to Bankruptcy Code §1322(b)(2). Now few debtors can modify mortgages against their principal residences under either chapter.

Thus the effect of the 1994 legislation may have been to overturn both of the holdings of *DeSeno*. Under current law, it may well be that a debtor filing Chapter 11 after a final judgment of foreclosure but before the sale *can reinstate* a home mortgage but *cannot modify* it!

Consumer debtors are eligible to file under Chapter 11. Even after the 1994 amendments, Chapter 11 relief remains in some respects more favorable to the debtor than Chapter 13 relief. Why don't more consumer debtors take advantage of Chapter 11? Part of the answer is that Chapter 11 is a considerably more expensive procedure. For some debtors, the cost is not justified; the total cost of reinstatement and cure under Chapter 13 is lower than the total cost of modification under Chapter 11. Other debtors would be better off in Chapter 11, but simply can't raise the cash to get there.

How much money are we talking about? The filing fee for Chapter 13 is $150 as of this writing; the filing fee for Chapter 11 is $1,000. By our rough estimate, an inexpensive fee for taking a mortgage reinstatement case through Chapter 13 would be about $1,500; an inexpensive fee for taking a mortgage modification case through Chapter 11 would be about $3,000.

C.   Binding Lenders in the Absence of a
Fixed Schedule for Repayment

As we noted in Assignment 54, many lending relationships lack a fixed schedule for repayment. Probably the most common of these is the line of credit
that is payable on demand. In that arrangement, borrowing and repayment
are expected to occur at the convenience of the debtor — unless the secured
creditor decides to call the loan. The debtor's right to cure and reinstate under
bankruptcy law is of no avail to debtors in such relationships. Cure and reinstatement only restores to the debtor contract rights the debtor enjoyed before
default. Debtors whose lines of credit were repayable on demand or at a
specific time that has passed have no contract rights that bankruptcy could
restore.

Such debtors are protected, if at all, only through their ability to modify the
claim or to use the respite of reorganization proceedings to find a willing
substitute lender. For modification to yield substantial benefits to the debtor,
there must be a substantial loan outstanding at the time of bankruptcy. The
automatic stay prevents secured creditors from trying to collect after a bankruptcy filing money they advanced to a debtor before the filing. But nothing
in bankruptcy law or practice requires a lender to make advances during
or after bankruptcy — even if the lenders have contracted to make those
advances. See, e.g., Bankr. Code §365(c)(2). If, as is often the case, the line
of credit lender simply waits until the debtor pays the line down and then
precipitates the bankruptcy by refusing to make further advances, the lender
has probably won the game.

Finding a substitute lender may not be out of the question. Many lenders
actively seek relationships with borrowers who are in bankruptcy. Some
demand a higher price. Some see a benefit to lending to debtors who are
stripping away their other debt and have good collateral to offer.

Problem Set 55

55.1.   How does reading Assignment 55 change your response to the situation presented in Problem 54.5? What do you expect Rebel to do if Second
National calls the loan without notice? Where is Second National going to
come out on this? Bankr. Code §§362(a) and (d), 363(a), (b)(1), (c), and (e),
1123(a)(5)(E), 1124.

55.2.   a.   David Walker (from Problem 54.4) has come up with alternatives for Teresa Revez. He now says the Bank can lend Teresa the $150,000 she
needs on either of two arrangements. The first is to lend her the money at
prime plus 2 percent on a demand note. The second is to lend her the money
at prime plus 3.25 percent on an arrangement that provides for 30 days' notice
prior to call if she is not then in default. Teresa wants your advice on choosing
between these options. Considering only these two, what do you recommend? Bankr. Code §§1123(a)(5)(E), 1124, and 1129(b)(2)(A)(i).

b.   Teresa's expression of concern about having the entire $150,000 out-
standing at such a high rate of interest, even when she did not need it,

prompted David Walker to sweeten the deal. Now the Bank is offering a line of credit for $150,000 on the same terms that they were offering to lend her $150,000 fixed. That is, she can choose between prime plus 2 percent on a demand note or prime plus 3.25 percent on a note with 30 days' notice before cancellation. Having this loan in the form of a line of credit entitles Teresa to pay back to the bank what she doesn't need, and draw it out again when she does need it. Under the options in part a of this problem, Teresa would have put the money she didn't need in a bank account at a relatively low rate of interest, so the savings offered by these line of credit options are substantial. Do you see any disadvantages? Which of the two line of credit arrangements seems more attractive?

55.3.   Ever since the market for single-family houses collapsed in the town where you practice, you've had a steady stream of debtors looking for ways to save their homes. The circumstances of two of them are described below.

Willard Spivak bought his home three years ago from Rolling Green Developers for $100,000. He financed the home with a 30-year conventional mortgage from Gateway Savings and Loan. The mortgage provides for repayment in equal monthly installments with interest at 8 percent per year. The principal amount of the loan was $80,000. Willard made 29 monthly payments of $587.02 each, and then missed the 30th and all subsequent payments. As of yesterday, he is seven months in arrears, a total of $4,109.14. Willard shows you each of the communications he has received from Gateway since he went into default. The first was a "Friendly Reminder"; the second and third were titled "Notice of Delinquency." The fourth was a letter from a law firm detailing the status of the loan and stating that if Willard did not bring the loan current within ten days, the bank would declare a default and accelerate the due dates of all payments. The next letter was from the same law firm, dated 23 days later. It stated that Gateway declared the loan in default, that the entire balance of approximately $84,000 was immediately due and payable, and that if Willard did not pay it within ten days, Gateway would foreclose. The last document Willard shows you is the foreclosure complaint and summons served by the sheriff on Willard yesterday, one month after the last letter. Willard says he is back at work now and has the money to resume payments on the mortgage, but he doesn't know where he can get $4,109 to make up the arrearage. When Willard called the bank recently, an officer told him that even if he *does* tender the arrearage now, the bank won't accept it. "You have to pay the whole $84,000," the officer told him. One of the reasons Gateway wants to get rid of this loan is that rates have risen since Gateway made it. Gateway currently charges 11 percent for the same kind of loan. (At that rate, Willard's monthly payment would have been $761.86 on the same loan.) The home is probably worth only about the amount of the loan, but Willard wants to keep it.

a.   What do you recommend? Bankr. Code §§1322(b)(5), 1322(c) and (d), 1325(b)(4), 1123(a)(5), 1123(b)(5), 1124, 1129(b)(2)(A).

b.   If Willard follows your recommendation, what is the minimum Willard must pay to keep the house and when will he have to pay it?

c.   Winona Williams bought her home three years ago for $100,000. Thinking that interest rates would go down in a few years, she financed her purchase with an $80,000 purchase-money mortgage from the seller, Marian Case. The terms are remarkably similar to the terms of Willard Spivak's mortgage — the loan is amortized over 30 years with interest at 8 percent per year, for a monthly payment of $587.02. The difference is that Winona's mortgage "balloons" at the end of five years — just two years from now. (The term *balloon* means that the entire balance becomes due.) Like Willard, Winona is seven months in arrears, a total of $4,109, and Marian Case has accelerated and commenced foreclosure. Winona's home is still worth $100,000 and she'd really like to hold on to it. What do you suggest? Bankr. Code §§1123(a)(5), 1123(b)(5), 1124, 1129(a)(11), 1129(b)(2)(A), 1322(b)(2), 1322(b)(5), 1322(c)(2), 1325(a)(5), 1325(a)(6), 1325(b)(4).

d. Would it help if Winona were to move out of the house, rent it to a tenant, and use that cash flow to rent another house for herself?

e. Willard Spivak, from part a of this problem, felt he couldn't afford your fees, so he didn't take your advice. Instead, he made a deal with Gateway. Under the deal, the amount of his arrearage was fixed at $6,000 ($4,109 plus Gateway's attorneys' fees) and Gateway gave him six months to pay it. In return, Willard agreed to an increase in the interest rate on the loan from 8 to 11 percent. Now Willard's six months is almost up. He has been making the regular monthly payments of $761.86 on the loan at the new interest rate, but hasn't been able to save anything toward the $6,000 payment that is about to come due. Realizing that he is about to default again, Willard is back to see you. Is there anything you can do for him? Bankr. Code §§1123(a)(5), 1123(b)(5), 1322(b).

55.4. a. In *Nobelman*, discussed in section B.3 of this assignment, American Savings held a mortgage in the amount of $71,000 against the debtors' condominium, which had a value of only $23,500. The Supreme Court held that the Nobelmans could not modify the unsecured portion of American Savings' claim. If you represented the Nobelmans at this point, what would you advise with regard to this condominium?

b. If you represented American Savings, what would you advise with regard to this condominium?

55.5. On reading Justice Stevens' one-paragraph concurring opinion in *Nobelman* (set forth in section B of this chapter), Congresswoman Martha Pepper has an idea. If denying modification of home mortgages can cause capital to flow into the home mortgage market, why can't denying modification of auto loans cause capital to flow into the auto market — and denying modification of business loans cause capital to flow into the business markets? The congresswoman is so excited by the whole idea that she is beside herself. "Maybe I've found the key to the nation's economic problems," she says with her characteristic modesty. Then she asks for your opinion. What do you tell her?

Chapter 17.   The Prototypical Secured Transaction

Assignment 56:   The Prototypical Secured Transaction

In Part One of this book, we have addressed various aspects of the relationship between a secured creditor and its debtor. In this assignment, we examine a specific example of such a relationship. The example we have chosen is a relationship between a boat dealer and its inventory lender. In preparing the description of this transaction, we were assisted by Deutsche Financial Services, a lender based in St. Louis, Missouri. The debtors, Bonnie Brezhnev and her corporation, Bonnie's Boat World, Inc., and their supplier, Shoreline Boats, are all fictional characters. But their relationships with Deutsche are not materially different from real relationships that others have with Deutsche and lenders like Deutsche.

While the relationships described in this assignment are typical of inventory lending, they are not typical of secured transactions generally. As you have already seen in earlier assignments, secured transactions come in a variety of forms. At one extreme, the secured transaction in which a consumer buys a color TV may be documented only by a half-page printed form signed when the debtor opens the charge account and a receipt issued for the particular sale. At the other extreme, the documentation for the financing of an office building or industrial plant may be hundreds or even thousands of pages in length. In its complexity, the transaction described in this assignment is perhaps about midway between those extremes.

We will discuss the strategies and motivations of both sides. The legal doctrine governing secured credit is best understood in relation to those strategies and motivations. But given the wide variety of circumstances in which creditors take security, it should come as no surprise that strategies and motivations differ from one kind of secured transaction to another and with the attitudes of different participants to the same kind of secured transaction. Thus, you should be cautious in attempting to generalize our prototype to other kinds of secured lending. To understand why a provision of Article 9 exists in the form it does, one must usually see how it operates in a variety of circumstances. At the same time, one must start somewhere, and we have chosen the context of inventory lending.

A.   The Parties

Deutsche Financial Services is among the largest commercial finance companies in the United States, with offices in 22 cities in the United States, Canada, and the United Kingdom. It lends against all kinds of business assets; a sister company is engaged in consumer finance. A substantial portion of its business is *floorplanning*, that is, financing the purchase of the inventory that is on a dealer's "showroom floor." The products financed by Deutsche's floorplanning program include computers, mobile homes, recreation vehicles, boats and motors, consumer electronics and appliances, keyboards and other musical instruments, industrial equipment, agricultural equipment, office machines, snowmobiles, and motorcycles.

Bonnie's Boat World, Inc. is a corporation invented by the authors of this book. Bonnie Brezhnev is a person invented along with the corporation to serve as its owner. She purchased Art's Boat World, Inc. about three months ago and changed the name to Bonnie's Boat World. The business is located on a commercial highway that passes within a few hundred feet of a lake. The boatyard, located on the narrow strip of land between the highway and the lake, consists of a small indoor showroom, sales offices, four acres of land surrounded by an eight-foot cyclone fence, a boat storage building, and a pier extending into the lake.

B. Deutsche Approves Bonnie's Loan

Dissatisfied with the lender who has been financing her inventory, Bonnie makes her first contact with Deutsche. She visits the local Deutsche office and meets with Paul Kaplan, a Deutsche loan officer. They discuss the boat business, Bonnie's plans for the future, the terms on which Deutsche makes loans, and a number of other subjects. Generally pleased, Bonnie takes the blank form of a loan application with her when she leaves. The application seeks a variety of information about Bonnie and her business, including current balance sheets, income statements, and income tax returns for both herself and the corporation. Because Bonnie has to bring some of the accounting records up to date, it takes Bonnie and her bookkeeper a little over a week to complete the application.

When Paul Kaplan receives the application, he immediately orders a credit report from Dun and Bradstreet (D & B). D & B has not previously reported on Bonnie or Bonnie's Boat World, so they have no information on either at the time they receive Deutsche's request. To get the information they eventually include in their report, D & B searches several public records, interviews Bonnie, and checks with some of the credit references she gives them. Paul arranges for all of the information he has obtained about Bonnie's to be entered into Deutsche's Expert Credit System, a computer system that uses artificial intelligence to simulate the analytical approach of senior loan officers. Based on the computer analysis and Paul's independent review of the application and credit report, Paul decides to recommend authorization of the loan.

Paul presents the loan application to his branch manager a few days later. Based on the size of the requested credit line, the branch manager has sufficient credit authority to approve the account alone. Although the branch manager has some concerns about Bonnie's relative inexperience in the retail boat business, the application is otherwise strong and the branch manager approves it. Paul calls Bonnie that same afternoon to tell her that the loan has been approved and to set a time for closing the transaction.

C.   Deutsche and Bonnie's Document the Loan

Just a few days after her inventory loan was approved, Bonnie returns to the offices of Deutsche to complete the documentation for the loan. She has already seen and discussed with her own lawyers the Agreement for Wholesale Financing (Security Agreement — Arbitration) that she will have to sign. Prior to this meeting, Richard Feynman, a Deutsche employee, has searched the Article 9 filing system to verify the name and address of the bank that financed the boats already in Bonnie's possession. He has visited Bonnie's Boat World and made a list of all the boats currently in the company's possession. While there, Richard examined the books and records of the business to see how they are kept. Satisfied with what he had seen and been told, Richard advises Paul that the loan is ready for closing.

When Bonnie arrives in his office, Paul has all of the documents on his desk. Bonnie and Paul go through them one by one, discussing and signing them. Four of these documents, the security agreement, a sample form statement of transaction, the financing statement, and the personal guarantee are relevant to an understanding of the security aspect of the transaction.

1.   Security Agreement and Statement of Transaction

Subject to a few omissions indicated, this is the full text of the security agreement Bonnie signs at the closing:

AGREEMENT FOR WHOLESALE FINANCING
(SECURITY AGREEMENT — ARBITRATION)

This Agreement for Wholesale Financing ("Agreement") is made as of <u>January 24, 2004</u> between Deutsche Financial Services ("Deutsche") and <u>Bonnie's Boat World, Inc.</u>, a CORPORATION ("Dealer"), having a principal place of business located at

12376 HIGHWAY 441
BLUE MOON, MO 63131

1. Subject to the terms of this Agreement, Deutsche, in its sole discretion, may extend credit to Dealer from time to time to purchase inventory from

Deutsche-approved vendors. Deutsche may combine all of Deutsche's advances to Dealer or on Dealer's behalf, whether under this Agreement or any other agreement, to make one debt owed by Dealer. Deutsche's decision to advance funds on any inventory will not be binding until the funds are actually advanced. Dealer agrees that Deutsche may, at any time and without notice to Dealer, elect not to finance any inventory sold by particular vendors who are in default of their obligations to Deutsche, or with respect to which Deutsche reasonably feels insecure.

2. Dealer and Deutsche agree that certain financial terms of any advance made by Deutsche under this Agreement, whether regarding finance charges, other fees, maturities, curtailments or other financial terms, are not set forth herein because such terms depend, in part, upon the availability from time to time of vendor discounts or other incentives, prevailing economic conditions, Deutsche's floorplanning volume with Dealer and with Dealer's vendors, and other economic factors which may vary over time. Dealer and Deutsche further agree that it is therefore in their mutual best interest to set forth in this Agreement only the general terms of Dealer's financing arrangement with Deutsche. Upon agreeing to finance a particular item of inventory for Dealer, Deutsche will send Dealer a Statement of Transaction identifying such inventory and the applicable financial terms. Unless Dealer notifies Deutsche in writing of any objection within fifteen (15) days after a Statement of Transaction is mailed to Dealer:

(a) the amount shown on such Statement of Transaction will be an account stated;

(b) Dealer will have agreed to all rates, charges and other terms shown on such Statement of Transaction;

(c) Dealer will have agreed that the items of inventory referenced in such Statement of Transaction are being financed by Deutsche at Dealer's request; and

(d) such Statement of Transaction will be incorporated herein by reference, will be made a part hereof as if originally set forth herein, and will constitute an addendum hereto.

If Dealer objects to the terms of any Statement of Transaction, Dealer agrees to pay Deutsche for such inventory in accordance with the most recent terms for similar inventory to which Dealer has not objected (or, if there are no prior terms, at the lesser of 16% per annum or at the maximum lawful contract rate of interest permitted under applicable law), but Dealer acknowledges that Deutsche may then elect to terminate Dealer's financing program pursuant to Section 12, and cease making additional advances to Dealer. Any termination for that reason, however, will not accelerate the maturities of advances previously made, unless Dealer shall otherwise be in default of this Agreement.

3. To secure payment of all Dealer's current and future debts to Deutsche, whether under this Agreement or any current or future guaranty or other agreement, Dealer grants Deutsche a security interest in all Dealer's inventory, equipment, fixtures, accounts, contract rights, chattel paper, instruments, reserves, documents and general intangibles, whether now owned or hereafter

acquired, all attachments, accessories, accessions, substitutions and replacements thereto and all proceeds thereof. All such assets are as defined in the Uniform Commercial Code and referred to herein as the "Collateral." All Collateral financed by Deutsche, and all proceeds thereof, will be held in trust by Dealer for Deutsche, with such proceeds being payable in accordance with Section 7.

4. Dealer represents that all Collateral will be kept at Dealer's principal place of business listed above, and, if any, the following other locations:

Dealer will give Deutsche at least 30 days prior written notice of any change in Dealer's identity, name, form of business organization, ownership, principal place of business, Collateral locations or other business locations.

5. Dealer will:

(a)   only exhibit and sell Collateral financed by Deutsche to buyers in the ordinary course of business;

(b)   not rent, lease, demonstrate, transfer or use any Collateral financed by Deutsche without Deutsche's prior written consent;

(c)   execute all documents Deutsche requests to perfect Deutsche's security interest in the Collateral;

(d)   deliver to Deutsche immediately upon each request, and Deutsche may retain, each Certificate of Title or Statement of Origin issued for Collateral financed by Deutsche; and

(e)   immediately provide Deutsche with copies of Dealer's annual financial statements upon their completion (which in no event shall exceed 120 days after the end of Dealer's fiscal year), and all other information regarding Dealer that Deutsche requests from time to time. All financial information Dealer delivers to Deutsche will accurately represent Dealer's financial condition either as of the date of delivery, or, if different, the date specified therein, and Dealer acknowledges Deutsche's reliance thereon.

6. Dealer will:

(a)   pay all taxes and fees assessed against Dealer or the Collateral when due;

(b)   immediately notify Deutsche of any loss, theft or damage to any Collateral;

(c)   keep the Collateral insured for its full insurable value under a property insurance policy with a company acceptable to Deutsche, naming Deutsche as a loss-payee and containing standard lender's loss payable and termination provisions; and

(d)   provide Deutsche with written evidence of such insurance coverage and loss-payee and lender's clauses.

If Dealer fails to pay any taxes, fees or other obligations which may impair Deutsche's interest in the Collateral, or fails to keep the Collateral insured, Deutsche may pay such taxes, fees or obligations and pay the cost to insure the

Collateral, and the amounts paid will be: (i) an additional debt owed by Dealer to Deutsche; and (ii) due and payable immediately in full. Dealer grants Deutsche an irrevocable license to enter Dealer's business locations during normal business hours without notice to Dealer to:

(A) account for and inspect all Collateral;
(B) verify Dealer's compliance with this Agreement; and
(C) examine and copy Dealer's books and records related to the Collateral.

7. Dealer will immediately pay Deutsche the principal indebtedness owed Deutsche on each item of Collateral financed by Deutsche (as shown on the Statement of Transaction identifying such Collateral) on the earliest occurrence of any of the following events:

(a) when such Collateral is lost, stolen or damaged;
(b) for Collateral financed under Pay-As-Sold ("PAS") terms (as shown on the Statement of Transaction identifying such Collateral), when such Collateral is sold, transferred, rented, leased, otherwise disposed of or matured;
(c) in strict accordance with any curtailment schedule for such Collateral (as shown on the Statement of Transaction identifying such Collateral);
(d) for Collateral financed under Scheduled Payment Program ("SPP") terms (as shown on the Statement of Transaction identifying such Collateral), in strict accordance with the installment payment schedule; and
(e) when otherwise required under the terms of any financing program agreed to in writing by the parties.

Regardless of the SPP terms pertaining to any Collateral financed by Deutsche if Deutsche determines that the current outstanding debt owed by Dealer to Deutsche exceeds the aggregate wholesale invoice price of such Collateral in Dealer's possession, Dealer will immediately upon demand pay Deutsche the difference between such outstanding debt and the aggregate wholesale invoice price of such Collateral. If Dealer from time to time is required to make immediate payment to Deutsche of any past due obligation discovered during any Collateral audit, or at any other time, Dealer agrees that acceptance of such payment by Deutsche shall not be construed to have waived or amended the terms of its financing program. Dealer agrees that the proceeds of any Collateral received by Dealer shall be held by Dealer in trust for Deutsche's benefit, for application as provided in this Agreement. Dealer will send all payments to Deutsche's branch office(s) responsible for Dealer's account. Deutsche may apply:

(i) payments to reduce finance charges first and then principal, regardless of Dealer's instructions; and
(ii) principal payments to the oldest (earliest) invoice for Collateral financed by Deutsche, but, in any event, all principal payments will first be applied to such Collateral which is sold, lost, stolen, damaged, rented, leased, or otherwise disposed of or unaccounted for. . . .

8. Dealer will pay Deutsche finance charges on the outstanding principal debt Dealer owes Deutsche for each item of Collateral financed by Deutsche at the

rate(s) shown on the Statement of Transaction identifying such Collateral, unless Dealer objects thereto as provided in Section 2. The finance charges attributable to the rate shown on the Statement of Transaction will:

(a)   be computed based on a 360-day year;
(b)   be calculated by multiplying the Daily Charge (as defined below) by the actual number of days in the applicable billing period; and
(c)   accrue from the invoice date of the Collateral identified on such Statement of Transaction until Deutsche receives full payment of the principal debt Dealer owes Deutsche for each item of such Collateral.

The "Daily Charge" is the product of the Daily Rate (as defined below) multiplied by the Average Daily Balance (as defined below). The "Daily Rate" is the quotient of the annual rate shown on the Statement of Transaction divided by 360, or the monthly rate shown on the Statement of Transaction divided by 30. The "Average Daily Balance" is the quotient of

(i)   the sum of the outstanding principal debt owed Deutsche on each day of a billing period for each item of Collateral identified on a Statement of Transaction, divided by
(ii)   the actual number of days in such billing period.

Dealer will also pay Deutsche $100 for each check returned unpaid for insufficient funds (an "NSF check") (such $100 payment repays Deutsche's estimated administrative costs; it does not waive the default caused by the NSF check). Dealer acknowledges that Deutsche intends to strictly conform to the applicable usury laws governing this Agreement and understands that Dealer is not obligated to pay any finance charges billed to Dealer's account exceeding the amount allowed by such usury laws, and any such excess finance charges Dealer pays will be applied to reduce Dealer's principal debt owed to Deutsche. The annual percentage rate of the finance charges relating to any item of Collateral financed by Deutsche shall be calculated from the invoice date of such Collateral, regardless of any period during which any finance charge subsidy shall be paid or payable by any third party. Deutsche will send Dealer a monthly billing statement identifying all charges due on Dealer's account with Deutsche. The charges specified on each billing statement will be:

(A)   due and payable in full immediately on receipt, and
(B)   an account stated, unless Deutsche receives Dealer's written objection thereto within 15 days after it is mailed to Dealer.

If Deutsche does not receive, by the 25th day of any given month, payment of all charges accrued to Dealer's account with Deutsche during the immediately preceding month, Dealer will (to the extent allowed by law) pay Deutsche a late fee ("Late Fee") equal to the greater of $5 or 5% of the amount of such finance charges (such Late Fee repays Deutsche's estimated administrative costs; it does not waive the default caused by the late payment). Deutsche may adjust the billing statement at any time to conform to applicable law and this Agreement.

9. Dealer will be in default under this Agreement if:

(a)   Dealer breaches any terms, warranties or representations contained herein, in any Statement of Transaction to which Dealer has not objected as provided in Section 2, or in any other agreement between Deutsche and Dealer;

(b)   any guarantor of Dealer's debts to Deutsche breaches any terms, warranties or representations contained in any guaranty or other agreement between the guarantor and Deutsche;

(c)   any representation, statement, report or certificate made or delivered by Dealer or any guarantor to Deutsche is not accurate when made;

(d)   Dealer fails to pay any portion of Dealer's debts to Deutsche when due and payable hereunder or under any other agreement between Deutsche and Dealer;

(e)   Dealer abandons any Collateral;

(f)   Dealer or any guarantor is or becomes in default in the payment of any debt owed to any third party;

(g)   a money judgment issues against Dealer or any guarantor;

(h)   an attachment, sale or seizure issues or is executed against any assets of Dealer or of any guarantor;

(i)   the undersigned dies while Dealer's business is operated as a sole proprietorship or any general partner dies while Dealer's business is operated as a general or limited partnership;

(j)   any guarantor dies;

(k)   Dealer or any guarantor shall cease existence as a corporation, partnership or trust;

(l)   Dealer or any guarantor ceases or suspends business;

(m)   Dealer or any guarantor makes a general assignment for the benefit of creditors;

(n)   Dealer or any guarantor becomes insolvent or voluntarily or involuntarily becomes subject to the Federal Bankruptcy Code, any state insolvency law or any similar law;

(o)   any receiver is appointed for any of Dealer's or any guarantor's assets;

(p)   any guaranty of Dealer's debts to Deutsche is terminated;

(q)   Dealer loses any franchise, permission, license or right to sell or deal in any Collateral which Deutsche finances;

(r)   Dealer or any guarantor misrepresents Dealer's or such guarantor's financial condition or organizational structure; or

(s)   any of the Collateral becomes subject to any lien, claim, encumbrance or security interest prior or superior to Deutsche's.

In the event of a default

(i)   Deutsche may at any time at Deutsche's election, without notice or demand to Dealer, do any one or more of the following: declare all or any part of the debt Dealer owes Deutsche immediately due and payable, together with all costs and expenses of Deutsche's collection activity, including, without limitation, all reasonable attorney's fees; exercise any or all rights under applicable law (including, without limitation, the right to possess, transfer and dispose of the Collateral); and/or cease extending any additional credit to Dealer (Deutsche's right to cease extending credit shall not be construed to limit the discretionary nature of this credit facility).

(ii) Dealer will segregate and keep the Collateral in trust for Deutsche, and in good order and repair, and will not exhibit, sell, rent, lease, further encumber, otherwise dispose of or use any Collateral.

(iii) Upon Deutsche's oral or written demand, Dealer will immediately deliver the Collateral to Deutsche, in good order and repair, at a place specified by Deutsche, together with all related documents; or Deutsche may, in Deutsche's sole discretion and without notice or demand to Dealer, take immediate possession of the Collateral together with all related documents.

(iv) Deutsche may, without notice, apply a default finance charge to Dealer's outstanding principal indebtedness equal to the default rate specified in Dealer's financing program with Deutsche, if any, or if there is none so specified, at the lesser of 3% per annum above the rate in effect immediately prior to the default, or the highest lawful contract rate of interest permitted under applicable law.

All Deutsche's rights and remedies are cumulative. Deutsche's failure to exercise any of Deutsche's rights or remedies hereunder will not waive any of Deutsche's rights or remedies as to any past, current or future default.

10. Dealer agrees that if Deutsche conducts a private sale of any Collateral by requesting bids from 10 or more dealers or distributors in that type of Collateral, any sale by Deutsche of such Collateral in bulk or in parcels within 120 days of

(a) Deutsche's taking possession and control of such Collateral; or
(b) when Deutsche is otherwise authorized to sell such Collateral;

whichever occurs last, to the bidder submitting the highest cash bid therefor, is a commercially reasonable sale of such Collateral under the Uniform Commercial Code. Dealer agrees that the purchase of any Collateral by a vendor, as provided in any agreement between Deutsche and the vendor, is a commercially reasonable disposition and private sale of such Collateral under the Uniform Commercial Code, and no request for bids shall be required. Dealer further agrees that 7 or more days prior written notice will be commercially reasonable notice of any public or private sale (including any sale to a vendor). If Deutsche disposes of any such Collateral other than as herein contemplated, the commercial reasonableness of such disposition will be determined in accordance with the laws of the state governing this Agreement.

11. Dealer grants Deutsche an irrevocable power of attorney to: execute or endorse on Dealer's behalf any checks, financing statements, instruments, Certificates of Title and Statements of Origin pertaining to the Collateral; supply any omitted information and correct errors in any documents between Deutsche and

Dealer; do anything Dealer is obligated to do hereunder; initiate and settle any insurance claim pertaining to the Collateral; and do anything to preserve and protect the Collateral and Deutsche's rights and interest therein. Deutsche may provide to any third party any credit, financial or other information on Dealer that Deutsche may from time to time possess.

12. Time is of the essence. This Agreement is deemed to have been entered into at the Deutsche branch office executing this Agreement. Either party may terminate this Agreement at any time by written notice received by the other party. If Deutsche terminates this Agreement, Dealer agrees that if Dealer:

(a) is not in default hereunder, 30 days prior notice of termination is reasonable and sufficient (although this provision shall not be construed to mean that shorter periods may not, in particular circumstances, also be reasonable and sufficient); or

(b) is in default hereunder, no prior notice of termination is required.

Dealer will not be relieved from any obligation to Deutsche arising out of Deutsche's advances or commitments made before the effective termination date of this Agreement. Deutsche will retain all of its rights, interests and remedies hereunder until Dealer has paid all Dealer's debts to Deutsche. Dealer cannot assign Dealer's interest in this Agreement without Deutsche's prior written consent, although Deutsche may assign or participate Deutsche's interest, in whole or in part, without Dealer's consent. This Agreement will protect and bind Deutsche's and Dealer's respective heirs, representatives, successors and assigns. All agreements or commitments to extend or renew credit or refrain from enforcing payment of a debt must be in writing. Any oral or other amendment or waiver claimed to be made to this Agreement that is not evidenced by a written document executed by Deutsche and Dealer (except for each Statement of Transaction that Dealer does not object to in the manner stated in Section 2) will be null, void and have no force or effect whatsoever. If any provision of this Agreement or its application is invalid or unenforceable, the remainder of this Agreement will not be impaired or affected and will remain binding and enforceable. If Dealer previously executed any security agreement with Deutsche, this Agreement will only amend and supplement such agreement. If the terms hereof conflict with the terms of any such prior security agreement, the terms of this Agreement will govern. Dealer agrees to pay all of Deutsche's reasonable attorneys fees and expenses incurred by Deutsche in enforcing Deutsche's rights hereunder.

13. Binding arbitration. [Editor's note: The two-page arbitration clause was omitted for lack of space in this reproduction. That clause provided that the parties would submit all disputes between them to binding arbitration through the National Arbitration Forum or the American Arbitration Association.]....

14. If Section 13 of this Agreement or its application is invalid or unenforceable, any legal proceeding with respect to any Dispute will be tried in a court of competent jurisdiction by a judge without a jury. Dealer and Deutsche waive any right to a jury trial in any such proceeding.

THIS CONTRACT CONTAINS BINDING ARBITRATION AND JURY WAIVER PROVISIONS.

Deutsche Financial Services Corp.	Dealer's Name: Bonnie's Boat World, Inc.
By: *Paul Kaplan*	By: *Bonnie Brezhnev*
Print Name: Paul Kaplan	Print Name: Bonnie Brezhnev
Title: Loan Officer	Title: President

[Editors' note: We have omitted the Dealer's certification that its Board of Directors adopted a specific resolution authorizing the corporation to enter into this financing arrangement with Deutsche.]

At the time she signs this agreement, Bonnie has not yet purchased any boats for Deutsche to finance. Deutsche disburses no money at this "closing" and there is no Statement of Transaction for Bonnie to approve. Paul shows Bonnie some information about the pricing of credit by Deutsche and a sample of a Statement of Transaction prepared on the basis of a hypothetical purchase (see Figure 56.1). The sequence of events that will occur when Bonnie buys some boats is discussed below.

FIGURE 56.1.
Statement of Transaction

RPT ID: H623A 40721
OFFICE: 01256015 DEUTSCHE FINANCIAL SERVICES STATEMENT OF TRANSACTION
DEALER: 50580

PAGE: 1
PRODUCT LINES
DLR INV
04 04

INVOICE#: 0148291
DATE OF NOTE: 07/13/1994

PLAN#	PLAN TITLE	MFG#	MANUFACTURER NAME	DIST#	DISTRIBUTOR NAME
0216-01	EAGLE PROGRAM II - 30 DAY FFP	0523	SHORELINE BOAT MFG	1406	BONNIE'S BOAT WORLD, INC.

PRODUCT DESCRIPTION	MODEL #	SERIAL #	MFG#	PRD	UNIT-ID	QTY	UNIT PRICE	AMOUNT
.	SPP	1 PAY	0523	808	6089402	1	15,566.58	15,566.58

**** FINANCE TERMS: - SCHEDULED PAYMENT PLAN -

PLAN #	CHARGE TYPE	DAYS/DATE	RATE/AMOUNT	DESCRIPTION
0216-01	FINANCE:	31 - 90	PRIME- 1.00%	PER ANNUM OF ADB
		91 -	2.4000 %	PER MONTH OF ADB
	FLAT:	31 -	.2500 %	OF BALANCE EVERY 1 MONTH(S)
	LATE RATE:		PRIME+ 5.50%	PER ANNUM OF ADB OF LATE PMT AMT
				DAY 1 IS DATE OF INVOICE

"PRIME" MEANS THE HIGHEST PRIME RATE OR REFERENCE RATE OF INTEREST PUBLICLY ANNOUNCED FROM TIME TO TIME BY CHASE MANHATTAN BANK, N.A., CHEMICAL BANK AND CITIBANK, N.A., AND SUCH RATE IN EFFECT ON THE LAST BUSINESS DAY OF ANY CALENDAR MONTH WILL BE PRIME FOR THE FOLLOWING CALENDAR MONTH, SUBJECT TO ANY MINIMUM PRIME.

****
* PRINCIPAL PAYMENTS DUE: *
****

02/04/2004 15,566.58

INVOICE TOTAL 15,566.58
TOTAL ITEM QUANTITY 1

BONNIE'S BOAT WORLD, INC.
12376 HIGHWAY 441
BLUE MOON, MO 63131

OFFICE ADDRESS
DEUTSCHE FINANCIAL SERVICES
P.O. BOX 502025
ST. LOUIS MO 63141 2025

DEUTSCHE FINANCIAL SERVICES

2. The Financing Statement

Bonnie also signs an authorization to file a financing statement for filing in the Uniform Commercial Code filing system of the state. The purpose of the financing statement is to give public notice that Deutsche claims a security interest in Bonnie's inventory (see Figure 56.2). We will discuss financing statements at greater length in Part Two of this book.

FIGURE 56.2.
U.C.C.-1 Financing Statement

UCC FINANCING STATEMENT
FOLLOW INSTRUCTIONS (front and back) CAREFULLY

A. NAME & PHONE OF CONTACT AT FILER [optional]

B. SEND ACKNOWLEDGMENT TO: (Name and Address)

Deutsche Financial Services
8251 Maryland Avenue
St. Louis, MO 63105

THE ABOVE SPACE IS FOR FILING OFFICE USE ONLY

1. DEBTOR'S EXACT FULL LEGAL NAME - insert only one debtor name (1a or 1b) - do not abbreviate or combine names

1a. ORGANIZATION'S NAME			
Bonnie's Boat World, Inc.			
1b. INDIVIDUAL'S LAST NAME	FIRST NAME	MIDDLE NAME	SUFFIX
1c. MAILING ADDRESS	CITY	STATE / POSTAL CODE	COUNTRY
12376 Highway 441	Blue Moon	MO 63131	USA

1d. SEE INSTRUCTIONS	ADD'L INFO RE ORGANIZATION DEBTOR	1e. TYPE OF ORGANIZATION Corporation	1f. JURISDICTION OF ORGANIZATION Missouri	1g. ORGANIZATIONAL ID #, if any 57-12345	NONE

2. ADDITIONAL DEBTOR'S EXACT FULL LEGAL NAME - insert only one debtor name (2a or 2b) - do not abbreviate or combine names

2a. ORGANIZATION'S NAME			
2b. INDIVIDUAL'S LAST NAME	FIRST NAME	MIDDLE NAME	SUFFIX
2c. MAILING ADDRESS	CITY	STATE / POSTAL CODE	COUNTRY

2d. SEE INSTRUCTIONS	ADD'L INFO RE ORGANIZATION DEBTOR	2e. TYPE OF ORGANIZATION	2f. JURISDICTION OF ORGANIZATION	2g. ORGANIZATIONAL ID #, if any	NONE

3. SECURED PARTY'S NAME (or NAME of TOTAL ASSIGNEE of ASSIGNOR S/P) - insert only one secured party name (3a or 3b)

3a. ORGANIZATION'S NAME			
Deutsche Financial Services Corp.			
3b. INDIVIDUAL'S LAST NAME	FIRST NAME	MIDDLE NAME	SUFFIX
3c. MAILING ADDRESS	CITY	STATE / POSTAL CODE	COUNTRY
8251 Maryland Avenue	St. Louis	MO 63105	USA

4. This FINANCING STATEMENT covers the following collateral:

Inventory, equipment, general intangibles

5. ALTERNATIVE DESIGNATION [if applicable]:	LESSEE/LESSOR	CONSIGNEE/CONSIGNOR	BAILEE/BAILOR	SELLER/BUYER	AG. LIEN	NON-UCC FILING

6. This FINANCING STATEMENT is to be filed [for record] (or recorded) in the REAL ESTATE RECORDS.   Attach Addendum   [if applicable] | 7. Check to REQUEST SEARCH REPORT(S) on Debtor(s) [ADDITIONAL FEE]   [optional] | All Debtors | Debtor 1 | Debtor 2

8. OPTIONAL FILER REFERENCE DATA

FILING OFFICE COPY — UCC FINANCING STATEMENT (FORM UCC1) (REV. 05/22/02)

3.   The Personal Guarantee

Although the loans contemplated by the agreement would be made to Bonnie's Boat World, Inc., Deutsche required that Bonnie personally guarantee repayment. Bonnie signed a one-page document to that effect at the closing.

Lenders such as Deutsche have at least two reasons for requiring personal guarantees from the owners of their corporate borrowers. First, if the borrower cannot repay the loan, the owners might. The guarantee gives the lender the right to obtain a judgment against the owners and proceed against their assets just as though the owners were the ones who had borrowed the money. In addition, personal guarantees can be, and sometimes are, secured by interests in property owned by the guarantors.

The second reason for a lender to take a personal guarantee is to assure, insofar as possible, that in the event of default, the lender will have the cooperation of the owners. When a corporate debtor becomes insolvent, the owners' interest in the business often becomes worthless. Unless the owners are personally liable for debts of the business, they may not care how much of the debt is repaid. Even if the owners have all of their wealth in the corporation and the corporation is hopelessly insolvent, if the owners are personally liable, they will continue to have an incentive to cooperate with the lender who holds the guarantee. Their incentive is to avoid or minimize the judgments that eventually might be taken against them. In the event of competition for the assets of the corporation, the owners are likely to be on the side of the creditor to whom they have given their personal guarantee. Even if the owners can discharge the personal guarantee through bankruptcy, the owners' desire to avoid the necessity of filing bankruptcy may also motivate them to repay.

D.   Bonnie's Buys Some Boats

With her floorplan line of credit in place, Bonnie is ready to go shopping. She contacts Shoreline Boat Manufacturing Company and arranges to become a Shoreline authorized dealer. Her choice is in part motivated by the fact that Shoreline is one of the dozen or so boat manufacturers who have signed a Floorplan Agreement with Deutsche.

1.   The Floorplan Agreement

The Floorplan Agreement provides that if Deutsche finances purchase of Shoreline Boats by dealers such as Bonnie's Boat World and then has to repossess those boats, Shoreline will buy them back at the full invoice price. These are the key terms of the Agreement:

FLOORPLAN AGREEMENT

To: Deutsche Financial Services
655 Maryville Centre Drive
St. Louis, Missouri 63141

We sell various products ("Merchandise") to dealers and/or distributors (collectively "Dealer") who may require financial assistance in order to make such purchases from us. To induce you to finance the acquisition of Merchandise by any Dealer and in consideration thereof, we agree that:

1. Whenever a Dealer requests the shipment of Merchandise from us and that you finance such Merchandise, we may deliver to you an invoice(s) describing the Merchandise. By delivery of an invoice we warrant the following:

   a. That we transfer to the Dealer all right, title and interest in and to the Merchandise so described contingent upon your approval to finance the transaction;
   b. That our title to the Merchandise is free and clear of all liens and encumbrances when transferred to the Dealer;
   c. That the Merchandise is in salable condition, free of any defects;
   d. That the Merchandise is the subject of a bona fide order by the Dealer placed with and accepted by us and that the Dealer has requested the transaction be financed by you; and
   e. That the Merchandise subject to the transaction has been shipped to the Dealer not more than 10 days prior to the invoice date.

If we breach any of the above-described warranties, we will immediately: (i) pay to you an amount equal to the total unpaid balance (being principal and finance charges) owed to you on all Merchandise directly or indirectly related to the breach; and (ii) reimburse you for all costs and expenses (including, but not limited to, attorney's fees) incurred by you as a direct or indirect result of the breach.

2. You will only be bound to finance Merchandise which you have accepted to finance (which acceptances will be indicated by your issuance of an approval number or a draft or other instrument to us in payment of the invoice less the amount of your charges as agreed upon from time to time) and only if:

   (i)   the Merchandise is delivered to the Dealer within 30 days following your acceptance;
   (ii)   you have received our invoice for such Merchandise within 10 days from the date of delivery of the Merchandise to the Dealer; and
   (iii) you have not revoked your acceptance prior to the shipment of the Merchandise to the Dealer.

3. Whenever you deem it necessary in your sole discretion to repossess or if you otherwise come into possession of any Merchandise, in which you have a security interest or other lien, we will purchase such Merchandise from you at the time of

your repossession or other acquisition or possession in accordance with the following terms and conditions:

    a.   We will purchase such Merchandise, regardless of its condition, at the point where you repossess it or where it otherwise comes into your possession;

    b.   The purchase price that we will pay to you for such Merchandise will be due and payable immediately in full, and will be an amount equal to (i) the total unpaid balance (being principal and finance charges) owed to you with respect to such Merchandise or our original invoice price for such Merchandise, whichever is greater, and (ii) all costs and expenses (including, without limitation, reasonable attorney's fees) paid or incurred by you in connection with the repossession of such Merchandise; and

    c.   We shall not assert or obtain any interest in or to any Merchandise acquired by us, until the purchase price, therefor is paid in full. . . .

    5. You may extend the time of a Dealer in default to fulfill its obligations to you without notice to us and without altering our obligations hereunder. We waive any rights we may have to . . . require you to proceed against a Dealer or to pursue any other remedy in your power. Our liability to you is direct and unconditional and will not be affected by any change in the terms of payment or performance of any agreement between you and Dealer, or the release, settlement or compromise of or with any party liable for the payment or performance thereof, the release or non-perfection of any security thereunder, any change in Dealer's financial condition, or the interruption of business relations between you and Dealer.

    6. We will pay all your expenses (including, without limitation, court costs and reasonable attorney fees) in the event you are required to enforce your rights against us. Your failure to exercise any rights granted hereunder shall not operate as a waiver of those rights. . . .

    8. Either of us may terminate this Agreement by notice to the other in writing, the termination to be effective 30 days after receipt of the notice by the other party, but no termination of this Agreement will affect any of our liability with respect to any financial transactions entered into by you with any Dealer prior to the effective date of termination, including, without limitation, transactions that will not be completed until after the effective date of termination.

Dated: <u>August 29</u>, <u>2003</u>

ATTEST:

<u>Shoreline Boat Company</u>

Alan R. Shoreline

By: <u>Alan R. Shoreline</u>

Title: <u>President</u>

Business Address:
Alachua, Florida
_____

_____

ACCEPTED:
Deutsche Financial Services

George Dobisky

By: George Dobisky
_____

Title: Division President
_____

_____

The advantage to Deutsche of this agreement is obvious. If Deutsche has to repossess Shoreline Boats from Bonnie's Boat World, Shoreline has agreed to buy them back for at least their full original invoice price. The advantages to Shoreline are also significant. With the Floorplan Agreement in place, Shoreline can offer qualified dealers nationwide 100 percent financing on the boats they buy from Shoreline, making the boats more attractive to dealers. Shoreline has to be ready to take the boats back if Bonnie's defaults, but if Shoreline financed the boats itself, Shoreline would have to do that anyway. If Shoreline financed the boats itself, it would bear much of the risk of boats being lost, stolen, or destroyed through dealer fraud. Under the Floorplan Agreement, Deutsche bears these risks.

Bonnie gets three advantages from this agreement. Because the repurchase agreement reduces Deutsche's risk of loss on resale after repossession, Deutsche can offer Bonnie's a larger line of credit and finance a larger portion of each purchase than a bank typically could. Additionally, Bonnie's may benefit from time to time from subsidies offered by Shoreline to Deutsche to provide dealers such as Bonnie's with periods when little or no interest accrues.

2.   The Buy

Bonnie contacts Shoreline and selects the five boats she wants. The total price of the boats is $55,000. In accord with the Floorplan Agreement, Shoreline contacts Deutsche to obtain approval of the purchase. Deutsche verifies from its records that both Bonnie's and Shoreline are in compliance with their agreements with Deutsche and that the purchase will not overdraw Bonnie's line of credit. Satisfied that everything is in order, Deutsche gives Shoreline an approval number for the purchase. (This is essentially the same thing that happens when you use your Visa card to buy a pair of shoes at the mall.) Shoreline ships the five boats to Bonnie and sends the invoice to Deutsche. Deutsche pays the $55,000 to Shoreline, recording it on their books as a loan to Bonnie's.

E. Bonnie's Sells a Boat

The morning after the Shoreline boats arrive in Bonnie's yard, William and Gladys Homer come to Bonnie's looking for the boat of their dreams. It turns out to be one of the five Bonnie's has just purchased from Shoreline. Bonnie's invoice price from Shoreline is $15,566.58; its invoice price to the Homers is $20,000. Bonnie's will have a gross profit on the sale of $4,333.42.

Arthur Dent, the Bonnie's salesman who helps the Homers pick out the boat, also helps them arrange their financing. Bonnie's has an arrangement with First State Bank under which First State finances 90 percent of the purchase price of a boat for any Bonnie's customer who qualifies. The Homers qualify and First State approves their boat loan on the same day they pick out the boat. The Homers write Bonnie's a check for $2,000, sign a security agreement and financing statement for First State, load the boat on their trailer, and drive off into a sunset filled with monthly payment coupons. On receipt of the security agreement and financing statement, First State deposits $18,000 to Bonnie's bank account.

If Bonnie's financed the purchase of these boats with Deutsche on a "pay-as-sold" basis, part of Bonnie's loan is now due. That is, ¶(7(b) of the Wholesale Financing Agreement provides that "Dealer will immediately pay Deutsche the principal indebtedness owed Deutsche on each item of Collateral financed by Deutsche (as shown on the Statement of Transaction identifying such Collateral)...when such Collateral is sold." In accord with this provision, Bonnie's sends Deutsche a check for $15,566.58 that same day. At the beginning of the next month, Deutsche will bill Bonnie's for the finance charges that accrued during the brief time this $15,566.58 loan was outstanding.

F. Monitoring the Existence of the Collateral

If Bonnie's had used the $15,566.58 it received from the Homers to pay other bills instead of sending it to Deutsche and Deutsche had then foreclosed, Deutsche's collateral would have been about that much less than its loan. If Bonnie repeated this diversion of funds enough times, Deutsche would soon have no collateral at all. How would Deutsche have discovered this developing problem?

The answer is that Deutsche will send a person to Bonnie's Boat World once every 30 to 45 days to verify the continuing existence of the collateral and check its condition. For the first such inspection, Deutsche assigns its most experienced floorchecker, Richard Feynman. Feynman arrives at Bonnie's Boat World unannounced, introduces himself to Bonnie, and goes to work.

Feynman has with him a list of all of the boats Deutsche has financed for Bonnie's, except those for which Deutsche has already received payment. For each boat, Feynman's list shows the make, model, and serial number. Feynman begins at one end of the fenced-in property and works his way to the other. For each boat he reads the make, model, and serial number from a metal plate attached to the boat, finds that boat on his list, and checks it off. He also notes the condition of the boat alongside the check mark.

When Feynman is finished, there are still two boats on his list he has not seen. He asks Bonnie about them. One, Bonnie tells him, was sold yesterday and delivered to the customer earlier this morning. Bonnie tells Feynman that she has already mailed the check to Deutsche for this boat. Feynman does not take Bonnie's word for that. Instead, he examines Bonnie's check ledger and verifies that Bonnie has written the check. He notes the existence of the purported check on his list; when the check arrives at Deutsche's offices, he will check the postmark on it. The other boat, Bonnie tells him, is out on the lake on a demonstration. It will be back in an hour or so if Feynman wants to drop by after lunch to check it, Bonnie suggests. Feynman explains to Bonnie that would be contrary to the established procedure for a floor check: All of the boats must be checked at the same time. Bonnie radios the missing boat and makes arrangements to rendezvous with it. Bonnie and Feynman take a second boat out, meet with the missing boat, and check it off on Feynman's list.

Why couldn't Feynman just stop back after lunch to look at the missing boat? The answer is that the registration plates are not a foolproof method for identifying a boat. Given time to do so, a dishonest debtor could remove the registration plate from a boat Feynman has already checked and substitute a counterfeit plate bearing the make, model, and number of a boat the debtor no longer owns. Feynman checks the boats all at the same time so that he does not have to rely solely on the registration plates; to a large degree, he relies on the number of boats he can see on the premises all at the same time. In addition, the floor check serves as a simulated repossession. Deutsche wants to know how much collateral they would have recovered had this been a real repossession. If it had been, Bonnie might never have told them the location of the missing boat.

Problem Set 56

56.1. As an attorney for Deutsche Financial Services, you have been asked to comment on the floor-checking procedures for a loan of $185 million against 160 million pounds of soybean oil stored in dozens of petroleum tanks in Bayonne, New Jersey. The procedure is as follows: The Deutsche floor checker shows up in Bayonne unannounced. With an employee of the debtor, Allied Crude Vegetable Oil Refining Corporation, the floor checker climbs the metal staircase that winds around the first tank. From any point along the circular walkway at the top of the tank, the floor checker can see (and taste) the oil. The checker sticks a 40-foot pole into the oil to test its depth. Then the floor checker and the employee move on to the next tank and do the same thing. The quantity of oil in each tank is determined by multiplying the depth of the oil by the surface area. Do you see any problems?

56.2.   What could the bank lenders in this story have done to protect themselves against the fraud perpetrated on them?

Miller Indicted on Bank Fraud

Calhoun (Illinois) News-Herald, Nov. 26, 2003 at page 1

After federal investigations were completed recently, Calhoun County Ford dealer Stephen Corbett Miller was accused in a federal indictment of defrauding five banks in an effort to retain funding to operate the dealership.

The grand jury indictment accuses Miller of executing a plan to defraud the Bank of Calhoun County, the Bank of Kampsville, Jersey State Bank, Central State Bank and Citizens Bank from 1993 through February 2003.

According to the indictment, Miller began working at Calhoun County Ford in 1954, before purchasing the dealership with a business partner in 1977. In 1993 the dealership began having financial problems. This allegedly led Miller to take part in several methods of deception to deceive the financial institutions to continue to lend money for the operation and inventory of the dealership.

The indictment states that Miller received financing commonly referred to as floor plan financing. In this type of financing, the inventory of the dealership's vehicles is issued to secure loans. The proceeds from the sales are then supposed to be forwarded to the financial institution within 10 days.

Miller also allegedly double collateralized vehicles. This was supposedly accomplished by using the same vehicles as collateral on two or more floor plan loans without disclosing that the vehicle had already been pledged as collateral.

Miller is also accused of making false statements to financial institutions when they arrived to conduct floor plan inventory checks. The institutions allegedly were told that the missing vehicles were on test drives or were out on loan to a customer whose vehicle was being serviced.

Not only did Miller allegedly make false statements to financial institutions, he supposedly practiced the same falsehoods with his customers. Customers who purchased vehicles from the dealership were allegedly told to return their vehicles for warranty or service work, at which time, the license plates were removed and the financial institutions were called to do a floor plan check on the missing vehicles.

The indictment also states that Miller obtained nominee loans involving the fictitious sales of automobiles, forged and falsified sales contracts for vehicles, in addition to financial contracts for those vehicles.

Miller also stands accused of obtaining vehicle loans on behalf of other individuals without their knowledge or consent. The proceeds of those loans were then allegedly utilized by Miller to pay the dealership's expenses.

56.3.   The law firm you work for is outside counsel to Archer Commercial Finance. For many years, Archer has insisted on personal guarantees from the individuals who own any closely held business they finance. Gordon Jamail, a department head at Archer, has proposed a change in policy. He reels off the names of four potential customers he says have gone to a competitor in the last month alone because by doing so they could avoid Archer's personal guarantee requirement. "The irony," Gordon says, "is that in nine out of ten cases, the judgment we might recover on a personal guarantee would be uncollectible. These people borrow from us because they've already put everything they have in the business." The president of Archer asks for your opinion. What do you tell her?

56.4. Three years after the events set forth in the reading, Bonnie Brezhnev comes to you for legal advice. For the past two years, the boat business has been lousy. During that time, she has put everything she has into the business, even to the extent of taking out a second mortgage on her home. Still short of working capital, she has been juggling boats, lying to the floor checker, and keeping phony records to back up her lies. On the floor check this morning she was five boats out of trust, a total of about $50,000. Deutsche has declared Bonnie's Boat World in default and demanded that she surrender the 20 Shoreline boats remaining in its possession. Over the past couple of weeks, Bonnie has come to the realization that the business cannot survive; what she wants now is to get out of the mess she is in.

a.   Bonnie asks you whether Deutsche has the right to the boats. Do they? See the Agreement for Wholesale Financing ¶9(iii); Floorplan Agreement ¶3; U.C.C. §§9-601(a), 9-609.

b.   If Bonnie surrenders the boats without a fight, what do you think will happen to her? U.C.C. §9-615(d)(2); 26 Ill. Stat. para. 9-315.01, set forth in section A.3. of Assignment 52.

c.   Does Bonnie have the power to keep these boats? If so, how? For how long?

d.   What advice do you give Bonnie? The Model Rules of Professional Conduct provide in relevant part:

> *Rule 4.4.* In representing a client, a lawyer shall not use means that have no substantial purpose other than to . . . delay or burden a third person.
> *Rule 1.2.* A lawyer shall not counsel a client to engage, or assist a client, in conduct that the lawyer knows is criminal or fraudulent . . . but a lawyer may discuss the legal consequences of any proposed course of conduct.
> *Rule 1.16.* A lawyer shall not represent a client . . . if the representation will result in violation of the rules of professional conduct or other law. . . .

56.5.   As an arbitrator for the American Arbitration Association, you have been assigned a case in which Deutsche seeks to enforce provisions of the Agreement for Wholesale Financing against a dealer who signed it five years ago and has been borrowing under it since that time. The dealer's attorney argues that the contract is "void for lack of consideration" and "illusory" because nowhere in it does Deutsche agree to make a loan or necessarily do anything else. What do you think of this argument? See Agreement for Wholesale Financing ¶1.

56.6.   Bonnie consults you prior to signing the agreement with Deutsche. What is your answer to each of the following questions?

a.   What interest rate will Bonnie pay on her outstanding balance? See Wholesale Financing Agreement ¶2 and Statement of Transaction.

b.   Will Deutsche have a security interest in Bonnie's lease of the boatyard? In her bank accounts? Wholesale Financing Agreement ¶3; U.C.C. §§9-109(a) and (d)(11) and (d)(13), 9-604, 9-102(a)(2) and (42), and 9-203(f).

c.   Would Bonnie violate her agreement with Deutsche by permitting an employee to take the boat for a demonstration ride? If she did, would that give Deutsche the right to call the loan? Wholesale Financing Agreement ¶¶5(b), 9; U.C.C. §§9-201(a), 9-601(a).

d.   Given that Shoreline has agreed, as part of the Floorplan Agreement, ¶3.b., to buy repossessed boats from Deutsche at the full amount owing on them, does that mean that Bonnie need not worry about a deficiency judgment on a repossessed boat? U.C.C. §§9-102(a)(59) and (71), 9-618, and Wholesale Financing agreement ¶10.

56.7.   It has been a year since Deutsche entered into this financing arrangement with Bonnie's Boat World. Deutsche is not happy with the arrangement, in part because Bonnie has been difficult to deal with and in part because the boat business has been bad and Deutsche would like to get out of it altogether. Bonnie's, however, is not in breach. Can Deutsche get out of this deal? If so, how does Deutsche do it? Wholesale Financing Agreement ¶¶2, 9(i) and 12. What will be the effect on Bonnie's?

Part Two
The Creditor-Third Party Relationship

Chapter 18. Perfection

Assignment 57: The Personal Property Filing Systems

A. Competition for the Secured Creditor's Collateral

In Part One of this book, we examined the relationship between a secured creditor and its debtor. We focused on how the rights of secured creditors to collect from the debtor differed from those of unsecured creditors. We also examined the procedures by which creditors obtained secured status and the contracts that created those rights.

In Part Two, we shift our focus to the relationship between a secured creditor and others who may claim the same collateral. Our approach remains pragmatic. We ask what the secured creditor must do to prevail over these new adversaries, how effective the secured creditor's rights against them are likely to be, and how expensive these new rights will be to obtain and to enforce.

Debtors sometimes participate in the struggle between their secured creditors and third parties. Other times they have already given up in exhausted resignation and do not care who gets the collateral. The issue now is the rights of a secured creditor against others who also have rights superior to those of the debtor.

Just as debtors come in many different types — consumers and businesses, hard-working but unfortunate people, and sleazeballs, wealthy and poor — so do their creditors. An individual debtor in financial trouble is likely to owe money to 20 or 30 creditors, including a home mortgage lender, several credit card issuers, a finance company, the phone company, several local department stores, an auto lender, a cable company, the family doctor, and so on. A business debtor may owe money to hundreds or even thousands of creditors, including banks, commercial lenders, current employees, retired employees, lessors, suppliers, customers, utility companies, and taxing authorities. Some of these creditors may not have acquired their status voluntarily. The creditor of an individual debtor may be the victim of an automobile accident or a custodial parent with the right to payments for child support. The creditor of a business debtor may be a government agency that has spent money to remove toxic waste from the debtor's property, a competitor injured by the debtor's illegal business practices, or the Internal Revenue Service. To complicate matters further, the third party who claims the secured creditor's collateral may not be a creditor at all. It may be someone who bought the collateral from the debtor or someone who claims to remain the owner because the debtor never completed the transaction in which the debtor bought the collateral.

A particularly slippery, imaginative, or unfortunate debtor can create a vivid array of contestants for its limited assets. These competitors may see the secured creditor's collateral (or what the secured creditor thought was its collateral) as their only source of recovery or merely as the most convenient or cost-effective one.

The law treats many of the contests over rights to collateral as questions of *priority*. This assignment briefly addresses what it means for one creditor to have priority over another. It also begins a discussion of how creditors obtain priority over one another. The latter discussion extends through the remaining assignments of Part Two, Chapter 18.

In Chapter 19 we examine what creditors who have priority must do to keep it. We consider the effect of the passage of time; the filing of bankruptcy; changes in the identity, use, and location of collateral; and changes in the identity and location of the debtor.

In Chapter 20 we examine the concept of priority in more detail. We look at how priority is implemented in both state law and bankruptcy procedures, and then use that reality to give further definition to the concept.

In Chapter 21 we explore competitions between secured creditors and others over collateral. We begin with lien creditors. Then we consider trustees in bankruptcy, other secured creditors, those who sold the collateral to the debtor, those who bought the collateral from the debtor, statutory lienors, and finally the federal government as tax-lien holder. As we examine these contests one by one, you will see how the rules for resolving them fit together (sometimes well and sometimes badly) to form a single system of lien priority based for the most part on the principle, "first in time is first in right." Along the way, the policies underlying secured credit should become clearer.

B.   What Is Priority?

In Part One of this book, we introduced the concept of a *lien*. A lien is a relationship between a debt and property that serves as collateral. If the debtor fails to pay the debt, the secured creditor can foreclose the lien, force a sale of the collateral, and have the proceeds of the sale applied to payment of the debt. We refer to this attribute of a lien as the secured creditor's *remedy*.

In Part Two, we will examine a second and perhaps even more important attribute of a lien: *priority*. If there is more than one lien against collateral, each will have a priority. Liens are commonly labeled "first," "second," "third," etc. (You may, for example, have heard of "second mortgages.") A lien with priority higher than another is referred to as the *senior* or *prior lien* and the other is referred to as the *subordinate* or *junior lien*. If the value of collateral is insufficient to pay all of the liens against an item of collateral, the junior liens yield to the senior ones.

To illustrate, assume that David owes Alice $7,000 and Betty $9,000. Each has a security interest (recall that a security interest is a type of lien) in David's BMW, which is worth $12,000. If Alice's lien has priority over Betty's lien and either is foreclosed, Alice will be entitled to $7,000 of the value of the BMW and Betty will be entitled to the remaining $5,000. Once the BMW has been liquidated and the proceeds distributed, Betty will be an unsecured creditor for the $4,000 balance owed to her.

(At this point, we pause to note the complexity of this scheme for resolving competition among creditors. Each creditor's lien is a relationship between an obligation and an item of collateral; priority is the relationship between these relationships. Don't be surprised if every implication of this complex scheme does not immediately spring to mind. It will come.)

While we usually think of priority as an attribute of a lien, priority can exist among creditors who do not have liens. For example, it is not uncommon for a large, publicly held company to raise some of its capital by borrowing from banks or insurance companies and some through the issue of unsecured bonds, or *debentures*. One term of the contract between the company and the purchasers of the bonds is that the bond debt is *subordinated* to the bank debt, which means that if the banks and the bondholders ever seek to satisfy their debts from assets of the debtor, the bondholders will take nothing until the banks have been paid in full. Even though the banks and the bondholders have contractually established priority between themselves, both remain unsecured.

Contracts establishing priority among unsecured creditors are relatively uncommon for the simple reason that debtors frequently encumber all of their assets with liens. Those liens have priority over all unsecured debts. When a debtor is in financial difficulty, even the most senior unsecured status is likely, in the metaphor popular among practitioners, to be "out of the money."

The system of lien priority is so fundamental a social and economic institution that many fail to realize that it is merely one of several ways that a legal system can resolve competition among creditors for the limited assets of a debtor. Some examples of other possible systems may help. First, such competitions could be resolved by allowing each competitor a pro rata share of the limited assets. Recall from Assignment 49 of this book that this is how competitions are resolved among unsecured creditors in bankruptcy. Second, competitions could be decided on the basis of the status of the competing creditors. Debts deemed more important, such as those owing to employees, taxing agencies, or widows and orphans, might be given higher priority, while less important ones, such as those owing to commercial creditors, might be assigned lower priority. Some of this kind of thinking is embodied in the distributional rules of Bankruptcy Code §§507(a) and 726(a) and in the various statutory lien laws in state law. Third, competitions over the value of a debtor's assets could be resolved by permitting competing creditors to trace and recover the value that each supplied to the debtor. But as the following case illustrates, the established legal system is comfortable with the idea that the winner takes all simply because it is secured, regardless of any competing social equities.

Peerless Packing Co. v. Malone & Hyde, Inc.

376 S.E.2d 161 (W. Va. 1988)

NEELY, JUSTICE.

Appellants are twelve companies that supply wholesale products to grocery stores. Appellee is also a wholesaler of grocery products, with operations covering the southeastern states. John Kizer was appellee's co-defendant below. This is an appeal from the trial court's award of a directed verdict for appellee.

Mr. Kizer...negotiated an agreement with appellee [to purchase the business of the former ADP store in Beckley]. Under this agreement, Mr. Kizer provided $50,000 for working capital that went into the purchase of inventory. Appellee allowed Mr. Kizer to use its trade name "PIC PAC," subleased the store to Mr. Kizer, sold him the store equipment for $200,000, and provided him with approximately $187,000 in additional inventory. In exchange, Mr. Kizer gave appellee a promissory note for approximately $387,000, plus interest, which was secured by a security interest in the present and after acquired inventory.

Appellee met all requirements of the Uniform Commercial Code (UCC) for perfecting its lien against the store's collateral and appellants do not challenge the technical validity of appellee's lien.

Mr. Kizer opened the store in November 1982. The store sold some goods in addition to those supplied by appellee. Many of these additional goods were supplied by the twelve appellant companies, who delivered the goods several times a week on open account credit extended to the store. None of appellants obtained purchase money security interests in the inventory supplied by them. Purchase money security interests could have given appellants priority over appellee's security interest in the inventory.

By March 1983, it was apparent to appellee that the store was not successful because it was meeting its obligations, in part, by reducing inventory. Also, one of Mr. Kizer's checks for the rent and note payments to appellee was returned for insufficient funds. Agents of appellee approached Mr. Kizer and told him that they were going to take the store back, and either he could voluntarily sign everything over to appellee, or "they would take everything he had." Mr. Kizer then signed a document presented by appellee called a Notice of Default and Transfer of Possession Agreement. This agreement transferred all of Mr. Kizer's rights in the store, equipment and inventory, and the balance of the store's bank account, about $64,000, to appellee. In return, appellee released Mr. Kizer from any liability, including personal liability for any deficiency, on the $387,000 note, the rent on the store and on an additional $54,000 [which was for groceries delivered by appellee and for which Kizer had not yet paid].

Appellee assumed ownership of the store and began operating it with Mr. Kizer as manager. Appellee sent a letter to the appellant vendors stating that appellee had realized on its security interest in the store's assets without assuming any liability to third parties, and would not pay any invoices for deliveries before 31 March 1988, the date appellee took ownership.

Appellants each sued Mr. Kizer for the unpaid accounts, and also sued appellee on a theory of unjust enrichment, with a claim for both compensatory and punitive damages. The cases were consolidated, and each appellant was granted default judgment before trial against Mr. Kizer, who discharged his obligation on the judgments in bankruptcy. At the close of appellants' case against appellee, appellee moved for a directed verdict, which the trial court granted.

I

...Appellants also contend that appellee was unjustly enriched by the transfer because appellee, knowing it was going to foreclose on the store, allowed appellants to continue to deliver goods for a week before appellee took over....

...Appellee contends that a theory of unjust enrichment is not applicable in a case that is governed by the UCC. Appellee argues that it was entitled to keep the collateral and that it got no more than it was owed by Mr. Kizer. In fact, appellee insists that it "lost" about $130,000 through the transfer.

The trial court agreed with appellee that an unjust enrichment claim is not applicable in a UCC case, and stated in its final order, in part,

> First, the Court concludes as a matter of law that the plaintiffs cannot maintain this action, which is governed by Article 9 of the UCC, on a theory of recovery grounded upon the equitable doctrine of unjust enrichment. Evans Products Co. v. Jorgensen, 421 P.2d 978 (Oregon, 1966). The Court agrees with the rationale of the Oregon Supreme Court at p. 983 that "[T]he purpose and effectiveness of the UCC would be substantially impaired if interests created in compliance with UCC procedure could be defeated by application of the equitable doctrine of unjust enrichment."

We agree with the trial court's order and affirm his ruling with regard to appellants' equitable unjust enrichment claim. As the Oregon Supreme Court pointed out in *Jorgensen*, cited by the trial court in the quote above, although the result of disallowing an equitable unjust enrichment claim in such a case may appear harsh, the unsatisfied creditors, (appellants in the case before us), could have protected themselves either by demanding cash payment for their goods, or by taking a purchase money security interest in the goods they delivered.[4]...

———

In the beginning, there were 13 unsecured creditors. One took a security interest. When the business failed, that one got everything, including goods sold to the debtor by the other 12 creditors and for which those 12 were not paid. That is the meaning of priority.

C.   How Do Creditors Get Priority?

Central to the system of lien priority is the idea that liens rank in the chronological order in which they were created. There are a few exceptions to this rule, but they are in favor of liens such as property taxes that secure relatively small, predictable obligations. The rationale of the lien priority system

---

4. We do not hold that an equitable claim for relief never lies in a case controlled by the U.C.C. As appellants point out, [U.C.C. §1-203 (Rev §1-304)] requires that "[e]very contract or duty within this chapter imposes an obligation of good faith in its performance or enforcement." Some courts have held that equitable claims raised under this section can change priorities explicitly provided in Article 9. However, most of these cases involve situations of virtually fraudulent conduct. The U.C.C. provides justice in the long run in large part through the certainty and predictability of its provisions, which should not be set aside absent truly egregious circumstances verging on actual fraud. In the case before us, even allowing appellants every favorable inference from their evidence, we do not believe they have presented evidence of such circumstances sufficient to disturb the priorities set by the provisions of Article 9.

depends heavily on the fact that once the priority of a lien is established, any lien created thereafter will be subordinate.

In a very general sense, priority by chronology makes it possible for a creditor to know, at the time it makes a loan, how it will fare in later competitions over the collateral. That is, it knows that it will rank behind liens already in existence and ahead of any liens created later. Because the liens it will rank behind are already in existence, the prospective lender can obtain information about them and, if necessary, contract with the holder regarding their disposition.

Of course, the mere fact that the prior liens exist does not itself assure that the prospective lender will be able to discover them or obtain needed information about them. There probably are liens against the inventory and fixtures in the grocery store where you shop, but to a person walking through the store, they are invisible. To assure that the prospective lender can discover a lien that will have priority over its own, the laws under which liens are created almost invariably condition the priority on the holder taking steps to make existence of the lien public and easily discoverable. The steps that must be taken differ with the type of lien, but nearly all include acts in one of four categories: (1) filing notice in a public records system established for that purpose, (2) taking possession of collateral, (3) taking control of collateral by means of the stake holder's agreement to hold for the secured creditor, or (4) posting notice on the property or where it will be seen by persons dealing with the property. The taking of whatever steps are required is generally referred to as *perfecting* the lien.

Secured parties usually choose to perfect their liens by public filing. But for particular kinds of property they may choose, or be required, to perfect by some other method. And recall from Assignment 43 that an unsecured creditor obtains an execution lien by reducing its claim to judgment, obtaining a writ of execution, and having the sheriff levy on the assets. Under the law of most states, the levy both creates the lien and perfects it by the sheriff's possession.

In the next four assignments we will discuss in more detail the actions that various kinds of creditors must take to perfect their liens in various kinds of collateral. For now, you can think of "perfection" as a series of steps that the holder of a lien must take to give public notice and thereby establish priority. Because priority is based on the time these steps were taken, it is important to document that time. To that end, the officers that receive notices for filing immediately stamp each with a date and time received. Similarly, the sheriff who seizes property pursuant to a writ of execution will immediately record the date and time of seizure. When disputes arise, the records of these officers can be used to prove these dates and times. Perfection sometimes can be accomplished in a manner that does not create a date-and-time-stamped public record. In that event, the secured creditor may have to prove the date and time by other evidence.

In the large majority of cases, the dates and times of perfection will determine the priorities of the liens. Notice that in the system thus created, the type of lien is unimportant. Except for the time of their perfection, one lien is the same as another. The assignment of dates and times of perfection makes it possible to quickly and simply determine the priorities among particular

Article 9 security interests, mortgages, federal tax liens, execution liens, judgment liens, construction liens, and any others.

As you might guess from the number of pages in the remainder of this book, the model we present here is an oversimplification of the system for perfecting and prioritizing liens. In the real world, the steps for perfecting a lien may be complicated. It may be difficult even to know what they are. The rules that determine priority among liens are made by diverse legislative bodies, and they are not always consistent. Not all priority follows the rule of first in time, first in right. But for now, this simple model will do.

D. The Theory of the Filing System

As we noted above, the filing system is the principal means used to communicate the possible existence of a lien from a creditor who has one to a creditor who is thinking of acquiring one. The filing system gives constructive notice, but it is intended to do more than that. In theory, at least, it is supposed to give actual notice to the later creditor. The difficulty in transmitting notice from the holder of a lien to the creditor who seeks to acquire one is that neither of these creditors has any way of knowing who the other is until it is too late for the communication to do any good.

The solution to this problem is for each creditor who obtains a lien to leave a "to whom it may concern" message. For an Article 9 security interest, that message is in the form of a *financing statement,* also known by its form number, a "U.C.C.-1." Each year, the creditors who take security interests leave millions of these messages in the filing system. And before they take their liens, many of these filers search the records to see whether prior secured creditors left messages for them.

For such a system to work, prospective creditors must know that the system exists and that there may be messages waiting in it for them. Of course, banks and most lawyers will have this kind of knowledge. But many consumers and small business people are not aware this system exists. (Neither are some law students who opted not to take this course.) Unsophisticated lenders often fail to claim their priority by filing; the result is that even later lenders will come ahead of them. Unsophisticated lenders often fail to discover a lien that is on the public record before they obtain their own; the result is that the lien they take will be subordinate to the lien already recorded. Either consequence can be disastrous to a lender who does not expect it. The advantages of a filing system come at a considerable human and economic cost.

The theory of the filing system has suffered considerably in implementation. As we will see in this and the subsequent chapter, filing systems are highly imprecise and difficult and expensive to use. Filing is relatively easy and failure to file creates a significant risk that the creditor's lien will be avoided by a trustee in bankruptcy. Searching is relatively difficult, and failure to search leads to adverse consequences only if the debtor previously granted a security interest to a competing creditor and fails to mention that fact on the loan application. As a result, many creditors are lax in searching, and some do not search at all. The following exchange is between Professor Ronald Mann and Joe DeKunder, vice president of NationsBank of Texas, N.A.

Mann: When you do take a pledge of the receivables, even on these really small transactions, do you do a U.C.C. search before you disburse the money?

DeKunder: Yeah, we do a U.C.C. search, yes. Now, I want to qualify that somewhat. We do have situations where we feel that we want to make an exception, and it's a timing factor. Let's say we make a small loan and we do this on blanket receivables, and we want to close that loan tomorrow, let's say — for whatever reason. It's a working capital loan and we want to get it done, and we determine that the search is going to be too lengthy in time, we'll do a post-search. We've already funded the loan, you know. We'll do a search after the fact, just to determine where we are. And frankly, we do that fairly frequently. Now I know that doesn't sound like the prudent thing to do, but what happens in effect is we determine often, just like I mentioned earlier, there are liens that need to be released. We determine sometimes that, obviously, there is nothing there. Sometimes, we are surprised. But at any rate, the post-search is done occasionally. Usually, in those situations we are comfortable with the customer. We are comfortable with the fact that we would make this unsecured and probably we're just taking this as a matter of control.

Mann: But you've done that and gotten burned?

DeKunder: We've done it and gotten burned, yes. . . . Many small business owners, to a degree, don't really understand, sometimes, that someone's even filed . . . a U.C.C. on their collateral. They'll be surprised, they'll say "gosh, I didn't know they did that." Well, you know the obvious question is "you apparently signed the papers." "Well, I didn't know. They never mentioned it. They never said anything about taking a blanket on my . . ." Sometimes what happens is that the blanket is already in place by that bank, the customer pays their loan off, they come back and they take another pledge but don't refile the U.C.C., but it's still in effect.

Mann: It's still there.

DeKunder: It's still there . . . and the borrower didn't know it. He didn't know that they would continue with that. I've had situations where the borrower is quite upset. They will call that other financial institution and say "I didn't know you were gonna . . ." And a lot of times they'll just go ahead and release it. Some of those things are mechanical in nature; it's like well, they didn't know it, we didn't know it, but it can be resolved if we work it out.

E.   The Multiplicity of Filing Systems

The task of a lender who would search for messages relating to the collateral, lend money, and leave a message of its own is vastly complicated by the fact that there is not just one message center, but many. With a few exceptions, each county in the United States maintains a real estate recording system in which not only real estate mortgages, but also Article 9 fixture filings are filed. See U.C.C. §9-501(a)(1). Many counties also maintain separate systems for property tax liens, local tax liens, and money judgments. All states except Georgia and Louisiana have state U.C.C. filing systems. See U.C.C. §9-501(a)(2). Georgia and Louisiana have local U.C.C. filing offices in each county, but the filings thus made can be searched through a statewide index. All states maintain certificate of title systems in which creditors can file notices of security interests in automobiles, and many states have separate certificate of title systems for boats and/or mobile homes. Some states maintain specialized systems for filing against particular kinds of collateral. For example, security interests in Florida liquor licenses are perfected by filing with the state agency that issues the licenses. The federal government maintains yet additional filing systems for patents, trademarks, copyrights, aircraft, and ship mortgages. International negotiations are under way for the creation of a world filing system for security interests in certain mobile property.

Although each of these systems is established by law and charged with keeping particular kinds of messages, the offices that keep the records have almost no communication with one another. If the secured creditor leaves its message in the wrong office, the message almost certainly will be ineffective. If the later lender searches only in the wrong office, it will miss whatever messages were left in the right office.

The statutes that create each of these systems specify, with differing degrees of clarity, the circumstances in which a message should be filed in that system. Usually the type of collateral is determinative. Thus, to decide which system is appropriate for a particular filing one might have to decide such weighty questions as whether particular collateral is a "ship" or a "boat," a "copyright receivable" or an "account," or a "motor vehicle" or "equipment." The definitions of controlling terms are often unexpected.

Ideally, there would be one and only one correct system in which to file notice of a particular security interest. But with both the state and national governments defining the boundaries of the systems, uncertainties and overlaps are inevitable. The following case both illustrates and discusses the kinds of problems that occur. Because the case arose under a prior version of Article 9, the language quoted by the court does not precisely match the sections indicated in the new section numbers we have inserted in brackets.

National Peregrine, Inc. v. Capitol Federal Savings and Loan Association of Denver (In re Peregrine Entertainment, Limited)

116 B.R. 194 (C.D. Cal. 1990)

ALEX KOZINSKI, UNITED STATES CIRCUIT JUDGE. Sitting by designation pursuant to 28 U.S.C. §291(b) (1982).

This appeal from a decision of the bankruptcy court raises an issue never before confronted by a federal court in a published opinion: Is a security interest in a copyright perfected by an appropriate filing with the United States Copyright Office or by a UCC-1 financing statement filed with the relevant secretary of state?

I

National Peregrine, Inc. (NPI) is a Chapter 11 debtor in possession whose principal assets are a library of copyrights, distribution rights and licenses to approximately 145 films, and accounts receivable arising from the licensing of these films to various programmers. . . .

In June 1985, Capitol Federal Savings and Loan Association of Denver (Cap Fed) extended to [NPI] a six million dollar line of credit secured by . . . NPI's film library. Both the security agreement and the UCC-1 financing statements filed by Cap Fed describe the collateral as "[a]ll inventory consisting of films and all accounts, contract rights, chattel paper, general intangibles, instruments, equipment, and documents related to such inventory, now owned or hereafter acquired by the Debtor." Although Cap Fed filed its UCC-1 financing statements in California, Colorado and Utah, it did not record its security interest in the United States Copyright Office.

NPI filed a voluntary petition for bankruptcy on January 30, 1989. On April 6, 1989, NPI filed an amended complaint against Cap Fed, contending that the bank's security interest in the copyrights to the films in NPI's library and in the accounts receivable generated by their distribution were unperfected because Cap Fed failed to record its security interest with the Copyright Office. NPI claimed that, as a debtor in possession, it had a judicial lien on all assets in the bankruptcy estate, including the copyrights and receivables. Armed with this lien, it sought to avoid, recover and preserve Cap Fed's supposedly unperfected security interest for the benefit of the estate.

The parties filed cross-motions for partial summary judgment on the question of whether Cap Fed had a valid security interest in the NPI film library. The bankruptcy court held for Cap Fed. NPI appeals.

II

A.   Where to File

The Copyright Act provides that "[a]ny transfer of copyright ownership or other document pertaining to a copyright" may be recorded in the United States Copyright Office. 17 U.S.C. §205(a). A "transfer" under the Act includes any "mortgage" or "hypothecation of a copyright," whether "in whole or in part" and "by any means of conveyance or by operation of law." 17 U.S.C. §§101, 201(d)(1). The terms "mortgage" and "hypothecation" include a pledge of property as security or collateral for a debt. In addition, the Copyright Office has defined a "document pertaining to a copyright" as one that "has a direct or indirect relationship to the existence, scope, duration, or identification of a copyright, or to the ownership, division, allocation, licensing, transfer, or exercise of rights under a copyright. That relationship may be past, present, future, or potential."

It is clear from the preceding that an agreement granting a creditor a security interest in a copyright may be recorded in the Copyright Office. Likewise, because a copyright entitles the holder to receive all income derived from the display of the creative work, see 17 U.S.C. §106, an agreement creating a security interest in the receivables generated by a copyright may also be recorded in the Copyright Office. Thus, Cap Fed's security interest could have been recorded in the Copyright Office; the parties seem to agree on this much. The question is, does the UCC provide a parallel method of perfecting a security interest in a copyright? One can answer this question by reference to either federal or state law; both inquiries lead to the same conclusion.

1. Even in the absence of express language, federal regulation will preempt state law if it is so pervasive as to indicate that "Congress left no room for supplementary state regulation," or if "the federal interest is so dominant that the federal system will be assumed to preclude enforcement of state laws on the same subject." Hillsborough County v. Automated Medical Laboratories, Inc., 471 U.S. 707, 713, 85 L. Ed. 2d 714, 105 S. Ct. 2371 (1985). Here, the comprehensive scope of the federal Copyright Act's recording provisions, along with the unique federal interests they implicate, support the view that federal law preempts state methods of perfecting security interests in copyrights and related accounts receivable.

The federal copyright laws ensure "predictability and certainty of copyright ownership," "promote national uniformity" and "avoid the practical difficulties of determining and enforcing an author's rights under the differing laws and in the separate courts of the various States." Community for Creative Non-Violence v. Reid, 490 U.S. 730, 109 S. Ct. 2166, 2177, 104 L. Ed. 2d 811 (1989). As discussed above, section 205(a) of the Copyright Act establishes a uniform method for recording security interests in copyrights. A secured creditor need only file in the Copyright Office in order to give "all persons constructive notice of the facts stated in the recorded document." 17 U.S.C. §205(c). Likewise, an interested third party need only search the indices maintained by the Copyright Office to determine whether a particular copyright is encumbered.

A recording system works by virtue of the fact that interested parties have a specific place to look in order to discover with certainty whether a particular interest has been transferred or encumbered. To the extent there are competing recordation schemes, this lessens the utility of each; when records are scattered in several filing units, potential creditors must conduct several searches before they can be sure that the property is not encumbered. It is for that reason that parallel recordation schemes for the same types of property are scarce as hen's teeth; the court is aware of no others, and the parties have cited none. No useful purposes would be served — indeed, much confusion would result — if creditors were permitted to perfect security interests by filing with either the Copyright Office or state offices.

If state methods of perfection were valid, a third party (such as a potential purchaser of the copyright) who wanted to learn of any encumbrances thereon would have to check not merely the indices of the U.S. Copyright Office, but also the indices of any relevant secretary of state. Because copyrights are incorporeal — they have no fixed situs — a number of state authorities could be relevant. Thus, interested third parties could never be entirely sure that all relevant jurisdictions have been searched. This possibility, together with the expense and delay of conducting searches in a variety of jurisdictions, could hinder the purchase and sale of copyrights, frustrating Congress's policy that copyrights be readily transferable in commerce.

This is the reasoning adopted by the Ninth Circuit in Danning v. Pacific Propel-ler. *Danning* held that 49 U.S.C. §1403(a), the Federal Aviation Act's provision for recording conveyances and the creation of liens and security interests in civil air-craft, preempts state filing provisions. 620 F.2d at 735-736.[8] According to *Dan-ning*,

> [t]he predominant purpose of the statute was to provide one central place for the filing of [liens on aircraft] and thus eliminate the need, given the highly mobile nature of aircraft and their appurtenances, for the examination of State and County records.

620 F.2d at 735-736. Copyrights, even more than aircraft, lack a clear situs; tan-gible, movable goods such as airplanes must always exist at some physical loca-tion; they may have a home base from which they operate or where they receive regular maintenance. The same cannot be said of intangibles. As noted above, this lack of an identifiable situs militates against individual state filings and in favor of a single, national registration scheme. . . .

The bankruptcy court below nevertheless concluded that security interests in copyrights could be perfected by filing either with the Copyright Office or with the secretary of state under the UCC, making a tongue-in-cheek analogy to the use of a belt and suspenders to hold up a pair of pants. According to the bankruptcy court, because either device is equally useful, one should be free to choose which one to wear. With all due respect, this court finds the analogy inapt. There is no legitimate reason why pants should be held up in only one particular manner: Individuals and public modesty are equally served by either device, or even by a safety pin or a piece of rope; all that really matters is that the job gets done. Registration schemes are different in that the way notice is given is precisely what matters. To the extent interested parties are confused as to which system is being employed, this increases the level of uncertainty and multiplies the risk of error, exposing creditors to the possibility that they might get caught with their pants down.

A recordation scheme best serves its purpose where interested parties can obtain notice of all encumbrances by referring to a single, precisely defined

---

8. Section 1403(a), which is similar in scope to section 205 of the Copyright Act, provides:

The Secretary of Transportation shall establish and maintain a system for the recording of each of each and all of the following:

(1) Any conveyance which affects the title to, or any interest in, any civil aircraft of the United States;

(2) Any lease, and any mortgage, equipment trust, contract of conditional sale, or other instru-ment executed for security purposes, which lease or other instrument affects the title to, or any interest in [certain engines and propellers];

(3) Any lease, and any mortgage, equipment trust, contract of conditional sale, or other instru-ment executed for security purposes, which lease or other instrument affects the title to, or any interest in, any aircraft engines, propellers, or appliances maintained by or on behalf of an air carrier. . . .

49 U.S.C. §1403(a).

recordation system. The availability of parallel state recordation systems that could put parties on constructive notice as to encumbrances on copyrights would surely interfere with the effectiveness of the federal recordation scheme. Given the virtual absence of dual recordation schemes in our legal system, Congress cannot be presumed to have contemplated such a result. The court therefore concludes that any state recordation system pertaining to interests in copyrights would be preempted by the Copyright Act.

2. State law leads to the same conclusion. [Editors' note: We omit this section of the opinion because the revision of Article 9 made significant changes in language and perhaps in substance. In the omitted section, the court concluded that express provisions of Article 9 yielded to the copyright filing system. The issue under new Article 9 would be slightly different: Did the filing provisions of the Copyright Act preempt the filing provisions of Article 9 with respect to copyrights? U.C.C. §9-109(c)(1).]

As discussed above, section 205(a) of the Copyright Act clearly does establish a national system for recording transfers of copyright interests, and it specifies a place of filing different from that provided in Article Nine. Recording in the Copyright Office gives nationwide, constructive notice to third parties of the recorded encumbrance. Except for the fact that the Copyright Office's indexes are organized on the basis of the title and registration number, rather than by reference to the identity of the debtor, this system is nearly identical to that which Article Nine generally provides on a statewide basis.[10] . . . .

The court therefore concludes that the Copyright Act provides for national registration and "specifies a place of filing different from that specified in [Article Nine] for filing of the security interest." [U.C.C. §9-311(a)(1).] Recording in the U.S. Copyright Office, rather than filing a financing statement under Article Nine, is the proper method for perfecting a security interest in a copyright.

. . . Compliance with a national registration scheme is necessary for perfection regardless of whether federal law governs priorities.[13] Cap Fed's security interest

---

10. Moreover, the mechanics of recording in the Copyright Office are analogous to filing under the U.C.C. In order to record a security interest in the Copyright Office, a creditor may file either the security agreement itself or a duplicate certified to be a true copy of the original, so long as either is sufficient to place third parties on notice that the copyright is encumbered. Accordingly, the Copyright Act requires that the file document "specifically identif[y] the work to which it pertains so that, after the document is indexed by the Register of Copyrights, it would be revealed by a reasonable search under the title or registration number of the work." 17 U.S.C. §205(c).

That having been said, it's worth noting that filing with the Copyright Office can be much less convenient than filing under the U.C.C. This is because U.C.C. filings are indexed by owner, while registration in the Copyright Office is by title or copyright registration number. See 17 U.S.C. §205(c).

This means that the recording of a security interest in a film library such as that owned by NPI will involve dozens, sometimes hundreds, of individual filings. Moreover, as the contents of the film library changes, the lienholder will be required to make a separate filing for each work added to or deleted from the library. By contrast, a U.C.C.-1 filing can provide a continuing, floating lien on assets of a particular type owned by the debtor, without the need for periodic updates. See [U.C.C. §9-204].

This technical shortcoming of the copyright filing system does make it a less useful device for perfecting a security interest in copyright libraries. Nevertheless, this problem is not so serious as to make the system unworkable. In any event, this is the system Congress has established and the court is not in a position to order more adequate procedures. If the mechanics of filing turn out to pose a serious burden, it can be taken up by Congress during its oversight of the Copyright Office or, conceivably, the Copyright Office might be able to ameliorate the problem through exercise of its regulatory authority. See 17 U.S.C. §702.

13. When a federal statute provides a system of national registration but fails to provide its own priority scheme, the priority scheme established by Article Nine . . . will generally govern the conflicting rights of creditors. Whether a creditor's interest is perfected, however, depends on whether the creditor recorded its interest in accordance with the federal statute. See U.C.C. §§[9-311(a) and (b)].

in the copyrights of the films in NPI's library and the receivables they have generated therefore is unperfected.[14]

In the second paragraph of Part II.A. of his opinion, Judge Kozinski states that "because a copyright entitles the holder to receive all income derived from the display of the creative work...an agreement creating a security interest in the receivables generated by a copyright may also be recorded in the Copyright Office." After all, what sense would it make to force secured creditors to file security interests in copyrights, but let them retain secret liens in the money produced by copyrights? None, as far as we can see. In what appears to us to be a dazzling disregard for system function, however, the Ninth Circuit held that an assignment of so much of the debtor's royalties as was necessary to pay certain debt was valid without being recorded in the Copyright Office, because it was not an assignment or mortgage of a copyright. Broadcast Music, Inc. v. Hirsch, 104 F.3d 1163 (9th Cir. 1997). Attempting to reconcile his opinion in *Broadcast Music* with *Peregrine*, Judge Schwarzer asserted that the assignment was absolute rather than in the nature of security. That argument, however, proves too much. Any mortgage of copyright receivables — or any other kind of receivables — can be described as an assignment absolute without changing its effect an iota. Taken literally, Judge Schwarzer's ruling would make recording against accounts receivable optional.

With regard to security interests in trademarks, Judge Kozinski states that a federal filing is not necessary to perfect; a state filing will do. In a more recent case, Joseph v. 1200 Valencia, Inc., 137 B.R. 778 (Bankr. C.D. Cal. 1992), the court held that a federal filing is not sufficient to perfect in a trademark. What makes the situation particularly interesting is that the Patent and Trademark Office accepts security agreements in trademarks for filing. There is obviously plenty of room for confusion here.

In the following case, the court notes the existence of three other federal filing systems, stating that two (aircraft and railroad) preempt the U.C.C. with respect to filing, but one (patents) does not.

---

14. The court also finds two trademark cases, TR-3 Indus. v. Capital Bank (In re TR-3 Indus.), 41 Bankr. 128 (Bankr. C.D. Cal. 1984), and Roman Cleanser Co. v. National Acceptance Co. (In re Roman Cleanser Co.), 43 Bankr. 940 (Bankr. E.D. Mich. 1984), aff'd mem. (E.D. Mich. 1985), 802 F.2d 207 (6th Cir. 1986), to be distinguishable. Both cases held that security interests in trademarks need not be perfected by recording in the United States Patent and Trademark Office. However, unlike the Copyright Act, the Lanham Act's recordation provision refers only to "assignments" and contains no provisions for the registration, recordation or filing of instruments establishing security interests in trademarks. The Copyright Act authorizes the recordation of "transfers" in the Copyright Office, and defines transfers as including "mortgages," "hypothecations" and, thus, security interests in copyrights.

In re: Pasteurized Eggs Corporation
(Pasteurized Eggs Corporation v. Bon Dente Joint Venture)
296 B.R. 283 (Bankr. D.N.H. 2003)

J. MICHAEL DEASY, BANKRUPTCY JUDGE.

. . . Section 544 of the Bankruptcy Code allows the Debtor to assume the role of a hypothetical lien creditor and avoid any unperfected security interest. See 11 U.S.C. §544(a)(1). Whether a security interest is perfected is generally a state law issue, even where the secured property is a patent. See *Cybernetic*, 252 F.3d 1039, 1043 (9th Cir. 2001). In *Cybernetic*, the Ninth Circuit held that a security interest in a patent was perfected where the assignor had complied with California UCC filing requirements but had not recorded the security interest with the PTO. There, the court concluded that Article 9 of California's UCC governs the method for perfecting a security interest in patents, as Article 9 applies to "general intangibles," which includes intellectual property.

The *Cybernetic* court further concluded that the Patent Act does not preempt the UCC with respect to perfection of security interests, because the Patent Act addresses filings only with respect to transfers in ownership but not with regard to security interests. The *Cybernetic* court underscored this point by noting that the Copyright Act does include such a provision. The court noted that "the Copyright Act governs any 'transfer' of ownership, which is defined by the statute to include any 'hypothecation.'" Black's Law Dictionary defines a "hypothecation" as the "pledging of something as security without delivery of title or possession." By contrast, the Patent Act does not refer to "hypothecation" or security interests. The court concluded that the inclusion of a security interest provision in the Copyright Act "is more evidence that security interests are outside the scope of [the Patent Act]."

In an earlier incarnation of *Cybernetic*, the Ninth Circuit Bankruptcy Appellate Panel pointed to aircraft and railroads as two additional areas in which Congress has established a federal filing system for liens. See Cybernetic Services, Inc. v. Matsco, Inc. (In re Cybernetic Services, Inc.), 239 B.R. 917, 922, nn.13, 14 (9th Cir. B.A.P. 1999). There, the Panel contrasts the Patent Act, which contains no provision regarding perfection of security interests, with statutes that clearly establish a federal filing system and therefore preempt state requirements. Regarding liens on aircraft, 49 U.S.C. §44107(a)(2) provides: "under §44108, the failure to file a security instrument with the FAA administrator precludes constructive notice of the existence of the security instrument and consequently limits the parties against whom it is valid. Regarding liens on railroad-related property, 49 U.S.C. §11301 provides that a "mortgage . . . or security interest in vessels, railroad cars, locomotives, or other rolling stock . . . shall be filed with the Board in order to perfect the security interest that is the subject of such instrument." Unlike the language in these statutes, the Patent Act does not contain any language regarding security interests, and therefore does not preempt state law. As such, perfection of a security interest in a patent requires filing a UCC-1 in accordance with state law. Filing a security agreement with the PTO does not perfect the security interest.

With modern computer technology, maintenance of thousands of isolated filing systems is no longer warranted. See LoPucki, Computerization of the Article 9 Filing System: Thoughts on Building the Electronic Highway, 55 Law & Contemp. Probs. 5 (1992), advocating a system in which every search covers all systems. By requiring filing against a corporation in the jurisdiction in which it is incorporated, new Article 9 has paved the way for joining the record of a U.C.C. filing against a corporation with the other records pertaining to that corporation. But the law has a tradition of staying behind the times, and we suspect that the consolidation across filing systems is still decades away.

F.   Methods and Costs of Searching

In many filing offices, only employees are permitted access to the records. In those systems, the lender or its lawyer must fill out a form precisely specifying the search requested and send it to the filing officer. In other filing offices a member of the public who knows how to do so can walk in and search the records or search them on the Internet. But most lenders and lawyers still choose not to deal directly with the filing office. Instead, they hire a "service company" to order or conduct the search for them.

The service companies are private businesses that serve as intermediaries between the lender or lawyer who needs a search and the filing office in which the search is conducted. Unlike many of the filing officers, who are government employees, the service companies will accept search requests by telephone and expedite them if necessary. If the service company has an office near the records to be searched, a company employee may go to the filing office and either conduct the search or order it "over the counter." If the service company does not have an office near the records, it may nevertheless provide the same service through a local correspondent. The local correspondent typically is an abstract company (known as a *title* or *escrow* company in some parts of the United States), a local U.C.C. search company, or an attorney.

The result is that, in most searches, the lender pays two fees: that of the filing officer and that of the service company. The filing officer's fee is usually specified by a state statute, and the service company's fee is determined by the service company or its correspondent. A typical fee for searching a single name would be about $50.[*] To search an additional name or a variation is likely to double the cost of the search. To search in an additional filing office is likely to double it again. About half the typical fee would go to the filing officer, the other half to the service company and its correspondent. If the search identifies relevant filings, the lender will usually wish to purchase copies. A typical search will turn up about ten pages of filings, although the actual number may vary from none to hundreds, depending on the complexity of

---

[*] The authors wish to express their thanks to Ed Hand of U.C.C. Filing and Search Services in Tallahassee, Florida, for the estimates of typical costs in this section.

the debtor's finances and distinctness of its name. Because filing officers typically charge about a dollar a page for making copies, the cost of copies can be considerable. Finally, many searches are conducted at remote locations on short notice, so the lender may also incur charges for overnight deliveries and the like.

Filing is usually a little cheaper than searching, but not much. The service company is likely to charge about $15 per filing and the filing officer may charge anywhere from about $5 to $25.

If the client is only an occasional user of the Article 9 filing system, the client will likely want the lawyer to arrange the necessary filings and searches. Involving even a relatively inexpensive lawyer (or an expensive one who delegates the task to a paralegal) can easily triple or quadruple the cost of filing or searching. On the other hand, a lender who deals with a particular filing office regularly may be familiar with the procedures of that office, have an account with the office, and perhaps even have the ability to search the records or make filings directly from a remote terminal. For such a lender, the cost of filing or searching in that particular office may be only a fraction of the cost the lender would incur working through a lawyer or a search company.

While the fees incurred by most filers and searchers may seem substantial to a student who is doing law school on $40 a day, they remain small in relation to the amounts of money involved in most commercial lending transactions. For this reason, a lawyer who is uncertain as to the filing office in which a particular search or filing should be made can often solve the problem by searching or filing in more than one system. The possibility has led some observers to advocate filing "everywhere," but that word tends to be used by people other than those paying the bills. We suggest that the issue of where to search and file is one that requires both a thorough knowledge of the law and the exercise of judgment in light of the likely cost and the amounts involved.

Problem Set 57

57.1. Leonard Drapkowski's only valuable possession is his Pontiac Firebird (lemon yellow, five-speed transmission, named "Honey"). The car is fully paid for and worth about $10,000. Leonard owes about that same amount to Felicia Steinberg, his ex-wife, for child support and alimony arrearages. He also owes a number of other debts, including $12,000 to his business partner, Bernie Keller, for money he borrowed from Bernie over the past few years. Six months ago, Felicia hired you to collect the arrearages for her. You obtained a judgment on the debt, but because Leonard was making the current support payments, the judge declined to hold him in contempt. When Leonard ignored the judgment, Felicia authorized you to have the sheriff seize Honey. In investigating the title to the Firebird, you learned that just over three months ago, Leonard signed a security agreement granting Bernie Keller an interest in Honey to secure the $12,000 debt. Leonard and Bernie went together to the Department of Motor Vehicles and immediately recorded notice of Bernie's lien on the certificate of title for the Firebird.

a.   Now where does Felicia stand? Uniform Motor Vehicle Certificate of Title Act §20(b). U.C.C. §§9-102(a)(52), 9-317(a)(2), and 9-311(b).

b.   Can you go ahead with the execution levy? If you can, should you? U.C.C. §9-401.

57.2.   Three Rivers Legal Services referred Sergio Morales to you. Sergio is a Salvadoran immigrant who has been in the United States a little over three years. For most of that time, he worked the graveyard shift at McDonald's, saving the money with which he hoped to start his own business. Five months ago, he found the opportunity he was looking for in an ad in a Spanish-language newspaper: a street vender cart with refrigeration for $2,000. Sergio paid the owner, Mark Winchell, $1,000 in cash, signed a promissory note for the balance, quit his job, and went into business for himself selling food and ice cream in the park. About two weeks ago, he received in quick succession (1) a notice that Winchell had filed for bankruptcy and (2) a letter from General Finance Company (GFC), demanding possession of the cart. Along with the GFC letter were copies of three documents. The first was Winchell's promissory note to GFC in the amount of $2,500. The second was a security agreement signed by Winchell more than a year ago granting GFC an interest in the cart to secure the note. The third was a financing statement bearing the date and time stamp of the Secretary of State U.C.C. division. U.C.C. §9-519(a)(2).

In your check of the public records, you found that GFC had done everything necessary to perfect their security interest months before Sergio bought the cart. When you asked Sergio why he had not searched the U.C.C. records before buying the cart, he told you sheepishly that he did not know such a thing existed.

The partner you work for says that if you take Sergio's case on a pro bono basis, the firm will support you. You like Sergio and would like to help him keep his cart and his dreams. But another lawyer in the firm who does lots of Article 9 work says that Sergio is not protected as a buyer under U.C.C. §9-320(a) because he did not buy in the ordinary course of business, and you accept your colleague's expertise. (You will study this point in greater detail in Assignment 69.) When you asked whether there was any other provision of Article 9 that might provide a defense, she said "No, the whole point of Article 9 is that people are supposed to check the records." You remember a favorite law professor having said that if a sympathetic client has a just case and good facts there's always some legal theory "to hang your hat on," but you also remember that the professor did not teach any commercial subjects. Sergio will be in to talk with you in the morning.

a.   What do you plan to tell him? See U.C.C. §§1-103 (Rev. §1-103(b)), 1-203 (Rev. §1-304), 9-201(a), 9-315(a)(1), and the footnote to the *Peerless Packing* case.

b.   If you discovered that GFC repossessed three vending carts in the past 12 months, each time from a defrauded buyer, would that help your case?

57.3.   As the most junior attorney in a firm that represents secured lenders you have been assigned to order U.C.C. filings and searches in anticipation of the client's lending against the collateral listed below. (The firm never mentioned this during their summer clerkship program.) In what filing system or systems will you make the filings and conduct the searches?

a.   Keith Pipes, an auto mechanic, has applied to your client, ITT Services, for a consumer loan to be secured by $5,000 worth of tools, which Pipes bought and paid for a couple of years ago to use at the service station he and his wife own and operate. See U.C.C. §§9-109, 9-310, and 9-501(a).

b.   Bernie Wolfson, an inventor who lives in San Diego, has applied to your client, a San Diego bank, for a $200,000 loan to be secured by a patent he obtained several years ago. U.C.C. §§9-311(a)(1), 9-109(c)(1).

c.   Your client is a New York bank that plans to lend $250,000 to famous author Nyl Ikcupol. The loan is to be secured by royalty payments Nyl receives from his New York publisher on the 119 books he has written. See U.C.C. §§9-102(a)(2), 9-109(a) and (c), 9-501(a). Reread the first few paragraphs of section II.A. of *National Peregrine*. If the Copyright Office charges a $20 fee for filing the transfer of a copyright, what do you estimate will be the cost to the client of filing in the Copyright Office? See *National Peregrine*, note 10. Will you be needing some searches as well?

d.   Your client is an Indiana bank planning to make a $300,000 working capital loan to an Indiana dealer in rare automobiles. The collateral will include (1) the dealer's inventory of automobiles, (2) some automobiles that are not for sale, (3) accounts receivable from the sale of automobiles, (4) all of the dealer's rights to its "American Originals" trademark. U.C.C. §§9-311(a)(2) and (d), Comment 4 to U.C.C. §9-311, U.C.C. §§9-501(a), 9-109(a) and (b), 9-102(a)(2), (33), (42), and (48); UMVCTA §§3, 4(a), and 20(a) and (b); *National Peregrine*, note 14 (dealing with trademarks).

57.4.   The lawyer who assigned the Indiana bank case to you specializes in real property work and isn't familiar with the U.C.C. He explains that the bank is concerned that the debtor might encumber the property at any time, even as the debtor is negotiating with your client. The lawyer asks which should be done first, the U.C.C. searches or the filings? U.C.C. §§9-502(d), 9-523(c).

Assignment 58: Article 9 Financing Statements: The Debtor's Name

In Assignment 57, we used the metaphor of leaving messages to explain the function of a filing system. For the system to work, the filer must leave the message in the correct system and the searcher must know to look for it in the same system. In this assignment we examine a closely related problem. Even if a filer and searcher go to the same filing system, that may still not be sufficient to ensure that the message is received. A single statewide or nationwide filing system will typically contain millions of messages. For the message to be received, the filer must not only leave it in the right system, the filer must leave it in the right "place" in that system, in such form that the searcher who finds it can realize its relevance. In this section we explore how the Article 9 filing system is designed and "where" messages must be left so they can be found later.

A. The Components of a Filing System

Several states now permit the electronic filing of financing statements and other records. To accommodate these "paperless" filings, the provisions of revised Article 9 are "media neutral." That is, they are written to be applied to paper filings, electronic filings, or any other sort of filing the future may hold. Thus the new term "record" is defined as "information that is inscribed on a tangible medium or which is stored in an electronic or other medium and is retrievable in perceivable form." Accordingly, the filing officer does not "stamp" the file number on a financing statement, the filing officer "assigns" the file number to a financing statement.

A filing system consists not only of the filed records but also of subsystems for (1) adding new records, (2) searching among the records, and (3) removing obsolete records. The subsystems for adding new records are relatively simple. The clerk who receives a filing typically assigns a date and time of filing, makes a copy, and returns the original to the filer with a receipt. Later, someone else in the clerk's office will index the copy and add it to the body of prior filings. In many filing systems, subsystems for removing obsolete records do not exist at all: The store of records simply grows each year. The subsystem for removing obsolete records from Article 9 filing systems is discussed in Assignment 61. In this assignment, we focus primarily on the subsystems that search for relevant records in the filing system.

For reasons more related to technology than law, search methods differ widely from one filing system to another. The introduction of new technologies for processing, storing, and searching the records results in important changes in the ways these systems operate. Each new technology spawns a new set of legal problems. For this reason, we think it is useful to understand the system at a broad conceptual level — to understand what the system is designed to do and the basic strategies for accomplishing its goals. This kind of understanding transcends any particular filing system and the technologies in use at the time. But students also need to know how particular technologies have been implemented in particular systems, because it is only in the particularity of those implementations that the system generates problems that require the attention of a lawyer. Law functions almost entirely as a facilitator of the technology of its day.

1. *Financing Statements*

The Article 9 filing system was designed and implemented before the era of the photocopier. Early filers had to furnish carbon copies of their financing statements to filing officers who had no means of creating additional copies. Searches were conducted among the actual pieces of paper that were filed. As photocopying came into wide use in the 1960s, some systems began making copies of filed financing statements. But many of the systems went directly from using carbon copies to microfilm as the medium for storing and using financing statements. Microfilm later gave way to microfiche. In both micromedia, the filing officer films and stores the financing statements in the order in which they are received. In most systems even today, the searcher who needs to examine a financing statement must spin through a reel of microfilm or find the right page on a microfiche. The searcher who wants a copy prints it directly from the microfilm or microfiche.

In the past few years, a few of the larger Article 9 filing systems have switched from microfilm or microfiche to computer storage of financing statements. These offices photograph the financing statements using a camera digitizer. The image can be stored on a disk drive or tape, retrieved electronically, and viewed on a computer screen. An important limitation of this new medium is that while the computers can reproduce the image of a financing statement, most understand it only as a picture. The computers cannot "read" the words. Thus, whether the current system uses microfilm, microfiche, or digital storage, it is usually impossible to search the text of financing statements in the way that one can search the text of court opinions on LEXIS or Westlaw. The system can provide a reproduction of the financing statement, but it does not provide a way to search its text.

Some systems permit electronic filing. The filer, usually a financial institution that files frequently, sets up an account in advance with the filing officer. It transmits each record electronically, in text format. On receipt, the filing officer charges the filing fee to the filer's account. The entire text of these records could be word-searched, but a search of less than all filings in the system has little commercial value; one could never be sure that relevant filings did not lurk in the remainder.

2. The Index

When a financing statement is filed, the filing officer assigns it a unique number, usually referred to as the *file number* or, in some local systems, the *book and page number*. The system uses this number as a means of identifying, indexing, and retrieving the statement.

To find a particular financing statement on microfiche or in electronic graphic images, one must have its number. For any person who already has a copy of the filed financing statement, this presents no problem. So, for example, a filer who wants a copy of the financing statement to prove the date and time of its filing to a court might order a certified copy of "file number 92-183849."

The typical searcher is a lender who contemplates making a secured loan to the debtor and who wants to discover whether there are prior recorded interests in the debtor's property. This subsequent lender comes to the filing system without a file number. It seeks not a particular financing statement, but any and all financing statements that might encumber the prospective collateral. What the typical searcher knows is the name of the prospective debtor and the proposed collateral. The searcher will be able to find the messages about earlier filed interests only if they are indexed by description of the collateral or the identity of the debtor.

A few kinds of filing systems index by a description of the collateral. The description often includes a number to add distinctness and make searching easier. One example is the *tract index* employed in some real estate recording systems. (Real estate systems are often referred to as "recording" systems rather than filing systems, but, for convenience, we sometimes use the term *filing systems* to encompass real estate as well as personal property systems.) Each tract of land in the county is assigned a unique number, and these numbers are written on maps. Searchers find the numbers on the maps and then search the index under the tract number.

The motor vehicle certificate of title system is another that indexes filings by description of collateral. Each motor vehicle is assigned a Vehicle Identification Number (VIN) at the time of manufacture or importation and a registration number at the time it is licensed for operation on the highways. A searcher can use either number to locate the certificate. All filed liens appear on the face of the certificate.

Both the real estate and motor vehicle filing systems can index by collateral because the collateral they govern has a stable identity. Tracts of land are split or consolidated infrequently, and, even when they are, the land in question remains easy to trace. Similarly, a motor vehicle usually retains its identity throughout its useful life. The system assigns a unique identification number to each tract or vehicle, making it possible to search by number. But for most kinds of collateral governed by the Article 9 filing system — think of tubes of toothpaste on the supermarket shelf or oil in the hands of a refinery — the assignment of identification numbers is impractical. Nor would it be practical to index directly by the description of collateral. A searcher who intended to lend money against oil in the hands of a refinery might find thousands of filings under "oil" and have little means for knowing which relate to the oil it plans to take as collateral. The filer who financed the inventory of a supermarket would have to list each type of collateral separately, resulting in thousands of separate notations in the index ("toothpaste," "bread," "milk"). Problems such as these make the indexing of Article 9 financing statements by collateral impractical. Article 9 filing officers index financing statements only by the name of the debtor.

U.C.C. §9-519(c) requires that the filing office index financing statements according to the name of the debtor. The index thus prepared typically will include the address of the debtor. The address is often helpful to searchers in distinguishing the debtor who is the subject of their search from other debtors with the same or similar names. Some filing officers include additional information in the index, such as the name and address of the creditor, the date of filing, or even a brief description of the collateral. Of course, the file number must be part of the index entry; the searcher consults the index to obtain the number and then uses the number to retrieve the financing statement.

Today, nearly all filing systems use computerized data management systems to generate the debtor name index. Employees of the filing officer enter the information to be included in the index from the face of the financing statement to the computer. Keyboards are the usual means of entry, although scanners are in use in some systems. A few systems permit electronic filing, which eliminates the need to enter filings so made.

3. Search Systems

Some computer systems sort the index entries alphabetically and print hard (paper) copies of the index. In such a system, the searcher interested in Smith, John, begins by locating the entries that begin with "S" and goes on from there. Anyone who has made significant use of the telephone directory of a large city is in a position to appreciate the subtle problems inherent in such a search. A misspelling early in a name can throw a name to a distant part of the directory where only a psychic could find it. The position of even a correctly spelled name can be affected by arbitrary, difficult-to-discover rules for alphabetizing. See, for example, Chemical Bank v. Title Services, Inc., 708 F. Supp. 245 (D. Minn. 1989) (secretary of state's search under the true name "Boisclair" would not discover a filing erroneously made under name "Bois Clair" because "there were at least seven filings between Bois Clair and Boisclair [on the printout of the index] on the date of the search in question").

In other computer systems, the same search is conducted electronically. Here the searcher enters a name such as "Smith, John" and the computer returns a list of matching entries. Some systems would consider only a financing statement listing the debtor as "Smith, John" to be a match. But others are programmed to recognize as equivalents names such as "Smith, J.", "Smith, Jack," or even "Smyth, John." The rules that determine what the program will consider equivalent are referred to as the "search logic" of the program. As you will see later in this assignment, the search logic can play a critical role in determining not only the results of searches, but also the outcomes of disputes. Some systems inform users of the particular search logic employed, while in other systems only those who manage the system have that information.

Another important difference among filing systems is in who is permitted access to the records to search. In some systems, only an employee of the filing officer can execute a search. The user of this kind of system typically is required to submit in writing the exact name or names under which the search is to be conducted. The filing officer may respond to the search request only after a delay of several days or even weeks. The quality of the search results in such a system are likely to vary with the ability and experience of the employee conducting it.

In other systems, members of the public can conduct their own searches. The immediate feedback thus available enables the user to vary the search until the results are as expected. For example, if the searcher knows there will be financing statements on file against the debtor, but none shows up on the search, the searcher can guess that there is some variation of the debtor's name that the searcher has not yet tried.

The filing officer creates a record that bears the record and file numbers assigned to each financing statement and the date and time of its filing. The financing statement is effective as of that moment, even though it may take a few days, or even a few weeks, for the filing officer to make the index entry. Thus, at any given time, there will be financing statements on file and effective that are not yet discoverable in a search of the index. Because in many filing systems the not-yet-processed documents were kept in an in-basket on someone's desk, these unindexed and therefore undiscoverable records have come to be known as *the basket*. Filing officers running small systems sometimes conduct or permit hand-searching of the basket in connection with a search of the index. But in a large system, there may be no way to discover financing statements in the basket except to wait for the filing officer to enter them.

By now it should be apparent that the debtor name index is of critical importance to the functioning of an Article 9 filing system. The vast majority of searchers can find the financing statements they seek only through that index. Moreover, they may be able to find the entries for those financing statements in the debtor name index only if the debtor's name shown on the financing statement is sufficiently similar to the debtor's name as they know it that the computer will return a match, or, if the search is on a hard copy index, the searcher will find the debtor's name and recognize it. Debtors' names as they appear in the index are the searchers' link to the financing statements on file.

B.   Correct Names for Use on Financing Statements

U.C.C. §9-506(a) provides that "a financing statement substantially complying with the requirements of [part 5 of Article 9] is effective, even if it includes minor errors or omissions, unless the errors or omissions make the financing statement seriously misleading." In the next section, we consider what kinds of errors are considered seriously misleading, but first we address a preliminary question: What is the "correct" name of a debtor that *ideally* would appear on the financing statement? The answer to this question is surprisingly complex.

The analysis begins with the U.C.C. §9-503 safe harbor. That section provides that a financing statement sufficiently provides the name of a registered entity only if it provides the name of the debtor indicated on the public record of the debtor's jurisdiction of origin. As to an individual or partnership, the financing statement must provide the "individual or organizational name of the debtor." U.C.C. §9-503(a)(4). A financing statement is not rendered ineffective by the inclusion of the debtor's trade name and use of a trade name alone does not sufficiently provide the name of the debtor. U.C.C. §§9-503(b) and (c). We discuss each of these four types of names separately.

1. Individual Names

The reference to "individual" names is to the names of human beings, as opposed to the names of artificial legal entities such as corporations, partnerships, or trusts. Unfortunately for all who deal with the filing system, our cultural and social practices are very tolerant of both variations and changes in individual names. An individual's birth certificate and college degree may indicate his name to be "Thomas Lawrence Smith," even though he never uses this form of his name on any other occasion. His friends may know him as "Bucky Smith," while his mother calls him "Tommy," but the line below his signature on documents is always "Thomas L. Smith," and his listing in the phone directory is under "T.L. Smith." If he wants to change any of these to "Tom Smith," most of us will consider that his prerogative and comply.

What is the legally correct name of this individual? Black letter law tells us that it is the name by which he is generally known, for nonfraudulent purposes, in the community. What community? Black letter law doesn't say, but the implication is that it might be a different community for different legal purposes. His birth certificate is not determinative. In other words, Tom has many names, but no single, unique identifier.

The naming problem is complicated by the fact that an individual can change his or her name. The individual can do so by filing a court action for that purpose. Divorce courts commonly include desired name changes in their decrees. But an individual can also change his or her name without legal action. All the individual need do is become generally known, for a nonfraudulent purpose, by a different name.

The implications for the Article 9 filing system are disconcerting. There may be no single version of an individual debtor's name that is "correct," and even if there is, it may be impossible to know for certain which version it is. To make matters even more complicated, more than one person may have precisely the same name. Together, these characteristics of individual names cause considerable confusion and uncertainty for both filer and searcher in the U.C.C. filing system. With regard to individual names, the indexing system is built on sand.

In re Kinderknecht (Clark v. Deere and Co.)
308 B.R. 71 (10th Cir. BAP 2004)

THURMAN, BANKRUPTCY JUDGE.

I.   BACKGROUND

It is undisputed that the debtor's legal name is "Terrance Joseph Kinderknecht." In addition, it is undisputed that the debtor is informally known as "Terry."

The debtor granted Deere security interests in two farm implements. Deere promptly filed financing statements in the appropriate place, listing the debtor as "Terry J. Kinderknecht."

Subsequently, the debtor filed a Chapter 7 petition. His petition, while signed by "Terry Kinderknecht," is filed under his legal name, "Terrance J. Kinderknecht."

The trustee in the debtor's Chapter 7 case commenced an adversary proceeding against Deere, seeking to avoid its interests in the debtor's farm implements pursuant to 11 U.S.C. §544(a)(1). . . .

II.   DISCUSSION

Section 84-9-503 reflects Kansas's adoption in 2000 of revised Uniform Commercial Code §9-503, recommended in 1998 by the National Conference of Commissioners on Uniform State Laws. Prior to that time, courts struggled with whether names, such as trade names, in a financing statement sufficiently provided the name of the debtor. U.C.C §9-503 . . . is meant to "clarify when a debtor's name is correct and when an incorrect name is insufficient." Official UCC Comment 4.h.

Although [U.C.C. §9-503] specifically sets parameters for listing a debtor's name in a financing statement when the debtor is an entity, it does not provide any detail as to the name that must be provided for an individual debtor — it simply states that the "name of the debtor" should be used. This could be construed, as it was by the bankruptcy court, as allowing a debtor to be listed in a financing statement by his or her commonly-used nickname. But, we do not agree with that interpretation because the purpose of [U.C.C. §9-503], as well as a reading of that section as a whole, leads us to conclude that an individual debtor's legal name must be used in the financing statement to make it sufficient under [U.C.C. §9-502(a)(1)].

As discussed above, [U.C.C. §9-503] is new, and it was enacted to clarify the sufficiency of a debtor's name in financing statements. The intent to clarify when a debtor's name is sufficient shows a desire to foreclose fact-intensive tests, such as those that existed under the former Article 9 of the UCC, inquiring into whether a person conducting a search would discover a filing under any given name. Requiring a financing statement to provide a debtor's legal name is a clear cut test that is in accord with that intent.

Furthermore, [U.C.C. §9-503], read as a whole, indicates that a legal name should be used for an individual debtor. In the case of debtor-entities, [U.C.C. §9-503(a)] states that legal names must be used to render them sufficient under

[U.C.C. §9-502(a)]. Trade names or other names may be listed, but it is insufficient to list a debtor by such names alone. A different standard should not apply to individual debtors. The more specific provisions applicable to entities, together with the importance of naming the debtor in the financing statement to facilitate the notice filing system and increase commercial certainty, indicate that an individual debtor must be listed on a financing statement by his or her legal name, not by a nickname.

Our conclusion that a legal name is necessary to sufficiently provide the name of an individual debtor within the meaning of [U.C.C. §9-503(a)] is also supported by four practical considerations. First, mandating the debtor's legal name sets a clear test so as to simplify the drafting of financing statements. Second, setting a clear test simplifies the parameters of UCC searches. Persons searching UCC filings will know that they need the debtor's legal name to conduct a search, they will not be penalized if they do not know that a debtor has a nickname, and they will not have to guess any number of nicknames that could exist to conduct a search. Third, requiring the debtor's legal name will avoid litigation as to the commonality or appropriateness of a debtor's nickname, and as to whether a reasonable searcher would have or should have known to use the name. Finally, obtaining a debtor's legal name is not difficult or burdensome for the creditor taking a secured interest in a debtor's property. Indeed, knowing the individual's legal name will assure the accuracy of any search that that creditor conducts prior to taking its secured interest in property.

Additionally, we note that although use of the Official Forms is not mandated, the language in the Financing Statement Form set forth in [U.C.C. §9-521] expressly states that the preparer should include the "DEBTOR'S EXACT FULL LEGAL NAME." This Form, which is meant to "reduce error," indicates to us an intent to increase certainty in the filing of financing statements by requiring a debtor's legal name. Our holding in this case will foster that intent.

By using the debtor's nickname in its financing statements, Deere failed to provide the name of the debtor within the meaning of [U.C.C. §9-503(a)], and its financing statements are not sufficient under [U.C.C. §9-502(a)]. Because the financing statements do not "sufficiently . . . provide the name of the debtor" under [U.C.C. §9-503(a)], they are "seriously misleading" as a matter of law pursuant to [U.C.C. §9-506(b)]. Furthermore, the undisputed facts in this case show that [U.C.C. §9-506(c)] does not apply in this case. That section saves a financing statement from being "seriously misleading" if a search of UCC filings "under the debtor's correct name, using the filing office's standard search logic, . . . would disclose a financing statement that fails sufficiently to provide the name of the debtor" in accordance with [U.C.C. §9-503(a)]. Included in the record before us are the results of a UCC search conducted by Deere's counsel in Kansas's official and unofficial UCC search systems. Under both systems, she found no matches for the debtor's legal name "Terrance," but numerous matches for his nickname "Terry" and the initial "T." Thus, a search of the debtor's "correct name" did not disclose a financing statement, and therefore, [U.C.C. §9-506(c)] does not apply. The result of Deere's UCC searches underscores the need for a clear-cut method of searching a debtor's name in UCC filings. The logical starting point for a person searching records would be to use the debtor's legal name. When a UCC search of the debtor's legal name does not provide any matches, parties in interest should be able to presume that the debtor's property is not encumbered, and they should not be charged with guessing what to do next if the legal name search does not result in any matches. Deere's financing statements, being seriously misleading, do not perfect its interest in the debtor's property and, therefore, the bankruptcy court erred in refusing to avoid its interests as against the trustee as a hypothetical lien creditor under 11 U.S.C. §544(a)(1).

In *Kinderknecht*, the parties were in agreement that "Terry" was merely a nickname. But keep in mind that "Terry" — like virtually any other nickname — can be a person's legal name.

2. Corporate Names

In the United States, corporations can be formed only by obtaining a *charter* or *certificate of incorporation* from the secretary of state of one of the 50 states. The federal government issues charters for a few kinds of corporations, such as national banks. The certificate will show the one and only legal name of the corporation. The corporation can change that name only by filing an amendment with the secretary of state. It follows that at any given time, a corporation has only a single correct name. By examining the certificate of incorporation on file with the Corporations division of the secretary of state, a searcher can discover the precise spelling of a corporate name, including the details of punctuation, hyphenation, and capitalization.

Two other characteristics of corporate names are of significance to the Article 9 filing system. First, in the large majority of states, the name must show that the entity is a corporation. It does that by including one of only a few permissible designators. The most common are "Corporation" or its abbreviation "Corp.," "Company" or its abbreviation "Co.," "Incorporated" or its abbreviation "Inc.," and "Limited Liability Company" or its abbreviation "L.L.C." If the corporation is formed for a particular purpose, such as to practice a licensed profession, alternative corporate designators may be required. For example, a corporation formed to practice law is a "Professional Association" or "P.A." under Florida law, a "Service Corporation" or "S.C." under Wisconsin law, and a "Profession Corporation" or "P.C." under California law. The primary significance of these rules for the Article 9 filing systems is that they make it possible to identify many names as not the names of corporations. For example, in the large majority of states, "McDonald's" cannot be a corporate name, but "McDonald's, Inc." can be. (California is an exception; it would permit the use of "McDonald's" as a corporate name.)

The other characteristic of the corporate naming system that is of significance to the Article 9 filing system is that no state will permit the formation of two corporations with the same name or confusingly similar names. (A name that differs from another only in its corporate designator is considered confusingly similar. If the state has already incorporated a McDonald's, Inc., it will refuse to incorporate a McDonald's Corporation.) Two corporations can have the same name only if they incorporate in different states. If one adds the state of incorporation to a corporate name, for example, "McDonald's, Inc., a Delaware Corporation," the result is a unique identifier. Together, these characteristics of corporate names make them more reliable and easier to use for filing and searching than individual names.

3. Partnership Names

A limited partnership is formed in much the same way as a corporation. The person causing it to be formed files papers with the secretary of state of one of the 50 states and the secretary issues a certificate. The certificate will contain the name of the limited partnership. The name generally must contain "Limited Partnership" or the abbreviations "Ltd." or "L.P." The secretary of state will not permit use of a name that is the same as, or confusingly similar to, that of a limited partnership already chartered by the state.

General partnerships are formed by contract, express or implied. No state registration is required or permitted. If there is a written partnership agreement, it may assign a name to the partnership. Regardless of the agreement among the partners, however, the legal name of a general partnership is the name by which it is generally known in the community. The name may, but need not, include some indication that the entity is a partnership. If Sally White and Grover Cleveland form a partnership, the name could be "White and Cleveland" (filed under "W"), "Sally White and Grover Cleveland" (filed under "S"), "White & Cleveland," "Realty Partners," or even "McDonald's."

Partnership names, like the names of individuals and corporations, can change over time. U.C.C. §9-507 contains rules dealing with the effects of these changes on filing and searching. Our discussion of the rules relating to name changes is in Assignment 62.

4. Trade Names

A "trade" or "fictitious" name is a name under which a person or entity conducts business that is not its legal name. For example, the purchaser of a McDonald's franchise may incorporate under a name like "McDonald's Restaurants of Atlanta, Incorporated." But if one visits the business premises, one sees only the name "McDonald's" in and about the golden arches. "McDonald's" is a trade name. Many trade names bear no resemblance to the name of the person or entity using them. For example, the Bernard Walker Corporation may do business as "Yellow Cab Company."

Trade names are the subject of several kinds of public record systems. The user of a trade name can register the name with a state or the federal government and thereby lodge a claim to exclusive ownership. Only a small portion of the trade names in use in the United States are so registered; most are simply adopted by a business without additional formality.

Most states have a "fictitious name" statute requiring that *every* person or entity doing business in a name other than its own file notice in a public record system provided for that purpose. Although the statutes typically make failure to file a misdemeanor, there are few prosecutions and no other effective penalties for not filing. Filing does nothing to preserve or to enhance the filer's claim to ownership of the trade name. As a result, most of these fictitious-name filing systems have fallen into disuse. Even large, publicly held companies that own and do business under many trade names do not file notices.

As a result, it can often be difficult to determine who or what is doing business under a particular trade name. The drafters of Article 9 deemed trade names too uncertain and too likely not to be known to the secured party or person searching the record to form the basis for a filing system. U.C.C. §§9-503(b) and (c) make clear that trade names are neither necessary nor sufficient to identify a debtor on a financing statement.

5.   The Entity Problem

The difficulty of determining the correct name of a legal entity is easily confused with a much more basic question: Who, or what, can have a name? That is, in the contemplation of the law, who or what will be recognized as a separate entity, capable of being a debtor and therefore capable of being the subject of an Article 9 filing? For example, assume that your search assignment was to determine whether the personal property of the law school in which you are studying is encumbered. Would you search under the name of the law school? The university? The board of regents or trustees that operate the university?

The U.C.C.'s answer to this question begins with the definition of "debtor" in §9-102(a)(28). A debtor is a "person." "Person" is defined in U.C.C. §1-201(30) (Rev. §201(b)(27)) to include an individual or an organization. "Organization" is defined in §1-201(28) (Rev. §1-201(25)) to include a variety of kinds of entities. The definition ends with the words "or any other legal or commercial entity." The apparent implication is that an entity might be a debtor under Article 9 and its name might show up on financing statements, even though it is not recognized as a *legal* entity for any other purpose.

C.   Errors in the Debtors' Names on
Financing Statements

Most searches are initiated by persons who intend to lend money to the debtor. They search to assure themselves that no one has perfected a prior security interest in the collateral. The search is conducted in the debtor name index and is for listings under the name of the debtor. If a search is conducted under the correct name of the debtor, it should discover any financing statement filed and indexed under that name. If the searcher has an incorrect name for the debtor, the search may fail to discover prior filings made and indexed under the correct name of the debtor. If the searcher lends money to the debtor pursuant to such a search, the searcher may later be surprised to find that its security interest is subordinate to undiscovered prior filings. If the searcher searches under the correct name of the debtor, but does not find the prior filing because the prior secured party listed an incorrect name for the debtor on its financing statement, the prior filing is ineffective. See U.C.C. §§9-503(a) and 9-506(a) and (c). Finally, if the search is made under the correct name of the debtor, but does not find prior filings made in the correct name of the debtor because the filing officer indexed the prior filings incorrectly, the prior filings are nevertheless effective. See U.C.C. §9-517. If the state has waived sovereign immunity for this purpose, the searchers have a cause of action against the filing officer.

Article 9 gives priority to the first creditor to file or perfect. Nothing in Article 9 requires that creditor to search for prior filings. A creditor that files its own financing statement second in time, an unsecured creditor who becomes a lien creditor after the prior creditor filed its financing statement, or a trustee appointed in the debtor's bankruptcy case can establish priority over the prior filer by demonstrating that the prior filing was "insufficient" because it did not "provide the name of the debtor." U.C.C. §§9-502(a) and 9-503. In fact, most cases in which the sufficiency of a financing statement is challenged are cases brought by trustees in bankruptcy or later lenders who did not search. When the sufficiency of the debtor's name as provided in the financing statement is challenged, the test is not whether the trustee or later lender *actually found* the financing statement, but whether a hypothetical search by the trustee or later lender under the correct name of the debtor *would have found* the financing statement. U.C.C. §9-506(c).

U.C.C. §9-506(c) tells us that this hypothetical search is conducted in the records of the filing office, under the debtor's correct name, using the filing office's standard search logic. Such a search might, for example, discover filings that a searcher could not discover using the search logic of LEXIS or Westlaw, or might fail to discover filings that a search could discover using the search logic of LEXIS or Westlaw. Most states have adopted filing office rules that explain to some degree the search logic employed. U.C.C. §9-526. But those explanations are not always comprehensive and the actual search logic may not be in accord with announced search logic. The only way to know for certain what the official search logic would discover is to conduct the search in the filing office system; those who search on LEXIS, Westlaw, or alternative systems are at risk for the differences.

Despite the vagaries of search logic, the particular search logic employed in a system determines what filing errors the system can overcome. Even the tiniest of errors in a name can prevent the matching of a filing to a search, rendering the filing insufficient or the search ineffective.

For example, in ITT Commercial Finance v. Bank of the West, 166 F.3d 295 (1999), the debtor's correct name was Compu-Centro, USA, Inc., but the secured creditor filed against Compucentro, USA, Inc. The court held the filing ineffective because a search under the correct name would not have retrieved the filing. (The search logic employed by the Texas Secretary of State treated the hyphen the same as a space. The search logic in most states ignores spaces, but the Texas search logic did not.)

Similarly, in In re Tyler, 23 B.R. 806 (Bankr. S.D. Fla 1982), the correct name of the debtor was Tri State Moulded Plastics, Inc. ("Moulded" spelled with a "u"), and the erroneous filing was against "Tri State Molded Plastics, Inc." The Florida bankruptcy court that decided the case held the error to be seriously misleading, because in the Ohio statewide filing system, where the financing statement was filed, searches could be conducted only by computer. In that system at that time, the erroneous filing would not have been discovered by a computer search of the index under the correct name.

Had the search in *Tyler* been conducted using a hard copy printout of the index, the erroneous filing would almost certainly have been discovered. To understand why this is so, look for Tri State Moulded Plastics, Inc. in the business section of your local telephone directory. Although the "Tri State" listings may be separated from the "Tri-State" or "Tristate" listings by the particular method of alphabetization used, it would be difficult to look in the place where Tri State Moulded Plastics, Inc. would be without seeing the listing for Tri State Molded Plastics, Inc. Once the searcher lays eyes on the latter name, it is easy to conclude that the searcher *ought* to suspect that it is merely a misspelling of the former name.

Such considerations, however, are now irrelevant in Article 9 filing and searching. Under U.C.C. §9-506(c), the test is to enter the correct name and apply the official search logic. Whatever is found is effective; whatever is not is ineffective. The drafters' motive for imposing this draconian rule was to eliminate the necessity for multiple searches. A searcher who knew the correct name could search under that name and be done with it.

Four years later, the Sixth Circuit did this:

In re Spearing Tool and Manufacturing Co., Inc. (United States v. Crestmark Bank)

412 F.3d (6th Cir. 2005)

COOK, CIRCUIT JUDGE.

I. BACKGROUND AND PROCEDURAL HISTORY

In April 1998, Spearing Tool and Manufacturing Co. and appellee Crestmark entered into a lending agreement, which granted Crestmark a security interest in all of Spearing's assets. The bank perfected its security interest by filing a financing statement under the Uniform Commercial Code, identifying Spearing as "Spearing Tool and Manufacturing Co.," its precise name registered with the Michigan Secretary of State. . . .

Meanwhile, Spearing fell behind in its federal employment-tax payments. On October 15, 2001, the IRS filed two notices of federal tax lien against Spearing with the Michigan Secretary of State. Each lien identified Spearing as "SPEARING TOOL & MFG. COMPANY INC.," which varied from Spearing's precise Michigan-registered name, because it used an ampersand in place of "and," abbreviated "Manufacturing" as "Mfg.," and spelled out "Company" rather than use the abbreviation "Co." But the name on the IRS lien notices was the precise name Spearing gave on its quarterly federal tax return for the third quarter of 2001, as well as its return for fourth-quarter 1994, the first quarter for which it was delinquent. For most of the relevant tax periods, however, Spearing filed returns as "Spearing Tool

& Manufacturing" — neither its precise Michigan-registered name, nor the name on the IRS tax liens.

Crestmark periodically submitted lien search requests to the Michigan Secretary of State, using Spearing's exact registered name. Because Michigan has limited electronic-search technology, searches disclose only liens matching the precise name searched — not liens such as the IRS's, filed under slightly different or abbreviated names.[3] . . . So Crestmark, unaware of the tax liens, advanced more funds to Spearing between October 2001 and April 2002.

On April 16, 2002, Spearing filed a Chapter-11 bankruptcy petition. Only afterward did Crestmark finally search for "Spearing Tool & Mfg. Company Inc." and discover the tax-lien notices. Crestmark then filed the complaint in this case to determine lien priority.

II. FEDERAL LAW CONTROLS WHETHER THE IRS'S LIEN NOTICE SUFFICED

When the IRS files a lien against a taxpayer's property, it must do so "in one office within the State . . . as designated by the laws of such State, in which the property subject to the lien is situated." 26 U.S.C. §6323(f)(1)(A). The Internal Revenue Code provides that the form and content "shall be prescribed by the [U.S. Treasury] Secretary" and "be valid notwithstanding any other provision of law regarding the form or content of a notice of lien." 26 U.S.C. §6323(f)(3) (emphasis added). Regulations provide that the IRS must file tax-lien notices using IRS Form 668, which must "identify the taxpayer, the tax liability giving rise to the lien, and the date the assessment arose." 26 C.F.R. §301.6323(f)-1(d)(2). Form-668 notice "is valid notwithstanding any other provision of law regarding the form or content of a notice of lien. For example, omission from the notice of lien of a description of the property subject to the lien does not affect the validity thereof even though State law may require that the notice contain a description of property subject to the lien." §301.6323(f)-1(d)(1).

The plain text of the statute and regulations indicates Form-668 notice suffices, regardless of state law. We therefore need only consider how much specificity federal law requires for taxpayer identification on tax liens.

III. THE NOTICE HERE SUFFICED

An IRS tax lien need not perfectly identify the taxpayer. The question before us is whether the IRS's identification of Spearing was sufficient. We conclude it was.

The critical issue in determining whether an abbreviated or erroneous name sufficiently identifies a taxpayer is whether a "reasonable and diligent search would have revealed the existence of the notices of the federal tax liens under these names." *Tony Thornton,* 791 F.2d at 639. In *Tony Thornton,* for example, liens identifying the taxpayer as "Davis's Restaurant" and "Daviss (sic) Restaurant" sufficed to identify a business correctly known as "Davis Family Restaurant." Id. In *Hudgins,* the IRS lien identified the taxpayer as "Hudgins Masonry, Inc." instead of

---

3. The search engine ignores various "noise words" and their abbreviations, including "Incorporated" and "Company," but not "Manufacturing" or "and."

by the taxpayer's personal name, Michael Steven Hudgins. This notice nonetheless sufficed, given that both names would be listed on the same page of the state's lien index. 967 F.2d at 977.

Crestmark argues, and we agree, that those cases mean little here because in each, creditors could search a physical index and were likely to notice similar entries listed next to or near one another — an option which no longer exists under Michigan's electronic-search system. So the question for this case becomes whether Crestmark conducted a reasonable and diligent electronic search. It did not.

Crestmark should have searched here for "Spearing Tool & Mfg." as well as "Spearing Tool and Manufacturing." "Mfg." and the ampersand are, of course, most common abbreviations — so common that, for example, we use them as a rule in our case citations. Crestmark had notice that Spearing sometimes used these abbreviations, and the Michigan Secretary of State's office recommended a search using the abbreviations. Combined, these factors indicate that a reasonable, diligent search by Crestmark of the Michigan lien filings for this business would have disclosed Spearing's IRS tax liens.

Crestmark argues for the unreasonableness of requiring multiple searches by offering the extreme example of a name it claims could be abbreviated 288 different ways ("ABCD Christian Brothers Construction and Development Company of Michigan, Inc."). Here, however, only two relevant words could be, and commonly are, abbreviated: "Manufacturing" and "and" — and the Secretary of State specifically recommended searching for those abbreviations. We express no opinion about whether creditors have a general obligation to search name variations. Our holding is limited to these facts.

Finally, we note that policy considerations also support the IRS's position. A requirement that tax liens identify a taxpayer with absolute precision would be unduly burdensome to the government's tax-collection efforts. Indeed, such a requirement might burden the government at least as much as Crestmark claims it would be burdened by having to perform multiple lien searches. "The overriding purpose of the tax lien statute obviously is to ensure prompt revenue collection." United States v. Kimbell Foods, Inc., 440 U.S. 715, 734-35, 59 L. Ed. 2d 711, 99 S. Ct. 1448 (1979). "To attribute to Congress a purpose so to weaken the tax liens it has created would require very clear language," which we lack here. *Union Central,* 368 U.S. at 294. Further, to subject the federal government to different identification requirements — varying with each state's electronic-search technology — "would run counter to the principle of uniformity which has long been the accepted practice in the field of federal taxation." Id. . . .

More importantly, the Supreme Court has noted that the United States, as an involuntary creditor of delinquent taxpayers, is entitled to special priority over voluntary creditors. Thus, while we understand that a requirement that the IRS comply with UCC Article 9 would spare banks considerable inconvenience, we conclude from Supreme Court precedent that the federal government's interest in prompt, effective tax collection trumps the banks' convenience in loan collection. . . .

Based strictly on the law, the Sixth Circuit could have gone either way. From a systems standpoint, however, the decision is a disaster. *Every* searcher wants to know about tax liens as well as U.C.C. filings. As the court acknowledged, the effect of its decision is that searches must be in not only the correct legal name of the debtor, but also in every variant that, if used by the IRS, would be effective. In a posting to the UCCLAW listserv, Seattle lawyer Richard L. Goldfarb captured the systems aspect of the case perfectly:

> The [court's] policy arguments are ridiculous. To understand this, one only needs to compare the situation filers and the IRS are in if the case goes either way. As decided by the Sixth Circuit, the IRS is of course sitting pretty, while filers are spending unnecessary time and money doing searches, checking the names used on IRS forms. . . . If the case goes the other way, the IRS loses its first position in the Spearing Tool bankruptcy, and the national office sends out a memo saying that all tax liens have to be filed in the true corporate name, some IRS personnel learn to use the internet, and everyone goes on their merry way. Overly burdensome? Hardly.

Problem Set 58

58.1.   Your client, Center Bank and Trust (CBT), plans to lend $2.5 million against equipment, inventory, and accounts receivable owned by McErny Leasing and Bob McErny, the owner of the company. How will you determine what names to search under? If Bob will be a source of information, what questions will you ask him? U.C.C. §§9-503, 9-102(a)(70), and 9-506.

58.2.   The law firm for which you work is located in the state capitol, near the office of the Uniform Commercial Code Division of the Secretary of State. One of the partners has given you these three names and asked you to do U.C.C. searches: (1) Susan Alexander, (2) John Phillip ("Jack") Smith, and (3) Tessie's Tire City. You already know that in this particular filing office, members of the public have access to a hard copy printout of the index. You cannot computer search the index directly, but you can submit a written request to search a particular name or names. The financing statements are on microfiche in the same office. How will you do these searches? (Keep in mind the old adage that when a partner gives you instructions, the partner doesn't want you to do what the partner told you to do, the partner wants you to do what the partner needs done.)

58.3.   In response to your written search request for filings against "John Phillip Smith," the secretary of state sent you a list of 112 financing statements filed against persons with the first name John and the last name Smith. Of those filings, one is against John P. Smith, three are against John Smith, one is against John Philip Smith, Jr., and the remaining 107 are against persons with middle initials other than P or middle names that don't begin with P. Which of the financing statements listed do you need to order and examine? U.C.C. §9-506(c).

58.4.   As the newest associate in the Office of the General Counsel of the Secretary of State, your first assignment is to make a recommendation regarding the search logic for a new computer program that will be used as the exclusive means of searching the U.C.C. filings. The computer consultants have asked two questions:

a.   When you get a request for "John Phillip Smith," which of the following should the computer program return? John P. Smith, J.P. Smith, J. P. Smith, John P. Smyth, John Phillip Smith, Jr., John Philip Smith, John Phillip Smith, Ltd.

b.   If the search is for a debtor at a particular address — for example, "John Phillip Smith, 333 Bush Street, San Francisco CA" — would it be helpful to report all filings against any debtors at that address? The consultants point out that such a system could overcome almost any error in the debtor's name, so long as the address is correct. U.C.C. §9-506(c).

58.5.   If the filing office receives an original financing statement on Wednesday, by what day must the filing office index it (and thereby render it searchable) to comply with U.C.C. §§9-519(a) and (h) and 9-523(c) and (e)? If the filing office complies with these sections, on what day would the last search go out that did not include reference to this financing statement? What happens if the filing office does not comply with these sections? U.C.C. §§9-524, Comment 8 to U.C.C. §9-523.

58.6.   Isabelle Sterling, the partner you work for, unexpectedly had to travel to Hong Kong. She left you the Tang Aluminum Products file for your client, Global Bank. Global will be lending Tang $1.9 million for its purchase of all of the assets of Argon, Inc. and taking a security interest in those assets. The closing is set for 16 days from today. The contract for purchase and sale, signed a week ago, provides for transfer of Argon's assets free and clear of liens and payment of the purchase price in "cash at closing."

a.   Assuming that the secretary of state is in compliance with U.C.C. §9-523(e), what do you do, and in what order? Can you be ready by the scheduled closing date? U.C.C. §9-523(c).

b.   Assuming that the filing office takes two weeks to process incoming filings to the point that they will show up on a search, that the filing office fixes the "as of" date and time by the state of the records when the search is run, that the filing office takes up to 24 hours to run an "expedited" search, and that the filing office faxes the search to the searcher immediately on completion, what do you do, and in what order? Can you be ready by the scheduled closing date?

58.7.   Sterling also asked you to run a U.C.C. search on John Phillip ("Jack") Smith. She thinks that Smith lives either in San Jose, California, or the San Jose suburb of Los Gatos. He also spends part of his time in Tucson or Golden Valley, Arizona. California U.C.C. filings are on LEXIS and Westlaw; Arizona filings are on the Internet at http://www.sos.state.az.us/scripts/ucc_search.dll. Be sure your method of searching will find all versions of the debtor's name that are "not seriously misleading." (Do not restrict your search to filings against persons in the cities mentioned. As you will learn in later assignments, filings made under an address correct at the time generally remain effective after a change of address and filings bearing an incorrect address may nevertheless be effective.) U.C.C. §9-506(c).

58.8.   If the Tri-State Moulded Plastics case (discussed at the end of section C of this assignment) arose in Arizona, what result? U.C.C. §§9-503(a)(1), 9-506(c). (Hint: Do the search yourself on the Arizona Secretary of State's Web site before you try to answer.)

Assignment 59: Article 9 Financing Statements: Other Information

A.   Introduction

Financing statements typically are written documents prepared on pre-printed forms. U.C.C. §9-521 contains a standard form for filing and amending the financing statement in hard copy, but Article 9 does not require its use. The secured party can use its own form or even file a copy of the security agreement as a financing statement. In some states, some financing statements may exist solely in electronic form.

In most states, it is now possible to file by filling in the blanks of the official form on the filing office's website. In states not yet set up for filing on the website the preferred method is probably to print the official form from the website of another state, fill in the blanks on the hard copy, and mail it to the filing office. Filers prefer the official form because the filing fee is typically lower when it is used and the filing office can refuse to accept the filing only for the limited reasons set forth in U.C.C. §9-516(b). Mandatory acceptance is no small advantage because filing officers historically have refused to accept a substantial percentage of all filings they have received.

U.C.C. §9-502(a) requires that three items of information be on an ordinary financing statement for the statement to be effective:

1. The name of the debtor
2. The name of the secured creditor
3. An indication of the collateral covered

U.C.C. §520(a) requires the filing officer to refuse to accept it unless it contains items 1 and 2 and these additional items:

4. The mailing address of the secured creditor. U.C.C. §9-516(b)(4).
5. The mailing address of the debtor. U.C.C. §9-516(b)(5)(A).
6. An indication of whether the debtor is an individual or a corporation. U.C.C. §9-516(b)(5)(B).

If the debtor is an organization, U.C.C. §9-516(b)(5)(C) also requires rejection of the financing statement unless it contains three additional items of information:

7. The type of organization (corporation, limited liability company, etc.)
8. The debtor's jurisdiction of organization
9. The debtor's organizational identification number

If a financing statement lacks any of these nine pieces of information, other than an indication of the collateral covered, see U.C.C. §9-516(b), the filing officer should refuse to accept it and communicate to the filer the reason for refusal and the date and time the record would have been filed. U.C.C. §9-520(b). The attempt at filing has accomplished nothing, but, notified of its failure, the filer has the opportunity to try again.

This does not mean that the filing officer should refuse filings that contain incorrect information — even if the incorrect information is implausible. The comment to U.C.C. §9-516 provides:

> Neither this section nor Section 9-520 requires or authorizes the filing office to determine, or even consider, the accuracy of information provided in a record. For example, the State A filing office may not reject under subsection (b)(5)(C) an initial financing statement indicating that the debtor is a State A corporation and providing a three-digit organization identification number, even if all State A organizational identification numbers contain at least five digits and two letters.

Generalizing on this example, it would seem that if the secured party fills in the key blanks on the financing statement, the filing officer must accept the filing almost irrespective of the content.

B. Filing Office Errors in Acceptance or Rejection

1. Wrongly Accepted Filings

If a filing officer mistakenly accepts a filing that contains items 1 through 3 on the above list, but is missing another item or items such that the filing officer was required to reject the filing pursuant to U.C.C. §§9-520(a) and 9-516(b), the filing is nevertheless effective. U.C.C. §9-520(c) and Comment 3 to that section. Why should a filing that the filing officer should have rejected have any effect at all? The answer can be derived from an understanding of how the system functions. First, while the omission might necessitate further inquiry, no one can be misled. The searcher who retrieves a financing statement with blank spaces in it knows it does not have the information that should have been in those blank spaces. The searcher can demand that the debtor provide the information or refuse to lend. Second, if the filing officer had rejected the filing, that would have given the filer the opportunity to correct its error. Because the filing officer accepted it instead, the filer likely will remain unaware of its error until it is too late to correct it. Thus, the effectiveness of the filing saves the filer from its error without inflicting much harm on searchers. Here, as in other decisions they had to make, the drafters were forced to choose between inflicting a burden on filers or searchers, choosing in this case to leave it to the searchers to investigate further.

2. Wrongly Rejected Filings

If the filing officer should accept an initial financing statement, either because it is correct or because the manner in which it is incorrect does not warrant rejection under U.C.C. §9-516 but the filing officer rejects it instead, the financing statement will not appear on the public record. Instead, the filing officer will stamp it with the date and time of the attempt to file and return it to the filer. U.C.C. §9-520(b). The attempt to file nevertheless perfects the underlying security interest sufficiently to defeat lien creditors. U.C.C. §9-516(d). This is so even though subsequent searchers have no access to the filing and no means of knowing it was made. The explanation for this anomalous result is that the drafters of Article 9 believed (as a matter of faith, not empirical reality) that lien creditors do not search the filing system and therefore cannot be prejudiced by the failure of the financing statement to appear. The non-filing is ineffective against purchasers who are prejudiced by the absence of the record from the filing system. (Recall that, when used in the U.C.C., "purchasers" includes secured parties. U.C.C. §§1-201(32) and (33) (Rev. §§1-201(b)(29) and (30)).) As a result, the drafters reasoned, giving this limited perfected status to security interests for which no filing is on record injures no one.

We will refer to security interests such as these — which are effective against lien creditors, but not sufficient to give constructive notice to purchasers — as "lien-perfected." We will refer to security interests for which the filings are sufficient to give constructive notice — and therefore bind even purchasers — as "purchaser-perfected."

C. Filer Errors in Accepted Filings

If a filer entirely omits from the financing statement a piece of information required in U.C.C. §9-516(b), the filing officer can and should reject the filing. U.C.C. §9-520(a). If the required piece of information is merely incorrect, however, that is insufficient reason for rejection. Filing officers are not required to read the filings and are specifically instructed not to evaluate the accuracy of any information contained therein. Properly accepted filings can, and frequently will, contain incorrect information. The effect of errors in the three pieces of information required for effectiveness is different from the effect of errors in the six pieces of information required only to qualify for filing.

1. Information Necessary Only to Qualify for Filing

The items of information numbered 4 through 9 in section A of this assignment are not necessary to the sufficiency of a financing statement. U.C.C. §9-502(a). If the information furnished in response to any or all of these items is merely erroneous (as opposed to omitted entirely), the financing statement qualifies for filing. Such a financing statement, however, will be of limited effectiveness.

Article 9 lumps these limited-effectiveness filings together with wrongly rejected and fully effective filings in the category of "perfected" filings. See, for example, U.C.C. §9-338, referring to limited-effectiveness filings as "perfected." That section provides that filings with incorrect U.C.C. §9-516(b)(5) information will be effective against lien creditors, bankruptcy trustees, and others ("lien-perfected"), but not against purchasers who give value and act in reasonable reliance on the incorrect information ("purchaser-perfected"). U.C.C. §9-338. Whether the drafters intended the conclusions in this subsection to apply to errors in the address of the secured party is unclear. U.C.C. §9-502 does not require the address for sufficiency, but Comment 9 to U.C.C. §9-516 excludes them from the errors that merely invoke U.C.C. §9-338.

To illustrate, assume that Firstbank files a financing statement against Debtor Corporation. In filling out the financing statement, Firstbank's employee correctly states the name of the debtor, Firstbank's own name, and the description of collateral. But the employee gives an incorrect address for the debtor, wrongly states that the debtor is a limited partnership, gives the wrong state of incorporation, and lists the wrong identification number for Debtor Corporation. Even if the filing officer notices these errors, the filing officer is required to accept the filing. The filing is fully effective against lien creditors, including the trustee in any bankruptcy Debtor Corporation later files. Only a purchaser who read the financing statement and gave value in reasonable reliance on the incorrect information could defeat Firstbank's filing.

To understand how a purchaser might give value in reliance on these kinds of information one must consider how searchers use the information. For example, searchers use the debtor's address as a means of determining whether a financing statement relates to their debtor or another debtor with the same name.

To illustrate the problem that may result, assume that First Bank is lending to John P. Smith, who lives in Los Angeles. First Bank conducts a search under that name, which returns 30 filings, all against "John P. Smith" at a San Francisco address. First Bank checks the San Francisco address and discovers that a person named John P. Smith — not First Bank's debtor — lives at that address. First Bank assumes that all 30 filings are against the John P. Smith who lives in San Francisco, and makes the loan. Commercial Finance — one of the 30 filers — in fact lent money to the John P. Smith who lives in Los Angeles. But the clerk who filled out Commercial Finance's financing statement erroneously put the address of the San Francisco John P. Smith on it. Commercial Finance's filing is lien perfected. Its security interest is subordinated to that of First Bank, however, because First Bank gave value in reasonable reliance upon the incorrect address. U.C.C. §9-338(1).

2. Required Information

The items of information specified in items 1 to 3 on the above list are necessary to the effectiveness of the financing statement. If the financing statement substantially complies with the requirement to specify these items, the financing statement will be effective despite "minor errors or omissions unless the errors or omissions make the financing statement seriously misleading." U.C.C. §9-506(a).

In Assignment 58, we considered what errors in the debtor's name will render the financing statement ineffective. Here we consider only errors in the name of the secured party and the indication of collateral. Our theme will be the same as with errors in the debtor's name. Whether an error in a particular item of information is "seriously misleading" depends in part on the function that information serves (or is thought to serve) in the search process. To decide whether errors in financing statement information render the statement seriously misleading, one must first understand why the information is supposed to be there and what impact its omission or distortion can be expected to have on the search process.

a. *Name of the Secured Party*   Searchers may need the name of the secured party for two reasons. First, if terminations statements, releases of collateral, or subordination agreements are needed to modify or eliminate prior filings to pave the way for the new loan, the name of the secured party on the financing statement tells the searcher who can or must authenticate them. Second, the searcher may need information from the secured party; the secured party's name on the financing statement assures the searcher that it is inquiring of the right person.

This second reason requires some elaboration. The Article 9 filing system is frequently described as a "notice filing" system. See Comment 2 to U.C.C. §9-502. That is, in contrast with the real estate recording system, where recording of the full text of the mortgage may be required, the Article 9 system requires only the recording of a notice of the possible existence of a security agreement. If the searcher wants to know the terms of the security agreement, the searcher is expected to inquire further outside the filing system. The searcher does that by requiring the debtor — typically a person who has applied to the searcher for a loan — to authorize the secured party to furnish information to the searcher. Unless otherwise agreed between the debtor and the secured party, a secured party has the right to respond to a request for credit information (as opposed to bank deposit information) from third parties, but no obligation to do so. The secured party ordinarily will do so, however, if the debtor so requests, either because of its ongoing business relationship with the debtor or because U.C.C. §9-210 requires the secured party to furnish certain information to the debtor on request. That is, if the secured party refuses to furnish information to the searcher, the debtor will make a formal request for it and the secured party will have to comply. Absent the name of the secured party on the financing statement, the searcher would be dependent on the debtor to tell the searcher of whom it should make these inquiries.

Once one understands that the function of the secured party's name on the financing statement is to unambiguously identify the holder of the security interest, one should realize that in some cases the secured party's address will be equally necessary. If the secured party's name is John P. Smith, without an address the debtor could steer searchers to any of the hundreds of John P. Smiths in the world. The debtor could easily defraud the searcher by steering the searcher to one who was not the secured party, but would claim to be.

b. *Description of Collateral*   The description of collateral in a financing statement is often identical to that in the security agreement, but that is not always so. For example, a secured creditor may contemplate lending money to the debtor to buy various items of equipment over a period of years. The secured creditor may file a financing statement indicating that the collateral is "equipment," and then, as the debtor buys each item of equipment, the secured creditor may require that the debtor authenticate a security agreement that describes the particular items of equipment. Under these circumstances, the secured creditor will have a perfected security interest in only the equipment described in the security agreements. See U.C.C. §§9-308(a) and 9-203(b)(3)(A). Other equipment owned by the debtor may remain unencumbered.

Formally, the legal standard for adequacy of a description of collateral in a financing statement is the same as that for a security agreement — that it "reasonably identif[y] the collateral." See U.C.C. §§9-108, 9-504. But given that the description of collateral in a financing statement serves functions different from the description in a security agreement, it should not be surprising if the legal standard is applied differently to the two kinds of descriptions. The most obvious difference is the one expressly acknowledged in the statute: "Super-generic" descriptions such as "all assets" or "all personal property" are valid in financing statements but not in security agreements. (The drafters give no clue as to their reasons for invalidating super-generic descriptions in security agreements, but it probably was to protect debtors who otherwise might not realize that they were granting such a broad interest. We are skeptical. We fail to see why a page-long string of categories of property should be any clearer to a debtor than the phrase "all property." We can see many reasons to think it might be less clear.)

U.C.C. §9-108 approves of any description that renders the collateral "objectively determinable." To give content to that phrase requires two inquiries. First, what meaning should be assigned to words in the description? When we encountered this issue with regard to descriptions in security agreements in Assignment 51, we concluded that the words should mean whatever the parties intended them to mean provided the intent was expressed objectively. The function of the financing statement, by contrast, is to put searchers on notice of the identity of the collateral. Here, it would make sense to give words their common meaning and to require that they make sense to complete strangers. The second inquiry is how much work can the drafters of the financing statement require of the searcher to link the description to the collateral? In the *Schmidt* case, discussed briefly in Assignment 51, reference in the description to the ACSC records in another government office required that the searcher (1) know where to look for the ACSC records and (2) go there and look. The court upheld the description. In the *Shirel* case, reference in the description to whether the item was purchased from the secured creditor department store required that the searcher (1) somehow obtain access to the records of the store and (2) examine those records. In the *Grabowski* case, the court expressed the traditional view that a filer's description can require a searcher to make inquiry of the secured creditor.

> In the case of a financing statement, a creditor may either describe its collateral by "type" or "category" as set forth in §9-108 or may simply indicate its lien on "all assets" of the debtor.
>
> This exceedingly general standard for describing collateral in a financing statement, which is new to the UCC under revised Article 9, is consistent with the "inquiry notice" function of a financing statement under previous law. A financing statement need not specify the property encumbered by a secured party's lien, but need merely notify subsequent creditors that a lien may exist and that further inquiry is necessary "to disclose the complete state of affairs." Uniform Commercial Code Comment 2 [§9-502]. In the present case, Bank of America filed a financing statement indicating it had a lien on the debtors' property consisting of "all inventory, chattel paper, accounts, equipment, and general intangibles." Despite the generality of the Bank's description, it was sufficient to notify subsequent creditors, including South Pointe, that a lien existed on the debtors' property and that further inquiry was necessary to determine the extent of the Bank's lien. For this reason, the Court finds no merit in South Pointe's argument that the description of the Bank's collateral was too general to fulfill the notice function of a financing statement under the UCC.

Grabowski v. Deere & Company (In re Grabowski), 277 B.R. 388 (Bankr. S.D. Ill. 2002).

The court in Teel Construction, Inc. v. Lipper, Inc., 11 U.C.C. Rep. Serv. 2d 667 (Va. Cir. Ct. 1990), took an even more permissive approach to an error in the financing statement description of collateral than did the court in *Grabowski*. In *Teel*, the financing statement described the collateral as furniture and inventory at a certain address. The address given was nonexistent; the furniture and inventory intended were at another address. The court nevertheless held the financing statement effective, because the particular searcher "knew where Lipper was located and . . . is required to make further inquiry of the secured party in order to determine whether a particular asset is covered by a security agreement."

If our description of *Teel* leaves you wondering just what the function of the description in a financing statement might be, you are not alone. In a classic article, Professor Morris Shanker suggested that descriptions of collateral — in both financing statements and security agreements — should be optional. Shanker, A Proposal for a Simplified All-Embracing Security Interest, 14 U.C.C. L.J. 23, 25-29 (1981). Under Professor Shanker's proposal, if the parties did not include a description, the security interest would reach all property of the debtor rather than none of it, as under current law. Cases like *Grabowski* and *Teel* require the searcher to inquire beyond the description in the financing statement anyway. The searcher can learn what collateral is encumbered from the secured party's statement under U.C.C. §9-210.

The duty to inquire further imposed in cases like *Teel* and *Grabowski* have their limit. In some cases, the description may be so specific as to exclude the possibility that the property in question could be collateral.

In re Pickle Logging, Inc.
(Deere Credit, Inc. v. Pickle Logging, Inc.)

286 B.R. 181 (Bankr. M.D. Ga. 2002)

JOHN T. LANEY, III, UNITED STATES BANKRUPTCY JUDGE.

FACTS

Pickle Logging, Inc. ("Debtor") is an Americus, Georgia based company doing business in the tree logging industry. In an effort to cure an arrearage to Deere Credit, Inc. ("Movant"), Debtor refinanced eight pieces of equipment. The refinancing was done with Movant.

On April 18, 2002, Debtor filed for Chapter 11 bankruptcy protection.... At a hearing held on August 16, 2002...the present issue was raised: whether Movant had a perfected security interest in one specific piece of equipment, a 548G skidder serial number DW548GX568154 ("548 G skidder"), which had been mislabeled in both the financing statement and the security agreement as a 648G skidder, serial number DW648GX568154. After hearing testimony from expert witnesses that a 548G skidder is substantially different in appearance, performance, and price from a 648G skidder, the court held that Movant did not have a perfected security interest in the 548G skidder because of the mislabeling. Therefore, Movant was an unsecured creditor as to the 548G skidder.... Movant has asked the court to reconsider....

CONCLUSIONS OF LAW

...The question is whether Movant's security interest in the 548G skidder is perfected despite the mislabeling on the security agreement and the financing statement.

Pursuant to [U.C.C. §9-203(b)(3)(A)], a security interest in collateral is not enforceable against the debtor or third parties unless the debtor has signed, executed, or otherwise adopted a security agreement that contains a description of the collateral. See also [U.C.C. §9-102(a)(7)]. The description of the collateral in the security agreement and the financing statement, if required, must comport with [U.C.C. §9-108(a)]. See also [U.C.C. §9-504(1)]. The description of collateral is sufficient if it reasonably identifies what is described. See [U.C.C. §9-108(a)]. "The question of the sufficiency of [a] description of [collateral] in a [recorded document] is one of law...." Bank of Cumming v. Chapman, 264 S.E.2d 201 (Ga. 1980).

Any number of things could be used to describe collateral and satisfy [U.C.C. §9-108(a)]. A physical description of the collateral, including or excluding a serial number, could be used so long as it "reasonably identifies what is described." The description merely needs to raise a red flag to a third party indicating that more investigation may be necessary to determine whether or not an item is subject to a security agreement. A party does not lose its secured status just because the description includes an inaccurate serial number. However, if the serial number is inaccurate, there must be additional information that provides a "key" to the collateral's identity.

Here, the description in the security agreement and the financing statement are identical. Both documents list a 648G skidder with the serial number DW648GX568154. There is nothing obviously wrong with the model number or the serial number. 648G is a model number for one type skidder sold by Movant. The serial number listed for the disputed skidder is in accordance with other serial numbers issued by Movant. . . .

According to testimony at the August 16, 2002 hearing, Debtor owned more than one of Movant's skidders, including at least two 548G skidders and at least two 648G skidders. There is nothing in either the financing statement or the security agreement that raises a red flag to a third party. A potential purchaser of the 548G skidder in dispute here could easily assume that the skidder is not covered by either the security agreement or the financing statement.

If just the model number was incorrect or if just the serial number was incorrect, the result may be different. It is apparent from the other items listed on the security agreement and the financing statement that the model number is reflected in the serial number. If the model number was not repeated in the serial number, then it would be apparent that something was wrong with one of the two numbers. At a minimum it should raise a red flag to a person of ordinary business prudence that further investigation is necessary. However, with both of the numbers reflecting a 648G skidder, there is nothing to indicate that there was a mistake.

Therefore, the court's order dated September 3, 2002 will not be changed. The 548G skidder is misdescribed in both the security agreement and the financing statement. The rights of Debtor, as a hypothetical lien creditor, are superior to the rights of Movant.

By cutting off the duty to inquire further, cases like *Pickle Logging* can save searchers a lot of time and expense. But for that to work, of course, all courts have to be on board.

D.   Authorization to File a Financing Statement

The purpose of a financing statement is to advise later lenders of the existence of a prior security interest. If a prior interest exists, the later lender may insist on different terms or decline to lend at all. Consequently, the presence of an incorrect or unauthorized financing statement in the filing system can interfere with the ability of the party named as debtor to borrow money.

To illustrate, assume that a financing statement discovered by State Bank in their search under "Teel, Inc.," showed "Alan Berkowitz" to be the secured party. Teel insisted that Berkowitz was not its secured creditor, but when State Bank contacted Berkowitz, he said he was. Even if State Bank believed Teel, the Bank might not be willing to make the loan, in the fear that its belief was wrong or that, even if it wasn't, the loan might involve the Bank in litigation with Berkowitz. Because of the uncertainty it creates, any filing that *might* encumber particular property makes that property difficult to sell or use as collateral. The title to possibly encumbered property is referred to as "clouded." Most lenders are reluctant to go forward until they can be certain that the title can be "cleared" and the "cloud lifted."

Prior to the revision, Article 9 provided that a financing statement was sufficient to perfect only if it was signed by the debtor. Even with that requirement in place, the filing of unauthorized financing statements was a significant problem. Prisoners, tax protestors, supporters of the Republic of Texas, and other political protestors realized how easy it was to cloud title to someone's property in the Article 9 filing system — or other filing systems — and filed bogus financing statements to accomplish that. Of course, the victim of a bogus filing could sue, prove the bogus nature of the filing, and have it declared invalid. See, e.g., United States v. Greenstreet, 912 F. Supp. 224 (N.D. Tex. 1996) (holding that the "political" filing of a financing statement by a farmer was ineffective because the alleged debtors had not signed it). But lawsuits are expensive and the victim cannot pass the cost on to a judgment-proof prisoner or protestor. Recognizing the ineffectiveness of the signature requirement in protecting public officials and others from bogus liens, in 1997 Texas enacted legislation making it a felony to file or refuse to release a "fraudulent lien."

At about the same time, the drafters of Article 9 were deciding to abandon the requirement of a signature on a financing statement. The immediate impetus was to facilitate electronic filing of financing statements by high-volume financial institutions. Electronic filings could include the signature of the debtor only if those filings included graphics. The U.C.C. filing offices were not up to that challenge.

The new system for the prevention of unauthorized filings is to work as follows. Before filing a financing statement, the secured creditor must obtain authorization from the debtor in an authenticated record. See U.C.C. §9-509(a)(1) ("A person may file [a] financing statement . . . only if the debtor authorizes the filing in an authenticated record."). To make it easy for the secured creditor to obtain such authorization, U.C.C. §9-509(b) provides that "By authenticating a security agreement, a debtor authorizes the filing of [a] financing statement covering the collateral described in the security agreement." Thus, all the creditor need do to obtain the right to file a financing statement is what it already had to do to become a secured creditor: Get the debtor to authenticate a security agreement.

If the person filing a financing statement is not authorized, the financing statement is ineffective. See U.C.C. §9-510(a). That alone, however, will not lift the cloud on title, because the would-be lender still has no way to assure itself that its would-be debtor did not authorize the filing. U.C.C. §9-518 allows the victim of a bogus filing to file a "correction statement" that will show up on searches. But the correction statement does not lift the cloud on title either. The bogus filing was ineffective without the correction statement and remains ineffective after it is filed. U.C.C. §9-518(c). The problem is that the would-be lender has no way to know that the bogus filing is unauthorized and therefore ineffective other than to know and trust its borrower.

With these changes, the Article 9 filing system now stands in stark contrast to the real estate system. Real estate systems typically require not only that the debtor sign the mortgage, but that the signature be both witnessed and *acknowledged*. The witnesses themselves must sign the mortgage. Acknowledgment is before a notary public or other official licensed by the state for that purpose. The notary is supposed to determine the identity of the person making the signature and place the notary's seal on the statement of acknowledgment. If the new, signatureless system of Article 9 is successful, the real estate system will probably come under pressure to follow the same path.

E. U.C.C. Insurance

Errors in filing and searching can put millions of dollars at risk. In real estate transactions, the roughly corresponding problems are often dealt with by purchasing title insurance. In recent years, some firms have begun offering a roughly analogous product under the name "UCC insurance." U.C.C. insurance, like title insurance, covers the risk of most kinds of errors in the filing and search processes.

Perhaps the most important difference between the two kinds of insurance stems from the fact that the U.C.C. system does not cover title to collateral. As a result, U.C.C. insurance does not insure against the possibility that the debtor does not own the collateral. It does, however, cover some aspects of attachment, perfection, and priority.

Problem Set 59

59.1. a. It's nearly 5:00 on Friday afternoon and you are working on an initial financing statement that *has* to be filed today. You know that the debtor is a Nevada corporation, but you just realized that you don't know its organizational identification number. You don't have time to get it. Would you be better off leaving the space for the number on the financing statement blank, or filling in the license plate number of your car? U.C.C. §§9-520(a) and 9-516(b)(5); Comment 3 to U.C.C. §9-516.

b. You filled in the license number of your car and sent the financing statement to the filing office. The filing office sent the financing statement back to you with a notice of rejection and instructions for obtaining the correct number. If you don't do anything else, are you perfected? U.C.C. §§9-308(a), 9-310(a) and (b), 9-502(a), 9-516(a), (b)(5), and (d), Comment 3 to U.C.C. §9-516.

c. Contrary to the facts of b, the filing office accepted your financing statement with the incorrect organizational identification number. Are you perfected? Do you need to take any further action? U.C.C. §§9-520(a) and (c), 9-338.

59.2. You represent Eric Bradford, a trustee in bankruptcy. One of the duties of a trustee is to examine the financing statements filed by secured creditors for irregularities. Bankruptcy Code §544(a) gives trustees the power to avoid security interests not sufficiently perfected to withstand attack by a lien creditor. That includes any that are unperfected and for which a required financing statement was not filed. See U.C.C. §9-317(a). In cases currently pending, Bradford noted the following irregularities in filed financing statements. Which of the cases should the trustee pursue? Identify any additional information that would help in your evaluation. U.C.C. §§9-502(a), 9-516(b), (d), 9-520(c), and 9-506.

a. The irregularity is the complete absence of any address for the secured party. The secured party's name is listed as "First National Bank of Wisconsin, N.A." The financing statement was filed in the Wisconsin statewide filing system. The secured party is a national bank with offices in several cities in Wisconsin. The debtor is a small business whose address is correctly stated on the financing statement. Comment 3 to U.C.C. §9-520.

b. The irregularity is an incorrect mailing address for the debtor, Jeffrey Adams. The address listed is for a different Jeffrey Adams, who is unrelated to the transaction in which the security interest was given.

c. The irregularity is the use of the secured creditor's trade name, Will's Furniture and Appliances, instead of its true name, Wardcorp, Inc. U.C.C. §§9-503(a), (b), and (c), Comment 2 to U.C.C. §9-506.

d. The irregularity is that the secured creditor's name is listed as "Elizabeth Warren" instead of the correct name, "Lynn M. LoPucki." The paralegal who filled out the financing statement said, "I don't know why I wrote Elizabeth Warren; I really meant to write Lynn M. LoPucki."

e. The irregularity is in the description of the collateral as "Pizza ovens, equipment, and fixtures located at 621 State Street, Madison, Wisconsin." The particular ovens, equipment, and fixtures covered by the security agreement have been at 514 East Washington Avenue, Madison, Wisconsin, at all relevant times. The debtor is Stoney's Pizza Parlour, Inc., a company that has operated stores at both locations at all relevant times. The creditor is Wisconsin State Bank. U.C.C. §§9-504, 9-108.

f. The irregularity is the complete absence of a description of collateral. The debtor is "Holiday Inn of Westport, Inc." and the creditor is Missouri State Bank. Correct addresses were given for both.

59.3. After three years of litigation, your client, Ron Smith, has won a judgment against his former employer, the Subterranean Circus, Inc. (SCI), in the amount of $26,000. SCI's lawyer says you might as well forget about collecting — the company has no unencumbered assets. Your U.C.C. search suggests otherwise. There are five financing statements, all showing Glacier Bank as the secured party. Each describes the collateral as "fixtures and equipment located at [a particular address]." The address of the SCI store on Trimble Avenue is not on any of the financing statements and there is no other public record showing any kind of lien against the fixtures and equipment located there. You know from talking with the landlord at the Trimble Avenue location that the fixtures and equipment were installed new and had never been used in any other store. Smith wants to levy on the Trimble Avenue store if the furniture and equipment there are not encumbered, but he is afraid of getting "bogged down in more litigation" if they are.

a. If Glacier Bank's security agreement includes as collateral the fixtures and equipment located in the Trimble Avenue store, is it possible that Glacier is perfected against them?

b.   What's your next move?

59.4.   You represent Glacier Bank. You get a telephone call from a respectable law firm that represents Ron Smith, a creditor with a $26,000 judgment against SCI, one of Glacier's borrowers. Smith wants to know if Glacier's security interest encumbers the equipment and leasehold at SCI's Trimble Avenue store. In fact, Glacier was supposed to have a security interest in the Trimble assets, but someone did a poor job of drafting.

a.   What do you say to the lawyer?

b.   Would the situation be different if the law firm's client was another bank that had a loan application from SCI? U.C.C. §9-210.

59.5.   Walter's Department Store (from problem 51.4) has been taking security interests in everything purchased from them on the store's credit card accounts. Last week, Walter's lost two riding lawn mowers that were collateral under their security agreements to neighbors of Walter's bankrupt customers. Unaware of Walter's security interests, the neighbors had purchased the lawn mowers from the debtors prior to bankruptcy. See U.C.C. §9-320(b). When you mentioned to Susie that Walter's would have won the cases had it filed financing statements, Susie asked you to look into doing just that on every Walter's credit card account. Specifically, Susie has the following questions for you.

a.   Does Walter's need permission from each of the thousands of customers involved to file these financing statements? U.C.C. §§9-509(a), (b), 9-510(a).

b.   What should Walter's use for a description of collateral? U.C.C. §§9-504, 9-108.

c.   Can you think of any practical problems that are likely to arise?

59.6.   When Pablo Escobar applied to Second National Bank to borrow money against his restaurant, Fisherman's Pier, the first thing the bank did was to file a financing statement on the form set forth in U.C.C. §9-521. The bank told Pablo they were filing the statement and Pablo said that was OK, but nobody thought to get him to sign it because the form has no place for a signature. The bank filed the financing statement on March 1 and conducted a search through that date. The search was clean, and the bank closed on the $320,000 loan on March 15. At the closing, Pablo signed a security agreement. Two days after the closing, Pablo disappeared. When the bank searched the title to Fisherman's Pier to prepare for foreclosure, it discovered a financing statement in favor of NationsBank that had been filed March 10. Further inquiry revealed that Pablo had borrowed $330,000 from NationsBank just before he disappeared. Second National Bank consults you because NationsBank has asked to see the authenticated record authorizing the filing of Second National's financing statement.

a.   Exactly what record would that be? U.C.C. §§9-502(d), 9-509(a) and (b), 9-510(a).

b.   Should Second National change its procedures? If so, how?

Assignment 60: Exceptions to the Article 9 Filing Requirement

For most kinds of security interests, perfection is accomplished by a public record filing. If the filing is not made, the security interest remains unperfected. But there are a number of exceptions to the filing requirement. In this assignment we explore several ways a secured creditor might perfect a security interest without filing.

There are essentially three other ways to perfect. First, a secured party can perfect a security interest in many kinds of collateral by taking possession of it. Second, a secured creditor may enjoy automatic perfection by operation of law in some kinds of collateral. Third, the secured creditor may give notice to or through some person or organization that controls the collateral.

Problems involving exceptions to the filing requirement can be analyzed in much the same way as filing problems. Begin by categorizing the collateral. Determine whether perfection will be governed by Article 9, the real estate recording statutes, or other law. Finally, examine that law to determine what, if anything, it requires of the creditor to perfect the security interest.

A. Collateral in the Possession of the Secured Party

1. The Possession-Gives-Notice Theory

Both Article 9 and real estate recording statutes recognize *possession* of some kinds of collateral as a substitute for public notice filing. The Article 9 exception appears in U.C.C. §§9-310(b)(6) and 9-313. The latter section permits perfection by taking "possession" of the collateral if the collateral is "negotiable documents, goods, instruments, money, or tangible chattel paper."

In functional terms, this exception to the filing requirement is grounded on two assumptions. First, a person who buys or lends against certain kinds of collateral (we will refer to this person as the *searcher*) will look at the collateral before disbursing its money. Second, looking at collateral in the "possession" of a secured party will alert the searcher to the possible existence of a security interest. We will refer to these two assumptions as the *possession-gives-notice theory*.

Under the possession-gives-notice theory, to require filing with regard to collateral in the "possession" of the secured party would be redundant. Possession would give actual notice to the diligent searcher. In accord with this theory, both Article 9 and real estate recording laws assume that when a secured party is in possession of the collateral, searchers will or should realize that the secured party may have an interest in the property. Based on that assumption, they provide that possession constitutes constructive notice to the searcher and treat the searcher essentially as if the searcher had actual notice of the interest.

To illustrate both the theory and its shortcomings, assume that Thomas Olszynski borrows money from the Seminole Bank & Trust company, using his cast iron lawn dog* as collateral. Olszynski drags the lawn dog to the loan closing (on a cart specially made for that purpose). The banker gives Olszynski a check for the loan proceeds and Olszynski turns the lawn dog over to the banker. The banker drags the lawn dog into the Bank's vault, unloads it from the cart, and places it among the bags of money. There it will remain until the loan is repaid or the lien foreclosed by sale. Although the Bank does not file a financing statement, the Bank will be perfected so long as it retains possession. If Olszynski manages to sell the lawn dog or borrow from some other lender using the lawn dog as collateral while it remains in the Bank vault, the law will have no sympathy for that buyer or lender. Had the buyer or lender demanded to see the lawn dog before buying it or lending against it, the buyer or lender would have discovered that it was in the Bank vault. Had they known that, the theory goes, they should have been able to figure out that the Bank had a security interest in it.

By positing a situation in which the secured party was clearly, unmistakably in possession of the collateral, the lawn-dog-in-the-vault example probably makes the possession-gives-notice theory appear more reasonable than it is. Even so, the theory stumbles on application of the second assumption: Searchers should be able to guess the meaning of the bank's possession. The facts of a litigated (but unreported) case illustrate the ambiguity. In that case, the debtor solicited investments in a solid gold statue. At all relevant times, the bank held the statue in its vault. The debtor told the investors that the bank was holding the statue for safekeeping. Some of the investors viewed the statue. They did not ask whether the bank claimed a security interest in the statue, and the bank did not tell them. Perhaps the particular employee who shepherded them into the room where they viewed the statue did not even know that the bank claimed an interest in it. The investors could see that the bank had immediate control of the statue, but that is hardly the equivalent of a sign that says, "This bank claims a security interest in this gold statue."

Because the investors in the gold statue case were relatively unsophisticated, possession did not make them actually aware of the bank's interest. But by operation of law, it constructively gave them notice. The bank prevailed in the case on the theory that the bank was perfected by possession of the statue. The case illustrates an important characteristic of the law governing secured transactions: It favors the relatively sophisticated parties who engage in these transactions repeatedly, at the expense of people who stumble occasionally into a system in which "everybody" knows things that they do not.

---

* For a pithy history of the cast iron lawn dog in the teaching of secured transactions, see John Ayer, An Unrepentant View of the Sale/Lease Distinction, 4 J. Bankr. L. & P. 291, 292 (1995).

2. What Is Possession?

Possession is an ethereal concept. One dictionary defines it as the "control or occupancy of property without regard to ownership," Webster's Ninth New Collegiate Dictionary 918 (1991), while another defines it as "The detention and control, or the manual or ideal custody, of anything which may be the subject of property, for one's use and enjoyment, either as owner or as the proprietor of a qualified right in it, and either held personally or by another who exercises it in one's place and name.... That condition of facts under which one can exercise his power over a corporeal thing at his pleasure to the exclusion of all other persons." Black's Law Dictionary 1047 (5th ed. 1979). The definition in Black's adds a level of sophistication by recognizing that it is not mere custody of the thing possessed, but "ideal custody." We take that to be a recognition that possession is not merely an observable fact, but in many situations depends ultimately on the legal right of the would-be possessor.

To illustrate, assume that Oneida Schwin is a law student who lives alone in a rented apartment. At the moment, she is in class. Is she in possession of the television set she owns and that sits on a table in her apartment? We have no doubt that she is. We don't think it matters that Bonnie the Burglar is immediately outside the door of the apartment or that the door is unlocked. Right now, Bonnie can more easily exercise power over the television than Oneida, but Oneida remains in possession. Why? Because Oneida has the *right* to control the television, while Bonnie does not. Oneida has possession not solely from power, but in large part from legal right.

Oneida probably remains in possession of the television even after Bonnie enters the living room. A searcher who knocks on the door and is greeted by a smiling Bonnie would almost certainly conclude that Bonnie is in possession of the television, but the searcher would be wrong. The law looks to legal right, not just physical fact, to determine who is in possession, and once we recognize this we can see that the law's definition of "possession" is at least in part circular. We look to possession to see who has rights and we look to rights to see who has possession.

The legal *right* to control is not determinative of possession. At the moment Bonnie picks up the television, the observable fact of physical control so overwhelms the legal right to control that we think most courts would say that possession has passed to Bonnie. Some courts would refer to this as "naked" possession to illustrate that few of the attributes of ideal possession had passed to Bonnie. (The word "naked" also spices up otherwise dull legal opinions.)

A secured party can possess collateral through an agent. See U.C.C. §9-313, Comment 3. Like ownership, agency might be invisible to the searcher. A case one of us litigated will illustrate. The author represented a plaintiff oil company that won the right to possession of a gasoline service station. The order was entered on a Friday afternoon, after the sheriff's office had closed for the weekend. The debtor, another oil company, remained in "possession" and continued to sell the inventory and collect the money. Author and client went to the station and saw that an employee of the debtor oil company was the only person on the premises. The employee had the keys to the building and he sat behind the counter. Was he in possession? The answer is no. The debtor oil company was in possession through him as their agent. Yet, given that the signs on the premises disclosed only the brand of gasoline sold, not the name of the defendant oil company, the true possessor would have been invisible to a searcher who happened by at that moment.

The client introduced himself to the employee, showed him the court's order for possession, and asked if he would like a new job (very much like his current job). Undoubtedly seeing the limited future in the position he then held, the employee said yes. The two agreed on terms, one of which was that the new job started immediately. As author and client walked back to their car, every condition observable to a searcher who looked at the premises was identical to what it had been before. The same employee sat beneath the same sign, collecting money from the same customers in the same way. But assuming the validity of the new employment agreement, the client's oil company was now in possession. Here again, possession shows itself to be a legal construct, not the observable fact some theorists posit it to be.

3.   Possession as a Means of Perfection

Depending on the type of collateral involved, possession may play any of three roles in the perfection of security interests. Possession is an alternative form of perfection for some types of collateral, an ineffective form for other types of collateral, and, as we discuss later in this section, the sole means of perfecting a security interest in money. U.C.C. §9-312(b)(3). If a debtor offers cash as collateral for a loan, the lender can perfect its security interest only by taking possession.

With regard to goods, instruments, tangible chattel paper, negotiable documents, and certificated securities, possession is an alternative to filing a financing statement. U.C.C. §§9-312(a), 9-313(a). Possession may appear to be *merely* an alternative means of perfecting. For goods, that is true, but for instruments, tangible chattel paper, negotiable documents, and certificated securities, perfection by possession is superior to perfection by filing. (One note before we go further: "Negotiable documents" include negotiable warehouse receipts, negotiable bills of lading, and similar documents, but the term does *not* include negotiable promissory notes. See U.C.C. §9-102(a)(30) and the definition of "document of title" in U.C.C. §1-201.)

Purchasers who subsequently take possession of these kinds of collateral generally take priority over secured creditors who previously perfected by filing. Possession and filing are both means of perfection, but perfection by possession trumps perfection by filing. U.C.C. §§9-330(d), 9-331(a). Filing is, however, fully effective against lien creditors and trustees in bankruptcy.

With respect to goods, while the rule that either form of perfection is acceptable is good news for the secured creditor who may find one method easier or cheaper than the other in a particular set of circumstances, it is bad news for the searcher who is trying to discover the previous security interest. The effect of such liberalization of the perfection requirement is to impose an additional burden on the searcher. Whenever the collateral subject to a security interest includes goods of any kind, the searcher must check both the filing system and the collateral itself.

For some kinds of collateral, perfection by possession is impossible. Security interests in accounts and general intangibles may be perfected only by filing or by some automatic perfection; they may not be perfected by possession. U.C.C. §9-313(a). At the most basic level, the rule may be explained by saying that these kinds of property are intangible and therefore incapable of being possessed, but the law can render intangible property tangible simply by recognizing some tangible object as the embodiment of the intangible rights. Thus the secured party who takes possession of a negotiable promissory note is regarded as having perfected in the right to payment it represents. U.C.C. §9-313(a). Similarly, the secured party who takes possession of a negotiable warehouse receipt or bill of lading is regarded as having perfected its interest in the goods in the warehouse or in the hands of the carrier. U.C.C. §9-312(c).

Notice the circular nature of this explanation: Because the law does not designate a particular document as the embodiment of the promise, the law does not recognize seizure of any document as perfecting the creditor's interest. It might seem that the law could easily resolve the problem by designating a particular document. For example, it might make the certificates issued by the state for liquor licenses or automobile titles the "physical embodiments" of liquor licenses and automobiles. Perfection could then be accomplished by taking possession of the certificates. In neither case would there be a competing document that might be seized by a competing creditor, yet in neither case has the law chosen to take this step.

To understand why the drafters of the law have not taken this step, one need only imagine that they did, for example, by designating the original certificate issued by the state to be the physical embodiment of a liquor license and decreeing that secured creditors can perfect by taking possession of the certificate. The problems that might arise would be numerous. What if the liquor laws of the state require that the original be posted on the debtor's premises? What if the state issues more than one original license? Or copies that cannot be distinguished from originals? If we shift from liquor licenses to accounts, we encounter the additional problem of what document to designate. Sales slips? The books of account? The computer file on which the accounts are recorded? And even if the law makes a decision, how does it get the word out to the millions who give or take security interests in accounts?

To avoid these kinds of problems, the law recognizes physical objects as embodying intangible rights only when business people do. Business practice plays the tune and the law dances, not the other way around.

Ultimately, the impossibility of perfection by possession in accounts and general intangibles results from the lack of any commercial function to be served. Those who want to perfect by taking possession of their debtors' accounts can require their debtors to obtain negotiable promissory notes from the account debtors. The use of negotiable warehouse receipts and bills of lading saves time and effort for those who use them; nobody has yet figured out a way to save significant time and effort by making liquor licenses or copyrights negotiable. If someone did, we suspect there would be pressure to recognize certificates as "embodiments" of these otherwise intangible rights.

By excluding the possibility of perfection by filing, Article 9 protects those who accept money from the possibility that a prior security interest was perfected by filing. The intent is to encourage free negotiability of money, unhampered by the need to conduct searches in the Article 9 filing system. Both "money" and "instrument" are carefully defined in the U.C.C., and refer only to specialized kinds of property. U.C.C. §§1-201(24) (Rev. §1-201(b)(24)) and 9-102(a)(47).

U.C.C. §9-312(a) permits the perfection of security interests in both instruments and chattel paper by filing. Given that chattel paper often includes instruments, see U.C.C. §9-102(a)(11), permitting the perfection of security interests by filing in either of these types of collateral might seem to interfere with their negotiability. But U.C.C. §9-330 protects the "purchasers" who take possession of chattel paper or instruments from security interests perfected in them by filing. Because "purchaser" is defined to include those who take a security interest in the chattel paper or instruments as well as those who buy them, the effect is to give priority to those who perfect by taking possession over those who perfect by filing. What good is a security interest perfected by filing in these kinds of collateral? It is easy to take and it beats the trustee in bankruptcy — which was probably the whole point of these complex provisions.

Negotiability — essentially the ability to treat the holder of an instrument or money as the owner of it — is of declining commercial importance. Advances in communications and data storage make it progressively easier to identify the source and ownership of funds. Under the old technology, there were many legitimate reasons for transactions in cash, bearer bonds, or notes endorsed in blank. Today there are few, with the result that such transactions are suspect and often regulated.

B.   Collateral in the Control of the Secured Party

Article 9 recognizes "control" of some kinds of collateral as a substitute for filing. They include deposit accounts, electronic chattel paper, investment property, and letter of credit rights. U.C.C. §9-310(b)(8). Because the rules differ slightly from one of these four types of collateral to another and each is in itself a substantial topic, we focus here on deposit accounts.

A "deposit account" is the type of property generally referred to as a bank account. See U.C.C. §9-102(a)(29). However, that definition excludes instruments, a term whose definition includes one type of bank account — a bank account represented by a certificate of deposit that can be transferred by indorsement and delivery to the transferee.

U.C.C. §9-104 indicates three ways that a secured party can take "control" of a deposit account. First, the secured party can be the bank in which the account is maintained. Second, the debtor, the secured party, and the bank can authenticate a record instructing the bank to comply with the secured party's instructions with regard to the account. Third, the secured party can become the bank's "customer" by putting the account in the name of the secured party. See U.C.C. §4-104 (defining "customer").

The control required to perfect in a deposit account is undermined by U.C.C. §9-104(b), which provides that the secured party's "control" is not abrogated by permitting the debtor to retain "the right to direct the disposition of funds from the deposit account." That is, the secured party is in "control" of the account even though the debtor can write checks on the account and perhaps withdraw the entire amount. The "control" specified in U.C.C. §9-104 is potential control, not actual control.

What kind of notice does "control" of a bank account give? If the account is in the name of the secured creditor, persons dealing with the debtor can hardly be misled. Anyone attempting to confirm the existence of the debtor's ownership of the account will discover the secured creditor's interest. If the secured party is the bank in which the debtor maintains the account, the drafters of Article 9 assert that "[n]o other form of public notice is necessary; all actual and potential creditors of the debtor are always on notice that the bank with which the debtor's deposit account is maintained may assert a claim against the deposit account." We doubt the drafters were naive enough to think that all or substantially all creditors actually know that a depositary bank can claim the account ahead of them. What they must mean is that they have declared the creditors to be on constructive notice of it.

Parties who wish to encumber a deposit account without putting other creditors on notice could do so by agreement. U.C.C. §9-104(a)(2) does not require that the agreement be filed or made public in any way. That section simply authorizes a secret lien.

C. Purchase-Money Security Interests in Consumer Goods

U.C.C. §9-309(1) creates an exception to the filing requirement for most purchase-money security interests in consumer goods. Security interests that meet the terms of this exception are considered "automatically" perfected. To understand this exception to the filing requirement, one must understand the two concepts from which it is constructed: (1) purchase-money security interest and (2) consumer goods. Each of these concepts is employed elsewhere in the law governing secured transactions, but this is as good a place to study them as any.

1. Purchase-Money Security Interest (PMSI)

U.C.C. §9-103(b)(1) defines "purchase-money security interest." Unfortunately, the definition is so tangled and complex as to be almost unreadable. The definition in former Article 9 was both clear and concise:

> A security interest is a "purchase money security interest" to the extent that it is
> (a) taken or retained by the seller of collateral to secure all or part of its purchase price; or

(b) taken by a person who by making advances or incurring an obligation gives value to enable the debtor to acquire rights in or the sue of collateral if such value is in fact so used.

We suggest you begin by mastering this definition before you try to deal with the new one in U.C.C. §9-103.

Purchase-money security interests arise in two situations, which correspond to the two subparagraphs of the definition in the preceding paragraph. In the simplest situation Pauline Reed buys a piano from Sweigert's Pianos for an agreed price of $2,000. She pays $100 down and signs a note promising to pay the remaining $1,900 to Sweigert's. If the note is secured by a security interest in the piano, it is a purchase-money security interest.

In the second situation, Reed makes application to Friendly Finance for a loan that will enable her to buy the piano. She signs a promissory note for $1,900 and a security agreement listing the piano she is about to purchase as collateral. Friendly lends her the $1,900 and she uses that money, together with $100 of her savings, to buy the piano from Sweigert's. In the most common form of this transaction, Friendly pays the $1,900 loan proceeds directly to Sweigert's or makes a check out to Reed and Sweigert's jointly to make sure the money is "in fact so used." Notice that from Reed's point of view, this transaction reaches the same end point as the simpler one: Reed pays $100 to own the piano subject to a $1,900 security interest. The difference is that in the first transaction, the seller of the piano became the secured creditor; in the second, a third party who provided the financing for the purchase became the secured creditor.

A secured party can easily lose the purchase-money status of its interest. If, for example, Reed deposits the $1,900 loan proceeds from Friendly to her bank account and then writes a $2,000 check to Sweigert's Pianos, a question may arise as to whether the loan proceeds were in fact used to buy the piano. Assume, for example, that before she deposited the check to her account, the account already contained $2,100 from her income tax refund and her monthly paycheck. Did Reed pay for the piano with the loan proceeds, her tax refund, or her monthly paycheck? That depends on the always somewhat uncertain rules for tracing money through bank accounts. To avoid that uncertainty, and, not incidentally, to prevent Reed from spending the loan proceeds on something other than the collateral, lenders who finance a purchase usually pay the loan proceeds directly to the seller for credit against the purchase price.

We will return to the subject of purchase-money security interests in Assignment 68.

2.   Consumer Goods

A purchase-money security interest is automatically perfected only in consumer goods. A PMSI in any other kind of goods must be perfected by the ordinary means required in the Code for the type of collateral. Thus, the classification as consumer goods becomes critical to determining whether perfection is automatic or whether the secured creditor needs to take some other steps.

U.C.C. §9-102(a)(23) tells us that "consumer goods" are "goods that are used or bought for use primarily for personal, family, or household purposes." It is not the nature of the goods but rather the use to which they are put or the purpose for which they are bought that determines their classification. The same computer might be "consumer goods" if the debtor uses it for family entertainment but "equipment" if the debtor uses it in business.

Courts and commentators all seem to agree that this exception from the filing requirement makes sense only when applied to consumer goods that are of relatively small value. Aside from those who finance the debtor's initial purchase of them, few lend against small-value consumer goods. Those who do rarely search in the filing system, because the amount of money at issue does not justify the expense. Given that filings against small-value consumer goods would be highly unlikely to achieve their purpose of alerting searchers to the existence of the prior lien, lawmakers have been reluctant to put purchase-money lenders to the expense of making them.

Unfortunately for the justification set forth in the preceding paragraph, there is nothing in the definition of "consumer goods" that assures that they will be of relatively small value. In the following case, the court confronted the problem that arises when the consumer goods are of substantial value and there has been no effective filing.

Gallatin National Bank v. Lockovich
(In re Lockovich)

124 B.R. 660 (W.D. Pa. 1991)

DONALD J. LEE, UNITED STATES DISTRICT JUDGE. . . .

The facts at issue are not in dispute. On or about August 20, 1986, John J. Lockovich and Clara Lockovich, his wife (Debtors), purchased a 22-foot 1986 Chapparel Villian III boat from the Greene County Yacht Club for $32,500.00. Debtors paid $6,000.00 to Greene County Yacht Club and executed a "Security Agreement/Lien Contract" which set forth the purchase and finance terms. In the Contract, Debtors granted a security interest in the boat to the holder of the Contract. Gallatin paid to the Yacht Club the sum of $26,757.14 on Debtor's behalf, and the Contract was assigned to Gallatin. . . .

The Debtors defaulted under the terms of the Security Agreement to Gallatin by failing to remit payments as required. Before Gallatin could take action, Debtors filed for relief under Chapter 11 of the Bankruptcy Code. [The Bankruptcy Court held that Gallatin failed to perfect its security interest in the boat and therefore was an unsecured creditor in the Chapter 11 bankruptcy.]

The issue on appeal is whether Gallatin must file a financing statement to perfect its purchase money security interest in the boat. Gallatin's position is that the boat is a consumer good as defined by the [Uniform Commercial Code, Article 9]. Because the boat was a consumer good subject to a purchase money security interest, Gallatin contends it was not required to file a financing statement in order to perfect its security interest. For the reasons below stated, we reverse the decision of the Bankruptcy Court and find that Gallatin has a valid security interest in the boat.

To perfect a security interest in collateral under the Code, [U.C.C. §9-501], a secured party must file a financing statement in the offices of the Secretary of the Commonwealth and the Prothonotary of the county in which the debtor resides. Under [U.C.C. §9-309], the Code permits several exceptions to the general rule depending upon the type of collateral. [The court then set out the provisions of U.C.C. §9-309(1).]

There are three significant problems in determining automatic perfection of purchase money interests in consumer goods. First, what is a purchase money security interest? Second, what are "consumer goods"? Third, can massive and expensive items qualify as consumer goods?

... It is undisputed in the instant case that the security interest held by Gallatin was a purchase money security interest, [so] therefore the first hurdle has been cleared.

... "Goods" are defined as "consumer goods" if they are used or bought for use primary for personal, family or household purposes. The goods are not classified according to design or intrinsic nature, but according to the use to which the owner puts them. Debtors have never maintained that the boat was used for anything other than for their personal use.

The question remaining for this Court is whether a $32,500.00 watercraft can be properly classified as consumer goods under [U.C.C. §9-309(1)] ... A Court of Common Pleas in Erie County, Pennsylvania, however, has held that a thirty-three (33) foot motor boat is not a consumer good. Union National Bank of Pittsburgh v. Northwest Marine, Inc., 27 U.C.C. Rep. Serv. 563, 62 Erie Co. L.J. 87 (1979). Though a lower court case is entitled to "some weight," it is not controlling.

It is apparent from the opinion of the Bankruptcy Court, and from the opinion of the court in *Northwest Marine*, that those courts perceive a void in the Code which does not address the problem of secret liens on valuable motorboats. The court in *Northwest Marine* stated that this void was "best filled by interstitial law-making by the court" until the Legislature acts to bridge the gap. Union National Bank of Pittsburgh v. Northwest Marine, Inc., 62 Erie Co. L.J. at 90.

We disagree. Determining what is a consumer good on an ad hoc basis leaves creditors with little or no guidelines for their conduct. Under the clear mandate of the Code, a consumer good subject to exception from the filing of financing statements is determined by the use or intended use of the good; design, size, weight, shape and cost are irrelevant. Should a millionaire decide to purchase the *Queen Mary* for his personal or family luxury on the high seas, under [U.C.C. §9-102(a)(23)] of the Code, the great Queen is nothing but a common consumer good. There need be no debate as to cost, size or life expectancy. Creditors must be confident that when they enter into a commercial transaction, they will play by the rules as written in the Code.

The Bankruptcy Court was also persuaded by Pennsylvania's history of disfavoring secret liens. It is undisputed that the Code's exemption of consumer goods from the burden of filing breeds the emergence of secret liens on such goods. Such secret liens, however, do not imperil the commercial world. Although the security interests described in [U.C.C. §9-309(1)] are perfected without filing, [U.C.C. §9-320(b)] provides that unless a financing statement is filed certain buyers may take free of a security interest even though perfected. [The court set forth the provisions of U.C.C. §9-320(b).]

This allows a secured party to file a financing statement, though one is not required for perfection, in order to insure that all buyers take subject to his security interest. At the same time, purchasers of consumer goods, who intend to maintain the characterization of such goods as consumer goods, are protected from hardships created by secret liens.

The Bankruptcy Court was also interested in protecting the reasonable expectations of subsequent creditors and purchasers. As above noted, a subsequent purchaser who intends to use the goods for personal, family or household purposes is protected by [U.C.C. §9-320(b)]. A subsequent purchaser with resale as its intent, such as the boat dealer in *Northwest Marine*, or a subsequent creditor, are, or should be, sophisticated in commercial dealings. They are charged with the knowledge of the contents of the Code, and should conduct themselves accordingly. A boat dealer is certainly aware when dealing with a consumer on the trade-in of a boat, that such boat could conceivably be subject to a purchase money security interest capable of perfection without filing. Likewise, a subsequent creditor is aware of the perils associated with accepting collateral which can clearly be subject to a secret lien.

Creditors, subsequent creditors and subsequent purchasers under the Code have options available to them that lend appropriate protection. To determine what protections are available to them "by interstitial law-making by the court" is more likely to defeat the intended simplification, clarification, and modernization of the law governing commercial transactions. . . .

There are two legislative solutions to the problem. One is to explicitly require the filing of security interests in motorboats.[2] The other approach, as done in some states, is to limit the value to which the exemption applies.[3] Durable, valuable "consumer goods" upon which a creditor is likely to rely for collateral, encompasses more than motorboats or mobile homes.[4] If motorboats or other expensive items are to be excluded from the dictates of [U.C.C. §9-309(1)], either via specific exemptions or a fixed ceiling price for consumer goods below which no financing statements are required, such determinations are necessarily for the Pennsylvania Legislature.

This Court, therefore, holds that Chapparel Villian III is a consumer good, and pursuant to [U.C.C. §9-309(1)] a financing statement was not required to be filed by Gallatin to perfect the security interest in the boat. Gallatin has a valid security interest in the boat. . . .

On appeal, the Third Circuit affirmed the decision in *Lockovich*, expressly endorsing Judge Lee's comment that "if motorboats or other expensive items

---

2. California requires a filing for a "boat required to be registered." See Cal. Com. Code §9-302(1)(d). Michigan requires a filing for a "vehicle, mobile home, or watercraft for which a certificate of title is required by the laws of this state." See Mich. Comp. Laws §440.9302(1)(d), Mich. Stat. Ann. §19.9302(1)(d).

3. Kansas ($1,000.00), Maryland ($1,500.00), Colorado ($250.00) and Wisconsin ($250.00) have imposed purchase price limitations above which automatic perfection is not allowed.

4. See Mayor's Jeweler's of Ft. Lauderdale, Inc. v. Levinson, 39 Ill. App. 3d 16, 349 N.E.2d 475 (1976) (a $10,000.00 diamond ring); Commercial Credit Equipment Co. v. Carter, 88 Wash. 2d 136, 516 P.2d 767 (1973) (a $24,000.00 airplane).

are to be excluded from the dictates of §9-309(1), . . . such determinations are necessarily for the Pennsylvania Legislature." Gallatin National Bank v. Lockovich (In re Lockovich), 940 F.2d 916 (3d Cir. 1991).

What if goods are bought with one use in mind, then put to a different use? U.C.C. §9-102(a)(23) is ambiguous on the point. White and Summers would allow the intended use at the time of purchase to control. They reason that such a rule enables the creditor to procure the debtor's written statement about his intended use at the time the loan is made, and perfect (or assume perfection) on that basis. In fact, security agreements often contain such a representation by the debtor. But this relaxation of the requirements for perfection puts additional burdens on the searcher. Under the White and Summers rule, the searcher who contemplates taking a security interest in a computer that has been used only in business is expected to consider the possibility that the computer initially was bought for personal use and is encumbered by an automatically perfected purchase-money security interest. The opposing view is that actual use should control classification of any goods put in use; the intent with which goods were bought should control only if the owner has not put them to use. Cases support each of these views.

D. Security Interests Not Governed by Article 9 or Another Filing Statute

Security interests in a variety of types of collateral are excluded from the coverage of Article 9. They include security interests in wage claims, U.C.C. §9-109(d)(3), insurance policies and claims, U.C.C. §9-109(d)(8), real estate interests, U.C.C. §9-109(d)(11), and non-commercial tort claims, U.C.C. §9-109(d)(12). The reasons for these exclusions vary. Security interests in wage claims, like other assignments of wages, are closely regulated in some states and prohibited in others. Security interests in insurance policies typically are "perfected" by notification to the insurance company and inclusion of the secured party as a "loss payee" on the policy itself. In the case of security interests in real estate interests, the purpose of the exclusion is to yield to an elaborate set of recording requirements found in real estate law. The drafters probably excluded non-commercial tort claims because granting security in them is controversial and their inclusion might have made adoption of revised Article 9 more difficult.

In the following case, the debtor owned a valuable lawsuit and several creditors sought to perfect liens against it. Ultimately all were successful, even the lawyers at Flynn & Stewart who filed an Article 9 financing statement to perfect a security interest that at the time was clearly not governed by Article 9. As you read the case, ask yourself what Flynn & Stewart ought to do next time they have to perfect in a non-commercial tort recovery.

Bluxome Street Associates v. Fireman's
Fund Insurance Co.

206 Cal. App. 3d 1149, 254 Cal. Rptr. 198 (Cal. Ct. App. 1988)

Opinion by STRANKMAN, J., with WHITE, P.J., and BARRY-DEAL, J. concurring....

I.   PROCEDURAL BACKGROUND AND
ISSUES ON APPEAL

In March 1987, a settlement was reached in a legal malpractice action entitled Woods v. Neisar in the Superior Court of the City and County of San Francisco. The settlement provided in part for payment of the sum of $582,500 to Eric H. Woods. This sum was put into a trust account of the law firm of Hassard, Bonnington, Rogers & Huber (Hassard Bonnington), Woods's attorneys in Woods v. Neisar. Hassard Bonnington, appellant Haas & Najarian, appellant Fireman's Fund Insurance Company (Fireman's Fund), and respondent Flynn & Stewart, among others, each claimed a lien on the settlement proceeds.

On May 6, 1987, Woods filed a motion for order establishing lien priorities and allowing distribution of proceeds. Following extensive briefing by all lien claimants and two hearings, the trial court ordered the $582,500 in settlement proceeds to be disbursed as follows: (1) $352,562.14, plus interest, to Hassard Bonnington, pursuant to a retainer agreement which provided for a lien in favor of Hassard Bonnington on any judgment or proceeds recovered in the litigation; (2) $72,500 plus interest to Charles Schilling; (3) the remainder (approximately $150,000) to respondent Flynn & Stewart. [The court concluded that Haas & Najarian and Fireman's Fund held valid liens against the settlement proceeds, but the prior liens consumed the entire settlement, rendering them worthless.]

Appellants Haas & Najarian and Fireman's Fund do not challenge the priority of the liens of Hassard Bonnington or Charles Schilling. Rather, they contend that their liens have priority over the lien of respondent Flynn & Stewart.... Flynn & Stewart contends that its lien was created prior in time to those of appellants and that, under the "first in time is first in right" rule, its lien takes priority....

III.   VALIDITY OF LIENS

[California] Civil Code section 2881, subdivision 1, provides that liens may be created by contract: "A lien is created: 1. By contract of the parties; or, 2. By operation of law." The liens of Flynn & Stewart and Haas & Najarian were valid contractual liens under this section.... The security agreement provides that Woods "grants to Flynn & Stewart, ... a security interest in any and all of the collateral," defined to include Woods's interest in Woods v. Neisar, to secure payment of a promissory note plus any additional amounts owing arising from the rendition of services by Flynn & Stewart to Woods. Such language describes a lien as defined by Civil Code section 2874....

...That Flynn & Stewart is a law firm and the purpose of the lien is to secure payment of attorney fees is immaterial to the creation and enforceability of the lien under Civil Code section 2881, subdivision 1. The lien would be enforceable, barring other factors, even if Flynn & Stewart were not a law firm and the obligation secured were not payment of legal fees. . . .

Fireman's Fund as well as Haas & Najarian next contend that the Flynn & Stewart lien is invalid because the California Uniform Commercial Code (UCC) financing statement filed by Flynn & Stewart incident to the security agreement was void ab initio and did not constitute notice of or perfect the lien.

The security agreement reflects the attorneys' belief that their security interest came within the purview of [Article] 9 of the UCC in that it provides that a UCC financing statement is to be filed with the California Secretary of State to perfect the lien. A financing statement was in fact filed with the Secretary of State.

We agree with appellants that [Article] 9 of the UCC does not apply to the Flynn & Stewart security interest or lien. The security agreement grants to Flynn & Stewart a lien on Woods's interest in a cause of action based upon legal malpractice — a tort cause of action. [U.C.C. §9-109(d)(12)] specifically provides that such lien is not covered by [Article] 9. . . . Because [Article] 9 of the UCC did not apply to Flynn & Stewart's security agreement or lien created thereby, the filing of the UCC financing statement did not operate to provide notice of or "perfect" the lien under [U.C.C. §9-501].

However, although the Flynn & Stewart lien was not perfected under the UCC, and, accordingly, was not entitled to the benefits accorded to a perfected security interest, it nevertheless was valid and enforceable, as discussed ante, under Civil Code section 2881, subdivision 1. . . .

Appellants' next contention is that the Flynn & Stewart lien is unenforceable because there was no notice of the lien. Unlike appellants, who filed written notices of lien in Woods v. Neisar, Flynn & Stewart filed no such notice.

Providing notice of a lien is a statutory prerequisite to the creation or enforceability of certain types of liens. For example, as explained below, the creation of an attachment lien on a litigant's interest in an action is dependent upon the filing of notice of the lien in that action. A judgment lien on real property is created by the recording of an abstract of judgment with the county recorder, and a judgment lien on personal property is created by the filing of notice thereof with the Secretary of State. A mechanic's lien is enforceable only if the claimant first gives notice under Civil Code section 3097, and then records the claim of lien within certain time constrictions.

As to a contractual lien under Civil Code section 2881 on a litigant's interest in a tort claim, however, we find no authority, statute, or case law which requires notice to create such lien. . . .

We conclude that appellants' contentions relating to the validity and enforceability of the Flynn & Stewart contractual lien have no merit.

The court decided that perfection of Flynn & Stewart's lien against Wood's lawsuit was not governed by Article 9 and no other California law established requirements for perfection. From there, the court could have reached any of three conclusions: (1) Flynn & Stewart were perfected because there was no law requiring them to do more than they did, (2) Flynn & Stewart were unperfected because there was no law specifying any means to perfect, or (3) the court could have established reasonable requirements for perfection, such as placing a notice of the lien in the court file. The court does not explain why it chose the first conclusion over the other two; other courts might choose differently.

E.   What Became of the Notice Requirement?

In this assignment, we have examined a variety of kinds of security interests that are excepted from the filing requirement. In some cases, the diligent searcher can discover these security interests by viewing or investigating the collateral, examining the court file, or making inquiry with a stakeholder such as a bank or insurance company. But in other cases, security interests will be effective against later interests even though the most diligent search would not lead to their discovery. Our most recent addition to this latter category is the automatically perfected purchase-money interest in consumer goods.

In earlier assignments, we noted a number of other situations in which a security interest might be effective, even though it would not be discovered on a diligent search. In later assignments, we will note more.

Prevailing theory holds that the priority granted earlier created interests is justified in part by the fact that those who accepted later interests did so with knowledge of the earlier interests or after choosing not to acquire such knowledge. In many cases, however, the availability of such knowledge is a legal fiction. We offer an alternative justification of these rules: They are principally rules that allocate losses that lawmakers do not consider worth avoiding.

Problem Set 60

60.1. What are the permissible ways to perfect in each of these items of collateral? Be prepared to describe the physical processes.

a.   The cash that comes into the debtor's cash register each day. U.C.C. §9-312(b)(3).

b.   A negotiable promissory note. U.C.C. §§9-102(a)(47), 9-312(a), 9-313(a).

c.   Money the debtor is keeping in a bank account. U.C.C. §§9-102(a)(29), 9-104, 9-312(b)(1), and 9-314(a) and (b).

d.   Shares of stock in General Motors, for which a certificate has been issued. U.C.C. §§8-102(a)(4), 8-106(b), 9-102(a)(49), 9-106(a), 9-312(a), 9-313(a).

e.   The obligations of customers of a used car lot to pay for the cars they purchased. The obligations are evidenced by promissory notes and security interests in the cars purchased. U.C.C. §§9-102(a)(11), 9-312(a), 9-313(a).

60.2. Last year, Ruth and Gene Canard sold their Turkey Burger franchise to Watson Family Restaurants, Inc. They received part of the purchase price in the form of a document titled "Contract for Payment." In the document, Watson promised to pay $500,000 in yearly installments at a stated interest rate. Your client, Casa Grande, is about to lend $300,000 to the Canards, secured by what they have from Watson.

a. How should Casa Grande perfect? U.C.C. §§9-102(a)(2), (42), (47), and (61), 9-310, 9-312(a), (b), 9-313(a), 9-330(d).

b. What if the document gives the Canards a security interest in the franchise and the Canards perfected that security interest properly at the time of the sale? U.C.C. §9-102(a)(11).

60.3. Instead of the "Contract for Payment" the Canards received in the previous problem, the Canards received only a negotiable promissory note that was an "instrument" within the meaning of U.C.C. §9-102(47). The Canards tell Casa Grande that they cannot give Casa Grande possession of the instrument because Garp Associates is holding it. Garp has a first security interest in the instrument, securing a debt to them in the amount of $60,000. Casa Grande is willing to make their loan as a second security interest, but they are not willing to risk being unsecured. What do you suggest? U.C.C. §§9-312(a), 9-313, including Comments 3 and 4, 9-330(d).

60.4. Chuck Kettering, former millionaire fallen on hard times, wants to borrow money from our client, Little Silverado Savings and Loan (LSSL). The loan officer is obviously uncomfortable with the loan and seems not to trust Kettering, but LSSL's president, Donald Paul, has been pressuring her to approve it. Paul argues that the appraisals show the collateral to be worth more than twice the amount of the loan, even at foreclosure prices. "If we get a clear U.C.C. search from both the county and the state, and we properly perfect our security interest in the collateral, and insure the collateral, what can go wrong?" The senior partner who advises the bank gave you the following list of proposed collateral and asked you to look into the possibility that there might be liens against the collateral that wouldn't show up on even a diligent search that included a viewing of the collateral. What do you advise? Are there other steps you might take to discover "automatically perfected" security interests? U.C.C. §§9-104, 9-309(1), 9-311(b), 9-313.

a. *A $20,000 mobile home.* It is located in a remote corner of Kettering's estate. State law does not allow for the issuance of a certificate of title for a mobile home.

b. *A rare book collection.* Valued at $1.5 million, the books are currently on display at the Library of Congress. If the Library were holding possession for someone who claimed a security interest in the books, would they have to tell the searcher? U.C.C. §9-210, 9-625(f) and (g).

c. *A Mercedes-Benz automobile.* The certificate of title shows no liens.

d. *A solid gold ingot and 20 unset diamonds.*

e. *Computer equipment.* The equipment cost about $40,000 at retail and is in Kettering's office, where he uses it principally to review stock quotations.

f. *A checking account.* The account is at Bank of the West and is in Kettering's name. The bank statements show no interest in favor of Bank of the West or anyone else.

60.5. Janet Dakin is in financial trouble. The only bright spot in her financial dealings is that her lawsuit against her former financial adviser, Adam Hershey, goes to trial next week. Adam was on pain killers for most of the three years he managed Janet's investments and the performance of Janet's investment portfolio shows it. In several instances, Adam promised to make particular investments for her but did not. During the three years, $2.5 million turned into $450,000. Adam has offered Janet $800,000 in settlement, but she thinks she can win more. In the meantime, Janet wants to borrow $100,000 from her brother, Will Dakin, using the lawsuit as collateral. Will asks what he should do to perfect. What do you tell him? U.C.C. §§9-109(d)(12), 9-102(a)(2), (13), (42).

60.6. When your client Sally loaned her friend Joe $5,000, she took possession of Joe's Rolex watch and gold chain as security. She did not file a financing statement and kept the items in her apartment. Now Joe has filed bankruptcy. Joe's trustee is suspicious of the transaction with Sally because it is completely undocumented. One of his arguments for voiding Sally's security agreement is that Sally was out of town for two weeks on the date Joe filed bankruptcy. During that time, Joe's mother was staying in the apartment where the watch and chain were located. (Joe's mother says she didn't even know the items were there.) Sally wants to know if there is anything to the trustee's argument. Is there? U.C.C. §§9-203(b)(3)(B), 9-310(b)(6).

60.7. Your client, Sabine Music Manufacturing (Sabine), wants to sell its electronic music tuning equipment to Jersey Music Associates, Inc. (Jersey) for $84,000, payable over seven years with no money down, with the equipment to serve as security for payment of the purchase price. Jersey wants to put the equipment to use immediately, but insists that no financing statement be filed. "Our bank lender will see it on the credit report and go nuts," says Bill Jersey, president of Jersey. Is there any way Sabine can do the deal without taking the risk of Jersey's bankruptcy? Bill Jersey suggests that he can put the music tuning equipment in a separate room, sublease the room to Sabine, and agree that the manufacturing equipment is "at all times in Sabine's possession." Bill, "as Sabine's agent, will control access to the room on behalf of Sabine, permitting Jersey workers to enter the room and use the equipment only as authorized from time to time by Sabine." All this will be in large print, on a sign posted on the door of the room. Sabine wants to do the deal, unless you tell them it won't work. Will it? U.C.C. §9-313(a).

Chapter 19. Maintaining Perfection

Assignment 61: Maintaining Perfection Through Lapse and Bankruptcy

In the preceding chapter, we discussed what secured parties must do to perfect their security interests. In this chapter we discuss what they must do to maintain that perfection over time and how they terminate perfection when it has served its purpose. We begin with the problem of termination.

A. Removing Filings from the Public Record

From the time it is placed on the public record, a filing or recording serves as constructive notice to the world that a security interest may be outstanding against property of the debtor. The theory is that searchers will discover the existence of a prior holder's interest by examining the public record, and then contact the holder of the prior interest for more information. Ultimately, such searchers must either come to terms with the holder of the prior interest or accept a subordinate position. The prior interest encumbers the property and clouds title to it.

When the debt is paid, both debtor and creditor typically will want to "remove" the filing from the public record. The debtor will want the filing off the record to clear its title to the property. The creditor will want the filing off the record so it won't be bothered by inquiries about property in which it no longer has an interest.

We put "remove" in quotation marks because many filing systems do not permit the literal removal of documents at the request of the parties. All one can do is *add* a document stating that the earlier document is no longer in effect. Nearly all real estate recording systems operate in this manner. Not surprisingly, some systems are growing in physical size at alarming rates.

1. Satisfaction

We begin our discussion of removal of filings with the real property system because it is simpler. When a real estate mortgage is paid, the mortgagee executes a document called a *satisfaction of mortgage* for recording. The satisfaction identifies the mortgage and states that it has been satisfied. Both the mortgage and the satisfaction of mortgage remain permanently in the recording system. It is important to realize that even if the debtor has paid the mortgage debt, the mortgage will continue to cloud the debtor's title until a satisfaction is recorded. The satisfaction assures persons who deal with the property in the future that the mortgagee will not make claims against it.

To understand the role that the satisfaction plays in a real estate transaction, consider the following example. Seller owns a beach house that is subject to a mortgage in favor of Western Savings in the amount of $80,000. Seller has contracted to sell the beach house to Buyer, free and clear of the mortgage, for $100,000 in cash. Seller, like most of us, does not have $80,000 with which to satisfy the mortgage; she must use the proceeds of sale to pay it. Buyer, like most of us, does not have the $100,000 he will use to pay the purchase price. He will borrow the money from Eastern Savings, using the beach house as collateral. Eastern Savings will, of course, insist that the title to the beach house be free and clear of liens before they will disburse the loan proceeds. But Western Savings will not remove their mortgage from the title until they are paid the $80,000 owing to them. A stalemate looms.

The standard solution to this problem is to set a *closing* — a gathering of all the parties so that they can make a simultaneous exchange of documents and money. At the closing, Eastern will pay the mortgage to Western, using $80,000 of the loan proceeds, and Western will simultaneously deliver a satisfaction of the mortgage to Seller. Seller will deed the property to Buyer. Buyer will sign a new mortgage for the amount of the loan proceeds and Eastern will record it immediately. The satisfaction is Western's assurance to Eastern that Western will make no further claims under the mortgage. Unless Seller can obtain this satisfaction of the old mortgage, Buyer cannot get the new mortgage he needs to pay the purchase price. The transaction will not *close* and the sale will fall through.

Because of the importance of the satisfaction, statutes in most states provide for imposition of a penalty on a secured party who fails to give one to a debtor who has fully paid the mortgage debt. The following statutes are typical:

Arizona Revised Statutes Annotated

(2005)

§33-712 LIABILITY FOR FAILURE TO ACKNOWLEDGE SATISFACTION

A. If any person receiving satisfaction of a mortgage or deed of trust shall, within thirty days, fail to record or cause to be recorded, with the recorder of the county in which the mortgage or deed of trust was recorded, a sufficient release, satisfaction of mortgage or deed of release or acknowledge satisfaction as provided in section 33-707, subsection C, he shall be liable to the mortgagor, trustor or current property owner for actual damages occasioned by the neglect or refusal.

B. If, after the expiration of the time provided in subsection A of this section, the person fails to record or cause to be recorded a sufficient release and continues to do so for more than thirty days after receiving a written request which identifies a certain mortgage or deed of trust by certified mail from the mortgagor, trustor, current property owner or his agent, he shall be liable to the mortgagor, trustor or current property owner for one thousand dollars, in addition to any actual damage occasioned by the neglect or refusal.

Florida Statutes Annotated

(2005)

§701.04   CANCELLATION OF MORTGAGES, LIENS, AND JUDGMENTS

Whenever the amount of money due on any mortgage, lien, or judgment shall be fully paid to the person or party entitled to the payment thereof, the mortgagee, creditor, or assignee, or the attorney of record in the case of a judgment, to whom such payment shall have been made, shall execute in writing an instrument acknowledging satisfaction of said mortgage, lien, or judgment and have the same acknowledged, or proven, and duly entered of record in the book provided by law for such purposes in the proper county. Within 60 days of the date of receipt of the full payment of the mortgage, lien, or judgment, the person required to acknowledge satisfaction of the mortgage, lien, or judgment shall send or cause to be sent the recorded satisfaction to the person who has made the full payment. In the case of a civil action arising out of the provisions of this section, the prevailing party shall be entitled to attorney's fees and costs.

2. Release

Mortgages frequently encumber more than one parcel of real property. If such a mortgage has not been paid in full but the secured creditor is willing to release some of the property from the mortgage lien, the secured creditor accomplishes this by executing a *release* for recording. Most secured creditors release collateral only to the extent they are required to do so by contract. The debtor typically bargains for the secured creditor's contractual obligation to release collateral before the loan is made.

Provisions requiring the release of collateral on partial payment of the loan are customary in financing the development of real estate subdivisions. For example, assume that High Point Development Company intends to purchase Blackacre, divide it into 100 residential building lots, build a road through it, install utilities, and sell the lots to contractors. Fidelity Savings lends High Point $700,000 to buy and improve the property. High Point does so, and begins offering the improved lots for sale. Linda Easterbrook, a professional home builder, is High Point's first customer. Easterbrook agrees to buy one of the lots for $25,000.

Easterbrook will almost certainly demand that she receive the lot free and clear of Fidelity's mortgage. Only then can she use it as collateral for the mortgage she will take out to finance construction of her house. Neither she nor her new lender want the risk that High Point will later default in payment of its mortgage and Fidelity will foreclose against the Easterbrook lot along with the others. But where will that leave Fidelity? The $25,000 that High Point will receive from the sale to Easterbrook will fall far short of the amount necessary to satisfy Fidelity's mortgage.

The usual accommodation between parties like these is that Fidelity will release the Easterbrook lot in return for a partial payment of its mortgage (a *paydown*). Fidelity's mortgage will probably contain a provision requiring it to give the release, contingent on High Point's payment of the *release price*. If the release price for the Easterbrook lot is, for example, $12,000, High Point will use proceeds of the sale to Easterbrook to pay that amount to Fidelity, reducing the balance owing Fidelity to $688,000. In return, Fidelity will sign a release of the Easterbrook lot, reducing Fidelity's collateral to 99 lots. Easterbrook will see that the release is recorded.

Notice that Fidelity's collateral-to-loan ratio improves as a result of the sale to Easterbrook. Before the sale, Fidelity has 100 lots as collateral for a $700,000 balance outstanding, a ratio of one lot per $7,000 of debt. After the sale, Fidelity has 99 lots as collateral for a $688,000 balance outstanding, a ratio of one lot per $6,949 of debt. High Point's $12,000 paydown on each lot sold will pay the debt in full before High Point sells all the lots. With each successive sale, Fidelity will be better assured of payment of the remaining balance.

Absent a release provision in a mortgage, the mortgagee is under no obligation to release collateral on partial payment of the mortgage — even if the debtor offers a paydown that will improve the lender's collateral-to-loan ratio. The mortgagee's only obligation is to execute a satisfaction when the debtor pays the entire balance owing on the mortgage debt. The same rule applies to security interests under Article 9.

3. Article 9 Termination and Release

If the debtor has paid the secured obligation and the secured party is not required by contract to lend more money, the debtor can demand that the secured party file a *termination statement* within 20 days. U.C.C. §9-513(c)(1). If the secured party fails to do so, the secured party becomes liable for actual damages and, in addition, a civil penalty of $500. U.C.C. §§9-625(b) and (e)(4). Upon the filing of a termination statement, the financing statement to which it relates ceases to be effective. U.C.C. §9-513(d).

Release of collateral from the coverage of a financing statement is accomplished by amending the financing statement. U.C.C. §9-512(a). As under real estate law, the secured party is obligated to file a termination statement upon full payment of the secured debt, but is not obligated to file an amendment deleting collateral on partial payment unless the secured party has contracted to do so.

A termination statement or amendment must identify, by its file number, the initial financing statement to which it relates. In addition, a termination statement must indicate that the identified financing statement is no longer effective. U.C.C. §9-102(a)(79). A termination statement or amendment becomes part of the financing statement to which it relates. See U.C.C. §9-102(a)(39). As a consequence, it appears that minor errors or omissions in the termination statement would be subject to the "seriously misleading" test of U.C.C. §9-506. That is, such errors would not render the financing statement — including the termination statement or amendment — ineffective unless errors make the financing statement seriously misleading.

U.C.C. §9-512 requires that an amendment (including a termination statement) identify "by its file number, the initial financing statement to which the amendment relates." Could an erroneous file number in the termination statement or amendment be a minor error that did not render the financing statement seriously misleading? Imagine, for example, that an amendment bore the wrong file number but contained the correct names and addresses of the debtor and the secured party, and correctly indicated the date and time of filing of the financing statement. If the filing officer noticed the problem at the time of filing, the filing officer could refuse to accept it pursuant to U.C.C. §9-516(b)(3)(B) and send it back to the filer. U.C.C. §9-520(b). The filer would correct the file number and refile. The problem would be solved. But what if the filing officer did not notice the problem, accepted the amendment for filing, created a record, and indexed the filing under the wrong financing statement? One possibility is that, although U.C.C. §9-506(c) would not literally apply, the courts would apply it by analogy. If a search of the records of the filing office under the debtor's correct name, using the filing office's standard search logic, would disclose the amendment, the erroneous number would not make the amendment seriously misleading. Another possibility is that this would be considered an indexing error rendering the amendment effective regardless of whether searchers could find it. U.C.C. §9-517. A third possibility is that the hypothetical could not arise. Both the financing statement and the amendment each contain both the file number and the debtor's name. See the official Amendment form in U.C.C. §9-521. By programming their computers to reject a filing unless both the file number and the name matched, the filing officer could prevent the error, rendering the legal issue moot. The point is that, when available, physical systems (here, the programming) are capable of addressing the same points addressed by law and will often provide superior solutions.

B. "Self-Clearing" and Continuation in the Article 9 Filing System

As we mentioned above, the real estate recording system is committed to keeping your deed to Blackacre for eternity. Documents are added to the system, but none are ever removed from it.

Perhaps cognizant of the record-storage problem confronting the real estate recording systems, the drafters of Article 9 opted for what they call a *self-clearing system*. Financing statements are effective for only five years. (A few states have adopted non-uniform amendments specifying longer periods.) Unless the secured party takes affirmative action by filing a *continuation statement* during the last six months of the five-year period, the financing statement "lapses." U.C.C. §9-515(a) and (c). Only about 30 percent of financing statements are terminated. Another 15 percent are continued. The remaining 55 percent are cleared by lapse. 11 Clark's Secured Transactions Monthly 7 (Jan. 1996). One year after a financing statement lapses, the filing officer can remove it from the records and destroy it. U.C.C. §9-522(a). As a result, an Article 9 filing system may contain only the financing statements filed or continued in the past six years.

Not all Article 9 filing systems are set up to take advantage of this self-clearing feature. Local systems are often integrated with the real estate recording systems in such a way that lapsed financing statements cannot be thrown away. But they lapse just the same.

To understand how the self-clearing feature of the Article 9 filing system works, think of the filed financing statements as each standing vertically on a conveyor belt. At the place where the moving belt begins its horizontal trip, the filing officer places newly filed financing statements on it. The belt carries the filings for six years, at which time they drop off the end into a paper shredder. At four and a half years, the filing statements enter the six-months-long segment of the belt in which they can be continued. If a continuation statement is filed while the financing statement is in this continuation "window," the filing officer pulls the financing statement off the conveyor belt, attaches the continuation statement to it, takes it to the beginning point, and puts it back on the belt, just like a newly filed financing statement.

What about the statements that are not continued? One might think that the conveyor belt should arrive at the paper shredder five years from the point of beginning — that is, as soon as it is out of the continuation window. If the filing officer could process continuation statements immediately on receipt, it probably should. But sometimes the filing officer gets a bit behind in the work. Even though a filing officer receives a continuation statement (and, of course, notes the date and time of filing on it) while the financing statement is in the six-months continuation window, the financing statement may be past the window by the time the filing officer begins looking for it. The conveyor belt extends for a year beyond the continuation window so that the financing statement will not reach the shredder before the busy filing officer can snatch it off the belt.

U.C.C. §519(h) requires that the filing officer index records within two days of their receipt by the filing officer. Why, then, does §9-522 require that the filing officer maintain lapsed records for a year after lapse? Perhaps the reason is that the drafters did not really expect filing officers to comply with U.C.C. §519(h). Filing offices traditionally have been one or two weeks behind in indexing new filings and in extreme cases have been more than four months behind. When such delays occur, the filing officers invariably blame their legislatures for not appropriating sufficient funds for the filing offices to carry the workload. No one can prove the filing officer wrong and no penalty is imposed for violating U.C.C. §519(h) anyway, making that provision what some refer to euphemistically as "aspirational."

Provided that the secured party files a continuation statement each time its financing statement passes through the continuation window, the financing statement can ride the conveyor belt for decades. Each time it passes the window, the filing officer attaches a new continuation statement and it gets thicker and thicker.

The secured party who wants to maintain the priority of its initial filing must continue that filing rather than simply file a new financing statement. The reason for this requirement may seem obvious, but it is not. Exactly what harm would it cause if a secured party, rather than filing a continuation statement as its earlier financing statement passed through the continuation window, simply filed another financing statement? The second financing statement would be on the belt before the first one reached the shredder. Anyone who searched before taking an interest in the collateral could discover the secured party's interest.

What more does the continuation statement tell them? Only that the priority date of the existing interest is earlier than they might otherwise have supposed. To illustrate, assume that Firstbank filed a financing statement in 1991 and filed a continuation statement in 1995. A search in 1997 would discover the 1991 financing statement with the continuation statement attached. The searcher would know that Firstbank's priority date was in 1991. Had Firstbank filed a second financing statement in 1995 instead of a continuation statement, the 1997 search would discover only the 1995 financing statement; the 1991 financing statement would, by that time, have met the paper shredder. The searcher might have no way of knowing that the 1991 filing was ever made.

So long as new filers entering the system know their own priority, what difference does it make whether the filing system continues to show the initial priority dates of the earlier interests? Perhaps not much. So long as each filer keeps a certified copy of its own filing, the shredding of the filing officer's copy will not prevent the parties from reconstructing the situation. Perhaps the continuation system is designed to guard against the forgery of backdated financing statements after a dispute has arisen. Perhaps a later filer will want to know the order of priority between earlier filers and not trust what they say. Whatever the reasons, U.C.C. §9-515 distinguishes between a continuation statement and a later-filed financing statement, and the courts generally enforce the distinction with a vengeance.

Worthen Bank & Trust Co., N.A. v. Hilyard Drilling Co. (In re Hilyard Drilling Co.)

840 F.2d 596 (8th Cir. 1988)

WOLLMAN, CIRCUIT JUDGE . . .

I

On April 25, 1979, [Hilyard Drilling Co. (Hilyard)] granted [the National Bank of Commerce of El Dorado (NBC)] a security interest in all of its existing and future accounts receivable, and the proceeds thereof. This security interest was perfected by the filing of appropriate financing statements on April 26, 1979.

On April 28, 1983, Paul C. Watson, Jr., [a vice president of Worthen Bank & Trust Co., N.A. (Worthen)] wrote a letter to Hilyard, which stated in relevant part:

> Confirming our telephone conversation, our Loan Committee has approved a renewal of your $550,000 equipment line and your $500,000 short-term working capital line on the following conditions:
>
> 1. That Worthen take a second lien position on accounts receivable . . .

> I do not think that any of these items present a problem to you since we have previously discussed these. I understand that you need to talk with [NBC] regarding the receivables. We acknowledge their first lien and would be happy to do so in writing so that it is clear to everyone that our lien is junior to theirs.

NBC never requested a written acknowledgment. On June 14, 1983, Hilyard granted Worthen a security interest in the same accounts receivable. Neither Worthen's loan documents nor the financing statements it filed on June 14, 1983, stated that Worthen's security interest was subordinate to NBC's security interest.

On July 8, 1983, in connection with the reworking of Hilyard's loans, NBC filed a new financing statement giving notice of its security interest in Hilyard's accounts receivable. NBC did not file a continuation statement within six months preceding April 25, 1984, the expiration date of its 1979 financing statement, as required by [U.C.C. §9-515(d)].

On July 6, 1984, Eugene G. Sayre, Hilyard's attorney, wrote a letter to Steven C. Wade, a commercial loan officer at Worthen, which stated in relevant part:

> The only matter which I want to make absolutely sure is clarified deals with 4.(a) on accounts receivable. Though the Loan Agreement does not reflect it, Hilyard Drilling Company, Inc., has previously made an assignment of its accounts receivable to the National Bank of Commerce of El Dorado, Arkansas. Thus, if the NBC in El Dorado has filed its financing statement and security agreement, Worthen Bank & Trust Company, N.A., would have a "second" position on these assets. As we have discussed, that was the intention of all parties concerned, as reflected in Paul Watson, Jr.'s letter to Ray Hilyard of April 28, 1983.

[Hilyard filed a Chapter 11 bankruptcy petition on January 25, 1985.] The schedule of assets filed in connection with Hilyard's Chapter 11 bankruptcy indicated that the debts to NBC and Worthen exceeded Hilyard's accounts receivable. Worthen filed a motion with the bankruptcy court for the determination of the priority of the security interests in Hilyard's accounts receivable. The bankruptcy court determined that Worthen's security interest was first in priority. On appeal, the district court affirmed the findings of the bankruptcy court. . . .

II

The effectiveness of a financing statement lapses five years from the date of filing, unless a continuation statement is filed prior to its lapse. [U.C.C. §§9-515(a), (c), and (d)]. Thus, unless NBC filed a continuation statement, its April 26, 1979, financing statement lapsed on April 25, 1984, prior to the filing of Hilyard's bankruptcy petition. NBC argues that its July 8, 1983, financing statement should be treated as a continuation statement under [U.C.C. §9-515(c)]. We disagree.

Under [U.C.C. §9-515(d)], a continuation statement must be filed within six months prior to the expiration of the original filing and "must be signed by the secured party, identify the original statement by file number and state that the original statement is still effective." [Editor's note: See U.C.C. §9-102(a)(27).]

NBC admits that its July 8, 1983, financing statement does not satisfy the specific statutory requirements for a continuation statement because it "was not filed within six months of the expiration of the original financing statement, it does not refer to the file number of that financing statement, and it does not state that the original financing statement is still effective." NBC nonetheless argues that its July 8, 1983, financing statement should be treated as a continuation statement because its failure to fulfill the requirements of [U.C.C. §9-102(a)(27)] is "harmless error," comparable to that addressed in [U.C.C. §9-506(a)].

Without determining whether the harmless error concept applies to [U.C.C. §9-102(a)(27)], the bankruptcy court found that NBC's July 8, 1983, financing statement did not substantially comply with the requirements for a continuation statement. This finding is not clearly erroneous.

Financing statements and continuation statements serve distinct and different purposes. A financing statement that does not refer to the original filing cannot suffice as a continuation statement. Bostwick-Braun Co. v. Owens, 634 F. Supp. 839, 841 (E.D. Wis. 1986). Compare In re Barnes, 15 U.C.C. Rep. Serv. 956, 962 (D. Me. 1974) (financing statement that specifically stated it was for "the purpose of continuing the Financing Statement filed with Town Clerk 5/1/67" provided the necessary linkage to original financing statement). NBC's failure to file a continuation statement cannot be considered harmless error, because the second financing statement gave no indication that it was filed for the purpose of continuing any other financing statement.

In addition, the fact that Worthen was aware of NBC's once-perfected security interest does not render harmless NBC's failure to file a proper continuation statement. "[S]ince the purpose of statutory filing requirements is, in most instances, to resolve notice disputes consistently and predictably by reference to constructive or statutory notice alone . . . consideration of a junior creditor's actual notice of a now lapsed prior filing by a competing senior creditor" is precluded. *Bostwick-Braun Co.*, 634 F. Supp. at 841.

III

NBC argues that even if its July 8, 1983, financing statement is not considered a continuation statement, its security interest is first in priority because it was continuously perfected from April 26, 1979, pursuant to [U.C.C. §§9-308(c) and 9-322(a)(1)]. . . .

To interpret [U.C.C. §9-308(c)] as providing that a security interest can be continuously perfected by consecutively filed financing statements contradicts the express language of [U.C.C. §9-515(c)]. [U.C.C. §9-308(c)] is applicable to security interests that are originally perfected in one way and then subsequently perfected in some other way, without an intermediate unperfected period. NBC, which initially perfected by filing, subsequently perfected in the same way, by filing, as opposed to "in some other way" as required by the statute. [U.C.C. §9-308(c)] is inapplicable to NBC's security interest in Hilyard's accounts receivable. . . .

Worthen's security interest had first priority pursuant to [U.C.C. §9-322(a)(1)]. NBC's April 26, 1979, financing statement lapsed due to its failure to file a continuation statement, leaving the underlying security interest unperfected. [U.C.C. §9-515(c)]. Following the lapse, the other perfected security interests in Hilyard's accounts receivable advanced in priority. Of the remaining perfected security interests, Worthen's interest had priority because it was first in time of filing or perfection.

———

In an earlier case, In re Hays, 47 B.R. 546 (Bankr. N.D. Ohio 1985), Production Credit Association (PCA) perfected its security interest by filing a financing statement in 1976. In 1981, PCA filed a second financing statement instead of the continuation statement it should have filed. In 1982, the Farmer's Home Administration (FmHA) filed a financing statement against the same collateral. After PCA's original 1976 financing statement expired, the court held that PCA was unperfected and awarded priority to FmHA. The court reasoned that by attempting to substitute a financing statement for a continuation statement, PCA had "disregard[ed] a positive legislative enactment." That rendered the second financing statement a nullity and left PCA unperfected even though it had a facially correct financing statement on file at all relevant times. The court cited the predecessor of U.C.C. §9-515(c), which used almost the same language:

> The effectiveness of a filed financing statement lapses on the expiration of the five-year period.... Upon lapse the security interest becomes unperfected, unless it is perfected without filing.

While the result in *Hays* is consistent with the language of U.C.C. §9-515(c), we see no harm to the system that could have been caused by allowing PCA's second financing statement to operate as a financing statement rather than as a continuation statement, giving PCA a 1981 priority date.

The courts have generally been harsh in their treatment of errors in the filing of continuation statements. When creditors file continuation statements after their financing statements have lapsed, the courts uniformly hold the continuation statements ineffective, even if no one was prejudiced by the error. See U.C.C. §9-510(c) (providing that "[a] continuation statement that is not filed within the six-month period prescribed by Section 9-515(d) is ineffective"). Some explain it doctrinally, saying that upon lapse of the financing statement there was no longer a filing to be continued. The result also can be explained through the imagery of the filing system as conveyor belt: By the time the filing officer processes a late-filed continuation statement, the financing statement might already have met its fate in the paper shredder.

It is more difficult to explain why a continuation statement filed too early should be ineffective. That is, nevertheless, the law. See, e.g., U.C.C. §9-510(c), Lorain Music Co. v. Allied Inv. Credit Corp., 535 N.E.2d 345 (1987) (continuation statement filed seven months before expiration of five-year period was ineffective; creditor lost his status as first perfected security interest holder when original statement expired).

To explore the problems early filing might create, assume that Firstbank files its financing statement on April 1, 1991, and then files a premature continuation statement on April 1, 1993. If the continuation statement were held effective, it would continue the filing to March 31, 2001. U.C.C. §9-515(e). Thus, there will be a period of more than six years between the filing of the continuation statement and the lapse of the filing. If we employ the image of the conveyor belt leading to the paper shredder, interrupted only when the filer jogs the filing officer to action by filing another continuation statement, the possibility looms that both financing statement and continuation statement will have gone to the shredder before March 31, 2001, while the filing remains effective.

We can only speculate, however, on the degree to which the actual systems employed to purge lapsed filings resemble the conveyor belt image we invoke. Nothing need go to the shredder unless the filing officer sends it. Because so many filed financing statements are preserved on microfilm or microfiche, we doubt that many filing officers actually destroy their only copy in the few years following lapse. (Whether these lapsed filings will show up on a search is another matter. The typical search request is only for presently effective filings. U.C.C. §9-523(c).)

The American Bar Association's Article 9 Filing System Task Force recommended elimination of the six-month prelapse period for filing continuation statements, saying that modern record keeping practices are able to accommodate early continuation statements with delayed effective dates. The Article 9 Study Group that preceded the Drafting Committee recommended that the Drafting Committee "give attention to existing problems in the following areas: (xix) expansion or removal of the 6-month prelapse period for filing continuation statements." Recommendation 11. Ignoring both groups, the Drafting Committee retained the six-month window, presumably merely as a trap for the unwary. It seems to serve no other function.

Upon lapse, the security interest "becomes unperfected" and "is deemed never to have been perfected as against a purchaser of the collateral for value." U.C.C. §9-515(c). This retroactive loss of priority does not apply in favor of a lien creditor (or the trustee in bankruptcy). Provided that the security interest was perfected at the time the lien creditor levied (or at the filing of the bankruptcy petition), the secured creditor retains priority over the lien creditor or trustee. See Comment 3 to U.C.C. §9-515. The security interest will, however, be subordinate to a lien creditor that levies after lapse and to the trustee in a bankruptcy filed after lapse.

C.   The Effect of Bankruptcy on Lapse
and Continuation

Under earlier versions of Article 9, there was confusion over the effect of bankruptcy on lapse and continuation. The confusion has now been resolved. A secured party must file continuation statements at five-year intervals to avoid lapse. No exception is made simply because the debtor has filed bankruptcy. See U.C.C. §9-515(c). The filing of continuation statements during the pendency of the bankruptcy case does not violate the automatic stay. Bankruptcy Code §§362(b)(3), 546(b)(1)(B).

Although the concept that the filing and searching game goes on even after the filing of a bankruptcy case is easy to grasp intellectually, secured creditors and lawyers never cease to be surprised by the resulting evaporation of their legal rights in the midst of litigation.

In re Schwinn Cycling and Fitness, Inc.
(Expeditors International of Washington, Inc. v. The Liquidating Trust)

313 B.R. 473 (D. Colo. 2004)

JUDGE EDWARD W. NOTTINGHAM.

FACTS

The parties have stipulated to the following undisputed facts. Appellant is a shipping company that shipped goods belonging to Debtor Schwinn Cycling and Fitness. The contract between appellant and debtor provided that appellant had a general lien and security interest in all of debtor's property in its possession, custody, or control.

On July 16, 2001, debtor filed a voluntary petition of bankruptcy under chapter 11 of the United States Bankruptcy Code. Within the twenty day time period preceding the petition date, appellant had in its possession some of debtor's goods. During this twenty day time frame, appellant transferred possession of these goods to the debtor who thereafter sold the goods. Thus, either shortly before or shortly after the petition date, debtor/debtor's bankruptcy estate had possession of the cash proceeds from the goods.

The parties agree that on and prior to the petition date, appellant held a perfected security interest in the goods and the proceeds from the goods. Appellant perfected its security interest by way of its actual or constructive possession of the goods. Appellant did not file a financing statement with respect to the goods within twenty days after it relinquished custody of the goods to the debtor. Pursuant to a Stipulation and Order in the bankruptcy proceedings, the debtor established a segregated cash collateral fund of $250,000 upon which appellant holds a replacement lien to the extent its lien and security interest in the goods and proceeds is valid and enforceable. . . .

ANALYSIS

At some point prior to the debtor's bankruptcy filing, appellant had a perfected security interest in the goods by possession. [U.C.C. §9-313(a)] ("a secured party may perfect a security interest in . . . goods . . . by taking possession of the collateral"). Appellant lost the perfected security interest by possession when it gave possession of the goods to debtor. [U.C.C. §9-313(d)] ("If perfection of a security interest depends upon possession of the collateral by a secured party, perfection occurs no earlier than the time the secured party takes possession and continues only while the secured party retains possession"). After it relinquished possession of the goods to the debtor, appellant had a temporarily perfected security interest in the goods under [U.C.C. §9-312(f)]. [U.C.C. §9-312(f)] provides that a perfected security interest in . . . goods in possession of a bailee . . . remains perfected for twenty days without filing if the secured party makes available to the debtor the goods or documents representing the goods for the purpose of:

(1) Ultimate sale or exchange; or
(2) Loading, unloading, storing, shipping, transshipping, manufacturing, processing, or otherwise dealing with them in a manner preliminary to their sale or exchange.

At the conclusion of this twenty day period, in order to still be perfected, the Uniform Commercial Code requires the secured party to perfect in another way, such as by filing or possession. [U.C.C. §9-312(h)] ("After the twenty-day period . . . expires, perfection depends upon compliance with this article"). Appellant did not do so.

Appellant argues, however, that it did not need to perfect the security interest after this time because the debtor's decision to file for chapter 11 protection during the interim resulted in its security interest being rendered permanently perfected. The Tenth Circuit comprehensively addressed this argument in the case of In re Reliance Equities. Inc., 966 F.2d 1338, 1341-45 (10th Cir. 1992), and this decision controls the result of this case regarding goods.

The issue before the Tenth Circuit in *Reliance* was whether the appellant held a perfected security interest in the proceeds from the sale of promissory notes under the former version of Colorado's codification of the Uniform Commercial Code. The *Reliance* appellant had a temporarily perfected security interest in the proceeds pursuant to . . . the precursors in relevant part to the current [U.C.C. §9-312(f-h)]. This temporary perfection expired before the *Reliance* appellant filed a financing statement. The *Reliance* debtor, however, filed for bankruptcy while the *Reliance* appellant's security interest was temporarily perfected. The *Reliance* appellant, accordingly, raised the identical argument that appellant raises here, arguing "that the perfected status of its security interest in proceeds continued indefinitely once bankruptcy proceedings began because the bankruptcy petition was filed during the ten-day period during which . . . it [had] an automatic perfected interest in the proceeds."

The Tenth Circuit rejected this argument, explaining that

[i]n this case, [appellant] did not file a financing statement. Rather, [appellant] relies upon temporary perfection under [U.C.C. §9-312(f)]. To freeze priorities upon the initiation of insolvency proceedings in an automatic perfection situation would contravene one of the principal purposes of the Bankruptcy Reform Act: to strike down secret liens.

The automatic perfection provisions . . . were designed to address particular short-term exigencies where creditors could not always be expected to perfect their security interests otherwise. The motivating reasons behind these sections do not logically extend throughout the duration of a potentially lengthy bankruptcy proceeding. The short and precise durations explicitly provided for by the automatic security provisions . . . are inconsistent with the concept urged upon us by [appellant] that a bankruptcy filing by the debtor should extend such security interests indefinitely. . . .

Moreover, we find it especially significant that [the provisions], which address short-term automatically perfected security interests, make no mention of an extension of the perfection period in the event insolvency proceedings are commenced.

This reasoning applies with the same force to the new temporary perfection rules found in [U.C.C. §9-312(f) and §9-313(d)]. Therefore, *Reliance* controls the outcome of this case. . . .

In another recent case, General Electric Capital Corporation v. Dial Business Forms, 341 F.3d 738 (8th Cir. 2003), the bankruptcy court confirmed a plan of reorganization that provided for the secured creditor to "retain [its] security interests and liens" in the property of the debtor. The plan further provided that a class of unsecured creditors "shall be secured by a subordinated interest" in the same assets. A few years later, the secured creditor's filing lapsed and the unsecured creditors claimed priority. The Court of Appeals rejected their claim, saying that a plan of reorganization "acts like a contract that binds the parties that participate in the plan," including those who voted against it. The court held that the reference to the unsecured creditors' interest as "subordinated" constituted a subordination agreement effective independent of the secured creditor's security interest. U.C.C. §9-339.

Problem Set 61

61.1. Your client, the Bank of East Palatka, perfected its $728,000 security interest in equipment owned by Horst Manufacturing by filing a financing statement on December 30, 2001. The bank filed a continuation statement on July 7, 2006. Today, March 22, 2010, Jan Swift, a loan officer from the bank, asks you the following questions:

a. Did the Bank file its prior continuation statement at the proper time? U.C.C. §9-515.

b. Swift wants to put on her calendar the time when she should file the next continuation statement for this filing. When will it be due?

c. A week after you answered those questions for Jan Swift, Horst Manufacturing filed a case under Chapter 11 of the Bankruptcy Code. Swift expects that the case will probably extend for about two years, but of course that time could vary. Swift would like to know if this changes your advice about the proper time for filing the Bank's next continuation statement. What do you tell her? Bankr. Code §362(b)(3); U.C.C. §9-515.

61.2. The discussion with Jan Swift reminded you that you did some U.C.C. closings in your early years of practice but hadn't yet realized the need to calendar your filings for continuation. You pulled the files and found that you filed one of the financing statements five years and two months ago on behalf of Juan Gomez. Gomez had sold his restaurant to The Cantina, Incorporated, and taken back a security interest in all of the restaurant equipment, including after-acquired property. The $60,000 note for the purchase price was amortized over 12 years, with a balloon payment at the end of six. A quick search in the filing system reveals that you're not the only one who didn't think about continuation; no continuation statement is on file for the financing statement you filed. What do you do now? U.C.C. §§9-102(a)(39), 9-509(b), 9-510(c), 9-515, 9-516(b)(7).

1025

61.3. Two weeks ago, the Wriggling Brothers Circus (founded by the great escape artists) filed under Chapter 11. This was of some concern to you, because your client, Mark Ryerson, holds a $120,000 first security interest in most of the assets of the circus. Associates Financial Partners (Associates) also holds a security interest in the same property, securing their loan for over $1 million. Both interests were created at the same time, about nine years ago. Ryerson's financing statement was filed first; Associates' later the same day. Both creditors filed continuation statements in a timely fashion.

Associates is represented by Millie Parker. When you spoke to Parker this morning about the bankruptcy case, she tweaked you by casually referring to Ryerson's interest as a "second." When you pointed out that Ryerson filed before Associates, she said that wasn't controlling because Associates had possession of the circus assets on the day the two filings were made. You can't remember anything about possession of the circus assets nine years ago, and neither can Ryerson. Would it matter if Parker were right about possession of the circus nine years ago? U.C.C. §§9-515, 9-308(c), 9-322(a)(1).

61.4. Philip Ghandi, a real estate broker, recently bought 16 lots in Brook Meadow, a residential subdivision, for $320,000. He financed the purchase with a $160,000 loan from Equity Investment Group (EIG) that is secured by a mortgage against the 16 lots. Ghandi has arranged to sell one of the lots for $30,000. When EIG learned about the sale, they told him that "of course, the entire proceeds of the sale must be applied against the mortgage." Ghandi says he can't do that, because there will be expenses of sale, including the fees of another broker involved in the deal that have to be paid. Ghandi would like you to "get tough with EIG, and free up some of this cash flow." What do you plan to say to EIG?

61.5. a. You represent Firstbank. The bank's security agreement covers 12 fork lifts, a stamping machine, and all "replacements or additions." The bank initially lent $400,000 to the debtor, Beaver Manufacturing, and the loan balance currently stands at $210,174. Beaver authorized, and Firstbank filed, an effective financing statement identifying the collateral as "equipment." Now Beaver is trying to borrow money against its drill presses. It wants Firstbank to put a release in the filing system for the drill presses and office furniture, neither of which is covered by Firstbank's security agreement. Firstbank does not want to give the release because it hopes to force Beaver to pay the loan off early or agree to a higher rate of interest. Firstbank's security agreement contains no provisions regarding release of collateral. Does Firstbank have to give Beaver the release? U.C.C. §§9-513, 9-512.

b. If Firstbank doesn't, will Beaver be able to assure another lender that it will have the first filed security agreement against the drill presses? Could Beaver solve its problem by demanding from Firstbank a written statement of collateral and showing it to the new lender? U.C.C. §§9-210, 9-401(b), 9-502(d), 9-322(a)(1).

61.6. Joe and Mary Suarez have contracted to sell their house and asked you to handle the closing. The first mortgage, originally given to First Florida Savings and Loan but now owned by Global Mortgage Service company of Newark, New Jersey, is to be paid in full at the closing.

Global has been very difficult to deal with. It was slow to respond to your request for an "estoppel letter" showing the balance owing on the mortgage.

When Global did respond, its number, $42,678, was suspiciously high. After a laborious comparison of the mortgage amortization schedule and the Suarezes' payment record, you concluded that the correct balance was $40,711: Global was demanding $1,967 more than what was owed them. When you finally got someone from Global to talk to you on the phone, you discovered that Global had failed to credit the Suarezes for two payments they had actually made (Mrs. Suarez showed you cancelled checks) and had charged the Suarezes' account with "administrative fees" not authorized by the mortgage. The final blow was a $350 fee for recalculating the account and sending you the estoppel letter. Such a fee is neither customary, nor provided for in the mortgage. Despite your protests, the Global representative will not make any change in the estoppel letter.

The mortgage contract provides that in the event of default, the Suarezes will pay the secured creditor's attorneys' fees and costs, but does not provide for the secured creditor to pay the Suarezes' attorneys' fees under any circumstances. The closing is scheduled for 40 days from today. If you don't have a satisfaction of mortgage from Global, your clients won't be able to convey marketable title to the buyers and the deal may fall through. Mike Schwartz, attorney for the buyer, says his client won't disburse the purchase price unless "there's a satisfaction from Global on the table." The sale price is at about the market, but the Suarezes don't want to lose the sale because it may take a lot of time to find another buyer and they fear that this buyer might sue them. What is your advice? If this property is in Florida, is there any way that the Florida satisfaction of mortgage statute might be of help? Would the Suarezes be better off or worse off if the property was in Arizona?

61.7. Assume that the sale in the previous problem had been of the Suarezes' business equipment rather than their residence, and therefore governed by Article 9. Would they be in a stronger or a weaker position? U.C.C. §9-513.

61.8. Harry Montague, a senior partner in your firm, heard that you took an advanced course in secured transactions in law school and has invited you to lunch. The governor recently appointed Harry to the National Conference of Commissioners on Uniform State Laws. (Surely you remember that bunch that shares control of the official text of the U.C.C. and the other uniform and model acts.) NCCUSL is considering revisions to Article 9. Harry didn't take secured transactions in law school and cheerfully admits that he knows nothing about the subject. Nonetheless, a NCCUSL committee of which Harry is a member is about to vote on a proposed amendment to U.C.C. §9-515 that would permit the filers of financing statements to choose the length of time for which they would be effective. The options would be 5, 10, 15, or 20 years. After that time, the secured parties could still file continuation statements. Harry, whose background is in real estate, doesn't see why there ought to be any time limit on the effectiveness of filings at all. If they need a limit on regular filings, Harry says, how come they don't need one on mortgages that reach fixtures? U.C.C. §9-515(g). Harry asks your opinion. What do you tell him?

Assignment 62: Maintaining Perfection Through Changes of Name, Identity, and Use

Communication in real time is hard enough. As we saw in earlier assignments, a secured creditor who attempts to name its debtor or describe the collateral in which it claims an interest may have difficulty finding the right words. In this assignment, we discuss the additional complexity that arises because communication through the filing system does not occur in real time.

The filer's message may be in the filing system for years before the searcher looks for it. In the interim, the circumstances that shaped the message may have changed. The debtor who comes to the searcher for a loan may have changed her name and address since the filer put its financing statement on file. If the debtor does not reveal the debtor's old name and address to the searcher, the searcher may have difficulty finding the financing statement that is on file. Collateral described accurately on the financing statement may have changed so drastically in use and appearance that even if the searcher finds the old financing statement it will be unable to link the collateral it sees to the description on the statement. Remember that one of the changes collateral can undergo is exchange for proceeds. The proceeds may neither look nor be anything at all like the original collateral described in the financing statement. For example, the financing statement may describe the collateral as "beans," but by the time the debtor seeks a loan from the searcher, the debtor may have traded the beans for a circus elephant.

One way to deal with this problem would have been to hold the financing statement ineffective if it would not have been effective as a new financing statement in the changed circumstances. That would have placed responsibility on the filer to monitor the circumstances, discover changes, and make appropriate amendments to the financing statement.

Another way to deal with the problem would have been to hold that an initially effective financing statement remained effective even though circumstances changed. That would have placed responsibility on the searcher to discover the previous circumstances of the debtor and the collateral and then search for statements filed effectively under those circumstances. By thorough investigation, the searcher might have been able to discover what changes had occurred and adjust its search to account for them.

The drafters of Article 9 chose to use a little of each approach, mixing them in a manner sufficiently complex to win them a place in both the law school curriculum and most state bar exams. In this assignment we explore that mix and raise questions about its impact: To what extent are both old filers *and* new searchers required to monitor the collateral, the debtor, or the public record to protect themselves? What is the cost of such monitoring? The cost of failing to monitor?

As you study the balance that has been struck between filer and searcher, you will be tempted to interpret each rule as placing an obligation on filers or searchers to do something. There is no harm in doing so, so long as you realize that in many situations real filers and searchers do not perform their obligations and can't realistically be expected to. These rules don't just tell filers and searchers what to do. In circumstances where losses are not worth the effort necessary to avoid them, the rules simply allocate those losses to the filers or searchers.

In this assignment, we focus on the three most important changes in circumstance: (1) changes of the debtor's name, (2) changes affecting the description of collateral, and (3) the conversion of the collateral into proceeds.

A. Changes in the Debtor's Name

Individuals, corporations, and other entities can, and sometimes do, change their names. If a debtor changes names between the time a filing is made against the debtor and the time a search for that filing is made, the change may — or may not — cause the communication to fail. To illustrate, assume that Adams Corporation borrows money from Firstbank in 2001 and gives Firstbank a security interest in all of Adams's assets. Firstbank perfects by filing. In 2002, Adams Corporation changes its name to Baker Corporation. Firstbank does not learn of the change of name, so it does not amend its financing statement to reflect it. In 2003, the corporation applies to Secondbank for a loan and offers the same assets as collateral. Secondbank, who does not discover the change of name either, conducts its search only under the name "Baker Corporation." Of course, the search does not discover Firstbank's filing.

That is not to say that Secondbank *could not* have discovered Firstbank's filing through a search. A corporate debtor's change of name is a matter of public record. Even without the debtor's cooperation, Secondbank could have discovered it by (1) insisting that the debtor prove its incorporation under the laws of some state or country, (2) searching the records of that state or country for changes of the debtor's name, and (3) having discovered that the debtor was previously named Adams Corporation, conducting its search in that name as well as in Baker Corporation.

By going to some extra trouble, Firstbank could also have prevented this failure of communication. If Firstbank had been sensitive to changes in its borrower, it might have noticed the change on the debtor's letterhead, checks, or bank accounts. Even if the debtor did nothing to publicize the change, Firstbank could have discovered it by periodically checking the corporate records of the state in which the debtor was incorporated. When it discovered the change, Firstbank could have amended its financing statement to reflect it. By these methods, Firstbank could have minimized the time during which its financing statement was indexed only under an obsolete name, but it could not have entirely eliminated it. For example, even if Firstbank checked the corporate records for borrower changes of name every four months, its filings could be indexed under former names for up to four months plus the time it took Firstbank to amend its filing.

Were Adams an individual instead of a corporation, the banks might have found it more difficult to discover her change of name from Juanita Adams to Juanita Baker. Evidence of the change might be in the records of any of thousands of courts or not in any public record at all. Either bank might have discovered the change by checking the debtor's driver's license or other identification, but only if they checked both before and after the change. Although discovery of an individual name change is likely to be more difficult than discovery of a corporate name change, once the creditor discovers the former the analysis for determining what action is required is the same as for the latter.

U.C.C. §9-507(c) provides that even though a change in the debtor's name renders a filed financing statement seriously misleading, the financing statement remains effective with regard to (1) collateral owned by the debtor at the time of the name change and (2) collateral acquired by the debtor in the first four months after the change. The seriously misleading financing statement is not, however, effective to perfect a security interest in collateral acquired by the debtor more than four months after the change.

Under this rule, a secured party that financed the purchase of a specific item of collateral (such as a boat) has no reason to concern itself with later changes in the debtor's name. On the other hand, a secured party that is financing the debtor's inventory of boats on a continuing basis should concern itself with changes in the debtor's name. The secured party's filing will not be effective against inventory the debtor acquires more than four months after the debtor changes its name. An inventory financier who fails to notice the debtor's name change for a period of a year might find that its filing is no longer effective against anything of real value.

The name-change rule of U.C.C. §9-507(c) potentially affects every searcher. Even though a search in the current, correct name of the debtor discovers no filings against the collateral, there may be a filing in the debtor's former name that remains effective against the proposed collateral. Depending on the amount of money at stake and the degree to which the searcher trusts the debtor, the searcher may want to investigate the possibility of changes in the debtor's name.

It may have occurred to you in reading the preceding paragraphs that there is one person who could easily keep track of the debtor's name and make sure changes have been promptly memorialized in amendments to the relevant financing statements — the debtor. Although this is true, it is not very helpful. Most security agreements do in fact contain a promise by the debtor to notify the secured party of the debtor's change of name as well as the other kinds of changes that affect the effectiveness of filings. Most debtors, particularly those who have decided to borrow twice against the same collateral, fail to give notice nevertheless. Their failure constitutes a breach of contract, for which they will have civil liability, but that is of little concern to most debtors. If they pay their debts, their lenders won't care whether they gave notice. If they do not pay their debts, their liability for their failures to give notice of their changes of name adds nothing of consequence to their liability on the debts themselves.

The situation would be different if the failure to give notice subjected the debtor to criminal prosecution or even rendered the debt nondischargeable in bankruptcy. They do not. To impose such penalties on a debtor without proof of fraudulent intent is entirely out of keeping with legal tradition in the United States. We live in a nation founded in large part by people who did not pay their debts in the places from which they came. Our tolerance for debtor misbehavior is relatively high in relation to the tolerance shown in other cultures. In spite of this tolerance, or perhaps because of it, the U.S. economy has done relatively well. Neither the criminal nor the bankruptcy authorities are likely to get exercised about a debtor's failure to comply with a contractual obligation by giving notice of a change in circumstances.

For all these reasons, the systems created under the laws governing security in the United States are designed to function without the cooperation of the debtor. Lenders are expected to fend for themselves. B.T. Lazarus v. Christofides, 662 N.E.2d 41 (Ohio App. 1996) illustrates the kind of vigilance required. In that case, the creditor took a security interest in the assets of B.T.L. Inc. The creditor delayed the filing of its financing statement for nearly four months after the signing of the security agreement. In the period between the signing and the filing, B.T.L. Inc. changed its name to Alma Marketing, Inc. The court held the filing ineffective.

You should not conclude from our comments that filers or searchers now stalk their debtors for evidence of changes of name. Changes of name are somewhat uncommon. In most instances, either the filer or the searcher will discover them without much effort and take appropriate action. But at the same time, you should realize that the filing system has no fail-safe mechanism for dealing with name changes. Some debtors, particularly those who change their names for the purpose of defrauding their secured lenders, will succeed in borrowing from a second lender who searches, but who does not discover the first lender.

Even though the governing rules are similar, it is important to distinguish changes of name, which are covered by U.C.C. §9-507(c), from the transfer of collateral to a new debtor, which is covered by U.C.C. §9-507(a). To illustrate the potential for confusion, assume that while doing business as a sole proprietor, Teresa Williams borrowed money against the equipment of her business. If Teresa later incorporates the business under the name Williams Electronics, Inc., that is not a change of name. That is the formation of a new entity, probably followed by a transfer of the collateral from Teresa to the corporation. The governing law would be U.C.C. §9-507(a). The financing statement filed against Teresa would be effective against the collateral in the hands of Williams Electronics.

B.   Changes Affecting the Description
of Collateral

If the collateral undergoes changes in its appearance, use, or location between the time a filing is made and a search for that filing is commenced, the changes may prevent the searcher from finding the filing or realizing its relevance. To understand these changes, begin by distinguishing two kinds.

Type 1 Changes. The first, which we will call a *type 1* change, is a change in circumstances that did not control the place of filing but that does make the collateral difficult for the searcher to identify as covered by the filing. For example, assume that Firstbank's security agreement correctly describes the collateral as "Coyote Loader, serial number 8203G45," that the debtor holds the loader as inventory at the time Firstbank files its financing statement, and that the financing statement describes the type of collateral as "inventory." Firstbank is perfected. Later, the debtor begins using the loader as equipment and seeks to borrow against it from Secondbank. Secondbank's search will discover Firstbank's financing statement, but Secondbank may not realize its significance. Secondbank is lending against equipment, and the filing they discover is only against inventory.

U.C.C. §9-507(b) addresses this example. That section provides that even if the change in circumstances has made the financing statement seriously misleading, the financing statement remains effective.

Type 2 Changes. A type 2 change in circumstances is one that is sufficient to affect the method of perfection that would have been appropriate for the initial filing. For example, assume that Dawson Lumber takes a security interest in lumber it sells to Michelle Pfeiffer and perfects by filing a financing statement in the office of the secretary of state. Later, Pfeiffer uses the lumber to build a hot tub that is attached to real property in such a manner that it becomes a fixture. U.C.C. §9-507(b) excuses the now-seriously-misleading description of collateral, but it does not excuse the failure to make a fixture filing. The same would be true of a financing statement that described automobiles on a dealer's lot as "inventory." If some of the automobiles are then used as equipment, U.C.C. §9-507(b) excuses the misdescription, but not the failure to require issuance of a certificate of title noting the security interest. U.C.C. §9-311(b).

In a case that illustrates this last point, Hart, who dealt in automobiles, obtained financing from Blue Ridge Bank for an automobile intended for his own personal use. The bank properly perfected its lien by notation on the certificate of title. Hart later swapped the automobile with another auto dealer. The court held that when Hart put his automobile up for sale it became part of his inventory and the bank's perfection lapsed.

> Even if Blue Ridge Bank had properly perfected its lien during a period of time in which the vehicle was a consumer good, such a lien would not remain perfected "during any period in which [the vehicle] is inventory." See [U.C.C. §§9-311(b) and (d)]. Generally...a security interest perfected by compliance with the certificate-of-title statute "remains perfected notwithstanding a change in the use or transfer of possession of the collateral," "except as otherwise provided in subsection (d)," i.e., during any period in which the collateral is inventory. If a security interest in collateral had been properly perfected while the collateral was a consumer good and, then, subsequently, use of the collateral changed to equipment, the security interest would remain perfected. If, however, the use of the collateral changes to inventory, compliance with the certificate of title statute does not remain effective. The first phrase of [U.C.C. §9-311(d)] states that "during any period in which collateral is inventory" the certificate of title statute is

inapplicable to perfect a security interest. The phrase "during any period" contemplates that collateral may be a consumer good (or equipment or farm products)
at one point in time, during which perfection under the certificate-of-title statute
is required and effective.

Blue Ridge Bank and Trust Co. v. Hart, 152 S.W.3d 420 (2005).

C. Exchange of the Collateral

When a debtor exchanges collateral for either property or cash, the effect is to
raise many of the same kinds of issues we discussed in the preceding section.
Recall from Assignment 52 that on sale, exchange, collection, or other disposition of collateral, a security interest continues in identifiable proceeds.
U.C.C. §§9-102(a)(64) and 9-315(a)(2). The holder of the security interest
will want (1) the security interest to be perfected in the proceeds and (2)
the perfection to be continuous from the creditor's initial filing. In this section, we examine what the secured creditor must do (if anything) to accomplish those two things.

1. Barter Transactions

Barter is the exchange of one commodity for another in a transaction in which
no cash is involved. The rules in U.C.C. §9-315(d)(1) governing perfection in a
barter exchange are different from the rules governing perfection in an exchange for cash that is then used to purchase the commodity. In this subsection we discuss only the barter transaction; the rules governing perfection in
cash proceeds and proceeds acquired with cash proceeds are discussed in the
next two sections.

   To understand when secured parties must take action to perfect their interests in proceeds, distinguish three types of barters. We refer to them as *type
0, type 1, and type 2* so we can retain the numbering from the previous section.
In a type 0 barter, the proceeds received by the debtor fall within the description of collateral in the already-filed financing statement. For example, assume that the security agreement described the collateral as "Coyote Loader,
serial number 8203G45" and the financing statement, properly filed only in
the office of the secretary of state, described the type of collateral as "loader."
The debtor trades the Coyote loader for a Caterpillar loader. The security
interest attaches to the Caterpillar loader as proceeds even without a statement to that effect in the security agreement. U.C.C. §9-203(f). The security
interest is perfected in the Caterpillar loader because the description "loader"
is broad enough to encompass it. (Recall that "A financing statement may be
filed before a security agreement is made. . . ." U.C.C. §9-502(d).) After this
type 0 barter, the secured creditor has a perfected security interest in the
new collateral on the basis of the description.

   A type 1 barter is an exchange of collateral for noncash proceeds where
those proceeds are property not covered by the description in the financing
statement but are property in which a security interest could be perfected by
filing in the office where the secured creditor's financing statement is already

on file. For example, the debtor's exchange of inventory for equipment would be a type 1 barter if the original financing statement covered only inventory. The equipment is not covered by the description in the financing statement, but the filing needed to perfect in equipment as original collateral would be made in the same filing office.

In a type 1 barter transaction, the secured party remains perfected without a new filing. The rule is contained in U.C.C. §9-315(d)(1). To illustrate, assume that the financing statement covers only inventory and the debtor trades inventory for a circus elephant that will not be inventory. The secured party remains perfected in the elephant without further action. We refer to thus rule as *the same office rule*.

The same office rule has potentially interesting implications for searchers. To illustrate, assume that Firstbank takes a security interest in the debtor's inventory and files a financing statement describing the collateral as "inventory." Later, the debtor trades some inventory for an elephant. Under the rule, Firstbank remains perfected against the elephant. When Secondbank conducts a search in preparation for lending against the elephant, which we assume is clearly and obviously not inventory, Secondbank finds only a filing against inventory. If, however, Secondbank is aware of the same office rule, it will realize that Firstbank may be perfected in the elephant and know that it cannot be sure that it will have the first recorded interest in the elephant without exploring how the debtor came to own the elephant.

To generalize from this example, any time a debtor has swapped collateral, the financing statement may encumber property not described in it. Unless the searcher knows that the debtor did not acquire the collateral in question in a swap transaction, the searcher cannot rely on the description of collateral in any financing statement.

A type 2 barter is an exchange of collateral for noncash proceeds of a type in which filing is required in a filing office other than the one in which the original collateral was perfected by filing. For example, if a debtor traded a Coyote Loader that it used as equipment for an automobile and an aircraft, that would be a type 2 barter. Security interests in equipment are perfected by filing in the office of the secretary of state; security interests in automobiles are perfected by recordation on the certificate of title by the Department of Motor Vehicles; security interests in aircraft are perfected by filing with the Federal Aviation Administration in Oklahoma City.

Type 2 barters do not invoke the exception created by U.C.C. §9-315(d)(1) from the Article 9 filing requirement. To be perfected in these proceeds at all, the secured party must refile. In the case of the automobile, the new filing will be in the Department of Motor Vehicles, so that the security interest will be noted on the certificate of title. For the aircraft, the new filing will be with the FAA in Oklahoma City. To be *continuously* perfected in the two items so that it has one perfection dating from the time of the filing on the original collateral, the secured party must make these filings within 20 days from the time the debtor receives the proceeds. U.C.C. §9-315(d)(3).

The rules for type 2 barters require more vigilance on the part of the secured creditor, and, consequently, less on the part of the subsequent searcher. The secured creditor must discover the type 2 barter and perfect in the proceeds within 20 days of the debtor's receipt of them. Unless the filer is in a relationship that warrants close physical monitoring of the collateral, the filer may not learn of the exchange in time. The subsequent searcher need only realize that the debtor may have encumbered proceeds in its possession for as long as 20 days before anything shows up on the public records.

To the extent Article 9 governs, the secured party does not need any additional authorization to file the financing statement necessary to perfect in the proceeds of collateral. U.C.C. §9-509(b)(2). Were such authorization required, some debtors would refuse to give it, thereby preventing their creditors from perfecting in the proceeds. Not requiring further authorization relieves creditors of the fear that their debtors can block them from reaching the proceeds of their own collateral. It also makes it possible for aggressive secured creditors to file financing statements erroneously claiming collateral as proceeds.

The following case illustrates the effect of the opposite rule. In this case, the debtor, who had given an Article 9 security interest, exchanged the collateral for proceeds not governed by Article 9, producing unexpected consequences.

National Bank of Alaska v. Erickson
(In re Seaway Express Corporation)
912 F.2d 1125 (9th Cir. 1990)

BEEZER, CIRCUIT JUDGE.

The National Bank of Alaska (NBA) appeals a decision of the Bankruptcy Appellate Panel (BAP), granting summary judgment to Erickson, trustee in the bankruptcy of Seaway Express Corp. (Seaway). NBA claims a priority interest in property owned by Seaway. The BAP rejected NBA's claim. We affirm.

I

During 1985-86, NBA provided a line of credit to Seaway secured by a credit agreement. Under the agreement, Seaway's credit line was set as a percentage of its inventory and "eligible" accounts receivable (accounts less than 90 days old). NBA eventually loaned Seaway over $9 million, of which at least $6 million remains owing. In exchange, Seaway granted NBA a security interest in all its inventory and accounts receivable, including any "proceeds" from the sale of either (outside the normal course of business). Seaway promised not to dispose of any of its secured assets without NBA's permission.

This dispute concerns an account receivable owed to Seaway by Anchorage Fairbanks Freight Service, Inc. (AFFS). By the end of 1985, AFFS owed Seaway in excess of $1 million. The account was over 90 days old and Seaway commenced legal action to collect it. In settlement, Seaway "sold" the account back to AFFS in exchange for a parcel of real property located in Auburn, Washington (the Auburn property). NBA was aware of the proposed settlement, but did not consent or object. After the transfer had been completed, NBA asked Seaway to record a deed of trust on the property in its favor. Seaway refused.

In February, 1986, Seaway declared bankruptcy under Chapter 11. It sold the Auburn property for approximately $1 million. The funds were placed in a segregated account. Seaway's bankruptcy was subsequently converted to Chapter 7, and Erickson was appointed the bankruptcy trustee.

NBA now claims it has a priority interest in the proceeds of the sale of the Auburn property . . . as "proceeds" from the sale of the AFFS account. . . .

II

A

NBA first argues that it had a perfected security interest in the Auburn property. We disagree.

Under its credit agreement with Seaway, NBA did have a perfected security interest in the AFFS account. Under the terms of the agreement and under the UCC, this interest continued in the "proceeds" of any unauthorized sale of the account. See [U.C.C. §9-315(a)]. NBA need only perfect its interest in the proceeds within [twenty] days of the sale. [U.C.C. §9-315(c),(d)(3)]. When perfection is impossible due to the actions of the debtor, such an interest may be deemed perfected.

NBA argues that under these principles, its interest in the Auburn property should be deemed perfected. It contends that the sale of the AFFS account was not authorized and that it attempted to perfect its interest in the Auburn property but was prevented by Seaway. We reject NBA's argument.

NBA concedes that by its terms the UCC does not extend to real property. See [U.C.C. §9-109(d)(11)]. NBA cites no case in which a perfected interest in UCC-covered goods has been extended to real property. Good reasons exist not to do so here. To "perfect" an interest in real property under Washington law, a party must record a deed signed by the grantor. An unrecorded interest in property is not binding on a subsequent purchaser in good faith. Such recording statutes are central to real property law.

We agree with the BAP that NBA's perfected security interest in the AFFS account did not extend to the Auburn property. . . .

AFFIRMED.

This case serves to remind secured creditors that while the Uniform Commercial Code gives them great protection by extending their security interests to proceeds, they nonetheless must make sure those security interests in proceeds are perfected. Here, the secured creditor's problem was that the law governing real estate recording did not contain a provision like U.C.C. §9-509(b)(2) allowing the secured creditor to perfect the security interest in the property into which it could trace its proceeds. The probable reason is that real estate financing is done parcel by parcel. When the debtor sells real estate, the secured party expects to be paid off or to remain secured by the same collateral in the hands of the buyer. It does not expect to leave its loan outstanding and trace the proceeds of its collateral. To put it another way,

National Bank of Alaska does not result from legislative policy but from legislative neglect. If the designers of the real estate recording system had thought about it, they almost certainly would have adopted a provision like U.C.C. §9-509(b)(2).

2. Collateral to Cash Proceeds to Noncash Proceeds

The debtor may exchange the original collateral for money, then use the money to buy collateral. Provided it can trace its value through both transactions, the creditor's security interest will reach the new property as proceeds of proceeds. U.C.C. §9-102(a)(12) and (64). In this section we consider the circumstances under which the original filing will give the secured creditor continuous perfection that extends to the new property.

In a type 0 change, the rule remains the same as it did in a barter transaction: The original filing remains effective to cover goods of the same description. To return to our earlier example, the security agreement described the collateral as "Coyote Loader, serial number 8203G45" and the financing statement, properly filed only in the office of the secretary of state, described the type of collateral as "loader." If the debtor sold the Coyote loader for cash and took that cash to buy a Caterpillar loader, the security interest would attach to the Caterpillar loader as proceeds and then would remain perfected because the description "loader" is broad enough to encompass it. U.C.C. §9-315(d)(3).

In a type 1 change, however, the exchange results in collateral that is no longer covered by the original description in the filing statement. Consider, again, the earlier example in which the security interest covered inventory and the debtor bartered the inventory for an elephant that would serve as the company's mascot. The creditor initially perfected in the inventory would remain continuously perfected in the elephant without taking any action. Now, assume instead that the debtor sold the inventory for cash and used the cash to buy the elephant. U.C.C. §9-315(d)(3) requires that the secured party file a financing statement to cover the new collateral. Unless the secured party accomplishes that within 20 days of the debtor's receipt of the new collateral, the perfection achieved by the filing is not continuous. If the second filing occurs within 20 days of the debtor's receipt of the new property, the second filing is effective as of the date of the first filing and perfection is continuous thereafter. If the second filing occurs after the end of the 20-day period, it dates only from the time it was made.

Type 2 changes are treated like type 1 changes. Recall that in a type 2 change the new property is of a type that requires filing in a different filing office. Here, also, the secured creditor must make the new filing within 20 days of the debtor's receipt of the collateral. To modify the earlier example, if a debtor sold its Coyote Loader for cash and used the cash to buy an automobile and an aircraft, a type 2 change has occurred. To be continuously perfected in the new property, the secured party must perfect on the certificates of title for the automobile and the aircraft within 20 days of the debtor's receipt of those items. See U.C.C. §9-315(d)(3).

3.   Collateral to Cash Proceeds (No New Property)

The debtor may simply sell the original collateral and keep the cash. U.C.C. §9-315(d)(2) grants secured parties continuous, perpetual perfection in identifiable *cash proceeds*. To illustrate the application of that subsection, again assume that Firstbank has a perfected security interest in inventory. The debtor sells some of the inventory for cash and deposits the cash in its bank account at Thirdbank. The bank account is "cash proceeds." U.C.C. §9-102(a)(9). Under the rule of U.C.C. §9-315(d)(2), Firstbank will remain perfected in it even if the money sits in the bank account for months or even years.

Problem Set 62

62.1.   Helen Monette is a compliance officer at Gargantuan Bank and Trust (GBT). Her job is to monitor the collateral securing loans outstanding from the Bank. Most of her work is devoted to verifying that collateral is physically in existence, but she occasionally encounters other problems. Currently, Monette is working with Bonnie Brezhnev, owner of Bonnie's Boat World Inc. (BBW). GBT finances BBW's inventory under a financing statement that describes the collateral as "inventory, accounts, and chattel paper." The agreement contains no restrictions on BBW's ability to finance equipment or real estate elsewhere. Today Monette called you with the following list of problems:

a.   On a routine inspection of collateral, Monette discovered that, contrary to the provisions of the security agreement prohibiting the use of inventory, Bonnie kept one of the boats at her house and used it personally. Monette warned her not to do it again, but now wonders: Assuming no transfer of ownership to Bonnie personally, did the interlude have any effect on perfection of the bank's security interest? U.C.C. §§9-506(a), 9-507(b).

b.   Assume that the facts in subpart a of this problem occurred in a jurisdiction that does not issue certificates of title for boats. If Bonnie transferred ownership of the boat from her corporation to herself before she took the boat home, what evidence would exist of that fact? If Bonnie did transfer ownership of the boat to herself, is GBT still perfected? U.C.C. §9-507(a).

c.   BBW traded one of the boats for a forklift. BBW now uses the forklift to move the boats in and out of storage. Monette says she assumes the forklift is "ours" because BBW bought it with our collateral, but wonders whether we need to do anything about perfection. Do we? U.C.C. §9-315(a) and (d).

d.   Would it make any difference if BBW bought the forklift in subpart c using cash it had received from a customer who bought a new boat? U.C.C. §§9-315(a) and (d).

e.   About a month ago, two of the boats in inventory suffered severe storm damage. The security agreement provided that BBW would insure the boats against storm damage and required that GBT be named as a loss payee on the policy. BBW bought the insurance, but for some reason GBT was not named as a loss payee. Since the storm, BBW changed insurers and GBT is named as a loss payee on the new policy. Monette wonders whether GBT has a perfected security interest in the claim against the former insurer and, if not, what GBT needs to do to get one. U.C.C. §§9-109(d)(8), 9-102(a)(64), 9-315(c) and (d), 9-203(f), 9-109(a).

62.2. Recently, Monette has been monitoring GBT's inventory loan to South West Appliance Corporation. In a routine check of corporate records, Monette discovered for the first time that six months ago the debtor changed its corporate name to South West General, Inc. Does Monette need to do anything to make sure GBT remains perfected in all its collateral? U.C.C. §§9-502(a)(1), 9-503(a)(1), 9-512, 9-507(c), 9-506, 9-509(b).

62.3. Although GBT has never had formal procedures for discovering its debtors' name changes, GBT's recent loss of a name-change case has Monette thinking about adopting some procedures. She has three questions:

a. How often would she have to check the corporate records to make sure she could amend GBT's financing statements in time to avoid loss of collateral? U.C.C. §9-507(c).

b. Does a continuation statement have to include the new name of a debtor that changed its name since the original filing? U.C.C. §§9-102(a)(27), 9-512(a), 9-516(b)(3) and (5), form for Amendments in U.C.C. §9-521.

c. In the investigation of a loan applicant, how old a change of name could be relevant? U.C.C. §9-515(e).

62.4. GBT is about to lend $500,000 to Russell Lair Enterprises (RLE), which operates a small chain of army/navy surplus stores. The loan is to be secured by an interest in substantially all the debtor's assets. The U.C.C. search came back clean, except for a financing statement filed by Suti, a manufacturer of cast iron lawn dogs. The financing statement describes Suti's collateral as "lawn dogs manufactured by Suti." On Helen Monette's physical inspection of the proposed collateral, Monette found only $25,000 worth of Suti lawn dogs. GBT does not care whether the lawn dogs are included in their collateral. Unless you advise otherwise, Monette proposes to go ahead with the loan, without clearing the Suti interest or inquiring further about it. But, first, Monette wants to know: Is there any way the Suti filing could encumber more than the lawn dogs? Is there any way it could be for more than $25,000? U.C.C. §9-315.

62.5. a. You represent October National Bank. ONB lent $1 million to Beaver Manufacturing, a local concern that produces and services commercial pumping equipment. The loan documents included a security agreement and financing statement, both of which describe the collateral as "equipment, inventory, accounts, chattel paper, general intangibles, fixtures, money, and bank accounts." You estimate the total value of all collateral at about $750,000. One of Beaver's assets is a bank account at Gargantuan Bank and Trust that contains $85,097. Does ONB have a security interest in the account? U.C.C. §§9-102(a)(29) and (64), 9-109(d)(13), and 9-203(a) and (b); Comment 16 to U.C.C. §9-109.

b. If ONB has a security interest in the bank account, is it perfected? U.C.C. §§9-104, 9-312(b)(1), 9-314, and 9-315(d)(2).

c. Does it matter that some of the proceeds have been in the account for as long as 45 days? U.C.C. §§9-315(c) and (d).

d. Does it matter if Beaver commingled $100 of its own money into the GBT account? U.C.C. §9-315.

Assignment 63: Maintaining Perfection Through Relocation of Debtor or Collateral

In previous assignments, we implicitly assumed that every secured transaction occurred within the boundaries of a single state. In this assignment, we relax that assumption and address the problems inherent in using state-based filing systems to keep track of commerce that flows freely from state to state.

A. State-Based Filing in a National Economy

In Assignment 57, we introduced a theory of the filing system. The filing system is a means for a secured creditor who takes a nonpossessory security interest in property of a debtor to communicate the existence of that security interest to others who may later consider extending credit to that debtor. We noted in that assignment that there is not one, but a multitude of filing systems. For a message left in a filing system to reach the later searchers for whom it is intended, the later searchers must be able to determine the correct filing system or systems in which to look. In Assignment 57, we examined how searchers made that determination as among state and federal filing systems specialized as to the type of collateral. In this assignment, we examine how searchers make that determination as among the statewide filing systems of the 50 states and those of foreign countries.

The rules that specify where to file and search are found in U.C.C. §§9-301 to 9-307. Those rules are framed as conflicts rules that determine the law applicable to "perfection, the effect of perfection or nonperfection, and priority." Because Article 9 has been adopted in all 50 states, the rules governing "the effect of perfection or nonperfection, and priority" are the same in all 50 states. Generally speaking, it does not matter whether the law of New York or New Mexico applies, because for all practical purposes, those laws are the same. In one important respect, however, they remain different. When the law of New York applies to require the filing of a financing statement in the Office of the Secretary of State, the reference is to an office in Albany, New York. When the law of New Mexico applies, the reference is to an office in Albuquerque, New Mexico. The principal impact of the rules in U.C.C. §§9-301 to 9-307 is to tell filers and searchers the state of the secretary of state's office in which they should file or search.

The rules in U.C.C. §§9-301 to 9-307 govern perfection by possession and perfection by control as well as perfection by filing. In exploring the impact of these sections, however, we deal almost exclusively with perfection by filing. Perfection by possession and perfection by control are likely to generate few interstate problems. When these kinds of perfection occur at all, they always occur in the right state.

B.   Initial Perfection

1.   At the Location of the Debtor

U.C.C. §9-301(1) states the general rule regarding the correct state in which to file a financing statement. While a debtor is located in a state, the local law of that state governs perfection of a nonpossessory security interest. (If the security interest is possessory, the more specific provision of U.C.C. §9-301(2) would override U.C.C. §9-301(1) and impose the law of the jurisdiction in which the collateral is located.) If the law of the state applies, §9-501(a)(2) will require filing in the statewide filing office of the state for non-real estate-related collateral.

U.C.C. §9-307 contains additional provisions specifying the locations of particular kinds of debtors. An individual debtor is deemed located at the individual's "principal residence." The term is not defined in the U.C.C. It is used in tax and bankruptcy law to refer to a building rather than a jurisdiction. One need not live in the building currently for it to qualify as one's principal residence.

Black's Law Dictionary defines "residence" as "Personal presence at some place of abode with no present intention of definite and early removal and with purpose to remain for undetermined period, not infrequently, but not necessarily combined with design to stay permanently." It states that "residence implies something more than mere physical presence and something less than domicile." Finally, Black's makes this distinction between residence and domicile: Residence means living in a particular locality, but domicile means living in that locality with the intent to make it a fixed and permanent home.

A "registered organization" is "an organization organized solely under the law of one State or the United States and as to which the State or the United States must maintain a public record showing the organization to have been organized." U.C.C. §9-102(a)(70). Virtually every corporation (profit or non-profit), limited partnership, limited liability company, service corporation, or professional association will qualify. The governments granting charters to such organizations are invariably required by law to maintain the necessary public record. While a few such organizations have managed to get charters from more than one government, that is extremely rare. If New York grants a corporate charter to "Acme Enterprises, Inc." and that corporation then applies for and obtains a charter in the same name from another state, the effect is to create a second corporation with the same name, not to obtain a second charter for the same corporation.

U.C.C. §9-307(e) provides that a registered organization that is organized under the law of a state is located in that state. (The provisions of U.C.C. §9-307(b) to the contrary expressly yield to the other provisions of U.C.C.

§9-307.) Thus, for example, a Delaware corporation is located in the state of Delaware — even though it may have no offices or employees in that state, do no business in that state, and have all of its extensive operations in Texas. This feature of the new law is deliberate. Because the appropriate state in which to file depends solely on place of incorporation — a matter of public record — the proper place for filing and searching can be determined solely from the public record. Neither filer nor searcher need be concerned with the location of the debtor's collateral or operations.

Early in the Article 9 revision process, the drafters decided to adopt a system in which filing would be in the jurisdiction in which the corporate debtor had its headquarters (referred to as *debtor-based* filing). Filing at the corporate debtor's place of incorporation (*incorporation-based* filing) was initially proposed in the law review article that follows. Empirical data showing that the switch to filing at the debtor's place of incorporation would move only about $3 million a year in filing fees to Delaware from the other 49 states established the political viability of the proposal. But from a systems standpoint, the most important feature of filing at the place of incorporation was placing the U.C.C. filings against a corporate debtor in the same jurisdiction as the corporate records on that debtor. By joining the two sets of files, the secretary of state could make possible a dramatic reduction in filing errors.

Lynn M. LoPucki, Why the Debtor's State of Incorporation Should Be the Proper Place for Article 9 Filing: A Systems Analysis

79 Minn. L. Rev. 577 (1995)

Filers who desire a high level of certainty that their filing was in fact made and properly indexed often conduct a post-filing search to verify that fact. In a collateral-based system, that search will show the filer's financing statement and any effective filings made prior to it in the jurisdiction against the debtor. But that search will tell the filer little about whether the filing is in the right jurisdiction. A debtor-based system has a considerable advantage in this regard. Most filers have sufficient information about their debtors to form some sort of expectation as to how many filings there will be against them. In ordinary circumstances, all of those filings will be made in the same office. If the filer's post-filing search reveals substantially fewer or more filings than expected, the filer can decide whether to investigate further. For example, failure of a post-filing search against a debtor that should have many filings to discover many filings indicates that the filer has filed in the wrong office. I will refer to this system characteristic as the "echo effect."

An incorporation-based system can both provide a strong echo and "trap" some kinds of errors in filings. Because both the corporation records and the statewide UCC filing records would be under the control of the same Secretary of State, the Secretary could link them electronically. Each time a UCC filing would be made against a corporate debtor, the computer could match the name of the debtor to the names of the corporations formed under the laws of the state. If there were no match, the filing would be erroneous. The system could notify the filer of that fact. If there were a match, the system could display a list of filings against the debtor, the equivalent of the echo effect available in a debtor-based system.[1]

The feedback advantages of an incorporation-based system do not depend on the existence of an automatic computer link between the corporate and statewide UCC filing records. If no such link existed, the filer still could telephone the corporation division of the Secretary of State's office to make the verification.

As increasing numbers of filings are made electronically, error trapping can sharply reduce the number of errors entering the filing system. Although error trapping could not eliminate errors in which the filer mistakes one corporation for another, it could eliminate filings on which the name does not match the name of any corporation formed in the state.

Some organizations are not incorporated. They include general partnerships and a variety of associations, both for profit and not for profit. U.C.C. §9-307(b)(2) deems such a debtor located at its place of business if it has only one and U.C.C. §9-307(b)(3) deems such a debtor located at its chief executive office if it has more than one place of business. U.C.C. §9-307(a) defines "place of business" to mean "a place where a debtor conducts its affairs." Comment 2 to that section adds "Thus, every organization, even eleemosynary institutions and other organizations that do not conduct 'for profit' business activities, have a 'place of business.'"

Determining the location of an organization's "chief executive office" may not be as easy as it sounds. The concept has proven problematic in a number of other contexts, including (1) filing against mobile goods and intangible property under former Article 9, (2) locating corporations for purposes of diversity jurisdiction in the federal courts, and (3) determining proper venue for corporate bankruptcies. In those contexts, courts developed what came to be known as the "nerve center" test: the organization is located in the place from which it is managed — regardless of the location of its operations. The place from which it is managed is its "nerve center," the place from which commands originate.

That place might not be much else. To illustrate, assume that San Antonio Hotel Corporation (Hotel) owns and operates the San Antonio Hotel in Texas. Jose Sanchez, who owns 100 percent of the stock of the corporation, is the chief executive officer. He lives in Tennessee and manages the 100-room San Antonio Hotel from there. Sanchez keep the books and records on a personal computer in his home. He makes all major decisions for the business, including those regarding the hiring and firing of employees. He is in touch daily with Hector Williams, the on-site manager in Texas. On these facts, a court would be likely to hold that the chief executive office of Hotel is in Tennessee.

---

1. The echo effect is stronger in an incorporation-based system because all effective filings against a debtor will be in the same system. In a debtor-based system, uncertainty about the location of the debtor will cause significant numbers of filers to make more than one filing, leading to the possibility of a false echo.

Finally, notice that "organization" is defined to include "two or more persons having a joint or common interest." Thus, if Alice Moore and Sara Wu are two farmers who share ownership of a tractor as tenants in common, they are an organization. As their organization has more than one place of business — their two separate farms — the proper place to perfect in the tractor is at their chief executive office. (They may be surprised to hear that they have one, but they do. See U.C.C. §9-307(b)(3).) The creditor is likely to solve the problem by filing at both places of business. U.C.C. §9-307(a).

2. At the Location of the Collateral

Recall that a fixture filing must be made in "the office designated for the filing or recording of a mortgage on the real property" to which the fixture is attached. U.C.C. §9-501(a)(1). The purpose of this rule is to keep all filings against a parcel of real property or the fixtures attached to it in the same set of records in the county where the land is located. The effect is that all filings and searches regarding a particular parcel of real property can be made in a single filing system — the real property records of the county in which the land is located.

The necessary effect is that those filings must sometimes be made in a state other than the state in which the debtor is located. For example, assume that Hotel Sierra Vista, Inc., a California corporation, is the owner of a free standing walk-in freezer. Regardless of where the freezer is located, non-fixture filings against it must be made in California. If the freezer is affixed to the Hotel property in Reno, Nevada, a fixture filing against the freezer must be made in the county real estate records in Reno.

U.C.C. §§9-304 to 9-306 specify the law applicable to the perfection and priority of security interests in deposit accounts, investment property, and letters of credit. Perfection in these kinds of property is by control of the collateral rather than by filing a financing statement. U.C.C. §9-314. As a consequence, these sections can never determine the proper states in which to file financing statements. The mostly simple and sometimes complex question of where an account, investment property, or letter of credit is located is beyond the scope of this book. Finally, the proper place to file against certificate of title property is reserved to Assignment 64.

C. Relocation of the Debtor

After the secured creditor has perfected its security interest in the collateral by filing in the state in which the debtor is located, the debtor may change its location to another state. An individual debtor would accomplish that by changing his or her *principal residence.* In most cases, such a change will be obvious: The debtor sells his or her house in the original state and a moving van takes the debtor's property to a new house in the destination state. Before the move, the debtor lived and worked in the original state; after the move, the debtor lives and works in the destination state. But many relocations will not be so tidy. Debtors may simultaneously have homes in two states and move back and forth between them. A debtor may own a home in one state but live in a rented home in another. Such a debtor may intend to return to the first state, may intend to remain permanently in the second, or may intend to move to a third. One must at least sometimes be physically present in a state to have one's *principal residence* there. But if a debtor is sometimes physically present in each of two or more states, the debtor's intentions become determinative. Those intentions may be difficult to discern and may change over time.

When an individual debtor changes his or her state of principal residence, the secured creditor who filed in the original state has four months in which to file in the destination state. U.C.C. §9-316(a)(2). If the secured creditor does not, the security interest becomes unperfected. U.C.C. §9-316(b). Security agreements usually require that the debtors declare their jurisdictions of principal residence and notify the secured parties of any changes in them. Experience tells us that debtors will often fail to comply with the latter requirement — particularly debtors who are already in financial difficulty. To protect against loss of perfection, secured creditors will have to discover changes of principal residence and respond.

No legal procedure exists to permit a registered organization to change the state in which it is organized. Lawyers have, however, developed strategies for accomplishing what amounts to the same thing. To illustrate, those in control of a corporation registered in Michigan can relocate the corporation to Florida by merging it into a corporation registered in Florida. After the merger, all of the assets owned by the Michigan corporation will be owned by the surviving Florida corporation. If, as is often the case, the Florida corporation was incorporated for the specific purpose of the merger and owns no assets except those acquired through the merger, the owners of the Michigan corporation can become the sole owners of the Florida corporation. After the merger, the Florida corporation will have precisely the same assets and the same owners that the Michigan corporation had before the merger. The effect will be the same as if the Michigan corporation had been permitted to change its state of incorporation to Florida.

Another strategy for accomplishing such a *reincorporation* is to register a new organization in the destination state and then transfer all of the assets of the existing organization to the new one. Both strategies — merger and sale of assets — reach precisely the same end. Which is employed will depend on the relative costs of the two transactions. Those costs are principally transfer taxes, attorneys' fees, and the costs of giving notice to interested parties.

If a debtor reincorporates by merger or sale of assets, U.C.C. §9-316(a)(3) will apply, giving the secured creditor one year in which to discover the merger and perfect in the destination state. The secured creditor's task in discovering the relocation by merger will usually be considerably easier than the secured creditor's task in discovering relocation by sale of assets or a debtor's change of principal residence. The merger will be a matter of public record, generally in both the original and the destination states. Because articles of merger must be filed in the states of incorporation of each of the merging entities, the secured creditor can discover a merger by monitoring the record of its debtor's incorporation in the original state.

If a debtor reincorporates by sale of assets, the transaction may be more difficult for the secured creditor to discover. Consider again the Michigan corporation that seeks to relocate to Florida. The Michigan corporation causes the formation of a new Florida corporation. The Michigan corporation then transfers all of its assets to the Florida corporation in return for all of the stock of the Florida corporation, and distributes the stock to its own shareholders. The Michigan corporation has no assets, but it may continue in existence. Nothing may occur on the corporate records of Michigan that would alert the monitoring secured creditor that the Michigan corporation no longer owns the collateral.

It is important to realize that reincorporation may be an entirely paper (or paperless) transaction. There may be no change whatsoever in the physical location of the assets or the conduct of the business. The new organization may do business under the same trade name in the same location, and even have the same name on its corporate charter. The only thing that necessarily has changed is the state of organization of the entity that owns the collateral.

An unregistered organization would move from one state to another by changing the location of its chief executive office. That might be an uprooting of an entire group of people, office machines, and records, and their transfer to a new address in another state. If it is, it will be easy to spot. But it may be nothing more than a move of the *chief executive officer* from one state to another. Today there are numerous examples of organizations being run by a chief executive officer who does not work in the same state as the officer's office staff. The drafters of revised Article 9 rejected location of the chief executive office as the place for filing against registered entities in part because of the ephemeral nature of the chief executive office in modern commerce. It remains the test for unregistered entities only for lack of a better alternative.

D.   Nation-Based Filing in a World Economy

When Grant Gilmore, the original draftsman of Article 9, proposed in the 1940s that there be "one big filing system," he meant one in each state. More than a half-century later, revised Article 9 implemented his proposal by eliminating county U.C.C. filing systems (but not county real property filing systems). Gilmore's slogan of "one big filing system" has long since been adopted by others who mean by it a single filing system for the entire United States, perhaps operated by the federal government. They were not taken seriously in the drafting of revised Article 9 for precisely the reasons that Gilmore lost his battle at the county level in the 1940s — filing offices are already in place at the state level and both jobs and political power would be shifted in the move to "one big filing system." The political reality seems to be that this kind of change can occur only when the old system is so hopelessly and obviously out of date that it has become a political embarrassment.

In the meantime, secured transactions have moved from the national level to the international, and the events of the last 50 years have begun to repeat themselves with respect to countries of the world rather than states of the United States. Secured loans from institutions in one country to borrowers in another are becoming routine. Lawyers are attempting to accompany their clients as the clients go international, but lawyers in the destination countries are resisting and struggling to defend their turf. Both lawyers and policymakers have become concerned with the laws of other nations on the subject of secured transactions.

Virtually every country in the world recognizes at least some security devices. This should not be surprising, given that, as we saw in Assignment 44, security devices can be constructed from the devices of ownership, contract, and option. London attorney Philip R. Wood, who has written extensively on differences in world financial laws, identifies a group of

> about 80 English-based states [that allow] a universal monopolistic security over all the assets of the debtor which:
> [1] reaches future assets, including assets coming into existence after the bankruptcy of the debtor;
> [2] imposes few formalities;
> [3] imposes no limits on who may take the security;
> [4] permits the security to cover all future debt without stating a maximum amount; and
> [5] allows the secured creditor privately to appoint a possessory manager to run the business without selling and allows private sales.

Wood classifies the United States, except for Louisiana, and Canada, except for Quebec, as within this group. Wood classifies France as the major trading power most hostile to security; a large group of "Franco-Latin" countries as having "limited security"; and a small but important group lead by Germany, Japan, and Russia as having "moderate security." The anti-security groups "allow security over land, but make it more difficult to take security over goods, receivables, investments and contracts." Those jurisdictions do so

> by prohibiting non-possessory security and by:
> [a] imposing onerous initial formalities and unrealistic taxes;
> [b] excluding security for future debt or revolving credits;
> [c] insisting on a maximum amount [of debt to be specified in the security agreement];
> [d] downgrading the security below priority creditors so that no-one knows what it is worth; and
> [e] placing obstacles in the way of enforcement, such as judicial public auction, compulsory grace periods and freezes on enforcement.

Philip R. Wood, Maps of World Financial Law 24-25 (1997).

Requirements for public filing of notice of security interests are less common outside the United States. Where they exist, they are of all four major types: filing at the location of the collateral, filing at the location of the debtor, filing at the place of incorporation, and notation on the certificate of title.

The choice of law rule in U.C.C. §9-301(1) applies among nations as well as among states. Comment 3 to U.C.C. §9-307 gives the following example:

Example 1.   Debtor is an English corporation with 7 offices in the United States and its chief executive office in London, England. Debtor creates a security interest in its accounts. Under subsection [9-307](b)(3), Debtor would be located in England. However, subsection (c) provides that subsection (b) applies only if English law conditions perfection on giving public notice. Otherwise, Debtor is located in the District of Columbia. Under Section 9-301(1), perfection, the effect of perfection, and priority are governed by the law of the jurisdiction of the debtor's location — here, England or the District of Columbia (depending on the content of English law).

While the reporters do not give an example going the other way, we submit the following:

Example 2.   Debtor is a Delaware corporation with 7 offices in England and its chief executive office in New York. Debtor creates a security interest in its equipment, which is located in England. Under subsection 9-307(e), Debtor would be located in Delaware. Under Section 9-301(1), perfection, the effect of perfection, and priority are governed by the law of the jurisdiction of Debtor's location — here, Delaware.

Of course, England may have something to say about the equipment as well. English law provides for filing of financing statements in the corporate records, but we don't know whether that includes *foreign* corporate records. If it does, the result is a relatively smooth fit of the U.S. and English systems. Secured creditors file where the debtor is located regardless of where the collateral is located. A misfit would occur only where the "English" debtor — meaning a debtor having its chief executive office in England — happened to be incorporated in another country. If English law did not allow for filing against foreign corporations in the foreign filing systems, the misfit would be more severe and the resulting system more complex. The creditor in Example 2 would have to file in Delaware to satisfy U.S. law and in England to satisfy English law.

As international secured transactions become more common, we think the participants will become less tolerant of such misfits. They will demand international coordination that eliminates the necessity for multiple filings in a single transaction. When that occurs, the issue will be the basis for coordination. Two seem to us plausible. Requiring filing in the country where the collateral is located gives power over the form of filing to the country that already has power over the collateral, assuring that once the formalities are satisfied, the security can be enforced. Requiring filing in the country of the debtor's incorporation offers the different set of advantages described above. Ironically, the one project seeking international cooperation with regard to filing that seems likely to succeed in the near future, the Unidroit Convention Relating to the Recognition and Enforcement of Security Interests in Mobile

Equipment, adopts neither of these approaches. Instead, it proposes to add yet another filing system devoted only to a narrow class of collateral.

Finally, it should be noted that revised Article 9 does not purport to reorder the world's filing systems. Although the text places no express limits on its application, Comment 3 to U.C.C. §9-307 notes:

> The foregoing discussion assumes that each transaction bears an appropriate relation to the forum State. In the absence of an appropriate relation, the forum State's entire UCC, including the choice-of-law provisions in Article 9 will not apply.

Problem Set 63

63.1. You have been assigned to file financing statements on behalf of your client, Firstbank, in connection with a loan in the amount of $250,000 to William Shatner, an inventor and professor of engineering. The collateral is the equipment, accounts, and inventory of Shatner Engineering, a small business located in Tucson, Arizona, that Shatner started before he began teaching. Shatner remains the sole owner of the business. Shatner's ex-wife, Louise Godfrey, runs the business on a day-to-day basis in return for a salary and a share of the profits, but Shatner himself makes all the big decisions. Shatner has a "permanent," tenured job at the University of Missouri in Kansas City. The school is in Missouri, three miles from the Kansas-Missouri state line. Shatner lives in an apartment on the Kansas side of the line, but is hunting for a house nearer the school — probably on the Missouri side of the line. During the summers, Shatner returns to the home he owns just outside of Tucson and spends his days working on the business. A friend of yours who knows Shatner well says Shatner intends to quit teaching in a few years, move to Hawaii, and operate the business from there. U.C.C. §§1-201(28) (Rev §1-201(b)(25)), 9-102(a)(28), 9-301, 9-307, 9-503(a)(4), 9-506(c), and Comment 2 to U.C.C. §9-307.

   a.   On the foregoing facts, in what states should you file?

   b.   What debtor names should be listed on each of the filings?

   c.   You just learned that three years ago Shatner formed a Nevada corporation under the name Shatner Engineering Products, Inc. Now where do you file?

   d.   Contrary to the facts initially given you, the business is unincorporated and Louise owns a one-third interest as a tenant in common. In what states should you file? What names should be listed on each of the filings?

63.2. a. What, if anything, should Firstbank do to monitor the location of these debtors? U.C.C. §9-316(a) and (b).

   b.   How would your answer change if the loan were for $25 million?

63.3.   Your client, Global Bank, is lending $1.9 million to Tang Aluminum Products to purchase the inventory, equipment, accounts, and general intangibles of Argon, Inc. The Bank will, of course, expect to receive a first security interest in those assets. You have been assigned to do the U.C.C. searches. What inquiries will you make? In what names will you search? In what filing systems? U.C.C. §§9-301(1), 9-307(a)-(e), 9-316(a), 9-507(a), and Comment 3 to U.C.C. §9-507.

63.4. Assume that Afghanistan law gives priority to the first security interest created and that the country has no filing system. Firstbank loans $1 million to Afghan, Inc., an Afghanistan corporation whose headquarters and operations are all in New York. Where is Firstbank required to file a financing statement? U.C.C. §§9-301, 9-307(b), (c), and (e), and Comment 3 to U.C.C. §9-307.

63.5. You are working for a politically connected firm in Wilmington, Delaware that does a lot of corporate work, including big bankruptcy cases that come from all over the United States. Carol Lynn Murphy, the youngest partner in the firm, explains that the firm got its start in the 1920s shortly after Delaware replaced New Jersey as the jurisdiction of choice for the incorporation of large public companies. The firm got a big boost in the early 1990s when the Delaware Bankruptcy Court began attracting the bankruptcy reorganization cases of those same large public companies. Today, Delaware is the place of incorporation for somewhere over half of all large public companies and the venue for somewhere over half of the bankruptcies of large public companies. Now that Article 9 provides for filing at the place of incorporation, Murphy envisions a third wave of prosperity for Delaware and the firm. The new law will bring only about $3 million in new filing fees to the state and the private profits from the increase in filing and searching activity will mostly be captured by service companies. But Murphy thinks there may yet be a gold mine in revised Article 9.

a. Murphy asks what you think would happen on the following facts. The other 49 states and the District of Columbia retain Article 9 as promulgated, but Delaware adopts a non-uniform amendment that excuses filing altogether. The Delaware law simply declares all security interests "perfected without filing." Cherokee, Inc., a Delaware corporation whose assets and operations are all located in New York, borrows money from a New York bank and grants the New York bank a security interest. The New York bank does not file a financing statement. A year later, Cherokee, Inc. files under Chapter 11 of the Bankruptcy Code in New York and seeks to avoid the New York bank's security interest as unperfected. U.C.C. §§9-301(1), 9-307.

b. Would a law that successfully excused some or all U.C.C. filings make Delaware a more or less attractive place for debtors to incorporate? Murphy notes a study by attorney Meredith Jackson, reported in Alces, Abolish the Article 9 Filing System, 79 Minn. L. Rev. 679, 690-691 (1995), indicating that the costs of filing and searching average about $25,000 for loans averaging in the range of $20 million to $70 million.

Assignment 64: Maintaining Perfection in Certificate of Title Systems

Each of the 50 states maintains a certificate of title system for motor vehicles. In each state, a motor vehicle certificate of title act enacted by the legislature governs that system. The most widely adopted certificate of title act is the Uniform Motor Vehicle Certificate of Title and Anti-theft Act (UMVCTA), which has been adopted in 11 states. In most states, a department with the name Department of Motor Vehicles, or something similar, operates the motor vehicle certificate of title system. We will refer to it as "the Department."

For the purpose of inclusion in this system, "motor vehicle" is defined as "a device in, upon, or by which a person or property is or may be transported or drawn upon a highway, except a device moved by human power or used exclusively upon stationary rails or tracks." UMVCTA §1(n). In other words, "motor vehicle" includes cars, trucks, buses, motorcycles, mobile homes, and the like. It does not include bicycles, trains, boats, or aircraft, even though some of these are vehicles that have motors.

For each motor vehicle in a system, the Department maintains a *certificate* that describes the vehicle and shows who owns it. When the system functions properly, there is one and only one certificate of title for any motor vehicle. A copy of a certificate appears later in this assignment. A certificate of title identifies the vehicle by Vehicle Identification Number (VIN), make, and model. It also identifies the owner and the holders of any liens against the vehicle by name and address. On the back of a certificate of title there is usually a form for transferring ownership of the vehicle.

Certificates of title are part of a complex system that serves a variety of purposes, most unrelated to secured credit. Certificates of title are part of the system by which the police identify the owner of a vehicle that is involved in an accident, lost, stolen, or used in the commission of a crime. Certificates of title are also used to transfer ownership of motor vehicles and to keep track of successive annual registrations and taxation of vehicles.

The reason we include an assignment dealing with certificates of title in this course is that for most kinds of property covered by a certificate of title, the face of the certificate is the proper place to record any security interest. (In certificate of title systems, security interests are referred to as *liens* and filing is referred to as *notation of the lien on the certificate of title*.) In all states, the certificate of title system is physically separate from the Uniform Commercial Code (UCC) filing system. Several states also maintain a separate certificate of title system for motorboats and/or mobile homes but those that do keep the boat and mobile home systems physically separate from the motor vehicle system.

FIGURE 64.1.
Sample Certificate of Title

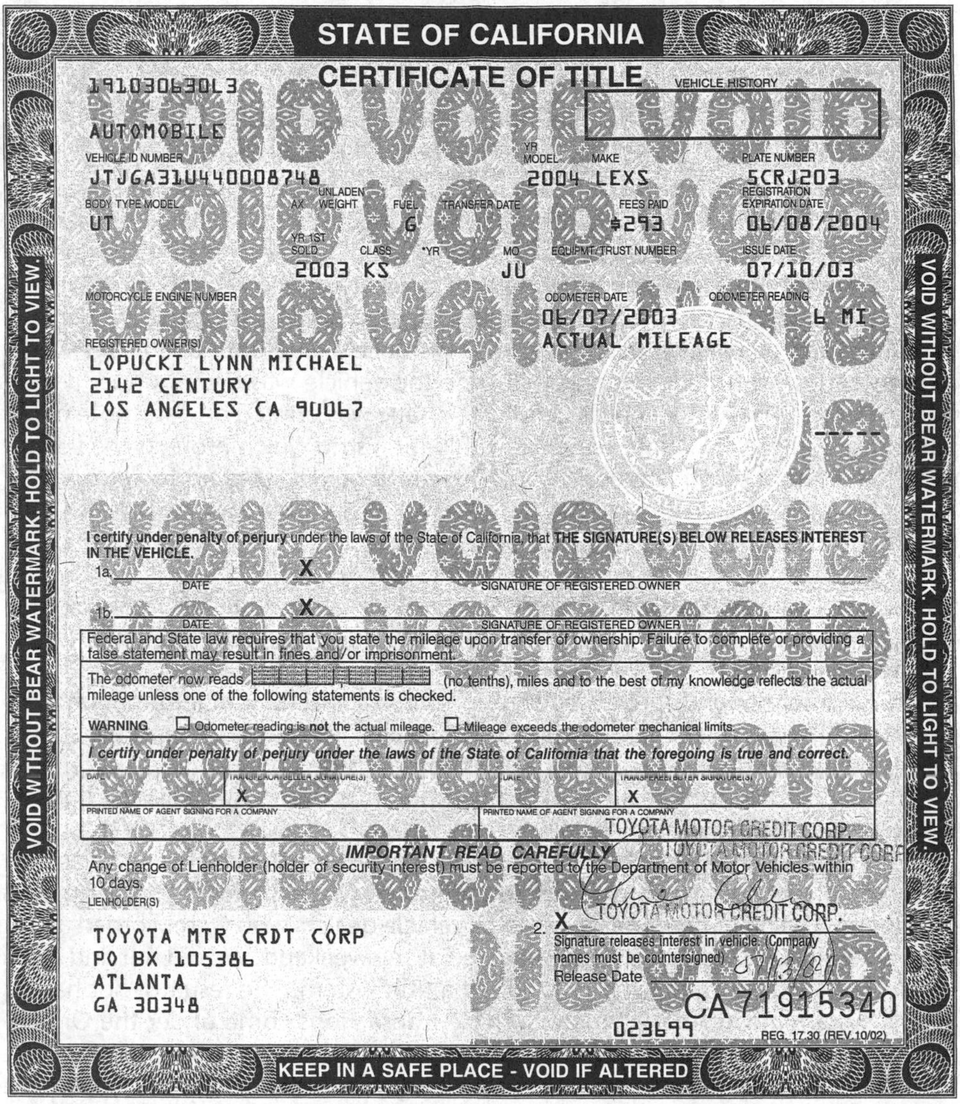
STATE OF CALIFORNIA
CERTIFICATE OF TITLE

1910306301L3 VEHICLE HISTORY
AUTOMOBILE

VEHICLE ID NUMBER	YR MODEL	MAKE	PLATE NUMBER
JTJGA31U440008748	2004	LEXS	5CRJ203

BODY TYPE MODEL	AX	UNLADEN WEIGHT	FUEL	TRANSFER DATE	FEES PAID	REGISTRATION EXPIRATION DATE
UT			G		$293	06/08/2004

YR 1ST SOLD	CLASS	YR	MO	EQUIPMT/TRUST NUMBER	ISSUE DATE
2003	KS		JU		07/10/03

MOTORCYCLE ENGINE NUMBER	ODOMETER DATE	ODOMETER READING
	06/07/2003	6 MI
	ACTUAL MILEAGE	

REGISTERED OWNER(S)
LOPUCKI LYNN MICHAEL
2142 CENTURY
LOS ANGELES CA 90067

I certify under penalty of perjury under the laws of the State of California, that THE SIGNATURE(S) BELOW RELEASES INTEREST IN THE VEHICLE.

1a. ______ X ______
DATE SIGNATURE OF REGISTERED OWNER

1b. ______ X ______
DATE SIGNATURE OF REGISTERED OWNER

Federal and State law requires that you state the mileage upon transfer of ownership. Failure to complete or providing a false statement may result in fines and/or imprisonment.

The odometer now reads ______ (no tenths), miles and to the best of my knowledge reflects the actual mileage unless one of the following statements is checked.

WARNING ☐ Odometer reading is not the actual mileage. ☐ Mileage exceeds the odometer mechanical limits.

I certify under penalty of perjury under the laws of the State of California that the foregoing is true and correct.

DATE	TRANSFEROR/SELLER SIGNATURE(S)	DATE	TRANSFEREE/BUYER SIGNATURE(S)
	X		X
PRINTED NAME OF AGENT SIGNING FOR A COMPANY		PRINTED NAME OF AGENT SIGNING FOR A COMPANY	TOYOTA MOTOR CREDIT CORP.

IMPORTANT READ CAREFULLY
Any change of Lienholder (holder of security interest) must be reported to the Department of Motor Vehicles within 10 days.

LIENHOLDER(S)
TOYOTA MTR CRDT CORP
PO BX 105386
ATLANTA
GA 30348

TOYOTA MOTOR CREDIT CORP
2. X TOYOTA MOTOR CREDIT CORP.
Signature releases interest in vehicle. (Company names must be countersigned)
Release Date 07/13/04

CA 71915340
023699
REG. 17.30 (REV. 10/02)

VOID WITHOUT BEAR WATERMARK. HOLD TO LIGHT TO VIEW.
KEEP IN A SAFE PLACE - VOID IF ALTERED

In the United States, security interests are perfected by notation on the certificate of title in all but a few states. In Canada, security interests in motor vehicles are filed in the personal property registration systems of the province (the equivalent of the Article 9 filing system in each state in the United States). There are no certificates of title for automobiles. In the late 1980s, New Zealand's Law Commission considered whether New Zealand should adopt a certificate of title system like that of the United States or permit perfection of security interests in motor vehicles by filing financing statements in the personal property filing system, as is done in Canada. The Commission sent a delegation to study and compare the U.S. and Canadian systems firsthand. The following excerpt is from their report:

New Zealand Law Commission,
Motor Vehicle Title Systems in
the USA and Canada

Preliminary Paper No. 6 (1988)

We give as an example of a Certificate of Title jurisdiction, Illinois. In Illinois, which has had such a system since the 1920s, the motor vehicle title system is a substantial operation with a large computer entry and checking staff. This seemed to be bigger than the registry staff for the whole Personal Property Security Registry in Toronto. The volume of new titles was approximately three million per year and on the day of our visit 27,000 new titles were issued. Many of these were updates of old titles where a transfer of ownership or change in a security interest had occurred. We were informed that the registry had 65 to 70 people working in two shifts and at present was not able to produce a title until about 3-4 weeks after a request was made. During that time the vehicle was driven under a temporary permit. The motor vehicle certificate of title was printed on bank note paper which was difficult to counterfeit and a lamination strip which protects the vehicle information from being altered, allows changes to be detected under retro-reflective light and is of such a form that the removal of the lamination will destroy the information. Before these security features were introduced, several hundred counterfeit or altered titles were discovered each year in Illinois. Since June 1978 when the security features were introduced there has been a continual decrease in counterfeit and altered titles. In addition to Certificates of Title there are separate certificates for junking and salvage.

Vehicle information is processed through the National Crime Information Center and LEADS Hot Check to determine whether a vehicle has been reported stolen. This is not entered on the register itself. Thousands of stolen vehicles have been identified since the implementation of a computerized title system. Illinois has had a title system for motor vehicles since the 1920s.

In the Canadian provinces there are no title systems for motor vehicles. We understand that such a system was considered in Ontario in the 1950s but was rejected as a result of pressure from motor vehicle dealers who were worried about being unable to confer title in a sale effected at the weekend. We did not find this a very convincing reason for the rejection of a title system. The result of not having such a system means that all motor vehicle transactions come under the Ontario Act. In Ontario over 90% of all transactions recorded under the Ontario Act are concerned with motor vehicles or the financing of motor vehicles or dealers. We understand that a similar proportion would apply in the other provinces.

Compared with this a title system takes the pressure off the Article 9 system. In the Article 9 registry in Illinois 600-700 financing statements were filed daily. There were two people working full time entering particulars on the computer and dealing with searches. The system had been computerized in 1972.

There was little doubt to us that the title system seemed to work well in practice and ease the pressure off the Article 9 system, as well as providing prospective purchasers of motor vehicles with notice of security interests without the need to undertake a search. This was due to the degree of specialization involved and in keeping the bulk of motor vehicles transactions off the Article 9 registry. The Canadian provinces have to contend with motor vehicles and a variety of other transactions. There is at the same time also a greater degree of uncertainty regarding the title to motor vehicles in Canadian provinces. While the problems concerned with title are cut down by a Personal Property Security Act they are not eliminated, because, though security interests can be ascertained from the register, the identity of the owner is not itself recorded. However, the ability to obtain searches of motor vehicles by reference either to the debtor or the identification number of the vehicle reduces this shortcoming somewhat.

The optimal system seems to us to be to have a title system for motor vehicles separate from an Article 9 system.

We estimate that new car financing alone results in about 12 million notations on certificates of title annually. That is about four times the number of initial U.C.C. financing statements filed annually.

Why then do certificate of title systems receive so little attention in law school courses in secured transactions? (At one of 27 assignments devoted to secured transactions a larger portion of this text than most others is devoted to certificates of title.) In part, it is because Article 9, as the product of an earlier generation of legal academics, has a certain cachet in legal academic circles. The motor vehicle certificate of title acts have far less lustrous histories. In part, certificate of title acts receive relatively little attention because the subject is narrow, the transactions routine, and the amounts of money in issue relatively modest. Although there is a small, steady flow of litigation emanating from the certificate of title system, the system has worked more smoothly than Article 9 and produced fewer problems.

Reference to this system as a "certificate of title" system implies that the certificate — the piece of paper issued by the state to the filer — has special importance such as that accorded negotiable instruments or documents. In a few states one can achieve some limited perfection merely by noting the lien on this piece of paper without sending the paper to the state. But with that minor exception, the implication is false. To perfect, the secured creditor must deliver to the Department its application for notation of its lien on the certificate of title.

The certificate for an automobile, motorboat, or mobile home does not control disputes over ownership of a vehicle. It is prima facie evidence of ownership, but if ownership is with a person other than the person shown on the certificate, the certificate is no impediment to proof of that fact. Owner liability statutes adopted in many states make the owner of a motor vehicle liable for the negligence of any person operating it with permission. But the "owner" for this purpose is the true owner, not the person whose name appears on the certificate of title as the owner. Thus, where *A* sells her car to *B*, turns over possession, but does not execute a transfer of the certificate of title so that the certificate remains in *A*'s name, *B* is nevertheless generally treated as the owner.

The certificate has similarly little direct importance in granting and perfecting security interests in motor vehicles. A security interest can be granted by any writing; it need not be noted on the certificate of title to be valid. As will be discussed shortly, strictly speaking, perfection is accomplished not by notation on either the owner's or the Department's copy of the certificate, but by application to the Department of Motor Vehicles for such a notation.

When an issued certificate of title differs from the Department's record of that certificate, the Department's record generally controls. The certificate of title system is best regarded as a filing system, closely analogous to the Article 9 filing system.

The certificate of title system has two principal advantages over the Article 9 system. First, the certificate of title system contains title as well as lien information. Searchers in the Article 9 system must determine from off-record sources who is the owner of the collateral they propose to finance. If they finance collateral not owned by their debtor, the true owner can reclaim it from them. In a certificate of title system, as in a real estate system, the chain of title is on the public record. A searcher can trace the debtor's title back to its source.

Probably the most important advantage of the certificate of title system is that each item of collateral is identified by two numbers. Every vehicle registered in a state has a license plate number that is unique within the state. Every vehicle also has a vehicle identification number (VIN) assigned at the time of manufacture and unique within the entire United States. Keep in mind that the ultimate purpose of nearly every search of a filing system is ultimately not to determine whether a particular *debtor* has filings against it, but to determine whether particular *collateral* has filings against it. In the Article 9 filing system, searches are conducted by the name of the debtor only because they cannot be conducted by an item of collateral. If an item of collateral has had more than one owner, the searcher must search under the name of each, with the result that multiple searches may be necessary to locate filings against a single item of collateral. The process of discovering former owners is imprecise, which means that Article 9 searching is imprecise as well. Conducting a search by a unique number assigned to the collateral, as can be done in a certificate of title system, eliminates the complexity and uncertainty of using the owner's (debtor's) name. Starting with the VIN number, the license number, *or* the name of the current owner, a searcher can immediately locate the certificate. On it will be every current piece of information in the system that relates to the particular vehicle.

Despite the powerful advantages of certificate of title systems, use is not likely to spread to very many kinds of collateral. To operate a certificate of title system, each item of collateral must be assigned a unique number. What made it worth doing this for motor vehicles was not the convenience of a smoothly operating filing system for security interests, but the vulnerability of motor vehicles to theft. Once the numbering system was adopted to control theft, the filing system simply took advantage of it.

The principal weakness of a certificate of title system is in its inability to deal with the addition of parts to, or the removal of parts from, the "whole" — that is, the object, such as the car or the boat, that is the subject of the system. This weakness restricts the use of certificate of title systems to objects, such as cars or boats, that are likely to remain essentially intact throughout their useful lives. The issues that arise when parts are added to or removed from collateral subject to a certificate of title are discussed in section B of this assignment.

A. Perfection in a Certificate of Title System

Article 9 applies to transactions that create security interests, and to the security interests thus created, in automobiles, boats, mobile homes, and other property subject to certificate of title systems. U.C.C. §9-109(a). However, U.C.C. §§9-311(a)(2) and (3) provide that "the filing of a financing statement otherwise required by this Article is not necessary or effective to perfect a security interest in property subject to [listed certificate of title statutes of this state]" or "a certificate of title statute of another jurisdiction under the law of which indication of a security interest on the certificate is required as a condition of perfection."

The certificate of title act specifies what the secured party must do to perfect. While these acts vary somewhat in their requirements, most are similar to the UMVCTA. UMVCTA §20 provides:

> A security interest is perfected by the delivery to the Department of the existing certificate of title, if any, an application for a certificate of title containing the name and address of the lienholder and the date of his security agreement and the required fee [and registration card]. It is perfected as of the time of its creation if the delivery is completed within ten (10) days thereafter, otherwise, as of the time of the delivery.

Notice that perfection occurs under this provision at the same moment it occurs under U.C.C. §§9-516(a) and 9-308(a), the moment when the filing officer receives the documents and the filing fee. UMVCTA §20 differs in two respects. First, the filing must include the existing certificate of title, if any. For the lien holder who anticipates the problem, unavailability of the certificate is not a serious problem. If the certificate is "lost, stolen, mutilated or destroyed or becomes illegible" the owner or legal representative of the owner is entitled to a replacement. Departments generally will accept both the application for a new title and the application for a lien on that title at the same time. Second, once made, the notation on the certificate of title relates back not just to the filing officer's receipt of the application but to the time of creation of the security interest. This second difference may soon disappear. The Legislative Note at the end of U.C.C. §9-311 advises that states with UMVCTA-type relation-back periods should amend their motor vehicle statutes to eliminate them.

When the Department issues a new certificate of title noting the existence of the lien, it mails the certificate to the secured party rather than to the debtor. UMVCTA §21(d). Until the lien is satisfied, only the secured party (whose name and address are shown on the face of the Department's copy of the certificate) has the right to apply for and obtain a duplicate certificate. UMVCTA §13. Ideally, this would make it impossible for a debtor to obtain release of the lien without the signature of the secured party. In fact, debtors or thieves sometimes manage to obtain "clean" certificates (that is, certificates showing no liens) from the Department where the lien is recorded or from the Department of another state. The erroneous issue of these certificates generates most of the litigation in this area.

Multiple liens against the same collateral pose a special problem in a certificate of title system. Assume that Ozzie Owner granted a security interest in his new Lexus to Firstbank. Later, Ozzie decides to grant a second interest to Larry Lender, who will loan him another $1,000. Larry's application for notation of his lien on the certificate must be accompanied by the existing certificate. But Ozzie, the person to whom he is lending the money, doesn't have the certificate. Firstbank has placed it in their vault for safekeeping. The solution is in UMVCTA §21(c). Larry makes application for notation of his lien on the certificate and gives it to Firstbank. Firstbank is then obligated to send the application and the certificate to the Department for processing. The Department issues a new certificate showing both liens and sends it to Firstbank, the holder of the first lien. UMVCTA §21(d).

The theoretical problems with such a system are numerous. Firstbank might refuse to forward the application because it doubts the authenticity of Larry's lien. Firstbank might have no doubts about authenticity, but might just be slow in sending the certificate. Firstbank might also go to the other extreme, releasing Larry's lien without Larry's authorization. Fortunately for the certificate of title system, such problems seldom arise in practice. Second and subsequent liens against motor vehicles are relatively uncommon. In fact, some states will record no more than two liens on the certificate because that is all that will fit on the form they use.

Searches can be requested by mail or, in most states, online. They can be by license number, VIN number, or owner's (debtor's) name. A few states prohibit name searches to prevent unwarranted invasions of privacy. Information on how to conduct searches in all 50 states is published by BRB Publications, Inc., in The MVR Book Motor Services Guide (2005).

B. Accessions and Removals

Just as personal property can be affixed to real property, creating a fixtures problem, one item of personal property can be affixed to another, creating an *accessions* problem. The accessions problem can occur with regard to property not covered by a certificate of title. For example, when the motor breaks on an industrial machine, the owner may repair the machine by installing a new motor. The new motor is an accession. The accessions problem causes the most difficulty, however, with regard to property covered by certificate of title systems. The certificate issued in a certificate of title system implicitly assumes that the collateral is a whole and is mortgaged as such; the certificate of title is not designed to deal with the possibility of mortgages against particular parts of that whole.

Examples of accessions to certificate of title property include radio equipment installed in an aircraft after it is sold by the manufacturer, the new tires installed on a car when the old ones wear out, or the camper top installed on the back of a pickup truck. In the typical accessions case, one creditor has lent against the accession while another has lent against the item to which it is affixed (referred to as the *whole*). The creditor secured by the accession, who may even be a purchase-money financier who perfected before the collateral was affixed, will expect to have priority in the accession over the creditor secured by the whole. In fact, *not* to give the accession-secured creditor priority would enable debtors to routinely defeat security interests just by affixing the collateral to a whole financed at some earlier time.

On the other hand, when a creditor secured by a car or truck repossesses its collateral, it does not expect accession-secured parties thereafter to strip the vehicle of its CB radio, let alone the tires, the engine, or the headlights. Yet in a system where accession lenders have priority, that might be a common occurrence. A repossessed car might look exactly like it did the day the secured creditor financed it, but the creditor's security interest might be subordinate to the suppliers of most of the parts. The creditor secured by the whole might well argue that this result too is absurd; a car lender cannot be expected to monitor repairs.

Just as with fixture problems, the courts that resolve accession problems divide affixed property into three categories: (1) that which is not sufficiently related to the whole to be considered part of it and therefore not an accession (e.g., a spare tire); (2) that which is so integrated into the whole that it is part of the whole for financing purposes (e.g., the mixer on the back of a cement truck); and (3) accessions, the property in between that is sufficiently affixed to be reached by a security interest in the whole, but not sufficiently integrated that it can no longer be the subject of separate financing (e.g., automobile tires).

Reexamine the certificate of title shown earlier in this assignment and you will see that it contemplates liens against the car but not against particular parts of the car. If secured parties are shown on the certificate, it is presumed that they have security interests in the entire car. There is no place for recording liens that cover only the radios, custom cabs, or motors. The accession-secured party can perfect its interest in the accession by filing in the Article 9 filing system, but probably only if it does so before the collateral becomes an accession. If perfection in an already-attached accession in the Article 9 system could defeat perfection in the whole in the certificate of title system, the creditor taking a security interest in property covered by a certificate of title statute would have to search in both systems. That may be why U.C.C. §9-311(a)(2) provides that "the filing of a financing statement . . . is not effective to perfect a security interest in property subject to [a certificate of title statute]."

U.C.C. §9-335(d) gives a security interest in the whole perfected by compliance with a certificate of title statute priority over a security interest in an accession to that whole — regardless of the order in which the two security interests were perfected and even though the security interest in the accession attached and became perfected before the accession was affixed and before the security interest in the whole was created. U.C.C. §9-335(e) bars the holder of the subordinate accessions interest from enforcing it, rendering it virtually worthless. To illustrate, assume that GMAC finances Dolly's purchase of a new automobile and perfects by notation on the certificate of title. After the warranty on the car expires, it becomes necessary to replace the engine. Joe's Garage sells Dolly a new engine on credit, takes a security interest in it, and perfects before installing the engine in the car. Under U.C.C. §9-335(d),

GMAC has the first security interest in the car, including the new engine. Joe's Garage has a second security interest in the engine. If Dolly fails to pay Joe's Garage, Joe's Garage cannot foreclose against or repossess the car, because it does not have a security interest in it. Joe's Garage cannot foreclose against or repossess the engine, because it does not have "priority over the claims of every person having an interest in the whole." U.C.C. §9-335(e). On a literal reading of the statute, this would be true even if the car were of sufficient value to satisfy both liens. What *can* Joe's Garage do? It can hope that GMAC will eventually force a sale of the property. If GMAC does, Joe's Garage can then make a claim against any proceeds of sale in excess of the obligation owing GMAC. Alternatively, Joe's Garage can sue as an unsecured creditor. Presumably, the same result would obtain if Joe's Garage sold the engine to Dolly under a contract that prohibited installment in a whole.

U.C.C. §9-335 facilitates the financing of automobiles, aircraft, boats, and other certificate of title property as wholes, and effectively makes it impossible to finance accessions — such as radio equipment or custom cabs — separately. The effect will be to favor those who mass-produce and finance standard units at the expense of those who attempt to customize them. The biggest losers will be those who finance items not intended to be used as accessions, but that are. Under U.C.C. §9-335, any secured creditor whose non-certificate of title collateral is affixed to some other secured creditor's certificate of title collateral effectively loses its interest.

C.   In What State Should a Motor Vehicle Be Titled?

The manufacturer of each motor vehicle assigns it a unique VIN number. The manufacturer also issues a *certificate of origin* for the vehicle, which contains both the make and model of the vehicle and the VIN number. While the certificate of origin functions in some respects like a certificate of title, a security interest cannot be perfected by notation on the certificate of origin. Instead, while a motor vehicle is inventory in the hands of a manufacturer or dealer, the certificate of title statute is inapplicable. UMVCTA §2(a)(2). Perfection of a security interest in the inventory of a car dealer is accomplished by filing a financing statement, U.C.C. §9-311(d), in the state where the car dealer is incorporated, U.C.C. §§9-301(1), 9-307(e).

Upon sale of the motor vehicle to the first user, the dealer delivers the certificate of origin. That user makes application for the first certificate of title based on the certificate of origin. UMVCTA §4. Once the certificate of title is issued, liens against the motor vehicle can be perfected only by notation on the certificate of title, except while the vehicle is owned by a used car dealer.

In what state should the vehicle be titled? UMVCTA §4(a) answers with the statement that "every owner of a vehicle which is in this state and for which no certificate of title has been issued by [this state] shall make application...for a certificate of title of the vehicle." Obviously, this statute cannot be read literally, or it might require two applications when a resident of Texarkana goes out for a cup of coffee. UMVCTA §2(a)(3) may at first glance seem to require titling in a state only if the owner is a resident of the state, but that section protects nonresidents only with regard to vehicles "not required by law to be registered in this state." A combination of case and statutory law requires registration of the vehicles of nonresidents when the nonresidents acquire regular places of abode in the state or use the vehicles in connection with a business in the state for more than a period established by the state. Those periods range from about 30 to 90 days in various states. Merely because a motor vehicle is supposed to be registered in the state does not necessarily mean that it is supposed to be titled there, but it usually does mean that.

The case reporters are full of cases in which owners titled their vehicles in states that are clearly inappropriate. Often, the motivation is to pay registration fees or sales tax in a state that charges a lower rate. These owners may be subject to fines or penalties levied by the state in which they should have titled the car. But the fact that their certificate of title is from the wrong state does not prevent it from being the proper place for a creditor to note the existence of its lien. Perfection can be lost when an owner obtains a second title, but in no case has a security interest in an automobile been held unperfected because the owner obtained the only certificate from the wrong state. See U.C.C. §9-303(a).

The point is illustrated in Hoffman v. Associates Commercial Corp., 228 B.R. 70 (1998). That case involved a truck that was garaged in Connecticut and used for transport between Connecticut and New York. Connecticut law required that the owner obtain a Connecticut title. Instead, the owner obtained a Maine title. Maine law authorizes the issuance of titles for vehicles that have no relationship to the state, and charges reduced fees and taxes. Perhaps not surprisingly, it has become a truck-title haven. (Titling in Maine is undoubtedly the "contemporary business practice" referred to in Comment 2 to U.C.C. §9-303.) The secured creditor perfected by notation on the Maine title. The debtor filed bankruptcy and the trustee challenged the secured creditor's perfection. The court noted that "[a]n owner's failure to register a vehicle required to be registered in Connecticut is an infraction. An owner's illegal conduct — not registering to avoid paying fees and taxes in Connecticut — does not, however, unperfect a creditor's otherwise validly perfected lien."

D.   Motor Vehicle Registration

Each of the 50 states levies a license tax on automobiles. Except as otherwise provided in reciprocity agreements, within some period after becoming a resident of a state or bringing a car into the state as a nonresident, the owner is required to *register* the car in the state. The owner pays the tax, obtains license plates (tags) from the state, and displays them on the vehicle as proof of payment of the tax and to identify the vehicle.

FIGURE 64.2.
Sample Vehicle Registration

The registration system in large part duplicates the function of the certificate of title system. A certificate of registration contains much the same information that appears on a certificate of title.

There are, however, some important differences between the two systems. First, liens cannot be perfected by notation on a certificate of registration. Second, the certificate of title system exists to keep track of ownership and liens, while the registration system exists to identify vehicles on the street and collect taxes. A vehicle should have only one certificate of title but may be required to have certificates of registration from every state in which the vehicle is operated. (Occasionally, you will see a semi-trailer truck on the highway displaying tiny license plates from as many as 20 states.) Third, not every movement of a motor vehicle that necessitates registration in the destination state also necessitates titling in the destination state. A motor vehicle can sometimes properly be titled in one state and registered in another. See UMVCTA §11.

E.   Maintaining Perfection on Interstate Movement of Collateral

1.   How It Is Supposed to Work

Marjorie Murphy, a resident of California who lives and works in California, owns a Toyota that is titled in that state. She still owes $10,000 on the car to the Upper Castro State Bank (UCSB). UCSB's lien is noted on the California certificate of title and the title is in the bank's vault. Murphy finds a better job in Georgia and makes the move, taking her car with her.

Georgia's version of the UMVCTA requires that Murphy make application to the Georgia Department of Motor Vehicles for a Georgia title and registration. UMVCTA §4(a). Murphy visits the web site of the Georgia Department and prints the forms. UMVCTA §6(c)(1) requires that Murphy's Georgia application be accompanied by her California certificate of title. Because UCSB has possession of the certificate, Murphy calls the Bank to ask for its cooperation. The Bank agrees to cooperate. UMVCTA §21(c). At the Bank's request, Murphy mails the application and fee, and the Bank forwards it with the certificate of title to the Georgia Department. UCSB's cover letter asks the Georgia Department to reflect UCSB's lien on the new certificate and to send the certificate directly to the Bank.

Upon receipt of the completed application, the Georgia Department issues a Georgia certificate of title with UCSB's lien noted on it. UMVCTA §9(a)(3). They keep the old California certificate of title on file and mail the new Georgia certificate of title to UCSB. UMVCTA §10. They mail the license plate and certificate of registration directly to Murphy. Using a flat-head screwdriver, Murphy attaches the license plate to the rear of her Toyota (Georgia uses only one license plate), puts the certificate of registration in the glove compartment, and the process is complete.

2. Some Things That Can Go Wrong

If the certificate of title systems worked the way they are supposed to, there would be one and only one certificate of title for each motor vehicle. The searcher would need only examine the face of that certificate to determine who had liens and as of what date those liens were perfected.

There are, however, three kinds of problems that commonly occur. The first is when a lien-laden certificate from State A is surrendered to the Department in State B and the Department inadvertently issues a "clean" certificate. Given that the State B Department had the State A certificate in its possession in this scenario, issuance of the clean certificate was almost certainly an error, although the error might have been encouraged by fraud. Having made that error, the Department almost certainly would have made a second by failing to mail the certificate back to the first lien holder who surrendered it. UMVCTA §21(d) requires mailing to the first lien holder *named* in the certificate, and there is no one named on the new certificate. It would be up to each lien holder to notice that the first lien holder had not received the new certificate as it should have and complain.

An even more frequent problem is that a Department issues a new certificate without obtaining surrender of the old one. This might occur when the owner of the vehicle certifies that the original certificate of title has been lost, stolen, or destroyed. UMVCTA §13. It might also occur when the Department excuses surrender under UMVCTA §11. The result is that two certificates are in existence, each arguably covering the vehicle.

U.C.C. §9-303(b) takes the position that when a subsequent certificate of title to property is issued by any state, prior certificates cease to cover the property. The law of the state issuing the most recent (second) certificate for the property governs. U.C.C. §9-303(c). Nevertheless, a security interest perfected by notation on the first certificate remains perfected permanently as against a lien creditor or a trustee in bankruptcy. See U.C.C. §9-316(d). But as against a purchaser for value — such as an Article 9 secured creditor — the security interest remains perfected for only four months after issuance of the second certificate. If the holder of the first lien fails to perfect on the second certificate during that four-month period, the first lien becomes unperfected as against that purchaser, whether the purchaser purchased before or after the end of the four-month period. See U.C.C. §9-316(e). (Remember that secured creditors are "purchasers," under Article 9. See U.C.C. §1-201(32), (33) (Rev. §1-201(b)(29) and (30)).) Thus, the trustee in a bankruptcy case commenced after issuance of the second certificate can be defeated by security interests noted on the first certificate before issuance of the second certificate and security interests noted on the second certificate.

Another possible solution to the two-certificates problem is for the state to revoke the improperly issued one, leaving the properly issued certificate to govern. The statutory basis for this solution is UMVCTA §26(a), which authorizes the revocation of a certificate that was "fraudulently procured or erroneously issued." To illustrate, assume that Firstbank perfects by notation on the certificate issued in Illinois. The debtor fraudulently obtains a clean certificate from Alabama and Secondbank perfects by notation on that certificate. Firstbank uses UMVCTA §26(a) to persuade the Alabama Department to revoke the second certificate. Secondbank's security interest remains valid because the revocation does not "in itself, affect the validity of a security interest noted on [the revoked certificate]." But Firstbank's security interest is also arguably valid because after revocation it is on the only remaining certificate. Notice that this is a *strategic* solution to the problem. The lawyer must take action to change the facts before raising the issue and arguing the law.

Some states permit a creditor that loses its lien as a result of filing office negligence to sue the filing officer who committed the error. Recovery is usually from a bond or insurance policy and limited in amount. See, e.g., Va. Code Ann. §46.2-219 (1996).

3. Movement of Goods Between Non-Certificate and Certificate Jurisdictions

Because all 50 states now have certificate of title systems for automobiles and trucks, the movement of automobiles and trucks between certificate and non-certificate jurisdictions has become far less a problem. Such movement remains a problem when automobiles and trucks are, for example, moved between the United States and Canada. In Canada, perfection of security interests in automobiles and trucks is accomplished by filing a financing statement. Because some states have certificate of title systems for boats and mobile homes, while others do not, the movement of boats and mobile homes between certificate and non-certificate states also remains a problem.

Certificate to non-certificate moves. Assume that Steve Harry, a resident of the state of Indiana, owns a boat. The boat is both registered and titled in Indiana.

Firstbank has a lien against the boat perfected by notation on the Indiana certificate of title. The bank has possession of the certificate.

Harry changes his principal residence to Idaho, a state that issues certificates of registration for boats but not certificates of title on which a security interest can be perfected by notation. In Idaho, filing in the U.C.C. filing system is necessary to perfect a security interest in a boat. Harry takes his boat with him.

Does Firstbank's security interest remain perfected after the move? The starting point for analysis is to determine whether the boat is still covered by the Indiana certificate of title after it is out of Indiana. First, U.C.C. §9-303(a) assures us that the movement of the goods and Harry's severance of his connections with Indiana are not impediments to continued coverage by the Indiana certificate. U.C.C. §9-303(b) states the two circumstances in which goods cease to be covered by a certificate of title. The first is that the title "ceases to be effective under the law of the issuing jurisdiction" (Indiana). No provision of Article 9 or the UMVCTA suggests that has happened. The second is that "the goods become covered subsequently by a certificate of title issued by another jurisdiction." We conclude that the boat remains covered by the Indiana certificate. U.C.C. §9-316(d) and (e) do not apply, so Firstbank's security interest remains perfected indefinitely.

Non-certificate to certificate moves. Now assume that Harry's change in principal residence is in the other direction, from Idaho to Indiana, and that prior to the move, Firstbank was perfected in Idaho by the filing of a financing statement. Upon Harry's arrival in Indiana, U.C.C. §9-301(1) makes Indiana law applicable. Under Indiana law, the filing of a financing statement is neither necessary nor effective to perfect in a boat. See U.C.C. §9-311(a)(2). However, Indiana U.C.C. §9-316(a)(2) preserves Firstbank's perfection for four months. To remain continuously perfected, Firstbank must cause an application for an Indiana certificate noting its security interest to be filed within the four-month period.

If Firstbank does not perfect in Indiana within the four-month period, its interest will be defeated by a purchaser who buys or takes a security interest during or after the four-month period. U.C.C. §9-316(b). Firstbank's interest will not be defeated by a lien creditor who levies within the four-month period. That section is ambiguous on its face with regard to a lien creditor who levies after the four-month period, but a member of the Drafting Committee tells us that the intent was that the secured creditor prevail.

Problem Set 64

64.1. a. Firstbank lends $65,000 to Kahled to purchase a teal blue Jaguar. Firstbank perfects by notation on Kahled's Wisconsin certificate of title and takes possession of the certificate. Kahled moves to Alabama and obtains a clean certificate of title from that state. One month after issuance of the new certificate, Kahled borrows $50,000 from Secondbank. Secondbank takes a security interest and perfects on the Alabama certificate. Six months after issuance of the new certificate, Kahled borrows $45,000 from Thirdbank. Thirdbank takes a security interest and perfects on the Alabama certificate.

Seven months after issuance of the new certificate, Kahled files bankruptcy. Is Firstbank perfected?

b. Change one fact: Firstbank learned of the issuance of the new certificate three months after issuance. Firstbank immediately demanded that Secondbank apply for notation of Firstbank's lien on the Alabama certificate. See UMVCTA §21(c). Secondbank promptly complied, and Firstbank's lien was noted on the Alabama certificate. As between Firstbank and Secondbank, who has priority? U.C.C. §9-316(d) and (e).

64.2. Babs lives in Missouri and owns a Nissan sedan that is titled in Missouri. United Missouri Bank financed her purchase of the car. It applied for the title, had its lien noted on it, and has possession of the certificate. Babs recently moved to New York without notifying the Bank of her move.

a. Four months have passed since her move and she has obtained neither a certificate of title nor a certificate of registration from New York. Is the Bank's security interest still perfected? If things continue as they are, how long will the Bank's security interest remain perfected? U.C.C. §§9-303, 9-316(d) and (e); UMVCTA §§2(a)(3), 4(a).

b. Suppose that Babs registers the car in New York and gets New York license plates a week after she arrives. The Bank still has the Missouri certificate of title and New York does not issue a certificate of title. Is the Bank still perfected? If so, how long will it remain perfected?

c. Suppose that Babs, rather than the Bank, is holding the Missouri certificate of title. A week after her arrival in New York, Babs applies for a New York certificate of title. She surrenders the Missouri title to the New York Department and tells them (falsely) that the Bank's lien has been satisfied. Ten days later, New York issues a clean certificate of title for the car. Is the Bank's lien still perfected? If so, how long will it remain perfected? U.C.C. §§9-303, 9-316(d) and (e); UMVCTA §§18(c), 26.

d. Suppose instead that Babs, frustrated at the thought of trying to involve the Bank in her title application in New York, gave the New York Department her affidavit stating that she lost her Missouri certificate of title and that it had no liens on it. The clerk issued a clean New York certificate. Is the Bank's lien still perfected? If so, how long will it remain perfected? U.C.C. §§9-303, 9-316(d) and (e); UMVCTA §26.

64.3. Your client, Missouri River Bank, was newly incorporated just a few months ago. The Bank plans to finance about a thousand automobiles each year. The Bank's plan is to lend only to Missouri residents, require that the cars it finances be initially titled and registered in Missouri, make sure the certificate of title carries a notation of the Bank's lien, and retain possession of the certificate. The Bank asks you if perfection according to its plan will be adequate to maintain perfection in cars owned by debtors who move out of the state. What is your answer? U.C.C. §§9-303, 9-316(d) and (e).

64.4. Shoreline Boats recently established Shoreline Credit Corporation (SCC) to finance the boats sold by Shoreline dealers at retail in 23 states.

a. SCC would like to know how it should perfect the purchase-money security interests it plans to take in the boats it sells. U.C.C. §§9-310(a) and (b), 9-311(a).

b. How should SCC protect itself against later movement or retitling of the boats? U.C.C. §§9-303, 9-309(1), 9-316(a), (b), (d), and (e). (In solving this problem, assume that the statute for titling boats is the same as UMVCTA.) Consider also the possibility that Shorelines's *debtors* may move out of state.

64.5.   Missouri River Bank plans to lend $130,000 to Coldwell Construction Company against a bulldozer already owned by Coldwell. Coldwell's offices are in Illinois. Coldwell tells you that the bulldozer is used on various construction sites, all of which are in Missouri. Your client, the Bank, asks what it should do to perfect this interest. U.C.C. §§9-301, 9-303, 9-307, 9-311(a); UMVCTA §§1, 2, 4, and 5. What is your answer? If you need additional information, where will you get it?

64.6.   Your client was recently injured in an automobile accident. The car that caused the accident was rendered inoperable. Before the police arrived, the driver removed the license plates from the car and fled the scene on foot. The accident report, which you obtained from the highway patrol, shows only the make and model of the car and the VIN. The police don't seem to be doing much to discover the name of the owner. Can you find it yourself, working only from the public records? Will your method discover the name of the owner if the car is from out of state? From Canada where no certificates of title are issued and the transfer of ownership of a motor vehicle is not recorded on any public record?

Chapter 20. Priority

Assignment 65: The Concept of Priority: State Law

This assignment explores in more depth what it means for a secured creditor to have priority. As should already be apparent, the order of priority among creditors can be crucial. Often, it spells the difference between effortless collection of the full amount of the debt and no possibility of collection at all. Reflecting the complexity and importance of priority, we devote the remainder of this book to it.

Because we often speak of priority as a right to be paid first, it may come as a surprise to realize that the "first" used here does not mean first in time. The holders of subordinate liens are often paid earlier in time than is the holder of the first lien. The actual meaning of priority is somewhat more difficult to describe. To say that one creditor has *priority* over another is to say that if the value of the collateral is sufficient to pay only one of them, the law requires that value be used to pay the one who has priority. The rules that award priority come into play whenever there is more than one interest in property. They include the rules governing foreclosure sales and the rules governing the rights of competing lien holders to possession of the property after default. We begin first with foreclosure sale procedure.

A. Priority in Foreclosure

Two basic principles govern the timing of the enforcement of competing liens against the same collateral. First, absent an agreement to the contrary, any lien holder may foreclose while the debtor is in default to that lien holder. The existence of a prior lien generally does not block the exercise of rights under a subordinate one. Second, no lien holder is compelled to foreclose. Each has the option to extend the debtor's time for payment or simply to forebear from exercising its remedy. A creditor whose priority is sufficient to guarantee that the debt will be paid may see no advantage in foreclosing, even though its debt is in default. Such a creditor may prefer to wait for others to expend the effort and money necessary to resolve the debtor's financial problems. To give effect to these two principles, sale procedures must provide for the possibility that the holders of liens against particular collateral might foreclose in any order, and that some might choose to rely on their security without foreclosing at all.

Notice the specific recognition of these two principles in this statute governing foreclosure:

§667-3. *Proceeds, How Applied.* Mortgage creditors shall be entitled to payment according to the priority of their liens, and not pro rata; and judgments of foreclosure shall operate to extinguish the liens of subsequent mortgages of the same property, without forcing prior mortgagees to their right of recovery. The surplus after payment of the mortgage foreclosed, shall be applied pro tanto to the next junior mortgage, and so on to the payment, wholly or in part, of mortgages junior to the one assessed.

Hawaii Rev. Stat. §667-3 (2005).

The holder of virtually any type of lien may foreclose, but the procedure for doing so varies with the type of lien. For example, one state statute may specify the procedure to foreclose a mortgage, another state statute may specify the procedure to enforce a state property tax lien, while a federal statute specifies the procedure for enforcement of a federal tax lien. Even for a particular type of lien, such as a mortgage on real property, the procedure may differ from state to state, or a single state may offer more than one procedure. Notwithstanding the many differences in detail, the general principles common to most foreclosure procedures can serve first as a means of understanding the sale process in the abstract and then as a frame of reference for understanding the sale process applicable to particular kinds of sales in particular jurisdictions. The principles that follow govern most judicial or foreclosure sales:

1. The sale discharges from the collateral the lien under which the sale is held and all subordinate liens. See U.C.C. §9-617(a). It does not discharge prior liens.
2. The sale transfers the debtor's interest in the collateral to the purchaser, subject to all prior liens. See U.C.C. §9-617(a). The holder of the prior lien cannot enforce the debt against the person who purchases at the foreclosure sale, because that person has not assumed the debt or agreed to pay it. But the holder of the prior lien can enforce the lien against the purchaser. Unless the debt underlying the prior lien is paid by the purchaser or someone else, the holder of the prior lien can foreclose.
3. The proceeds of sale are applied first to the expenses of sale, then to payment of the lien under which the sale was held, then to payment of subordinate liens in the order of their priority. See U.C.C. §9-615(a). The remaining surplus, if any, is paid to the debtor. See U.C.C. §9-615(d)(1). Unsecured creditors do not share in the distribution; their remedy is to levy on the surplus in the hands of the debtor.
4. The debt underlying each lien is reduced by the amount paid to the lien holder from the sale, but the balance remains owing. The lien holder is then entitled to a judgment against the debtor for the deficiency, unless there is a statute providing otherwise. See U.C.C. §9-615(d)(2).

To illustrate the operation of these rules, assume that a debtor's vacation home is subject to a first mortgage lien in the amount of $50,000 and a second mortgage lien in the amount of $30,000. Both mortgages are in default and it is the holder of the first mortgage that forces the sale. The value of the collateral is not yet specified, because it will be determined by bidding at the public auction sale. Sophisticated bidders at the sale would understand that:

1. The mortgage sale will discharge both liens so that the purchaser will own the vacation home free and clear of them.
2. The sheriff will use the first proceeds of sale to pay the expenses of sale.

3. The sheriff will pay the next $50,000 to the first mortgage holder.
4. The sheriff will pay the next $30,000 to the second mortgage holder.
5. The sheriff will pay any remaining balance to the debtor (ignoring the claims of unsecured creditors).

For example, if the amount bid at the sale was $100,000 and the costs of sale were $1,000, the sheriff would pay the costs of sale, pay both mortgage holders in full, and then pay the surplus of $19,000 to the debtor.

If instead the amount bid was $60,000 the sheriff would pay the costs of sale and the debt owing the first mortgagee in full, and pay the remaining $9,000 toward the debt owing the second mortgagee. The holder of the second mortgage could continue to pursue the debtor for the $21,000 deficiency, but the lien of the second mortgage would be discharged from the vacation home and the purchaser would take the home free and clear of both mortgages.

The result is different if it is the holder of the second mortgage that forces the sale. In that event:

1. The mortgage sale discharges only the second mortgage lien; the purchaser will take "subject to" the first mortgage.
2. The sheriff will use the first proceeds of sale to pay the expenses of sale.
3. The sheriff will not pay anything to the first mortgage holder, but will pay the next $30,000 to the second mortgage holder.
4. The sheriff will pay any remaining balance to the debtor.

A bidder who understands this difference will, of course, want to adjust for it. One likely adjustment is to stop bidding at $50,000 less than the bidder thinks the house is worth, reserving that amount to pay the first mortgage after the sale is complete. So, for example, if the bidder thought the home was worth $60,000 free and clear, it would bid only up to $10,000 at the sale. The sheriff would apply the $10,000 first to the expenses of sale and then to the second mortgage debt.

What happens if the purchaser at the foreclosure sale does not pay a mortgage to which it takes subject? Although the purchaser is not liable on the debt, the debtor is. But the debtor is not likely to pay a debt to avoid a foreclosure of a lien against someone else's property. If no one pays the first mortgage, the first mortgage holder can foreclose and almost certainly will do so. Purchasers usually choose to pay the mortgage debt.

Sophisticated bidders at a sale under a second mortgage sometimes arrange with the first mortgagee, before they bid, that if they buy the property they will assume the first mortgage. The deal might call for the bidder to cure any default in the first mortgage and then pay in accord with its original terms, or to pay on new terms negotiated between the parties. The actual terms are not governed by legal rules; they are negotiated in the shadow of what would happen in the absence of agreement. If no deal is struck, the prospective bidder might choose not to bid, or might bid and, if successful, pay the first mortgage.

Not surprisingly, not all bidders at judicial sales understand the rules of priority. Sometimes an unsophisticated bidder bids what he or she considers to be the value of the property, without deducting the amounts to cover the prior liens. To continue with the earlier example, a bidder who values the vacation home at $60,000 might bid the full $60,000, failing to account for the $50,000 mortgage outstanding, rather than bid only $10,000. Such a bid establishes the value of the property as $110,000 (a $60,000 bid for the debtor's interest in the property, subject to a $50,000 mortgage). This bidder is unlikely to learn of the first mortgage in time to correct the mistake. Once the sale is complete, it is unlikely that the purchaser can rescind on the basis of a unilateral mistake; judicial sales are one of the few places in the American economy where the rule of caveat emptor still applies. (See the discussion on the enforceability of judicial sales, even over bidder mistakes, back in Assignment 46.)

B.   Reconciling Inconsistent Priorities

While the rules governing foreclosure sales and priority in proceeds discussed in the preceding section are typical of many, they are not universal. In some sale procedures the purchaser takes free of all liens against the property and proceeds of sale are distributed first (after payment of the expenses of sale) to the holder of the first lien. Such procedures are relatively rare for two reasons. First, they deprive the holders of senior liens of their option not to foreclose. In such a system, a small subordinate lien could force the liquidation of a large first mortgage. Second, a procedure that required payment of the first lien first would require some mechanism for identifying and giving notice to the holder of that lien so that the holder could protect its rights by bidding at the sale. That in turn would further complicate the foreclosure proceedings.

When legislatures create the procedures governing foreclosure and priority in the collateral, their attention is often focused on a particular type of creditor whom they wish to prefer or a dispute between two types of creditors that they wish to resolve. For example, many state legislative staffs have been called on to draft rules that resolve priority disputes between competing execution liens. But if the dispute is between execution liens and security interests, that subject is covered by the Uniform Commercial Code and therefore considered within the jurisdiction of the drafters of the Code. The legislature must eventually pass on the rule, but it will be in a different year, in the context of a bill proposing adoption of a set of amendments to the Uniform Commercial Code that cover many other subjects as well. Rules governing priority between execution liens or security interests and federal tax liens are beyond the power of the state legislature altogether, because those rules are enacted by Congress as part of the Internal Revenue Code. Priorities are granted in many other kinds of legislation. It should be obvious that in such a system, conflicting rules can be adopted. They often are.

Because all of these liens compete for the value of the same collateral, the conflicts eventually must be resolved. As the courts resolve them, they fuse diverse sets of state and federal statutes into a single system of priority. In the resulting system, all the schemes of foreclosure and distribution have one feature in common: Those creditors whose liens are discharged by the sale share in the proceeds of sale in the order in which their liens have priority. Without this feature, the system of lien priority would no longer be functional.

Mortgages usually have priority over judgment liens for the simple reason that when a debtor has judgment liens against his or her property, no one will make a mortgage loan to the debtor. Although the opinion does not explain how the mistake was made, in the following case Bank Leumi Trust made mortgage loans to Joseph Liggett even after his ex-wife Helen Liggett had perfected a judgment lien against his property. The mortgage was subordinate to Helen's lien, but senior to a lien later acquired by Cosden Oil. When Helen forced a sale of the property pursuant to her lien, Cosden Oil argued that even though Bank Leumi Trust's mortgage would be discharged, Bank Leumi Trust could not share in the proceeds of sale. Cosden's argument was supported by the clear language of the statute:

> §5236(g) *Disposition of Proceeds of Sale.* After deduction for and payment of fees, expenses and any taxes levied on the sale, transfer or delivery, the sheriff making a sale of real property pursuant to an execution shall, unless the court otherwise directs,
>   1. distribute the proceeds to the judgment creditors who have delivered executions against the judgment debtor to the sheriff before the sale, which executions have not been returned, in the order in which their judgments have priority, and
>   2. pay over any excess to the judgment debtor.

Had the court not decided that this was a situation in which it should "otherwise direct," Bank Leumi Trust's mortgages would have been discharged, but Bank Leumi Trust would not have been paid from the proceeds of sale. Their mortgages would have been worthless and the proceeds would have gone to Cosden Oil's subordinate lien. This was a possibility that the New York legislature did not address in drafting the statute. The court took the only reasonable course under the circumstances — it ordered otherwise.

Bank Leumi Trust Co. of New York v. Liggett

496 N.Y.S.2d 14 (N.Y. App. Div. 1985)

MEMORANDUM DECISION.

. . . This case presents an issue of first impression, whether CPLR 5236(g) establishes priority of judgment creditors over mortgages which have been recorded prior to the judgments.

Joseph and Mylene Liggett purchased real property located at 6 Riverview Terrace in Manhattan in September 1974. The following year, the Liggetts transferred the property to Mylene individually. Joseph's first wife Helen Liggett subsequently prevailed in an action for moneys due under their 1970 separation agreement, and obtained a jury verdict of $388,472. In February 1980, Helen commenced a separate action to enforce her judgment in the matrimonial action by setting aside the conveyance of the Riverview Terrace property as fraudulent. She filed a notice of pendency against the property in conjunction with the second lawsuit. The following month a judgment ("the 1980 judgment") was entered in her favor for $508,129, including interest, against Joseph.

Between November 1980 and November 1981, petitioner Bank Leumi Trust Company of New York (Bank Leumi Trust) took successive mortgages on the Riverview Terrace property to secure the amounts of $550,000, $70,000 and $400,000. In February 1982, respondent Cosden Oil & Chemical Company (Cosden Oil) obtained and entered a $144,154 judgment against Joseph.

In September 1983, Helen won partial summary judgment in her action for fraudulent conveyance. By judgment resettled in February 1984, the sheriff was directed to sell the property and to make "distribution out of such proceeds to any judgment creditors in accordance with CPLR 5236(g) in the order of their statutory priority" ("the 1984 judgment"). This court denied petitioner's motion for a stay of the sheriff's sale and to intervene on that appeal. We affirmed the judgment (109 A.D.2d 642). Leave to appeal was denied by this court and the Court of Appeals.

Subsequent to the denial of the motion to intervene, Bank Leumi Trust commenced this proceeding pursuant to CPLR 5239. Only respondents Helen Liggett and Cosden Oil appeared in opposition. Special Term rejected petitioner's application to vacate the 1984 judgment. The court also denied and dismissed the remainder of the petition, which sought a declaration that Bank Leumi Trust had a right to share in the distribution of the proceeds of the sheriff's sale with judgment creditors in the order of priority of its recorded mortgages. Special Term held that CPLR 5326 did not contemplate participation by mortgagees since, on its face, it provides that only judgment creditors share in the distribution of proceeds. It relied upon the fact that petitioner bank's lien, which was junior to Helen's judgment, would be wiped out by the sale. It also interpreted the provision "unless the court otherwise directs" to require a showing of exceptional or unusual circumstances warranting departure from the statutory method of distribution. The dismissal was without prejudice to the petitioner's rights to share in any surplus remaining after distribution of the proceeds of the sheriff's sale to judgment creditors. On June 4, 1985, this court granted the petitioner a stay of the distribution of the proceeds of the sheriff's sale pending appeal, except as to respondents.

Bank Leumi appeals only from that portion of Special Term's order which denied its application insofar as it sought a declaration that its mortgages have priority in the distribution of proceeds from the sale over subsequently entered judgments. It concedes the validity of the 1984 judgment and the seniority of Helen Liggett's lien. We disagree with Special Term and reverse for the reasons set forth below.

Special Term misapprehended the issue presented here. This case is unusual since Cosden Oil's judgment is, like petitioner's mortgages, junior in time to the 1980 judgment. Both liens, not just the petitioner's, will be wiped out in the judicial sale. (CPLR 5203(a)(2).) Since there are other judgment creditors in addition to Cosden Oil, junior in time to petitioner, petitioner's mortgages cannot ride through this sale with the purchaser at the sale taking subject to the lien of its mortgages. Cosden Oil has refrained from executing on its judgment in hopes of utilizing the 1980 judgment to gain an advantage over Bank Leumi Trust. Therefore, the real issue is the right to share in the surplus proceeds between petitioner's 1980-1981 mortgages and Cosden Oil's 1982 judgment.

It has long been established that first-in-time priority obtains as between mortgages and judgments. CPLR 5203, not CPLR 5236, contains the substantive provisions concerning the priorities of competing judgment creditors with respect to realty. CPLR 5203 does not purport to determine all priorities among all categories of liens.

It is manifest from the legislative history and the language "unless the court otherwise directs" that CPLR 5236 simply establishes the procedural mechanism for the sale which converts realty into money to pay liens. The purpose of first enacting and later amending CPLR 5239, was, inter alia, to provide a procedural device by which lienors, other than judgment creditors, could stake their claims against the subject property, and have the validity and priority of all liens, including their own, judicially determined prior to a judicial sale. According to Professor Siegel, who recommended the amendment, which resulted from a study made at the request of the Committee to Advise and Consult with the Judicial Conference on the CPLR, the new language, "unless the court otherwise directs":

> recasts the subdivision to permit the court to "otherwise direct" the distribution of the proceeds of the sale when it appears to the court that someone other than those specified in the subdivision has an interest superior to the specified persons. Thus, whenever it appears that, e.g., a lien creditor (whether by way of judgment or mortgage or tax lien or mechanic's lien, etc.) has an interest superior to a judgment creditor (who would ordinarily share in the proceeds under present 5236(e) merely by issuing an execution), the court may apply the proceeds to the superior interest first. Siegel, The Sale of Real Property Pursuant to an Execution Under the CPLR, 10th NY Jud Conf Rep, pp.120, 148 [1965].

Respondent Cosden Oil contends that Bank Leumi is barred by CPLR 6501, which binds a person whose encumbrance is recorded after filing of a lis pendens in all proceedings taken in that action "to the same extent as if he were a party." This contention overlooks that in this respect Cosden Oil is in the same position as petitioner bank, both having liens junior to Helen Liggett's. The 1984 judgment should not be deemed final on the issue of priority as between Cosden Oil and Bank Leumi Trust, who were not parties to that action, where there was no opportunity to raise that issue as between these parties.

All concur.

How did the court know that this was a case in which it should disregard the distributions specified in the statute? The answer has to be that the court knew how the system was supposed to work, and knew it would not work that way if the court ordered the distributions specified.

C. The Right to Possession Between Lien Holders

As we previously discussed, one of the basic principles underlying the system of priority is that any lien holder is free to foreclose at any time. But what happens if two lien holders decide to foreclose at the same time? Some courts require that junior lien holders surrender possession to senior lien holders, effectively giving seniors the right of way.

The Grocers Supply Co. v. Intercity Investment Properties, Inc.

795 S.W.2d 225 (Tex. Ct. App. 1990)

CANNON, J. . . .

The facts are undisputed. On February 3, 1989, Grocers Supply perfected a security interest exceeding $600,000 to secure its inventory financing of The Grocery Store, Inc. and Cedric Wise. On March 6, 1989, Intercity Investments obtained a judgment in the county court against The Grocery Store, Inc. and Cedric Wise for approximately $36,000 and on June 22, 1989, the county court issued a turnover order. Grocers Supply was not a party to that suit.

On July 12, 1989, the constable, accompanied by three attorneys for Intercity, levied writs of execution obtained by Intercity on The Grocery Store and took possession of the inventory of groceries, equipment, and other items described in the inventory to the writ of execution. The attorneys for Intercity were aware of the prior recorded security interest of Grocers Supply but did not contact Grocers Supply. Upon learning of the execution on The Grocery Store inventory, appellants filed this action on July 17, 1989, to determine their rights in the property, resulting in the judgment from which this appeal is taken . . . .

In its first cross-point, Intercity contends the trial court erred in awarding possession of the seized property to Grocers Supply. Intercity argues that both Tex. R. Civ. P. 643 and [U.C.C. §9-401] expressly authorize execution against collateral, the sale of which is subject to the existing encumbrance. Appellant argues that when confronted with facts almost identical to those in this case, a Florida court held that [U.C.C. §9-401] does not exempt collateral from execution and that it may be seized and sold by the judgment creditor, subject to the secured party's lien. Altec Lansing v. Friedman Sound, Inc., 204 So. 2d 740 (Fla. Dist. Ct. App. 1967). Intercity also cites First Natl. Bank of Glendale v. Sheriff of Milwaukee County, 34 Wis. 2d 535, 149 N.W.2d 548 (Wis. 1967), wherein the Wisconsin Supreme Court reached the same conclusion. Based upon these two cases, Intercity reasons this is the majority rule. We agree with Grocers Supply that the precedential effect of *Altec Lansing* is highly questionable because of the later case of Brescher v. Assoc. Fin. Serv. Co., 460 So. 2d 464 (Fla. Dist. Ct. App. 1984), in which the court made it clear that the "secured party, upon default by a debtor, may recover possession of a chattel by replevin from a sheriff who has taken possession thereof under execution." Id. at 465.

Texas' version of the Uniform Commercial Code provides that "unless otherwise agreed a secured party has on default the right to take possession of the collateral." [U.C.C. §9-609(a)]. It appears that, with the exception of Wisconsin, other states considering the issue have consistently held that the right of a prior perfected creditor to take possession of its collateral is superior to any right of a mere judgment creditor and that the prior perfected secured creditor may regain possession of the collateral from an officer who has levied on the property at the direction of a judgment creditor. We agree with this interpretation. To hold otherwise would be to take away from the perfected security interest holder the important right of repossession of the collateral.

The security agreement between Grocers Supply and The Grocery Store clearly provided that a judgment against the debtor, or the levy, seizure, or attachment of the collateral constituted a default and upon the occurrence of any of those events, "the entire obligation becomes immediately due and payable at secured party's option without notice to debtor." We hold the right of Grocers Supply, as a prior secured creditor, to take possession of its collateral was superior to the right of Intercity, a mere judgment creditor, and that Grocers Supply could regain possession of the collateral from the constable who had levied on the property....

In its second cross-point, Intercity contends the trial court erred in adjudging against it the transportation and storage costs incurred. Intercity argues that since such costs are not specifically authorized by rule or statute, and since they are not taxable as costs of court, adjudging those costs against Intercity was unauthorized and improper. We disagree. As stated above, the evidence shows that Intercity knew of Grocers Supply's security interest before it seized the collateral, yet they failed to notify appellant before taking action. Intercity's action caused Grocers Supply to incur the additional expense of $24,113.00 in order to recover its collateral. Since someone had to pay this expense, it is appropriate that the one causing the injury be ordered to pay. As pointed out by Grocers Supply, the Oregon Court of Appeals and the Utah Supreme Court have held that a secured creditor with a right of possession of the collateral after default may maintain an action for conversion against one who exercised unauthorized acts of dominion over the property to the exclusion of the creditor's rights. We believe these authorities are sound and support the court's award of the storage and transportation costs....

We modify the judgment and order that The Grocers Supply Co., Inc. have judgment against Intercity Investment Properties, Inc. for $24,113.00, such sum being the amount which The Grocers Supply Co., Inc. paid to discharge the warehouseman's lien on the property seized under the writs of execution.

As modified, we affirm the judgment of the trial court.

Other courts have addressed the issues raised in *Grocers Supply*. As the court here noted, some have reached different conclusions. But *Grocers Supply* is not alone in holding that when junior and senior lien holders clash, the senior has the right of way. When the courts so conclude, where does this leave the junior creditor? If it cannot seize property of the debtor and force a sale merely because the holder of a senior lien whose debt is in default objects, what can it do to collect its debt? If the answer is that it cannot collect until the senior lets it, a junior lien is next to useless. The point has not gone unnoticed.

Frierson v. United Farm Agency, Inc.

868 F.2d 302 (8th Cir. 1988)

[Merchants held a first security interest in collateral owned by United Farm Agency, Inc. (UFA). When Frierson levied on the collateral, Merchants demanded that Frierson return the collateral to UFA.] With respect to Merchants' and UFA's arguments under Article 9 of the Uniform Commercial Code, see [U.C.C. §9-101], et seq., we agree with the district court. As the district court stated:

> Most secured loans provide for numerous events which constitute default, many of which are technical in nature and are inserted in the loan documents to enable the lender to declare the note in default when even a relatively minor problem arises with the loan or the debtor. Thus, at any given time many secured loans are technically in default, but are never treated as such by secured creditors. In addition, a secured party will occasionally, as Merchants has done in this case, ignore a default which is more than just a technical default. If a secured creditor with a security interest over all the debtor's property is permitted to rely on a default, whether technical or not, to prevent another creditor from executing on the debtor's property, while treating the loan as not in default when dealing with the debtor and others, severe inequities would result. . . . Such an approach would be against both the spirit and the letter of the Uniform Commercial Code.

672 F. Supp. at 1276.

Merchants cannot refuse to exercise its rights under the security agreement, thereby maintaining UFA as a going concern, while it impairs the status of other creditors by preventing them from exercising valid liens. Allowing Merchants to do so would fly in the face of all Article 9, which is premised on the debtor's ability to exercise rights in the property. See [U.C.C. §9-401]. Regardless of whether the funds in question are viewed as collateral or as proceeds, Article 9 requires that Frierson take the remaining funds subject to Merchants' security interest if the bank refuses to exercise its remedies under the code. [U.C.C. §9-315(a)]. Merchants' security interest in the funds will continue, and Merchants can trace and recapture when it chooses to declare the loan in default and accelerate the debt.

U.C.C. §9-401 does not say that an unsecured creditor who has obtained a judgment against the debtor can levy on collateral encumbered by another creditor's security interest. It merely says that the issue "is governed by applicable law other than this article." The most obvious feature of that other law will be statutes authorizing judgment creditors to levy on the debtor's property. Those statutes make no exception for encumbered property.

We think there are at least two ways to reconcile *Grocers Supply* with U.C.C. §9-401. The first is the reasoning in *Frierson*: The right of the senior to possession is not the right to possession for the purpose of leaving the debtor in business and frustrating collection by junior lien holders. The senior lien holder must foreclose or stand aside so junior lien holders can do so. The second begins with the observation that *Grocers Supply* requires the junior lien holder to surrender possession to the senior, but it does not bar the junior from continuing with the sale. Under some sale procedures at least, property can be sold even though it is not physically present.

Problem Set 65

65.1.   Your client, Katherine Kinski, has investigated an upcoming fore-closure sale for the purpose of bidding at it. The sale is being conducted by the sheriff under a final judgment of foreclosure in favor of John Gottleib on a mortage securing a debt in the amount of $10,000. The judgment specifically forecloses a subordinate mortgage in the amount of $29,000, but makes no mention of a senior mortgage in the amount of $17,000. Kinski has examined the property and concluded that she is willing to pay up to $25,000 to own the property free and clear of all liens. The sheriff's expenses in conduct-ing the sale are $200. How much should Kinski bid at the sale? Compare U.C.C. §9-617(a).

65.2.   A 2000 Rolls Royce automobile worth $75,000 was seized by the sheriff under a writ of execution on an $8,000 judgment. The car is subject to a first security interest in the amount of $60,000 and a second in the amount of $30,000. Both secured creditors are aware of the sale; neither has objected or demanded possession of the collateral. The expenses of con-ducting the sale are estimated at $200. If all bidders understand the sale procedure, what do you expect will be the highest bid at the sale? Compare U.C.C. §9-617(a).

65.3.   You represent Diamond Head National Bank, which holds a first security interest against some mobile equipment owned by Henry Walker, securing a debt in the amount of $27,000. Walker is current on his payments. Diamond Head considers the loan very safe because, even at a sheriff's auction sale, the Bank is confident the equipment would bring at least $40,000. From friends at the Club, you have heard that Walker is in financial difficulty and the holder of some kind of second lien is forcing a sale of the equipment.

a.   If this information is correct, is there any reason for Diamond Head to be concerned? U.C.C. §§9-611(c)(3), 9-617(b), 9-625(b).

b.   Can Diamond Head protect its position by purchasing the equipment at the sale? U.C.C. §9-615(a).

c.   Can Diamond Head prevent the sale? U.C.C. §§9-609(a), 9-401.

d.   Assuming that the creditor forcing this sale was an Article 9 secured party, was Diamond Head entitled to receive notice of this sale? U.C.C. §9-611 and Comment 4 to that section.

65.4.   You had never intended to get so intimately involved in debtor-creditor relations, but a friend needs to borrow $10,000 from you. She is willing to give you a second mortgage against the house she recently bought for $120,000. The house is subject to an $80,000 first mortgage and appears to be easily worth more than $90,000.

a.   If your friend defaults on the $10,000 loan and you have to look to the house for repayment, what will you do?

b.   Will taking that action assure recovery of your $10,000?

c.   What will happen if your friend makes the payments on your mortgage, but defaults in payments under the first mortgage?

d.   Can you protect yourself against default under the first mortgage by a provision in your loan or mortgage agreement?

65.5.   After the decision in *Grocers Supply*, Bob Gorman, president of Intercity Investments, directed the sheriff to surrender possession of The

Grocery Store inventory to Grocers Supply and paid Grocers Supply $24,000 in satisfaction of the judgment. Gorman discharged the attorneys who represented Intercity in the execution and came to you for advice on how to collect Intercity's $36,000 judgment against The Grocery Store and Cedric Wise. It appears that after its victory in court, Grocers Supply instructed the sheriff to return the inventory to The Grocery Store, the sheriff has done so, and The Grocery Store is back in business. Wiser from his earlier experience, Gorman contacted Grocers Supply and told them that he intended to execute on the inventory again to enforce his judgment. Grocers Supply objected, saying that they preferred that the inventory remain in place, and threatened that if Gorman executed "it will just be a repeat of the earlier case." Gorman thinks the inventory is worth more than enough to pay both liens, and Grocers Supply is only objecting in order to protect The Grocery Store. "If they can do this," Gorman says, "any debtor with a co-operative secured creditor can beat its judgment creditors." What do you tell Gorman?

65.6. Your firm has just picked up a new client, Fidelity Mortgage. Fidelity is an Alaska lender that frequently lends against real property, taking a first mortgage in the property. You review Fidelity's current standard loan documents and you notice they say nothing about property taxes, which may range anywhere from 1 to 3 percent of the value of the property each year. Alaska Stat. §29.45.300 has a provision of the type common in most U.S. jurisdictions: "Property taxes, together with penalty and interest, are a lien upon the property assessed, and the lien is prior and paramount to all other liens or encumbrances against the property." If they are not paid within two years, the state forecloses the property tax lien and the property is sold to the highest bidder at auction. The proceeds of sale are applied first to the tax and then to subordinate liens.

a. If one of Fidelity's debtors fails to pay property taxes and the state forecloses, what is the effect on Fidelity's mortgage?

b. If such a foreclosure is already under way against one of Fidelity's mortgagors, what can Fidelity do to protect itself?

c. What suggestions do you have for reforming Fidelity's standard form contract?

65.7. You represent Commercial Finance, a commercial lender. It holds a second mortgage in the amount of $2.3 million against an industrial plant. (That amount includes principal, interest, attorneys' fees, and the estimated costs of conducting the mortgage foreclosure sale.) The plant is the only asset of the debtor, Industrial Manufacturers, Inc. (Industrial). The principals of Industrial have personally guaranteed payment of the mortgage debt, but it is unclear whether any deficiency against them will be collectible. The foreclosure of Commercial's mortgage is complete and the sale is set for next week. The first mortgage in the amount of $4.1 million in favor of City State Bank is in default, but the bank has not yet begun to foreclose. Commercial has asked you to prepare the bidding strategy for the upcoming sale. It believes that if the property were marketed and sold privately, it would bring between $4.2 million and $5.6 million, with the most likely resale price being about $5 million. Commercial estimates its out-of-pocket costs of buying, holding, and reselling the plant at $200,000, and an additional $300,000 of interest and attorneys' fees will accrue on the first mortgage during the time it would take to resell the plant. How much should Commercial bid at the sale? Organize your answer by assuming a resale of the property for exactly $5 million, then explain how the numbers change if the property actually brings more or less.

Chapter 21. Competitions for Collateral

Assignment 66: Lien Creditors Against Secured Creditors: The Basics

In Assignment 57, we introduced a crude model of priority among liens. That model ranked liens chronologically in the order in which they were perfected. In Assignment 65, we refined the model by noting that the rules governing priority among the various kinds of liens are contained in diverse bodies of law. To list just a few, Congress determines the priority of tax liens, a complex superstructure of organizations controls the priority rules contained in the U.C.C., and state legislatures control priority among judgment liens. The courts are left to deal with the resulting inconsistencies. In this series of assignments, we examine these rules as they were written, one competition at a time.

Along the way, we will consider the effects of two circumstances that have spawned their own special rules of priority: future advances and purchase-money status. As to future advances, the principal issue is whether the priority date of a later advance should be the date of that advance or the date of the earlier transaction in which the future advance was contemplated. As to purchase-money status, the principal issue is what steps a later purchase-money lender must take to have priority over competing liens perfected earlier. We will see that the rules governing future advances and purchase-money lending, like the rules governing priority generally, differ from one competition to another.

In this assignment, we discuss three competitions, all involving lien creditors. They are (1) lien creditor against lien creditor, (2) lien creditor against Article 9 secured party, and (3) lien creditor against real estate secured party.

A. How Creditors Become "Lien Creditors"

The prototypical lien creditor is an unsecured creditor who won a judgment against the debtor, obtained a writ of execution, and then obtained a lien by levying on specific property of the debtor. U.C.C. §9-102(a)(52) defines "lien creditor" somewhat more broadly as including any "creditor who has acquired a lien on the property involved by attachment, levy or the like."

Like execution, *attachment* is a legal process in which the plaintiff in litigation obtains a writ and delivers it to a sheriff, marshal, or other law enforcement officer, who then levies on property of the debtor. In a few jurisdictions, "attachment" is virtually a synonym for "execution." But in most, the distinction between attachment and execution is that an attachment occurs before judgment is entered, while execution occurs afterward. As you might expect, property seized pursuant to attachment is not immediately sold; it is held by the sheriff pending the outcome of the litigation.

Two other procedures by which an unsecured creditor may obtain lien creditor status are worthy of mention. *Garnishment* is the process by which a judgment creditor in most states reaches debts owing from a third party to the debtor or property of the debtor that is in the hands of a third party. The garnishing creditor becomes a lien creditor at the moment the writ of garnishment is served on the third party. In many jurisdictions, an unsecured creditor can garnish before obtaining a judgment in certain kinds of cases, subject to numerous statutory and constitutional restrictions. However, garnishment of wages held by an employer is prohibited prior to judgment in all states and even after judgment in a few.

The second procedure worth mentioning is the recordation of a judgment for money damages. In nearly all states, recordation of a money judgment in the real property recording system creates and perfects a lien against all real property owned by the debtor within the county. The judgment lien thus created will also reach any such property that the debtor later acquires while the judgment lien remains perfected.

Also, in a growing minority of states, including both California and Florida, a judgment creditor can record its judgment — or a notice of it — in the Uniform Commercial Code filing system or a separate statewide system, and thereby create and perfect a lien against personal property of the debtor.

Judgment Liens on Real and Personal Property
Cal. Civ. Proc. Code (2005)

§697.310

(a) Except as otherwise provided by statute, a judgment lien on real property is created under this section by recording an abstract of a money judgment with the county recorder.

§697.510

(a) A judgment lien on personal property described in Section 697.530 is created by filing a notice of judgment lien in the office of the Secretary of State pursuant to this article.

§697.530

(a) A judgment lien on personal property is a lien on all interests in the following personal property that are subject to enforcement [of a money judgment] at the time the lien is created if a security interest in the property could be perfected under the Commercial Code by filing a financing statement at that time with the Secretary of State:

(1) accounts receivable
(2) chattel paper
(3) equipment

(4)   farm products
(5)   inventory
(6)   negotiable documents of title

The filing officer indexes the notice of judgment lien thus filed in the same system with financing statements. A search of the Article 9 filing system will disclose the existence of the judgment.

Last, but certainly not least, a trustee in bankruptcy, including a debtor in possession under Chapter 11, has the rights of a hypothetical ideal lien creditor — essentially a lien creditor with no debilitating history or knowledge — who obtained a lien on all property of the debtor on the date of the filing of the bankruptcy case. For example, even if none of the debtor's creditors could prevail over an unrecorded mortgage because all knew about it, the debtor's trustee, as an ideal lien creditor, could prevail over it. See Bankr. Code §544(a). By statute the trustee has the rights of an ideal lien creditor, which are exercised on behalf of all the general creditors. We alert you to their existence now, because they lend added significance to the subject of this assignment. You must first know the rights of a lien creditor to calculate the rights of a trustee in bankruptcy.

B.   Priority Among Lien Creditors

The rules governing priority among competing lien creditors are generally found in state statutes. They set up a first-come, first-served system. That is, the first creditor to take the legally designated crucial step has the first lien, the second to take that step has the second lien, and so forth. The laws generally award a lien priority as of one of four dates; we list them roughly in their frequency of use.

1.   *Date of levy.*   The reference here is to the date on which the sheriff or other officer took possession of particular property. Some states honor only actual physical possession by the sheriff; others consider various kinds of constructive or symbolic possession adequate. In some jurisdictions, the sheriff actually hauls moveable property back to a warehouse maintained for the purpose of holding property subject to a lien. In others, it may be adequate for the sheriff to post a notice on or about the property stating that the property is in the sheriff's possession.

2.   *Date of delivery of the writ.*   A writ of execution, attachment, or garnishment typically is issued by the clerk of the court on the request of a creditor who is entitled to it. The creditor then delivers the writ to the sheriff. In a minority of states, including Illinois, writs of execution rank in the order in which they are delivered to the sheriff with instructions for levy on the property in issue. In all or nearly all of these states, the

lien comes into existence only on levy and may then be said to "relate back" to the date of delivery to the sheriff. This means that if two executions are delivered to the sheriff but only one is levied, then only the one levied is a lien. If and when the other execution is levied, it will have priority as of the date the creditor delivered the writ to the sheriff.

3. *Date of service of a writ of garnishment.*   Service is the delivery of the writ by the sheriff to the garnishee, which is typically a bank or an employer.

4. *Date of recordation of judgment.*   The date will be the date the judgment is delivered to the filing or recording officer. (In the large majority of states, this rule gives liens only in real estate.)

In a competition between writs of execution, the majority rule gives priority to the first to levy on the particular property. For example, in California, "A levy on property under a writ of execution creates an execution lien on the property from the time of levy...." Cal. Civ. Proc. Code §697.710 (West 1994). Recall that a *levy* occurs when the sheriff takes possession of property pursuant to a writ of execution or attachment.

Under the minority rule, priority depends on the order in which the writs were delivered to the sheriff. The following statute illustrates the minority rule.

Preference Between Writs of Execution

Ohio Revised Code, §2329.10 (2005)

When two or more writs of execution against the same debtor are delivered to the officer to whom they are directed on the same day, no preference shall be given to either of such writs. If a sufficient sum of money is not made to satisfy all such executions, the amount made shall be distributed to the several creditors in proportion to the amounts of their respective demands. In all other cases the writ of execution first delivered to the officer shall be the first satisfied. The officer shall indorse on every writ of execution the time when he received it. This section does not affect any preferable lien which a judgment on which execution issued has on the lands of the debtor.

It is important to keep in mind that the priority rules for lien creditors are the creatures of state legislatures, and that diversity is great. To answer any particular question, it is nearly always necessary to consult the applicable statute.

C.   Priority Between Lien Creditors and Secured Creditors

Priority between a lien creditor and a nonpurchase-money Article 9 secured creditor depends on whether the lien creditor "becomes a lien creditor" before the secured creditor does either of two things: (1) perfects its security interest or (2) files a financing statement and complies with U.C.C. §9-203(b)(3).

Article 9 defines "perfection" in a highly technical manner. U.C.C. §9-308(a). A security interest is perfected only after it has attached and the "applicable steps required for perfection" have been taken. If, for example, the step taken to perfect is to file a financing statement, perfection will occur at the time of attachment or of filing, whichever is later. The important thing to notice here is that filing and perfection are not the same thing; they may or may not occur simultaneously.

The lien creditor's priority date in this context is the date on which the lien creditor "becomes a lien creditor." U.C.C. §9-317(a)(2). In states that follow the majority rule regarding priority among execution creditors, an execution creditor becomes a lien creditor at the time of the levy. In states that follow the minority rule, an argument can be made that the execution creditor becomes a lien creditor upon delivery of the writ to the sheriff. But in most of those states, there exists either a statute or dicta to the effect that even though priority dates from delivery of the writ, the lien comes into existence only upon levy.

People v. Green

22 Cal. Rptr. 3d 736 (Cal. App. 2004)

RICHLI, J., with RAMIREZ, P.J., and WARD, J., concurring.

Penal Code section 186.11 (section 186.11) is sometimes known as the "Freeze and Seize Law." It defines an "aggravated white collar crime enhancement." When such an enhancement applies, it allows the trial court, before trial, to enjoin the defendant from disposing of assets; it then allows the trial court, after trial, to levy on those assets to pay restitution to victims.

FACTUAL AND PROCEDURAL BACKGROUND

On July 6, 2000, sheriff's deputies executing a search warrant seized items from Douglas Green. These items included those at issue in this appeal: two cars, a motorhome, a boat and boat trailer, a jet ski and jet ski trailer, three all-terrain vehicles, a computer, various computer peripherals, a digital camera, a copier, a fax machine, four two-way radios, and $10,900 in cash. We will refer to these collectively as "the property." . . .

On August 15, 2000, a complaint was filed charging Green with grand theft, burglary, and forgery. Green retained attorney Lawrence Buckley to defend him. When Buckley asked for a $25,000 retainer, Green told him "he did not have access to that much money because the Sheriff had taken all of his money and personal property." They therefore agreed that Buckley would have an attorney's lien against the seized property for $25,000.

. . . Buckley . . . filed a motion on Green's behalf for the return of any seized items that were not contraband or evidence. . . . The People . . . filed [an] opposition to the motion which stated, "Pursuant to Penal [C]ode section 186.11[, subdivision](e)(1), the Court is requested to preserve those items of value siezed [sic] pursuant to the search warrant." . . . On August 3, 2001 . . . at least with respect to the property involved in this appeal, the trial court denied Green's motion for the return of seized items. . . .

On August 29, 2001, in exchange for legal services in this case and in certain civil cases, Green gave Buckley a promissory note for $80,000. He also signed a written security agreement, purporting to give Buckley a security interest in the property and its proceeds, to secure the note and any other present or future debts. Buckley filed a "Notice of Lien," asserting a lien on the property for $80,000 in attorney fees and costs.

On September 12, 2001, Buckley filed a UCC-1 financing statement listing the property and its proceeds. However, he was unable to perfect his security interest in the cash because the sheriff had possession of it. See [U.C.C. §§9-312(b)(3), 9-313(a), (c), (f)]. Likewise, he was unable to perfect his security interest in the vehicles because the sheriff had possession of the title documents. See [U.C.C. §9-311(a)(2)]; Veh. Code, §§6300-6303, 9919-9922.

On October 11, 2001, following a jury trial, Green was found guilty as charged; all enhancements were found true. On October 25, 2001, Green entered into a plea bargain, pursuant to which the jury verdict was vacated: Green pleaded no contest to two counts of forgery, one count of conspiracy, and one count of grand theft; he admitted the white collar enhancement with respect to the conspiracy count; and he was sentenced to seven years in prison. The trial court ordered Green to pay restitution to the victims as follows: $95,661.41 to MBNA America (MBNA), $93,330 to Washington Mutual, and $59,800 to Wells Fargo. As part of the plea bargain, Green agreed that the property could be sold and the proceeds could be used for restitution. . . . [The sheriff sold the property.] The net proceeds of the auction were $33,426.95.

The People then filed a motion for a hearing concerning the disposition of the proceeds. . . . The trial court found insufficient evidence that the property had been purchased with stolen funds: "[L]ogically, you would assume that given the business that Mr. Green did or the . . . legitimate business he didn't do, . . . most of his income must have come from these . . . illegitimate businesses. . . . But nobody has been in a position to go and trace all of these sources of money from which he secured the Seedoos [sic], the boats, the cars, and all that. . . . And absent being able to do that, nobody is able to conclusively prove that all of these items came from the money that was stolen from the victims in these cases."

COMPLIANCE WITH PENAL CODE SECTION 186.11

The People plainly did not file a proper petition. The only kind of petition section 186.11 permits is a petition for "a temporary restraining order, preliminary injunction, the appointment of a receiver, or any other protective relief necessary to preserve the property or assets." §186.11(e)(2). Because the property had already been seized pursuant to the search warrant, the People felt there was no need to petition for protective relief.

The only property, however, that may be levied on pursuant to section 186.11 is property that is subject to a preliminary injunction. . . . No petition, no preliminary injunction; no preliminary injunction, no levy. . . .

THE VALIDITY OF BUCKLEY'S SECURITY INTEREST

This brings us to the People's contention that Buckley's security interest was not perfected. We discuss this contention solely as to the vehicles and the cash; as to all of the other property, it was perfected, by Buckley's UCC-1. . . .

A restitution order is enforceable as a money judgment. Pen. Code, §§1202.4(i), 1214(b). Generally speaking, a judgment creditor can obtain an execution lien by levying on personal property of the judgment debtor. Code Civ. Proc., §697.710. Alternatively, with respect to a few specific kinds of personal property, a judgment creditor can obtain a judgment lien by filing a notice of lien with the Secretary of State. Code Civ. Proc., §§697.510, subd. (a), 697.530, subd. (a). Either type of lien has priority over an unperfected security interest. [U.C.C. §9-317(a)(2).]

Under the Uniform Commercial Code, upon default, a secured party has the right to immediate possession of the collateral, including proceeds. [U.C.C. §§9-607(a)(2), 9-609(a)(1), (b)(1), (b)(2).] A perfected security interest has priority over an unperfected security interest. [U.C.C. §9-322(a)(2).] An unperfected security interest, however, is not null and void. Among other things, it has priority over an unsecured creditor's claim. [U.C.C. §9-201(a).]

As far as we can tell from the record, none of the victims had levied on the property or filed a notice of judgment lien. Accordingly, when the trial court held a hearing to determine the disposition of the proceeds, the victims were still just unsecured creditors. They had no right to any particular property. Buckley, by contrast, had the immediate right to possession of the proceeds of the property, up to the amount he was owed; whatever that was, it exceeded the proceeds.

It follows that the trial court should have awarded all of the proceeds to Buckley.

People v. Green demonstrates the importance of procedure to the priority scheme. The People seized Green's assets and demanded that the court retain them for restitution purposes before Green granted a security interest to Buckley. But seizures and demands are not enough to create rights in unsecured creditors: The unsecured creditors must levy.

Would the People have prevailed over the secured creditor if their compliance with procedure had been flawless? In a footnote to People v. Green, the court suggests not:

> Section 186.11 gives the People no way to prevent the dissipation of assets before a complaint or indictment has been filed. Here, for example, by July 6, 2000, when the search warrant was executed, Green knew the police were on to him. On August 15, 2000, he retained Buckley and made his first attempt to apply the property to Buckley's legal fees. Yet it was not until February 26, 2001, when the People filed an amended complaint with aggravated white collar crime enhancements, that they were in a position to obtain injunctive relief.

In other words, if criminals give their lawyers Article 9 security interests before they are indicted and the lawyers file financing statements, the lawyers will come ahead of the victims. The scheme won't work if the collateral are shown to be the proceeds of crime, but that, as People v. Green illustrates, is a difficult showing to make.

People v. Green is unusual in that a lien creditor and a secured creditor took the steps to assure their priority in a piece of collateral at about the same time. Most competitions for priority between lien creditors and secured creditors involve no race to the courthouse or the filing office and no close measurement of which party completed the necessary tasks first. Instead, most U.C.C. §9-317(a)(2) cases will involve either a trustee in bankruptcy or a creditor who took the steps necessary to become a lien creditor against the property. (Recall that every bankruptcy filing immediately gives the trustee the rights of an ideal lien creditor that levied at the moment of the filing of the petition.) After becoming a lien creditor, that person asserts that the apparently prior secured creditor failed to properly perfect its interest. The claim is often based on a defect in the secured creditor's filing. The issue is not when the secured creditor perfected, but whether the secured creditor perfected at all.

D. Priority Between Lien Creditors and Mortgage Creditors

Priority between lien creditors and mortgage creditors is governed by real estate law. Real estate law generally gives priority to the first lien created, and then reverses the result only if the failure to perfect offends the state's recording statute. In most states, a judgment lien creditor against real property is not entitled to the benefit of the recording statute. The result is that a mortgage granted before the judgment creditor became a lien creditor by recording its judgment has priority over the judgment lien, even though the judgment lien was the first lien perfected.

E. Purchase-Money Priority

As we mentioned previously, the fundamental principle underlying the system of priority among liens is that liens rank in the order in which they become public. Because the liens that will have priority are already public, one who contemplates taking a lien can evaluate the priority it will have before accepting it.

When a second-in-time interest takes precedence over an earlier interest, the cognoscenti describe the second secured creditor as "priming" the first. One of the most frequent events of priming occurs with *purchase-money security interests* (PMSIs), which may be granted and perfected long after the competing liens they prime. PMSIs are an exception to the fundamental principle of first in time is first in right, but the exception is not nearly so broad as it at first appears. In the context of competition between security interests and lien creditors the exception is brief and unlikely to cause difficulty for the holders of earlier interests. Under the rule stated in U.C.C. §9-317(e), a PMSI can prime a lien creditor's interest only if the PMSI comes into existence and attaches to the collateral before the creditor obtains its lien against that collateral. If the PMSI attaches first, the holder of the PMSI has a 20-day grace period in which it can perfect and thereby defeat a lien that came into existence between the dates of attachment and perfection of the PMSI. That 20-day grace period runs from the debtor's receipt of delivery of the collateral. This means that if a debtor buys property on secured credit and the lien creditor levies on the property before the secured creditor perfects its interest, the lien creditor will prevail unless the secured creditor perfects its interest within 20 days of the time the debtor received delivery of the property. The effect is that a purchase-money secured creditor that went public later can defeat a lien creditor who went public up to 20 days earlier.

The reason for allowing a 20-day grace period is to facilitate sales of personal property on secured credit. The grace period makes it possible for the seller to give immediate delivery to the buyer, without first filing its financing statement. Absent the grace period, purchase-money secured sellers might feel the need to file before delivery. The result might be to delay sale transactions.

The benefits of the grace period do not come without cost to the system. Relation back of the PMSI might surprise and disappoint the lien creditor who levied on the debtor's new property after running a U.C.C. search and finding it apparently free and clear. But the injury is likely to be relatively minor. Through its unsuccessful levy on the property, the lien creditor may have suffered additional expense and delay, but no lien creditor is likely to advance additional funds to the debtor on the basis of the deceptively clear title. Lien creditors who are concerned about the possibility of secret purchase-money liens might choose to delay their levies for 20 days after the debtor acquires new property to see if a PMSI shows up on the public record. But we don't think that will happen often. Lien creditors are usually in a hurry to establish their priority. Probably most will levy and wait to see if a purchase-money secured party files later.

Problem Set 66

66.1.   The local credit bureau reported today the entry of a judgment in the amount of $125,000 in favor of Sheng Electronics, an unsecured creditor of Conda Copper. Conda Copper also owes a $50,000 unsecured obligation to one of your clients, RFT Enterprises. Billy Williams, the owner of RFT, is concerned that by the entry of this judgment, Sheng will obtain priority in Conda's assets. "I have been patient with Conda, and they haven't," says Williams. "Why should my account be subordinated to theirs?" Can you think of a way that Williams could get priority over Sheng? U.C.C. §§9-317(a) and 9-201(a).

66.2.   Melinda Hu is in financial difficulty. Her friend, Phyllis Goldman, decides to lend her $20,000, which is to be secured by scaffolding and construction equipment owned by Melinda and located in Melinda's construction yard. On March 7, Melinda signs a financing statement, security agreement, and promissory note, but Phyllis does not disburse the money. Phyllis files the financing statement that same day and orders a search. On March 10, the sheriff levies on the equipment pursuant to a writ of execution in favor of Star Plastering. On March 11 Phyllis receives from the filing officer the report of her expedited search showing Phyllis's interest to be the first filed against the equipment.

a. As matters now stand, is Phyllis perfected? U.C.C. §§9-308(a), 9-203(b).

b. If Phyllis makes the $20,000 loan despite the levy, will she have priority over Star in the equipment? U.C.C. §9-317(a).

66.3. Your client, National Business Credit (National), specializes in asset-based lending to small businesses that are in financial distress. All of National's loans are nonpurchase-money loans secured by tangible personal property. All are made in a state with clear precedent that a creditor "becomes a lien creditor" only when the sheriff takes actual physical possession of the property levied on. Because many of its debtors are high-risk, National wants to make sure its procedures are perfect. Ned Williams, head of the loan department, explains the theory under which National operates: "First, we get our own financing statement on file. Then we search to make sure no one filed ahead of us and we check the collateral to make sure it's in the possession of the debtor. Typically, we disburse within two weeks of the time we file and within a few days after we receive the search report." Ned wonders if, aside from an error in the search or physical verification, "there's any way an execution creditor could come ahead of us." What do you tell him? U.C.C. §§9-317(a)(2), 9-308(a). If there is a problem, what should he do about it?

66.4. Assume that the state in which National lends adopts statutes identical to California Code of Civil Procedure §§697.510 and 697.530 (set forth in section A of this assignment), but its law otherwise remains the same. Should National change its loan procedure? U.C.C. §9-317(a)(2).

66.5. Assume that the state in which National lends adopts a statute identical to Ohio Revised Code §2329.10 (set forth in section B of this assignment), but its law otherwise remains the same. Should National change its loan procedure? U.C.C. §9-317(a)(2).

66.6. Bonnie Brezhnev, who recently purchased Bonnie's Boat World (BBW), calls to ask your advice. Earlier in the day, BBW sold a $35,000 Bayliner Boat to Edith Jones. BBW ran an "instant" credit check, which missed the fact that Edith's former husband, Orville, held an unrecorded judgment against her in the amount of $22,000 for unpaid alimony and child support. Edith paid $3,500 of the purchase price of the boat by check and signed a promissory note for the balance. Along with the note she signed a security agreement and a financing statement in favor of BBW. Edith immediately took possession of the boat and the documents landed in the in-basket of BBW's bookkeeper for processing.

As a result of some good detective work, Orville and a sheriff's deputy were waiting a block away when Edith rolled out of BBW's yard with the boat in tow. Orville and the sheriff followed her to the marina. As soon as she stopped, the sheriff levied on the boat and took possession of it.

Bonnie has two questions. First, can she get the boat back from the sheriff today? (The security agreement Edith signed provides that any levy on the collateral constitutes a default.) Second, is there anything else Bonnie should do? See The Grocers Supply Co. v. Intercity Investment Properties, Inc., in Assignment 65. See also U.C.C. §§9-102(a)(23), 9-308(a), 9-309(1), 9-317(a) and (e), 9-609.

66.7. Bonnie Brezhnev calls back with some bad news and some good news. The bad news is that she checked the documents after her earlier conversation with you. Edith signed the financing statement but not the security agreement. The space for the signature on the security agreement is blank. The good news is that Edith is at this very moment sitting in Bonnie's office, willing to sign the security agreement if you say it is okay. "I'd rather you got the boat than that #\@$%&*," Edith tells Bonnie. What do you tell Bonnie? U.C.C. §9-317(e).

66.8. You are a member of the U.C.C. Drafting Committee. The committee is considering a proposal to incorporate provisions permitting judgment creditors to obtain liens by filing their judgments in the statewide U.C.C. filing systems. The provisions are similar to California Civil Procedure Code §§697.310 and 697.530 set forth in section A. Do you think such provisions are in the public interest? Why or why not?

66.9. a. Debtor grants a real estate mortgage to *M*, who does not record. *C* levies on the real estate. As between *M* and *C*, who has priority?

b. Assume the facts are the same as in *a*, except that the collateral is personal property and Article 9 governs. As between *M* and *C*, who has priority? U.C.C. §9-317(a).

Assignment 67: Lien Creditors Against Secured Creditors: Future Advances

A. Priority of Future Advances: Personal Property

As we discussed in Assignment 51 of this book, secured creditors often continue to disburse money to their debtors after the initial loan transaction. For example, the secured party with an interest in the debtor's inventory and accounts receivable may advance additional funds each time the debtor acquires additional inventory or accounts. Similarly, the lender who finances construction of a building may make advances (referred to as *draws*) as the building reaches particular stages of completion.

Of course, most of the secured parties who make these advances would be unwilling to do so if their interest securing them might be subordinate to a lien creditor who levied on the collateral before the secured creditor made the advance. Such a secured party theoretically could protect itself against that possibility by repeating its search for lien creditors before making each new advance and refusing to make the advance if one has intervened. That would, however, be expensive. Instead, U.C.C. §9-323(b) gives future advances priority over the lien, provided the creditor making the advance does not have knowledge of the lien. The rule enables a secured creditor to conduct one search at the time it begins its lending relationship with the debtor and make future advances without fear of lien creditors of whom the secured creditors do not have actual knowledge.

But the exception for future advances made without knowledge of the lien is not the only exception in U.C.C. §9-323(b) in favor of secured parties who continue to make advances. The section provides two other exceptions. First, every secured advance made within 45 days after the lien's creation is entitled to priority over the lien, even if the secured creditor making the advance knows of the lien's existence. Second, every advance made "pursuant to commitment entered into without knowledge of the lien" is similarly protected. U.C.C. §9-323(b)(2). Knowledge at the time of the advance, even if the advance is more than 45 days after the lien's creation, does not prevent the lender making the advance from having priority, provided the advance is made pursuant to a commitment made when the creditor did not have knowledge of the lien.

The reason for giving priority to advances made by the secured party with actual knowledge of the lien during the 45 days after its creation is technical. As Comment 4 to U.C.C. §9-323 makes a weak attempt to explain, only by giving unconditional priority over lien creditors to secured creditors' future advances made during the 45-day period could the drafters qualify those future advances for the maximum priority over IRS tax liens available under the Tax Lien Act, 26 U.S.C. §§6321 et seq. Keep in mind, however, that the provision enables secured creditors to prevail over lien creditors in these circumstances; it is not restricted just to beating out the IRS.

The exception in favor of advances made "pursuant to a commitment entered into without knowledge of the lien" is considerably more difficult to justify. The secured creditor who makes advances pursuant to commitment can do so knowing of the lien and secure in the knowledge that its security interest will prevail over the lien. To illustrate the justifications for the exception and give you the opportunity to evaluate the arguments, we present our discussion in the form of a debate between a bank and a lien creditor.

Bank: The same reasons that warrant a priority for advances we make without knowledge of the lien also warrant a priority for advances we *commit* to make without knowledge of the lien. The appropriate time to consider our state of knowledge is when we commit; at the time of the advance, we have no choice.

Lien Creditor: That is simply not true. Suffering a judgment lien is nearly always a default under the bank's security agreement, so once you know of a lien, you are not obligated to make further advances. Yet U.C.C. §9-102(a)(68) defines "pursuant to commitment" such that these optional advances are pursuant to commitment. In nearly every instance where you make an advance "pursuant to commitment" with knowledge of the lien, you had the right to refuse it.

Bank: But for us to refuse to make advances pursuant to commitment because you became a lien creditor in the interim, we would have to know you did. Without the "pursuant to commitment" exception, we would have to search before making each advance.

Lien Creditor: Not so. You could lend without searching even if the "pursuant to commitment" exception did not exist. The "without knowledge" exception in U.C.C. §9-323(b) would still protect you against liens you did not know about. The "pursuant to commitment" exception only comes into play when you know of the lien and make advances anyway.

Bank: But you can easily destroy our protection under the exception, merely by notifying us of your levy. We'd have to stop making future advances and the debtor's business would be history.

Lien Creditor: What's wrong with that?

Bank: Many of these businesses can be saved if we continue to make advances.

Lien Creditor: You're not the right ones to make that decision. You have priority in the debtor's assets for the amounts you already advanced. In most cases, you are going to get paid whether or not the debtor's business survives. It is more likely our money than yours that is at risk in the decision on whether to continue the business. We are the ones with the right incentives to make the decision whether the business should continue or not — but the law gives you the power to decide.

> *Bank:* Who has the right incentives will vary from case to case. But we are the ones with the big money at stake. A lone tort creditor or supplier shouldn't be able to sabotage a multimillion dollar lending relationship.
>
> *Lien Creditor:* If you can make discretionary advances against any property we lien and take it from us, how are we *ever* supposed to get paid?
>
> *Bank:* Who said you were supposed to get paid?

B.   Priority of Nonadvances: Personal Property

Most security agreements provide that in the event of default, the debtor will pay the secured creditor's reasonable costs of collection, including attorneys' fees. In complex transactions, the debtor often agrees to pay many other kinds of expenses that may be incurred by the secured creditor before or after default. Do these *nonadvances* qualify for priority over lien creditors under U.C.C. §9-323(b)? In the following case, the court addresses that question.

Uni Imports, Inc. v. Exchange National Bank of Chicago

978 F.2d 984 (7th Cir. 1991)

CRABB, DISTRICT JUDGE. . . .

FACTS

On August 12, 1987, Exchange National Bank and Aparacor, Inc. executed a document entitled "Security Agreement," which granted Exchange a security interest in Aparacor's assets at Exchange. On October 9, 1987, the two executed a note due April 30, 1988, which incorporated the security agreement and established a revolving line of credit of up to $7.2 million for Aparacor and related entities. After the note expired, Exchange continued to make advances of funds without an additional written agreement.

On November 18, 1988, UNI obtained a $66,000 judgment against Aparacor in the United States District Court for the Central District of California. UNI registered the judgment in the United States District Court for the Northern District of Illinois. On January 12, 1989, UNI tried to enforce the judgment against Aparacor's assets at Exchange by delivering a writ of execution to the United States Marshals Service. The marshals service served the writ on Exchange the following day, but Exchange refused to turn over any of Aparacor's assets, contending that it had priority status.

Exchange continued to advance money to Aparacor. . . . By February 26, 1989 (45 days after Exchange had been served with the writ), the principal balance of Aparacor's loan had grown to approximately $2.8 million from a balance of approximately $780,000 as of January 12, 1989. Between February 26, 1989 and March 2, 1989, Exchange advanced an additional $274,000 to Aparacor. . . . Between March

2 and May 31, 1989, Exchange made additional payments of over $2 million as follows:

Advances to Assignee	$ 636,595
Payment of Sales Commissions	419,080
Payment of Real Estate Taxes	728,753
Payment of Interest under	27,056
Modification Note to Mar. 2	
Payment of Mechanics' Lien	2,200
Payment of Legal Fees	30,708
Letter of Credit Draws	277,716
Miscellaneous	19,326
TOTAL	$2,141,438

After . . . March 2, 1989, Exchange credited to Aparacor's outstanding balance the following: credit collections from accounts receivable, $2,584,638.21; proceeds from the sale of real estate and equipment, $1,414,287.30; and proceeds from the application of a certificate of deposit, $51,203.00, for a total of $4,050,128.51.

On September 27, 1990, UNI petitioned the district court for turnover of Aparacor's assets in the possession of Exchange. The court granted the petition and this appeal followed. UNI's $66,000 judgment has not been satisfied. Aparacor still owes $938,553.78 to Exchange. . . .

OPINION

When a person in need of money borrows a lump sum secured by specific collateral, such as real estate, the question of priorities between the lender and any subsequent person who obtains a judgment against the borrower is relatively straightforward: the judgment creditor's interest is subordinate to the lender's, so long as the lender has obtained and perfected a security interest in the borrower's realty before the lien attaches. This straightforward situation becomes complicated when the borrower wants a line of credit rather than a lump sum loan and when the collateral is a constantly changing one in the form of inventory or accounts receivables. Scholars and practitioners have debated whether the lender's security interest in the collateral attaches from the outset, that is, from the first advance under the line of credit (the "unitary" theory), or whether each advance gives rise to a new security interest, each of which arises no earlier than the time the creditor extends value (the "multiple" theory). . . .

[U.C.C. §9-323(b)] rests on the assumption that the multiple theory is operative for future advances, that is, each advance gives rise to a new security interest, which arises when the creditor extends value. See Dick Warner Cargo Handling Corp. v. Aetna Business Credit, 746 F.2d at 133:

> Sections [9-323(b) and (d)] generally accepted Coogan's conclusion that security interests relating to advances created subsequent to the intervention of a third party as lien creditor or purchaser should be subordinated to the interest of the third party.

Section [9-323(b)] applies to situations in which there is a "perfected" security interest in existence when the judgment lien attaches. (Perfection occurs when a debtor signs a security agreement containing a description of the collateral, value has been given and the debtor has rights in the collateral. [U.C.C. §9-203(b)(2)].) Under [§9-323(b)], future advances are protected (1) in all cases for 45 days following attachment of the lien; (2) beyond 45 days if the secured party makes the advance without knowledge of the lien; and (3) beyond 45 days if the secured party is committed to make advances, provided the commitment was entered into without knowledge of the lien. . . .

Left unanswered by the drafters of [§9-323(b)] was the question of the treatment of the other parts of a secured obligation such as interest and collection expenses. Were these different parts of the obligation subsumed by the term "advances" (and treated identically) or did they give rise to their own security interests and, if so, did those security interests arise when value was given or at the outset when the obligation was entered into? In the only case to address this issue, Dick Warner Cargo Handling Corp. v. Aetna Business Credit, 746 F.2d 126 (2d Cir. 1984), the Court of Appeals for the Second Circuit concluded that the separate parts of the obligation were not intended to be treated as advances. Although the court did not say so explicitly, in effect it treated such obligations as giving rise to their own security interests, at least some of which arose with the execution of the financing agreement. . . .

In *Dick Warner*, [the secured party, Aetna Business Credit and its borrower, Best Banana, entered into a security agreement that obligated Best Banana to indemnify Aetna for various expenses that Aetna might have to incur in connection with the loan and to reimburse Aetna for its expenses in enforcing or protecting its security interest or its other rights in the transaction. Best Banana defaulted under the agreement, Dick Warner obtained an execution lien against the collateral, and then Aetna incurred expenses that Best Banana was obligated under the security agreement to reimburse].

The Second Circuit held that Aetna's interest in the [collateral] had priority over Dick Warner's lien, based on Best Banana's undertaking in the original financing agreement to reimburse Aetna for attorneys' fees and other expenses it might incur in defending against suits such as Dick Warner's. According to the court, the drafters of [§9-323(b)] did not intend to include such expenditures by the lender in the term "advances" because the lender's obligation to advance funds to the borrower differs from the lender's obligation for expenses in connection with the loan, such as attorneys' fees. Expenditures in the latter category

> do not constitute "advances" as that term is commonly used; in the ordinary meaning of language, "advances" are sums put at the disposal of the borrower — not expenditures made by the lender for his own benefit.

Id. at 130. The Second Circuit suggested use of the term "nonadvances" for the debtor's obligation to pay interest and indemnify the lender for various expenses it has incurred. The court held that a lender that perfects its security interest with respect to such obligations is entitled to protection against a subsequent lien creditor. In other words, the lender is entitled to priority reimbursement insofar as a prior-perfected security interest secures a nonadvance obligation relating to a transaction prior to the levy, like that of the debtor to pay interest or even to reimburse the creditor for attorneys' fees incurred reasonably and in good faith with respect to loans made prior to the imposition of the lien or otherwise protected by it.

Id. at 134. The court took the view that the drafters of [§9-323(b)] never intended to include nonadvance obligations under this section. Thus, although for the purpose of the section, advances were treated as multiple (giving rise to a new security interest with each new advance), the treatment of future "nonadvance" obligations was not affected by the new [§9-323(b)]. Such obligations retained their unitary character, relating back to the original agreement. They continued to have priority over a later judicial lien if they had been undertaken before the lien attached, even if they did not mature until after attachment. The court acknowledged that a straightforward reading of [§9-323(b)] would not support such an interpretation, but concluded that it was what the drafters must have meant and that any other result "would be so plainly unreasonable and inconsistent with commercial practice that such an interpretation must be avoided." *Dick Warner*, 746 F.2d at 134.

The result reached in *Dick Warner* is not wholly convincing. As a general rule, security interests under Article 9 do not arise until value is extended. The court does not explain satisfactorily why it should be different for "nonadvances." Although protecting nonadvances benefits revolving credit lenders and thus, presumably improves debtors' chances of obtaining such loans, it does so at the cost of squeezing out lien creditors. One can reasonably ask whether it is fair or commercially useful to strike the balance in favor of the financier. After all, the lender in these situations has a close and continuing relationship with the debtor, enabling him to supervise and control all of the debtor's transactions, whereas the judgment lien creditor may well be an involuntary creditor of the debtor. See Grant Gilmore, The Good Faith Purchase Idea and the Uniform Commercial Code: Confessions of a Repentant Draftsman, 15 Ga. L. Rev. 605, 627 (1981) ("The financing assignee, who serves a useful function in providing working-capital loans is not an ignorant stranger. . . . He does not need to be insulated, as a matter of law, from the risks of the transactions in which [his borrowers] engage. Because he can investigate, supervise, and control, he should be encouraged to do so and penalized if he has not done so.") The drafters of the 1972 amendment noted this unfairness with respect to future advances:

It seems unfair to make it possible for a debtor and secured party with knowledge of the judgment lien to squeeze out a judgment creditor who has successfully levied on a valuable equity subject to a security interest, by permitting later enlargement of the security interest, by an additional advance, unless that advance was committed in advance without such knowledge. [Footnote omitted.]

U.C.C. §9-312 (1972) Reasons for 1972 Change. Ironically, the possibility of squeeze-out posed by future advances is less than for nonadvance value. Future advances have the positive value of enlarging the estate; reimbursing the secured creditor for nonadvance value only depletes the estate. In *Dick Warner*, for example, Best Banana was obligated to pay Aetna a $7500 minimum monthly charge. Aetna had no incentive and no apparent obligation to stop the running of the charge, other than the declining [value of the collateral].

Nonetheless, the *Dick Warner* result is endorsed by the Permanent Editorial Board for the Uniform Commercial Code. . . . In light of [the Board's] commentary and the holding of the Second Circuit, we conclude that the Illinois courts would hold [nonadvances not to be advances for purposes of §9-323(b)]. This conclusion is not the end of the inquiry in this case, however. It remains to be determined just which non-advance payments and expenditures have priority under UNI's lien. Neither *Dick Warner* nor the Permanent Editorial Board's commentary can be read as giving priority to every expense claimed by a secured creditor, whenever incurred and for whatever purpose. [The court went on to distinguish nonadvances relating to advances made before the levy (which have the priority of the first advance) from nonadvances relating to advances made after the levy (which have only the priority of the future advance).]

Uni Imports gives the secured creditor's nonadvances — typically interest, attorneys' fees, and expenses of collection accruing on the debt owing to the secured creditor — the priority of the advances to which they relate, unrestrained by U.C.C. §9-323(b). The result is that after a levy, the prior secured debt continues to grow in amount, each day reducing a little of what the levying creditor will ultimately collect. The 45-day limit does not apply. Grant Gilmore's complaint was that the rule encourages secured creditors carelessly to leave their secured debts outstanding even after default — provided only that the collateral is worth more than the debt owing to the secured creditor. When secured creditors do that they themselves incur no risk, but their non-advance accruals eventually eliminate any equity from which junior creditors might recover.

C. Priority of Future Advances and Nonadvances: Real Property

The law governing real estate transactions is even more tolerant of future advances made after a lien creditor perfects an interest in the collateral. In the following case, the Supreme Court of Mississippi explains what is generally considered the modern view, and compares it with U.C.C. §9-323(b).

Shutze v. Credithrift of America, Inc.
607 So. 2d 55 (Miss. 1992)

ROBERTSON, J.

I

This is a lien priority case. The holder of a second deed of trust securing future advances made such an advance after a junior creditor had enrolled his judgment and perfected his lien. The Chancery Court enforced the future advance clause and assigned its lien a priority relating back to the recording of the original deed of trust, priming the judgment lien.

We affirm on this issue....

II

In the early 1980s, Hobart W. Gentry, Jr., and Georgia C. Gentry owned Lot 53 of Rosewood Heights Subdivision to the City of Hattiesburg, Mississippi, commonly known by street number as the residence at 1105 North 34th Avenue. At all times relevant hereto, this property has been subject to the lien of a deed of trust, the beneficiary of which was Deposit Guaranty Mortgage Company and its predecessors in interest. The Deposit Guaranty lien was a conventional, residential first mortgage.

The first of today's combatants is Credithrift of America, Inc. On April 8, 1981, the Gentrys negotiated a second mortgage, home equity loan with Credithrift, borrowing the sum of $23,679.36. The Gentrys executed and delivered a second deed of trust conveying a security interest in the 34th Avenue property to Ben Hendrix, trustee for the benefit of Credithrift, and this deed of trust was duly recorded in the land records of Forrest County, Mississippi. Of considerable consequence, this deed of trust contains a future advance clause, in legal colloquia sometimes a "dragnet clause," which reads as follows:

> In addition to the indebtedness specifically mentioned above and any and all extensions or renewals of the same or any part thereof, this conveyance shall also cover such future and additional advances as may be made to the Grantor, or either of them, by the beneficiary....

The clause went on to provide that the conveyance in trust secured

> any and all debts, obligations, or liabilities, direct or contingent, of the grantor herein, or either of them, to the beneficiary, whether now existing or hereafter arising at any time before actual cancellation of this instrument on the public records of mortgages and deeds of trust, whether the same be evidenced by note, open account, overdraft, endorsement, guaranty or otherwise.

Nothing in any of the papers obligated Credithrift to make any future advances. ...

Enter Thomas E. Shutze, our other combatant. Shutze resides in Lamar County, Mississippi, and apparently had business dealings with the Gentrys, the nature of which is not disclosed in the record, nor is it important, except that on September 20, 1984, the County Court of Forrest County entered a judgment in favor of Shutze and against Hobart W. Gentry, Jr., in the original principal sum of $4,541.78. This judgment was duly enrolled in Forrest County on October 23, 1984, and its lien thereupon acquired the powers our law provides.

Re-enter Credithrift — eleven months later. By this time, the Gentrys had reduced their indebtedness to Credithrift to $11,215.13. On August 23, 1985, the Gentrys again refinanced — "renewed" — their loan with Credithrift and executed a new note in the principal sum of $14,150.26, repayable in installments at interest. The future advance — "the new money" — the Gentrys received was $2,784.13. Credithrift again regarded the renewal and advance as within the dragnet clause of the 1981 deed of trust which it in no way canceled or released, although it did take the precaution of a new deed of trust.

Over the next several years, the Gentrys struggled financially. It appears they made their payments to Credithrift through the Spring of 1988. At some point thereafter, they abandoned all and left for the West Coast and are believed in Reseda, California. Their creditors immediately resorted to the 34th Avenue residence to satisfy their respective debts.

No one questions that Deposit Guaranty Mortgage Company held a good, valid and perfected first lien and security interest by virtue of its 1978 deed of trust. Second mortgage holder Credithrift and judgment lien creditor Shutze, however, litigated below regarding their respective rights, and particularly the priority thereof with regard to Credithrift's future advance of $2,784.13 made after Shutze perfected his judgment lien. . . .

III

Future advance clauses are enforceable according to their tenor. Accepting their creative and constructive role in a credit economy and, as well, freedom of contract, we have upheld such clauses for more than a century. The point has been repeatedly litigated since, and we have repeatedly ruled, incident to a secured transaction, the debtor and secured party may contract that the lien or security interest created thereby shall secure other and future debts which the debtor may come to owe the secured party. Such clauses are treated like any other provisions in a contract and will be enforced at law subject only to conventional contract defenses, e.g., fraud, duress, and the like, none of which are present here.

We noted the practical rationale for such clauses in Newton County Bank v. Jones, 299 So. 2d 215 (Miss. 1974).

> When inserted in a deed of trust, such a clause operates as a convenience and an accommodation to [borrowers]. It makes available additional funds without [their] having to execute additional security documents, thereby saving time, travel, loan closing costs, costs of extra legal services, recording fees, et cetera.

Newton County Bank, 299 So. 2d at 218. And so Whiteway Finance Co., Inc. v. Green, 434 So. 2d 1351 (Miss. 1983), but repeats the obvious when it says matter-of-factly, as between the parties, " 'dragnet clauses' are valid and enforceable in Mississippi."[1]

There can be no question but that, vis-à-vis the Gentrys, the lien or security interest Credithrift held in the 34th Avenue residence secured all sums the Gentrys owed Credithrift through and including the 1985 refinancing, renewal and new advance.

---

1. The term "dragnet clause" connotes breadth of reach and is thought something much more than a conventional future advance clause. Future advances are one sort of debt included within dragnet clauses. All such clauses are enforced by reference to their language and law and not their label.

IV

A

Shutze accepts all of this but argues, instead, it proves little regarding the conflicting priorities issue he tenders. More specifically, Shutze concedes the 1981 deed of trust established Credithrift's priority the moment it was recorded, regarding of like priority the 1983 renewal and refinancing and any other indebtedness within the dragnet's reach, up until October of 1984. Shutze's point is that on October 23, 1984, he enrolled his judgment to the tune of some $4,541.78 plus interest and that, from and after that date, he held by law a lien on all of Gentry's property in the county. He argues further that his judgment lien is entitled to priority as of the date of enrollment, and in this he is correct. Credithrift does not dispute this. Indeed, our question is not which lien came first. All admit that the lien of Credithrift's April 8, 1981, deed of trust has priority over Shutze's October 23, 1984, judgment lien. . . .

The more difficult question concerns the 1985 future advance of $2,784.13. Witczinski v. Everman, 541 Miss. 841, 846 (1876), though decided a good while back, speaks perceptively to the point.

> A mortgage to secure future advances, which on its face gives information as to the extent and purpose of the contract, so that a purchaser or junior creditor may, by an inspection of the record, and by ordinary diligence and common prudence, ascertain the extent of the encumbrance, will prevail over the supervening claim of such purchaser or creditor as to all advances made by the mortgagee within the terms of such mortgage, whether made *before or after* the claim of such purchaser or creditor arose. [Emphasis supplied.]

The *Witczinski* future advance clause was far less elaborate than Credithrift's but was nevertheless held "enough to show a contract that . . . is to stand as a security . . . for such indebtedness as may arise from future dealings between the parties," by reason of which the Court held it "sufficient to put a purchaser or encumbrancer on inquiry. . . ." *Witczinski*, 51 Miss. at 846. . . .

[F]or priority purposes, the lien securing the future advance takes its date from the recording of the original deed of trust and by operation of law reaches forward to secure the advance made after intervening rights became perfected. The reason we permit this is the same we found in *Witczinski* . . . almost 120 years ago. . . . Third parties dealing with the debtor . . . Thomas E. Shutze in today's case — are given notice by the public record that the recorded lien secures any future advances. Those third parties are charged at their peril to inquire of the debtor and prior secured creditors. The device of a subordination agreement or notice to terminate may be available but, failing some legally effective contract or notice rearranging rank, third parties cannot be heard to complain when the original secured creditor's future advances are accorded the priority its publicly recorded instrument imports.

Nothing said here turns on the fact that in 1985, at the time of its last advance to the Gentrys, Credithrift had no actual knowledge of Shutze's judgment nor the lien thereof. We quite agree with the point Shutze stresses on appeal, that the Circuit Court erred when it held Credithrift prevailed by reason of its lack of actual knowledge. Shutze's enrolled judgment became notice to the world from and after

October 23, 1984, and the fact that Credithrift did not know of it in no way affects Shutze's rights. Where Shutze fails is in his inability to see that Credithrift's lien was perfected three-and-a-half years prior to his judgment lien and, by reason of the dragnet clause, Credithrift's lien reaches forward and secures the 1985 renewal and advance. Credithrift's dragnet clause had been a matter of public record since 1981, and under *Witczinski* and progeny would-be creditors such as Shutze were charged with knowledge thereof and with a duty of diligent inquiry regarding further details, before doing business with Gentry whether on open account or otherwise.

All of this makes perfectly good sense in today's world. Our citizens and their secured creditors need the flexibility dragnet clauses provide. The demands of our agricultural credit economy are as great as in the days of *Witczinski*. . . . Draws on construction loans and disbursements under lines of credit are other common examples of future advances businessmen need and secured lenders make. Second mortgage home equity loans are a more recent area of need. Many Mississippians need to borrow substantial sums with which to educate their off-spring and to borrow by the semester as tuition payments become due. They and their lenders need the security of the knowledge that their priority position will remain fixed to the date of the original deed of trust or security agreement, so that they can save "time, travel, loan closing costs, costs of extra legal services, recording fees, et cetera," as in Newton County Bank v. Jones, 299 So. 2d at 218. There is no reason our law should demand new title searches incident to each advance. Any other view could imperil the student's education in mid-stream. The same may be said for opportunities our citizens pursue in many other areas of social and economic life. The public records system each county maintains affords third parties full opportunity for knowledge which, if pursued with diligence, protects such third parties from being blind-sided. And because they will know we mean what we say, creditors do not have to record a new deed of trust every time a future advance is made which, if nothing else, avoids cluttering up the land records.

B

There is another dimension. The Uniform Commercial Code as originally enacted in Mississippi treated the priority of liens securing future advances the same as our cases noted above. Effective July 1, 1986, we amended our law to limit the lien's priority (though not its enforceability) to future advances made within forty-five days of perfection of an intervening lien or without actual knowledge of the new lien. [U.C.C. §9-323(b)]. This enactment does not directly reach real estate secured transactions. [U.C.C. §§9-109(a) and 9-109(d)(11)]. It does, however, pronounce the public policy in an area on its face indistinguishable in principle from real estate secured transactions. Dragnet clauses legally identical to Credithrift's abound in personal property security agreements across this state. We perceive no good reason why this legal language should have one meaning and effect where the security is personalty and an altogether different meaning and effect where the security is realty. We sharpen the point when we see dragnet clauses in mixed security agreements, where the collateral is a combination of real and personal property and a single dragnet clause says all collateral stands to secure all future advances.

If we imported [U.C.C. §9-323(b)] into our law of real estate secured transactions, we would cut back the reach of the dragnet clause. We need not take that step today, for Credithrift prevails even under the UCC. The Chancery Court found as a fact that, at the time of its 1985 refinancing and advance, Credithrift "had no actual notice of [Shutze's] judgment." ... The point for the moment is, given the findings of fact, Credithrift prevails even under amended [U.C.C. §9-323(b)] if we enforced it by analogy.

Obtaining a judicial lien against personal property is generally a more intrusive process than obtaining one against real property. The usual means of obtaining a judicial lien against personal property is for the sheriff to take possession of the property by levy. Both the debtor and the lien creditor are likely to know that the lien has been created and there is a good chance the secured creditor will find out as well. The usual means of obtaining a judicial lien against real estate is for the creditor to record its judgment in the real estate records. Unless the lien creditor thereafter conducts a search, it will not know whether its lien attached to any property of the debtor. While the debtor typically will know that the judgment was entered, it is unlikely to discover that the judgment was recorded until it tries to sell or borrow against the property. It is thus perhaps more understandable that the real estate system should give absolute protection to the prior mortgagee, while the personal property system gives only limited protection to the holder of the prior security interest.

Even with regard to real property, not all jurisdictions follow the *Shutze* view. The *Shutze* court gave Credithrift's future advance priority over the earlier judgment, even though Credithrift was not obligated to make it. Surely that court would reach the same result with regard to a future advance the mortgagee was obligated to make. Other jurisdictions refuse priority to such *optional* advances made by the mortgagee with knowledge of a subsequent lien, but give priority to *obligatory* advances. This distinction between "optional" and "obligatory" advances is similar to the U.C.C. distinction between advances made "pursuant to commitment" and those that are not.

Problem Set 67

67.1. Mortgagor borrows $50,000 from Mortgagee, and executes a note and mortgage that state that future advances up to an additional $25,000 may be made by Mortgagee in the future. However, Mortgagee has no obligation to make such advances. The mortgage also states that it secures interest at 10 percent per annum and Mortgagee's attorneys' fees in any collection action. Thereafter *J* obtains a judgment for $100,000 against Mortgagor and properly records it so as to impose a lien on Mortgagor's real estate. Mortgagee has actual knowledge of this lien. Then Mortgagee lends and Mortgagor accepts an additional $25,000 advance. Mortgagor defaults on the loan, owing the full balance and $10,000 in interest. After default,

Mortgagee incurs $5,000 of attorneys' fees that are recoverable against Mortgagor under the terms of the mortgage. As between Mortgagee and J, who has priority in the real property?

67.2. Debtor borrows $50,000 from Secured Party and executes a note and security agreement that state that future advances up to an additional $25,000 may be made by Secured Party in the future. However, Secured Party has no obligation to make such advances. The security agreement also states that it secures interest at 10 percent per annum and Secured Party's attorneys' fees in any collection action. Secured party perfects. Thereafter, J obtains a judgment for $100,000 against Debtor and becomes a lien creditor by levying on the collateral. Secured Party has actual knowledge of the lien. Sixty days after the levy, Secured Party lends and Debtor accepts an additional $25,000 advance. Debtor defaults on the loan, owing the full balance and $10,000 in interest. Secured Party incurs $5,000 of attorneys' fees that are recoverable against Debtor under the terms of the security agreement. As between Secured Party and J, who has priority in the personal property? U.C.C. §9-323(b).

67.3. A year ago, Carol Dearing lent $1,000 to her friend, Bob Muzzetti. Bob gave her a security interest in his 32-foot Bayliner boat, (worth about $32,000), and saw that her financing statement was duly filed. Business Credit Associates (BCA) recently recovered a judgment against Muzzetti in the amount of $45,000. Yesterday, March 1, they levied on the boat. It now sits in the Sheriff's compound, behind an eight-foot cyclone fence that is topped with concertina wire.

Now Bob is back to ask another favor of Carol. What Bob wants is an additional advance of $31,000. Bob's lawyer, John Sung, says that the advance will protect the boat from judicial sale. "Even if they go through with the sale, they won't get anything," he says. Carol, who has been your client for years, asks whether this will work. What do you tell her? U.C.C. §9-323(b).

67.4. Assume that instead of representing Carol Dearing, you represent BCA in its attempt to collect the $45,000 judgment. You assess the value of the boat at $32,000. The sheriff's sale is set for March 29, just a few days from now. In preparation for bidding at the sale, you conducted a U.C.C. search and discovered Carol Dearing's financing statement. Because you believe that a deficiency judgment against Muzzetti may be collectible, you don't want to bid higher than the value of Muzzetti's equity in the boat. But to know how much that is you need know the amount secured by Dearing's interest.

When you called Dearing, she said she would have to consult her attorney before giving you that information. Although she said she would call you back, you have not heard from her.

a. How do you plan to get the information? U.C.C. §9-210.

b. If you can't get the information, what will be your bidding strategy at the sale? U.C.C. §9-323(b) and (d).

67.5. You represent Sheng Electronics (from Problem 66.1). In preparing to levy, you ran a U.C.C. search on Conda Copper, the judgment debtor. Your search turned up three financing statements filed a little over three months ago. Each names a different secured party and describes the collateral as "all of the assets of Conda Copper." From your discovery earlier in the case, you know that at the time of those filings Conda Copper was in such bad financial condition that you doubt anyone would have been stupid enough to lend them money unsecured.

   a.   What do you think is going on? U.C.C. §§9-317(a) and 9-323(b).
   b.   What should you do?

Assignment 68: Secured Creditors Against Secured Creditors: The Basics

In this assignment we examine the rules governing priority among Article 9 security interests. These rules appear in U.C.C. §9-322. As we discuss them, keep in mind that they do not apply to competitions between Article 9 security interests and other kinds of liens except agricultural liens. If the competitor is a lien creditor, a real estate mortgagee, or a tax lien, to give but three examples, you must look to rules other than those in U.C.C. §9-322. Because the rules governing priority among different kinds of liens are spread among several bodies of law, priority is a subject that must be learned one competition at a time.

A. The Basic Rule: First to File or Perfect

The basic rule governing priority among security interests is in U.C.C. §9-322(a)(1). Between the holders of two security interests in the same collateral, the first to file or perfect has priority. In other words, the priority date of a security interest is the earlier of the dates on which the secured party filed with respect to the interest or perfected it. As between two security interests, the one with the earlier priority date has priority. The holder who gains priority by first filing or perfecting retains it so long as the holder remains continuously filed or perfected. U.C.C §9-322(a)(1).

To illustrate the basic rule, assume that on December 1, Bank1 files a financing statement against collateral the debtor already owns, but neither lends money nor enters into a security agreement with the debtor. So far, Bank1 remains unperfected, because its security interest has not attached. U.C.C. §9-308(a). On December 5, Bank2 files a financing statement against the same collateral and perfects by entering into a security agreement with the debtor and lending money. On December 10, Bank1 perfects by entering into a security agreement with the debtor and lending money. Bank1 has priority, because Bank1 filed *or* perfected (it filed on December 1) before Bank2 filed or perfected (it filed and perfected on December 5).

The explanation for this complex rule is itself complex, and not entirely satisfactory. The drafters sought by this rule to "[protect] the filing system." The concept is explained in Comment 5 to U.C.C. §9-322. Given the rule, a secured party could file a financing statement before either lending or agreeing to lend, U.C.C. §9-502(d), search the filing system at its leisure (or perhaps, more to the point, at the leisure of the filing officer) to make sure its financing statement was the first on file, and then lend without worrying that a competing security interest had been perfected in the interim.

The trouble with this explanation is that it justifies a "first to file" rule rather than the "first to file or perfect" rule of U.C.C. §9-322(1)(a). The reference to "perfection" was probably added as an afterthought to deal with the situation in which one of the competitors perfected without filing — that is, automatically or by taking possession. In all probability, the drafters acted without malice in adopting the "first to file or perfect" language — they just wanted to cover all cases with a single pronouncement.

To illustrate the operation of the rule, assume that US Bank and Trust (USBT) contemplates lending against assets already owned by, and in the possession of, Davis Industries. USBT files a financing statement on September 1. USBT waits for the Secretary of State to process all filings through September 1, which the Secretary of State manages to do by September 15. Knowing that its priority date against competing security interests will be the date of its September 1 filing, USBT also knows that any filing with priority over its own is now in the index and discoverable. USBT orders its search for filings against Davis Industries. The search report it receives on September 22 shows its filing to be the only one on record against Davis as of the effective date of the search, September 1.

Because the rule is first to file or *perfect*, USBT must also view the collateral to make sure it is not in the possession of the holder of a competing security interest. The ideal time to conduct this inspection would be at the moment USBT files on September 1. That inspection would ensure absolutely that no competing creditor had priority over USBT by virtue of filing or perfection by possession.

If USBT conducts the visual inspection on September 7, there is the possibility that the competing creditor was perfected by possession until September 6 and relinquished possession on that day only after filing a financing statement. The competing creditor would be continuously perfected, U.C.C. §9-308(c), but its financing statement would not show up on USBT's search because the search would only cover the period through September 1. Neither secured creditors nor their lawyers are likely to lose much sleep over such a possibility — unless a *very* large amount of money is at issue.

Notice that U.C.C. §9-322(a) assigns priority without reference to either creditor's state of mind. The drafters intend that the first to file or perfect have priority even if the first knows that the debtor intended that another creditor have priority and even if the first believed itself to be subordinate at the time it filed or perfected. White and Summers explain:

Note that [§9-322(a)] is a "pure race" statute. That is, the one who wins the "race" to the court house to file is superior without regard to the state of his knowledge. The section nowhere requires that the victor be without knowledge of its competitor's claim. [Example 1 in comment 4 to §9-322] illustrates the irrelevance of knowledge under the subsection. One justification for that rule is the certainty it affords. Under [§9-322(a)] no disappointed secured creditor can trump up facts from which a compassionate court might find knowledge on the part of the competitor. If the competitor filed or perfected first, as the case may be, that's the end of it; this party wins even if it knew of the other party's prior but unperfected claim.

James J. White & Robert S. Summers, Uniform Commercial Code §24-3 (5th ed. 2000).

U.C.C. §9-325 sets forth an important exception to the rule of first to file or perfect. That section subordinates security interests perfected against a transferee to those perfected against the transferor. To illustrate, assume that Firstbank takes a security interest against all equipment of DebtorTee, including after-acquired property, and perfects by filing a financing statement on March 1. On April 1, Secondbank takes a security interest in all of the assets of DebtorTor and perfects by filing a financing statement. On May 1, DebtorTor sells an item of equipment — an automated chicken scratcher — to DebtorTee. Because Secondbank did not authorize the sale free and clear of its security interest, the interest continues to encumber the chicken scratcher in the hands of DebtorTee. Firstbank's security interest attaches to the chicken scratcher pursuant to the after-acquired property clause. Firstbank is perfected in the chicken scratcher because its financing statement is sufficiently broad to cover it.

Which of the two banks has priority? Simply applying the rule of U.C.C. §9-322(a)(1), it would seem that Firstbank has priority: It filed against the chicken scratcher before Secondbank did. But U.C.C. §9-325 gives priority to Secondbank, because Secondbank perfected in the chicken scratcher before DebtorTor sold it to DebtorTee.

Even without U.C.C. §9-325, someone who understood how the Article 9 system of priority functioned would have realized the necessity for the §9-325 exception. Security interests rank in order of perfection so that lenders can discover the security interests to which they will be subordinate. If a lender to DebtorTor could be subordinate to a security interest filed earlier against DebtorTee, that lender's search could not discover prior competing interests. The lender could not search for filings against DebtorTee because even DebtorTor may not yet have identified DebtorTee as a potential transferee.

B. Priority of Future Advances

In competitions between Article 9 secured creditors, the rule regarding future advances is essentially the rule you saw applied between a mortgage holder and a lien creditor in Shutze v. Credithrift of America in Assignment 67. Provided only that the secured creditor's financing statement "covers the collateral," all advances made by the secured creditor to the debtor have priority as of the filing of the financing statement. This rule is implicit in U.C.C. §9-322(a)(1).

To illustrate, reconsider the scenario in which Bank1 files a financing statement against collateral owned by the debtor, Bank2 files and perfects in the same collateral, and Bank1 then perfects by taking a security interest in the collateral and making an advance against it. We concluded that Bank1's interest had priority over Bank2's interest because Bank1 was the first to file or perfect. If Bank1 later makes additional advances against the collateral, those advances will have the same priority as the first. They will have priority over Bank2's security interest.

The justification for this priority under Article 9 is the same given for the priority of future advances in real estate law. Bank1's filing put Bank2 on notice of the possible existence of a security interest that might secure future advances, so Bank2 should not be heard to complain if such advances are made. An important function of an Article 9 financing statement is to put searchers on notice of present and future interests that may prime the one they intend to take. So long as searchers understand the rule regarding priority of future advances, the financing statement will in fact convey notice to searchers. The understanding is that one who takes a second security interest agrees to take subject to the amount outstanding under the first filing and any future advances the holder of the first may later make.

This justification is less persuasive under Article 9 than under real estate law. Under real estate law, the future-advance clause must appear in the mortgage and the mortgage must be recorded. To gain actual notice of the possibility of future advances, one need only know how to search and how to read. Under Article 9, only the financing statement need be on the public record. Rarely will it mention the existence of the future-advance clause in the security agreement. In fact, the security agreement containing the future-advance clause need not yet be in existence. To realize the possibility of future advances under Article 9, one must know a little law as well as how to search and read.

An important function of the future-advance rule under Article 9 is to relieve the lender who will make future advances from the necessity to file and search in conjunction with each advance. The same is true in the real estate system. In both systems, once the lender achieves priority with regard to its security interest, it can make future advances secure in the knowledge that they will have that priority.

Who would take a second security interest in a system in which the first can increase without limit? The takers fall essentially into three categories: (1) lenders who do not understand the future-advance rule, (2) creditors who hope to benefit from their second interest but do not advance funds in reliance on it, and (3) lenders who protect themselves against future advances by contract with the holder of the first interest. U.C.C. §9-339.

Subsection (a) of U.C.C. §9-322 refers to the priority of a "security interest." Ironically, the security interest whose priority date is fixed by filing may not yet be in existence at the time. The filing has the effect of reserving priority for whatever security interest the debtor later grants in favor of the filer — limited, of course, by the description of collateral in the financing statement.

Can a single financing statement secure more than one such interest? To illustrate the problem, assume that the debtor gives the bank a security interest in the debtor's inventory of auto parts. The parties file a financing statement describing the type of collateral as "inventory" and the bank advances funds under the first promissory note and security agreement. Later, the debtor gives the bank a security interest in the debtor's inventory of automobiles and the bank advances funds under a second promissory note and security agreement. The parties do not file a second financing statement. On these facts, both advances have priority as of the filing of the financing statement.

See U.C.C. §§9-322(a) and 9-502(d). A single financing statement is adequate to perfect any number of security interests, to the limits of the description of collateral in the financing statement.

C.   Priority in After-Acquired Property

Recall from Assignment 51 that Article 9 permits the grant of a security interest in property the debtor does not yet own. The security agreement can describe the collateral to be acquired specifically ("John Deere tractor bearing serial number 5843F877Y99") or in general terms ("any inventory or equipment the debtor acquires in the future"). Debtors who grant security interests in after-acquired property often do not even contemplate acquiring any property of the kind described. If the debtor later acquires property that fits the description in the security agreement, the security interest attaches. U.C.C. §9-203(b).

If the description of collateral is broad enough to cover the after-acquired property, the filing covers it. As against other Article 9 secured creditors of the debtor, the after-acquired lender's priority dates from the time of its filing. U.C.C. §9-322(a)(1). To put it another way, a security interest has the same priority with respect to after-acquired property that it has with respect to the original collateral.

To illustrate, assume that Bank1 files a financing statement on April 1 against the equipment of Davis Industries and Bank2 files such a financing statement on April 5. On April 11, Davis Industries signs a security agreement granting a security interest in equipment, including after-acquired equipment, to Bank2. Bank2 makes an advance. On April 15, Davis Industries signs such a security agreement in favor of Bank1 and Bank1 makes an advance. On April 10, Davis Industries acquires its first and only item of equipment, a Giant Mashing Machine. On these facts, Bank1 has priority over Bank2 in the Giant Mashing Machine. Under U.C.C. §9-322(a)(1), Bank1's priority dates from the filing of its financing statement.

The most common commercial use of after-acquired property clauses is in inventory-secured financing. The typical debtor is continually selling inventory and replacing it with new inventory. If an inventory-secured lender's interest did not reach property acquired after the initial loan transaction, in a few days or a few weeks little collateral would remain. The debtor and creditor could solve this problem without the use of an after-acquired property clause: They could simply enter into a new security agreement every time a new shipment of inventory arrived. That would be cumbersome. Instead, nearly all inventory loan agreements provide that after-acquired inventory will serve as collateral for all amounts outstanding under the loan. The lender perfects its interest in both currently owned and after-acquired inventory by the filing of a single financing statement.

Many regard the validation of after-acquired property clauses as the most important innovation in Article 9. They argue that modern-day inventory lending could not exist without the use of after-acquired property clauses and that without such lending, the overall level of economic activity would be considerably lower. To understand the factual assertions on which their argument is based, consider the example of Sally Raj, who is planning to open a stereo store in a small shopping center. Sally estimates the cost of the inventory the store will need to open at $100,000. She has $100,000 that she has raised through savings and unsecured borrowing from friends, but she will have to use nearly all of that money to rent and furnish store space, hire employees, and get the business under way. How will she buy the inventory she needs? Most suppliers of inventory for stereo stores are themselves short of working capital. They will sell their products on credit, even unsecured credit, but they are unwilling to "carry" a debtor for more than 30 to 60 days after the sale. They want to be paid quickly so they can reinvest the money in their own business. If all of Sally's suppliers would sell on 30 to 60 days' credit, if they would sell her enough to adequately stock the store, and if Sally could sell all of that inventory for cash quickly enough to pay her suppliers when due, Sally would not need inventory financing. But that is a lot of "ifs."

Most people in Sally's situation find it necessary to seek an inventory loan from a bank or finance company. We discussed inventory lending at some length in Assignment 56. The lender will take a security interest in the debtor's inventory (which may be nothing at the time the loan is closed), including after-acquired inventory. A common arrangement would be for the bank to lend 60 percent of the cost of the inventory. The bank chooses this particular level of financing because it is the level at which the bank feels "secure" — that is, the bank estimates that in the event of default on the loan, they could take possession of the inventory, sell it, and net about 60 percent of its cost.

Each time a new shipment of inventory arrives, Sally sends proof of its arrival to the bank and the bank deposits 60 percent of the invoice amount to Sally's bank account. Each day the business is open, Sally deposits all of the proceeds from sale of inventory to the same bank account, and the bank takes an amount equal to what they lent against the items of collateral that have been sold. From time to time, an employee of the bank might stop by the stereo store to make sure there is as much inventory there as the bank thinks there is. So long as Sally's revenues are sufficient to pay her debts as they fall due, the bank is always fully secured, Sally has sufficient inventory, and the suppliers get paid on time. If her revenues are insufficient, the bank can make itself whole by selling the inventory and Sally and the suppliers will have to take the hit. That is the very meaning of priority.

D.   Priority of Purchase-Money
Security Interests

1.   *Purchase-Money Security Interests Generally*

Under U.C.C. §9-324(a), a purchase-money security interest in collateral other than inventory has priority over a conflicting security interest in the same collateral if the purchase-money security interest is perfected not later than 20 days after the debtor receives possession of the collateral. To illustrate, assume Bank1 files its financing statement against the equipment of Davis Industries on February 1. On July 1, Preferred Micro Sales, Inc. (PMSI) sells a computer to Davis Industries, delivers possession, and retains a purchase-money security interest. On July 20, PMSI perfects by filing a financing statement. Under U.C.C. §9-324(a), PMSI has priority over Bank1 with regard to the computer.

The rules regarding the priority of purchase-money security interests on their face may seem to violate the principle of first in time, first in right. The after-acquired lender files before, and attaches simultaneously with, the purchase-money lender, yet the purchase-money lender gets priority.

But the purchase-money lender is "first" in another important sense: It either supplied the collateral or made advances "to enable the debtor to acquire...the collateral." U.C.C. §§9-103(a) and (b). The purchase-money lender could have made its interest first by insisting that a straw man take title to the collateral and grant a perfected purchase-money interest, before the collateral was transferred to the debtor. The debtor then would have taken title subject to an already perfected purchase-money security interest, the after-acquired lender's security interest would have attached only at that time, and we would not have thought of the after-acquired lender as having been "first in time." See U.C.C. §9-325(a). Purchase-money priority can be understood as recognizing that, in the sense described here, the purchase-money lender has a relationship with the collateral before the after-acquired lender does. The purchase-money priority rule merely excuses the purchase-money lender from going through a straw man transaction to prove it.

The priority of purchase-money security interests is often justified on another basis. It enables companies like Preferred Micro Sales to sell and deliver immediately without having to check the public record. Provided that Preferred Micro Sales files within 20 days of the day the debtor receives possession, it will have priority over any earlier filings against the debtor that might exist.

As you have seen in other contexts, any easing of the burden on filers is likely to increase the burden on searchers. The 20-day grace period in U.C.C. §9-324(a) is no exception. Because it exists, anyone lending against noninventory collateral in the possession of the debtor must consider the possibility that (1) the debtor obtained possession of the collateral in the past 20 days and (2) the holder of one or more purchase-money security interests in the collateral has not yet filed a financing statement, but will do so before the end of that 20 days. One way for the searcher to remedy this problem is to verify the debtor's possession of the collateral and then wait 20 days beyond the basket period before searching.

Commentators on Article 9 have advanced yet another justification for the rules establishing purchase-money priority:

> A more modern justification for purchase money priority may be found in a desire to protect the *debtor* from the initial secured creditor's overreaching. If the security agreement with the first creditor contained a blanket description of the debtor's assets, including after acquired collateral and a broad definition of debt, the debtor would become virtually indentured to the initial secured creditor. If that

creditor refused to lend more money and also refused to grant a subordination agreement, the debtor would be unable to borrow to finance the purchase
of a new asset from a second creditor willing to lend only against a security interest
in that very asset having priority over the first creditor. The purchase money priority rule in effect frees the debtor from the reach of the first security agreement.

Speidel, White & Summers, Secured Transactions Teaching Materials, 205
(West 1987).

We disagree. Many, if not most, debtors *are* virtually indentured to their
initial secured creditor. The security agreement they signed makes anything
they buy collateral and makes the attachment of any other lien to the collateral a default, whether it is a purchase-money lien or not. Default, at the
option of the secured party, generally leads to catastrophe for the debtor.
Thus a properly indentured debtor cannot take advantage of purchase-
money financing over the objection of his or her master.

We think the rule permitting purchase-money priority is better explained
as a default rule that governs only if the parties make no agreement to the
contrary. Not every secured party chooses to indenture its borrowers and not
every secured party who indentures its borrowers chooses to enforce the indenture. A secured party may be willing to tolerate the debtor's acquisition of
additional collateral through purchase-money financing because it increases
the aggregate value of the secured party's collateral. That is, without having to
advance additional funds, the secured party gets a second security interest in
new collateral the debtor might not otherwise have been able to acquire. To
the extent that the new property is used to produce income for the debtor, it
also increases the likelihood that the first secured creditor will eventually be
repaid.

More than one creditor may have a valid purchase-money security interest
in the same collateral. For example, Mary Parker wants to buy some well-
drilling equipment for $10,000. The seller is willing to sell the equipment
for $2,000 cash-down and accept a promissory note secured by a purchase-
money security interest for the $8,000 balance. But Mary does not have
$2,000. She borrows the $2,000 down payment from Firstbank, giving Firstbank a security interest in the well-drilling equipment. Provided that Mary
uses the $2,000 to make the down payment, both Firstbank and the seller have
security interests that qualify for purchase-money priority. Both their interests
would have priority over any nonpurchase-money security interest Mary
granted in the same collateral.

U.C.C. §9-324(g)(1) gives the seller's purchase-money security interest priority over cash-lender Firstbank's purchase-money security interest. The rationale for this priority is stated in Comment 13 to U.C.C. §9-324. "[T]he law
is more sympathetic to the vendor's hazard of losing [well-drilling equipment]
previously owned than to the third party lender's risk of being unable to
collect from an interest in the [well-drilling equipment] that never previously
belonged to it." (Not much of a rationale, is it?)

Had both competing purchase-money security interests been in favor of
lenders rather than sellers, U.C.C. §9-324(g)(2) would have referred the
issue of priority to be determined under U.C.C. §9-322(a). That section
gives priority to the first to file or perfect — which may come as a surprise

to a PMSI lender that thinks it has a 20-day "grace period" in which to file and assure itself complete priority.

2. Purchase-Money Security Interests in Inventory

The 20-day grace period for the filing of a PMSI in U.C.C. §9-324(a) does not apply when the property sold will be inventory in the hands of the buyer. This exception is designed to accommodate the customs and practices in inventory financing. Most inventory financing is extended on the understanding that the inventory-secured lender's lien will be the only lien against inventory owned by the debtor. Within days, or even hours, of the arrival of a new shipment of inventory, the inventory-secured lender will make advances against it. The inventory-secured lender will do so on proof that the debtor is in possession of the inventory, without investigating whether the debtor has paid for it. (In fact, the understanding is usually that the debtor will *not* have paid for the inventory at the time it borrows against the inventory.) The inventory-secured lender may or may not require the debtor to use the loan proceeds to pay for the inventory, but the understanding is that the debtor will grant no PMSIs in it.

If these understandings applied to all inventory financing, a flat prohibition on PMSIs in inventory would have been appropriate. But some inventory lenders are willing to allow their debtors to take advantage of some purchase-money secured financing. Even these more tolerant lenders must, of course, have some way of knowing that others are financing some of the debtor's inventory. Inventory-secured lenders do not want to lend in reliance on collateral that is fully encumbered by a prior interest.

To protect against such double borrowing, it is not enough that the inventory lender learn of the purchase-money secured financing. The inventory lender must learn of the financing before disbursing against the collateral. If a purchase-money secured lender against inventory could, like its noninventory counterpart, obtain priority by filing a financing statement 20 days after delivery, the debtor would have (and spend) its double financing long before the inventory lender learned of the conflict.

These special needs of inventory financiers are reflected in the special rules in U.C.C. §9-324(b). These rules permit purchase-money priority in inventory only on these conditions:

1. The purchase-money financier must perfect no later than the time the debtor receives possession of the collateral, and
2. The purchase-money financier must give advance notice to the inventory lender that it expects to acquire a purchase-money security interest in inventory. To give this notice the purchase-money lender first searches the filing system for the names and addresses of all secured parties with a filing against inventory of the type it plans to sell. The lender then sends the notice to each of the inventory lenders. Like a financing statement, the notice expires at the end of five years. The purchase-money supplier can avoid expiration by repeating the notice at intervals of less than five years.

As Comment 3 to U.C.C. §9-324 explains,

> The notification requirement protects the inventory financier [against attempts by the debtor to borrow from both inventory financier and supplier against the same collateral]: If he has received notification, he will presumably not make an advance; if he has not received notification...any advance he may make will have priority.

Most important, the protection comes without necessity for the inventory lender to search the filing system before making each advance.

If the security agreement prohibits liens against inventory other than the lien of the inventory lender, a notification pursuant to U.C.C. §9-324(b) is a notification to the inventory lender that the debtor is about to go into default. To avoid that, debtors typically refuse to grant purchase-money security interests to their suppliers. The suppliers typically have little choice but to sell on unsecured credit and hope that the debtor pays.

E.   Purchase-Money Priority in Proceeds

Assume that a seller manages to acquire purchase-money priority in property of the debtor. What happens when the debtor exchanges the collateral for proceeds? Of course, the seller must take whatever action is required under U.C.C. §9-315(d) to continue its perfection in the proceeds. But will it have purchase-money priority over a competing security interest perfected by an earlier filing against the debtor naming those proceeds as original collateral?

Generally speaking, the answer is yes. Purchase-money priority under U.C.C. §9-324(a) extends to the "collateral or its proceeds." To illustrate the operation of this rule, assume that Bank1 has perfected a security interest in the equipment of Davis Industries and Bank2 has perfected a security interest in the accounts of Davis Industries. Seller sells a piece of equipment to Davis Industries, retaining a PMSI. Seller perfects within the 20-day grace period of U.C.C. §9-324(a), thereby obtaining priority over Bank1. Davis later sells the piece of equipment to Buyer, resulting in an account owing from Buyer to Davis that is proceeds of the equipment. Seller has a security interest in the account as proceeds of the sale of its collateral. U.C.C. §9-315(a)(2). In addition, Seller's purchase-money priority flows through to the account, giving Seller priority over Bank2's earlier filing against "accounts." U.C.C. §9-324(a).

The rule that purchase-money status flows through into proceeds is subject to an important exception. The exception, found in U.C.C. §9-324(b), is that purchase-money status in inventory flows only into chattel paper, instruments, and cash proceeds. The limitation prevents purchase-money status from flowing into other kinds of proceeds, most notably accounts. Even the flow-throughs of purchase money status into chattel paper, instruments, and cash deposits are themselves limited by the provisions of U.C.C. §§9-327 and 9-330. Those provisions protect purchasers of the chattel paper or instruments and secured parties with control of the deposit account into which the cash proceeds are deposited.

The reason for the exception was to facilitate account financing. To understand the perceived necessity for the exception, assume that Davis Industries had no financing statements on file against it when it approached Bank1 for a loan against its accounts receivable. Absent the exception, the unencumbered accounts would not have been adequate collateral for a loan in any amount. Bank1's fear would be that after it perfected its security interest and advanced funds against the accounts, Bank2 would make a purchase-money loan against inventory. As Davis Industries converted the inventory to accounts through sales, Bank2's purchase-money priority would flow through into the accounts, priming Bank1's lien. By limiting Bank2's purchase-money status in the proceeds of inventory to just the chattel paper, instruments, and cash proceeds, the exception arguably makes it possible for Bank1 to lend against Davis's accounts.

A later purchase-money inventory lender can protect itself against the possibility that such an account lender exists. The inventory lender would know of the account lender from the outset, because the account lender would have filed a financing statement before the inventory lender entered the picture. (If the inventory lender filed first, it could have filed against both the inventory and the accounts, and would have had priority over the later account lender on that basis.) The inventory lender can refuse to lend unless the debtor arranges to pay the inventory lender upon sale of the inventory. The obvious source of that payment is the advance made by the account lender each time a new account comes into existence. The arrangement can provide for the account lender to pay an appropriate portion of each advance directly to the inventory lender.

F. Priority in Commingled Collateral

Collateral is *commingled* when it is mixed with other property. Commingling may occur when the debtor deposits cash collateral to a bank account that also contains funds that are not proceeds. It may occur when a debtor mixes corn purchased from one supplier with corn purchased from another, or it may occur when a debtor manufactures a car using steel purchased from one supplier and aluminum purchased from another.

The commingling of funds in a bank account was discussed in Assignments 52 and 53. Here we discuss the commingling of goods. Distinguish two situations. The first is where the identity of the collateral is lost by commingling as the collateral becomes part of a product or mass. The effect is that the security interest "continues in the product or mass." U.C.C. §9-336(c). For example, assume that Firstbank holds a security interest in a shipment of potassium nitrate that the debtor combines with other chemicals to manufacture fertilizer. Under U.C.C. §9-336(c), Firstbank's security interest continues in the resulting shipment of fertilizer even though the potassium nitrate constitutes only a small part of the fertilizer.

If more than one security interest attaches to a product or mass as a result of commingling, the interests rank equally and share in the proportion that the cost of each party's contribution bears to the total cost of the product or mass. For example, assume that Farmer Green sells wheat to Processing Co. for $20,000 and Farmer Brown sells wheat to Processing Co. for $80,000. Processing Co. commingles the two shipments. Further assume that Farmer Green's wheat is subject to a security interest in favor of PCA in the amount of $20,000 and Farmer Brown's wheat is subject to a security interest in favor of WestBank in the amount of $20,000. PCA and WestBank have equal priority in the commingled wheat and are entitled to a pro rata distribution of the proceeds of its sale. PCA will be entitled to 20 percent of any proceeds from the sale of the commingled wheat; WestBank will be entitled to 80 percent. If Processing Co. sells the commingled wheat for $10,000, PCA will be entitled to $2,000 and WestBank will be entitled to $8,000.

The second situation is where the identity is not lost, as where a replacement part is installed in a machine. (The identity of the replacement part is not lost because we can still see the part and perhaps take it back out of the machine.) As we saw in Assignment 64, such a replacement part is an *accession*. If the secured party has taken a security interest in only the replacement part, U.C.C. §9-335 will apply. The secured party's interest will continue to be perfected, and will have priority over later-perfected interests in the whole. But the accession-secured party's remedies may be severely impaired by U.C.C. §9-335(e). Under that section, any secured party with priority over the accession-secured party is entitled to prevent removal of the accession from the whole. For example, assume that Firstbank has a security interest in a generator that is perfected by filing against the debtor and that the debtor installs the generator in a machine. Firstbank continues perfected in the generator. If Secondbank perfects in the machine after installation of the generator, Firstbank's interest has priority over Secondbank's. U.C.C. §§9-335(c), 9-322(a). What if Secondbank perfected its interest in the machine before Firstbank perfected in the generator? Again, U.C.C. §9-335(c) refers us to other provisions of Part 3 of Article 9. Firstbank will have priority in the generator if its security interest is purchase-money, see U.C.C. §9-324(e); otherwise Secondbank will have priority, see U.C.C. §9-322(a)(1).

Problem Set 68

68.1. In late July, Dawgs & More (Dawgs) applied to Bank One for a loan against its lawn dog manufacturing equipment. Without committing to make the loan, on August 1 Bank One filed a financing statement against Dawgs showing the equipment as collateral. Also in late July, Dawgs applied for a similar loan from Bank Two. On August 5, Bank Two approved the loan and filed a financing statement against Dawgs showing the equipment as collateral. Bank Two and Dawgs signed a security agreement on August 5 and Bank Two advanced funds to Debtor. On August 7 C-Dogs, a supplier and judgment creditor of Dawgs, became a lien creditor by levying on the equipment. On August 10, Bank One received the report of their U.C.C. search showing their financing statement to be in first position. They approved the loan to Dawgs. Bank One and Dawgs signed a security agreement, and Bank One advanced funds against the equipment. As soon as the check from Bank One cleared, the owner of Dawgs wired the Bank One loan proceeds to Freeport in the Bahamas, where they paused only long enough to join the proceeds from the Bank Two loan, and then continued on to places unknown. Who has priority in the equipment? U.C.C. §§9-203(b), 9-308(a), 9-317(a), 9-323(b), 9-322(a)(1).

68.2. A year ago, Centurion National Bank loaned Flight Analysis, Inc. $250,000, took a security interest in "flight simulation equipment," and filed a financing statement using those words as the description of collateral. Centurion filed its financing statement on September 21. A few days ago, Centurion learned for the first time that First National Bank had filed a financing statement against the same collateral on July 21 of the same year. Centurion's chief loan officer, Harley Davidson, sees what is coming and is scrambling for a way out. He recalls that Centurion took and perfected a security interest in some flight simulation equipment owned by Pilots Unlimited, including after-acquired equipment, and perfected that interest by filing a financing statement on March 21 of last year describing the collateral as "flight simulation equipment." Harley now proposes to get Flight Analysis to sell its flight simulation equipment to Pilots Unlimited. Harley figures that once Pilots Unlimited owns the collateral, "Centurion will be first because we will have the earliest financing statement on file that covers the collateral." Will this work? U.C.C. §§9-322(a)(1), 9-325, and 9-507.

68.3. A year ago, George Sol Estes borrowed $7,500 from Octopus National Bank (ONB) to purchase a computer for his dry cleaning business. The security agreement he signed at that time provided that the collateral would consist of the computer and any "substitutions, replacements or accessions." The security agreement contained no provision regarding future advances, because none was contemplated at the time. ONB filed a financing statement indicating that the collateral was "equipment."

ONB has just approved a $40,000 line of credit for George, to be secured by the dry cleaning equipment in his shop. Molly Parker, the loan officer at ONB, tells you that she knows she must prepare a new security agreement, but wonders if she must also file a new financing statement. U.C.C. §§9-322(a)(1), 9-502(d).

68.4. a. A year ago, Carol Dearing lent $1,000 to her friend, Bob Muzzetti. Bob gave her a security interest in his 32-foot Bayliner boat and saw that her financing statement was properly filed in accord with the law of the state. About a month later, Business Credit Associates (BCA) lent Muzzetti $45,000, taking a security interest in several items of collateral, including the boat. BCA also filed an effective financing statement. Muzzetti fell behind in his payments to BCA and yesterday, March 1, BCA repossessed the boat. The boat now sits in the repo agent's compound, behind an eight-foot cyclone fence that is topped with concertina wire.

Now Bob is back to ask another favor of Carol. What Bob wants is an additional advance of $31,000 "to protect the boat from sale by BCA and prevent BCA from collecting." Carol, who has been your client for years, asks whether this will work. What do you tell her? U.C.C. §§9-322(a)(1), 9-609(a).

b.   Assume that Carol had filed a financing statement against Bob before BCA repossessed, but Bob had not authorized a security agreement and Carol had not lent any money. Would the scheme work under these circumstances? Comment 4 to U.C.C. §9-322.

68.5.   On the heels of its bad experience with Bob Muzzetti, your client, BCA, has sensed the need for a change in the way it does business. While its high-risk lending remains profitable overall, BCA does not want to continue being victimized by the likes of Bob Muzzetti and Carol Dearing. Restricting its loans to first security interests is not a practical solution because nearly all of BCA's borrowers have given security interests in their collateral and the creditors who have taken them want to retain their current priority until they are paid. Is there anything else you can suggest? U.C.C. §9-339.

68.6.   Harley Davidson is under a lot of pressure in his job at Centurion National Bank. Davidson's freewheeling lending policies have generated a number of "nonproducing assets." (To put it as politely as possible.) "One more," Harley says, "and I may no longer be viable in my current position."

Harley tells you this in the context of a discussion of the Paul Grumman loan. Until yesterday, Grumman's deteriorating financial condition looked like it would be the bale of straw that broke the camel's back. Centurion's loan to Grumman is in the amount of $150,000 and is unsecured. The financial statements Grumman has given Centurion from time to time have always shown Centurion's principal competitor, First National Bank, as the holder of a $1.5 million security interest in all of Grumman's assets (principally equipment, inventory, and accounts). In the event of liquidation, Harley is sure the assets will yield less than $1.5 million. Two weeks ago, desperate for ideas, Harley ran a U.C.C. search under Grumman's name.

Yesterday, a miracle happened. Harley received the Secretary of State's search report in the mail. The certificate, which Harley has laid gently on the desk in front of you, shows no filings against Paul Grumman. Harley says he is sure that the assets are in Grumman's possession and that "Paul Grumman" is the correct name of the debtor — sure enough to bet his career on it.

To seize his opportunity, Harley has tentatively cut a deal with Grumman. Centurion is to advance an additional $100,000 to Grumman. In return, Grumman will grant a security interest in favor of Centurion that will secure both the $150,000 advance already outstanding and the new $100,000 loan. "The way I figure," Harley says, "that will leave us with a $250,000 first on almost a million five in collateral."

The bankruptcy expert in your firm tells you that the old $150,000 advance will remain vulnerable as a preference for 90 days, but the new $100,000 advance will not. From her point of view, Centurion has something to gain and nothing to lose by making the new loan — *provided that Centurion will have priority over First National*. Harley would like you to give your opinion that Centurion will have priority. If Harley loses his job, you worry that the firm may not be able to hang onto Centurion's business, perhaps putting your job in jeopardy as well.

a.   Is there any way that First National could have an effective financing statement that doesn't show up on an official search in the state in which

Grumman's business is located? U.C.C. §§9-316(a) and (b), 9-338, 9-502(d), 9-506(c), 9-507(a), 9-515(c), 9-516(d), 9-517.

b. How can you find out if such a financing statement exists, without shooting yourself in the foot? U.C.C. §9-322(a)(1) and Comment 4 to that section. For example, what if you search under "Gruman" (an incorrect spelling) and find First National's filing?

c. What should you do?

d. Is there an ethical issue here?

68.7. Sara Wisnewski has been manufacturing high-quality speakers for audio systems since 1979. Her speakers are among the best available and her prices are reasonable. For the past few years, orders have been running in excess of her manufacturing capacity and she has been unable to fill all she receives from dealers.

At the same time, she has been losing a considerable amount of money on bad debts. In your initial conference, she told you about a case in which she sold $15,000 worth of speakers to a dealer, who promptly filed bankruptcy. The dealer still had most of her speakers in stock when it closed its doors, but the bankruptcy court gave them to the inventory lender. Sara literally ended up having to buy her own speakers back from the bank to fill other orders. Her attorney in the bankruptcy case explained to her that "the bank got the speakers because they had the first security interest."

a. Sara thinks she should have the first security interest and she'd like you to tell her what she needs to do to get it. What do you tell her? U.C.C. §§9-102(a)(48), 9-324(a) and (b).

b. What problems do you foresee? What can Sara do about them?

68.8. Harley Davidson, who is still hanging on at Centurion National Bank, has made an appointment with you to discuss a letter he received from Mark Kauffman, attorney for Weil's Feed and Seed (WFS). For years, WFS has been the only feed supplier to Harley's borrower, the now-defunct Murray Cattle Company. Now WFS has surprised the bank by claiming a security interest "of equal priority with the bank" in Murray's cattle and its inventory of manure, and a prior security interest in the feed on hand. WFS has a financing statement on file against Murray, but WFS filed it two years after Centurion's and it covers only "feed." Harley says he is sure that WFS never served a §9-324 notification on the bank.

Kauffman's letter contains copies of WFS's security agreement and financing statement. His argument is that when the cattle ate the feed, WFS's collateral became part of the "mass" (the cow) and, some time later, part of the collateral became the "product" (the manure). Kauffman cites U.C.C. §9-336. Harley wants to know if he should take the Kauffman letter seriously or whether "it's just a bunch of bull****." What do you tell him? U.C.C. §§9-102(a)(34) and (48), 9-324.

68.9. Your new client, the Equitable Lending Group (ELG), specializes in high-risk, high-profit lending. It lends to debtors in possession under Chapter 11 and buys nonperforming loans from other institutions and restructures them. ELG is now interested in a new lending concept and would like your opinion on it. Harley Davidson, who recently moved to ELG from his position at Centurion and brought ELG to you, explains a typical case.

Silicon Microchip (SM) is a manufacturer of computer components. Its business is fundamentally sound, but the company is overburdened with debt. First National Bank has a perfected security interest in its inventory and accounts, worth about $600,000, securing First National's loan in the amount of $825,000. The SM-First National relationship is currently in a holding pattern while the parties attempt to renegotiate. While they are doing that, ELG wants to finance SM's acquisition of new inventory and have purchase-money priority over First National in both the inventory and the accounts that arise when that inventory is sold. Harley says he can handle the problem of monitoring the collateral, but wants you to tell him whether ELG can get the priority it seeks without agreement from First National. Harley says the folks at First National will be "mad as hell" when they see what ELG is doing, but "they're so conservative they'll still be having meetings about it six months from now. In the meantime, we'll be making six points over prime. As long as we've got first priority, it's zero risk." Can ELG get priority? U.C.C. §§9-324, 9-401(b).

Assignment 69: Buyers Against Secured Creditors

A. Introduction

Because debtors typically are in possession of the property that is subject to a security interest, the debtor may decide to raise a little cash by selling the property. In this assignment we look at property that goes out the debtor's door and may or may not fall out of that spell.

Secured creditors have a variety of expectations about possible sale of their collateral by the debtor. The bank that lends against the inventory of a retail store typically expects the debtor to sell the collateral and apply the proceeds to payment of the debt or the purchase of new inventory that will serve as collateral. The insurance company that provides financing for an apartment building may expect the debtor to sell the building without paying off the loan, but, if so, the insurance company expects that its mortgage will continue to encumber the building in the hands of its new owner. The finance company that makes a car loan may expect the debtor to repay the loan in full as a condition of selling the car. All these scenarios share two characteristics. First, the secured creditor recognizes that the debtor has the right to sell the collateral. Security does not interfere with the free alienability of property. See U.C.C. §9-401. Second, the secured creditor expects to be protected as to the *value* of its interest. The protection may be in the form of a lien on the proceeds the debtor receives from the buyer, a continuing lien on the collateral in the hands of the buyer, payment of the loan, or some combination of these protections.

Buyers have a variety of expectations as to what, if anything, they must do to make sure they get good title to what they buy. The consumer who buys a refrigerator from a store in the mall does not expect to search the public records, but does expect to be protected against preexisting security interests. This expectation of protection without search is not limited to consumers: After all, Sears doesn't search the U.C.C. records when it buys refrigerators from a manufacturer or wholesaler either. But buyers of real estate have a very different set of expectations. Even the young couple buying their first home are likely to be aware of the expectation that there must be a search of the real estate records and, if there is not, they may find that the property they buy could be saddled with mortgages that others were supposed to pay. The buyer of a negotiable instrument does not expect to search public records, but probably knows that it must take possession of the instrument at the time it buys or risk taking subject to a security interest in favor of the person who does have possession.

It is possible to view these expectations as the product of law. When doing that, we might say, for example, that the buyer of real estate must search because the law subjects its title to mortgages of record, including those of which the buyer is not aware. But it may be more useful to view the law as the product of these expectations. When doing that, we might say that the law subjects the buyer's title to mortgages of record because the custom of searching is so strong that the buyer *should* know of them.

B. Buyers of Real Property

The general rule resolves the competition between buyer and mortgagee on the basis of first in time. That is, if the mortgage was created before the debtor sold the property to the buyer, the buyer takes subject to the mortgage. If the sale takes place first, it will be free of a later mortgage granted by the debtor-seller. A recording statute may reverse either of these results. One who buys in good faith, for value, without notice of an unrecorded mortgage may take free of it under the recording statute. Similarly, one who takes a mortgage in good faith, for value, without notice of an unrecorded deed may have priority over the rights of the buyer pursuant to the recording statute. If a mortgage is recorded before the debtor sells the property, its priority over the rights of the purchaser is pretty much absolute. All purchasers of real property are expected to search the public record, are deemed to have notice (*constructive notice*) of duly recorded mortgages, and take subject to them. No exceptions are recognized for sales in the ordinary course of business or even sales to consumers.

To illustrate, assume that Bob Mason sees a magazine ad for five-acre tracts of land in the Rocky Mountains. He calls the Mountain Development offices in Denver and they send a salesman to Bob's home in New York. In good faith, Bob pays the salesman $20,000 in return for a deed that recites conveyance of lot 237 "free and clear of all liens and encumbrances." Unknown to Bob, American Finance holds a first mortgage against Mountain's entire inventory of lots, including lot 237, to secure a $1.2 million loan American made to Mountain Development. American recorded their mortgage in Colorado before Bob purchased the lot. Bob is an innocent purchaser for value, but he nevertheless takes lot 237 subject to the $1.2 million mortgage. Although Bob did not search the public record and therefore did not know of the mortgage before paying his money, the law regards that as his fault, not his virtue. Consumer Bob, like every other purchaser of real property, is expected to search, and takes with constructive notice of all duly recorded mortgages.

If the mortgage exists but remains unrecorded at the time Bob buys lot 237, the recording statute of the state will govern the validity of the mortgage against Bob. Real estate recording statutes apply to conveyances by deed to purchasers, as well as conveyances to lenders by mortgage.

The applicable statute may be a pure *race statute*, such as the North Carolina statute. It may be a *notice-race statute*, such as the New York statute. In either case, Bob will prevail so long as he records his deed before American records its mortgage. If the statute is a pure *notice statute*, such as the Massachusetts statute, Bob will prevail even if American records after Bob buys but before Bob records. (Remember, this is a buyer against an unperfected security interest.) Thus, in general, a bona fide purchaser of real estate for value will take free of a prior unrecorded mortgage if that purchaser records before the mortgage holder.

Had Bob contacted a lawyer, the lawyer would have recommended a search of the public records before Bob paid for the land. The search would have discovered the mortgage. It then would have been up to the debtor, Mountain Development, to obtain a release of lot 237 from American's mortgage. Bob would simply have refused to pay the purchase price until the record title to lot 237 was clear.

The importance of searching title has become so much a part of real estate purchases and sales that in every state some group — usually lawyers or title companies — routinely handles sales, checking all the paperwork to make certain that liens have been properly cleared from the property before the purchase money is released to the seller. Title searches also explain why it takes so much longer to buy a home than it takes to buy a car or a stereo, even when the latter sales are financed and the goods are valuable.

C. Buyers of Personal Property

The general rule governing sales of encumbered personal property is essentially the same as the general rule governing sales of real estate: Buyers take subject to encumbrances of record. The personal property rule is reflected in U.C.C. §§9-201 and 9-315(a). The former section provides that "a security agreement is effective ... against [subsequent] purchasers." The latter provides that even in the absence of a provision to that effect, "a security interest continues in collateral notwithstanding sale." The personal property rule is, however, subject to considerably more exceptions than is the corresponding rule of real property law.

1. The Authorized Disposition Exception:
U.C.C. §9-315(a)(1)

The *authorized disposition exception* appears in U.C.C. §9-315(a)(1). The security interest does not continue in the collateral if "the secured party authorized the disposition free of the security interest."

This exception is broader than may at first appear. First, the exception does not depend for its operation on equities in favor of the buyer. It can apply in favor of a buyer who did or did not search the public record. It can apply in favor of a buyer who knows or does not know of the security interest or the secured creditor's authorization to sell.

Second, the authorization to sell need not be express. In numerous cases, the courts have held that a secured creditor who knew that the debtor was making sales of collateral in violation of provisions of the security agreement thereby waived the provisions and "authorized" the sale so that the buyer took free of the security interest. For example, in Gretna State Bank v. Cornbelt Livestock Co., 463 N.W.2d 795 (Neb. 1990), the bank held a security interest in the debtor's cows and hogs, which were farm products under U.C.C. §9-102(a)(34). The security agreement expressly prohibited sale of the collateral without the prior written consent of the bank. The debtor sold some of the cattle without written consent and the bank sued the buyer. The court held that the bank's security interest did not continue in the cattle after their sale because the sale was "authorized" within the meaning of U.C.C. §9-315(a)(1). The court relied on the fact that the debtor previously had sold cattle and hogs without the bank's written consent on numerous occasions, the bank knew about many of those sales, and the bank had not objected to them or rebuked the debtor for having made them. The court concluded that the bank had thereby waived the security agreement provision requiring its consent to sales and authorized such later sales as the debtor might make. This problem would rarely arise with regard to inventory, for reasons presented in the next section.

For the authorized disposition exception to apply under revised Article 9, the authorization must be to dispose of the collateral free of the security interest. This element of the authorization also can be express or implied.

But revised Article 9 leaves unresolved a split of authority as to conditional authorizations. To illustrate, assume that Gretna State Bank holds a security interest in cattle owned by Cornbelt Livestock Co. Gretna authorizes Cornbelt to sell 30 head of cattle free of Gretna's security interest, but only on the condition that Cornbelt immediately pay the proceeds of sale to Gretna as a payment on the loan. Cornbelt sells the cattle to Butler, receives the proceeds from Butler, but does not pay them to Gretna. In an action by Gretna to enforce its security interest in the cattle now owned by Butler, the courts split. Some treat the disposition as authorized; others do not. The courts are more likely to treat the disposition as authorized if Butler does not know of the condition, but that factor is not determinative.

In the case that follows, the secured creditor expressly authorized the sale, but only on the condition that the loan be paid in full. The court holds the condition binding on the purchaser, even though the secured creditor agreed to withhold knowledge of the condition from the purchaser.

RFC Capital Corporation v. EarthLink, Inc.

55 U.C.C. Rep. Serv. 2d 617 (Ohio App. 2004)

KLATT, J., BOWMAN and PETREE, JJ., concur.

[RFC loaned $12 million to Internet Commerce & Communications, Inc. ("ICC"), a publicly traded company that provided internet access, among other internet services, to its customers.] To secure the loan, ICC granted RFC a security interest in, among other assets:

All of [ICC's] customer base, which shall include but not be limited to all of [ICC's] past, present and future customer contracts, agreements, lists, documents, computer tapes, letters of agency or other arrangements, any customer list relating thereto and any information regarding prospective customers and contracts, agreements, goodwill and other intangible assets associated with any of the foregoing. . . .

[In late 2000, ICC was in financial trouble and agreed to sell the customer base to EarthLink for a "bounty" of $190 per customer.] ICC represented that it had 97,000 customers who could transfer to EarthLink. Thus, if all 97,000 customers transferred to EarthLink and paid for two months of service, EarthLink would pay ICC a total of $18,430,000.

[Cliff Bryant, EarthLink's Director of Acquisitions] asked if RFC knew of the proposed sale of the customer base, and Mr. Hanson assured him that RFC knew of the sale and had agreed to release the collateral. . . . [A]t the time ICC and EarthLink executed the EarthLink Agreement, RFC was considering the release of its security interest, but it had not agreed to do so.

After RFC's financial review of ICC, RFC drafted the "Second Amendment to the Loan and Security Agreement" ("Second Amendment") to address the sale of the customer base. RFC and ICC executed the Second Amendment on April 2, 2001. Section 11 of the Second Amendment provided that:

> The Lender hereby consents to the sale of the Purchased Accounts by [ICC]. Upon the performance by [ICC] and [its wholly owned subsidiary] of all their obligations under the Loan Agreement and this Amendment, the Lender agrees to release its security interest in the Purchased Accounts.

. . . Neither ICC nor RFC informed EarthLink of the Second Amendment. In fact, Mr. Hanson forbade RFC from contacting EarthLink. Despite RFC's knowledge that EarthLink expected the customer base to be delivered free and clear of any security interest, RFC followed Mr. Hanson's instructions. . . .

Ultimately, only 25,144 former ICC customers paid EarthLink for either dial-up or web hosting service for two consecutive months. Because EarthLink had paid for 40,000 customers, but only received 25,144 customers, EarthLink determined that it did not owe ICC any further payments. . . .

On May 24, 2002, RFC filed suit against EarthLink, alleging conversion, tortious interference with a contractual relationship, unjust enrichment, impairment of RFC's security interest, and a right to an accounting. RFC claimed that, as a secured party, it was entitled to a recovery from EarthLink because EarthLink took and damaged its collateral without obtaining a release.

The case was submitted to the jury, which found EarthLink liable and awarded RFC $6 million. On June 23, 2003, the trial court entered judgment for RFC in the amount of $6 million plus post-judgment interest. EarthLink then filed this appeal. . . .

EarthLink contends that RFC expressly authorized the release of its security interest when it consented to the sale of the customer base in the Second Amendment. We disagree. . . .

In [U.C.C. §9-315] the UCC drafters [made] it explicit . . . that a security interest continues in collateral "unless the secured party authorizes the disposition *free of the security interest*. . . . " Construing the two sentences of Section 11 together, we conclude that RFC authorized the sale of the customer base, but made that collateral subject to its security interest until ICC performed its contractual obligations. Because RFC retained its security interest, despite its consent to the sale, the customer base remained encumbered as long as ICC's contractual obligations went unperformed. . . .

EarthLink [also] contends that the condition RFC imposed upon the release of its security interest (i.e., ICC's performance of its contractual obligations) was ineffective against EarthLink because satisfaction of the condition was outside of EarthLink's control. Consequently, EarthLink reasons that, even though ICC did not perform its contractual obligations, RFC's security interest was released.

As EarthLink points out, there is a split in authority regarding whether a conditional consent cuts off a secured party's interest in the collateral. The line of authority EarthLink relies upon holds that, "a condition imposed on an authorization to sell is ineffective, unless performance of the condition is within the buyer's control." Production Credit Assn. of Baraboo v. Pillsbury Co., 392 N.W.2d 445, 448 (Wis. 1986) [additional case citations omitted]. These courts reason that a condition requiring performance only the seller can provide is not a "real" condition because it "makes the buyer an insurer of acts beyond its control." First Natl. Bank & Trust Co. of Oklahoma City v. Iowa Beef Processors, Inc., 626 F.2d 764, 769 (10th Cir. 1980). Under this view, the third party purchaser who agreed to no condition has superior rights over the secured party who permitted the collateral to be placed on the market.

Not surprisingly, RFC directs us to the contrary line of authority, which holds that regardless of the nature of the condition, "no authorization exists where the debtor fails to satisfy the conditions of the creditor's conditional consent." Northern Commercial Co. v. Cobb, 778 P.2d 205, 208 (Alaska 1989) [additional case citations omitted]. These courts reason that the UCC does not prevent a secured party from attaching a condition or limitation to its consent. Further, these courts maintain that a buyer can protect itself by searching UCC filings to ascertain whether a security interest exists and then contacting the secured party to determine whether there are any conditions attached to the consent.

After reviewing the authority on each side of this issue, we are persuaded that any and all conditions a secured party places upon its consent must be satisfied for the consent to be effective. We do not agree with the reasoning of First Natl. Bank & Trust Co. of Oklahoma City, *supra*, and its progeny that a conditional consent should be construed as a full authorization of a release because the condition is out of the buyer's control. Rather, we hold that it is the buyer, who has the power to ascertain any potential conditions prior to sale and the status of those conditions, that must bear the consequences of purchasing another's collateral.

By giving the secured party the power to authorize the release of the security interest, the UCC places the secured party in a superior position over a third party purchaser. Thus, the onus is on the third party purchaser to determine if a security interest exists and ensure that the secured party fully authorizes the release of that security interest. If the third party purchaser does not conduct a search of UCC filings or does not obtain a release, it must bear the risk and/or burden of buying potentially encumbered collateral.

This burden, however, is relatively light. When purchasing goods that are subject to a security interest, the buyer must simply communicate with the secured party disclosed in the UCC filing to determine what conditions, if any, the secured party has placed upon its consent to a release. If a secured party discloses that it will only consent if the seller satisfies a condition (whether it be a condition precedent or subsequent to the release), the buyer can then investigate the likelihood of the condition occurring, value the collateral in the context of the potentially ongoing security interest and generally assess the risk of going forward with the transaction. If the buyer determines that the risk presented by the conditional consent is too high, it can decide not to consummate the deal. While the condition may only be in the seller's power to satisfy, the decision to purchase the collateral is totally within the buyer's power.

In the case at bar, RFC agreed to release its security interest in the customer base "upon the performance by [ICC] . . . of all [its] obligations under the Loan Agreement and [the Second] Amendment." This provision reflected RFC's consistently-held position that it would only release its security interest if ICC either paid off or paid down the loan. ICC, however, did not satisfy either of these conditions. Therefore, RFC never authorized the release of its security interest in the customer base.

EarthLink's ignorance of the condition contained in the Second Amendment until after it transferred ICC's customers to its system and its inability to satisfy the condition itself are not significant factors in our analysis. By not obtaining a full release of RFC's publicly-disclosed security interest, EarthLink assumed the risk that the customer base would remain encumbered by that security interest.

The court seems to be saying that EarthLink should have searched the U.C.C. records, discovered RFC Capital's security interest, and insisted on a release of that interest before paying the purchase price. The problem with that interpretation of the "unless" clause in U.C.C. §9-315(a)(1) is that it seems the clause would never apply to any case at all.

2. The Buyer-in-the-Ordinary-Course Exception: U.C.C. §9-320(a)

Every purchaser of real estate is expected to search the public records before paying the purchase price and is deemed to have notice of what it would have found. The same is not true for buyers of most kinds of personal property. An obvious example is the shopper at a grocery store. To charge such a buyer with constructive notice of what the buyer would have found on a search of the public records under the name of the grocery store would be absurd. One might think that the distinction in what the law expects of a real estate shopper and a personal property shopper results from the difference in the amounts of money involved. Perhaps the amounts typically involved in the two kinds of transactions contributed to the decision to make the real/personal distinction. But we think the distinction is principally an accident of history perpetuated by custom. Some real estate purchases involve only a few hundred dollars, but the system expects a search; some personal property purchases involve millions of dollars, but the system does not. In addition, a search is expected for some kinds of personal property, including automobiles, aircraft, and intellectual property. Whatever the reason, the system does not require those who buy and sell most kinds of personal property in the ordinary course of business to play the search-and-file game.

The ordinary course of whose business? Under U.C.C. §9-320(a), a buyer in the ordinary course of business can take free of a security interest created by its seller. "Buyer in the ordinary course of business" is defined in U.C.C. §1-201(9) (Rev. §1-201(b)(9)). "Buying" is "in the ordinary course" only if it is "from a person in the business of selling goods of that kind." Thus, the buy must be in the ordinary course of the *seller's* business, not the *buyer's* business. To illustrate, assume that Linda Westerbrook buys and sells used traffic lights. State Street Bank holds a perfected security interest in her inventory. When she sells a traffic light to Peter Kollander (who knows nothing about how Linda finances her business) and installs it in his living room, the sale is in the ordinary course of Linda's business, U.C.C. §9-320(a) applies, and Peter takes free of State Street's security interest. When Linda buys a used traffic light from Disney World, U.C.C. §9-320(a) does not apply. This buy is in the ordinary course of Linda's business. Selling traffic lights is not in the ordinary course of Disney World's business, although it may sell a traffic light from time to time. Linda would not take free of a security interest granted by Disney World to its bank.

In the foregoing example, it was a consumer buyer who took free of a security interest granted by his seller. U.C.C. §9-320(a) is not limited to consumer buyers. If Linda sold one of her traffic lights to Neiman Marcus, for display or for resale, Neiman Marcus would be a buyer in the ordinary course of Linda's business, and they would take free of the State Street Bank security interest.

The buyer's knowledge. U.C.C. §9-320(a) protects a buyer in the ordinary course of business "even though the buyer knows of [the security interest's] existence." U.C.C. §1-201(9) (Rev. §1-201(b)(9)) limits "buyer in the ordinary course of business" in a manner that may at first seem to contradict U.C.C. §9-320(a). One cannot be a buyer in the ordinary course if one knows "that the sale to him is in violation of the...security interest of a third party." Comment 3 to U.C.C. §9-320 explains: "Reading the definition together with the rule of law results in the buyer's taking free if the buyer merely knows that a security interest covers the goods but taking subject if the buyer knows, in addition, that the sale violates a term in an agreement with the secured party." In other words, merely knowing that Neiman Marcus has granted a security interest in its inventory should not prevent shopper Edith Parker from taking free of the security interest under U.C.C. §9-320(a). Many, if not most, businesses that sell goods from inventory have granted security interests in their inventories. Those security agreements almost invariably authorize the debtors to sell the collateral free and clear of the security interests. U.C.C. §9-320(a) entitles Edith to assume that is true of every merchant's inventory security agreement until she learns otherwise.

As we noted above, some inventory security agreements impose conditions on the sale of collateral. For example, a bank that finances the inventory of a yacht dealer may want to be involved in and scrutinize every sale. The security agreement employed in such a relationship may prohibit sales of yachts from inventory except with the express written consent of the bank for sale to the particular buyer. A customer who knows that this dealer has inventory financing will not be bound by this sale condition if it does not know of it, but will be bound if it does. If the customer knowingly buys in violation of the condition, the customer takes subject to the bank's security interest.

"Created by his seller." Assume that First National Bank holds a security interest in all personal property owned by Disney World, including its single traffic light, to secure a loan in the amount of $90 million. Disney World sells the traffic light to Linda in a sale that is not in the ordinary course of Disney World business. As previously noted, Linda takes subject to First National's security interest. Not realizing that the traffic light is encumbered, Linda sells it to Neiman Marcus. Does Neiman Marcus take free of First National's security interest under U.C.C. §9-320(a)? The answer is no. Although Neiman Marcus is a buyer in the ordinary course of business, under U.C.C. §9-320(a), it only takes free of "a security interest created by [its] seller," Linda Westerbrook. It does not take free of security interests created by her predecessors in title.

The effects of this limitation of U.C.C. §9-320(a) become even more surprising when Neiman Marcus decides to sell vintage traffic lights as a Christmas special from their store in the Galleria Mall. When Christmas shopper Edith Parker buys one as a gift for her husband George, both may be in for a surprise. The traffic light inside their gift-wrapped package may have a $90 million perfected security interest firmly attached to it. Should Disney World default on its debt to First National, the Bank may hunt George down and repossess the traffic light. (One of us heard a GMAC representative refer to this as "going knocking on doors.")

The farm products exception. U.C.C. §9-320(a) affords no protection to those who buy farm products. But the federal Food Security Act provides parallel protection. That law provides:

> Except as provided in subsection (e) and notwithstanding any other provision of Federal, State, or local law, a buyer who in the ordinary course of business buys a farm product from a seller engaged in farming operations shall take free of a security interest created by the seller, even though the security interest is perfected; and the buyer knows of the existence of such interest.

7 U.S.C. §1631(d) (2005). The exceptions in subsection (e) of §1631 provide farm lenders with various ways of notifying prospective buyers of their security interests. The security interests of lenders who do give notice continue in the collateral notwithstanding sale. The result is that farm lenders can preserve their security interests somewhat more easily than nonfarm lenders. The details of the Food Security Act system are, however, outside the scope of this book. For our purposes it is sufficient to see that the farm products exception of U.C.C. §9-320(a) may not be much of an exception at all.

When does a buyer become a buyer? At the moment a bankruptcy petition is filed or the moment that a secured creditor takes possession of its collateral, there typically will be persons who have contracted to buy some of the collateral but who have not yet completed their transactions. If such a person is a "buyer" within the meaning of U.C.C. §9-320(a), the person will take free of the inventory lender's security agreement and be able to keep what was bought. If the person has paid part of the purchase price, the person will get credit for that part, and owe the balance. If the person is not yet a "buyer," the person is merely an unsecured creditor of the seller for any part of the purchase price paid and for the benefit of the bargain the person has lost. Particularly if the person has paid part of the purchase price in advance, the moment when the person becomes a "buyer" within the meaning of U.C.C. §9-320(a) can be of tremendous importance. As the following case illustrates, there are many permutations of this problem and much remaining uncertainty.

Daniel v. Bank of Hayward

425 N.W.2d 416 (Wis. 1988)

SHIRLEY S. ABRAHAMSON, J. . . .

This case presents the following issue: When does a retail purchaser who makes a down payment on a motor vehicle but does not take title to the vehicle become a "buyer in ordinary course of business" under [U.C.C. §1-201(9) (Rev. §1-201 (b)(9))] and [U.C.C. §9-320(a)] to prevail over the security interest of the motor vehicle dealer's floor plan financier? . . .

In Chrysler Corp. v. Adamatic, 59 Wis. 2d 219, 208 N.W.2d 97 (1972), this court concluded that a purchaser becomes a buyer in ordinary course of business when he or she takes title to the goods. . . . We conclude that the purchasers in this case became buyers in ordinary course of business when the vehicle was identified to the contract. To the extent that our decision in the *Chrysler* case is inconsistent with our decision in this case, we overrule the *Chrysler* case.

The facts in the record are undisputed. Joseph and Marijane Daniel, the purchasers, entered into a motor vehicle purchase contract in May 1983 with Don Hofstadter, Inc., a motor vehicle dealership in the City of Hayward. The purchasers agreed to purchase a 1984 Chevrolet van which had not yet been manufactured and to trade in the older motor home. According to the contract, the cash price of the vehicle was $12,077.55; the trade-in allowance was $8,675.55; and the amount the purchasers owed on delivery was $3,402.00. The contract described the motor vehicle and its various accessories but did not set forth the vehicle identification number because the vehicle had not been manufactured when the contract was signed.

The purchasers signed over title to their existing motor home and delivered the home to the dealership. The dealership sold the motor home on or about June 6, 1983. The record does not reflect how much the dealership received on the sale of the motor home, and it is not clear whether the Bank received any of the proceeds.

The dealership did its financing, including floor plan financing on new vehicles, with defendant Bank of Hayward (Bank). The floor plan financing operated as follows: There was a master note in the original sum of $150,000 dated April 19, 1982. When the dealership would order a new vehicle from General Motors, the Bank would receive a copy of that order. Prior to GM's delivery of the new vehicle to the dealership, GM would send the Bank a sight draft which included the vehicle identification number. The Bank would then prepare an individual floor plan note in the amount of the draft and the dealership would sign it. When the individual note was signed by the dealership, the Bank would pay GM. GM would then send the Manufacturer's Statement of Origin (MSO) to the Bank which retained the MSO. Because the MSO is necessary to obtain title to the motor vehicle, the Bank effectively controlled delivery of title to the retail purchaser and ensured itself of being paid. This procedure was unusual. Ordinarily, GM would send the MSO directly to the dealership. The Bank used the unusual procedure in this case because it was concerned about the financial status of the dealership.

On September 30, 1983, the Bank received a sight draft from General Motors for the van the purchasers had ordered. The dealership executed a floor plan note in the amount of $9,905.22 to pay General Motors for a 1984 Chevrolet van, I.D. No. 1GCGG35M6E7105325. The parties agree that the van bearing this identification number is the vehicle the purchasers ordered. The Floor Plan Note conveyed a security interest in the van to the Bank on September 30, 1983.

Sometime on Friday, October 21, 1983, the Chevrolet van was delivered to the dealership. On Saturday, October 22, 1983, the Bank discovered that its debtor, the dealership, was removing used vehicles from the lots. Because these used vehicles were collateral for the Bank's loans, the Bank called all loans and secured the lot so that no vehicles could be removed. The purchasers' Chevrolet van was among the new vehicles on the lot when the Bank took possession of the dealership's premises.

On October 24, 1983, the purchasers went to the dealership to complete the purchase of the van. . . .

The Bank was willing to release the van only if the purchasers paid in full the Bank's interest in the van pursuant to the Floor Plan Note, namely, $9,905.22. According to their contract with the dealership, the purchasers did not owe the dealership $9,905.22. By virtue of the trade-in, the purchasers owed the dealership only $3,402.00. Because the purchasers needed the van to go to Florida, they [paid] $9,905.22 . . . and they then took title to and possession of the van. They brought this action against the Bank to recover damages "to the extent of the overpayment together with consequential damages including interest on the monies that plaintiff had to borrow to meet the extorted demands of the bank, actual attorney's fees incurred and a great inconvenience all to their damage in the sum of $15,000."

As we stated previously, the sole question in this case is: When do purchasers who make a down payment under a contract for sale and have not taken title to the vehicle achieve the status of buyer in ordinary course of business? If the purchasers in this case became buyers in ordinary course of business prior to the Bank's seizing the van, their interest in the van takes priority over the Bank's perfected security interest.

We examine first the relevant provisions of the Wisconsin Uniform Commercial Code. [U.C.C. Article 9] establishes a priority system for determining the rights of parties who claim competing interests in secured property. As a general rule, the holder of a perfected security interest has an interest in the secured property which is superior to the interests of the debtor, unsecured creditors of the debtor and subsequent purchasers of the secured property. [U.C.C. §9-201] thus protects the secured creditor. The Code provides, however, exceptions to the rule that the secured creditor has priority over purchasers of the collateral. A principal exception to the rule is found in [U.C.C. §9-320(a)], captioned "protection of buyers of goods," which permits a buyer in ordinary course of business as defined in [U.C.C. §1-201(9) (Rev. §1-201(b)(9))] to take free of a security interest created by the seller. The Code thus recognizes a potential conflict between the buyer in ordinary course of business and the seller's secured creditor and attempts to seek a fair accommodation between the two. [The court set forth the provisions of U.C.C. §9-320(a).] [U.C.C. §9-320(a)] severs the inventory lender's security interest in favor of the buyer in ordinary course of business. In order to prevail over the Bank's perfected security interest, the purchasers in this case must qualify as buyers in ordinary course of business, as that term is defined in [U.C.C. §1-201(9) (Rev. §1-201(b)(9))]. [The court set forth the provisions of U.C.C. §1-201(9) (Rev. §1-201(b)(9)).] The exception for a buyer in ordinary course of business accommodates the interests of all parties. Buyers desire to be free of the lender's interest after they have committed themselves to paying for the goods. A buyer cannot easily determine how the seller finances its inventory, nor can the buyer afford to negotiate subordination agreements with the seller's lenders for each purchase made. Secured creditors at some point expect to surrender their security interest in the goods and look to the proceeds of a sale for repayment of the loan. The secured creditor thus depends on the goods being sold. The secured lender expects a constant flow of inventory in and out of the seller's possession; it is usually in the business of lending funds and is in a better position to take precautions against the loss of its security.

Although the Code protects the buyer in ordinary course of business, the Code provides no explicit guidance to the question presented in this case, namely when does a purchaser under a contract for sale achieve the status of buyer in ordinary course of business. There are at least five possible dates on which a purchaser may be viewed as having achieved the status of buyer in ordinary course of business: (1) the date of initial contract; (2) the date the goods are identified; (3) the date title passes to the purchaser; (4) the date the purchaser gets delivery; and (5) the date the purchaser accepts the goods.[1]

Relying on Chrysler Corp. v. Adamatic, 59 Wis. 2d 219, 208 N.W.2d 97 (1973), the Bank maintains that the purchasers can not become buyers in ordinary course of business who take free of the seller's secured creditor until the purchasers take title or delivery of the van. Because the purchasers in this case did not take title or delivery, the Bank contends that the purchasers do not take free of its interest as the dealership's secured creditor....

We have reconsidered our analysis in *Chrysler* and are persuaded by the reasoning of the commentators and courts which have, since our decision in Chrysler Corp. v. Adamatic, addressed the issue presented in this case. The commentators and courts have, for the most part, opted for an earlier date than the date that title passed as the time when a purchaser achieves the status of a buyer in ordinary course of business.

We conclude that we erred in relying on the date of transfer of title as the date on which a purchaser becomes a buyer in ordinary course of business. Reliance on the concept of title is contrary to the thrust of the Uniform Commercial Code and the commentary. The drafters of the Uniform Commercial Code tried to avoid giving technical rules of title a central role in furthering the policies of the Uniform Commercial Code. See [U.C.C. §§2-401, 9-202]. Although title questions may be of significance in determining some issues under the Code, we conclude that

---

1. In similar but not precisely the same fact situations, several courts have adopted dates ranging from initial contract through identification.

reliance on title to interpret [U.C.C. §9-320(a)] is an unduly narrow and technical interpretation. . . .

Courts have overwhelmingly rejected a definition of buyer in ordinary course that focuses on whether title has passed. These courts reason that the inventory financier is better able to guard against the risks inherent in this type of financing than is the average retail buyer because the financier is more knowledgeable and has the resources to guard against the risks. These courts conclude that placing the burden on the buyer would inhibit retail sales.

Furthermore, focusing on the words "in ordinary course," these courts reason that a court must consider the substance of the transaction; a court must look to the customary manner in which sales are made in the seller's business and to the expectations of the buyer under the contract. The language "in ordinary course" indicates deference to commercial practice and is consistent with the purposes and policies underlying the Code "[t]o permit the continued expansion of commercial practices through custom, usage and agreement of the parties." [U.C.C. §1-102(2)(b) (Rev. §1-103(a)(2))]. If it is customary in the seller's business to sell goods in a particular manner (e.g., seller and purchaser enter into a contract for sale and purchaser makes a down payment), then the court may find that the purchaser who makes a down payment without taking title is a "buyer in ordinary course of business."

The purchasers in this case ask the court to reject the title or delivery date in this case and adopt an "identification" date as the date on which they became buyers in ordinary course of business. The purchasers rely on [U.C.C. §2-501(1)], which provides that a buyer obtains a special property interest on identification. [U.C.C. §2-501(1)] provides:

> The buyer obtains a special property and an insurable interest in goods by identification of existing goods to which the contract refers even though the goods so identified are nonconforming and he has an option to return or reject them. Such identification can be made at any time and in any manner explicitly agreed to by the parties. In the absence of explicit agreement identification occurs:
>
>   (a) When the contract is made if it is for the sale of goods already existing and identified;
>   (b) If the contract is for the sale of future goods . . . when goods are shipped, marked or otherwise designated by the seller as goods to which the contract refers. . . .

The purchasers argue that adoption of the identification date strikes a fair balance between the interests of the buyer in ordinary course and the secured party. The purchasers argue that once the goods have been identified they have an insurable interest in the goods and can maintain an action against a third party who has injured them through his or her dealings with the goods. The purchasers reason that their interest at identification justifies considering them buyers in ordinary course at that time.

The purchasers conclude that they became buyers in ordinary course of business when the van became identified to the contract, that is, when it was produced or when GM sent the Bank the sight draft including the vehicle identification number. We need not decide in this case which is the appropriate date of identification. Whichever date, the purchaser would prevail over the Bank. Because the purchasers do not ask this court to adopt the date of contract as the triggering date for transforming the purchasers to buyers in ordinary course, we need not decide this issue.

We merely hold today that the purchasers became buyers in ordinary course of business when the goods became identified to the contract. We rest our decision on the circumstances surrounding the transaction in this case and the manner in which sales are made in this industry.

This case presents the situation that [U.C.C. §9-320(a)] was designed to address. The purchasers were ordinary retail consumers purchasing a vehicle from a dealership, an entity in the business of selling vehicles. The purchasers made a down payment and signed a contract. The Bank as financier of the inventory authorized the sale of the inventory. It was only through the sale of the inventory that the Bank would receive cash from the dealership to repay the loan. The Bank knew of the purchasers. The Bank knew of the purchase order and paid the manufacturer for the vehicle in question on September 30, 1983.

In its amicus brief the Wisconsin Bankers Association states that protecting the purchasers in this case will make a security interest in inventory an unworkable concept. The position we adopt today is the position most courts have adopted, concluding that the floor plan financier can guard against the risks. The Bank was in a better position than the purchasers to guard against the risk of loss. Most retail purchasers probably have never heard of the Uniform Commercial Code and would not know how to go about protecting their interest. The Bank, on the other hand, is in the business of lending money and has access to information about how to protect itself, as best it can, against risk of loss. Accordingly, under the facts of this case, we hold that the purchasers were buyers in ordinary course of business upon identification of the merchandise to the contract. The purchasers assert that the van had been identified to the contract before the Bank took over the dealership's premises and that their interest prevails over the Bank's. Because it is unclear whether the Bank disputes the date of identification, this issue may have to be resolved in remand. . . .

The judgment of the circuit court is reversed and the cause remanded.

In First National Bank of El Campo v. Buss, 143 S.W.3d 915 (2004), several buyers each bought used automobiles from Greg's Auto Sales. Each paid for the vehicle and took possession of it. The buyers completed title applications and left them with the dealer. Unbeknownst to the buyers, the titles were in the hands of First National Bank, Greg's inventory lender. FNB refused to surrender the titles without payment. The Texas certificate of title act "declared that the non-transfer of certificates of title renders the sale void." The Texas Court of Appeals held that the buyers were buyers in the ordinary course of business under Article 9 and that the provisions of Article 9 were in conflict with and superseded the provisions of the certificate of title act.

After *Daniel*, the drafters revised U.C.C. §1-201(9) (Rev. §1-201(b)(9)) to add that "[o]nly a buyer that takes possession of the goods or has a right to recover the goods from the seller under Article 2 may be a buyer in ordinary course of business." The Comment to that section identifies U.C.C. §§2-502 and 2-716 as the law identifying the buyers who do not take possession but still can qualify as buyers in ordinary course of business.

Sales of goods in the possession of the secured party. Daniel v. Bank of Hayward illustrates that a buyer in the ordinary course of business can defeat the inventory lender's security interest without taking possession of the goods. In that case, the seller-debtor, Don Hofstadter, Inc., had possession. What if, instead, the Bank of Hayward had possession of the vehicle at the time the Daniels purchased it? Could the Daniels still have bought the vehicle in the ordinary course of business and taken free of the Bank's now doubly perfected security interest? If so, it would seem to be virtually impossible for a secured creditor to prevent its debtor from selling collateral free of the creditor's security interest. Even collateral resting in the bank's vault would not be safe. On the other hand, the Wisconsin Supreme Court determined that the Daniels were buyers in the ordinary course of business even though they had never seen the van they bought. For all the Daniels knew, their van might have been in the Bank's vault.

Tanbro Fabrics Corp. v. Deering Milliken, Inc., 350 N.E.2d 590 (N.Y. 1976), illustrates both the problem and the solution. The secured creditor, Deering, had possession of 267,000 yards of a certain fabric as security for an account owing from Mill Fabrics, the debtor, to Deering. Mill Fabrics sold the fabric to Tanbro. Tanbro was familiar with the industry practice of leaving goods in the possession of the seller's seller as security and hence did not find it unusual to be buying fabric the seller did not possess. Tanbro paid the purchase price to Mill Fabrics. Mill Fabrics promptly went belly-up without paying Deering. Deering refused to give the fabric to Tanbro and Tanbro sued. The court held that Tanbro was a buyer in the ordinary course of Mill Fabric's business and that Tanbro therefore took free of Deering's security interest.

Some of the drafters of former Article 9 were apoplectic over *Tanbro Fabrics*. Although they never managed to overturn that decision, the drafters of revised Article 9 have. U.C.C. §9-320(e) provides somewhat mysteriously that "Subsections (a) and (b) do not affect a security interest in goods in possession of the secured party under Section 9-313." Comment 8 explains that U.C.C. §9-320(e) "rejects the holding of *Tanbro Fabrics Corp. v. Deering Milliken* ... and, together with Section 9-317(b), prevents a buyer of collateral from taking free of a security interest if the collateral is in the possession of the secured party." The Comment makes explicit reference to the fact that under U.C.C. §9-313, a secured party may be in possession of collateral that is in the physical possession of a third party.

3. The Buyer-Not-in-the-Ordinary-Course Exception: U.C.C. §§9-323(d) and (e) and 9-317(b)

Those who buy goods outside the ordinary course of business have no exemption from the search-and-file game. They are expected to search the U.C.C. records and are charged with constructive notice of the filings they would have found. The result is that in a sale not authorized by the secured creditor, the buyer not in the ordinary course takes subject to any security interest that is perfected, but has priority over unperfected ones. This hierarchy of interests is reflected in U.C.C. §§9-323(d) and (e) and 9-317(b).

To illustrate, assume that Thomas Redding plans to open a frozen yogurt store. He needs a walk-in cooler to refrigerate the yogurt mix. He spots one for $2,000 in the newspaper want ads. The owner, Peter's Pizzas, used the cooler to store food and drinks in connection with its pizza business, but the business closed a few weeks ago. Because Peter's is not in the business of selling coolers, the sale of this cooler to Redding will not be a sale in the ordinary course. Redding will take subject to any perfected security interest in the cooler, including even some future advances Peter's might receive from its lender after Redding's purchase. U.C.C. §§9-323(d) and (e). For that reason, Redding is well advised to search the public record before paying the $2,000 purchase price.

If, instead, Redding bought his cooler from Paul's Restaurant Supply, a company that sells, among other things, used coolers, he would not have been expected to search the public record. He would have taken free of any security interest given by Paul's Restaurant Supply. U.C.C. §9-320(a).

4.   The Consumer-to-Consumer-Sale Exception: U.C.C. §9-320(b)

When a sale is outside the ordinary course of business, even consumer buyers are expected to play the search-and-file game. Assume, for example, that Steve Waldoch offers to sell his riding lawn mower to Thomas Redding for $600. If Sears holds a security interest in the lawn mower that is perfected by filing and Sears has not authorized the sale, Redding will take subject to it. Redding is not protected by U.C.C. §9-320(a) because Waldoch does not deal in lawn mowers. See U.C.C. §1-201(9) (Rev. §1-201(b)(9)). Redding is not protected by U.C.C. §9-320(b) because of the exception in that section in favor of secured parties who have filed a financing statement. Ordinary people would consider it absurd that Redding be expected to search the public record before buying a lawn mower in a garage sale. But you should realize by now that the drafters of Article 9 were not ordinary people.

We refer to the exception in U.C.C. §9-320(b) as the consumer-to-consumer-sale exception[*] because the exception applies only if the goods are consumer goods in the hands of the seller before the sale and consumer goods in the hands of the buyer after the sale. The requirement that the goods be held for personal, family, or household purposes of the seller prior to the sale is contained in the main part of section (b); the requirement that they be held for personal, family, or household purposes of the buyer after the sale is contained in subsection (b)(3). The buyer in a consumer-to-consumer sale is protected from an automatically perfected purchase-money security interest (PMSI) in consumer goods. Thus, if Sears had not filed a financing statement in the illustration given in the previous paragraph, but instead relied on its PMSI protection from U.C.C. §9-309(1), the consumer-to-consumer-sale exception of U.C.C. §9-320(b) would apply to permit Redding to take free of Sears' perfected security interest. Given that consumers such as Redding are not going to

---

[*]Some think it is better remembered as the garage sale exception.

search the U.C.C. records, we can think of no good reason for letting them take free of automatically perfected interests, but not interests perfected by filing. But that is how the rule reads.

Problem Set 69

69.1. Davis Department Store sold a combination TV-stereo-VCR-pop-corn popper to Beavis on credit for $1,925. Beavis paid no money down, but signed a promissory note, security agreement, and financing statement. Davis filed the financing statement in the statewide U.C.C. records. The security agreement provided that Beavis "agrees not to sell the collateral." Six months later, Beavis lost his job at the meat processing plant and moved to Tennessee. Before leaving, he held a garage sale at which he sold the entertainment unit to his friend Butthead for $960. Butthead didn't know about the security agreement with Davis Department Store and (wouldn't you know it?) made the mistake of paying by check. Davis identified Butt-head as the buyer from Beavis's checking account records. Davis asks whether it is entitled to repossess the entertainment unit from Butthead. If so, do they have to refund his $960? U.C.C. §§1-201(9)(Rev. §1-201(b)(9)), 9-315(a), 9-320, 9-401(b).

69.2. Your client, University City Bank (UCB), has a security interest in the inventory of Sound City, Inc. Sound City sells sound systems at retail to consumers and businesses. The security agreement between UCB and Sound City authorized sales only in the ordinary course of business, prohibited sales on credit, and required that "Debtor deposit all proceeds of sales of collateral to Debtor's account #937284 at University City Bank." UCB perfected the security interest by filing a financing statement. On October 20, Sound City, Inc. filed under Chapter 7 of the Bankruptcy Code. The trustee abandoned the inventory, the debtor surrendered it to UCB, and UCB sold it and applied the proceeds to the inventory loan. A deficiency of $36,000 remains owing to UCB on the Sound City loan. Through discovery, you learned of the following transactions that took place before the filing of the bankruptcy petition:

a. Sound City sold a sound system to Rhonda Fried for $12,000. Rhonda paid $2,000 in cash and signed a negotiable promissory note for the remaining $10,000. There is no evidence that she knew of the restrictive provisions of the security agreement. Sound City deposited Rhonda's check to an account with a bank other than UCB and used the money to pay a utility bill. About a month later, Sound City sold the Rhonda note for $9,200. UCB has been unable to determine what Sound City did with the proceeds. Is UCB entitled to repossess the sound system from Rhonda? U.C.C. §§9-315(a), 9-320, 9-323(d) and (e), 1-201(9) (Rev. §1-201(b)(9)).

b. George Paulos is a lawyer who has been representing Sound City for several years. As of July 17, Sound City owed George $16,458 for legal services rendered in two employment discrimination suits. George agreed to accept a $14,000 sound system as partial payment and Sound City installed it in his home. Is UCB entitled to repossess the sound system from George? U.C.C. §§1-201(9) (Rev. §1-201(b)(9)), 9-315, 9-320, 9-323(d) and (e).

69.3.   Alecia Card bought a used 1992 "Lindy Delux Housecar" (the Lindy) from the used car lot of Sunrise R.V. She paid for the recreational vehicle with a $23,000 cashier's check and drove it home. The salesman at Sunrise assured her that she would receive title to the Lindy directly from the Division of Motor Vehicles within two weeks. When the title did not arrive as promised, Alecia complained to Sunrise.

Eventually she learned the history of the Lindy. A man named Kenneth Eddy purchased it from All Seasons R.V. over a year ago. Eddy granted All Seasons a security interest in the Lindy to secure a part of the purchase price. In the security agreement, Eddy agreed "not to transfer any interest in the vehicle." A few weeks ago, Eddy violated the security agreement by trading the Lindy to Sunrise R.V. (Sunrise) for another recreational vehicle. At the time he sold the Lindy to Sunrise, Eddy still owed All Seasons $17,000 of the purchase price. Sunrise bought the Lindy subject to that lien and agreed to pay it. Instead, Sunrise deposited Alecia's $23,000 to its operating account and spent the money on rent and other expenses. Alecia also learned that Eddy did not notify All Seasons that he was selling to Sunrise and did not obtain All Seasons' permission to sell.

a.   Alecia wants to sue to remove All Seasons' lien from the title to the Lindy. How good is her case? U.C.C. §§9-315(a), 9-320(a).

b.   If Alecia had insisted on seeing the certificate of title for the Lindy before she paid her $23,000, what would she have learned? See U.C.C. §9-311(d) and Comment 4 to that section; form for motor vehicle certificate of title in Assignment 64.

69.4.   Alecia Card is back to see you for the fourth time since you represented her in the *All Seasons* case. Although she is a bright, energetic, friendly person, she has been asking questions that seem . . . well, a little too basic. Even before today, you had been suspecting that Alecia might be showing signs of paranoia. In your meeting this morning, Alecia explained that she has been shopping for a piano, has found a reconditioned one she likes for $5,000 at American Piano Company in the Galleria Mall, and would like you to "represent her at the closing." Covering your surprise, you told her that most people who buy things in the mall just represent themselves. "Yes," she replied matter-of-factly, "but they haven't been through what you and I have." You told her you'd think about it and give her a call this afternoon.

a.   Is there anything to her fears? U.C.C. §9-320(a).

b.   Can the problem be dealt with by a thorough search of the public records? U.C.C. §9-507(a), including Comment 3.

c.   Should you recommend a psychiatrist or try to deal with this yourself? If you try to deal with it yourself, what will you say to Alecia and what will you do to get ready for the "closing"?

d.   Is this a problem that is unique to used goods, or could it occur with respect to new goods as well?

69.5.   Would the Daniels still prevail over Bank of Hayward under the penultimate sentence of U.C.C. §1-201(9) (Rev. §1-201(b)(9))? That is, would the Daniels have "a right to recover [the van] from the seller under Article 2"? See Comment 9 to U.C.C. §1-201.

69.6.   Charles Hayward, president of the Bank of Hayward, was really angry about the Bank's loss in the *Daniel* case. Fresh from a meeting of bankers in which they all grumbled about "the end of inventory financing," he would like your advice on damage control. The Bank finances several motor vehicle dealerships. Before the *Daniel* case, the Bank sent inspectors out at unpredictable times to physically inspect the inventory. Each inspector carried a list of vehicle ID numbers for the vehicles against which the Bank had lent money. As the inspector found each vehicle on the lot, the inspector checked it off on the list. If a dealer could not satisfactorily account for all of the vehicles on the list, the Bank would consider calling the loan.

a. "After *Daniel*," Charles says, "the presence of a vehicle on the lot means nothing. The dealer could already have sold it and been paid for it. The lot could be full of vehicles, but every one of them sold to a prepaying buyer." Do you agree?

b. "Under *Chrysler*," Charles says, "we controlled delivery of the title to the retail purchaser by holding the MSO. Now the buyer doesn't need title; they can just sue us for it." Is he right?

c. The *Daniel* court said that "The bank...is in the business of lending money and has access to information about how to protect itself, as best it can, against risk of loss." Charles wants to know how the Bank can protect itself. What do you suggest?

69.7. Charles Hayward, president of the Bank of Hayward, is back. He would like your opinion of "a great new scheme" he just heard about at a meeting of bankers. The bills of lading for new vehicles will provide that from the moment of identification of a new vehicle to a dealer's contract for sale until the vehicle actually arrives on the dealer's lot, the manufacturer and the carriers will hold possession of the vehicle as agents for the bank that finances the dealer's inventory. That way, Hayward says, buyers like the Daniels won't be entitled to vehicles on which they have made down payments unless those vehicles actually arrive on the dealers' lots before repossession.

a. Is Hayward right? U.C.C. §§9-313(a) and (b), 9-315(a) and (c), 9-317(b), 9-320(a) and (e).

b. Is there any way the Bank can use U.C.C. §9-320(e) to prevail even as to vehicles actually delivered to the dealer's lot?

c. What advice would you give to people like the Daniels who want a car custom-made for them, but are faced with the inevitable demand from the dealer for a substantial down payment?

69.8. Robert and Edward Sherrock are partners in Sherrock Brothers, a Toyota dealership. Ed tried to call you early this afternoon, but you were in a meeting and he was unable to get through. Your secretary took a lengthy message and now relates it to you. Ed called from Dover Motors, the Toyota dealership in a nearby city. He bought two cars from Dover and made arrangements to pay for them by transfer of funds later this afternoon. Dover agreed to keep the cars for a few days until Sherrock Brothers could send a couple of drivers to move them. After he left Dover's lot, Ed had second thoughts. He had heard some rumors that Dover was in financial difficulty, so he called you to find out if it's okay to leave the cars there till he gets back from Chicago in two days. Actually, you were on your way out of town as well. Does this have to be dealt with now? U.C.C. §§9-320, 1-201(19) (Rev. §1-201(b)(20)), 2-103(1)(b), 2-102, 2-403(2) and (3). Consider two possibilities:

a.   Dover sells the two cars to buyers in the ordinary course of business and then files bankruptcy.

b.   Dover files bankruptcy and Dover's inventory lender claims the cars.

69.9.   Frances Foster runs a small company that manufactures musical instruments and sells them directly to retail stores. The company has suffered substantial losses when customers have filed for bankruptcy and inventory lenders have seized and sold some of Foster's instruments. Frances has tried to get security interests to protect her sales, but her customers refuse, noting that they would be in violation of their inventory loan agreements. She has another idea to protect herself.

Deutsche Credit Corporation will finance the inventory of her corporation, Foster Musical Manufacturing Corporation (Manufacturing), under a security agreement that provides for release of collateral only when Deutsche is paid. Frances proposes to set up a separate corporation, Foster Musical Marketing Corporation (Marketing). Manufacturing will sell the inventory to Marketing subject to Deutsche's security interest. Marketing will sell the inventory to retail stores. U.C.C. §9-320(a). The retail store will not take free of Deutsche's lien because it was created by Manufacturing, not "the buyer's seller" (Marketing). The retail stores won't know the instruments are subject to Deutsche's security interest, but that won't make any difference to them provided they pay what they owe. If they don't, justice will prevail. Deutsche will repossess the instruments and Frances will buy them back from Deutsche. Best of all, Frances does not have to rely on purchase-money status to beat the retail store's inventory lender, so she does not have to comply with U.C.C. §9-324(b). Will this work? U.C.C. §§1-102(3) (Rev. §1-302), 9-315(a), 9-322(a), 9-325, 9-507(a), 9-602.

Table of Cases

Italics indicate principal cases.

1143

Table of Statutes, Regulations, and Restatements

Index